New Testament
History, Culture, and Society

A Background to the
Texts of the New Testament

Lincoln H. Blumell, editor

Published by the Religious Studies Center, Brigham Young University, Provo, Utah, in cooperation with Deseret Book Company, Salt Lake City.
Visit us at rsc.byu.edu.

Printed in the United States of America by Sheridan Books, Inc.

DESERET BOOK is a registered trademark of Deseret Book Company.
Visit us at DeseretBook.com.

Cover and interior design by Emily V. Strong.

ISBN: 9781944394769

Library of Congress Control Number: 2019933783

For Bruce and Jean

parentibus fidelibus et devotis

חֲנֹךְ לַנַּעַר עַל־פִּי דַרְכּוֹ גַּם
כִּי־יַזְקִין לֹא־יָסוּר מִמֶּנָּה:

—Proverbs 22:6

Contents

The Apostle Paul, General Epistles, and Revelation

New Testament Issues and Contexts

The Text of the New Testament

After the New Testament

Acknowledgments

Given the size and scope of this volume, there are various persons who deserve mention for their contributions. The first is Scott C. Esplin, publications director of the Religious Studies Center, who deserves special thanks for overseeing the review of this work and for expediting this project. His competence, professionalism, oversight, and attentiveness to this project have ensured not only that it has been published on a very tight schedule but also that the overall quality of the volume has been greatly enhanced. Along the same lines, special thanks should be extended to the editors and staff at the RSC, including Don L. Brugger, R. Devan Jensen, Shirley S. Ricks, Emily V. Strong, Brent R. Nordgren, Joany O. Pinegar, Breanna Anderl, Ashlin Awerkamp, Emily Cook, and Abigail Crimm, who collectively performed a myriad of tasks so that this volume could see the light of day. A special thanks should also be extended to Zakarias D. Gram, who read the entire manuscript at an early stage in the project and helped to significantly reduce the number of infelicities. Additionally, Camille Fronk Olson and Dana M. Pike, the previous and current chair of the Department of Ancient Scripture, deserve thanks for all of their support for this project. Finally, very special thanks go to my wife, Melissa, and our four children, Luke, Grace, Charlotte, and Claire, for all their patience and love during the time in which this project was underway.

Introduction

The New Testament is a compilation of twenty-seven texts written by various authors who labored under differing circumstances and dealt with a variety of issues and interests. While these texts were written during the first century AD, it was not until the fourth century that they collectively achieved canonical status and were viewed as authoritative in matters pertaining to religious belief and practice. Thus, for more than sixteen hundred years this corpus has been the foundation of Christianity despite the countless ways it has been read and interpreted over the centuries.

Many twenty-first-century readers access these texts only via translation and live in lands far removed geographically and culturally from first-century Judea and other parts of the Roman world where much of the New Testament is set. For them, approaching these texts can be fraught with challenges. Accordingly, this volume is designed as a study companion that will help elucidate the text, history, culture, and society associated with the New Testament so as to provide modern readers with greater insight. Though this volume stands at more than eight hundred pages, it is not intended to serve as a comprehensive introduction, for that would require a treatment many times this length. Rather, it is more of a handbook that readers can consult topically to supplement their study of the New Testament.

The forty-three chapters herein range from the law of Moses and the intertestamental period to the First Jewish Revolt of AD 66–73 and the canonization of the New Testament. The opening section, "Jewish Background of the New Testament," covers a host of topics, including the law of Moses, the intertestamental period, the Jerusalem temple, the Dead Sea

Scrolls, rabbinic literature, notions of messianism in ancient Judaism, and modes of Jewish hermeneutics. There is also an image-laden chapter that provides a virtual tour of Jerusalem and the Temple Mount in the New Testament period. The array of topics in this section thus introduces readers to the larger Jewish context of the New Testament—scriptural, extrascriptural, and archaeological. The next section, "Greco-Roman Background of the New Testament," expands the focus to survey the larger Greco-Roman world. Chapters cover Roman law, Greek and Roman philosophy and religion, Judea as a Roman province, and the First Jewish Revolt against Rome. Section 3, "Jesus and the Gospels," begins by illuminating aspects of Jesus's ministry, death, and resurrection and introduces readers to the canonical and noncanonical gospels. Following a lengthy review of Jesus's mortal ministry in light of biblical and Restoration scripture are chapters on atonement theologies, economics in the first century, and a geographic survey of Jesus's ministry.

Section 4, "The Apostle Paul, General Epistles, and Revelation," devotes much attention to the life and letters of the apostle Paul and discusses the remaining writings of the New Testament. This is followed by "New Testament Issues and Contexts," with chapters pertaining to women, family and marriage, clothing, worship, baptism, nonverbal communication, and prostration as they relate to the New Testament. Section 6, "The Text of the New Testament," examines this book of scripture from a variety of perspectives. In addition to surveying the Joseph Smith Translation and tracing how the New Testament text is employed in Restoration scripture, the chapters also cover textual criticism, the King James translation, and the Greek text underlying the King James New Testament. The concluding section, "After the New Testament," deals with early Christianity in the post–New Testament period and the canonization of the New Testament.

Given the breadth and depth of this volume, there is something for anyone who wants to gain a deeper understanding of the texts and background of the New Testament. While employing academic scholarship, this wide-ranging collection by more than three dozen specialists is written for readers who are nonspecialists. Chapters define technical vocabulary and include maps, tables, and images. Also, a list of further readings at the end of most chapters can be consulted for additional sources. As there is nothing quite like this volume for Latter-day Saint students of the New Testament, it is hoped that *New Testament History, Culture, and Society* will be a welcome addition to the personal libraries of those who are seeking a deeper engagement and understanding of the New Testament.

Lincoln H. Blumell, editor

Part 1
Jewish Background of the New Testament

Between the Testaments

The History of Judea between the Testaments of the Bible

Joshua M. Matson

The four centuries that precede the Common Era are known by a variety of names. The Jews refer to this time as the Second Temple period, emphasizing the return of the faith's central sacred space. Protestant Christians often refer to this time as the intertestamental period, acknowledging the interlude between the faith's two primary collections of sacred text. Orthodox Christians and Catholics prefer the deuterocanonical period, highlighting the production and acceptance of additional religious texts such as the Apocrypha. In recent years, some Christians have also named it the Four Hundred Silent Years, suggesting a lack of prophetic activity between the prophet Malachi and the New Testament apostles. The varied names of this period serve as a fitting introduction to a time that attempted to bridge gaps in the historical and religious record but was fraught with division.

The biblical record reveals little concerning the events of these four centuries. Only the books of Ezra, Nehemiah, Haggai, Zechariah, and Malachi are explicitly contemporaneous with events following the Babylonian exile. Malachi, composed around 420 BC, completes the record of the Old Testament, leaving a considerable gap of commentary on the political, social, and religious developments in the time between the conclusion of the Old Testament and the beginning of the New Testament. While various historical sources shed additional light on the history of this period in Judea, recent discoveries such as the Dead Sea Scrolls and a renewed appreciation and acceptance for noncanonical Jewish literature have added a considerable amount of information pertaining to the Jewish history that preceded the

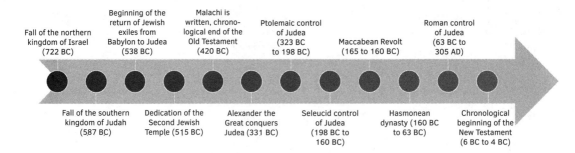

Table 1. Timeline between the Old and New Testaments.

events of the New Testament. From these historical sources, we can bridge the gap between the testaments of the Bible.

The Period of Destruction and Exile (721–538 BC)

Prior to the destruction of the northern Israelites in 722 BC and the exile of Jews from Judah in 587 BC, divisions existed among the Israelite people. The books of 1–2 Kings and 2 Chronicles preserve the history of this division between the northern kingdom of Israel and the southern kingdom of Judah. These kingdoms divided themselves along lines of political, social, economic, and religious ideologies. Beginning in the late tenth century BC, tension abounded as these separate kingdoms attempted to navigate the shifting geopolitical landscape of Israel. While the southern kingdom of Judah outlasted the northern kingdom by a century and a half, ultimately both fell to domineering world powers that imposed on them their forms of conquest. These conquests began the diaspora, or the displacement of Jewish people from the land of Judea.

The Assyrian conquest of the northern kingdom of Israel is well documented in the histories of the Old Testament (2 Kings 15:29 and 17:3–6) and in Assyrian inscriptions. Conquering Israel in 722 BC, the Assyrians destroyed Samaria, the capital of the northern kingdom, and imposed their method of exile on the Israelites by scattering nearly all the inhabitants of the ten northern tribes throughout the vast Assyrian Empire. A mass return of these Israelite exiles to Judea following the fall of the Assyrian Empire is not found among the biblical or historical record, and these tribes are often designated as the lost ten tribes of Israel in later religious texts. These lost tribes dispersed themselves throughout the world in many ways in the following centuries. The Assyrian conquest of the kingdom of Israel foreshadowed the events of the Babylonian conquest of the kingdom of Judah a century later.

The Babylonian conquest of the southern kingdom of Judah is similarly documented in the histories and prophetic literature of the Old Testament (2 Kings 25:8–12; 2 Chronicles 36:17–21) and the Babylonian Chronicles. Jeremiah and Ezekiel are the primary prophetic commentators of the events that are described in the histories of 2 Kings and 2 Chronicles. The Babylonian model of conquest differed from that of the Assyrians, but not radically. Instead of scattering the inhabitants of Judah throughout the empire, the Babylonians focused on exiling waves of Judahite elites over a twenty-year period. First in 606 BC and again in 587 BC, Babylonians carried members of the priestly and royal families of Judah away into captivity. The captivity of 587 BC differed from its predecessor in that the Babylonians employed a greater level of destruction by razing the walls of Jerusalem, burning the city, and destroying the temple. In response to the destruction of the city and their central place of worship, the people of Judah in exile remained largely intact and were left to reflect on unfulfilled promises, mourn the loss of their promised land, and devise new ways in which to continue to practice their religion.

While the biblical record focuses primarily on the captivity of the inhabitants of the northern and southern kingdoms, the non-elites who remained in the land of Judea after 587 BC are almost completely lost in the narrative of exile (2 Kings 25:12). The peasantry and those situated in villages and towns throughout the countryside of Judea faced many of the same challenges as the exiles. Left to themselves for a half century, these inhabitants devised their own mechanisms to cope with unfulfilled promises and developed new practices for their religion. These decisions would become a focal point in divisions in the period following the exile and in the New Testament (Ezra 4:4; 9:1).

The experiences of the elites taken into Babylon dominate the narrative of exile found in both biblical and historical records. Babylonian traditions heavily influenced exiled elites' responses to the loss of their cultural, religious, and political identity. Because exiles could meet in congregations in Babylon, local synagogues appear to have replaced the temple as the central place of worship. Aramaic replaced Hebrew as the primary language spoken by the people (Ezra 4:7). The Jewish calendar was replaced by the Babylonian. New narratives, including some found in the additional Old Testament writings named the Apocrypha, focus on individuals faithfully living the Mosaic law in exile rather than dwelling in a land of promise (see especially Daniel and Esther). These changes occurred in almost every Jewish community throughout the Babylonian empire.

Jewish communities also held vehemently to the traditions that made them a peculiar people. These communities attributed their failure to remain faithful to God as the primary factor in their captivity. The communities of exiles instituted a religious reform to combat a similar captive fate in the future. These reforms are made manifest in the records produced by the returned exiles. Everyday life appears to have been viewed through the lens of exile, and the religious perspective of the southern kingdom of Judah focused on returning to the genesis of Jewish culture, religion, and politics. Exclusive monotheism (Nehemiah 9:6), a renewed adherence to the Mosaic law (Nehemiah 8:2–18), an abhorrence for intercultural marriage (i.e., exogamy, Ezra 9), and a greater commitment to the institutions of the Aaronite priesthood and the Davidic monarchy became trademarks of Jewish identity shortly after the exiles' return from Babylon. These ideologies likely developed during the period of exile but flourished once the Jewish communities returned to Judea.

Returning from Exile and Judea under Persian Rule (538–331 BC)

The Persian Empire approached conquered peoples differently than the Assyrian and Babylonian Empires did. When the Persians defeated the Babylonians in the mid-sixth century BC, they allowed those exiled under Babylonian rule to return to their original lands and maintain a degree of political, cultural, and religious autonomy. In 538 BC the Persian king Cyrus the Great authorized the rebuilding of the Jerusalem temple and allowed the sacred vessels for the temple to be returned to the city. Coupled with the autonomy that they were granted by the Babylonians, some Jewish communities of the Babylonian exile began to return to Jerusalem, although many remained in Babylon despite Cyrus's edict (Ezra 1:4–6). These communities intended to carry out their reforms in the promised land free from the divisions and strife that had plagued them before the exile. Unsuspectingly, however, they found the land they were returning to inhabited by peoples who had different religious, cultural, and political expectations from their own (Ezra 9:1). The reestablishment of these reformed Jewish communities would take more than a hundred years to be realized.

The return of the Jewish communities from exile proved divisive almost immediately. The ʿam haggôlâ (people of the deportation/exile) desired to distinguish themselves from the people they found in the land. The ʿam haʾaretz (people of the land) inhabited the countryside and villages in Judea and were the descendants of the peasantry that remained in the land during the Babylonian exile (2 Kings 25:12). The "adversaries of Judah and Benjamin" (Ezra 4:1–3) settled in the parts of the old northern kingdom of Israel following the Assyrian exile and may have had a connection with the Samaritans. The Edomites were the descendants of Esau who moved into Judea following the Babylonian exile because of political pressure from neighboring kingdoms. The people of the exile, being the descendants of those who originally composed the noble and priestly classes, felt entitled to the land and positions of leadership in the newly autonomous region. These elites progressively imposed themselves as the new aristocracy.

The exiles who returned to their promised land moved quickly to regain control of Judea from the people of the land, the adversaries of Judah and Benjamin, and the Edomites. The introduction of new religious and political practices developed in Babylon by the people of the exile and the syncretism of religion and culture by the people already in Judea resulted in contention. Different cultural histories also contributed to this outcome. Haggai, Zechariah, Ezra, and Nehemiah preserve partial histories of this period from the perspective of the returnees from the exile. These records recount the disputes that led to the eventual dividing of Judea into three distinctive regions during the fifth century BC. The people of the land remained in the villages and countryside of Judea as subjects to the people of the exile and vocally opposed the political and religious reforms instituted by the returned exiles, including the building of the Jerusalem temple (Ezra 4:4–5). The adversaries of Judah and Benjamin inhabited the vacated northern territories of Ephraim and Manasseh. Later generations renamed this land Samaria, after the central city of the northern kingdom, and named the people Samaritans. Like the reference to "Samaritans" in 2 Kings 17:29, it is un-

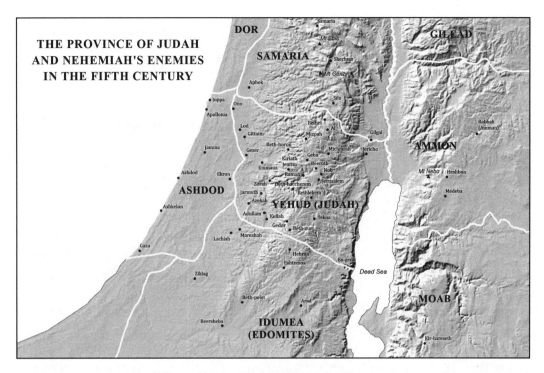

Map of postexile Judea. Map by ThinkSpatial.

certain if this is a reference to the same group discussed in the New Testament, as the term is employed to describe both the inhabitants of Samaria and members of the religious group. While the origination and connection of the Samaritans that appear in the New Testament with these settlers in Samaria is unclear, the tensions exhibited at this early period, as well as confrontations discussed below, illustrate why there would be great animosity between Jews and Samaritans in Jesus's day. Making the cultural landscape even more diverse were the Edomites who inhabited the southern region of Judea, which was later named Idumea (Ezekiel 36:5). Ultimately, the people of the exile regained control of the land of Judah and the city of Jerusalem, but only after a lengthy period of reconstruction and consolidation.

After gaining control of the region, the people of the exile focused on rebuilding the temple in Jerusalem. The books of Haggai and Zechariah were written during this period, while Ezra recounts these events from a later perspective. These accounts are fragmentary and unclear on the chronology of rebuilding the temple. The Jerusalem community, under the political direction of the governor Zerubbabel (a descendant of the old royal house of David) and the religious direction of the high priest Jeshua, rebuilt the altars and structure of the temple, establishing Jerusalem as the center of the religious hierarchy. This temple was only a shell of the former one built by Solomon, but its establishment centered the religious activities of Judea in Jerusalem for the returned exiles. The dedication of the temple in 515 BC brought religious centrality back to Jerusalem (Nehemiah 12:27–13:3). After the mysterious disappearance of Zerubbabel, Jeshua reappropriated the office of high priest into a central political figure appointed by the ruling nation, creating a small priestly temple-state that received autonomy from the Persian Empire. These events created religious centrality in Jerusalem, but the city remained a place of insecurity with voids in religious and political law.

After nearly a century of reinstatement in Judea, the people of the exile continued to wrestle with the other inhabitants of Judea to restore Jerusalem to its former glory. Aware of the instability in the city and region, Persian kings appointed Nehemiah and Ezra to return to Jerusalem to usher in the restoration of the social, political, cultural, and religious community that had once thrived within its walls. While the sequence of events in the fifth century BC is still unclear, Ezra and Nehemiah sought to reestablish political and religious stability. Strict adherence to the law of Moses, the paying of tithes, Sabbath day observance, and laws against intermarriage with those outside the community were among the laws instituted during this time, and they played a prominent role in the history of the Jewish people throughout the period. Additionally, Ezra, acting as a scribe and priest within the Jerusalem community, initiated the study of Torah, or the Law contained in the first five books of the Old Testament, ushering in a distinct period of studying religious texts among the Jewish people.

Jewish communities took various approaches to authoritative religious texts following the exile. Although all Jewish communities at the time accepted the Torah, they disputed the authoritative nature of other Jewish texts. Throughout the Second Temple period, authoritative religious texts (primarily the Torah) played an important role in shaping Jewish communities and their interpretation of the Law, with each Jewish community maintaining a different opinion of what constituted authoritative scripture. However, groups like the Samaritans interpreted these authoritative texts very differently than the Jews in Jerusalem did. Unlike other Jewish communities of the Second Temple period, the Samaritans adhered only to their own version of the Torah (known as the Samaritan Pentateuch) with divergent traditions. One such tradition was the belief that the properly designated location for a central place of worship was Mount Gerizim, not Mount Ebal or, as later dictated, Jerusalem (see Samaritan Pentateuch, Deuteronomy 27:4). This belief was further manifested at this time by the building of a temple. While concern about the proper interpretation of authoritative texts elevated tensions in Judea during the time of Malachi (420 BC), it served as a primary indicator of each Jewish community's identity during the Hellenistic period. Judea maintained near-complete autonomy throughout the remainder of the dominance of the Persian Empire in the eastern Mediterranean area. Religious communities took advantage of this autonomy.

The biblical and historical records are silent regarding Judea and the events of the next century and a half. Although the Persians engaged in a variety of political and cultural entanglements, the inhabitants of Judea were primarily unaffected by them. This autonomy would be maintained throughout the Persian period but diminished with the overthrowing of the Persian Empire by Alexander the Great and the introduction of Hellenism to Judea.

The Hellenization of Judea (331–164 BC)

As mentioned above, the biblical record is silent about events that occurred after the fifth century BC, requiring scholars to look to other sources to create a history of the period. The writings of Flavius Josephus are one prominent source scholars refer to when discussing the history of the Second Temple period. Josephus was a Roman Jew who lived during the first century AD. A political diplomat, military general, and historian, Josephus wrote extensively about the history of the Jewish people. While Josephus wrote other works, *Jewish Antiquities* and *Jewish War* are valuable histories that preserve information about the time between the Old and New Testaments. *Antiquities* preserves a history of the Jewish people from the creation of the world to the days of Gessius Florus, the Roman procurator of Judea from AD 64 to AD 66. Most of the early chapters of this work are drawn from the history presented in the Old Testament. *Jewish War* overlaps with *Antiquities* and preserves a war history of the Jewish people from the rule of the Seleucid king Antiochus IV Epiphanes (175–164 BC) to the aftermath of the destruction of the Jewish temple (AD 70). Many of the things that are known to scholars today about the intertestamental period are based on the histories of Josephus and the Maccabean histories included in the Apocrypha.

Alexander the Great rapidly conquered the Persian Empire through military campaigns between 334 and 324 BC. Alexander gained control of the region of Judea between 333 and 331 BC with a series of campaigns in the western border of the Persian Empire.[1] Alexander is credited with attempting to unify his conquered empire with the spread of Hellenism (Greek culture and language). The spread of Hellenism through the region of Judea, and to Jews throughout the diaspora, marked a period of shifting ideals and manifestations within Judaism.

Hellenism spread throughout Jewish communities in various ways. Greek became the preferred language of the elite throughout the empire, although Hebrew and Aramaic remained in general use among the inhabitants of Judea. The Hebrew scriptures were translated into Greek in Egypt and utilized throughout the empire. Hellenistic structures like the gymnasium and the stadium became the social centers of communities, even in Jerusalem. Some Jewish inhabitants removed the distinguishing mark of circumcision through a variety of methods, including an operation known as *epispasm*. Others, including some high priests, took Greek names.[2] Education of elite citizens emphasized Hellenistic culture over traditional Jewish history. Jewish communities adopted and fought against Hellenism to varying degrees. While some communities believed that the adoption of some elements of Hellenistic culture did not weaken Jewish identification, others became outraged and rose in rebellion against it.

The inhabitants of Judea found themselves in a precarious political situation following the death of Alexander the Great in 323 BC. Immediately following his death, Alexander's generals divided the conquered lands among themselves. These generals began dynasties that determined the destinies of various lands throughout the empire. The Ptolemies in Egypt and the Seleucids in Syria-Mesopotamia governed the people living in Judea for almost two hundred years. Originally, the Ptolemies ruled Judea. Under Ptolemaic control, the inhabitants of Judea experienced a change in imperial protocol. While the Persians had allowed a great degree of autonomy to the people of Judea, the Ptolemies constructed a large bureaucracy that wielded considerable political power. On the whole, Jews in Judea and Egypt flourished under Ptolemaic control and had a certain degree of autonomy.

Located on the border between these two dynasties, Judea observed battles between the Ptolemies and the Seleucids that penetrated community dynamics. These battles forced individuals and communities to take sides, hoping that their side would prevail and reward them for their loyalty. High priests, now the preeminent position of authority and power among the Jewish people in Judea, aligned themselves with outside forces for political gain, appointment, and advancement. In 198 BC the Seleucids wrestled control of Judea away from the Ptolemies.

Under Seleucid rule, the Jewish communities in Judea experienced a lessening of religious and political autonomy. While the Seleucids approached ruling their territories through cooperation with established elites, these elites often failed to cooperate with those who had opinions differing from those within the Seleucid hierarchy. In Judea the Seleucids provided financial and political incentives to the elites of high priestly families in exchange for loyalty to Syrian rulers and the implementation of hellenization. As individuals obtained the position of high priest by bribery, rather than lineage, and Jewish communities disputed the appropriate degree of hellenization allowed by the Jewish law, considerable divisions arose among the Judean people. The Maccabean histories, found in the Apocrypha as 1 and 2 Maccabees, preserve an account of the events surrounding this period.

According to the Maccabean narrative, the ascension of Antiochus IV Epiphanes to the throne of Seleucid Syria marked the decisive moment in the divisive atmosphere in Judea between Jews and Hellenistic rulers. Around 175 BC Antiochus raised taxes on the inhabitants of Judea to fund his failed military campaigns into Egypt. Additionally, Jason, a highly hellenized Jew, successfully bribed Antiochus to appoint him to the position of high priest. Three years later, Menelaus, a highly hellenized Jew devoid of priestly lineage, acquired the position from Jason. In 167 BC Antiochus collaborated with the hellenized Jewish elite in Jerusalem to convert the Jerusalem temple into a pagan shrine. Some sources, including 1 and 2 Maccabees, suggest that Antiochus instituted these changes to force Greek culture, religion, and language on the inhabitants of Judea (1 Maccabees 1:10–15). Scholars of the Second Temple period debate Antiochus's motives and the extent of his forced reform. However, the results of Antiochus's decisions are undisputed because they led to a revolution in Judea against Hellenistic rule.

A Period of Revolt and Restitution (165–160 BC)

Mattathias, a priest from outside Jerusalem, together with his five sons, led the revolt against Hellenistic rule. Employing guerrilla-style tactics, the rebels attempted to drive the Seleucids out of Judea and reinstate political, cultural, and religious autonomy to the region (1 Maccabees 2:1–14). Mattathias and his supporters initiated their assaults on the villages and towns of Judea in 167/166 BC. This tactic isolated Jerusalem from the rest of Judea. Mattathias left control of the revolt in the hands of his sons when he died in 166/165 BC.

Judas, one of Mattathias's sons who was given the new name of Maccabeus or Maccabee ("fighter" or "hammer"), became the primary leader of the rebellion (1 Maccabees 3:1–9). Under Judas's leadership, the revolutionaries defeated the Seleucid forces near the city of Jerusalem in 164 BC.[3] Following their victory, they easily regained control of the city. Almost immediately, Judas's followers focused on purifying and rededicating the temple in Jerusalem. Future generations commemorated the events of this rededication with the festival of Hanukkah. Around the same time the revolutionaries gained control of Jerusalem, Antiochus died, igniting a succession crisis in the Seleucid Empire. The Jews took advantage of the political instability, and what began as a fight for religious freedom became an all-out war for Jewish independence.[4]

After restoring the temple in Jerusalem and appointing a high priest whom they believed to be the rightful successor to the position (a decision that would further divide other Jewish communities who did not agree), Judas and his followers focused on forcing the Seleucids out of Judea. Judas marshaled a series of successful military campaigns throughout Judea in the following years. In 160 BC, however, Judas was killed by Seleucid forces, creating a leadership crisis among the rebelling Jews. Disoriented by their defeat, Judas's forces retreated to the countryside of Judea. The Seleucids quickly regained control of Jerusalem and appointed Alcimus, a highly hellenized Jew outside the lineage of the high priestly families, to the position of high priest. The revolutionaries regrouped and appointed Jonathan, one of Judas's brothers, as their new leader. In 159 BC Alcimus died, and Jonathan led a successful campaign to regain Jerusalem.[5]

While Jonathan ruled as a general for the ensuing years, in 152 BC he tactfully negotiated with the Seleucid rulers and obtained an appointment to be high priest in Jerusalem. The official recognition of Jonathan by the Seleucids began a period of autonomous rule like that enjoyed under the Persians. Descendants of the family of Mattathias officiated in the role of both political leader and high priest for over a century, creating the Hasmonean dynasty.[6] Although Jonathan was not from a high priestly family line, he convinced the Jewish people that he and his posterity would maintain the position of high priest only until the advent of another prophet who could successfully identify a rightful successor (1 Maccabees 14:41). This change in religious practice, coupled with the divisions throughout Judaism over Hellenism and the revolt against it, led to the creation of various Jewish factions, including the Pharisees, Sadducees, and Essenes.[7] These groups constantly contended with one another over religious and political matters. Some of these religious factions, including the community that authored some of the Dead Sea Scrolls, moved away from Jerusalem to establish their own religious communities, free from the rule of the Hasmoneans.

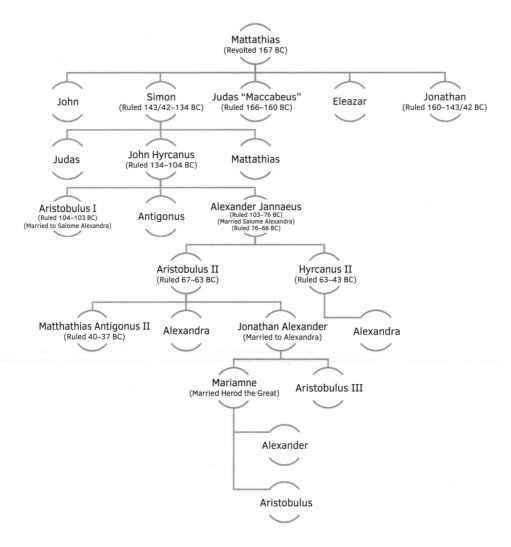

Table 2. Hasmonean family tree.

The Hasmonean Dynasty (160–63 BC)

Political instability in the Seleucid Empire ensured that the beginnings of the Hasmonean dynasty were anything but ideal and smooth. The Seleucids engaged in various internal battles between claimants to the throne. Although Jonathan and his family had been granted autonomous authority in Judea, the Seleucid claimants persuaded him to participate in numerous military campaigns to maintain that autonomy.[8] During one of these campaigns, those antagonistic to the Hasmoneans and the claimant they supported killed Jonathan, leaving the Jewish state without a leader. The Jerusalem assembly appointed Simon, the last remaining brother of Judas, as ethnarch (ruler of the people) and high priest.[9]

Simon continued the campaign for Judean independence. One of the claimants to the Seleucid throne, Demetrius II, made concessions with Simon and the Jewish people in 142 BC in exchange for their support in obtaining control of the empire. Complete Jewish independence was among these concessions. In 141 BC Simon led a successful campaign against one of the final remaining Greek and highly hellenized Jewish communities at the Acra fortress, marking the beginning of Jewish independence (1 Maccabees 13:52–14:15).

Jewish independence preceded the restitution of the Jewish state to lands that were part of Davidic and Solomonic kingdoms in earlier times. Simon's son-in-law orchestrated Simon's assassination in 135 BC, leaving the throne of Judea and the position of high priest in the control of Simon's son John Hyrcanus. Although Antiochus VII, the ruler of the Seleucids, attempted to regain some of the lands the Hasmoneans had captured during the revolts, Hyrcanus negotiated a deal with the Seleucids to maintain autonomy in Judea in exchange for tribute payments for the cities in their control. This agreement ensured that Hyrcanus reigned for over twenty years and allowed him to lead military campaigns to restore the borders of the old kingdom.[10] Among these campaigns, Hyrcanus annexed Idumea in the south and persuaded the inhabitants to convert to Judaism. He also moved to the north and acquired Galilee and Samaria. In Samaria, he destroyed the temple on Mount Gerizim, causing a final divisive blow between the Samaritans and the Jews. Hyrcanus died in 104 BC, leaving the throne to his son Aristobulus I.[11]

Aristobulus I ruled over Judea for only a year but changed the Hasmonean state for the remainder of the dynasty. After gaining control of Judea, Aristobulus continued to push the boundaries of the Hasmonean state toward those that existed during the kingdoms of David

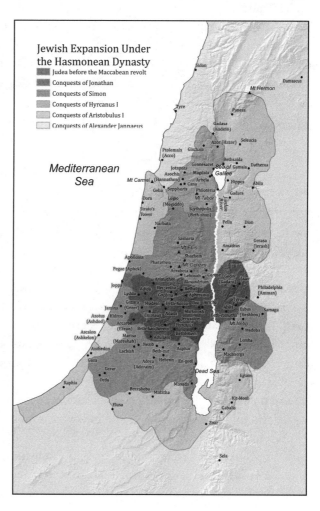

Map of the expansion of the Hasmonean Empire.
Map by ThinkSpatial.

and Solomon. Further, Aristobulus took upon himself the title of king.[12] Previous rulers in the dynasty had avoided the title for a variety of reasons, but now the rulers would be known as both priests and kings. This development reflected and molded Jewish expectations of the coming messianic age and proved divisive among the various Jewish factions throughout Judea.

Aristobulus's heir to the throne, his brother Alexander Jannaeus, furthered the divide in Judea during his twenty-seven year reign. Jannaeus continued to expand the borders of the Hasmonean state, attaining the borders of the earlier kingdom of Solomon, and took upon himself the title of king. Jannaeus faced a rebellion from the Pharisees and other Jewish factions because of his support for the Sadducees and his adoption of many Hellenistic practices. These internal conflicts soon spilled over into civil war.[13] The opponents of Jannaeus solicited the help of Demetrius III, a rival to the Seleucid throne, and engaged in a lengthy series of battles. Jannaeus ultimately prevailed and executed eight hundred of his opponents during a victory feast in Jerusalem. Following Jannaeus's death in 76 BC, his wife Alexandra Jannaea Salome became queen. This form of succession, from husband to wife, resembled that of other Hellenistic kingdoms.[14] The dynasty that started as a defense of religious freedom and independence against Hellenistic rule now resembled Hellenism itself.

Salome reigned masterfully from 76 to 67 BC and facilitated further divisions among the Judeans. She shifted the religious alliances of the crown and aligned herself with the Pharisees, a move that angered the Sadducees, who had been supported by her husband. Salome's support for the Pharisees included placing them among the ruling class of the society. Further, Salome installed her son Hyrcanus II to the position of high priest and expanded the power of the Sanhedrin, a ruling body of religious leaders. This move granted the Sanhedrin power to pronounce judgment in religious matters that had previously been reserved for the high priest. Salome's death signaled the beginning of a civil war between Hyrcanus II and his brother Aristobulus II and began the decline of the Hasmonean dynasty.[15]

The civil war between Hyrcanus and Aristobulus introduced the Romans into political matters in Judea. Aristobulus almost immediately seized the throne from Hyrcanus. After the bitter takeover, Hyrcanus fled to Petra and allied himself with Rome's eastern opponents, the Nabateans. Convinced that his brother would continue to pursue him until his death, Hyrcanus led a joint assault on Jerusalem with his newfound allies. During the fierce battle, both Hyrcanus and Aristobulus appealed to Rome for intervention.[16] The Romans conquered the remnants of the Seleucid Empire in the seventies BC and began to expand throughout the eastern Mediterranean. Rome intervened and expelled the Nabateans, opening the way for Aristobulus to again prevail over his brother. Eventually, the Roman general Pompey interrogated both brothers to decide who should reign. Aristobulus and his supporters made numerous fateful mistakes, so the Romans sided with Hyrcanus and assigned him to the positions of high priest and ethnarch, revoking the title of king and taking control of the Hasmonean kingdom.[17] Again, the inhabitants of Judea found themselves under the control of a foreign power.

Roman Rule through the Herodian Dynasty (63 BC–AD 70)

Roman rule over Judea began in a way that divided the Jewish people from their new overseers religiously and geographically. Following the intervention of the Romans in the civil war between Hyrcanus and Aristobulus, Pompey explored the Temple Mount in Jerusalem. Curiously, Pompey visited the holy of holies, which he had heard was void of any cultic objects.[18] Jewish communities joined together to express their anger over the insensitivity of this Roman ruler. Additionally, although Hyrcanus II ruled over Jerusalem and the temple-state, the Romans divided the remaining lands that had been part of the Hasmonean kingdom and restored independence to each region. In this realignment, the Samaritans, Idumeans, and other Jewish and non-Jewish regions of the eastern Mediterranean were placed under the control of the Roman proconsul of Syria.

The realignment of the region lasted through the life of Pompey. Following Pompey's death in 48 BC, Hyrcanus II obtained the support of Julius Caesar. Caesar appointed Antipater, the trusted advisor of Hyrcanus, to the position of governor of Judea and reconfirmed the position of high priest upon Hyrcanus with added political powers. Furthermore, Caesar returned lands that had been realigned by Pompey to the jurisdiction of Judea. For the remainder of Caesar's reign, the remnants of the Hasmoneans controlled Judea with little intervention from the Romans.[19]

Caesar's death in 44 BC triggered another period of instability throughout the Mediterranean. In Judea, Aristobulus II's son Antigonus seized the opportunity to take back control of the region and establish an independent kingdom. Antigonus allied with Rome's primary opponent in the East, the Parthians, and attacked Hyrcanus in Judea. After capturing Jerusalem, the forces of Antigonus killed Antipater and imprisoned Hyrcanus. Antigonus proclaimed himself king of Judea and attempted to reestablish the autonomy of the Hasmonean dynasty. However, the Romans appointed Herod, one of Antipater's sons, to establish their own dynasty over Judea.[20]

Herod stands as an example of the complex worlds of Judea in the final century before Christ. Herod's family is situated at the crossroads of the old and the new in many ways, bridging divides and creating new ones. Herod presented his ancestry as deriving from the tribe of Judah and the Babylonian exile. His grandfather and father were Idumeans and converts to Judaism. Both acquired social status and position in the Hasmonean state under Salome and Hyrcanus II. Herod's mother came from a Nabatean family that likely aligned themselves with Hyrcanus in his campaign to regain the throne from his brother. Herod married Mariamne I, the granddaughter of both Aristobulus II and Hyrcanus II. Herod's marriage tied him directly to the Hasmonean royal line. Ultimately, Herod's father, Antipater, appointed Herod governor of Jerusalem in 47 BC. The assault by Antigonus in 44 BC limited Herod's original appointment, but political allegiances reinstated him.

The Romans grew tired of the Hasmonean struggles to regain autonomous power in Judea and looked for a suitable replacement. Herod's knowledge of the political system of the Romans and the Jews, as well as his ability to maintain both systems, made him an ideal candidate for appointment. Herod's lineage, however, prevented him from being accepted by the Jews as a legitimate heir to the position of high priest. Instead, Rome proclaimed Herod king of Judea, Galilee, and Perea in 40 BC, and together they recaptured Jerusalem from Antigonus and the Parthians in 37 BC. Herod's appointment was not an autonomous kingship, but the role of a client king. Herod and his descendants occupied such positions in Judea until almost AD 100.

Herod's rule over Judea mirrored that of the Hasmoneans and those that ruled an independent Judea before them. The support Herod received from the overseeing Romans distinguished him from the earlier kingdoms. Herod expanded the borders of Judea to the size that had been obtained by the Hasmoneans. Herod fortified these borders by erecting fortresses throughout the region. Additionally, he initiated an extensive building project to rebuild the Tomb of the Patriarchs and the capital of Samaria and to construct new cities. Herod's renovations to the Jerusalem temple returned the sacred edifice to the glory and prestige that it had enjoyed in the days of Solomon. Herod also engaged in construction projects that were clearly Hellenistic. In Jerusalem, Herod constructed a theater, an amphitheater, a hippodrome, temples to foreign deities, and a golden eagle above the gate to the temple. The Jews in Judea oscillated in their support for their complicated client king.

Herod executed laws and judgment in erratic ways to preserve his position of power. He ordered that Aristobulus III, a high priest of Jerusalem and the brother of his wife Mariamne, be drowned so that he could appoint a less established family to the high priesthood. This appointment, and the consistent appointing and disposing of high priests, ensured loyalty to Herod and prevented the possibility of revolt by the temple-state. Similarly, he executed his wife Mariamne and two of her sons to prevent familial conflict between the children he fathered from his ten wives that could jeopardize his authority in the eyes of the Romans. Ultimately, following Herod's death in 4 BC, the Romans left the region of Judea in control of his descendants.

Herod's posterity who ruled over Judea play a central role in the narrative of the New Testament. Rome appointed Herod's son Archelaus ethnarch of Judea. Archelaus's brother, Antipas, became the tetrarch (ruler of a quarter) of Galilee. Philip, the half brother of Archelaus and Antipas, became the tetrarch of the gentile region of Iturea on the eastern side of the Jordan River. The history of New Testament Judea predominantly occurs in the areas ruled by these three sons of Herod. Archelaus's inability to control the region of Judea in a manner similar to that of Archelaus's father led to his removal in AD 6. Instead of appointing another ethnarch, Rome installed a prefect of equestrian rank over Judea. Pontius Pilate served as the fifth prefect over Judea. Shortly after his rule, the title of governor was changed to that of procurator and the Jews were again limited to controlling the temple-state while others controlled the political landscape of Judea.

Two of Herod's grandsons appear prominently in Judea throughout the New Testament narrative. Rome exiled Antipas in AD 37 and appointed Agrippa I, Herod's grandson by Mariamne, first as heir to Philip's tetrarchy and then in AD 39 expanded his rule over Antipas's tetrarchy. Additionally, Rome allotted the expanse of Judea to mirror the borders of previous kingdoms. Following Agrippa I's death in AD 44, Rome reinstated their own rulers over Judea because Agrippa II was too young to rule in his father's stead. In AD 50 the Romans appointed Agrippa II as overseer of the kingdom of Chalcis in the north. Additionally, the Romans appointed Agrippa II as high priest, whereupon he deposed the Sadducee high priest Ananus, adding to the tumultuous tension between Jews and Romans that would eventually erupt in rebellion. These revolts ultimately led to the temple's destruction in AD 70 and the removal of the Jews from Judea.

Conclusion

A brief overview of the history of the Second Temple period highlights that this was a time of divisiveness within Judaism. Jewish communities of this period were at odds with those who ruled over them. These tensions, especially against the Hellenistic rulers that followed an age of autonomy under Persian rule, grew as Jewish communities experienced constant fluctuation between autonomy and oppression. Additionally, Jews frequently found themselves at odds with one another. From the earliest days of their return from exile, the Jews of this period struggled to create a cohesive identity, holding to traditions and adaptations that were at the core of their uniqueness, no group wanting to sacrifice its identity at the cost of another. This history emphasizes the consistent attempts made by Jewish communities and outside leaders to bridge the divides that existed in the social, cultural, political, and religious aspects of their time. It also emphasizes that while attempts were made to bridge these divides, those bridges frequently were adorned with the peculiarities of those in power at the cost of those who were not. Although the biblical sources for this period are scarce, the historical record reveals that seeds planted within the Old Testament history grew in adversity and sprouted roots of discord and contention among the Jews that span throughout the text of the New Testament.

⥲

Joshua M. Matson is a PhD candidate in religions of western antiquity at Florida State University.

Further Reading

Brown, S. Kent, and Richard Neitzel Holzapfel. *Between the Testaments: From Malachi to Matthew*. Salt Lake City: Deseret Book, 2002.

Goodman, Martin. "Jewish History, 331 BCE–135 BCE." In *The Jewish Annotated New Testament*, edited by Amy-Jill Levine and Marc Zvi Brettler, 507–13. New York: Oxford, 2011.

Grabbe, Lester L. *A History of the Jews and Judaism in the Second Temple Period*, vol. 4. New York: Bloomsbury Academic, 2006.

Holzapfel, Richard Neitzel, Eric D. Huntsman, and Thomas A. Wayment. *Jesus Christ and the World of the New Testament*. Salt Lake City: Deseret Book, 2006.

Notes

1. Josephus, *Antiquities* 11.6.
2. Josephus, *Antiquities* 12.5.

3. Josephus, *Jewish War* 1.1.

4. Josephus, *Antiquities* 13.7.

5. Josephus, *Jewish War* 1.2.

6. The origin of the name *Hasmonean* is a point of uncertainty among scholars. The term originates in the histories of Josephus and may not have been used prior to his written histories. For Josephus, the name pays homage to an ancestor of Mattathias named Hašmônay, who was a descendant of Joiarib (see *Jewish War* 1.36 and *Antiquities* 11.111 and 20.190, 238). This name would be significant since it would tie Mattathias and his children into a priestly line of the Aaronite priesthood. An alternative scholarly opinion is that the name *Hasmonean* is linked to the village of Hesbon (see Joshua 15:27), making the reference perhaps a link to Mattathias's ancestral home. A final opinion among scholars is that the name *Hasmonean* is taken from the Hebrew "Ha Simeon," a reference to the tribe of Simeon, one of the twelve tribes of Israel.

7. Josephus, *Antiquities* 18.1.

8. Josephus, *Antiquities* 13.5.

9. Josephus, *Antiquities* 13.6.

10. Josephus, *Antiquities* 13.8.

11. Josephus, *Antiquities* 13.10.

12. Josephus, *Antiquities* 13.11.

13. Josephus, *Antiquities* 13.13.

14. Josephus, *Antiquities* 13.16.

15. Josephus, *Antiquities* 14.1.

16. Josephus, *Antiquities* 14.3.

17. Josephus, *Jewish War* 1.6.

18. Josephus, *Jewish War* 1.7.

19. Josephus, *Antiquities* 14.8.

20. Josephus, *Antiquities* 14.9.

2

The Law of Moses

An Overview

Daniel L. Belnap

During the last week of his life, Christ was confronted by a group of Jewish authorities who asked him, "Master, which is the great commandment in the law?" (Matthew 22:36). Christ's answer, that one should love God with all one's heart, soul, and might (Deuteronomy 6:5), as well as one's neighbor as oneself (Leviticus 19:18), was then followed by the assertion "On these two commandments hang all the law and the prophets" (Matthew 22:40). Clearly, in Christ's day the law of Moses was regarded as providing crucial instruction regarding one's behavior both with one's fellow man and with God, and as such was a subject of much interest. In fact, references to the law can be found throughout the New Testament, not only in the teachings of Christ but also in the Pauline writings where there is considerable engagement with it.

For many modern readers of the New Testament, what constituted the law and what it exactly was is not altogether clear. For example, the law is periodically associated with the "tradition of the elders" (Matthew 15:2; Mark 7:3, 5) even though Christ separates the two, and this association can create some confusion.[1] Moreover, because the law was "fulfilled" with the resurrection of Christ (3 Nephi 15:4–5), there is the assumption that the law no longer has any significance or meaning and therefore does not need to be understood. While there might be some merit to these claims, complete ignorance of the law almost certainly ensures that one will not be able to fully appreciate, or even comprehend, most of the Old Testament and a large portion of the New Testament. With that in mind, this opening chapter seeks to provide an introduction and overview of the law of Moses so that one may more fully appreciate its significance and be better equipped to understand its use in the New Testament. Furthermore, even though the law has been superseded by the law of the gospel, since it served as a "schoolmaster" (Galatians 3:24), a knowledge of the law can still offer insights into the manner by which God interacts with his children.

The Law of Moses and Biblical Redaction

Perhaps the single most significant insight about the law at the time of the New Testament is that it was not a monolithic, unified text or system but rather a cobbling together of a number of older legal and cultic traditions. The law had its origin in the Exodus tradition of ancient Israel and is spread across the books of Exodus, Leviticus, Numbers, and Deuteronomy. Though one can find reference to God's law prior to this event (see Genesis 26:5), the first mention of the law associated with Moses is found in Exodus 13:9. The events surrounding this reference recount the first Passover with both Exodus 12 and 13 providing instructions as to how and when it was to be performed. The parallel but distinct set of instructions highlights one of the challenges to Old Testament study: redaction (the process of editing multiple sources) and multiple authors.[2]

Like the Book of Mormon, the Bible in its current form is best understood to consist of original authorial writing as well as redacted text, the latter being earlier biblical text that has been edited or commented on by later editors. But unlike the Book of Mormon, it is not clear who exactly these later editors were. Moreover, we are even unsure who some of the original authors were. The first five books of the Old Testament, for instance, are ascribed to the hand of Moses himself, yet the Deuteronomy epilogue describes Moses in the third person and speaks of him being a prophet unparalleled in all of Israelite history: "And there arose not a prophet since in Israel like unto Moses" (Deuteronomy 34:10). This verse is a clear example that, at the very least, part of Deuteronomy has been edited/redacted at some point, presumably with a fair amount of Israelite history having passed to make such an observation. Since the early twentieth century, biblical scholarship has suggested that there are four primary "schools" that authored the first five biblical books.[3]

The earliest of these sources is designated as "J" because of the prominent use of the divine epithet *Jehovah* (*YHWH* in Hebrew). This source is primarily understood to be narrative in nature, meaning that J recounts the early biblical narratives, highlighting those associated with the covenant.[4] The second source is designated as "E" because of its use of the divine epithet *Elohim* (most often rendered as "God" in the KJV). Like J, E is also narrative in nature, the difference between the two being their supposed origin, with J associated with the southern kingdom of Judah and E associated with the northern kingdom of Israel.[5] The third source is "D," or the Deuteronomist. This source is believed to make up most of the historical texts of the Bible from Deuteronomy through Kings. The dating for this source is later, perhaps around the sixth century BC, and a hallmark of this source is that it tends to emphasize God's sovereignty and is highly skeptical of human kingship; consequently, in this source the law plays a fundamental role in Israel's relationship with God. The final, and supposedly latest source, is "P," or the Priestly source. As the designation for this source suggests, it is presumed to have been written from the priestly point of view and is concerned with those issues and subjects associated with priestly duties. Thus, P is believed to be the source behind Leviticus as well as the other instruction having to do with the temple practice in the early books of the Old Testament.

Of course, the assigning of biblical text to one of the presumed sources is by no means as clear-cut as some have supposed. The book of Genesis for instance, because of its narrative structure, is presumed to have primarily J material, but some of the narratives are thought to be from E while Genesis 1 is supposedly a P addition. Similarly, Numbers is mostly J but overlaid with a P redactor. This type of overlapping of sources has led some to go even so far as to dissect a single verse, assigning individual clauses to the different schools, thus resulting in one verse supposedly evidencing authorship and redaction by three or more of the schools.[6] More recently, some have suggested that E should no longer be considered a source, but merely another J tradition,[7] with others saying that the whole process of transmission reveals the hand of a Book of Mormon–like single redactor and therefore one cannot know for sure what is original to a particular school and what is redaction.[8]

To the casual reader, this parsing of traditions may seem like nothing more than an academic exercise, and there is some merit to this observation, particularly since there is no actual text that demonstrates these hypothetical schools existed. Yet the value of the approach is that it reveals places where the Old Testament clearly did have multiple traditions. Moreover, it provides a general chronology to the text and can help in determining which of the various traditions is older. So even if the actual schools are not correct, meaning there really is not a J or an E, it is clear that there was an older text and that somebody somewhere and sometime worked on that text and redacted it. Consequently, this can help us to better understand the formation of the law that is scattered across the texts of Exodus, Leviticus, Numbers, and Deuteronomy and preserves three similar but distinctive law codes: the Covenant Code, the Holiness Code, and the Deuteronomic Code.

The Covenant Code

According to biblical tradition, the law of Moses was not given until Moses and the camp of Israel arrived at Sinai following the exodus from Egypt, at which point Moses ascended the mountain and received a promise that if Israel obeyed God's voice and kept his covenant, they would be blessed and become a "kingdom of priests" (Exodus 19:6). Contingent upon Israel's acceptance, they were told to prepare themselves for the space of three days, after which God would come down "in the sight of all the people" (Exodus 19:11). Three days later, the text describes an epiphany in which God descended on Sinai. Moses is again called to ascend the mountain a second time, receiving the instruction comprising Exodus 20–23. Referred to as the "Covenant Code" because of its relationship with the covenantal events of Exodus 19 and 24, as well as the specific reference to the *sēfer ha brît*, or "book (writing)" of the covenant," this legal instruction is considered by many to be the oldest of the Israelite legal traditions.[9]

The collection itself is composed of three types of law: apodictic, casuistic, and participial.[10] Apodictic laws may be characterized by their unconditionality, their use of the second person, and they often lack a penalty for violation of a said law. These laws may either be prescriptive, meaning that they indicate positive commandments ("thou shalt"), or prohibitive ("thou shalt not"). As such, the Ten Commandments are the most emblematic of this type of law. Because of their absolute nature, apodictic commandments are understood to be divine decrees, representing the voice of God directly. This is reinforced by the biblical tradition in which they were written down in stone by the finger of God (Exodus 31:18).

While the apodictic laws are, by their very nature, relatively straightforward, the casuistic and participial laws set out a general precept and then provide varying cases that determine whether the individual's behavior is allowed or not.[11] These cases address two primary aspects of Israelite life: civic interaction and cultic participation. Regarding the first aspect, particular focus is placed on avoiding social conflict, such as interactions between household members (including male and female servants), accidental or intentional property damage (including damage to moveable property such as livestock), and legal procedures. The last of these, legal procedures, are given special consideration, as injunctions are given concerning false reports, false charges, the acceptance of bribes, and the like (Exodus 23:1, 6–8). It is within this context that we can place the famous *lex talionis*, or "eye for eye" formulation (Exodus 21:24, 26). The principle highlights the significance that just recompense should play if one causes harm or injury to another or their property.[12] As the astute reader will quickly note, there is no actual eye exchanged for an eye, but a series of recompenses based on whether the act was intentional or not. Thus, for instance, if one strikes the eye of one's servant, then that servant is now free (Exodus 21:26–27).

The code also establishes protections for a number of marginalized groups, including the poor, families that have lost husbands and fathers, and the stranger, or those who were not a part of the house of Israel, whom Israel was told expressly not to "vex" or oppress. Though the text is not explicit concerning their economic states, the context of Israel's instructions suggests that these groups were generally understood to be economically in need.[13] Thus, the Covenant Code addressed their poverty; for example, the Sabbatical Year, established in Exodus 23, left all produce for the poor. Yet the law sought to do more than simply provide aid for the poor; it also sought to preserve the dignity of the marginalized groups. One intriguing instance is the legal precept found in Exodus 22:26–27, which relates what one did if another offered his "raiment" (cloak) as a pledge to repay: "If thou at all take thy neighbour's raiment to pledge, thou shalt deliver it unto him by that the sun goeth down: For that is his covering only, it is his rainment for his skin: wherein shall he sleep?" The reason for doing so seems obvious—as the text states, the return of the cloak is required so that the individual has some means of warmth or protection while sleeping at night. Yet there is greater significance to the precept when one realizes that clothing plays an important social role as well, particularly as one of the primary ways in which individuals define themselves.[14]

Though many have noted the role of clothing in identification, such as priestly and royal costumes, the act of clothing, or investiture, is as significant in that it indicates the ability of an individual to make a definition. Thus, clothing specifies who we believe we are, while the act of clothing displays the power to define oneself and not be defined by others.[15] For the poor, giving the cloak, the last possession one has, as a pledge must have been a humbling experience. Returning the cloak would have reinforced the worth of any such individual, both to the owner and the returner.[16]

As the above examples demonstrate, the precepts of the law were more than mere restrictions. Their emphasis on personal responsibility for the welfare of oneself and others suggests that they were grounded, at least originally, in an effort to teach Israel their divinely appointed obligations for both themselves and their fellow man, creating the conditions whereby they could fulfill the covenant established between them and God.[17]

The Holiness Code

The Holiness Code, the second code in terms of placement but not necessarily in terms of composition, may be understood as the legal instruction comprising Leviticus 17–27 and the sacrificial instructions that make up Leviticus 1–7.[18] Though the sacrificial instruction is not the same type of instruction as the legal principles described later, its central place within Israel's worship highlights the importance of personal righteousness, as well as worthiness and holiness, and forms the basis of the later legal material. In light of this, understanding the sacrificial forms becomes important to better understand the powerful, even spiritual, relationship that Israel believed was possible with God and was reflected in the legal traditions.

Sacrifices fall into two primary categories: (1) freewill offerings and (2) reparation offerings. Within each category there were about three or four different sacrificial forms, or manners, by which sacrifice was performed. The first category, freewill offerings, included Leviticus 1 and 2, which are specifically about the ʿolāh, or an offering of flesh, and minḥāh sacrifices, or an offering of grain. That grain offerings would be so prominently discussed as viable sacrifices may be surprising for some, but in fact minḥāh offerings were integral parts of the sacrificial system overall, while also making it possible for all Israelites, regardless of their economic state, to make an offering. The following describes the three most significant sacrificial forms: the burnt offering, the sin offering, and the peace offering.

First offering type: The burnt offering

The burnt offering, or ʿolāh offering, was so named because following the slaughter of the animal and offering up of specific elements of the animal's corpse, all of the animal was then placed on the altar and consumed by fire, with the smoke of the offering ascending up (ʿolāh) to heaven (Leviticus 1:5–13). As for the meaning of the sacrifice itself, the text simply states that if it is done properly and willingly, then it will be accepted in order to "make atonement" for the individual (Leviticus 1:4). What "making atonement" means is not explicitly explained. The Hebrew verb *kpr* has been translated as "to purify, to cleanse, to cover, to reconcile," which spans a number of different meanings.[19] This study will revisit the different uses of atonement later. For now it is enough to note that, at some level, atonement lies at the heart of the ʿolāh offerings.

Second offering type: The sin offering

The second sacrificial form, commonly known as the "sin offering," may be further divided into two subforms, the *hattʾāt* and *ʾāshām*, or "uncleanliness" and "trespass" offerings (for the *hattʾāt*, see Leviticus 4:1–5:5; for the *ʾāshām*, see Leviticus 5:6–6:6). These offerings, as their names imply, reconcile or repair one's spiritual state after having become unclean. Here sin may be understood as fitting within one of three categories: (1) intentional sins that may be recompensed only through the death of the individual; (2) unintentional sins; and (3) sins that one intended but can be recompensed through another means, that is, the *hattʾāt* and *ʾāshām* offerings. As for the offerings themselves, they may be noted by their unique use of the offering's blood (as opposed to the burnt and peace offerings), as some of the blood was daubed on different items within the tabernacle or temple, particularly the altar (Leviticus 4:6–7, 17–18, 25; 5:9; 16:14–15, 18–19). As with burnt offerings, these offerings made atonement possible with forgiveness given to the individual of wrongdoing. The latter promise is unique to the *hattʾāt* offering and suggests that "making atonement" may be understood in more than one way, as burnt offerings did not lead to forgiveness but did effect atonement.

How these sacrifices effected atonement may be implied by the manipulation of the blood, as the blood covered the items in the sacred space. In the Holiness Code, Israel is commanded to never ingest blood—blood being the "life" of a being (Leviticus 10–14). If one assumes the same symbolic parameters for the blood of a sacrifice, then the life of the animal is being placed on the altar and transformed, becoming clean through this interface. If the animal can be understood as representing the offerer, then the animal's blood may represent the offerer's life, which has been transformed by the ritual experience. Part of this experience requires the priest to partake of some of the flesh of the animal to effect atonement, which may demonstrate that in the forgiving and cleansing process, the offerer is not alone, because the process is shared and experienced with the priest as well.[20]

Third offering type: The peace offering

The third sacrificial form is the *shelāmîm*, or "peace" offering, and it may be divided into two subforms as well: the *tôdāh* offering, also known as a "thanksgiving" offering, and the "vow" or "voluntary" offering, which completes or finishes the vow process and is given as an acknowledgement of the fulfilling or completing of the vow (Leviticus 3; 7:11–21). This sacrifice may be distinguished from the others by the consumption of the animal by the offerer. Unlike the ʿolāh and *hattʾāt/ ʾāshām* sacrifices, once the priest has offered the portion of the animal dedicated to God (namely, the blood and some of the internal viscera such as the fat), the offerer then takes the rest of the animal home to consume there. There is a time restriction to the consumption: the animal has to be consumed within one or two days depending on whether it is a thanksgiving or vow offering (Leviticus 7:15–17). Nothing may be preserved or saved; thus the *shelāmîm* offering was a shared experienced with friends, family, or neighbors who often helped in the consumption of the sacrifice. Of the three sacrificial forms, the peace offering is perhaps the most intriguing because it is not intended to overcome a negative condition. Instead, it acts to enhance a positive event, whether that was the completion of a project (e.g., the construction of the temple) or the fulfilling of a vow. The communal nature of this sacrificial form, in light of its function, suggests that the peace offering was the highest offering that could be offered.[21]

All of the sacrificial forms can have christological interpretations, the *hatṭ'āt/'āshām* offerings being the most readily interpreted in this manner. The Book of Mormon makes it quite clear that recognizing Christ's supernal act of atonement was an essential part of the rituals of the law of Moses. In his discourse to the priests, the prophet Abinadi declared that the purpose of the law and rituals was to facilitate Israel's remembrance of God and their duty to him: "Therefore there was a law given them, yea, a law of performances and of ordinances, a law which they were to observe strictly from day to day, to keep them in remembrance of God and their duty towards him" (Mosiah 13:30). Earlier, Nephi made it clear that the law directed one toward Christ (2 Nephi 25:23–30). Nephi's father, Lehi, explained in particular the relationship between the Atonement and rituals of Moses, calling Christ's act a "sacrifice for sin," that is, a sin offering.

Christ's supernal act is certainly reflected in the sin offering, of which the explicit purpose is to bring about forgiveness through the individual's offering. Just as the blood of the sin offering covers the items of the tabernacle, thereby reconciling the individual represented by the offering, Christ's blood covers us, reconciling us to his Father. Similarly, the burnt offering represents all that he offered to bring about reconciliation as well as what we are expected to offer for this reconciliation. It may also highlight another important part of the atonement process, namely, our need to offer all in order to receive that salvation. As for the peace offering, its function to enhance the positive events of ancient Israel suggests an aspect of the Atonement that is often not recognized, that being the joy of God and Christ when positive events happen—perhaps even their desire to share that joy.

The precepts

The Holiness Code, following the sacrificial instruction, can best be understood as consisting of precepts that governed Israel's cultic behavior. While it contains many of the same moral and ethical commandments as the Covenant Code, it also emphasizes cultic regulations such as the eating of the *shelāmîm* offerings, the prohibition against consuming blood, and the proper (and only) place to offer burnt offerings. Associated with the direct cultic regulations are repeated injunctions to not engage in any way with foreign worship systems (Leviticus 19:4). Similarly, mourning rites for the dead such as tattooing, cutting, shaving, and the cutting of hair are prohibited (Leviticus 19:27–28). Divinatory specialists such as those who associate or seek guidance from "familiar spirits" are specifically highlighted as improper (Leviticus 19:31; 20:27). While not directly cultic, the Holiness Code is the first law code to designate clean and unclean animals, further stating that only animals that have been slaughtered are acceptable for consumption (Leviticus 20:25). While these precepts may seem somewhat arbitrary, they indicate that Israel was expected to maintain a certain set of behaviors that would allow them to participate in tabernacle service.

This is especially true regarding the moral and ethical elements of the Holiness Code. While many of the precepts are similar to the proper social behavior exemplified in the Covenant Code, the specific and explicit association of these with holiness suggests a completely new understanding. The term *holy* is actually translated from two related Hebrew terms: *qodesh* and *qādôsh*. Unlike Indo-European languages, Hebrew does not have vowel letters, but derivations of the root, with subsequent nuances to the general meaning of the term, are demonstrated through the use of prefixes, suffixes, and the vowel sounds. Thus, even though *qodesh* and *qādôsh* stem from the same root, *qdsh*, the different vowel sounds suggest different nuances between the two.[22]

Of the two, *qādôsh* is much more common, being used 468 times in the Hebrew Bible (Old Testament), and is used to describe a number of things such as the clothing of the priests, the animals offered for sacrifice, and the instruments used in the tabernacle. The term *qādôsh*, on the other hand, is used only 106 times, and the items considered *qādôsh* are much more limited. Chief among them is God, "the Holy One" (*qādôsh*). Certain locations where God may be present are also *qādôsh*, though the sanctuary itself is *qodesh*. In Numbers 5:17, the running water used in the rite to discern whether a woman has been committing adultery is referred to as *qādôsh*. However, the second most common usage of *qādôsh* describes the potential state of mortals.

Though both terms stem from the same root, for the most part there is no overlap in usage. Instead, those things that are considered *qādôsh* are differentiated from those things that are *qodesh* in that *qādôsh* items possess a dynamic quality, or the "ability to move things (or people) into, or at least toward, the realm of the divine."[23] It is for this reason that God is *qādôsh*. As Moses clarifies elsewhere, God's primary responsibility is to "bring to pass the immortality and eternal life of man," a process of movement from a lesser state into the ultimate divine state (Moses 1:39). This dynamic quality lies at the heart of the use of *qādôsh* in the law of Moses, for throughout Leviticus the precepts are established with the injunction that Israel be holy (*qādôsh*), "for I the Lord your God am holy (*qādôsh*)."[24] In other words, Israel was expected to be made up of individuals who moved others toward the divine state, as God himself did.[25]

In this context, the specific instruction to avoid gossip, not harbor hidden enmity (a precept that Christ himself emphasizes in the Sermon on the Mount), and not exact vengeance (Leviticus 19:16–18) suggests that the Holiness Code sought to encourage moral behavior above and beyond the other law codes, which, for instance, allowed for absolute justice. Perhaps even more striking are the similarities between these precepts and the characteristics of those who may "abide in the [Lord's] tabernacle" and who shall dwell in the "holy hill" of the Lord as noted in Psalm 15:1. There a righteous person is described as one who "speaketh the truth in his heart, . . . that backbiteth not with his tongue" (Psalm 15:2–3), does not engage in usury, and keeps his oaths. Perhaps, then, it is not surprising that it is in the Holiness Code that the commandment to "love thy neighbour as thyself" is found (Leviticus 19:18). Likewise, of equal significance is the commandment to recognize the stranger as "one born among you, and thou shalt love him as thyself" (Leviticus 19:34). These two injunctions, perhaps the defining characteristics of those God had chosen to be "holy," will also become primary injunctions of Christ himself.

The Holiness Code also includes a section of precepts specifically for the priests. Among other things, these include injunctions regarding the type of woman a priest can marry, the physical requirements that may restrict priesthood service, and restrictions regarding contact with corpses (Leviticus 21–22). While these rulings may seem particularly restrictive and out of step with modern mores, they highlight the extraordinary responsibility that the priest had with the rest of Israel. They were to be held to a higher standard, representing a divine purity and thus necessitating their need to be in that state of purity.[26]

Deuteronomic Code

The last of the three codes, in terms of placement within the canon, is the Deuteronomic Code that comprises the book of Deuteronomy.[27] The biblical text itself states that Deuteronomy was understood to be the last set of instructions given by Moses to Israel before their entrance into the promised land (Deuteronomy 1:1; 31:1–2; 34:1–5). Though some have questioned the historical accuracy of this, it does suggest that the Old Testament compilers recognized that Deuteronomy was a later text. A close review of the laws provided in Deuteronomy suggests familiarity with both the Covenant Code and elements of the Holiness Code, with the Deuteronomic Code revising or modifying the earlier legal and cultic precepts.[28]

With that said, Deuteronomy contains a number of differences with the other two law codes. First, the deuteronomic text shows a striking similarity to ancient Near Eastern treaty texts. These texts defined the relationship between greater political entities, such as the Egyptian, Hittite, or Assyrian polities, and the lesser kingdoms that were their vassal states. These relationships were established through assigning specific responsibilities to the two, oftentimes a brief history of the two parties and their interaction with one another, curses and blessings detailing the consequences of improper and proper behavior, and instruction by which the treaty was to be periodically read in order to remind the parties that the relationship was still in force. The appearance of all these characteristics in Deuteronomy suggests that this law code could be understood as the "treaty" between Israel and God, which needed to be reiterated as Israel entered into the promised land.[29]

Another significant difference between the Deuteronomic Code and the others is its recognition of the Israelite community as a city.[30] While the Covenant Code appears to address a population primarily rural in nature, Deuteronomy alludes to urban concerns as well. For instance, in Deuteronomy 17:1–5, the city's social structure is explicitly mentioned in a law explaining what one should do if reports of potential false worship in a given city emerge. Other instruction concerns what to do if a city is captured in a military conflict (see 18:10–20). This code also reflects the political structure of kingship by explicitly stating that the king must have a copy of the law with him at all times and know it well (Deuteronomy 17:14–20). While cities of refuge, so designated to avoid improper blood revenge, appear in Numbers, their placement within both the geography of Israel and its social structure are fleshed out in Deuteronomy 19. Deuteronomy also incorporates the duties of judges and elders into the civic regulations, suggesting the greater social complexity of urban life. While the appointment of judges was noted in the Covenant Code, in Deuteronomy the political class of the "elders" is explicitly mentioned and takes a prominent role in the juridical duties (Deuteronomy 19:12; 21:2–6, 19–20; 22:15–18; 25:7–9).[31] Finally, cultic restrictions in Deuteronomy emphasize that Israel was to worship in only one place, presumably the temple in Jerusalem, an emphasis known within biblical studies as "cultic centralization" (Deuteronomy 12:1–14, 26–27; 18:1–8).[32]

In terms of legal instruction, like the Covenant and Holiness Codes, the Deuteronomic Code makes it clear that Israel was not to engage in foreign worship, including alternative divinatory practices. The Deuteronomic Code also emphasized the importance of caring for the marginalized, again expanding on earlier, more generalized principles. Thus, Deuteronomy establishes that the third-year tithe was expressly for the Levites, strangers, fatherless, and widowed (14:28–29) and that the festivals that Israel was to celebrate were to be occasions in which all individuals could rejoice alongside the Israelites by virtue of Israelite hospitality. These responsibilities were to reflect divine characteristics, God himself declaring in Deuteronomy 10:17–18 that he watched over the fatherless and the widowed and loved the stranger, and that therefore Israel too was "to love" the stranger, a principle found in the Holiness Code.

These social obligations are also foundational for a number of Christ's teachings, as well as the characteristics of one who is seeking the "kingdom of God" according to Jacob (Jacob 2:18–19). James summed up Christian discipleship as visiting the "fatherless and widows in their affliction" (James 1:27), suggesting that the Mosaic precepts simply reflect the law of God regardless of the manner in which that law may be found. It is in this context that one can place one of the more unique precepts in Deuteronomy, namely that one could take young birds or even nests, but not the mother (Deuteronomy 22:6–7). Though ostensibly about birds, the law suggests that one should always provide the opportunity for the return and regrowth of all creatures.

Like the Holiness Code, the Deuteronomic Code was concerned with cultic matters, demonstrating particular concern for improper mixing. The list of clean and unclean animals is expanded and associated by type, while elsewhere Israel was told not to mix different seed types in the same field, or plow the field with different types of animals, or wear clothing made of different types of cloth (Deuteronomy 14:3–20; 22:9–11). Making sure that one ate only slaughtered meat and that one did not boil a kid in its mother's milk may be included in this concern (Deuteronomy 14:21). Such specifications may seem arbitrary, but they appear to have emphasized the role of assigning things to a proper order, perhaps even reflecting the initial creation process in which objects and entities were delineated from one another and assigned their proper place within creation as a whole.[33] If this is the case, then the separation laws provided a way for Israel to engage in the creation process. This concern may influence one of the more difficult precepts of Deuteronomy, namely, the injunction to "smite them, and utterly destroy them," meaning the communities inhabiting the land before Israel's arrival (Deuteronomy 7:1–2; 9:3; 20:16–18).

While many of the injunctions in the law codes are understandable, perhaps even reflecting our own moral and ethical sensibilities, the injunction requiring the annihilation of entire communities is hard to reconcile. Because of the extreme nature of the commandment, some have suggested that it represents a later addition, reflecting an Israel that "could have been"—that is, strong, unwavering, and powerful in the face of adversity. Israel's actual experience was less than this, as noted by the Assyrian and Babylonian captivities. Moreover, the actual archaeological evidence suggests that Israel did not truly engage in this behavior all the time but appears to have often lived more or less in harmony with their Canaanite neighbors. Yet it is also possible that the injunction was original, at least to the earliest version of Deuteronomy. If this is the case, then the injunction represents a continuation of the creative process.

In this cosmology, the creation is the work of God instituting order and meaning using unorganized elements. Forces that would seek to upend or tear down that order and structure would therefore be going against the will of God. In this perspective, if the Canaanite and other native populations did not recognize the sovereignty of Israel's God and instead actively sought to emphasize their own deities, thereby leading Israel to fall, then it would be better to wipe them out, just as God did to the inhabitants before the Flood.[34] Christ himself would teach a similar principle when he declared that if the "right hand offend thee, cut it off" (Matthew 5:30). While this is not a direct comparison, similarity in principle may be recognized. Finally, the reader would do well to remember that this injunction does not stand isolated but appears in a code that also explicitly repeats again and again the importance of treating the stranger with respect. Thus, it appears to represent an extreme measure. Regardless, the injunction remains one of the more difficult laws to understand and comprehend for the modern reader.

Again, as with the two other law codes, Deuteronomy also addresses the legal aspects of Israelite interaction, noting the importance of fair and impartial judgments. The concern for legal fairness is found throughout the code. Deuteronomy 19:15–21 presents a series of precepts about the importance of accurate witnessing, noting that there must be at least two witnesses and that if a false witness is discovered then that individual shall have done to him what he had hoped would have been done to the falsely accused (this is the context of Deuteronomy's use of the talionic "eye for an eye"). As noted earlier, Deuteronomy gave greater judicial authority to other entities beyond the aggrieved parties. But with that said, Israel was still expected to overcome differences without resorting to the authorities, with

Deuteronomy 17:8–13 enjoining aggravated parties to reach out to authorities only as a last resort. More significantly, Deuteronomy makes it explicit that one was not held accountable for another's actions: "The fathers shall not be put to death for the children, neither shall the children be put to death for the fathers; every man shall be put to death for his own sin" (Deuteronomy 24:16). Thus, the legal environment of the deuteronomic law may be understood as one in which individuals were to be fair, impartial, and held accountable for themselves while seeking the welfare of those around them.

Later Developments and Consolidation

Outside these three more or less intact codes, one can find further legal instruction. Numbers, in particular, contains portions of both Deuteronomic and Holiness Codes.[35] When exactly these three early law codes were canonized and understood as the singular "law" is difficult to ascertain. Certainly one can see the attempt to consolidate, as the final redaction of these texts claims Moses as the voice for all three of them, even though all three show earlier revisions. A possible early consolidation may be noted by reference to the "book of law" found in Deuteronomy and later deuteronomic texts. Second Kings 22 recounts the reconstruction of the temple following a period of misuse and disuse. In the cleanup efforts, a "book of the law" was found in the temple, whereupon Josiah had the book read to all of Judah[36]—many believe this book to be Deuteronomy. If so, then reconciliation of these different traditions had begun, or at least was believed to have begun, before the Babylonian exile.[37]

Yet it is in the exile that consolidation and canonization appears to have truly made progress. The book of Ezra recounts the priest Ezra's return to Jerusalem and the rebuilding of the temple. According to the text, Ezra was a "scribe in the law of Moses" (Ezra 7:6), suggesting that at the time when Ezra was written, ca. 400–350 BC, the legal texts were comprehensively known as "the law of Moses." This would indicate that the consolidation process had reached a formative stage by which the law of Moses was conceived as an entirety; by the time the Septuagint was compiled around 280 BC, the five books of Moses appear to have become a "canon." While the centuries immediately preceding Christ's ministry continued to evidence redaction, by the time of his ministry the law of Moses was now understood as the combined legal texts found within the books of Exodus, Numbers, Leviticus, and Deuteronomy.

Conclusion

Following the death and resurrection of Christ, Paul, writing to the saints in Galatia, declared that the law had been a "schoolmaster" to Israel (Galatians 3:24), bringing them to Christ. While it may be tempting, as modern readers, to understand this solely as reflecting the sacrificial practices, it no doubt included the moral and ethical teachings as well. Adherence to those principles, expressly meant to lead the Israelite to holiness, taught the Israelite how to be like God himself. This may explain why Christ rarely condemned practice of the law, but merely the traditions that had arisen around it. In fact, time and time again, it appears that Christ referred to the principles of the law, restoring the law to its place as divine schoolmaster.

From the Sermon on the Mount to his sermons during the last week of his ministry, Christ frequently demonstrated that the principles in the Mosaic law regarding conduct with one's neighbor were simply the law of God—and that may in fact be the most appropriate way to understand the law of Moses. Regardless of the dispensation or the tradition, the law of God is the law of God. While we no longer need to keep all aspects of the law of Moses, the principles of hospitality, holiness, and social responsibility endure and continue to define what it means to be a Saint.

≈

Daniel L. Belnap is an associate professor in the Department of Ancient Scripture at Brigham Young University.

Further Reading

Boecker, Hans Jocham. *Law and Administration of Justice in the Old Testament and Ancient East.* Minneapolis: Augsburg, 1980.

Carmichael, Calum M. *The Origin of Biblical Law: The Decalogue and the Book of the Covenant.* Ithaca, NY: Cornell University Press, 1992.

Hiers, Richard H. *Justice and Compassion in Biblical Law.* New York: Continuum, 2009.

Morrow, William S. *An Introduction to Biblical Law.* Grand Rapids, MI: Eerdmans, 2017.

Thielman, Frank. *The Law and the New Testament: The Question of Continuity.* New York: Crossroad, 1999.

Westbrook, Raymond. *Everyday Law in Biblical Israel: An Introduction.* Louisville, KY: Westminster John Knox, 2009.

Notes

1. Found in the New Testament narrative concerning the eating with unwashed hands, the phrase references the Jewish oral traditions that had accumulated around the written law. Though not a part of the written law, these traditions had been given legitimacy by presenting them as instruction passed on orally through the preceding generations. Codified and written in the Jewish Mishnah around the third century AD, these traditions included a history of their formation (see m. Avot 1:1: "Moses received the Torah at Sinai, and transmitted it to Joshua, and Joshua transmitted to the Elders, and the Elders to the Prophets, and the Prophets to the members of the Great Assembly. They said three things: be deliberate in judgment, raise up many disciples, and make a fence for the Torah"). Christ's criticism is that already by the New Testament era, these traditions, which were meant to preserve and protect the law (i.e., the fence), had been elevated to the status of the law itself, thus creating tensions in the performance of both the law and the tradition. For more on these particular New Testament passages, see John Nolland, *The Gospel of Matthew*, The New International Greek Testament Commentary (Grand Rapids, MI: Eerdmans, 2005), 609–15; also Adela Yarbo Collins, *Mark*, Hermenia Commentary Series, ed. Harold W. Attridge (Minneapolis: Fortress, 2007), 344–49.

2. William Johnstone, "The Two Theological Versions of the Passover Pericope in Exodus," in *Text as Pretext: Essays in Honour of Robert Davidson*, ed. Robert P. Carroll (Sheffield, England: JSOT, 1992), 160–78.

3. Biblical scholarship refers to this approach to the Bible as the documentary hypothesis within the larger methodological approach known as source criticism. Discussion on this approach can be found in any introductory study to the Bible. For an excellent introduction to source criticism, see Pauline A. Viviano, "Source Criticism," in *To Each Its Own Meaning: An Introduction to Biblical Criticisms and Their Application*, ed. Steven L McKenzie and Stephen R. Davis (Louisville: Westminster John Knox, 1999), 35–57. For a Latter-day Saint approach, see David Bokovoy, *Authoring the Old Testament: Genesis–Deuteronomy* (Salt Lake City: Greg Kofford Books, 2014). For excellent summaries of biblical criticism topics in general, see Richard N. Soulen, *Handbook of Biblical Criticism* (Louisville: John Knox, 2011).

4. See Albert de Pury, "Yahwist ("J") Source," in *Anchor Bible Dictionary*, ed. David Noel Freedman (New York: Doubleday, 1992), 6:1012–20, for more on the nature of this source. For more detail see John Van Seters, *The Yahwist: A Historian of Israelite Origins* (Winona Lake, IN: Eisenbrauns, 2013).

5. De Pury, "Yahwist ("J") Source," 6:1012–20.

6. This type of dissection was more common in the early to mid-twentieth century. For a critique of this type of hyper parsing, see Joel S. Baden, "Why Is the Pentateuch Unreadable?," in *The Formation of the Pentateuch*, ed. Jan C. Gertz, Bernard M. Levinson, Dalit Rom-Shiloni, and Konrad Schmid, Forschungen zum Alten Testament 11 (Tubingen, Germany: Mohr Siebeck, 2016), 243–51, esp. 245–47.

7. This is the stance of most European pentateuchal scholarship. Joel Baden, a scholar from the United States, has rebutted this, suggesting that E should in fact still be understood as a viable source; see Joel S. Baden, "Continuity between the Gaps: The Pentateuch and the Kirta Epic," in *Formation of the Pentateuch*, 283–92.

8. This particular approach is known as redaction criticism and arises from the "gaps" within a given pentateuchal narrative, meaning that the lack of certain elements within a biblical narrative (such as the period of time between Isaac and Rebekah's marriage and the birth of the sons) suggests that there were not coherent, complete sources but fragments or pieces of given traditions and that, therefore, one can only trace the text to a redactor. For a rebuttal see Baden, "Continuity between the Gaps."

9. While this is the consensus, like much of biblical studies, it is not accepted by all. For a contrasting position, see John Van Seters, *A Law Book for the Diaspora: Revision in the Study of the Covenant Code* (New York: Oxford University Press, 2003).

10. William S. Morrow, *An Introduction to Biblical Law* (Grand Rapids, MI: Eerdmans, 2017), 74–76.

11. Casuistic laws often demonstrate an "if-then" structure and reflect case-by-case precepts. Participial laws use a participial to refer to the participants and may be understood as hybrids of casuistic and apodictic laws (see Morrow, *Introduction to Biblical Law*, 73–74).

12. Ze'ev W. Falk, *Hebrew Law in Biblical Times: An Introduction* (Provo, UT: Brigham Young University Press and Eisenbrauns, 2001), 73–77.

13. See David L. Baker, *Tight Fists or Open Hands? Wealth and Poverty in Old Testament Law* (Grand Rapids, MI: Eerdmans, 2009), 136–93.

14. Susan B. Kaiser, *The Social Psychology of Clothing and Personal Adornment* (New York: Macmillan, 1985), 216–17: "There are two important functions to clothes in nonverbal communication. First, they help us to negotiate identities, as we present our situated identities or roles, moods, values, and attitudes to one another. Second, they help us to define situations, that is, to socially construct the basis for our interactions."

15. Malcolm Bernard, *Fashion as Communication* (London: Routledge, 2002), 39: "Clothing and fashion, as communication, are cultural phenomena in that culture may itself be understood as a signifying system, as the ways in which a society's beliefs, values, ideas and experiences are communicated through practices, artefacts, and institutions; . . . fashion, clothing and dress are the artefacts, practices, and institutions that constitute a society's beliefs, values, ideas and experiences. According to this view, fashion, dress and clothing are ways in which people communicate, not only things like feeling and mood, but also the values, hopes and beliefs of the social groups of which they are members. They are, then, the ways in which society is produced and reproduced."

16. Note that in Exodus 22:27, one reason for returning the cloak is because the Lord is "gracious." Interestingly, there is an extrabiblical text that describes a scenario where the individual's cloak was not found. On an ostraca (pottery sherd with writing on it) from the area of Yavneh-Yam, Israel, the following text was found: "Let my lord, the governor, hear the word of his servant! Your servant is a reaper. Your servant was in Hazar Asam, and your servant reaped, and finished, and he has stored (the grain) during these days before the Sabbath. When your servant had finished the harvest, and had stored (the grain) during these days, Hoshavyahu came, the son of Shobi, and he seized the garment of your servant, when I had finished my harvest. It (is already now some) days (since) he took the garment of your servant. And all my companions can bear witness for me—they who reaped with me in the heat of the harvest—yes, my companions can bear witness for me. Amen! I am innocent from guilt. And he stole my garment! It is for the governor to give back the garment of his servant. So grant him mercy in that you return the garment of your servant and do not be displeased." For more on this text, see J. H. Tigay, "A Talmudic Parallel to the Petition from Yavneh-Yam," in *Minhah le-Nahum: Biblical and Other Studies Presented to Nahum M. Sarna in Honour of His 70th Birthday*, ed. Marc Zvi Brettler and Michael Fishbane (Sheffield: JSOT, 1993), 328–33; F. W. Dobbs-Allsopp, "The Genre of the Meṣad Hashavyahu Ostracon," *BASOR* 295 (1994): 49–55.

17. John I. Durham, *Exodus*, Word Biblical Commentary 3, ed. Bruce M. Metzger (Waco, TX: Word, 1987), 337: "The Book of the Covenant is a kind of theological rule for life in the Presence of Yahweh. Its concern is how to serve Yahweh, and him alone; . . . it is a rule for life in Yahweh's presence that links the narrative of Yahweh come to Israel with the narrative of Israel's approach to Yahweh by providing the rule by which such an approach can be made by such a people to such a God."

18. The dating for these two sections is complicated. See Morrow, *Introduction*, 110–17, for a brief summary.

19. B. Lang, "רפכ," in *Theological Dictionary of the Old Testament*, ed. Gerhard Kittel and Gerhard Friedrich, trans. Geoffrey W. Bromiley (Grand Rapids, MI: Eerdmans, 1971), 7:288–303.

20. The unique use of the blood in the atoning process associated with the sin offering has been noted extensively. For more see Jacob Milgrom, *Leviticus 1–16*, Anchor Bible (New York: Doubleday, 1991), 3:226–307. A good review is Yitzhaq Feder, *Blood Expiation in Hittite and Biblical Ritual: Origins, Context and Meaning* (Atlanta: Society of Biblical Literature, 2011). See also Nicole J. Ruane, *Sacrifice and Gender in Biblical Law* (Cambridge: Cambridge University Press, 2013), 130–45.

21. Nobuyoshi Kiuchi, "Spirituality in Offering a Peace Offering," *Tyndale Bulletin* 50, no. 1 (1999): 23–31.

22. Ringgren, "שדק," in *Theological Dictionary of the Old Testament*, 12:521–45.

23. E. Jan Wilson, *"Holiness" and "Purity" in Mesopotamia*, Alter Orient und Altes Testament 237 (Neukirchen-Vluyn: Neukirchener, 1994), 87–88. For more discussion on the distinction of these terms, see Gaye Strathearn, "'Holiness to the Lord' and Personal Temple Worship," in *The Gospel of Jesus Christ in the Old Testament*, ed. D. Kelly Ogden, Jared W. Ludlow, and Kerry Muhlestein (Provo, UT: Religious Studies Center, Brigham Young University; Salt Lake City: Deseret Book, 2009), 219–32.

24. Leviticus 19:2; see 11:44–45, 20:7, 21:8; Deuteronomy 7:6; 14:2; 28:9.

25. Biblical scholar Jonathan Klawans considers this in his article "Pure Violence: Sacrifice and Defilement in Ancient Israel," *Harvard Theological Review* 94, no. 2 (2001): 135–57: "Jon D. Levenson . . . has argued that the biblical narrative of tabernacle (and temple) construction take on a cosmic significance. . . . In so doing, Levenson demonstrates that the priestly traditions understand tabernacle and temple construction as an act of *imitatio Dei*. If the building of the temple can be understood as an act of *imitatio Dei*, and if the process of preparation for the rituals that will take place there can be understood likewise, can this concept help us to better understand at least some aspects of ancient Israelite animal sacrifice?" (p. 145).

26. For more on the Holiness Code and its relationship to the rituals, see Leigh M. Trevaskis, *Holiness, Ethics and Ritual in Leviticus*, Hebrew Bible Monograph 29 (Sheffield, England: Sheffield Academic Press, 2011).

27. The title "Deuteronomy" is Greek, reflecting the usage of this Greek noun in the Septuagint of Deuteronomy 17:18, meaning "second law."

34

28. See Morrow, *Introduction*, 200–206, for a brief summary concerning dating. The lack of land concern in the Holiness Code is one of the primary reasons for the later dating of P. See also Moshe Weinfeld, *The Place of the Law in the Religion of Ancient Israel* (Leiden, Netherlands: Brill, 2004), 77–80.

29. For more on the covenant-treaty pattern, see George E. Mendenhall, *Law and Covenant in Israel and the Ancient Near East* (Pittsburgh: Biblical Colloquium, 1955); and Dennis J. McCarthy, "Covenant in the Old Testament: The Present State of Inquiry," *Catholic Bible Quarterly* 27, no. 3 (1965): 217–40. A more recent example is Kenneth A. Kitchen and Paul J. N. Lawrence, *Treaty, Law and Covenant in the Ancient Near East* (Wiesbaden, Germany: Harrassowitz, 2012).

30. Don C. Benjamin, *Deuteronomy and City Life: A Form Criticism of Texts with the Word City ('îr) in Deuteronomy 4:41–26:19* (Lanham, MD: University Press of America, 1983).

31. Timothy M. Willis, *The Elders of the City: A Study of the Elders-Laws in Deuteronomy* (Atlanta: Society of Biblical Literature, 2001).

32. Rannfrid I. Thelle, *Approaches to the "Chosen Place": Accessing a Biblical Concept* (London: T&T International, 2012). See also Bill T. Arnold, "Deuteronomy and the Law of the Central Sanctuary *noch einmal*," *Vetus Testamentum* 64 (2014): 236–48.

33. Mary Douglas, *Purity and Danger: An Analysis of Concepts of Pollution and Taboo* (London: Routledge and Kegan Paul, 1978).

34. The Hebrew term for this utter annihilation is *ḥerem*. For more on the relationship between *herem* and creation, see Philip D. Stern, *The Biblical Ḥerem: A Window on Israel's Religious Experience* (Atlanta: Scholars Press, 1991). See also Yair Hoffman, "The Deuteronomistic Concept of Ḥerem," *Zeitschrift für die alttestamentliche Wissenschaft* 111, no. 2 (1999): 196–210. Interestingly, the concept of *herem* appears in the Book of Mormon. Alma 16 describes the destruction of Ammonihah in language reminiscent of the utter destruction associated with *herem*. Helaman 6 describes a *herem* in which the Gadianton robbers are utterly destroyed out of Lamanite territory. In the latter case the utter destruction comes about through the preaching of the word of God.

35. See Numbers 5–6; 9:1–14; 19; 27; and 35.

36. Erik Eynikal, *The Reform of King Josiah and the Composition of the Deuteronomistic History* (Leiden, Netherlands: Brill, 1995).

37. One of the evidences used for this perspective is the Ketef Hinnom inscriptions. In 1979, during excavations of a series of tombs west of the City of David, two silver amulet scrolls were found that contained portions of what is known as the "priestly blessing" recorded in Numbers 6:23–27. The scrolls themselves have been dated to a preexilic origin (late seventh–early sixth century BC). For more on this inscription, see Gabriel Barkay, Andrew G. Vaughn, Marilyn J. Lundberg, and Bruce Zuckerman, "The Amulets from Ketef Hinnom: A New Edition and Evaluation," *Bulletin of the American Schools of Oriental Research* 334 (2000): 41–70.

3

Jerusalem, the Holy City
A Virtual Tour of the City in the New Testament Period

Tyler J. Griffin

"He who has not seen the Temple of Herod has never seen a beautiful building."[1]

Few cities have attracted more attention, from more people, for a longer period of time than Jerusalem.[2] For Jews and Muslims, this city is esteemed as a promised land, filled with holy sites integrally important to their religions and identities as a people. On the same rock where Jewish tradition holds that Abraham nearly sacrificed his son Isaac (the rock inside the holy of holies, where the ark of the covenant rested; Genesis 22), Muhammad is believed to have ascended into heaven. For Christians, the central importance of Jerusalem is manifested by Jesus's personal presence in the city. It was in and around Jerusalem that Jesus was presented in the temple as an infant, taught the learned men as a twelve-year-old, cleansed the temple, taught the peo-

Figure 1. View of Temple Mount in Virtual New Testament App (facing west-southwest).

ple, healed the sick, suffered in Gethsemane, was condemned, suffered and died on the cross, then became the first to rise from the dead. Though two thousand years have passed since these events occurred, Christians continue to visit the city so they can walk in his footsteps. By combining the latest archaeological and historical research with modern technology, we are now able to create a virtual reconstruction of the city and its environs as they possibly appeared at the time of Christ. This chapter offers readers a virtual tour of sorts as it attempts to peel away nearly two thousand years of geographic and structural changes now visible in the present city.

The Setting for the City

To begin, it is worthwhile to start with an overview of the geographic setting for Jerusalem and how that affected its inhabitants and visitors in the New Testament period. The city is located approximately 40 miles (65 km) east of the Mediterranean Sea and about 100 miles (160 km) south of the Sea of Galilee. In the New Testament, Jewish people traveled between Jerusalem and Galilee using one of two main routes, through Samaria or through the deep Jordan River Valley.[3] The latter route took much longer and required a steep climb from

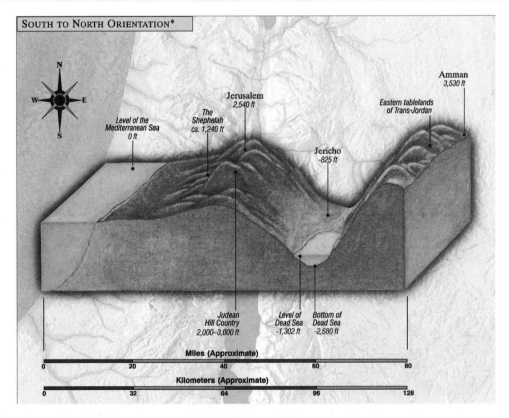

Figure 2. Elevations of the Holy Land.

Jericho (nearly 900 feet below sea level) through a dry and desolate wilderness before arriving in Jerusalem (2,540 feet above sea level).

At the time of Jesus, the large city walls encircled an area just under one square mile in size. For perspective, compare the three Google Earth images on the right depicting an outline of the old city walls superimposed over three modern-day locations of today, the campus of Brigham Young University (BYU), the area between the Lincoln and Washington Memorials in Washington, DC, and a portion of Central Park in New York City.

The city walls encircled two large hills, Mount Moriah (also known as Temple Mount) and Mount Zion, the higher hill to the southwest. These were separated by the Tyropoeon Valley (i.e., "valley of the cheesemakers") running between them from north to south. Two steep valleys outside the walls, the Hinnom on the west and south and the Kidron on the east, helped create a natural defense for the city. Jerusalem was nearly surrounded by taller hills and mountains around much of its perimeter, including the Mount of Olives directly to the east. The photograph in figure 4, taken from the BYU Jerusalem Center on Mt. Scopus (looking southwest) shows the golden Dome of the Rock situated on the summit of Mount Moriah.

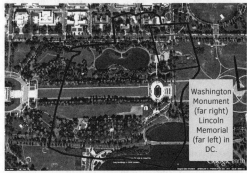
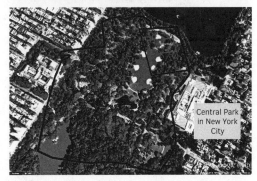

Figure 3. Comparison of relative size: ancient Jerusalem with three US locations today.

Note how low the Dome of the Rock sits compared with the hills and mountains encircling most of the city. Psalm 125:2 describes this geographic setting for the Holy City: "As the mountains are round about Jerusalem, so the Lord is round about his people from henceforth even for ever."

The main regions of the city mentioned in the New Testament are labeled and discussed as follows:

Figure 4. View of the Dome of the Rock (top center left) from Mount Scopus.

- Temple Mount
- Kidron Valley and the Mount of Olives
- The Lower City (City of David)
- The Upper City (Mount Zion)
- The northern quarries, gardens, and pools

The Temple Mount

Figure 5. Significant regions of Jerusalem.

The temple dominated the city. Its trapezoid shape covered over 169,000 square yards (more than twenty-six American football fields).[4] The platform was covered by many structures and courtyards, including the sanctuary of the Holy Place and holy of holies, the Royal Stoa (a large portico structure covering the southern end of the platform), and the Antonia Fortress (in the northwest corner of the platform).

Figure 7 shows the southwest corner of the temple. The spacious plaza and monumental staircases leading up to the temple were big enough to accommodate the large numbers of pilgrims who would pour into the city during important festivals. The stair treads on the large staircases were built at inconsistent depths, perhaps to require visitors to the Temple Mount to ascend with greater care and reverence.[5] Geographically, this was the center of the city. Markets lined the plaza to the south and the busy street to the west of the temple. The Wailing Wall, or Western Wall, of the temple is located approximately 550 feet (165 meters) to the north of this southwest corner. Today, faithful Jewish worshippers congregate there

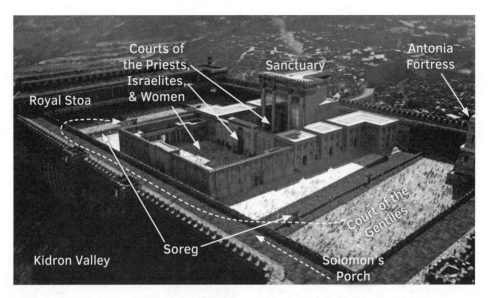

Figure 6. View of Temple Mount, facing southwest, with Mount Zion in the background.

to offer prayers because that is as close as they can get to the physical location of the ancient holy of holies.

People could enter the temple through various gates, including the double and triple gates on the south—Robinson's Arch, Barclay's Gate, Wilson's Arch—and Warren's Gate on the west. From atop the southwest pinnacle (upper-left corner of figure 7), a priest would sound a trumpet to signal important events such as the beginning and ending of the Sabbath and daily sacrifices each morning and afternoon.[6] It was likely from that point or the southeast pinnacle (far right side of figure 7) where Jesus was tempted by Satan to cast himself down (Matthew 4:5–7).

Everything on the Temple Mount was designed to symbolize approaching the presence of God, which emanated from within the holy of holies (the highest place on the mount). All non-Jews (Gentiles) were allowed to ascend onto the platform, but they were not allowed to pass through a stone fence of latticework called the Soreg. This 500-cubit-square border separated the outer porticoes from the inner courts.

A portion of this Soreg can be seen as a faint line between the Royal Stoa and the temple in figure 9. Openings in the Soreg were clearly marked with inscriptions in Greek and Latin warning all Gentiles that they would be responsible for their own deaths if they entered the gates (compare Acts 21:28–30).[7]

Figure 7. Southern façade of the temple with large plaza and markets.

Figure 8. View from atop the place of the trumpeter on the southwest pinnacle (facing south), and a view from above the southeast corner of the temple (facing west).

Consider the depictions of Jesus cleansing the temple in the context of the monumental size of the Temple Mount and the number of pilgrims that frequented Jerusalem during festivals such as Passover. It is hard to know exactly how many money changers and sellers of sacrificial animals were involved or where they were located on the mount when Jesus confronted them and expelled them.

Figure 9. View of the Temple Mount from atop the southeast end of the Royal Stoa (facing northwest).

Unlike the Gentiles, all Jews could pass through the Soreg, cross the large stone courtyard, and enter the large square enclosure called the Court of the Women, depicted on the right in figure 9 and seen from the ground level in figure 11.

This court contained four large chambers in each of its corners, one for sorting wood to be used on the altar (northeast corner), one for those taking a Nazarite vow (southeast corner), one for oil and wine to be used in the temple (southwest corner), and one for lepers to wash themselves before being presented before the priests (northwest corner).[8] The Court of the Women also contained the treasury, which consisted of thirteen trumpet-shaped boxes for donations as depicted in the foreground of figure 11 (Mark 12:41–44).

Figure 10. The Soreg, or wall of partition, with inscriptions warning the Gentiles not to pass through the gates or they would be killed.

Figure 11. Interior view of the Court of the Women (facing southwest).

Figure 12. Nicanor Gate and 15 semi-circular steps on the west end of the Court of the Women.

Figure 13. The inner side of the Nicanor Gate with the Court of the Israelites separated from the Court of the Priests by a one-cubit-tall step.

Figure 14. The Court of the Priests (facing southwest) with the altar on the left and the sacrificial area on the right.

The innermost part of this court contained fifteen semicircular steps leading up to the large Nicanor Gate.[9] Levites would stand on these steps, play their instruments, and sing psalms. The Nicanor Gate was located at the top of these steps. Only Jewish men were allowed to pass through the gate into the Court of the Israelites, but they were not allowed to proceed beyond the one-cubit-high step into the Court of the Priests.

There were twenty-four distinct groups of priests who would officiate at the temple for one week at a time, thus ensuring that the special occasions (e.g., Passover, Pentecost, Tabernacles, Hanukkah; see Luke 1:5–9) would systematically rotate through each of the groups from year to year.[10]

Sacrificial animals were killed in the area north of the altar (Leviticus 1:11). Because of the large number of animals slain in the temple, especially during one of the annual feasts, a steady supply of water was required for the priests to wash themselves and keep their courtyard clean. A continuous flow of fresh water was piped in from Solomon's Pools, located south of Bethlehem.[11] The priestly courtyard was built in such a way that water could

Figure 15. View of the Antonia Fortress from the Court of the Gentiles (on the left) and view looking down into the courtyards from the steps of the Antonia.

be flooded over the stones and then collected into an underground drainage system that channeled the sacrificial fluids and waste down into the Kidron brook, which eventually emptied into the Dead Sea.

A series of steps led from this courtyard up to a porch on the eastern face of the Sanctuary. This porch contained a giant vine with grapes and leaves made out of pure gold. The wooden door into the Sanctuary was covered with a colorful outer veil that could be pulled aside. The holy place contained three sacred furnishings: the candelabra (or menorah), the altar of incense, and the table of shewbread (Hebrews 9:2). A large veil hung from floor to ceiling and wall to wall, separating the Holy Place from the holy of holies. Only the high priest could pass through the veil, one time each year, on the Day of Atonement (Yom Kippur; Hebrews 9:7). He would sprinkle blood on the rock escarpment where the ark of the covenant had been placed during Solomon's time. At Jesus's crucifixion, this veil was ripped from top to bottom (Mark 15:38; Matthew 27:5; Luke 23:45), symbolically signifying that he was *the* High Priest who would be going into the presence of God and opening the gate of heaven for all who would choose to enter as well (Hebrews 9–10).

The Antonia Fortress was a large structure built in the northwest corner of the Temple Mount. It was built as a northern fortress for the city and Temple Mount. It also housed the Roman garrison in charge of keeping the peace in the temple. Roman soldiers pulled Paul away from an angry crowd in the Court of the Gentiles and brought him here, to the "castle" (Acts 21:30–37), where from the stairs he addressed the crowd below.

Kidron Valley and the Mount of Olives

Jesus's triumphal entry began in the region of Bethany and Bethphage, just over the Mount of Olives to the east of Jerusalem. He ascended the mount and then descended into the steep Kidron Valley before riding triumphantly into Jerusalem (Matthew 21:6–11; Mark 11:7–11; Luke 19:35–38; John 12:12–18).

This mountain forms part of the border between the fruitful plains and hill country to the west and the desolate Judean wilderness that slopes sharply down toward Jericho, the

Figure 17. View of the southern portion of the Kidron Valley with tombs carved into the limestone face of the Mount of Olives, facing southeast.

Figure 16. East of Jerusalem. The temple was aligned in such a way that it formed a straight line with the summit of the Mount of Olives.

Figure 18. View of Temple Mount from the Mount of Olives (facing west), just before sunset.

Jordan River Valley, and Dead Sea to the east. Jesus often resorted to the Mount of Olives (John 18:2; Luke 22:39).

From here he delivered the famous Olivet Discourse to his disciples (Matthew 24; Joseph Smith—Matthew), wherein he foretold the complete destruction of the temple and revealed many things that would occur at the hands of the Romans (AD 70) and many signs that would be shown before his second coming. It was also from this mountain that Luke tells us that Jesus ascended to heaven following his forty-day post-Resurrection ministry (Acts 1:1–11).

Near the northern end of the Kidron Valley, at the base of the Mount of Olives, was a grove of olive trees and a working olive press (called a *gethsemane*) located inside a cave. The night before Jesus's crucifixion, after the Last Supper with his apostles, he invited them to leave the Upper Room with him (John 14:31). Jesus continued to teach them as they made their way up the Kidron Valley (John 15–16). Right before entering Gethsemane, he paused to offer his intercessory prayer (John 17).

Figure 19. View of the temple's eastern gate (the Golden Gate) from the Kidron, just outside Gethsemane looking up the hill toward the west. The tip of the Dome of the Rock can be seen in the center of the photo.

The Lower City (City of David)

In earlier Old Testament times, Jerusalem was limited to the region known as the Lower City (the outlined region in figure 22). As time passed, various kings and leaders kept expanding the reach of the city to the north and the west. The Gihon Spring was the only source of fresh water in the city during biblical times. In the time of Isaiah, Hezekiah built a tunnel through solid rock, connecting the fresh water from this spring to the pool of Siloam, which sits at the lowest point of elevation in the city, near the main southern entrance into the city.

Right before his death, King David directed his son Solomon to be placed on David's mule and taken to the Gihon Spring. There he was anointed king of Israel before riding triumphantly into the city to sit upon his father's throne (1 Kings 1:32–35).

Figure 20. Olive trees in Gethsemane today.

Figure 21. Modern entrance into the cave that housed the oil press (Gethsemane) in Jesus's day.

Figure 22. The Lower City, or City of David.

Centuries after this event, Jesus was seen riding into Jerusalem, on "the foal of an ass," amid shouts of hosanna from the Kidron Valley, and the leaders of the Jews did not miss the significance of the symbolism (Mark 11:7–10; Matthew 21:9–11; John 12:12–19).[12] They demanded that Jesus stop the crowds from declaring him the son of David, heir to his throne (Matthew 21:15–16; Luke 19:39–40).

Another feature of the Kidron Valley was an extensive garbage dump dating to the first century.[13] The odors from this giant refuse pile, combined with the animal waste tainting the brook Kidron (by-products of temple sacrifices) would have made this lower part of the

Figure 23. The pool of Siloam, a large public pool for ritual washing (*mikvah*). Fresh water could also be gathered from a small feeder pool on the left.

Kidron Valley very unpleasant, especially at Passover when so many lambs were being killed and bled out in the temple.

Another story involving this part of the city took place in John 9. On that Sabbath day, Jesus left the temple and encountered a blind man. Jesus made spittle clay, anointed the man's eyes, and commanded him to go wash in the pool of Siloam. There were many other sources of water situated much closer to the temple, but Jesus required the blind man to walk a great distance, down a steep path with many steps, on the Sabbath day in order to reach Siloam and wash.

The Upper City (Mount Zion or the Western Hill)

The Upper City is so designated because of its higher elevation in relation to the other parts of the city. This was where Jerusalem's elite built their homes, most of which were opulent in comparison with the poorer class of dwellings in the Lower City. Visitors to Jerusalem today can see a few homes and structures that date back to the time of Christ, including the Palatial Mansion and the Burnt House of the Katros family.[14]

Herod built a large palace on the highest point of the Western Hill, such that he could look down into the temple courtyards to the east. Within these fortified walls, he built two castle-like palaces, each with its own lavish accommodations for hundreds of guests. The walls also encompassed extensive water features, gardens, vineyards, extravagant furnishings, and a large barracks for soldiers assigned to protect the palace.[15]

For added fortification, he built three towers on the northern end of the palace (these can be seen in figure 26 as the features of highest altitude in the city). Herod named the

Figure 24. View of the Upper City (facing west) from the pool of Siloam.

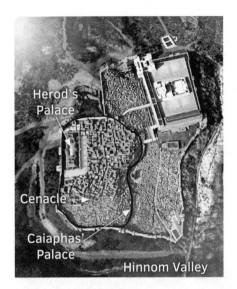

Figure 25. The Upper City, Mount Zion, or the Western Hill.

towers Phasael (after his brother), Hippicus (after a friend), and Mariamne (after one of his wives).

The Cenacle, or traditional Upper Room site, would be located near the bottom left corner of figure 27. The current Cenacle was not constructed until the twelfth century, but it is possibly built over the ruins of the original site where Jesus shared his last supper with the apostles, washed their feet, and introduced the sacrament. Other possibilities for the location of the Upper Room include other parts of the Upper City or any large, open room on a top floor of one of the many structures built in step-wise fashion into the steep hillside that separates the Lower City from the Upper City (as depicted running down the middle of figure 28). The traditional site, Akeldama, where Judas Iscariot was buried after hanging himself (Matthew 27:8; Acts 1:19), would be located in the far right-hand side of figure 27 in the Hinnom Valley.

St. Peter in Gallicantu (i.e., "cock's crow") is the traditional site of Caiaphas's Palace, where Jesus was taken following his arrest in Gethsemane to be judged of the leaders of the Jews: Caiaphas (the high priest), Annas (Caiaphas's father-in-law), and the Sanhedrin (the authoritative body of Jewish leaders). This palace would have been located near the southern

Figure 26. View from the southwest corner of the city looking north. Mount Zion is on the left with Herod's Palace. Mount Moriah is on the right.

edge of the steep hill separating the Upper from the Lower City (near the middle of figure 27).

On Jesus's final night he left the Upper Room, likely from one of the southern parts of the city, walked up the Kidron Valley, endured the agonies of Gethsemane, and was taken back down the valley, into the city, and up the hill to Caiaphas's Palace. After being condemned by the Sanhedrin, he was taken to be judged by Pilate. Even though long-standing tradition places the judgment and scourging experiences in the Antonia Fortress, it would have been more likely for Pilate to have been staying in the more luxurious accommodations of Herod's Palace at the time. Pilate sent Jesus to be judged by Herod Antipas (Herod the Great's son, the Roman-appointed ruler in Galilee and Perea who was in Jerusalem at the time; Luke 23:7–12). Herod sent him back to Pilate, where he was ultimately condemned, scourged, and sent away to be crucified.

Figure 27. View of the southern part of the Upper City in the foreground and the Lower City in the background with the Hinnom Valley on the right.

Figure 28. View of the Upper City on the right with the priestly mansions in the foreground and Herod's Palace in the background. The Lower City is shown on the left.

The Northern Quarries, Gardens, and Pools

The pool of Bethesda is the site of the miracle recorded in John 5. It is described as a pool near the sheep market with five porches. After many centuries of confusion over the meaning of this description, two large pools were discovered north of the Temple Mount in a region known as Bezetha.[16] The five porches refer to the covered porticoes surrounding the four sides of the pools, plus one dividing them down the middle. The northern pool was a large collecting pool for fresh water. The southern pool was a large *mikvah* (ritual bath) for Jewish purity rituals. A sluice gate could be opened between the two pools, and water would rush down into the southern pool from the freshwater supply of the higher northern pool.

This part of Jerusalem was known as a gathering place for many who were sick and infirm. During the time of Christ, or shortly thereafter, a Greco-Roman healing center was built in this same area. These ancient hospitals were called *asclepeions*, being named after the Greek god of healing and well-being, Asclepius. In the King James Version of the Bible, John 5:4 states that "an angel went down at a certain season into the pool, and troubled the water; whosoever then first after the troubling of the water stepped in was made whole of whatsoever disease he had." This verse, however, is absent from all early manuscripts of the New Testament. It was added much later, perhaps to explain the lame man's frustration at having "no man, when the water is troubled, to put me into the pool" (John 5:7).

Figure 29. The northern regions of Jerusalem.

Because of heavy public usage of a large *mikvah* (like the one in figure 31 and the pool of Siloam), the water would likely have become extremely dirty and contaminated. When an infusion of fresh water was introduced into the pool through the sluice gate, the sick folk would rush to be the first ones into the pool, believing they would be healed. Jesus bypassed all the traditions of the day and simply commanded the man to take up his bed and walk, even though it was the Sabbath day (John 5:8–9). This event led to Jesus's first major confrontation in the Gospel of John with the leaders of the Jews in the temple later that day (John 5:10–47).

There has been much debate over the location of Calvary, or the "place of the skull," where Jesus was crucified, buried, and then resurrected (Mark 15:22; Matthew 27:33; John 19:17). The majority of the Christian world views the Church of the Holy Sepulchre as the site for Golgotha. The traditions for this location date back many centuries. Helena, Emperor Constantine's mother, paid for a church to be constructed over the site in the early fourth century.

Since 1867, however, many Protestants and other Christian groups believe that Gordon's Calvary, or the Garden Tomb, is where these events took place. One argument advanced for this site is the skull-like rock near the actual tomb.

Figure 30. The dividing walkway between the north and south pools.

Figure 31. View looking down at the first-century *mikvah*.

Figure 32. A skull-like image in the rock near the Garden Tomb.

Interpretation of the "skull" passages could also simply mean a place where death occurred and not be dependent on a physical characteristic of the surrounding land. Both locations would have been outside the walls of the city in that day (John 19:20). Both would have been near a road into the city. Both locations also had gardens nearby: "Now in the place where he was crucified there was a garden; and in the garden a new sepulchre, wherein was never man yet laid" (John 19:41; see also Matthew 27:60). The Church of the Holy Sepulchre was an active quarry in the first century, whereas the Garden Tomb, based on its style and design, seems to have been carved hundreds of years before the time of Christ. There could have been other tombs in the vicinity of the Garden Tomb, however, that were newly carved by Joseph of Arimathea. The critical point is not exactly *where* these events happened but that somewhere in this region Jesus Christ was crucified on a cross, laid in a tomb, and rose triumphant over the grave three days later.

Conclusion

While it is not essential for a disciple of Christ to physically travel to the Holy Land to gain a testimony of the divinity of his life and mission, a better understanding of the setting where those events unfolded adds a richness and new dimension to one's faith in Christ. Since travel to Israel is not feasible for most Christians in the world today, digital reconstructions of the city allow everyone to visually and virtually immerse themselves in the world of Jesus and his disciples. These experiences allow a student of the scriptures to better understand what they are reading as they gain a perspective in scope and scale of the places where these events took place.

∼

Tyler J. Griffin is an associate professor in the Department of Ancient Scripture at Brigham Young University.

All of the 3-D images included in this chapter are screenshots from an app called Virtual New Testament. Visit virtualscriptures.org to download the app for Mac or PC. Search for "Virtual

New Testament" in the Apple or Google Play stores to download the app to your smart phone or smart device (Android devices and iPhones/iPads).

Further Reading

Bahat, Dan. *The Carta Jerusalem Atlas.* Jerusalem: Carta, 2011.

Galbraith, David, D. Kelly Ogden, and Andrew C. Skinner. *Jerusalem: The Eternal City.* Salt Lake City: Deseret Book, 1996.

Ogden, D. Kelly. *Biblical and Modern Geography of the Holy Land.* Jerusalem: Jerusalem Center for Near Eastern Studies, 1985.

Richman, Chaim. *The Holy Temple of Jerusalem.* Jerusalem: Temple Institute, 1997.

Ritmeyer, Leen. *The Quest: Revealing the Temple Mount in Jerusalem.* Jerusalem: Carta, The Lamb Foundation, 2006.

Ritmeyer, Leen, and Kathleen Ritmeyer. *The Ritual of the Temple in the Time of Christ.* Jerusalem: Carta, 2002.

Ritmeyer, Leen, and Kathleen Ritmeyer. *Secrets of Jerusalem's Temple Mount.* Washington, DC: Biblical Archaeology Society, 1998.

Shanks, Hershel. *Jerusalem's Temple Mount: From Solomon to the Golden Dome.* New York: Continuum, 2007.

Notes

1. Babylonian Talmud Baba Bathra 4a.
2. For a brief discussion of the significance of Jerusalem, and more importantly, the Temple Mount, see Hershel Shanks, *Jerusalem's Temple Mount: From Solomon to the Golden Dome* (New York: Continuum International, 2007), 1–7.
3. There is a long-standing tradition that Jews would rarely or never pass through Samaria. More recent scholarship calls that tradition into question. Jesus himself passed through Samaria in John 4 and Luke 9:51–56; 17:11. Other Jews in the New Testament also pass through Samaria in Acts 8:5, 14–15, 25, 26; 15:3. Additionally, Josephus, the ancient Jewish historian, clearly stated, "It was the custom of the Galileans, when they came to the holy city [Jerusalem] at the time of the festivals, to take their *journeys through the country of the Samaritans*" (*Antiquities* 20.118; emphasis added).
4. See quick statistics on the Herodian Temple Mount walls in Leen Ritmeyer, *The Quest: Revealing the Temple Mount in Jerusalem* (Jerusalem: Carta, 2006), 20. The surface area of the Temple Mount is 1,520,638.2 square feet, or 168,959.8 square yards. For comparison, a US football field is 360 feet long (including the endzones) and 160 feet wide for a total of 6,400 square yards. On the ancient Temple Mount, 26.4 football fields could fit (168,959.8 / 6,400).
5. See Shanks, *Jerusalem's Temple Mount*, 79, "The alternating depths of the stair treads forced pilgrims to slow their pace while approaching the holy area." See also Ritmeyer, *Quest*, 65: "The thirty steps, partly cut into the rock and partly built of large stones, were laid alternately as steps and landings, thus conforming to the slope of the mountain and assuring a reverent ascent."
6. For more details on the trumpeting stone, see Ritmeyer, *Quest*, 57–60.
7. See Ritmeyer, *Quest*, 346–47.
8. See Ritmeyer, *Quest*, 352–54.
9. See Ritmeyer, *Quest*, 354–56.
10. See Chaim Richman, *The Holy Temple of Jerusalem* (Jerusalem: The Temple Institute and Carta, 1997), 20.
11. See Ritmeyer, *Quest*, 62.
12. The triumphal entry was a common event in Jewish (and Roman) culture when a king returned from battle to show that he was victorious over the enemy. See Joshua 6; 1 Samuel 18:6–7; 2 Samuel 6:1–5, 12–17;

1 Kings 1:32–40; 8:1–61; Nehemiah 12:31–43; Esther 6:7–12; Psalm 68:24–27; Zechariah 9:9. See also Josephus, *Jewish War* 7.123–157; Plutarch, *Aemilius* 33–35; Dio Cassius 63.4.1–5.2. See further T. E. Schmidt, "Mark 15.16–32: The Crucifixion Narrative and the Roman Triumphal Procession," *New Testament Studies* 41, no. 1 (January 1995): 1–18; and H. S. Versnel, *Triumphus* (Leiden, Netherlands: Brill, 1970).

13. See the discussion regarding the recent findings of the ancient garbage dump in the Kidron Valley at https://www.ritmeyer.com/2017/12/29/jerusalems-garbage/.

14. See https://www.haaretz.com/archaeology/priestly-quarter-of-ancient-jerusalem-found-on-mt-zion-1.5409239.

15. Josephus's description of Herod's Palace: "[The King's palace] was completely enclosed within a wall 30 cubits high, broken at equal distances by ornamental towers, and contained immense banqueting-halls and bedchambers for a hundred guests. The interior fittings are indescribable—the variety of the stones (for species rare in every other country were here collected in abundance), ceilings wonderful both for the length of the beams and the splendor of their surface decoration, the host of apartments with their infinite varieties of design, all amply furnished, while most of the objects in each of them were of silver or gold. All around were many circular cloisters, leading one into another, the columns in each being different, and their open courts all of a greensward; there were groves of various trees intersected by long walks, which were bordered by deep canals, and ponds everywhere studded with bronze figures through which the water was discharged and around the streams were numerous cots for tame pigeons" (*Jewish War* 5.176–181).

16. See https://www.biblicalarchaeology.org/daily/biblical-sites-places/jerusalem/the-bethesda-pool-site-of-one-of-jesus%E2%80%99-miracles/ for a description of the archaeology at the site.

4

The Temple of Herod

David Rolph Seely

The First Temple/Solomon's Temple

After King David conquered Jerusalem, Solomon built his splendid temple in ca. 966 BC (1 Kings 5–9; 2 Chronicles 2–4) on the top of a hill that was traditionally considered to be the site of Mount Moriah, where Abraham nearly sacrificed his son Isaac (2 Chronicles 3:1; Genesis 22:2). When Solomon dedicated his temple he declared, "I have surely built thee an house to dwell in" (1 Kings 8:13). In Hebrew the temple is referred to as the *beth Yahweh* "house of the Lord," *har habayit* "mountain of the house [of the Lord]," or *hekhal* "palace," indicating that the primary function and symbolism of the ancient Israelite temple was to represent where God dwelt in the midst of his people. The ark of the covenant in the holy of holies represented the throne of the Lord, who was described as dwelling "between the cherubim" (1 Samuel 4:4; 2 Samuel 6:2). In addition to representing the presence of God, the temple represented the covenant that bound the Lord to his people (Leviticus 26:11–12), since the ark of the covenant contained the Ten Commandments written on stone tablets (Exodus 25:16).[1] According to Deuteronomy 12, after the temple was built all sacrifices were to be done only at the Jerusalem temple. Thus, the temple was a central religious, political, social, cultural, and economic institution in ancient Israel, and beginning in the days of Hezekiah and Josiah it was the only place where the ancient Israelites, under the authorization of the priests and Levites, worshipped the Lord God through sacrifices and offerings and pilgrimage. It was also a central place for fasting, prayer, and singing hymns. The sac-

Looking northwest to the Temple of Herod.

rifices, offerings, and furnishing of the Israelite temples such as altars, basins, veils, candle-
sticks, incense altars, tables for shewbread offerings, and the priestly clothing were familiar
to the gentile cultures surrounding Israel.[2] The Israelite temples were unique in that they had
no image of their deity.

Solomon's temple is known as the First Temple, and it was the temple familiar to Isaiah,
Jeremiah, Ezekiel, and Lehi—prophets who warned the people that unless they repented and
kept the covenant, the Lord would allow their enemies to destroy Jerusalem and scatter the
people. After many generations of apostasy the Lord allowed the Assyrians to conquer and
deport the northern kingdom of Israel in 722. Judah, in spite of the reforms of Hezekiah and
Josiah, also continued to disobey the covenant, and in ca. 586 BC the Lord allowed Nebuchadnezzar and the Babylonians to capture Jerusalem and destroy the temple and take many
of the people into exile.[3]

The Second Temple/Zerubbabel's Temple

In ca. 539 BC Cyrus the Persian conquered Babylon and granted permission to the Jews
along with other exiled peoples living in Babylon to return to their homes. Cyrus granted
the Jews permission to take back to Jerusalem the temple vessels that had been captured by
the Babylonians and rebuild their temple (2 Chronicles 36:22; Ezra 1). Led by Zerubbabel,
the Jews eventually rebuilt the temple (called Zerubbabel's temple) and rededicated it in ca.
515 BC (Ezra 5–6); that temple would stand until ca. 20 BC, when Herod dismantled it and
built a new temple in its place. The phrase "Second Temple" is a designation used for both
Zerubbabel's and Herod's temples.[4]

The people returning from exile sought to restore temple worship by erecting a replica
of Solomon's temple on the Temple Mount. However, because of poverty they were unable
to adorn it with the wealth and splendor of the First Temple. The book of Ezra records that

at the dedication of Zerubbabel's temple, those who had seen the First Temple wept (Ezra 3:12). Nevertheless, the temple and the Temple Mount were enhanced by wealthy donations and by additional building projects through the Persian and Hellenistic periods.

Zerubbabel's temple enjoyed a long period of relative tranquility from ca. 515 to 198 BC under the Persians and the Ptolemies based in Egypt. This period would end in 198 BC when the Seleucids, based in Syria, defeated the Ptolemies and took control of Yehud/Judea. Eventually, by order of the Seleucid king Antiochus Epiphanes IV (reigned 175–164 BC), Judaism was deemed illicit and Antiochus desecrated the temple by offering sacrifices to foreign gods and to himself on its altar (1 Maccabees 1:20–63). While some of the Jews acquiesced, most were outraged. In 168 BC the Jews, led by members of the family known as the Maccabees, revolted and against overwhelming odds defeated the Seleucids (1:64–4:35). Upon taking back the Temple Mount, Judas and his men set about cleansing the temple in preparation for restoring the sacrifices. In ca. 165 BC the Maccabees rededicated the temple, an event commemorated by the Feast of Dedication, or Hanukkah (4:36–59; John 10:22). The Maccabees (a Hebrew nickname meaning "hammer"), also known as the Hasmoneans (family name), established an independent Jewish nation led by a Hasmonean king that enjoyed its independence until 63 BC, when the Romans captured Jerusalem. Josephus, a first-century-AD Jewish writer, recounted that Pompey, the conquering general, made it a point to enter into the holy of holies of the temple and was amazed to see that the rumors of there being no image to the god of Israel were true. Pompey arranged for the cleansing of the temple and the resumption of temple service under Roman rule.[5]

Herod's Temple (ca. 20 BC–AD 70)

Herod (reigned ca. 40–4 BC) was one of the great builders of antiquity; his goal in rebuilding the temple was to create one of the most magnificent buildings in his day and in the process to try to please his subjects, the Jews. Herod began to build his temple in ca. 20 BC, and it was not completed until ca. AD 63. According to Josephus, Herod believed that building the temple would be a task great enough "to assure his eternal remembrance."[6] Herod's temple was one of the wonders of the ancient world—a beautiful building and a marvel of engineering. Josephus, who was an eyewitness of the temple, reported, "The exterior of the building lacked nothing that could astound either mind or eye. . . . To approaching strangers it appeared from a distance like a snow-clad mountain; for all that was not over laid with gold was of purest white."[7]

Ancient sources pertaining to Herod's temple include the writings of Josephus (ca. AD 37–100)[8] and Philo (ca. 20 BC–AD 50)[9]—both eyewitnesses of the temple—and tractates in the Mishnah: Middot ("measurements"), Tamid ("the permanent sacrifice"), Yoma ("the Day of Atonement"), and Shekalim ("the shekel dues").[10] While there is no archaeological evidence of the temple proper, there are many architectural and archaeological evidences of the Temple Mount, including several important inscriptions.[11]

Josephus records that Herod, in the eighteenth year of his reign (20–19 BC), gave a speech to the people in which he proposed to rebuild Zerubbabel's temple in gratitude for the fact that he had, "by the will of God, brought the Jewish nation to such a state of prosperity as it has never known before."[12] His envisioned rebuilding project was a delicate operation since it would involve the complete demolition of Zerubbabel's temple and the expeditious building of the new temple.[13] In order to assuage the fears of the people that he would not build the new temple after demolishing the old one, in consultation with religious leaders Herod first prepared all the necessary materials for his temple. Next, he allegedly appointed ten thousand men to rebuild the temple and specifically trained a thousand priests as builders and stonemasons so they would be able to carry out the construction in the inner courts of the temple where nonpriests would not be allowed to enter.[14] For the erection of the altar, Herod followed the biblical prescription (Exodus 20:22) and used stones quarried nearby not touched by iron.[15] The temple proper was built in a year and a half and the surrounding porticoes and courtyards in eight years.[16] However, construction on the whole complex continued for more than eighty years from the time it was begun and was only completed in AD 63 (compare John 2:19).[17]

From the descriptions preserved in Josephus and the Mishnah, correlated with the remains and the excavations around the Temple Mount, it is possible to reconstruct what the mount and the temple looked like with some degree of confidence.[18] The dimensions of Herod's temple are given in cubits and/or *stadia* in the ancient sources; while the length of a cubit probably varied through time, most believe that the cubit used in the building of the temple was the long cubit. For the sake of convenience, this study will describe the measurements of the temple in terms of feet and meters, usually based on the long cubit of about 21 inches.[19]

Looking west to the Temple Mount from the Mount of Olives.

Herod's temple mount

Solomon's temple and Zerubbabel's temple, including the Hasmonean additions, were confined to the top of the hill called Mount Moriah, bounded on the east and south by the Kidron Valley and to the west by the Tyropoean Valley. The temple faced east toward the Mount of Olives. To the north of the mount was the Roman Antonia Fortress, and to the west and south was the city of Jerusalem. In order to enlarge the sacred platform, Herod expanded the area of the Temple Mount to the south and west by adding fill and erecting a series of arched vaults. He thus doubled the size of Solomon's temple mount.[20] According to the Mishnah, Solomon's temple mount was a square of 500 cubits on each side (861 feet/262.5 meters), or about 17 acres (Middot 2:1). When completed, Herod's temple mount was a trapezoid-shaped walled platform 1,550 feet (472 meters) long north to south, and about 1,000 feet (304 meters) wide east to west.[21] It measured about 144,000 meters square, or 36 acres. Scholars have noted that this was one of the largest sacred precincts in the ancient world. It was twice as large as Trajan's Forum in Rome and three and a half times more extensive than the combined temples of Jupiter and Astarte-Venus at Baalbek. In fact, it was about the same size as the Neo-Babylonian Marduk temple complex in Babylon.[22]

Herod's temple precinct was demarcated by fences and gates into concentric rings of successive holiness. The outer courtyard was called the Court of the Gentiles—here all nations were invited to come and worship the Lord. This space was open to Jews and Gentiles. Around the perimeter of the Court of the Gentiles was a portico where people could gather and teach or be taught. Along the south wall (some believe along the east wall) of this court was a long colonnaded porch forming a basilica-like room running east and west with rows of 162 beautiful columns with Corinthian capitals. Called the Royal Stoa, it is probably Solomon's porch of the New Testament (John 10:23). The Court of the Gentiles was separated by a wall from the court where only Israelite men and women were permitted to go. Gentiles were forbidden from entering this inner court. Posted around this barrier were signs warning Gentiles not to pass on pain of death. Two of these signs have been found—one contained the entire inscription reading "No Gentile shall enter inward of the partition and barrier around the Temple, and whoever is caught shall be responsible to himself for his subsequent death."[23] Apparently temple officials were given the right to enforce this ban on foreigners in this sacred space. The seriousness of the offense of Gentiles crossing the barrier is dramatized by the story in Acts where Paul was falsely accused of bringing non-Jews past this enclosure and the mob attempted to kill him (Acts 21:27–32). The temple proper was approached from the east by passing through the Court of Women—where men and women could go to observe the sacrifices through the gate. A long narrow court stood between the Court of the Women and the altar called the Court of the Israelites; there only Jewish men could go. Beyond that court only the priests and Levites could serve in the area around the altar; only the priests could enter the temple, and only the high priest could enter the holy of holies once a year.

Archaeological evidence has determined that there were eight gates to Herod's temple mount from the surrounding city: one in the east, two in the south, four in the west, and one

Temple of Herod looking northwest from the Court of the Gentiles.

in the north. Archaeological remains of ritual baths, or *mikvahs*, have been excavated near several of these gates, indicating that the Jews would ritually purify themselves before coming onto the Temple Mount. The most common entrance for pilgrims coming to the temple were the two splendid gates in the south, called the Double Gate and the Triple Gate, that were approached by a monumental stairway.

The temple and temple worship

Herod's temple represented the house of the Lord and was the center of Israelite worship as legislated in the Old Testament and enhanced by centuries of Jewish tradition.[24] Temple worship consisted of a complex series of sacrifices and offerings that could only be offered at the temple. Additionally, the temple was the focal point of the Jewish festivals, including the three pilgrimage festivals that all Jews throughout the world were required to celebrate at the temple in Jerusalem.

The temple proper was situated near the middle of the inner courtyard, facing east, and surrounded by a wall. Jewish men and women could pass from the east through the Beautiful Gate (Acts 3:2) to enter a square courtyard in front of the temple called the Court of the Women, where, Josephus records, "[we] who were ritually clean used to pass with our wives."[25] Just inside this gate, chests were placed for the collection of monetary offerings, such as the two mites offered by the widow (Luke 21:1–4). Four large lampstands were erected in this court, each with four bowls, to light the temple—especially at the Feast of Tabernacles.

Men and women congregated in the Court of the Women to observe through the gate the priests offering the sacrifices at the altar and to receive the priestly benediction. Here Jewish men and women could participate in temple worship through prayer, fasting, and hymns. Proceeding to the west, Israelite men climbed fifteen curved stairs and entered into

Court of the Women looking west to the Nicanor Gate, Court of the Israelites, and Court of the Priests.

the narrow Court of the Israelites separated from the Court of the Priests by a line in the pavement. Standing in the Court of the Israelites, one could see the large stone altar 40 feet [12 meters] square and 15 feet [4.5 meters] high[26] upon which the priests offered the sacrifices. A ramp led to the top of the altar that had horns at the four corners. The priests offered regular daily offerings at the temple on behalf of all Israel and also assisted in the many offerings brought by individuals to the temple. Under the law of Moses there were five major sacrifices (Leviticus 1–7). The burnt offering was the sacrifice of an animal that was completely burned on the altar—the smoke symbolized the offering ascending into heaven. In addition to the burnt offering, the sin offering and trespass offering were connected with the offering of blood for atonement from sin and ritual impurity (Leviticus 17:11). The meal offering was offered for thanksgiving. The peace offering represented a communal meal—divided into three portions: one given to the Lord, one given to the priests, and one taken home and eaten by the offerer. To the north of the altar was the Place of Slaughtering, where the sacrificial animals were butchered and skinned. Between the altar and the temple was a large bronze laver providing water for washing. Each of the priests ritually washed their hands and feet before and after officiating at the temple (Exodus 30:20–21).

According to the Mishnah, Herod's temple was 100 cubits (172 feet/52.5 meters) long, wide, and high (Middot 4:6) and was divided like Solomon's temple into three rooms: the porch, the Holy Place, and the holy of holies.[27] The gold-covered facade of the temple was imposing. On the east wall of the Holy Place, visible through the portal of the temple, was an elaborate gate to the Holy Place. Josephus says there were pillars on either side of the gate but does not specify how many. Early depictions on coins and in synagogues depict four columns with two on each side. Josephus further describes "a golden vine with grape-clusters hanging from it" that was placed above the door and wound itself around the pillars.[28] This vine was decorated with the costly gifts brought to the temple and was described in the Mishnah: "A golden vine stood over the entrance to the sanctuary, trained over the posts; and whosoever gave a leaf, or a berry, or a cluster as a freewill-offering, he brought it and the priests hung it

Court of the Priests.

thereon" (Middot 3:8). On the stairs leading up to the doors of the temple the priests would daily gather to recite the priestly benediction on the people (Numbers 6:23–27).

A large veil of several colors hung in front of the doors at the entrance to the Holy Place. Passing through the veil, one entered the Holy Place. The Holy Place and the holy of holies together comprised one large rectangular room completely covered with plates of gold separated only by the veil of the temple. In the Holy Place there were three furnishings: the table for the bread of the presence (shewbread); the seven-branched lampstand, or menorah; and the incense altar. Each week the tribes of Israel offered twelve loaves of bread to the Lord on the table, and at the end of the week the priests ate them on the Sabbath. This symbolized a sacred meal shared by the offerer, the Lord, and the priest. The menorah is described as being shaped like a tree consisting of a central axis and three branches on each side, making seven branches in all. At the top of each branch was a cup filled with olive oil that functioned as a lamp. Because of its form, the menorah is often associated with the tree of life.[29] The lamp was the only source of light in the temple. Each day the priests entered the Holy Place to light and trim the lamps and to light the incense. The golden altar of incense stood next to the veil of the temple. Incense was expensive and was thus seen as a sacrifice, and the sweet odor helped to counteract the smells of sacrifice at the temple. It also effectively created an otherworldly environment suggesting the presence of God. In the scriptures the burning of incense symbolized prayer (Psalm 141:2; Revelation 5:8; 8:4). In the New Testament, Zecharias was officiating at the incense altar, with a prayer in his heart, when Gabriel appeared to him to announce the birth of John the Baptist (Luke 1:5–23).

Separating the Holy Place from the holy of holies was another veil. The veil of the temple consisted of two curtains hung about 18 inches apart. The outer curtain was looped up on the south side, and the inner one on the north side provided a corridor for the high priest to walk through on the day that he entered the holy of holies so that no one else could see into the holy of holies. The holy of holies was a square-shaped room 20 cubits (34.4 feet/10.50 meters) in width and length with a height of 40 cubits (69 feet/21 meters) (Middot 4:7). The

The Holy Place with Menorah (left), Altar of Incense (center), and Table for the Bread of Presence (right).

interior was covered with plates of beaten gold. In the tabernacle and Solomon's temple, the original focal point of the worship of Israel was the ark of the covenant, which was covered by the mercy seat with two cherubim representing the throne of God and designating his presence. In the Second Temple the holy of holies was empty since the ark of the covenant and the cherubim had disappeared in the course of the destruction of Solomon's temple in 586 BC.[30] Rabbinic tradition identified a stone on the floor of the holy of holies, rising to a height of three finger breadths, as the "foundation stone" (*eben shetiyyah*)—the very stone with which the creation of the world began (Mishnah Yoma 5:1). On the Day of Atonement in Old Testament times, the high priest sprinkled the blood of the sacrifice on the mercy seat of the ark in order to make atonement. In Herod's temple the high priest sprinkled the blood of the sacrifice on this stone. The Mishnaic tractate Middot relates that in the upper story of the holy of holies were openings through which workmen could be let down in boxes to assist in the maintenance of this space (Middot 4:5).

The festivals

The most important holy day in ancient Israel was the Sabbath (Saturday), and this day was celebrated by changing the twelve loaves of the bread of the presence, with the priests eating the week-old bread, and by offering a double sacrifice at the temple. According to biblical law (Exodus 23; 34; Deuteronomy 16), three times a year all Jewish males were required to appear "before the Lord" (i.e., at the temple). The three festivals are Passover, Shavuot (Weeks/Pentecost), and Tabernacles (Booths). At these festivals the Jews celebrated and renewed their covenantal relationship with the Lord and expressed thanksgiving by prayer, feasting, sacrifices, and offerings. Philo of Alexandria (ca. 20 BC–AD 50) described the significance of these annual pilgrimages:

> Countless multitudes from countless cities come, some over land, others over sea, from east and west and north and south at every feast. They take the temple for their port as a general haven and safe refuge from the bustle of the great turmoil of life, and there they seek to find calm weather, and released from the cares whose yoke has been heavy

upon them from their earliest years, to enjoy a brief breathing-space in scenes of genial cheerfulness.[31]

The temple had a function for each of these festivals. At Passover, which celebrated the exodus from Egypt, the Passover lambs were sacrificed at the temple and then taken to the homes, where the festival was celebrated by families. Fifty days later at the Festival of Weeks, or Pentecost (compare Acts 2), which celebrated the first harvest, individuals brought first-fruit offerings to the temple to be offered on the altar. The Feast of Tabernacles commemorated the wanderings in the wilderness, and the people were commanded to live for seven days in booths and to eat each day the bounty of the harvest with thanksgiving. In addition, a procession was held with the waving of palm branches, ethrog (citron fruit), and lulav (palm branch with myrtle and willow branches). Based on descriptions in extrabiblical Jewish traditions (Mishnah Sukkah "The Feast of Tabernacles" 4–5), an elaborate procession of water was held in conjunction with Tabernacles in which the priests drew water from the Siloam pool and brought it up in a happy procession to pour on the altar of the temple (compare John 7). At this festival the four great menorahs in the Court of the Women were lit, illuminating the whole of Jerusalem.

The most solemn yearly festival celebrated at the temple was the Day of Atonement, described in Leviticus 16. This festival was held on the tenth day of the seventh month, which began with Rosh Hashanah initiating the fall new year, four days before the Feast of Tabernacles. On this day the high priest led Israel in a series of sacrifices that would atone for sin and ritual impurity through the ritual of the two goats. One goat would be sacrificed, and upon the head of the other goat the sins of the people would be pronounced. This goat, known as the "scapegoat," would be sent into the wilderness. Then the high priest, as the climax of this ritual, was able to enter into the holy of holies to sprinkle the blood of the sacrifice on the floor, thus effecting the forgiveness of sin and ritual impurity and resulting in reconciliation, or at-one-ment, between God and humans.

Clothing of the high priest

While serving in the temple, the priests wore special clothing consisting of pantaloons, a white robe, an embroidered belt, and a round hat. In addition, the high priest wore four additional vestments (Exodus 28:3–43). First, he wore a long blue robe with embroidered pomegranates and golden bells hanging from the bottom. Next, he wore an apron called an ephod that encricled the body and was held in place by two shoulder straps, each bearing an onyx stone inscribed with the names of six tribes of Israel (28:6–10). Connected to the ephod was a breastplate containing twelve stones representing the twelve tribes of Israel (28:15–28). Thus, when the high priest officiated at the temple, he did so bearing the tribes of Israel symbolically before the Lord. An embroidered flap of the breastplate folded behind, forming a pouch wherein the high priest kept the divinatory instruments (the Urim and Thummim), representing the means of inquiring and receiving the will of the Lord. Finally, he wore a hat (called a turban) and a pure gold plate inscribed "Holiness to the Lord" (28:36–38).

Symbolism of the temple

The biblical descriptions of the furnishings of the temple rarely specify the symbolic meaning of the temple or its furnishings. However, in the Hellenistic-Roman period, Philo and Josephus set forth various interpretations giving cosmic significance to various aspects of the temple. Philo interpreted the high priestly clothing as representing the cosmos—the violet robe representing the air, the embroidered flowers the earth, and the pomegranates the water. Similarly, Josephus interpreted the seven lamps of the menorah as the seven planets, the twelve loaves of the bread of the presence as the circle of the year and the Zodiac, and the thirteen spices of the incense on the incense altar as coming from the sea and the land and signifying "all things are of God and for God."[32] Likewise, Josephus ascribed cosmic significance to the veil at the entrance of the temple: "The scarlet seemed emblematical of fire, the fine linen of the earth, the blue of the air, and the purple of the sea; the comparison in two cases being suggested by their color, and in that of the fine linen and purple by their origin, as the one is produced by the earth and the other by the sea. On this tapestry was portrayed a panorama of the heavens, the signs of the Zodiac excepted."[33] He also described the holy of holies: "In this stood nothing whatever: unapproachable, inviolable, invisible to all."[34]

The New Testament and the Temple

The temple is a central feature in the Gospel narratives of the life and ministry of Jesus. The Gospel of Luke opens in the temple with the appearance of the angel Gabriel to the priest Zacharias as he was officiating at the incense altar in the Holy Place (Luke 1:5–24), and the Gospel of Luke ends with a note that the disciples of Jesus, after his ascension, "were continually in the temple, praising and blessing God" (Luke 24:53). Forty days after the birth of Jesus, Mary and Joseph took him to the temple to offer the burnt and sin offerings as prescribed by the law of Moses (Leviticus 12:6–8), and there they met Anna and Simeon, who both proclaimed Jesus's messiahship (Luke 2:28–38). The only story of the youth of Jesus in the Gospels recounts how as a twelve-year-old, after being left behind in Jerusalem following the Passover feast, he was found by his parents conversing with the elders at the temple (Luke 2:41–52). And as part of the temptations, Jesus was transported by the Spirit (JST) to "a pinnacle of the temple" where Satan tempted him to throw himself off so that the angels would come and save him (Luke 4:9–11; Matthew 4:5). The Gospel of John records that Jesus cleansed the temple at the outset of his ministry as a symbol that he came in power and with authority, and Jesus used this occasion to teach of his eventual death and resurrection from the dead (John 2:13–25). Following this cleansing of the temple, the Jews asked Jesus for a sign of his authority. According to the Gospel of John, "Jesus answered and said unto them, Destroy this temple, and in three days I will raise it up. Then said the Jews, Forty and six years was this temple in building, and wilt thou rear it up in three days? But he spake of the temple of his body" (John 2:19–22).

Throughout his ministry Jesus came to Jerusalem each year to celebrate Passover. He regularly taught and healed at the temple (Matthew 21:14–15). In the temple precincts he observed the widow offering her alms and taught the lesson of the widow's mite (Mark 12:41–44). During the Feast of Dedication (Hanukkah), John records that Jesus taught in the porch of Solomon (John 10:22). According to the Synoptic Gospels (Matthew, Mark, and Luke), Jesus cleansed the temple at the end of his ministry. During the passion week, Jesus went to the temple, whose precincts were crowded with tens of thousands of pilgrims who had come to Jerusalem to celebrate Passover. There he made a whip and drove out those "that sold and bought in the temple, and overthrew the tables of the money-changers, and the seats of them that sold doves" (Matthew 21:12; Luke 19:45–47). Jesus explained his act by quoting Jeremiah 7:11: "My house shall be called the house of prayer; but ye have made it a den of thieves" (Matthew 20:13). More than six hundred years earlier, Jeremiah had come to the temple and had warned Israel that their unrepentant hypocrisy and sin would bring the destruction of the temple by the Babylonians. Jesus's reference to Jeremiah was thus an ominous foreshadowing of the future destruction of the temple by the Romans if the people did not repent. And finally, at the moment when Jesus died on the cross, the veil of the holy of holies in the temple was rent in two (Luke 23:45), symbolizing that through his atonement all would be able to enter into the presence of God.

The Gospel of John specifically portrays Jesus as a fulfillment of some of the symbols of the temple and its festivals. A passage at the beginning of John describes Jesus as the tabernacle when it says "and the Word was made flesh, and dwelt among us" (John 1:14). Here the English word *dwelt* is derived from the Greek verb *skēnoō* used in reference to the Old Testament tabernacle with the literal meaning "he tabernacled" or "pitched his tent" among us. Thus, through Jesus, God came to dwell among his people just as God had made his presence known among his people anciently in the tabernacle, in which he could "dwell among them" (Exodus 25:8). When John the Baptist first saw Jesus, he announced him as "the Lamb of God, which taketh away the sin of the world" (John 1:29), an allusion to the sacrifice of the lambs at the temple. And in the Gospel of John, Jesus is crucified on the cross on the day of Passover, when the paschal lambs were being sacrificed at the temple (19:31–37).[35] The Feast of Tabernacles included a ceremony of drawing water from the Siloam pool and pouring it on the altar of the temple and also of lighting the four great menorahs in the Court of the Women. Jesus may have been comparing himself to these symbols of water and light when in the context of this festival (7:2) he taught: "He that believeth on me, as the scripture hath said, out of his belly shall flow rivers of living water" (7:38), and also "I am the light of the world" (8:12).

Following the death of Jesus, the book of Acts records that the apostles and followers of Jesus continued to teach and worship at the temple. A pivotal event occurred fifty days after the death of Jesus during the pilgrimage feast of Pentecost, in which many Jews had come to Jerusalem to offer up to God their firstfruit harvests at the temple. On that day the Holy Spirit descended on the apostles like a mighty wind and tongues of fire, causing them to speak in tongues. Three thousand people followed Peter's invitation to repent and be baptized in the name of Jesus Christ—fulfilling the symbols of Pentecost as the firstfruit harvest of Christianity (Acts 2). Acts describes the early saints as "continuing daily with one accord in the temple" (2:46). Following Pentecost, Peter and John healed the lame man at the temple (Acts 3) and continued to teach the good news of the resurrected Jesus at the temple, leading to their arrest and imprisonment (4:1–3).

The sanctity of the temple for the earliest Christians is further reflected in a number of stories recorded in Acts. Paul and the other apostles prayed and worshipped at the temple, performing the required purification rituals and offering sacrifice there (Acts 21:26). Paul insists that he never "offended" "against the temple," implying he accepted its sanctity (25:8). Indeed, Paul's second vision of Christ occurred at the temple (22:14–21), strongly suggesting the continued special sanctity of the temple where God still appeared to men.

The Epistle to the Hebrews explains the atonement of Jesus Christ in terms of the temple. Hebrews 8–9 portrays Jesus as the high priest and explains his act of reconciliation between God and humans in terms of the ritual of the Day of Atonement when the high priest would take the blood of the sacrifice into the holy of holies and sprinkle it on the mercy seat, thereby reconciling God and his children (Leviticus 16). In Hebrews this atonement occurred not in the temple on earth but in the heavenly temple made without hands: "For Christ is not entered into the holy places made with hands, which are the figures of the true; but into heaven itself, now to appear in the presence of God for us" (9:24).

The book of Revelation contains John the Revelator's vision of the New Jerusalem. In this vision John looked for the temple in this heavenly city and then said, "And I saw no temple therein: for the Lord God Almighty and the Lamb are the temple of it" (21:22). In this vision the ultimate fulfillment of the temple was realized by the continuing presence of the Father and the Son in the heavenly city.

The Temple in First-Century Judaism and Christianity

The Roman general Pompey conquered Jerusalem in 63 BC, and Judea became a vassal state to Rome. Herod the Great ruled as a loyal subject to Rome, and yet the splendid temple he erected generally enjoyed a fiercely defended autonomy broken only by incidents when Roman rulers demanded the erection of images of themselves or their pagan gods and required the Jews to worship them.[36] As a symbol of this balance of power under Roman rule, a daily sacrifice was offered for the welfare of the Roman emperor at the temple consisting of two lambs and an ox. The sacrifice was initiated and financed by Augustus but was defiantly abandoned at the beginning of the Jewish Revolt in AD 66.[37]

The major sects of Judaism and early Christianity had their own distinctive relationships to the institution of the temple and its priesthood and rituals. The Sadducees were the aristocratic priestly families who controlled and administrated many aspects of the temple. When the temple was destroyed, the Sadducees lost the foundation of their livelihood and their base of power among the people. While priestly traditions survived for a time in the synagogue traditions, eventually the Sadducees without a temple were eclipsed by the Pharisees.

The Pharisees did not oppose participation in the temple in spite of their opposition to the control of the Sadducees. The Pharisees, however, owed their allegiance to oral law and thus found their relationship with the temple more flexible. Through oral law they would be able to forge religious practices that could survive without the temple. A Jewish legend records how Rabbi Johanan ben Zakkai, who found himself trapped in Jerusalem during the Roman siege, realized the temple was going to be destroyed. He had himself hidden in a coffin in order to leave the city. He was taken before the military commander Vespasian, who eventually became a Roman emperor. The rabbi asked Vespasian to give him Yavneh, a city where he founded a rabbinical academy that preserved the Sanhedrin and the ongoing process of oral tradition that would result in the publication of the Mishnah (Babylonian Talmud Gittin 56).

Eventually the sect of the Pharisees transitioned into Rabbinic Judaism, which became mainstream Judaism to the present day. With time Pharisaic Judaism was able to promote institutions that continued worship in the absence of the sacrificial system of the temple. A well-known story in the Midrash tells of Rabbi ben Zakkai, who, when walking by the ruins of the temple, said to his disciple, "My son, do not be grieved, for we have another atonement that is just like it. And which is it? Acts of loving-kindness, as it is said, 'For I desire loving-kindness, and not sacrifice' [Hosea 6:6]" (*Avot de-Rabbi Natan* 4.21).[38] With time, other rabbis noted that prayer, study, and acts of loving-kindness are, like sacrifice, pleasing to the Lord.[39]

The Samaritans claimed to be remnants of the northern ten tribes. They preserved an ancient tradition in their version of the Torah called the Samaritan Pentateuch that commanded the temple be built on Mount Gerizim. According to Josephus, the Samaritans built their temple there sometime in the period of Alexander the Great,[40] and it remained a center of their religious community and a competing temple to the Jerusalem temple until the Samaritan temple was destroyed by the Hasmonean king John Hyrcanus in 129 BC.[41] The age-old conflict between the Jews and Samaritans was exacerbated by the Jewish refusal to allow the Samaritans to help with the rebuilding of Zerubbael's temple in ca. 515 BC. The destruction of the Samaritan temple in 129 BC was another one of the defining incidents leading to the division and continued animosity between the Jews and Samaritans as reflected in the New Testament. This dispute over the temple provides the background of the conversation Jesus had with the Samaritan woman in John 4. To this day Samaritans continue to live near Mount Gerizim and offer the yearly Passover sacrifice in the vicinity of their temple site.

Most scholars believe that the Qumran community reflected in the Dead Sea Scrolls were the Essenes (see chapter 7 herein). According to ancient historians, as well as some of the documents from Qumran, the Essenes believed that the Jerusalem priesthood that administered the temple was corrupt and that the sacrificial system and the calendar were also corrupt. Thus, while the Essenes passionately believed in the temple, they did not participate in its rituals in Jerusalem. Some scholars argue that Essenes saw themselves as a community representing the temple.[42] While they may have rejected the Jerusalem temple in their time, they had a strong belief in and love for the institution of the temple. One of the significant finds in the Dead Sea Scrolls is the Temple Scroll, believed by the Qumran sect to be scripture that describes the plans and the legal requirements for a future eschatological temple.[43]

Christians initially continued worshipping at the Jerusalem temple and living the law of Moses, but eventually it became clear, following the Council of Jerusalem, that one did not have to become a Jew to become a Christian (Acts 15; compare Galatians 2); therefore most Christians began to distance themselves from the temple. Following the destruction of the temple in AD 70, Christianity generally adopted the point of view that the church was a temple. Based on passages of scripture in the writings of Paul—such as "Know ye not that ye are the temple of God, and that the Spirit of God dwelleth in you?" (1 Corinthians 3:16) and "For we know that if our earthly house of this tabernacle were dissolved, we have a building of God, an house not made with hands, eternal in the heavens" (2 Corinthians 5:1)—Christians came to view the individual believer and the church as a community of believers functioning as the new temple of God.[44]

Destruction of the Temple

In the final week of his ministry, speaking to the apostles on the Mount of Olives, Jesus prophesied the destruction of the temple: "Verily I say unto you, there shall not be left here, upon this temple, one stone upon another that shall not be thrown down" (Joseph Smith—Matthew 1:3; compare Matthew 24:1–2). In this prophecy Jesus also quoted the prophecy of Daniel of the "abomination of desolation" connected with the destruction of Jerusalem and the desecration of the temple, and he advised those who wished to be preserved to "stand in the holy place" and "flee into the mountains" (Joseph Smith—Matthew 1:12–13; compare Matthew 24:15–16). Eusebius recounted that the saints in Jerusalem were spared from the destruction of Jerusalem by fleeing across the Jordan River to Pella.[45]

The temple became the focal point of the conflict between the governing Romans and the vassal Jews that lasted from AD 66 to 70 when Titus and the Roman armies besieged and destroyed Jerusalem and the temple. As Jesus had prophesied, the temple was burned and destroyed, leaving a pile of rubble. The historian Josephus recorded the Roman destruction following the burning of the temple: "Caesar ordered the whole city and the temple to be razed to the ground." He further noted that the city "was so thoroughly laid even with the ground by those that dug it up to the foundation, that there was left nothing to make those that came thither believe it had ever been inhabited."[46] The Jews were eventually driven from Jerusalem and were left without a temple.

Many of the furnishings of the temple were destroyed, though several of the implements—the trumpets, the table of the bread of the presence, and the lampstand—were preserved and taken to Rome, where their images were captured in the relief on the Arch of Titus in Rome built to commemorate Titus's triumph. Various implements from the temple, including the menorah and the shewbread table, were preserved for many years in Rome in Vespasian's Temple of Peace.[47]

The final echo of the temple in the Roman period is found in the Bar Kokhba revolt. Simon Bar Kokhba ("son of the star") was a Jewish claimant to the title of "Messiah" who led an unsuccessful revolt against the Romans in AD 132–35. He issued coins depicting the façade of the temple, suggesting that the rebuilding of the sacred building was an integral part of Bar Kokhba's rebellion. Bar Kokhba was heralded as the Messiah by numerous prominent Jewish rabbis, including Akiba, and thus many Jews gathered to his rebellion. The devastating defeat of Bar Kokhba led to the banning of Jews from even living in Jerusalem.

The destruction of the temple was pivotal for Jews and Christians alike. For the Jews the temple of Herod was a tangible symbol of their religion that made it possible to fulfill the laws of sacrifice in the law of Moses. With its destruction came the loss of the center of their religion, and Judaism would have to develop ways of worship to replace or compensate for the rituals and ordinances—most notably sacrifice and the celebration of the festivals— that could formerly be done only at the temple. Christians would have to decide what their proper relationship was to the temple—whether they needed an actual earthly building or if Jesus had in some way done away with the need for a physical temple. However, both Jews and Christians would continue to read and study the canonical books of their religions, including the prophecies in the Old Testament about the future restoration and rebuilding of the temple. Amos prophesied, "In that day I will raise up the tabernacle of David that is fallen, . . . and I will build it as in the days of old" (Amos 9:11). Ezekiel has a vision of the future temple complete with the plans in Ezekiel 40–48. And Isaiah prophesied, "And it shall come to pass in the last days, that the mountain of the Lord's house shall be established in the top of the mountains, . . . and many people shall go and say, Come ye, and let us go up to the mountain of the Lord, to the house of the God of Jacob" (Isaiah 2:2–3).

❦

David Rolph Seely is a professor in the Department of Ancient Scripture at Brigham Young University.

Notes

1. According to Deuteronomy 31:24–26, a scroll containing the law was also placed beside the ark of the covenant.

2. Many aspects of temple worship were common in ancient Near Eastern cultures. For a typology of some of these features, see John M. Lundquist, "What Is a Temple?: A Preliminary Typology," in *The Quest for the Kingdom of God: Studies in Honor of George E. Mendenhall*, ed. H. B. Huffmon, F. A. Spina, and A. R. W. Green (Winona Lake, IN: Eisenbrauns, 1983), 205–19.

3. For a review of the history and theology of the Israelite temples, see Menahem Haran, *Temples and Temple Service in Ancient Israel* (Oxford: Clarendon Press, 1978); Margaret Barker, *The Gate of Heaven: The History and Symbolism of the Temple in Jerusalem* (London: SPCK, 1991); William J. Hamblin and David Rolph Seely, *Solomon's Temple in Myth and History* (London: Thames & Hudson, 2007); and John M. Lundquist, *The Temple of Jerusalem: Past, Present, and Future* (Westport, CN: Praeger, 2008).

4. A collection of the extrabiblical sources for the Second Temple can be found in C. T. R. Hayward, *The Jewish Temple: A Non-Biblical Sourcebook* (New York: Routledge, 1996).

5. Josephus, *Antiquities* 14.70–73; see also Tacitus, *Histories* 5.11–12. Quotations of Josephus's works throughout are taken from *Josephus*, Loeb Classical Library edition, trans. H. St. J. Thackery, Ralph Marcus, Allen Wikgren, and L.H. Feldman (Cambridge, MA: Harvard University Press, 1926–64).

6. Josephus, *Antiquities* 15.380.

7. Josephus, *Jewish War* 5.222–223.

8. Josephus was from a priestly family and therefore claimed to have intimate knowledge of Herod's temple. He wrote two lengthy and sometimes parallel descriptions of the temple and the Temple Mount in *Antiquities* 15.380–425 and *Jewish War* 5.184–247.

9. Philo's references to the temple are found scattered throughout his writings. A convenient collection can be found in Hayward, *Jewish Temple*, 108–41.

10. A reputable English translation of the Mishnah can be found in Herbert Danby, *The Mishnah* (Oxford: Oxford University Press, 1933).

11. Descriptions and analysis of the textual and archaeological data relating to the Temple Mount can be found in Benjamin Mazar, *The Mountain of the Lord* (Garden City, NY: Doubleday, 1975); Lee I. Levine, *Jerusalem: Portrait of the City in the Second Temple Period (538 B.C.E–70 C.E)* (Philadelphia: The Jewish Publication Society, 2002); Leen Ritmeyer, *The Quest: Revealing the Temple Mount in Jerusalem* (Jerusalem: Carta, 2006); and Eilat Mazar, *The Complete Guide to the Temple Mount Excavations* (Jerusalem: Shoham Academic Research and Publication, 2012). An excellent description of the history of the Temple Mount is Oleg Grabar and Benjamin Z. Kedar, eds., *Where Heaven and Earth Meet: Jerusalem's Sacred Esplanade* (Austin: University of Texas Press, 2010).

12. Josephus, *Antiquities* 15.383.

13. A historical review of Herod's rebuilding the Second Temple can be found in Ehud Netzer, *The Architecture of Herod the Great Builder* (Tübingen, Germany: Mohr Siebeck, 2006), 137–78; reprinted in paperback by Grand Rapids, MI: Baker Books, 2006.

14. Josephus, *Antiquities* 15.390–391.

15. Josephus, *Jewish War* 5.225.

16. Josephus, *Antiquities* 15.420–421.

17. Josephus, *Antiquities* 20.219.

18. In Josephus and elsewhere in ancient sources, the Greek word *temenos* is used to describe the sacred precinct containing a temple. The King James Version of the New Testament uses the English term *temple* to translate two different Greek words: *naos*, which means "house" and refers to the temple proper, and *hieron*, which means "sanctuary" and refers to the whole temple complex. Usually the reader can tell from the context which meaning is intended.

19. The descriptions in Josephus and the Mishnah occasionally show discrepancies. For a discussion and possible solutions to these discrepancies see Ritmeyer, *Quest*, 139–45.

20. Ritmeyer, *Quest*, 168, 233.

21. Mazar, *Mountain of the Lord*, 119.

22. Lundquist, *Temple of Jerusalem*, 103–4.

23. Elias J. Bickerman, "Warning Inscription of Herod's Temple," *Jewish Quarterly Review* 37 (1946/47): 387–405.

24. For an overview of the temple and temple worship at the time of Jesus, see Alfred Edersheim, *The Temple: Its Ministry and Services as They Were at the Time of Jesus* (Grand Rapids, MI: Kregel, 1997); Randall Price, *Rose Guide to the Temple* (Torrance, CA: Rose Publishing, 2012); and Leen and Kathleen Ritmeyer, *The Ritual of the Temple in the Time of Jesus* (Jerusalem: Carta, 2002).

25. Josephus, *Antiquities* 15.418.

26. Josephus, *Jewish War* 5.225; and Middot 3:1.

27. There are some discrepancies in the ancient sources about the dimensions of Herod's temple. See Ritmeyer, *Quest*, 77–400, for a complete description of the temple according to the Mishnah.

28. Josephus, *Antiquities* 15.395.

29. Leon Yarden, *The Tree of Light* (Ithaca, NY: Cornell University Press, 1971), 35.

30. The last mention of the ark is from the time of Josiah (2 Chronicles 35:3). Because no mention is made of the ark of the covenant in the list of furnishings taken by the Babylonians to Babylon following the destruction in 586 BC (2 Kings 25:13–17; Jeremiah 52:17–23), most scholars presume the ark was destroyed by the Babylonians when they destroyed the temple. Scholars and others have suggested many speculative theories about the ark being lost, hidden, or taken away before its destruction. For example, an apocryphal book says that Jeremiah hid the ark in Mount Nebo (2 Maccabees 2:4–8). For a scholarly review of these theories, see John Day, "Whatever Happened to the Ark of the Covenant?," in *Temple and Worship in Biblical Israel*, ed. John Day (New York: T&T Clark, 2007), 250–70.

31. Philo, *On the Special Laws* 1.69. Quotations of Philo are taken from *Philo*, Loeb Classical Library, trans. F. H. Colson (Cambridge, MA: Harvard University Press, 1937–62).

32. Josephus, *Jewish War* 5.216–218.

33. Josephus, *Jewish War* 5.213.

34. Josephus, *Jewish War* 5.219.

35. In the Synoptic Gospels the Last Supper is a Passover meal (Matthew 26:17; Mark 14:12; Luke 22:1–15); however, in John the Last Supper took place before Passover (13:1), and therefore Jesus may have been crucified on the day of Passover.

36. For example, the emperor Caligula (AD 37–41) demanded his statue be erected and worshipped in the temple courtyards, resulting in a widespread Jewish revolt. See the accounts in Philo, *On the Embassy to Gaius* 188, 198–348; and Josephus, *Antiquities* 18.261–309; *Jewish War* 2.184–203.

37. Philo, *On the Embassy to Gaius* 157, 317–319.

38. As quoted in Jonathan Klawans, *Purity, Sacrifice, and the Temple: Symbolism and Supersessionism in the Study of Ancient Judaism* (Oxford: Oxford University Press, 2009), 205.

39. For a complete discussion of the relationship between prayer, study, and acts of loving-kindness and temple sacrifice, see Klawans, *Purity, Sacrifice, and the Temple*, 203–11.

40. Josephus, *Antiquities* 11.310–311.

41. Josephus, *Antiquities* 13.254–256. For a report of the excavations of the alleged temple site on Mount Gerizim, see Yitzhak Magen, "Bells, Pendants, Snakes and Stones," *Biblical Archaeology Review* 36, no. 6 (November/December 2010): 26–35.

42. Bertil Gärtner, *The Temple and the Community in Qumran and the New Testament: A Comparative Study in the Temple Symbolism of the Qumran Texts and the New Testament*, Society for New Testament Studies Monograph Series (Cambridge: Cambridge University Press, 2005).

43. Yigael Yadin, *The Temple Scroll: The Hidden Law of the Dead Sea Sect* (New York: Random House, 1985); Johann Maier, *The Temple Scroll: An Introduction, Translation, and Commentary* (London: Bloomsbury, 2009); and Adolfo Roitman, *Envisioning the Temple* (Jerusalem: The Israel Museum, 2003).

44. For a comprehensive discussion of how Christians interpreted scripture in regard to the temple, see G. K. Beale, *The Temple and the Church's Mission: A Biblical Theology of the Dwelling Place of God*. New Studies in Biblical Theology (Downers Grove, IL: InterVarsity, 2004).

45. Eusebius, *Ecclesiastical History* 3.5.3.

46. Josephus, *Jewish War* 7.1.3.

47. Steven Fine, *The Menorah from the Bible to Modern Israel* (Cambridge, MA: Harvard University Press, 2016), 4.

5

Messianism and Jewish Messiahs in the New Testament Period

Trevan G. Hatch

The terms *Messiah* and *Christ* are widely used today and are employed almost exclusively by Christians in reference to Jesus. Modern Christians, including Latter-day Saints, associate a litany of notions, implications, and expectations with these titles. *Messiah*, or *mashiach* in Hebrew, is synonymous with *Christ*, or *christos* in Greek, both meaning "one who is anointed" (with oil). What, however, were the deeper meanings and implications of these terms in Jesus's day? How did Jews in the first centuries BC and AD interpret Old Testament passages regarding a messiah, and what were their expectations of a future messiah? When some of Jesus's followers viewed him as *the* Messiah, what would they have initially expected him to accomplish? Were any figures during the New Testament period, other than Jesus, considered to be the Messiah by their followers? This chapter will address these questions with the primary goal of understanding the broad messianic context of the New Testament period and situating Jesus within it.

Origins of "Messiah"

In the first century, Jesus's followers referred to him as "Messiah," "Son of God," "Son of David," and "Son of Man"; his adjudicators also referred to him, mockingly, as "King of the Jews."[1] Christians typically see these terms as referring to a divine being who came in human form to provide salvation to humanity. When and where did this notion of messiah originate, and how do the titles "Son of God," "Son of David," "Son of Man," and "King of the Jews" relate, if at all, to the general idea of "messiah"?

Conceptions of "messiah" among Jews in the first centuries BC and AD are rooted in the ideology of kingship of earlier Israelite eras. The primary leaders in ancient Israel, particularly priests and kings, were anointed with oil.[2] The Hebrew Bible is replete with references to Israelite kings being anointed, usually by prophets.[3] Israelite kings were frequently called "the Lord's anointed"—or "the Lord's messiah" in Hebrew and "the Lord's christ" in Greek.[4] In the early Israelite literature that came to form a part of our Bible, the root *mšh*, meaning in its various forms "to anoint" or "anointed one," did not seem to denote an awaited, future agent of God who would come to deliver Israel from their enemies in the end of days, or a messianic era. "Anointed ones" were simply Israel's kings—and, during certain time periods, priests.[5] Even one non-Israelite king, Cyrus of Persia, was called "his anointed" (Isaiah 45:1), the only explicit reference to this title in all of Isaiah.

The Israelite king was not only a messiah but a "son of God." Surrounding Near Eastern cultures—Canaanite, Egyptian, Mesopotamian, and Ugaritic—influenced Israelite conceptions of kingship. Ancient Near Eastern kings were thought by some to be divine—specifically to be sons of God.[6] Old Assyrian and Egyptian kings were thought to have attained divine status at or before birth. King Piankhi of Egypt (eighth century BC), for example, stated, "I am he who was fashioned in the womb and created in the divine egg, the seed of the god being in me."[7] In contrast, Hittite and Canaanite kings attained godhood at death.[8] Like their neighboring nations, early Israelite texts described the king in relation to Deity, or even as a deity himself. For example, many Near Eastern gods and kings were associated with shepherd imagery—"Good Shepherd" (Egyptian), "Noble Shepherd" (Sumerian), "Shepherd of mankind" (Hittite), and "Wise Shepherd" (Assyrian).[9] In Israelite literature, just as God was identified as a shepherd of Israel,[10] so too was the king.[11] The god-king rhetoric in Israelite texts seems to be most pronounced in Psalms. Both Jehovah (i.e., Yahweh) and King David will rule the sea (Psalm 89:9, 25), and the enemies of both Jehovah and David will be scattered (Psalm 89:10, 22–23). More explicitly, King David is Jehovah's "begotten" son (Psalm 2:7), and his "firstborn" (Psalm 89:26–27), who will sit at God's "right hand" (Psalm 110:1). The idea that Israelite kings—particularly those during the golden age of Israel's monarchy—were both messiahs and sons of God shaped views of *the* Messiah for later Jews. But what about Israelites before the exile to Babylon—did they believe that the king was a divine being? Was a "son of God" viewed as an earthly, human figure or a supernatural being? Scholars continue to debate this question, in part because of the paucity of source material. The primary scholarly conclusions are (1) Israelite kings were viewed as divine; (2) Israel's god-king rhetoric was not meant to be literal but was metaphorical court language; or (3) Israel's kings were adopted into the divine fold at their coronations but were not seen as Jehovah's literal divine sons.[12]

It seems that early Israelites during the height of the monarchy tended to describe the king in terms that suggested divinity or at least a very close association between the king and Deity. Later authors, it appears, rejected this idea, which is most apparent during the exile and postexile, when the king's role was corrupted and less significant (Ezekiel 34).[13] Regardless of whether Israelites viewed their kings as literal or metaphorical sons of God before the exile, later Jews interpreted the kingship passages in different ways, leading to a diversity of messianic expectations in the age of Jesus, as we will see below. As far as the association between the Messiah and the end of days, the late Joseph Fitzmyer, a Catholic priest and professor at The Catholic University of America, concluded that the "idea of [messiah] as an awaited or future anointed agent of God in the end time [was a] late development" in Israelite religion.[14]

Before continuing, let us briefly consider whether the Book of Mormon sheds light on the question of how Israelites before the exile understood the nature of "Messiah" and "Son of God." The word *Messiah* is used twenty-seven times, twenty-three of which are in 1–2 Nephi. *Son of God* is mentioned fifty times, primarily in Alma (twenty-three times). *Son of man* is mentioned only once, in 2 Nephi 8:12 (from Isaiah chapter 51); however, this verse refers to humans. The term *Son of David* is never used. The Book of Mormon posits the following regarding the Messiah: (1) he would be the future redeemer of humankind (1 Nephi 10:4–5; 2 Nephi 1:10; 2:6); (2) the Son of God was the Messiah (1 Nephi 10:17); (3) he would come in the fulness of time, also called the meridian of time (2 Nephi 2:26); (4) he would be slain and rise from the dead (1 Nephi 10:11; 2 Nephi 25:14). Thus, while the Book of Mormon does show that God revealed to preexilic Israelite prophets details regarding the role of Jesus as the Messiah, the extent to which these conceptions were fully understood by larger Israel is not altogether clear from preexilic source materials. Furthermore, much of the information in these verses, as well as those referring to the Son of God, was *revealed* to Lehi and Nephi and written several decades after they left Jerusalem.

A third title relevant to messiah is "Son of David." Although an "anointed one" in ancient Israel was associated with kings generally, it was primarily used in the Hebrew Bible in relation to the Davidic dynasty of the southern kingdom of Judah. In 2 Samuel 7, God, via the prophet Nathan, covenants with David that his offspring would be God's "son" (2 Samuel 7:14) and would establish an everlasting throne and kingdom (7:16). This idealized Davidic dynasty continues through the prophetic books of the Hebrew Bible and intensifies when the nation is either threatened by foreign enemies or the throne is not held by a Davidic king. For example, Isaiah speaks of a future king who will have authority and who will bring endless peace to the throne and kingdom of David (Isaiah 9:6–7). Hosea prophesies that for a time Israel will be without a king but that eventually God will once again restore the Davidic line to the throne (Hosea 3:4–5; compare Amos 9:11; Isaiah 55:3; Jeremiah 23:5). During the exile after the Davidic king had been dethroned, Ezekiel prophesies that "David" will again be Israel's "shepherd" (Ezekiel 34:23–24; compare 37:22–25).

In sum, early Israelite kings were known as messiahs, or "anointed ones," who were also "sons of God"—terms most closely associated with the Davidic dynasty. It is not entirely clear from the prophetic books whether this future, idealized Davidic kingdom would be led by an earthly king, like David and Solomon, or had expanded into a body of general expectations that included a figure who would be a divine agent of God and savior of Israel.

It seems that before the Second Temple period (ca. 200 BC–AD 70) such expectations of a divine messianic figure were not fully formed and articulated.

"Messiah" in the Second Temple Period

After Persia conquered Babylonia and King Cyrus permitted Jews to return to Judea in 538 BC, the returnees were prohibited from reestablishing an autonomous state. Jews were kingless not only during Persian rule (539–332 BC) but also during Hellenistic (i.e., Greek) domination of the region until 142 BC. During most of this four-hundred-year span there seems to be a reduced emphasis on a royal messiah figure who will restore Israel. Language once associated with Israel's kings in times past (e.g., "anointed one" and "son of God") seemed to be transferred to the high priest, the leading head among the Jewish people.[15]

In the second century BC, expectations of a king-deliverer started to expand. The major reasons include the following. First, oppression from Greek overlords intensified, culminating in the desecration of the temple (164 BC). Second, when Jewish guerrilla fighters wrested Judea and the temple away from the Greeks, the Jewish Hasmonean dynasty (142–63 BC) controlled the throne; the problem for many Jews, however, was that the Hasmoneans were not from the Davidic line. Thus, the anticipated Davidic king would not come through the Hasmonean dynasty. Third, the high priesthood was usurped and corrupted by non-Aaronide (i.e., those not descended from Aaron) wealthy aristocrats. The Jewish populace witnessed attacks on their religion and temple cult from all sides, including from within.

The morale of the young autonomous Jewish nation worsened and messianic expectations intensified when the Romans, with the help of some Jews, swept in and dethroned the Hasmonean dynasty in 63 BC. Rome eventually appointed an illegitimate (i.e., half-Jew) ruler in the region. Herod, with approval from Rome, ruled with an iron fist. According to Josephus, Herod executed numerous people that he suspected opposed him. Among these were his brother-in-law (the high priest), his mother-in-law, his second wife, three of his sons, and three hundred military leaders.[16] Corruption and violence did not escape the populace, even after Herod died. On many occasions the crowds protested a perceived injustice against them. Pontius Pilate, the Roman governor of the region (ca. AD 26–36), brought into Jerusalem (and possibly into the temple complex) "Caesar's effigies" with approval of the priestly class. When the masses discovered the busts, a "multitude" demanded that Pilate remove them.[17] On another occasion, priests permitted Pilate to use funds from the temple treasury to pay for an aqueduct to Jerusalem. When a protest ensued, Pilate dispatched soldiers to disperse the crowds by threatening to kill them.[18] In the face of this oppression and corruption, a more intense messianic fervor spread. In these two centuries before the ministry of Jesus, Jews experienced a widespread expectation of *the* Messiah's appearance, who would be a Davidic king come to liberate Israel by throwing off its yoke of imperial bondage. By the time Jesus started his ministry, and in the decades after his ministry was completed, messianic expectations were high.

Perhaps the earliest passage during this time period that illustrates the shift in messianic expectations is in the book of Daniel, which many scholars believe dates to the early Second Temple period.[19] Here we encounter another messianic title, the "Son of Man." This term comes from the Hebrew *ben adam* and the Aramaic *bar enosh*, both meaning a "person" or "human being." The plural in Hebrew *b'nei adam* typically meant "humankind."[20] In chapter 7, Daniel describes seeing a vision of four great beasts, probably referring to Babylon, Media, Persia, and Greece. Daniel then saw the Ancient of Days on his throne and another figure alongside, who defeated and judged these nations:

> As I watched in the night visions, I saw one like a human being coming with the clouds of heaven. And he came to the Ancient One and was presented before him. To him was given dominion and glory and kingship, that all peoples, nations, and languages should serve him. His dominion is an everlasting dominion that shall not pass away, and his kingship is one that shall never be destroyed. (Daniel 7:13–14 NRSV)[21]

The figure in this passage is one *like* a son of man, meaning a divine figure who looked like a human. He will have authority and will be worshipped by all people. Note also the language tying this figure to the Davidic kingship ideal, that he will be a king whose kingdom will be everlasting. The "clouds of heaven" link this figure to the Deity, according to several passages in the Hebrew Bible (Exodus 34:5; Psalm 104:3; Isaiah 19:1). Scholars have debated the precise interpretation of this Son of Man figure in Daniel; however, it seems that he had the appearance of a human and was a divine royal figure destined to defeat Israel's foreign enemies.

A later text, the book of 1 Enoch, dating to the late first century BC or early first century AD,[22] also includes material about the Son of Man:

> I saw the One to whom belongs the time before time. And his head was white like wool, and there was with him another individual, *whose face was like that of a human being.* . . . This [is the] Son of Man whom you have seen, [he] is the One who would remove the kings and the mighty ones from their comfortable seats and the strong ones from their thrones. (1 Enoch 46:1–4)
>
> At that hour, that Son of Man was given a name, in the presence of the Lord of the Spirits, the Before-Time; even before the creation of the sun and the moon, before the creation of the stars, he was given a name in the presence of the Lord of the Spirits. . . . All those who dwell upon the earth shall fall and worship before him. . . . And he has revealed the wisdom of the Lord of the Spirits to the righteous and holy ones, for he has preserved the portion of the righteous because they have hated and despised this world of oppression (together with) all its ways of life and its habits and it is his good pleasure that they have life. . . . For they [the wicked kings and landowners] have denied the Lord of the Spirits and his Messiah. (1 Enoch 48:2–10)
>
> Thenceforth nothing that is corruptible shall be found; for that Son of Man has appeared and has seated himself upon the throne of his glory; and all evil shall disappear from before his face. (1 Enoch 69:29)[23]

We learn from these texts that expectations of a divine messianic figure had expanded in the few centuries before Jesus's ministry. The heavenly figure in Daniel who looked *like* a son of man was later called "Son of Man" in the book of 1 Enoch. According to these Jewish authors, this figure was a premortal being who was closely associated with God, would have dominion over all earthly kingdoms, would be worshipped by all people, would judge the wicked and overthrow his enemies, would establish an everlasting kingdom, and would be the "Messiah."

Alongside these Son of Man traditions is a litany of other messianic traditions in several early Jewish texts. Perhaps the most prominent theme among these texts regarding the Messiah is that he will descend from the tribe of Judah through David. Genesis 49 and Isaiah 11 served as the primary texts for this idea: "The sceptre shall not depart from Judah, nor a lawgiver from between his feet, until Shiloh come; and unto him shall the gathering of the people be" (Genesis 49:10 KJV; compare JST Genesis 50:24); "And there shall come forth a rod out of the stem of Jesse, and a Branch shall grow out of his roots" (Isaiah 11:1 KJV). Many Jews during this time period interpreted these passages messianically. For example, a Genesis commentary text discovered in cave 4 at Qumran held that this future Judahite king will be the "Righteous Messiah, the Branch of David."[24] The *Psalms of Solomon*, a text from the mid-first century BC, harks back to 2 Samuel 7 where God promised David that his offspring will be God's son (7:14) and he will establish an everlasting throne (7:16): "See, Lord, and raise up for them their king, the son of David, to rule over your servant Israel in the time known to you, O God. . . . And their king shall be the Lord Messiah."[25]

Another emergent messianic theme in early Jewish texts is that the Messiah would have ultimate authority and be praised by all people. In this authoritative role, the Messiah would be charged with judging the wicked and punishing Israel's enemies. Several Qumran texts, for example, posit that "heaven and earth shall listen to His Messiah,"[26] rulers of Israel will "sit before him,"[27] and others "will be handed over to the sword when the Messiah . . . comes."[28] In the *Psalms of Solomon* the Messiah will "lead the righteous" and "will have gentile nations serving him under his yoke"; he will "expose officials and drive out sinners."[29] In the *Sibylline Oracles*, another first-century-BC text, "God will send a King . . . who will stop the entire earth from evil war, killing some, imposing oaths of loyalty on others."[30] The expectation of a warrior messiah who will fight Israel's foreign enemies may have been justified based on Isaiah 45:1, which reads, "Thus says the Lord to *his anointed*, to Cyrus, whose right hand I have grasped to *subdue nations before him*."

It seems clear from the sources that it was during this period—the first two centuries before Jesus's ministry—that the idea of a divine agent of God who would redeem Israel became more widely accepted, or at least more apparent, among the Jewish population, although some earlier texts are foundational for such beliefs (Isaiah 9 and 32; Zechariah 14). Whatever earlier Israelites believed about the nature of the future agent of God who would destroy the wicked and redeem Israel, it is clear that by the time Jesus started his ministry many Jews had high expectations of the one they called "Messiah," "Son of God," or "Son of Man." What used to be generic terms in earlier centuries referring to kings ("messiah" and "son of God") or human beings ("son of man") were later understood as titles for one special individual who would redeem Israel. This divine agent of God would not just be *a* messiah, but *the* Messiah.[31]

Before proceeding to discuss messiah figures during the late Second Temple period, including Jesus himself, it is useful to recap what we find in pre-Christian, Jewish texts regarding messianic expectations leading up to the ministry of Jesus. These texts present the following expectations of the Messiah among many early Jews:

- He would be a premortal, divine figure
- All people would worship him
- He would be a king
- He would reestablish the Davidic dynasty
- His kingdom would be everlasting
- He would have authority over all nations
- He would lead Israel
- He would judge the wicked and overthrow Israel's foreign enemies
- He would be associated with righteousness

Note one expectation lacking in these texts: the notion that the Messiah would be subdued, humiliated, and killed by his enemies. The one text that seemed to suggest that the Messiah would be killed is 4 Ezra: "For my son the Messiah shall be revealed with those who are with him, and those who remain shall rejoice four hundred years. And after these years *my son the Messiah shall die*, and all who draw human breath."[32] In this ambiguous text, the Messiah will not be humiliated and killed by his enemies but will die along with everyone else after four hundred years ("one thousand years" in the Arabic version). Further, this text dates to the late first century AD and may not tell us much about messianic expectations in the two centuries preceding Jesus's ministry. Some may challenge the conclusion that early Jews did not expect a suffering, defeated messiah by pointing to the suffering servant passage in Isaiah 53. Perhaps the most contested verses in all of the Hebrew Bible are the following:

> He is despised and rejected of men; a man of sorrows, and acquainted with grief: and we hid as it were our faces from him; he was despised, and we esteemed him not. Surely he hath borne our griefs, and carried our sorrows: yet we did esteem him stricken, smitten of God, and afflicted. But he was wounded for our transgressions, he was bruised for our iniquities: the chastisement of our peace was upon him; and with his stripes we are healed. All we like sheep have gone astray; we have turned every one to his own way; and the Lord hath laid on him the iniquity of us all. He was oppressed, and he was afflicted, yet he opened not his mouth: he is brought as a lamb to the slaughter, and as a sheep before her shearers is dumb, so he openeth not his mouth. (Isaiah 53:3–7 KJV)

Ancient Jewish commentators disagreed on the nature of the "servant" here in Isaiah. Some interpreted it as referring to the Messiah, others to Israel. Although Abinadi interprets Isaiah 53 as referring to Jesus (Mosiah 14:1–15:1), it seems that this messianic prophecy for Jews in the Near East was overshadowed by the many other expectations of a victorious messiah in the two centuries leading up to Jesus's ministry. Thus, in pre-Christian Jewish texts of the Second Temple period the notion that the messiah was to suffer and die was virtually nonexistent.[33] In fact, when Jesus first tells the apostles that part of his mission will include suffering and dying, Peter immediately reproaches him and says, "This must never happen to you" (Matthew 16:22). We must note that Daniel 9 refers to an "anointed one" who will be "cut off and shall have nothing" (9:26), but it is ambiguous whether this passage suggests that the anointed one will be humiliated and ultimately killed. Could it be that this figure will be defeated for a time and then conquer his foes? We just do not know. What we can say is that the few passages like this in Daniel 9 are overshadowed a great deal in other early Jewish texts by a victorious messiah.

That messianic expectations for Jews near the time of Jesus generally did not include a suffering, dying messiah is crucial to understanding the events immediately following Jesus's death. One must also remember that not all Jews held a normative set of beliefs about the Messiah's divine status—whether he would be divine or mortal—nor did all Jews uniformly expect the Messiah to accomplish a specific set of tasks. The various Jewish texts predating Jesus posited a multiplicity of messianic expectations as well as ideas about the divine status of a future messiah. Daniel Boyarin, a scholar of early Jewish literature, noted the disparate messianic beliefs among early Jews:

> There are many variations of traditions about this figure in the Gospels themselves and in other early Jewish texts. Some Jews had been expecting this Redeemer to be a human exalted to the state of divinity, while others were expecting a divinity to come down to earth and take on human form; some believers in Jesus believed the Christ had been born as an ordinary human and then exalted to divine status, while others believed him to have been a divinity who came down to earth. Either way, we end up with a doubled godhead and a human-divine combination as the expected Redeemer.[34]

Messianic-Like Activity in the First Century AD

After Herod died in 4 BC, the region of Judea and Galilee appears to have experienced an increase in persons asserting kingship who at the same time may have had messianic pretensions. Prior to Herod's death, hope of a conquering messiah seemed to be idealistic; in the first century AD, however, the realization of the Messiah had become more concrete, especially in response to Roman authoritarian and militaristic governing style. Josephus detailed approximately a dozen figures in the first century alone—with many more mentioned in passing—who acted in ways that might have caused the populace to view them as possible messianic candidates. He explained that many of these figures were declared "king" by their followers, thus becoming a nuisance to Roman authorities.[35] The Jerusalem temple bureaucrats and the Roman officials attempted to quash any movement led by a "king," especially those who sought to wrest control of the region away from the Romans and the temple establishment.

One such figure was Judas from Sepphoris, a town in Galilee about five miles from Nazareth. In the wake of Herod's death, Judas gathered a sizable following and besieged several royal armories. He subsequently targeted others who had royal aspirations, probably because he himself had his eye on the throne.[36] The same year, Simon of Perea put a diadem on his head and declared himself king. With a group of followers, he proceeded to burn several royal properties, including the palace at Jericho. Roman soldiers eventually intercepted and beheaded him.[37] During the next few years, Athrongeus, a man known as a shepherd, declared himself king and went about killing Roman soldiers and Jewish royalists until Roman authorities captured him.[38]

A few decades later, John the Baptist established such a large following that he was imprisoned and eventually beheaded after challenging Herod Antipas. Josephus recorded that Herod Antipas was particularly concerned that John's power and influence with the populace would lead to a rebellion. Approximately ten years after John the Baptist's death, another figure gained a large following among the Samaritans, a people closely related to the Jews, both ideologically and geographically. Samaritans awaited a figure like Moses who would restore the ancient temple. This Samaritan prophet promised to show his followers the holy vessels that Moses supposedly buried on Mount Gerizim. Pilate and his infantry attacked the group, killing some and arresting others.[39] Roughly a decade later, a prophet, Theudas, who was alleged to have performed miracles, led a group to the Jordan River. He had promised to divide the waters as did Joshua. Before the group arrived at the river, Roman authorities attacked them, killing many and beheading Theudas.[40] At this same time, a Judas from Gamala in Galilee gathered a group and revolted against Rome in order to establish national independence. The group eventually perished, according to Acts 5:37; Josephus did not explain Judas's fate, but we learn that two of his sons were crucified during Tiberius Alexander's tenure (AD 46–48) in consequence of the rebellion. Judas's other son, Menahem, also had kingly aspirations like his father.[41]

A few years later, an unnamed Egyptian prophet gathered a large group on the Mount of Olives. He claimed that Jerusalem's walls would fall on his command, allowing the multitude to enter the city. The Roman authorities rushed to the Mount of Olives and killed or arrested over six hundred people.[42] The prophet escaped and never appeared in Jerusalem again; however, when the apostle Paul made his last trip to Jerusalem a short time later, Roman authorities mistook him for the Egyptian prophet: "You are not the Egyptian who recently stirred up a revolt and led the four thousand assassins out into the wilderness?" (Acts 21:38). This prophet seemed to be motivated by the messianic prophecies in Zechariah 14 that speak of a divine warrior figure who would descend from heaven and stand on the Mount of Olives before entering Jerusalem. The goal of this divine figure would be to overthrow the foreign enemies of Israel.

Another figure who challenged the authorities in Jerusalem was Jesus ben Ananias. In AD 62 he went about in the temple complex during the Feast of Tabernacles (i.e., Sukkoth) proclaiming judgment upon Jerusalem. His shouts included direct quotations from Jeremiah 7, precisely the same block of scripture that Jesus of Nazareth used when he accused priests of turning the temple into a "den of robbers" (Jeremiah 7:11). Like Jesus of Nazareth, this Jesus was arrested by Roman authorities and whipped until his flesh wore away, exposing his bones.[43] A few years later, Menahem, son of the aforementioned Judas of Gamala, entered Jerusalem as a "king" wearing royal garb. With an armed group, he managed to kill the high priest and then occupy the Roman barracks. He was eventually captured, dragged into a public space, and tortured to death.[44] Within a few years of Menahem's defeat, two other figures from near Galilee—John of Gischala and Simon bar Giora (rivals of one another)—attempted to take control of Jerusalem and reign as king. John was eventually caught and imprisoned for life, and Simon was carried off to Rome, where he was executed.[45]

The actions of these individuals illustrate the tension between popular figures asserting some kind of kingship, with perhaps messianic overtones, and Roman authorities.[46] A few observations from these twelve cases provide some context for Jesus's ministry. First, Galilee was the locale of several first-century-AD figures who not only promoted themselves as "king" but could have also potentially had messianic pretensions. However, it needs to be pointed out that our primary source, Josephus, who details all these stories, never alleges that any one of these individuals, nor their followers, ever explicitly assumed the title of "Messiah" or "Christ," or received the title from their followers—Jesus, on the other hand, is the only person ever mentioned in Josephus where both he and his followers adopted the titles "Messiah" and "Christ."[47] Second, a number of these figures seemed to gain support from segments within the Jewish populace and were met with punishment by Roman soldiers.[48]

First-Century Figures with Monarchic, and Possibly Messianic, Aspirations

> Judas of Sepphoris (4 BC)
> Simon of Perea (4 BC)
> Athrongeus the Shepherd (4–2 BC)
> Samaritan Prophet (AD 35)
> Theudas (AD 45)
> Judas of Gamala (40s AD)
> Unnamed Egyptian (50s AD)
> Jesus ben Ananias (AD 62)
> Menahem of Gamala (AD 66)
> John of Gischala (late 60s AD)
> Simon bar Giora (late 60s AD)

Jesus as a Messianic Candidate

How did Jesus compare to the messianic expectations of the first centuries BC and AD? Did Jesus's lukewarm followers see him as the Messiah? Did even his closest followers, his disciples, uniformly recognize him as the Messiah? If so, did they refer to him as such? By the time the Gospel writers were putting pen to paper, so to speak, they had already established in their minds the fact that Jesus was, indeed, the Messiah, and their written accounts were an attempt to demonstrate this truth to others.

During Jesus's ministry, his role as the Messiah was not always clear-cut for his followers; there seemed to be some ambiguity at times. Perhaps a reason for this confusion was that Jesus sometimes seemed to avoid the term *Messiah* or *Christ*. In fact, Jesus infrequently referred to himself as such, except on occasion. For example, the singular occasion when Jesus acknowledged outright that he was the Messiah to someone outside his close circle was to the Samaritan woman. When Jesus spoke with her alone about salvation, she claimed she was waiting for the Messiah and that he would reveal such things when he came. Jesus replied, "I am he" (John 4:26). Later, when another nonapostle, the high priest, asked Jesus in private whether he was the Messiah, Jesus acknowledged that he was, according to the Gospel of Mark (14:61). However, his response in Matthew and Luke is more ambiguous. In Matthew, Jesus responded, "You have said so" (26:64); in other words, "that is your way of putting it."[49] In Luke, Jesus responded, "If I tell you, you will not believe; and if I question you, you will not answer" (22:67–68).

Jesus was more forthright with some of his closest disciples, but even in those cases he either hedged or told them to keep quiet. When Nathanael first met Jesus he said, "Rabbi, you are the Son of God! You are the King of Israel!" (i.e., the Messiah). Jesus responded, "Do you believe because I told you that I saw you under the fig tree? You will see greater things than these" (John 1:49–50). Again, Jesus hesitated to just say, "Yes, I'm the Messiah." At Caesarea Philippi, Jesus asked his closest disciples about his reputation—how people talked about him. They answered that some thought he was Elijah or a prophet. Jesus then asked his disciples what they thought of him, to which Peter answered, "You are the Messiah." Jesus then "sternly ordered" them (*epitimēsas* in Greek, also meaning "rebuke") not to tell anyone about his messiahship (Mark 8:28–30; Luke 9:19–21; Matthew 16:13–20). Perhaps Jesus refrained from referring to himself directly as "Messiah" in public because of the baggage it had accumulated over the centuries, as illustrated previously. Note that when one group in Galilee attempted to make Jesus their "king," he fled alone into the hills (John 6:15). It seems that Jesus, according to the New Testament, preferred "Son of Man" as a self-designation.

The accounts detailing the last week of Jesus's life and the immediate aftermath of his death are illustrative for understanding messianic expectations both of the first century broadly and of Jesus's messiahship specifically. When Jesus entered the vicinity of Jerusalem at the end of his ministry, he went first to the Mount of Olives. By the first century, the Mount of Olives was firmly entrenched within Jewish messianic lore. His first act after arriving on the mount, according to the Synoptic Gospels, was obtaining a donkey.[50] This deliberate act was meant to highlight Jesus's messiahship. Note that Matthew 21 quotes Zechariah 9: "Tell the daughter of Zion, Look, your king is coming to you, humble, and mounted on a donkey, and on a colt, the foal of a donkey" (Matthew 21:5; compare John 12:15). The keyword here is *king*. The notion that the Messiah would come riding on a donkey reflects earlier Israelite precedent. For example, according to Genesis 49:10–11, the future ruler of the tribe of Judah will bind "his foal to the vine and his donkey's colt to the choice vine." Israel's kings, David and Solomon, rode donkeys on the Mount of Olives in relation to their roles as king (2 Samuel 16:1–2); Solomon rode his down the Kidron Valley, at the base of the Mount of Olives, where he was anointed king over Israel (1 Kings 1:32–37). King Solomon's royal procession was accompanied by people shouting, "Long live King Solomon!" (1 Kings 1:39). Similarly, Jesus's followers held a procession for him as he rode the donkey from the Mount of Olives to the east gate of Jerusalem (Matthew 21:2–9; Mark 11:1–10; Luke 19:29–44; John 12:12–19) while they shouted, "Hosanna! Blessed is the son of David. Blessed is the king who comes in the name of the Lord!"[51] Jesus and his followers undoubtedly had messianic expectations in mind.

Jesus's procession from the Mount of Olives to the east gate of Jerusalem was deliberate, based on passages in Ezekiel and Zechariah. According to these texts, a messianic figure will descend from heaven to the summit of the Mount of Olives and then enter Jerusalem (Ezekiel 43:1–5; Zechariah 14). Once Jesus entered Jerusalem via the east gate, he cleansed the temple as prescribed in Zechariah (14:21). Jesus's activities are similar to the three-part structure in Zechariah 14, referring to the future divine messianic figure: (1) he arrives on the Mount of Olives, (2) he pronounces judgment on Israel, and (3) he enters Jerusalem and cleanses the temple. Thus, Zechariah 14 served as a type of guide to Jesus's messianic activity on the Mount of Olives. Cleansing the temple was an act of rebellion that set Jesus on a collision course with the temple establishment and Roman authorities, who saw him, like other messianic figures of the first century, as a rabble-rousing messiah aspirant who must be silenced and punished.

Jesus also pronounced judgment upon Jerusalem multiple times during the last week of his ministry. While on the Mount of Olives, he said to Jerusalem, "The days will come upon you, when your enemies will set up ramparts around you and surround you, and hem you in on every side. They will crush you to the ground, you and your children within you, and they will not leave within you one stone upon another" (Luke 19:43–44). He also cursed a fig tree (Mark 11:12–14, 20–25), which, according to earlier Israelite texts was a symbol of Judah and Israel (Micah 7:1–6; Jeremiah 8:13).[52] Thus Jesus's cursing of the fig tree on the Mount of Olives near Bethpage, meaning "house of unripe figs," was a pronouncement of judgment upon Jerusalem and Israel.[53] A third pronouncement was embedded in Jesus's so-called Olivet Discourse on the Mount of Olives—a discourse that included prophecies of the temple's destruction, wars, famines, persecution, desolation, the coming of the Son of Man, and parables of judgment (Matthew 24–25; Mark 13; Luke 21:5–37; compare Joseph Smith—Matthew). Finally, while at the temple complex, Jesus pronounced judgment upon Jerusalem and dared to prophesy of the temple's destruction in the presence of temple priests (Mark 11:15–18; 12:1–12; 14:56–59; John 2:19).

Jesus's activities during the few days leading up to his arrest demonstrate that he satisfied several expectations of a messiah prescribed in Jewish texts in the two centuries before Jesus's ministry. Jesus was viewed by his followers as the divine figure in Zechariah 14, people worshipped him as he entered Jerusalem, they referred to him as king and Son of David, he pronounced judgment upon Israel, and his activities suggested his status of judge and new leader of Israel. Like many of his contemporary messianic figures introduced previously, Jesus was arrested, mocked, and punished by the authorities for being a messiah, or the "king of the Jews" (Mark 15:26).

Because Jesus was killed by his enemies, which was not a widespread messianic expectation in the early first century AD, some Jews who thought he might be the Messiah would have abandoned such hope after the Crucifixion, including perhaps some of Jesus's close followers. For example, two nonapostle followers of Jesus were "sad" as they walked to Emmaus after Jesus's execution. They mentioned to the disguised Jesus that he was a great "prophet" who had just been killed, adding, "But we had *hoped* that he was the one *to redeem Israel*" (Luke 24:21, emphasis added; see verses 13–20). Even after the resurrected Jesus met with his apostles in Galilee, some still "doubted" (Matthew 28:16–20), most likely concerning Jesus's role as the Messiah in relation to their previous messianic expectations. Some of Jesus's actions, particularly near the end of his ministry, suggested to many within his larger Galilean circle that he may be the Messiah. While Jesus's messiahship would eventually become obvious to his disciples at some point after his resurrection, it was not always as clear to his followers during his actual ministry. When Jesus was arrested, humiliated, tortured, and killed by the authorities, it seemingly shattered messianic hopes for some of Jesus's followers. However, after his resurrection and additional time with the apostles, wherein he further instructed them (Acts 1:1–3), the belief that he was indeed the Messiah became much clearer. Following the Resurrection, Peter began to preach the notion that Jesus was the Messiah and that he suffered and died on account of salvation (Acts 2:14–26; 3:11–26; 4:1–22). Likewise, the letters of the apostle Paul, which were written within a few decades of the Resurrection (ca. AD 45–65), are replete with references to Jesus being the Messiah/Christ who suffered death and was resurrected. However, it is also clear from these same letters that the idea of a suffering, crucified messiah, notwithstanding the resurrection, was still "a stumblingblock" (1 Corinthians 1:23 KJV) to Jews since it was quite different from commonly held notions at the time.

❧

Trevan G. Hatch is the ancient scripture, religious studies, and philosophy specialist in the library at Brigham Young University.

Further Reading

Collins, Adela Yarbro, and John J. Collins. *King and Messiah as Son of God: Divine, Human, and Angelic Messianic Figures in Biblical and Related Literature*. Grand Rapids, MI: Eerdmans, 2008. This source is a bit denser than the Fitzmyer source, but it is not a burden to read. Unlike the Fitzmyer source, the authors include a conclusion section at the end of each chapter to keep the reader on track. They also dedicate significant space to explaining other terms associated with *Messiah*, including *Son of Man* and *Son of God*.

De Jonge, Marinus. "Messiah." In *The Anchor Bible Dictionary*, vol. 4, edited by David Noel Freedman, 777–88. New York: Doubleday, 1992. This source provides an authoritative but brief treatment of the Messiah in the Old Testament, early Jewish literature, and early Christian literature.

Fitzmyer, Joseph A. *The One Who Is to Come.* Grand Rapids, MI: Eerdmans, 2007. Fitzmyer's volume is an academic yet accessible source for examining the notions of "Messiah" in Jewish antiquity. The book walks the reader through the Hebrew Bible, the Septuagint, early Jewish writings, and the New Testament. In some key places, he slows down to spend time on significant developments or texts, like the book of Daniel.

Lucass, Shirley. *The Concept of the Messiah in the Scriptures of Judaism and Christianity.* London: Bloomsbury, 2011. This volume is the most recent of these sources. The layout is similar to the others, but Lucass positions her ideas in relation to authors that wrote before her. Thus, one can get a feel for earlier ideas and scholarship by reading this book.

Notes

1. The Gospels and Acts use *Messiah* sixty-three times, *Son of God* twenty-eight times, *Son of Man* eighty-four times, and *King of the Jews* seventeen times.
2. Exodus 28:41; 30:30; 40:13; Leviticus 7:35; 16:32; Numbers 3:3; 35:25. The Old Testament provides only one example of a prophet being anointed—the case of Elijah being commanded to anoint Elisha (1 Kings 19:15–16; compare 2 Kings 9:1–3, 6, 12).
3. 1 Samuel 9:9, 16; 10:1; 15:1, 17; 16:1–3, 12–13; 2 Samuel 12:7; 22:51; 23:1; 1 Kings 1:34, 39, 45; 19:15–16; 2 Kings 9:1–3, 6, 12; 25:4–6.
4. 1 Samuel 16:6; 24:6, 10; 26:9, 11, 16, 23; 2 Samuel 1:14, 16; 19:21; Psalm 2:2; 18:50; 20:6; 28:8; 89:39, 51; 132:10.
5. Joseph Fitzmyer, *The One Who Is to Come* (Grand Rapids, MI: Eerdmans, 2007), 8–25.
6. Adela Yarbro Collins and John J. Collins, *King and Messiah as Son of God: Divine, Human, and Angelic Messianic Figures in Biblical and Related Literature* (Grand Rapids, MI: Eerdmans, 2008), 1–10.
7. Cited in Henri Frankfort, *Kingship and the Gods: A Study of Ancient Near Eastern Religion as the Integration of Society and Nature* (Chicago: University of Chicago Press, 1948), 42.
8. Shirley Lucass, *The Concept of the Messiah in the Scriptures of Judaism and Christianity* (London: Bloomsbury, 2011), 45–47.
9. See Jeffery Jay Niehaus, *Ancient Near Eastern Themes in Biblical Theology* (Grand Rapids, MI: Kregel, 2008), 39; Andrew C. Cohen, *Death Rituals: Ideology and the Development of Early Mesopotamian Kingship* (Leiden, Netherlands: Brill, 2005), 123; Trevor Bryce, *The Kingdom of the Hittites* (Oxford: Oxford University Press, 2005), 20; and Sennacherib Prism, column 1, line 3, translation at http://www.kchanson.com/ANCDOCS/meso/sennprism1.html.
10. Genesis 49:24; Psalm 23:1–4; 28:9; 80:1; 95:7; 100:3; Ezekiel 34:11–31.
11. 2 Samuel 5:2; 7:7–8; 1 Kings 22:17; Psalm 78:70–71; Ezekiel 34:1–10.
12. For the various arguments, see Collins and Collins, *King and Messiah as Son of God*, 1–25.
13. Collins and Collins, *King and Messiah as Son of God*, 10–47; Lucass, *Concept of Messiah*, 66–121.
14. Fitzmyer, *One Who Is to Come*, 8.
15. Lucass, *Concept of Messiah*, 122–43.
16. Josephus, *Antiquities* 15.50–56, 222–236, 247–251, 365–372; 16.392–394.
17. Josephus, *Antiquities* 18.55–57.
18. Josephus, *Antiquities* 18:60.
19. It is believed, according to some scholars, that the book of Daniel was produced in the early second century BC, simultaneous with Greek persecution under Antiochus Epiphanes IV (175–164 BC). See, for example, John J. Collins, *Daniel: A Commentary on the Book of Daniel* (Minneapolis: Fortress, 1993), 1–38; Daniel Smith-Christopher, "Daniel (Book and Person, Hebrew Bible/Old Testament)," in *Encyclopedia of the Bible and Its Reception* (Berlin: De Gruyter, 2013), 6:86–94.
20. Ezekiel, for example, is addressed as "son of man" nearly one hundred times in the book of Ezekiel.

21. Throughout I use the New Revised Standard Version (NRSV) for the biblical quotations except as otherwise indicated.

22. Collins and Collins, *King and Messiah as Son of God*, 87.

23. E. Isaac, "1 Enoch: A New Translation and Introduction," in *The Old Testament Pseudepigrapha*, ed. James H. Charlesworth (New York: Doubleday, 1983), 1:34–36, 49.

24. 4Q252 5.1–4, translation from Michael Wise, Martin Abegg Jr., and Edward Cook, *The Dead Sea Scrolls: A New Translation* (New York: HarperSanFrancisco, 2005), 355.

25. Psalms of Solomon 17:21, 32, in Charlesworth, *Old Testament Pseudepigrapha*, 2:667.

26. 4Q521 frags 2 + 4 ii 1, translation from Wise, Abegg, and Cook, *Dead Sea Scrolls*, 531.

27. 1QSa 2.14–15, translation from Wise, Abegg, and Cook, *Dead Sea Scrolls*, 140.

28. CD 19.10–11, translation from Wise, Abegg, and Cook, *Dead Sea Scrolls*, 59.

29. Psalms of Solomon 17:26–36, in Charlesworth, *Old Testament Pseudepigrapha*, 2:667–68.

30. Sibylline Oracles 3:652–54.

31. This is similar to how we use the term *prophet* today. Although there are many prophets, when "the Prophet" is used, most assume reference to either Joseph Smith Jr. or the current President of the Church.

32. 4 Ezra 7:28–30, in Charlesworth, *Old Testament Pseudepigrapha*, 1:537; emphasis added.

33. Collins and Collins, *King and Messiah as Son of God*; Lucass, *Concept of Messiah*; and Fitzmyer, *One Who Is to Come*.

34. Daniel Boyarin, *The Jewish Gospels: The Story of the Jewish Christ* (New York: The New Press, 2012), 34.

35. Josephus, *Antiquities* 17.10.8.

36. Josephus, *Antiquities* 17.10.5; *Jewish War*, 2.4.1.

37. Josephus, *Antiquities* 17.10.6; *Jewish War*, 2.4.2.

38. Josephus, *Antiquities* 17.10.7; *Jewish War*, 2.4.3.

39. Josephus, *Antiquities* 18.4.1.

40. Josephus, *Antiquities*, 20.5.1; Acts 5:36.

41. Josephus, *Antiquities* 18.1.1.

42. Josephus, *Antiquities* 20.8.6.

43. Josephus, *Jewish War* 6.5.3.

44. Josephus, *Jewish War* 2.17.8–10.

45. Josephus, *Jewish War* 2.19.2; 2.20.6; 2.21.1; 4.6.1; 4.7.1; 4.9.4–5; 6.9.4; 7.1.2; 7.2.2; 7.5.3–6.

46. For a more detailed treatment of popular prophet and messiah figures in the first century, see Craig A. Evans, *Ancient Texts for New Testament Studies: A Guide to the Background Literature* (Peabody, MA: Hendrickson, 2005), 431–43; and Richard A. Horsley and John S. Hanson, *Bandits, Prophets and Messiahs: Popular Movements in the Time of Jesus* (Harrisburg, PA: Trinity Press International, 2007), 88–187.

47. Josephus, *Antiquities* 18.63; 20.200.

48. Thus, Jesus's actions as a prophet and messianic candidate would not have alienated him from the Jewish populace as much as Christian commentators have claimed for two millennia in an attempt to demonize Jews; rather, Jesus would have encountered opposition *primarily* from Roman authorities and Roman-sympathizing Jewish temple bureaucrats.

49. Fitzmyer, *One Who Is to Come*, 138.

50. Jesus's first act according to the Gospel of John was raising Lazarus (John 11).

51. See Matthew 21:9; Mark 11:9–10; Luke 19:37–38.

52. William Telford, *The Barren Temple and the Withered Tree: A Redaction-Critical Analysis of the Cursing of the Fig-Tree Pericope in Mark's Gospel and Its Relation to the Cleansing of the Temple Tradition* (Sheffield, England: JSOT, 1980), 132–56, 176–204.

53. The account in Matthew agrees in part with both Luke and Mark. Like Luke, Matthew positions Jesus's procession into Jerusalem and the cleansing of the temple on the same day. Like Mark, Matthew contains the curse of the fig tree, but only after Jesus cleanses the temple, whereas Mark has Jesus cursing the tree before the cleansing of the temple.

6

Jewish Hermeneutics in the New Testament Period

Matthew L. Bowen

Too often, believers in Jesus of Nazareth as Messiah, including some Latter-day Saints, have historically viewed him and his earliest followers as standing outside of and apart from Judaism. Likewise, Jesus's modes of teaching and dialogue as described in the New Testament Gospels have too often been treated as having no precedents or analogues within Judaism. The textual evidence of the New Testament itself, viewed within the historical, cultural, and religious context of first-century Judaism, confirms that the opposite is true in both cases.

Jesus may not have enjoyed (or needed) a traditional pharisaic or scribal education ("How knoweth this man letters, having never learned?" John 7:15),[1] but he taught, discoursed, and debated using rhetorical and hermeneutical (interpretive) methods commonly used among his contemporaries. Jesus's earliest disciples and interpreters also employed contemporary Jewish hermeneutics. Luke preserves Paul's assertion that though he was a Jew of the diaspora ("born in Tarsus [of] Cilicia"), he had been "brought up in this city [Jerusalem] at the feet of Gamaliel, and [had been] taught according to the perfect manner of the law of the fathers" (Acts 22:3) as a Pharisee.[2] We should thus expect to see Paul using these hermeneutical methods, and indeed we see him doing so.

In this chapter I will explore Jesus's use of several traditional Jewish modes of scriptural exegesis, argumentation, and interpretation as preserved in the New Testament Gospels, as well as the inclusion of these hermeneutical modes by early church leaders and writers such as Paul, Peter, James, and the author of Hebrews. I will begin with the hermeneutical and argumentation methods sometimes called the seven *middôt* or "rules" of Hillel. As Strack and Stemberger point out, these "seven *middôt* of Hillel were not invented by Hillel but constitute a collation of the main types of argument in use at that time."[3] In other words, although the codification of these "rules" is sometimes attributed to Hillel by tradition, they represent some of the most important ways that the scriptures were being used and means by which arguments were being made within intra-Jewish religious discussions. To conclude, I will cite several important examples of *māšāl* (parables), paronomasia, and gematria, which also surface in significant instances in the New Testament.

"Lighter and Weightier" and "Weightier and Lighter" (*Qal wāḥômer* and *ḥômer wĕqal*, Hillel Rule #1)

The Gospels record that Jesus frequently employed a form of what was described in the latter rabbinic period as *qal wāḥômer*, a form of *argumentum a minore ad maius*, or an argument from the "light" (or lesser) to the "heavy" (or greater). In other words, one begins from a minor premise and moves to a major one. By Jesus's time this mode of argumentation already enjoyed a long history of use within the Hebrew Bible. For example, Deuteronomy records Moses as stating, "Behold, while I am yet alive with you this day, ye have been rebellious against the Lord; and *how much more* after my death?" (Deuteronomy 31:27; emphasis added).

Matthew records several outstanding examples of Jesus's use of "lighter and weightier" and "weightier and lighter." His use of this method of reasoning often emphasized the value of human life. In the Sermon on the Mount, Jesus described the Father's providence thus: "Behold the fowls of the air: for they sow not, neither do they reap, nor gather into barns; yet your heavenly Father feedeth them. *Are ye not much better than they*?" (Matthew 6:26; emphasis added). Jesus also extends this line of argumentation to the Father's power to clothe the disciples as they ministered to the people.[4] "And why take ye thought for raiment? Consider the lilies of the field, how they grow; they toil not, neither do they spin: And yet I say unto you, That even Solomon in all his glory was not arrayed like one of these. Wherefore, if God so clothe the grass of the field, which to day is, and to morrow is cast into the oven, *shall he not much more clothe you*, O ye of little faith?" (Matthew 6:28–30; emphasis added).[5] The fowls of the air and the grass of the field represent the "lighter" (*qal*) in these analogies, while Jesus's disciples represent the "weightier" (*ḥômer*). If the Father takes care to provide food for birds, his disciples must know that he will provide them needed food as they do his work. If the Father clothes the lilies and the grass, the disciples can further rest assured that they will have sufficient clothing while they proclaim the gospel: "Wherefore, seek not the things of this world but seek ye first to build up the kingdom of God, and to establish his righteousness, *and all [such] things shall be added unto you*" (JST Matthew 6:38; emphasis added).

Later in the Sermon on the Mount, Jesus returns to lighter and weightier argumentation to emphasize the Father's accessibility and willingness to answer prayers: "Ask, and it shall be given you; seek, and ye shall find; knock, and it shall be opened unto you. . . . Or what man is there of you, whom if his son ask bread, will he give him a stone? Or if he ask a fish, will he give him a serpent? *If ye then, being evil, know how to give good gifts unto your children, how much more shall your Father which is in heaven give good things to them that ask him?*" (Matthew 7:7–11; emphasis added). Jesus's disciples, being comparatively "evil," represent the lighter, while the Father, the supreme embodiment of goodness, represents the weightier. Even evil human beings know how to give good gifts to their children. The Father's good gifts, as a manifestation of his supreme goodness, are beyond compare. Luke's interpretive rendition of this lighter and weightier argument replaces "good things" with "the Holy Spirit" (Luke 11:13), suggesting that the gift of the Holy Ghost constitutes one of the greatest of the Father's good gifts. Luke records that Jesus gave a similar but even more elaborate lighter and weightier explanation of God's willingness to answer the prayers of the elect in the parable of the unjust judge (18:1–8). If an unjust judge, because of a widow's persistent "troubl[ing]" him, would "avenge her, lest by her continual coming she weary [him]," how much more will "God avenge his own elect, which cry day and night unto him, though he bear long with them?" (18:6–7).

In yet another lighter and weightier argument, Jesus extols the value of human life—and thus the lives of his disciples—as of supernal value: "Are not two sparrows sold for a farthing? and one of them shall not fall on the ground without your Father ["and not one of them is forgotten before God," Luke 12:6]. But the very hairs of your head are all numbered. Fear ye not therefore, *ye are of more value* than many sparrows" (Matthew 10:29–31; emphasis added; compare Luke 12:6–7).

Two additional examples of the lighter and weightier method revolve around the value of human life. These, however, are relative to the daily application of Torah. Matthew, utilizing Mark's record, illustrates that questions regarding proper Sabbath observance followed hard on Jesus throughout his ministry. Jesus boldly uses the healing of a man in a synagogue in Capernaum[6] to clarify that alleviating human suffering did not violate Mosaic Sabbath restrictions—quite the contrary. Jesus's words and actions as preserved in Matthew 9:2–8, Mark 2:1–13, and Luke 5:18–26 constitute as visible and emphatic an example of this method as one could wish for to assert his divine "power" or (better) "authority" (Greek *exousia*).

In that episode, Jesus begins by declaring that the man's sins are forgiven, knowing full well that this will immediately raise questions of "authority" (*exousia*) among the religious leaders present. When the scribes question this action, Jesus makes it the *qal* ("lighter") aspect of his forthcoming analogy with the question, "For whether [which] is easier, to say, Thy sins be forgiven thee, or to say, Arise, and walk?" This sets up the imminent healing as the *ḥômer* ("weightier") aspect of his argument. Of course, anyone can *say* "thy sins be forgiven thee," a statement that requires no immediate, demonstrable proof. However, the validity of a statement like "Arise, and walk" rests on proof following. The sick man "rising" and "departing" to his house confirms not only Jesus's command "Arise, take up thy bed, and go," but also his assertion that the man's sins were forgiven. This miracle also makes a powerful statement about the purpose of divine authority and the Sabbath: both are given to humankind to improve the quality of human life (compare John 10:10).

One of Jesus's most significant uses of lighter and weightier and weightier and lighter arguments in the interpretation of scripture occurs following his good shepherd sermon in John 10, in a debate with religious leaders, perhaps within the precincts of the temple. The religious leaders intend to stone Jesus for the allegedly blasphemous claim "I and my Father are one" (10:30). The crux of Jesus's argument in verses 32–36 centers on his quotation and interpretation of Psalm 82:6 ("Ye are gods; and all of you are children of the most High").[7] Psalm 82, like all the Psalms, presumably constituted a temple hymn—a hymn sung or performed in the Jerusalem temple. Whoever its original addressees (i.e., divine beings, rulers, etc.), Jesus's circumlocution "them . . . unto whom the word of God came" reflects an anthropological interpretation of the psalm—that is, its addressees were human beings, perhaps Israelites (compare the "noble and great ones" of Abraham 3:22; compare also Doctrine and Covenants 138:55). Jesus's argument runs thus: the weightier claim is to be a "god" or "gods" (Hebrew *'ĕlōhîm*; Greek *theos, theoi*) rather than to be a/the "son of God" (the lighter claim). Psalm 82:6 addresses certain human beings as gods. If the unbreakable scripture called those human beings gods, Jesus cannot be rightly charged with blasphemy. On the surface Jesus's argument is weightier and lighter, yet on another level it represents a lighter and weightier argument: any humans that might be called gods are subordinate to Jesus as Son of God, if that title is rightly understood. But Jesus may have also hinted at the exalted view of humanity that John makes explicit at the outset of his Gospel: "But as many as received him, to them gave he power to become the sons [*tekna*, "children"] of God, even to them that believe on his name" (John 1:12).[8]

Indeed, Jesus intended (and intends) his disciples to become "even as I am" (3 Nephi 28:10), as additional lighter and weightier examples emphasize. Matthew records Jesus saying to his disciples: "It is enough for the disciple that he be [become, *genētai*] as his master, and the servant as his lord. If they have called the master of the house *Beelzebub, how much more* shall they call them of his household?" (Matthew 10:25; emphasis added). The name *Beelzebub* ("Lord of the flies") constitutes a dysphemism[9] for *Beelzebul* ("Lord of the lofty abode").[10] In other words, if the contemporary religious leaders in Judea and Jerusalem have labeled Jesus "Satan," they can hardly label his disciples anything worse. Yet they are to become as he is. According to John, Jesus offers similar lighter and weightier counsel to his disciples on the final night of his mortal ministry (John 15:18–20).

Paul, an erstwhile Pharisee, also frequently employed lighter and weightier arguments. For example, Paul extols God's love and the power of Jesus Christ's atonement before and after we apply it: "But God commendeth his love toward us, in that, while we were yet sinners, Christ died for us. *Much more then*, being now justified by his blood, we shall be saved from wrath through him. For if, when we were enemies, we were reconciled to God by the death of his Son, *much more*, being reconciled, we shall be saved by his life" (Romans 5:8–10; emphasis added). If the love of God is evident in the formulation (and foreordination) of the plan of salvation and the provision of Jesus Christ as our Savior, even before we have faith in him or repent ("when we were yet without strength," Romans 5:6), how much more that love becomes evident as we activate the blessings of Christ's atonement by obeying his doctrine (Articles of Faith 1:4).

Paul employs a lighter and weightier analogy again a few verses later to push this argument even further, this time using Adam and the Fall: "Nevertheless death reigned from Adam to Moses, even over them that had not sinned after the similitude of Adam's transgression, who is the figure of him that was to come. But not as the offence, so also is the free gift. For if through the offence of one many be dead, *much more* the grace of God, and the gift by grace, which is by one man, Jesus Christ, hath abounded unto many" (Romans 5:14–15; emphasis added). Paul compares Adam with Christ on a lighter and weightier analogy to again extol the power of Christ's atonement and the grace made available thereby—the *weightier*. Paul considers it a foregone conclusion that physical and spiritual death came upon the whole human race through Adam's transgression or offense—the *lighter*. If Adam's "disobedience" (Romans 5:19), a human act, had that kind of power and efficaciousness on "many," how much more must Jesus's atonement, a divine act, have upon "many."[11]

Paul later applies the lighter and weightier method to Israel and those Jews who had not yet accepted Jesus as Messiah: "Now if the fall of them be the riches of the world, and the diminishing of them the riches of the Gentiles; *how much more* their fulness?" (Romans 11:12; emphasis added); "For if thou wert cut out of the olive tree which is wild by nature, and wert graffed [grafted] contrary to nature into a good olive tree: *how much more* shall these, which be the natural branches, be graffed [grafted] into their own olive tree?" (Romans 11:24; emphasis added). As Joseph Fitzmyer notes, "Israel's disbelief is only temporary" and partial.[12] Indeed, "Israel has stumbled over Christ but it has not fallen down completely so that it cannot regain its footing."[13] He further observes, "Paul hints at the untold benefits of the world that would come with the full acceptance of Jesus as Messiah by the Jews; if their action has so far resulted in such incredible benefits, then what will their full acceptance mean?"[14] Lehi, Nephi, Jacob, Zenos, Isaiah, and many other prophets had some idea.[15]

In 2 Corinthians 3:7–11, Paul uses lighter and weightier reasoning to argue that if the heavenly ministrations that were concomitant with the institution of the law of Moses were glorious, how much more so Christ's heavenly ministrations. The author of Hebrews argues much the same thing in the same way in Hebrews 9:11–14 and 12:18–26.

Some additional examples of Paul's use of lighter and weightier methods occur in Paul's analogy of the church to the body (1 Corinthians 12:22), in his plea to the Philippian saints to "work out [their] own salvation with fear and trembling" (Philippians 2:12), and in his efforts to persuade Philemon to allow his use of Onesimus, an escaped slave, for the furtherance of the work of the gospel (Philemon 1:16). The author of Hebrews, too, appeals extensively to this mode of argumentation (Hebrews 2:1–4; 9:11–14; 10:28–29; 12:9, 18–26).

"Equal Statute" (*Gĕzērâ šāwâ*, Hillel Rule #2)

Arland Hultgren cites Paul's use of "the so-called *Gezera Shawa* principle, which became codified in later rules for biblical interpretation."[16] "According to that principle," he states, "two texts using the same word can be brought together, and what is taught in the one can be applied to the other as well."[17] We see Jesus, Paul, Matthew, Mark, and others make extensive use of *gĕzērâ šāwâ* ("equal statute") throughout the New Testament.

Though not one of the original twelve, Mark was one of Jesus's early disciples, an early church leader, a possible tradent and interpreter of Peter,[18] and probably a Jew. Mark wrote to a largely gentile and Roman audience, as evident in his explanation of Jewish customs and inclusion of Latinisms.[19] However, Mark uses the equal statute exegetical technique to fashion a very Jewish introduction to his Gospel, which begins with Jesus's baptism by John the Baptist: "The beginning of the gospel of Jesus Christ, the Son of God; as it is written in the prophets, Behold, I send my messenger before thy face, which shall _prepare_ thy _way_ [*kataskeuasei tēn hodon sou*] *before thee*. The voice of one crying in the wilderness, _Prepare ye the way_ [*hetoimasate tēn hodon*] *of the Lord*, make his paths straight" (Mark 1:1–3; emphasis added).

Using equal statute, Mark first quotes a portion of Malachi 3:1: "Behold, I will send my messenger, and he shall *prepare the way before me* [*ûpinnâ-derek lipānāy*, clear the way before me]: and the Lord, whom ye seek, shall suddenly come to his temple, even the messenger of the covenant, whom ye delight in: behold, he shall come, saith the Lord of hosts." He then joins part of Isaiah 40:3: "The voice of him that crieth in the wilderness, *Prepare ye the way of the Lord* [*pannû derek yhwh*], make straight in the desert a highway for our God" (emphasis added).

Mark's use of equal statute transforms Isaiah's and Malachi's separate prophecies into a single prophecy that he applies to—or is fulfilled in—John the Baptist. This equal statute on the specific term *prepare*—the same in Hebrew, though differing in Greek—and on the expression *the way* to describe John the Baptist's mission, including the baptism of Jesus, takes on particular significance because the way *is* the doctrine of Christ,[20] and repentance and baptism is the gate. Mark thus appears to suggest what Nephi makes more explicit after his father saw and described "a prophet who should come before the Messiah, to prepare the way of the Lord" (1 Nephi 10:7; compare 10:8): "For he is the same yesterday, today, and forever; and *the way is prepared* for all men from the foundation of the world, if it so be that they repent and come unto him" (1 Nephi 10:18; emphasis added).

Matthew and Mark offer a climactic example of Jesus's use of equal statute during the last week of the Savior's life. Matthew, clearly writing to a Jewish audience, depicts Jesus using this method in an exchange between a lawyer of the Pharisees and Jesus after the latter had defeated the Sadducees on a question about marriage designed to entrap him (Matthew 22:23–33). Jesus's equal statute response, as recorded in Matthew 22:36–40, adjoins the apodictic commandment from Deuteronomy, "And thou shalt love [*wĕ 'āhabtâ*] the Lord thy God with all thine heart" (Deuteronomy 6:5), to the lesser-quoted apodictic commandment from the priestly Holiness Code, "but thou shalt love [*wĕ 'āhabtâ*] thy neighbour as thyself" (Leviticus 19:18). Jesus then declared that "on these two commandments hang all the law and the prophets" (Matthew 22:40). Luke 10:27 tells this account or the account of a similar encounter differently, attributing the joining of the two Torah passages to the lawyer who was testing Jesus and describes the exchange as a setup for Jesus's parable of the good Samaritan.

Regardless of whether the two accounts represent the selfsame event or two entirely separate events, the juxtaposition of Deuteronomy 6:5 and Leviticus 19:18 on the equal statute principle unquestionably constitutes the foundation of both accounts. If Luke's account in Luke 10 depicts a separate event, it would suggest that this particular equal statute constituted something of a commonplace in the discourse of the religious leaders in Jesus's time. Matthew's and Mark's accounts are clear in their attribution of this equal statute to Jesus himself.

Thus, in the context of first-century-AD Judaism, the Pharisee lawyer's question and Jesus's response about the great commandment in the law represent an intra-Jewish attempt to better understand the Torah and its ethical application in daily Jewish life. The "first and great commandment" to wholeheartedly "love the Lord thy God" in Deuteronomy 6:5 constitutes a part of the so-called Shema (šĕmaʿ), which begins in Deuteronomy 6:4 ("Hear [šĕmaʿ], O Israel, the Lord is our God, the Lord is one"). Indeed, Mark's account includes a part of Deuteronomy 6:4 ("The first of all the commandments is, Hear, O Israel; The Lord our God is one Lord"). To this day, the Shema remains one of Judaism's most important creedal texts.

We should note in addition that Jesus's citation of Leviticus 19:18 in Matthew 22:34–40 and Mark 12:28–34—as a commandment summarizing the whole law (Torah)—may originate with Hillel the Elder, a noted Jewish religious authority who lived during the time of Jesus's adolescence (ca. AD 10). Hillel is reported to have said, "Whatsoever is distasteful to you, do not do to your neighbor: this is the whole Law altogether [dʿlk sny lḥbrk lʾ tʿbyd zw hyʾ kl htwrh kwlh]" (Babylonian Talmud Shabbat 31a, my translation). Hillel's declaration constitutes a precedent for and a probable basis of the Savior's Golden Rule: "Therefore all things whatsoever ye would that men should do to you, do ye even so to them: for this is the law [Torah] and the prophets" (Matthew 7:12; compare Luke 6:31). Consequently, when Jesus added Leviticus 19:18 as the "second [great commandment] like unto" Deuteronomy 6:5, he imported or invoked contemporary Jewish discourse on the ethical weight of Leviticus 19:18.

All of the foregoing helps us better understand the significance of James's description of the commandment to love thy neighbor as thyself as the "royal law," which if we fulfill, we "do well" (James 2:8). Paul, too, writing to a mixed Jewish and gentile audience at Rome, declared adherence to Leviticus 19:18 to be the fulfillment of Torah in Romans 13:8–9 (see further below).

Jesus's use of equal statute to place the vertical cultic dimension ("Love the Lord thy God") atop the horizontal ethical obligation ("Love thy neighbor," as emphasized by Hillel) thus suggests the means par excellence of demonstrating love of God: to love one's neighbor. Or, as King Benjamin put it: "When ye are in the service of your fellow beings ye are only in the service of your God" (Mosiah 2:17). Service (Hebrew ʿăbōdâ) is a temple word in the foregoing context,[21] and the most important temple service that can be rendered is that rendered on behalf of someone who cannot act "in their own *propria persona*" (Doctrine and Covenants 128:8)—that is, for and in behalf of themselves. Notably and appropriately, Mark and Matthew situate Jesus's teaching, of which this *gĕzērâ šāwâ* constitutes a part, in the temple. Love of God and neighbor—pure charity—stands at the heart of all appropriate temple activity.

Jesus's equal statute involving Deuteronomy 6:5 and Leviticus 19:18 thus implies what Nephi's declaration makes explicit: "The Lord God hath given a commandment that all men should have charity, which charity is love. And except they should have charity they were nothing. Wherefore, if they should have charity they would not suffer the laborer in Zion to perish" (2 Nephi 26:30). Or as Paul summarizes it: "Now the end of the commandment is charity out of a pure heart, and of a good conscience, and of faith unfeigned" (1 Timothy 1:5).

Mark and Matthew also both preserve an exchange with some of the Pharisees over the traditional hand washings stipulated in the oral law wherein Jesus used equal statute to criticize the contemporary traditional practice of Corban, a perversion of temple service (Mark 7:9–13; Matthew 15:1–9). Jesus's critique joins the apodictic Decalogue command-ment "Honour thy father and thy mother" (Exodus 20:12; Deuteronomy 5:16) to the casu-istic penalty for cursing one's parents, "he that curseth his father, or his mother, shall surely be put to death" (Exodus 21:17; Leviticus 20:9). Jesus does this on the basis of the words *father* and *mother* and probably secondarily on *honor* and *curse* as binary antonyms. In so doing, Jesus emphasizes that through the tradition of Corban—the practice of declaring the service that one might render to parents a temple gift—the Pharisees were at once failing to honor their parents, a grievous sin of omission, and actively cursing their parents, an even worse sin of commission and a capital offense. Jesus cites this as an outstanding example of the hypocrisy of some contemporary traditional practices among some Pharisees and their adherents ("many such like things do ye," Mark 7:13).

For his part, the apostle Paul, a self-described "Israelite [from] the tribe of Benjamin, a Hebrew of Hebrews, [and] as touching the law, a Pharisee" (Philippians 3:5), employs equal statute in several instances. Arguably the most significant of these occurs in Romans 4, where Paul expounds the doctrine of justification and why Abraham was justified—set in a right relationship with God—by faith rather than by works (Romans 4:3–8).

There Paul brings together Genesis 15:6 ("And he [Abraham] believed in the Lord; and *he counted it* [Hebrew *wayyaḥšĕbehā*; Greek *elogisthē*] to him for righteousness"; emphasis added) and Psalm 32:1–2 ("Blessed is he whose transgression is forgiven, whose sin is cov-ered. Blessed is the man unto whom the Lord *imputeth* [Hebrew *yaḥšōb*; Greek *logisētai*] not iniquity," 31:2 LXX; emphasis added) on the basis of the Hebrew word *ḥāšab* or Greek *logizō*. Joseph A. Fitzmyer writes, "Thus both witnesses, Abraham and David, show that the OT itself supports Paul's thesis of graced justification through faith. In this way his teaching 'upholds' the Law."[22]

Paul uses another equal statute that sees two prophecies of Isaiah as fulfilled in Jesus Christ and his rejection by some of his Israelite contemporaries: "For they stumbled at that stumblingstone; as it is written, Behold, I lay in Sion a stumblingstone and rock of offence: and whosoever believeth on him shall not be ashamed" (Romans 9:32–33). This equal statute joins Isaiah 8:14 ("And he shall be for a sanctuary; but for a stone of stumbling and for a rock of offense to both the houses of Israel") to Isaiah 28:16 ("Behold, I lay in Zion for a foundation a stone, a tried stone, a precious corner stone, a sure foundation: he that believeth shall not make haste"). Paul brings Israel's past rejection of Jehovah, the stone of Isaiah 8:14, into the present as the rejection of Jesus as Messiah and identifies him with the Zion stone—that is, "the stone laid by Yahweh in (the eastern hill of Jerusalem on which the Temple was built) [and] a symbol of salvation for those who trusted in him."[23]

Peter taught the need to become "lively [living] stones" coming to Christ to be built as part of a spiritual temple (1 Peter 2:6–8). In so teaching, he uses an equal statute that is very similar to Paul's. Peter's equal statute joins together Isaiah 28:14 ("Behold, I lay in Zion for a foundation a stone"), Psalm 118:22 ("The stone which the builders refused is become the head stone of the corner"), and Isaiah 8:14 ("he shall be . . . for a stone of stumbling and for a rock of offence"). Paul and Peter mutually interpret these passages and apply them to Jesus on the basis of words translated as "stone." Luke cites Jesus using Psalm 118:22 and Isaiah 8:14–15 together in Luke 20:17–18, again on the basis of *stone* (Greek *lithos*; Hebrew *'eben*) as a shared term (see further below). Taken together, these examples suggest that these Old Testament passages were linked together by Jesus's earliest followers, who saw their fulfillment in him. Jacob's use of these passages in Jacob 4:15–17 further suggests that this interpretive scriptural reading well preceded New Testament times.[24]

The author of Hebrews uses equal statute christologically in several instances. For example, he creates an equal statute in Hebrews 1:5 as a part of a larger "building of a family" (*binyan 'āb*) in Hebrews 1:3–8 (see below). Hebrews joins Psalm 2:7 LXX and 2 Samuel 7:14 LXX together to emphasize Jesus's divine sonship. Hebrews 1:6–7, quoting Deuteronomy 32:43 LXX and Psalm 96:7 LXX on the basis of "angels" (Greek *angeloi*), is another example. Apart from Jesus's parables and use of the lighter and weightier method, equal statute is arguably the most prominent Jewish hermeneutical/rhetorical mode in the New Testament.

The related hermeneutical method of *heqeš* ("comparison"), which Strack and Stemberger describe as a "less strictly controlled *topical analogy*,"[25] juxtaposes and mutually interprets scriptures on the basis of shared concepts or contents, rather than strictly on a lexical basis. Paul's "stringing together" Psalm 14:1–3 (53:2–4), 5:10, 140:4, 10:7, 36:2, and Isaiah 59:7–8 in Romans 3:10–18—all "linked by the mention of parts of the body: throat, tongue, lips, mouth, feet, [and] eyes"[26]—might constitute an example of this practice (Romans 9:12–19). Jesus's implicit linking of Isaiah 56:7 to Jeremiah 7:11 might constitute equal statute, comparison, or something in between: "And he taught, saying unto them, Is it not written, My house shall be called of all nations the house of prayer? [Isaiah 56:7] but ye have made it a den of thieves [Jeremiah 7:11]" (Mark 11:17).

"Building of a Family" (*Binyan 'āb*, Hillel Rules #3 and #4)

"Building of a family," or *binyan 'āb*, is a hermeneutical mode that, in the words of Aaron M. Gale, "entails using one Torah passage to reach a conclusion regarding another."[27] In other words, this interpretive mode allows one scriptural passage to serve as an authoritative lens for interpreting and applying another. Gale identifies the expression "have ye not read" as a "rabbinic formula"[28] pertaining to the "building of a family." Jesus's use of this formula signals that an authoritative ruling using scripture—usually a "building of a family"—is forthcoming.

"Building a family from a single scripture" (Binyan 'āb mikkātûb 'eḥād)

Strack and Stemberger gloss the simplest form of this hermeneutical mode, *binyan 'āb mikkātûb 'eḥād*, as literally the "'founding of a family' (*ab* short for *bet ab*) 'from a single Scripture text.'"[29] All three Synoptic evangelists offer a possible example of "building a family from a single scripture." Jesus uses a vineyard parable clearly based on Isaiah's song of the vineyard (Isaiah 5:1–7) to criticize the contemporary religious leadership in Jerusalem (Matthew 21:33–46; Mark 12:1–2; Luke 20:9–18). He then offers an interpretation of this Isaiah-based parable: "And *have ye not read* this scripture; The stone which the builders rejected is become the head of the corner: This was the Lord's doing, and it is marvellous in our eyes?" (Mark 12:10–11; emphasis added).

Jesus offers an interpretation of his vineyard parable (and thus also a contemporary application for Isaiah 5:1–7) by quoting Psalm 118:22–23 from the Hallel (Psalms 113–118), one of ancient Israel and Judah's most important temple hymns. Matthew's and Luke's accounts go even further, with Jesus turning the building of a family from a single scripture into an equal statute, with Jesus also invoking Isaiah 8:14–15 on the basis of the shared word *stone* (Hebrew *'eben*; see Matthew 21:42; Luke 20:18), a homonym of the Hebrew word *bēn*, "son." The power of Jesus's teaching, using this parable and Psalm 118:22–23 (and Isaiah 8:14–15), must have been amplified by its temple setting.

All three Synoptic evangelists preserve an even more lucid example of this interpretive method (Matthew 22:24–33; Mark 12:18–27; Luke 20:27–38). The Sadducees, who rejected the doctrine of a physical resurrection[30] and anything beyond the Torah (or Pentateuch, the five books of Moses), challenged Jesus with a question involving the Deuteronomic statutes regarding levirate marriage. The scenario, wherein seven brothers marry the same wife, was an attempt at *reductio ad absurdum*. Daniel J. Harrington writes: "The Sadducees based their rejection of the resurrection on the silence of the Pentateuch about it. They cite a passage from Deuteronomy 25:5–10 that they think will be irrefutable proof for their position and attach to it an application designed to reduce to absurdity those who favor belief in the resurrection."[31]

Jesus responds by building a family from a single scripture using Exodus 3:6, 15–16. As recorded by Mark, the Savior states: "And as touching the dead, that they rise: have ye not read in the book of Moses, how in the bush God spake unto him, saying, I am the God of Abraham, and the God of Isaac, and the God of Jacob? He is not the God of the dead, but the God of the living: ye therefore do greatly err" (Mark 12:26–27).[32] Earle Ellis writes: "God is not the God of the dead, and yet in Exodus 3:14 he affirmed a continuing covenant relationship with dead Abraham. Therefore, he must intend to raise Abraham out of death, and from this conclusion one may infer the resurrection of all the dead who have a similar covenantal relationship."[33] In other words, Abraham is not dead, but his spirit lives. As Bruce Chilton, Darrell Bock, and Daniel Gurtner's appendix notes: "from this one text one further may infer as Jesus did (Mark 12:16; Matthew 22:31; Luke 20:37) the truth of the general resurrection."[34] This accords well with JST Mark 12:32 (emphasis added): "He is not therefore the God of the dead, but the God of the living; *for he raiseth them up out of their graves.*" Harrington further observes, "Exod 3:6, 15–16, where Yahweh is identified as the God of the fathers of Israel, is from the Pentateuch and so must be taken seriously by the Sadducees."[35] Jesus thus adroitly and powerfully builds a family from a single scripture to teach and testify of the reality of a literal bodily resurrection.

"Building a family from two scriptures" (Binyan ʾāb miššĕnê kĕtûbîm)

Regarding this second form of building a family, Wilhelm Bacher writes: "By means of this exegetical norm, a specific stipulation found in only one of a group of topically related biblical passages is applied to them all. Thus, the main passage bestows on all others a common character which combines them into a family."[36] Arguably the best example of this extended hermeneutic from the Gospels is Jesus's exchange with the Pharisees about his disciples' Sabbath observance. Notably, Jesus quotes Hosea 6:6 ("For I desired mercy, and not sacrifice; and the knowledge of God more than burnt offerings") at least twice as the doctrinal or theological basis for using contemporary hermeneutical modes. The first of these occurs in Matthew 9:13, where Jesus uses Hosea 6:6 to reinforce the parable of the physician. Matthew 12:1–8 records that he uses "building a family" again when asserting his own authority with regard to the Sabbath in another intra-Jewish debate with the Pharisees.

Regarding the events depicted in Matthew 12:1–8, Gale explains Jesus's "building a family from two scriptures" thus: "Jesus responds by arguing that other Jews violated Sabbath laws when they were in need. Matthew makes the need clear in 12.1 by adding to Mark 2.23 that the disciples were hungry. Matthew's Jesus is thus depicted as utilizing Jewish exegetical methods to create new authoritative rulings."[37] Jesus uses the example of David and others eating the bread of the presence (shewbread) in need in 1 Samuel 21:6 (and Leviticus 24:7–8) and the offering of Sabbath sacrifice in Numbers 28:9–10 to build the principle that humanitarian considerations supersede normal Sabbath rules.

Another clear example of Jesus's building a family from two or more scriptures emerges in Matthew 19:3–8 when the Pharisees test Jesus on the Mosaic legislation regarding divorce. Gale observes that here "Jesus cites Genesis 1.27 [and] 2.24 to issue an authoritative decision regarding another [passage], Deut 24.1–4."[38] Jesus builds a doctrine from Genesis 1:27 ("So God created man in his own image, in the image of God created he him; male and female created he them") and Genesis 2:24 ("Therefore shall a man leave his father and his mother, and shall cleave unto his wife: and they shall be one flesh") that God intended marriage to be permanent. When the Pharisees respond by invoking Deuteronomy 24:1–4, Jesus explains that Moses gave the divorce provision. The pre-Mosaic historical context of the first marriage makes it weightier than the Mosaic divorce provision (see further below). Latter-day Saints should appreciate the power of the Savior's teaching here: if God regards marriage as ideally permanent, death and hell will not prevail against it in eternity (Matthew 16:16–19).

In 1 Corinthians 9:9–14 Paul, too, builds a doctrine or principle regarding full-time ministers of the gospel from two unrelated scriptural passages. Ellis explains Paul's building a family from two scriptures thus: "From the commands to unmuzzle the working ox (Deut 25:4) and to give the temple priests a share of the sacrifices (Deut 18:1–8) one may infer the general right of ministers of the gospel to a living (1 Cor 9:9, 13)."[39] Ellis additionally sees James, often thought to be James the brother of Jesus, building on the examples of Abraham in Genesis 22:9–19 and Rahab (Joshua 2:1–16) "to establish the general principle that genuine faith is manifest by works" in James 2:22–26.[40] James may have been responding to Paul's *dābār halāmēd mē'inyānô* ("argument from the context") on justification in Galatians 3 that also rests on Genesis 22 (see below).

The author of Hebrews elaborately builds a family from two (or more) scriptures using seven blocks of biblical passages in Hebrews 1:5–13[41] in order to establish the general principle or doctrine of Jesus's superiority to the angels. It begins with an equal statute involving Psalm 2:7 and 2 Samuel 7:14 in Hebrews 1:5 on Greek *huios* ("son"),[42] then adds a second equal statute on a blending of Deuteronomy 32:43 LXX, Psalm 96:7 LXX [97:7] (that privileges the word "angels" [*angeloi*] over "sons of God" [*huioi theou*] in the former and "gods" in the Hebrew MT of the latter), and Psalm 103:4 LXX all on the basis of the word *angels*. He then quotes Psalm 44:7 LXX [45:6], which addresses the Davidic king as "God," and then Psalm 101:26–28 LXX [102:25–27], which extols God's permanence. He crowns the whole building of a family with Psalm 109:1 LXX [110:1], which declares the Davidic king enthroned at God's right hand. This building of a family from two (or more) scriptures thus stands as an impressive rhetorical description of Jesus's status as Son of God to a believing Jewish audience.

"The General and the Particular, the Particular and the General" (*Kĕlāl ûpĕrāt ûpĕrāt ûkĕlāl*, Hillel Rule #5)

The hermeneutical method *kĕlāl ûpĕrāt ûpĕrāt ûkĕlāl*—"the general and the particular, the particular and the general"—is the "qualification of the general by the particular, and the particular by the general."[43] Returning to Jesus's exchange at the temple with other Jewish religious authorities, we should note how Matthew reports that Jesus appended to his equal statute on Deuteronomy 6:5 ("Thou shalt love the Lord thy God") and Leviticus 19:18 ("thou shalt love thy neighbour as thyself") the statement "On these two commandments hang all the law and the prophets." Jesus thus "summed up in one 'general' commandment all of the 'particular' commandments (Mark 12:38–34; Matthew 22:34–40)."[44] In so doing, he makes his equal statute into an example of the particular and the general as well.

Similarly, Paul wrote to the Roman saints: "Owe no man any thing, but to love one another: for he that loveth another hath fulfilled the law. For this, Thou shalt not commit adultery, Thou shalt not kill, Thou shalt not steal, Thou shalt not bear false witness, Thou shalt not covet; and if there be any other commandment, it is briefly comprehended in this saying, namely, Thou shalt love thy neighbour as thyself" (Romans 13:8–9). Here too, as Ellis notes, "the particular commandments are apparently regarded as illustrative examples of the general."[45]

"Something Similar to This in Another Passage"/"Exposition by Means of a Similar Case" (*Kayyôṣēʾ bô bĕmāqôm ʾaḥēr*, Hillel Rule #6)

The name of the hermeneutical mode *kayyôṣēʾ bô bĕmāqôm ʾaḥēr* denotes "something similar to this in another passage"[46] or "exposition by means of a similar case."[47] It functions similar to *gĕzērâ šāwâ*, "but it is less strictly limited."[48] Jesus seems to use this tool as recorded in Matthew 19:16–22. When the rich young man asks what "good thing" will qualify him for eternal life, Jesus responds, "if thou wilt enter into life, keep the commandments" (19:17). The rich young man then asks "which?" (19:18), and Jesus adumbrates the Decalogue commandments of Exodus 20:12–26 ("Thou shalt do no murder, Thou shalt not commit adultery, Thou shalt not steal, Thou shalt not bear false witness, Honour thy father and thy mother"), adjoining the commandment "love thy neighbor as thyself" from Leviticus 19:18 (Matthew 19:18–19). When the rich young man responds, "All these things I have kept from my youth; what lack I yet?" (Matthew 19:20), Jesus adds an allusion to Jehovah's commandments to Abraham in Genesis 17:1 ("walk before me, and be thou perfect [Hebrew *tāmîm*; *amemptos* LXX]), saying, "If thou wilt be perfect [Greek *teleios* = Hebrew *tāmîm*], go and sell that thou hast, and give to the poor, and thou shalt have treasure in heaven: and come and follow me" (Matthew 19:21; compare 5:48). In so doing, Jesus not only sums up the meaning of the commandments of Exodus 20:12–26 in Leviticus 19:18 (a similar passage), but also infers that one becomes "perfect" in keeping all the commandments with an Abrahamic sacrifice (compare "the works of Abraham"; John 8:39; Doctrine and Covenants 132:32). Abraham proved himself willing to walk with God and even part with Isaac, but the rich young man would not part with temporal wealth for his neighbor to walk with Jesus.

Ellis sees Paul using something similar to this in another passage in Galatians 3:8 and 3:16[49] where he argues for the justification of the Gentiles through faith from the Abraham cycle: "And the scripture [Genesis 12:3], foreseeing that God would justify the heathen through faith, preached before the gospel unto Abraham, saying, In thee shall all nations be blessed" (Galatians 3:8); "Now to Abraham and his seed were the promises made [Genesis 22:18]. He saith not, And to seeds, as of many; but as of one, And to thy seed, which is Christ" (Galatians 3:16). Paul resolves and expounds the meaning of Genesis 12:3, "And I will bless them that bless thee, and curse him that curseth thee: and in thee shall all families of the earth be blessed," by alluding unmistakably to Genesis 22:18: "And in thy seed shall

all the nations of the earth be blessed; because thou hast obeyed my voice." Ellis writes, "The prophecy in Gen[esis] 12:3 that all nations shall be blessed in Abraham may, in light of the analogous passage in Gen[esis], be understood of Abraham's seed and thus of Messiah (Gal 3:8, 16)."[50]

"Argument from the Context" (*Dābār halāmēd mēʿinyānô*, Hillel Rule #7)

Strack and Stemberger describe *dābār halāmēd mēʿinyānô* as "the 'argument from the context' of a biblical statement"[51] or, literally, "a word of instruction from its context."[52] For example, after building a family, Jesus argues from historical context regarding the original meaning of the divorce statute in Deuteronomy 24:1 when he adds, "Moses because of the hardness of your hearts suffered you to put away your wives" (Matthew 19:8; compare 5:1). Israel during Moses's time had been hardhearted (see, e.g., Psalm 95:7–11) like Jesus's opponents.

In Romans 4:9–24, Paul extends the equal statute involving Genesis 15:6 and Psalm 32 into an argument from the context when he mentions Abraham's circumcision as described in Genesis 17, which effectively situates his whole argument of justification by faith within a pre-Israelite and pre-Mosaic law time frame. In Galatians 3, probably written in roughly the same time period as Romans and wherein Paul also invokes Genesis 15:6 (Galatians 3:6), Paul makes a similar argument from the context in Galatians 3:17 when he states: "And this I say, that the covenant, that was confirmed before of God in Christ, the law, which was four hundred and thirty years after, cannot disannul, that it should make the promise of none effect." Regarding these two instances of "argument from context," Ellis summarizes Paul's argument thus: "That righteousness was reckoned to Abraham (Gen 15:6) before he was circumcised (Gen 17:10f.) enables him to be the father of both Jewish and (uncircumcised) gentile believers (Rom 4:10f.). Equally, because the covenant promise was established with Abraham (Gen 22:18) before the Mosaic Law (Exod 12:40), it has validity independent of that law (Gal 3:17)."[53]

"Parable" (*Māšāl*)

Parables, proverbs, taunt-songs, and allegories fall under a single Hebrew term—*māšāl*: a "likening" or "comparison."[54] The Hebrew Bible contains a substantial number of these, whether or not each is formally called *māšāl* in the text. Nathan's juridical parable[55] against David in 2 Samuel 12 constitutes one of these. The text designates Isaiah's taunt-song or proverb against the king of Babylon ("Lucifer") in Isaiah 14:4–20 a *māšāl*, but Isaiah 5:1–7, 27:2–6 (2–11), and 28:23–29 would also fit that designation. Ezekiel uses the *māšāl* in Ezekiel 17:2–20 and 24:3–5. Jotham's parable of the trees in Judges 9:7–20 represents another excellent example. The canonical Proverbs have been collectively labeled with the incipit title *mišlê* (i.e., *mišlê šĕlōmô*, "Proverbs of Solomon," Proverbs 1:1).

Charles W. Hedrick notes that "Rabbinic parables are considerably more numerous than the number of OT parables. Around 2,000 have been estimated to exist in rabbinic literature."[56] Although most of these have been dated to centuries later than Jesus, it is interesting to note that many "are introduced similar to the ways parables in the NT are introduced. For example, 'to what may the parable be likened to . . .' or 'I will set forth a parable; to what may the parable be likened, to. . . .' A very few use simply 'as' or 'like.'"[57]

The latter observation is striking when we consider the Book of Mormon's best example of a *māšāl* or parable—and may be the best example of an extended *māšāl* ever written—Zenos's "allegory" in Jacob 5, which begins with the words "I will liken thee." In Hebrew, that phrase would constitute a form of the verb *māšāl*. Nephi, perhaps using Zenos as his model, turns the scriptures themselves more broadly into parables by likening[58] them or interpretively mapping them onto himself and his people.[59] Jacob, the brother of Nephi, likens Isaiah 49:22–52:2 to the Nephites as an extended parable about their situation.[60]

As noted above, Jesus too sometimes formally designated his sayings as parables with the formula "whereunto shall I liken" (see, e.g., Matthew 11:16; Luke 7:31; 13:20). Jesus's parables constitute an indispensable and incomparable aspect of his teaching. Since the criteria for what officially constitutes a parable are somewhat arbitrary, totals for the number of Jesus's parables in the New Testament vary.

Paul uses the *māšāl* form when he likens the Hagar-Ishmael and Sarah-Isaac story to the Sinai covenant with the law of Moses and the covenant promises made available through Jesus Christ. He maps this story onto the early church Judaizers who wanted to make gentile converts (including Paul's converts at Galatia) fully conform to the requirements of the law of Moses: "For it is written, that Abraham had two sons, the one by a bondmaid, the other by a freewoman. But he who was of the bondwoman was born after the flesh; but he of the freewoman was by promise. *Which things are an allegory*: for these are the two covenants; the one from the mount Sinai, which gendereth to bondage, which is Agar. For this Agar is mount Sinai in Arabia, and answereth to Jerusalem which now is, and is in bondage with her children. But Jerusalem which is above is free, which is the mother of us all" (Galatians 4:22–26; emphasis added). To be clear, Paul is not privileging Christianity over Judaism— an anachronistic notion. As Mark Nanos states, "Paul saw himself wholly within Judaism, as one who was assigned a special role in the restoration of Israel and the nations (Rom 11.1–15; Gal 1.13–16)."[61]

Paul then employs *heqeš* ("comparison") when he applies Isaiah 54:1 to Sarah, Abraham's barren wife, and thus metaphorically to his gentile converts as well: "For it is written, Rejoice, thou barren that bearest not; break forth and cry, thou that travailest not: for the desolate hath many more children than she which hath an husband. Now we, brethren, as Isaac was, are the children of promise" (Galatians 4:27–28). Paul views the Judaizers as "bondsmen" who want to put the gentile converts ("the children of . . . the free," 4:31) into bondage and their demands as persecution: "But as then he that was born after the flesh persecuted him that was born after the Spirit, even so it is now" (4:29). Paul also allegorizes or "likens" the Genesis story for the solution: "Nevertheless what saith the scripture? Cast out the bondwoman and her son: for the son of the bondwoman shall not be heir with the son of the freewoman" (4:30). As Fitzmyer puts it, "Paul bids the Galatians rid themselves of the Judaizers—and, ironically enough, obey the Torah itself."[62]

One final example that we should mention here is Hebrews 9:1–9, wherein the author uses the wilderness tabernacle (including Holy Place and holy of holies), its appurtenances (the menorah, table, shewbread, cherubim, ark with its mercy-seat [Hebrew *kappōret*, place of atonement], etc.), its Mosaic ordinances (sacrifices, applying blood, etc.), and the ministrations of the Aaronic priests and high priest as a "figure for the time then present." In other words, according to the author, it all constituted a kind of parable *prefiguring* Jesus Christ and his high priestly service, including his atonement, for the whole human family.

Punning and Explanatory Punning (Paronomasia and Polyptotonic Etiology)

The prophecy of Jesus's birth in Matthew 1:20–21 echoes the form and content of two specific birth prophecies in the Hebrew Bible: the divine/angelic prophecies of the births of Abraham's sons, Ishmael and Isaac. The biblical text uses wordplay to give etiological explanations (explanations of origin) for both names, both being divinely foreordained.

An angel instructs Hagar that she should give her son the name Ishmael: "And the angel of the Lord said unto her [Hagar], Behold, thou art with child, and shalt bear a son, and shalt call his name *Ishmael* [*yišmā ʿēl* = "May God hear" or "God hath heard"]; because *the Lord hath heard* [*šāma ʿ yhwh*] thy affliction" (Genesis 16:11; emphasis added). The angel explains Ishmael's naming in terms of the Semitic/Hebrew verb *šāma ʿ*, "hear," "hearken," "obey." The divine onomastic element - *ʾēl* is here identified with Jehovah.

God himself foreordains the name Isaac similarly: "Then Abraham fell upon his face, *and laughed* [*wayyiṣḥāq*], and said in his heart, Shall a child be born unto him that is an hundred years old? and shall Sarah, that is ninety years old, bear? And Abraham said unto God, O that Ishmael might live before thee! And God said, Sarah thy wife shall bear thee a son indeed; and thou shalt call his name *Isaac* [*yiṣḥāq*]: and I will establish my covenant with him for an everlasting covenant, and with his seed after him" (Genesis 17:17–19; emphasis added).

The angel's foreordination of Jesus's name in Matthew 1:20–21 employs similar wordplay on cognate terms (polyptoton): "But while he thought on these things, behold, the angel of the Lord appeared unto him in a dream, saying, Joseph, thou son of David, fear not to take unto thee Mary thy wife: for that which is conceived in her is of the Holy Ghost. And she shall bring forth a son, and thou shalt call his name *JESUS* [Greek *Iēsoun* (*Iēsous*) < Hebrew *yēšûa ʿ*]: for *he shall save* [Greek *sōsei* = Hebrew *yôšîa ʿ*] his people from their sins" (Matthew 1:20–21; emphasis added). In explaining Jesus's name in terms of "saving" or "salvation," Matthew uses wordplay that works in Hebrew and Greek. The Hebrew/Aramaic form of Jesus's name is *yēšûa ʿ*, which derives from the same root as *yěšû ʿâ*, "salvation," meaning to "save." Jesus's statement to the woman of Samaria, "salvation is of the Jews" (John 4:22) may constitute an identification of himself with the servant "Israel" of Isaiah 49:6 (emphasis added): "I will also give thee for a light to the Gentiles, that thou mayest be *my salvation* [yĕšûātî] unto the end of the earth" (compare Isaiah 49:3).

Jeremiah 23:2 famously employs a pun on the Hebrew terms *rāʿâ* (to "feed" or to "pasture")[63] and *rōaʿ* ("corruption, vice, evil"):[64] "Therefore thus saith the Lord God of Israel against *the pastors that feed* [hārōʿîm hārōʿîm] my people; Ye have scattered my flock, and driven them away, and have not visited them: behold, I will visit upon you the *evil* [rōaʿ] of your doings, saith the Lord" (emphasis added; compare Jeremiah 22:22 and 1 Nephi 21:1). The initial pun is a play on cognate terms (polyptoton): "the *pastors* that *pasture* my people." However, these same Hebrew consonants can be turned into a paronomasia—a play on sounds or meaning—and be read as *hārōʿîm hārāʿîm*, "the evil shepherds."[65] Jesus appears to have this passage and pun in mind when he states: "I am the *good shepherd*: the good shepherd giveth his life for the sheep"; "I am the *good shepherd*, and know my sheep, and am known of mine" (John 10:11, 14; emphasis added). Jesus's title "the good shepherd" creates a pun by inverting an older scriptural pun.

Most Latter-day Saint readers are at least passingly familiar with Jesus's pun on the surname or nickname Peter, preserved in Greek as follows: "And I say also unto thee, That thou art <u>Peter</u> [Greek *petros*], and upon this <u>rock</u> [petra] I will build my church; and the gates of hell shall not prevail against it" (Matthew 16:18; emphasis added). Fitzmyer suggests, probably correctly, that "Peter" and "rock" would have both been *kêpāʾ* if Jesus spoke to Peter in Aramaic.[66] As Chrys C. Caragounis suggests, by using slightly different terms in Greek—*petros* and *petra*—"the author very neatly preserved the same stem and hence the 'same' general sense in the main elements, thus creating an elegant word-play, while at the same he markedly distinguished the two main terms as to their meaning and specific referents. The result was an exceptionally good and effective word-play."[67]

Paul employs an elegant Old Testament–style wordplay in Ephesians 3:14–15: "For this cause I bow my knees unto the *Father* [patera] of our Lord Jesus Christ, Of whom the whole *family* [patria] in heaven and earth is named" (emphasis added). In this case the word rendered family (*patria*) literally derives from the Greek word for Father (*pater*). The result is a pun that beautifully emphasizes God the Father's universal fatherhood, including the entire human family. The pattern of God's paternity can (or should be) evident in every "family."

Gematria

One of the best-known examples of New Testament *gematria* is attested in the genealogy for Jesus offered in Matthew 1. Matthew subdivides Jesus's genealogy into three sets of fourteen generations: Abraham to David, David to the Babylonian exile, and the exile to Jesus. As numerous commentators have pointed out, the number fourteen can be written with the Hebrew letters *daleth* (4)-*waw* (6)-*daleth* (4)—i.e., DVD, or the consonants in the name David. Matthew has to play with the genealogy somewhat to arrive at the requisite number fourteen. Gale writes, "The genealogy omits five kings (Ahaziah, Joash, Amaziah, Jehoiakin, and Zedekiah) to make the numbers add up to fourteen."[68]

Moreover, the numbers three and seven are also significant here. M. Eugene Boring notes that "after the number seven . . . in the Bible the number three is used most frequently in a symbolic or sacral sense."[69] The number three in Hebrew numerology symbolizes completeness (compare the tripartite universe—celestial, terrestrial, telestial). Seven—Hebrew *šeba'*—also symbolizes completeness (*šeba'* is also a homonym of *śb'*, which denotes satiation, abundance, or fullness).

Later in Matthew's Gospel, this symbolism emerges again in Jesus and Peter's discussion of forgiveness that Jesus uses as a gematria: "Then came Peter to him, and said, Lord, how oft shall my brother sin against me, and I forgive him? till seven times? Jesus saith unto him, I say not unto thee, Until seven times: but, Until seventy times seven" (Matthew 18:21–22). The number four hundred and ninety (490) is a gematria for *TMYM* (*tāmîm*), "perfect."

Gale notes that Matthew uses "the same phrasing" as Genesis 4:24 LXX.[70] If Cain shall be avenged sevenfold, truly Lamech seventy and sevenfold (Genesis 4:24; Moses 5:48). That account (Genesis 4; Moses 5:16–59) tells how Cain committed the unpardonable sin and how Lamech follows in his footsteps as the master of murder for profit, as works of darkness spiraled out of control in the human family. If seven and seventy-seven constitute symbols of vengeance and an absence of forgiveness in that account, Jesus makes it a symbol of perfect forgiveness.

Far and away the most famous and lucid example of gematria in the New Testament occurs in Revelation 13:16. John's gematria resembled what the Greeks called *isopsephy*.[71] The book of Revelation, which also abundantly uses the number seven as a symbol of completion,[72] uses the number six in a distinctly negative way: "Here is wisdom. Let him that hath understanding count the number of the beast: for it is the number of a man; and his number is Six hundred threescore and six" (Revelation 13:16). The "number of the beast" totals "666," or as some ancient witnesses have it, "616."[73] Boring writes: "Of the numerous explanations, the most cogent is that the author is interpreting the current or soon-to-come Roman emperor in terms of the Nero redivivus myth and that 666 is a gematriac cryptogram for NERO using the numeric values of *nrwn qsr* [וזרנ רסק] = Nero Caesar in Hebrew: נ = 50; ר = 200; ו = 6 נ = 50; Q = 100; S = 60; R = 200, which total 666]. This understanding is supported by the fact that some manuscripts read 616."[74] Therefore, this number should not be seen as constituting a prophecy to be fulfilled in any other person or entity (even our least favorite politicians). Boring thus also rightly notes that "later explanations referring the 'number of the beast' to figures present or expected in the interpreter's time have no basis in the biblical text."[75]

Conclusion

Apart from Jesus's extensive use of forms of the *māšāl* ("parable"), lighter and weightier and equal statute by far constitute the commonest hermeneutical modes and modes of argumentation in the New Testament. However, as I have attempted to show here, the New Testament also attests strong examples of building of a family (in both forms) and the other rules or methods attributed to Hillel (the general and the particular/the particular and the general, something similar to this in another passage, and argument from context).

Even texts that are normally regarded as having been written to largely gentile audiences, such as Paul's letters to the Romans and Galatians, employ distinctly Jewish hermeneutics (like equal statute, something similar to this in another passage, and argument from context). Ironically, in Galatians 3, as part of a letter to an audience largely composed of gentile converts and inveighing against Judaizing members of the church, Paul makes some of his most Jewish arguments. All of this probably suggests that early gentile members of the church became familiar with at least some of these modes of discourse, interpretation, and argumentation from the synagogue (which many attended as God-fearers) even if they had heard rhetorical techniques similar to those used in the wider Hellenistic world.

Recognizing these hermeneutical and argumentation modes and their use in the New Testament, we are better prepared to appreciate and understand the intra-Jewish debates and discussions not only ongoing throughout Jesus's mortal ministry, but also present in the texts of Acts, Revelation, and the New Testament epistles. Thus, we can truly describe the whole New Testament, with the so-called "Old" Testament, as, using Nephi's words: "the book [that] proceeded forth from the mouth of a Jew" (1 Nephi 13:33–34). Recognizing and understanding these modes can also help us better "respect the words of the Jews," which Nephi mentions in the same verse as a prerequisite to eternal life (2 Nephi 33:14).

∽

Matthew L. Bowen is an assistant professor of religious education at Brigham Young University–Hawaii.

Further Reading

Bateman, Herbert W. *Early Jewish Hermeneutics and Hebrews 1:5–13*. New York: Peter Lang, 1997.

Blumell, Lincoln H., and Thomas A. Wayment. "The 'Number of the Beast': Early Christian Isopsephies and Revelation 13:18." In *Book of Seven Seals: The Peculiarity of Revelation, Its Manuscripts, Attestation, and Transmission*, edited by Thomas J. Kraus and Michael Sommer, 119–35. Tübingen, Germany: Mohr Siebeck, 2016.

Boring, M. Eugene. "Numbers, Numbering." In *The New Interpreter's Dictionary of the Bible*, edited by Katharine Doob Sakenfeld, 4:294–95. Nashville: Abingdon, 2009.

Ellis, E. Earle. *The Old Testament in Early Christianity: Canon and Interpretation in Light of Modern Research*. Eugene, OR: Wipf and Stock, 2003.

Evans, Craig A. "Prophet, Sage, Healer, Messiah, and Martyr: Types and Identities of Jesus." In *Handbook for the Study of the Historical Jesus*, edited by Tom Holmen and Stanley E. Porter, 1217–43. Leiden, Netherlands: Brill, 2011.

Fitzmyer, Joseph A. "Romans." In *The New Jerome Biblical Commentary*, edited by Raymond E. Brown et al., 830–68. Englewood Cliffs, NJ: Prentice-Hall, 1990.

Gale, Aaron M. "The Gospel According to Matthew." In *The Jewish Annotated New Testament: New Revised Standard Version Bible Translation*, edited by Amy-Jill Levine and Marc Zvi Brettler, 1–54. New York: Oxford University Press, 2011.

Hedrick, Charles W. "Parable." In *New Interpreter's Bible Dictionary*, edited by Katharine Doob Sakenfeld, 4:368–77. Nashville: Abingdon, 2009.

Hultgren, Arland J. *Paul's Letter to the Romans: A Commentary*. Grand Rapids, MI: Eerdmans, 2011.

Strack, H. L., and Günter Stemberger. *Introduction to the Talmud and Midrash*. Translated by Markus Bockmuehl. Minneapolis: Fortress, 1996.

Notes

1. JST Matthew 3:25: "And it came to pass that Jesus grew up with his brethren, and waxed strong, and waited upon the Lord for the time of his ministry to come. And he served under his father, and he spake not as other men, neither could he be taught; for he needed not that any man should teach him."

2. Paul offers his full Pharisaic credentials in Philippians 3:4–6 (compare also Romans 11:1).

3. H. L. Strack and Günter Stemberger, *Introduction to the Talmud and Midrash*, trans. Markus Bockmuehl (Minneapolis: Fortress, 1996), 17.

4. Compare JST Matthew 6:25–27.

5. Or, "*how much more* will he not provide for you, if ye are not of little faith?" (JST Matthew 6:34; emphasis added).

6. Mark locates this miracle at Capernaum (near Nazareth, Jesus's hometown). Matthew prefaces the miracle with a general statement, "and [he] came into his own city." Luke does not offer a precise location, but does say that religious leaders were present "out of every town of Galilee," indicating the general location. All three Gospel writers place this miracle very early in Jesus's ministry.

7. For some recent Latter-day Saint treatments of John 10 and Psalm 82, see Daniel C. Peterson, "'Ye Are Gods': Psalm 82 and John 10 as Witnesses to the Divine Nature of Humankind," in *The Disciple as Scholar: Essays on Scripture and the Ancient World in Honor of Richard Lloyd Anderson*, ed. Stephen D. Ricks, Donald W. Parry, and Andrew H. Hedges (Provo, UT: FARMS, 2000), 471–594; David Bokovoy, "Ye *Really* Are Gods: A Response to Michael Heiser concerning the LDS Use of Psalm 82 and the Gospel of John," *FARMS Review* 19, no. 1 (2007): 267–313; and Daniel O. McClellan, "Psalm 82 in Contemporary Latter-day Saint Tradition," *Interpreter: A Journal of Mormon Scripture* 15 (2015): 79–96.

8. Compare McClellan, "Psalm 82," 93.

9. Dysphemism = the deliberate pejorative (negative) alteration of a name. See, for example, Paul Y. Hoskisson, "Dysphemisms," *Insights* 31, no. 2 (2011): 2–3.

10. Compare Aaron M. Gale, "The Gospel According to Matthew," in *The Jewish Annotated New Testament: New Revised Standard Version Bible Translation*, ed. Amy-Jill Levine and Marc Zvi Brettler (New York: Oxford University Press, 2011), 20.

11. As a Hebraism, *many* can sometimes mean—or almost mean—"all" in some contexts. For example, Jesus states: "The Son of man came not to be ministered unto, but to minister, and to give his life *a ransom for many*" (Matthew 20:28; Mark 10:45; emphasis added). This does not delimit the scope of the Savior's atonement. This idiom occurs in 2 Nephi 29:9: "And I do this that I may *prove unto many* that I am the same yesterday, today, and forever" (emphasis added).

12. Joseph A. Fitzmyer, "Romans," in *The New Jerome Biblical Commentary* (Upper Saddle River, NJ: Prentice Hall, 1990), 860.

13. Fitzmyer, "Romans," 860.

14. Fitzmyer, "Romans," 860.

15. See especially 1 Nephi 10:12–14; 15:12–20; 19:24–21:26; 2 Nephi 6–10; Jacob 4–6.

16. Arland J. Hultgren, *Paul's Letter to the Romans: A Commentary* (Grand Rapids, MI: Eerdmans, 2011), 182.

17. Hultgren, *Paul's Letter to the Romans*, 182.

18. Irenaeus in the second century (*Against Heresies* 3.1) wrote: "After [Peter and Paul's] departure, Mark, the disciple and interpreter of Peter, did also hand down to us in writing what had been preached by Peter" (from Alexander Roberts and William Rambaut, trans., *Ante-Nicene Fathers,* ed. Alexander Roberts, James Donaldson, and A. Cleveland Coxe [Buffalo, NY: Christian Literature, 1885], 1:414). Eusebius quotes Papias quoting John the Elder: "This also the elder used to say. Mark, indeed, having been the interpreter of Peter, wrote accurately, howbeit not in order, all that he recalled of what was either said or done by the Lord. For he neither heard the Lord, nor was he a follower of his, but at a later date (as I said) of Peter, who used to adapt his instructions to the needs [of the moment], but not with a view to putting together the Dominical oracles in orderly fashion: so that Mark did no wrong in thus writing some things as he recalled them. For he kept a single aim in view: not to omit anything of what he heard, nor to state anything therein falsely." Eusebius, *Ecclesiastical History* 3.39.14–15 (in *Eusebius: Ecclesiastical History and the Martyrs of Palestine*, trans. Hugh J. Lawlor and John E. Oulton [London: SPCK, 1954], 1:101).

19. See, for example, Barry D. Smith, *Introducing the New Testament: A Workbook* (Moncton, NB, Canada: Crandall University, 2010), 58. See further Adam Winn, *The Purpose of Mark's Gospel: An Early Christian Response to Roman Imperial Propaganda* (Tübingen, Germany: Mohr Siebeck, 2008), 80–83.

20. See Noel B. Reynolds, "The Gospel of Jesus Christ as Taught by the Nephite Prophets," *BYU Studies* 31 (Summer 1991): 31–50; Reynolds, "The True Points of My Doctrine," *Journal of Book of Mormon Studies* 5, no. 2 (1996): 26–56; see also Reynolds, "How to Come unto Christ," *Ensign*, September 1992, 7–13; Reynolds, "The Gospel According to Mormon," *Scottish Journal of Theology* 68, no. 2 (May 2015): 218–34; and Reynolds, "The Gospel According to Nephi: An Essay on 2 Nephi 31," *Religious Educator* 16, no. 2 (2015): 51–75.

21. Donald W. Parry, "Service and Temple in King Benjamin's Speech," *Journal of Book of Mormon Studies* 16, no. 2 (2007): 42–47, 95–97.

22. Fitzmyer, "Letter to the Romans," 842.

23. Fitzmyer, "Letter to the Romans," 858.

24. See Matthew L. Bowen, "'I Have Done According to My Will': Reading Jacob 5 as Temple Text," in *The Temple: Ancient and Restored: Proceedings of the 2014 Temple on Mount Zion Symposium*, ed. Stephen D. Ricks and Donald W. Parry (Salt Lake City: Interpreter Foundation and Eborn Books, 2016), 235–72; Bowen, "'He Shall Add': Wordplay on the Name Joseph and an Early Instance of *Gezera Shawa* in the Book of Mormon," *Insights* 30, no. 2 (2010): 2–4 (especially p. 3); and Bowen, "Onomastic Wordplay on Joseph and Benjamin and *Gezera Shawa* in the Book of Mormon," *Interpreter: A Journal of Mormon Scripture* 18 (2016): 255–73. Fitzmyer, "Letter to the Romans," 858, notes that "the Essenes of Qumran also applied Isa 28:16 to themselves looking upon their community as a temple."

25. Strack and Stemberger, *Introduction to the Talmud and Midrash*, 19.

26. Fitzmyer, "Letter to the Romans," 839.

27. Gale, "Gospel According to Matthew," 2.

28. Gale, "Gospel According to Matthew," 35. For an outstanding example of building a family from one scripture, see Matthew 21:9–16.

29. Strack and Stemberger, *Introduction to the Talmud and Midrash*, 19.

30. The Sadducees' rejection of the Resurrection is mentioned in Matthew 22:23, Mark 12:18, and Acts 23:8.

31. Daniel J. Harrington, "The Gospel According to Mark," in *The New Jerome Biblical Commentary*, 622.

32. Matthew 22:31–33 records Jesus's response slightly differently: "But as touching the resurrection of the dead, have ye not read that which was spoken unto you by God, saying, I am the God of Abraham, and the God of Isaac, and the God of Jacob? God is not the God of the dead, but of the living. And when the multitude heard this, they were astonished at his doctrine."

33. E. Earle Ellis, *The Old Testament in Early Christianity: Canon and Interpretation in Light of Modern Research* (Eugene, OR: Wipf and Stock, 2003), 88.

34. Bruce D. Chilton, Darrell L. Bock, and Daniel M. Gurtner, eds., "Appendix I," in *A Comparative Handbook to the Gospel of Mark: Comparisons with Pseudepigrapha, the Qumran Scrolls, and Rabbinic Literature* (Leiden, Netherlands: Brill, 2011), 538. Craig A. Evans, "Prophet, Sage, Healer, Messiah, and Martyr: Types and Identities of Jesus," in *Handbook for the Study of the Historical Jesus*, ed. Tom Holmen and Stanley E. Porter (Leiden, Netherlands: Brill, 2011), 1227, uses almost identical language: "From this one text and its inference one may further infer, as Jesus did (Mark 12:26), the truth of the general resurrection."

35. Harrington, "Gospel of Mark," 622.

36. Wilhelm Bacher, *Die exegetische Terminologie der jüdischen Traditionsliteratur*, 2 vols. (Leipzig: Hinrichs, 1899–1905; repr., Nachdruck: Hildesheim, 1965), 1:9. Translation cited in Strack and Stemberger, *Introduction to the Talmud and Midrash*, 19.

37. Gale, "Gospel of Matthew," 2.

38. Gale, "Gospel of Matthew," 2.

39. Ellis, *Old Testament in Early Christianity*, 90.

40. Ellis, *Old Testament in Early Christianity*, 90.

41. For a lengthy treatment, see Herbert W. Bateman, *Early Jewish Hermeneutics and Hebrews 1:5–13* (New York: Peter Lang, 1997), passim.

42. King Benjamin does something similar in Mosiah 5:7–9. See also Bowen, "Onomastic Wordplay on Joseph and Benjamin," 255–73; Matthew L. Bowen, "Becoming Sons and Daughters at God's Right Hand: King Benjamin's Rhetorical Wordplay on His Own Name," *Journal of the Book of Mormon and Other Restoration Scripture* 21, no. 2 (2012): 2–13.

43. Strack and Stemberger, *Introduction to the Talmud and Midrash*, 19.

44. Chilton, Bock, and Gurtner, "Appendix I," 530–31.

45. Ellis, *Old Testament in Early Christianity*, 90.

46. Strack and Stemberger, *Introduction to the Talmud and Midrash*, 20.

47. Robert G. Hamerton-Kelly, "Some Techniques of Composition in Philo's Allegorical Commentary with Special Reference to *De Agricultura*: A Study in the Hellenistic Midrash," in *Jews, Greeks, and Christians: Religious Cultures in Late Antiquity: Essays in Honor of William David Davies*, ed. Robert G. Hamerton-Kelly and Robin Scroggs (Leiden, Netherlands: Brill, 1976), 50.

48. Strack and Stemberger, *Introduction to the Talmud and Midrash*, 20.

49. Ellis, *Old Testament in Early Christianity*, 90.

50. Ellis, *Old Testament in Early Christianity*, 90.

51. Strack and Stemberger, *Introduction to the Talmud and Midrash*, 20.

52. Craig A. Evans, "Midrash," *Dictionary of Jesus and the Gospels: A Compendium of Contemporary Biblical Scholarship*, ed. Joel B. Green, Jeannine K. Brown, and Nicolas Perrin, 2nd ed. (Downers Grove, IL: InterVarsity, 2013), 590.

53. Ellis, *Old Testament in Early Christianity*, 90.

54. Strack and Stemberger, *Introduction to the Talmud and Midrash*, 28: *māšāl* as "'parable', allegorical interpretation."

55. See Uriel Simon, "The Poor Man's Ewe-Lamb: An Example of a Juridical Parable," *Biblica* 48, no. 2 (1967): 207–42. For a recent treatment of Nathan's parable, see Joshua Berman, "Double Meaning in the Parable of the Poor Man's Ewe (2 Sam 12:1–4)," *Journal of Hebrew Scriptures* 13 (2013): article 14, 1–17 (online).

56. Charles W. Hedrick, "Parable," *New Interpreter's Bible Dictionary* (Nashville: Abingdon, 2009), 4:369.

57. Hedrick, "Parable," 369.

58. See 1 Nephi 19:23; 2 Nephi 11:8. In 2 Nephi 11:8, Nephi invites his audience to "liken" Isaiah 2–14 to themselves—that is, to make Isaiah 2–14 a parable of their own lives and that of the whole human family: "Now these are the words, and ye may liken them unto you and unto all men."

59. John Gee and Matthew Roper, "'I Did Liken All Scriptures unto Us': Early Nephite Understandings of Isaiah and Implications for 'Others' in the Land," in *Fullness of the Gospel: Foundational Teachings of the Book of*

Mormon (Salt Lake City: Deseret Book; Provo, UT: Religious Studies Center, Brigham Young University, 2003), 51–66.

60. For an excellent treatment of Jacob's speech in 2 Nephi 6–10 and his use of Isaiah material, see Daniel Belnap, "'I Will Contend with Them That Contendeth with Thee': The Divine Warrior in Jacob's Speech of 2 Nephi 6–10," *Journal of the Book of Mormon and Restoration Scripture* 17, no. 1–2 (2008): 20–39.

61. Mark D. Nanos, "Paul and Judaism," in *The Jewish Annotated New Testament: New Revised Standard Version Bible Translation*, ed. Amy-Jill Levine and Marc Zvi Brettler (New York: Oxford University Press, 2011), 552.

62. Joseph A. Fitzmyer, "The Letter to the Galatians," in *The New Jerome Biblical Commentary*, 788.

63. Ludwig Koehler and Walter Baumgartner, *The Hebrew and Aramaic Lexicon of the Old Testament* (Leiden, Netherlands: Brill, 2001), 1256.

64. *Hebrew and Aramaic Lexicon*, 1256.

65. Strack and Stemberger, *Introduction to the Talmud and Midrash*, 29.

66. Joseph A. Fitzmyer, "Aramaic Kepha and Peter's Name in the New Testament," in *To Advance the Gospel: New Testament Studies* (New York: Crossroad, 1981), 112–14.

67. Chrys C. Caragounis, *Peter and the Rock* (Berlin: de Gruyter, 1989), 90.

68. Gale, "Gospel According to Matthew," 3. He further notes that "Matthew lists only thirteen generations for the last set."

69. M. Eugene Boring, "Numbers, Numbering," *The New Interpreter's Dictionary of the Bible* (Nashville: Abingdon, 2009), 4:298.

70. Gale, "Gospel According to Matthew," 34.

71. Lincoln H. Blumell and Thomas A. Wayment, "The 'Number of the Beast': Early Christian Isopsephies and Revelation 13:18," in *Book of Seven Seals: The Peculiarity of Revelation, Its Manuscripts, Attestation, and Transmission*, ed. Thomas J. Kraus and Michael Sommer (Tübingen, Germany: Mohr Siebeck, 2016), 119–35; and Lincoln H. Blumell, *Lettered Christian: Christians, Letters, and Late Antique Oxyrhynchus* (Leiden, Netherlands: Brill, 2012), 46.

72. See, for example, Revelation 1:4, 11–16; 2:1; 3:1; 4:7; 5:1–6; 8:1–6; 10:3–4, 7; 11:13, 15; 13:1; 15:1, 6–8; 16:1, 17; 17:1, 3, 7, 9–11; 21:9.

73. Compare Blumell, *Lettered Christians*, 46.

74. Boring, "Numbers, Numbering," 299. He continues: "Since John elsewhere uses names in Hebrew letters symbolically (9:11; 16:16), this explanation would have been understood by contemporary readers. Suetonius (*Nero* 39) had already used gematria in explaining Nero's name; its number in the Greek system is 1005, the total of the numerical value of the letters in *Nerōn idian mētera apekteine* (Νέρων ἰδίαν μητέρα ἀπέκτεινε, meaning "Nero killed his own mother")."

75. Boring, "Numbers, Numbering," 299.

7

The Dead Sea Scrolls and the New Testament

Dana M. Pike

S ince their initial discovery in 1947, the Dead Sea Scrolls have generated a great deal of interest, ranging from responsible scholarly inquiry to public sensationalism.[1] During the years 1947–1956, local Bedouin and eventually archaeologists found scrolls and primarily scroll fragments (many thousands of them) in eleven caves proximate to the small archaeological site of Qumran, near the northwest shore of the Dead Sea. Stories of the initial discovery of major scrolls by Bedouin cousins in what is now called Qumran Cave 1 vary in certain details and have been often recounted, as have stories about the intrigue involved in the authentication of the scrolls and the Israeli acquisition of most of them. Therefore, these accounts are not repeated here.[2]

Additional Jewish texts from the first two centuries AD have also been discovered in other caves and sites along the western Dead Sea, such as Wadi Murabbaʻat, Nahal Hever, and Masada. These texts are sometimes also included under the broad designation Dead Sea Scrolls. As valuable as these are in their own right, the focus of this chapter is on the texts found in the eleven caves near Qumran.

Since the Dead Sea Scrolls are Jewish religious documents, one may wonder why they are discussed in this volume on the New Testament or, for that matter, why knowing something about them can benefit Latter-day Saints in their study of the New Testament. There are actually several significant reasons for this. What follows includes brief comments on the Dead Sea Scrolls themselves and the Jews responsible for their placement in caves near the Dead Sea, plus a more extended discussion of the ways in which these texts help provide

View of the area at Qumran. Courtesy of Lincoln H. Blumell.

a greater context for the people and beliefs recorded in the Christian New Testament, with particular attention given to claims made about possible connections between the Jewish Qumran Community and John the Baptist or Jesus, and to claims about possible connections between the Dead Sea Scrolls and the New Testament. These include messianic titles and expectations, as well as particular passages in the Dead Sea Scrolls that sound quite similar to passages and concepts in the New Testament.

It is worth emphasizing at the start that *no* New Testament passages occur in the Dead Sea Scrolls and the Jewish group that settled at Qumran was not Christian.[3] These are *Jewish* religious texts collected and studied by certain Jews at the turn of the era. But they do have much to offer for our study of the Christian New Testament.

Introducing the Scrolls, Qumran, and the Essenes

The majority of the surviving Dead Sea Scrolls were copied between about 250 BC and AD 60. Dating is established by comparative paleographic analysis (the study of their handwriting styles) and carbon-14 dating. The vast majority of the surviving textual material divides broadly into three categories: (1) copies of texts that became known as biblical (meaning the Hebrew Bible, the Christian Old Testament), (2) copies of religious texts more widely read among Jews of the time but that never became part of the biblical canon, and (3) copies of texts that appear to be unique to the sect of Jews who lived at Qumran and elsewhere at the turn of the era, which are thus called sectarian texts. The process of the formation of the biblical canon had not completely occurred by this point in time, so referring in what follows to certain texts as "biblical" must be understood to be somewhat anachronistic.[4]

The assertion is often made that portions of all the texts in the Hebrew Bible were found in the caves around Qumran except for the book of Esther. Although true, this basic statement ignores the important fact that several other biblical books are hardly represented at all. For example, remains of only one manuscript each have been found of Chronicles, Ezra, and Nehemiah, and portions of only two manuscripts each survive for Joshua, Proverbs, and Ecclesiastes. While some of this is no doubt attributable to accidents of preservation, scholars see the number of surviving biblical texts as providing a relative indicator of what books of scripture were more important to the community. Clearly, the covenantal, legal, and prophetic content of the following books were highly regarded by the Qumran community, given the remains of thirty-six different manuscript copies of Psalms, thirty of Deuteronomy, twenty-one of Isaiah, twenty of Genesis, and seventeen of Exodus.

Two prime examples of popular religious texts that did not become part of the standard biblical canon, but which are well attested in the Qumran caves and are also known from elsewhere, are Jubilees and 1 Enoch. Jubilees, thought to have been composed in the early to mid-second century BC, presents a revelation from God, given by an angel to Moses on Mount Sinai, that relates certain events from the creation of the earth to the Israelite exodus from Egypt, divided into fifty separate forty-nine-year segments.[5] Jubilees was previously known only through a partially surviving Latin translation and a full version in Ethiopic. Five of the eleven Qumran caves yielded the remains of what appear to be fifteen copies of Jubilees, indicating not only the popularity of this work in the Qumran community, but also that it may have been regarded as scripture by them.

The lengthy and complex work known as 1 Enoch recounts various revelations given to Enoch, about whom the Bible preserves so very little (compare Genesis 5:24; Hebrews 11:5; Jude 1:14; none of the content of 1 Enoch is quite like the Enochic material in the Latter-day

Qumran Cave 4. Courtesy of Lincoln H. Blumell.

Saint Book of Moses). Prior to the discovery of a number of fragments in Qumran cave 4, 1 Enoch was known from surviving portions in Greek and primarily from the full version in Ethiopic, as well as a New Testament use of 1 Enoch 1:9 in Jude 1:14–15. The remains of eleven copies of 1 Enoch, all written in Aramaic and all discovered in cave 4, as well as evidence of important calendrical and other influences from 1 Enoch, suggest the important influence of this document, particularly during the earlier portion of the Qumran community.

Fragments of other texts from the Qumran caves, such as the Wisdom of Ben Sira (a.k.a. Sirach/Ecclesiasticus) and Tobit, were previously known from their inclusion in the Greek Septuagint, as part of the books referred to as the Apocrypha.

The better-preserved and better-known sectarian texts include the Rule of the Community (1QS, plus portions from cave 4; the "Q" indicates Qumran, the number preceding it indicates in which of the eleven caves the text was found, and the letter or number that follows the "Q" identifies the particular text from that cave). This work provides important information about the community (the *yahad*, in Hebrew), such as its purpose and organization, its dualistic view of the world and how its members fit into it, rules for admittance into the community, and so on. The War Scroll or War Rule (1QM, plus portions from cave 4) foretells the eschatological war between the "Sons of Light" and the "Sons of Darkness," including extensive information regarding the weapons and instruments that should be used, culminating in the destruction of the evil forces that have opposed God's rule. Other sectarian texts include hymns, such as those preserved in 1QHodayot, and the *pesharim*, which are commentaries on portions of certain biblical books, such as Isaiah (3Q4; 4Q161–64), Habakkuk (1QpHab), and Psalms (1Q16; 4Q171, 173).

The Dead Sea Scrolls are thus of enormous value for studying the variety of beliefs and practices of Jews in the land of Israel at the turn of the era, all part of the stream of traditional Mosaic religion as it existed at that time. They are also of great value for studying the text and transmission of the Hebrew scriptures, since they not only preserve the oldest copies of these texts but also demonstrate the textual similarities to and differences from what became the traditional text of the Hebrew scriptures after about AD 100, but which was previously best known from Hebrew manuscripts dating to the tenth and eleventh centuries AD. The scrolls also have value for studying the Hebrew and Aramaic languages at the turn of the era, as well as scribal practices in making and copying documents.

Given this assortment of texts, and given that these copies of manuscripts were produced by a variety of scribes over a period of about three centuries, it is commonly accepted that many of these texts were *brought to* Qumran from elsewhere and that many, especially the sectarian ones, were *copied at* Qumran. It is these latter texts that provide much of the information about the Qumran community's organization, views, and identity.

Qumran and Its Inhabitants

Qumran itself is located on a terrace between rocky cliffs to the west and the Dead Sea to the east. It preserves the remains of a number of walled rooms, a tower, and several cisterns and *miqvaot* (ritual bathing pools; *miqveh/mikvah* is singular). Although the site was known for centuries, its primary excavation was only formally undertaken in 1951–1956, after the initial discovery of scrolls in nearby caves, which themselves were also excavated (subsequent, less extensive excavations have also been undertaken at Qumran, its cemetery, and in nearby caves).[6] Following minor occupation in the eighth to seventh centuries BC, the site appears to have been uninhabited for centuries. Early assessments and publications placed the first major habitation by the Jewish community in about 150 BC, but many scholars now revise this downward to about 100 BC. Members of this community appear to have utilized this site, with a few short-lived interruptions because of an earthquake and other factors, until AD 68, when Roman soldiers camped at Qumran as part of the larger Roman effort to suppress the First Jewish Revolt (AD 66–70; see chapter 14 herein). Surviving artifacts include pottery, coins, and other small-scale finds. No scrolls or fragments were found "in" Qumran; they all come from nearby caves.

Based on the small size of the site, most archaeologists presume that the community generally consisted of about one hundred to two hundred people. The most likely scenario is that the site itself served as a community center, which members of the community entered daily for ritual purification, worship, study, instruction, and group meals. Few if any of them appear to have actually lived in the buildings, but rather in caves and tents in the surrounding area. Alternative proposals for Qumran's function include a fortress, a trading center, and a country villa, but these views have attracted few proponents, and the available evidence best supports the original view that it was a religious community center.

The identity of the inhabitants of Qumran is related to the purpose of the site (overviewed above) and to the scrolls found in the surrounding caves. Despite occasional claims to the contrary, it is untenable to detach the Qumran inhabitants from the scrolls found nearby; these are the remains of their collection. Most scholars generally continue to accept that Jewish Essenes inhabited Qumran on the basis of a confluence of claims about the locations and practices of Essenes found in the writings of authors such as Philo, Pliny the Elder, and Josephus, plus the related contents in some of the Qumran scrolls and the nature of the archaeological remains at the site. As best we can tell, the Jewish sect called the Essenes emerged as a distinctive force in the mid- to late second century BC, about the same time that the better-known and more influential Pharisee and Sadducee sects began to emerge (these more prominent groups receive much attention in the New Testament and elsewhere). The term *sect* when used for ancient groups is not pejorative, as it often is today. It connotes a small subset of a religious tradition, the beliefs and practices of which mark it as distinct from and as the self-declared correct and legitimate successor to the greater tradition from which it separated itself.

The available documentary evidence suggests there was variety among the Essenes scattered throughout the land of Israel. The Jewish men who gathered to the wilderness community at Qumran (never completely isolated from its greater surroundings) seem to have embraced a celibate lifestyle and were required to participate in a two-year initiation process, which if successfully completed resulted in their handing over all their possessions and allowed them to participate in the community meals and decisions. The hierarchy of this group consisted of priests. The community was also composed of Levites and non-Levitical Jews. They had strict rules regarding obedience and purity, emphasizing repentance and regular ritual self-immersion (*not* Christian baptism), holiness, and spiritual preparation for the great last battle. There may well have been other, similar separatist-oriented communities of Essenes of which we lack knowledge. Quite different were the Essenes who lived in groups in cities and towns and who had families and private property. It is still not clear how to reconcile the differences between these two broad portions of the sect, nor how they viewed each other.

Surviving evidence indicates that the Qumran Essenes believed they lived in the last days, that they constituted the true remnant of Israel with whom God had renewed his covenant, and that ancient prophecies would be fulfilled with and through them in their day. They believed they were predestined by God to be his "Sons of Light," as opposed to all the "Sons of Darkness," and would successfully fight alongside their soon-to-return messiah(s). This passage from their Rule of the Community (1QS 8.3–10), in describing expectations for the community and its initiates, nicely captures their view of their important role in the last days, to serve as a replacement for the polluted temple and to atone for the land as they awaited the coming of their messiah(s):

> They are to preserve faith in the land with self control and a broken spirit, atoning for sin by working justice and suffering affliction. They are . . . true witnesses to justice, chosen by God's will to atone for the land and to recompense the wicked their due. They will be . . . a fortress, a Holy of Holies for Aaron, all of them knowing the Covenant of Justice and thereby offering a sweet savor. They shall be a blameless and true house in Israel, upholding the covenant of eternal statutes. They shall be an acceptable sacrifice, atoning for the land and ringing in the verdict against evil, so that perversity ceases to exist. When these men have been grounded in the instruction of the Yahad for two years—provided they be blameless in their conduct—they shall be set apart as holy in the midst of the men of the Yahad.[7]

The Dead Sea Scrolls and the New Testament[8]

In the seven decades since their discovery, the relationship between the scrolls and the New Testament and early Christianity has garnered a great deal of attention. Early claims were made that the contents of the Dead Sea Scrolls would destroy Christianity because Christianity would no longer be viewed as unique and that the Vatican had conspired to hide scrolls seen as problematic (neither of these claims is true). More recent claims include conjecture that a few passages from the New Testament are preserved on small fragments from cave 7, which contained only fragments written in Greek; that the Gospel accounts were really written in code to secretly convey the identity of John the Baptist and Jesus with figures mentioned in the scrolls; and that there was an Essene temple on Mount Carmel, where Joseph and Mary were married.[9] These and similar claims require convoluted readings of the scrolls and have usually resulted in sensational media attention, but they have no legitimate support in the scrolls themselves nor acceptance among most scroll scholars.

Rather than further recounting and refuting such claims in more detail, what follows is an overview of possible intersections and interesting overlaps between the Dead Sea Scrolls, John the Baptist, Jesus, and the New Testament. Similarities in the community's and Christians' use of titles and biblical scripture passages are readily apparent. Space permits only the more obvious highlights.

New covenant

Central to the Qumran Essene community's existence was its sense of self-identity. They referred to themselves as the true remnant of Israel, with whom God had made a new or renewed covenant. For example, the Damascus Document emphasizes a "new covenant" (e.g., CD 6.19; 8.21), and the Rule of the Community instructs that initiates into the community be brought into this covenant with God, which was renewed annually (1QS 1.16–2.25). For these Essenes, the renewed covenant had a Mosaic orientation. However, the use of the phase "new covenant" in the New Testament is generally understood by Christians to move beyond the Mosaic era to a new dispensation (e.g., Luke 22:20; 1 Corinthians 11:25; 2 Corinthians 3:6; Hebrews 8:8–10), which Latter-day Saints associate with Melchizedek priesthood ordinances. Both the Qumran community and the early Christians drew on the prophecy of a future new covenant found in Jeremiah 31:31–33: "Behold, the days come, saith the Lord, that I will make a new covenant with the house of Israel, and with the house of Judah: Not according to the covenant that I made with their fathers in the day that I took them by the hand to bring them out of the land of Egypt. . . . But this shall be the covenant that I will make with the house of Israel." Thus, in this and other instances, both groups used the same prophetic passage but applied it differently, each to their own movements.

John the Baptist

The New Testament never specifically mentions the Essenes, but some scholars have connected John the Baptist with the Qumran community, and the introductory film shown at Israel's Qumran National Park confidently depicts John as associating with and then leaving the community. Reasons for this include Qumran's location and the New Testament statements that following his birth and blessing, John "was in the deserts [or wilderness] till the day of his shewing unto Israel" (Luke 1:80). And John, with his priestly lineage, was active during his ministry in the southern Jordan River Valley (Mark 1:4, 9; John 1:28), not that many miles from the priest-directed community at Qumran. Furthermore, some authors postulate that John's baptizing effort was impacted by the ritual self-immersion regularly practiced at Qumran, even though there are distinct differences and though self-immersion was practiced by other Jews in Jerusalem and elsewhere in the land. John also warned about coming judgments (Matthew 3:10; Luke 3:9). But during his ministry, John did not retreat to the wilderness to prepare for the arrival of the messiah(s), as the Qumran community had done; rather, he went out to preach the message of preparation. While it is possible, and even likely, that John the Baptist knew of and had some interaction with Essenes near the Dead Sea, significant differences exist in his message and practices. His reliance upon the Qumran community cannot be substantiated.

Perhaps the most fascinating intersection is that the New Testament depicts John fulfilling Isaiah 40:3 as the voice in the wilderness preparing the way for Jesus: "As it is written in the prophets, Behold, I send my messenger before thy face, which shall prepare thy way before thee [Malachi 3:1]. The voice of one crying in the wilderness, Prepare ye the way of the Lord, make his paths straight [Isaiah 40:3]" (Mark 1:2–3; Matthew 3:3). The Qumran Rule of the Community uses this same passage from Isaiah to present the community as preparing the way of the Lord by their separating from the impure Jewish priestly leaders in Jerusalem and going into the wilderness to live and teach God's law in preparation for the imminent (to them) eschatological battles: "When such men as these come to be in Israel, conforming to these doctrines, they shall separate from the session of perverse men to go to the wilderness, there to prepare the way of truth, as it is written, 'In the wilderness prepare the way of the Lord, make straight in the desert a highway for our God' [Isaiah 40:3]" (1QS 8.12–16). Thus, again, the Qumran community and early Christians understood and employed the same prophetic passage in different ways.

Jesus and the Gospel accounts

As with John, links have been asserted between the Qumran community and Jesus, even though the New Testament depicts Jesus interacting with Pharisees and Sadducees but not with Essenes (of whom he must have been aware). Jewish followers gathered around Jesus, just as they had around the community's leader, the Teacher of Righteousness, but Jesus was not Qumran's Teacher, as some have claimed.

Many scholars suggest that Jesus's statement in Matthew 5:43–44 betrays awareness of the Essenes. In presenting a series of antitheses, Jesus states, "Ye have heard that it hath been said, Thou shalt love thy neighbour, and hate thine enemy. But I say unto you, Love your enemies." The injunction to love one's neighbors is clearly specified in Leviticus 19:18. But as commentators now regularly observe, the encouragement to hate one's enemies is found nowhere in the Hebrew scriptures or other early Jewish texts, except those from Qumran. For example, the Instructor [*maskil*] was to teach the community members "to love all the Children of Light [the Qumran community and those who believed similarly]—each commensurate with his rightful place in the council of God—and to hate all the Children of Darkness [other Jews and all Gentiles], each commensurate with his guilt and the vengeance due him from God" (1QS 1.9–11). Although this is a possible connection, the account of Jesus's sermon does not include any other uniquely Essene-oriented statements.

An obvious parallel between the Dead Sea Scrolls and the New Testament is a messianic emphasis, a complex phenomenon among Jews and Christians at the turn of the era.[10]

The New Testament preserves several references to Jesus as a royal Davidic messiah (e.g., Matthew 1:1; 22:42; Luke 1:32; 2:11); a priestly messiah after the order of Melchizedek, not Aaron (e.g., Hebrews 3:1; 5:5–6; 8:1); a prophetic messiah (Deuteronomy 18:18–19; Acts 3:2–23); and as a suffering, atoning messiah (e.g., Isaiah 53:4–6; Matthew 20:28; Luke 22:19–20; 23:39–46; Acts 8:30–35; Romans 5:10). The Qumran texts teach of a separate Prophet and two messiahs who will come as part of the last days, the age in which they thought they lived: "They shall govern themselves using the original precepts by which the men of the Ya-had began to be instructed, doing so until there come the Prophet [Deuteronomy 18:15–18] and the Messiahs of Aaron and Israel" (1QS 9.10–11; see, e.g., CD 12.23–13.1). The messiah of Aaron was a priestly messiah of the Aaronic, not Melchizedek, order. The nonpriestly messiah of Israel, as indicated elsewhere, was viewed as the royal messiah, a descendant of David (e.g., 4Q252 5.3: "until the Righteous Messiah, the Branch of David, has come"). At least many in the community therefore believed in multiple messianic figures with different roles, especially royal and priestly functions (i.e., from a Christian perspective, they fragmented the various roles of Jesus, the true Messiah, among separate individuals); their messiahs were not imagined to be fully divine, and their messiahs would come with power and bring a new order to the earth (not unlike what Latter-day Saints and other Christians expect Jesus to do at his second coming). However, after the coming of their messiahs this new order would be based on a pure form of the law of Moses.

Finally, a few comments on some of the Dead Sea Scrolls passages that have attracted much attention in relation to Jesus and the New Testament will have to suffice for this overview.

4Q246

This fascinating composition, popularly dubbed the "Son of God" text, is written in Aramaic and was copied late in the first century BC. Three immediately obvious parallels exist between phrases in this text and Gabriel's annunciation to Mary about her future son Jesus, as found in Luke's Gospel account: he "will be called The Great" (4Q246 i 9; Luke 1:32), "he will be called the Son of God" (4Q246 ii 1; Luke 1:35), and "they will call him the son of the Most High" (4Q246 ii 1; Luke 1:32). Because 4Q246 is incomplete, we do not know to whom these phrases refer in that text. Various scholarly opinions range from a human king and the Jews collectively to an angel and one of the messiahs. Whoever this figure is in 4Q246, some form of Lukan dependence on this earlier text from Qumran has been claimed. However, in the Hebrew scriptures God, kings, and others are described as "great" (e.g., Deuteronomy 10:17; 2 Samuel 7:22; 2 Kings 18:19), God is called the "most high" (e.g., Genesis 14:18–20; Psalm 7:17; 47:2; 57:2), and kings descended from David were designated God's "son" (2 Samuel 7:14; Psalm 2:7; 89:26–27). Thus, it is most likely that 4Q246 and the prophecy in Luke 1 were utilizing phrases and concepts from older Israelite texts to designate a divinely sanctioned deliverer, Jesus in the case of Luke 1, without positing direct dependence. Nevertheless, the concentration of similarities in these two passages is striking.

4Q285

Labeled the "Book of War," this poorly preserved Hebrew text originally gained attention because it was claimed that fragment 7 (originally labeled 5) supported the notion that some Jews in the first century BC believed in a dying messiah, a view that is otherwise attested only in Christian documents, not in Jewish ones. The Hebrew text includes the messianic title "Branch of David," and the key word in question is *whmytw*, which can represent either "and they put (him, the messiah) to death" or "and he (the messiah) will cause him (someone else) to die." Scholars now confidently prefer the latter reading, as evidenced in this translation (the portions in brackets are restorations): "[This is the] Branch of David. Then [all forces of Belial] shall be judged, [and the king of the Kittim shall stand for judgment] and the Leader of the congregation—the Bra[nch of David]—will have him put to death. [Then all Israel shall come out with timbrel]s and dancers" (4Q285 frag 7.3–5). Drawing as it does on portions of Isaiah 10 and 11, this text describes the future success of a royal messiah vanquishing his enemies; it does not prophesy of a dying one.

4Q521

This fragmentary Hebrew text, also copied in the first century BC, has been labeled the "Messianic Apocalypse" because it describes a future messianic age. Most relevant here is the enumeration of messianic signs that are remarkably similar to those associated with Jesus in the New Testament. For example, for the Qumran community a coming messiah "will honor the pious upon the th[ro]ne of His eternal kingdom, setting prisoners free, opening the eyes of the blind, raising up those who are bo[wed down]. . . . For He shall heal the critically wounded, He shall revive the dead, He shall send good news to the afflicted, He shall sati[sfy the poo]r, He shall guide the uprooted, He shall make the hungry rich; . . . the Reviver [rai] ses the dead of His people. Then we shall [giv]e thanks and relate to you the righteous acts of the Lord . . . thos[e destined to d]ie. And He shall open [the graves]" (4Q521 f2 ii+4.7–13; and f7+5 ii 6–9).

Several of these phrases are also found in Luke 4:16–21, which reports Jesus's reading from Isaiah 61:1–2 and applying that prophecy to himself, and in Luke 7:21–22, which reports Jesus instructing John the Baptist's disciples about himself: "And in that same hour he cured many of their infirmities and plagues, and of evil spirits; and unto many that were blind he gave sight. Then Jesus answering said unto them, Go your way, and tell John what things ye have seen and heard; how that the blind see, the lame walk, the lepers are cleansed, the deaf hear, the dead are raised, to the poor the gospel is preached." Luke's Gospel account (compare Matthew 11:2–5) depicts Jesus as already demonstrating these messianic capabilities mentioned in Isaiah 35:5–6 and 61:1–2 during his mortal ministry, including restoring the dead to mortal life, although the actual resurrection of dead individuals had to wait until after Jesus's own resurrection. 4Q521 presents an unnamed messiah doing similar things, including raising the dead, thus representing an additional witness to certain messianic expectations some Jews had in Jesus's day, but in both cases based on earlier prophecies in the Hebrew scriptures.

4QMMT (4Q393–399)

As currently understood, this text provides important insights into the thinking of the Qumran community, illuminating at least some of the reasons they separated themselves from priestly leaders and others in Jerusalem. Only fragments of multiple copies of this work were found in Qumran cave 4. Despite the inherent problems of its fragmentary nature, this text has generated great interest for its display of the community's views on some ritual and purity matters and for its potential value for studying the New Testament. *MMT* is an abbreviation for the Hebrew phrase *miqsat ma'ase ha-torah*, "some of the works of the law," which occurs in the epilogue of MMT. This phrase occurs in its Greek form, *erga nomou*, in Paul's letters to the Galatians and the Romans. In 4QMMT the author/leader claims that "we have written to you [an opposing priestly leader or someone who has left the community] some of the works of the Law, those which we determined would be beneficial for you and your people" (C 26–27, 4Q398 f14_17ii.3). These "works" seem to be the particular aspects of the greater law of Moses highlighted earlier in the text. Alignment with these works as part of the law, it is claimed, "will be reckoned to you as righteousness, in that you have done what is right and good before Him" (C 31, 4Q398 f14_17ii.7). By way of contrast, Paul proclaims, "Knowing that a man is not justified by the works of the law, but by the faith of Jesus Christ, even we have believed in Jesus Christ, that we might be justified by the faith of Christ, and not by the works of the law: for by the works of the law shall no flesh be justified" (Galatians 2:16; compare 3:2–3; Romans 3:20–28). Taken in the context of other statements in Qumran sectarian texts that emphasize God's graciousness and the need for human repentance (e.g., 1QS 10.20–23; 11.10–15), the claim in 4QMMT cannot be superficially contrasted with Paul's statements. However, it appears that Paul was countering a widespread view that reliance on keeping the Mosaic law was the basis for salvation, a view that allowed no place for the fundamental role of Jesus Christ as Redeemer and our need to exercise faith in him and his saving powers.

11QMelchizedek (11Q13)

Given the paucity of information about the priest Melchizedek in the Old Testament (Genesis 14) and the use of this name as a title in Psalm 110:4, it is no surprise that several early Jewish and Christian texts variously expanded the role of Melchizedek, creating a complex of competing views about him and his significance. 11QMelchizedek, for example, depicts him as a semidivine being who will come from God in the last days to execute judgment against the wicked and deliver the righteous. The Epistle to the Hebrews in the New Testament cites Melchizedek primarily to highlight a priesthood greater than Aaron's (as do a few other noncanonical works), thus emphasizing that Christ's Melchizedek priesthood was greater than Aaron's, which was associated with the law of Moses (Hebrews 5; 7). Hebrews 7:3 clearly indicates Melchizedek is "like" but different from Jesus Christ: "but [Melchizedek was] made like unto the Son of God; [and] abideth a priest continually." Thus, again, the Qumran community and early Christians employed passages of Hebrew scripture to present their own particular views.

Wrapping Up / Making Sense

Despite the fact that no New Testament manuscripts were found among the Dead Sea Scrolls, some people have claimed that John or Jesus had some connection with the Qumran community. Even with interesting parallels, there are striking differences demonstrating that neither John nor Jesus was an Essene, and although presumably aware of the Qumran community, they were separate from it. Jesus, from a Latter-day Saint perspective, was uniquely the divine Son of God in the flesh, and he (and his followers) thus uniquely applied the contents of the law and prophecies in Hebrew scripture to himself.

But even in this, the overlaps in scripture passages and interpretations indicate that Jesus and his followers were not isolated from their context. Most Jews, including those who became Christians, were familiar with and had faith in Jehovah, the Mosaic law, and the Israelite prophetic writings. Many Jews in Jesus's time were looking for a messianic deliverer and a priestly leader and based their expectations on prophecies in the Hebrew scriptures and in additional texts produced between Malachi and John the Baptist that reworked earlier scriptures.

However, for Latter-day Saints, Christianity did not just "develop" from Jewish roots. Jesus's ministry and resurrection inaugurated a new gospel dispensation. Nevertheless, Jesus's efforts, and those of his apostles and earliest followers, took place in a particular historical time and place that involved Jewish religious forces and factors, some of which bear an interesting resemblance to what is in the New Testament. So even though the Dead Sea Scrolls are not Christian texts, they share an assortment of interesting similarities with Christian writings in the New Testament and can be fruitfully employed to better understand the world of Jesus and his earliest Jewish followers.

❧

Dana M. Pike is a professor of ancient scripture and ancient Near Eastern studies at Brigham Young University.

Further Reading

Translations of the Dead Sea Scrolls

Abegg, Martin G., Peter W. Flint, and Eugene C. Ulrich. *The Dead Sea Scrolls Bible: The Oldest Known Bible*. San Francisco: HarperSanFrancisco, 1999.

Vermes, Geza. *The Complete Dead Sea Scrolls in English*, rev. ed. New York: Penguin Putnam, 2004.

Introductions to the Dead Sea Scrolls

(Note: Newer works are generally preferable since their authors have had access to more recent and more accurate information. For recent, responsible overviews of the scrolls and their significance, see the following.)

Collins, John J. *The Dead Sea Scrolls, A Biography*. Princeton: Princeton University Press, 2013.

VanderKam, James C., and Peter W. Flint. *The Meaning of the Dead Sea Scrolls: Their Significance for Understanding the Bible, Judaism, Jesus, and Christianity*. San Francisco: HarperSanFrancisco, 2002.

Latter-day Saint approaches to the scrolls

Parry, Donald W., and Dana M. Pike, eds. *LDS Perspectives on the Dead Sea Scrolls*. Provo, UT: Foundation for Ancient Research and Mormon Studies, 1997.

Parry, Donald W., and Stephen D. Ricks. *The Dead Sea Scrolls: Questions and Responses for Latter-Day Saints*. Provo, UT: Foundation for Ancient Research and Mormon Studies, 2000.

Pike, Dana M. "The Dead Sea Scrolls and Latter-day Saints: Where Do We Go from Here?" *Studies in the Bible and Antiquity* 2 (2010): 29–48.

Notes

1. There are several recently published, reputable books on the Dead Sea Scrolls. Some examples are listed under "Further Reading" and in the notes that follow. Since space is limited here, interested readers are advised to consult these for further information. Additionally, pictures of many of the Dead Sea Scrolls fragments, along with introductory comments, are now available online through the Israel Antiquities Authority at http://www.deadseascrolls.org.il/home. Lastly, the official publication series for the scrolls is *Discoveries in the Judaean Desert* (New York: Oxford, 1955–2010). See also Donald W. Parry and Emanuel Tov, eds., *The Dead Sea Scrolls Reader*, 2nd expanded ed., 2 vols. (Boston: Brill, 2014).

2. For details of the discovery and early work on the scrolls, see Weston W. Fields, *The Dead Sea Scrolls: A Full History*, vol. 1 (Boston: Brill, 2009).

3. See, for example, Peter W. Flint, *The Dead Sea Scrolls* (Nashville: Abingdon, 2013), 184–85.

4. The Hebrew scriptures had not been completely limited to the Old Testament biblical canon as we now have it until about AD 100–150, at least beyond the traditional core of the Law, the Prophets, and the Psalms (Luke 24:44). The Qumran community, for example, appears to have accepted books such as Jubilees, 1 Enoch, and the Temple Scroll as authoritative, although these compositions never became part of the traditional biblical canon.

5. The name *Jubilees* derives from the concept, found in the Bible, that under the Mosaic law every fiftieth year was a "jubilee" year.

6. See Jodi Magness, *The Archaeology of Qumran and the Dead Sea Scrolls* (Grand Rapids, MI: Eerdmans, 2003).

7. Unless otherwise noted, quoted translations of nonbiblical Qumran texts are from Accordance, "Qumran Non-biblical Manuscripts: A New English Translation (QUMENG)," version 4.2, which is based on *The Dead Sea Scrolls: A New English Translation*, ed. Michael O. Wise, Martin G. Abegg Jr., and Edward M. Cook (New York: HarperCollins, 2005).

8. In addition to chapters on this topic in the introductory volumes cited in "Further Reading," there are also books that specifically address the possible connections between the Dead Sea Scrolls and the New Testament and early Christianity. Although of uneven quality, see, for example, Joseph A. Fitzmyer, *The Dead Sea Scrolls and Christian Origins* (Grand Rapids, MI: Eerdmans, 2000); and James Charlesworth, *Jesus and the Dead Sea Scrolls* (New Haven: Yale University Press, 1992).

9. Due to space limitations, interested readers are encouraged to find reputable publications that overview these and other such theories. See, for example, James C. VanderKam and Peter W. Flint, *The Meaning of the Dead Sea Scrolls: Their Significance for Understanding the Bible, Judaism, Jesus, and Christianity* (San Francisco: HarperSanFrancisco, 2002); and Flint, *Dead Sea Scrolls*, 311–30.

10. For an extensive review of this topic, see John J. Collins, *The Scepter and the Star: Messianism in Light of the Dead Sea Scrolls*, 2nd ed. (Grand Rapids, MI: Eerdmans, 2010).

8

Rabbinic Literature and the New Testament

Avram R. Shannon

The New Testament is made up of a series of books that are, in many ways, hybrid texts. Like the works of Philo of Alexandria (ca. 20 BC–AD 50) and Josephus (ca. AD 37–100), early Jewish authors who composed their works in Greek, the New Testament texts are written in Greek but from a Jewish background. They are not translation literature but reflect both Greek and Jewish ideas and vocabulary.[1] Because of this, an attempt to understand these texts in a first-century context often involves an appeal to both Greek or Hebrew/Aramaic lexicography and cultural or legal norms. On the Hebrew side, this appeal is usually to the Old Testament, to texts found at Qumran and around the Judean desert (Dead Sea Scrolls), and to the complex literature of the rabbinic movement, those Jewish teachers who taught and promulgated an oral law after the fall of the Jewish temple. It is this last literature, that of the rabbis, that will be the subject of this chapter. While some Latter-day Saint studies have sought to elucidate the life and teachings of Jesus by reference to either the Old Testament or the Dead Sea Scrolls,[2] none have ever seriously considered rabbinic literature as another lens through which to view his ministry; and even though this literature is later and can be fairly esoteric, it does have the potential to enhance our understanding in certain areas.

Though it probably goes without saying, it is important to remember that Jesus and his earliest followers were Jews who lived in a decidedly Jewish context and that Jesus's mortal ministry was specifically to the house of Israel (Matthew 15:21–28). It is only after the Resurrection that the gospel message was taken in earnest to non-Jews (Acts 10). In fact, many of the ideas in Christianity that seem universal, such as the existence of a messiah, are

Jewish notions that the earliest Christians brought to their non-Jewish converts. The original twelve apostles were all Jews, as were Paul and Barnabas and the vast majority of the earliest Christian leaders. This means that Judaism is the essential matrix that Christianity and the New Testament grew out of; because of this, understanding Judaism can help us better comprehend the background and the activities in the New Testament.

Judaism was not, however, a monolith—either in the ancient world or now. It represented a complex series of interrelated ethnic, religious, ritual, and political ideals that were expressed in various ways. These expressions were so varied that some scholars of ancient Judaism have preferred to talk about "Judaisms" rather than "Judaism."[3] The diversity in ancient Judaism is visible in the New Testament with groups such as the Pharisees and the Sadducees. These ancient Jewish groups had very different approaches to the temple, the law of Moses, and the scriptures. It can, therefore, be helpful when talking about Judaism and its relationship to the New Testament to remember that Judaism, in both its ancient and modern varieties, was a broad spectrum. Thus, a simple comparison between the New Testament and Judaism, however that is understood, is problematic.

Rabbinic Judaism has rich connections to the New Testament: Jesus is called "rabbi" (John 1:38, 49; 3:2; 6:25), Paul claims as a teacher the rabbinic sage Gamaliel (Acts 22:3), and there are even places where the New Testament and rabbinic literature share similar readings of biblical text. What is more, both the New Testament and rabbinic literature arose out of the world of Second Temple Judaism—the Judaism that flourished between the third century BC and the second century AD while the Second Jewish temple stood—and both rabbis and the New Testament are connected to the Pharisees. These connections make comparing the New Testament and rabbinic literature a fruitful exercise.

The present chapter is therefore a brief comparison of the New Testament with what is often called Rabbinic Judaism.[4] It first contains a brief description of this form of Judaism and the texts that expressed it. Rabbinic Judaism serves as the basis for almost all other forms of subsequent Judaism, including even most forms of contemporary Judaism. It is characterized by the literary and legal output of a variety of men known as "sages" and "rabbis." These men were educated, self-aware, and articulate, and so their discussions on the Bible, the law of Moses, and Jewishness serve as some of our best evidence for ancient Judaism broadly. In particular, the sages of Rabbinic Judaism promulgated an oral law, which connects to the New Testament "tradition of the elders" (Matthew 15:2). The rabbinic traditions, however, derive from a later time than the New Testament, and often from a different social context, so that the evidence provided by the ancient rabbis must be used judiciously, especially in connection to the New Testament.

In this chapter, I illustrate the connection between Rabbinic Judaism and the New Testament with three worked examples. My first example is the trial of Jesus, where rabbinic literature has been appealed to as a tool against Judaism. My second example shows how the rabbinic notion of messengers and agency can help explain the New Testament idea of apostle. Finally, I discuss how the author of Hebrews shares certain scriptural reading principles with the rabbinic sages. These examples show that Rabbinic Judaism is best utilized for conceptual comparisons and is less useful for specific historical or legal comparisons.

Rabbinic Literature

To begin,[5] something needs to be said about the terms *rabbi* and *rabbinic*. *Rabbi* is a Hebrew term that means "master" or "teacher." Although "master" is a legitimate translation, it is in the sense of a student/teacher relationship instead of an owner/slave relationship. The ancient rabbis' preferred term for themselves collectively was the *sages*.[6] In contrast to current usage, the rabbis of rabbinic literature were not primarily associated with the synagogue and were not usually leaders in the synagogue. Rather, their primary locale was in the schoolhouse. In this context, rabbinic literature refers to the variety of texts produced by these sages. In addition, *rabbi*, and its variations,[7] seems to have been a common title for Jewish religious leaders in the ancient world and was not limited to the producers of rabbinic literature.[8] In fact, the only two individuals called "rabbi" in first-century-AD documents are John the Baptist (John 3:26) and Jesus Christ.[9]

Rabbinic Term	Definition
Rabbi	teacher, master
Sage (*ḥakham*)	the preferred term of self-identification by the ancient rabbis
Halakhah	Jewish legal discussions; discourse on how to live the law of Moses and the commandments
Aggadah	those parts of rabbinic literature that are not specifically concerned with understanding and interpreting law; not halakhah
Gemara	later rabbinic discussion on the Mishnah; Mishnah plus Gemara equals Talmud
Midrash	Jewish biblical interpretation

In considering what constitutes Rabbinic Judaism, one should note that what we are interacting with in the modern age is largely a product of literature. While there are definitely archaeological remains from the rabbinic period (roughly 200 BC–AD 600), they are next to impossible to pin to any specific rabbinic discussion, and in some cases contradict the rulings found in the sources of rabbinic literature.[10] Any discussion of Rabbinic Judaism is, therefore, ultimately rooted in a discussion of the literature that the sages produced. But this literature is multivaried and complex, containing songs, prayers, homilies, legal rulings, legends, myths, jokes, biblical interpretations, and many other types of writing. Its diversity makes its connection to the New Testament richer but also more difficult to use responsibly.

Rabbinic literature can be divided into two broad categories, even if there is some overlap. These two types are "halakhic," or legal, texts and "aggadic" texts, a term that is difficult to define, since aggadic texts cover everything that is not halakhic. Since the ancient rabbis were primarily concerned with legal notions, legal discussions have a prominent place in rabbinic discourse. Halakhah is basically a series of discussions on *how* to keep the commandments. It might be something akin to what Latter-day Saints call "application." For instance, the scriptures usually outline what the Lord wants done, but not always *how* to do it. An example of this is the command to keep the Sabbath day holy, found in Exodus 20:8–11 (Deuteronomy 5:12–16). While this passage forbids working on the Sabbath, it does not explicitly define what work was, and so it was largely left to the individual living the Sabbath to figure that out.[11] In the Gospels, Jesus and the Pharisees seem to have frequently disagreed on the proper way to observe the Sabbath (Matthew 12:1–13; John 5).[12] These discussions on how to live the commandments are the core of rabbinic legal discussion, which served as the foundation of rabbinic literature.

The rabbinic sages believed that God delivered to Moses *two* laws on Mount Sinai: a written and an oral law.[13] A famous passage in rabbinic literature reads, "Moses received the Law on Mount Sinai, and transmitted it to Joshua. Joshua transmitted to the Elders, who transmitted it to the Prophets. The Prophets transmitted it to the Men of the Great Assembly."[14] Thus, in addition to the written law, which is the five books of Moses (Genesis through Deuteronomy), the sages believed there was an additional oral law that was transmitted through Joshua and the elders of Israel.[15] This was transmitted to the prophets, which showed that the ancient sages saw themselves in continuity with the writings of the prophets. The bulk of the oral law defines ways to apply the law of Moses. Thus, the written law gave the commandments of God, and the oral law contained discussions and explorations on *how* to live those commandments.[16] The acceptance of the oral law is an integral part of early rabbinic self-understanding.

Rabbinic Text	Date	Brief Description
Mishnah	compiled about AD 200	the earliest compilation of rabbinic halakhah; the base text for Rabbinic Judaism
Tosefta	compiled after the Mishnah, but likely before the two Talmuds	a collection of rabbinic traditions that date from the mishnaic period but were not included in the Mishnah
Jerusalem or Palestinian Talmud	compiled about AD 400	Gemara on the Mishnah by Palestinian sages
Babylonian Talmud	compiled about AD 600	Gemara on the Mishnah by the Babylonian sages; contains large amounts of halakhic and aggadic material
Midrashim	dates range from about AD 350 to 1100	collections of Jewish biblical interpretations; these are often arranged by a biblical book and use distinctive interpretive techniques; derives mostly from Palestinian sources

These oral laws were finally collated and edited around AD 200 by a Jewish leader named Judah the Prince. This collection is known as the Mishnah, from a Hebrew word that means "to repeat, or recite."[17] The Mishnah is, therefore, the Recitation of the Law. It is the foundational document of what came to be called Rabbinic Judaism, building on the written Law found in the Bible. The Mishnah is divided into six "orders," called in Hebrew *sedarim*, that are arranged thematically. These orders cover agricultural laws (*Zeraim*), laws about festivals (*Moed*), damage and punitive laws (*Neziqin*), laws about women's issues (*Nashim*), temple laws (*Qodashim*), and laws dealing with impurity (*Toharot*). The various mishnaic orders are then subdivided into various tractates, dealing with a specific aspect of the law. Like the Pauline Epistles in the New Testament, mishnaic tractates are arranged according to length, from longest to shortest. The Mishnah is the closest to the New Testament temporally and geographically and is thus one of the most privileged places for comparing the New Testament and rabbinic literature.

The interpretation of the law and the scriptures is an ongoing process, and so the Mishnah is not the final word on the oral law. After the codification and compilation of the Mishnah in the third century, the ancient Jewish sages began to comment on and clarify the laws recorded in the Mishnah. This commentary was known as *Gemara*, an Aramaic word meaning "study." The Gemara, which was largely composed in Aramaic (as opposed to the Mishnah, which was composed in Hebrew), was (and is) read alongside the original Mishnah. These two elements together—Mishnah plus Gemara—constitute the Talmud.

There are, in fact, two Talmuds, which are distinguished by the location where they were compiled. One Talmud was compiled in the Holy Land and is known as the Jerusalem or Palestinian Talmud (ca. fourth century AD). It had much less influence on the development of Jewish thought and practice and is completely preserved in a single manuscript dating to the thirteenth century. The Talmud compiled in the Jewish communities that stayed in Babylon after the Babylonian captivity is known as the Babylonian Talmud (ca. sixth century AD).[18] Of the two Talmuds, the Babylonian Talmud is the more authoritative. When referencing simply the "Talmud," the Babylonian Talmud is generally meant. The two Talmuds are based on the same underlying Mishnah but differ in interpretations and the sages quoted.[19] If the Mishnah is the foundational text of Rabbinic Judaism, then the Talmud is the edifice. The study of Torah, both in the Bible and in the Talmud, is one of the great commandments in Judaism.

It is not, however, the sum total of Jewish thought or practice. The other type of rabbinic literature is aggadah. This broad category covers everything the sages write and speak about that does *not* cover application of the laws and commandments found in the scriptures. It comes from an Aramaic word that means "tellings." A key part of aggadah is midrash, which is Jewish biblical interpretation. Midrash is a complex literature that is rooted in the biblical text but encourages expansion and interpretation where the Bible is sparse.[20] Although the ancient sages were deeply entrenched in the biblical text, they were not promulgators of a kind of *sola scriptura*. It would be a mistake to understand the Talmud as being primarily biblical interpretation, although the Bible is never far from the thoughts of the sages. The sages did engage in biblical interpretation in both literary and legal ways and collected these interpretations. The earliest midrashic texts deal with legal matters and the application of the law, while later midrashic collections are concerned with answering questions raised by the biblical narratives. All the midrashic collections are later than the codification of the Mishnah, and most of them are contemporaneous with the traditions in the Talmud. This places them many hundreds of years later than the New Testament. Although this limits their usefulness in *directly* understanding the New Testament, these traditions can still provide insight, especially into the methods and ways in which ancient Jews understood and interpreted the Bible.

The midrashic form of biblical interpretation involves a very close reading of the biblical text but does so in ways and following a logic that can sometimes be different from traditional post-Enlightenment modes of thinking.[21] In order to be midrash, a story or legal interpretation must be connected to the biblical text that provides the basic parameters for a given rabbinic interpretation.[22] This is one of the clear ways in which midrash differs from the Mishnah and Talmud, which are not based on the biblical text. Midrashic interpretation is driven by what may be termed "rough places" in the text. The midrashic exercise is extremely attuned to questions such as repetitions and apparent omissions. Midrash serves as a way of filling in those blanks.

The sages themselves spoke about various interpretive principles that guided the formation of midrash.[23] It seems that in many cases these principles were after-the-fact rationalizations of already-extant midrashic exegesis.[24] A few broad principles stand out. The first is the "omnisignificance" of the biblical text—every portion of the text has meaning for every other part.[25] The next is that every word has meaning, and even when words are repeated by the biblical text, the rabbis will derive meaning out of the repetition.[26] Thus, in Genesis 22:11, when the angel says "Abraham, Abraham," the rabbinic sages must address why the name is said twice. Although these assumptions seem illogical to us in our present interpretive world, the New Testament authors' assumptions about the Bible more closely resemble the rabbinic perspective than they do modern notions.

Rabbinic Literature and the New Testament

With this brief background of the texts that comprise Rabbinic Judaism, we turn to how Rabbinic Judaism intersects with the New Testament. Composed by an erudite and self-reflective class of ancient Jews, rabbinic literature represents one of the best windows into the world of thought and practice of the Jews of the New Testament era. This portion of the chapter first looks broadly at the connections between rabbinic literature and the New Testament, as well as some of the pitfalls to be aware of in using the two literatures to understand one another.

The New Testament Gospels present Jesus in ways that connect him and his ministry to the sages and the literature they produced. In fact, the Gospels show Jesus involved in legal and halakhic discussions with other Jews in Jerusalem and the Galilee.[27] These discussions are places where Jesus's teachings and style find parallels in rabbinic literature, but sometimes these parallels can be overstated.[28] Nonetheless, there are fruitful places for comparison. An example is in the parables that Jesus employs. Although many of them are unique to Jesus, employing parables is not unique to Jesus's teaching style. In fact, there is a parable in the Babylonian Talmud that closely accords to one of Jesus's parables:

> R. Yohanan b. Zakkai said: This may be compared to a king who summoned his servants to a banquet without appointing a time. The wise ones adorned themselves and sat at the door of the palace. ["For,"] said they, "is anything lacking in a royal palace?" The fools went about their work, saying, "can there be a banquet without preparations?" Suddenly the king desired [the presence of] his servants: the wise entered adorned, while the fools entered soiled. The king rejoiced at the wise but was angry with the fools. "Those who adorned themselves for the banquet," ordered he, "let them sit, eat and drink. But those who did not adorn themselves for the banquet, let them stand and watch." R. Meir's son-in-law said in R. Meir's name: Then they too would [merely] look as being in attendance. But both sit, the former eating and the latter hungering, the former drinking and the latter thirsting, for it is said, Therefore thus saith the Lord God, Behold, my servants shall eat, but ye shall be hungry: behold, my servants shall drink, but ye shall be thirsty: [behold, my servants shall rejoice, but ye shall be ashamed:] behold, my servants shall sing for joy of heart, but ye shall cry for sorrow of heart. (Babylonian Talmud Shabbat 153b)[29]

This parable shares parallels with the parable of the wedding banquet in Matthew 22:1–13—especially with the notion of wearing proper clothing for the feast. The sage telling this parable, Yohanan b. Zakkai, dates to around the destruction of the Second Temple in AD 70, making him a little later than Jesus but roughly contemporaneous. This does not mean, of course, that Jesus and Yohanan b. Zakkai are using the same parable or that one is dependent on the other. Rather, it suggests that the parables of Jesus were part and parcel of the broader Jewish world from which rabbinic literature emanated.

In addition, the Mishnah represents itself as containing materials that derive from the Second Temple period. Thus, the Mishnah quotes traditions and legal opinions from sages who lived during the New Testament period. The authors of the New Testament mention at least one of these sages (Gamaliel)[30] by name. According to Acts, Paul claims to have been a disciple of this sage: "I am verily a man which am a Jew, born in Tarsus, a city in Cilicia, yet brought up in this city [Jerusalem] at the feet of Gamaliel, and taught according to the perfect manner of the law of the fathers, and was zealous toward God, as ye all are this day" (Acts 22:3). Gamaliel is also mentioned earlier in Acts, where Luke mentions him approvingly.[31] According to traditional Jewish understanding, Gamaliel was a grandson of Hillel, one of the earliest and greatest of mishnaic teachers.[32] This gives Paul, in his own way, a rabbinic pedigree. This allows scholars, with some caution, to posit similar, if not identical, legal positions underlying some of the questions and discussion taken up by the New Testament authors and editors.

There are also connections between nonlegal rabbinic material and the New Testament, especially in the Epistles. In many ways the Epistle to the Hebrews represents a clear example of something like midrashic material in the New Testament. Hebrews shares a number of assumptions with the sages who produced rabbinic literature and the biblical midrashim. The most important assumption is what is often called the "omnisignificance" of the biblical text. This is the notion that the scriptures are all interconnected, and that it is, therefore, possible to use scriptures from one place in order to explain a usage in another place. Where this differs most strongly from modern conceptions is how these connections are brought about. For ancient readers, a single word can signal a connection that is to be made between two verses in disparate scriptural places, because the notion of omnisignificance ignores book and chapter boundaries. This process of bringing two verses together is known as "verbal analogy." The ancient rabbinic sages called this principle *gezera shawa* (see chapter 6 herein).[33] The author of the Epistle to the Hebrews uses a number of verbal analogies to make its point. Words such as *son*, *today*, and *swear an oath* are found in numerous passages in Hebrews, such as Hebrews 1:2 and 1:5, and are brought together to illustrate several points, such as the superiority of the Son of God over everything else, including the law of Moses and the immediacy of God's salvation.

Example 1: Difficulties with the trial of Jesus

One instance where rabbinic literature has been used to further understand the New Testament, but where there are very real difficulties in how that literature was deployed, is the trial of Jesus. The notion that the trial of Jesus was illegal is something that has pervaded Latter-day Saint thinking since at least James E. Talmage's *Jesus the Christ*. Latter-day Saints, building from Talmage, found support in a book by Walter M. Chandler, an American lawyer and politician.[34] The evidence mustered for the illegality of the trial of Jesus comes from various parts of rabbinic literature, without any real regard for questions of when and where the various laws and quotations are coming from. Because the trial of Jesus has been used so much for anti-Semitic purposes, it is especially important to handle the rabbinic sources judiciously.[35]

The Mishnah represents, in many ways, a utopian law code—in other words, the Mishnah represents the way that the sages understood the law of Moses and how they wanted it interpreted but not necessarily how it was actually lived. The most obvious example of this is the large amount of space dedicated to the administration and regulation of the Jerusalem temple.[36] The temple had been destroyed for over 130 years by the time the Mishnah was collated, but it still contained regulations on how to administer the sacrifices and what the proper rules for vows and other temple-focused laws from the law of Moses were.

The regulation of capital punishment is a crucial example of probable utopian laws that has direct bearing on the trial of Jesus. It is unclear from our sources whether the Jews living under Roman control had the power to execute capital punishments. Mishnah Sanhedrin, the mishnaic tractate on legal judgments and courts, presumes that the rabbis retain the biblical power to enact punishment for capital crimes. The mishnaic tractate of Sanhedrin covers many issues of rabbinic jurisprudence, including the sentencing of crime according to the biblical mandate. Mishnah Sanhedrin 7:6 states, "Four forms of execution were transmitted to the [rabbinic] court: stoning, burning, decapitation, and strangulation."[37] The Mishnah then lists various ways in which these executions were to be performed. The Mishnah, drawing on biblical laws, presumes that it has the power to perform executions. The New Testament, however, makes an opposite claim. The contradiction is likely because of the utopian nature of much of the Mishnah's laws—they are describing the world as they wished it to be. In John 18:31 the leaders of the Jews tell Pilate, "It is not lawful for us to put any man to death."[38] This passage is useful precisely because it lays out what appears to be a direct contradiction between a rabbinic source on the one hand and the New Testament on the other. Because of this, it shows the danger in using the Mishnah to explore the illegality of the trial of Jesus. Thus, the connection between the legal world described by the sages and the legal situation of Jesus's trial is tenuous at best.

This has been recognized by Latter-day Saint scholars in recent years. Dana M. Pike notes, "Claims that Jesus' 'trial' was illegal because it violated Mishnaic regulations have no historical basis and are best avoided."[39] Likewise, in their study companion to Talmage's *Jesus the Christ*, Thomas Wayment and Richard Holzapfel state, "Scholars today realize that the Jewish sources used by earlier scholars to identify the illegalities of the trial come from a later period than the New Testament and, therefore, likely do not give an accurate portrayal of first-century Jewish practice. The Gospels do not accuse the Jewish council of illegalities, so we assume there are none to report."[40] This acknowledgment is an important step in helping us better understand how to use the New Testament and rabbinic literature in making comparisons. If rabbinic literature is read *only* for its connection to the New Testament, it is possible to make grave mistakes and overstatements.

Example 2: The Jewish understanding of apostles as agents

Once again, this is not to say that there is no place for exploring connections between rabbinic literature and the New Testament. There are, in fact, a number of instances where concepts from both literatures meet and allow for a better understanding. One place where rabbinic literature seems to have explanatory power is in examining the New Testament notion of apostles and apostleship. The Greek word *apostolos* is a nominative form deriving from the verb *apostellein*, which means "to send out." According to the *Theological Dictionary of the New Testament*, its classical reference is to naval expeditions.[41] The Hebrew word with the most obvious corollary to the Greek *apostolos* is *šeliaḥ*. This word is the passive participle of the Hebrew root *š/l/ḥ*, which means "to send." This word, therefore, like the Greek, has the meaning of "sent one" or "messenger." We shall see, however, that in a rabbinic context, including in a community or synagogal context, the word usually means "agent."

The Hebrew word *šeliaḥ* has already been examined in connection with *apostolos* by previous scholars.[42] As part of his discussion of the relationship between Hebrew *šeliaḥ* and Greek *apostolos*, K. H. Rengstorf observes, "It must be emphasized most strongly that Jewish missionaries, of whom there were quite a number in the time of Jesus,[43] are never called *šeliaḥ*."[44] He also notes, however, that "the Gk. gives us . . . the form of the NT concept; the *šeliaḥ* of later Judaism provides the content."[45] The emphasis of the section in *Theological Dictionary of the New Testament* remains primarily on traveling and preaching the word.[46] The difficulty here is that although this scholar acknowledges the existence and importance of a Jewish notion of *šeliaḥ*, the emphasis remains on how the apostleship came to be understood in later Christianity. Thus, the apostles are viewed primarily in their missionary aspect. This is even maintained while quoting halakhic positions presupposing that a given *šeliaḥ* is not traveling. If we are to compare the rabbinic notion of *šeliaḥ* to our understanding of *apostle*, then it is necessary to get beyond the etymology of the word to its actual legal and cultural referent in a Jewish context. This involves looking beyond assumptions of what *apostle* already means in a Christian context.

Rabbinic sources emphasize the agency and authority of the *šeliaḥ*. In fact, the standard dictionary for rabbinic literature gives the definition of this word as "deputy, agent."[47] An examination of the uses of this word in mishnaic sources illustrates this. In Mishnah Gittin 4:1, which discusses the serving of a divorce decree to a woman, we read, "If a man sends[48] a divorce decree to his wife, and he reaches the agent (*šeliaḥ*) [before it gets to the woman], he may annul it." The legal idea here is not specifically in the sending of the message but in the authority of the sending.[49] The core legal idea here is that the agent has the full authority of the man who sent him.

The mishnaic reference that is, in many ways, paradigmatic for a discussion on how rabbinic literature can help explain some of the ideas behind the office of apostle is Mishnah Berakhot 5:5. Berakhot is the tractate on prayers and benedictions, and this particular passage refers to the "messenger or agent of the congregation" using the term *šeliaḥ*. This "messenger of the congregation" is someone who is deputized by the congregation in order to say prayers on behalf of the congregation. The paragraph states: "As for the one who prays and errs, it is a bad omen for him, and if he were the 'agent (*šeliaḥ*) of the congregation,' it is a bad omen for them, since 'A person's agent is as himself'" (Berakhot 5:5). As noted, the context of this paragraph in the Mishnah makes it clear that this is not referring even to someone who has been sent away on behalf of the congregation. This is someone who has been authorized to act on behalf of the community to say their prayers. This simple fact illustrates the danger of a simple etymological explanation of words. Although it is true that the word *šeliaḥ* derives from the Hebrew root meaning "to send," it is clear in this passage that actual traveling is not necessary for them to exercise their functions. In this rabbinic context, the important aspect is the notion of agency and authorized representation. This becomes especially apparent when the anonymous Mishnah quotes from what was apparently a proverb about the connection between a person and their agent.

This sense is also visible behind the concept of "apostle" in Christianity of the first century. This is not to suggest that the notion of travel and sending of messages is not present in New Testament usage, but to show that rabbinic literature gives another perspective on the evidence and assumptions about what is behind some of the vocabulary in the New Testament.

The Gospel of Matthew, traditionally considered to be the most Jewish of the New Testament Gospels, has this to say: "And he called to him his twelve disciples and gave them authority over unclean spirits, to cast them out, and to heal every disease and every infirmity" (Matthew 10:1–2). The Gospel then lists the names of the twelve disciples. Following this, they are sent out (the Greek here comes from the same root as *apostle*) on a preaching mission (Matthew 10:7). The aspect that qualifies the twelve disciples to be apostles, however, is not their being sent out, but their being given authority over unclean spirits and the attendant power to heal. The emphasis in Matthew is not on their traveling but on their power. They are certainly sent out from Jesus, but their function seems to have been more than messengers of Jesus. This suggests that a Hebrew/Jewish notion of *šeliaḥ*, and the concept of "authorized representative," is behind part of the conception of apostles in Matthew.

The Acts of the Apostles, generally understood as a sequel to the Gospel of Luke, often refers to apostles. In Acts 8, Philip (not the apostle) teaches and converts a number of people in Samaria (8:4–13). After this, Acts records: "Now when the apostles at Jerusalem heard that Samaria had received the word of God, they sent to them Peter and John" (8:14). The implication of this verse is that the apostles, as a body, are staying in Jerusalem and that they send out Peter and John. For the purposes of the present argument, what is important is that Peter and John are not sent to preach or proselytize in Samaria. That work had already been done by Philip. According to Acts, upon arriving in Samaria, Peter and John "prayed for them [Philip's converts] that they might receive the Holy Spirit" (8:15). In other words, Peter and John's purpose in this passage is not to act as preachers in a foreign area. On the contrary, their purpose is to bestow the Holy Spirit. As soon as this is accomplished, they return to Jerusalem, although they do preach on the way back (8:25).

It is thus clear that, as with Hebrew *šeliaḥ*, the Greek *apostolos*, although coming from a word that clearly means the "sent one," does not *necessarily* have primary reference to traveling missionary work. This is further illustrated by the recording in Acts of the Jerusalem Council in Acts 15. According to this chapter, the admission of non-Jewish converts to the Christian community had raised certain questions about the relations of these converts to the Jewish practice of the law, circumcision in particular.[50] The halakhic question was strenuous enough that a delegation was sent from Antioch, including Paul and Barnabas (who had been identified as apostles in Acts 14:14). According to Acts 15:4: "When they [the delegation] came to Jerusalem, they were welcomed by the church and the apostles and the elders, and they declared all that God had done with them." In this section, as in other places in Acts, *apostles* seems to indicate a body that is centered in Jerusalem and is not traveling, as there is no sense in this passage in Acts that the apostles need to be summoned back to Jerusalem for this conference.

Example 3: Using Midrash to understand Hebrews

Of all of the New Testament authors, the author of Hebrews is the most likely to use methods of biblical interpretation that are similar to those used by the sages in creating midrash. Techniques like verbal analogy (the rabbinic *gezera shawa*) are deployed by the author of Hebrews in various ways and places within the text of the letter to the Hebrews. It should be noted, however, that many of these principles also appear in the Greek world, and so we do not need to look specifically to the rabbinic sages for these types of interpretation.[51] The sages are using Jewish-Greek methods of interpretation that would later be codified by the rabbinic sages producing midrash.

Like much of the New Testament, the Epistle to the Hebrews is heavily based in the scriptures of the Old Testament. Unlike those books, however, the author of Hebrews often builds scripture into fairly complex interpretive schemes that can be characterized as something like early midrashim. They lack some of the characteristics of later midrashim—such as the presence of multiple interpretations to a single verse—and, of course, the substance of the interpretations has a decidedly Christian bent, but they do provide unique and interesting perspectives on ancient scripture. Hebrews 3:1–8 presents one such interpretive strand, building on Numbers 12:6–8, in which the greatness of Moses among prophets is discussed. The context in Numbers is of a disagreement in precedence from Miriam and Aaron against Moses. God chastises them and says, "And he said, Hear now my words: If there be a prophet among you, I the Lord will make myself known unto him in a vision, and will speak unto him in a dream. My servant Moses is not so, who is faithful in all mine house. With him will I speak mouth to mouth, even apparently, and not in dark speeches." The author of Hebrews uses this verse as part of his larger point on the superiority of Jesus over all the other prophets.

He does so by emphasizing notion of the "house," referring here to the household. The word *house*, Greek *oikos*, appears six times in Hebrews 3:2–6. It forms the backbone for the point that the author of Hebrews is trying to make. The point here is that Moses is part of the household but is, as the verse quoted indicates, a member of the household as a faithful servant or slave. According to Hebrews 3:2, Jesus is also faithful, like Moses, but 3:6 indicates that he is, as the son, not just faithful in the house, but actually over the house. Moses was a faithful slave to God *in* the household, but Jesus is a faithful son *over* the household. Even though they are described in similar fashions, the passage actually serves to highlight their different roles rather than elide them. This is reinforced by Hebrews 3:3, where the author appears to mix his metaphors a little bit and moves from a household metaphor to an architectural one. The point remains, however, that Moses must be inferior to Jesus because Jesus built the house, while Moses is only a member of it, no matter how faithful.

One of the most important things to recognize when working through midrash and midrashic-type interpretation is how the interpreted verse interacts with the surrounding verses. This is one of the places where the interpretation in this passage of Hebrews has some of the greatest affinity with the rabbinic art of midrash. On the one hand, from a modern perspective, like the rabbis the author of Hebrews is much concerned with context. On the other hand, they would often bring ideas from verses surrounding the quoted verse. That seems to be the case here. The whole point of identifying Moses as faithful in God's household is to make a comparison with him to Miriam and Aaron and, by extension, to all other Israelite prophets. Moses was superior to those prophets because, even though a slave, he was a member of the household. The implication here is that other prophets, including

Aaron and Miriam, although important servants of God, do not share the same status as Moses. The midrashic logic extends this even further by bringing in notions of sonship and households. Just as Moses is superior in the house (i.e., over the other prophets), so, as son over the house, is Jesus superior to Moses. The midrashic logic defines the whole argument.

Conclusion

Jesus Christ and his immediate followers were Jews who initially lived and preached in a largely Jewish world. The New Testament is, therefore, in many ways a product of Judaism and Jewish thinking. In order to better understand the New Testament, it is useful to have some understanding of ancient Judaism; rabbinic literature, in all its varieties, represents one of the richest bodies of literature for enhancing that understanding. The rabbinic sages were articulate thinkers about the scriptures and what it meant to be Jewish, and their comments, thoughts, and interpretations produced an abundant treasure of material on an enormous variety of texts. Much of their teachings are rooted in their desire for halakhah and application, for understanding *how* to live the commandments of God, but because of their belief that all things could be found in Torah, their commentary on Torah contains all kinds of material.

The ink that has been spilled over the trial of Jesus and the illegality of it shows the importance of not pushing the connection between the New Testament and rabbinic literature. The whole point of using rabbinic literature to show illegality was to drive home notions of the perfidy of the Jews. Using the Mishnah and the Talmud in this way ignores the historical realities of both the earliest Christians and the rabbis. It represents the dangers in viewing Rabbinic Judaism as a kind of magic bag for Christian interpreters to take out whatever they like and make it fit into their preconceived mold.

On the other hand, the notion of apostles as agents provides a place where rabbinic literature points to an ancient understanding that might otherwise have been lost. Christian interpretation of apostles and the apostleship has highlighted their missionary and traveling functions and the fact that they were "sent out." Although this is understandable, especially in the Greek linguistic context that the New Testament is situated in, it leaves open certain questions, such as why Acts presents the apostles as staying primarily in Jerusalem, if they are predominantly to be understood as traveling missionaries. The rabbinic equivalent to apostle, *šeliaḥ*, which carries notions of agency, without specifically requiring travel, provides evidence that something similar could be behind the New Testament apostleship. In this case, rabbinic literature does not provide direct evidence, but instead provides another avenue of understanding.

This is even more the case with midrash and midrash-type interpretations in the Epistle to the Hebrews and other places in the New Testament. The midrashim date to centuries after the composition of the New Testament. In this case, it is not the actual midrashic collections that prove helpful in understanding the New Testament. Instead, it is seeing the ways in which the New Testament authors and editors and the producers of rabbinic literature, including midrash, shared similar assumptions and interpretive tools. There is no *specific* midrash comparing what the author of Hebrews does with Jesus, Moses, and their position in God's household. But the type of comparison and the assumptions that underlie it are a well-established part of rabbinic thinking. Learning how the sages thought about the scriptures and their methods of interpretation provides insight into how the New Testament authors and editors are interacting with the scriptures.

While there are other places and categories where rabbinic literature relates to the New Testament, such as in Paul's discussion of idolatry in Romans (2:27–28) and comparisons of identity and Israel (9:3–14), these examples show both the advantages of using rabbinic literature for comparison as well as the care that should be taken when working with that literature. As with the worked examples presented in this chapter, it is important to take rabbinic literature on its own terms. Rabbinic literature is not simply a source to mine for information about Jesus and the apostles but is a real and complex literature with its own rules and traditions. Even with that being said, it still represents one of the best sources for understanding how ancient Judaism thought on its own terms. Because Jesus and his followers were Jews, this provides a valuable window of understanding into the ancient worldview that produced the New Testament.

❧

Avram R. Shannon is an assistant professor in the Department of Ancient Scripture at Brigham Young University.

Further Reading

Holtz, Barry W., ed. *Back to the Sources: Reading the Classic Jewish Texts.* New York: Simon and Schuster, 1986. This very useful volume has a chapter introducing nonspecialists and nonacademics to the various original sources within Judaism. It contains chapters on the Talmud, on Midrash, and even on Jewish readings of the Bible. It is written by specialists in a very engaging and down-to-earth style. Each of the chapters has further reading as well.

Strack, H. L., and Günther Stemberger. *Introduction to the Talmud and Midrash.* Translated and edited by Markus Bockmuehl. Minneapolis: Fortress, 1996. This is the best single volume on rabbinic literature. It has a somewhat scholarly tone but includes discussions of all the major sources and manuscripts for rabbinic literature. It is especially useful when dealing with some of the more obscure aspects of rabbinic literature, like the various midrashic collections.

Danby, Herbert, trans. *The Mishnah.* Peabody, MA: Hendrickson, 2012. Originally published by Oxford University Press in 1935, this single-volume translation of the Mishnah is an indispensable resource for reading rabbinic literature in its original context. The mishnaic traditions are closer to the time period of the New Testament than other rabbinic sources; therefore, the Mishnah is one of the most useful of the rabbinic sources to study on its own. Danby provides numerous notes and explanations for nonspecialists.

Notes

1. Some scholars have suggested Aramaic or Hebrew originals for at least some of the Gospels, Matthew in particular. See James R. Edwards, *The Hebrew Gospel and the Development of the Synoptic Tradition* (Grand

Rapids, MI: Eerdmans, 2009). Although this tradition is persistent, and a Semitic background has been suggested for all four of the Gospels, it remains a minority view in current New Testament scholarship.

2. See especially Donald W. Parry and Dana M. Pike, *LDS Perspectives on the Dead Sea Scrolls* (Provo, UT: Foundation for Ancient Research and Mormon Studies, 1997). For specific examples, see Edward J. Brandt, "The Law of Moses and the Law of Christ," in *Sperry Symposium Classics: The Old Testament*, ed. Paul Y. Hoskisson (Provo, UT: Religious Studies Center, Brigham Young University; Salt Lake City: Deseret Book, 2005), 133–53; Andrew C. Skinner, "The Dead Sea Scrolls and Latter-day Truth," *Ensign*, February 2006, https://www.lds.org/ensign/2006/02/the-dead-sea-scrolls-and-latter-day-truth; James H. Charlesworth, "Messianism in the Pseudepigrapha and the Book of Mormon," in *Reflections on Mormonism: Judaeo-Christian Parallels*, ed. Truman G. Madsen (Provo, UT: Religious Studies Center, Brigham Young University, 1978), 99–137; and Ann N. Madsen, "Melchizedek at Qumran and Nag Hammadi," in *Apocryphal Writings and the Latter-day Saints*, ed. C. Wilfred Griggs (Provo, UT: Religious Studies Center, Brigham Young University, 1986), 285–95.

3. See, for example, Jacob Neusner, "Messianic Themes in Formative Judaism," *Journal of the American Academy of Religion* 52 (1984): 357–74. Neusner was one of the great promulgators of this approach, since it fits his "documentary" approach where every ancient Jewish text represented an independent philosophical worldview. For a critique of this approach that still allows for the diversity of belief and practice in ancient Judaism, see Daniel Boyarin, "Beyond Judaisms: Meṭaṭron and the Divine Polymorphy of Ancient Judaism," *Journal for the Study of Judaism* 41 (2010): 323–65.

4. The best overall scholarly discussion of rabbinic literature remains H. L. Strack and Günter Stemberger, *Introduction to the Talmud and Midrash*, trans. Markus Bockmuehl (Minneapolis: Fortress, 1996). An extremely accessible introduction to the various genres in Jewish literature is Barry W. Holtz, ed., *Back to the Sources: Reading the Classic Jewish Texts* (New York: Touchstone, 1984; repr., Simon and Schuster, 1986).

5. The overview in this chapter must be brief, and so only the barest sketch of rabbinic literature may be given. The reader interested in more in-depth discussion is directed to the further reading selections at the end of this chapter.

6. Hebrew *ḥakhamim*, sing. *ḥakham*.

7. Rabbinic literature gives us *rab* and *rabban* as alternatives, although these are usually reserved for specific individuals or families.

8. Shaye J. D. Cohen, "Epigraphical Rabbis," *Jewish Quarterly Review* 72 (1981): 1–17; and Hayim Lapin, "Epigraphical Rabbis: A Reconsideration," *Jewish Quarterly Review* 101 (2011): 311–46.

9. Matthew 26:25, 49; Mark 9:5; 11:21; 14:45; John 1:38, 49; 3:2; 4:31; 6:25; 9:2; 11:8. These are the references in Greek. In English the term appears only in John. This is a choice on the part of the KJV translators and probably represents a slight anti-Semitic bias.

10. Stuart S. Miller, "'Epigraphical' Rabbis, Helios, and Psalm 19: Were the Synagogues of Archaeology and the Synagogues of the Sages One and the Same?," *Jewish Quarterly Review* 94 (2004): 27–76; Miller, "The Rabbis and the Non-existent Monolithic Synagogue," in *Jews, Christians and Polytheists in the Ancient Synagogue: Cultural Interaction during the Graeco-Roman Period*, ed. Steven Fine (London: Routledge, 1999), 57–70; and Jodi Magness, "Helios and the Zodiac Cycle in Ancient Palestinian Synagogues," in *Symbiosis, Symbolism, and Power of the Past: Canaan, Ancient Israel and Their Neighbors from the Late Bronze Age through Roman Palaestina*, ed. W. G. Dever and Seymour Gitin (Winona Lake, IN: Eisenbrauns, 2003), 363–89.

11. There are specific precedents given in other parts of the law, such as the specific command to not light fire in Exodus 35:3 and the story of the man stoned for gathering wood on the Sabbath in Numbers 15:32–36. These (relatively few) examples aid in the halakhic process but do not give definite solutions to most of the legal discussions.

12. These ideas are not unique to ancient Judaism. The debate surrounding the proper way to keep the Sabbath day continues in Latter-day Saint discourse to this day.

13. For further discussion on the written law of Moses and its relationship to the New Testament, see chapter 2 herein.

14. Mishnah Avot 1:1. Available in English translation in Herbert Danby, *The Mishnah* (Oxford: Oxford University Press, 1933), 446.

15. This is a reference to the seventy elders who went up to the mountain with Moses and Aaron in Exodus 24:1.

16. For further discussion on the oral law of Judaism, see Avram R. Shannon, "Torah in the Mouth: An Introduction to Jewish Oral Law," *Religious Educator* 19, no. 1 (2018): 139–59.

17. Strack and Stemberger, *Introduction to the Talmud and Midrash*, 124 (see note 4). Strack and Stemberger point out here that basically everything we know about the compilation of the Mishnah derives from a letter from AD 987, written by Sherira Gaon.

18. It is often referred to as the *Bavli*, after the Hebrew word for "Babylonian."

19. Christine Elizabeth Hayes, *Between the Babylonian and Palestinian Talmuds: Accounting for the Halakhic Difference in Selected Sugyot from Tractate Avodah Zarah* (Oxford: Oxford University Press, 1997).

20. For more information on the processes of midrash, including discussion of how it relates to Latter-day Saint modes of thinking, see Avram R. Shannon, "Mormons and Midrash: On the Composition of Expansive Interpretation in Genesis Rabbah and the Book of Moses," *BYU Studies Quarterly* 54, no. 2 (2015): 15–34.

21. Howard Eilberg-Schwartz, "Myth, Inference, and the Relativism of Reason: An Argument from the History of Judaism," in *Myth and Philosophy,* ed. Frank Reynolds and David Tracy (Albany: State University of New York, 1990), 247–85; and Naomi Janowitz and Andrew J. Lazarus, "Rabbinic Methods of Inference and the Rationality Debate," *Journal of Religion* 72, no. 4 (1992): 491–511.

22. According to Irving Jacobs, the rabbinic sages "acknowledged plain meaning—*as they perceived it*—to be the boundary within which the midrashic process was obliged to function." Irving Jacobs, *The Midrashic Process* (Cambridge: Cambridge University Press, 1995), 3; emphasis in original.

23. Menahem I. Kahana, "The Halakhic Midrashim," in *The Literature of the Sages*, vol. 2, ed. Shmuel Safrai, et al. (Assen, Netherlands: Royal Van Gorcum, 2006), 3–107, esp. 13–15.

24. For an accessible English discussion of Midrash and its workings, see Barry W. Holtz, "Midrash," in *Back to the Sources: Reading the Classic Jewish Texts*, ed. Barry W. Holtz (New York: Touchstone, 1984), 177–211.

25. James Kugel, "Two Introductions to Midrash," *Prooftexts* 3 (1983): 131–55, esp. 144.

26. James Kugel, *The Idea of Biblical Poetry: Parallelism and Its History* (Baltimore: Johns Hopkins University Press, 1998), 96–134.

27. This has led many authors to write numerous chapters on Jesus's perspective on the law of Moses. See E. P. Sanders, *Jewish Law from Jesus to the Mishnah* (Minneapolis: Ausburg Fortress, 2016), 1–134; John P. Meier, *A Marginal Jew: Rethinking the Historical Jesus*, vol. 4 (New Haven: Yale University Press, 2009), esp. 26–73; and Chaim Saiman, "Jesus' Legal Theory: A Rabbinic Reading," *Journal of Law and Religion* 23 (2007/2008): 97–130. These citations merely scratch the surface on what is something of a cottage industry in New Testament studies. It should be noted that many studies of Jesus's relationship to the law are written from a perspective of Paul's statements in Galatians 3.

28. For example, one biblical scholar has connected the boats in Mark 4:36 to the Jonah story and a tradition that there were many boats with Jonah. The problem with connecting this particular Jonah tradition with the New Testament is that it comes from Yalkut Shimoni, a midrashic compilation from the Middle Ages. It *may* reflect earlier traditions, but it is essentially impossible to say. See Joel Marcus, *Mark 1–8* (New York: Doubleday, 2002), 333.

29. Soncino Translation. This is available online at http://halakhah.com/shabbath/shabbath_153.html.

30. Called Gamliel in rabbinic literature.

31. This is likely out of cognizance of his position as Paul's teacher. Since Luke was probably Paul's student, this would make him part of Gamaliel's line of tradition. On this point, see Jacob Neusner and Bruce D. Chilton, "Paul and Gamliel," in *In Quest of the Historical Pharisees*, ed. Neusner and Chilton (Waco, TX: Baylor University Press, 2007), 175–223.

32. This tradition is historically unreliable. See Strack and Stemberger, *Introduction*, 67.

33. See the discussion in Saul Lieberman, *Hellenism in Jewish Palestine* (New York: Jewish Theological Seminary, 1950; repr. in combined edition in 1994), 58–61.

34. Walter M. Chandler, *The Trial of Jesus from a Lawyer's Standpoint* (New York City: Federal Book Company, 1925). Steven W. Allen's *The Illegal Trial of Jesus* (Mesa, AZ: Legal Awareness Series, Inc, 2005) is essentially a recapitulation of Chandler's arguments.

35. See John W. Welch, "Latter-day Saint Reflections on the Trial and Death of Jesus," *Clark Memorandum* (Fall 2000): 2–14.

36. The relationship between the temple laws and the Mishnah is explored in Jacob Neusner, "Map without Territory: Mishnah's Laws of Sacrifice and Sanctuary," *History of Religions* 19 (1979): 103–27. The use that the sages of the Mishnah turn the temple narratives to is examined in Naftali Cohn, *The Memory of the Temple and the Making of the Rabbis* (Philadelphia: University of Pennsylvania, 2012).

37. Author's translation, with a Hebrew text taken from Sefaria.org.

38. Although it should, of course, be further noted that Stephen is stoned for blasphemy at Acts 7:57–58.

39. Dana M. Pike, "Before the Jewish Authorities," in *The Life and Teachings of Jesus Christ: From the Last Supper to the Resurrection*, ed. Richard Neitzel Holzapfel and Thomas A. Wayment (Salt Lake City: Deseret Book, 2003), 210–68, 225.

40. Richard Neitzel Holzapfel and Thomas A. Wayment, *Jesus the Christ Study Guide* (Salt Lake City: Deseret Book, 2014), 164.

41. Rengstorf, "ἀπόστολος," *Theological Dictionary of the New Testament*, 407–45, esp. 407. See also Hermann Vogelstein, "The Development of the Apostalate in Judaism and Its Transformation in Christianity," *HUCA* 2 (1925): 99–123. Vogelstein sees the notion of "apostle" reaching back into biblical times at least as far back as the Chronicler.

42. "ἀπόστολος," *Theological Dictionary of the New Testament*, 407–45; and Francis H. Agnew, "The Origin of the NT Apostle-Concept: A Review of Research," *Journal of Biblical Literature* 105 (1986): 75–96, esp. 79–82. Agnew outlines the various objections to the association of *šeliaḥ* with *apostle* but notes that the one term is legal, while the other is religious, in a rabbinic context. This is not a reasonable distinction from an ancient perspective.

43. This is according to Matthew.

44. "ἀπόστολος," *Theological Dictionary of the New Testament*, 418.

45. "ἀπόστολος," *Theological Dictionary of the New Testament*, 421.

46. "ἀπόστολος," *Theological Dictionary of the New Testament*, 429,

47. Marcus Jastrow, *Dictionary of the Targumim, Talmud and Midrashic Literature*, 1583.

48. Hebrew: *š/l/ḥ*

49. It should perhaps be noted that the verb *šalaḥ* has a reference to divorce in Deuteronomy 24:1. It may be coincidence, but in the interest of bringing these two literatures together, Rabban Gamaliel I is the named sage quoted in Gittin 4:2.

50. Circumcision was seen as the distinctive mark of Judaism in this period, although other ancient peoples practiced circumcision. The ancient Greeks believed the foreskin to be one of the most attractive parts of the male body, and so in the Hellenistic/Roman world, the Jewish lack of a foreskin marked them as barbarous. See Frederick Mansfield Hodges, "The Ideal Prepuce in Ancient Greek and Rome: Male Genital Aesthetics and Their Relation to Lipodermos, Circumcision, Foreskin Restoration and Kynodesme," *Bulletin of the History of Medicine* 75 (2001): 375–405. The circumcision of non-Jewish converts was, therefore, a major question in how nascent Christianity was placing itself vis-à-vis its Jewish and Roman environment. This is not simply an ancient phenomenon. See Sander L. Gilman, "Decircumcision: The First Aesthetic Surgery," *Modern Judaism* 17 (1997): 201–10.

51. This may be seen in the discussion in Saul Lieberman, *Hellenism in Jewish Palestine* (New York: Jewish Theological Seminary, 1950; reprinted in combined edition with *Greek in Jewish Palestine* in 1994), 58–61.

Part 2

Greco-Roman Background of the New Testament

9

Judea as a Roman Province, AD 6–66

Michael R. Trotter

Shortly after Jesus's triumphant entry into Jerusalem on Palm Sunday, a group of ill-in-tentioned Pharisees sought to discredit the Savior by publicly asking him a question they believed could not be answered without either causing him serious trouble with Roman authorities or offending a significant portion of his followers: "What thinkest thou? Is it lawful to give tribute unto Caesar, or not?" (Matthew 22:17; see Mark 12:14; Luke 20:22).[1] Although the question may seem innocent, the installment of a Roman official as governor of Judea had caused a deep political divide between Jews who supported Roman administrative oversight and Jews who viewed Roman leaders as their oppressors. Jesus avoided the political repercussions of the question by pointing to the image of Caesar imprinted on a coin (denarius) and saying, "Render therefore unto Caesar the things which are Caesar's; and unto God the things that are God's" (Matthew 22:21; see Mark 12:17; Luke 20:25). Without understanding the political tension caused by Rome's intervention in Judea at this time, we cannot fully appreciate the nefarious nature of this question and the wisdom of Jesus's answer.

This exchange between Jesus and the Pharisees illustrates how understanding Rome's involvement in Judean politics can enhance our comprehension of the New Testament. This chapter will discuss the Roman political activities in Judea from AD 6 to 66 and how the Jews responded to Rome's intervention. Chronologically describing how Roman authority in Judea grew and transformed during this period, while giving special consideration to the significant Roman officials portrayed in the New Testament, will illuminate Rome's influence on first-century Christians.

Herod "the Great" as a Client King of Rome

When the Savior was born in the village of Bethlehem (Matthew 2:1–10; Luke 2:1–7), he was born into a kingdom ruled by Herod the Great. Although Herod was the reigning king of the Jews, his position as monarch depended entirely on the will of the Roman emperor and the Roman senate. Herod began his political career as a *procurator* of Galilee serving under Hyrcanus II, the Jewish high priest who ruled as *ethnarch* (literally "ruler of the nation"). When Hyrcanus II was captured during a Parthian invasion in 40 BC, however, Herod was forced to flee to Rome to beg for assistance. With the help of powerful friends, such as Mark Antony, Herod was proclaimed king of Judea by the Roman senate and given sufficient military support to reclaim his new kingdom from the Parthians.[2] By 37 BC, Herod had successfully expelled the Parthians from Jerusalem and established his authority over the territories of Judea, Galilee, Perea, and Idumea.[3] Herod's kingship was later confirmed by the emperor Augustus in 30 BC, and his territory was expanded to include Gadara, Hippos, Samaria, Gaza, Anthedon, Joppa, and Strato's Tower.[4]

Because Herod was the ruler of an independent kingdom, his territory was not considered part of the Roman Empire. However, this technicality did not prevent Roman officials from regulating Herod's rule; if Herod did anything to displease the Roman senate, the senate could inflict disciplinary actions against him. Consequently, Herod was considered a client king of Rome, that is, an independent monarch accountable to Rome for the administration of his kingdom. Client kings were permitted to rule as they saw fit provided they maintained peace in their territories, did not attempt to interfere in foreign affairs without prior Roman approval, and rendered service to the Roman Empire when called upon. In return for complying with these requirements, the client king's position as ruler would be secured indefinitely.

Client kings were not required to collect and pay taxes to Rome, although they often gave Roman officials extravagant gifts to earn their favor.[5] This policy of not collecting taxes from client kingdoms poses some problems for understanding the Gospel of Luke's account of the birth of Jesus. Luke 2:1–3 states: "And it came to pass in those days, that there went out a decree from Caesar Augustus, that all the world should be taxed. . . . And all went to be taxed, every one into his own city."[6] According to the author of the Third Gospel, Joseph brought Mary to Bethlehem in order to register to pay a tax. If the Gospel of Matthew is correct in placing the birth of Jesus toward the end of Herod's reign, however, the emperor Augustus would have had no authority to collect taxes from Herod's territory. Some scholars have attempted to clarify this inconsistency by identifying the census mentioned in Luke 2 with the Roman census of AD 6/7, which was conducted long after the death of Herod when a portion of his original kingdom had been incorporated into the Roman Empire.[7] Consequently, Luke's reference to a Roman taxation in Judea and Galilee around the time of Jesus's birth cannot be readily reconciled with the known governmental structure of the time. Unless new historical evidence that reconciles this inconsistency emerges, the exact circumstances surrounding Joseph and Mary's journey to Bethlehem must remain obscure.

As a client king of Rome, Herod was forced to maintain a delicate balance between pleasing his Roman patrons and pleasing his Jewish subjects, many of whom considered Roman culture an affront to traditional Jewish life. Herod, however, maintained this political balance by portraying himself as a Roman to the Romans and a Jew to the Jews. In his predominantly gentile territories, Herod commissioned numerous building projects to honor the Romans and their culture. For example, on the site of Strato's Tower he built a massive coastal city that he named Caesarea in honor of the emperor, and he erected multiple temples to honor Augustus across his kingdom, including the extravagant temple in the heart of Sebaste.[8] Additionally, he rebuilt the Pythian Temple of Apollo at Rhodes at his own expense after the original temple was destroyed by a fire.[9] By embracing Roman culture and flattering his Roman patrons in these ways, Herod was able to secure his throne.

Although he promoted Roman culture in the pagan cities of his kingdom, Herod also sought to respect the customs of the Jewish cities in his territory to some extent. For instance, in these cities he ensured that all coinage was devoid of images in keeping with the law of Moses.[10] His most significant attempt to please the Jewish people, however, was the extravagant renovation and expansion of the Jerusalem temple, which he accomplished using only priestly builders.[11] The construction of this costly endeavor, which began in ca. 20 BC and took decades to complete, was still ongoing during the ministry of Jesus (John 2:20). Herod's renovation of the temple was so exquisite that rabbis would later say, "Whoever has not seen Herod's building, has never seen anything beautiful."[12]

Despite Herod's efforts to appease his Jewish subjects, he often aroused their animosity by attempting to impose Roman culture on them. When he built a theater and a hippodrome in Jerusalem, many Jews were upset because these Roman institutions were considered distinctly un-Jewish and directly "in opposition to Jewish customs."[13] On another occasion Herod installed a large golden eagle, a symbol closely associated with the Roman Empire, over the gate of the temple, causing many devout Jews of the city to recoil in horror.[14]

The hostility with which some of Herod's Jewish subjects regarded him on account of his pro-Roman policies made him paranoid of any potential Jewish uprising that might threaten his throne. This paranoia motivated him to use extreme and often brutal means of securing his position, as can be seen in the Gospel of Matthew's account of his ordering the murders of Bethlehem's infants shortly after the birth of Jesus (2:1–16). Some scholars have questioned the validity of this event because it cannot be corroborated by any evidence outside the Gospel of Matthew.[15] While it must be conceded that Matthew 2 is the only known account of this tragic event, the paranoia and brutality that Matthew attributed to Herod can also be seen in Josephus's descriptions of him. For example, according to Josephus, when the Hasmonean high priest Aristobulus began to be celebrated and revered among the Jews, Herod had him murdered because he feared the Jews would want to make him king.[16] He also executed his own sons Alexander, Aristobulus, and Antipater because he believed they were plotting to take his throne.[17] Additionally, Josephus reports that on his deathbed Herod ordered all the prominent men of Judea be imprisoned in the hippodrome and executed as soon as he passed away, so that all the Jews would weep when he died (although this com-

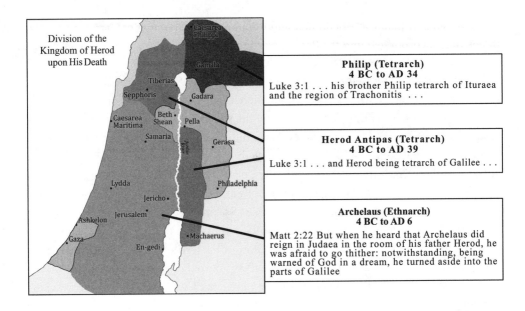

Division of the Kingdom of Herod upon his death. Map by ThinkSpacial.

mand was not obeyed).[18] While the account of Herod in Matthew 2:1–16 cannot be corroborated by evidence outside the New Testament, the description of his character in this passage fits well with the portrait offered by Josephus.

By the end of Herod's life, the attitudes of his subjects toward the Romans were varied and often polarized; in gentile cities, such as Caesarea Maritima, Roman culture was embraced and celebrated, while in predominantly Jewish cities, such as Jerusalem, Roman influence was commonly regarded with suspicion or open disdain.

The Division of Herod the Great's Kingdom

Upon the death of Herod in the spring of 4 BC, his final testament divided the kingdom into three territories with the stipulation that three of his sons, Archelaus, Antipas, and Philip, each be given one of these territories to rule over. Because Herod was a client king of Rome, however, only the Roman emperor had the authority to confer the kingdom on another, regardless of what Herod's will stipulated. Consequently, shortly after Herod's death each of his remaining three sons went before Emperor Augustus to request that his father's will be disregarded since both Archelaus and Antipas claimed to be the sole heir of Herod's kingdom.

Ultimately, Augustus decided to respect the essentials of Herod's will and divided the kingdom among all three sons: Archelaus was awarded the territories of Judea, Samaria, and Idumea with the title ethnarch (a rank lower than king although with similar administrative functions); Antipas was given the territories of Galilee and Perea, with the rank of tetrarch (a rank lower than ethnarch but with similar administrative responsibilities);[19] and Philip was made tetrarch over Batanea, Trachonitis, and Auranitis, while the cities of Gaza, Gadara, and Hippos were incorporated into the Roman province of Syria.[20]

The Ethnarchy of Archelaus and the Beginning of Roman Rule

When Joseph, the adoptive father of the Lord, learned of Herod's death and that "Archelaus did reign in Judea in the room of his father Herod, he was afraid to go thither" (Matthew 2:22), that is, from Egypt back to Bethlehem. Joseph thus decided to settle in the village of Nazareth, which was under the jurisdiction of Herod Antipas in the territory of Galilee.

Although little is known regarding Archelaus's reign, Joseph's fear of living under his rule appears to have been well-founded. Josephus reports that Archelaus's rule was so oppressive that the Jews and Samaritans could not bear "his cruelty and tyranny." Consequently, both groups sent delegations to the Roman emperor to accuse the ethnarch of violating the imperial command "that he conduct himself fairly with respect to the affairs pertaining to [his people]."[21] When Augustus heard the accusations against Archelaus, he immediately summoned the Judean ethnarch to Rome. Archelaus's defense before the emperor was insufficient, however, and after stripping Archelaus of his title and territories, the Roman emperor exiled him to Vienna to live out the remainder of his life in disgrace.[22]

Instead of dividing Archelaus's kingdom between Antipas and Philip, in AD 6 Augustus made Judea, Samaria, and Idumea an official province of Rome.[23] The Romans first instituted the provincial system of government in 241 BC when they acquired Sicily in the First Punic War. Finding it impractical to govern a nation outside Italy from Rome, they appointed one man invested with *imperium*, or administrative and military authority, to govern Sicily as a representative of Rome. Each Roman governor was given command of the military forces stationed in the province and was charged with maintaining peace and collecting taxes throughout his assigned territory. Because governors were given limited administrative resources, they typically did not impose a new administrative system upon their subjects; rather, they tended to act as supervisors over the indigenous governing systems operating in their respective territories.[24] By the time Judea was made a province in AD 6, governors, known as prefects (Latin *praefectus*), were appointed by the emperor and given *imperium*, which among other things granted them jurisdiction over criminal proceedings of Roman citizens in their territories and the right to assume jurisdiction over local criminal proceedings as needed.[25] In the case of the province of Judea, this imperium also gave the prefect the right to appoint and dismiss the Jewish high priest as he saw fit.

With Judea now being directly governed by a Roman prefect, the collection of taxes became a point of tension among the Jews of the province. While tetrarchs and ethnarchs collected taxes from their subjects, these taxes were not technically given to the Romans; rather, taxes were paid to the tetrarch or ethnarch, and he would then give the Roman emperor a "gift" from his own treasury funds. However, with Judea now a province of Rome, the collected taxes were officially paid to the emperor for the glory of the empire.[26] There were two main taxes levied on provinces in the Roman Empire: an income tax known as the *tributum soli* and a head tax called the *tributum capitis*, or poll tax.[27] Unlike the taxes required by traditional Jewish custom, such as the temple tax,[28] the *tributum soli* and the *tributum capitis* were deeply resented by many Jews who regarded them as nothing more than compulsory ransom payments to their oppressors. By the time of Jesus's ministry, there was a deep divide between Jews who willingly paid Roman taxes and those who saw these taxes as an affront to God and the covenant people. As a result, the former were commonly seen as traitors to traditional Judaism, while the latter were regarded as unfaithful subjects of Rome; to support one was to betray the other. It was with this political context in mind that a cunning Pharisee deviously asked Jesus, "What thinkest thou? Is it lawful to give tribute unto Caesar, or not?" (Matthew 22:17; see Mark 12:14; Luke 20:22).

In addition to the increased tension caused by the Roman taxation of Judea, Jewish-Roman relations were considerably strained by the actions of Roman governors who were ignorant of Jewish religious practices. Unlike previous rulers of Judea, the Roman prefects often did not grasp how seriously the Jews took their religious laws and had difficulty understanding how seemingly routine actions, such as displaying the image of the emperor, could kindle the ire of their Jewish subjects.

Roman Prefects (*praefecti*) of Judea ca. AD 6–41	
ca. AD 6–9	Coponius
ca. AD 9–12	Marcus Ambilibus
ca. AD 12–15	Annius Rufus
ca. AD 15–26	Valerius Gratus
ca. AD 26–36	Pontius Pilate
ca. AD 36–37	Marcellus
ca. AD 37–41	Marullus

Despite this lack of an in-depth comprehension of Jewish customs, the Roman administrators who ruled Judea from AD 6 to 41 generally went to great lengths to preserve the indigenous laws of their Jewish cities. Unlike much of the Roman Empire, the province of Judea was not required to worship the emperor; instead the emperor asked only that the Jews make burnt offerings to God on his behalf.[29] Likewise, with the exception of Pontius Pilate,[30] the Romans seem to have made a sincere effort to respect the Jewish law forbidding images. For example, when the Syrian legate Vitellius was bringing an army to Nabatea, he agreed to lead his soldiers around Judea so that the banners bearing the image of the emperor would not pass through Jewish cities.[31]

In addition to generally respecting Jewish customs, Roman prefects of Judea allowed Jewish cities to have a certain degree of autonomy in enforcing local Jewish laws. Although the Roman governor was ultimately responsible for the military, financial, and judicial administration of the province, in general the Sanhedrin (the governing body of the Jews led by the high priest) had authority to enforce Jewish law and arbitrate legal disputes in Jewish cities, provided the crime in question was not political in nature, since such crimes were seen as attempts to interfere with Roman interests and were therefore under the jurisdiction of the Roman governor. Because one could become a Roman citizen only by performing a notable service to the Roman Empire or by being the child of a Roman citizen, most Jews living in Judea fell under the jurisdiction of the Sanhedrin and its subsidiary tribunals.[32] However, the Sanhedrin's authority among the Jews was not absolute. For example, although the Sanhedrin was legally empowered to enforce the observance of Jewish customs, as will be discussed below, it could not legally carry out capital punishment.

Despite the privileges extended to the Jews by their Roman governors, some saw Roman rule as "an insult to the rights of God's chosen people who instead of paying tribute to the emperor in Rome should themselves have been called to rule over the pagan world."[33] Consequently, tension arose between the Jews and their Roman administrators, and organized Jewish resistance groups began to form. Shortly after Coponius was made the first governor of Judea in AD 6, Judas of Gamala, also called "Judas the Galilean," and a Pharisee named Zadduk began to teach that the tribute levied on Judea by Rome was nothing other than the Roman enslavement of the Jewish people. Accordingly, they made it their mission to incite the Jews to revolt against Rome. While neither Judas nor Zadduk succeeded in mounting a significant revolt, Josephus states that the Jewish people "would receive the message which they would speak with pleasure . . . and the nation was further infected with [their] preaching."[34] The antiestablishment message of Judas and Zadduk eventually became so popular that some Jews formed a widespread anti-Roman political party known as the Zealots.[35] Famous for their radical ideas and passionate calls for political change, the Zealots prized liberty above all else and recognized God alone as the legitimate ruler of the Jews.[36]

This political tension between the Jews and their Roman overlords during the early decades of the first century serves as the narrative context for many events described in the Gospels. One representative example is the trial of Jesus, to which we now turn.

The Political Dynamics of the Trial of Jesus

As the popularity of Jesus grew, the chief priests and scribes "feared him, because all the people was astonished at his doctrine" (Mark 11:18). The Gospel of John, however, clarifies that the Jewish leaders feared Jesus's increasing popularity not simply because they rejected his teachings, but because they viewed him as a serious political threat as well. Shortly after Lazarus was raised from the dead, the chief priests and Pharisees convened to decide how Jesus should be handled. During this meeting the Jewish leaders discussed the political danger the Savior posed to the Jewish people, saying, "If we let him thus alone, all men will believe on him: and the Romans shall come and take away both our place and nation" (John 11:48). Before the Savior's earthly ministry, the Roman Empire had established an administrative system in Judea that granted the high priest power to generally oversee religious and political affairs among the Jews. However, as noted earlier, the Roman governor possessed the authority to appoint and dismiss the high priest as he pleased; if the high priest failed to maintain peace or refused to support Roman interests, he was replaced with someone more conformable to the Roman agenda. Jewish leaders apparently feared that Jesus was going to upset the status quo. Unlike the high priest and his associates, the Savior was not constrained by any need to support Roman interests. If Jesus became influential enough to challenge the high priest's authority, then the Roman governor might deem the high priest incapable of maintaining peace and supporting Roman interests in the region, a situation that would result in the dismissal of the established Jewish leadership. In order to secure their positions and, as they perceived it, the political stability of their nation, the Jewish leaders decided Jesus had to die (John 11:49–53).

The political situation between the Jews and the Romans also influenced the manner in which the Jewish leaders brought about the death of the Savior. The Gospels report that Jesus was forced to appear before at least one Jewish judiciary council that declared him worthy of death but did not officially sentence him to death. The exact nature of this council is unclear because each Gospel account describes it somewhat differently.[37] Matthew relates that Jesus was brought before a "council" (Sanhedrin) of the chief priests and elders who sought false witnesses to justify putting him to death (Matthew 26:59). After many witnesses were produced who could not corroborate each other's false accusations, Jesus was accused of threatening to destroy the temple and rebuild it in three days (26:60–61; compare John 2:19). Although this false accusation served as the initial charge against Jesus, as his interrogation progressed the charge against him became blasphemy. When the high priest asked Jesus if he claimed to be the Son of God, he answered: "Thou has said: nevertheless I say unto you, Hereafter shall ye see the Son of man sitting on the right hand of power, and coming in the clouds of heaven" (26:64). Considering Jesus's response blasphemous, the council proclaimed him worthy of death and beat him violently before sending him to be examined by Pilate (26:65–68).

The account of this council in the Gospel of Mark generally corroborates the account given in the Gospel of Matthew. Both agree that Jesus was brought before a judiciary council composed of the chief priests and elders of the Jews and that they sought false witnesses to accuse him (Matthew 26:59; Mark 14:55–56), both agree that Jesus was eventually accused of threatening to destroy the temple and rebuild it in three days (Matthew 26:60–61; Mark 14:57–59), and both agree that Jesus was judged worthy of death because he declared that they would see the Son of Man sitting at the right hand of power (i.e., God) and coming in heavenly clouds (Matthew 26:64; Mark 14:62).

The Gospel of Luke recounts the event slightly differently, however. Luke states that instead of being taken directly to the judiciary council, Jesus was first taken to the house of the high priest, where he was mocked and beaten (Luke 22:54, 63–65). The Savior then remained at the high priest's residence until the following morning when the chief priests, elders, and scribes convened a council to decide his fate (22:66). Unlike the accounts given in Matthew and Mark, Luke omits any mention of false witnesses or beatings during the council. Instead the council first asked if Jesus was the Messiah (22:67). When the Savior refused to answer the question, the council asked if he claimed to be the Son of God (22:67–70). Although Jesus did not explicitly confirm or deny being God's Son, his lack of a denial and his general unwillingness to cooperate were used by the council to justify his execution (22:70–71).

The account in the Gospel of John differs significantly from those in the Synoptic Gospels. According to John, after Jesus was arrested he was led to the house of Annas, a man who had served as high priest from AD 6 to 15 and was the father-in-law of the current high priest, Caiaphas (John 18:13).[38] While it is not clear who attended this meeting, it does not appear to have been a formal judiciary council but rather an informal inquiry, since the current high priest was not present and no chief priests or elders are mentioned.[39] However, it does not appear to have been a private conversation since others, including Peter and an unnamed disciple of Christ, were allowed to enter Annas's court while Jesus was being questioned (18:15–16). The interrogation appears to have been brief; Annas asked Jesus about his disciples and his teachings, and Jesus responded by suggesting Annas ask his disciples about his teachings since he always taught them publicly (18:20–21). Jesus was then bound and sent to Caiaphas, who sent him to stand trial before Pilate (18:24, 28). Although the Gospel of John does not describe a formal trial of Jesus on this night, it must be remembered the author of this Gospel had described a prior council held by the chief priests and Pharisees in John 11:47–54, where it was decided that Jesus was worthy of death.

While scholars have variously explained the differing accounts of the Savior's appearance before the Jewish authorities,[40] it suffices here to show that the Gospels agree the Savior was compelled to appear before Jewish authorities who believed he was guilty of a crime (perhaps blasphemy) and worthy of death but who stopped short of passing a formal death sentence against him. Rather than impose the death sentence themselves, the Jewish leaders delivered Jesus to Pilate for trial, hoping the Roman governor would execute the punishment they had already determined he deserved.

It is commonly assumed that the Jewish leaders were forced to deliver Jesus to Pilate for trial because only the Roman governor had the authority to inflict capital punishment. For example, James E. Talmage wrote, "In strict accuracy we cannot say that the Sanhedrists sentenced Christ to death, inasmuch as the power to authoritatively pronounce capital sentences had been taken from the council by Roman decree."[41] The assertion that the Jewish authorities could not legally execute Jesus primarily relies on two pieces of evidence. The first is a statement made by Josephus indicating that Coponius became the first Roman governor of Judea "after he received authority to govern from Caesar, including the infliction of capital punishment."[42] The second piece of evidence is a statement attributed to the Jewish leaders in John 18:31, which states, "It is not lawful for us to put any man to death." Taken together, these statements imply that only the Roman governor possessed the authority to sentence Jesus to death.

Other events also imply the Jews lacked legal authority to inflict capital punishment. For example, Josephus records that in AD 62 when the sitting governor of Judea, Festus, died and his replacement was en route to the province, the Jewish high priest, Annas II, convened the Sanhedrin and decreed that a group of Christians, including James the half brother of

Jesus, be stoned to death "as violators of the law."[43] A group of outraged citizens complained to Albinus, the newly appointed governor of Judea, about Annas II's behavior "because it was not lawful for Annas to convene the Sanhedrin without his knowledge."[44] If, as Josephus says, the Sanhedrin could not be convened legally without Roman approval, it would not have been able to legally pass a death sentence without similar authorization.[45]

The Jewish authorities may have had political reasons for wanting Pilate to give the official death sentence, however. The Gospels of Mark and Luke record multiple occasions when the chief priests and scribes sought to lay hands on Jesus but restrained themselves because "they feared the people" (Mark 12:12; Luke 20:19; 22:2). Since Jesus had a large group of followers who might have come to his defense, the Jewish leaders could not move against him openly without risking a public protest or riot. If such a tumult were to arise, the Jewish leaders would lose the support of many Jews and the favor of Pilate for failing to maintain peace in the region. By having Pilate pass the death sentence against Jesus, the Jewish leaders could deflect his disciples' blame onto Pilate while simultaneously forcing the prefect to take responsibility for any ensuing tumult.

The political situation of the time also heavily influenced the Savior's trial before Pilate. While each of the Gospel writers depicts the trial somewhat differently, they all depict Pilate as ordering Jesus's crucifixion largely as a result of the cries of the angry mob. While the Gospels of Mark and Luke subtly reference Pilate's interest in appeasing the mob by stating that the "loud voices" of the crowd "prevailed" and that the Roman governor was "willing to content the people" (Luke 23:23; Mark 15:15), the Gospel of Matthew unambiguously states that Pilate capitulated to the mob's demands because "a tumult was made" by them (Matthew 27:24). As stated previously, Roman prefects were responsible for maintaining peace within their provinces. Pilate may have feared that if this tumult were to escalate into a full-scale riot, the emperor might deem him incapable of keeping the peace in his Jewish territories and recall him, especially since he already had a poor track record of successfully de-escalating Jewish tumults.[46]

The Gospel of John also describes the Jewish mob accusing Pilate of disloyalty to Rome: "The Jews cried out, saying, If thou let this man go, thou art not Caesar's friend: whosoever maketh himself a king speaketh against Caesar" (John 19:12). Although no threat was made to report this accused disloyalty to Caesar, it may reasonably be assumed that such a threat was implied, since after hearing this response Pilate immediately agreed to the crowd's demand. Furthermore, Pilate seems to have been prudent to take even the implication of such a threat seriously, since when a Samaritan delegation formally complained to Vitellius, the Syrian legate, about Pilate's conduct in AD 36, Pilate was removed from his post and recalled to Rome.[47]

As can be seen from the preceding analysis of the arrest and trial of Jesus, the political situation between the Jews and Romans significantly influenced the manner in which Jesus's death was brought about. While the politics of first-century Judea may explain *how* the Savior was killed, it should not be assumed that this political situation explains *why* he was killed. The Savior himself gave the reason for his death: "My Father sent me that I might be lifted up upon the cross; and after that I had been lifted up upon the cross, that I might draw all men unto me . . . to stand before me, to be judged of their works, whether they be good or whether they be evil—and for this cause have I been lifted up" (3 Nephi 27:14–15). Christ suffered death in order to fulfill his divine purpose; the political situation in Judea merely influenced the way this purpose was accomplished.

Herod Agrippa I and the Reestablished Kingdom of Judea

The political situation generally continued in this way until the advent of Herod Agrippa I, who began changing the political landscape of the region in AD 37. A grandson of Herod the Great, Agrippa spent much of his early life chasing after the political success enjoyed by his grandfather. Although he failed to win the favor of the emperor Tiberius, he managed to become friends with the future emperor, Gaius Caligula (AD 37–41). Agrippa made a grievous political misstep, however, by publicly proclaiming that he wished the aged Tiberius would die soon so that his friend Caligula might ascend the imperial throne. When Agrippa's statement was reported to the emperor, Tiberius had him imprisoned for disloyalty.[48] Agrippa remained in prison until Tiberius's death in March of AD 37, when Caligula became emperor of the Roman Empire. Remembering the loyalty of his unfortunate friend, Caligula released Agrippa from prison and conferred upon him the territory of the late Herod Philip along with the title of king.[49]

Agrippa's appointment as king did not sit well with Herod Antipas, who continued to rule the client kingdom of Galilee and Perea as tetrarch, a lesser rank than that of a king. Having governed his tetrarchy successfully for decades, Antipas decided the time was right to petition the emperor for a promotion to the rank of king. When Agrippa heard of Antipas's ambition, he sent an envoy to the emperor formally accusing Antipas of disloyalty to Rome. Upon hearing from both Antipas and Agrippa, Caligula sided with his longtime friend and permanently exiled Antipas to Gaul. Caligula also added Galilee and Perea to Agrippa's kingdom in ca. AD 40 as a reward for his loyalty.[50]

When Caligula was assassinated in January of AD 41, Agrippa once again saw the opportunity to extend his political influence. In the chaos that followed the emperor's murder, Claudius and the Roman senate both possessed formidable armies, and both initially claimed the right to rule the empire. As tensions mounted between the two parties, Agrippa was selected to help resolve the situation, and he exerted all of his influence to ensure that Claudius would become the next emperor.[51] When Claudius was ultimately accepted as emperor by the senate thanks in part to Agrippa's efforts, the new emperor expressed his gratitude by confirming Agrippa's kingdom and expanding his territory to include Judea and Samaria.[52] With these additions to Agrippa's kingdom, the Roman province of Judea was officially dissolved and the former kingdom of Herod the Great was essentially restored to his grandson.

Agrippa enjoyed the support of Rome throughout his reign and appears to have been popular among his Jewish subjects as well. Although he embraced Roman culture when he was among Romans, he devoutly observed Jewish law when he was in Judea. Josephus states that "dwelling continuously in Jerusalem was pleasant for him and he preserved the practices of his country in purity. Through everything he kept himself pure and no day passed by him which was lacking the lawful sacrifices."[53] Agrippa was also praised for defending Jewish culture against Roman influence. When Caligula commanded that a statue of himself be erected inside the Jerusalem temple, the predictable Jewish outrage immediately followed. Upon hearing of the situation in Judea, Agrippa intervened with Caligula on behalf of the Jews. Two different accounts exist that describe Agrippa's intervention: Philo of Alexandria states that Agrippa sent a letter to the emperor convincing him to follow the precedent set by past Roman emperors and revoke his command to install the statue, while Josephus states that Agrippa won Caligula's favor by throwing an extravagant banquet for the emperor, who then agreed to revoke his command as a token of gratitude for Agrippa's generosity.[54] Although Philo and Josephus give very different descriptions of Agrippa's intervention, both credit him with protecting the sanctity of the Jerusalem temple from Roman defilement.

Agrippa also attempted to win the favor of his Jewish subjects by trying to suppress the nascent Christian movement. As Christianity began to spread throughout the Mediterranean world, "Herod [Agrippa] the king stretched forth his hands to vex certain of the church . . . because he saw it pleased the Jews" (Acts 12:1, 3). In his quest for greater approval, Agrippa beheaded the apostle James (the brother of John) and sentenced Peter to death, although the latter miraculously escaped from custody before the sentence could be carried out (Acts 12:2–19). While his persecution of Christians brought Agrippa the support of the Jews, some later Christian writers contend that he suffered an excruciating death as divine retribution for his actions against the apostles.[55] According to Acts 12, shortly after Peter's escape Agrippa was addressing a crowd from Tyre and Sidon when the crowd proclaimed that he spoke with the voice of a god rather than the voice of a mortal man (12:20–22). "And immediately the angel of the Lord smote him, because he gave not God the glory: and he was eaten of worms, and gave up the ghost" (12:23).[56]

The End of the Jewish Kingdom and the Return of Roman Rule

The sudden death of Agrippa had significant political consequences for the inhabitants of his kingdom. Because Agrippa's son, Herod Agrippa II, was too young to assume his father's throne, Claudius decreed that Agrippa's territory become an imperial province governed directly by Roman procurators. Unlike the Roman prefects who governed Judea and Samaria before Agrippa, however, the procurators failed to understand the critical role that Jewish religious practices played in maintaining peace in the predominately Jewish province.

Cuspius Fadus, who served as the first procurator of the new Judean province from ca. AD 44 to 46, quickly ran afoul of Jewish custom when he attempted to take possession of the high priest's vestments, a tactic that had previously been employed by Roman prefects. Many Jews saw this as a violation of their religious rights and sent a delegation to Claudius to protest Fadus's actions. After consulting with Agrippa II, Claudius determined that Fadus should not take possession of the vestments.[57] Although Fadus accepted the emperor's decision, the incident did little to diffuse the tension between the Jews and their Roman administrators.

Roman Procurators (*procuratores*) of Judea ca. AD 44–66	
ca. AD 44–46	Cuspius Fadus
ca. AD 46–48	Tiberius Alexander
ca. AD 48–52	Ventidius Cumanus
ca. AD 52–60	Antonius Felix
ca. AD 60–62	Porcius Festus
ca. AD 62–64	Albinus
ca. AD 64–66	Gessius Florus

Relations between the Jews and Romans continued to decline when Ventidius Cumanus became procurator of the Judean province in ca. AD 48. Resentment turned into open hostility when a Passover celebration at the Jerusalem temple was interrupted by a Roman soldier who exposed himself and made indecent gestures during the sacred proceedings.[58] An angry crowd of Jews immediately went to Cumanus and demanded that the offending soldier be punished. When members of the crowd began throwing stones at the Roman soldiers, Cumanus called for reinforcements. The arrival of additional soldiers caused the crowd to panic, however, and thousands[59] of Jews were purportedly trampled to death as the crowd frantically fled.[60]

The Jews and Romans clashed over Jewish custom again when Cumanus plundered a handful of Jewish villages that had been accused of aiding robbers. During the enforcement of the punishment, however, a Roman soldier publicly destroyed a Torah scroll.[61] Enraged by the contempt shown to their most sacred writings, the Jews immediately complained to Cumanus, who executed the offending soldier when he saw a revolt was about to break out.[62]

Although Cumanus was able to pacify the Jews in this instance, the relationship between the Jews and the Romans continued to deteriorate because of the procurator's corrupt practices. The most serious instance of administrative corruption came at the end of Cumanus's administration when some Galilean Jews were murdered in a Samaritan village. Since Cumanus had accepted a bribe from the Samaritans, he refused to punish the offending village.[63] Unwilling to allow the Samaritans to go unpunished, a large group of armed Jews invaded Samaria and destroyed several villages. Cumanus then rushed to Samaria with an army and defeated the Jewish vigilantes.[64] After the Jews and Samaritans both complained to the legate of Syria, the case was referred to the emperor, who sided with the Jews and exiled Cumanus for his actions.[65]

Any hopes that affairs between the Jews and Romans might improve with the removal Cumanus proved vain when Antonius Felix was appointed as his replacement in ca. AD 52.[66] The Roman historian Tacitus states that instead of learning from the mistakes of his predecessor, Felix governed the Judean province like a man who "believed he could commit any evil deed with impunity."[67] Felix earned the ire of the Jews by his scandalous marriage to Drusilla, a Jewish noblewoman who had left her husband to marry Felix. In addition, the new procurator's administration inspired the formation of numerous anti-Roman factions. During this time a particularly violent faction known as the *sicarii* began to spread throughout the province, assassinating anyone they believed supported the Roman administration, including the high priest Jonathan, whom they murdered as he officiated in the temple.[68] Besides the sicarii, false prophets attempted to incite a revolt against the Romans by leading large groups of Jews into the desert, where they claimed God would reveal to them the signs of their freedom. Felix regarded such religious groups as insurrectionists and sent Roman soldiers to forcibly disperse their gatherings and execute the so-called prophets.[69]

The imprisonment of the apostle Paul in Caesarea Maritima, described in Acts 23–24, took place toward the end of Felix's administration. Perhaps because of Felix's scandalous personal life and corrupt administration, Paul found it prudent to teach the unjust procurator of "righteousness, temperance, and judgment to come" (Acts 24:25). Despite Paul's powerful message, Felix desired a bribe in exchange for the apostle's release; because Paul refused to bribe the Roman governor, he remained in prison for the remainder of Felix's rule (24:26–27). When Felix's replacement, Porcius Festus, arrived in ca. AD 60, the new procurator deemed it wise to review Paul's case himself. Herod Agrippa II, who had risen to some prominence in the years since his father's passing,[70] requested permission to participate in the investigation as well, although it is unclear if he was involved in an official capacity or simply to satisfy his own curiosity (25:22). After Festus and Agrippa II had thoroughly questioned Paul, both declared that the apostle had done "nothing worthy of death or of bonds" (26:31). But Festus was not able to acquit Paul of any wrongdoing because by this time the apostle had exercised his right as a Roman citizen to plead his case before the emperor, effectively removing the case from Festus's jurisdiction.

After only two years in office, Festus died suddenly and was replaced by Albinus in ca. AD 62, and according to Josephus "there was no form of wickedness which he omitted."[71] Allegedly more concerned with making a profit than governing the province, Albinus instituted a policy that allowed imprisoned criminals to be set free provided an appropriate ransom was paid to the procurator.[72] Because of Albinus's refusal to punish those who violated the law, Josephus states that bandits and sicarii wreaked havoc throughout the province.[73]

The situation only grew worse when Gessius Florus became procurator of Judea in AD 64; Josephus observed that Florus's administration was so corrupt that Albinus seemed "a most excellent man by comparison."[74] According to the Jewish historian, Florus made no effort to conceal his corruption, going so far as offering the plunderers and robbers of the province protection provided they gave him a portion of the spoils.[75] Consequently, Florus's tenure proved to be the straw that broke the camel's back. Unwilling to tolerate these abuses any longer, the Jewish people revolted against Rome in AD 66, "thinking it was better to be destroyed quickly [by revolting] than be destroyed little by little [under Roman governors]."[76]

Conclusion

The writings of the New Testament cannot be fully grasped without understanding the political tension that existed between the Jews and the Romans during the first half of the first century. Rather than being founded in a vacuum, the Christian movement emerged from a preexisting political climate that the Savior and his apostles had to navigate as they established his church. The dynamic and often chaotic political atmosphere of first-century Judea contextualizes the New Testament and sheds light on the motivations of those portrayed in it. Whether clarifying how the Savior's original audience understood his words "Render therefore unto Caesar the things which are Caesar's" (Matthew 22:21; see Mark 12:17; Luke 20:25) or explaining how he could be condemned to die by a governor who believed he had done nothing worthy of death, the New Testament narrative cannot be separated from the political climate of the time without losing important background information. The political turmoil of Roman-ruled Judea was the nutrient-rich soil in which the church of Christ took root. As cultures clashed and the future of Judea became increasingly uncertain, the gospel of Jesus Christ became a beacon of hope for thousands of faithful Christians who, even in these trying circumstances, felt "peace, from him which is, and which was, and which is to come" (Revelation 1:4).

❧

Michael R. Trotter is a doctoral student of Christianity in antiquity at the Department of Theological Studies at Saint Louis University.

Further Reading

Huntsman, Eric D. "The Roman World Outside Judea." In *The Life and Teachings of the New Testament Apostles: From the Day of Pentecost Through the Apocalypse*, edited by Richard Neitzel Holzapfel and Thomas A. Wayment, 97–116. Salt Lake City: Deseret Book, 2010. This article gives a useful overview of provinces in the Roman Empire. In addition to discussing the Roman administrative system of first-century Judea, Huntsman illustrates how the Roman provincial system influenced the ministry of the apostle Paul as Christianity spread beyond the borders of Judea.

Pike, Dana M. "Before the Jewish Authorities." In *From the Last Supper Through the Resurrection*, ed. Richard Neitzel Holzapfel and Thomas A. Wayment, 210–68. Vol. 3 of *The Life and Teachings of Jesus Christ*. Salt Lake City: Deseret Book, 2003. Pike provides an in-depth analysis of Jesus's appearance before the Jewish authorities on the night of his arrest as described in the Gospels. The relationship between the Jewish authorities and the Roman governor of Judea is discussed at length, and relevant scholarly approaches to the topic are included.

Richardson, Peter. *Herod: King of the Jews and Friend of the Romans*. Minneapolis: Fortress, 1999. As a biography of Herod the Great, this book discusses the career and personal life of the Judean king in detail. Although Herod is the primary subject of the book, Richardson also provides a useful overview of client kingdoms in the Roman Empire as well as an in-depth discussion of the New Testament portrayals of Herod and his sons.

Schürer, Emil. *The History of the Jewish People in the Age of Christ (175 B.C.–A.D. 135)*. Revised and edited by Geza Vermes, Fergus Millar, and Matthew Black. 4 vols. Edinburgh, Scotland: Bloomsbury, 1973. This work provides an in-depth discussion of religious and political affairs in Judea from the rise of the Hasmonean dynasty in the second century BC to the Bar Kokhba revolt in the second century AD. Although this work goes far beyond the time frame of the New Testament, it includes a detailed summary of the interactions between the Jews and Romans before the Jewish Revolt in ca. AD 70 that is helpful in reconstructing the political context of the New Testament.

Notes

1. Although the KJV translates the word κῆνσον as "tribute," the term is better translated as "taxes." See Walter Bauer, *A Greek-English Lexicon of the New Testament and Other Early Christian Literature*, 3rd ed., ed. and trans. Frederick William Danker (Chicago: University of Chicago Press, 2000), 542.
2. See Flavius Josephus, *Jewish Antiquities* 14.14.4–5 (381–389); and *Jewish War* 1.14.4 (282–285).
3. Some ancient historians disagree on the specific territories Herod initially received from Rome; for a brief discussion of these disagreements, see Peter Richardson, *Herod: King of the Jews and Friend of the Romans* (Minneapolis: Fortress Press, 1999), 131.
4. See Josephus, *Antiquities* 15.6.7 (195), 15.7.3 (217); and *Jewish War* 1.20.3 (396).
5. For a more detailed discussion of client kings, see David C. Braund, "Client Kings," in *The Oxford Classical Dictionary*, 3rd ed., ed. Simon Hornblower and Antony Spawforth (Oxford: Oxford University Press, 1996), 348–49.
6. The KJV translates the word ἀπογράφεσθαι as "to be taxed"; however, the word literally means "to be registered [for a tax]" (Bauer, *Greek-English Lexicon*, 108). Thus, Luke seems to be describing a census that was taken in preparation for collecting taxes.
7. See Emil Schürer, *The History of the Jewish People in the Age of Christ (175 B.C.–A.D. 135)*, rev. and ed. Geza Vermes and Fergus Millar (Edinburgh, Scotland: Bloomsbury, 1973), 1:399–427. All attempts to connect this census with the birth of Jesus have failed because Joseph and Mary lived in Galilee and "there was no moment in the lifetime of Jesus when Roman tribute was raised in Galilee, which was part of the tetrarchy [i.e., client kingdom] of Herodes Antipas" and therefore not part of the Roman Empire. See Fergus Millar, *The Roman Near East 31 B.C.–A.D. 337* (Cambridge, MA: Harvard University Press, 1993), 46.
8. See Josephus, *Antiquities* 15.8.5 (292–298), 15.9.6 (331–341); and *Jewish War* 1.21.2 (403), 1.21.5–8 (408–415); compare Pliny the Elder, *Natural History* 5.14.
9. See Josephus, *Jewish War* 1.21.11 (424).
10. See Schürer, *History of the Jewish People*, 1:312.
11. See Josephus, *Antiquities* 15.11.1–7 (380–424); and *Jewish War* 1.21.1 (401); compare Schürer, *History of the Jewish People*, 1:311–13.
12. Schürer, *History of the Jewish People*, 1:308; compare Babylonian Talmud Sukkah, 51b; and Baba Batra, 4a.
13. Josephus, *Antiquities* 15.8.1 (268).
14. See Josephus, *Antiquities* 17.6.2 (151).
15. See, for example, Richardson, *King of the Jews*, 295–98; Jan Willem van Henten, "Matthew 2:16 and Josephus' Portrayals of Herod," in *Jesus, Paul, and Early Christianity: Studies in Honour of Henk Jan de Jonge*, ed. Rieuwerd Buitenwerf, Harm W. Hollander, and Johannes Tromp (Leiden, Netherlands: Koninklijke Brill NV, 2008), 101–21; and Geza Vermes, *The True Herod* (New York: Bloomsbury, 2014), 42.
16. See Josephus, *Antiquities* 15.3.3 (51–55); and *Jewish War* 1.22.2 (437).
17. See Josephus, *Antiquities* 16.11.2–7 (361–394), 17.7.1 (184–187); and *Jewish War* 1.27.2–6 (538–551), 1.32.1–5 (622–640), 1.33.7 (663–664).
18. Josephus, *Antiquities* 17.6.5 (174–179); and *Jewish War* 33.6 (659–660).
19. For more on the distinctions between ethnarchs and tetrarchs in the Roman Empire, see Schürer, *History of the Jewish People*, 1:333–34.
20. Josephus, *Antiquities* 17.11.4 (317–320); and *Jewish War* 2.6.3 (94–97).
21. Josephus, *Antiquities* 17.13.2 (342); compare *Jewish War* 2.7.3 (111).
22. See Josephus, *Antiquities* 17.13.2 (343–344); and *Jewish War* 2.7.3 (111).

23. There was some confusion among ancient authors about whether Judea was a distinct province or whether it was part of the province of Syria. For example, Josephus, in *Antiquities* 18.1.1, states that Judea was added to the province of Syria. Schürer has shown this statement to be inaccurate, however, by pointing out that Judea was governed by its own prefect and that the Syrian legate could interfere with Judean affairs only in times of extreme difficulty (*History of the Jewish People*, 1:357–61).

24. See H. F. Jolowicz and Barry Nicholas, *Historical Introduction to the Study of Roman Law*, 3rd ed. (Cambridge: Cambridge University Press, 1972), 67.

25. See Peter Garnsey, "The Criminal Jurisdiction of Governors," in *Journal of Roman Studies* 58 (1968): 51–59.

26. The taxes imposed on Judea by the Romans should not be confused with the customs that were exacted by collection agents known as publicans. In client kingdoms and provinces alike, customs were collected at every territorial border by publicans who leased the right to collect them from the client king or governor in exchange for an agreed-upon amount of money. Should a publican's revenue exceed the amount of the payment stipulated in the lease, he was entitled to keep the excess; however, if a publican collected less than the agreed-upon amount, he was responsible to pay the difference. Because publicans' livelihoods depended on the amount of money they collected from travelers, they were commonly considered corrupt and were notorious for their unethical practices. It was for this reason that Jesus was criticized for eating with "publicans and sinners" (Mark 2:16). By the time Judea became a Roman province in AD 6, taxes were collected by Roman officials while customs continued to be collected by publicans (see Schürer, *History of the Jewish People*, 1:375). Although many Jews despised paying customs because of the corrupt tactics associated with publicans, the payment of customs did not seem to inspire the same anti-Roman sentiment that the payment of taxes did. For more on the differences between tax and customs collections in Judea, see Schürer, *History of the Jewish People*, 1:373–76.

27. See Schürer, *History of the Jewish People*, 1:401–2.

28. The temple tax was an annual half-shekel payment required of every male Israelite over the age of twenty. The tax was first revealed to Moses during the children of Israel's forty-year sojourn in the wilderness for the intended purpose of maintaining the tabernacle and later the Jerusalem temple (Exodus 30:11–16). Because it was commanded in the law of Moses, the payment of the temple tax was considered a sacred duty and was required of all Jewish males who were of age regardless of their geographical proximity to Jerusalem and the temple. Josephus recounts how the Jewish men of the city of Nisibis in Mesopotamia collected the temple tax locally before sending it to Jerusalem under the care of armed guards (*Antiquities* 18.9.1 [312–313]). For more on the temple tax, see Schürer, *History of the Jewish People*, 2:271–72.

29. See Josephus, *Against Apion* 2.77; and Philo of Alexandria, *On the Embassy to Gaius* 23 (157), 40 (317).

30. See Josephus, *Antiquities* 18.3.1 (55–59); and *Jewish War* 2.9.2–3 (169–174).

31. See Josephus, *Antiquities* 18.5.3 (120–122).

32. For more on the judicial practices of Judea from AD 6 to 41, see Schürer, *History of the Jewish People*, 1:376–78.

33. Schürer, *History of the Jewish People*, 1:378.

34. Josephus, *Antiquities* 18.1.1 (6); compare *Jewish War* 2.8.2 (118).

35. While the Zealots would later play a critical role in inciting the Jewish Revolt against Rome in AD 66, it is unknown how active the party was in Judea and Galilee during the ministry of Jesus. Luke 6:15 identifies one of Jesus's apostles as "Simon called Zelotes," which might be better translated as "Simon who is called a Zealot." It is not clear whether this means Simon was a member of the Zealot political party, however, because Matthew 10:4 and Mark 3:18 call Simon a "Canaanite," which is the Greek transliteration of the Aramaic word *qanā'nā*, meaning "enthusiast." Although it is possible that Luke 6:15 is referring to the Zealot political party, it is also possible that the verse is describing the zeal or enthusiasm with which Simon lived. See Eric D. Huntsman, "Galilee and the Call of the Twelve Apostles," in *The Life and Teachings of Jesus Christ*, ed. Richard Neitzel Holzapfel and Thomas A. Wayment, vol. 1, *From Bethlehem Through the Sermon on the Mount* (Salt Lake City: Deseret Book, 2005), 227.

36. Josephus, *Antiquities* 18.1.6 (23).

37. For a detailed discussion of the differences between the Gospel accounts of Jesus's appearance before the Jewish authorities, see Dana M. Pike, "Before the Jewish authorities," in Holzapfel and Wayment, *Life and Teachings of Jesus Christ*, vol. 3, *From the Last Supper Through the Resurrection* (Salt Lake City: Deseret Book, 2003), 214–26.

38. See Josephus, *Antiquities* 18.2.1 (26), 18.2.2 (34).

39. In connection with John 18:19 ("The high priest then asked Jesus of his disciples, and of his doctrine") some confusion exists as to whether Jesus was interrogated by Annas, the former high priest, or by Caiaphas, the high priest at the time. See, for example, James E. Talmage, *Jesus the Christ: A Study of the Messiah and His Mission according to Holy Scriptures both Ancient and Modern* (Salt Lake City: Deseret Book, 1981), 622, 643–44. John 18:24, however, states, "Now Annas had sent him bound unto Caiaphas the high priest." The Greek particle *oun*, which the KJV translates as "Now," denotes the continuation of a narrative and is better translated here as "Then" (Bauer, *A Greek-English Lexicon*, 736), making it clear that Annas was the one speaking to Jesus.

40. For a brief overview of the theories scholars have employed to reconcile the differences in the Gospel accounts of Jesus's appearance before the Jewish authorities, see Pike, "Before the Jewish authorities," 224–25.

41. Talmage, *Jesus the Christ*, 627.

42. Josephus, *Jewish War* 2.8.1 (117).

43. Josephus, *Antiquities* 20.9.1 (200).

44. Josephus, *Antiquities* 20.9.1 (202).

45. It is unclear, however, how closely Jewish leaders followed this law. Some evidence in the New Testament suggests they sometimes carried out death sentences without seeking Roman approval. For example, John 8:1–11 recounts how Jesus saved the life of an adulterous woman whom the scribes and Pharisees were about to stone to death. Although many scholars believe this story is almost certainly a later interpolation (e.g., Bruce M. Metzger and Bart D. Ehrman, *The Text of the New Testament: Its Transmission, Corruption, and Restoration*, 4th ed. [Oxford: Oxford University Press, 2005], 319–21), it nevertheless seems to preserve an earlier tradition that Jewish leaders at least occasionally attempted to carry out capital punishment. Additionally, Stephen was tried before a judiciary council presided over by the high priest and was stoned to death by those present (Acts 6:11–7:60). Since there is no evidence in the text or otherwise suggesting that Stephen's execution had received prior Roman approval, it is reasonable to assume that those who carried out the sentence did not obtain Roman permission first. Although some scholars have explained these inflictions of capital punishment by Jewish leaders as lynchings or actions that were not officially sanctioned by law (see Raymond Brown, *The Death of the Messiah: From Gethsemane to the Grave* [New York: Doubleday, 1994], 1:369–71), it is evident that Jewish leaders possessed means of inflicting the death penalty without Roman approval, even if those means were not technically legal.

46. See Josephus, *Antiquities* 18.3.1–2 (55–62); *Jewish War* 2.9.2–4 (169–177); and Philo, *On the Embassy to Gaius* 38 (299–305).

47. See Josephus, *Antiquities* 18.4.1–2 (85–89).

48. See Josephus, *Antiquities* 18.6.6–7 (179–204); and *Jewish War* 2.9.5 (178–180).

49. See Josephus, *Antiquities* 18.6.10 (237); and *Jewish War* 2.9.6 (181).

50. See Josephus, *Antiquities* 18.7.1–2 (240–252); and *Jewish War* 2.9.6 (181–183).

51. See Josephus, *Antiquities* 19.4.1–6 (236–273); and *Jewish War* 2.11.2–5 (206–214).

52. See Josephus, *Antiquities* 19.5.1 (274–275); *Jewish War* 2.11.5 (215–216); and Dio Cassius, *Roman History* 60.8.2–3.

53. Josephus, *Antiquities* 19.7.3 (331).

54. See Philo, *On the Embassy to Gaius* 36–42 (276–333); and Josephus, *Antiquities* 18.8.7–8 (289–302).

55. See Eusebius, *Ecclesiastical History* 2.10.

56. Josephus gives an account of Agrippa's death that differs from the description given in Acts in some key details. In Josephus's account the crowd mistook Agrippa for a god because his royal robe illuminated in the sunlight. An owl then appeared above him as a divine omen that God was displeased with him for not

correcting the crowd's erroneous proclamation. Herod then became violently ill and died in agony five days later (*Antiquities* 19.8.2 [343–350]). Although Josephus's account disagrees with Acts 12:20–23 on the details of Agrippa's death, both agree on a general narrative: Agrippa addresses the crowd and is mistaken for a god, a divine manifestation appears when he does not correct the crowd, and he is immediately struck down with a divinely inspired illness that results in his death.

57. See Josephus, *Antiquities* 20.1.1–2 (6–14).

58. See Josephus, *Antiquities* 20.5.3 (108); and *Jewish War* 2.12.1 (224).

59. The number of Jews who perished is unknown; in *Jewish War* 2.12.1 (227) Josephus states that more than thirty thousand Jews died, while in *Antiquities* 20.5.3 (112) he puts the number at twenty thousand.

60. See Josephus, *Antiquities* 20.5.3 (109–112); and *Jewish War* 2.12.1 (224–227).

61. See Josephus, *Antiquities* 20.5.4 (115), and *Jewish War* 2.12.2 (229).

62. See Josephus, *Antiquities* 20.5.4 (116–117); and *Jewish War* 2.12.2 (230–231).

63. See Josephus, *Antiquities* 20.6.1 (119).

64. See Josephus, *Antiquities* 20.6.1 (120–122); and *Jewish War* 2.12.3–5 (232–236).

65. See Josephus, *Antiquities* 20.6.2–3 (125–136); and *Jewish War* 2.12.5–7 (238–246).

66. While Josephus states that Felix was Cumanus's successor, Tacitus, in *Annals* 12.54, suggests that Cumanus served as procurator of Galilee at the same time Felix was procurator over Samaria and Judea. For a detailed discussion of the differing accounts, see Schürer, *History of the Jewish People*, 1:459–60.

67. Tacitus, *Annals* 12.54.

68. See Josephus, *Antiquities* 20.8.5 (162–165); and *Jewish War* 2.13.3 (254–257).

69. See Josephus, *Antiquities* 20.8.6 (167–168); and *Jewish War* 2.13.4 (258–260). Paul was mistakenly accused of being one of these false prophets in Acts 21:38.

70. Although Agrippa II had been deemed too young to inherit Agrippa I's kingdom at the time of his father's death, he went on to enjoy a relatively prosperous career in the decades that followed. Having successfully ingratiated himself with several powerful figures in Rome, Agrippa II was initially awarded some smaller territories in his father's former kingdom. When Herod of Chalcis died in ca. AD 50, his territory and administrative powers were given to Agrippa II by the emperor Claudius, including the authority to appoint the high priest of Jerusalem, which had previously been given to Herod of Chalcis after Fadus was deemed unfit to retain possession of the high priest's vestments (see Josephus, *Antiquities* 20.1.3 [15], 20.5.2 [104]). In AD 53 Agrippa II gave up the territory of Chalcis in exchange for being put over the larger territories of Batanaea, Trachonitis, Gaulanitis, and Abila (see Josephus, *Antiquities* 20.7.1 [138]; and *Jewish War* 2.12.1 [223]). Following the death of Claudius in AD 54, the emperor Nero augmented Agrippa II's territory further by awarding him a portion of Galilee containing the important cities of Tiberius and Tarichea, as well as a portion of Perea containing the city of Julias and its fourteen surrounding villages (see Josephus, *Antiquities* 20.8.4 [158–159]; and *Jewish War* 2.13.2 [252]).

71. Josephus, *Jewish War* 2.14.1 (272).

72. See Josephus, *Jewish War* 2.14.1 (273).

73. See Josephus, *Antiquities* 20.9.3 (208–210); and *Jewish War* 2.14.1 (274–276).

74. See Josephus, *Jewish War* 2.14.2 (277).

75. See Josephus, *Antiquities* 20.11.1 (255); and *Jewish War* 2.14.2 (278).

76. Josephus, *Antiquities* 20.11.1 (257).

10

Roman Law Relating to the New Testament

John W. Welch

Behind the events and teachings presented in every book of the New Testament stand three large cultural, political, and legal worlds—Jewish, Greek, and Roman. Several conspicuous Roman names and Latin expressions in the New Testament—including *Rome, Romans, Caesar Augustus, Tiberius, Pilate, mile, centurion, denarius, kodrantēs* (*quadrans,* or mite)—alert readers that in the background of just about every public institution or legal encounter in the world of Jesus and his disciples stood Roman laws, Roman order, Roman authorities, and Roman civilization. Although Roman law is not overtly mentioned or applicable in much of the New Testament, some awareness of Roman culture, religion, politics, and law is essential in order to understand the daily life of people in the worlds of the New Testament.[1]

Certain Roman legal rules and conventions figure significantly in New Testament texts. But because all ancient civilizations ordinarily faced similar problems of family and economic life, their laws often addressed common legal problems in comparable ways. Thus, one should not assume that Jewish, Greek, or Roman laws always differed markedly from one another. While drawing attention to certain similarities, this chapter will emphasize legal regulations or practices that are characteristically Roman, highlighting what set Roman and Jewish law apart.

Roman Values and the Law

Roman jurisprudential values emphasized practicality, empire, and security of wealth and position. In Latin the main word for "law" is *lex* (derived from the verb *lego*, "I read" or "I select"), and thus Roman law fundamentally pertained to written materials to be read and used as practical administrative and economic tools.[2] In this sense, for both the Romans and the Jewish Sadducees, law was based in written texts or published decrees read aloud at public convocations, although not all Jews saw the law exactly that way, such as the Jewish Pharisees, who embraced the wider range of law including traditional oral interpretations.

The Romans, Greeks, and virtually all ancient peoples believed in their pantheons of deities, seeing their main gods, such as Jupiter or Zeus, as the source of justice and law. The Jews likewise saw their god, Jehovah, as the author and revealer of their scriptural bodies of law. Their preeminent word for "law," *torah*, was linguistically connected with the idea of God's teaching and instruction. Their laws zealously protected their unique worship of a single god and guarded their distinctive religious and temple practices.

Romans were known for their pragmatism. The originality of ideas was often less important than their utility, whatever the source; they readily borrowed architecture, art, and language from the Etruscans, the Greeks, or other peoples. For example, mastering the enormously practical use of the Etruscan arch allowed Romans to build aqueducts, bridges over major rivers, and large domed public buildings. Effective city planning and the building of amphitheaters, marketplaces, forums, roads, chariots, armor, tools, and equipment brought political peace and prosperity throughout the Mediterranean world, allowing Roman law to dominate for about five centuries. To promote and maintain that stability, Roman administrators and lawyers were pragmatically accommodating, allowing considerable latitude to conquered or allied peoples—notably the Jews in the first century—to govern themselves, but only so long as they participated in the economic life of the empire (especially paying taxes, tributes, and tolls) and caused little trouble.

Before the New Testament era, the Roman Empire established a provincial system—a type of federalized government—headquartered and normally expertly administered by a central imperial government and efficiently managed by legates and governors in the various provinces. Smooth administration of the Roman Empire grew out of Rome's ancient Twelve Tables of the Law and ultimately resulted in a very sophisticated body of law codes that enshrined thousands of rules of Roman law that provided uniformity and regularity throughout the empire and for centuries in Europe thereafter.[3] The Roman genius for organization and executive efficiency is manifested no better than in the Roman army, with its legions divided into "centuries" of up to one hundred soldiers each. The ability of these units to move adroitly in three flanks of soldiers allowed these highly trained Roman forces to dominate less organized battle formations of opponents or insurgents. In the New Testament centurions are mentioned as being present in Capernaum, Caesarea, and Jerusalem. Their presence supported a baseline of law and order.

In civic life the empire engendered enormous respect among the Romans. Duty to one's country was the apex of good citizenship, the empire being called "the common parent of us all, than which nothing can be greater or sweeter."[4] Jewish jurisprudence also celebrated community and central ethnic values but, above all, God, with a main emphasis on preserving Jewish religious uniqueness.[5] The Roman emphasis on community and empire was in marked contrast to the Greeks, who prized individuality and liberty.

The Roman system of governance created and protected enormous fortunes in the hands of a few aristocrats. Entrenched networks of patrons and their clients created and reentrenched lifelong senators, indomitable coalitions, vast agricultural estates, and family power brokers. Even more than in Greece, Roman civilization, military power, and economic infrastructure were built on the backs of slaves, some of whom were treated well but most of whom were captives of war or the victims of other misfortunes of life. Slavery was a very conspicuous and common part of Roman life and throughout the ancient world, except among the Jews, whose law prohibited one Jew from holding another Jew as a slave for more than six years. Modern estimates suggest that between two and three million slaves lived in Italy alone during New Testament times.[6] Slaves performed a wide array of jobs, and they were considered the absolute property under the strict control of the head of the household. Roman slaves could be subjected to the worst of conditions and were exposed to inhumane punishments with impunity. To be sure, some were well educated and could be treated well, even saving enough personal money to buy their own freedom. But as long as they were slaves, they had no legal rights or recourse.

Fundamentally, Jews and early Christians found themselves at odds with several cultural and legal values of the Romans (and Greeks), although they were not in a position to dramatically change the public order. For example, injured slaves in the Jewish world were granted freedom (Exodus 21:26–27), and the New Testament required masters and slaves to treat each other with kindness and obedience (1 Peter 2:13–18). The apostle Paul admonished all to be subject to the higher powers and rulers (Romans 13:1–7), and Christian doctrine sublimated subjection and slavery in making strong metaphorical points warning about the sinner's being enslaved by sin and about the righteous absolutely belonging to Jesus as redeemer and master.

Administrative Law

Administratively, the Roman Empire was divided into provinces, each of which was ruled by a single Roman magistrate. The most important provinces were governed directly by the emperor through his chosen legates, while less important provinces were controlled by proconsuls under the direction of the Senate. The least important provinces, such as Judea (which became a province in AD 6), were governed by a *praefectus* from the equestrian class, below the senatorial class but above the level of the ordinary plebs. The leader of these provinces was given authority from the emperor to hear and adjudicate cases involving Roman citizens and, when necessary, non-Romans.[7] Gallio in Corinth (Acts 18) and Sergius Paulus in Paphos (Acts 13) were provincial rulers who exercised such powers, and for this reason Paul (who was a Roman citizen) was brought to court before them.

Each province had a capital city that was its seat of local legal, military, and economic power. Many provincial Roman capitals are mentioned in the New Testament, including Caesarea Maritima (Judea), Antioch (Syria), Tarsus (Cilicia), Paphos (Cyprus), Ephesus (Asia), Philippi (Macedonia), and Corinth (Achaia). Other cities in the Eastern Roman Empire were of strategic, economic, or intellectual importance to the Romans (such as Athens and Alexandria). The constitutions of these cities varied widely. Some were Roman cities with typical Roman architecture and legal structures, while others were "free" cities that retained their own constitutions, enjoyed certain tax exemptions and other privileges, and preserved their regional character while remaining part of the empire (notably Thessalonica and Corinth).[8] For many reasons Paul's missionary journeys largely focused on these powerful cities. As a Roman citizen, he knew his way around these places, he was respected and protected there, and from those legal centers his influence could reach far and wide.

In each of these provincial capitals, interactions with Roman law figure prominently in the New Testament. In Caesarea, Paul exercised his legal right to appeal in person to the Roman emperor (Acts 23–27). In Antioch, the Christians were for the first time called Christians, which may reflect a legal recognition of the church by the provincial governor of Syria as a legally constituted society (Acts 11:26). In Paphos, the Roman governor Sergius Paulus brought Paul into a legal hearing regarding the conduct of a magician (Acts 13:6–12), for not only was the regulation of magic and divination of great concern to the Romans, but under Jewish law as well all members of the Sanhedrin and legal experts were expected to be able to distinguish between acceptable practices of divination or wonder-working from conduct that ran contrary to the public order.[9] In Philippi, Paul was arrested under Roman law for interfering with the business of a man in the Roman forum who was there selling the fortune-telling services of a girl, perhaps a devotee of Apollo, the Roman god of revelation (Acts 16:16–40). In Thessalonica, Paul was taken before a Roman tribunal and accused of leading people to believe in gods other than those normally approved by Roman law, which may mean that Paul's teachings were seen as degrading the Roman imperial cult (Acts 17:5–9). In Corinth, Paul prevailed against his Jewish accusers when the governor Gallio refused to take jurisdiction over their Jewish complaints under Roman law (Acts 18:1–18). In Ephesus, Roman law permitted and local authorities oversaw the burning of illegal books of magic after Paul had exposed the workings of the sons of Sceva (Acts 19:13–19).

Roman Judea

Although Jerusalem was not the Roman capital of Judea, Roman power and pressures were also strongly felt and exercised there.[10] In the east generally, Rome faced a complex situation during the early first century, with the Parthians, Nabateans, and others standing as possible competitors if not actual intruders or invaders. At the time of Jesus, Rome had not yet pushed into the Euphrates Valley or into the lower Danube and Dacia, and in Syria and along the vulnerable eastern Mediterranean coast, Rome adopted a general practice of forming alliances with local rulers as client kings, such as King Agrippa (Acts 26). While Rome was always the dominant party in these alliances, the local rulers were given a high degree of autonomy but also were held strictly accountable. Lacking the manpower to manage this area, the Romans left the administration of the region largely in the hands of local authorities who could rely on Roman power to back them up. This system was used for over a century.

Whenever a local leader failed to control the population and satisfactorily keep the peace, Rome would break off that relationship and form a new alliance, as it did when the Parthians invaded Jerusalem: Hyrcanus, who had been installed as high priest by Pompey, was removed; and with Roman aid Herod reconquered Judea, was given the title of King of the Jews by the Romans, and soon ruled a fairly substantial and important client state. These client kings were seen more as allies or "friends" than as subjected subservients, as the word *philoi*, used in designating these treaty partners, indicates (see, for example, Luke 23:12).[11]

At the opening of the New Testament, Judea and Galilee were under the rule of Herod the Great as parts of a single kingdom. Herod was a Roman citizen and was under the control of the emperor, Augustus Caesar. So long as Herod kept order in his kingdom, remained loyal to Rome, and provided a buffer against enemy states, he remained in control of his client state. But after Herod's death, the kingdom of Judea was divided by Rome into three tetrarchies ruled by three of Herod's sons—Archelaus (over Judea), Herod Antipas (over Galilee and Perea), and Philip (over the northern area east of the Jordan). In the north, Herod Antipas remained in control of the Galilee during the entire lifetime of Jesus; but in the south, not long after taking power over Judea, Archelaus was removed by Augustus because of complaints about his rule in AD 6. The fear expressed by Caiaphas and the Jewish leaders—that the Romans would remove them from their positions of power and take away their "place" if they did not restrain the wonder-workings of Jesus (John 11:48)—was obviously based in real-life political experiences.

Soon Judea came under the full control of Rome as an imperial province controlled by a *praefectus*, as noted earlier. Pontius Pilate was one such equestrian prefect, sent to Judea to rule in ca. AD 26. While Judea was not as large as many other Roman provinces, it was territorially crucial enough to justify specific Roman attention.[12] Pilate mostly allowed the Jewish leaders to govern the Jewish people. He interfered—sometimes violently (Luke 13:1)—only when Jewish dissidents became unruly or when Roman citizens were adversely affected.

Apart from a brief interlude when Herod Agrippa was installed as its local king (AD 41–44), Judea remained, until the outbreak of the Jewish War in AD 66, under the control of equestrian prefects or procurators, including Felix and Festus, before whom the apostle Paul would appear after he was taken into protective custody in the temple precinct by Roman guards stationed in the Antonia Fortress. Being a Roman citizen, Paul was transferred to Caesarea, the provincial headquarters, for legal hearings in the Roman palace there as certain Jews brought legal complaints against him (Acts 21–25).

Roman Citizenship

Perhaps the most powerful legal words in New Testament times were "I am a Roman citizen." During the time of Paul, it is estimated that only 1 or 2 percent of the population in the eastern Mediterranean world under Roman control enjoyed the distinctively powerful status of Roman citizenship.[13] Because noncitizens had no claim on rights or protections from Rome, citizenship was highly coveted. A Roman citizen had access to and was under the protection of Roman law. Citizenship entailed special rights and privileges, including public rights of voting and serving in public office, private rights of being a party in a lawsuit and of marriage that granted citizenship to one's children, and property rights of making a will, transferring property, or entering into contracts.[14] Roman citizens at this time were also exempted from poll taxes, physical abuse during interrogation, corporal punishment without trial, and the more excruciating forms of capital punishment (such as crucifixion or exposure to wild beasts). They also had the right to be represented by an advocate and to appeal to the emperor in person concerning any capital charges against them.[15] Almost all Jews—along with all other noncitizens—in the early Christian era were precluded from any of these legal benefits.

In the first century, Roman citizenship could be inherited, received as a result of great service to the empire or emperor, or obtained by favoritism. Paul was a Roman citizen by birth, which tells us that at least one of his ancestors received Roman citizenship before Paul was born. In his family were tentmakers, a profession whose members made many important heavy-cloth items such as army tents, ship sails, store awnings, grain sacks, and canopies for theaters or athletic games. Scholars speculate that Paul's father may have helped supply Romans during their military campaigns in Cilicia near Tarsus (Paul's hometown) and was therefore rewarded with the highly coveted status of Roman citizenship.[16]

Paul utilized his citizenship at crucial moments during his life. After being imprisoned in Philippi, he used his Roman citizenship to get local magistrates to publicly apologize for holding him without a proper trial (Acts 16:35–39). When the Sanhedrin plotted to kill Paul and brought charges against him, Felix, the Roman governor, protected Paul (Acts 23). After two years, Paul exercised his legal right as a citizen to require Festus, the new governor, to send him to Rome to appeal his case before the emperor himself (Acts 25:10–12). Understanding the enviable powers and privileges of Roman citizenship, Paul's readers would have been impressed when he declared them to be "fellowcitizens with the saints, and of the household of God" (Ephesians 2:19).[17]

Being a Roman citizen facilitated Paul's many travels. He made free use of Roman roads, ports, protections, facilities, and currency. Paul is estimated to have traveled nearly ten thousand miles during his missionary journeys.[18] Throughout the Roman Empire generally, people traveled extensively by both land and sea. Such vast legal and practical freedom of travel would not be known again until much later in European history.[19] Although Roman toll collectors sat in customhouses to collect tolls from travelers and levy tariffs on goods being transported into and out of different areas, as a Roman citizen, Paul could pass those toll stations without charge. As a Roman citizen, he also could transport money across provincial boundaries to support the church in Judea and elsewhere. In towns, travelers usually stayed with relatives or friends who legally vouched for them (as seen in Paul's travels in Acts 16:12–15; 17:5; 21:16; 28:7, 14), though roadside inns and way stations were used outside of towns. For practical reasons, many of Paul's missionary activities occurred in homes in cities along major roadways.[20]

Family Law

Marriage and family laws were important in all ancient civilizations. Every Roman was expected to marry and produce children. Men normally married in their late twenties, women in their mid-to-late teens. Legally, a Roman marriage was an agreement that the couple entered into in front of their family—some of whom served as witnesses—and it usually included the husband presenting a ring to his new wife as a promise of fidelity.[21] The bride's family protected her by preserving her inheritance rights and giving her control over the testamentary disposition of her property. Many Roman funerary monuments reflect the hope that the married couple and family will remain together in the afterlife (see chapter 30 herein). In New Testament times, adultery was prosecuted in a public, criminal court, but the law applied only to married women, and the punishment consisted of banishment and confiscation of one-third of the woman's property.[22]

Under Jewish law, marriages were also highly valued, but in somewhat different ways. Prenuptial agreements were arranged by the mother and father of the prospective groom in negotiation with the prospective bride's family, sometimes years before the actual event. The marriage included a gift or dowry from the groom's family to the bride's family, and the marriage covenant was completed when the bride was taken into the groom's home. The entire village would be involved in the ceremony, with a social and religious leader signing the marriage contract in front of the entire village, who served as witnesses.[23] In the Old and New Testaments, the marriage relationship was legally and religiously cherished (Matthew 19:4; 1 Corinthians 11:11; Ephesians 5:25), and adultery was treated as a serious legal infraction, with both the man and the woman being held worthy of death (Deuteronomy 22:22).

Divorce was more acceptable in Roman law than in Jewish law. A Roman divorce could be "achieved without formalities, simply by a definite cessation of the common life of the consorts, initiated by common agreement or by one of them."[24] Under the law of Moses, divorce was permitted but with certain restrictions (see Deuteronomy 21:14; 22:29; 24:1–4). Jesus took a strong position, comparing divorce to adultery (unfaithfulness), except in cases of sexual infidelity of a spouse (Matthew 5:31–32). Peter and Paul used various conceptions of marriage, divorce, and remarriage in describing the faithful life of a Christian (Romans 7:1–6; 1 Corinthians 7:2–4; 11:7, 11; Ephesians 5:22–25, 33; 1 Peter 3:1–2, 5–7).

Adoption in the Roman world consisted of a person (usually a son) coming under the paternal power of a new family head and thereby inheriting all of the same rights and entitlements of natural-born children.[25] Adoption often took place for political reasons, such as to secure a successor (as with Claudius's adoption of Nero) or to preserve a family name, and adoption made the adoptee a new person in a legal sense. "This was a new birth. A new life had begun. . . . In the eyes of the law, [the adoptee] was no longer the person he had been. He was a new man."[26] Full legal adoption, however, was not used in Jewish law. In writing to the Christians in Rome, Paul used the Roman precept of adoption in an extended metaphor about redemption from sin, salvation from past fatherlessness, and the commencement of a new life, under a new name, grafted into God's household of Israel (Romans 8:12–17; 11:23).[27]

Regarding the family laws of inheritance, various complex forms of testamentary disposition were recognized. A Roman will (*testamentum*) was typically a unilateral disposition that could take effect immediately in part and then fully upon death of the testator. A *testamentum* could be changed by later versions before the death of the testator.[28] A Jewish will (*matenat bari*) irrevocably transferred immediate use of property to a beneficiary, but full ownership passed only on the death of the donor.[29] Powers of heirs over their future interests could be limited by rights of the father during his lifetime, and some wills made in anticipation of death were revocable upon the testator's recovery. Lifetime gifts to some heirs could sometimes preclude them from a later share in the father's estate, a situation potentially at play in Jesus's parable of the prodigal son.[30] Paul may have had either Jewish, Greek, or Roman laws in mind when he used the metaphor of an inheritance in comparing God's promises to Abraham concerning the blessings that would extend to his seed (as well as the Gentiles) and cannot now be annulled or amended (Galatians 3:15).

Religious Freedom

As a general rule, the Romans allowed local laws and customs to remain in place after they had conquered a people. Roman law still always ruled the day, but it allowed a good deal of latitude regarding the cultural and religious sensibilities of local individual peoples living in regions far enough away from Rome. Jews, for example, were at first exempt from the requirement to worship Roman deities so that they could keep their covenant to worship only the God of Israel. Instead of emperor worship, some Jews would offer sacrifices at the temple on behalf of (but not to) the emperor.[31] Despite this accommodation, Herod the Great built a number of temples to the emperor and sponsored the imperial cult at numerous places in Judea.[32] Also during the first century BC, because Jews had provided military help particularly to Julius Caesar and Octavian, the Julian laws exempted Jewish soldiers, who served in the Roman army as auxiliaries, from normal military duties on Sabbath days.[33]

But religious freedoms gave way when the Roman order was threatened. During New Testament times, astrologers, magicians, and followers of Egyptian religions were legally expelled from the city of Rome.[34] Worried about illegal divination activities, especially those that might incite political unrest, Tiberius required many people to leave Italy or to renounce their superstitions.[35] Outside of Italy, various popular religious groups such as the cults of Dionysus, Isis, Sarapis, and Mithras, as well as the Jews in Judea and Galilee, were allowed to operate freely. But things changed for the Jews midway through the first century AD, when some kind of disturbance led to the expulsion of Jews from Rome under the official Edict of Claudius in ca. AD 49.[36] Any broad tolerance toward the Jews ended throughout the empire with the uncontrollable outbreak of the Jewish Revolt in AD 66. In these developments, some Christians were undoubtedly caught up in the conflagrations. While problems and legal responses must have varied from one province to another, by the late first century some Roman governors executed Christians who would not deny their faith.[37] One of the reasons for this general change in religious climate was the rise of the imperial cult in the first century.

In the reign of Augustus, the first Roman emperor, during whose lifetime Jesus was born, the practice known as emperor worship began. Worshipping the emperor involved the building of temples and making sacrifices and offering prayers. Roman citizens were expected to worship the emperor (though not exclusively as the only deity).[38] Past and present emperors or their *genius* (or watchful spirit)[39] were worshipped or entreated as divinely powerful beings. This presented a serious problem for most Jews, who tenaciously held that the one true God alone should be worshipped, and also for most Christians, who believed that prayers should be offered only in the name of Jesus. At first, Jews were largely exempt from the requirement to worship the emperor, though at times this exclusivity caused serious tensions.[40] Some commentators argue that the book of Revelation should be read in light of the imperial cult and that the worshipped "beast" in chapter 13 refers to the worship of the Roman emperor.[41] A related problem came up in the debate over whether food sacrificed to idols was appropriate for Christians to consume (Acts 15:29; 1 Corinthians 8:1–11; Revelation 2:14, 20). Earlier, in Jesus's own time, serious legal debates could be easily sparked just by asking the question, What should one render unto Caesar? (see Matthew 22:21). Such "rendering [or returning] unto Caesar" could take the forms of taxes, sacrifices, prayers, or devotions, which Christians in the mid-first century were advised to accommodate (Romans 13:1–7).

Taxation

Like all other peoples, the Jews paid various taxes to the Romans and to local rulers. The most famous New Testament instance is the tax mentioned in Luke 2:1: "There went out a decree from Caesar Augustus, that all the world should be taxed." This could refer to the tax initiated by Quirinius and mentioned by Josephus (*Antiquities* 18.1.1:2–3), but such censuses were a common way to assess the tax responsibility of any area (see chapters 9 and 13 herein). Jews could expect to pay to the Romans an annual head tax for each adult male, property taxes, sales taxes, inheritance taxes, and transit tolls. Taken together, Roman imperial, regional, and local taxes, in addition to the annual temple tax and tithing requirements, could total as high as 50 percent of all production in Judea.[42] Such taxes could often prompt outcries and divisions among the Jews, sometimes becoming violent. Those who defied Roman tax collectors could pay for it with their lives (e.g., Judas the Galilean, mentioned in Acts 5:37). This, as well as the distaste for publicans or tax collectors in general, is likely the backdrop for the question posed to Jesus about taxation (Matthew 22:17; Mark 12:14; Luke

20:22). "Publicans," at least in Jerusalem, worked for the Romans as invested tax agents. Used ambiguously in the New Testament, this term can also refer to a tax collector for a local client king (like Philip in the northern Galilee). Often local cities were contracted to collect taxes that would be paid to the Roman Empire. Those in charge of such collections, called "chief" tax collectors, would work directly for the Romans (as apparently Zacchaeus did, mentioned in Luke 19:2), but their employees or assistants did not (such as those mentioned in Matthew 5:46; 9:10; 10:3).[43] Jesus's association with such people (like Zacchaeus in Luke 19:1–10) shows his willingness to mingle with people of every social station.

Business Law

As with many other facets of daily life, the legal and business worlds provided rich metaphors that were used by New Testament speakers and writers, especially the savvy apostle Paul, to teach gospel principles by way of analogy. Especially because of his Roman citizenship and educational interest in the law, Paul often drew on technical judicial concepts or legal practices to authoritatively express religious or theological points. Because Roman law provided the dominant legal norms throughout the cities and church communities among which he labored, several of his metaphors came from important areas of Roman law, especially laws from the business world.

Paul used the Roman law of guarantees (i.e., legal contracts securing a business transaction) to instruct Christians about the role of Christ as a surety, reliably binding them together as a people and also to God (2 Corinthians 1:21–22). Paul spoke of having a seal stamped by God upon a person, the use of official seals being a common administrative practice in the ancient world to indicate ownership or authorization, notably by Roman officials.[44] The business practice of an initial installment payment or down payment as a token of goodwill and firm intent was used to represent the gift of the Holy Spirit that prefigures the final full deliverance of the promised goods of salvation.[45]

Laws of indebtedness stand behind many New Testament teachings of transgression and forgiveness. People could fall into debt for a number of reasons: having too many mouths to feed, unreliable rainfall and crop yields, famines, and so on. Under Roman law, a debtor could have his money taken away against his will,[46] and if one failed to pay a debt, he could be sued or even sold into slavery. Debts were not simply monetary either. One could owe or be obliged to perform certain actions. To be a debtor involved a legal obligation to one's creditor, and violating such an obligation was more than a civil law matter; it was also punishable under criminal law. If the creditor chose to (and he was under no obligation to do so), a debtor could pay an amount other than initially owed to the creditor or perform some other service to remove the debt.[47] Or a person could buy the debt and redeem the debtor from its obligations (or impose new ones). Paul uses the concept of debt, obligation, and redemption as metaphors to explain Christ's grace and our obligations to him.[48] For those who accept only "the law," they are obliged to keep every commandment or suffer the penalties. God offers redemption from this law as an act of grace through Jesus Christ because "Christ hath redeemed us from the curse of the law" (Galatians 3:13). As a result, the Christian "owes" it to God to live according to his commandments—"we are debtors" (Romans 8:12).

Financial institutions were important in the running of the empire, not just as places to deposit or borrow money. In Roman culture, sometimes the services of a bank were fulfilled by wealthy individuals or families, who could provide loans or insure deposits. Deposits were given to a depository who would watch over the money and return it when the depositor demanded it, usually without any remuneration.[49] In some cases, deposits could earn interest in a bank or could be put to work in lucrative but risky ventures, such as financing shiploads of produce or in financing major tax-collecting responsibilities. This may be the legal backdrop for the parable of the talents in Matthew 25, where the unfaithful servant is chastised for not taking advantage of opportunities to return to his master more than was deposited with him. Amounts as large as one, two, or five talents would seem to involve major projects on a large Roman scale. A talent was not a coin but a large ingot of metal, weighing from fifty to ninety-two pounds—variations occurred from one century to another and from one land to another. One talent of gold was an enormous sum, let alone the ten-thousand-talent debt owed by the unjust steward to his lord (Matthew 18:24).[50]

In general, Roman business law did not recognize true agency, in which an agent can enter into legally binding contracts on behalf of a principal.[51] Agency risked the dilution of powers of fathers over their sons, the blurring of rights of citizens in preference to noncitizens, and the weakening of the status of free men and women over slaves. This Roman rule stood in stark contrast with the Jewish view that readily recognized agency, a legal practice that perhaps derived from the power of prophets sent as agents to speak and act for God, or from the privileges of priests acting at the temple on behalf of the people in offering atoning sacrifices. In the New Testament, apostles were literally "sent forth—*apostellō*," with authority to speak and act in the name of their principal, or master, Jesus.

A contribution of Roman law was its recognition of a number of different types of contractual arrangements. In particular, a *societas* was a contract between two or more people to invest money or goods and to share profits and losses, and the contract was formed simply through the consent of the parties.[52] The partners would share in the profits and losses equally unless they agreed that the shares would be divided in some other way (perhaps reflecting the unequal contributions of different partners).[53] Another common contract was known as the *locatio conductio*, which stipulated the type of work that a laborer would do and for what pay. Like the *societas*, it was formed by consent of the parties, but it involved no sharing of profits or losses. The laborer agreed to a wage and then performed the work, regardless of the gains for the employer or the wages given to other workers.[54] Roman laws governing funerary associations uniquely recognized the durability of these legal arrangements surviving beyond the lifetimes of their members. Such organizational provisions were useful models in shaping the legal status of early Christian communities and their collective concepts of unity and holding property or assets for the common good.

High Crimes

For the most part, Roman law allowed local rulers a fair amount of autonomy in dealing with common crimes by noncitizens. Roman law dealt with the conduct of citizens and issues concerning loyalty to the empire, but otherwise local rulers could govern in the way they saw fit. When the behaviors of noncitizens were serious enough, high crimes affecting Roman interests would be dealt with by a Roman governor or prefect, who alone had the power to hear and decide cases on behalf of the emperor, an authority known as the *cognitio extra ordinem*.[55] In Judea the Sanhedrin for the most part dealt with the crimes committed by Jewish people, though there was some legal ambiguity surrounding the scope of its jurisdiction.[56] This explains some of the confusion during the trial of Jesus, where he was brought before the Sanhedrin, Herod Antipas, and Pontius Pilate. During his missionary journeys, Paul was often tried by the rulers of cities who had the legal power to decide whether any crime was committed and then dole out a sentence. For example, Paul was brought before Gallio in the province of Achaia in Acts 18 because of his missionary activity in Corinth. Gallio had the power to decide whether any action should be taken by Roman authorities and Roman law, but he decided that the issue was an internal Jewish dispute and therefore took no jurisdiction over the matter. Paul utilized this legal distinction to his advantage during his travels, as he moved from city to city after charges had been brought against him, forcing his Jewish accusers to deal with new magistrates and differing local laws.[57]

Roman rulers took strong action against any threatening or disrespectful conduct "committed against the Roman people and its security."[58] Such matters were dealt with under the law of treason (*crimen maiestatis*). In Jesus's day, the law of *maiestas* condemned not only outright revolts or insurgencies but also treasonous conversation or expressions, the selling of a statue of the emperor for money, or "spreading slanderous stories in the army with a seditious intent," if such conduct was directed against "the deified Augustus, [his wife] Livia while she lived, and [his son] Tiberius."[59] The potential penalty for such offenses was death.[60] Mourning the death of anyone convicted of active treason was forbidden, and the name of the convict was blotted out of records and public memory under a decree of disgrace (*damnatio memoriae*).[61] In a similar fashion, the disciples of Jesus were prohibited by Jewish authorities from speaking in his name or of his memory following his death (Acts 4:17–18). The law of *maiestas* may also explain why the Jewish chief priests (wrongly) thought they could get Pilate to take action against Jesus.[62] Letting him lay a miraculous spell on the emperor or speak "against Caesar" would certainly make Pilate no friend of Caesar (John 19:12),[63] and such also would comprise an accusation of *maiestas*.[64]

Magic and sorcery were also very serious concerns of the Roman state. Under Roman law, wonder-working or having a demon spirit was a serious offense. Jewish law had similar concerns, especially when such powers were presented as signs of divine approval or as miraculous wonders that encouraged people to follow gods other than Jehovah (Exodus 22:18; Leviticus 20:27; Deuteronomy 13:1–12). In Roman law and religion, "only a king [emperor] possessed the necessary magic power . . . [due to] the rightful king's closeness to the gods," and his status "was revealed by the gods through a sign (especially through the flight of birds)."[65] In Roman legal terminology, *maleficus* is "common parlance for 'magician'"[66] and "commonly denotes a sorcerer."[67] Its Latin cognate *maleficium* (Greek *kakopoiia*) is sometimes synonymous with *magia* (magic). The practice of magic was a capital offense when "performed with an evil intention to harm or defraud another."[68] At the time of Jesus, in AD 11, certain forms of spell casting or use of supernatural powers had become punishable by death. Tacitus, Suetonius, Ulpian, and Cassius Dio confirm that foreign sorcerers (*magi*) and their confederates were executed in Rome at this time, while Roman citizens who persisted in these practices were expelled from Italy.[69] Tiberius, however, "pardoned those who petitioned him and promised that they would give up their craft."[70] Later Roman law would specify that the punishment for enchanters or spellbinders was crucifixion.[71] Such Roman and Jewish laws might stand behind the chief priests' answer to Pilate that they had found Jesus to be an evil-worker (*kakourgos* or *kakopoios*)[72] and also behind Jesus's affirmation that his realm was not a kingdom "of this world" (John 18:36).

Brigands were a third serious threat to the social order of the ancient world. More than mere thieves, these bands of robbers attacked and plundered especially the elites, often appearing during times of heavy taxation, high debt, famine, or political crisis.[73] They operated openly, violently, and often with the support and protection of poor, rural peoples. Their numbers in some cases could swell into the thousands, and they had their own codes of conduct and hideouts from which they could launch raids to disrupt local governments and commerce. Because Roman law treated them as outlaws, they could be dealt with harshly (normally executed) under martial law or with no trial at all.[74] Herod, for example, went to great lengths to kill a large and particularly disruptive group of brigands (along with their families) who were hiding in caves in the countryside.[75] The fact that such brigands were popular among some antiestablishment segments in the general population helps explain the call from some to release Barabbas the robber before the crucifixion of Jesus (John 18:40).[76]

Judicial Procedures

Actual Roman trials appear rarely, if ever, in the New Testament. Jesus admonished his followers to settle legal arguments quickly out of Roman or Herodian courts, which were typically handled by a single judge who had the power to require litigants to pay "the uttermost farthing" (*kodrantēs*, a Greek loanword for the Latin *quadrans*, Matthew 5:26). This mention of the Roman farthing in this text may be a signal to Christians to keep out of Roman courtrooms. In his parable of the persistent widow, apparently set in Galilee, Jesus praised a woman who kept entreating a judge in a city to exonerate her from her accuser (Luke 18:1–8), but the story gives no information about what judicial action this god-fearing judge (perhaps a Roman) actually took. Paul scolded church members in Corinth for going to court "before the unjust," likely the Romans (1 Corinthians 6:1), because such judicial proceedings began with libations to the Roman gods, and the oaths required of litigants and witnesses had to be sworn in the name of Roman deities, all of which would be unseemly, if not impossible, for a Jewish or Christian litigant.

Even though Paul stood in the presence of Roman authorities with judicial powers, as far as is known he never was actually tried in a Roman court. For example, in Thessalonica Paul's host Jason was taken before the "rulers of the city," who required Jason to post a security bond, whereas Paul and Silas never were tried but slipped away at night to Berea (Acts 17:5–10). Paul was accused by Sosthenes before the Roman governor Gallio in Corinth, but the cause of action was dismissed on substantive jurisdictional grounds—as not being a matter of Roman law—and then Sosthenes was beaten before Gallio's rostrum (or judicial platform, *bēma*) for having brought a legally groundless matter before the Roman magistrate (Acts 18:12–17). Hearings concerning Paul's behavior in Jerusalem were conducted by the Roman governors Felix and Festus in Caesarea, but Paul was never tried there because he petitioned that his case be removed to Rome to be heard before the emperor.

Likewise, what happened with Jesus before Pilate was more like a final sentencing hearing than an actual trial. All that happened, legally or illegally, on that occasion in the early morning before the crucifixion of Jesus Christ will probably never be known, but nothing like a normal, full Roman trial seems to have been held in Jesus's case. As far as the Jewish leaders were concerned—at least according to the Gospel of John—Caiaphas had issued a ruling of the "council" (John 11:47, *sanhedrion*) by speaking, "not of himself" (11:51) but as the high priest, that Jesus should die as a deceptive wonder-worker leading people to follow him (11:47, 50; 12:11; see Deuteronomy 13:1–12). On that occasion, a few weeks before his entry into Jerusalem, Jesus was convicted *in absentia*, in an *ex parte* proceeding suitable in abnormal, emergency cases involving robbers, traitors, or evil-workers leading people to follow other gods or ways of worship. Thus, all that remained was to plan how they would apprehend him (John 11:53, 57), along with his putative accomplice Lazarus (12:10), as well as how, when, and by whom he should be executed. Thus, when Jesus was taken from the Garden of Gethsemane to Caiaphas, there was no need for a retrial. Jesus was asked questions about his teachings and his followers and may have been given a chance to recant, which, if true, he refused. When the chief priests then took Jesus to Pilate, they apparently hoped that the Roman prefect would show deference to the Sanhedrin's decision and carry out the execution. Pilate, however, chose not to call any additional witnesses or to undertake any further judicial investigation.

Although the rowdy multitude tossed out accusations against Jesus that any Roman would have taken seriously—causing public uproar, encouraging tax evasion, and calling himself a king (Luke 23:2)—Pilate preferred not to get dragged into the fray. Instead, showing legal regard for the possible *in personem* jurisdiction that Herod Antipas, tetrarch of Galilee, might have under Roman law over the life of one of Herod Antipas's residents, Pilate sent Jesus to the Palace of Herod. Antipas, in turn, shrewdly showed his deference to Rome by not taking the case and sending Jesus back to Pilate. In this way and on that day, Antipas and Pilate become "friends" (*philoi*, Luke 23:12), the term likely referring to their thereby becoming nonmilitary, political allies under Roman law in an *amiticia foedus*.

Having already allowed a detachment of Roman soldiers to accompany the temple guards who had arrested Jesus earlier that night, Pilate allowed those combined soldiers to continue forward. They crucified Jesus, instead of Barabbas, on one of the crosses already planned by the Romans to be used that day for three outlaw robbers. Under both Roman and Jewish law, all executions were to take place publicly and without delay.[77] Crucifixion was a particularly brutal form of execution that was almost always reserved as punishment for the most serious crimes (see chapter 5 herein).[78] People condemned to crucifixion were normally beaten and then required to carry the cross upon which they would be crucified (in line with the Gospel accounts). While crucifixion is normally associated with the Romans—who used it regularly—it was apparently widespread in various forms and cultures throughout the ancient world.[79]

Attentive readers of the New Testament can see that Roman legal matters affected many social and political situations in the New Testament. In Judea, as elsewhere in the empire, Roman authorities were content to allow local populations a considerable degree of self-rule, and often Jewish and Roman practices had much in common. Where significant conflicts arose in matters involving security, the public order, or the economy, however, Roman law and authority normally took strong precedence.

***

John W. Welch, author, editor, and professor of law at Brigham Young University, has taught courses on ancient legal systems in the scriptures since 1980.

Further Reading

Borkowski, Andrew, and Paul du Plessis. *Textbook on Roman Law.* 3rd ed. Oxford: Oxford University Press, 2005.

Buss, Septimus. *Roman Law and History in the New Testament.* London: Rivingtons, 1901.

Frakes, Robert M. "Roman Law." In *Encyclopedia of the Bible and Law*, edited by Brent A. Straw, 245–56. Oxford: Oxford University Press, 2015.

Jeffers, James S. *The Greco-Roman World of the New Testament Era: Exploring the Background of Early Christianity*, 259–91. Downers Grove, IL: InterVarsity, 1999.

Nippel, Wilfried. *Public Order in Ancient Rome.* New York: Cambridge University Press, 1995.

Rapske, Brian M. "Roman Rule in Palestine." In *Encyclopedia of the Historical Jesus*, edited by Craig Evans, 523–29. New York: Routledge, 2008.

Sherwin-White, Adrian N. *Roman Society and Law in the New Testament.* Oxford: Clarendon, 1963.

Welch, John W. "Miracles, *Maleficium*, and *Maiestas* in the Trial of Jesus." In *Jesus and Archaeology*, ed. James H. Charlesworth, 349–83. Grand Rapids, MI: Eerdmans, 2006.

Welch, John W. "How Rich Was Paul? . . . And Why It Matters." In *Bountiful Harvest: Essays in Honor of S. Kent Brown*, edited by Andrew C. Skinner, D. Morgan Davis, and Carl W. Griffin, 425–53. Provo, UT: Neal A. Maxwell Institute for Religious Scholarship, 2011.

Notes

1. See generally Robert M. Frakes, "Roman Law," in *Encyclopedia of the Bible and Law*, ed. Brent A. Straw (Oxford: Oxford University Press, 2015), 245–56; and Septimus Buss, *Roman Law and History in the New Testament* (London: Rivingtons, 1901).

2. *Oxford Latin Dictionary*, s.v. "lex."

3. Andrew Borkowski and Paul du Plessis, *Textbook on Roman Law* (Oxford: Oxford University Press, 2005), 30–31.

4. M. L. Clarke, *The Roman Mind: Studies in the History of Thought from Cicero to Marcus Aurelius* (New York: Norton, 1968), 13.

5. Graydon F. Snyder, *Judaism and Christianity in First-Century Rome*, ed. Karl P. Donfried and Peter Richardson (Grand Rapids, MI: Eerdmans, 1998), 89. In a study analyzing Jewish and Christian symbols in early Rome, one finds that "according to the data available, it is clear that Jewish enculturation of Roman culture was slight."

6. David J. Williams, *Paul's Metaphors: Their Context and Character* (Peabody, MA: Hendrickson, 1999), 111.

7. See generally Wilfried Nippel, *Public Order in Ancient Rome* (New York: Cambridge University Press, 1995).

8. See further James S. Jeffers, *The Greco-Roman World of the New Testament Era: Exploring the Background of Early Christianity* (Downers Grove, IL: InterVarsity, 1999), 259–91.

9. Adolf Berger, *Encyclopedic Dictionary of Roman Law* (Philadelphia: American Philosophical Society, 1953), 572–73. See further John W. Welch, "Miracles, *Maleficium*, and *Maiestas* in the Trial of Jesus," in *Jesus and Archaeology*, ed. James H. Charlesworth (Grand Rapids, MI: Eerdmans, 2006), 365–75.

10. See generally Brian M. Rapske, "Roman Rule in Palestine," in *Encyclopedia of the Historical Jesus*, ed. Craig Evans (New York: Routledge, 2008), 523–29.

11. L. I. Levine, "Herod the Great," in *Anchor Bible Dictionary*, ed. David Noel Freedman (New York: Doubleday, 1992), 3:163.

12. Jeffers, *Greco-Roman World*, 128.

13. See Simon Goldhill, *Being Greek under Rome: Cultural Identity, the Second Sophistic, and the Development of Empire* (New York: Cambridge University Press, 2001).

14. Paul Van Warmelo, *An Introduction to the Principles of Roman Law* (Cape Town, South Africa: Junta, 1976), 45.

15. See further Peter Garnsey, *Social Status and Legal Privilege in the Roman Empire* (Oxford: Clarendon Press, 1970); and A. N. Sherwin-White, *The Roman Citizenship* (Oxford: Clarendon Press, 1973).

16. John W. Welch, "How Rich was Paul, and Why It Matters?," in *Bountiful Harvest: Essays in Honor of S. Kent Brown*, ed. Andrew C. Skinner et al. (Provo, UT: Neal A. Maxwell Institute for Religious Scholarship, 2011), 425–53.

17. See further Williams, *Paul's Metaphors*, chap. 6.

18. Ronald F. Hock, *The Social Context of Paul's Ministry: Tentmaking and Apostleship* (Philadelphia: Fortress, 1980), 27.

19. Jeffers, *Greco-Roman World*, 34–35.

20. Jeffers, *Greco-Roman World*, 37.

21. Williams, *Paul's Metaphors*, 52, 83.

22. Berger, *Encyclopedic Dictionary*, s.v. "Adulterium"; Andrew Borkowski and Paul du Plessis, *Textbook on Roman Law*, 3rd ed. (Oxford: Oxford University Press, 2005), chap. 5, esp. 129–30.

23. See Bruce J. Malina and Richard L. Rohrbaugh, *Social Science Commentary on the Synoptic Gospels* (Minneapolis, MN: Fortress, 1992), 28–30.

24. Berger, *Encyclopedic Dictionary*, s.v. "Divortium."

25. Berger, *Encyclopedic Dictionary*, s.v. "Adoptio."

26. Williams, *Paul's Metaphors*, 64.

27. Williams, *Paul's Metaphors*, 65.

28. Berger, *Encyclopedic Dictionary*, s.v. "Testamentum"; Borkowski, *Textbook on Roman Law*, chap. 8.

29. Bernard S. Jackson, "Why the Name *New Testament?*," *Melilah: Manchester Journal of Jewish Studies* 9 (2012): 92.

30. Bernard S. Jackson, *Essays on Halakhah in the New Testament* (Leiden, Netherlands: Brill, 2008), 111–50.

31. Jeffers, *Greco-Roman World*, 102.

32. Josephus, *Jewish War* 1.407.

33. Josephus, *Antiquities* 14.10.1–8.

34. For a listing of various legal actions against astrologers (among others), see Frederick H. Cramer, *Astrology in Roman Law and Politics* (Chicago: Ares, 1996), 233–48.

35. Mary Beard, John North, and Simon Price, *Religions of Rome: A History* (Cambridge: Cambridge University Press, 1996), 1:230–31.

36. Acts 18:1–2; Suetonius, *Life of Claudius* 25.4; Cassius Dio, *Roman History* 60.6.6–7.

37. Beard, North, and Price, *Religions of Rome*, 1:237.

38. See further Ralph Martin Novak, *Christianity and the Roman Empire: Background Texts* (Harrisburg, PA: Trinity Press International, 2001), appendix C, esp. 267–71.

39. Jeffers, *Greco-Roman World*, 101.

40. For example, when Pilate introduced busts of the emperor into Jerusalem and caused an uproar; see Josephus, *Antiquities* 18.3.1:55 and *Jewish War* 2.9.2:169; and Tacitus, *Histories* 2.89, 4.62.

41. For example, Steven J. Friesen, *Imperial Cults and the Apocalypse of John: Reading Revelation in the Ruins* (Oxford: Oxford University Press, 2001).

42. John W. Welch and John F. Hall, *Charting the New Testament* (Provo, UT: Foundation for Ancient Research and Mormon Studies, 2002), chart 2-6.

43. Malina and Rohrbaugh, *Social Science Commentary on the Synoptic Gospels*, 82–83.

44. 2 Corinthians 1:21–22; see further Williams, *Paul's Metaphors*, 180.

45. Williams, *Paul's Metaphors*, 179–80.

46. Justinian, *Digest* 50.116.108.

47. Berger, *Encyclopedic Dictionary*, s.v. "Datio in solutum."

48. Williams, *Paul's Metaphors*, 180–84.

49. Williams, *Paul's Metaphors*, 184–85.

50. This is likely the amount of money in the treasury at the temple in Jerusalem. See John W. Welch, "Herod's Wealth," in *Masada and the World of the New Testament*, ed. John F. Hall and John W. Welch (Provo, UT: BYU Studies, 1997), 79.

51. Borkowski, *Textbook on Roman Law*, 284.

52. Berger, *Encyclopedic Dictionary*, s.v. "Societas"; Borkowski, *Textbook on Roman Law*, 286–90.

53. J. Paul Sampley, *Pauline Partnership in Christ: Christian Community and Commitment in Light of Roman Law* (Philadelphia: Fortress, 1980).

54. Berger, *Encyclopedic Dictionary*, s.v. "Locatio conductio."

55. A. N. Sherwin-White, *Roman Society and Roman Law in the New Testament* (Oxford: Oxford University Press, 1963), 1–23.

56. Sherwin-White, *Roman Society and Roman Law*, 24–47.

57. Jeffers, *Greco-Roman World*, 155; Acts 17:5–10.

58. Justinian, *Digest* 48.4.1.1.

59. R. S. Rogers, *Criminal Trials and Criminal Legislation under Tiberius* (Middletown, CT: American Philosophical Association, 1935), 79, 83, 88, 99, 130.

60. Cramer, *Astrology in Roman Law and Politics*, 249.

61. Rogers, *Criminal Trials*, 116, 140.

62. Welch, "Miracles, *Maleficium*, and *Maiestas*," 349–83.

63. G. Lohfink, in *The Last Day of Jesus* (Notre Dame, IN: Ave Maria, 1984), 50, suggests that Pilate himself was at risk of being accused of *maiestas populi Romani*.

64. S. Légasse, in *The Trial of Jesus* (London: SCM, 1997), identifies *maiestas* as the reason for the death of Jesus, concluding: "Jesus was executed for having laid claim to royal power over his own people. Such a claim . . . fell under the accusation of *crimen maiestatis populi romani*." Légasse thinks, however, only in terms of political sedition or treason.

65. Wolfgang Kunkel, *An Introduction to Roman Legal and Constitutional History*, trans. J. M. Kelly, 2nd ed. (Oxford: Clarendon, 1973), 13–14.

66. Smith, *Jesus the Magician*, 41.

67. Berger, *Encyclopedic Dictionary*, 573.

68. Berger, *Encyclopedia Dictionary*, 572–73.

69. Cramer, *Astrology in Roman Law and Politics*, 238.

70. Suetonius, *Tiberius* 36.

71. Smith, *Jesus the Magician*, 75, citing *Sententiae Receptae Paulo Tributae* 23.15–18.

72. John W. Welch, "The Legal Cause of Action against Jesus in John 18:29–30," in *Celebrating Easter*, ed. Thomas A. Wayment and Keith J. Wilson (Provo, UT: Religious Studies Center, Brigham Young University, 2007), 157–76.

73. Malina and Rohrbaugh, *Social Science Commentary on the Synoptic Gospels*, 157.

74. Bernard S. Jackson, "Some Comparative Legal History: Robbery and Brigandage," *Georgia Journal of International and Comparative Law* 1, no. 1 (1970): 61–86.

75. See Josephus, *Jewish War* 1.311.

76. See Kent P. Jackson, "Revolutionaries in the First Century," *BYU Studies Quarterly* 36, no. 3 (1996): 129–40; and John W. Welch, "Legal and Social Perspectives on Robbers in First-Century Judea," *BYU Studies Quarterly* 36, no. 3 (1996): 141–53.

77. Berger, *Encyclopedic Dictionary*, s.v. "Poena," "Poena capitalis."

78. Berger, *Encyclopedic Dictionary*, s.v. "Crux."

79. See David W. Chapman and Eckhard J. Schnabel, *The Trial and Crucifixion of Jesus* (Tübingen, Germany: Mohr Siebeck, 2015); and Gunnar Samuelsson, *Crucifixion in Antiquity* (Tübingen, Germany: Mohr Siebeck, 2013).

11

Greco-Roman Philosophy and the New Testament

Bryce Gessell

When we read the New Testament, we enter a world that is in many ways foreign to us: the most important events happened two millennia ago, they took place in a distant land, and they were lived by people whose society contrasts sharply with our own. While these barriers do not stop us from feeling the power of Christ's words in the Sermon on the Mount, for example, he still spoke those words at a particular time and place to a particular group of people. As Nephi put it, he spoke "unto men according to their language" (2 Nephi 31:3). Language is more than just a form of communication—it is a way of seeing the world and one's place in it (see 1 Nephi 1:2). In this chapter, I will use the word *language* in Nephi's broad sense. The more we know about the language of the New Testament, the more we will draw from the fertile richness of its pages.

This chapter considers the *philosophical* part of that language. Philosophy embraces some of the deepest questions we can ask: What is existence, and how do existing things relate to each other? How do we come to know the world? How should we live in that world and with one another? Though it is not possible to deal with the nuances of any one philosopher here, this chapter will offer an overview of the major Greco-Roman philosophies before, during, and shortly after the time of Christ. By familiarizing ourselves with the philosophical languages spoken among these groups, we will see how their answers to deep questions form an essential part of the New Testament and our reading of it.

The Beginning: Ancient Greek Philosophy

Western philosophy begins with a group of thinkers in Miletus, an ancient city located in modern-day Turkey.[1] The "Milesians"—Thales (ca. 600 BC), his pupil Anaximander (ca. 610–546 BC), and Anaximenes (ca. 585–528 BC)—were interested in questions about what the world was made of and how it worked.[2] Instead of relying on gods and fate to explain things, however, the Milesians began to answer their questions in terms of natural principles. Thales, for example, thought that the primary constituent of all existing things was water: "from water come all things and into water do all things decompose."[3] Anaximenes, on the other hand, took air to be the most fundamental element. Other figures with alternative views arose elsewhere, such as Heraclitus of Ephesus (ca. 500 BC), Empedocles of Acragas (ca. 495–435 BC), and Democritus of Abdera (ca. 460–370 BC).[4]

The general name for these early philosophers is "Presocratic," but that term is somewhat misleading. Though the Milesians did in fact precede Socrates, other Presocratic authors were his contemporaries. And while these early theorists tend to answer philosophical questions in many different ways, they share a commitment to certain *methods* for answering. Rather than appealing to supernatural beings, they are more likely to use natural phenomena in explaining the world; thus they are commonly called "natural philosophers." Natural philosophy is the ancestor of modern science—it is a way of approaching the world that uses causes within the natural world in order to explain it. The departure from mythology toward a more scientific sort of investigation is one of the early marks of Western philosophical inquiry.

Socrates, Plato, and Aristotle—the major voices of Greek philosophy—followed the early natural philosophers. There are no more important philosophers in the ancient world than these three. We will, however, cover them only briefly here, for they were not so directly influential in the New Testament world as their later notoriety might suggest.

Socrates (469–399 BC)[5]

A one-time soldier in the Peloponnesian War, Socrates lived his later years in Athens. He wandered the city looking to engage (or trap, depending on whom you asked) its citizens in conversation on ethical topics such as the nature of piety or love. His Socratic method consisted of asking questions designed to attack or defend a certain point of view or to establish accepted principles in some investigation. He considered himself a "gadfly" who took up the responsibility of stirring the state and its people into action.[6] He was eventually charged with impiety and corruption of Athens's youth; he was found guilty and executed.

We know of Socrates from works by Plato, Xenophon, and (to some extent) the playwright Aristophanes. Since Socrates wrote nothing himself, it can be difficult to tell which views in these works really belonged to the historical Socrates and which belonged to the authors themselves.[7]

Plato (424–347 BC)[8]

Plato was Socrates's disciple and established his own school in Athens called "the Academy." He wrote voluminously on virtually every topic in philosophy. His texts are mostly dialogues, or conversations, between a main speaker (often Socrates) and his companions (sometimes called "interlocutors"). He held that the world we now inhabit is a shadow of a higher, more perfect, and unchanging reality—the world of the "Forms." Mundane objects are what they are because they "participate in," or stand in some relation to, certain Forms. A dog is a dog, for instance, because it participates in the form Dog; the same is true for humans, chairs, and other things. The objects we know and experience daily are but imperfect copies of more genuine realities.

For Plato, the function of philosophy is to free the soul from the prison of the body in order for it to contemplate the Forms more directly. His allegory of the cave may be one way of thinking about this process.[9] By gaining knowledge, we free ourselves from the deceptive and harmful images of things experienced in bodily reality. Philosophy gradually leads our soul from captivity as we begin to grasp the real nature of existence. The truest light—the Form of the Good—illuminates us upon our leaving the cave. For Plato, our souls had knowledge before birth and will outlast our bodies after death.

Aristotle (384–322 BC)[10]

Aristotle in turn was Plato's student at the Academy. Following Plato's death, Aristotle began to tutor Alexander the Great but later returned to Athens to found his own school of philosophy, the Lyceum. Aristotle also wrote on many topics and developed systematic theories in logic and science. Unlike Plato, however, Aristotle did not believe that higher forms of knowledge required the soul to apprehend the Forms. He saw knowledge as a result of information gained about the external world from the senses. On this view, more general knowledge comes from the mind's capacity to abstract away

Plato (left) and Aristotle (right), as depicted in Raphael's The School of Athens (1510-1511). Plato's gesture toward the heavens and Aristotle's toward the earth are thought to represent the different approaches they took to explaining the natural world. Plato holds a copy of the Timaeus, his dialogue on cosmology and natural philosophy; Aristotle carries his Ethics, likely the Nicomachean Ethics, a work on virtue and happiness.

from particular truths in order to grasp universal ones, as it appreciates the essences of various objects.

In Raphael's painting *The School of Athens*, Plato is shown talking to Aristotle with his finger pointing upward, while Aristotle responds by gesturing toward the world below. This famous image illustrates the different approaches these philosophers are thought to have taken on questions about the world and humanity.

Early Greek philosophy in conclusion

The language of Western philosophy begins with the thinkers we call the "Presocratics" before moving to their Athenian successors, including Plato and Aristotle. These figures introduced many of the terms, methods, and problems that are fundamental to the practice of philosophy. In many ways, the philosophical shifts discussed below—and much of Western philosophy in general—stem from questions and answers proposed by Plato and Aristotle.[11] As we will see, this is as true for religion as it is for philosophy.

Hellenistic Philosophy, Wisdom, Epicureanism, and Stoicism

After the major figures of Greek philosophy, we begin to find movements and philosophical doctrines more directly associated with the New Testament. We also begin to see greater development of philosophical terms and concepts that will eventually impact Christian theology. In a familiar passage from the book of Acts, we read about Paul encountering certain philosophical movements:

> And they that conducted Paul brought him unto Athens: and receiving a commandment unto Silas and Timotheus for to come to him with all speed, they departed. Now while Paul waited for them at Athens, his spirit was stirred in him, when he saw the city wholly given to idolatry. Therefore disputed he in the synagogue with the Jews, and with the devout persons, and in the market daily with them that met with him. Then certain philosophers of the Epicureans, and of the Stoicks, encountered him. And some said, What will this babbler say? other some, He seemeth to be a setter forth of strange gods: because he preached unto them Jesus, and the resurrection. And they took him, and brought him unto Areopagus, saying, May we know what this new doctrine, whereof thou speakest, is? For thou bringest certain strange things to our ears: we would know therefore what these things mean. (For all the Athenians and strangers which were there spent their time in nothing else, but either to tell, or to hear some new thing.) Then Paul stood in the midst of Mars' hill, and said, Ye men of Athens, I perceive that in all things ye are too superstitious. For as I passed by, and beheld your devotions, I found an altar with this inscription, TO THE UNKNOWN GOD. Whom therefore ye ignorantly worship, him declare I unto you. (Acts 17:15–23)

Here Paul meets adherents of two philosophical groups, the Epicureans and the Stoics. Both groups play a critical role in the philosophical background of the New Testament.

These systems of thought belong to an era known today as the Hellenistic period. In ancient Greek, the country of Greece was known as *Hellas* (Ἑλλάς). Though Plato and Aristotle were also Greek, we use the term *Hellenistic philosophy* to refer to the period following Aristotle.[12] The period is worth looking at in greater detail.

Hellenistic philosophy

Hellenistic philosophy includes much more than Epicureanism and Stoicism. The Cynics, for example, began a philosophical movement around the time of Plato, before the beginning of the Hellenistic period.[13] Antisthenes (445–365 BC), their alleged founder, was a contemporary of Plato and was, like Plato, a student of Socrates. Later Cynics developed a philosophy of life based on virtue and harmony with nature. The goal of a Cynic was εὐδαιμονία (*eudaimonia*), "happiness." Vanity (τῦφος, *tuphos*) stands in the way by clouding the mind with delusion. A life free from corrupting influences like bodily temptations, wealth, and social power eliminate vanity and lead to *eudaimonia*. The Cynic lifestyle was sometimes taken to ascetic extremes, most famously by the eccentric Diogenes of Sinope (404–323 BC), sometimes called "Diogenes the Dog" (the Greek word for "cynic" meant "dog-like"). A famous (and perhaps apocryphal) story shows his philosophical commitments in action. Diogenes used a cup to drink out of the river but one day came across a child drinking with his hands. Disgusted with himself, Diogenes cast away his cup and exclaimed, "A child has beaten me in plainness of living." He threw his bowl away in a similar manner upon seeing a child eat on a piece of bread instead of a plate.[14]

A critical feature in much of Hellenistic philosophy is a shift away from natural philosophy and issues about the general properties of existing things (called "metaphysical" issues). This shift brought a renewed emphasis on ethics and ways of living life. In Plato, Aristotle, and many of the Presocratics, we find philosophers asking questions about the world and its place in the universe: their interests range from inquiries about the tiniest constituents of matter to the earth's place in the cosmos as a whole.

As we will see below, many Hellenistic philosophers are willing to address questions about the natural world. Like Plato and Aristotle, they have ideas about what causes things to happen in nature, and some of these ideas are comprehensive and systematic. But their purpose in offering such explanations is not necessarily to gain an understanding of the world for its own sake. Rather, in many cases these post-Aristotelian philosophers take an interest in nature in order to frame and justify their own views about how to live. The qualities of divinity, the way we gain knowledge about our environment, the way we reason—all these issues matter in determining the correct approach to personal conduct.

A major part of this shift toward ethics is the influence of Socrates. Though he left no written record, Socrates's self-conscious reflection on moral issues—and his stubborn commitment to his ideals—had a long-lasting effect on Greek philosophers. The Hellenistic focus on proper conduct parallels the emphasis of Christ himself and his apostles in much of New Testament scripture. In the Gospels, Christ says nothing about whether the earth goes around the sun or whether atoms are the fundamental building blocks of everything else, but on nearly every page we find guidance about how to see ourselves and relate to others.

Hellenistic philosophy is a rich tradition with many branches to explore.[15]

Worldly wisdom and philosophy in the New Testament

We began this section by quoting Paul's experience in Acts 17. The New Testament addresses Greek philosophy in other ways as well, though they are not always so obvious. The first chapter of 1 Corinthians is a good example. After greeting the church at Corinth and praising Christ, Paul begins a denunciation of the world and its learning:

> For the preaching of the cross is to them that perish foolishness; but unto us which are saved it is the power of God. For it is written, I will destroy the wisdom of the wise, and will bring to nothing the understanding of the prudent. Where is the wise? where is the scribe? where is the disputer of this world? hath not God made foolish the wisdom of this world? For after that in the wisdom of God the world by wisdom knew not God, it pleased God by the foolishness of preaching to save them that believe. For the Jews require a sign, and the Greeks seek after wisdom: But we preach Christ crucified, unto the Jews a stumbling block, and unto the Greeks foolishness; But unto them which are called, both Jews and Greeks, Christ the power of God, and the wisdom of God. Because the foolishness of God is wiser than men; and the weakness of God is stronger than men. For ye see your calling, brethren, how that not many wise men after the flesh, not many mighty, not many noble, are called: But God hath chosen the foolish things of the world to confound the wise; and God hath chosen the weak things of the world to confound the things which are mighty. (1 Corinthians 1:18–27)

The key word in the passage is *wisdom*, or σοφία (*sophia*). According to Paul, God will "destroy the *wisdom* of the wise"; despite the Greeks' seeking for it, this worldly wisdom is not enough to know God. Paul chooses his words carefully in this passage. The Greek word φιλοσοφία (*philosophia*) is a combination of the words *philo-* ("love") and *-sophia* ("wisdom"); therefore, philosophy is literally the "love of wisdom." Paul describes the Greeks as wisdom-seekers, but he has in mind their tendency toward philosophy and worldly knowledge. Perhaps he would have said of the Hellenistic philosophers of his day, as we read in 2 Timothy, that they were "ever learning, and never able to come to the knowledge of the truth" (2 Timothy 3:7; see Acts 17:21).

In connection with the criticism of worldly wisdom in 1 Corinthians 1, we find the New Testament's only use of the Greek word φιλοσοφία ("philosophy") in Colossians 2:

> As ye have therefore received Christ Jesus the Lord, so walk ye in him: Rooted and built up in him, and stablished in the faith, as ye have been taught, abounding therein with thanksgiving. Beware lest any man spoil you through philosophy and vain deceit, after the tradition of men, after the rudiments of the world, and not after Christ. (Colossians 2:6–8)

Here we see a marked split between two ways of viewing philosophy. For Plato, the acquisition of knowledge through philosophy was the key to liberating the soul from the prison of the body. Before philosophy, one's soul was "imprisoned in and clinging to the body, and . . . it is forced to examine other things through it as through a cage and not by itself, and . . . it wallows in every kind of ignorance."[16] The true course is to be a person "who has truly spent his life in philosophy" and so will be "of good cheer in the face of death and . . . very hopeful that after death he will attain the greatest blessings yonder."[17]

In contrast to Plato, Paul warns against the seductive power of the sorts of philosophies the Greeks used to seek truth. He claims that these worldly manners of thought, handed down in the teachings of men, may "spoil" us. The way we use *spoil* today gives a misleading impression of the meaning in this verse. The Greek word is a form of συλαγωγέω (*sulagōgeō*), which means "to gain control of by carrying off as booty . . . in imagery of carrying someone away from the truth into the slavery of error."[18] Note the powerful reversal of the Platonic metaphor. Leaving Plato's cave and ascending to the light and truth required philosophy; on Paul's interpretation, it is as though philosophy takes one *away* from the light and back down into the darkness (see 2 Corinthians 4:5–6; Ephesians 5:14). Once again Paul has chosen his words with great care and foresight. Just before his warning about philosophy, he reminds his audience that only "in [Christ] are hid all the treasures of wisdom (σοφία, *sophia*) and knowledge" (Colossians 2:3). The love of wisdom, separated from the treasure of Christ, leads to nothing but ignorance.

Returning now to Paul's encounter with the Epicureans and Stoics, on meeting Paul, some of these philosophers said that he seemed "to be a setter forth of strange gods," while others asked themselves, "What will this babbler say?" (Acts 17:18). The epithet *babbler* is σπερμολόγος (*spermologos*), an insult made to one who unsystematically gathers pieces of information to create a patchwork view of the world.[19] The term seems to be an inside joke. Both Plato and Aristotle were comprehensive philosophers: their ideas reached from the smallest bits of matter to the largest bounds of the universe and touched on almost everything in between. Both the Epicureans and the Stoics inherited this Greek concern with system-building. At least at the time they spoke to Paul, Christian thought must have seemed to those at Mars' Hill as hardly even worth being called a patchwork. To see how fledgling Christianity differed from these Hellenistic views, let's take a closer look at both schools of thought.

Epicureanism

Like other movements in Hellenistic philosophy, the principal aims of Epicureanism involved morality: they concerned the way one should live. Epicurus (341–270 BC), the school's founder, was born about two decades after Aristotle. Some of Epicurus's original writings have survived, detailing his ideas about physics, astronomy, and ethics.[20] He divided philosophy into three groups: *Canonic* (Logic), the treatment of which comprises the introduction to his system; *Physics*, which deals with nature; and *Ethics*, which treats life and conduct. The hallmark of Epicurean physical theory is atomism, which posited indivisible, fundamental particles whose interactions give rise to the objects and events we experience (the earliest atomists, Leucippus and Democritus, date back to the fifth century BC). Experience itself is the arbiter of truth, which forms a philosophical view of knowledge now called "empiricism."[21]

In contemporary usage the adjective *epicurean* describes a person who is preoccupied with sensual pleasures, but this use of the term is not faithful to Epicurean ethical theory. Epicureanism was a form of *hedonism*—the idea that pleasure is the ultimate good—but the "pleasures" Epicurus had in mind were not necessarily the same as the sensual pleasures of the body we often think of when we hear the epithet. In fact, Epicurus tended to describe the good life in *negative* terms—that is, as the absence of mental distress and physical pain. This state, called ἀταραξία (*ataraxia*) or "ataraxy," is the goal of life for Epicurus. Intense physical pleasures might even bring their own kind of trouble, for we feel distress at not having them after getting a taste of what they are like.

Epicurus's emphasis on what is *material*, or made of matter, led him to claim that the soul too is made of atoms. The physical soul was an important part of Epicurus's teachings on death. The soul cannot last forever because it is made of material things; therefore it is not immortal, and concerns about immortality should not motivate us any one way in action: "a right understanding that death is nothing to us makes the mortality of life enjoyable, not by adding to life an illimitable time, but by taking away the yearning after immortality."[22] Epicurus, however, was not an atheist. He told Menoeceus, the recipient of his letter on ethics, that he should "believe that God is a living being immortal and blessed. . . . For verily there are gods, and the knowledge of them is manifest; but they are not such as the multitude believe."[23] Common notions of God are impious and false, in fact, and only a true understanding of the divine could help one live the correct kind of life. That true understanding characterizes God as an untroubled being, uninvolved in human cares and concerns.

Epicurus died in 270 BC, but his philosophical system long outlived him. Philodemus (110–40 BC) and Lucretius (99–55 BC) were two important figures in the later Epicurean tradition. The latter's only surviving work is a poem called *On the Nature of Things* (*De rerum natura*). This text discusses atoms and the void they move in, criticizes religion, and extols simple goods, thereby covering the crucial issues in Epicureanism as well as many other topics.[24] Epicureanism following Lucretius enjoyed a prominence that lasted several hundred more years.

The Epicureanism alive in the time and regions of the New Testament was more or less the same as the traditions outlined by Epicurus himself. The book of Acts tells us that these Epicureans, or those that knew them, had erected an altar with the inscription "TO THE UNKNOWN GOD" (17:23). Such a god is not exactly the god of Epicurus, who affirmed that god was known to some degree. But the spirit of the inscription fits the mindset of Epicurean philosophy. Paul's speech to these philosophers emphasizes the personal nature of God and his involvement in human affairs: "God . . . made the world and all things therein" (17:24); God "hath made of one blood all nations of men for to dwell on all the face of the earth" (17:26); in God "we live, and move, and have our being" (17:28).[25] Attributing characteristics like these to a divine being represented exactly the kind of common and superstitious notions of divinity that Epicurus had railed against. In a similar vein, Paul then mentions the Judgment and the Resurrection: "Because he hath appointed a day, in the which he will judge the world in righteousness by that man whom he hath ordained; whereof he hath given assurance unto all men, in that he hath raised him from the dead" (17:31). Verse 32 reports the reaction among his listeners—"some mocked: and others said, We will hear thee again of this matter" (see 17:18 as well). It may be that these two groups correspond to the Epicureans and Stoics, respectively.[26] The Epicurean philosophers gathered on Mars' Hill may have been familiar with Christian doctrine, and their derisive reaction typified the Epicurean attitude toward most religions. In particular, they could not have accepted resurrection from the dead. Epicurean ideas on the soul demanded that it be paired with a body in order to perceive, and without the body the soul's atoms could not maintain their continuity as a soul. The atoms would disperse into nothingness, and the soul would cease to exist. For Epicureans, the dispersal of the soul's atoms is the end of life, with no possibility of reassimilation to a past identity.

Two hundred years or so after Paul, Epicureanism began to give way to other philosophical systems, including Neoplatonism and Christianity itself. The influence of Epicurus's thought is far-reaching, however, especially in comparison to some other Hellenistic philosophies. Pierre Gassendi, a French philosopher in the first half of the seventeenth century, brought Epicurus's ideas to prominence once again in his 1649 book *Animadversiones*. Ironically, one of Gassendi's main motivations was to reconcile Epicureanism with the Christian notion of God.

Stoicism

The other philosophers mentioned in Acts 17 are the Stoics. Stoicism as a Hellenistic school of philosophy began with Zeno of Citium (334–262 BC), who was born twelve years before the death of Aristotle. Because Zeno's original writings are lost, our knowledge of his views comes from reports made by later writers. In Zeno's case, however, these reports are sometimes extensive. We know, for example, that he wrote a lengthy work called the *Republic*, perhaps as a response to Plato's dialogue of the same name. One commentator said that Zeno's *Republic* can "be summed up in this one main principle: that all the inhabitants of this world of ours should not live differentiated by their respective rules of justice into separate cities and communities, but that we should consider all men to be of one community and one polity, and that we should have a common life and an order common to us all, even as a herd that feeds together and shares the pasturage of a common field."[27]

Like other Hellenistic systems, Stoicism encompassed a range of doctrines on the natural world, but these served as a means to support and encourage the more important ethical views. We now understand the word *stoic* to refer to a person who is resolute in the face of pain or opposition. Unlike *epicurean* and perhaps *cynic*, our modern term *stoic* does preserve some of the original meaning of the philosophical doctrine. For Stoic philosophers, the ethical ideal is the sage (σοφός, *sophos*, the adjective form of the Greek noun for "wisdom"—thus "the wise man"). A sage makes correct judgments, or judgments in accordance with nature, in order to understand the world correctly. Correct understanding frees the sage from passions, or dominant emotions, which would otherwise destroy his happiness. As one Stoic author put it, "It is not things themselves that disturb men, but their judgements about things. . . . Whenever we are impeded or disturbed or distressed, let us blame no one but ourselves, that is, our own judgements."[28] Therefore, a sage actively creates a life by a process of ἄσκησις (*askēsis*), "training" or "practice," in order to apprehend the world correctly, make appropriate judgments, and live in accordance with reason.

Although we have few actual writings of the early Stoics, Stoicism flourished among some later Roman authors, many of whose works have survived: Seneca (4 BC–AD 65), Epictetus (AD 55–155), and Marcus Aurelius (AD 121–180) are three of them.[29] These authors, especially Epictetus and Seneca, lived during the New Testament period.

We also see Stoic influence in many important concepts and terminology of Christian scripture. For the Stoics, the λόγος (*logos*, "word, account, reason") is the universal reason that is basic to all existence. This same word appears in prominent passages of the New Testament, most notably at the beginning of John (1:1), where Christ is referred to as the λόγος (*logos*). Other important terms, such as πνεῦμα (*pneuma*, "breath, spirit") and ἀρετή (*aretē*, "virtue, excellence"), have an important history in Stoicism as well as in Greek philosophy more broadly.

Let us return to Acts 17 one last time. Earlier we saw that, on hearing of the resurrection of the dead, the Epicurean and Stoic philosophers had two different reactions. The Epicureans mocked Paul's doctrine because their atom-based physics precluded any possibility of a resurrection. The Stoics, on the other hand, reacted differently: "We will hear thee again of this matter" (17:32), they said. Stoicism was also a materialist philosophy and held that God was an active principle inherent in all of nature. This version of theism is sometimes called "pantheism," from the Greek word πᾶν (*pan*), which means "all" or "everything": everything is God. God therefore exists *in* this world, not outside or apart from it; we also exist as parts of the divine whole, and so perhaps a sort of resurrection could be possible.[30]

In this section we have taken only a brief tour through the many branches of Hellenistic philosophy, two of which—Epicureanism and Stoicism—are particularly important for the New Testament era. We saw that the common language of these branches was *moral* philosophy. While they did attempt to supply answers to questions about the nature of existence, the essence of matter, and our access to reality, their primary goal was to outline the proper way to live. We have also had a glimpse at some of the influence Hellenistic philosophy had on the languages and events of the New Testament itself. Paul's meeting at Mars' Hill is the most obvious case, but other concepts and discussions, such as σοφία (*sophia*, "wisdom") or Paul's exhortation against certain philosophies in Colossians 2, witness how far Greek learning extended into early Christianity.[31]

Roman Philosophy and Plotinus

The New Testament was written at a time when the ancient Mediterranean world was dominated by Rome. The Roman Empire reached far and wide and even included Jerusalem in the Roman province of Judea. In Paul's extensive missionary travels, he never ventured outside the empire's borders. While the geographic boundaries of the Roman Empire were relatively clear, the boundaries of what we now call "Roman philosophy" were less so. For example, in discussing the major Hellenistic philosophies, we have already named a number of important Roman philosophers: Philodemus, Lucretius, Seneca, and Marcus Aurelius. The lines between Roman philosophers and Greek and Hellenistic philosophies became blurred as Roman thinkers presented Greek philosophy in their own work, albeit from a different perspective. To this group could also be added Marcus Tullius Cicero (106–43 BC), known for his involvement in Roman politics and literature. He dealt with many philosophical issues across a prolific corpus, treating friendship, laws, divinity, and other topics. His work is a good guide to both the Roman reception of Greek philosophy and the later dissemination of Hellenistic thinking in other authors.[32]

Even though many "Roman" philosophers were in some ways carrying on the traditions of some Hellenistic schools, talking about Roman philosophy can still be useful. For one, the early Christian era points toward a changing understanding of the relationship between Christianity and philosophy. In some of the writings of Paul, we saw a deliberate warning against Greek philosophy and an implicit criticism of certain Greek philosophical ideas. These ideas spanned the duration of the New Testament, but by the time we come to later thinkers of the Roman period, we have left the events of the New Testament behind. There is still far more to say about those events, however, and their relation to philosophy. The flourishing of Roman thought helps us understand the roots and development of other philosophical systems. Some of these were to outlast Epicureanism and Stoicism, both of which lost favor in the decades following Paul.

In fact, these new Roman philosophical developments were in part a return to the important Greek thinkers of the past. From the time of Plato and Aristotle, there had always been Platonists and Aristotelians. Several hundred years after their deaths, though, there began a more conscious revival of their thinking. The most important figure in this evolution of ancient philosophy was Plotinus (ca. AD 204–270). Plotinus lived at the beginning of a period we now call "late antiquity," which continued into the medieval era. In considering Plotinus and other philosophers of late antiquity, we venture beyond the limits of the New Testament. This discussion will help us understand, however, how the languages of the New Testament combined with philosophy to have a powerful effect on later thinkers.

In a series of works called the *Enneads*, which were compiled by his student Porphyry, Plotinus outlined an original philosophical system based on the metaphysical teachings of Plato.[33] Some of these teachings are already familiar to us: Plato believed that the Forms made up true reality and that they inhabited a world apart from this one. True knowledge was apprehension of the Forms. Accordingly, Plotinus's system contained three basic parts—the "One" or the "Good," intellect, and soul. The One is the most fundamental part of all reality and, like the principles of some Presocratics, is the explanation for the other phenomena we observe. The One is not a compound of anything but is simple. It must be simple if we are to use it as a ground to explain everything else, for if it were not simple, we would have to explain its existence in terms of some other thing. The other two principles of Plotinus's system, the intellect and the soul, are derivations from the One.

Plotinus's *Enneads* contain discussions of ethical topics, with chapters titled "On True Happiness," "On Beauty," "On Love," and so on. But with his doctrines on the One, Plotinus is noteworthy for his role in refocusing philosophical questions on metaphysical issues. This new focus, in a sense just a return to the concerns of Plato and Aristotle, would last long into the medieval period (and in some ways continues even today). Nowhere is this more true than in Neoplatonism, the philosophical school founded by Plotinus, in which later stages of Christian theology saw a more conscious evolution in step with philosophical thinking. Below we will explore some of these connections as well.

Neoplatonism

For the intellectual world following the New Testament, the most important strain of thought we have yet to discuss is Neoplatonism. Plotinus is the founder of this school, which carries on Plato's interest in questions concerning the fundamental nature of reality and our relationship to it. The term *Neoplatonism* is a modern one, however. Historians use it to designate developments in Platonic thought after the death of Plato and his closest followers in Athens.

We may wonder, though, why understanding Neoplatonism matters for the New Testament. After all, Plotinus lived long after Christ, the apostles, and Paul; his views could not have had any effect on the philosophers who gathered to hear Paul at Mars' Hill, for example. Yet there are good reasons to discuss Neoplatonism in this context. One is that it is the most important philosophical influence on post-apostolic Christian thought until Thomas Aquinas in the thirteenth century. Another reason is that Neoplatonism was also a major player in the larger world in which the New Testament, as we know the text today, was shaped. Knowing a little about the philosophical language of those who shaped it will prepare us to explore many important issues, such as the role of philosophy and theology in determining why the New Testament exists in its current form.

Using the ideas of Plato as a base, Neoplatonist philosophers undertook to rationalize many ancient doctrines and produce perhaps the widest-ranging and deepest system of thought then developed. We should also note that the two main views *rejected* by Neoplatonism were Epicureanism and Stoicism. Neoplatonic thinking had a decidedly mystical slant; this mysticism de-emphasized the importance of the body and empirical reality in general, which did not fit well with the materialism of the two most important Hellenistic movements. More fundamental than body was mind—that is, νοῦς (*nous*, "intellect"). The cause of intellect traces back to the One. Like Platonism, Neoplatonism is not an idealist philosophy, idealism being the theory that ideas or mental reality are the only things that exist.

For Neoplatonists, matter exists and derives its existence from an emanation of the One. For some Neoplatonist thinkers, matter was also related to the existence of evil. This view stands in contrast to other strands of Neoplatonism in which moral depravity is not due to passive matter but instead is possible in the human soul itself.

Following Plotinus we find multiple developing branches of Neoplatonism. Plotinus's student Porphyry (AD 234–305) gathered Plotinus's writings into the *Enneads*, and he also wrote original works in some areas of natural philosophy. One piece worth noting here is Κατὰ Χριστιανῶν (*kata christianōn*), or *Against the Christians*.[34] By Porphyry's time, the Christian religion was already spreading widely and there were many new converts and established believers throughout the Roman Empire. *Against the Christians* assailed the burgeoning movement on all fronts, from ad hominem attacks against Christ and the apostles to philosophical critiques of the nature of God and the Resurrection. Fellow second-generation Neoplatonist Iamblichus (AD 245–325) took a different course, writing mostly on mathematics.[35]

Porphyry's polemic illustrates one side of a broader development in early Neoplatonism. On the one hand, Porphyry and others used philosophy to criticize Christian doctrine as well as the habits and customs of the believers. But other Neoplatonists were beginning to concern themselves more with reconciling the two systems. The appeal of Neoplatonism to an interested Christian thinker would have been obvious. The similarity between the One of Neoplatonic metaphysics and the Christian God spoken of in the Bible is readily apparent; once that connection is made, the believer gains access to many other useful philosophical resources, including some dealing with the mind, the soul, and their relation to God. Neoplatonism also emphasizes spiritual or mental reality over and above bodily reality, which in some ways coheres with the New Testament's emphasis on what lies beyond this earth. In fact, unlike Epicureanism and other Hellenistic views, Neoplatonism already had all the pieces in place to unite with many theological ideas in early Christianity. It would not be long after Paul's death before Christians had turned a full 180 degrees in their attitude toward Greek philosophy.

As a living philosophical movement, Neoplatonism lasted well into the medieval period. Like Epicureanism, it even played a role in seventeenth-century philosophy, this time among the so-called "Cambridge Platonists." More importantly for our purposes, it influenced some of the earliest Christian philosophers, a few of whom we will meet briefly in the final section.

Conclusion

Christianity continued to develop in step with philosophy. Neoplatonism emerged with the work of Plotinus in the third century AD, following a group of Christian philosophers and theologians known now as the "church fathers." These figures, such as Irenaeus (second century AD), Clement of Alexandria (AD 150–215), Tertullian (AD 155–240), and Origen (AD 184–253), contributed to an enormous body of theological literature written in both Greek and Latin. Others played an equally fundamental—and generally more orthodox—role in the development of Christian theology, like Ambrose (AD 340–397), Jerome (AD 347–420), and Augustine of Hippo (AD 354–430). Augustine in particular had wide philosophical influence that extends far beyond Christianity. Although the church fathers agree among themselves on certain issues within Christian theology, there is still great variation among their views. Though they are not part of the Greco-Roman background of the New Testament proper, they still belong both to the background that many readers bring to the text and to the history of New Testament interpretation that has developed around them.

In this chapter we have discussed the philosophical language of the New Testament world. This language has many dialects: from its beginnings in the Presocratics and its flowering in ancient Greece to the Hellenistic philosophers and their intellectual heirs, a few long-running philosophical movements had an outsized impact on the New Testament. The most important of these are Epicureanism and Stoicism, which Paul encountered directly and which run as an undercurrent beneath many scriptural passages.

Given the influence of Greek and Roman thinking in the early communities of Christianity, it may be surprising that we do not see even more explicitly philosophical material in Paul's letters or the Gospels. We have seen how Paul warily treats some of these issues, worrying always that the influence of worldly wisdom will spill over into the minds and hearts of the faithful. What might he have thought when later theological developments began to fold many ideas of Greek and Roman thinking into Christianity itself? The legacy of the church fathers and other thinkers witnesses the checkered history of the interaction between Christian doctrine and philosophy—an interaction that began within the philosophical milieu of the Roman Empire and continues today.

Though not often articulated or appreciated, Latter-day Saint thought encompasses many interesting and important philosophical positions in dialogue with both the scriptures and other movements in Christian thought. The more we understand the language of these positions and how they relate to each other, the more we can value and live the beautiful system of thought given fullest expression in Joseph Smith and his successors.

⥺

Bryce Gessell is a PhD student at Duke University studying the history and philosophy of science.

Notes

1. Western philosophy is not the only philosophical movement of this time; both Chinese philosophy and Buddhism can claim ancient origins. For an accessible exploration of these topics, see Bryan W. Van Norden, *Introduction to Classical Chinese Philosophy* (Indianapolis: Hackett, 2011).
2. For Presocratic primary sources in English and Greek, see Daniel W. Graham, ed., *The Texts of Early Greek Philosophy: The Complete Fragments and Selected Testimonies of the Major Presocratics* (Cambridge: Cambridge University Press, 2010); and S. Marc Cohen, Patricia Curd, and C. D. C. Reeve, eds., *Readings in*

Ancient Greek Philosophy from Thales to Aristotle (Indianapolis: Hackett, 1995). References to Presocratic philosophers are made with Diels-Kranz numbers (see tinyurl.com/gessellNT04).

3. Graham, *Texts of Early Greek Philosophy*, 29.

4. See Graham, *Texts of Early Greek Philosophy*.

5. For Socrates, Plato, and Aristotle, as well as most other figures discussed in this chapter, more comprehensive introductions to their lives and thought are found in the Internet Encyclopedia of Philosophy (iep.utm.edu) and Stanford Encyclopedia of Philosophy (plato.stanford.edu).

6. Plato, *Apology* 30e.

7. This is called the "Socratic problem." See tinyurl.com/gessellNT05 for further discussion.

8. For Plato's primary sources in English, see John M. Cooper, ed., *Plato: Complete Works* (Indianapolis: Hackett, 1997); quotations in this chapter are from this edition. Greek editions can also be found in the Oxford Classical Texts series as well as in the Loeb Classical Library (loebclassics.com). Greek and English versions of many of Plato's works are available for free online at the Perseus Project (perseus.tufts.edu). References to Plato's works are made with Stephanus numbers (tinyurl.com/gessellNT06).

9. Plato, *Republic* 514a–520a.

10. For Aristotle's primary sources in English, see Jonathan Barnes, ed., *The Complete Works of Aristotle: The Revised Oxford Translation* (Princeton, NJ: Princeton University Press, 1984). The standard Greek editions of his work are part of the Oxford Classical Texts series; see also the Loeb Classical Library (loebclassics.com). As with Plato, the Perseus Project (perseus.tufts.edu) hosts free versions of Aristotle's work in both Greek and English. References to Aristotle's works are made with Bekker numbers (tinyurl.com/gessellNT07).

11. Alfred North Whitehead, an early-twentieth century philosopher and mathematician, wrote that "the safest general characterization of the European philosophical tradition is that it consists of a series of footnotes to Plato." *Process and Reality*, ed. David Ray Griffin and Donald W. Sherburne (London: Free Press, 1978).

12. More precisely, the Hellenistic age begins with the death of Alexander the Great in 323 BC and ends with the Roman victory at Egypt in 30 BC.

13. Unlike the works of the more prominent philosophers like Plato and Aristotle, most of the original writings of the Cynic philosophers are now lost. We know about them through the descriptions of other writers. For a discussion of the available sources and translations of many important Cynic texts, see Robert Dobbin, *The Cynic Philosophers: From Diogenes to Julian* (London: Penguin, 2012).

14. Both stories are reported in Diogenes Laërtius, *Lives of Eminent Philosophers* (see next note).

15. Other important philosophical systems of this period are the Skeptics (also called Pyrrhonism), the Cyrenaics, and the Hellenistic Judaism of Philo of Alexandria. As with the Cynics, we do not possess many original sources from authors in the Hellenistic period. Diogenes Laërtius, who lived several hundred years after Christ, gathered many philosophical doctrines and stories in his *Lives of the Eminent Philosophers*. Both the Greek text and an English translation of *Lives* are available online as part of the Loeb Classical Library (loebclassics.com). A recent English edition of textual fragments with commentary is A. A. Long and D. N. Sedley, *The Hellenistic Philosophers* (Cambridge: Cambridge University Press, 1987). For Philo, see Charles Duke Yonge, *The Works of Philo* (Peabody, MA: Hedrickson Publishers, 1995).

16. Plato, *Phaedo* 82e.

17. Plato, *Phaedo* 63e.

18. See συλαγωγέω in Frederick William Danker, *A Greek-English Lexicon of the New Testament and Other Early Christian Literature* (Chicago: University of Chicago Press, 2001). This work, sometimes called "BDAG" for the initials of current and former editors, is one of the most authoritative lexicons for New Testament Greek.

19. See σπερμολόγος in Danker, *Greek-English Lexicon of the New Testament*.

20. The tenth book of Diogenes Laërtius's *Lives*, cited earlier, deals with Epicurus (see tinyurl.com/gessellNT08). This work contains the original sources, which are letters Epicurus wrote to some of his followers. See also Cyril B. Bailey, *Epicurus: The Extant Remains* (Oxford: Clarendon Press, 1926), tinyurl.com/gessellNT03;

and Long and Sedley, *Hellenistic Philosophers*. Tim O'Keefe, *Epicureanism* (Durham, UK: Acumen, 2010), is a good introduction to Epicureanism in general.

21. The main opposition of empiricism is "rationalism," or the idea that we have knowledge that is somehow independent of sense experience.

22. Diogenes Laertius, *Lives* 10.124.

23. Diogenes Laertius, *Lives* 10.123.

24. For an English translation of *De rerum natura*, see tinyurl.com/gessellNT02.

25. Paul continues in the same verse: "as certain also of your own poets have said, For we are also his offspring." Here he quotes from the Stoic poet Aratus (315–240 BC), who wrote a long work called *Phenomena*.

26. This view is based on the Greek μὲν . . . δὲ construction in Acts 17:32, along with a parallel to verse 18, where the philosophers are first mentioned. See Jerome H. Neyrey, "Acts 17, Epicureans, and Theodicy: A Study in Stereotypes," in David L. Balach, Everett Ferguson, and Wayne A. Meeks, eds., *Greeks, Romans, and Christians: Essays in Honor of Abraham J. Malherbe* (Minneapolis: Fortress, 1990). The possibility has also been suggested by other authors.

27. See Plutarch, *On the Fortune or the Virtue of Alexander* (tinyurl.com/gessellNT01). Other early Stoic authors include Cleanthes and Chrysippus. See Long and Sedley, *Hellenistic Philosophers*, for texts and background on Cleanthes, Chrysippus, and other Stoic philosophers.

28. Epictetus, quoted in Long and Sedley, *Hellenistic Philosophers*, 418.

29. For primary sources of these authors, see the Loeb Classical Library (loebclassics.com). For collected fragments, see Long and Sedley, *Hellenistic Philosophers*.

30. Human beings, consisting of a "heavy" body and a "light" soul—though both are material—have a kind of personal identity during life. Upon death, our still-existent parts return to form part of the whole once again, but we are no longer differentiated by an identity. It may have been the identity-preserving nature of the Resurrection—as opposed to the weaker, impersonal "immortality" of typical Stoicism—that piqued the interest of these philosophers. The last important Stoic philosopher was Marcus Aurelius. By his time, Stoicism had dropped most of its interest in questions about the natural world and was focused exclusively on ethics. The original Stoic division of knowledge into logic, physics, and ethics still existed, but Aurelius's writings were more personal in nature. His *Meditations*, sometimes called *To Himself*, was a series of reflections on his life and duty as an emperor and adherent of Stoic philosophy. See tinyurl.com/gessellNT09 for the *Meditations*, in addition to the sources cited earlier.

31. Other passages with possible Greek philosophical influences include Romans 1–2 and 2 Peter 3. For an introduction to these issues along with a discussion of Stoicism in several apocryphal texts, see Tumoas Rasimus, Troels Engberg-Pedersen, and Ismo Dunderberg, eds., *Stoicism in Early Christianity* (Grand Rapids, MI: Baker, 2010).

32. See tinyurl.com/gessellNT10 and tinyurl.com/gessellNT11 for works by Cicero.

33. The *Enneads* are available online in the Loeb Classical Library (loebclassics.com).

34. Some of this material is online; see tinyurl.com/gessellNT12. A better source is R. Joseph Hoffmann, ed. and trans., *Porphyry's Against the Christians* (Amherst, NY: Prometheus Books, 1994).

35. For texts and interpretation of Iamblichus, see tinyurl.com/gessellNT13.

12

Greco-Roman Religion and the New Testament

Grant Adamson

Early Christians regularly defined themselves not only in relation to their fellow Jews but also in relation to the many other inhabitants of the ancient Mediterranean world and the Near East. The need first became acute with the launch of gentile missions during the years after the crucifixion and resurrection of Jesus. This chapter discusses references to Greco-Roman religion in the New Testament as a feature of early Christian self-definition.

Gentiles and Gentile Missions

The term *Greco-Roman* is academic shorthand for two civilizations that overlapped in space and time: that of ancient Greece during the archaic, Hellenic, and Hellenistic periods; and that of ancient Rome during the periods of monarchy, republic, and empire. The two civilizations were multicultural, extending far beyond such cities as Athens, Sparta, or Rome itself on the Italian peninsula. Thus the term applies to Greeks and Romans proper along with numerous subordinates. In that sense, early Christians and their fellow Jews can be classified as Greco-Roman to the extent they were influenced by Hellenistic culture one way or another and lived within the boundaries of the Roman Empire. In a somewhat more restricted sense, scholars may use *Greco-Roman* to signify anyone or anything non-Christian and non-Jewish. It can therefore be interchangeable with *gentile* and *pagan*, which are far from neutral terms.

When the different authors of the various books of the New Testament wanted to refer to non-Jews, sometimes they referred to them as "Greeks" or "Hellenes" (e.g., Acts 16:1), and only occasionally did they refer to them as "Romans" (e.g., Acts 28:17). Most often they referred to them simply as "Gentiles" (e.g., Acts 4:27). Christians also came to refer to non-Jews and non-Christians as "pagans," but that was much later, long after the New Testament was written. The English word *pagan* comes from the Latin adjective *paganus* (plural *pagani*); it means someone "from the countryside," or a "peasant." In a military context it could also mean "civilian."[1] The term was used in classical Latin before Christianity, but ancient Romans did not self-identify as pagans. Christians developed that identification for them beginning in the fourth century AD in an effort to characterize them as being either unrefined or outside the ranks of the "army of Christ."[2] Much later still, Christians living in the Latin West (Italy, Gaul, Britain) used the term *heathen* as an English equivalent of *pagan*.[3] But because it tends to be derogatory, as well as anachronistic, scholars normally avoid the term.[4] As for *pagan* and *Gentile*, there is debate, but many scholars still use those terms even though the former is also anachronistic to earliest Christianity—not to mention with regard to ancient Greece and Rome in the centuries BC.

The New Testament authors wrote in Greek (a prime example of the influence of Hellenistic culture), and in Greek the underlying words for "Gentiles" are *ethnē* (singular *ethnos*) and *ethnikoi* (singular *ethnikos*); *ethnē* literally means "nations."[5] In Latin the equivalents are *gentes* (singular *gens*) and *gentiles* (singular *gentilis*).[6] Like the term *pagan*, *Gentile* is not an insider designation. As used by Christians, the term can be overtly pejorative, and it assumes a non-Greek, non-Roman point of view that Christianity largely inherited from earlier Judaism. Very broadly speaking, ancient Israel saw itself as God's chosen people or nation. Everyone else belonged to "the nations," *goyim* in Hebrew (singular *goy*); for hellenized Jews who could no longer comprehend Hebrew or Aramaic, *goyim* was rendered as *ethnē* in Greek versions of Jewish scripture known as the Septuagint, the versions of scripture that the New Testament authors were familiar with.[7] The supposition was that Israel worshipped the one true God and everyone else worshipped idols. There were some efforts to proselytize non-Israelites before Christianity came along, and a number of Jews even anticipated that Gentiles would be welcomed in at the end of time. But for the most part, Jews kept to themselves, and their religion was for them. In Jesus's day the boundary between Jews and non-Jews was physically drawn in the architecture of the Jerusalem temple, where Gentiles were limited to the outer court and occupied the least holy space surrounding the inner courts for Jewish women, Jewish men, and Jewish male priests.[8] Certain Jewish believers in Jesus, most notably the (former) Pharisee Paul, defied the distinction between Jews and Gentiles while still seeing themselves as the chosen people or nation of God.

All twenty-seven books of the New Testament were written after Christians decided to start preaching to non-Jews in earnest, and the authors of the books have provided accounts of multiple gentile missions. In his letter to the Galatians, Paul claims he was called directly by God through revelation, not by the original apostles or any other mortal agent. Moreover, he says the original apostles, such as Peter, were involved in a mission to Jews, not

Gentiles (Galatians 1:1, 11–2:10). According to the book of Acts, however, the gospel was first taken to non-Jews when Philip preached to the Samaritans, and then when he taught an Ethiopian who had traveled to Jerusalem (8:4–40). Next was Paul's conversion on the road to Damascus in Syria, but according to Acts, he did not preach to Gentiles right away;[9] Peter preceded him. Upon seeing a vision and hearing a divine voice, Peter, not Paul, visited the house of a Roman army commander, Cornelius, in Caesarea Maritima. Peter had him and his household baptized, thereby formally launching the gentile mission in the region of Judea, Samaria, and Galilee (10; 11:1–18; 15:6–21). Acts states that it was later that Paul and his companions, headquartered in Syrian Antioch, took the gospel to Gentiles elsewhere. Even then Paul did not do so until after two things had occurred: first, he was commissioned and set apart by his peers in Antioch who included "Simeon that was called Niger, and Lucius of Cyrene, and Manaen" (13:1–3); second, Jews repeatedly rejected his message as he went throughout Asia Minor (modern Turkey), Greece, and eventually the empire's capital (13:46–48; 14:27; 18:4–6; 28:24–28). After those events, at last he preached to Gentiles. Such is the story in the book of Acts, which is not the same story Paul himself told in Galatians.

However exactly the decision was made to start preaching to non-Jews, some Christians were not supportive of gentile missions or else disagreed as to how the missions ought to be run. This should not be surprising. It was hardly a foregone conclusion that Jesus and his disciples would preach to non-Jews. For instance, according to the Gospel of Mark, when a Greek Syrophoenician woman asked Jesus to heal her daughter, he said, "Let the children first be filled: for it is not meet to take the children's bread, and to cast it unto the dogs" (7:27). According to Matthew, he also said he was "not sent but unto the lost sheep of the house of Israel" (15:24), which matches the Matthean version of Jesus's call and commission of the original apostles: "Go not into the way of the Gentiles, and into any city of the Samaritans enter ye not: but go rather to the lost sheep of the house of Israel" (10:5–6). Again according to Matthew, Jesus updated the mission to include non-Jews after his resurrection (28:18–20; compare Luke 24:47; Acts 1:8). But that information reflects what Christians decided some years later. Both Mark and Matthew as well as Luke–Acts were written in light of post-Easter developments, after Paul's opening revelation. Paul wrote in the late 40s, 50s, and early 60s AD, and according to him the original apostles were still involved in a mission to Jews, not Gentiles. Mark was probably written in the late 60s or 70s, Matthew in the 70s or 80s, and Luke–Acts in the 80s or 90s.[10]

At any rate, the decision to preach to Gentiles was controversial even among Christians. Their missionizing brought them into closer contact as well as conflict with the diverse religious practices and beliefs of the peoples of the ancient Mediterranean and Near East. As missionaries preached to Gentiles besides their fellow Jews, they had to determine what they wanted their converts to do and not do, to believe and not believe, in order to become Christians like them. Paradoxically, wherever the similarities were already too close they had to distinguish themselves from those they were trying to missionize. The process of preaching, then, was simultaneously one of defining Christianity.

New Testament References to Greco-Roman Religion

With perhaps a rare exception or two, the authors of the New Testament came from Jewish backgrounds; they were not gentile converts, though, to be sure, they narrated the conversion stories of several non-Jews. Justin Martyr's account may be the earliest autobiographical record of gentile Christian conversion, and it dates to the middle of the second century. In his case, he converted from Greek philosophy, Platonism in particular.[11] Therefore the New Testament authors did not write as former worshippers of Greek and Roman gods and goddesses; they wrote as Judeo-Christians. At best their references to non-Jewish, non-Christian religion are mildly sympathetic, at worst dismissive or outright condemnatory, either way communicating more about themselves than about Gentiles. Greeks and Romans do not speak in these references; the voices are generally those of the New Testament authors.

Most of the references to Greco-Roman religion are in the letters of Paul and the book of Acts. By no means passive, they work to establish a series of distinctions between the one true God and false deities, inspiration and possession, and religion and magic. To better understand these distinctions that involve Jews as well as Gentiles, it is necessary to read references to Greco-Roman belief and practice together with references to Judaism.

The one true God versus false deities

Consistent with his Jewish background, in his letters Paul counts idolatry among the many sins for which he thinks unconverted Gentiles will be liable to incur divine wrath. Part of his gospel message to non-Jews was that they should turn away from idols, toward the worship of the one true God instead, thereby avoiding the imminent doom that otherwise awaited them. For Paul the true God was living, which suggests that idols were not, though Paul does ultimately posit metaphysical existence behind the statues and images of Greek and Roman divinities, namely demons. The true God is the immortal creator, but idols have been fashioned after mortal creation: figures shaped like humans, birds, quadrupeds, and reptiles (1 Thessalonians 1:9–10; 1 Corinthians 6:9–11; Romans 1:18–32, esp. 18–25).

These ideas in Paul's letters are elaborated in a speech attributed to Paul in the book of Acts, where he waxes philosophical in the company of Athenian intelligentsia. Remarking on their many idols, if not their superstition, he tells them that they do not actually know God. They think God resides in the holy places they build for him, that he requires their sacrifices and other offerings, and that their representations of him in precious metal and stone are both adequate and accurate. But God transcends all these, Paul tells the Athenians while inviting them to repent before the coming judgment (Acts 17:16–31).

On the basis of his letters, it is not always obvious precisely how Paul wanted Gentiles to turn away from idols. Statues and other artistic representations of the many non-Jewish gods and goddesses were ubiquitous in the Roman Empire, and there was no separation of church and state then, as there is in some modern societies. Throughout the provinces and cities, in public temples and shrines, as well as in private households, sacrifices and offerings were made to this or that deity represented by his or her image. The idea that Gentiles worshipped beast-shaped gods and goddesses is a stereotype accurate enough in Egypt and other ancient Near Eastern civilizations, but not true of Romans, who sometimes mocked them for it. In fact, starting long before Christianity, Greek philosophers as well as other critics questioned popular beliefs that the divine was anthropomorphic and that divinities and their images were one and the same. In sacrifices and offerings in both Greek and Roman religions, usually just a portion of the animal sacrificed at the altar was placed on the fire to be burned for the god or goddess. The rest of the meat went to the priests and celebrants, and anything that remained was sold. Meat was not the only food offering; there were also offerings of grain and wine.[12]

In 1 Corinthians, Paul flatly tells the saints not to consume food offered to idols, because it has been sacrificed to demons and participation in demon worship is wholly incompatible with belief in Jesus: "Ye cannot drink the cup of the Lord, and the cup of devils: ye cannot be partakers of the Lord's table, and of the table of devils" (10:21; a better translation than "devils" would be "demons," as in the NRSV). Paul's reasoning seems to be in line with monotheistic and aniconic passages from the Hebrew Bible or Old Testament stating that God stands alone and yet is jealous of worship directed at any other deity or representation thereof (10:6–22; compare Deuteronomy 4; 5:6–8; 32:16–21). Incidentally, according to the book of Acts, the Jerusalem Council led by Jesus's brother James also ruled that gentile converts not eat food offered to idols (15:19–21).[13]

Nevertheless in the same epistle to the Corinthians, Paul makes allowances. He tells the Corinthians not to worry about asking whether the meat they buy in the market or that is served to them as guests in the houses of Gentiles has been sacrificed to idols. They could eat it regardless. But if somebody points out that it has been sacrificed to a non-Jewish, non-Christian deity, then Paul instructs them not to eat it. The rationale here has to do with grouping the saints into strong and weak adherents. The strong know that idols are nothing and that it is faith rather than food that matters most. The weak do not understand yet, and until they do they should not eat sacrificial food. To help the weak, neither should the strong eat when the weak are around and watching. At least hypothetically, though, the strong could walk into a Greek or Roman temple and eat and drink there with gentile worshippers, so long as the weak were not nearby to be upset (see 1 Corinthians 10:23–11:1; also 1 Corinthians 8; Romans 14).

The issue was not Jewish dietary regulations and the catalog of clean and unclean animals in Jewish scripture, though there could be overlap. For instance, along with sheep and cattle, pigs were one of the animals that Greeks and Romans often sacrificed, and of course eating pork was prohibited by Jewish law. Paul was and is (in)famous for disregarding aspects of the law, such as the requirement of circumcision for males, which he even vehemently opposed in some of his writing (Galatians 5:2–12; Philippians 3:2–4). When it came to food, he was prepared to say everything was clean, and thus believers in Jesus, whether from a Jewish or gentile background, need not keep kosher. But once more, at the same time, he did not want anyone to be bothered, and it all hinged on the knowledge and conscience of the strong and weak.

Despite his flexibility, Paul was clearly opinionated, and though his behavior made sense to him, he was met with anger from all sides. In his letters he enumerates the hazards and violence he experienced, but he does not go into detail (2 Corinthians 11:21–29). In the book of Acts, there is an account of a riot in Ephesus that resulted from his preaching against idols and Greco-Roman deities. The Greek goddess Artemis (KJV Diana) could be amalgamated with other local goddesses throughout the Roman Empire, and her Ephesian temple was renowned, a wonder of the ancient Mediterranean world.[14] In Acts the silversmiths selling figurines of the temple feel threatened by Paul. As one of them is said to have put it, "Not alone at Ephesus, but almost throughout all Asia, this Paul hath persuaded and turned away much people, saying that they be no gods, which are made with hands: so that not only this our craft is in danger to be set at nought; but also that the temple of the great goddess Diana should be despised, and her magnificence should be destroyed, whom all Asia and the world worshippeth" (19:26–27; see 23–27). Some of Paul's companions are pushed and pulled around by the ensuing mob, while Paul is at a safe distance. After a couple of hours of chaos, a city official has to disperse the crowd and remind them of civil order and due process (19:28–41). Embellishments are to be expected in Acts as in any literature, even the Greco-Roman genre of history, but this is precisely the kind of negative response Paul sometimes undoubtedly encountered. Some Gentiles converted and turned away from idols; others did not. To them Paul's preaching might easily have been perceived as an attack on their religion, cultural identity, and in some instances their immediate livelihood.

It would be one thing for Paul to have run afoul of Greco-Roman religious rivals by jeopardizing their monetary interests, another for him to have undermined the well-being of the empire and the legitimacy of imperial rule, which were thought to rest, in no small degree, on the traditional pantheon and the cultivation of their favor and protection through traditional worship; in ancient Rome, political peace and stability came from the gods. What is more, several Hellenistic kings and queens and not a few Roman emperors and empresses themselves—especially in the eastern half of the Roman Empire—were given divine honors, like gods and goddesses, in their own lifetime, not just after death.[15] In his letter to the Romans, Paul tells the saints in the capital city to "be subject unto the higher powers. For there is no power but of God: the powers that be are ordained of God" (13:1; a better translation than "higher powers" would be "governing authorities," as in the NRSV). Paul even goes so far as to tell them to give honor to their rulers (13:2–7). It is doubtful, though, that he would have approved sacrifices and offerings made to an emperor or king as a divinity. That would have blurred the distinction between the one true God and false deities, be they idols, demons, or human beings. Note how Paul positions the one true God atop government, thereby maintaining the legitimacy of Roman rule in the eyes of Judeo-Christians.[16] From his preaching against idols, his audience might have arrived at the perilous conclusion that demons were controlling the empire and thus that they should not support imperial administration. Paul reassures them that their God is in charge. This would have allowed for sacrifices and offerings to be made to the Lord on behalf of the emperor, rather than to the emperor as deity—a key difference.

The writings of an older contemporary, another Greek-speaking Jew, Philo of Alexandria, provide an instructive parallel. Alexandria, in Roman Egypt, was home to many Jews and of course to non-Jewish Egyptian Greeks, or Greco-Egyptians. Relations were so strained in the 30s AD that both sent embassies to the emperor Gaius, nicknamed Caligula, in Rome. The Greeks alleged that the Jews would not sacrifice in affairs of state. Philo headed up the Jewish embassy, and according to his telling of events he and the rest of the Jewish delegation unanimously insisted that they had sacrificed hundreds of animals on multiple occasions during Caligula's reign: upon his rise to power, to give thanks for his improved health after a keen sickness, and in the hopes of his success in battle. Their insistence, however, did not satisfy the emperor. According to Philo, Caligula wanted the Jews to sacrifice to him, not merely on his behalf. This visibly terrified the Jewish ambassadors.[17]

Paul may have been of the same mind as Philo: willing to sacrifice on a ruler's behalf, if the sacrifices and offerings were made to the Lord according to Jewish practice. For centuries, ancient Israelites ritually slaughtered animals at their altars. They eventually stopped after the Jerusalem temple was destroyed in AD 70 and never rebuilt (Samaritans, by contrast, sacrifice on Mount Gerizim to this day). But the temple was still there when Paul was alive. He and the original apostles would have participated with their fellow Jews in sacrifices and offerings even after the crucifixion and resurrection of Jesus, whether it was the daily rites, those of the Sabbath, or the major pilgrimage festivals.[18] Paul had no reason to oppose Jewish sacrifice made to the one true God of Judaism and Christianity on behalf of the Roman emperor. But he almost certainly would have resisted any form of ruler worship.

In the book of Acts, the gentile error of worshipping human beings is a narrative theme, from the worship of government authorities to holy men and wonder-workers. The subject is initially introduced with the conversion of the centurion Cornelius and the launch of the gentile mission in Judea, Samaria, and Galilee. When Cornelius encounters Peter, he prostrates himself (10:24–25). Peter corrects him and says, "Stand up; I myself also am a man" (10:26; a better translation than "man" would be "mortal," as in the NRSV). The subject is addressed again with the death of Herod Agrippa I (a grandson of Herod the Great), who ruled Palestine AD 41–44 as a Jewish client king appointed by Rome. In Acts, after his speech to the people of Tyre and Sidon (in modern Lebanon), they cheer that they have listened to a deity, not a human being (12:20–22). Then Herod dies: "And immediately the angel of the Lord smote him, because he gave not God the glory: and he was eaten of worms, and gave up the ghost" (12:23). The subject is broached for a third time with the missionary journey of Paul and Barnabas from Syrian Antioch to Lystra (near Konya in modern Turkey). While preaching there, Paul heals a man in front of a sizable audience. The people who witness the miracle think that Paul and Barnabas are the Greek gods Hermes and Zeus respectively (14:8–12; KJV Mercurius and Jupiter). As with the goddess Artemis, these deities could be amalgamated with other local gods throughout the Roman Empire, and their worship, especially the worship of Zeus, was widespread. In Acts, as the Lystran priest of Zeus prepares to offer sacrifice to Barnabas and Paul, they are horrified and yell, "Sirs, why do ye these things? We also are men of like passions with you, and preach unto you that ye should turn from these vanities unto the living God, which made heaven, and earth, and the sea, and all things that are therein" (14:15; see 13–18; a better translation than "men of like passions with you" would be "mortals just like you," as in the NRSV). The common denominator in each of these instances is that Gentiles are prone to venerate humans, and the point is that anyone whom Gentiles might try to worship should decline obeisance and should defer to the one true God. Peter and Paul and Barnabas defer, whereas Herod Agrippa does not. This Judeo-Christian view of Greco-Roman religion is a trope. Greeks and Romans did not understand themselves to be worshipping mere mortals; they believed, some more than others, that their rulers, heroes, holy men, and healers could be divine. Moreover, they believed that their immortal gods and goddesses could appear on earth disguised as mortals.

Worth noting is that ancient Judaism also had a tradition of theophanies and angelophanies, including the belief that the one true God or his angels might be disguised temporarily among humans—a tradition that facilitated early Christian belief that Jesus pre-existed as a divine being and that he descended from heaven and was incarnated.[19] Over the centuries of late antiquity and on into the Middle Ages, Jesus's godhood and incarnation became one of the major doctrines separating mainstream Christianity from Rabbinic Judaism and Islam. For many Greeks and Romans, however, those teachings would have been relatively unobjectionable; they were accustomed to the idea of a deity appearing as a human being on earth, even the idea that the son of a god might be born to a human mother (virgin birth is another topic).[20] The potential offense to Gentiles was the exclusivity of Christian doctrine: that Jesus alone was God made manifest and that his incarnation within a negligible territory of the empire was a singular event of universal consequence.

Inspiration versus possession

The distinction between the one true God and false deities is fundamental in New Testament references to Greco-Roman religion. It brings with it a further distinction: protagonists are inspired by the one true God, that is, by his Spirit; antagonists are possessed by some other false spirit or demon. In Paul's epistles, the communities of saints he describes are charismatic, exercising numerous spiritual gifts such as prophecy and speaking in tongues. Paul describes and prescribes the activity of multiple prophets and prophetesses even in one gathering of saints. He gives instructions for weighing and testing prophecy, and he lists the discernment of spirits itself as a spiritual gift (1 Thessalonians 5:19–22; 1 Corinthians 11:2–16; 12:4–11; 14:1–33, 37–40; esp. 12:10; 14:29).[21] So in these charismatic communities it must have been accepted that some utterances might be false, coming from a source besides the Spirit of the one true God. Presumably that is how Paul would have categorized Greco-Roman prophecy and divination, but he does not talk about gentile oracles, seers, prophets, or prophetesses in his letters, and so he does not say that they were possessed by the wrong spirit.

The closest Paul comes to discussing gentile possession is in his general statements about the lives of gentile converts before they believed in Jesus. Things become complex, though, because he makes analogous statements about the former life of Jewish converts as well. In his epistle to the Galatians, he employs metaphor to explain what he regards to be the expiration of aspects of Jewish law. The metaphor he uses is that of a juvenile's status before maturity and inheritance: "Even so we, when we were children, were in bondage under the elements of the world: but when the fulness of the time was come, God sent forth his Son, made of a woman, made under the law, to redeem them that were under the law, that we might receive the adoption of sons [and daughters]" (4:3–5; a better translation than "elements" would be "elemental spirits," as in the NRSV). It is difficult to be sure, but Paul is apparently referring to the former life of both Jewish and gentile converts as servitude. By the "elemental spirits" of the world or cosmos, he may mean the angels through whom the law of Moses was added to God's will or testament (3:6–29), as if these angels surreptitiously changed the promises and blessings to Abraham and his seed after God gave them. Shifting from the first person *we* to the second person *you*, Paul also means the divinities of Greco-Roman religion. This is clear from the statement he makes a few verses later. Addressing the Galatian saints who had begun to observe Jewish law more rigorously at the encouragement of some of Paul's Jewish-Christian competitors, he writes, "Howbeit then, when ye knew not God, ye did service unto them which by nature are no gods," a patent reference to gentile deities and religious statuary. "But now, after that ye have known God, or rather are known of God, how turn ye again to the weak and beggarly elements, whereunto ye desire again to be in bondage? Ye observe days, and months, and times, and years. I am afraid of you, lest I have bestowed upon you labour in vain" (4:8–11; again a better translation than "elements" would be "elemental spirits," as in the NRSV). To judge from these two statements in his letter to the Galatians, it seems that Paul was not averse to classifying Judeo-Christian angels and Greco-Roman deities together as "elemental spirits" when it suited his purposes in arguing with his co-religionists over how gentile missions ought to be run (e.g., whether male converts should be circumcised or not). Saying that someone is enslaved to idols and the elemental spirits of the cosmos is, in a measure, proximate to saying they have been possessed.

Paul makes another statement about the former life of gentile converts in 1 Corinthians. This time he may have something else in mind, and the context is, in fact, gifts of the Spirit, or charismata: "Now concerning spiritual gifts, brethren [and sisters], I would not have you ignorant. Ye know that ye were Gentiles, carried away unto these dumb idols, even as ye were led. Wherefore I give you to understand, that no man [or woman] speaking by the Spirit of God calleth Jesus accursed: and that no man [or woman] can say that Jesus is the Lord, but by the Holy Ghost" (12:1–3). The thought here is difficult to grasp. Perhaps the Corinthian saints had wanted to know whether correct information (Jesus is Lord) could ever come from a false spirit or from outside the community. Writing in reply, Paul reminds them of their former life as pagans, and in so doing he resorts to a Judeo-Christian cliché of gentile religion, that is: Gentiles worship idols, and idols of stone and wood are not living and cannot say anything. But then without acknowledging it, Paul seems to proceed on the assumption that idols—or, more correctly, the demonic spirits behind them—do speak. A person inspired by the Spirit of the one true God would not utter incorrect information;

that oracular content would have to come from a false spirit. Whereas anyone who utters correct information, whether as a member of the community or not, is not possessed by an idolatrous spirit or demon; that content would have to come from the Spirit of God. Hence, membership in the community is not altogether definitive. Correct content is the important thing. And the source or origin of an utterance simply follows its content: someone who curses Jesus is possessed; someone who calls Jesus Lord is inspired.

If that is what Paul was thinking in 1 Corinthians, it may be difficult to reconcile that idea with an account in the book of Acts, where he happens upon a girl in Philippi who has a Pythian spirit, or in other words a divinatory spirit of the oracle of the Greek god Apollo (16:16). Apollo's foremost oracle was at Delphi, and the oracle herself, the Pythia, was a woman through whom the deity was supposed to answer questions. There were other oracles in the ancient Mediterranean, large and small, as well as a host of freelance practitioners of divination and prophecy of various kinds, not to mention official priests who interpreted the entrails of sacrificial animals, the flight of birds, and so on.[22] Some of these freelance practitioners are known to have had children working for them as mediums.[23] According to Acts, the girl in Philippi "brought her masters much gain by soothsaying" (16:16), which is entirely plausible. The girl begins accompanying Paul and his associates, rightly shouting day after day to the people around: "These men are the servants of the most high God, which shew unto us the way of salvation" (16:17). For whatever reason, Paul is aggravated after a while, and in Jesus's name he expels the Pythian spirit from the girl. Since she would not be able to tell fortunes any longer, this infuriates the practitioners she was working for, and Paul and Silas end up in prison (16:17–24). The account here suggests that the source or origin is what is definitive, not content. The information that the girl uttered was correct. Nevertheless, the source of that declaration, according to Acts, was not the Spirit of the one true God; it came from another spirit that Paul cast out of her, like the many other evil or unclean spirits and demons in Luke–Acts that must be driven from the sick and disabled (see Luke 4:31–36; 6:17–19; 8:1–3, 26–39; 9:37–43; 11:14–26; Acts 5:16; 8:6–7; 19:11–16). Thus, the girl was not an inspired gentile prophetess whose utterances could be tolerated as a complement to the gospel message—she was possessed.

The Paul of Galatians and 1 Corinthians could see himself as a liberator of sorts, bringing freedom to Gentiles who had been "in bondage under the elements of the world," who "did service unto them which by nature are no gods," and who had been "carried away unto these dumb idols, even as ye were led" (Galatians 4:3, 8; 1 Corinthians 12:2). But when it came to physical slavery, Paul equivocated (see Philemon; 1 Corinthians 7:17–24).[24] Whatever the situation of physical slaves in his epistles, in the book of Acts the girl with a Pythian spirit is not said to have been freed from her owners. Nothing is recorded regarding what happened to her next. The spotlight is on Paul, and the upshot is that his religious rivals, the practitioners of divination and prophecy in Philippi, were financially motivated, just as the silversmiths in Ephesus.

Religion versus magic

Along with the worship of idols, in his letters Paul counts sorcery as a sin. He cautions the Galatians against it and a broad range of other types of misconduct (5:19–21). The inventory of transgressions may be a set list, so this is not automatically evidence of saints practicing magic in Galatia. But some of Paul's gentile converts likely did practice what he would have considered sorcery. Almost no one ever says that the rituals they are performing are anything other than religious. Typically, religion is what insiders say they do, and sorcery and magic are labels they apply to the religious practices of outsiders.[25]

The distinction between religion and magic is established again and again in Acts. First, in Samaria there is Simon the magician. The Samaritans are said to have regarded him as "the great power of God" (8:10). He is supplanted by the evangelist Philip, who impresses everyone, Simon included, with exorcisms and healings. For his profiteering Simon is denounced by Peter, who arrives with John to confer the Spirit on the Samaritans after their baptism (8:4–24). Second, on the island of Cyprus there is the magus Bar-Jesus, that is, "son of Joshua." He is also known as Elymas and is described as "a certain sorcerer, a false prophet, a Jew" (13:6). He battles Barnabas and Paul over the potential convert Sergius Paulus, a Roman provincial governor. In a dramatic display of superiority, Paul blinds Elymas, thus vanquishing him and securing the governor's conversion (13:4–12). Third, in Ephesus there are "certain of the vagabond Jews, exorcists," said to be "sons of one Sceva, a Jew, and chief of the priests" (19:13–14; a better translation than "vagabond" would be "itinerant," as in the NRSV). As they attempt to imitate Paul's success and cast out evil spirits in Jesus's name, one evil spirit possessing a man tells them it recognizes Jesus and Paul; it does not recognize the sons of Sceva. The possessed man then attacks and injures the sons of Sceva, who run away. At the news, scores of Ephesians are converted and give up magic themselves by burning their expensive spellbooks (19:11–20).

All of the named magicians in these passages are Jewish or else Samaritan, perhaps because the foundations of magic were associated with Judaism in Greco-Roman imagination. For one, Pliny the Elder, a Roman statesman and Latin author of the first century AD, wrote in his encyclopedia that along with Zoroaster and the Persian magi, Moses and the Jews were responsible for bringing magic to Greece and Rome.[26] The author of Luke–Acts may be playing on Greco-Roman imagination as he distances himself and Christianity from the practice of magic. Be that as it may, there are many unnamed and privately practicing gentile sorcerers among the converts who burn their books in Ephesus.

In these passages from Acts, Christians are defined more than non-Christians and their rituals are described. Philip, Peter, John, Paul, and the increasing tally of believers are distinct from sorcerers and magicians because they are affiliated with the one true God and his Spirit, not the alternative. They perform signs and miracles; they don't practice magic, nor are they looking to make money (Acts 5:1–11). All this is in contrast to Simon and Elymas and the sons of Sceva. When Simon learns that Peter and John have the ability to cause God's Spirit to enter into someone by placing their hands on the person, he wants to buy the power from them, like a transaction between businesses, presumably so that he could then sell their product and service to his clients in Samaria. His offer to Peter assumes that the original apostles care about revenue just as he does and just as he would if they wanted to purchase his trade secret. Peter condemns him and suggests that Simon's wickedness may not be forgivable (8:14–24). Paul is even harsher on Elymas. The unstated reason that Elymas is on Cyprus in the presence of the Roman provincial governor (13:7) is that the governor paid him for his consultations. He cannot lose his best customer, so he strives to prevent the governor from believing Barnabas and Paul (13:8). Although Paul's curse of blindness on Elymas is temporary, the words leave little hope of salvation for him: "Thou child of the devil, thou enemy of all righteousness, wilt thou not cease to pervert the right ways of the Lord? And now, behold, the hand of the Lord is upon thee, and thou shalt be blind, not seeing the sun for a season" (13:9–11). The curse not only shows Paul to be the winner of the contest, it also lets the governor know that Elymas has been operating by the forces of evil. As for the sons of Sceva in Ephesus, they do not want to buy Paul's ability to drive bad spirits out the way Simon wanted to buy Peter and John's power; the sons just try to mimic it, using the potent name of Jesus in their exorcisms. The attempt backfires, however. Use of the name in and of itself is not enough (19:11–16). The lesson that the people of Ephesus seem to learn from this is that their valuable spellbooks are actually worthless given that Jesus is more effective than any other deity they could pray to or invoke. And even if Jesus's name were added to invocations in their books, the prayers would not work on the lips of non-Christians, just as the exorcisms of the sons of Sceva failed. Another option, then, would have been for gentile converts to keep and Christianize their spellbooks, but the author of Luke–Acts has them burn them as a gauge of their conversion (Acts 19:17–20).

However many tomes of magic the converted Ephesians may have destroyed, that sort of literature still survives. Most manuscripts come from Roman Egypt because the arid climate has preserved them. The bulk of them were copied in the 200s and 300s AD, though transcribed from even older manuscripts. They are specific to the regional culture there, having been written in a combination of Greek, Demotic, and Coptic (the latter two are stages of the Egyptian language, Coptic being the final hellenized form of Egyptian that employs the Greek alphabet and Greek loanwords). The manuscripts are also thoroughly representative of ritual practices from across ancient Greece and Rome. Not only do they represent what may have been in the spellbooks of Paul's Ephesian converts, but some of the rituals they contain are similar to the signs and miracles performed by Christians in Acts.[27]

In these manuscripts, for example, are escape spells. One such spell is "a sacred rite for acquiring an assistant" or junior god who, once summoned, "frees from bonds the person chained in prison, he opens doors, and causes invisibility."[28] In another manuscript there is a prayer and invocation that "loosens shackles, makes invisible."[29] Yet another contains a charm to release one from bonds. The instructions read, "If you want to do something spectacular and want to free yourself from danger, stand at the door and say the spell, and having said it, go out, adding: 'Let the bonds of him, NN (supply the name), be loosened, and let the doors be opened for him, and let no one see him. . . .'" *NN* is a placeholder where the practitioner is to substitute his or her name or the name of the person for whom the ritual is being performed. The instructions continue: "When the bonds break, say: 'I thank you, lord, [because] the holy spirit, the unique one, the living one, has [released] me.'"[30] That manuscript also prescribes wearing an all-purpose gemstone amulet set in a ring: "Anyone can open doors and break chains and rocks if he touches them with the stone, that is, the gem, and says the name written below," the name carved on the amulet, on the underside against the finger of the person wearing it.[31] Yet another manuscript contains prayers and invocations, songs and chants "for release from bonds" and "to open doors."[32] And another also contains a "charm to open a door."[33]

In Acts, Peter and Paul both escape from jail, Peter more than once. He and the rest of the original apostles are arrested and imprisoned in Jerusalem by the Jewish high priest, Sadducees, and temple police (5:17–26). Peter is incarcerated again by Herod Agrippa I (12:6–11). And Paul and Silas are jailed by city officials in Philippi (16:19–40). They all escape incredibly, sometimes getting away unnoticed as though they were concealed from view even walking in front of the guards. Divine messengers aid Peter, like the assistant or junior god who "frees from bonds the person chained in prison, he opens doors, and causes invisibility," mentioned in the manuscript quoted above. According to Acts, the first time Peter and the rest were imprisoned, "the angel of the Lord by night opened the prison doors" (5:19). The second time, after much prayer for him by members of the church, an angel appeared to Peter, "his chains fell off from his hands," and "the iron gate . . . opened to them of his [the gate's, its] own accord" (12:5, 7, 10). Paul and Silas were not assisted by an angel, but while they "prayed, and sang praises unto God," a tremor rattled the prison "and immediately all the doors were opened, and every one's bands were loosed" (16:25–26). Even though the author of Luke–Acts has distinguished between Christian signs and miracles on the one hand and magic on the other, similarities are present—from jail escapes and healings to exorcisms and protection against snakebites (28:1–6). Such affinities belie the author's own efforts to define Christianity as something separate from Greco-Roman religion.

Conclusion

Nearly two millennia after the launch of its gentile missions in the mid-first century AD, Christianity is now the largest religion on the planet. Recent statistics estimate that almost one-third of the global population is Christian.[34] The traditional religious practices and beliefs of many ancient Mediterranean and Near Eastern peoples, to say nothing of cultures and societies missionized later, either are totally gone or else have been absorbed and transformed by Christianity and other religions. But discussion of New Testament references to ancient Greco-Roman religion still has relevance for our day, not least because it highlights the question of how to treat those who belong to different religions (or to none at all), be they family, friends, neighbors, coworkers, or acquaintances. While some passages from the New Testament are relatively inclusive (Galatians 3:28; compare 2 Nephi 26:33), others are not. At almost any moment, Latter-day Saints have the opportunity to interact with people who hold a variety of different religious beliefs. Thus, our challenge is to remain true to our individual convictions while showing respect and love for those whose beliefs are different from our own (compare Articles of Faith 1:11).

⁓

Grant Adamson is a lecturer in the Department of Religious Studies and Classics at the University of Arizona.

Further Reading

Beard, Mary, John North, and Simon Price. *Religions of Rome*. 2 vols. Cambridge: Cambridge University Press, 1998. The first volume is a roughly chronological survey. The second is a collection of primary texts in English translation, arranged by topic. Both focus on the Roman Republic and especially the Roman Empire, so they are narrower in scope but more detailed than Johnston's edited volume.

Ferguson, Everett. *Backgrounds of Early Christianity*. 3rd ed. Grand Rapids, MI: Eerdmans, 2003. This book features an introductory chapter on Hellenistic-Roman religions. It is topically arranged, and all words from ancient languages are transliterated.

Johnston, Sarah Iles, ed. *Religions of the Ancient World: A Guide*. Cambridge, MA: Harvard University Press, 2004. Boasting an interdisciplinary team of some 140 contributors, this book is highly comparative, focusing not only on ancient Greece and Rome but also on Egypt, Mesopotamia, Israel, and so forth. The book is arranged by topic and includes chapters that summarize the history of each culture and its religion. Ancient languages are transliterated.

Klauck, Hans-Josef. *The Religious Context of Early Christianity: A Guide to Greco-Roman Religions*. Trans. Brian McNeil. Edinburgh, Scotland: T&T Clark, 2000. This book covers many of the same topics as Ferguson's chapter, plus philosophy, but at greater length and engaging more with European scholarship. It is arranged topically, with Greek words often left untransliterated.

Notes

1. *Oxford Latin Dictionary*, ed. P. G. W. Glare (Oxford: Oxford University Press, 1996), 1282, s.v. "pāgānus."
2. For a summary of evidence and scholarship, see Michele R. Salzman, "Pagans and Christians," in *The Oxford Handbook of Early Christian Studies*, ed. Susan Ashbrook Harvey and David G. Hunter (Oxford: Oxford University Press, 2008), 187.
3. OED Online, Oxford University Press, http://www.oed.com, s.v. "heathen."
4. For example, following the precedent of older English translations, the translators of the King James Version of the Bible, published in 1611, frequently used *heathen* in the books of the Old Testament and even sometimes in the books of the New (Matthew 6:7; 18:17; Acts 4:25; 2 Corinthians 11:26; Galatians 1:16; 2:9; 3:8). The term is also found in the Book of Mormon (2 Nephi 26:33; 3 Nephi 13:7; 21:21), Doctrine and Covenants (45:54; 75:22; 90:10), and Pearl of Great Price (Abraham 1:5, 7). By contrast, the translators of the New Revised Standard Version of the Bible, published in 1989, have avoided *heathen* altogether in both the Old and New Testaments, opting instead to use the term *Gentile* and occasionally the term *pagan*.
5. *A Greek-English Lexicon of the New Testament and Other Early Christian Literature*, ed. Frederick William Danker, 3rd ed. (Chicago: University of Chicago Press, 2000), 276–77, s.v. "ἐθνικός," "ἔθνος."
6. *Oxford Latin Dictionary*, 759–60, s.v. "gens," "gentilis."
7. Ronald E. Clements and G. Johannes Botterweck, "גוי," in *Theological Dictionary of the Old Testament*, ed. and trans. G. Johannes Botterweck, Helmer Ringgren, and John T. Willis (Grand Rapids, MI: Eerdmans, 1975), 2:426–33; and Bertram and K. L. Schmidt, "ἔθνος, ἐθνικός," in *Theological Dictionary of the New*

Testament, ed. and trans. Gerhard Kittel and Geoffrey W. Bromiley (Grand Rapids, MI: Eerdmans, 1964), 2:364–72.

8. See Everett Ferguson, *Backgrounds of Early Christianity*, 3rd ed. (Grand Rapids, MI: Eerdmans, 2003), 538–39, 546–51, 562–65.

9. Paul's preaching to Gentiles is foreshadowed in Acts 9:15 but only commences in Acts 13:46–47.

10. On Paul, his chronology, and the disputed authorship of some of the letters attributed to him, see Raymond E. Brown, *An Introduction to the New Testament* (New Haven, CT: Yale, 1997), 422–45. For theories of how the Gospels were composed, particularly the Synoptic Gospels of Mark, Matthew, and Luke, see Brown, *Introduction to the New Testament*, 100–125.

11. Justin Martyr, *Dialogue with Trypho* 3–8.

12. See Ferguson, *Backgrounds of Early Christianity*, 188–93; Hans-Josef Klauck, *The Religious Context of Early Christianity: A Guide to Greco-Roman Religions*, trans. Brian McNeil (Edinburgh, Scotland: T&T Clark, 2000), 12–23; Sarah Iles Johnston, ed., *Religions of the Ancient World: A Guide* (Cambridge, MA: Harvard University Press, 2004), 325–69 (esp. 340–46) and 598–621 (esp. 614–19); and Mary Beard, John North, and Simon Price, *Religions of Rome* (Cambridge, MA: Cambridge University Press, 1998), 2:148–66.

13. But in Galatians 2:10 Paul seems to preclude any such ruling, and he was an eyewitness, writing before the author of Luke–Acts.

14. See Ferguson, *Backgrounds of Early Christianity*, 198–99.

15. See Ferguson, *Backgrounds of Early Christianity*, 199–212; Klauck, *Religious Context of Early Christianity*, 250–330; Johnston, *Religions of the Ancient World*, 547–63 (esp. 556–61); and Beard, North, and Price, *Religions of Rome*, 1:140–49, 2:222–28, 253–59.

16. Other examples are Josephus, *Jewish Antiquities* 11.332–339, for the Jewish legitimization of Alexander the Great and his contingent of Jewish soldiers; and Eusebius, *Ecclesiastical History* 8.13; 9.9, for the Christian legitimization of the emperor Constantine and his engagement in civil war.

17. Philo, *On the Embassy to Gaius* 355–57, quoted in Beard, North, and Price, *Religions of Rome*, 2:259.

18. See Ferguson, *Backgrounds of Early Christianity*, 555–67; Klauck, *Religious Context of Early Christianity*, 12; and Johnston, *Religions of the Ancient World*, 547–63 (esp. 333–36).

19. Some of the go-to examples are the appearance of God and angels in Genesis 18 and the appearance of the angel Raphael in the book of Tobit.

20. One go-to example is the conception and birth of the emperor Augustus as son of the god Apollo: Suetonius, *Lives of the Caesars* 2.94.4, quoted in *Documents for the Study of the Gospels*, 2nd ed., ed. David R. Cartlidge and David L. Dungan (Minneapolis, MI: Fortress, 1994), 133.

21. Arguably, 1 Corinthians 14:34–35 was not written by Paul but added by an interpolator.

22. See Ferguson, *Backgrounds of Early Christianity*, 213–22; Klauck, *Religious Context of Early Christianity*, 177–209; Johnston, *Religions of the Ancient World*, 370–91 (esp. 383–90); and Beard, North, and Price, *Religions of Rome*, 2:166–93.

23. See Johnston, *Religions of the Ancient World*, 385, referencing the Greco-Egyptian ritual papyri, such as PGM IV.88–93, 850–929; PGM V.1–53; PGM VII.348–58, 540–78; and PDM xiv (throughout).

24. There is no equivocation in the disputed Pauline Letters, which perpetuate and reinforce slavery. See Ephesians 6:5–9; Colossians 3:22–4:1; 1 Timothy 6:1–2; Titus 2:9–10.

25. Latter-day Saints should be able to appreciate this in their own modern church history. For instance, most members of the Church would not say that Joseph Smith practiced magic; they would say that the seer stones he gazed into while seeking buried treasure and translating the gold plates of the Book of Mormon were "instruments" and "sacred objects." See "Book of Mormon Translation," Gospel Topics, https://www.lds.org/topics.

26. Pliny, *Natural History* 30.2.

27. English edition of the manuscripts: Hans Dieter Betz, trans. and ed., *The Greek Magical Papyri in Translation, Including the Demotic Spells*, 2nd ed. (Chicago: University of Chicago Press, 1992); hereafter *Greek Magical Papyri*.

28. PGM I.96–133, *Greek Magical Papyri*, 5–6.

29. PGM V.458–89, *Greek Magical Papyri*, 109–10.

30. PGM XII.160–78, *Greek Magical Papyri*, 159–60.

31. PGM XII.270–350, *Greek Magical Papyri*, 163–65.

32. PGM XIII.288–96, 327–34, 1064–75, *Greek Magical Papyri*, 180–81, 195.

33. PGM XXXVI.312–20, *Greek Magical Papyri*, 277.

34. See "The Changing Global Religious Landscape," Pew Research Center, April 5, 2017, http://www.pewforum .org/2017/04/05/the-changing-global-religious-landscape/. In some countries the Christian population is much more. The United States is approximately 70.6 percent Christian, including 46.5 percent Protestant, 20.8 percent Catholic, and 1.6 percent Latter-day Saint. See "America's Changing Religious Landscape," Pew Research Center, May 12, 2015, http://www.pewforum.org/2015/05/12/americas-changing-religious-landscape/.

13

The Cares of This World
Roman Economics and the New Testament

John Gee

A parable is a hypothetical story told for comparison, often with hyperbole for effect.[1] It could have actually taken place but need not have since the important point is the comparison. Jesus employed parables both to teach truth and to obscure his teachings, and while the parables were the open teachings of Jesus, their interpretation was given in private to his disciples.[2] At times Jesus's parables drew on information that was unstated—not because it was secret or sacred but because everyone was already familiar with it. Jesus's first-century audience took a number of basic facts for granted and could understand (better than a modern reader) where he was exaggerating for effect. Since the parables of Jesus assume a number of facets about first-century society, in particular about economic life, the parables and the world of the New Testament in general can be much better apprehended through a cursory understanding of some of the economic realities of the day. To this end, this chapter will provide a cursory overview of economics in the Roman Empire.

Macroeconomics of the New Testament

To begin, it is important to remember that the New Testament took place in the Roman world, a complex society that functioned in ways that are sometimes similar to modern society and sometimes very different. The Roman Empire ruled over anywhere from 50 to 80 million inhabitants, of which about 5 million were Roman citizens[3] who had special privileges like exemption from certain taxes and the right to receive the grain dole.[4] Looked at as a business, the Roman Empire had income and expenditures. The income principally consisted of taxes and other revenues. The expenditures were largely to maintain building projects, the military, the welfare state, and the bureaucracy. It is estimated that the Roman government in the first century needed 825,000,000 sesterces every year to run,[5] though this amount could come either in kind or in coin. To obtain the income needed to run the empire, "imperial tribute was demanded based on the principle of obtaining as much as possible with the least effort."[6]

Death and Taxes

Rome collected a large number of diverse taxes. These could consist of poll taxes, property taxes, trade taxes, and commodity tariffs. While most of our information about taxes comes from Roman Egypt, which might not have been treated the same as neighboring Judea, it is effectively the best and often the only evidence we currently possess.

Poll taxes

The Roman Empire taxed its subjects for simply being alive. Augustus increased the taxes in coin by increasing the rate of the poll tax (λαογραφία, *laographia*), also called a capitation or head tax.[7] This was a tax levied on all subjects of the Roman Empire who were not Roman citizens, although scribes and certain priests were exempt.[8] To account for the poll tax, occasional censuses were taken[9] (every fourteen years starting in AD 33/34, irregularly before that)[10] and all listed were required to pay the poll tax yearly. Families of the deceased were required to continue to pay the poll tax for the deceased unless the death of the individual was officially recorded. The tax rate was 3–5 denarii/year for urban dwellers and 10 denarii/year for rural dwellers.[11] This rate seems to have held throughout New Testament times since the rate of the poll tax did not increase until the short reign of Nerva (AD 96–98).[12] Another capitation tax was levied on areas, and all inhabitants of a particular area had to pay their share of the tax.[13] This latter tax was used either to pay for the construction and renovation of statues of the emperor or to cover the tax share owed by tax dodgers.[14] Jews also paid a tax for the maintenance of the temple in Jerusalem (Mark 12:41–42; Luke 21:1–2).[15] After the destruction of the temple, Vespasian confiscated this revenue for other purposes.[16]

Property taxes

Property taxes were assessed both in coin and in kind. Farmers in Egypt paid a tax in coin on any type of farmland to pay for dike maintenance. In general, grain farmers paid a property tax of 1/26 of an artaba of wheat (about 1.25 liters) per aroura of land (2756.25 meters^2, an area of a square 52.5 meters on each side, roughly half the size of the playing area of an American football field). Rates for property tax on private land ranged from 1 to 2 artabas per aroura. Cultivation of government land was assessed at a higher rate, between 1 and 7 artabas per aroura, along with an agreed-upon rent (compare Luke 20:22; Romans 13:6–7), a 1 percent rent, and a 1.5 percent rental fee.[17] Since the grain yield was generally 4.64–13.00 artabas of wheat per aroura in Egypt (Judea would have yielded less), the taxes might take a significant portion of the crop, or even all of it in times of poor harvest. Surtaxes were assessed if individuals paid with barley instead of wheat, if individuals borrowed their seed from the government, or if more revenue was needed.[18] Because it was cheaper to ship grain from one end of the Mediterranean to the other than it was to cart it 75 miles overland,[19] a shipping charge was added to the taxes, with different rates assessed for government and private land. "The accumulation of such supplements and fees was a serious burden on the cultivators."[20] It is little wonder that taxation was a serious issue in Jesus's day (Matthew 17:24; 22:17; Mark 12:14–15; Luke 20:22; 23:2; Romans 13:6–7). The government could also compel farmers to sell their grain (after taxes) to the government at a price below market value or to cultivate otherwise uncultivated lands; the responsibility for larger tracts were spread over several villages, requiring villagers to take care of lands in addition to their own. Villages were also assessed a tax of a certain amount of straw per year. The Roman emperor did not want officials to overdo taxes; when his prefect, Aemilius Rectus, told Tiberius (AD 14–37) that there was a large surplus in tax revenues, Tiberius responded that he wanted his sheep (i.e., his subjects) sheared, not flayed.[21] Roman citizens in Italy, however, were exempt from land taxes.[22]

Grains such as wheat and barley are staple crops, and because the Romans needed to feed people, it made sense to collect taxes in kind. Because wine, olive oil, and other cash crops were lucrative items readily sold on the market, Romans typically collected property taxes on vineyards, date orchards, and gardens in cash. They leveed a charge for surveying the land—40 drachmas per aroura for vineyards and 20 drachmas per aroura for date orchards and vegetable gardens. Property taxes on cash crops were 1,500 copper drachmas (= 5 silver drachmas) per aroura for vegetable gardens and 3,000 copper drachmas per aroura (= 10 silver drachmas) for vineyards, equaling about a tenth of the production. A surtax was additionally charged on all cultivated land of 2,000 copper drachmas (= 6 silver drachmas and 4 obols) per aroura. Vineyards were taxed an additional 8 drachmas per aroura for the wine tax (οἴνου τέλος).[23]

Proper assessment of taxes in kind called for standardized measures. The modius measure was a standard capacity measure for grain, small seeds, and oil, equal to 8.733 liters (and thus a mere quarter of a US bushel).[24] This is the term Jesus uses when he talks of putting a candle (actually a lamp) under a bushel (Matthew 5:15; Mark 4:21; Luke 11:33), since the bushel was not a woven basket but a modius. Because this bronze vessel[25] had to hold liquids, it would be watertight and thus airtight. Placing a lamp under one of these measures would not just dim the light but cut off the oxygen as well, thus putting the lamp out in short order.

Dry Measures		
Measure	**Capacity**	**Choinix per measure**
choinix	0.98 liters	1
modius	8.733 liters	9
artaba	39.2 liters	40
Liquid Measures		
Measure	**Capacity**	
chous	2.9 liters	
keramia	unknown	

Property owners also had to register with the government to be taxed.[26] Joseph and Mary came to Bethlehem because of the need "to register" for taxation purposes (Luke 2:1). They could have registered for the poll tax anywhere, so they may have owned property in Bethlehem if they needed to travel there. If they owned property in Bethlehem, they probably stayed on their own property. The term translated "inn" at Luke 2:7 (καταλύμα, *kataluma*) could simply refer to a temporary dwelling place[27] (at Luke 22:11 it designates a guestchamber needed for the Last Supper). Since the upper story was full, the family stayed on the ground floor, where animals were often kept.[28]

Trade taxes

While the majority of people in ancient society were involved in agriculture, some plied a trade instead. Practitioners of a trade paid a yearly tax for engaging in that trade. For example, bakers and oil merchants were taxed at the rate of 8 drachmas a month, while brickmakers were required to pay a yearly tax of 80 drachmas (which means that in some cases they would need to sell 8,000 bricks a year just to cover their taxes). Fishmongers paid 4 drachmas a month, or 48 drachmas per year.[29]

Commodity tariffs

The Romans also taxed certain commodities. For example, fishermen like Peter, James, John, and Andrew had to pay one-quarter of their catch in taxes. This was in addition to the taxes they had to pay on their boats, which could amount to 625 drachmas and 4 obols per annum. Rent on a boat could run 540 drachmas per year. Bread sellers also had to pay one-quarter of their sales in taxes. The same rate was paid by painters. Private baths had a higher rate: one-third of the gross receipts. There was also a 2 percent sales tax. There was a 10 percent tax on the sale of real estate that would have had to be paid if the rich young man had actually sold all he had (Luke 18:18–23).[30]

Tax collection

Each year government officials made an estimate of the tax revenues for the upcoming year. Taxes were collected by renting out or selling the taxes to tax farmers or tax collectors (publicans).[31] Each year in each tax district, the tax farmers bid for the tax revenues, which went to the highest bidder. If at the end of the year these revenues exceeded the winning bid, the tax farmer made a profit. If, however, the revenues were less than the winning bid, the tax farmers had to pay the difference to the state. Tax farmers were thus required to present securities worth more than their bid. The tax farmers could hire as many tax collectors as they wished, but they were required to pay the tax collectors a fixed wage, which was deducted from the tax revenues. They could hire more tax collectors to ensure a thorough collection of taxes, but the expense would cut into their profits. "Most of them were wealthy landowners, a necessary requirement since holders of government contracts had to offer land as security for the fulfillment of terms."[32] The tax collectors hired scribes to keep their accounts.[33] Scribes thus became an indispensable part of the bureaucracy. Tax collectors' records were open to higher officials, and they made at least annual reports.[34] Tax collectors were especially concerned with collecting delinquent taxes and could use force or seizure to do so,[35] which could lead to abuses since "the logic of tax-farming dictated a certain amount of ruthless extraction."[36] This is why John the Baptist told the tax collectors, "Exact no more than that which is appointed you" (Luke 3:13). If the taxes exceeded their estimates, they would of course keep the surplus, which explains why publicans were so hated (Matthew 9:10–11; 11:19; 18:17; 21:31–32; Mark 2:15–17; Luke 5:29–30; 7:34; 15:1–2; 18:10–14; 19:2–7). Once the tax was collected, it was shipped to Rome, preferably by boat since that was the least expensive means of transportation. The Egyptians paid their taxes to Rome in grain. It took thousands of ships to transport the grain from Egypt, the largest supplier of grain, to Rome.

The apostle Matthew came from the ranks of the publicans (Matthew 10:3). Insofar as he fit into the mold of a Roman publican, he would have been literate in Greek and had substantial property and income (compare Luke 19:2). His literacy would have made him a prime candidate to write an account of the life of Jesus. It is somewhat surprising that, given his background, Matthew was not in charge of the finances among Jesus and his apostles, but that Judas was (John 12:6; 13:29).

In the Roman world, gold coins started to be used in 46 BC, after the Romans had siphoned off the precious metals of the Mediterranean and the gold coins of "Macedon, Carthage, Ptolemaic Egypt, and Gaul had ceased to circulate."[37] Gold coins became the norm when one wanted to convey large sums of money, to more easily conceal one's money, or to trade outside the Roman Empire.[38] Otherwise, silver coins (drachma, denarius, and stater/tetradrachma) were used. Augustus also minted a number of bronze coins (the *as*) that, smaller than their predecessors, caused their predecessors to increase in value.[39] In AD 56 Nero took over the mint by placing it under prefects of his own choosing.[40] Nero also began minting coins that were smaller. "When it was in the Emperor's interest to debase the coinage beginning with Nero, he did so without thought for the economic consequences."[41] So Nero flooded Egypt with debased tetradachmas.[42]

In the King James Bible, a number of different terms for monetary units are used. The following are monetary terms that occur in the New Testament:

King James Term	Transliteration	Greek	References
farthing	*assarion*	ἀσσάριον	Matthew 10:29; Luke 12:6
farthing	*kodrantēs*	κοδράντης	Matthew 5:26; Mark 12:42
mite	*lepton*	λεπτόν	Mark 12:42; Luke 12:59; 21:2
penny (pence)	*dēnarion*	δηνάριον	Matthew 18:28; 20:2, 9–10, 13; 22:19; Mark 6:37; 12:15; 14:5; Luke 7:41; 10:35; 20:24; John 6:7; 12:5; Revelation 6:6
piece of money	*statēr*	στατήρ	Matthew 17:27
talent	*talanton*	τάλαντον	Matthew 18:24; 25:15–16, 20, 22, 24–25, 28; Revelation 16:21

Different monetary systems were used in different parts of the Roman Empire. The Roman monetary system was based on the silver denarius. Egypt was personal property of the Roman emperor, and one way it was kept separate was through the use of a separate monetary system. In addition, documents kept in Hebrew and Aramaic often used a different monetary system even if it was directly equivalent to the Roman monetary system.

It was the taxpayers throughout the empire, including those in Egypt, who supplied the bulk of the revenues demanded by Rome.[43] One option if one could not pay taxes was to flee. By the time of Jesus, the Romans began to encounter the Egyptian phenomenon of *anachoresis*, the deliberate fleeing of the land by the peasants to avoid paying taxes.[44] By AD 19 we already encounter declarations by family members officially averring that individuals had fled without leaving property and therefore their remaining family could not be liable for taxes.[45] "Under the Romans fugitives became also more numerous, and flights more frequent and widespread. No longer the peasants alone, but the propertied middle-class, to escape the crushing liturgies which sapped their personal fortunes, also had recourse to this expedient."[46] The practice would later play a role in Christian monasticism; anchorite monasticism takes its name directly from the practice.

When people fled taxes, they were reported to the village scribe, the *komogrammateus*, and then to the *strategos*. The village scribe entered their names into the annual list, while the *strategos* officially declared the fugitives outlaws. They were left with one of two options: fleeing to a city "where they could hope to be swallowed up in the large and heterogeneous population, or they joined together in robber bands and led a vagabond, marauding life."[47] These robber bands play a role in Judea and Galilee as well. Barabbas (which is a patronymic, Bar-Abbas, son of Abbas) was a robber (John 18:40), guilty of leading a rebellion against the government (Matthew 27:16–26; Mark 15:7, 11, 15; Luke 23:18–19), precisely what Jesus was accused of. Jesus was crucified between two robbers (Matthew 27:38, 44; Mark 15:27; Luke 23:32, 39–41) who were not petty thieves but rather brigands or bandits.

With a diminishing tax base and an increased demand for government handouts, the Romans were faced with a problem. "The obvious remedy for the evil was to lighten the tax burden of the peasants; but as such a remedy stood in direct antithesis to the Roman policy of squeezing the greatest possible revenues of grain and money from the country, the administration characteristically evaded the issue and bent its efforts, not to solving the problem proper, but to insuring the fisc against any loss in revenue. . . . Instead of a reduction in taxes, however, the government preferred whenever possible to grant a moratorium, which did not involve any diminution of its revenue. Another type of concession, finally, was the amnesty for fugitives." Because Roman government policy did not try to solve the problem of *anachoresis*, but rather was aimed at keeping revenue up, the *komogrammateus* conscripted other people to farm the abandoned land. "The result of applying this policy to the problem in question might have been foreseen: the number of fugitives at large in the country increased steadily, and the problem facing the administration became steadily more acute."[48]

The Romans were inflexible when it came to collecting taxes, and special surcharges were added when the emperor needed more money for travel or armies. In times when grain was scarce because of famine elsewhere, the government forced the farmers to sell their wheat at low prices when the market price was much higher.[49]

The Roman government's large income was acquired by numerous compulsory means, backed by the punitive might of the empire. The income was necessary because the outlays were large.

Great and Spacious Buildings

One way the Roman Empire spent all the tax revenue flowing in was to hire lots of people. "Unskilled workmen were enrolled or impressed in gangs, and craftsmen and semiskilled workers were organized according to their specialties into corporations or guilds (neither term is very satisfactory)."[50] All these workers were employed in monumental construction projects that demanded lots of labor.

The Romans are famous for their large public works projects that provided work for artisans and, when completed, things to keep life comfortable for the elites, and sometimes for the general populace. They built temples, harbors, theaters, amphitheaters, circuses, aqueducts, and baths all over the Roman world.

Augustus claimed that he "found Rome a city of brick and left it a city of marble."[51] He could do so because of the wealth he had extracted from Egypt. When Augustus defeated Anthony and Cleopatra, he seized Egypt's fortunes, an amount estimated in the neighborhood of a billion sesterces.[52] "When he brought the treasures of the Ptolemies to Rome at his Alexandrian triumph, so much cash passed into private hands that the interest rate on loans dropped sharply, while real estate values soared."[53] The withdrawal of that much capital impeded the economic recovery of Egypt.[54]

Behold a Royal Army

Another large expenditure of the Roman Empire was the maintenance of its considerable standing army. These are the soldiers that John the Baptist asked to "do violence to no man" (Luke 3:14). One result of the Roman civil wars that ended with Augustus was a standing professional army of volunteers.[55] This was a contrast to Roman policy in the Republic when Roman conquests were often left to fend for themselves since "the profits from empire were not going to be squandered on providing demanding, and potentially expensive, services to imperial subjects."[56] To man a committed professional army required the men to be volunteers rather than conscripts, which meant inducements to recruit, train, and retain them.[57] This required adequate pay, which in turn placed a heavy financial burden on the state.[58] Thus John the Baptist counseled the soldiers to "be content with your wages" (Luke 3:14). Part of the remuneration was providing all their basic necessities,[59] including, of course, feeding them.

Since Egypt supplied more grain than Rome itself could use, the excess was used to feed troops in northern Europe.[60] In fact, it was precisely the acquisition of Egypt that allowed Rome to pursue military expansion into northern Europe.[61] The grain supplies could be shipped via water to places where the empire wanted to concentrate its resources.

The Farmer on the Dole

Although the emperor spent tax money building monuments to his glory and keeping the subjects in line, he also had to keep the citizens in line, and that was not cheap either. The emperor had other means of subduing the populace besides the army: bread and circuses, which kept the people fed and entertained.[62]

Securing food supply was important for the Caesars not just because they needed to feed the army but more because they needed to feed the Roman citizens. "Filled with palaces, monuments, and slums, [Rome] was a city of contrasts where splendor and squalor existed side by side. Short of space, Rome had expanded vertically as well as horizontally, and much of the population lived in multistoried tenements. Most housing was poorly built, and the collapse of apartment houses was not uncommon. Yet, since living space was at a premium, rents were high. Fires were frequent and destructive. Although the city contained many large public baths, sanitation was poor. Congested and noisy, Rome had grown without planning, and its streets were narrow and winding—a factor that aided rioters."[63] Though the Romans had earlier fought wars to aid their farmers, by the time of Jesus, Rome had lost the ability to feed itself from the surrounding territory and so had come to rely on commodities from Africa, Sicily, and Sardinia[64] until the acquisition of Egypt and the taxes on its grain allowed the Caesars to placate the Roman citizens with a massive welfare program. The typical entitlement welfare payment to an adult Roman male was 5 *modii* of wheat a month, which translates into about 3,000–3,500 calories per day with the ideal caloric intake of 3,300 calories per day.[65] While an individual Roman could live on that amount of food, it was insufficient for a family and would not help pay the rent or clothe the naked.[66]

Augustus acknowledged that the dole discouraged Italian agriculture (there was no impetus to work hard to raise food when one did not have to) but continued to supply the dole as an entitlement lest another politician wrest support from him by promising the dole or reinstating it.[67] This created a vicious cycle in which Rome, deprived of any incentive to feed itself, was perpetually unable to do so and thus completely dependent on the hard labor of others. Paul was a Roman citizen (Acts 16:37–38; 22:25–29; 23:27) and thus was entitled to receive the dole but worked as a tentmaker (Acts 18:3), thus setting an example to the other saints of laboring with his own hands (1 Corinthians 4:11–12; Ephesians 4:28; 1 Thessalonians 4:11).

Corrupt Bureaucracy

For the typical citizen, the face of the Roman Empire was the bureaucracy. The Roman government paid a quarter of its tax revenue to maintain the bureaucratic apparatus. There were a number of good and high-minded officials in the Roman Empire, but there were also many corrupt officials. The structure of the empire was designed for honest individuals but invited corruption since it favored those who were "rich, partisan, sought after by many, and feared by most."[68] Because it is the "nature and disposition of almost all men" (Doctrine and Covenants 121:39) to abuse their power, this is what the typical individual encountered in the Roman government. This aspect of society forms an element of a number of parables and teachings of Jesus: unjust judges (Luke 18:1–8), dishonest scribes (Matthew 23:1–33), and unjust stewards (Luke 16:1–9) abound in the New Testament. Jesus warned his followers that "they shall deliver you up to councils; and in the synagogues ye shall be beaten: and ye shall be brought before rulers and kings for my sake" (Mark 13:9; compare Luke 21:12; Acts 4:5–6; 16:19–24), just as he himself was (Luke 24:20; Acts 3:17). This would even be considered an act of piety: "whosoever killeth you will think that he doeth God service" (John 16:2). Pilate was, in some ways, merely a typical Roman official who had not the courage to do what was right rather than what was politically expedient (Luke 23:4).

In theory, corrupt officials could be charged with crimes and punished accordingly, but this process was corrupt too. Informers (*delatores*) would accuse rich individuals of disloyalty to the emperor; the accused would be sold as slaves or exiled, and their property would be confiscated by the emperor, though accusers would sometimes suffer the same fate.[69] In AD 33 the Roman money changers were charged with irregularities in their exchanges between silver and copper coins. There is no question that they were making money on the deals since that was the reason they were in business, and there was good money to be made (Matthew 25:16–17, 27).[70] They tried to turn the tables on their accusers by calling for immediate repayment of all outstanding loans to them, requiring people to sell their property to cover the debt, flooding the market with property and causing the real estate prices to plummet. Tiberius intervened with an interest-free loan of 100,000,000 sesterces to those whose reputation and honor were threatened.[71]

Microeconomics of the New Testament: A Farmer's Life

As vast and expansive as the empire's economy was, the empire itself accounted for only an estimated 5–10 percent of the total economic activity in the empire. Most of the activity took place on the individual and local level.[72] The other way to look at the economic situation in the New Testament is from the point of view of the individual Roman subject, who usually lived in a rural area.

From the farmer's point of view, his principal task is growing enough food to feed his family. The life of a farmer is tied to the land and the seasons, and so are the religious festivals. Though Judea has early and later rains (Deuteronomy 11:13–17; Jeremiah 5:24), it lies in a liminal zone around the 100 mm isohyet on the borderline between having enough rainfall for crops or not; it depends on the year. The Galilee and the Jezreel valley fair better.[73] Around middle to late October the early rains come. Between December and March come the later rains, and 75 percent of the rainfall comes at that time.[74] When Jesus said that God "sendeth rain on the just and on the unjust" (Matthew 5:45), he was referring to rain as a blessing, not a curse.

The year begins in the spring.[75] The Passover begins on the full moon of that month,[76] right after the flax and barley are harvested. Seven weeks later is the Feast of Weeks or Firstfruits (Pentecost), after the wheat harvest, and offerings of a sheaf of wheat and new flour figure prominently.[77] The episode when the disciples went through the grain on the Sabbath must have occurred at this time of year (Matthew 12:1–8; Mark 2:23–28; Luke 6:1–5). Seven weeks later was the completion of the grape harvest.[78] Seven weeks after that coincided with the end of the olive harvest.[79] This was the time of the Feast of Tabernacles (Sukkot), which followed the Day of Atonement. It also coincided with Rosh Hashanah, which was considered the beginning of the year because after that time the fields were plowed in preparation for sowing in time for the early rains.

Independent farmers needed to figure out how to get their grain to the threshing floors; those farming government land could use government animals. At the threshing floor a government agent would assess the tax and collect the best of the grain. Farmers of government land would have to pay a fee for the government to transport their taxes in grain to storage granaries. Farmers might also be assessed a storage fee. When the grain was deposited in the granary, the granary overseer or his scribe would issue a receipt.[80] The farmer himself would have his own granary and would want it to be large enough for his own needs (Luke 12:17–18).

Since the harvest was likely to be sixfold at best (tenfold in Egypt),[81] the farmer needed to keep at least one-sixth of the crop for seed corn. When Jesus talked of those who accepted the gospel as seeds producing thirty, sixty, and a hundredfold (Matthew 13:8, 23), he was talking about the least productive adherent as producing at a rate that was unheard of in the ancient world, five times as much as a good harvest.

Grain was a staple crop that grew best in well-watered flat places. Hillsides were more amenable to grapes and olives, which were cash crops fetching a much higher price than grain. One large farm allocated five-sevenths of the land to grain and the other two-sevenths to grapes.[82] About 90 percent of the wine was sold, though the poorer grade was used as wages for the day laborers.[83] Extra grain would be sold to others, such as bakers who would turn the grain into bread that could be sold to nonfarmers. The disciples who mentioned to Jesus the idea of buying 200 denarii of bread to feed five thousand men—not counting women and children (Mark 6:37; John 6:7)—knew that 200 denarii would buy about forty-eight hundred loaves.[84]

Besides grain, grape vines and a number of fruit trees were grown, including sumachs, carob, walnuts, almonds, pistachios, pomegranates, olives, date palms, figs, wild figs, white figs, sycamore figs, peaches, pears, apples, hawthorn, medlars, pippins, quinces, and citrons.[85] Figs appear in a number of scriptures (Matthew 7:16; 21:19–21; 24:32; Mark 11:13, 20–21, 28; Luke 6:44; 13:6–7; 21:29; John 1:48–50). Carob, used as a food for smaller livestock,[86] appears in the parable of the prodigal son because the husks of the carob pod are what the son feeds the swine and wishes that he himself could eat (Luke 15:16).

Animals were used both as beasts of burden and a source of income. Prices between animals varied significantly, as with horses (448–2,800 drachmas),[87] fatted calves (330 drachmas),[88] sheep (120 drachmas),[89] and goats (80 drachmas).[90] Chickens (2 drachmas)[91] were worth more than doves (1–3 obols).[92] Thus, in the parable of the prodigal son the older brother notes that the father has killed the fatted calf, an extremely expensive animal, when the father had never allowed him a comparatively cheaper animal for a feast (Luke 15:29–30). The offering of turtledoves or pigeons by Joseph and Mary (Luke 2:24) is indicative of their lowly financial status.

Plowing, sowing, and harvesting were all hard work shouldered by the farmer and his family. Sometimes, like at harvesttime, more hands were needed (Matthew 9:37–38; Luke 10:2). Two sorts of additional labor were available: slaves and hirelings.

Romans could own slaves. It is estimated that the Roman army took some fifteen thousand to twenty thousand individuals per year as slaves and sent them to be sold,[93] a number further swollen by those sold into slavery because of debt. Essentially free for the feeding once they were purchased, slaves were denied a number of privileges, such as wearing rings. Wearing a golden ring was a sign of equestrian status and prohibited by law for the children or grandchildren of freed slaves.[94] So when the father of the prodigal son gives his son a ring (Luke 15:22), he is indicating his status as a son and not making him a slave, or servant, as the son proposed (Luke 15:19, 21). Purchasing slaves did not come cheaply; they were much too expensive for the typical farmer. Hiring extra hands for a day or two was a less expensive solution.

Wages for a day laborer in Egypt during the first century were 20–40 drachmas per month. At an exchange rate of 4 drachmas to the denarius,[95] that would be about 4.4 denarii a month, or 0.2–0.4 denarii per day. In Jesus's parable of the laborers (Matthew 20:1–15), the payment of those who worked all day was about two and a half to five times the going rate. While the laborers of the parable who worked only an hour were certainly getting paid much more for the amount of time, those who worked for a day were getting almost a week's worth of wages for a single day of work. This is something that Jesus's audience all knew. The point of the parable is somewhat lost if one does not realize how generous the householder was being in the first place. A drachma could be worth as much as a week's worth of wages, and so it was definitely worth sweeping out the house to find such a coin (Luke 15:8–9).

Living within one's means was important. Going into debt was a problem because the loan typically had to be paid back with interest in a year,[96] or upon demand: "any time that you tell me (*bkwl zmn dy tmr ly*)."[97] This explains why in the parable of the unforgiving servant the debts could be demanded as payment without warning (Matthew 18:23–35). The amounts owed in the parable are telling—100 denarii was a substantial sum, but a talent was 2,500 denarii. And 10,000 talents was the equivalent of 60,000,000 sesterces, enough to run the whole Roman bureaucracy and army in Egypt for five years.[98] We have records of wealthy individuals who earned half a talent a month,[99] but even at that rate it would take 1,667 years to earn that much money. A talent would take a day laborer 6,000 to 36,000 days, or 16 to 98 years, to earn. That is a tremendous amount of money to simply bury in the ground (Matthew 25:18). A typical person would not feel slighted at being entrusted with a whole talent (25:24–27), which was more money than most people would ever see in their lives. In the parable of the two debtors (Luke 7:41–43), one of the debtors owed 50 denarii, which was about two months' worth of wages, but the other owed ten times as much. Other debts were of very trivial amounts (11:5–6).

Both loans and labor agreements could be drawn up in contracts, the language of which is often used in the New Testament. The term translated as *faith*, πίστις, can mean many things in a legal context: "'oath', 'safe-conduct', 'credit', 'guarantee for a credit', 'personal surety', 'trust' are only some among its possible legal meanings."[100] "Whenever one of the parties in a reciprocal agreement anticipates his own performance or liability, we can say that he acts "ἐν πίστει" ("in faith"), such as "by issuing the documents without having actually received the loan" or otherwise "acting on trust."[101] The Christian demonstrates faith by acting on the terms of the covenant even though blessings promised by God may not be apparent. Most contracts commonly start with the party writing the contract specifying agreement with the terms of the contract (ὁμολογῶ). Most translations of the Bible give this term as *confess* rather than a word that would convey the contractual meaning, which those in New Testament times would have recognized.

Conclusion

How the economy of that day worked is not stated in the New Testament because it did not need to be, but it is essential to understanding and appreciating the scriptures and the life and teachings of Jesus. A knowledge of economic realities in the time of Jesus changes how we read the New Testament.

Appendix: Prices

Most of our knowledge about prices in the Roman Empire comes from Egypt.[102] Prices in Egypt tended to be a bit lower than comparable prices in Judea, partly because Egypt was largely built along the river Nile and thus had access to an inexpensive means of transportation, while Judea was inland and goods had to be priced to account for the more expensive transportation of hauling items overland by caravan. The following is a list of the price ranges for various commodities in Egypt in the period AD 20–70.[103]

Commodity	Price Range	Notes
Food		
barley	4–16 drachmas/artaba[104]	The cost of barley was generally 40–50 percent less than wheat.[105]
beer	1.5 obols/keramion to 1 drachma for 2 chous[106]	
bread	1 obol/loaf[107]	
cumin	7 drachmas/artaba[108]	
dates	8 obols for 3 metra to 28 drachmas for 10 artaba 8 metra[109]	
figs	1.5 obols for 100 figs[110]	
fish (θρίσσα)	1 obol[111]	
fish (λάτος)	17 obols[112]	
fish (κορακίνος)	19 for 20 obols[113]	
fish (φάγρος)	3 obols[114]	
myrrh	2/3–1+ drachma[115]	amount unknown
oil (ἔλαιον)	4 drachmas 2 obols/chous to 9 obols/chous[116]	
salt (ἅλς)	1.5–2.5 obols/metron[117]	price depended on quality
wheat	4.4–13.8 drachmas/artaba[118]	
wine	2 drachmas 2 obols to 10 drachmas/keramion[119]	
Fabric and Clothing		
cloak or toga	20 drachmas[120]	This was an outer wrap.
coat, clothes, or robe	4–12 drachmas[121]	This was a basic garment that looked something like a T-shirt that went down to the knees.
mantle (φαινόλης)	10 drachmas[122]	
wool, raw	16 drachmas/fleece[123]	
wool, thread	1.4–2 drachmas/stathmia[124]	Apparently it took 4 stathmia to make a robe (χιτών).[125]
Real Estate		
apartment	120–600 drachmas[126]	The price is normally to purchase one floor of a multistory building.

cultivatable land	28 drachmas/aroura[127]	purchased, not rented
date palm orchard	1,000 drachmas/aroura[128]	purchased, not rented
land	154–600 drachmas/aroura[129]	purchased, not rented
land for building	124–240 drachmas[130]	purchased, not rented; area not specified
olive orchard	600 drachmas/aroura[131]	purchased, not rented
rent of mill	160 drachmas/year[132]	
rent of oil press	40 drachmas for 7 months to 300 drachmas/year[133]	
vineyards +	100–675.55 drachmas/aroura[134]	purchased, not rented
Labor/Wages		
bricklayer (πλινθευτής) +	12 obols for 2 days[135]	
carpenter (τέκτων) +	1–2 drachmas/day[136]	
laborer, daily	1–6 obols/day[137]	
laborer, monthly	12–20 drachmas/month[138]	
mason	1–40 drachmas/wall[139]	
priest (of Souchos) +	344 drachmas/year[140]	
publican (assistant tax collector) +	200–252 drachmas/year[141]	
stonemason (λαξός) +	28–40 drachmas[142]	
Slaves		
female slave, 4 years old	2,000 drachmas[143]	
female slave, 8 years old	640 drachmas[144]	
female slave with child	1,100 drachmas[145]	
female slave with two children	1,800 drachmas[146]	
male slave −/+	900–1,200 drachmas[147]	
Animals		
calf +	330 drachmas[148]	
camel	72–168 drachmas[149]	
chickens	2 drachmas[150]	
cow +	120 drachmas[151]	
donkey, female +	56–244 drachmas[152]	
donkey, renting	3 obols–4 drachmas/day[153]	
dove	1–3 obols[154]	
goat	80 drachmas[155]	
horse	448–2,800 drachmas[156]	

ox, rented	4 obols–4 drachmas/day[157]	A yoke of oxen would be double.
pig (swine)	8–12 drachmas[158]	
sheep +	120 drachmas[159]	
Transportation		
ship	100–2,231 drachmas[160]	purchase price for ship
3 donkeys and 2 drivers	5 obols[161]	
33 donkeys for two days	39 drachmas[162]	price of carrying 100 artabas of wheat
man carrying over land	3–4 obols[163]	

John Gee is the William (Bill) Gay Research Professor and senior research fellow at the Neal A. Maxwell Institute for Religious Scholarship at Brigham Young University.

Further Reading

Bang, Peter Fibiger. "Predation." In *The Cambridge Companion to the Roman Economy*, edited by Walter Scheidel, 197–217. Cambridge: Cambridge University Press, 2012.

Drexhage, Hans-Joachim. *Preise, Mieten/Pachten, Kosten und Löhne im römischen Ägypten bis zum Regierungsantritt Diokletians*. St. Katharinen, Germany: Scripta Mercaturae Verlag, 1991.

Gee, John, and Daniel C. Peterson. "Graft and Corruption: On Olives and Olive Culture in the Pre-Modern Mediterranean." In *The Allegory of the Olive Tree*, edited by Stephen D. Ricks and John W. Welch, 186–247. Salt Lake City: Deseret Book and Foundation for Ancient Research and Mormon Studies, 1994.

Rickman, G. E. "The Grain Trade under the Roman Empire." *Memoirs of the American Academy in Rome* 36 (1980): 261–75.

Yardeni, Ada. *Textbook of Aramaic, Hebrew and Nabataean Documentary Texts from the Judean Desert and Related Material*. Jerusalem: The Hebrew University, 2000.

Notes

1. R. Dean Anderson Jr., *Glossary of Greek Rhetorical Terms* (Leuven, Belgium: Peeters, 2000), 86–87.
2. It is telling that of the many parables of Jesus, only three have interpretations associated with them.
3. Hans Kloft, *Die Wirtschaft der griechisch-römischen Welt* (Darmstadt, Germany: Wissenschaftliche Buchgesellschaft, 1992), 198.
4. A. N. Sherwin White, *The Roman Citizenship* (Oxford: Clarendon, 1973), 234, 171–72.
5. Peter van Minnen, "Agriculture and the 'Taxes-and-Trade' Model in Roman Egypt," *Zeitschirft für Papyrologie und Epigraphik* 133 (2000): 208.
6. Peter Fibiger Bang, "Predation," in *The Cambridge Companion to the Roman Economy*, ed. Walter Scheidel (Cambridge: Cambridge University Press, 2012), 201.
7. Sherman L. Wallace, *Taxation in Egypt from Augustus to Diocletian* (Princeton: Princeton University Press, 1938), 116, 343; and J. Grafton Milne, "The Ruin of Egypt by Roman Mismanagement," *Journal of Roman Studies* 17 (1927): 4.
8. Wallace, *Taxation in Egypt*, 119–20.

9. Bang, "Predation," 208.

10. Roger S. Bagnall and Bruce W. Frier, *The Demography of Roman Egypt* (Cambridge: Cambridge University Press, 1994), 2; and Wallace, *Taxation in Egypt*, 96–98.

11. Wallace, *Taxation in Egypt*, 121–22, 126–27.

12. Wallace, *Taxation in Egypt*, 347.

13. Wallace, *Taxation in Egypt*, 135–36.

14. Duncan Fishwick, "Statues Taxes in Roman Egypt," *Historia: Zeitschrift für Alte Geschichte* 38, no. 3 (1989): 335.

15. Mishnah Shekalim 1:1–4:9. According to the Mishnah, the woman who threw in her offering was not required to contribute anything (Shekalim 1:5). The following uses are listed for the temple tax: the purchase of offerings (Shekalim 4:1); the purchase of wine, oil, and flour (Shekalim 4:3); the purchase of gold to plate the temple and the purchase of service utensils (Shekalim 4:4); and the wages of craftsmen working on the temple (Shekalim 4:6).

16. Wallace, *Taxation in Egypt*, 170–76.

17. Wallace, *Taxation in Egypt*, 40–41, 71–72.

18. Wallace, *Taxation in Egypt*, 11–15.

19. G. E. Rickman, "The Grain Trade under the Roman Empire," *Memoirs of the American Academy in Rome* 36 (1980): 261–62.

20. Wallace, *Taxation in Egypt*, 41.

21. Dio Cassius, *Roman History* 57.10.5; Wallace, *Taxation in Egypt*, 31; Bang, "Predation," 208; Andrew Monson, "Rule and Revenue in Egypt and Rome: Political Stability and Fiscal Institutions," *Historical Social Research* 32, no. 4 (2007): 264.

22. Bang, "Predation," 201.

23. Wallace, *Taxation in Egypt*, 47–64.

24. L. A. Moritz, *Grain-Mills and Flour in Classical Antiquity* (Oxford: Clarendon, 1958), 221, 90.

25. R. P. Duncan-Jones, "The Size of the Modius Castrensis," *Zeitschrift für Papyrologie und Epigraphik* 21 (1976): 59–60.

26. Wallace, *Taxation in Egypt*, 13.

27. Geneviève Husson, *OIKIA: le vocabulaire de la maison privée en Égypte d'après les papyrus grecs* (Paris: La Sorbonne, 1983), 13–353.

28. William G. Dever, *The Lives of Ordinary People in Ancient Israel* (Grand Rapids, MI: Eerdmans, 2012), 131; and Kenneth E. Bailey, *Jesus Through Middle Eastern Eyes* (Downers Grove, IL: IVP Academic, 2008), 28–30.

29. Wallace, *Taxation in Egypt*, 191–208.

30. Wallace, *Taxation in Egypt*, 219–28.

31. See the description in Josephus, *Jewish Antiquities* 12.4.4.

32. Bang, "Predation," 203.

33. B. P. Muhs, *Receipts, Scribes, and Collectors in Early Ptolemaic Thebes* (Leuven, Belgium: Peeters, 2011), 220; and Wallace, *Taxation in Egypt*, 36–37.

34. Wallace, *Taxation in Egypt*, 37.

35. Wallace, *Taxation in Egypt*, 37–38.

36. Bang, "Predation," 205–10, quotation on 207.

37. Christopher Howgego, "The Supply and Use of Money in the Roman World 200 B.C. to A.D. 300," *Journal of Roman Studies* 82 (1992): 2, 5, 10.

38. Howgego, "Supply and Use of Money in the Roman World," 11–12.

39. Michael Crawford, "Money and Exchange in the Roman World," *Journal of Roman Studies* 60 (1970): 44.

40. Shelagh M. Bond, "The Coinage of the Early Roman Empire," *Greece and Rome* 4, no. 2 (1957): 151.

41. Crawford, "Money and Exchange in the Roman World," 48.

42. J. G. Milne, "The Roman Regulation of Exchange Values in Egypt: A Note," *Journal of Egyptian Archaeology* 16 (1930): 169.

43. Van Minnen, "Agriculture and the 'Taxes-and-Trade' Model in Roman Egypt," 210.

44. Wallace, *Taxation in Egypt*, 136.

45. Naphtali Lewis, "Μερισμος Ανακεχωρηκοτων: An Aspect of Roman Oppression in Egypt," *Journal of Egyptian Archaeology* 23 (1937): 68–69.

46. Lewis, "Aspect of Roman Oppression," 63–64.

47. Lewis, "Aspect of Roman Oppression," 63–69.

48. Lewis, "Aspect of Roman Oppression," 67–73.

49. Wallace, *Taxation in Egypt*, 339.

50. William L. MacDonald, *The Architecture of the Roman Empire* (New Haven, CT: Yale University Press, 1982), 1:144.

51. Quoted in J. B. Ward-Perkins, *Roman Imperial Architecture* (New Haven, CT: Yale University Press, 1981), 21.

52. Wallace, *Taxation in Egypt*, 343.

53. Suetonius, *Divus Augustus* 41.1.

54. Wallace, *Taxation in Egypt*, 343; and Milne, "Ruin of Egypt by Roman Mismanagement," 3.

55. M. Rostovtzeff, *The Social and Economic History of the Roman Empire*, 2nd ed. (Oxford: Clarendon, 1957), 40.

56. Bang, "Predation," 201.

57. Rostovtzeff, *Social and Economic History of the Roman Empire*, 40.

58. Rostovtzeff, *Social and Economic History of the Roman Empire*, 40.

59. Crawford, "Money and Exchange in the Roman World," 45.

60. Michael Fulford, "Territorial Expansion and the Roman Empire," *World Archaeology* 23, no. 3 (1992): 301.

61. Fulford, "Territorial Expansion and the Roman Empire," 301.

62. Martial, *De Spectaculis* 1.6–13, 17–24, 26–27, 30–34, 37.

63. Thomas W. Africa, "Urban Violence in Imperial Rome," *Journal of Interdisciplinary History* 2, no. 1 (1971): 4–5.

64. Rickman, "Grain Trade under the Roman Empire," 263.

65. Rickman, "Grain Trade under the Roman Empire," 262; and Hans-Joachim Drexhage, *Preise, Mieten/ Pachten, Kosten und Löhne im römischen Ägypten bis zum Regierungsantritt Diokletians* (St. Katharinen, Germany: Scripta Mercaturae Verlag, 1991).

66. Africa, "Urban Violence in Imperial Rome," 6; Rickman, "Grain Trade under the Roman Empire," 262.

67. Suetonius, *Divus Augustus* 42.3; and Monson, "Rule and Revenue in Egypt and Rome," 255.

68. Pliny, *Letters* 1.5.15.

69. Martial, *De Spectaculis* 1.4–5.

70. For Jewish regulations, see Mishnah Shekalim 2:1.

71. Crawford, "Money and Exchange in the Roman World," 46.

72. Bang, "Predation," 202.

73. William G. Dever, *Beyond the Texts: An Archaeological Portrait of Ancient Israel and Judah* (Atlanta: SBL, 2017), 62–63.

74. Dever, *Beyond the Texts*, 66, 70–71.

75. 11Q19 (11QTemple-a) XIV:9–10.

76. 11Q19 (11QTemple-a) XVII:6–7.

77. Leviticus 23:9–22; 11Q19 (11QTemple-a) XVIII:10–XIX:9.

78. 11Q19 (11QTemple-a) XIX:11–XXI:10.

79. 11Q19 (11QTemple-a) XXI:12–XXII:16.

80. Wallace, *Taxation in Egypt*, 33–40.

81. Rickman, "Grain Trade under the Roman Empire," 261.

82. Van Minnen, "Agriculture and the 'Taxes-and-Trade' Model in Roman Egypt," 214.

83. Van Minnen, "Agriculture and the 'Taxes-and-Trade' Model in Roman Egypt," 214.

84. P.Aberd. 67; P.Mich. 2.123, 124, 127, 128; SB 12.11004; and Drexhage, *Preise, Mieten/Pachten, Kosten und Löhne*, 29.

85. A number of different crops are mentioned in the Mishnah. Specific references in this chapter have been omitted for space reasons.

86. Mishnah Shabbath 24:2.

87. BGU 11.2112; PSI 6.729; and Drexhage, *Preise, Mieten/Pachten, Kosten und Löhne*, 297, 300.

88. BGU 3.986; and Drexhage, *Preise, Mieten/Pachten, Kosten und Löhne*, 302.

89. P.Bad. 2.19a (AD 110); and Drexhage, *Preise, Mieten/Pachten, Kosten und Löhne*, 303.

90. P.Strassb. 2.118; and Drexhage, *Preise, Mieten/Pachten, Kosten und Löhne*, 305.

91. P.Mich. 2.121; and Drexhage, *Preise, Mieten/Pachten, Kosten und Löhne*, 310.

92. P.Oxy. 4.736; SB 16.12515; and Drexhage, *Preise, Mieten/Pachten, Kosten und Löhne*, 312.

93. Bang, "Predation," 201–2.

94. White, *Roman Citizenship*, 331.

95. Sítta von Reden, "Money and Finance," in *The Cambridge Companion to the Roman Economy*, ed. Walter Scheidel (Cambridge: Cambridge University Press, 2012), 275.

96. Wadi Murabba'at 18, in Ada Yardeni, *Textbook of Aramaic, Hebrew and Nabatean Documentary Texts from the Judean Desert and Related Material* (Jerusalem: The Hebrew University, 2000), 1:15; 2:[19]; and Klaus Beyer, *Die aramäischen Texte vom Toten Meer* (Göttingen: Vandenhoeck & Ruprecht, 1984), 306–7. The fifth added for interest is restored by Beyer and though reasonable is not certain. Beyer did not indicate that the word was damaged or reconstructed.

97. XHev/Se 49, in Yardeni, *Textbook of Aramaic, Hebrew and Nabatean Documentary Texts*, 1:17; 2:[19]; and Wadi Sdeir, in Yardeni, *Textbook of Aramaic, Hebrew and Nabatean Documentary Texts*, 1:19; 2:[20].

98. Wallace, in *Taxation in Egypt*, 344, estimates this at 11.3 million sesterces per year. Van Minnen ("Agriculture and the 'Taxes-and-Trade' Model in Roman Egypt," 209) estimates 22 million drachmas per year.

99. O.Uppsala VM 1285, in Sten Wångstedt, *Ausgewählte demotische Ostraka aus der Sammlung des Victoria-Museums zu Uppsala und der Staatlichen Papyrussammlung zu Berlin* (Uppsala, Sweden: Norblads Bokhandel, 1954), 156; Ursula Kaplony-Heckel, "Rund um die thebanischen Tempel (Demotische Ostraka zur Pfründen-Wirtschaft)," in *Res Severa Verum Gaudium*, ed. Friedhelm Hoffmann and Heinz-Josef Thissen (Leuven, Belgium: Peeters, 2004), 298; and Ursula Kaplony-Heckel, *Land und Leute am Nil nach demotischen Inschriften, Papyri und Ostraka* (Wiesbaden, Germany: Harrassowitz, 2009), 1294. For the date, see John Gee, "Horus Son of Osoroeris," in *Mélanges offerts à Ola el-Aguizy*, ed. Fayza Haikal (Cairo: Institut Français d'Archéologie Orientale, 2015), 169–78.

100. José Luis Alonso, "Πίστις in Loan Transactions: A New Interpretation of P. Dion. 11–12," *Journal of Juristic Papyrology* 42 (2012): 29.

101. Alonso, "Πίστις in Loan Transactions," 29.

102. Walter Scheidel, "Real Wages in Early Economies: Evidence for Living Standards from 1800 BCE to 1300 CE," *Journal of the Economic and Social History of the Orient* 53 (2010): 428.

103. If data is not available from that time period, the nearest available price is noted with a plus sign (+) indicating a date later than the time period and a minus sign (–) indicating a date earlier than the time period.

104. P.Mich. 2.127; PSI 12.1263; SB 6.9017; and Drexhage, *Preise, Mieten/Pachten, Kosten und Löhne*, 25.

105. Drexhage, *Preise, Mieten/Pachten, Kosten und Löhne*, 26–27.

106. P.Tebt. 2.401; SB 8.9699 (AD 78/9); and Drexhage, *Preise, Mieten/Pachten, Kosten und Löhne*, 43.

107. P.Aberd. 67; P.Mich. 2.123, 124, 127, 128; SB 12.11004; and Drexhage, *Preise, Mieten/Pachten, Kosten und Löhne*, 29.

108. P.Fay. 101 (18 BC); and Drexhage, *Preise, Mieten/Pachten, Kosten und Löhne*, 41.

109. P.Mich. 2.127; and Drexhage, *Preise, Mieten/Pachten, Kosten und Löhne*, 36.

110. P.Mich. 2.123; and Drexhage, *Preise, Mieten/Pachten, Kosten und Löhne*, 36.

111. P.Mich. 2.123; and Drexhage, *Preise, Mieten/Pachten, Kosten und Löhne*, 52.

112. P.Mich. 2.123; and Drexhage, *Preise, Mieten/Pachten, Kosten und Löhne*, 52.
113. P.Mich. 2.123; and Drexhage, *Preise, Mieten/Pachten, Kosten und Löhne*, 52.
114. P.Mich. 2.124; and Drexhage, *Preise, Mieten/Pachten, Kosten und Löhne*, 53.
115. P.Oxy. 4.736; and Drexhage, *Preise, Mieten/Pachten, Kosten und Löhne*, 392.
116. P.Oxy. 4.736, 739, 819; 8.1143; P.Strasb. 7.763; and Drexhage, *Preise, Mieten/Pachten, Kosten und Löhne*, 47.
117. P. Mich. 5.245; and Drexhage, *Preise, Mieten/Pachten, Kosten und Löhne*, 41.
118. P.Mich. 2.123, 127; P.Oxy. 47.3352; 49.3488; and Drexhage, *Preise, Mieten/Pachten, Kosten und Löhne*, 13–14.
119. P.Mich. 2.123, 124, 127; SB 16.12515; and Drexhage, *Preise, Mieten/Pachten, Kosten und Löhne*, 61, 64.
120. Aeg. 65 (1985): 3.11 (4 BC); and Drexhage, *Preise, Mieten/Pachten, Kosten und Löhne*, 355.
121. P.Mich. 5.346a; P.Oxy. 2.267; 41.2971; and Drexhage, *Preise, Mieten/Pachten, Kosten und Löhne*, 355.
122. P.Oxy. 4.736; and Drexhage, *Preise, Mieten/Pachten, Kosten und Löhne*, 355.
123. P.Mich. 2.123; and Drexhage, *Preise, Mieten/Pachten, Kosten und Löhne*, 352.
124. P.Mich. 2.127; SB 12.10947; and Drexhage, *Preise, Mieten/Pachten, Kosten und Löhne*, 352.
125. Basically a T-shirt shaped garment that went down to one's knees.
126. P.Mich. 5.235; P.Oxy. 1.99; 34.2720; and Drexhage, *Preise, Mieten/Pachten, Kosten und Löhne*, 79, 84.
127. SB 5.7599; and Drexhage, *Preise, Mieten/Pachten, Kosten und Löhne*, 135.
128. P.Hamb. 1.97 (AD 104/5); and Drexhage, *Preise, Mieten/Pachten, Kosten und Löhne*, 137.
129. BGU 2.379; CPR 1.1 (AD 83/4); P.Hawara 166; P.Mich. 2.121; P.Ross.Georg. 2.14 (AD 81/95); ZPE 37 (1980): 207 (AD 81); and Drexhage, *Preise, Mieten/Pachten, Kosten und Löhne*, 129, 141, 148.
130. P.Lond. 2.140; P.Oxy. 2.330; and Drexhage, *Preise, Mieten/Pachten, Kosten und Löhne*, 139.
131. BGU 2.379; and Drexhage, *Preise, Mieten/Pachten, Kosten und Löhne*, 137.
132. P.Ryl. 2.167; and Drexhage, *Preise, Mieten/Pachten, Kosten und Löhne*, 99.
133. P.Aberd. 181; P.Mich. 2.123; SPP 22.173; W.Chrest. 176; and Drexhage, *Preise, Mieten/Pachten, Kosten und Löhne*, 101.
134. P.Lugd.Bat. 6.3 (AD 92); SB 14.11399 (second century); and Drexhage, *Preise, Mieten/Pachten, Kosten und Löhne*, 136.
135. SB 8.9699 (AD 78/9); and Drexhage, *Preise, Mieten/Pachten, Kosten und Löhne*, 123.
136. P.Oxy. 18.2190 (first century); SB 6.9494 (second century); 14.11958 (AD 117); and Drexhage, *Preise, Mieten/Pachten, Kosten und Löhne*, 123.
137. P.Oxy. 6.985; SB 8.9699; and Drexhage, *Preise, Mieten/Pachten, Kosten und Löhne*, 413–14.
138. P.Oxy. 6.985; SB 8.9699; 12.10947; and Drexhage, *Preise, Mieten/Pachten, Kosten und Löhne*, 425.
139. O.Bodl. 2.1755 (second century); O.Bruss.Berl. 71 (second century); O.Strassb. 701 (second century); P.Serap. 61 (second century), 65 (second century); P.Tebt. 2.402 (AD 172); SB 14.11958 (AD 117); and Drexhage, *Preise, Mieten/Pachten, Kosten und Löhne*, 120.
140. BGU 1.337 (AD 140); SPP 22.183 (AD 138); and Drexhage, *Preise, Mieten/Pachten, Kosten und Löhne*, 430.
141. P.Fay. 35 (AD 150/1); P.Lond. 2.306 (AD 145); and Drexhage, *Preise, Mieten/Pachten, Kosten und Löhne*, 430.
142. P.Mil.Vogl. 7.307 (second century); and Drexhage, *Preise, Mieten/Pachten, Kosten und Löhne*, 125.
143. BGU 3.987; and Drexhage, *Preise, Mieten/Pachten, Kosten und Löhne*, 259.
144. P.Oxy. 2.263; and Drexhage, *Preise, Mieten/Pachten, Kosten und Löhne*, 259.
145. P.Gen. 22; and Drexhage, *Preise, Mieten/Pachten, Kosten und Löhne*, 259.
146. P.Oxy. 2.375; and Drexhage, *Preise, Mieten/Pachten, Kosten und Löhne*, 259.
147. BGU 4.1128 (14 BC); 4.1114 (5 BC); P.Oxy. 38.2856 (AD 91/2); and Drexhage, *Preise, Mieten/Pachten, Kosten und Löhne*, 261.
148. BGU 3.986; and Drexhage, *Preise, Mieten/Pachten, Kosten und Löhne*, 302.
149. BGU 1.89; 3.912; and Drexhage, *Preise, Mieten/Pachten, Kosten und Löhne*, 287–88.
150. P.Mich. 2.121; and Drexhage, *Preise, Mieten/Pachten, Kosten und Löhne*, 310.
151. P.Bad. 2.19a (AD 110); and Drexhage, *Preise, Mieten/Pachten, Kosten und Löhne*, 302.

152. P.Fay. 92 (AD 126); P.Lond. 2.466 (AD 143); SPP 22.22 (AD 142); and Drexhage, *Preise, Mieten/Pachten, Kosten und Löhne*, 283.

153. SB 8.9699; and Drexhage, *Preise, Mieten/Pachten, Kosten und Löhne*, 313–14.

154. P.Oxy. 4.736; SB 16.12515; and Drexhage, *Preise, Mieten/Pachten, Kosten und Löhne*, 312.

155. P.Strassb. 2.118; and Drexhage, *Preise, Mieten/Pachten, Kosten und Löhne*, 305.

156. BGU 11.2112; PSI 6.729; and Drexhage, *Preise, Mieten/Pachten, Kosten und Löhne*, 297, 300.

157. SB 8.9699; and Drexhage, *Preise, Mieten/Pachten, Kosten und Löhne*, 316–17.

158. P.Ryl. 2.134, 140; and Drexhage, *Preise, Mieten/Pachten, Kosten und Löhne*, 306–7.

159. P.Bad. 2.19a (AD 110); and Drexhage, *Preise, Mieten/Pachten, Kosten und Löhne*, 303.

160. BGU 4.1157 (13 BC), 1179 (10 BC); P.Lond. 3.1171 (8 BC); P.Oxy. 45.3250; P.Oxy.Hels. 14; and Drexhage, *Preise, Mieten/Pachten, Kosten und Löhne*, 327, 330.

161. SB 8.9699; and Drexhage, *Preise, Mieten/Pachten, Kosten und Löhne*, 343.

162. Drexhage, *Preise, Mieten/Pachten, Kosten und Löhne*, 349.

163. SB 8.9699; and Drexhage, *Preise, Mieten/Pachten, Kosten und Löhne*, 343.

14

The First Jewish Revolt against Rome

Jared W. Ludlow

When Jews of the Roman province of Judea initiated a revolt against Rome in ca. AD 66, the results were catastrophic and had lingering effects on both Jews and Christians. While the revolt occurred some three decades after the lifetime of Jesus, it is nonetheless important for understanding the development of early Christianity and the text of the New Testament. There are also significant connections between the First Jewish Revolt and some of the prophecies in the New Testament, most notably the Olivet Discourse recorded in Matthew 24 (compare Mark 13; Luke 21:5–37; Joseph Smith—Matthew). This chapter will review the major impetuses for the Jewish Revolt, summarize its major events and figures, and sketch its lasting impacts on both Judaism and Christianity.

Josephus the Jewish Historian

The Jewish historian Josephus (ca. AD 37–100) is the primary source for the events leading up to and during the Jewish Revolt. Born in Jerusalem as Joseph ben Matthias, he was a son of a priest and a descendant of the Hasmoneans. He was well educated, having spent time learning from ascetic groups such as the Essenes. When he was twenty-six years old, he traveled to Rome and was impressed with its size and grandeur as the dominant regional power. He became an important writer and scholar, somewhat bridging the gap between the Jews and Romans. By the end of his career, he had written four key works: *Jewish Antiquities*, a summary of Jewish history for the non-Jewish world; *The Life of Flavius Josephus*, his autobiography; *Against Apion*, an apologetic work defending Jewish belief against aspects of Greek thought; and *Jewish War*, the key account of the Jewish Revolt. While his eyewitness account of the revolt is a vital source of information, a number of historians have come to question his motives and agenda since he began the war as a Jewish general in the Galilee but later surrendered to the Romans and became a Roman citizen and friend of Titus and Vespasian—Roman generals during the revolt and later emperors of the Roman Empire. His traitorous actions raise suspicions about his purpose and reliability in writing his later account of the revolt, *Jewish War* (*Bellum Judaicum*). Many are quick to accuse him of enriching himself on a project of Roman propaganda;[1] however, eminent Josephus scholar Steve Mason believes this perspective may misinterpret Josephus's intentions. While Josephus did gain some advantages from his close work with the Romans, he did not necessarily gain much more than others in similar situations. Other Jews also received Roman citizenship, and teachers regularly received a stipend, accommodation, and relief from taxation. In addition to these common benefits, Josephus did receive some land in Judea, but nothing extravagant.[2] While Josephus's work was flattering toward Vespasian and Titus (such deference was common among contemporary historians), Mason argues that it was not written merely as propaganda. Rather, having been on both sides of the conflict, Josephus uniquely knew issues from both camps and seems to be trying to strengthen his fellow Jews facing increasing tension from the extreme patriotism in Rome. It "appears to be a coherent response to a hostile postwar situation for Judeans in the 70s."[3]

Causes of the Jewish Revolt

What caused the Jewish Revolt? It is nearly impossible to point to one precipitating factor, so a review of various causes leading up to the outbreak of war is necessary. Of course, there never would have been a Jewish revolt if the Romans under Pompey had not conquered the region in 63 BC and incorporated Judea into the Roman Empire. In any event, the Jews did not rebel until more than 130 years later. While they could have resisted Roman rule and taxation from the beginning, many Jews from the time of Roman arrival until the revolt accommodated themselves to the Romans.[4] In fact, the Romans initially ruled the area under a local vassal king, Herod (see Matthew 2; Luke 1). Herod bears responsibility for bringing a new elite to power while effectively ending the old order under the Hasmoneans, the descendants of the great Maccabees whose zealousness ignited Jewish aspirations for independence and religious revival.

This new elite worked closely with the Romans, thereby sowing seeds of disapproval among other Jewish groups and segments of the Jewish populace. These seeds germinated for several decades until they burst forth from the soil of discontent as Jews turned against their fellow Jews who they felt had betrayed their traditions and leadership. Thus, some see the revolt in a lengthy trajectory of zeal for God against those deemed disloyal to him, a kind of holy war. From Phineas in Moses's time (Numbers 25:6–11), to the Maccabees preceding the Roman arrival, to the Zealots of the revolt (the Zealots are also known variously as the

Fourth Philosophy, *sicarii*, and Jewish nationalists),[5] this defensive attitude out of loyalty to God and his commandments led to strong militaristic responses. As part of this religious zeal, some looked for a messiah or deliverer who could liberate the people from the Romans as the Maccabees had done earlier against the Greeks. Yet this catalyzing religious zeal does not explain why the revolt broke out when it did, especially since the group that came to be known as "Zealots" was actually opposed by many religious leaders in Jerusalem, such as the high priests.[6] Why did it take more than a century after Roman arrival for the Jews to revolt?

For a chronologically closer cause of the revolt, some scholars point to the inept, corrupt, and harsh Roman procurators stationed over Judea in the first century—especially those following the death of the Herodian ruler Herod Agrippa I in AD 44 (see Acts 12). When Jewish-pagan hostilities throughout Judea grew stronger, especially in Caesarea Maritima, rebellion naturally followed. Primary texts recount the procurators' injustices and insensitivity toward the Jews, which built up Jewish frustration at not having their interests protected. This brewing frustration fed into the hands of extreme religious/nationalistic Zealot leaders in Jerusalem, like Eleazar, who felt emboldened enough to withhold the daily sacrifice for the emperor.[7] When the Roman auxiliary garrison was massacred in Jerusalem, Emperor Nero had little choice but to respond with force[8] administered by Vespasian and then Titus.

Besides these political conflicts with the government, there were plenty of issues with Jewish society that fed the discontent. The later rabbinic literature highlights societal hatred and ills, such as a breakdown of values and materialistic concerns, as major causes for the revolt.[9] Other socioeconomic factors exacerbated by a famine in AD 48 (Acts 11:28), heavy taxation, and population increase—all of which put greater demand on resources—led to higher incidents of brigandage, a greater rift between the rich and poor, and economic instability.[10] In addition, several general causes played a role in the backdrop to this conflict: the presence of Roman officials, the tension between Jewish tradition and Greco-Roman influence (Hellenism), and messianic expectations. According to the Roman writer Suetonius, as well as Josephus, these messianic expectations included an oracle, or the belief spread throughout the Orient that it was time for someone arising from Judea to rule the world. The inhabitants of Judea took this to refer to themselves, but in hindsight it was interpreted as portending Vespasian's rise to emperor.[11] Beyond these general causes, more immediate causes fanned the flames of these latent general issues and led to a violent rebellion. These immediate causes included tension between Roman procurators and Jewish leaders, economic strife, and inner-Jewish strains. What proved to be different with this revolt compared to the earlier Maccabean revolt in 167 BC and the later Bar Kokhba revolt in AD 132 was the lack of organization, planning, and leadership. A review of pivotal moments in the Jewish/Roman relationship and their concomitant effect on early Christians will illuminate the mounting frustration and discontent and the resulting disorganization that precipitated the Jewish Revolt against Rome in the mid-first century.

Roman/Jewish Relations

By AD 66 the Jews had been under varying forms of Roman control for over a century. With the exile and death of most of the Herodian family, Roman officials had increasingly become the face of occupation in the land. Gessius Florus (reigned ca. AD 64–66), installed as procurator of Judea by Nero in AD 64, exacerbated tensions between the Jewish and local Hellenistic communities. Rather than listening to Jewish complaints of harassment and discrimination and impartially addressing them, he often punished the accusers and profited thereby.[12] The last straw for many Jews came when Florus took seventeen talents from the Jerusalem temple treasury.[13] Jewish protests of his theft led to the arrest of Jewish leaders, thousands of whom were whipped and even crucified despite many of them holding Roman citizenship.[14] Despite efforts by the Herodian elite (Berenice and Agrippa II, see Acts 24–26) to prevent escalation and to seek more just treatment by Florus, their calls went unheeded and eventually the crowds turned against them, expelled them from Jerusalem, and burned their palaces.[15] The Jewish population of Jerusalem exploded in anger at Florus's actions and the Zealot leaders capitalized on this opportunity to rally the populace to their side.

The Zealots, perhaps originating in protests over Quirinius's tax reform in AD 6, had been seeking to expel the Romans so they could be solely under God's rule. Josephus also referred to some rebels as *sicarii*, or "dagger-men" or "dagger-wielders," because their secret assassinations terrorized their fellow countrymen (in hopes they would join the fight against the Romans) as well as the Romans.[16] Menahem ben Yehuda and Eleazar ben Ya'ir were key Zealot leaders. Eleazar, a priest, had been primarily responsible for halting the daily sacrifice to the emperor.[17] He was supported by the lower priests and revolutionary leaders against the traditional high priestly authorities, thus turning it partly into a class struggle. Eleazar was able to take control of the temple and lower city of Jerusalem, thereby shutting out the high priests from the temple. Menahem came from a father and grandfather who both also zealously resisted the Romans and Herodians. When the revolt began, he led some forces to Masada along the Dead Sea and attacked a Roman garrison there, capturing a large cache of weapons.[18]

Emboldened from his victory, Menahem marched toward Jerusalem, took over the Antonia Fortress with its forces from Herod Agrippa II, and besieged Herod's Palace and towers. The attack on the Roman garrison in Jerusalem was matched by a gentile attack on Jews in Caesarea that resulted in twenty thousand deaths.[19] Various cities suddenly ignited in Jew-versus-Gentile attacks throughout the Galilee and Golan and along the Phoenician coast (the area under Herod Agrippa II largely escaped these violent outbursts). Menahem, who had early successes against the Romans, may have become too overbearing with royal pretensions and was killed by fellow revolutionaries. Jewish infighting continued as various leaders vied for control of the city and the revolt, particularly between moderates (who were primarily aristocratic Jerusalemites that were more cosmopolitan and pro-Roman and wanted to capitulate to Rome) and resisting Zealots. (Keep in mind that this narrative is told and propagated by Josephus, who may have colored the story with his agenda and personal bias. While scholars largely accept Josephus's narrative, it behooves us to remember the anti-Zealot perspective from which he wrote.)

Roman Military Response to the Revolt

The Romans responded to these initial Zealot victories by sending military reinforcements from Syria.[20] What was expected to be an easy Roman victory (the initial march into Jerusalem was successful) turned into disaster when the Romans suddenly retreated toward the coast and were ambushed near Beth Horon, losing some six thousand troops and a significant amount of equipment.[21] There was now no turning back for the Jews, and many pro-Roman Jews fled Jerusalem. On the other side, the Romans had to reassess their response and decided to send in a very strong military force under the experienced leadership of Vespasian.

Vespasian came from an equestrian family and gained fame as a military leader in the conquest of Britain.[22] Following his military victories in Britain, Vespasian spent time governing in Africa, managing his finances on his estate, and even hiding from Emperor Nero for fear of his life. Eventually, he was selected to lead a sizeable army to put down the revolt in Judea. Alongside his son Titus and four legions, Vespasian began the counterattack in the Galilee. While this region was not where the recent unrest had started, it made strategic sense for the Romans coming from the north to secure that region first. The Jews knew what was happening and worked to defend the Galilee region. Many Galileans fought because of hatred for the large, gentile-influenced cities there such as Sepphoris and Tiberias. Older settlements resented newer ones, and the indigenous population held animosity toward the foreigners. Yet even with these sentiments, there was no unanimity on war with Rome. When war did finally break out, Jews were little match, especially on the battlefield, for the initial brunt of Vespasian's forces. One of the local generals, Josephus, prepared the city of Yodfat (or Jotapata), and though they held out for forty-seven days (the third-longest siege of the revolt after Jerusalem and Masada), the Jews there eventually fell in bloody defeat and enslavement. It was at this point that Josephus defected to the Romans and began chronicling the war from the other side.[23]

With the fall of Galilee, thousands of refugees and Zealots fled to Jerusalem, and by late spring of AD 68, all the areas around Judea—Perea and Idumea—were securely in Roman hands. Yet right when the revolt could have been snuffed out, Nero died and a succession crisis broke out in Rome, thereby also ending Vespasian's mandate for leading the war in Judea. A nearly two-year reprieve for the Jerusalem inhabitants came as Rome faced its own struggle over leadership, with Vespasian ultimately coming out on top and marching into Rome as its next emperor in AD 69. Meanwhile, the Jewish leadership of the revolt suffered its own conflicts, becoming bifurcated between moderates ruling in Jerusalem and revolutionaries trying to upend Roman control and influence. The Zealots spread terror throughout the city as the moderates made efforts to stem their tide.[24] The Zealots then invited the Jews of Idumea to join them. Butchery among the populace, including moderate leaders and the high priest, ensued. Those who could escape deserted Jerusalem. At this high point of Zealot control, their coalition fell apart with various groups controlling different parts of the city and temple complex.

Siege of Jerusalem

In the midst of such revolutionary discombobulation, the Roman siege of Jerusalem continued under the leadership of Vespasian's son Titus. During the seven-month siege by four Roman legions, the Zealots became more desperate in their efforts to turn their compatriots to their cause and even resorted to burning the city's food supply to force others to join the fight. With little food and under siege, the inhabitants of Jerusalem starved, tried to escape, or waited for the inevitable end. Josephus described in ghastly detail the effects of the siege:

> The Jews, unable to leave the City, were deprived of all hope of survival. The famine became more intense and devoured whole houses and families. The roofs were covered with women and babies too weak to stand, the streets full of old men already dead. Young men and boys, swollen with hunger, haunted the squares like ghosts and fell wherever faintness overcame them. To bury their kinsfolk was beyond the strength of the sick, and those who were fit shirked the task because of the number of the dead and uncertainty about their own fate; for many while burying others fell dead themselves, and many set out for their graves before their hour struck. In their misery no weeping or lamentation was heard; hunger stifled emotion; with dry eyes and grinning mouths those who were slow to die watched those whose end came sooner. Deep silence enfolded the City, and a darkness burdened with death.[25]

With great difficulty, the Roman forces finally regained control of the Antonia Fortress and turned their sights on the temple. Titus offered peace overtures to the Jewish forces inside the temple complex, allowing some, particularly from the upper classes and priestly families, to leave. Owing to a lack of animals, the Jews, for the first time during the revolt, discontinued their daily sacrifices at the temple. Josephus describes Roman leaders discussing whether they should destroy the temple or leave it as a monument to the Roman victory,[26] but it is unclear whether Titus intended to destroy the temple or whether its destruction simply happened in the course of the battle. Fighting continued mercilessly with great losses on both sides. The Roman battering rams failed against the massive stones surrounding the temple. Fire was finally set to the temple gates, leading to the eventual destruction of the magnificent sanctuary in AD 70. (According to the Jewish calendar, this happened on the 9th of Av, traditionally the same day Solomon's temple was destroyed by the Babylonians and commemorated as Tisha B'Av, one of the saddest days in the Jewish calendar.) The Romans finally overcame the weakened Jewish forces, and a bloodbath ensued with incredible carnage throughout the city. Josephus said that around the altar "the heap of corpses grew higher and higher, while down the Sanctuary steps poured a river of blood and the bodies of those killed at the top slithered to the bottom."[27] Eventually the Romans were able to dismantle the

Overturned stones on west side of Temple Mount.
Courtesy of Lincoln H. Blumell.

temple, destroy the temple complex, and push the massive stones off the Temple Mount and onto the market street below, where they still rest. The destruction of the Jerusalem temple was devastating for the Jewish community and led to a new worship focus by the rabbis without the temple and its associated cultic system—what came to be known as Rabbinic Judaism.

The rest of Jerusalem proceeded to fall into Roman hands as the Romans rejected any bids for surrender and burned large sections of the city. Only the rebel-held Masada proved challenging for the Romans, but eventually it fell, culminating in a mass suicide among the remaining rebels;[28] and by this last gruesome act thus ended the first Jewish Revolt against Rome.

View of Roman siege ramp of Masada (left) and Roman base camp (top center left).
Courtesy of Lincoln H. Blumell.

New Testament Prophecies of the Temple's Destruction

Although the Jewish Revolt and subsequent destruction of the Jerusalem temple happened three decades after the time of Jesus, the New Testament records significant prophecies and teachings of Jesus about the fate of this magnificent edifice. These prophecies were even brought back during Jesus's trial in an attempt to find Jesus's words inflammatory and revolutionary when one witness claimed, "This fellow said, I am able to destroy the temple of God, and to build it in three days" (Matthew 26:61). After one visit to the Temple Mount, Jesus made the ominous declaration to his apostles that not one stone of the temple would be left upon another, but rather they would be thrown down (see Matthew 24:2; Joseph Smith—Matthew 1:2–3; Luke 21:6). Naturally concerned, the apostles later asked Jesus, "When shall these things be? And what shall be the sign of thy coming, and of the end of the world?" (Matthew 24:3). It seems they wondered if the two events went together: the destruction of the temple and Jesus's return leading to the end of the world. Their questions led to a lengthy response by Jesus now recorded in Matthew 24 (compare Mark 13; Luke 21) and sometimes referred to as the "Olivet Discourse" because it was delivered on the Mount of Olives. This chapter underwent a major revision as part of the Joseph Smith Translation project and was eventually canonized in the Pearl of Great Price as Joseph Smith—Matthew.[29]

One of the major results of Joseph Smith—Matthew is the reordering of some verses so that everything before verse 21 deals with the time period immediately following Jesus's ministry while everything after verse 21 prophesies of events connected with Jesus's second coming and the end of the world. Verse 21 functions as the transitionary verse that separates these events: "Behold, these things I have spoken unto you concerning the Jews; and again, *after* the tribulation of those days which shall come upon Jerusalem . . . " (emphasis added).

Following verse 21, Jesus warns of tribulation and destruction that will come upon the Jews and Jerusalem. Jesus talks about false Christs and false prophets who would lead to great iniquity and persecution of the righteous. Perhaps here he is alluding to the leaders of the Zealots and others who led the people astray through their charismatic but misguided leadership. Josephus alleges that some of the Jewish leaders' claims misled the people and were responsible for thousands of deaths. "There was formed another group of scoundrels, in act less criminal but in intention more evil, who did as much damage as the murderers [the *sicarii*] to the well-being of the City. Cheats and deceivers claiming inspiration, they schemed to bring about revolutionary changes by inducing the mob to act as if possessed, and by leading them out into the desert on the pretense that their God would show them signs of approaching freedom." Josephus then describes how various groups of people followed these leaders into the wilderness only to be brutally killed when government officials responded to their rebellions.[30] Later on, Josephus pinned the responsibility of thousands of deaths within the city to false prophets when the Roman soldiers set fire to the cloister where thousands, including women and children, had sought refuge and either burned to death or died jumping headlong from the structure.

> Their destruction was due to a false prophet who that very day had declared to the people in the City that God commanded them to go up into the Temple to receive the signs of their deliverance. A number of hireling prophets had been put up in recent days by the party chiefs to deceive the people by exhorting them to await help from God, and

so to reduce the number of deserters and buoy up with hope those who were above fear and anxiety. . . . So it was that the unhappy people were beguiled at that stage by cheats and false messengers of God.[31]

It is certain that because of all these factions and false leaders, the violent actions and cruel treatment of even their fellow Jews surely witness that the love of many waxed cold as Jesus said it would (see Joseph Smith—Matthew 1:10). Josephus included many descriptions of the extremes Jerusalem inhabitants would go to take food from their family members and neighbors.[32] Any who tried to desert to the Romans faced even worse circumstances. Josephus stated that "the entire City was the battleground for these plotters and their disreputable followers, and between them the people were being torn to bits like a great carcass. Old men and women, overwhelmed by the miseries within, prayed for the Romans to come, and looked forward to the war without, which would free them from the miseries within."[33] Josephus's summary statement captures the awful situation: "To give a detailed account of their outrageous conduct is impossible, but we may sum it up by saying that no other city has ever endured such horrors, and no generation in history has fathered such wickedness."[34]

Within the Olivet Discourse, Jesus also reiterates a prophecy from Daniel about the "abomination of desolation," which seems to point toward a time when the temple reaches such corruption that it will be destroyed: "When you, therefore, shall see the abomination of desolation, spoken of by Daniel the prophet, concerning the destruction of Jerusalem, then you shall stand in the holy place" (Joseph Smith—Matthew 1:12; this prophecy seems to have multiple fulfillments; it is repeated again among the signs of Jesus's second coming in verse 32: "And again shall the abomination of desolation, spoken of by Daniel the prophet, be fulfilled"). The only way to avoid the impending destruction, Jesus taught, is to stand in the holy place—not the Jerusalem temple, because it will be destroyed, but places designated by God for spiritual and physical refuge. In the Olivet Discourse, Jesus commands those who are in Judea to flee into the mountains and not return to take anything from their houses (1:13–15). It will be a time of great tribulation "on the Jews, and upon the inhabitants of Jerusalem, such as was not before sent upon Israel, of God, since the beginning of their kingdom until this time; no, nor ever shall be sent again upon Israel" (1:18). But as terrible as those sorrows will be, the Lord will shorten their days for the elect's sake according to the covenant so not everyone will be destroyed (1:19–20). Although the Christian community would survive and continue, some of its key leaders—like Peter and Paul—met martyrs' deaths in Rome during the time of the Jewish Revolt as Nero used Christians as scapegoats for some of the problems he faced in the capital. It truly was a time of severe tribulation for the early Christian community.

Doctrine and Covenants 45

It is interesting to note that a revelation very similar to Joseph Smith—Matthew was given again in our day through the Prophet Joseph Smith. Now canonized as section 45 of the Doctrine and Covenants, this revelation likewise warns against not being prepared for the end, but it goes on to promise great things for the righteous. Yet even this revelation seems connected to the reordered version found in Joseph Smith—Matthew: "And now, behold, I say unto you, it shall not be given unto you to know any further concerning this chapter, until the New Testament be translated, and in it all these things shall be made known; wherefore I give unto you that ye may now translate it, that ye may be prepared for the things to come" (Doctrine and Covenants 45:60–61). Joseph Smith commenced the Joseph Smith Translation project on Matthew 24 the day after section 45 was received, March 8, 1831. Thus, for the Saints of this last dispensation, this prophecy provides signs of future events while also strengthening hope in the fulfillment of prophesied promises in the face of strong persecution. Section 45 also strengthened connections between past, present, and future since it represented continuation of God's eternal plan that had been revealed before Christ, by Christ to his first apostles, and now through the Prophet Joseph Smith. It is simply the everlasting gospel manifest in different dispensations. Regardless of the time period, the message is the same: steadfastness in Christ brings God's blessings and helps avoid the harsh, but just punishment for sinners. But just as Jesus's early apostles and followers relied on this prophecy for guidance, the Saints of Joseph Smith's day relied on the Joseph Smith Translation version of this prophecy for the full picture of future events associated with Jesus's second coming.

Impact of the Jewish Revolt on Early Christians

The early Christians in Jerusalem were not willing participants in the Jewish Revolt against Rome but were caught up in the turmoil because of their proximate location and their similarities to Jews. In Roman eyes there was probably little to distinguish them from the Jews. According to early Christian tradition recorded by Eusebius of Caesarea[35] and Epiphanius,[36] the Christian inhabitants of Jerusalem fled around the beginning of the revolt and made their way east across the Jordan River and north to Pella, one of the cities of the Decapolis.

> The members of the Jerusalem church, by means of an oracle given by revelation to acceptable persons there, were ordered to leave the City before the war began and settle in a town in Peraea called Pella. To Pella those who believed in Christ migrated from Jerusalem; and as if holy men had utterly abandoned the royal metropolis of the Jews and the entire Jewish land, the judgement of God at last overtook them for their abominable crime against Christ and His apostles, completely blotting out that wicked generation from among men.[37]

This flight could have been in response to Jesus's prophetic injunction to flee during the destruction of Jerusalem (Matthew 24:16). While these early Christian sources were earlier deemed reliable, some scholars today question their veracity.[38] They doubt that the Christians were able to move freely through the land when the Romans were suppressing a rebellion, and it is unclear why they would be freely received by a Greek city. Josephus also recounted that Pella had already been destroyed,[39] so where were they arriving? Instead, some scholars believe these traditions were invented by early Jewish Christians in an effort to strengthen their legitimacy by drawing direct connections with Jerusalem's Christian

Relief from the Arch of Titus showing the spoils of the Jerusalem siege. Courtesy of Lincoln H. Blumell.

community. If they did not flee to Pella, it leaves open the question of what happened to the Christians in Jerusalem and whether they perished alongside their Jewish neighbors.

In some early Christian sources it appears that the Christians returned to Jerusalem after the Roman destruction in AD 70. Eusebius lists the bishops of the Jerusalem community up until Hadrian (ca. AD 132), all of whom had Jewish background: James, Simeon, Justus, Zacchaeus, Tobias, Benjamin, John, Matthias, Philip, Seneca, Justus, Levi, Ephrem, Joseph, and Judas.[40] Following the Second Jewish Revolt in AD 132, the list of bishops reveals gentile backgrounds.

Conclusion

The First Jewish Revolt in ca. AD 66 was an enormously tragic event for the Jewish people and the city of Jerusalem, resulting in the loss of many lives and the destruction of the temple. The Jews sought for independence from the Romans who had been their overseers for over a century. Various factors combined to ignite the rebellion in AD 66—corrupt procurators, economic struggles, breakdown of values, heavy taxation, religious fervor, and inner-Jewish factional strife. Encouraged by an early victory against a Roman army, the Jews may have become overly confident that their revolt could succeed. But a much stronger army was sent against them; there was nothing the Jews could do to stop it. Fractured leadership and lack of planning and organization doomed the revolt. The revolt became a violent nexus between religious zeal and politics. What had begun as hope for God's deliverance and liberation from the Romans turned into a catastrophe, with failures on the battlefield and the love having waxed cold among the people. Furthermore, the temple was desecrated by revolutionaries long before the Romans further desecrated and destroyed it.

From a Christian perspective these events were significant because of prophecies recorded in the New Testament regarding future tribulations among the Jews and the loss of the temple. The Olivet Discourse is one of the most important and lengthy prophecies by Jesus about both impending and distant future events. Joseph Smith's revision of this discourse, now known as Joseph Smith—Matthew, helps clarify the time frame of the events and associated signs. It provides a window on not only the events surrounding the Jewish Revolt but also future events pertaining to the Second Coming. Just as the early Christians had to heed the words of the prophecy and flee to holy places to avoid the "abomination of desolation," so true Christians in the last days will need to stand in holy places for refuge. In such a manner, the elect of the covenant and those who are steadfast will be blessed even in the midst of great tribulation.

✦

Jared W. Ludlow is a professor in the Department of Ancient Scripture at Brigham Young University.

Further Reading

Cohen, Shaye. "Roman Domination: The Jewish Revolt and the Destruction of the Second Temple." In *Ancient Israel: A Short History from Abraham to the Roman Destruction of the Temple*, edited by Hershel Shanks, 205–35. Washington, DC: Biblical Archaeology Society, 1988.

Goodman, Martin. *The Ruling Class of Judaea: The Origins of the Jewish Revolt against Rome*, A.D. 66–70. New York: Cambridge University Press, 1987.

Jackson, Kent P. "The Olivet Discourse." In *The Life and Teachings of Jesus Christ, Volume Two: From the Transfiguration through the Triumphal Entry*, edited by Richard Neitzel Holzapfel and Thomas A. Wayment, 318–43. Salt Lake City: Deseret Book, 2006.

Josephus. *The Jewish War*. Translated by G. A. Williamson. London: Penguin Books, 1981.

Mason, Steve. *A History of the Jewish War*, A.D. 66–74. New York: Cambridge University Press, 2016.

Seely, David R. "The Olivet Discourse." In *Studies in Scripture, Volume Five: The Gospels*, edited by Kent P. Jackson and Robert L. Millet, 391–404. Salt Lake City: Deseret Book, 1986.

Notes

1. E.g., Eric D. Huntsman, "The Reliability of Josephus : Can He Be Trusted?," *BYU Studies Quarterly* 36, no. 3 (1996): 392–395; and Henry St. John Thackeray, *Josephus: The Man and the Historian* (New York: Jewish Institute of Religion Press, 1929).

2. Flavius Josephus, *The Life of Flavius Josephus* 417–429.

3. Steve Mason, "Josephus and Judaism," in *The Encyclopedia of Judaism*. ed. Jacob Neusner, Alan J. Avery-Peck, and William Scott Green (Leiden, Netherlands: Brill, 1999), 2:546–63, esp. 547–53. For one of the most comprehensive treatises on the revolt, see Steve Mason, *A History of the Jewish War, A.D. 66–74* (Cambridge: Cambridge University Press, 2016).

4. For some of these issues, see Martin Goodman, *The Ruling Class of Judaea: The Origins of the Jewish Revolt against Rome, A.D. 66–70* (New York and Cambridge: Cambridge University Press, 1987).

5. See Josephus, *Antiquities* 18.1.9–10; and Josephus, *Jewish War*, trans. G. A. Williamson (London: Penguin Books, 1981) 2.13.254–255.

6. See Lincoln H. Blumell and Haley Wilson-Lemmon, "Zealots," in *T&T Clark Encyclopedia of Second Temple Judaism*, ed. Loren T. Stuckenbruck and Daniel M. Gurtner (forthcoming).

7. See Josephus, *Jewish War* 2.17.409–410.

8. See Josephus, *Jewish War* 2.17.452–455.

9. See *Yoma* 9b.

10. See Goodman, *Ruling Class of Judaea*, 1–3.

11. See Suetonius, *Life of Vespasian* 4.5; Josephus, *Jewish War* 6.5.312–313.

12. See Josephus, *Jewish War* 2.14.277–279, 292.

13. See Josephus, *Jewish War* 2.14.293–295.

14. See Josephus, *Jewish War* 2.14.305–308.

15. See Josephus, *Jewish War* 2.17.425–426.

16. See Josephus, *Jewish War* 2.13.254–257.

17. See Josephus, *Jewish War* 2.17.409–410.

18. See Josephus, *Jewish War* 2.8.433–434.

19. See Josephus, *Jewish War* 2.18.457.

20. See Josephus, *Jewish War* 2.18.510.

21. See Josephus, *Jewish War* 2.19.551–555.

22. Suetonius, *Life of Vespasian* 4.1–2.

23. See Josephus, *Jewish War* 3.7.387–392.

24. See Josephus, *Jewish War* 4.10–11.162–195.

25. Josephus, *Jewish War* 5.12.512–515.

26. See Josephus, *Jewish War* 6.5.249–253.

27. Josephus, *Jewish War* 6.4.259.

28. See Josephus, *Jewish War* 7.9.389–401.

29. Joseph Smith—Matthew adds nearly 450 new words, roughly a 50 percent increase in text size, but there is only one verse (55) which has no correlation in the King James Bible and three verses are repeated.

30. Josephus, *Jewish War* 2.13.258–263.

31. Josephus, *Jewish War* 6.5.285–288.

32. See Josephus, *Jewish War* 5.10.429–434; 5.12.515–516.

33. Josephus, *Jewish War* 5.1.27.

34. Josephus, *Jewish War* 5.10.442.

35. Eusebius, *Ecclesiastical History* 3.5.3.

36. Epiphanius, *Refutation of All Heresies* 29.7; *On Weights and Measures* 15.

37. Eusebius, *The History of the Church from Christ to Constantine*, trans. G. A. Williamson (New York: Dorset Press, 1984), 111. Epiphanius also addresses this flight in the context of discussing the heretical Ebionites: "from there [Pella] it originated after the migration from Jerusalem, after all the disciples had settled in Pella, because Christ had told them to leave Jerusalem and to depart, since it was about to suffer siege" from *Panarion* 29.7.8; see also 30.2.7.

38. For an overview of this issue, see Craig Koester, "The Origin and Significance of the Flight to Pella Tradition," *Catholic Biblical Quarterly* 51, no. 1 (1989): 90–106.

39. See Josephus, *Jewish War* 2.181.1.

40. See Eusebius, *Ecclesiastical History* 4.7.

Part 3
Jesus and the Gospels

15

The Life of Jesus of Nazareth
An Overview

Andrew C. Skinner

J esus of Nazareth is not just *the* central figure of the New Testament, he is its *sine qua non.*
A proper overview, then, of the life of Jesus would require considerable space; a detailed
account of his life would fill more books than "the world itself could . . . contain," as the
testimony of the Beloved Disciple states (John 21:25). However, in a volume like this we
must be content with a survey of the most important events, starting at the beginning and
agreeing that some matters deserve more attention than others. The Gospels of Matthew and
Luke begin with announcement and birth narratives. John's Gospel takes readers back to the
premortal existence when Jesus was the firstborn spirit son of a divine father (see Doctrine
and Covenants 93:21), which is the only proper way to truly comprehend the significance of
Jesus's mortal life.[1]

The prologue to John's Gospel (John 1:1–18) begins by declaring that the premortal
Jesus was the "Word" (Greek *logos*). One definition of "the Word" is "messenger of salvation"
(Doctrine and Covenants 93:8), the agent of God the Father, the one who put into effect all
the terms and conditions of the Father's plan. This harmonizes well with the concept of *logos.* In our present language words act as a messenger between individuals. Similarly, Jesus
Christ acts as the mediator, medium, or messenger of his Father. Jesus's life and teachings are
the perfect expression of the Eternal Father's mind and will.[2]

In John 1:1, John implies, though does not explicitly state, that the premortal Jesus was
Jehovah, the Great I Am, come to earth.[3] John merely says that "the Word was with God
and the Word *was* God" (emphasis added). However, John knew as a Jew that there was no

other way to take his assertion than that Jesus was Jehovah—the one true God of Israelite religion (Deuteronomy 6:4). The terms *Jehovah* (Exodus 6:3) and *I Am* (Exodus 3:13–15) are related, the first derived from the verb "to become, to bring into being" and the second from the associated verb "to be, to exist."[4] Thus, the premortal Jesus of Nazareth was the eternally existing God of Israel.

According to John, the premortal Jesus was also the maker of "all things" (1:3). Latter-day revelation confirms John's witness with greater detail, explaining that Jesus Christ "created the heavens and the earth, and all things that in them are" (3 Nephi 9:15), as well as "millions of earths like this [one]" (Moses 7:30). But even more spectacular than his infinite creative power is his infinite redemptive power—he is able to save all that he creates (Doctrine and Covenants 76:42).

With the birth of Jesus, God himself physically entered history—the "Lord Omnipotent who reigneth, who was, and is from all eternity to eternity, [came] down from heaven among the children of men, and [dwelt] in a tabernacle of clay" (Mosiah 3:5). This is known in Latter-day Saint theology as the "condescension of God" (1 Nephi 11:26–33).

John the Baptist

Luke reports that the announcement of the Advent was preceded six months earlier by the angel Gabriel's announcement to Zacharias that the son his wife, Elizabeth, would deliver in her old age, John the Baptist, would be an Elias[5]—a servant who would prepare the way for the coming of the awaited Messiah (1:16–17). All of the Gospels indicate that this is exactly what John did once he reached maturity[6]—"preaching the baptism of repentance for the remission of sins" (Luke 3:3), quoting Isaiah 40:3 ("prepare ye the way of the Lord, make his paths straight," Matthew 3:3), and boldly declaring to the religious leaders of his day that his baptisms by water were a foreshadowing of the baptisms by fire and the Holy Ghost to be performed by Jesus, "who coming after me is preferred before me" (John 1:27; compare Luke 3:16).

A significant aspect of John's ministry of preparation appears to have been the training of future disciples of Jesus. So powerful a teacher was John that during his ministry he gathered followers or disciples who called him "Rabbi" (John 3:26), literally "my great one" or "my master." John taught these disciples to look ultimately for the Messiah and then urged them to transfer their allegiance from himself to Jesus (Matthew 11:1–5). He knew he was sent to prepare Jesus's disciples and said to them, "He [Jesus] must increase, but I must decrease" (John 3:30).

Some of those who were first disciples of John and later of Jesus became members of the original Twelve. Andrew, the brother of Peter, is specifically mentioned by name and shown to have influenced his brother: "Again the next day after John stood, and two of his disciples; and looking upon Jesus as he walked, he saith, Behold the Lamb of God! . . . One of the two which heard John speak, and followed him, was Andrew, Simon Peter's brother. He first findeth his own brother Simon, and saith unto him, We have found the Messias, which is, being interpreted, the Christ" (John 1:35–41).[7]

We are not sure how many of the original twelve were first disciples of John the Baptist, but a statement attributed to Peter, the chief apostle, has been seen to imply that several, if not all, were initially followers of John the Baptist and trained by him. After Judas Iscariot's death, Peter met with 120 disciples and instructed them that a replacement for the vacancy in the quorum of the twelve must be filled according to special criteria, including having been with the original twelve from the time of John's baptism onward (Acts 1:21–22).[8]

It would be impossible to understand the ministry of Jesus or his early church, as depicted in the New Testament, without understanding John the Baptist. So powerful and long-lasting was John's influence in Judaism of Jesus's and Paul's day that it was still being felt many years after his death (Acts 19:2–5).

Mary and Joseph in Nazareth

Luke states that Mary was a virgin living in Nazareth of the Galilee at the time of Gabriel's announcement of her impending conception (1:26). The Book of Mormon prophet Nephi adds that she was "exceedingly fair" (1 Nephi 11:13). The word *fair* in the King James Old Testament is primarily translated from one of two Hebrew terms: *tov* ("good," meaning "good to look at," as in Genesis 6:2) or *yapheh* ("beautiful"). The tradition of Mary's physical beauty became well established in early Christianity and persisted.[9]

Nazareth was small and insignificant biblically, the only major Christian site not mentioned in the Old Testament, the writings of the historian Josephus, or the Talmud. Archaeologist James F. Strange put the estimated size of Nazareth at under sixty acres, most of which "was empty space in antiquity." He estimated the population of Nazareth at the time of Jesus to be "a maximum of about 480."[10] Others think it was even fewer. The statement of one of Jesus's early disciples summarizes Nazareth's reputation at the time. When Philip first reported to Nathanael that he and others had "found him, of whom Moses in the law, and the prophets, did write [i.e., the Messiah], Jesus of Nazareth," Nathanael retorted, "Can there any good thing come out of Nazareth?" (John 1:45–46). If Jesus "descended below all things" (Doctrine and Covenants 88:6), this might well include the place where he grew up.

That Mary, and subsequently the holy family, lived in poor circumstances is made clear by Luke's report of the temple offering made by Mary and Joseph when Jesus was presented in the temple at forty days of age (2:22–24). As provided by the Mosaic law, the poor who could not afford a larger animal for the sacrificial offering could give a pair of turtledoves or two young pigeons (Leviticus 1:14; 5:7; 12:8).

Mary and Joseph Betrothed

Mary's faith and courage are demonstrated by her response to the divine announcement of her forthcoming motherhood: "My soul doth magnify the Lord, and my spirit hath rejoiced in God my Saviour" (Luke 1:46–47). This personal hymn of praise (verses 46–55, known as the Magnificat) is one of four such hymns preserved in Luke 1–2.[11] Indeed, we cannot even imagine what Mary learned about God, his majesty, glory, and personality, about the wonder of new life, conception, birth, and motherhood.

Mary was espoused, or betrothed, to Joseph at the time of her conception (Matthew 1:18), a circumstance much more binding than modern engagement to be married. Marriage customs in New Testament times derived from Mosaic laws and practices, exemplified in the Old Testament. Marriage between a young man and a young woman was typically arranged and agreed on between heads of the respective families.[12] Negotiations focused on, but were not limited to, the size of the *mohar* (the "bride price"; see Genesis 34:12; Exodus 22:17; 1 Samuel 18:25). Once the marriage was agreed on, the wedding consisted of two stages: betrothal and a separate celebration. Betrothal was legally and religiously more significant than the subsequent celebration, after which cohabitation actually began. Betrothal was regarded as finalization of a solemn agreement. It carried the force of a covenant to be honored between God-fearing parties (Genesis 2:24; Ezekiel 16:8; Ephesians 5:21–33). Legal action was required to dissolve a betrothal (Deuteronomy 24:1). Mosaic law also recognized the changed status of a man after betrothal by excusing him from military service until after the wedding celebration (Deuteronomy 20:7).

Though betrothed couples were regarded as husband and wife legally (Deuteronomy 22:23–24), between the time of betrothal and the celebration that inaugurated cohabitation, a strict code of chastity was enforced (Matthew 1:18, 25). At the time of betrothal the young man took legal, but not physical, possession of the young woman. Nonetheless, Mosaic law still referred to the woman as a wife, and unfaithfulness during the period of betrothal (espousal) could be punished by death (Deuteronomy 22:23–24).

Joseph's Righteousness

Thus, when Mary was found to be pregnant after a three-month visit to her relative Elizabeth (Luke 1:56; Matthew 1:18), Joseph did not want to have Mary stoned or exposed to public disgrace and therefore determined to divorce her quietly by signing the necessary legal document, called in Hebrew a *sefer keritut* (Deuteronomy 24:1), later called a *get*.[13] Only after the test of his character was he instructed in a dream by an angel to complete the marriage process.

As a result of Jesus's extraordinary conception, the idea of illegitimacy was perpetuated by uninformed sources and caused both Mary's and Jesus's reputations to suffer (and probably Joseph's) throughout their lives. Respected Roman historian Michael Grant wrote that the unusual circumstances surrounding Jesus's birth "led to subsequent Jewish stories of Jesus' illegitimacy, which persisted for centuries."[14] It is possible that we see these charges of illegitimacy surface in John's Gospel when certain Jews responded to Jesus's charge of not being the spiritual heirs of Abraham, which he leveled sometime after the Feast of Tabernacles: "They answered and said unto him, Abraham is our father. Jesus saith unto them, If ye were Abraham's children, ye would do the works of Abraham. But now ye seek to kill me . . . : this did not Abraham. Ye do the deeds of your father. Then said they to him, We be not born of fornication; we have one Father, even God" (John 8:39–41).

Birth

The Holy Ghost came upon Mary "to prepare her for admittance into the divine presence," because "no man or woman can live in mortality and survive the presence of the Highest except by the sustaining power of the Holy Ghost."[15] Latter-day Saint theology affirms the doctrine of the virgin birth, but not immaculate conception (Alma 7:10).[16] "From Mary, a mortal woman who had never had sexual relations with any man (Luke 1:34), Jesus inherited mortality, including the capacity to die; from God, the immortal Man of Holiness, Jesus inherited immortality, the capacity to live forever. He is the Son of God, and he is God the Son."[17] John reported Jesus himself testifying that "as the Father hath life in himself; so hath he given to the Son to have life in himself" (5:26).

Both Matthew and Luke place the birth of Jesus at Bethlehem of Judea, south of Jerusalem. Luke is the only Gospel writer who relates his narrative to specific dates of world history. He says Caesar Augustus (27 BC–AD 14), the first and one of the greatest of the Roman emperors, called for a taxing or census enrollment, which first occurred when Quirinius was Roman governor of Syria (2:1–7). Both assertions of location and time have been called into question by some notable scholars.[18] While Luke's association of the Roman census with Quirinius may present historical problems,[19] Alma 7:10 points to Bethlehem as the place of the Nativity.

After giving birth, Mary wrapped Jesus in cloths and placed him in a manger "because there was no room for them in the inn" (Luke 2:7). The Joseph Smith Translation changes *inn* to *inns*. The Greek word *kataluma* can be translated as "inn," "guest room," or "room."[20] Some have wondered if Joseph and Mary might have sought lodging with relatives in the area since their family history clearly ties back to King David and his city, Bethlehem (Luke 2:4; 1 Samuel 16:1, 11–12), and it is possible to translate Luke 2:7 as "laid him in a manger because they had no space in the room(s)." But Luke does not tell readers where, precisely, the birth occurred. Second-century-AD Christian apologist Justin Martyr states: "Since Joseph had nowhere to lodge [*katalyein*] in that village, he lodged in a certain cave near the village; and while they were there, Mary brought forth the Messiah and laid him in a manger, where the magi from Arabia came and found him."[21] We note, however, that these magi apparently came later since the family was by that time living in a "house" (Matthew 2:11). In addition, the early church father Origen, who was very familiar with the land of Israel from personal visits, wrote: "If anyone wants further proof to convince him that Jesus was born in Bethlehem, . . . he may observe that in agreement with the story in the Gospel about Jesus' birth, the cave at Bethlehem is shown where he was born, and the manger in the cave where he was wrapped in strips of cloth."[22]

The traditional site of that cave is inside the Church of the Nativity in Bethlehem, commissioned in the fourth century by St. Helena, mother of Constantine. The traditional manger is carved out of stone, and the exact spot of the birth is marked by a fourteen-point silver star, representing the three groupings of fourteen generations in Jesus's genealogy according to Matthew (1:17).

There is tremendous symbolism associated with Bethlehem, a name meaning "house of bread" in Hebrew. It is a fitting location for the Advent of the "Bread of Life" (John 6:35). His birth was attended by angels and later by good shepherds, who were keeping watch over their sheep.

Infancy

In accord with Jewish practice, Jesus was circumcised when eight days old as a sign that identified him as a member of the Abrahamic covenant (Genesis 17:10–12; compare JST Genesis 17:11–12). Circumcision was itself a symbol of the Lord's greater desire—to circumcise one's heart, meaning to conform to and live according to God's will (Deuteronomy 10:16; 30:6).

At forty days of age, Jesus was taken to the temple in Jerusalem to be presented to his Father and be redeemed or ransomed according to the Mosaic law (Exodus 13:13; Numbers 18:15). By the Lord's decree, every firstborn son belonged to him (Exodus 13:2; 34:19). This ritual of ransoming was a symbolic reliving of the Passover,[23] where the male child was redeemed from full-time servitude to God by a five-shekel payment (Numbers 3:47–48). Later, the tribe of Levi became the Lord's special possession instead of the firstborn males—but the ransoming ceremony was kept (3:45).

Matthew's Gospel describes the visit of *magi*, "wise men from the east" who followed a star to find the new king of the Jews (Matthew 2:1–2). The term *magi* or *magoi* used in the Greek text of Matthew points to a Persian origin. *Magi* refers to Zoroastrian priests.[24] Perhaps these noble visitors were descendants of Jewish priests who were taken to Babylon as part of the exile in 586 BC and subsequently came under Persian rule and culture when Cyrus the Great conquered the region (539 BC), and who stayed there (as the majority of the Jewish exiles did) instead of returning to Judea beginning in 538 BC. It is not hard to see how Jewish priests in the Persian Empire would be categorized with priests of Zoroastrianism under the general rubric *Magi* and make astrology or star watching part of their priestly function. After all, a very early prophecy of the appearance of the Messiah states that "there shall come a Star out of Jacob, and a Sceptre shall rise out of Israel" (Numbers 24:17).

We do not know how many wise men visited the holy family, nor do we know how long after Jesus's birth they arrived. Their visit is backdrop to Herod's treachery,[25] followed by dreams of warning given to the wise men and to Joseph, the flight of the holy family to Egypt, the slaughter of the innocents in and around Bethlehem, and the return of Joseph, Mary, and Jesus ultimately to their permanent residence of many years in Nazareth (Matthew 2:12–23). Matthew presents the holy family's physical departure out of Egypt as fulfillment of Hosea 11:1 —"I . . . called my son out of Egypt" (compare Matthew 2:15).

Growing to Maturity

We possess scant details of Jesus's maturation and young adult years from canonical sources. The Joseph Smith Translation of the Bible provides an important note:

> And it came to pass that Jesus grew up with his brethren, and waxed strong, and waited upon the Lord for the time of his ministry to come. And he served under his father, and he spake not as other men, neither could he be taught; for he needed not that any man should teach him. And after many years, the hour of his ministry drew nigh. (JST Matthew 3:24–26)

There exists a genre of apocryphal stories about Jesus's boyhood called "hidden life" stories, which are found in noncanonical sources like the *Infancy Gospel of Thomas*, "which recounts 'the mighty childhood deeds of our Lord Jesus Christ,' between ages five to twelve."[26]

Luke's report of Jesus's appearance at the Jerusalem temple when twelve years old serves as a bridge between his infancy and public ministry accounts.[27] In the temple precinct we see Jesus as a prodigy, teaching and answering questions from the doctors of the law, who were astonished at his insights (JST Luke 2:46–47). Among the Jews of the rabbinic period, such a performance would fit the ideal model of the rabbinic prodigy or scholar-genius—the *ilui* or enlightened one.[28] But as is made clear by Luke, Jesus was not a genius, not a rabbinic prodigy. He was, and he *knew* he was by age twelve, the literal Son of God the Father (2:49). In Luke's account we also learn that Jesus was well rounded in his development—in wisdom, stature, favor with God, and favor with man, or in other words, intellectually, physically, spiritually, and socially (2:52).

Opening Events of Jesus's Public Ministry

The Gospel of Mark introduces his account of the earthly ministry of Jesus of Nazareth by using the Greek word *euangelion*, "good news" or "good tidings," translated as "gospel" in the King James Version: "The beginning of the gospel [good news] of Jesus Christ, the Son of God" (Mark 1:1). This closely parallels a Roman proclamation dated to around 9 BC that speaks of the birth of Caesar Augustus (emperor from 27 BC to AD 14) as "the beginning of good tidings for the world."[29] One gets the sense that Mark was trying to persuade Roman audiences that Jesus is the real ruler and bearer of good tidings.

Luke associates the beginning of Jesus's public ministry with his baptism:

> Now when all the people were baptized, it came to pass, that Jesus also being baptized, and praying, the heaven was opened, and the Holy Ghost descended in a bodily shape like a dove upon him, and a voice came from heaven, which said, Thou art my beloved Son; in thee I am well pleased. *And Jesus himself began to be about thirty years of age,* being (as was supposed) the son of Joseph, which was the son of Heli." (3:21–23; emphasis added)[30]

The doctrinal significance of Jesus's baptism is powerfully described in the Book of Mormon, particularly in 2 Nephi 31. But several years after Jesus's mortal ministry, the apostle Paul reminded disciples in equally powerful terms of baptism's symbolic link to Jesus's death, burial, and resurrection (Romans 6:3–6). In a way, Jesus's own baptism was a reminder to him of his ultimate purpose in mortality—the atoning sacrifice.

Luke's mention of Jesus being about thirty years old has reference to the legal age of maturity in Jewish society (Luke 3:23), the age at which Aaronic priests completed their five-year apprenticelike preparation and fully entered into their ministerial responsibilities in the tabernacle and, later, the temple (Numbers 4:3, 47; 8:24). A famous section of the Mishnah Pirqe Aboth 5:24, outlines the various phases a man's life should follow: "At five years the age is reached for the study of Bible, at ten for the study of Mishnah, at thirteen for the fulfillment of the commandments, at fifteen for the study of Talmud, at eighteen for marriage, at twenty for seeking a livelihood, at thirty for full strength."[31] Age thirty was thus generally recognized as the time when one moved from preparation to full engagement with one's life's work.

The statement from *Pirqe Aboth* naturally raises a question about Jesus's marital status. The scriptures say nothing about it. It is obvious, however, that Jewish religion and culture commended marriage and family life to one and all and looked with disfavor upon normal adult unmarried men. For example, Mishnah tractate Kiddushin 4:13 stipulates that "an unmarried man may not be a teacher of children."

Temptations

Immediately after his baptism, Jesus was led by the Spirit into the wilderness to commune with his Father (JST Matthew 4:1; Mark 1:12). The location of this special communion was the wilderness of Judah, on the western side of the Dead Sea.[32] After Jesus had been with his Father and fasted forty days, he was naturally hungry. Satan used this juncture of vulnerability to attack and tempt Jesus—to get him to use his power to satisfy personal appetites, to appeal to his vanity, and ultimately to obey someone other than his Father. The key phrases each begin with the proposition "if" (Matthew 4:3, 6, 9). This same tactic would be used in the last hours of Jesus's mortal life on the cross when the rulers of the people and the Roman soldiers goaded Jesus: "He saved others; let him save himself, *if* he be Christ. . . . And the soldiers . . . saying, *If* thou be the king of the Jews, save thyself" (Luke 23:35–37; emphasis added). The temptations leveled at Jesus—to use his power for personal gratification rather than advancing God's will and to submit to the will of the adversary—affect all disciples and get at the heart of whom we submit to, whom we worship, who we are, and *whose* we are. In each circumstance Jesus responded to Satan by quoting scripture (Matthew 4:4, 7, 10).

The significant change of JST Matthew 4:1 regarding Jesus's original reason for being in the wilderness ("to be with God" versus the KJV, "to be tempted of the devil") is exceptionally enlightening and helps to answer the question raised by scholars about whether the "wilderness" in this context is to be viewed negatively or positively: "Is it to be understood negatively as a place of demons (compare 1QM 1) where creation has been cursed (Isaiah 13:19–22; Ezekiel 34:25; Luke 11:24–28) or positively as a place restored to a new creation by the coming of the messianic age (Isaiah 11:6–9; 32:14–20; 40:3; 65:25; Hosea 2:18; compare the pre-Fall paradise of Genesis 1:26–28)?"[33]

The reading of the Joseph Smith Translation shows that the Holy Ghost did not purposely lead Jesus to the devil to be tempted. Rather, the Holy Ghost led Jesus to the Father, to a higher spiritual environment, which is one of the purposes of the Holy Ghost.[34] The wilderness experience foreshadows the Millennium and harks back to the paradise of Eden. A hallmark of the earth's paradisiacal condition was the presence of God, and that was the environment of Jesus's forty-day wilderness sojourn. The whole earth will return to that state at the second coming of Christ.[35]

At some point early in his ministry, Jesus started to extend initial calls to specific individuals to transfer their allegiance from John the forerunner to himself, to become his disciples, and to join him in the work of his messianic ministry. John's record indicates this began the day after Jesus's baptism when John identified Jesus as the Messiah, the Lamb of God, to his own disciples. On this occasion Jesus gave Peter a new name, *Kepha'* in Aramaic, *Petros* or Peter in Greek (John 1:35–42). The Joseph Smith Translation interprets Simon's new name as "a seer or a stone"—perhaps intending for us to think metaphorically of "seer stone" and thus of one who would receive revelation for the post-Resurrection church. John then reports that the next day Jesus headed north to the Galilee where Philip and Nathanael formally became disciples when Jesus demonstrated his powers of seership in calling Nathanael (John 1:43–51). John's Gospel does not take into account Jesus's forty-day fast and subsequent temptation. Thus, with our present state of information, it is not possible to lay out the exact chronology of Jesus's early ministry and harmonize the Gospels with certainty.

In Galilee

Back in the Galilee at the beginning of his public ministry, in the village of Cana, Jesus performed the first of many recorded miracles—the turning of water into wine at a wedding celebration (John 2:1–11). Jesus and at least five of his new followers who had accepted the invitation to discipleship were "called" to attend a marriage (2:2). It appears from the role his mother occupied that it was a member of Jesus's family who was being married, as she had responsibility to provide refreshment for the guests. Jesus accommodated his mother's request for more wine by producing more than one hundred gallons (2:6).[36]

The significance of this miracle is manifold. The episode shows that Jesus was no social recluse: He participated in a marriage feast. He was obedient to his mother's wishes to make more wine in order to make people happy. He performed the miracle to teach his disciples about his power and strengthen their faith in him (John 2:11). He foreshadowed the Atonement: just as the best wine (symbolic of his blood) came at the end of the feast (2:10), so his greatest sacrifice came at the end of his ministry. He also taught the concept of timing by declaring his "hour [had] not yet come" (2:4), meaning that the time to openly and grandly proclaim his messianic kingship had not yet come. He did not want to preempt the time needed to perform all those events that needed to be accomplished before an announcement stirred up tremendous and irreversible controversy.

In Jerusalem with Nicodemus

Jesus left the Galilee for Jerusalem to attend Passover—the first of his public ministry (John 2:13–25). John reports that on this occasion Jesus cleansed the temple, attempting to re-institute some semblance of reverence and order. The area of his activity centered around those locales in the temple precinct where the money changers and animal merchants had permission to pursue their ventures—the Court of the Gentiles and Solomon's porch—and not the temple itself. It is striking, from the perspective of hindsight, that in his rebuke Jesus refers to the temple as "my Father's house" (2:16). Later, during the last week of his life, he cleansed the temple again, but this time referred to it as "my house" (Matthew 21:12–13). And a few days after that, while in the temple precinct just before he delivered the Olivet Discourse (Matthew 24), he referred to it as "your house"—"your house is left unto you des-olate" (23:38). We see a progressive distancing of the temple from God the Father.

While in Jerusalem at this juncture, Jesus had a nighttime encounter with Nicodemus, a Pharisee and ruler of the Jews (John 3:1).[37] Jesus taught him a key doctrine of the kingdom of God: spiritual rebirth and the necessity of baptism and receipt of the gift of the Holy Ghost (3:3–8). In John's account of this episode we learn important things about Jesus—he was called "Rabbi," known as a teacher come from God, recognized as a miracle-worker, and linked with godly righteousness in the minds of at least some Jewish leaders. That Nicode-mus became a profound disciple is seen in two subsequent events reported by John: Nico-demus's defense of Jesus in front of his Pharisaic colleagues (7:50–51) and his help with the burial of Jesus's body after the Crucifixion (19:39–42). Nicodemus is identified forever after his nighttime encounter with Jesus as he who came to Jesus by night (7:50; 19:39).

During this time, as the Synoptic Gospels report, John the Baptist was imprisoned by Herod Antipas. Josephus placed this incarceration at the fortress of Machaerus, east of the Dead Sea.[38] Herod Antipas, son of Herod the Great, was tetrarch of Galilee and Perea (Luke 3:19–20). John had been testifying powerfully of Jesus as well as baptizing. Again, we are struck by his complete absence of self-importance, pride, and self-interest, as well as by his fearless declaration of the truth in the face of Herod's wicked behavior (Matthew 14:3–5; Mark 6:17–20). It was this courageous pursuit of the truth at all hazards that resulted in John's beheading.

Return to the Galilee

Jesus left Judea for the Galilee once again, but by taking a route through Samaria. Here he had his famous encounter with the woman at the well (John 4:4–42). The lessons from this episode are powerful. Though he was a Jew, possessing the status of rabbi, he nevertheless spoke directly to a woman who was a Samaritan, thereby abrogating the narrow-minded social conventions and prejudices of the day. Jesus carefully led the woman to the realization that he was the Messiah, culminating in his powerful self-declaration "I that speak unto thee am he" (4:26).

As a result of the Samaritan woman's newfound testimony, which she bore to her neighbors, "many of the Samaritans of that city believed on him for the saying of the woman" (4:39). But then the Samaritans besought Jesus "that he would tarry with them: and he abode there two days. And many more believed because of his own word; and said unto the woman, Now we believe, not because of thy saying: for we have heard him ourselves, and know that this is indeed the Christ, the Saviour of the world" (4:40–42). These verses describe the converting power of a single testimony, the essence of the way the gospel of Jesus Christ spread.

Back in the Galilee, Jesus went to his hometown synagogue, where his messianic witness was rejected by the people, as already noted (Luke 4:16–30). Jesus would be rejected in Nazareth a second time, which caused him amazement on account of the people's unbelief (Mark 6:1–6). Rejection was a major element of his brief life; even his own half brothers did not believe in him while he lived in mortality (John 7:5). And so he left Nazareth and "came and dwelt in Capernaum"—"his own city" from that time on (Matthew 4:13; 9:1).

Sermon on the Mount

Luke's accurate chronological sequence of events places the time of the sermon immediately after the choosing of the Twelve, when a great multitude of people from Judea, Jerusalem, and the seacoast of Tyre and Sidon came to hear Jesus and to be healed of their infirmities (6:17–19).[39] Matthew says the sermon was delivered on a "mountain" (5:1; 8:1), while Luke places it on a "plain" (6:17).

It is important for us to understand the intended audience. It was not the multitude in general. Rather, it was Jesus's disciples—particularly the Twelve Apostles—for whom the sermon was given. Matthew notes that when he saw the multitudes, "he went up into the mountain: and when he was set, *his disciples* came unto him" (Matthew 5:1; emphasis added). As a training session for the apostles, the Sermon on the Mount was multifaceted: it was the keynote address of the restoration of the gospel in Jesus's day (JST John 1:26–28), describing how the Mosaic law was fulfilled and what was restored or new to the Jews (Matthew 5:17–18, 21–44); it was a discourse on perfection (5:48); it was a description of the characteristics possessed by those who will inherit eternal life (5:3–12)[40]; hence it was a description of Jesus's own character and attributes and the constitution for a perfect life[41]; it was a reintroduction of God the Father (and his nature), whose existence had been obscured in the Judaism of Jesus's day, to the disciples (6:1–34; 7:7–11); and it was an instructional session on how to teach the Jews, especially the leaders (JST Matthew 7:9–11).

The content Jesus presented in the sermon was noted by people who were also listening, for they "were astonished at his doctrine." And his method was different from that of other rabbis, "for he taught them as one having authority, and not as the scribes" (Matthew

7:28–29). Jesus did not cite precedent nor quote previous teachers and authorities. He was the authority.

Both Matthew and Luke report that when Jesus finished the sermon he headed east to Capernaum, where he performed more miracles, including the healing of the centurion's servant (likely the centurion's own child). Capernaum stood on a branch of an ancient highway called the Via Maris, thus making it an important station between districts from which to collect taxes and house a Roman garrison led by a centurion. Though a Gentile, this centurion was a man of unequaled faith in Jesus of Nazareth as Messiah. In fact, Jesus marveled and said he had "not found so great faith, no, not in Israel" (Matthew 8:10).

Capernaum became known as a place of miracles. Jesus seems to have performed more miracles in Capernaum than anywhere else. Sadly, in the end it was precisely because of all the miracles witnessed, but without any corresponding repentance (Matthew 11:20), that Jesus leveled harsh judgment against Capernaum and two other towns, Chorazin and Bethsaida. To the inhabitants of Capernaum he declared: "And thou, Capernaum, which art exalted unto heaven, shalt be brought down to hell: for if the mighty works, which have been done in thee, had been done in Sodom, it would have remained until this day. But I say unto you, That it shall be more tolerable for the land of Sodom in the day of judgment, than for thee" (11:23–24).

Miracles

The miracles Jesus performed constitute a major element of and reason for his messianic ministry.[42] They are not ancillary to it. The Gospels present several accounts of Jesus's miracles but do not contain many of his own comments about them. However, he said, "I cast out devils by the Spirit of God" (Matthew 12:28) and perform miraculous events "with the finger of God" (Luke 11:20). Apparently, he was self-aware of his unusual power, for he said that he had "done among [the people] the works which none other man did" (John 15:24). And it appears that Jesus regarded his miracles as evidence of his messiahship and divine sonship. When messengers from John the Baptist came to Jesus asking if he were the one they should look for (meaning the Messiah), Jesus responded by curing "many of their infirmities and plagues, and of evil spirits; and unto many that were blind he gave sight" (Luke 7:20–21). He then told the disciples of John that they in turn should go tell the Baptist what things they had seen and heard, namely, "how that the blind see, the lame walk, the lepers are cleansed, the deaf hear, the dead are raised, to the poor the gospel is preached" (7:22).

Indeed, there was an acknowledgement among many of the people who believed on Jesus that he looked like the Messiah precisely because of his miracles, for they asked, "When Christ cometh, will he do more miracles than these which this man hath done?" (John 7:31). Some Jewish leaders also recognized that Jesus's works were extraordinary and could only have been performed by the power of God (3:2; compare 11:47).

The purposes for which Jesus performed miracles tell us much about his ministry and his personality. Perhaps the fundamental reason that Jesus performed miracles was to help those in need. He saw suffering and was filled with compassion. This godly love, one would argue, was the very essence of his personality. The First Epistle of John declares that "God is love" (1 John 4:8). Jesus and his Father are the embodiment of pure, perfect love (Greek, *agape*), translated in the King James Version as "charity" in Paul's famous instruction to the Corinthian saints on love (1 Corinthians 13). In other words, of all the perfect attributes that make up their personalities and characters, it is love that molds, shapes, informs, mediates, and invigorates the rest.[43]

Examples of Christ's compassion abound in the Gospels. At a time when Jesus departed to a desert place to be alone after hearing of John the Baptist's beheading, he saw a great multitude following him and "was moved with compassion toward them, and . . . healed their sick" (Matthew 14:12–14). He then multiplied five loaves of bread and two fish to feed five thousand men, plus women and children, because they were hungry and he was compassionate. This miracle is recounted in all four Gospels, suggesting its impressive aspects to the disciples and its pivotal nature (Matthew 14:16–21; Mark 6:33–44; Luke 9:11–17; John 6:5–14).

Three times we know of, Jesus brought deceased individuals back to life (the widow's son in Luke 7:11–18, Jairus's daughter in Mark 5:35–43, and his friend Lazarus in John 11:1–46). In all three instances the Savior's compassion is obvious, and it is specifically mentioned in the raising of the widow's son (Luke 7:13). Perhaps most touching is the tenderness Jesus displayed toward the daughter of Jairus, a scene interestingly interrupted by Jesus healing the woman with the issue of blood (Mark 5:25–34). But when messengers from Jairus's house came reporting the death of Jairus's daughter and asking why Jairus was still bothering the Master, he reassured the synagogue ruler, encouraging him to not be afraid but to "only believe" (Mark 5:36). Jesus ignored the commotion outside Jairus's house as well as the spiritual immaturity of those who "laughed him to scorn" (Mark 5:40). Always the mentor, Jesus took the chief apostles inside the house and restored the twelve-year-old girl to life. But what Jesus said is the focal point of the episode.

Of the four Gospels, Mark preserves the most Aramaic phrases used by Jesus. It does so in Mark 5:41. Though the King James Version interprets Jesus's declaration, "Talitha cumi," as "Damsel, I say unto thee, arise," the phrase could better be rendered as "Little one, get up,"[44] a great example of the kindness Jesus had for those around him. Jesus was one who not only wept (John 11:35) but also, stirred by a sensitive soul, exuded great tenderness for those for whom he also felt pain.

Jesus demonstrated he had power over physical death and thus foreshadowed his resurrection. He also showed he had concern for healing the soul (making glad those who were devastated by the vicissitudes of life) as well as the physical body (Mark 2:1–12). By performing miracles, Jesus sought to elevate the thoughts of those who benefitted from his power and to cause them to realize their spiritual infirmities and ultimate dependence on Deity (Matthew 21:18–21; Mark 2:1–11). Thus, Jesus sometimes performed miracles to give evidence of his divine mission and power so that truth seekers would believe in him and believers would be strengthened in their faith. His miracles taught his disciples that he was the creator and master of the elements and forces of nature. He walked on water (Matthew 14:25–26), calmed storms on the Sea of Galilee (Mark 4:35–41), and cast out evil spirits and controlled them at his will (1:23–27; 9:17–29).

On occasion Jesus performed miracles to expose the narrow, contracted, elitist, and self-righteous views of some of the scribes, Pharisees, and Sadducees he encountered (Mark 3:1–6; Luke 13:10–17; 14:1–6). Therefore, sometimes the miracles Jesus performed made his opponents all the more antagonistic and desirous of killing him for their own selfish purposes (John 11:46–48). He refused to give the Pharisees a sign to prove who he was (Matthew 12:38–39; Mark 8:11–21; Luke 11:16, 29). However, Jesus never performed miracles for selfish purposes; he emphatically refused to turn stones into bread after his lengthy fast (Matthew 4:3–4), and he would not come down from the cross and save himself (Mark 15:29–32).

Parables

As a teacher, Jesus adapted to the situation at hand and used a variety of methods: he appealed to precedent in the scriptures (Matthew 12:1–8); he quoted from the scriptures (John 10:34); he taught forthrightly with authority and usually did not cite secondary sources (Matthew 7:28–29); he candidly corrected error (Matthew 22:29); he used questions, sometimes bargained by means of questions (Luke 10:25–28; Matthew 21:23–27); he sometimes appeared to change the subject (John 8:3–11; Matthew 22:29–33); he posed problems (Matthew 22:41–46); and he used irony, even sarcasm (Matthew 23:15, 27).

Jesus used parables extensively (Matthew 13). At a certain point in his ministry he taught only through parables (Mark 4:34). Great teachers throughout history have used parables—extended metaphors and allegories—to get across their messages. Among the greatest teachers of Israel were the Tannaitic rabbis (roughly AD 10–200), who used stories in their instruction. Jesus of Nazareth was, in part, a product of his culture and time and drew on a somewhat common stock of stories and illustrations as he taught. The codification of Jewish oral tradition and law, the Midrash and Talmud collections, contain many parables and hortatory narratives involving sowing, harvesting, farming, building, stewards, landlords, tenants, and peasants. There are rabbinic stories of hidden treasure, a Pharisee and a publican, a prodigal son, a feast given to the poor but meant for others, and so on. In short, many of the stories told by Jesus were familiar to the great Jewish teachers of that period, but their uniqueness came in the way Jesus used them. As one author put it, Jesus did not invent the form of teaching known as parables, nor even the specific components of the stories, but under his transforming touch, the water of the parables, as it were, became the richest wine.[45]

Many of these parables were delivered in the Galilee. This is the setting for Matthew 13, which records more parables than does any other single chapter of scripture. When Jesus was sitting by the Sea of Galilee one day, great multitudes gathered around him "so that he went into a ship, and sat; and the whole multitude stood on the shore. And he spake many things unto them in parables" (13:2–3). Based on interpretive commentary by Joseph Smith,

Latter-day Saints believe the parables of Matthew 13 have both an ancient and a modern application. Regarding the latter, Joseph Smith taught that their deepest meaning is found only when the parables are seen as an organic whole and "afford us as clear an understanding upon the importance of the gathering [of Israel] as anything recorded in the Bible."[46] In Joseph Smith's mind, the parables illustrate how the gospel came to be restored in the dispensation of the fulness of times.

The other major location where some of the best-known parables of Jesus were delivered was across the river Jordan in the district of Perea during the last year of Jesus's ministry. These are recorded only by Luke and include the parables of the wedding feast (14:7–11), the great supper (14:12–24), the lost sheep (15:1–7), the lost coin (15:8–10), the prodigal son (15:11–32), the unjust steward (16:1–13), and the rich man and Lazarus (16:19–31).

Feeding of the Five Thousand

Jesus spent much time in the Galilee pursuing his ministry, teaching "throughout every city and village" (Luke 8:1). He was accompanied by the apostles and by women who "ministered unto him of their substance" (8:3). These are some of the unsung heroes of the early church, who continued to follow and support Jesus, including Mary Magdalene and Joanna the wife of Chuza, Herod's household steward (24:1, 10).

About one year before the Crucifixion, word reached Jesus that John the Baptist had been executed by Herod Antipas. He crossed the Sea of Galilee alone by ship to reach a desolate place (Greek *eremon topon*), undoubtedly to mourn John's death and privately honor him. But when crowds managed to follow, he felt compassion for them and turned from his personal solitude to heal their sick. This further led to the feeding of the great multitude by multiplying the meager number of loaves and fishes.

Immediately afterward, Jesus compelled the apostles to go on ahead to the other side of the lake, sent the crowds away, and went up to a mountain again by himself to pray (Matthew 14:22–23). One of the reasons Jesus sent away the multitude was because some of the men wanted to "take him by force, to make him a king" (John 6:15), and that was contrary to Jesus's plan. During the fourth watch of the night (about 3–6 a.m.), Jesus met up with his disciples in the ship by walking on the water and helping Peter do the same. When the apostles saw him walking toward them, they cried out in fear, supposing they had seen a spirit. But as on other occasions, Jesus calmed them as he also commanded them: "Be of good cheer; it is I; be not afraid" (Matthew 14:27).

Fear seems to have been a frequent companion of several of the early disciples. On more than one occasion Jesus offered words of counsel to serve as a powerful antidepressant (e.g., "be of good cheer," John 16:33) as well as a reminder of the destructive effects of fear and the positive effects of faith ("Why are ye so fearful? how is it that ye have no faith?," Mark 4:40).

Bread of Life Discourse

The next day Jesus and his apostles sailed over to Capernaum. People who were part of the miracle of the loaves and fishes also went to Capernaum seeking Jesus somewhat impertinently, not because they were spiritually enriched and wanted to live better lives. Rather, they had gotten a free meal and were seeking another (JST John 6:26). Jesus told them not to work for temporal sustenance but for that spiritual food that brings eternal life. He testified that such was the work of God. However, the response of his listeners betrayed their real interest: "What sign shewest thou then?" (John 6:30).

This set the stage for one of the most powerful and pivotal sermons of Jesus's ministry, the Bread of Life, though only John records it (John 6:29–58). Jesus would never again be as popular as he was after the feeding of the five thousand. After the sermon his popularity plummeted, for "many of his disciples went back, and walked no more with him" (John 6:66).[47] In addition, two other results of the discourse are significant. First, a powerful testimony was elicited from Peter that paralleled and foreshadowed his great confession at Caesarea Philippi (Matthew 16:13–16). When Jesus asked the Twelve if they would also go away, the chief apostle replied, "Lord, to whom shall we go? thou hast the words of eternal life. And we believe and are sure that thou art that Christ, the Son of the living God" (John 6:67–69). Second, Jesus alluded to his future betrayer, Judas Iscariot, one of the Twelve, though none of the apostles knew this (6:70–71).

Caesarea Philippi and North

Refusing to go to Jerusalem just yet because certain Jews sought to kill him, Jesus continued his ministry in the Galilee (John 7:1). He rebuked scribes and Pharisees for hypocrisy—namely, using their oral tradition to skirt certain precepts of the Mosaic law, particularly responsibility to look after parents (Matthew 15:1–9; Mark 7:1–13). During this period, he and his disciples made an excursion to the coastal region of Tyre and Sidon (ancient Phoenicia, modern Lebanon) and interacted with a gentile woman whose daughter was "grievously vexed with a devil" (Matthew 15:22).

The mother's plea for help was initially rebuffed by Jesus, who reminded both the woman of Canaan and his disciples that he was sent only to "the lost sheep of the house of Israel" (Matthew 15:24). But the woman's worshipful humility, persistence, and cleverness caused Jesus to relent,[48] cure her daughter, and commend the tenacious mother for her faith (15:25–28).

This episode was the only time we know of when Jesus went to that northern seacoast. According to Mark's Gospel, Jesus returned from the region of Tyre and came through Sidon to the lake of Galilee (Mark 7:31). This route has been equated with "the trunk road from Tyre to the region of Caesarea Philippi."[49] Perhaps Jesus took this route to stop at Caesarea Philippi and use the geology of the region as a graphic visual aid to teach a profound lesson.

Caesarea Philippi sits at the bedrock base of Mount Hermon, the tallest mountain in the region. Standing somewhere near this bedrock base, which visually dominates the area,

Jesus asked the Twelve who men said he was. He then asked them who they believed he was. This elicited Peter's powerful witness: "Thou art the Christ, the Son of the living God" (Matthew 16:16). Jesus identified the source of Peter's knowledge—revelation from the Father that Jesus was the Messiah—and in turn proclaimed Peter's identity and role: "And I say also unto thee [pointing to Peter, as we suppose], That thou art Peter (Greek, *petros*, "small rock"), and upon this rock (Greek *petra*, "bedrock") I will build my church [pointing to the bedrock base of Mount Hermon, as we suppose]" (16:18). Peter was not the foundation of the church; the revelation that Jesus was Messiah was the foundation. Other passages in scripture speak of Jesus Christ as the rock and foundation of a disciple's faith (1 Corinthians 10:4; Helaman 5:12; Doctrine and Covenants 6:34; Moses 7:53).

Jesus then promised that the keys of the kingdom and the sealing power would be given to Peter and the other apostles so that whatever they caused to be bound or loosed on earth would also be effective in heaven (Matthew 16:19). That the keys and sealing power are references to the full authority of the priesthood is made clear in Restoration scripture and the statements of modern prophets.[50]

Transfiguration

According to Matthew and Mark, Jesus's promise of the bestowal of priesthood keys and sealing power was fulfilled six days after events at Caesarea Philippi. At this time he was transfigured (Greek, *metemorphothē*; compare "metamorphosis") before his chief apostles (Mark 9:2), and the ancient prophets Moses and Elijah "appeared in glory" with him and spoke "of his decease which he should accomplish at Jerusalem" (Luke 9:31). In fact, Peter, James, and John were also transfigured or else they could not have withstood the glory manifested before them (Moses 1:11). Luke 9:28 places this event after "eight days."

The reason for the visitation of Moses and Elijah on the holy mount was explained by Joseph Smith: "The Savior, Moses, and Elias, gave the keys to Peter, James, and John, on the mount, when they were transfigured before him."[51] A parallel event occurred in Latter-day Saint history in 1835 in the Kirtland Temple with Joseph Smith and Oliver Cowdery present:

> Moses appeared before us, and committed unto us the keys of the gathering of Israel from the four parts of the earth, and the leading of the ten tribes from the land of the north. . . . After this vision had closed, another great and glorious vision burst upon us; for Elijah the prophet, who was taken to heaven without tasting death, stood before us, and said . . . the keys of this dispensation are committed into your hands; and by this ye may know that the great and dreadful day of the Lord is near, even at the doors. (Doctrine and Covenants 110:11, 13, 16)[52]

After this event, Jesus continued his Galilean ministry with teaching and healing the people (Matthew 17:14–27).

Later Judean Ministry

The transfiguration event seems to have occurred as the Feast of Tabernacles approached. The chief apostles wanted to craft three tabernacles for Jesus, Moses, and Elijah as the ancient prophets departed, which suggests they recognized the approach of the feast (Luke 9:33). Since the festival was almost upon them and Jesus was still in the Galilee after the Transfiguration, he was chided by his half brothers for not going to Jerusalem to attend the festival, which they said he should have done if he was really the Messiah. Jesus did finally slip into Jerusalem amid popular discussions about him (John 7:11–12).

The Feast of Tabernacles was a seven-day festival, and Jesus taught in the Jerusalem temple precinct during its celebration (John 7:14, 28). Tabernacles was the most joyous of all the celebrations and commemorations of the Jewish liturgical calendar. It marked the end of one agricultural cycle and the beginning of another. Thus, each day of the feast a procession of priests participated in the drawing-of-water ceremony by going down to the Siloam pool to draw water, return to the temple, walk around the altar of sacrifice with a choir chanting from Psalms 113–118 (messianic in their content), and pour out the water as a libation at the time of the morning sacrifice.[53] On the last day of the feast, "the great day of the feast," Jesus did something remarkable. He stood, perhaps as the libation was being poured out, and declared that if anyone came to him and drank, out of their bellies would "flow rivers of living water" (John 7:37–38). Such action must have been an amazing spectacle as Jesus began to announce more formally and publicly his divine sonship.

Earlier in his ministry Jesus had declared to a Samaritan woman at Jacob's well that he was the giver of "living water" (John 4:10). Later, after the conclusion of the Feast of Tabernacles, Jesus, the Living Water, sent a blind man down to the Siloam pool—the same pool used in the drawing-of-water ceremony—to wash in that living water[54] and be healed. On that same occasion (Feast of Tabernacles) Jesus declared himself also to be the "light of the world" (John 9:5). Thus, John emphasized two themes that were very important to him personally—Jesus was the living water and Jesus was the light of the world (John 4:10; 7:38; 1:4, 9; 8:12; compare Revelation 7:17; 21:6).

Judea to Perea

The late fall season of the last year of Jesus's public ministry witnessed him teaching and continuing the organization of the church. He appointed seventy men, spoke of himself as the Good Shepherd, and proclaimed the existence of other sheep—not of the land of Israel—who would hear his voice (John 10:14–16). This prophecy was fulfilled when the resurrected Jesus visited the Nephites (3 Nephi 15:21–24). While in Judea, Jesus also taught the parable of the good Samaritan (Luke 10:25–37) and visited the home of Martha, Mary, and Lazarus in Bethany, discussing spiritual priorities with them (10:38–42).

As winter commenced and the Feast of Dedication (Hanukkah) was celebrated, Jesus was in the temple precinct, instructing the Jews. Significantly, he taught the doctrine of theosis (becoming like God) by quoting Psalm 82:6 ("Ye are gods") in response to the accusation of blasphemy—that being a man he made himself God (John 10:22–39). This, the ultimate purpose of the Father's plan, was clearly affirmed by Jesus. He then left Jerusalem and went to Perea to escape persecution and deliver the powerful parables mentioned above.

The episode that brought Jesus back to Judea after several weeks in Perea was the death of his close personal friend, Lazarus. When word reached Jesus in Perea that Lazarus was sick, he purposely waited two days before going to aid him (John 11:1–6). Perhaps he taught the parable of the rich man and Lazarus during those two days, outlining conditions in the spirit world, including the great gulf separating the righteous from the wicked (Luke 16:19–31).[55] Of course, Jesus knew that Lazarus would die in the interim, affording Jesus the opportunity to teach about his resurrection—the most crucial, pivotal event of the Christian faith—and to foreshadow it by raising Lazarus from the grave. To Mary, the sister of Lazarus, he declared, "I am the resurrection, and the life: he that believeth in me, though he were dead, yet shall he live" (John 11:25).

The results of raising Lazarus were both gratifying and despicable. On the one hand, many Jews who witnessed the miracle Jesus performed "believed on him" (John 11:45). On the other hand, reports of the miracle caused the chief priests and Pharisees to convene a council to decide what to do about Jesus. Their concern was selfish at heart: "If we let him thus alone, all men will believe on him: and the Romans shall come and take away both our place and nation" (11:48). At Caiaphas's suggestion the decision was to put Jesus to death (11:49–53). Equally contemptible was the chief priests' effort to murder Lazarus (12:10). Those responsible for the administration of what was supposed to be the holiest place on earth—the Jerusalem temple—were the very ones who wanted to get rid of both the miracle-worker and the living evidence of the miracle. Therefore, Jesus left the area with his disciples, went to the small village of Ephraim northeast of Jerusalem, and waited for Passover while both the chief priests and Pharisees sought his whereabouts in order to arrest him (11:54–57).

Triumphal Entry

Six days before Passover, the last one of his mortal life, Jesus returned to Bethany to the house of Simon the leper, where Martha, Mary, and Lazarus lodged. Mary anointed him with spikenard, a costly extract from India. Judas Iscariot objected, his fraudulent practices in danger of being exposed "because he was a thief; as keeper of the money bag, he used to help himself to what was put into it" (John 12:6 NIV). But Jesus defended Mary, her act of devotion and humility foreshadowing his burial anointing (12:1–8). All four Gospels contain an account of a woman anointing Jesus, but at different times during his ministry.[56]

The next day, Sunday, Jesus made his triumphal entry into Jerusalem on a young donkey (JST Matthew 21:5), publicly indicating he was a king, just as Solomon had ridden to his coronation on King David's mule (1 Kings 1:38). Jesus's entry into the city of kings on a young donkey symbolized peace and royalty and fulfilled prophecy (Zechariah 9:9). Had he entered the city riding a horse, an entirely different meaning would have been implied—

warfare and conquest.[57] He was a different kind of Messiah than expected but will someday be seen riding a white horse to inaugurate the Millennium, to "judge and make war" and ultimately subdue "all enemies under his feet" at his second coming (Revelation 19:11–16; Doctrine and Covenants 58:22).

All four Gospels record the triumphal entry, indicating its pivotal nature. Jesus was greeted with the Hosanna Shout (Matthew 21:9).[58] Great messianic fervor and expectation had filled Jerusalem; "all the city was moved" (21:10). Some believed he was the long-awaited Messiah, others were probably undecided, and still others may have lost faith in him when he turned to the temple and cleansed it instead of the Antonia Fortress (21:12–15). Jesus went back to Bethany, where apparently he lodged the next few nights (21:17).

This Passover week was a whirlwind of activity for Jesus and his disciples. He cursed the fig tree near the village of Bethphage (Hebrew, "house of figs") for a variety of reasons, all centering on his identity in the face of Judaism's rejection of him and his teachings (Matthew 21:17–22). He instructed daily in the temple (Luke 22:53; Mark 14:49) and presented three parables on the need for repentance and not hypocrisy (Matthew 21:28–22:14). He chastised the scribes and Pharisees and uttered a significant lament over Jerusalem and its inhabitants (23:1–37). He delivered an important sermon, the Olivet Discourse, concerning the last days, the signs of the times, and the inauguration of the Millennium (JST—Matthew; Matthew 24). And he finished his time with his apostles by instituting two new ordinances and providing unequaled instruction in an upper room during the Passover meal (Matthew 26:17–30; Luke 22:1–38; John 13:1–17:26).

Sacrament Instituted

The Synoptics tell a backstory: two days before the Passover celebration the chief priests, scribes, and elders met in the palace of Caiaphas the high priest and finalized the secret plot to take Jesus and kill him (Matthew 26:2–5; Mark 14:1–2; Luke 22:2). Satan entered into Judas, who covenanted with the Jewish leaders to betray his master for thirty pieces of silver—the price of a slave at that time. Luke reports this chilling development as occurring during the Passover preparations. John places it during the Last Supper (13:27).

After the Passover plot was in place, Jesus's own preparations for the Festival of Unleavened Bread were carried out by his delegated representatives. The traditional Passover meal is referred to as the Seder (Hebrew, "order, arrangement") and evokes images of elaborate preparations of special foods, special dining arrangements, and specific recitations presented throughout the evening. Jesus sent Peter and John to secure the location of the Seder meal—a home with a furnished upper room owned by an unnamed disciple of Jesus (Luke 22:7–13).

At the appointed time, thousands of paschal lambs began to be slaughtered within the Jerusalem temple precincts. Josephus indicated that the lambs were to be slain between the ninth and eleventh hours of the day[59] (from about three to five o'clock in the evening) as Jesus and the apostles prepared for their own paschal commemoration.

We have every reason to believe the Seder meal proceeded in the traditional manner—up to a point. They sat around a *triclinium*, a three-sectioned, low-lying table, against which participants reclined on left elbows with feet pointed away from it. The first cup of wine was blessed and drunk. Hands were washed as a blessing was recited. Bitter herbs, symbolic of the bitterness of Egyptian bondage, were eaten—dipped in sour broth made of vinegar and bruised fruit, both messianic symbols. The origins of Passover were likely recounted by the leader of the Seder service—in this instance, Jesus. The lamb was then placed on the table or, if already on the table, was acknowledged, and the first parts of the Hallel (Psalms 113 and 114) were sung. The second cup of wine was blessed and drunk.

It may have been at this point that something extraordinary happened. According to the Gospel of Luke, instead of breaking the unleavened bread of Passover and reciting the traditional blessing, Jesus "took bread, and gave thanks, and brake it, and gave unto them, saying, This is my body which is given for you: this do in remembrance of me" (Luke 22:19). The disciples must have sat in stunned silence. Such a thing as this had never been done before. Such a comment as Jesus had made would have been totally inappropriate—unless, of course, the commentator really was the Messiah.

From this point, a typical Passover dinner usually proceeded at a leisurely pace until everything was eaten and the atmosphere of celebration increased. But the apostles of the Lamb had just eaten a piece of bread and a fragment of lamb not in remembrance of the events of the first Passover (Exodus 12:8), but in remembrance of the Bread of Life and the Lamb of God. Ordinarily, after the dinner portion of the Seder celebration was completed, the third cup of wine, the "cup after supper"—what the rabbis also called "the cup of blessing"—was mixed with water and then blessed and drunk in an atmosphere of celebration. The Gospel of Luke, however, perhaps referring to this cup, describes the scene in the Upper Room with solemn brevity and poignancy: "Likewise also the cup after supper, saying, This cup is the new testament in my blood, which is shed for you" (Luke 22:20).

The new ordinance replaced the old system of animal sacrifice in which a priest ritually slaughtered an offering on behalf of the covenanter. It did away with any priestly intermediary as well as almost all outward aspects of the old system of blood sacrifice. What Jesus said explicitly to the Nephites he said by inference to the apostles during the Last Supper: "And ye shall offer up unto me no more the shedding of blood; yea, your sacrifices and your burnt offerings shall be done away. . . . And ye shall offer for a sacrifice unto me a broken heart and a contrite spirit" (3 Nephi 9:19–20). The same two aspects of sacrifice that the Lord commanded the Nephites to offer in place of animals are the very things Jesus, the Lamb of God, experienced during his agony in the Garden of Gethsemane and on the cross at the moment he died: Jesus experienced a contrite ("crushed") spirit in the garden and a broken heart on the cross.[60]

If the activities of the evening had concluded with only the establishment of the sacrament, the night would still have been far spent. But, as it turned out, the evening was far from over. As Jesus and his apostles remained together after the meal, another powerful ordinance was instituted—the washing of the feet—and many powerful and important teachings were also delivered by the Master. Jesus concluded his final teaching moments on this night of nights by offering what has come to be known as the great high priestly prayer or the great Intercessory Prayer. All of these key events after the Last Supper are recorded in the New Testament uniquely by John (13–17). They include, among other things, instruction on the First and Second Comforters, a powerful discourse on love, and prophecies about the fate of the apostles.

Jesus instituted the ordinance of the washing of the feet as "a holy and sacred rite, one performed by the saints in the seclusion of their temple sanctuaries."[61] It appears to be an ordinance of ultimate approbation by the Lord and, in a fascinating way, stands in direct contrast to the ordinance of the dusting off of the feet, which seems to be the ultimate earthly ordinance of condemnation by the Lord.

That Jesus performed the ordinance of the washing of the feet for his closest friends is another indication of his attempts to prepare them for the coming spiritual onslaught in Gethsemane as well as to teach them further about his role in fulfilling the law of Moses. "He that has washed his hands and his head, needeth not save to wash his feet, but is clean every whit; and ye are clean, but not all. Now this was the custom of the Jews under their law; wherefore, *Jesus did this that the law might be fulfilled*" (JST John 13:10; emphasis added).

John's Gospel further tells us that after the washing of the feet, Jesus said to his apostles: "Now is the Son of man glorified, and God is glorified in him. . . . Little children, yet a little while I am with you. Ye shall seek me: and as I said unto the Jews, Whither I go, ye cannot come. . . . Simon Peter said unto him, Lord, whither goest thou? Jesus answered him, Whither I go, thou canst not follow me now; but thou shalt follow me afterwards" (John 13:31–36). Here Jesus speaks as though his looming agony in Gethsemane and the suffering on the cross are a foregone conclusion. Jesus's statement also appears to be a prophecy clearly foreshadowing Peter's future. According to tradition, Peter was later crucified head downward for the cause of his Master because he felt unworthy to die in the exact manner of Jesus.[62]

The four Gospels are not clear as to exactly when Judas Iscariot left the Seder dinner to consummate his betrayal, only that he did so after Jesus identified him as the betrayer (John 13:23–30). Was that before the washing of the feet or before the sacrament was instituted? Nor do we know at what moment Jesus and the apostles left the Upper Room to proceed to the Garden of Gethsemane. John 14:31 reports Jesus saying to the group after his instruction on the two Comforters, "Arise, let us go hence." Indeed, the opening content of John 15, Jesus's discourse on the True Vine, suggests an outdoor setting because of the readily visible images of vines or vineyards outside Jerusalem's walls. Others have been less definitive in assigning a location to all the teachings found in John 14–17.

However we view the sequence of scenes, we know that at some point before the end of the Passover experience, Jesus and his apostles concluded by singing together. "And when they had sung an hymn, they went out into the mount of Olives" (Mark 14:26). Likely, this hymn was the last part of the great Hallel, a magnificent set of messianic psalms (Psalms

115–18) whose thinly veiled meanings testify of Jesus Christ. One authority has stated that this hymn was preparation for Jesus's greatest test, which began in Gethsemane.[63]

Gethsemane

Each of the Gospels contributes to our understanding of events in the Garden of Gethsemane. John tells us that this garden was located across the Kidron brook and that Jesus often visited there with his apostles. Therefore, Judas knew where to find Jesus so that he could be arrested by the temple police (John 18:1–2).

Mark describes the immediate intensity of Jesus's suffering once inside the garden in the presence of Peter, James, and John. His sadness was so great it caused him to think of death (14:33–34). The phrase "sore amazed" in the King James Version is translated from the Greek *ekthambeisthai*, which Jerome Murphy-O'Connor argues is better rendered "terrified surprise."[64] This reaction may be attributed to the uniqueness of this experience. Jesus had never sinned nor felt its effects. So profound was the pain that Jesus asked the Father to rescue him from the experience if possible, but reaffirmed his commitment to do his Father's will (14:35).

Perhaps looking for relief or distraction but certainly possessing concern for the welfare of the apostles, Jesus got up from a prostrate position, found Peter asleep, asked him to stay alert, went back and offered up the same prayer, and again found the apostles asleep. The Joseph Smith Translation describes the concomitant intense struggle the apostles themselves were facing at the same time Jesus was suffering so intensely:

> And they came to a place which was named Gethsemane, which was a garden; and the disciples began to be sore amazed, and to be very heavy, and to complain in their hearts, wondering if this be the Messiah. And Jesus knowing their hearts, said to his disciples, Sit ye here, while I shall pray. And he taketh with him, Peter, and James, and John, and rebuked them, and said unto them, My soul is exceeding sorrowful, even unto death; tarry ye here and watch. (JST Mark 14:36–38)

Luke's unique contribution is twofold. First, an angel from heaven is sent to strengthen Jesus in his extremity (22:43). Second, Luke reports that Jesus's agony became so intense that he prayed even "more earnestly" and bled from every pore (22:44). Scholars point out that this passage has questionable textual support, it being a later insertion, and that even if viewed as credible, the words "his sweat was as it were [or became like] great drops of blood falling down to the ground" refer to a comparison, not an actual reality.[65] Latter-day Saint theology appeals to Restoration scripture for clarification in the matter.

The Book of Mormon prophet King Benjamin is quite clear that Jesus would suffer so much, "even more than man can suffer, except it be unto death," that blood would indeed come "from every pore" (Mosiah 3:7). Even more important is the testimony of the very participant himself. Jesus Christ declared in a latter-day revelation that he, God himself, suffered so much pain it caused him "to tremble because of pain, and to bleed at every pore, and to suffer both body and spirit" (Doctrine and Covenants 19:18).

The source of Jesus's hemorrhage is a subject in itself and has been addressed in various articles by modern-day physicians.[66] There may indeed be a documented medical condition known as hematidrosis, whereby one can literally sweat blood, but the ultimate cause was spiritual. Brigham Young stated that it was the withdrawal of the Father's powers of light and life in Gethsemane that caused Jesus to sweat blood. President Young said, "If he [Jesus] had had the power of God upon him, he would not have sweat blood; but *all* was withdrawn from him, and a veil was cast over him."[67]

Matthew's Gospel implies that Jesus's suffering was relentless. He prayed the same prayer three times, afterward getting up to check on the apostles. Matthew's report helps readers to appreciate Jesus's resistance to Satan's onslaught in the garden that awful night, as James E. Talmage eloquently described:

> Christ's agony in the garden is unfathomable by the finite mind, both as to intensity and cause. . . . He struggled and groaned under a burden such as no other being who has lived on earth might even conceive as possible. It was not physical pain, nor mental anguish alone, that caused him to suffer such torture as to produce an extrusion of blood from every pore; but a spiritual agony of soul such as only God was capable of experiencing. . . . In that hour of anguish Christ met and *overcame all the horrors that Satan, "the prince of this world," could inflict*. . . . [It was a] supreme contest with the powers of evil [John 14:30].[68]

Arrest, Trial, and Crucifixion

Jesus was arrested in Gethsemane after he had identified himself and Judas had confirmed that identification with a kiss (John 18:3–8; Matthew 26:49; Luke 22:47). The irony of the scene was prophetically captured by Proverbs 27:6: "Faithful are the wounds of a friend, but the kisses of an enemy are deceitful" (compare Matthew 26:40). Peter tried to stop the arrest by use of the sword but was chastised by Jesus, citing his ability to call twelve legions of angels (literally seventy-two thousand) to his defense if he desired (John 18:10–12; Matthew 26:51–54). Jesus was taken first to Annas, former high priest (AD 7–15) and father-in-law to the current high priest, Joseph ben Caiaphas (AD 18–36). Though no longer acting as officiating high priest, he was still called high priest (Luke 3:2; John 18:19) since the title and some responsibilities of the high priest were retained until death.[69] Annas interrogated Jesus, mistreated him, and then sent him to Caiaphas (John 18:13–24).

Jesus was next examined by Caiaphas and then the council of the Jews. He endured insults, false witnesses, illegal proceedings, significant physical abuse, and finally treatment reserved for slaves and the lowest members of the social order (Matthew 26:57–68).[70] As all this was going on in the residence of Caiaphas, Peter was out in the courtyard denying he was one of Jesus's associates (Matthew 26:69–75).

Having been declared guilty of blasphemy and worthy of death by Caiaphas, the chief priests, and elders of the people, Jesus was bound and delivered to Pontius Pilate, Roman prefect or governor (Matthew 26:65–66; 27:1–2).[71] Pilate became involved because, as the Jewish leaders reminded the governor, "It is not lawful for us to put any man to death" (John 18:31). According to F. F. Bruce, "the right of jurisdiction in capital cases was most jealously reserved by provincial governors" and permission to exercise it "a very rare concession."[72] However, the future case of Stephen before the high priest and chief priests raises questions (Acts 6:9–15; 7:1, 54–60). Jesus's first appearance before Pilate resulted in his being sent to Herod Antipas, who was in Jerusalem for Passover, because Pilate found nothing from a Roman standpoint to warrant Jesus's conviction of a capital offense. One senses that because Pilate was already in political trouble over his governance of the Jews in Judea, he wanted someone else to have to deal with Jesus.[73] Herod Antipas is the only person we know of to have spoken with Jesus face-to-face but received in return complete "disdainful" silence (Luke 23:4–12). Jesus's dislike of Herod Antipas was manifest on an earlier occasion when he called him a "fox" (13:32). In the end, Herod also found nothing in Jesus worthy of condemnation. But because of this episode Herod and Pilate became friends, having before been at odds.

Jesus was sent back to Pilate, who again declared Jesus's innocence to the public and proposed to chastise and release Jesus but was met with protests. Readers are struck by the number of times Pilate proclaimed Jesus's innocence and tried to release him (John 18:28–38; Luke 23:4, 13–14). Pilate then proposed another way of fulfilling the Passover custom of releasing one prisoner of the people's choosing—pit Jesus against such a notorious criminal that they would logically choose to release Jesus when compared with a convicted murderer, insurrectionist, and robber (Matthew 27:15–17; Mark 15:6–10; Luke 23:16–17; John 18:40). But the chief priests stirred up the people to call for the release of Barabbas and the crucifixion of Jesus (Matthew 27:20–22; Mark 15:11–14; Luke 23:18–22; John 18:40). Adding to Pilate's woes was the strong marital admonition of his wife to leave Jesus alone because she had suffered many things in a dream because of him (Matthew 27:19).[74]

The circumstance of Barabbas's release and Jesus's condemnation is so thick with irony that it can be cut with the proverbial knife. The given name of Barabbas was also Yehoshua, or Jesus. An ancient variant reading of the text of Matthew 27:16–17 preserves the full name: "Jesus Barabbas." And the early church theologian Origen (died ca. AD 254) implied that the full name appeared in most of the manuscripts of his day. The term *Barabbas* means, literally, "son of [Aramaic, *bar*] the father [Aramaic, *abba*]." Jesus *was* the true and literal Son of the Father. The angry, stirred-up mob chose to release one Jesus over the other, chose to release one son of the father, rather than the true Son of the Father. Barabbas was the fulfillment of the ritual scapegoat of the sacrificial rites performed on the Day of Atonement—the animal led to the wilderness and released; Jesus of Nazareth was the fulfillment of the goat sacrificed on the temple altar as the sin offering representing the guilt of the people (Leviticus 16:7–22).

Jesus was scourged, mocked, forced to carry his cross to Golgotha, and crucified. Pilate had tried once more to free Jesus, but then resorted to ritual handwashing to try to absolve himself of guilt over the execution of an innocent man (John 19:1–15; Matthew 27:24–32).[75] Pilate may have come to a genuine belief in Jesus as a holy man, if not the Jewish Messiah, for when chided by the chief priests about the superscription he penned and placed on the cross, "Jesus of Nazareth, King of the Jews," he responded curtly, "What I have written I have written" (John 19:19–22).

Jesus uttered seven final statements while on the cross, which in one way or another illuminate his character.

1. "Father, forgive them; for they know not what they do" (Luke 23:34).
2. "Verily I say unto thee, To day shalt thou be with me in paradise" (Luke 23:43).
3. "Woman, behold thy son! . . . Behold thy mother!" (John 19:26–27).
4. "My God, my God, why hast thou forsaken me?" (Matthew 27:46; Psalm 22:1).
5. "I thirst" (John 19:28).
6. "It is finished" (John 19:30).
7. "Father, into thy hands I commend my spirit" (Luke 23:46; Psalm 31:5).

John 19:30 must be read in concert with JST Matthew 27:50 ("Father, it is finished, thy will is done") to appreciate the ultimate significance of Jesus's death on the cross. This inspiring change to the text brings us back full circle to the promise made by Jesus in our premortal existence to accomplish the Father's will (Moses 4:2), which fulfillment came only after all things had been accomplished.

Jesus's remarkable selflessness is magnified against the backdrop of bodily torture and anguish produced by crucifixion. Mark's Gospel tells us Jesus was nailed to the cross at about nine o'clock in the morning and hung on the cross until around three o'clock in the afternoon (15:25, 34). The unnatural and contorted position of his body on the cross was foreseen by one of Israel's ancient psalmists and expressed in poetic form (Psalm 22:14). Indeed, Psalm 22:1–20 constitutes an amazingly accurate descriptive prophecy of the specific occurrences associated with Jesus's crucifixion and ought to be read in tandem with the Gospel accounts. Crucifixion was one of the most brutal and horrible forms of execution ever invented. The Romans did not devise it, but raised it to an art form. However, even the Romans themselves protested its use. The first-century-BC Roman statesman Cicero said that no word could be found to adequately portray this "cruelest and most disgusting punishment."[76] Crucifixion was applied especially to slaves in the Roman Empire—a motif seen in the way Jesus was treated by all those who incarcerated him.[77] Several descriptions by physicians and scholars have been penned over the years, illuminating the kind of pain, torture, and slow death that constituted crucifixion.[78] Thus, crucifixion was practiced as much for deterrence as for punishment, as the Roman writer Quintilian (ca. AD 35–95) indicated: "Whenever we crucify the guilty, the most crowded roads are chosen, where the most people can see and be moved by this fear. For penalties relate not so much to retribution as to their exemplary effect."[79]

As soon as Jesus was mercifully released from mortality through physical death, he continued his ministry in the world of spirits (Doctrine and Covenants 138). But there were other occurrences as a result of the Crucifixion: nature convulsed as prophesied (1 Nephi 19:12), an earthquake occurred, there was a period of darkness, and the veil of the temple was torn apart from top to bottom (Matthew 27:51; Mark 15:38; Luke 23:45). Jesus was buried in a new tomb by two disciples, members of the Sanhedrin, Joseph of Arimathea (owner of the tomb) and Nicodemus. They begged for possession of the body from Pilate, who had guards placed at the tomb, with the faithful women from Judea and Galilee left to witness the burial and plan for its completion following the Sabbath (Matthew 27:57–66; Mark 15:42–16:1; Luke 23:50–56; John 19:38–42).

The Resurrection

The first mortals to learn that something unusual and powerful had taken place at the site where the body of Jesus was buried were the sentinels placed there to make sure disciples could not steal the body and make it appear as though Jesus had risen from the dead after three days, as he had prophesied. A great earthquake occurred as two angels came from heaven and rolled back the stone from the tomb entrance, causing the guards to shake and collapse like dead men from fear (Matthew 28:2–4; JST Matthew 27:62–66).

Next came Mary Magdalene and other women to the tomb in the dawning hours of Sunday morning to anoint the body of Jesus. But they saw the stone rolled away and in the tomb the two angels, with countenances like lightning, who announced the resurrection of Jesus: "Why seek ye the living among the dead? He is not here, but is risen: remember how he spake unto you when he was yet in Galilee, saying, The Son of man[80] must be delivered into the hands of sinful men, and be crucified, and the third day rise again. And they remembered his words" and so put into motion events that would result in the worldwide Christian faith we see today (JST Matthew 28:3–5; Luke 24:3–8).

Though John's Gospel presents a slightly different scenario of events that resurrection morning,[81] the ultimate result is the same: many hundreds of witnesses saw for themselves the resurrected Jesus alive, with a tangible body of flesh and bone. The first was apparently Mary Magdalene (John 20:11–18), followed by the other women (Matthew 28:9–10; Mark 16:9–12), then two disciples at Emmaus (Luke 24:13–35), then Simon Peter (24:34), then ten of the Twelve in a closed-door session where the gift of the Holy Ghost was given (John 20:19–23; Luke 24:36–48), and on and on.

In the words of New Testament scholar Bruce Metzger,

> The evidence for the resurrection of Jesus Christ is overwhelming. Nothing in history is more certain than that the disciples believed that, after being crucified, dead, and buried, Christ rose again from the tomb on the third day. . . . The most obvious proof that they believed this is the existence of the Christian church. . . . Never were hopes more desolate than when Jesus of Nazareth was taken down from the cross and laid in the tomb. Stricken with grief at the death of their Master, the disciples were dazed

and bewildered. Their mood was one of dejection and defeat, reflected in the spiritless words of the Emmaus travelers, 'We had hoped that he was the one to redeem Israel' (Luke 24:21). . . . [Yet] fifty-some days after the crucifixion the apostolic preaching of Christ's resurrection began in Jerusalem with such power and persuasion that the evidence convinced thousands.[82]

More importantly, not only did the ancient disciples believe that Jesus was resurrected, there exist modern disciples who possess that sure witness. Regarding Jesus of Nazareth, Ezra Taft Benson once said, "He lives! He lives with a resurrected body. There is no truth or fact of which I am more assured, or know better by personal experience, than the truth of the literal resurrection of our Lord."[83] By his resurrection, along with all his life and ministry, Jesus of Nazareth showed himself to be Jesus the Christ.

❧

Andrew C. Skinner is a professor of ancient scripture and ancient Near Eastern studies at Brigham Young University.

Further Reading

Brown, Raymond E. *The Birth of the Messiah: A Commentary on the Infancy Narratives in the Gospels of Matthew and Luke.* Anchor Bible Reference Library. Updated ed. New York: Doubleday, 1999.

———. *The Death of the Messiah.* 2 vols. Anchor Bible Reference Library. New York: Doubleday, 1998.

McConkie, Bruce R. *The Mortal Messiah.* 4 vols. Salt Lake City: Deseret Book, 1979–1981.

Notley, R. Steven. *In the Master's Steps: The Gospels in the Land.* Jerusalem: Carta, 2015.

Ogden, D. Kelly, and Andrew C. Skinner. *Verse by Verse: The Four Gospels.* Salt Lake City: Deseret Book, 2006.

Stein, Robert H. *Jesus the Messiah: A Survey of the Life of Christ.* Downers Grove, IL: InterVarsity, 1996.

Talmage, James E. *Jesus the Christ.* With revised and updated notes by Lincoln Blumell, Gaye Strathearn, and Thomas Wayment. Springville, UT: Cedar Fort, 2015.

Notes

1. Boyd K. Packer inferred that a lack of understanding about the premortal existence is "like one who enters a theater just as the curtain goes up on the second act . . . , making it difficult to figure out who relates to whom and what relates to what" ("The Play and the Plan," CES fireside for college-age young adults, May 7, 1995, 2). So it is with our understanding about Jesus of Nazareth. Note the January 2000 official declaration by the First Presidency and Quorum of the Twelve Apostles entitled "The Living Christ: The Testimony of the Apostles," which begins by discussing Jesus's premortal activity. Two principal Latter-day Saint treatises on the life of Jesus Christ, both written by apostles, begin by discussing Jesus's activity in our premortal existence. See James E. Talmage, *Jesus the Christ* (Salt Lake City: Deseret Book, 1986), and Bruce R. McConkie, *The Promised Messiah* (Salt Lake City: Deseret Book, 1995).

2. Stephen E. Robinson and H. Dean Garett, *A Commentary on the Doctrine and Covenants* (Salt Lake City: Deseret Book, 2004), 3:180–81.

3. However, in John 8:58 Jesus unequivocally proclaims that he is Jehovah. That the Jews understood this is clear from their response, which was to stone him.

4. Francis Brown, S. R. Driver, and Charles A. Briggs, *A Hebrew and English Lexicon of the Old Testament* (Oxford: Clarendon, 1976), 217–18, 226.

5. The term *Elias* is used in several ways in scripture: a messenger who appeared in the Kirtland Temple, committing the keys of the dispensation of the gospel of Abraham (Doctrine and Covenants 110:12); the Greek form of the name Elijah; a name-title of one who performs a preparatory work, that is, a forerunner, such as John the Baptist (JST John 1:21–38); a name-title of one whose mission it is to commit keys and powers in this dispensation of the fulness of times, such as Noah or Gabriel (Doctrine and Covenants 27:6–7) or John the Revelator (77:9, 14); and a name-title for Jesus Christ as a restorer (JST John 1:28).

6. John undoubtedly began his ministry at age thirty, when priests and Levites typically began their full-time service in the temple (Numbers 4:3, 47), but we know even less about John's formative years and preparation than Jesus's. See Joan E. Taylor, *The Immerser: John the Baptist within Second Temple Judaism* (Grand Rapids, MI: Eerdmans, 1997), 12, who says of John: "That John had a social context is a reality overlooked by most of the primary literary material about him. In the Lucan narrative, he appears in the wilderness completely alone—untaught, unmarried, his old father and mother surely dead, without connection to any place, relatives, or sects. At the start of Mark's Gospel, he is both adopted by the church and separated from his Jewish context. He stands 'at the beginning of the good news of Jesus the Messiah, the Son of God' (Mark 1:1), as the messenger who will prepare his way (Mark 1:2; cf. Mal. 3:1; Isa. 40:3). John has no background; he simply appears (cf. Matt. 3:1)."

7. The famous Synoptic scene, perhaps near Capernaum, also shows Jesus walking by the Sea of Galilee and calling these disciples to follow him, promising them that he would make them "fishers of men. And straightway they forsook their nets, and followed him" (Mark 1:17–18). "Fishers of men" is an Old Testament figure of speech (Jeremiah 16:16), sometimes viewed negatively (e.g., Micah 7:2). But here Jesus uses it positively, asking the disciples' assistance in the noble cause of drawing converts ("out of the waters of this world into the next of the eschatological life of the age to come" [Samuel Tobias Lachs, *A Rabbinic Commentary on the New Testament* (Hoboken, NJ: KTAV, 1987), 59]). Later, Jesus refers to the kingdom of heaven as a net cast into the sea that gathers every kind of follower (Matthew 13:47).

8. Robert J. Matthews, *A Burning Light: The Life and Ministry of John the Baptist* (Provo, UT: Brigham Young University Press, 1972), 38.

9. The Piacenza Pilgrim, traveling in the Holy Land in the sixth century AD, related the following about his visit to Nazareth: "The house of Saint Mary is now a basilica, and her clothes are the cause of frequent miracles. The Jewesses of that city are better looking than any other Jewesses in the whole country. They declare that this is Saint Mary's gift to them, for they also say that she was a relation of theirs." Quoted in Jerome Murphy-O'Connor, *The Holy Land: An Oxford Archaeology Guide to Earliest Times to 1700*, 5th ed. (Oxford: Oxford University Press, 2007), 424.

10. James F. Strange, "Nazareth," *Anchor Bible Dictionary*, ed. David Noel Freedman (New York: Doubleday, 1992), 4:1050. See also Eric Meyers and James F. Strange, *Archaeology, the Rabbis, and Early Christianity* (Nashville: Abingdon, 1981), 56.

11. The other three are the Benedictus of Zacharias (Luke 1:68–79), the Gloria in Excelsis Deo of the angels (2:14), and the Nunc Dimittis of Simeon (2:29–32).

12. Madeleine S. Miller and J. Lane Miller, *Harper's Encyclopedia of Bible Life* (Edison, NJ: Castle Books, 1996), 98–99.

13. The term *get* appears to come from the Akkadian *gittu* and then into late Hebrew as *get*. The essential part of the bill of divorcement is very short: "You are now permitted to all men."

14. Michael Grant, *Jesus, An Historian's Review of the Gospels* (New York: Charles Scribner's Sons, 1977), 70.

15. Melvin J. Ballard, *Sermons and Missionary Services of Melvin Joseph Ballard*, comp. Bryant S. Hinckley (Salt Lake City: Deseret Book, 1949), 167.

16. Immaculate conception is the dogma that from the moment of her conception the Virgin Mary was free from all stain of original sin by the grace of God and the merits of Jesus Christ. The earliest proponents of

this idea appear to be the early church fathers Justin Martyr and Irenaeus, who regarded Mary as the new Eve to correspond with Jesus Christ as the new or second or last Adam (1 Corinthians 15:45). The dogma was officially defined by a papal bull decree in 1854: "Ineffabilis Deus," Pope Pius IX. See F. L. Cross and E. A. Livingstone, eds., "Immaculate Conception of the BVM," *The Oxford Dictionary of the Christian Church*, 2nd ed. (Oxford: Oxford University Press, 1984), 682–93.

17. Robert L. Millet, Camille Fronk Olson, Andrew C. Skinner, and Brent L. Top, *LDS Beliefs: A Doctrinal Reference* (Salt Lake City: Deseret Book, 2011), 653.

18. As to the place of Jesus's birth, see Raymond E. Brown, *The Birth of the Messiah* (New York: Doubleday, 1979), 513: "The overwhelming evidence to the contrary has made the thesis that Bethlehem was *not* the historical birthplace of Jesus the *communis opinion* of New Testament scholarship." The majority rejecting Bethlehem opt for Nazareth; a few others opt for Capernaum. As for the time of birth and historical problems associating it with Quirinius's governorship, see again Raymond Brown's brief summary, *Birth of the Messiah*, 395.

19. "Publius Sulpicius Quirinius was made legate of Syria in A.D. 6"—a chronological problem in matching up Jesus's birth sometime around 6 BC. Again, see Brown, *Birth of the Messiah*, 395, but Brown does admit that the Greek of Luke 2:2 permits other translations, one of which would resolve Luke's accuracy issue: "This census was earlier than the one . . . " or "This census was before the governorship of . . . "

20. See the discussion in Robert H. Stein, *Jesus the Messiah, A Survey of the Life of Christ* (Downers Grove, IL: InterVarsity, 1996), 74–75.

21. Justin Martyr, *Dialogue* 77:5, quoted in Brown, *Birth of the Messiah*, 401.

22. Origen, *Against Celsus* 1:51, quoted in Brown, *Birth of the Messiah*, 401.

23. Stein, *Jesus the Messiah*, 76.

24. See the discussion in Brown, *Birth of the Messiah*, 167.

25. Herod's order to kill all children in the area that were under two years old provides evidence that upwards of two years had transpired between Jesus's birth and the arrival of the magi, as well as the fact that Matthew now refers to Jesus as a small boy or toddler.

26. Raymond E. Brown, *An Introduction to the New Testament* (New York: Doubleday, 1997), 234 (quoting from the *Infancy Gospel of Thomas*).

27. It also bespeaks an interest on Luke's part, seen in both his Gospel and the book of Acts, about the role of the temple in the early church. Jesus and his family had probably gone to the temple in obedience to the command that all males of the covenant appear before the Lord three times a year, for the Feast of Unleavened Bread (Passover), the Feast of Harvest or First Fruits (Shavuot or Weeks), and the Feast of Ingathering (Succoth or Tabernacles), as described in Exodus 23:14–17.

28. David Flusser, *Jesus*, trans. Ronald Walls (New York: Herder and Herder, 1969), 18.

29. Millar Burrows, "The Origin of the Term 'Gospel,'" *Journal of Biblical Literature* 44, nos. 1–2 (1925): 21.

30. Jesus was baptized by John in the Jordan River at a locale known as Bethabara, Hebrew for "house or place of the ford" (John 1:28; 1 Nephi 10:9), traditionally identified with a site east of Jericho, north of the place where the Jordan empties into the Dead Sea. There John was also interviewed by a delegation of Levites and priests from Jerusalem and declared Jesus to be the Messiah and an Elias who would restore all things (JST John 1:20–34).

31. The Mishnah is the codification of Jewish oral law discussed by the early or Tannaitic rabbis and is the core of the Talmud (both Babylonian and Palestinian).

32. That Jesus entered the wilderness immediately after his baptism argues for this region since Bethabara (baptism site) is nearby.

33. Stein, *Jesus the Messiah*, 105.

34. *True to the Faith: A Gospel Reference* (Salt Lake City: The Church of Jesus Christ of Latter-day Saints, 2004), 82.

35. See Articles of Faith 1:10: "Christ will reign personally upon the earth; and . . . the earth will be renewed and receive its paradisiacal glory."

36. Each of the six stone pots held two to three firkins. A firkin is about nine gallons.

37. The pervasive nature of Hellenism, even in Jewish culture, is seen in the very name of this Jewish leader. The name Nicodemus is Greek, meaning "victory of the people."

38. Josephus, *Jewish Antiquities* 18.119. However, some scholars doubt the location, believing Josephus's account to be unreliable. See, for instance, R. Steven Notley, *In the Master's Steps: The Gospels in the Holy Land* (Jerusalem: Carta, 2014), 18.

39. Matthew mentions a multitude in connection with the sermon coming from Galilee, the Decapolis (a ten-city league mostly Gentile), Jerusalem, Judea, and the region across the Jordan (Perea).

40. Of the Beatitudes, for example, President Harold B. Lee said, "Jesus is actually describing the qualities of an exalted person." Harold B. Lee, *Decisions for Successful Living* (Salt Lake City: Deseret Book, 1973), 21.

41. Again, Harold B. Lee: "These declarations of the Master are known in the literature of the Christian world as the Beatitudes and have been referred to by Bible commentators as the preparation necessary for entrance into the kingdom of heaven. For the purposes of this discussion may I speak of them as something more than that as they are applied to you and me. They embody in fact the constitution for a perfect life." *Decisions for Successful Living*, 21.

42. For a powerful, succinct discussion about Jesus's miracles, see Robert J. Matthews, "The Miracles of Jesus," *The Instructor*, May 1967, 211–12.

43. See *Lectures on Faith* (Salt Lake City: Deseret Book, 1985), 43.

44. See Mark 5:41 NRSV.

45. George A. Buttrick, *The Parables of Jesus* (New York: Harper and Brothers, 1928), xiii.

46. Manuscript History of the Church, November 16, 1835, Book B1 (September 1, 1843–November 2, 1838), 643–51.

47. Reasons for disciples leaving Jesus are found in the sermon's content, which may be broken down into three parts: first, Jesus testified he was the Bread of Life (John 6:32–41); second, the people were told to stop murmuring and turn to Jesus (6:41–50); and third, Jesus then foreshadowed the sacrament in very unappealing language (6:51–58).

48. The exchange centered on the Greek word *kunariois*, a diminutive that means "puppy" or "little dog," as in a household pet. The woman turns the term to her advantage. *A Lexicon Abridged from Liddell and Scott's Greek-English Lexicon* (Oxford: Clarendon, 1976), 399.

49. Notley, *In the Master's Step*, 51.

50. See Doctrine and Covenants 7:7; 128:8–14; 132:7; Joseph F. Smith, *Gospel Doctrine* (Salt Lake City: Deseret Book, 1939), 136; and D. Kelly Ogden and Andrew C. Skinner, *Verse by Verse: The Four Gospels* (Salt Lake City: Deseret Book, 2006), 331–32.

51. *Teachings of Presidents of the Church: Joseph Smith* (Salt Lake City: The Church of Jesus Christ of Latter-day Saints, 2007), 105.

52. Other happenings of a sacred nature transpired on the mount that are not recorded in the New Testament. One of these was a vision of the future transfiguration of the earth itself "according to the pattern which was shown unto mine apostles upon the mount; of which account the fulness ye have not yet received" (Doctrine and Covenants 63:21). Jesus taught the apostles about Elias and John the Baptist (Matthew 17:10–13), the latter of whom JST Mark 9:3 informs us was present as Elias on the mount to support his cousin as turbulent challenges were increasing in magnitude and pace for Jesus.

53. Beth Uval, "Streams of Living Water," *Jerusalem Perspective* 49 (October–December 1995): 7–8.

54. The term *living water* is a multifaceted concept possessing several meanings. The Bible contains references to the concept of living water. Jehovah was the fountain of living water (Jeremiah 2:13). Living water was salvation (Isaiah 12:3; 2 Nephi 22:3). Literally speaking, living water is running water, or water originating in the earth (springs and rivers) or its atmosphere, as in rainwater, that is regarded as being from God. Living water has a purifying and cleansing function (Leviticus 14:5–6, 50–52; 15:13). Thus, living water is an apt metaphor for Jesus—the Lamb that will lead to the living fountains of water (Revelation 7:17) for eternal

life. God will give to everyone who thirsts water from the fountain of the water of life (Revelation 21:6). In Judaism living water refers to the ritual immersion bath, or *mikveh*.

55. We know that the parable was given in Perea. Since the only two places where Lazarus is mentioned in the four Gospels is, one, in connection with the parable that speaks of Lazarus dying and, two, the report of Lazarus's actual death and being raised to life, it seems logical that the timing of the parable coincided with Lazarus's death.

56. Matthew and Mark place the anointing two days before Passover, John six days before, and Luke much earlier, during a feast in Galilee. See Matthew 26:6–13; Mark 14:3–9; John 12:1–3; Luke 7:36–50.

57. The symbolism of the donkey on the one hand and the horse on the other is ably treated in James E. Talmage, *Jesus the Christ* (Salt Lake City: Deseret Book, 1961), 516–17.

58. The Hosanna Shout is of ancient origin and has been uttered on different occasions to welcome the Lord to various locations: to Jerusalem (Matthew 21:9), to the American continent (3 Nephi 11:16–17), and to modern temples (Doctrine and Covenants 109:7–9). The Hebrew word *hosanna*, which means "save now," comes from Psalm 118:25, one of the messianic psalms of the Hallel (Psalms 113–18).

59. Josephus, *Jewish War* 6.423–425, trans. H. J. Thackeray, Loeb Classical Library (Cambridge: Harvard University Press, 1990). He also claimed that the number of Passover lambs slain during a single Passover season reached an incredible 255,600.

60. See Dana M. Pike, "3 Nephi 9:19–20: The Offering of a Broken Heart," in *Third Nephi: An Incomparable Scripture*, ed. Gaye Strathearn and Andrew C. Skinner (Salt Lake City: Deseret Book and Neal A. Maxwell Institute for Religious Scholarship, 2010).

61. Bruce R. McConkie, *Doctrinal New Testament Commentary* (Salt Lake City: Deseret Book, 2002), 1:708.

62. Eusebius, *Ecclesiastical History* 3.1.2.

63. Boyd K. Packer, "Inspiring Music—Worthy Thoughts," *Ensign*, January 1974, 28.

64. Jerome Murphy-O'Connor, "What Really Happened at Gethsemane?" *Bible Review* 14:2 (April 1998), https://www.baslibrary.org/bible-review/14/2/13, 4.

65. Stein, *Jesus the Messiah*, 215. On the issues associated with Luke 22:43–44 see, for example, Bart D. Ehrman and Mark A. Plukett, "The Angel and the Agony: The Textual Problem of Luke 22:43–44," *Catholic Biblical Quarterly* 45 (1983): 401–16. They argue that the verses in question are "an interpolation made early in the second century" (401).

66. For example, see William D. Edwards, Wesley J. Gabel, and Floyd E. Hosmer, "On the Physical Death of Jesus Christ," *Journal of the American Medical Association* 225, no. 11 (March 21, 1986): 1455–56.

67. *Journal of Discourses*, 26 vols. (London: Latter-day Saints' Book Depot, 1854–86), 3:205–6; emphasis added.

68. James E. Talmage, *Jesus the Christ*, 613; emphasis added.

69. Mishnah Horayot 3:4.

70. Andrew C. Skinner, "Two Crucified Men: Insights into the Death of Jesus Christ of Nazareth," in *Bountiful Harvest: Essays in Honor of S. Kent Brown*, ed. Andrew C. Skinner, D. Morgan Davis, and Carl Griffin (Provo, UT: Neal A. Maxwell Institute for Religious Scholarship, 2011), 374–79.

71. R. Steven Notley, "Pontius Pilate: Sadist or Saint?," *Biblical Archaeology Review* 43, no. 4 (July/August 2017): 43–45. The historicity of Pontius Pilate is beyond question. In 1961 an Italian archaeological team, excavating the Herodian theater in ancient Caesarea Maritima, found a limestone block with an engraved, four-line inscription containing the name of Pontius Pilate and his title "prefect of Judea." This suggests that Pilate was a prefect, not a procurator. He was the fifth prefect, appointed after Coponius (AD 6–9), Ambivius (AD 9–12), Rufus (AD 12–15), and Gratus (AD 15–26). Initially, in the Roman Empire prefects were officials with military responsibilities and procurators were officials with financial responsibilities primarily. In Egypt and the eastern portion of the Roman Empire there were no procurators before AD 41, the beginning of Claudius's reign (AD 41–54).

72. F. F. Bruce, *New Testament History* (New York: Doubleday, Galilee Book, 1969), 200.

73. The Pilate inscription also may help to explain how the Jewish leaders could maneuver Pilate into giving them what they wanted concerning Jesus. The inscription indicates Pilate was dedicating the Tiberium, a building in Caesarea, to Tiberius in order to ingratiate himself with the emperor. Pilate seems to have gotten in trouble with the emperor over incidents that provoked protests from his subjects and highlighted his poor judgment and leadership. Thus, when Pilate tried to have Jesus released, the Jews responded, "If you release [Jesus], you are no friend of Caesar!" (John 19:12; translation mine). For more on Pilate's complex personality, see the succinct summary in R. Steven Notley, *Jerusalem: City of the Great King* (Jerusalem: Carta, 2015), 42. He cites Philo and Josephus, who wrote of Pilate's reputation for brutality, inflexibility, stubbornness, cruelty, venality, violence, robbery, abusive behavior, and savage ferocity.

74. Because of her defense of Jesus, Pilate's wife was later honored as a saint in the Greek Orthodox Church. See Paul J. Achtemeier, ed., *Harper's Bible Dictionary* (San Francisco: Harper and Row, 1985), 559.

75. The assessment of Elder Neal A. Maxwell emphasizes what some writers are reluctant to acknowledge— Pilate had the ability to insist on Jesus's release: "Pilate sought to refuse responsibility for deciding about Christ, but Pilate's hands were never dirtier than just after he had washed them." Neal A. Maxwell, "Why Not Now?," *Ensign*, November 1974, 13.

76. Cicero, *Against Verres* 2.5.165.

77. Cicero, *Against Verres* 2.5.169.

78. C. Truman Davis, "A Physician Testifies about Crucifixion," *Review of the News*, April 14, 1976, 37; Edwards, Gabel, and Hosmer, "On the Physical Death of Jesus," 1460; Joseph Zias and Eliezer Sekeles, "The Crucified Man from Giv'at ha-Mivtar—A Reappraisal," *Biblical Archaeologist*, September 1985, 190.

79. Quintilian, *Declamations* 274, as cited in Gerald G. O'Collins, "Crucifixion," *Anchor Bible Dictionary*, 1:1208.

80. The phrase "son of man" is used in the Old Testament to describe simply a man (Numbers 23:19; Job 25:6; Psalms 8:4; 80:17) and is found some ninety times in Ezekiel. In Daniel 7:13–14 the "Son of man" is portrayed as a heavenly figure, entrusted by God with authority, glory, and power. In the Gospels the phrase is Jesus's most common title for himself, used eighty-one times, and only by Jesus of himself. That it is a messianic title seems obvious from Matthew 12:8 and Mark 8:31, where it is juxtaposed with Peter's declaration that Jesus of Nazareth is the Christ. Later Christians in the early church used the title of Jesus, as demonstrated by Stephen (Acts 7:56).

81. The conflicts presented by the difference in the Synoptic accounts versus John's account are able to be reconciled. See, for example, Thomas M. Mumford, *Horizontal Harmony of the Four Gospels in Parallel Columns* (Salt Lake City: Deseret Book, 1976), 163n260.

82. Bruce Metzger, *New Testament*, 126–27.

83. Ezra Taft Benson, "Five Marks of the Divinity of Jesus Christ," *Ensign*, December 2001, 12.

16

The Mediator of the New Covenant

Robert L. Millet

Jesus Christ came into the world to save sinners (1 Timothy 1:15). Because Adam and Eve transgressed by partaking of the forbidden fruit, they were cast from the Garden of Eden and from the presence of the Lord, resulting in spiritual death (i.e., separation from God). Consequently, blood, sweat, opposition, bodily decay, and, finally, physical death entered the world. Even though the Fall was a vital part of the great plan of the Eternal God[1]—as much a foreordained act as Christ's intercession (1 Peter 1:20)—our state, including our relationship to and contact with God, changed dramatically. The plight of the human family rested in the sobering truth that "all have sinned, and come short of the glory of God" (Romans 3:23).

The Need for Mediation

All mortals desperately need help. Those who are lost need to be found. Those who are fallen need to be lifted up. Theologian John Stott has written that "Christianity is rescue religion. It declares that God has taken the initiative in Jesus Christ to deliver us from our sins."[2] Elder Boyd K. Packer reminded us painfully that "each of us, without exception, one day will settle [our] spiritual account. We will, that day, face a judgment for our doings in mortal life and face a foreclosure of sorts. . . . Each of us lives on a kind of spiritual credit. One day the account will be closed, a settlement demanded. However casually we may view it now, when that day comes and the foreclosure is imminent, we will look around in restless agony for someone, anyone, to help us."[3]

Jesus was sent by the Father to show us the way back home. He is able to do so because he *knows* the way; indeed, he *is* the way (John 14:6). We can have total trust and confidence in him and rely completely upon his merits, mercy, and grace. This is what it means to have faith *in* Christ. We simply cannot be saved *in* our sins, nor can we merit anything of ourselves (Alma 11:37; 22:14). In the words of the apostle Paul, "by the deeds of the law there shall no flesh be justified" (Romans 3:20; see 2 Nephi 2:5). Because of our fallen nature, we must be justified—forgiven, pardoned, and placed once again in a proper relationship with God our Heavenly Father. We cannot fix the damaged relationship on our own, but Jesus can. Through his advocacy and mediation he is able to effect a reconciliation with God. In short, God reconciles fallen men and women to himself by Jesus Christ (2 Corinthians 5:18).

President Joseph Fielding Smith explained that "all revelation since the fall has come through Jesus Christ, who is the Jehovah of the Old Testament. In all of the scriptures, where God is mentioned and where he has appeared it was Jehovah who talked with Abraham, with Noah, Enoch, Moses and all the prophets." Now note this important principle: "*The Father has never dealt with man directly and personally since the fall, and he has never appeared except to introduce and bear record of the Son.*"[4] Hence, Jesus Christ is our *mediator* with God the Eternal Father.

A mediator is a "go-between" person, an intermediary between two parties, an arbitrator, one who intervenes to resolve a conflict or, in some cases, to ratify a covenant. In the Old Testament, Abraham was a mediator between God and the corrupt people of Sodom and Gomorrah. In spite of their gross wickedness, he pleaded for divine mercy in their behalf—to spare them from destruction—if he could identify but ten righteous persons in those cities (Genesis 18:22–32). Moses also served as a mediator on behalf of the children of Israel. Jehovah declared that because of their wandering rebellion he would destroy the people and basically start all over.

After Moses discovered that the Israelites had built and worshipped a golden calf, he said to the people: "Ye have sinned a great sin: and now I will go up unto the Lord; peradventure [perhaps] *I shall make an atonement for your sin.*" Other translations render this passage as "secure pardon for your sin" (Exodus 32:30 Revised English Bible) or "clear you of your sin" (Exodus 32:30 The Message: The Bible in Contemporary Language). Then, speaking to the Lord, Moses declared: "Oh, this people have sinned a great sin, and have made them gods of gold (32:31)." Now note this tender plea, a touching act of mediation: "Yet now, if thou wilt forgive their sin—; and *if not, blot me, I pray thee, out of thy book which thou hast written*" (Exodus 32:32; emphasis added).

The Epistle to the Hebrews opens as follows: "*God, who at sundry times and in divers manners spake in time past unto the fathers by the prophets*, hath in these last days spoken unto us by his Son, whom he hath appointed heir of all things, by whom also he made the worlds; who being in the brightness of his glory, and the express image of his person, and upholding all things by the word of his power, when he had *by himself purged our sins*, sat down on the right hand of the Majesty on high" (Hebrews 1:1–3; emphasis added). John Stott observed that this passage "brings together the two major spheres of mediation, in which God has taken action through Jesus Christ, which we usually call 'revelation' and 'redemption.' That is, God has both spoken to our ignorance through Jesus Christ, and dealt with our sins through Jesus Christ." Stott concluded that "in the sphere of revelation Jesus was a prophet greater than Moses, and in the sphere of redemption he was a priest greater than Aaron."[5]

The Mediator: Man, but More than Man

Jesus the Christ stands in a most unusual position as a member of the divine family of God. He had a dual inheritance. First, he was the son of Mary, and from her he inherited *mortality*, the flesh, including the capacity to die. Jesus needed to be mortal to understand and appreciate the challenges of being a human being. Indeed, "in all things it behoved him to be made like unto his brethren" (Hebrews 2:17). He went out into a fallen world and, day by day, encountered pain, affliction, temptation, infirmity, or weakness, "that his bowels may be filled with mercy, according to the flesh, that he may know according to the flesh how to succor his people according to their infirmities" (Alma 7:11–12). Second, he was also the Son of God, the Almighty Elohim, and from him he inherited *immortality*, the capacity and power to live forever. The Lord stated it plainly when he taught: "Therefore doth my Father love me, because I lay down my life, that I might take it again. No man taketh it from me, but I lay it down of myself. I have power to lay it down [through his mortal inheritance], and I have power to take it again [through his immortal inheritance]. This commandment have I received of my Father" (John 10:17–18).

The Savior's co-inheritance was absolutely necessary. Look carefully at the words of the angel to King Benjamin as he spoke of the condescension of Jehovah: "And lo, he shall suffer temptations, and pain of body, hunger, thirst, and fatigue, *even more than man can suffer*, except it be unto death" (Mosiah 3:7; emphasis added) He also prophesied: "And lo, he cometh unto his own, that salvation might come unto the children of men even through faith on his name; and even after all this *they shall consider him a man*, and say that he hath a devil, and shall scourge him, and shall crucify him" (Mosiah 3:9; emphasis added). Truly, Jesus of Nazareth was a man, but he was so much more than a man. Had he not had immortality within him, he could not have endured the suffering of Gethsemane and Golgotha, he could not have had the power to forgive sin and effect a mighty change in those who came to him by faith, he could not have raised himself from the tomb, from death to everlasting life.

Jesus Christ is *holy*. Charles E. Jefferson, pastor of the Broadway Tabernacle in New York City in the early years of the twentieth century, wrote:

> What do we mean by holiness? We mean wholeness, full-orbed perfection. . . . Let us think about the sinlessness of Jesus. . . .
>
> The men who were nearest to [Jesus] got the idea that he was without sin. . . . Now these men were with Jesus. They ate with him, drank with him, slept with him, they saw him in all conditions and in all moods, and under varying circumstances. They saw him hungry, angry, stern, surprised, disappointed, amazed, yet they believed that in him there was no sin. . . .

The reason we are drawn to him is because we feel instinctively that he is far above us, a man without a sin. It is this which gives the Christian church its power. The Christian church has but one perfect possession, that is Jesus. The creed of the church is not perfect, its phrases were formed by the blundering mind of man. The Bible is not perfect, it is not inerrant, it has many a flaw. The church itself is imperfect, stained through and through with sin; but Jesus of Nazareth, the head of the church, is stainless. And because he is without sin, the church will come off triumphant.[6]

Nevertheless, Jesus was subject to temptation. It was possible for him to sin. The Son of God was not spared the tauntings, buffetings, and allurements of the father of lies; Jesus knew from firsthand experience that Lucifer was, as Joseph Smith explained, an "actual being from the unseen world, who had such marvelous power as I had never before felt in any being."[7] Some have supposed that the Savior's confrontation with Lucifer in the Judean desert following our Lord's baptism was the extent of his temptation (Matthew 4:1–11; Luke 4:1–13). This is definitely not the case. It is the Gospel writer Luke who offered this point of clarity: "And when the devil had ended all the temptation, he departed from him *for a season*" (Luke 4:13; emphasis added). Indeed, Jesus was "in all points tempted as we are, yet without sin" (Hebrews 4:15). "For in that he himself hath suffered being tempted, he is able to succor them that are tempted" (Hebrews 2:18; see Doctrine and Covenants 62:1).

We know from scripture that some of the prophets like Noah (Moses 8:27) and Job (Job 1:1) were "perfect."[8] That is, they were upright, whole, faithful, dependable before God, people of integrity, and steadfast in their quest to know the Lord and keep his commandments. Their lives were complete, and their faith in God was mature. Because we know they were human, however, we know also that they had at various times in their lives been guilty of sin, but had repented and been forgiven.

Jesus was different: we can say of him what can be said of no other person to inhabit earth—he was totally and completely innocent, had never taken a backward step, had never taken a moral detour, had never committed sin. In speaking to students at a Brigham Young University fireside, Elder Bruce R. McConkie stated: "We have to become perfect to be saved in the celestial kingdom. But nobody becomes perfect in this life. Only the Lord Jesus attained that state, and *he had an advantage that none of us has.* He was the Son of God, and *he came into this life with a spiritual capacity and a talent and an inheritance that exceeded beyond all comprehension what any of the rest of us was born with.*"[9] In short, Jesus was in many ways just as we are. And yet he possessed innate powers, divine attributes, and heavenly qualities that no other mortal being possessed. Jesus himself said: "For he whom God hath sent [speaking of himself] speaketh the words of God: for God giveth him not *the Spirit* by measure, for he [the Spirit] *dwelleth in him, even the fullness*" (JST John 3:34; emphasis added). As Joseph Smith taught: "Where is the man that is free from vanity? None ever were perfect but Jesus; and why was He perfect? Because He was the Son of God, and *had the fullness of the Spirit,* and greater power than any man."[10]

The Messenger of the Covenant

Jesus is our mediator in that he is the "Messenger of the Covenant." In speaking through Malachi, Jehovah proclaimed: "Behold, I will send my messenger, and he shall prepare the way before me: and the Lord, whom ye seek, shall suddenly come to his temple, even the messenger of the covenant, whom ye delight in: behold, he shall come, saith the Lord of hosts" (Malachi 3:1). One way of looking at the phrase "Messenger of the Covenant" is to see Jesus as the preeminent Prophet, the great Word of the Father, the consummate dispenser of truth. Jesus was also a restorer in his day, a legal administrator, one charged by the Father to deliver priesthood powers and keys to his appointed servants. Joseph Smith taught that Jesus "was greater than John [the Baptist], because He held the keys of the Melchizedek priesthood and kingdom of God, and had before revealed the priesthood of Moses."[11] On another occasion the Prophet said, "Jesus was then the legal administrator and ordained his apostles."[12]

In other words, Jesus Christ was the Messenger of the *gospel covenant*. Joseph Smith revealed one of the grand truths of the Restoration when he explained that "the kingdom of God was set up on the earth from the days of Adam to the present time. Whenever there has been a righteous man on earth unto whom God revealed His word and gave power and authority to administer in His name, and where there is a priest of God . . . , there is the kingdom of God."[13]

One of the principal reasons for our Lord's incarnation was to reveal the Father to men and women on earth. Jesus made it very clear that his Father is greater than he is (John 14:28); that "there is none good but one, that is, God" (Matthew 19:17); that God is the "Father of lights" (James 1:17); that he (Christ) came to earth to do the will of the Father (John 6:38); that the message of salvation is first and foremost "the gospel of God" (Romans 1:1; 1 Thessalonians 2:2, 8; 1 Peter 4:17); that the Father, through the Son, is reconciling the world to himself (2 Corinthians 5:18–20); and that God is in Christ, manifesting himself to the world (Hebrews 1:3; John 14:9).

Elder Jeffrey R. Holland taught that "in all that Jesus came to say and do, including and especially in His atoning suffering and sacrifice, *He was showing us who and what God our Eternal Father is like*, how completely devoted He is to His children in every age and nation. *In word and in deed Jesus was trying to reveal and make personal to us the true nature of His Father, our Father in Heaven*." Elder Holland went on to explain that many Christians "feel distant from the Father, even estranged from Him, if they believe in Him at all. And if they do believe, many moderns say they might feel comfortable in the arms of Jesus, but they are uneasy contemplating the stern encounter of God. . . . In that sense Jesus did not come to improve God's view of man nearly so much as He came *to improve man's view of God* and to plead with them to love their Heavenly Father as He has always and will always love them. The plan of God, the power of God, the holiness of God, yes, even the anger and the judgment of God they had occasion to understand. But the love of God, the profound depth of His devotion to His children, they still did not fully know—until Christ came."[14]

Our Lord and Savior did not, however, come to earth simply to make known certain matters, as important as they are. He came "not only to teach but to save, not only to reveal God to human beings, but also to redeem human beings for God. This is because our major problem is not our ignorance but our sin and guilt."[15]

The Mediator of a Better Covenant

Following the translation of Moses, the keys of the Melchizedek priesthood were taken from the generality of the people and the Aaronic priesthood became the priesthood of administration from the days of Aaron's sons to the coming of John the Baptist, a period of almost a millennium and a half. As given in modern revelation, because the children of Israel "hardened their hearts and could not endure his [Jehovah's] presence," the Lord "swore that they should not enter into his rest while in the wilderness, which rest is the fulness of his glory. Therefore, he took Moses out of their midst, and the Holy Priesthood also" (Doctrine and Covenants 84:24–25). William Clayton recorded the following remarks from Joseph Smith: "All priesthood is Melchizedek; but there are different portions or degrees of it. That portion which brought Moses to speak with God face to face was taken away; but that which brought the ministry of angels [the Aaronic] remained. All the prophets had the Melchizedek priesthood and were ordained by God himself."[16]

Spiritually unprepared Israel was given a lesser gospel, a preparatory gospel, including the laws and statutes of what we know as the law of Moses. This was "a law of performances and of ordinances, a law which they were to observe strictly from day to day, to keep them in remembrance of God and their duty towards him" (Mosiah 13:30). This preparatory or lesser gospel was thus administered by a lesser priesthood, the priesthood of Aaron. When Jesus came, however, he restored the higher or Melchizedek priesthood, and with it the everlasting gospel. In this final dispensation, the Savior declared, "Blessed are you for receiving mine everlasting covenant, even the fulness of my gospel, sent forth unto the children of men, that they might have life and be made partakers of the glories which are to be revealed in the last days" (Doctrine and Covenants 66:2; see 1:22; 45:9; 49:9; 133:57).

Hence from the days of Moses to the coming of Christ, the people were given the Mosaic covenant, and with the advent of the Lord came the new and everlasting covenant. It is everlasting in the sense that it was had from the beginning, as Joseph Smith taught. It is new at any given time in that it has been restored anew through the Lord's authorized legal administrators. Therefore, some six hundred years before what we know as the meridian of time, God spoke through Jeremiah: "Behold, the days come, saith the Lord, that *I will make a new covenant* with the house of Israel, and with the house of Judah: not according to the covenant that I made with their fathers . . . , which covenant they brake, . . . but this shall be the covenant that I will make with the house of Israel; after those days, saith the Lord, I will put my law in their inward parts, and write it in their hearts; and will be their God, and they shall be my people" (Jeremiah 31:31–33; emphasis added).

This prophecy was, of course, fulfilled with the coming of the Son of God, he who called all men and women under the Mosaic covenant to a higher righteousness, a righteousness consisting not of good deeds alone but also a religion of the heart, as Jeremiah learned. In other words, the restoration of the everlasting gospel in the meridian of time made Jesus "the mediator of a better covenant" (Hebrews 8:6). Through the sufferings and death of Christ, there is effected a "redemption [from] the transgressions that were under the first testament [covenant]," and by this means "they which are called might receive the promise of eternal inheritance" (Hebrews 9:15). In this manner, Jesus became the "mediator of the new covenant" (Hebrews 12:24).

Mediation through Prayer

A significant aspect of revealing God the Father to the people of earth is revealing how the children of God are to communicate meaningfully with the Father. The Savior himself was very clear regarding the order of prayer: we are to pray to God the Father in the name of Christ the Son. In his last supper, Jesus taught the Twelve: "And whatsoever ye shall ask *in my name*, that will I do, that the Father may be glorified in the Son. If ye shall ask any thing *in my name*, I will do it" (John 14:13–14; emphasis added). In describing the nature of their call and divine authorization, the Lord stated, "Ye have not chosen me, but I have chosen you, and ordained you, that ye should go and bring forth fruit, and that your fruit should remain: that *whatsoever ye shall ask of the Father in my name*, he may give it you" (John 15:16, emphasis added; see 16:23–24, 26).

The risen Lord offered similar counsel to the Nephites when he explained, "Therefore ye must always pray unto the Father in my name" (3 Nephi 18:19). And now note this vital qualification upon having those requests granted: "And whatsoever ye shall ask the Father in my name, *which is right, believing that ye shall receive*, behold it shall be given unto you" (3 Nephi 18:20, emphasis added; see 18:23, 30). The Savior then instructed his Nephite twelve to teach the same order of prayer to the people to whom they would minister: "And the twelve did teach the multitude; and behold, they did cause that the multitude should kneel down upon the face of the earth, and should pray unto the Father in the name of Jesus" (3 Nephi 19:6). This same counsel has been offered to Latter-day Saints in modern revelation (Doctrine and Covenants 14:8; Moses 7:59).

Now, to say that we are to pray to our Father in heaven in the name of the Son is *not to say that our prayers somehow go through Christ*. The scriptures speak otherwise. To be sure, Christ is the way to the Father (John 14:6), and his is the only name by which salvation comes to the children of God (Acts 4:12); he is our Advocate with the Father, our Intercessor in the courts of glory. Our prayers, however, go directly to God our Father. Indeed, we are entitled to "*come boldly unto the throne of grace*, that we may obtain mercy, and find grace to help in time of need" (Hebrews 4:16; emphasis added).

Someone has noted that "a true doctrine of the mediation of Jesus Christ is the ground of Christian assurance. Only when we come to God—through Jesus Christ, who died for us—can we come with boldness instead of timidity, with confidence instead of fear."[17] The great prophet Enoch, some three thousand years before Christ came to earth, was commanded to pray to the Father in the name of the Only Begotten Son; "thou hast . . . commanded me that I should ask in the name of thine Only Begotten; thou hast made me, and given unto me *a right to thy throne*, and not of myself, but *through thine own grace*" (Moses 7:59; emphasis added).

"We pray to the Father, not the Son," a modern apostle observed; "but according to the laws of intercession, advocacy, and mediation, our answers come from the Son." Or, stated in a slightly different way, "proper prayers are made to the Father, in the name of the Son, by the power of the Holy Ghost. *The Father answers prayers, but he does it through the Son*, into whose hands he has committed all things." Finally, proper prayers "are not made to Moses, the mediator of the Old Covenant, nor to Jesus, the Mediator of the New Covenant, nor to the Holy Spirit of God."[18] In summary, we pray to God, the Eternal Father, in the name of our Mediator, Jesus Christ, and we strive to do so by the power of the Holy Ghost.

The Mediator Intercedes and Advocates

Earlier in this chapter I mentioned that no woman or man is saved by virtue of their own merits, deeds, or accomplishments, no matter how impressive they may be. We are saved because of the merits, mercy, and grace of Jesus Christ. Since he was perfect, having committed no sin and the law of justice having no claims upon him (Hebrews 7:26–27), the sinless one was in a unique position with regard to our Heavenly Father, the Man of Holiness (Moses 6:57). Jesus was and is in a position to make certain claims upon the Father, to request of the Almighty what no one of us would ever be in a position to request. His righteousness and holiness enabled and empowered him to be able to "claim of the Father his rights of mercy which he [Christ] hath upon the children of men. . . . For he hath answered the ends of the law, and *he claimeth all those who have faith in him*" (Moroni 7:27–28; emphasis added). By faith in Jesus Christ, we who have been guilty of violating God's law are in a position to lean upon and draw strength and forgiveness from the one who did in reality live that law perfectly. We are redeemed by the righteousness of our Redeemer (Romans 10:1–4; see also 2 Nephi 2:3).

For one thing, because of our Lord's perfection and his complete faithfulness to the laws of God, he is able to extend his righteousness to us. Now whether a person believes that Jesus *imputes* his righteousness to us (a Protestant perspective, a legal declaration describing one's *standing* before God) or *imparts* his righteousness to us (a Roman Catholic perspective describing an actual change in one's *state* or nature), or some of each, as in numerous Protestant-Catholic rapprochements since the Second Vatican Council, what is abundantly clear in the scriptures is that our Savior can change us, can both elevate our standing before God and sanctify our soul. Christ "is able also to save them to the uttermost [perfectly] that come unto God by him, seeing *he ever liveth to make intercession for them*" (Hebrews 7:25; emphasis added). In speaking of those who inherit the celestial kingdom, the revelation states, "These are they who are just men [and women] *made perfect through Jesus the mediator of the new covenant*, who wrought out this perfect atonement through the shedding of his own blood" (Doctrine and Covenants 76:69; emphasis added). Thus, people who come unto Christ with full purpose of heart are "perfected in him" (Moroni 10:32).

The apostle Paul explained that "if any man be in Christ, he is a new creature: old things are passed away; behold, all things are become new. And all things are of God, who hath reconciled us to himself by Jesus Christ. . . . For he [God the Father] hath made him [Christ] to be sin for us, who knew no sin; that we might be made the righteousness of God in him" (2 Corinthians 5:17–18, 21). This is what New Testament scholars and Christian leaders have through the years called the "great exchange" or the "great reversal." In addition, however, Paul is explaining that Jesus came to earth *to exchange with us*. It is as though the Redeemer says to each of those who yearn for cleansing and for rest, "Come unto me, and I will take your sin. On the other hand, I will convey my righteousness to you."

What an exchange! The late Roman Catholic scholar Richard John Neuhaus put it this way: "It was not simply that [Jesus] bore the consequences of sin, but . . . he was made to *be* sin [see 2 Corinthians 5:21, above]. The great reversal reverses all of our preconceptions." Now note the following significant insight: "*God must become what we are in order that we might become what God is.* To effectively take our part, he must take our place." Also, Christ "became what by right he was not, so that we might become what by right we are not. This is what Christians through the ages have called the 'happy exchange.' This exchange, this reversal, is at the very epicenter of the story of our redemption."[19]

One Christian theologian, Donald Bloesch, described the continuing nature of the exchange in this way: "The exchanged life is an ongoing reality and not simply a change in our status before God. It is characterized by the substitution of Christ's humility for our vanity, his courage for our fear, his love for our bitterness, his power for our weakness, his holiness for our sin."[20]

One of the most moving and instructive models or analogies used by the prophets to explain the Messiah's saving labor is the law court setting. We are guilty of offenses against the law, and Jesus Christ offers to serve as our defense attorney. "My little children, these things write I unto you, that ye sin not," declared John the Beloved. "But if any man sin and repent, we have an advocate with the Father, Jesus Christ the righteous" (JST 1 John 2:1). Note the following inspired language of the Prophet Joseph Smith from the dedicatory prayer of the Kirtland Temple: "Thou art gracious and merciful, and wilt turn away thy wrath when thou lookest upon the face of thine Anointed" (Doctrine and Covenants 109:53). "I am Christ," the Lord said in an earlier revelation, "and in mine own name, *by the virtue of the blood which I have spilt, have I pleaded before the Father for them*" (Doctrine and Covenants 38:4; emphasis added).

Jesus was fully human, meaning there was nothing about his human nature or his divine powers that would prevent him from experiencing all of the trials and traumas, the disappointments and delights of mortality. In addition, he was an infinite and eternal being (Alma 34:14) possessed of perfect love for each of us, which allowed him to have perfect empathy.

"Wherefore in all things it behoved [Christ] to be made like unto his brethren, that he might be a merciful and faithful high priest in things pertaining to God, to make reconciliation for the sins of the people. For in that he himself hath suffered being tempted, he is able to succor them that are tempted" (Hebrews 2:17–18; see Alma 7:11–13; Doctrine and Covenants 62:1).

Ours, however, is definitely a different kind of law court. Normally the defense might seek to provide evidence that the accused had a sterling reputation in the community, that the crime for which he is charged is simply incongruous with the esteem with which he is held by those who know him best, that over a period of thirty years he has built a solid and enviable reputation as a city councilman, Little League coach, Scout leader, and volunteer fireman. But what would we make of a defense attorney whose opening remarks went something like the following: "Your honor, I would recommend most strongly, in order to save the time of the court and the money of taxpayers, that this charge be dismissed." The judge might answer, "On what grounds?" The attorney's reply: "Because of my outstanding record as a defense attorney!" The judge: "Come again?" "Well, your honor," the confident advocate continues, "I think if you check my record you will see clearly that I have never lost a case. I am an outstanding lawyer. I really do think it would be wise to dismiss these proceedings."

Now, if the defense attorney were not fined heavily for contempt of court, he would certainly be laughed out of the courtroom. Perhaps both. Why? Because the innocence or guilt of the accused is absolutely unrelated to the competence or effectiveness of his lawyer. In fact, one of the reasons why the Savior's atonement can be described as "infinite and eternal" is that it defies human (mortal) law and logic. The touch of Jesus's hand, the depth and breadth and unspeakable power of his mediation, defies what you and I understand about justice and mercy and right and wrong and restitution and punishment. Turning briefly to the Book of Mormon, we note Amulek's words to the errant Zoramites: "It is expedient that there should be a great and last sacrifice; yea, not a sacrifice of man, neither of beast, neither of any manner of fowl; for *it shall not be a human* [mortal] *sacrifice*; but it must be an infinite and eternal sacrifice. Now there is not any [typical mortal] man that can sacrifice his own blood which will atone for the sins of another. Now, if a man murdereth, behold will our law, which is just, take the life of his brother? I say unto you, Nay. But the law requireth the life of him who hath murdered; therefore there can be nothing which is short of an infinite atonement which will suffice for the sins of the world" (Alma 34:10–12; emphasis added).

C. S. Lewis has written: "Among [the] Jews there suddenly turns up a man who goes about talking as if He was God. He claims to forgive sins. He says He has always existed. He says He is coming to judge the world at the end of time. . . . Now unless the speaker is God, this is really so preposterous as to be comic. We can all understand how a man forgives offenses against himself. You tread on my toes and I forgive you, you steal my money and I forgive you. But what should we make of a man, himself unrobbed and untrodden on, who announced that He forgave you for treading on other men's toes and stealing other men's money? . . . He told people that their sins were forgiven, and never waited to consult all the other people whom their sins had undoubtedly injured. He unhesitatingly behaved as if He was the party chiefly concerned, the person chiefly offended in all offenses. This makes sense only if He really was the God whose laws were broken and whose love is wounded in every sin."[21]

Conclusion

"The fundamental principles of our religion," Joseph Smith taught, "are the testimony of the Apostles and Prophets, concerning Jesus Christ, that He died, was buried, and rose again the third day, and ascended into heaven; and *all other things which pertain to our religion are only appendages to it*."[22] That singular principle puts everything else into proper perspective. If there had been no atonement of Jesus Christ, it would matter precious little to know that we lived before we were born into mortality, that all those who do not have an opportunity to hear the message of salvation in this life will have that privilege in the postmortal spirit world, that there are degrees of glory hereafter, that through those keys of the priesthood known as the sealing power, families may be linked and bound together everlastingly. In other words, if there had been no Atonement, no amount of good on our part or deep and profound doctrine could make up for the loss. "Salvation could not come to the world," the Prophet Joseph declared, "without the mediation of Jesus Christ."[23]

Elder Boyd K. Packer spoke of these solemn matters in a related way. "Truth, glorious truth, proclaims there is . . . a Mediator," he testified. "Through him mercy can be fully extended to each of us without offending the eternal law of justice." Now notice what Elder Packer had to say about this key doctrine: "*This truth is the very root of Christian doctrine. You may know much about the gospel as it branches out from there, but if you only know the branches and those branches do not touch that root, if they have been cut free from that truth, there will be no life nor substance nor redemption in them*."[24] In other words, Christ is the divine center: his life and atoning sacrifice, his advocacy and mediation, together with his bodily resurrection from the dead, give meaning and purpose to everything else we do and believe.

Because God our Heavenly Father devised a plan for the regeneration of fallen mortals, we can have hope. Because, as an essential part of that great plan of happiness, Jesus the Redeemer was sent to earth to provide a system of redemption and reclamation for all who would receive it, we can rejoice. And because he has bridged the divide between fallen, mortal humanity and a holy, glorified, and exalted God, our souls can rest.

⁂

Robert L. Millet is a professor emeritus in the Department of Ancient Scripture at Brigham Young University.

Further Reading

Bloesch, Donald. *Jesus Christ: Savior and Lord*. Downers Grove, IL: InterVarsity, 1997.

Brown, Raymond E. *The Death of the Messiah*, 1:117–234. New York: Doubleday, 1994.

Holland, Jeffrey R. "Where Justice, Love, and Mercy Meet." *Ensign*, May 2015.

———. "None Were with Him." *Ensign*, May 2009.

McConkie, Bruce R. "The Purifying Power of Gethsemane." *Ensign*, May 1985.

Millet, Robert L. *The Atoning One*, 59–96. Salt Lake City: Deseret Book, 2018.

Stott, John. *Life in Christ*. Wheaton, IL: Tyndale House, 1991.

Notes

1. Elder Orson F. Whitney taught, "The Fall had a twofold direction—downward, yet forward. It brought man into the world and set his feet upon progression's highway." *Cowley and Whitney on Doctrine*, comp. Forace Green (Salt Lake City: Bookcraft, 1963), 287.
2. John Stott, *Basic Christianity* (Grand Rapids, MI: Eerdmans, 1999), 81.
3. Boyd K. Packer, "The Mediator," *Ensign*, May 1977, 54–55.
4. Joseph Fielding Smith, *Doctrines of Salvation*, comp. Bruce R. McConkie (Salt Lake City: Bookcraft, 1954), 1:27; emphasis added.
5. John Stott, *Life in Christ* (Wheaton, IL: Tyndale House, 1991), 12.
6. Charles E. Jefferson, *The Character of Jesus* (New York: Thomas Y. Crowell Company, 1908), 326, 331, 332–333, 334.
7. Joseph Smith—History 1:16.
8. In KJV Job 1:1, Job is described as "perfect," but other translations translate the original word as "blameless" (e.g., New Revised Standard Version).
9. Bruce R. McConkie, "Jesus Christ and Him Crucified," *1976 BYU Devotional Speeches of the Year* (Provo, UT: BYU Press, 1977), 399; emphasis added.
10. *Teachings of Presidents of the Church: Joseph Smith* (Salt Lake City: The Church of Jesus Christ of Latter-day Saints, 2007), 53; emphasis added; cited hereafter as *Joseph Smith*.
11. *Joseph Smith*, 83.
12. *The Words of Joseph Smith: The Contemporary Accounts of the Nauvoo Discourses of the Prophet Joseph*, ed. Andrew F. Ehat and Lyndon W. Cook (Provo, UT: BYU Religious Studies Center, 1980), 235; punctuation corrected.
13. *Joseph Smith*, 82.
14. Jeffrey R. Holland, "The Grandeur of God," *Ensign*, November 2003, 70–71; emphasis added..
15. Stott, *Life in Christ*, 16.
16. *Words of Joseph Smith*, 59.
17. Stott, *Life in Christ*, 18.
18. Bruce R. McConkie, *The Promised Messiah: The First Coming of Christ* (Salt Lake City: Deseret Book, 1978), 335, 557, 558; emphasis added.
19. Richard John Neuhaus, *Death on a Friday Afternoon: Meditations on the Last Words of Jesus from the Cross* (New York: Basic Books, 2000), 30–32; emphasis added.
20. Donald Bloesch, *Jesus Christ: Savior and Lord*, Christian Foundations series (Downers Grove, IL: InterVarsity, 1997), 160.
21. C. S. Lewis, *Mere Christianity* (New York: Touchstone, 1996), 55.
22. *Joseph Smith*, 49; emphasis added.
23. *Joseph Smith*, 48.
24. Packer, "Mediator," 56; emphasis added.

17

The Synoptic Gospels
Matthew, Mark, and Luke

Alan Taylor Farnes

Most readers of the New Testament begin with the book of Matthew. After completing it, they tend to proceed to Mark, the next Gospel in canonical order. But upon encountering Mark, they may be surprised to discover that it shares a high degree of material with Matthew. For example, Mark 1:2 begins the story of John the Baptist, but this story was already covered in Matthew 3:13–17. Continuing, they discover that Luke also shares a high degree of material with both Mark and Matthew. Why this repetition? Why does the New Testament begin with three Gospels that essentially tell the same story about Jesus?

Careful readers, however, will notice that Mark tells the story of John the Baptist slightly differently than Matthew does and that Luke has yet more differences. At Jesus's baptism in Mark 1:10, for example, the Gospel of Mark speaks of "the Spirit like a dove descending upon him," whereas Matthew's account reads "the Spirit of God descending like a dove, and lighting upon him" (Matthew 3:16). Luke is different still: "the Holy [Spirit][1] descended in a bodily shape like a dove upon him" (Luke 3:22). Here we have three different Gospels with three slightly different renderings of an event at Jesus's baptism.

These are small and seemingly inconsequential changes, but we must nonetheless ask why they were made. Since most scholars believe that Mark was the first Gospel to be written, it is commonly held that both Matthew and Luke employed Mark as a source in their respective Gospels.[2] Consequently, the books of Matthew, Mark, and Luke are referred to as the "Synoptic" Gospels (the word *synoptic* comes from a Greek word meaning "to see together" or "from the same point of view"). While the Gospel of John shares a small amount of material with the Synoptic Gospels (such as Jesus's baptism, implied at John 1:28–34), it differs enough from the Synoptics to be in a class of its own (see chapter 18 herein).[3] In this study I will discuss the individual nature of the Synoptic Gospels and provide an overview of their respective authors, the potential dates of their composition, and their intended audiences. I will also discuss the "Synoptic problem," or the attempt to determine which of the Synoptic Gospels was written first and the exact nature of dependence among the Synoptics as far as this can be determined.

Dating and Authorship of the Synoptic Gospels

Scholars disagree about when these books were written. Whether the Synoptic Gospels were written before or after AD 70 (when the Jerusalem temple was destroyed by the Romans) during the siege of Jerusalem (see chapter 14 herein) is a matter of interpretation. As will be discussed in detail below, some commentators claim that the Synoptics show definite signs of knowing that the temple was destroyed, while other scholars respond that this awareness is due to Jesus's ability to prophesy of future events. Other chronological clues are less determinative for the dating question. For Latter-day Saints, who accept Jesus's prophetic ability, any claimed awareness of the temple's destruction or the presence of later events in the Gospels does not necessarily prove they were written after the fact. Thus, while scholarly endeavors to date the Synoptic Gospels have merit, they are largely based on assumptions that Latter-day Saints do not always share. Of course, such speculation has little theological bearing on the Gospels.

The question of Gospel authorship is similarly complex, with many variables and assumptions at issue in any given argument. For instance, some scholars argue that Matthew, one of Jesus's original twelve apostles as inferred from Matthew 9:9, wrote the Gospel of Matthew, while others claim it was written by a later figure and that the ascription to Matthew was made by later Christians who could not have known the author's identity. While such authorship issues have dominated in academia, for Latter-day Saints they need not have a dominating role in theological discussions of the Gospels. Here the words of I. Howard Marshall are helpful: "If the Gospel rests on sound tradition faithfully recorded, the name of its author is of secondary importance."[4]

Some might retort that the Gospels must have been written by the original apostles so that their words can be trusted because they were eyewitnesses. But, only two of the four Gospels claim to have been written by eyewitnesses (Matthew and John). The other two, Mark and Luke, make no claim to apostolic authority; furthermore, Luke explicitly states that he was not an eyewitness of Christ's ministry (Luke 1:2). Thus, the Gospels need not have been written by eyewitnesses to be trustworthy and reliable. Consider an analogy from the Book of Mormon: Latter-day Saints believe the Book of Mormon to be the word of God. But who "wrote" the vast majority of the Book of Mormon? Mormon and Moroni served as editors, redactors, and authors but lived hundreds of years after most of the events that they chronicled. Yet Mormon and Moroni used eyewitness records as sources for compiling the

Book of Mormon. Latter-day Saints do not question the veracity, reliability, or trustworthiness of the Book of Mormon, even though it was compiled some four hundred years after most of the events took place, largely because Latter-day Saints accept that Mormon and Moroni used eyewitness testimony as sources while compiling the record and did so with the aid of the Holy Ghost. Consequently, Mormon's and Moroni's editorial processes may not have been dissimilar to some of those employed by non-eyewitness writers of the New Testament Gospels as they sought to compile narratives that would convince their readers that Jesus was the Christ and the Son of God.

The Synoptic Gospels as Individual Testimonies

Latter-day Saints often conflate the three Synoptic Gospels in an attempt to tell the life of Jesus as one simple story. Indeed, most Latter-day Saint biblical reenactments, such as Christmas nativity plays, are by necessity harmonizations of the Synoptics since only in Matthew's Gospel, for example, do we find the wise men (Matthew 2:1–12) and only in Luke's Gospel do we learn about the shepherds (Luke 2:8–18). Yet in nativity plays the wise men and the shepherds usually appear side by side—a conflation of events not supported by the record. However much we may want a single Gospel that encapsulates Jesus's life and teachings into one simple narrative, we do not have one. Instead we have four Gospels that describe Jesus's life in different ways and, importantly, with different purposes in mind. Attempting to flatten the Gospels into one can do a disservice to the narrators' individual testimonies, perspectives, and purposes.[5]

While there are reasons that one could probably read the Synoptics as a harmony (such as seeing one coherent story of Jesus and obtaining an overall perspective on who he was), the impossibility of creating an accurate harmony—one that does not contain obvious contradictions or favor one Gospel account over another—suggests that this method of study has less merit than approaching the Gospels as individual accounts. Only after we understand what each Gospel says on its own can we responsibly attempt to place the pieces together to form a more coherent whole. When we do so, however, we must be aware of and honest about the differences and contradictions among the Synoptic accounts.

Gospel of Mark

If the aim is to understand what the Gospel of Mark has to say about Jesus—who he was, what he was like, what he taught, and so on—the reader should read Mark for Mark's sake, that is, without reference to the other Gospels. If the aim is to gain a more complete picture of what the entire New Testament has to say about Jesus, the reader could forgo reading Mark altogether since much of it is repeated in other Gospels. Reading Mark for Mark's sake provides insight into what this earliest Gospel writer thought about Jesus (most New Testament scholars accept that Mark's Gospel was written first, at least before Matthew and Luke).[6] As twenty-first-century Christians, we take for granted these books called "Gospels" that tell the story of Jesus's life and preserve his teachings. However, before the author of

Mark began composing his work, there were no such accounts that we know of. Mark's attempt to gather and record the disparate accounts of Jesus's ministry into one Gospel was an innovation that quickly caught on, yet the book is sometimes ignored or even disparaged because it is the shortest Gospel and, as noted earlier, contains only 7 percent unique material. But that fact is a testament to the book's genius: only 7 percent of it is unique precisely because Matthew and Luke thought highly enough of Mark's Gospel to borrow 93 percent of its material.

It is important to remember that the New Testament exists in manuscripts that are not original copies but rather much later handwritten copies that were preserved by early Christians. While the Gospels were probably written in the generation after Jesus, the earliest extant fragments date to more than a century after his death and resurrection. For example, the earliest extant text of the Gospel of Mark is preserved in a manuscript from about the middle of the third century AD.[7] While this manuscript is a collection of the other New Testament Gospels and Acts as well, it is most likely that the Gospel of Mark first circulated as a single Gospel.[8]

While most scholars accept that Mark wrote the Gospel bearing his name, the question of the authorship deserves more analysis. For example, who was Mark and whence the title "Gospel of Mark"? A person in the New Testament identified as John Mark is described as the son of Mary, whose house served as a meeting place for Christ's disciples: "[Peter] came to the house of Mary the mother of John, whose surname was Mark; where many were gathered together praying" (Acts 12:12). Later in this same chapter we are told that John Mark accompanied Paul and Barnabas on a missionary journey (12:25; 13:5). John Mark soon left his companions and returned to Jerusalem (13:13). That something like abandonment or desertion occurred here is underscored by the text.[9] In Acts 15 John Mark is the subject of a sharp debate between Paul and Barnabas. Barnabas wanted John Mark to accompany them on the next leg of their mission, but Paul "thought not good to take him with them, who departed from them" (15:38).[10] We also find the name Mark elsewhere in the New Testament. In Colossians 4:10 Paul identifies someone named Mark as the cousin of Barnabas, and in 2 Timothy 4:11 Paul says Mark is profitable for the ministry. Further, in Philemon 1:24 Mark is listed as a "fellowlabourer" of Paul, and in 1 Peter 5:13 the author calls a person named Mark his "son."[11]

Moreover, a second-century bishop of Hierapolis named Papias mentions someone named Mark in connection with this Gospel: "Mark became Peter's interpreter and wrote accurately all that he [Peter] remembered, not, indeed, in order, of the things said or done by the Lord. For he [Mark] had not heard the Lord, nor had he followed him, but later on, as I said, followed Peter."[12]

Is it possible that all these mentions of Mark and John Mark concern the same person? Joel Marcus, a renowned scholar of the Gospel of Mark, argues that is the case.[13] While this is a distinct possibility, we must keep in mind that John and Mark were, respectively, some of the most popular Hebrew and Roman names, so it would not be surprising to find multiple people named John or Mark in the New Testament.[14] Nonetheless, many believe that the John Mark mentioned in the New Testament is the same person who wrote the Gospel of Mark.[15] Joel Marcus goes on to assert the likelihood that this same Mark was indeed the author because any later person attempting to ascribe the Gospel falsely to someone would probably have chosen a famous apostle from the New Testament rather than an obscure person who appears therein only a couple of times.[16]

The most significant signposts that scholars use to date the Gospel of Mark are its mention of the impending destruction of the temple (13:1–2), "the abomination of desolation" (13:14), and the flight to the mountains (13:14). Those who belonged to the Jerusalem church did indeed flee to Pella or elsewhere, the temple was indeed destroyed, and there was some kind of abomination. Mark may have been writing after these events associated with the Jewish War (AD 66–73) occurred (that is, post-AD 70), or perhaps he wrote just before them with a sense of foreboding about what was to come. Of course, if Jesus prophesied of these events, then the events of AD 70 no longer serve as *the* defining point for dating the Gospel. One argument that Mark composed his Gospel before AD 70 is that it "does not reflect the kind of detail expected when one looks back on that event."[17]

Another signpost used to date the Gospel of Mark is found in Mark 15:21, where Simon of Cyrene carries Jesus's cross. Simon is introduced to the reader as "the father of Alexander and Rufus." Many claim that Simon's children are mentioned because Alexander and Rufus were known to the hearers of Mark's Gospel.[18] While these signposts show that Mark was written within one or two generations of Jesus's ministry, they are not as helpful for pinpointing an exact year or small span of time during which Mark wrote.

Concerning the intended audience of the Gospel of Mark, Gaye Strathearn and Frank Judd demonstrate that "internal evidence strongly suggests that the Gospel of Mark was written for a gentile, or non-Jewish, audience."[19] They show that Mark routinely interprets Aramaic phrases that Matthew leaves untranslated. For example, in Mark 5:41 Jesus says to Jairus's daughter "Talitha cumi," which is then translated as "Damsel, I say unto thee, arise." Likewise, in 7:34 Jesus says, "Ephphatha," which Mark translates as "Be opened." Lastly, on the cross Jesus cries, "Eloi, Eloi, lama sabachthani?" and Mark translates the statement for his readers (15:34). Strathearn and Judd conclude that "if Mark's audience were Jewish and spoke Aramaic, there would be no need for such explanations."[20] Here we see that Mark intended to write to a non-Jewish audience and so provided explanations of Aramaic phrases.

Gospel of Matthew

Matthew seems to have been the second Gospel written and has a different presentation and focus than Mark's Gospel. Surviving early Christian sources suggest that Matthew and John were the most popular of the four Gospels based on how much they were quoted and copied.[21] Strathearn and Judd note that Matthew's account was probably referenced in 2 Peter and James, and early Christians such as Ignatius and a second-century handbook called the Didache also quoted Matthew.[22]

Because Matthew's primary purpose was to convince his readers that Jesus was the promised Messiah of the Old Testament, an intended Jewish audience seems most likely. According to Strathearn and Judd, "Internal evidence from the Gospel itself seems to confirm that the intended audience was Jewish. Unlike Mark, Matthew does not explain Jewish concepts for his audience."[23] Matthew quotes extensively from the Old Testament to show how Jesus fulfilled Old Testament prophecy. He also presents Jesus as a new Moses figure—a new lawgiver. Just as Moses gave the law to Israel in the book of Exodus, Jesus fulfilled the law and gave a higher law to his people. Matthew incorporates scripture from the Old Testament so well that Davies and Allison remark that "our author was, there can be no doubt, some sort of scholar."[24] Framing the Sermon on the Mount to mirror Moses's story at Sinai, Matthew says that Jesus "went up into a mountain" (*anebē eis to oros*) to give his sermon (Matthew 5:1), which matches the Septuagint version of Exodus 19:3, where Moses goes up into a mountain (the exact same Greek phrase is used) before receiving the Ten Commandments. Notably, whereas Moses finds God atop the mountain, in Matthew's account Jesus goes up into the mountain to find himself at the top of it, thus becoming both the law originator and the law deliverer, thereby surpassing Moses in divine authority.

In order to fully convince Jewish Christians that Jesus is the Messiah, Matthew includes ten "formula quotations"[25] that follow a pattern similar to the one found in Matthew 1:22–23: "Now all this was done, that it might be fulfilled which was spoken of the Lord by the prophet, saying, . . . " These formula quotations were intended to show that Jesus was the Messiah prophesied of in the Old Testament. While Mark has quotations like this from the Old Testament (see, for example, Mark 1:2–3), they are not nearly so numerous.

There are two main theories concerning who wrote the Gospel of Matthew: (1) Matthew, Jesus's apostle, as indicated in Matthew 9:9, and (2) a later person, with the ascription to Matthew added sometime later. There is no need to be wedded unnecessarily to traditional theories of authorship concerning the Gospels, because whoever wrote them used eyewitness testimony as sources for compiling their narratives. While Latter-day Saints generally hold to traditional authorship in the Church, such a position concerning Matthew poses a few challenges based on the evidence at hand. For example, if Matthew was written by the apostle Matthew, why would such an eyewitness have relied so heavily on another source, namely Mark, who was not an eyewitness? On the other hand, if Matthew was called at some later point in Christ's ministry (Matthew 9:9), this might account for why he could have relied on Mark, especially if the source behind Mark was Peter.[26]

As has been shown, dating the Synoptic Gospels is often educated guesswork, and this is especially true for Matthew and Luke. Scholars readily admit that dating Matthew is largely dependent on Mark's date and is therefore a relative date. Since Matthew uses Mark as a source, scholars guess that it may have taken Mark's Gospel about a decade to circulate and become popular enough for Matthew to use it as a source. Since most date Mark sometime from AD 65 to AD 74, Matthew is therefore dated sometime after that. According to Davies and Allison, "Matthew was almost certainly written between AD 70 and AD 100, in all probability between AD 80 and 95."[27] Another reason for their dating is that, as mentioned above, Matthew was known to Ignatius and the Didache and therefore could not have been written later than AD 100.[28]

Strathearn and Judd summarize well the overall themes and goals of the Gospel of Matthew: "Matthew, therefore, highlights the truth that God is with his people. Jesus's coming to earth was the fulfillment of a plan that had been in place from the very beginning. Israel may have rejected their God, but he had not rejected his people, even though the Gentiles would have a place in his kingdom. Instead of coming as a judge, which he will do at the end of time, God first sent his Son to teach and heal his people, both physically and spiritually."[29]

Gospel of Luke

Luke's Gospel, while borrowing heavily from Mark, is quite different from Mark as well as from Matthew. First, Luke is the only evangelist to explicitly state his goals, intentions, and motivations for penning his Gospel.

> Forasmuch as many have taken in hand to set forth in order a declaration of those things which are most surely believed among us, even as they delivered them unto us, which from the beginning were eyewitnesses, and ministers of the word; it seemed good to me also, having had perfect understanding of all things from the very first, to write unto thee in order, most excellent Theophilus, that thou mightest know the certainty of those things, wherein thou hast been instructed. (Luke 1:1–4)

This passage has many important elements, and we are fortunate that Luke opens up and invites us behind the curtain to see him at work. Luke tells us first that "many" have already attempted to write such Gospels. Here he is undoubtedly referencing Mark and could also be referring to Matthew. It is also possible that Luke is referring to other Gospels or sources not presently in the New Testament canon (see discussion below). Marshall asserts that Luke's purpose was to "give an historical account which would form the basis for a sound Christian faith on the part of those who had already been instructed, perhaps imperfectly or incompletely, in the story of Jesus."[30]

Luke says that he is writing "unto" (KJV) or "for" (NRSV) someone whom he refers to as "most excellent Theophilus" (Luke 1:3). Marshall claims that Theophilus was the patron, or financier, of Luke's project;[31] François Bovon adds that Theophilus was "not an abstraction, but a historical person."[32] Bovon is responding to the assertion that since *Theophilus* means "friend of God," Luke is directing his work to any "friend of God" and that Theophilus was not a real person but rather a symbol of each believer in Christ. While Bovon is probably correct that Theophilus was a historical figure and the patron of Luke's effort, we should allow room for more than one meaning: "Because *Theophilus* means 'friend of God,' we can also apply it to ourselves as we read Luke's writings—we are also friends of God who are being invited to seek the truth about the Savior in Luke's Gospel."[33] That Luke could have intended this multivalence is not an unreasonable conjecture. Additionally, while Luke tells us that he is writing *for* Theophilus, the internal evidence of the text suggests that he is writing *to* "educated Gentiles, Hellenistic Jews, and Christians unsettled by rumors."[34]

It is worth noting here that Luke wrote a two-volume work: Luke and Acts (see Acts 1:1). These two accounts can be read together as one large work. Luke's Gospel primarily concerns the life and ministry of Jesus Christ, while the principal purpose of Acts was to show the culmination and spread of Jesus's good news.

Like Mark, the Gospel of Luke does not claim any apostolic authority and is written anonymously (Luke's name does not appear in Acts either). Marshall comments, "The Gospel itself is anonymous and contains no information which would enable us to identify its author."[35] The author of Luke–Acts, however, is somewhat revealed in Acts 16:10–17, 20:5–15, 21:1–18, 27:1–37, and 28:1–16, where the narration suddenly shifts from third person to first person plural: "And after he had seen the vision, immediately *we* endeavored to go into Macedonia, assuredly gathering that the Lord had called *us* for to preach the gospel unto them" (16:10; emphasis added). These "*we*-passages," as they are called, imply that the author of Luke–Acts accompanied Paul on some of his missionary journeys, although this clue is not determinative of Lukan authorship.

A person named Luke is mentioned elsewhere in the New Testament in the letters of Paul. Interestingly, in two of these instances Luke is mentioned along with Mark. In Colossians 4:14 we read, "Luke, the beloved physician, and Demas, greet you," suggesting that someone named Luke was traveling with Paul. In 2 Timothy 4:11 we read, "Only Luke is with me. Take Mark, and bring him with thee: for he is profitable to me for the ministry." Lastly, we find Luke in Philemon, where he is again mentioned alongside Mark: "Marcus, Aristarchus, Demas, Lucas, my fellowlabourers" (Philemon 1:24). This gives us two possibilities for authorship: the Gospel of Luke could have been written by someone named Luke who was a missionary companion of Paul and is the same person mentioned in the Pauline Epistles, or a later person recognized that the anonymous author was a companion of Paul and chose to name him after Luke (or Lucas). The latter scenario is unconvincing. Moreover, there is no strong argument against Luke himself being both the author of the Gospel and a missionary companion of Paul.

As early as AD 200 manuscripts bore the title "Gospel according to Luke." Early tradition likewise attests that this Gospel was written by someone named Luke. If Papias mentioned Luke, as he did Mark and Matthew, then his comments did not survive. Instead the first extant mention of Luke by an early Christian author is Irenaeus, who discussed all four Gospels around the end of the second century AD. Of Luke he said, "Luke also, the companion of Paul, recorded in a book the gospel preached by Paul."[36] Marshall concludes, "In short, the best hypothesis is still that the Gospel was composed by Luke."[37]

Dating the Gospel of Luke is similar to dating Matthew's since Luke clearly uses Mark as a source and enough time must have passed since its publication and circulation for Luke to have received and read it. If Luke used Matthew, Luke's Gospel must also have been written later. Bovon dates Luke–Acts to sometime between AD 80 and 90,[38] Strathearn and Judd agree with Bovon,[39] and Marshall tentatively suggests ca. AD 80.[40]

Luke's Gospel is characterized by vivid parables that show rather than tell. For example, when Jesus is asked "Who is my neighbour?" (Luke 10:29), he relates the classic parable of the good Samaritan. It is in Luke where we find many other memorable and didactic parables such as the prodigal son, the lost sheep, and the lost coin. Of Luke's purpose in writing, Marshall notes, "His task was to provide [his audience] with such an account of the story of Jesus as would enable them to see that the story with which they had already become partially acquainted was a reliable basis for their faith. Thus, his work was probably intended for members of the church."[41]

The Synoptic Problem

It is commonly accepted in biblical scholarship that Mark was written first and Matthew and Luke used Mark as one of their sources. The question that arises is how to account for material that is shared by Matthew and Luke but not found in Mark. This forms the basis of the so-called Synoptic problem. Over the centuries various solutions have been offered, many rather complicated. Today the majority of scholars find two theories most tenable. The Two Source Theory (or Q Theory)[42] postulates that Matthew and Luke had access to Mark and another source that

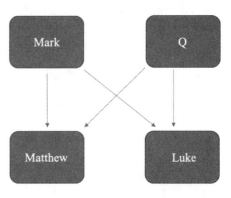

Table 1. Two Source Theory or "Q" Theory.

is now lost. This lost source has been called "Q," short for the German *Quelle,* meaning "source." It is conjectured that Matthew and Luke both had access to Q and Mark while writing their Gospels. To clarify, Q is a hypothetical document that has never been found and has been reconstructed only by identifying passages shared by Matthew and Luke but absent in Mark. While this postulation addresses most of the big issues of the Synoptic problem, it is not without its shortcomings. A main objection to the Q Hypothesis is that it is merely a hypothesis: the Q document is entirely conjectural, and no document has been found that matches what we would expect Q to look like.

The other proposed solution that has a large scholarly following is the Farrer-Goulder Hypothesis, named after its early proponents. This hypothesis claims that Mark wrote first, then Matthew wrote using Mark as a source, and finally Luke wrote his Gospel using both Mark and Matthew as sources. The current champion of this position is Mark Goodacre.[43] Many younger scholars are attracted to this solution because they see it as the simplest solution, passing Occam's razor. Under this solution there is no need to postulate or reconstruct hypothetical ancient documents; rather, all the sources needed are in the New Testament.

One weakness of the Farrer-Goulder Hypothesis, however, is that if Luke copied Matthew, he broke up many of Matthew's beautiful sermons like the Sermon on the Mount and replaced them with less elegant ones. What would motivate Luke to do that? Additionally,

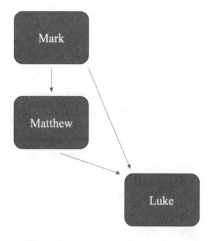

Table 2. The Farrer-Goulder Hypothesis.

proponents of Q argue that Matthew and Luke display "alternating primitivity," or places where Matthew or Luke seems to have the more primitive account. For the Farrer-Goulder Hypothesis to work, Matthew must predate Luke in order for Luke to use Matthew as a source. But Q theorists argue that it is not clear whether Matthew or Luke was written earlier and that both display alternating primitivity, as evident in the Sermon on the Mount and the Sermon on the Plain. Matthew 5:3 reads "Blessed are the poor in spirit," but Luke reads only "Blessed be ye poor" (Luke 6:20). Q theorists argue that Luke displays a more primitive account of this saying and that it could not be dependent on Matthew. If Luke were copying directly from Matthew, then Luke would not have a saying that appears to be more primitive than Matthew's.[44] Here we see that any solution to the Synoptic problem is fraught with challenges and that scholars will likely never fully agree on a solution.

The solution to the Synoptic problem is, of itself, of no significant theological importance. Whether or not Q existed or Luke knew and used Matthew does not affect one's testimony of Jesus as Savior. However, what has been done with Q could have an effect on one's faith negatively. Thomas Wayment observes that "conclusions drawn from [Q] are influencing the faith of thousands and altering the way the New Testament is taught and preached throughout the world."[45] Q can become dangerous because, as a hypothetical document, it can be reconstructed in many ways to say many things. And if Q did exist, it would have been one of the earliest Christian documents, and what it did or did not contain would be extremely important for the origins of the Christian faith. Wayment continues: "Q has become something unwieldy—a beast with a spirit of its own. Q scholars want to alter our understanding of who Jesus was and present to us a Jesus who did no miracles, did not anticipate His death, did not understand He was the Messiah, and did not leave behind an organized church. The Jesus of Q is essentially a scholar's Jesus who wandered the countryside and taught using conventional wisdom. He had no power to save Himself, and He had no power to save others. Scholars call this the Jesus of history, whereas we worship the Jesus of faith."[46]

Because Q can indeed be made to say whatever a given scholar wants it to say, it should be treated cautiously. Yet it remains possible that a lost sayings source could have been a source for Matthew and Luke. Q does not necessarily depict Jesus in a negative light, but it can construe him negatively depending on how it is reconstructed. So Wayment concludes: "We do not object to the possible use of sources by the Evangelists, and we expect that if such sources were available to them in the earliest years of the Church, they would make good use of them. We object, however, to what is being said concerning the items that those early sources did not contain, and we openly question whether such a document actually existed. The problem lies not necessarily in Q but in what Q has become."[47]

Conclusion

As I hope to have shown, there can be much merit in reading Matthew, Mark, and Luke individually as separate witnesses. Mark, who was likely a companion of Paul, innovatively crafted an account to convince his hearers that Jesus was the Son of God. On the other hand, Matthew likely wrote his account shortly after and used Mark as a source while writing to Jewish people in order to convince them that Jesus was the promised Messiah of the Old Testament. Likewise, Luke also wrote after Mark, using Mark as a source and writing primarily to gentile members of the church to strengthen them in their newfound faith. As we read each Gospel individually, we can gain an appreciation for their individual merits, purposes, and testimonies. It can be tempting at times to group them together as one narrative, but as Strathearn and Judd remind, "students and teachers have much to gain by considering how each Gospel highlights individual aspects of the Savior's ministry and paints an individual portrait of the Savior."[48]

Alan Taylor Farnes is an independent scholar of New Testament manuscripts whose research primarily focuses on how scribes copied the New Testament text.

Further Reading

Mark

Marcus, Joel. *Mark 1–8*. London: Yale University Press, 2000.

———. *Mark 8–16*. London: Yale University Press, 2009.

Matthew

Davies, W. D., and Dale C. Allison. *The Gospel According to Saint Matthew*. 3 vols. Edinburgh, Scotland: T&T Clark, 1988–91.

Luke

Bovon, François. *Luke 1*. Minneapolis: Fortress, 2002.

———. *Luke 2*. Minneapolis: Fortress, 2013.

———. *Luke 3*. Minneapolis: Fortress, 2012.

Synoptic problem

Goodacre, Mark. *The Synoptic Problem: A Way Through the Maze*. London: Sheffield, 2001. Freely available online at https://archive.org/details/synopticproblemw00good.

Notes

1. The King James Version here reads "the Holy Ghost," but the word translated in Luke 3:22 as "ghost" is the same word used in Mark 1:10 for "spirit"—*pneuma*. The KJV translators translated *pneuma* in two different ways: "spirit" and "ghost." When we keep in mind that Luke's version could actually read "Holy Spirit," we

realize that Luke has added here only one word, not two, to Mark's account. In Greek, Luke has actually added two words—*to hagion*—but the *to* simply means "the" and is unimportant when translated.

2. For a brief overview of the direction of borrowing among the Synoptics, see Mark Goodacre, *The Synoptic Problem: A Way Through the Maze* (London: Sheffield, 2001), 16–24. This topic will be discussed at length below.

3. Robert L. Millet has provided a useful chart showing the percentage of agreement among the four Gospels: Only 7 percent of Mark's material is unique to Mark, meaning Matthew and Luke borrowed 93 percent of Mark's material but left 7 percent untouched. The Gospel of Matthew is 42 percent unique to Matthew while sharing 58 percent of material with other Gospels. The Gospel of Luke contains 59 percent unique material and shares 41 percent with other Gospels. On the other hand, the Gospel of John has 92 percent unique material and shares only 8 percent of material with the other Gospels. Robert L. Millet, "The Testimony of Matthew," in *Studies in Scripture, Volume Five: The Gospels*, ed. Kent P. Jackson and Robert L. Millet (Salt Lake City: Deseret Book, 1986), 49.

4. I. Howard Marshall, *The Gospel of Luke* (Exeter, England: Paternoster, 1978), 33.

5. See Gaye Strathearn and Frank F. Judd Jr., "The Distinctive Testimonies of the Four Gospels," *Religious Educator* 8, no. 2 (2007): 59–60, for more perspectives on the disadvantages of reading the New Testament Gospels as a harmony.

6. For more evidence that Mark was written before Matthew and Luke, see Goodacre, *Synoptic Problem*, 56–83.

7. Most New Testament manuscripts are dated paleographically, or according to their handwriting style. The earliest surviving text of the Gospel of Mark is preserved in a manuscript called Papyrus 45, or P[45], dating to around AD 250. Containing some of Matthew, Mark 4–9 and 11–12, and some of Luke, John, and Acts, it is badly damaged throughout.

8. As the first Gospel written, Mark had no need for a title bearing the author's name since those who used the account knew who authored it. It was only after other Gospels were written and collected into a single volume that the need to distinguish them one from another became important. That the manuscripts do not carry the title "Mark" until the fourth century AD could largely be attributed to the fragmentary nature of our earliest manuscripts, for the places on most of them where titles would be found are damaged and lost. Nonetheless, early Christian writers attest that a Gospel called Mark had been written. Irenaeus, writing in the late second century, mentions all four Gospels by name (Irenaeus, *Against Heresies* 3.1.1). So it seems clear that by the end of the second century all four Gospels had been written, were known by the names Matthew, Mark, Luke, and John, and were in circulation.

9. The word used to describe John Mark's departure is *apochōreō*. While this word can simply mean "to leave," it can also mean "to desert." This word is used only two other times in the New Testament, and both times it describes a negative aspect of leaving. So Acts 13:13 supports the idea that John Mark may have abandoned Paul and Barnabas and left that particular ministry.

10. This time the author of Acts uses a different Greek word to describe John Mark's departure—*apostanta* (from *aphistēmi*), which should sound familiar since it comes from the same root as the English word *apostasy*. This word gives an even stronger sense that John Mark did not originally leave his companions on good terms—or at least that Paul thought so. And so Acts 15 reports that Paul would not work with John Mark and that Barnabas and John Mark went to preach in Cyprus while Paul chose Silas to accompany him. This is the last we hear of John Mark in Acts. While it is clear there was some bad blood between Paul and John Mark, it is also clear that John Mark, while he may have deserted Paul, did not desert the faith but began another missionary effort with Barnabas.

11. On the identity of Mark who is referred to as a "son" of Peter, see Paul J. Achtemeier, *1 Peter* (Minneapolis: Fortress, 1996), 355: "It appears more likely, however, that the phrase is figurative, pointing to one for whose entrance into the Christian faith Peter was responsible, as seems, for example, also to have been the case of Paul with Timothy. Yet the language of Paul is different, reducing the certainty of such a conclusion."

12. Eusebius, *Ecclesiastical History* 3.39.15; as found in Joel Marcus, *Mark 1–8* (London: Yale University Press, 2000), 21–22. Papias's writings have not survived but are preserved and passed on only through other writers, mainly the fourth-century Christian historian Eusebius of Caesarea.

13. See Marcus, *Mark 1–8*, 18.

14. "Mark was one of the commonest names in the Roman Empire, as well-known personages such as the emperor Marcus Aurelius or the general Marcus Antonius ('Mark Antony') attest." Marcus, *Mark 1–8*, 17–18; see Achtemeier, *1 Peter*, 355.

15. See S. Kent Brown, "The Testimony of Mark," in *Studies in Scripture, Volume Five: The Gospels*, ed. Kent P. Jackson and Robert L. Millet (Salt Lake City: Deseret Book, 1986), 61–64; and Strathearn and Judd, "Distinctive Testimonies," 61.

16. See Marcus, *Mark 1–8*, 17–18.

17. Brown, "Testimony of Mark," 67.

18. See Brown, "Testimony of Mark," 66.

19. Strathearn and Judd, "Distinctive Testimonies," 61.

20. Strathearn and Judd, "Distinctive Testimonies," 61.

21. See Peter M. Head, "Some Recently Published NT Papyri from Oxyrhynchus: An Overview and Preliminary Assessment," *TynBul* 51, no. 1 (2000): 17.

22. See Strathearn and Judd, "Distinctive Testimonies," 81–28.

23. Strathearn and Judd, "Distinctive Testimonies," 65.

24. W. D. Davies and Dale C. Allison, *The Gospel According to Saint Matthew* (Edinburgh, Scotland: T&T Clark, 1988), 1:144.

25. For a more complete discussion of formula quotations, see Davies and Allison, *Matthew*, 3:573–77.

26. The earliest manuscript bearing the title "According to Matthew" is dated to around AD 200. As with Mark, it is not until we get to the grand majuscules of the fourth century, such as Codex Sinaiticus and Codex Vaticanus, that we finally find the full text of Matthew preserved.

27. Davies and Allison, *Matthew*, 1:138.

28. Davies and Allison, *Matthew*, 1:130.

29. Strathearn and Judd, "Distinctive Testimonies," 69.

30. Marshall, *Luke*, 40.

31. Marshall, *Luke*, 39.

32. François Bovon, *Luke 1* (Minneapolis: Fortress, 2002), 9. See also Strathearn and Judd, "Distinctive Testimonies," 69: "Because the name *Theophilus* was common among both Jews and Gentiles in the Greco-Roman world, most scholars conclude that Theophilus was a real person whom Luke knew personally."

33. Strathearn and Judd, "Distinctive Testimonies," 69.

34. Bovon, *Luke 1*, 9.

35. Marshall, *Luke*, 33.

36. Irenaeus, *Against Heresies* 3.1.1; as found in Bovon, *Luke 1*, 9.

37. Marshall, *Luke*, 34.

38. Bovon, *Luke 1*, 9.

39. Strathearn and Judd, "Distinctive Testimonies," 69–70.

40. Marshall, *Luke*, 34–35.

41. Marshall, *Luke*, 35.

42. For more information on the Q Hypothesis, see John S. Kloppenborg Verbin, *Excavating Q: The History and Setting of the Sayings Gospel* (Minneapolis: Fortress, 2000).

43. For more information on the Farrer-Goulder Hypothesis, see Mark Goodacre, *The Synoptic Problem: A Way Through the Maze* (London: Sheffield, 2001); Mark Goodacre, *The Case Against Q: Studies in Markan Priority and the Synoptic Problem* (Harrisburg, PA: Trinity Press, 2002); and Mark Goodacre and Nicholas Perrin, eds., *Questioning Q: A Multidimensional Critique* (Downers Grove, IL: InterVarsity Press, 2004).

44. Goodacre does have a retort for the problem of alternating primitivity. See Goodacre, *Synoptic Gospels*, 133–40 (he addresses the saying "Blessed are the poor in spirit" directly on pages 136–38). Additionally, in this case Q scholars rely on a theory claiming that a shorter reading is usually the earlier reading. This is an outdated theory that has largely been discarded.

45. Thomas A. Wayment, "A Viewpoint on the Supposedly Lost Gospel Q," *Religious Educator* 5, no. 3 (2004): 106.

46. Wayment, "Lost Gospel Q," 113–14.

47. Wayment, "Lost Gospel Q," 114. Michael Goulder, one of the main champions of the Farrer-Goulder Hypothesis, echoed Wayment's sentiments that Q can be made to say anything, as is evident in the title of one of Michael D. Goulder's articles: "Is Q a Juggernaut?," *Journal of Biblical Literature* 115, no. 4 (1996): 667–81.

48. Strathearn and Judd, "Distinctive Testimonies," 77.

18

The Gospel of John

Eric D. Huntsman

The Gospel of John, often characterized as a Gospel written to and for those who already believed in Jesus Christ, stands apart in content and style from the three Synoptic Gospels (Matthew, Mark, and Luke). Sometimes referred to in scholarly circles as "The Fourth Gospel," it contains material not found in the others. Unlike Matthew and Luke, which follow the basic chronological and geographic progression of Mark that culminates in a single visit to Jerusalem, John portrays Jesus as traveling from Galilee to Jerusalem several times, suggesting a ministry of two or three years. Passing over miracles, parables, and sermons recorded in the Synoptics, John relates other powerful acts and teachings of Jesus that focus largely on his divine identity and mission.[1]

John also differs strikingly in style and approach. In terms of genre, as a "gospel," it is close to the Synoptics. Like them, it is an interesting combination of ancient biography, history, and theological reflection. Nevertheless, John also has much in common with classical drama.[2] Filled with dialogues and scenes that draw in the reader, it effectively paints characters that present models of different types of responses, positive and negative, to Jesus with which readers can identify.[3] This Gospel is also the most symbolic, teaching at many levels and rooting believers in every age more firmly in their faith. Above all, John's Christology— that is, how it portrays Jesus and his saving work—is more developed than that of the Synoptics. Whereas Mark demonstrates that Jesus is God's son by having the Father proclaim it at his baptism (Mark 1:11) and Matthew and Luke show that he was divinely conceived and miraculously born in their infancy narratives (Matthew 1–2; Luke 1–2), John reveals Jesus as the Divine Word who was together with God from the beginning (John 1:1). Throughout the text, John consistently portrays Jesus as a divine and majestic figure.

The Gospel according to John has long been appealing to Latter-day Saint readers because of its symbolism and high Christology, which are similar to that of the Book of Mormon and the revelations of Joseph Smith in the Doctrine and Covenants. Indeed, many of its images and ideas, and even some of its language, appear in other Restoration scripture, influencing the way we talk about important doctrinal concepts.[4] Many Latter-day Saints, however, are not familiar with the host of scholarly issues—such as questions concerning its authorship, compositional history, and thematic questions—surrounding the study of John. A deeper understanding of these issues will help us better interpret and apply the Fourth Gospel and be more appreciative of its symbolism, theology, and literary power.

The Beloved Disciple: Author or Source?

Like the other Gospels, the Gospel of John is formally anonymous, meaning that its text never directly identifies its author.[5] Such anonymity, which is different from the epistolary conventions of the New Testament letters, may seem particularly unusual to Latter-day Saint readers, who are accustomed to the regular self-designation of Book of Mormon authors. It was not unusual for other biblical books, however, especially those of the Old Testament. In the case of the Gospel of John, the original audience may have already known the author's identity, and perhaps he did not want to highlight his own role in a narrative intended to focus on the Savior. In addition, the name *John*, by which the Fourth Gospel is identified, never appears in the text except in reference to John the Baptist. Instead, our knowledge about the author—or perhaps the source behind the original author—is based on internal evidence from the text itself and from suggestions by early Christian authors in the post-apostolic period. While the compositional history of the Gospel of John may be more complicated than many readers are aware, the text has as its foundation the testimony of an important eyewitness of Jesus and his ministry.

Although the Fourth Gospel never identifies its author by name, it has more direct references to its ultimate source than do any of the Synoptic Gospels. An editorial addition at the very end of the Gospel maintains, "This is the disciple which *testifieth* of these things, and *wrote* these things: and we know that his testimony is true" (John 21:24; emphasis added). While this passage seems to suggest that this disciple was the author of the text, it could mean that he caused his witness to be written by a scribe or other intermediary. As biblical scholar Raymond Brown has emphasized, anciently there was often a difference between the *author* (from the Latin *auctor*, or "authority") and the actual *writer*.[6] Another possibility is that the disciple wrote his earlier recollections, which a final author or editor used to produce the text as we have it now. This testifying figure had been twice identified earlier in John 21 as the unnamed disciple "whom Jesus loved" (21:7, 20). The setting was a post-Resurrection appearance of the risen Lord to seven disciples at the Sea of Galilee. Three of these—Simon Peter, Thomas, and Nathanael—are directly named, two are described as the sons of Zebedee, and the remaining two are not identified. The Gospel of John never mentions either of the sons of Zebedee by name, though we know from the Synoptics that their names were James and John. Because James was martyred in AD 44, long before the Gospel was written, presumably either John or one of the two unnamed followers of Jesus was "the disciple whom Jesus loved."

This beloved disciple figure had previously appeared at the Last Supper (John 13:23) and at the foot of the cross (19:26), where he also bore record of the blood and water that flowed from Jesus's side after his death (19:24–25). If he had also been the unnamed disciple who accompanied Peter to Caiaphas's house after the arrest of Jesus (18:15–16), then he was a firsthand witness of many of the Savior's final hours in the second half of the Gospel.[7] This disciple was also with Peter when they heard from Mary Magdalene that Jesus's tomb was empty, and together the two apostles ran to see for themselves that Jesus's body was no longer there (20:2–10). Some scholars also identify the Beloved Disciple with the unnamed disciple of John the Baptist who, along with Andrew, was one of the first to begin following Jesus (1:35–40). Regardless, the first half of the Gospel bears many indications that it, too, came from an eyewitness,[8] and there are other indirect indications in the text that the source or author was a Jew from the Holy Land at the time of Jesus. These include his detailed knowledge of Jewish terms and customs and his accurate descriptions of the geography of the Holy Land and the city of Jerusalem.[9]

The Beloved Disciple—whether he was the actual writer or the original witness whose testimony lay behind the final text—is not the only unnamed figure in the Gospel of John. Other anonymous characters include the mother of Jesus (John 2:1–12; 19:25–27), the woman at the well in Samaria (John 4), and the man born blind (John 9). By not naming them, John allows them to serve not only as historical figures but also as literary types with whom readers can identify. The result is that this original witness not only serves as a type or representative for all disciples who come to know Jesus, but also allows us to compare ourselves to him, stressing that we, too, are loved by the Lord.[10]

Not surprisingly, several early Christian sources identified the apostle John as the author of the Fourth Gospel. John, along with Peter and James, was one of the Twelve whom the Synoptics portrayed as being closest to Jesus (see Mark 5:37; 9:2; 14:33; and parallels). In addition, John and Peter were associated together in Acts 3–4 and 8, much as the Beloved Disciple and Peter were in the final scene of John 21 and in earlier scenes such as 13:21–30 and 20:2–10. Irenaeus supported this identification in the mid-second century, writing, "John, the disciple of the Lord, who also had leaned upon his breast, did himself publish a Gospel during his residence at Ephesus in Asia."[11] Likewise, another early authority, Clement of Alexandria, wrote, "But, last of all, John, perceiving that the external facts had been made plain in the Gospel, being urged by his friends and inspired by the Spirit, composed a spiritual Gospel."[12]

On the other hand, Papias, another early Christian source, provided ambiguous evidence that we could read as suggesting that another early disciple, also named John but not the apostle, wrote the Fourth Gospel.[13] In addition to this "John the Elder," who might also be connected with 1 and 2 John, modern commentators have made a number of other suggestions for the Beloved Disciple. These range from Lazarus, Philip, and an unknown disciple (any of whom could have been one of the two unnamed and otherwise unidentified figures of John 21:2) to other candidates such as Nathanael, Thomas, Judas (not Iscariot), or John Mark.[14] While the conventional identification of John the son of Zebedee as the author has long remained the accepted one, some have noted that it might have been encouraged by the tendency to attribute Christian texts to apostolic authorship, real or putative, to give them more authority.[15] Others, however, have stressed that because such early Christian sources were relatively close to the time of the composition of the Gospels, these writers may well have preserved legitimate, well-known traditions regarding their authorship.[16] In this case, the identification of John as "the Beloved" is still a real possibility, one that Latter-day revelation and tradition support.

Compositional History and the Purpose of the Gospel

For various reasons, scholars see the text as having gone through several stages of development. Later editors may have thus reworked and revised the original witness, and perhaps even an early draft of the Gospel. Such theories of compositional history see the Beloved Disciple as an eyewitness who served as the original source for the Fourth Gospel. He either shared this orally with his own students or perhaps wrote an early draft, which a later author reworked. This Gospel, along with other texts attributed to John, such as the epistles that bear his name and perhaps the book of Revelation, may have received final editing as part of a collection of Johannine works.[17] Latter-day Saints can certainly understand how this kind of compositional history can occur, being familiar with how discourses such as those of King Benjamin or Amulek were recorded by others, collected with one set of records, and then finally abridged and edited by Mormon (see Mosiah 2–5; Alma 34).[18]

One indication of this compositional history is seen in the fact that all references to the Beloved Disciple are in the third person. While there are ancient parallels for authors referring to themselves impersonally in this way, it seems unlikely that an author who studiously avoided naming himself would regularly call himself "the disciple whom Jesus loved." Rather, this phrase might indicate a later editor's understanding of the relationship that the original "author" had with the Lord, or it might reflect the honor and affection the editor and the first audience felt for this witness. Additionally, for homiletic reasons the final editor may have decided to use the anonymous source as a type to represent all disciples who used the text to better love and be loved by Jesus.

Such compositional history helps to reconcile the conventional understanding that many Latter-day Saints have regarding the authorship of the Gospel of John with the observations that other scholars have made about the text. Early Latter-day Saints leaders accepted the tradition that the apostle John wrote the Fourth Gospel, and later authorities and commentators have generally accepted the traditional identification without much analysis.[19] This propensity is understandable because Latter-day revelations seem to confirm that

John wrote it (see Doctrine and Covenants 7; 77:1–15; 88:141; see also 1 Nephi 14:18–27 and Ether 4:16, which directly link the book of Revelation with John). In particular, Doctrine and Covenants 7:1–3, a revelation that seems to have been received because of a discussion that Joseph Smith and Oliver Cowdery had about the fate of the apostle John, directly equates John with the "the disciple whom Jesus loved" in John 21:20–23.[20]

Nevertheless, Joseph Smith's understanding of the apostle John's role in the Gospel of John is not in conflict with the proposition that John, as the Beloved Disciple, was the source but not necessarily the final author or editor of the text. In fact, the renaming of the Gospel of John in Joseph Smith's New Translation (popularly known as the Joseph Smith Translation or JST) to "The Testimony of St. John" accords rather well with the fact that this may be a text based upon an original source's witness.[21] As Frank Judd has described this possible scenario, "Unlike the Gospel of Mark, it is not the scribe or compiler who received the credit for authoring the Gospel of John. Instead, the apostolic eyewitness and source of the information received the credit."[22]

A staged compositional history also helps explain certain questions about the dating of the Gospel and the nature of its original and intended audiences. The developed theology of John and post-apostolic references to its composition combine to suggest that it was written later than the Synoptics. Scholars frequently suggest a date in the AD 90s, placing it between Luke, usually assumed to be the last of the Synoptics written, and the appearance of the earliest manuscript evidence for the text, which dates to the early second century. On the other hand, the lack of any reference to the destruction of Jerusalem in AD 70, present tense statements in the description of the pool of Bethesda in John 5:2, and the fact that it seems to be unaware of the other Gospels could be taken to suggest an earlier date of composition.[23] These two different views might be reconciled by suggesting that the original material from the Beloved Disciple, whether transmitted orally or in written form, took shape earlier but that the final edition that we now have dates to the end of the first century AD.

Similarly, such a compositional history can help resolve conflicting possibilities regarding the original audience of the Gospel of John. The stated purpose of this Gospel is broad: "And many other signs truly did Jesus in the presence of his disciples, which are not written in this book: but these are written, *that ye might believe that Jesus is the Christ, the Son of God*; and *that believing ye might have life through his name*" (20:30–31; emphasis added; compare 1:7). While this passage could have been written by a later editor, it nonetheless reflects very well the testimony that we would have expected from the apostle John or some other original witness of Jesus Christ. Still, many scholars have noted that certain episodes seem to reflect the situation of a particular Christian community in the late first century as much as they do the situation at the time of Jesus. One of the most frequently cited examples revolves around the story of the man blind from birth whom Jesus healed in John 9. Jesus's opponents in the Jewish leadership threatened him and his parents with being "put out of the synagogue" (9:22; compare 12:42; 16:2), something that many scholars feel might have been a sadly familiar experience to many Jewish Christians who were expelled from their synagogues later in the first century.

The resolution may be that the original source, and even the first author, had a simple, theological purpose for the text but the final editor tailored it for his audience, emphasizing and perhaps adapting descriptions to fit the situations that he and his readers faced. For a modern audience, however, perhaps a more important point is how we should interpret and apply the stated purpose of John 20:30–31 that readers "might believe that Jesus is the Christ, the Son of God." Because of the theological depth of the Fourth Gospel, commentators both within and without The Church of Jesus Christ of Latter-day Saints see John as a Gospel written for believers.[24] On the other hand, editorial asides and explanations seem to suggest that some readers did not know certain details of Jesus's ministry or some points of doctrine. Additionally, deep theological, almost philosophical, reflections might have been intended for educated non-Christian readers.

Interestingly, the textual evidence for the phrase "might believe" is divided. Some manuscripts read *pisteuēte*, a present subjunctive that means "continue to believe" or "keep believing," a reading that would suggest the text was meant to help readers deepen their faith. Others, however, read *pisteusēte*, an aorist subjunctive form that suggests beginning to believe or coming to faith.[25] Regardless of which reading best reflects the original, perhaps we should assume a broad audience for the Gospel. Like the Book of Mormon that was written for the Lamanites, the rest of the house of Israel, and the Gentiles—in effect, for everyone— the Gospel of John is a powerful testimony of Jesus Christ that can bring all readers to know that Jesus is the Son of God. Having faith in this, they can then lay hold of his great gift of eternal life.

Themes and Structure

The central purposes of the Gospel of John—to bring readers to a knowledge that Jesus is the Christ, the Son of God, and to help them have eternal life through his name—are reflected in two of its major emphases. The first is its high Christology, which shows that Jesus is the Divine Word made flesh and that as the Incarnate Word he always said and did the will of the Father. The second is an emphasis on the response of people to Jesus, particularly of the disciples who choose to follow him and believe in his name. While much of the "the world" rejects him, those who come to know him, either through the witness of others or their own encounters with him, are given the power to become the children of God, passing from spiritual death to life even while in the world (John 1:12; 3:16–17; 5:24; 10:10; 11:25–26). These emphases are frequently seen in dualistic terms as the Gospel presents its major themes such as life and death, light and darkness, spirit and flesh, the world above and the world below, truth and falsehood, and love and hatred. Such terms in John are also broader and more inclusive than the words sometimes mean otherwise. For instance, *life* does not just refer to biological functioning. Rather, it is the fuller, spiritual type of existence that believers can experience as they are waiting for eternal life in the next world. Likewise, *light* is more than what is visible from the sun or a fire; it represents spiritual truth, illumination, and the enlivening power of the Spirit.[26]

John's primary focus on Jesus and its secondary attention to believers unfolds in the structure of the Gospel as these themes are developed and applied. The Gospel is divided into four major parts (see table 1): a prologue (John 1:1–51); a major division focusing on the ministry of Jesus (2:1–11:57); another division focusing on Jesus's final week, culminating in his passion and resurrection (12:1–20:31); and an epilogue (21:1–25). The prologue is an introduction that first presents Jesus in cosmic and thematic terms and then provides the first template of how his disciples come to believe in and follow him. John first presents Jesus in what is often called the *Logos* Hymn (1:1–18), because *logos* is the Greek term for "word" as well as a wide semantic range of related concepts. Echoing the opening of the creation story when God brought forth first light and then all of creation by speaking (Genesis 1:3–2:3), John describes Jesus as the Word, representing God's will, plan, and intent as well as the means by which he communicates and interacts with his creation. Set "in the beginning," the *Logos* Hymn establishes that even before his birth, Jesus was with God, divine, and the source of light (1:1–5). Becoming flesh, the Word is rejected by many of his own people but accepted by his own creation, and those men and women who receive him become God's children by believing in his name (1:9–14). The hymn in some ways serves as an overture, introducing the Gospel's Christology and major themes. As such, it helps interpret the explication of these themes as they appear later in the text.[27]

Poetic whenever it speaks of the Word, the hymn also interweaves prosaic descriptions of the first witness of the light, the prophet John (1:6–8, 15), known as "the Baptist" in the Synoptics.[28] In the Fourth Gospel his primary role is to bear witness of the Word. After being introduced in the hymn, John is the first figure in the second part of the introduction (1:19–51), where he is the first in a chain of witnesses when he declares to two of his own followers that Jesus is the Lamb of God (1:29, 39). As they then go and find others who become Jesus's first disciples, they set the pattern that becomes the template for those who hear

Table 1. Outline of the Gospel of John

- Prologue (1:1–51)
  » *Logos* Hymn (1:1–18)
  » The first witnesses and disciples (1:19–51)
- Book of Signs (2:1–11:57)
  » First signs and dialogues (2:1–4:54)
  » Signs and discourses in the context of Jewish feasts (5:1–10:42)
  » The raising of Lazarus and its aftermath (11:1–57)
- Book of Glory (12:1–20:31)
  » Setting the scene for the Passion (12:1–12:50)
  » The Last Supper and the farewell discourses (13:1–17:26)
  » Crucifixion, death, and burial (18:1–19:42)
  » Resurrection (20:1–29)
  » Purpose of the Gospel (20:30–31)
- Epilogue (21:1–25)
  » Resurrection appearance to seven at the Sea of Galilee (21:1–15)
  » Jesus and Simon Peter (21:15–19)
  » The fate and testimony of the Beloved Disciple (21:20–25)

the testimony of another and then "come and see" (1:39) that Jesus is the Master, the Messiah or Christ, the Son of God, and the King of Israel.[29]

The first major division of the Gospel after its prologue chronicles Jesus's miraculous and symbolic acts as well as his conversations with individuals and his speeches before groups during the course of his ministry (2:1–11:57). This ministry lasts two or three years, depending on how many Passover festivals are mentioned (2:13, 6:4, and 11:55 refer specifically to Passover, but 5:1 refers to an unspecified feast often taken to be a Passover). Sometimes called "the Book of Signs" because of seven miraculous signs that Jesus performs in it, this section also contains seven discourses.[30] Both signs and discourses focus more on who Jesus is and simultaneously on individuals who either accept or reject him. The first signs and dialogues comprise a discrete unit, framed by miracles performed in the Galilean town of Cana (2:1–4:54). These all stress the theme of newness, particularly the new life that Jesus has come to bring. The next collection of signs and discourses occurs in the context of Jewish feasts, including the weekly festival of the Sabbath and the annual celebrations of Passover, Tabernacles, and Dedication (5:1–10:42). In this section, Jesus's actions and teachings reveal him as the fulfillment of the Jewish law and expectations. Finally, a dramatic episode centering on the death and raising of Jesus's friend Lazarus demonstrates that Jesus is the resurrection and the life, strengthening the faith of his followers even as this seventh miraculous sign rallies the Jerusalem establishment against him (11:1–57).

The Gospel's second major division is often called "The Book of Glory" because John frequently describes the saving death and resurrection of Jesus as the means by which he is both glorified and glorifies the Father.[31] The title is apt, especially for Latter-day Saint readers, because in Restoration scripture the Lord directly declares, "For behold, this is my work and my glory—to bring to pass the immortality and eternal life of man" (Moses 1:39). After setting the scene for the Passion with Mary of Bethany's anointing of Jesus and the triumphal entry (John 12:1–12:50), this section moves to an account of the Last Supper and Jesus's final discourses to his disciples (13:1–17:26). While recounting his last hours with his earthly friends, the scenes and words are profoundly intimate and draw in and also speak to modern believers. They are followed, however, by the strikingly painful scenes of Jesus's trial, crucifixion, death, and burial (18:1–19:42), which are ameliorated by his resurrection appearances, first to Mary Magdalene (20:11–18) and then to the eleven apostles (20:19–29). Each moves from grief to hope with the news of the empty tomb and then to joy with the witnesses of the risen Lord. Thomas, the last to gain this testimony, echoes the description of the Divine Word from the prologue with his own declaration, "My Lord and my God" (20:28).

The style of the epilogue (21:1–25) may suggest that it was a later addition; it certainly resumes a narrative that seemed to end with the programmatic statement of John 20:30–31. With its final resurrection appearance to seven disciples at the Sea of Galilee (21:1–14), it provides another witness to the reality of Jesus's rising. Jesus's loving dialogue with Peter not only provides the leader of the Twelve with a chance to proclaim his love three times after his earlier threefold denial, it also shifts the story of Jesus to the future of his church, which

Peter will lead and care for (21:15–19). The epilogue finally closes with a focus on the fate and testimony of the Beloved Disciple (21:20–25). Throughout the four parts of the Gospel and in each of their subsections, the Beloved Disciple's witness shines powerfully, showing Jesus as the source of life, light, and truth and encouraging readers to come to Christ and believe in his name.

The Divine Word Made Flesh

When the prologue declares, "And the Word was made flesh, and dwelt among us" (John 1:14), it connects Jesus with *YHWH*, or Jehovah, who had earlier dwelt with his people in the wilderness. This is done through the Greek term *eskēnōsen* (KJV "dwelt"), which literally means "pitched his tent" and recalls the ancient tabernacle in which Jehovah had dwelt after the Exodus. From that point on, John's portrayal of Jesus is that of Jehovah only thinly veiled in flesh as he walks and works among his people. He knows the will of the Father perfectly and knows all things even before they happen (3:11; 7:29; 8:55; 10:15; 13:1–3; 18:4; 19:28). Further, he knows all men and women, seeing into their hearts and knowing which have been given to him by God (5:42; 6:37–39; 17:9, 11, 24). He also rarely tires or acts like a normal man. In fact, when he gets tired and thirsty in John 4:6–7, it only seems to be a way for him to initiate his conversation with the Samaritan woman, and he never drinks the water she draws or eats the food that his disciples later offer him. Similarly, when he thirsts on the cross, he does so to fulfill the prophecy of Psalm 69:21 (John 19:28–29).

Perhaps the most revealing way in which John's text implies that Jesus is in fact Jehovah is through its use of what are called "I Am" statements. The Greek phrase *egō eimi* was used in the Septuagint, or Greek translation of the Old Testament, to render the phrase "I Am that I Am" (Hebrew, *'eyeh 'ašer 'eyeh*), by which Jehovah had identified himself to Moses (Exodus 3:14; compare Isaiah 43:25; 46:4; 51:12). It is also close to the root meaning of the name-title *YHWH*, which comes from the Hebrew verb *to be*. John's Gospel has Jesus use the phrase *egō eimi*, or "I am," more frequently than do the Synoptics. Often these are in predicated situations, that is, when Jesus says that he is *something*. While there is no other way to express this in Greek or English, in seven instances Jesus uses the expression to equate himself with a christological title or symbol, such as "I am the bread of life" (John 6:35) or

---

Table 2. "I AM" (egō eimi) Statements in John

- "I am the bread of life" (6:35, 41, 48)
- "I am the light of the world" (8:12)
- "I am the door of the sheep" (10:7, 9)
- "I am the good shepherd" (10:11, 14)
- "I am the resurrection and the life" (11:25)
- "I am the way, the truth, and the life" (14:6)
- "I am the true vine" (15:1)

Absolute "I AM" statements: 4:26; 6:20; 8:24, 28, 58; 13:19; and 18:5

"I am the good shepherd" (10:11, 14), that are reflective of his divine role (see table 2). More significantly, however, are seven absolute "I AM" sayings, where *egō eimi* appears without a predicate. While the King James Version sometimes provides the predicate *he*, yielding "I am he," these passages are better read as an appositive to the main clause. For instance, "I that speak unto thee am he" (4:26) can be read, "I AM, the one who speaks to you."[32]

Another important way that John stresses Jesus's divinity is through his statements that Jesus not only is the source of life for all mankind but also has power over life and death for himself: "Therefore doth my Father love me, because I lay down my life, that I might take it again. No man taketh it from me, but I lay it down of myself. I have power to lay it down, and I have power to take it again" (John 10:17–18). In accordance with the high Christology of John, Jesus in the Fourth Gospel carries his own cross all the way to Golgotha (19:17), not needing the help of Simon of Cyrene, and accomplishes the atoning sacrifice on his own. Unlike the Synoptics, which portray the Jewish leaders and the Romans as taking Jesus's life and the Father raising him from the dead, Jesus gives up his own life (19:30), and the disposition of his grave clothes in the Fourth Gospel's resurrection narrative (20:6–7) suggests that Jesus has taken it up again on his own.[33]

Signs and Discourses

Jesus's divinity is revealed throughout the Fourth Gospel in his actions and his words. Both his miracles and many of his symbolic actions are "signs" (Greek, *sēmeia*) that symbolize who he is and what he came to do. Likewise, even the way he speaks reveals his divinity and focuses on his mission.[34] The most common Greek word in the Synoptics for "miracle" is *dynamis*, or "mighty deed," indicating the great thing he does for those whom he blesses. On the other hand, the narrator of this Gospel consistently uses the word *sēmeion*. Although this word is usually translated simply as "miracle" in our King James Version, the Greek word choice emphasizes that in the Fourth Gospel the miracles are primarily signs that reveal something about Jesus himself.

John records far fewer miracles than the Synoptics, with seven in the first major section of his gospel, the Book of Signs (see table 3), and a final sign, the miraculous catch of 153 fish, in the epilogue. However, each is significant for what it reveals about Jesus. The changing of water into wine at the wedding at Cana (John 2:1–11) is more than just a miracle of provision. Instead, it reveals Jesus as Jehovah. Just as the Divine Word had first created, or

---

Table 3. Seven Miraculous Signs in John

- Water to wine (2:1–11)
- Healing the nobleman's son (4:46–54)
- Healing the man at the pool of Bethesda (5:1–18)
- Feeding the five thousand (6:1–15)
- Walking on water (6:1–15)
- Healing the man born blind (9:1–41)
- The raising of Lazarus (11:38–44)

organized, the world, the Incarnate Word reorganizes. Establishing this correspondence, the healings of the nobleman's son (4:46–54), the man at the pool of Bethesda (5:1–18), and the man born blind (9:1–41) can be seen as acts of divine reorganization, restoring infirm bodies to their correct, whole state. Yet the symbolism is often even deeper. Because of the symbolic correspondence in this Gospel of water to divinity and spirit on the one hand and wine and blood to mortality on the other, the changing of water to wine can also be seen as a symbol of the incarnation as the Divine Word becomes the man Jesus. Similarly, the infirm healed by Jesus can be types of fallen men and women, making Jesus's restoration of them symbols of his atoning work. In John, the feeding of the five thousand (6:1–15) and Jesus's walking on water (6:16–21) are directly connected to the first Passover and the Exodus, revealing him as Jehovah who parted the Red Sea and fed his people with manna. Now, as Jesus, he can feed us (temporally and spiritually) and still the storms in our lives. The seventh and crowning miracle in the Book of Signs is the raising of Lazarus (11:38–44), showing not only Jesus's power over death but foreshadowing his own resurrection and the ability to raise all of us from spiritual as well as physical death.[35]

Some of Jesus's nonmiraculous acts can also be seen as signs. For instance, the cleansing of the temple, which occurs earlier in Jesus's ministry in John than it does in the Synoptics, is less about the temple than it is a foreshadowing of the death of Jesus's body (John 2:13–22). After this episode, some Jews in Jerusalem begin to believe in Jesus "when they saw the miracles [Greek *sēmeia*] which he did" (2:23). Likewise, Nicodemus may have had this action in mind as well when he said, "We know that thou art a teacher come from God: for no man can do these miracles [*sēmeia*] that thou doest, except God be with him" (3:2). Such figurative actions are similar to some of the symbolic performances of prophets such as Isaiah and Ezekiel (see, for example, Isaiah 20:26; Ezekiel 3:1–4; 4:9–17; 24:15–27), suggesting some other actions, either performed by Jesus or performed for him, are what we could call "enacted signs."[36] These could include the anointing of his feet by Mary of Bethany (John 12:3–8), the triumphal entry (12:12–16), Jesus's washing the feet of his disciples (13:4–17), and his being lifted upon the cross itself (3:14; 8:28; 12:32; 19:16–37).

The words of Jesus in John also differ in style, and often in focus, from those recorded by the Synoptics. As the Incarnate Word, Jesus speaks differently than mortals, using what biblical scholar Raymond Brown describes as a semipoetic divine speech, which his listeners often misunderstand, perhaps reflecting that the words of God can be understood only by the Spirit.[37] Whereas Mark primarily preserved parables and short teaching sayings, to which Matthew and Luke added longer sermons, John presents long discourses of Jesus, seven in the Book of Signs, and the Farewell Discourses to his disciples in the Book of Glory (see table 4). The first of Jesus's speeches, the Discourse on the New Birth (3:1–15) and the Discourse on the Water of Life (4:7–26), are set as dialogues with Nicodemus and a woman from Samaria. As such, they present very personal interactions and conversations with Jesus that readers can identify with. Framed by the signs of the new wine at the wedding at Cana and the newly healed nobleman's son, being born from above (Greek *anōthen*; KJV "again")

Table 4. Seven Discourses in John

- The New Birth (3:1–15)
- The Water of Life (4:7–26)
- The Divine Son (5:17–47)
- The Bread of Life (6:35–58)
- The Life-Giving Spirit (7:16–52)
- The Light of the World (8:12–59)
- The Good Shepherd (10:1–18)

Also, the Farewell Discourses (14:1–16:33), the Intercessory Prayer (17:1–26), and the final dialogue with Peter (21:15–19)

in John 3:3 and the water springing up to everlasting life in 4:14 both symbolize the eternal life that Jesus came to bring.

Jesus delivers his other discourses in the Book of Signs to groups of people. The Discourses on the Divine Son (5:17–47), the Life-Giving Spirit (7:16–52), the Light of the World (8:12–59), and the Good Shepherd (10:1–18) were delivered in Jerusalem, often to hostile crowds, to whom he nonetheless boldly declared who he was and what he had come to do. Jesus gave the Bread of Life Discourse (6:35–58) in Galilee to a mixed group. Jesus first addressed this discourse to the crowds who had recently seen the miracle of the feeding of the five thousand, describing himself as the Divine Word come down from heaven, which represented both the manna and the law that God had given the Israelites in the wilderness. He then spoke more specifically to "the Jews," which John frequently used as a term for the religious elite who were often at odds with Jesus.[38] To this group, who should have better understood the symbolism he was using, he declared why it was necessary for people to symbolically eat his flesh and drink his blood in order to obtain eternal life. Finally, after some of his own disciples stopped following him because of this "hard saying" (6:60), he spoke with Peter and the Twelve, who confessed their faith, declaring that he had words of eternal life and that they believed that he was the Christ, the Son of the living God (6:68–69).

Discipleship in John

Another major emphasis of the Fourth Gospel, how people respond to Jesus, is seen in the reaction of people to his signs and discourses. Although groups of people, including disappointed crowds and the religious leadership opposed to Jesus, often rejected him, by and large the Gospel of John focuses on individual responses to Jesus. These are the ones who, picking up a theme established in the prologue, receive him and believe on his name (John 1:14). This individual focus explains John's emphasis on discipleship. In the ancient world, discipleship was not only about learning from a teacher; it was also about striving to become like a master. In the other Gospels, the primary model of discipleship is usually the Twelve. John, on the other hand, refers to the Twelve only a few times. He never provides a full list of the Twelve, and the word *apostle* does not occur in the English translation of this Gospel at all (the Greek word *apostolos* does appear in John 13:16, where it is used in such a nontechnical sense that the KJV simply renders it "he that is sent"). Andrew, Simon Peter, and Philip appear in 1:19–51 as individuals coming to Christ. Each of these apostles appears later, as do Thomas and the two Judases, but the Twelve only appear explicitly as a group at the end of the Bread of Life Discourse, at the Last Supper and the following Farewell Discourses, and, minus Judas, in the Upper Room after Jesus's resurrection (John 6:67, 70; 13:18; 15:16, 19; 20:19–29).

The result is that rather than being limited to a smaller group of chosen special witnesses, discipleship appears more broadly as something with which all readers can identify.[39] To this end, the Gospel of John develops a number of other, non-apostolic disciples, such as Lazarus, Martha, Mary, and perhaps Nathanael, who, although he is often associated with the Synoptic figure of Bartholomew, is presented differently in John. The variety of characters and the different trajectories of their walks with Jesus make them valuable models for readers today. Most of the characters in John are presented as encountering Jesus and then needing to make a faith-decision as to whether and how to follow him.[40] Andrew, for instance, was already an earnest believer who readily followed Jesus when he received the witness of another. Nicodemus, well-to-do and well educated, first struggled to understand and accept Jesus but seems to have accepted him in his death. The Samaritan woman was an outsider with a questionable past who was nonetheless open to the truth. Peter and Thomas were devoted but impulsive disciples: at times each slipped or questioned, but both went on to have great faith. Martha and Mary were devoted friends of the Lord whose faith was tested at a time of great loss.[41] These and other characters can serve as different models for discipleship, but perhaps the most significant is the Beloved Disciple himself. This figure never wavers in his devotion and was a witness of some of the most pivotal moments in the narrative: he leans on Jesus's bosom at the Last Supper, stands at the foot of the cross, and runs to find the empty tomb (John 13:23; 19:26; 20:1–8).

The Lamb of God

The declaration of John the Baptist that Jesus is the Lamb of God (John 1:29, 36) provides one of the central themes of the second major division of the Fourth Gospel, the Book of Glory. This association of Jesus with the Passover lamb explains many of the unique features of the Passion narrative in John that differ from the versions presented by the Synoptics. First, it helps explain differences in the timing of the Last Supper and the Crucifixion. Whereas the Synoptics portray the Last Supper as a Passover meal (Matthew 26:17–20; Mark 14:12–17; Luke 22:1, 7–14), in John the festival began at sunset *after* Jesus died on the cross (John 18:28; 19:31, in which the preparation day was likely the day when the Passover was prepared). Reconciling John with the Synoptics on this matter is not easy. One possibility is that the Synoptics are correct but John moved the Passover to the next evening for literary reasons so that Jesus's death on the cross was taking place even as the paschal lambs were being sacrificed in the temple. On the other hand, John's version bears more historical verisimilitude, since it was unlikely that an arrest, trial, and execution would have taken place during the festival itself, something that the Jewish leaders had explicitly said they wanted to avoid (Mark 14:2; parallel Matthew 26:5). In this case, perhaps the Synoptics had moved the timing of the Passover to underscore the feast's similarity with the sacrament, the institution of which they record but John does not. A third possibility is that Passover actually occurred after the Crucifixion but Jesus, knowing he would be dead before it was celebrated, held a symbolic Passover meal with his friends a day early.[42] Instead of the institution of the sacrament, the Gospel of John includes an account of the washing of the disciples' feet (13:3–17).

Paschal imagery and the high Christology of John may also explain other differences in the Fourth Gospel's Passion narrative, which lacks any reference to Jesus's suffering in the Garden of Gethsemane and provides different details about the Crucifixion. This may be because the Passover lamb was not primarily a vicarious sin offering but rather a sacrifice that brought the hope of new life to the children of Israel, who were passed over by the angel of death because of the lamb's blood. Perhaps rather than seeing Jesus shoulder the crushing burden of sin in Gethsemane and carry it to the cross, where he died as a vicarious sacrifice for sin, John focused on Jesus's death as a source of life. Passing over reference to Jesus's feeling abandoned by the Father, with whom he is always at one with in John, this account has Jesus declare "It is finished" and voluntarily "g[i]ve up the ghost" (John 19:30). Then, just as the blood of the paschal lambs was spread on the doorframes of the Israelites in Egypt, so the blood of the Lamb of God pours on the wood of the cross when a soldier pierces Jesus's side with a spear to make sure he is dead. Linked with the blood is a stream of water (19:34), recalling the fountain of living water of John 4:10 and the rivers of living water of John 7:38. To complete the Passover imagery, John 19:36–37 stresses that the soldiers did not break Jesus's legs, a requirement of the paschal lamb being that none of its bones could be broken.[43]

With Jesus's death on the cross, Nicodemus, who was confused by his first encounter with Jesus (3:1–15) and timid in his support for Jesus in a later meeting of the Jewish leadership (7:45–53), came out in the open after the Crucifixion to help Joseph of Arimathea bury Jesus (19:38–42). At last recognizing the Lamb of God as the King of Israel, he brought a royal weight of spices to honor Jesus. Through this action he seems to have at last understood the sign that Jesus had prophesied to him at their first meeting: "And as Moses lifted up the serpent in the wilderness, even so must the Son of man be lifted up: That whosoever believeth in him should not perish, but have eternal life" (3:14–15).

Abundant and Eternal Life

The paschal emphasis on escaping death and obtaining new life picks up the theme that was established in the prologue: "In him was life" (John 1:4). Indeed, one of the most famous and beautiful passages of the Gospel of John is the witness that "God so loved the world, that he gave his only begotten Son, that whosoever believeth in him should not perish, but have everlasting life. For God sent not his Son into the world to condemn the world; but that the world through him might be saved" (3:16–17). As with many of the themes in the Gospel of John, life is a broad concept, referring to biological activity, the nature of life in this world, and the promise of eternal life in the world to come. In his Discourse on the Good Shepherd, Jesus had testified, "I am come that they might have life, and that they might have it more abundantly" (10:10). Meaning "to an extent remarkable or extraordinary," *abundantly* (Greek *perisson*) refers to a richer, deeper life such as that suggested by the good wine of Cana, the living water of Samaria, or the flowing rivers promised by Jesus. It suggests a spiritual quality of life here on the earth that anticipates the everlasting life promised by the death and resurrection of Jesus.

In John, Jesus stresses that such life is available here and now, a concept called realized eschatology. Eschatology is literally the "study of the end," and usually eschatology is future, referring to the blessed state that will accompany the end of the world and the advent of God's kingdom. Yet Jesus at times speaks of our future state as if it can be realized now. For instance, in his Discourse on the Divine Son he declares, "Verily, verily, I say unto you, He that heareth my word, and believeth on him that sent me, *hath everlasting life*, and shall not come into condemnation; but *is passed* from death unto life" (5:24; emphasis added). By using present and present perfect tenses here, he suggests that believers have eternal life and have passed from death to life now. Similarly, in his famous declaration to Martha that he is the resurrection and the life, Jesus says, "Whosoever liveth and believeth in me shall never die" (11:26). Because many believers in Jesus die (indeed, Martha's brother Lazarus has just died), the suggestion seems to be that the death Jesus is talking about is spiritual death, making the raising of Lazarus that follows this scene as much a symbol of the spiritual rebirth of people who come to Christ as it is an anticipation of a future resurrection.[44]

Of course, in John, Jesus teaches future eschatology also, as when he spoke of the coming day when "all that are in the graves shall hear his voice, and shall come forth; they that have done good, unto the resurrection of life; and they that have done evil, unto the resurrection of damnation" (5:28–29). Yet eternal life is more than just the immortal, never-ending life that follows the Resurrection. As Latter-day Saint doctrine teaches, it is having the kind of life that God and Christ have in their presence for eternity, for "this is life eternal, that they might know thee the only true God, and Jesus Christ, whom thou hast sent" (17:3).

⁓

Eric D. Huntsman is a professor in the Department of Ancient Scripture and the coordinator of the Ancient Near Eastern Studies Program at Brigham Young University.

Further Reading

Bauckham, Richard. *Gospel of Glory: Major Themes in Johannine Theology.* Grand Rapids, MI: Baker Academic, 2015.

Blomberg, Craig L. *The Historical Reliability of John's Gospel: Issues and Commentary.* Downer's Grove, IL: InterVarsity, 2001.

Brown, Raymond E. *An Introduction to the Gospel of John.* Edited by Franic J. Moloney. New York: Doubleday, 2003.

Culpepper, R. Alan. *John, The Son of Zebedee: The Life of a Legend*. Minneapolis: Fortress, 2000.

Edwards, Ruth B. *Discovering John: Content, Interpretation, Reception*. Grand Rapids, MI: Eerdmans, 2015.

Griggs, C. Wilfred. "The Testimony of John." In *The Gospels*, edited by Kent P. Jackson and Robert L. Millet, 109–26. Vol. 5 of *Studies in Scriptures*. Salt Lake City: Deseret Book, 1986.

Huntsman, Eric D. "'And the Word Was Made Flesh': A Latter-day Saint Exegesis of the Blood and Water Imagery in the Gospel of John." *Studies in the Bible and Antiquity* 1 (2009): 51–65.

———. *Becoming the Beloved Disciple: Coming to Christ through the Gospel of John*. Springville, UT: Cedar Fort, 2018.

———. "The Lamb of God: Unique Aspects of the Passion Narrative in John." In *"Behold the Lamb of God": An Easter Celebration*, edited by Richard Neitzel Holzapfel, Frank F. Judd Jr., and Thomas A. Wayment, 49–70. Provo, UT: Religious Studies Center, Brigham Young University, 2008.

Koester, Craig R. *Symbolism in the Fourth Gospel: Meaning, Mystery, and Community*. Minneapolis: Fortress, 2003.

Morris, Leon. *The Gospel according to John*. Revised edition. Grand Rapids, MI: Eerdmans, 1995.

Skinner, Christopher W. *Reading John*. Eugene, OR: Cascade Books, 2015.

Notes

1. Leon Morris, *The Gospel according to John*, rev. ed. (Grand Rapids, MI: Eerdmans, 1995), 43–45; Craig L. Blomberg, *The Historical Reliability of John's Gospel: Issues and Commentary* (Downer's Grove, IL: InterVarsity, 2001), 19, 53–56; Raymond E. Brown, *An Introduction to the Gospel of John*, ed. Francis J. Moloney (New York: Doubleday, 2003), 90–104; and Richard Bauckham, *Gospel of Glory: Major Themes in Johannine Theology* (Grand Rapids, MI: Baker Academic, 2015), 185–201.

2. Brown, *Introduction to the Gospel of John*, 284–91; Blomberg, *Historical Reliability of John's Gospel*, 20, 57–61; and Richard Bauckham, *The Testimony of the Beloved Disciple* (Grand Rapids, MI: Baker Academic, 2007), 16–21.

3. Colleen M. Conway, *Men and Women in the Fourth Gospel: Gender and Johannine Characterization* (Atlanta: Society of Biblical Literature, 1999), 42–45; Christopher W. Skinner, *Characters and Characterization in the Gospel of John* (Bloomsbury, IL: Bloomsbury T&T Clark, 2013), xvii–xxxii; and Eric D. Huntsman, *Becoming the Beloved Disciple: Coming unto Christ through the Gospel of John* (Springville, UT: Cedar Fort, 2018), 8-12 and passim.

4. For instance, see Blake T. Ostler, "The Development of the Mormon Concept of Grace," *Dialogue* 24, no. 1 (1991): 57–84; Eric D. Huntsman, "The King James Bible and the Doctrine and Covenants," in *The King James Bible and the Restoration*, ed. Kent P. Jackson (Salt Lake City: Deseret Book, 2011), 182–96; and Nicholas J. Frederick, "Line within Line: An Intertextual Analysis of Mormon Scripture and the Prologue of the Gospel of John" (PhD diss., Claremont Graduate School, 2013).

5. See Frank F. Judd Jr., "Who Really Wrote the Gospels? A Study of Traditional Authorship," in *How the New Testament Came to Be*, ed. Kent P. Jackson and Frank F. Judd Jr. (Provo, UT: Religious Studies Center, Brigham Young University; Salt Lake City: Deseret Book, 2006), 123–40.

6. Raymond E. Brown, *The Gospel according to John*, vol. 29, Anchor Bible Series (New York: Doubleday, 1966), lxxxvii. See also Richard Bauckham, *Jesus and the Eyewitnesses: The Gospels as Eyewitness Testimony* (Grand Rapids, MI: Eerdmans, 2006), 358–63.

7. R. Alan Culpepper, *John, the Son of Zebedee: The Life of a Legend* (Minneapolis: Fortress, 2000), 56–72.

8. Brown, *Gospel according to John*, xcii–xciv; Morris, *Gospel according to John*, 10–12; Bauckham, *Jesus and the Eyewitnesses*, 127–29, 390–93, 402; and Cornelis Bennema, *Encountering Jesus: Character Studies in the Gospel of John* (Milton Keynes: Paternoster, 2009), 299–30.

9. Brown, *Introduction to the Gospel of John*, 200–201; Morris, *Gospel according to John*, 8–10; and Blomberg, *Historical Reliability of John's Gospel*, 27–28.

10. David Beck, "The Narrative Function of Anonymity in the Fourth Gospel," *Semeia* 63 (1993): 153–55; Richard Holzapfel, Eric D. Huntsman, and Thomas A. Wayment, *Jesus Christ and the World of the New Testament* (Salt Lake City: Deseret Book, 2006), 126–27; Huntsman, *Becoming the Beloved Disciple*, 8–12; and Huntsman, "John: The Disciple Whom Jesus Loved," *Ensign*, January 2019, 18–23.

11. Irenaeus, *Against Heresies* 3.1.1; see also 2.22.5 and 3.3.4.

12. Quoted in Eusebius, *History of the Church* 6.14.7.

13. Bauckham, *Jesus and the Eyewitnesses*, 420–23.

14. Culpepper, *John, The Son of Zebedee*, 72–85; and Ruth B. Edwards, *Discovering John: Content, Interpretation, Reception* (Grand Rapids, MI: Eerdmans, 2015), 25–32.

15. Blomberg, *Historical Reliability of John's Gospel*, 37–40; Brown, *Introduction to the New Testament*, 10–11; and Edwards, *Discovering John*, 49–53.

16. Bauckham, *Jesus and the Eyewitnesses*, 264–318.

17. Brown, *Introduction to the Gospel of John*, 62–78.

18. Holzapfel, Huntsman, and Wayment, *Jesus Christ and the World of the New Testament*, 128.

19. See, for instance, C. Wilfred Griggs, "The Testimony of John," in *The Gospels*, ed. Kent P. Jackson and Robert L. Millet, vol. 5, *Studies in Scripture* (Salt Lake City: Deseret Book, 1986), 109–11; John D. Claybaugh, "What the Latter-day Scriptures Teach about John the Beloved," in *The Testimony of John the Beloved: The 27th Annual Sidney B. Sperry Symposium* (Salt Lake City: Deseret Book, 1998), 16–20; and Brian L. Smith, "The Witness of John," in *The Testimony of John the Beloved*, 266–67.

20. See Frank F. Judd Jr. and Terry L. Szink, "John the Beloved in Latter-day Scripture (Doctrine and Covenants 7)," *The Doctrine and Covenants, Revelations in Context,* ed. Andrew H. Hedges, J. Spencer Fluhman, and Alonzo L. Gaskill (Provo, UT: Religious Studies Center, Brigham Young University, 2008), 90–107.

21. Significantly, though printed Latter-day Saint editions of the KJV Bible note that *Gospel* should be changed to *Testimony* for all four Gospels, the actual JST manuscripts do so only for Matthew and John. See Scott H. Faurling, Kent P. Jackson, and Robert J, Matthews, eds., *Joseph Smith's New Translation of the Bible: Original Manuscripts* (Provo, UT: Religious Studies Center, Brigham Young University, 2004), 234; and Kevin L. Barney, "The Joseph Smith Translation and Ancient Texts of the Bible," *Dialogue* 19, no. 3 (Fall 1986): 88. This could support the idea that these were in fact "apostolic testimonies" or, as I have suggested here, literary texts based on apostolic testimonies.

22. Judd, "Who Really Wrote the Gospels?," 134.

23. Griggs, "Testimony of John," 111; Brown, *Introduction to the Gospel of John*, 206–15; and Blomberg, *Historical Reliability of John's Gospel*, 42–44;

24. The Latter-day Saint Bible Dictionary, for instance, maintains, "[John wrote] to members of the Church who already had basic information about the Lord. His primary purpose was to emphasize the divine nature of Jesus as the Only Begotten Son of God in the flesh" (s.v. "Gospels," 683), and Raymond Brown in his Anchor Bible commentary wrote, "This is a Gospel designed to root the believer deeper in his faith" (*Gospel of John*, lxxviii).

25. Bruce R. Metzger, *A Textual Commentary on the Greek New Testament*, 2nd ed. (Stuttgart: German Bible Society, 1994), 219–20. See Blomberg, *Historical Reliability of John's Gospel*, 62–63.

26. Craig R. Koester, *Symbolism in the Fourth Gospel*, 2nd ed. (Minneapolis: Fortress, 2003), 141–43, 171–74; and Bauckham, *Gospel of Glory*, 119–29.

27. Christopher W. Skinner, *Reading John* (Eugene, OR: Cascade Books, 2015), 8–31.

28. Huntsman, *Becoming the Beloved Disciple*, 132–34.

29. Huntsman, *Becoming the Beloved Disciple*, 16–25.

30. Brown, *Introduction to the Gospel of John*, 300–307; and Edwards, *Discovering John*, 170–71.

31. Brown, *Introduction to the Gospel of John*, 307–15; and Edwards, *Discovering John*, 171.

32. Bauckham, *Testimony of the Beloved Disciple*, 243–50; Bauckham, *Gospel of Glory*, 195; and Skinner, *Reading John*, 70–78.

33. Eric D. Huntsman, "The Lamb of God: Unique Aspects of the Passion Narrative in John," in *"Behold the Lamb of God": An Easter Celebration*, ed. Richard Neitzel Holzapfel, Frank F. Judd Jr., and Thomas A. Wayment (Provo, UT: Religious Studies Center, Brigham Young University, 2008), 60–62.

34. Eric D. Huntsman, "Jesus on Jesus: John 5 and 7," in *Perspectives in Mormon Theology: Scriptural Theology*, ed. James E. Faulconer and Joseph M. Spencer (Salt Lake City: Greg Kofford Books, 2015), 69–80.

35. Eric D. Huntsman, *The Miracles of Jesus* (Salt Lake City: Deseret Book, 2014), 3, 15–25, 52–55, 96–100, 112–18, 135–36.

36. Koester, *Symbolism in the Fourth Gospel*, 79–82, 127–34.

37. Brown, *Introduction to the Gospel of John*, 284–92. See also Skinner, *Reading John*, 68–95.

38. For a discussion of John's use of the expression "the Jews" (Greek *hoi Ioudaioi*), see Huntsman, *Becoming the Beloved Disciple*, 41–42, 78, 86–87n13.

39. Huntsman, *Becoming the Beloved Disciple*, 5–8.

40. Bennema, *Encountering Jesus*, 103.

41. Huntsman, *Becoming the Beloved the Disciple*, 53–65, 89–100, 106–19.

42. Huntsman, "Lamb of God," 54–56.

43. Huntsman, "Lamb of God," 59–64.

44. Huntsman, *Miracles of Jesus*, 115–17; and Huntsman, *Becoming the Beloved Disciple*, 93, 101.

19

Noncanonical Gospels

Jason R. Combs

As a young BYU undergraduate majoring in ancient Near Eastern studies, I was fascinated with extrabiblical texts. My initial fascination was born out of the teachings of The Church of Jesus Christ of Latter-day Saints that more scripture is yet to come (2 Nephi 29:12–13; Articles of Faith 1:9) and that truth can be found in a noncanonical text (Doctrine and Covenants 91:1). When I discovered that these texts were called *apocryphal*, from the Greek word for "hidden" or "secret," my interest grew all the more. What Latter-day Saint wouldn't want to read a secret ancient text about Jesus? And if there is evidence within such a text that would support the idiosyncrasies of contemporary Latter-day Saint beliefs and practices, I thought, all the better! What I did not realize at the time was that the importance of these texts lay outside their ostensible parallels to our current beliefs and practices. I also did not realize that these "hidden" texts number in the hundreds and that most are readily available in English translation.[1]

This chapter will show how the apocryphal gospels provide us with unique insight into the world of early Christians. In particular, we will see that some Christians were not content with the four Gospels that would eventually become part of our New Testament. As Christianity developed and faced new challenges, some imaginative Christians wrote new gospels to deal with those challenges or to present new theological understandings of Christ. Before I introduce some of the important apocryphal gospels, however, it may be helpful to discuss the terminology used to describe noncanonical texts and to review the history of Latter-day Saint engagement with these texts.

Key Terminology

Noncanonical, extracanonical, apocryphal, and *pseudepigraphal* are all terms used to describe texts written by Jews and Christians that include some of the same people, places, themes, and genres of the Bible but are not included in our Bible today. Yet none of these terms is perfect, and each one can be misleading if not properly understood. The terms *noncanonical* and *extracanonical* designate texts existing outside the authoritative books, or canon, of Christian scripture (Latter-day Saints prefer the term *standard works*). So it would make sense for Latter-day Saints, Protestants, or Roman Catholics, for instance, to refer to 1 Enoch or Jubilees as noncanonical since they do not appear in the editions of the Old Testament embraced by those faiths. We instantly realize how imprecise the designation "noncanonical" is when we discover that the Ethiopian Orthodox Church includes 1 Enoch and Jubilees in their Old Testament canon.

What's more, at the time that many extracanonical texts were written, the canon we know today did not exist. Christians, at least as early as the second century AD, began to develop traditions around the proper use of texts; certain books were accepted for public use and others for private use.[2] Yet strict practices distinguishing between authoritative and unauthoritative texts—that is, between canonical and noncanonical—continued to develop well into the fourth century and beyond (see chapter 43 herein on canonization).[3] In the first century AD, for instance, the New Testament book of Jude quotes as authoritative—as if it were canon—a noncanonical tradition about Moses (Jude 1:9) and the noncanonical book of 1 Enoch (see Jude 1:14–15, quoting 1 Enoch 1:9). A list of canonical books from perhaps as early as the late second century AD, called the Muratorian Fragment, includes the Apocalypse of Peter in addition to the Apocalypse of John (Revelation) as authoritative, though it acknowledges that "some of us are not willing that the [Apocalypse of Peter] be read in church."[4] The term *noncanonical* is therefore anachronistic.

The terms *apocryphal* and *pseudepigraphal* are also used to describe extracanonical literature. The English word *pseudepigrapha* (singular, pseudepigraphon) comes from the Greek adjective *pseudēs* (ψευδής) meaning "false" and the noun *epigraphē* (ἐπιγραφή) meaning "title" or "ascription"; it designates a text that is falsely titled or ascribed to someone who did not write it. And the English word *apocrypha* (singular, apocryphon) comes from the Greek adjective *apocryphos* (ἀπόκρυφος), which means "hidden" or "secret." This term was used in a positive way by some Christians in antiquity to describe special esoteric teachings. For instance, one noncanonical text is titled Apocryphon of John or Secret Teaching of John. Other Christians, however, used the term *apocrypha* pejoratively to describe texts they considered dangerous. For instance, Irenaeus of Lyons, a late second-century Christian, describes texts he deems heretical as "an untold multitude of apocryphal and spurious writings, which they [heretics] have composed to bewilder foolish men and such as do not understand the letters of Truth."[5]

Today it has become common to distinguish between noncanonical texts relating to the Old Testament and those relating to the New Testament by labeling the former as "Old Testament Pseudepigrapha" and the latter as "New Testament Apocrypha." This distinction is artificial and somewhat imprecise because most of the New Testament Apocrypha are also pseudepigraphal, or falsely ascribed. For instance, the correspondence between Paul and the Roman philosopher Seneca was written by neither Paul nor Seneca. Yet the author writes as if he were both of them.[6] Regardless, in this chapter I follow the standard practice of referring to collections of texts that incorporate New Testament figures and narratives as New Testament Apocrypha.

One more distinction must be made about the term *apocrypha*. The New Testament Apocrypha should not be confused with the collection of texts found in some Bibles, often between the Old and New Testaments, labeled "Apocrypha" or "Deuterocanon." The biblical collection called the Apocrypha includes such books as Tobit, Judith, Wisdom of Ben Sira (Ecclesiasticus), 1 and 2 Maccabees, and additions to the biblical book of Daniel. These are Jewish works mostly written in the centuries after the Old Testament books had been completed and prior to the birth of Jesus. Since these texts have more in common with the Old Testament than the New Testament, some of them also appear in collections of the Old Testament Pseudepigrapha. What set them apart originally from the rest of the Old Testament was their language: whereas the Old Testament was written predominantly in Hebrew, the books of the Apocrypha were written mostly in Greek.[7] Since the Old Testament used by most early Christians was entirely Greek, those texts that now form the Apocrypha were used by some early Christians as authoritative scripture. As Tony Burke notes in his introduction to New Testament Apocrypha, "It wasn't until the early sixteenth century that a Bible was printed that was arranged [in such a way] that the books set apart from the Old and New Testaments acquired the name 'Apocrypha.' The influential King James Version followed suit, but most modern Protestant Bibles omit the texts entirely."[8] Today the Apocrypha appears primarily in Roman Catholic and Greek Orthodox Bibles and is labeled "Deuterocanonical" to designate it as a secondary (*deutero-*) canon of scripture.[9]

History of Latter-day Saint Engagement with Apocryphal Texts

In the twentieth century, Latter-day Saint engagement with apocryphal texts focused on ancient parallels to the idiosyncrasies of modern beliefs. For instance, BYU professor Hugh Nibley began his book *The Message of the Joseph Smith Papyri* by suggesting, "There are countless parallels, many of them very instructive, among the customs and religions of mankind, to what the Mormons do."[10] In particular, he argued, "the Near East . . . is littered with the archaeological and living survivals of practices and teachings which an observant Mormon may find suggestively familiar."[11] For Nibley, noncanonical texts were not to receive the same standing as the standard works; there exists a "world of difference between [them]."[12] He insisted that extracanonical texts were merely pale imitations of the truth.[13] Nevertheless, Nibley believed that ancient parallels to the contemporary scripture, theology, and practice of The Church of Jesus Christ of Latter-day Saints could be instructive for Latter-day Saints today.[14] Other Latter-day Saint authors went further with the identification of ancient parallels and argued that these in fact demonstrated the veracity of modern beliefs.[15]

Mining ancient texts for parallels to the modern beliefs and practices of Latter-day Saints can, however, be problematic. In an important article about Latter-day Saint approaches to apocryphal texts, Stephen Robinson offers this caution: "The apocrypha do often prove that ideas peculiar to the Latter-day Saints in modern times were widely known and widely believed anciently, but this is not the same as proving that the ideas themselves are true, or that those who believed them were right in doing so, or that they would have had anything else in common with the Latter-day Saints."[16] In order to demonstrate the dangers of searching through apocryphal texts for evidence supporting modern Latter-day Saint beliefs, Robinson draws our attention to the Hymn of the Pearl from the apocryphal Acts of Thomas:

> Particularly annoying is the practice of "proof-texting" from the apocrypha, that is, of selecting certain passages to prove a particular point while ignoring its context and the rest of the text. For example, I have heard it argued that the Acts of Thomas supports LDS theology because it contains a beautiful poem called the Hymn of the Soul, or Hymn of the Pearl, which teaches the doctrine of premortal existence. But the Acts of Thomas also teaches a transubstantiationist view of the Eucharist, that celibacy is the goal of all Christians, that sexual intercourse is evil, and that baptism was performed by sprinkling. . . . Is it not dishonest to represent an apocryphal book as being firm evidence for the truth when it agrees with us, and yet quietly look the other way when it does not? The truth is that it's just as easy to support Catholicism or Lutheranism or Calvinism by proof-texting the apocrypha as it is to prove our views. It's all a matter of which passages one decides to use.[17]

We should take care that our search for truth does not lead us to proof-texting. Section 91 of the Doctrine and Covenants, although it addresses only that collection of texts in the Bible called the Apocrypha, affirms that truth can be found in a noncanonical text.[18] Yet there is a difference between discovering truth and discovering ostensible evidence to support what we already believe to be true—the former opens our minds to new understanding; the latter lulls us away into the false security that we already know all we should ever need to know.[19] Apocryphal writings are valuable to Latter-day Saints regardless of their similarity to or difference from the doctrine proclaimed in the Church today. We ought to liken to ourselves the command given to Joseph Smith that wisdom and understanding should be sought in all good books and that we should obtain a knowledge of history (Doctrine and Covenants 88:118; 90:15; 93:53).[20]

Survey of Important Apocryphal Gospels

The remainder of this chapter focuses on a small subsection of New Testament Apocrypha, the apocryphal gospels. In the canonical New Testament today there are four Gospels, yet one recent collection of extracanonical gospels contains nearly forty distinct entries.[21] Some of these entries are nothing more than short fragments of what once might have been gospels of equal length to canonical Mark or even Matthew. Nevertheless, the number is indicative of the great diversity of gospel accounts that were written during the early centuries of Christianity. This chapter will focus on four important extracanonical gospels: the Gospel of Peter, the Gospel of Thomas, the Gospel of Mary, and the Infancy Gospel of Thomas.

In what follows, I will show, first, how some of the apocryphal gospels were used as though they were canonical and, second, how the apocryphal gospels were either passed down through the ages or rediscovered in modern times. Then, we will turn our attention to the questions of purpose and function: Why did people write gospels in the names of Peter, Thomas, or Mary? To answer this ques-

> ### Select Noncanonical Gospels
> with approximate dates of origin
>
> Gospel of the Ebionites (early 2nd cen.)
> Gospel of the Hebrews (early 2nd cen.)
> Gospel of Judas (mid 2nd cen.)
> Gospel of Mary (2nd cen.)
> Gospel of Nicodemus (early 5th cen.)
> Gospel of Peter (mid 2nd cen.)
> Gospel of Philip (3rd cen.)
> Gospel of the Savior (late 2nd cen.)
> Gospel of Thomas (early 2nd cen.)
> Infancy Gospel of Thomas (early 2nd cen.)
> Papyrus Egerton 2 (late 2nd cen.)
> Papyrus Oxyrhynchus 840 (early 3rd cen.)
> Proto-Gospel of James (mid 2nd cen.)

tion, I will show how these writings (1) participated in the second-century debate over the legitimacy of various Christian groups, (2) adopted the authority of first-century figures to address second-century problems, and (3) used that authority to answer questions about material missing from the earliest record, such as Jesus's childhood. In the process of exploring these issues, we will see how the apocryphal gospels reveal the variety of ways that early Christians interpreted and continued to develop their unique religious traditions in dialogue with the scripture and traditions of the past.

The Gospel of Peter

An example of canonical use

Manuscript evidence suggests that in the second century the Gospels of Matthew, Mark, Luke, and John were used publicly, whereas extracanonical gospels were generally read in private.[22] Yet some Christian communities did engage with apocryphal texts publicly as though they were authoritative scripture. For instance, we learn from Eusebius's *History of the Church* that some Christians in the town of Rhossus, Syria, used the Gospel of Peter as an authoritative text.[23] In fact, when Serapion, the bishop of Antioch, Syria, visited the church in Rhossus in the early third century AD, he approved their use of the Gospel of Peter without reading a page—it was, after all, the Gospel of Peter, and if the great apostle Simon Peter had written a gospel, of course it was appropriate to read! Later, Serapion had a change of heart when he learned that some Christians in Rhossus were using passages from the Gospel of Peter to support what he considered to be false teachings. They were teaching that Christ was fully divine, but not fully human, and that during his mortal ministry he only appeared to be mortal.[24] When Serapion learned that this was being taught from the Gospel of Peter, he studied that gospel himself, identified the problematic passages, and wrote a letter to the church of Rhossus. Eusebius includes a quotation from that letter: "I have been able to go through the book and draw the conclusion that while most of it accorded with the authentic teaching of the Savior, some passages were spurious additions. These I am appending to my letter."[25] Unfortunately, Eusebius does not quote the offending passages from the Gospel of Peter. For Eusebius, writing in the early fourth century AD, the Gospel of Peter was a forgery and had no place among the authoritative scriptures of Christendom.[26] For Serapion, however, even after discovering problematic passages, he did not forbid its use; "most of it," he wrote, "accorded with the authentic teaching of the Savior."[27] Today we have a better idea regarding which passages might have offended Serapion and Eusebius. Even though these Christians did not find the text worthy of preservation, others did, and it has been rediscovered in our own age.

Discovery and identification

Some apocryphal gospels have been passed down through the ages in a similar fashion to the New Testament Gospels.[28] Yet others were lost to time only to be rediscovered through archaeological excavations or by mere happenstance. The Gospel of Thomas, Gospel of Truth, and Gospel of Philip, for instance, were discovered at Nag Hammadi, Egypt, in 1945 when a small group of Bedouin were digging for fertilizer and happened upon a skeleton buried next to a large sealed earthenware jar full of leather-bound books (codices).[29] The stories of this discovery and of the codices' journey into the hands of a Coptic Christian priest and finally the Coptic Museum are full of scandal and intrigue.[30] Some key details remain sketchy. Suffice it to say, the discovery of the "Nag Hammadi library," as it is now called, was a watershed for our understanding of ancient Christian history—it has provided insight into forms of Christianity previously known only through the accounts of their theological opponents.[31] Despite its significance for scholars of Christian history, public knowledge of this discovery was eclipsed one year later by the discovery of the Dead Sea Scrolls.

The discovery of the Gospel of Peter was similarly important. Before its discovery about 130 years ago, little was known regarding its contents since Eusebius had failed to quote any part of it. In the winter of 1886–87, French archaeologist M. Grébant was digging near Akhmîm, Egypt, a town on the shore of the Nile in the center of Egypt (Upper Egypt) and to the northwest of Nag Hammadi and Luxor. He was excavating a portion of an ancient Christian cemetery with graves dating from the eighth to twelfth centuries AD when he discovered a small book (codex), no bigger than most modern cell phones today, that had been buried alongside an eighth-century monk.[32] The book was a collection of texts. One of them was clearly identifiable as a gospel even though it began and ended mid-sentence. It contained an account of Jesus's trial by Herod Antipas and Pilate and an account of his crucifixion, burial, and resurrection, but it did not match any previously known gospels.

This gospel was soon identified as the Gospel of Peter, the same gospel discussed by Eusebius in his *History of the Church*.[33] Although it did not contain a title, portions of it were written in first person. For instance, after the crucifixion and death of Jesus, the author writes, "I and my companions were grieving and went into hiding" (26). Then, after the story about the women discovering an empty tomb, the author continues, "But we, the twelve disciples of the Lord, wept and grieved; and each one returned to his home, grieving for what had happened. But I, Simon Peter, and my brother Andrew, took our nets and went off to the sea. And with us was Levi, the son of Alphaeus, whom the Lord . . . " (59–60).[34] There the Akhmîm fragment ends, but not before the author identifies himself as Simon Peter.

The conclusion that this was the same Gospel of Peter discussed by Eusebius also comes from evidence within the text. Scholars have identified at least two passages that could lend themselves to the sort of "heretical" interpretation that Serapion, and later Eusebius, lobbied against. First, in the Gospel of Peter, immediately before Jesus dies, he shouts from the cross words that echo Mark 15:34 and Matthew 27:46: "And the Lord cried out, 'My power, O power, you have left me behind!' When he said this, he (*or it*) was taken up" (19). The wording of this passage could have allowed some Christians to draw a distinction between the divine Christ and the human Jesus. For those who have always heard the words *Jesus* and *Christ* together as though they formed a single name, this idea may sound strange. Yet, according to Irenaeus, the late second-century Christian and chronicler of heresies (heresiologist), at least one group of Christians believed that there was a distinction between the human being, Jesus, and a divine being that possessed Jesus, called Christ.

> [Cerinthus] proposes Jesus, not as having been born of a virgin—for this seemed impossible to him—but as having been born the son of Joseph and Mary like all other men, and that he excelled over every person in justice, prudence, and wisdom. After his baptism Christ descended on him in the shape of a dove from the Authority that is above all things. Then he preached the unknown Father and worked wonders. But at the end Christ again flew off from Jesus. And Jesus indeed suffered and rose again from the dead, but Christ remained impassible, since he was spiritual.[35]

It is possible, therefore, that Christians with a similar understanding of Jesus's humanity and Christ's divinity could have understood the passage in the Gospel of Peter where Jesus cries out about a "power" leaving him behind as describing the divine Christ leaving behind the body of the human Jesus to die on the cross alone.[36]

A second passage that could have troubled Serapion and later Eusebius appears in the account of the Resurrection. The Gospel of Peter is the only extant gospel that provides an account of Jesus leaving the tomb after his resurrection.

> But during the night on which the Lord's day dawned, while the soldiers stood guard two by two on their watch, a great voice came from the sky. They saw the skies open and two men descend from there; they were very bright and drew near to the tomb. That stone which had been cast before the entrance rolled away by itself and moved to one side; the tomb was open and both young men entered. . . . [Then] they saw three men emerge from the tomb, two of them supporting the other, with a cross following behind them. The heads of the two reached up to the sky, but the head of the one they

were leading went up above the skies. And they heard a voice from the skies, "Have you preached to those who are asleep?" And a reply came from the cross, "Yes." (Gospel of Peter 35–37, 39–42).[37]

The narrative seems to imply that the two "men" or "young men" who entered the tomb were angels and that the third person who exited the tomb with them was Jesus resurrected. That it was Jesus is implied not only because he had been buried in that tomb but also because he is shown to be superior to the two "men": the angels' heads only reached the sky, but Jesus's head reached beyond. The representation of these angels and Jesus being extraordinarily tall borrows from Greek and Roman depictions of the gods. Throughout Greek and Roman literature, gods often reveal their divinity by manifesting themselves with extraordinary height.[38] Yet the height of Jesus and the angels is not the only unordinary aspect of this account. Jesus and the angels are followed by a walking, talking cross. Although this certainly seems strange to us today, the idea that an inanimate object could become miraculously animated is not entirely unheard of in antiquity. In some Greek and Roman accounts of divine manifestations, the gods take on the forms of inanimate objects and come to life. In the Homeric Hymn to Dionysus, for example, the god appears first in disguise as a prince and then manifests himself as a lion, a bear, a vine, and a flood of wine.[39] If Christians were reading the account of the Resurrection in the Gospel of Peter as similar to such Greek and Roman accounts of pagan gods, then they likely interpreted the walking, talking cross to be another manifestation of Jesus.[40] With the manifestation of Jesus as both extremely tall and in the form of a cross, it is clear how some Christians could have read this account to suggest that Jesus's body was not an ordinary human body.

Although neither this account nor the passage about Jesus's cry from the cross would have compelled the reader to see Jesus as a being who was not fully human, it is clear how someone could interpret them in that way. And this was sufficient to suggest to scholars that the fragment they discovered in Akhmîm was the same text read by Eusebius and Serapion.

Question of authorship

The two passages from the Gospel of Peter reviewed above may be sufficiently different from the four canonical Gospels to convince most Christians today that the Gospel of Peter was not actually written by Jesus's disciple Simon Peter. And there is evidence that the Gospel of Peter was written after the four canonical Gospels had been composed and circulated.[41] The Gospel of Peter seems to weave together the author's memories of stories from the early (canonical) Gospels, with some unique twists and new stories.[42] For instance, the Gospel of Peter includes the involvement of Herod Antipas in Jesus's trial, which is unique to the account in Luke 23:7–12 (Gospel of Peter 1–5). Then the Gospel of Peter adds a narrative explanation for why Jesus's legs were not broken (14), a detail found elsewhere only in John 19:31–33. The Gospel of Peter also includes an earthquake following Jesus's death (21), which is otherwise found only in the Gospel of Matthew 27:51, 54. In the Gospels of Matthew and Mark, a Roman soldier declares at Jesus's death that he "truly . . . was the

Son of God" (Mark 15:39; Matthew 27:54), but in the Gospel of Peter this proclamation is postponed until after soldiers guarding Jesus's tomb witness his resurrection (45). Whoever wrote the Gospel of Peter seems to have fashioned a new Gospel from his memory of those written previously. But why?

If the Gospel of Peter was not written by Simon Peter, then who wrote it and why did the author claim to be Peter? It is impossible to say who wrote the Gospel of Peter, but something can be said about why the author would write in the name of Simon Peter.[43] First, it should be acknowledged that the author could have believed that he was accurately representing Peter's "Gospel." According to 2 Esdras 14, the biblical scribe Ezra received a revelation from God that allowed him to accurately reproduce the Torah, the five books of Moses, after every copy had been burned. No reader of 2 Esdras 14 would have understood this chapter to mean that Ezra forged the Torah. Rather, under inspiration, Ezra faithfully re-produced the original. Similarly, when Tertullian, a Christian living in Carthage in the early third century, suggested that the book of 1 Enoch had been destroyed in the Flood and then miraculously and accurately reproduced by Noah, Tertullian was not suggesting that Noah was a forger.[44] Regardless of how the authors of apocryphal literature understood their work, the result of attributing a text to a famous figure from the earliest period of Christian history was to claim that figure's authority for the text. This was one of the most common purposes for the forgery of all sorts of documents in antiquity. As Bart Ehrman argues in his study of ancient forgeries, "The single most important motivation for authors to claim they were someone else in antiquity . . . was to get a hearing for their views. If you were an unknown person, but had something really important to say and wanted people to hear you . . . one way to make that happen was to pretend you were someone else, a well-known author, a fa-mous figure, an authority."[45] By writing in the name of Simon Peter, the author of the Gospel of Peter claimed for his gospel the authority of Jesus's premier apostle. Of course, Peter was not the only early disciple who was held in high esteem by the second century. So it should come as little surprise that the authority of other early disciples was likewise co-opted in the writing of other apocryphal gospels.

The Gospels of Thomas and Mary

Authority in the second century

The question of who had authority within the early Christian church was a matter of debate in many congregations from the earliest period of Christian history.[46] In one of Paul's let-ters to the saints of Corinth, he describes such a debate: "Now this I say, that every one of you saith, I am of Paul; and I of Apollos; and I of Cephas; and I of Christ" (1 Corinthians 1:12). This debate continued into the second century with some Christians promoting one apostle over another.[47] We already saw how the Gospel of Peter claims the authority of the chief apostle, Simon Peter. Other Gospels, however, promoted other apostles as the foremost authority on Christ and his message. Here we will consider the Gospel of Thomas and the Gospel of Mary.

The Gospel of Thomas, in contrast to the Gospel of Peter, calls into question the knowledge of Peter and promotes Didymus Judas Thomas as the Lord's special apostle. The Gospel of Thomas includes a passage that echoes Matthew 16:13–20, Mark 8:27–30, and Luke 9:18–21, wherein Jesus questions his disciples regarding his identity. In the Synoptic Gospels, it is Peter who responds properly by identifying Jesus as the Messiah or Christ. In the Gospel of Thomas, however, Peter's answer is wrong. "Jesus said to his disciples, 'Make a comparison and tell me: who am I like?' Simon Peter said to him, 'You are like a righteous angel.' Matthew said to him, 'You are like a wise philosopher.'" After both Peter and Matthew attempt unsuccessfully to answer the Lord's question, Thomas declares, "Teacher, my mouth cannot let me say at all what you are like." Although Jesus corrects Thomas's honorific address by explaining, "I am not your teacher," he also declares that Thomas has rightfully "drunk and become intoxicated from the bubbling spring that I myself have measured out." The author makes it clear that Thomas provided the best answer of the three, because Jesus next leads Thomas away from the other apostles to give him special instruction: "[Jesus] took him, withdrew, and said three sayings to him." When Thomas returns to his companions, they all desire to know what the Lord had revealed. Thomas's response once again sets him apart as the chosen apostle: "Thomas said to them, 'If I tell you one of the sayings he said to me, you will take up stones and cast them at me, and fire will come out of the stones and burn you'" (Gospel of Thomas 13).[48] This brief narrative demonstrates to the readers of Thomas's gospel that he has superior authority and insight into the message of Jesus, supporting the promise made at the beginning of the gospel: "These are the hidden sayings that the living Jesus spoke and Didymus Judas wrote down" (preface to the Gospel of Thomas).[49] According to the Gospel of Thomas, Didymus Judas Thomas is clearly the most authoritative witness of Jesus Christ and his message.[50]

Another Gospel that includes a narrative intended to elevate one particular church leader over others is the Gospel of Mary. As the fragmentary Gospel begins, the Savior is providing his final words of instruction to his apostles. He then departs and the apostles weep. They cry not because their Savior has departed but because they fear his command to go forth and preach: "How can we go to the gentiles and preach the gospel of the kingdom of the Son of Man? If they did not spare him, how will they spare us?" (9).[51] It is Mary Magdalene who rises to inspire them and call them to action: "Do not weep or grieve or be of two minds, for his grace will be with all of you and will protect you" (9).[52] In the discussion that follows, the apostles listen intently as Mary shares with them special teachings that the Lord had revealed to her alone: "Mary replied, 'What is hidden from you I will tell you.' And she began speaking these words to them. 'I,' she said, 'saw the Lord in a vision and said to him, 'Lord, I saw you in a vision today.' He answered me, 'You are blessed, because you do not falter at seeing me. For where the mind is, there is the treasure'" (10). Even though the Gospel, as it exists today, is missing large portions of Mary's visionary experience, the apostles' response to her remains intact. After Mary finishes revealing the Savior's special teachings,

Andrew responds, "Say what you will about what she has said, but I do not believe that the Savior said these things" (17). Next, Peter addresses his fellow apostles, "Did [the Savior] really speak with a woman secretly from us, not openly? Should we turn about, too, and all listen to her? Did he choose her over us?" (17). The scene is ironic since the Gospel of Mary answers each of Peter's questions with a resounding "Yes!" The Savior did speak to Mary secretly, the apostles should listen to her, and Jesus chose her over them—they wavered; she did not. At the end of the Gospel of Mary, it is Levi who comes to Mary's defense:

> Levi responded and said to Peter, "Peter, you are always angry. Now I see you disputing with this woman like the adversaries. If the Savior made her worthy, who are you then, for your part, to cast her aside? Surely the Savior knows her full well. That is why he has loved her more than us. Let us rather be ashamed, and put on the perfect human and bring it forth for ourselves, just as he commanded us; and let us preach the Gospel, laying down no rule or law other than what the Savior has spoken." When Levi said these things, they began to go out to teach and proclaim. (Gospel of Mary 18–19)

In the Gospel of Mary, Mary Magdalene is clearly the most authoritative witness of Jesus Christ and his message. The other disciples must humble themselves and listen to her.

New theological ideas and questions

As with the Gospel of Peter, the Gospel of Thomas and the Gospel of Mary are not actually the writings of the historical disciples Thomas and Mary.[53] These Gospels adopted the authority of Thomas and Mary, important figures in the first century of Christian history, in order to present new theological ideas or address theological questions that came to the fore during the second century.

The Gospel of Thomas, unlike the canonical Gospels, presents a Jesus who saves primarily through his teachings.[54] There is no atoning sacrifice in the Gospel of Thomas, no narrative of his death or bodily resurrection; Thomas's Jesus is a revealer of wisdom. Yet much of the Gospel of Thomas sounds like the canonical Gospels. In fact, two recent studies have independently and convincingly argued that the author of the Gospel of Thomas copied numerous passages from the canonical Gospels.[55] The Gospel of Thomas, even more directly than the Gospel of Peter, shows signs of reliance on the earlier Gospels now found in our New Testament. For instance, compare the unique saying of Jesus in Luke 14:26–27 to Gospel of Thomas 55:

> Whoever comes to me and does not hate father and mother, wife and children, brothers and sisters, yes, and even life itself, cannot be my disciple. Whoever does not carry the cross and follow me cannot be my disciple. (Luke 14:26–27 NRSV)

> Jesus said, "Whoever does not hate his father and his mother cannot be a disciple of mine; and whoever does not hate his brothers and his sisters and take up his cross the way I do, he will not be worthy of me." (Gospel of Thomas 55)

This is only one example of the numerous parallels between the New Testament Gospels and the Gospel of Thomas. So why copy the sayings of Jesus from the canonical Gospels but leave out the climactic narratives of Jesus's death and resurrection? Mark Goodacre has argued, "The Gospel of Thomas' genius is that it conveys its radical difference from the Synoptic Gospels by hiding its theology in words and images it derives from them."[56] In other words, the Gospel of Thomas borrows not only the authority of Thomas to present its unique theology but also the authority of earlier Gospels already accepted by many Christians.

The Gospel of Mary does not evince the same dependence on the canonical Gospels as the Gospel of Thomas. And yet it likewise borrows the authority of an important figure from first-century Christianity in order to address a new audience in the second century. Karen King, in her study of the Gospel of Mary, explains: "The Gospel of Mary seems most concerned with challenges to the truth of its teaching by other apostles within the Christian community. . . . Those challenges were basically of two kinds: 1) the rejection of new teachings based on prophecy or private revelation, and 2) gender."[57] As the church grew and certain leaders attempted to create unity and consistency through the assertion of hierarchical authority from Rome or from other major metropolises, individual claims to "prophecy or private revelation" became problematic.[58] In this context, female authority was also viewed as increasingly problematic. By the end of the second century, Tertullian rails against Christians who allowed women to teach and perform ordinances in the church: "'It is not allowed for a woman to speak in church', but also neither to teach, nor to baptize, nor to offer [the Eucharist], nor to claim a share of any male function, much less of priestly office, for herself."[59] In one instance, Tertullian complains that Christians are justifying this behavior by appealing to an apocryphal text that he insists is a forgery:

> But if certain Acts of Paul, which are falsely so named, claim the example of Thecla for allowing women to teach and to baptize, let men know that in Asia the presbyter who compiled that document, thinking to add of his own to Paul's reputation, was found out, and though he professed he had done it for love of Paul, was deposed from his position. How could we believe that Paul should give a female power to teach and to baptize, when he did not allow a woman even to learn by her own right? Let them keep silence, he says, and ask their husbands at home.[60]

Although the Gospel of Mary does not make any claims about women's authority to baptize, it nevertheless participates in this debate over women's authority within the church, which came to the fore in the second century.[61] Like the Gospel of Thomas, the Gospel of Mary also borrows the authority of a key figure from the earliest century of Christian history in order to address new theological ideas and questions relevant in the second century.

Filling in the Blanks: The Infancy Gospel of Thomas

Sometimes apocryphal gospels also address questions about what is missing from the earliest Christian records. For instance, none of the earliest Gospels has much to say about what Jesus was like as a child. Mark and John say nothing about Jesus's early life. Matthew includes Jesus's birth in Bethlehem and a brief account about a journey to and from Egypt, but says nothing about Jesus's childhood. Luke also describes Jesus's birth and includes only a brief account about Jesus and his parents visiting Jerusalem for Passover when he was twelve (Luke 2:41–51). In Luke, the rest of Jesus's childhood is summarized by the statement "And Jesus increased in wisdom and stature, and in favour with God and man" (Luke 2:52; see 2:40). Certainly Christians must have wondered what Jesus was like as a child. Indeed, at least one apocryphal gospel was written in part to satisfy that curiosity: the Infancy Gospel of Thomas. This infancy gospel ends in the same way as Luke's childhood narrative of Jesus: it tells the story of Jesus's time in the Jerusalem temple as a twelve-year-old boy and concludes with the summative statement "And Jesus grew in wisdom and stature and grace" (19.5).[62] Leading up to that story, the Infancy Gospel of Thomas includes accounts of Jesus's youth, beginning with him as a precocious and somewhat temperamental five-year-old child (2.1). One story tells how Jesus was walking through his village when another child, running past, bumped into him.

> Jesus was aggravated and said to him, "You will go no further on your way." Right away the child fell down and died. Some of those who saw what happened said, "Where was this child born? For everything he says is a deed accomplished!" The parents of the dead child came to Joseph and blamed him, saying, "Since you have such a child you cannot live with us in the village. Or teach him to bless and not to curse—for he is killing our children!" (Infancy Gospel of Thomas 4.1–2)

Christians today would likely balk at the idea that Jesus, even as a child, could have been so vengeful and violent. One might ask, How could a believing Christian, even in antiquity, ever imagine Jesus cursing and killing other children? For some time, even scholars of the Infancy Gospel of Thomas concluded that the Gospel must have been heretical because Jesus's "actions were . . . 'violent and vindictive,' 'bizarre and completely spiteful,' or 'offensive and repulsive.'"[63] Yet, as Stephen J. Davis suggests in his study of these accounts, "just because a story appears peculiar to our eyes does not mean that it would have been equally out of sync with the (diverse and often fractious) sensibilities and expectations of ancient readers."[64] This particular story seeks to demonstrate that, even in his youth, Jesus's words were powerful and he ought to be revered as the Lord (Infancy Gospel of Thomas 9.3; 17.2)—otherwise one might face dire consequences.[65]

The depiction of Jesus in the Infancy Gospel of Thomas is based in part on traditions of Jesus as an adult. For instance, another story from this gospel suggests that the rivalries and controversies of Jesus's adulthood had begun already in his youth. When the young Jesus was playing by a stream and made some pools of water, another boy approached, took a willow branch, and used it to scatter the water.

> Jesus was irritated when he saw what happened, and he said to him: "You unrighteous, irreverent idiot! What did the pools of water do to harm you? See, now you also will be

withered like a tree, and you will never bear leaves or root or fruit." Immediately that child was completely withered. Jesus left and returned to Joseph's house. (3.2–3)

The child who had scattered the pools of water is identified at the beginning of the story as "the son of Annas the scribe" (Infancy Gospel of Thomas 3.1).[66] In context Annas's son was not merely acting out of childish spite, but stood with those who had accused the five-year-old Jesus of "doing what is forbidden on the Sabbath" (2.3–4). It was the Sabbath when Jesus had formed those pools of water from a flowing stream, "things he ordered simply by speaking a word" (2.1). Jesus had then used those pools to make "some soft mud and [fashion] twelve sparrows from it," which at his command came to life and flew away chirping (2.4). The actions of the scribe's son against the child Jesus in the Infancy Gospel of Thomas mirror the harsh reactions of scribes and Pharisees toward Jesus as an adult in the canonical Gospels.[67]

Conclusion

Latter-day Saints can sometimes imbue ancient Christian apocryphal texts with an air of mystery. Despite the meaning of the term *apocryphal*, these texts today are neither hidden nor secret—nor do they provide exclusive access to esoteric or deep doctrines of The Church of Jesus Christ of Latter-day Saints. In fact, the apocryphal gospels themselves reflect a practice in antiquity that is somewhat similar to this modern pursuit of esoteric teachings. Whereas some Latter-day Saints have searched through ancient texts in order to piece together evidence supporting the unique beliefs and practices of the Church in the twentieth and twenty-first centuries, some ancient authors reworked the traditions of the earliest Christian texts in order to support their own unique beliefs and practices in the second century AD. This second-century engagement with early Christian authorities resulted in part in the creation of the apocryphal gospels. In other words, even though the apocryphal gospels do not provide evidence to legitimize our modern beliefs, they do reveal that the desire to legitimize contemporary beliefs by appealing to ancient authorities is not unique to Latter-day Saints.

These writings are valuable to Latter-day Saints regardless of their similarity to or difference from the doctrine proclaimed in the Church today. Apocryphal gospels provide us with unique insight into the world of early Christians. In particular, we have seen that some Christians were not content with only those four Gospels that would eventually become canonical. As Christianity developed and faced new challenges, some imaginative Christians wrote new gospels to deal with those challenges, to present new theological understandings of Christ, or to address gaps of knowledge in the earliest accounts. As historical artifacts of some of the earliest Christian traditions, we ought to read them. Indeed, we ought to "become acquainted with all good books" (Doctrine and Covenants 90:15)—especially those found at the foundations of Christianity.

Jason R. Combs is an assistant professor in the Department of Ancient Scripture at Brigham Young University.

Further Reading

Burke, Tony. *Secret Scriptures Revealed: A New Introduction to the Christian Apocrypha.* Eerdmans, 2013. Currently the best and most up-to-date introduction to New Testament Apocrypha.

Ehrman, Bart D. *Lost Christianities: The Battles for Scripture and the Faiths We Never Knew.* New York: Oxford University Press, 2003. An accessible introduction to the world of the New Testament Apocrypha. This book focuses on important developments in the history of early Christianity and situates key apocryphal texts within that history.

Ehrman, Bart D., and Zlatko Plese. *The Other Gospels: Accounts of Jesus from Outside the New Testament.* Oxford: Oxford University Press, 2013. The most recent English translation of all early apocryphal gospels that survive in Greek, Latin, and Coptic manuscripts.

Elliott, J. K. *The Apocryphal New Testament: A Collection of Apocryphal Christian Literature in an English Translation.* Revised ed. Oxford: Oxford University Press, 1993. An English translation of most of the earliest apocryphal gospels, acts, letters, and apocalypses related to the New Testament.

Meyer, Marvin, ed. *The Nag Hammadi Scriptures: The Revised and Updated Translation of Sacred Gnostic Texts.* New York: HarperOne, 2007. An English translation of ancient gnostic writings discovered in 1945 near Nag Hammadi, Egypt, that include some New Testament Apocrypha. This book features essays by top scholars on the different forms of gnostic belief represented by these texts.

Notes

1. See the further readings listed above.
2. Tony Burke, *Secret Scriptures Revealed: A New Introduction to the Christian Apocrypha* (Grand Rapids, MI: Eerdmans, 2013), 14. See also Scott D. Charlesworth, *Early Christian Gospels: Their Production and* Transmission, Papyrologica Florentina 47 (Florence, Italy: Edizioni Gonnelli, 2016), passim.
3. Burke, *Secret Scriptures Revealed*, 144.
4. Bruce M. Metzger, *The Canon of the New Testament: Its Origin, Development, and Significance* (Oxford: Clarendon, 1987), 305–7; see also 191–201. This list may be as late as the fourth century AD; see Metzger, *Canon of the New Testament*, 193. Yet the point remains that practices distinguishing between official and unofficial texts continued to develop well into the fourth century and beyond.
5. Irenaeus, *Against Heresies* 1.20.1. The edition used here is Dominic J. Unger, trans., rev. John J. Dillon, *St. Irenaeus of Lyons, Against the Heresies, Book 1*, Ancient Christian Writers 55 (New York: Newman, 1992); hereafter Irenaeus, *Against Heresies*.
6. For the text of the Letters of Paul and Seneca, see J. K. Elliott, *The Apocryphal New Testament: A Collection of Apocryphal Christian Literature in an English Translation*, rev. ed. (Oxford: Oxford University Press, 1993), 547–53. For a discussion of the Letters of Paul and Seneca as pseudepigraphal, see Bart D. Ehrman, *Forged: Writing in the Name of God—Why the Bible's Authors Are Not Who We Think They Are* (New York: HarperOne, 2011), 90–92.
7. Some Old Testament books were written in part in Aramaic (i.e., Ezra and Daniel), and some of the Apocrypha may have been originally written in Hebrew and then translated to Greek (i.e., Wisdom of Ben Sira).
8. Burke, *Secret Scriptures Revealed*, 7.
9. For more on the biblical Apocrypha, see Timothy Michael Law, *When God Spoke Greek: The Septuagint and the Making of the Christian Bible* (Oxford: Oxford University Press, 2013), 58–74.

10. Hugh Nibley, *The Message of the Joseph Smith Papyri: An Egyptian Endowment* (Salt Lake City: Deseret Book, 1975), xii.

11. Nibley, *Message of the Joseph Smith Papyri*, xii.

12. Nibley, *Message of the Joseph Smith Papyri*, xii. Regarding the Egyptian Book of Breathings, which was the focus of his study, Nibley argued that "the Egyptians did not have the real thing, and they knew it." See Nibley, *Message of the Joseph Smith Papyri*, xii.

13. For instance, regarding what Nibley called the "Egyptian Endowment," he said, "In the words of Abraham, Pharaoh, 'being a righteous man,' was ever 'seeking earnestly to imitate that order established by the fathers in the first generations, in the days of the first patriarchal reign' (Abraham 1:26), for he 'would fain claim [the priesthood]' (1:27)." Nibley, *Message of the Joseph Smith Papyri*, xii–xiii.

14. Nibley, *Message of the Joseph Smith Papyri*, xiii. For an important recent critique of Nibley's approach to identifying ancient parallels to modern Latter-day Saint beliefs, see Taylor Petrey, "Siding with Heretics: Evaluating Hugh Nibley Today," *Studies in the Bible and Antiquity* 7 (2015): 66–70.

15. For example, see Eugene Seaich, *Ancient Texts and Mormonism: The REAL Answer to Critics of Mormonism, Showing that Mormonism is a Genuine Restoration of Primitive Christianity* (Sandy, UT: Mormon Miscellaneous, 1983).

16. Stephen E. Robinson, "Lying for God: The Uses of Apocrypha," in *Apocryphal Writings and the Latter-day Saints*, ed. C. Wilfred Griggs (Provo, UT: Religious Studies Center, Brigham Young University, 1986), 148.

17. Robinson, "Lying for God," 147–48. For more on the challenges associated with identifying parallels between texts or religious groups, see Samuel Sandmel, "Parallelomania," *Journal of Biblical Literature* 81 (1962): 1–13; and Jonathan Z. Smith, *Drudgery Divine: On the Comparison of Early Christianities and the Religions of Late Antiquity* (Chicago: University of Chicago Press, 1990).

18. In Doctrine and Covenants 91, Joseph Smith receives a revelation about the biblical Apocrypha. He learns that "there are many things contained therein that are true ... [and] there are many things contained therein that are not true" (91:1–2) This revelation also promises that "whoso is enlightened by the Spirit shall obtain benefit therefrom" (91:5). See Robinson's caution about applying Doctrine and Covenants 91 to other collections of texts, such as "the Pseudepigrapha, the Dead Sea Scrolls, the Nag Hammadi Codices, or the New Testament apocrypha," in Robinson, "Lying for God," 154n59.

19. Joseph Smith himself saw in extracanonical texts the opportunity for new insight and theological reflection. See Thomas A. Wayment, "Joseph Smith's Developing Relationship with the Apocrypha," in *Approaching Antiquity: Joseph Smith and the Ancient World*, ed. Lincoln H. Blumell, Matthew J. Grey, and Andrew H. Hedges (Provo, UT: Religious Studies Center, Brigham Young University; Salt Lake City: Deseret Book, 2015), 331–55.

20. "Indeed, the apocrypha do have great value, but not because they teach Mormonism; for by and large they do not. . . . I want to affirm the importance of the apocryphal literature for our understanding of biblical history, of biblical languages, and of the background of the biblical books themselves. There is much valuable information here for the Latter-day Saints if we understand the texts for what they really are and use them appropriately." Robinson, "Lying for God," 148.

21. See Bart D. Ehrman and Zlatko Plese, *The Other Gospels: Accounts of Jesus from Outside the New Testament* (Oxford: Oxford University Press, 2013).

22. Charlesworth, *Early Christian Gospels*, passim.

23. Eusebius, *History of the Church* 6.12. For a translation of Eusebius's *Ecclesiastical History*, see G. A. Williamson, *Eusebius: The History of the Church from Christ to Constantine*, rev. ed., ed. Andrew Louth (London: Penguin, 1989). References to Eusebius's *History* hereafter use this translation. For an introduction to the role of Peter in early Christian apocryphal literature, written for a Latter-day Saint audience, see Nicholas J. Frederick, "Peter in the Apocryphal Tradition," in *The Ministry of Peter, the Chief Apostle*, ed. Frank F. Judd Jr., Eric D. Huntsman, and Shon D. Hopkin (Provo, UT: Religious Studies Center, Brigham Young University; Salt Lake City: Deseret Book, 2014), 337–59.

24. This view on the nature of Christ is sometimes called "docetism"—from the Greek *dokein* (δοκεῖν), meaning "to seem" or "to appear." For more on the various perspectives held by second-century Christians about the nature of Jesus Christ, see my article "'Christ' after the Apostles: The Humanity and Divinity of the Savior in the Second Century," in *Thou Art the Christ, the Son of the Living God: The Person and Work of Jesus in the New Testament*, ed. Eric Huntsman, Lincoln Blumell, and Tyler Griffin (Provo, UT: Religious Studies Center, Brigham Young University, 2018), 303–34.

25. Eusebius, *History of the Church* 6.12.6.

26. Eusebius, *History of the Church* 3.3.2; 3.25.6. It should be noted that Eusebius also calls into question the authenticity of 2 Peter; see Eusebius, *History of the Church* 3.3.1; 3.25.3.

27. Eusebius, *History of the Church* 6.12.6.

28. For instance, the Infancy Gospel of Thomas, which will be discussed below, was quite popular; it survives in different forms in multiple languages. See Ehrman and Plese, *Other Gospels*, 3–7.

29. The Gospel of Thomas will be discussed below.

30. Bart D. Ehrman, *Lost Christianities: The Battles for Scripture and the Faiths We Never Knew* (New York: Oxford University Press, 2003), 51–55; but see the recent analysis of discovery narratives in Mark Goodacre, "How Reliable is the Story of the Nag Hammadi Discovery?," *Journal for the Study of the New Testament* 35 (2013): 303–22.

31. For instance, Irenaeus tells us that Valentinus was a heretic, but in the Nag Hammadi library we find the Gospel of Truth, which likely provides us with Valentinus's own theology. See David Brakke, *The Gnostics: Myth, Ritual, and Diversity in Early Christianity* (Cambridge, MA: Harvard University Press, 2010), 100–104.

32. The average size of a page was 13 x 16 cm. There were sixty-six total pages. For more on this book, see Ehrman, *Lost Christianities*, 16–17. For an academic analysis, see Paul Foster, *The Gospel of Peter: Introduction, Critical Edition and Commentary* (Leiden, Netherlands: Brill, 2010), 43–55.

33. For a detailed academic overview of the history of scholarship on the fragmentary Gospel of Peter, see Foster, *Gospel of Peter*, 7–38.

34. This is where the manuscript ends, but the missing story could have been something like the account from John 21:1–14.

35. Irenaeus, *Against Heresies* 1.26.1.

36. Ehrman, *Lost Christianities*, 18.

37. Ehrman and Plese, *Other Gospels*, 199.

38. For instance, see the Homeric *Hymn to Demeter* 275–80. For an accessible English translation, see Apostolos N. Athanassakis, *The Homeric Hymns: Translation, Introduction, and Notes* (Baltimore, MD: Johns Hopkins University Press, 1976), 9. For an academic study of the common characteristics of Greco-Roman epiphanies, including manifestation of enormous height, see H. S. Versnel, "What Did Ancient Man See When He Saw a God? Some Reflections on Greco-Roman Epiphany," in *Effigies Dei: Essays on the History of Religions*, ed. Dirk van der Plas (Leiden, Netherlands: Brill, 1987), 42–55.

39. For additional examples, see Jason Robert Combs, "A Walking, Talking Cross: The Polymorphic Christology of the Gospel of Peter," *Early Christianity* 5 (2014): 207–9, 213–15.

40. Combs, "Walking, Talking Cross," 215–19.

41. See Raymond E. Brown, "The Gospel of Peter and Canonical Gospel Priority," *New Testament Studies* 33 (1987): 321–43. Crossan argues that an earlier, hypothetical form of the Gospel of Peter, which he calls the "Cross Gospel," would have predated some of our canonical Gospels. See John Dominic Crossan, *The Cross That Spoke: The Origins of the Passion Narrative* (San Francisco: Harper and Row, 1988).

42. See Brown, "Gospel of Peter and Canonical Gospel Priority," 321–43.

43. Although it is impossible to say who wrote the Gospel of Peter, sometimes there is evidence for the authorship of apocryphal texts. For instance, Tertullian claims to know the author of the apocryphal Acts of Paul. See Tertullian, *On Baptism* 17.5.

44. Tertullian, *On the Apparel of Women* 1.3.1.

45. Ehrman, *Forged*, 31.

46. See also, for example, 2 Corinthians 11:4–5, 13; Galatians 1:6–8; 3 John 9–10.

47. For more on claims to authority in the second century, see Elaine Pagels, "Visions, Appearances, and Apostolic Authority: Gnostic and Orthodox Traditions," in *Gnosis: Festschrift für Hans Jonas*, ed. Barbara Aland and Ugo Bianchi (Göttingen, Germany: Vandenhoeck und Ruprecht, 1978), 415–30.

48. Trans. Ehrman and Plese, *Other Gospels*.

49. Trans. Ehrman and Plese, *Other Gospels*.

50. Regarding Gospel of Thomas 13, Goodacre suggests, "As well as legitimizing the role of *Thomas*'s alleged author, the exchange cleverly situates the book over against Christian Gospels that are already becoming authoritative by virtue of their popularity and greater antiquity"—referring specifically to the Gospel of Mark and Gospel of Matthew. See Mark Goodacre, *Thomas and the Gospels: The Case for Thomas's Familiarity with the Synoptics* (Grand Rapids, MI: Eerdmans, 2012), 178–79.

51. Unless otherwise indicated, all quotations of the Gospel of Mary are from Ehrman and Plese, *Other Gospels*.

52. On the Gospel of Mary being the Gospel of Mary Magdalene rather than the Gospel of Mary, Jesus's mother, see Karen L. King, *The Gospel of Mary of Magdala: Jesus and the First Woman Apostle* (Santa Rosa, CA: Polebridge, 2003), 205n58.

53. Both date to the second century AD. On the date of the Gospel of Mary, see King, *Gospel of Mary of Magdala*, 183–84. On the date of the Gospel of Thomas, see Goodacre, *Thomas and the Gospels*, 154–71.

54. For an introduction to the theology of the Gospel of Thomas written for a popular audience, see Elaine Pagels, *Beyond Belief: The Secret Gospel of Thomas* (New York: Random House, 2003). For a recent academic commentary, see Simon Gathercole, *The Gospel of Thomas: Introduction and Commentary* (Leiden, Netherlands: Brill, 2014), 144–75.

55. See Goodacre, *Thomas and the Gospels*; and Simon Gathercole, *The Composition of the Gospel of Thomas: Original Language and Influences*, Society for New Testament Studies Monograph Series 151 (Cambridge: Cambridge University Press, 2012).

56. Goodacre, *Thomas and the Gospels*, 192.

57. King, *Gospel of Mary of Magdala*, 87. See also Ann Graham Brock, "What's in a Name: The Competition for Authority in Early Christian Texts," *Society of Biblical Literature Seminar Papers* 37 (1998): 106–24; and Ann Graham Brock, *Mary Magdalene, the First Apostle: The Struggle for Authority*, Harvard Theological Studies 51 (Cambridge, MA: Harvard University Press, 2003).

58. Pagels, "Visions, Appearances, and Apostolic Authority," 415–30; Christine Trevett, *Montanism: Gender, Authority, and the New Prophecy* (Cambridge; New York: Cambridge University Press, 1996); Laura Nasrallah, *An Ecstasy of Folly: Prophecy and Authority in Early Christianity*, Harvard Theological Studies 52 (Cambridge, MA: Harvard University Press, 2003).

59. Tertullian, *On the Veiling of Virgins* 9. Translation adapted from Geoffrey D. Dunn, trans., *Tertullian* (London: Routledge, 2004), 109; see also Tertullian, *Prescription against Heretics* 41.5. For more on women and baptism, see Ross Kraemer, *Her Share of the Blessings: Women's Religions among Pagans, Jews, and Christians in the Greco-Roman World* (New York: Oxford University Press, 1992), 181.

60. Tertullian, *On Baptism* 17. The edition used here is Ernest Evans, trans., *Tertullian's Homily on Baptism* (London: SPCK, 1964), 37. For a translation of the apocryphal Acts of Paul and Thecla, see J. K. Elliott, "The Acts of Paul," in *The Apocryphal New Testament: A Collection of Apocryphal Christian Literature in an English Translation*, ed. J. K. Elliott (Oxford: Oxford University Press, 1993), 351–88.

61. By the end of the second century, Ross Kraemer notes, "the debate over women's leadership in early Christian communities became particularly acute around the question of women's authority to baptize." Kraemer, *Her Share of the Blessings*, 181.

62. Unless otherwise indicated, all quotations of the Infancy Gospel of Thomas are from Ehrman and Plese, *Other Gospels*.

63. Stephen J. Davis, *Christ Child: Cultural Memories of a Young Jesus* (New Haven, CT: Yale University Press, 2014), 6, 224n8. Kristi Upson-Saia suggests that the original narratives were anti-Christian but were later adopted and adapted by Christians. See Upson-Saia, "Holy Child or Holy Terror? Understanding Jesus' Anger in the Infancy Gospel of Thomas," *Church History* 82, no. 1 (2013): 1–39.

64. Davis, *Christ Child*, 7.

65. Davis, *Christ Child*, 64–91, especially 87–91. On the Christology of the Infancy Gospel of Thomas as closer to the Gospel of John than the Synoptics, see Reidar Aasgaard, *The Childhood of Jesus: Decoding the Infancy Gospel of Thomas* (Cambridge, England: James Clarke, 2010), 153, 155–56. The depiction of Jesus as already fully cognizant of his power and divinity even as a child is also represented in the account of Jesus as a twelve-year-old in the Jerusalem temple. In Luke the young Jesus is discovered "sitting in the midst of the doctors, both hearing them, and asking them questions" (2:46). In the Infancy Gospel of Thomas, Jesus is the teacher: "After the third day they found him sitting in the temple in the midst of the teachers, both listening and asking them questions. Everyone was attending closely, amazed that though a child, he silenced the elders and teachers of the people, explaining the chief points of the Law and the parables of the prophets" (19.2). This same tendency, to present the young Jesus as similar to the adult Jesus, is also seen in the Joseph Smith Translation of Luke 2:46 (see footnote *c* of Luke 2:46 in the Latter-day Saint edition of the Bible; for an alternative view, see Doctrine and Covenants 93:12–14). On the types of changes Joseph Smith made to the Bible, see Scott H. Faulring, Kent P. Jackson, and Robert J. Matthews, eds., *Joseph Smith's New Translation of the Bible: Original Manuscripts* (Provo, UT: Religious Studies Center, Brigham Young University, 2004), 8–11.

66. Rendered in the Greek *Paidika* as "Annas the high priest"; see Davis, *Christ Child*, 64. For Annas the high priest in the canonical Gospels, see Luke 3:2; John 18:13, 24; and Acts 4:6.

67. For examples of scribes and Pharisees reacting to Jesus's actions on the Sabbath in the canonical Gospels, see Matthew 12; Mark 2–3; Luke 6; and John 5.

20

The Atonement

Noel B. Reynolds

J esus Christ came into a world already well supplied with a rich variety of beliefs and practices related to atonement, redemption, and sacrifice. His exit three decades later established a dramatically new set of beliefs and practices that would inspire literally billions of followers over the next two millennia. While the cultural context of the ancient Mediterranean world provided New Testament and other early Christian writers with a variety of metaphors they could use to explain Christ's atonement, the resulting texts do not give us a clear, unitary view. Almost six centuries earlier and a hemisphere away, the Nephite prophets recorded visions and revelations that foretold Christ's coming and atonement in detail and that now provide us with an enlarged and more consistent understanding. Finally, the revelations given to Joseph Smith in the early nineteenth century add considerable detail about the afterlife made possible by the Atonement. Because the prophetic motivation has always been to promote the salvation of souls, the scriptural accounts of atonement tend to mix explanations of how the Atonement works with explanations of how men and women can pursue its blessings in their lives.

Biblical Accounts of the Atonement

New Testament writers consistently and vigorously testify that Jesus Christ atoned for the sins of all people and has provided for their resurrection from the dead. In so doing they point to historical facts, the things he did to accomplish this—to his sufferings during his crucifixion and his resurrection. Some of these writers also offer explanations or characterizations of that atonement intended to illuminate how it was possible or how it works. The various explanations offered are not identical or even always consistent with each other but vary somewhat between writers or sometimes even within the pages written by the same person. The overall impression we get from reading these testimonies of the Atonement is the deep conviction of the writers and their desires to help their readers understand and appreciate all dimensions of its contributions—even though they themselves may not understand it fully or believe that their readers will be able to comprehend its full implications. Book of Mormon writers had the same motivation and faced the same challenges while contributing an even richer collection of testimonies and explanations than what we find in the Bible.

In comparison with the King James Version of the New Testament, which uses any form of the word *atone/atonement* only once (Romans 5:1), the Book of Mormon features thirty-nine instances of the word that accurately reflect its much more frequent direct discussion of the topic. These discussions are distributed throughout the book from the teachings of Lehi and Nephi in the beginning to the concluding comments of Mormon and Moroni at the end and include treatments of atonement-related concepts such as *expiation, propitiation*, and *redemption* that carry more of the load in the New Testament.

The long scholarly tradition of biblical interpretation has produced quite a number of competing explanations for the Atonement. For convenience, I will follow the helpful division of these into five categories that has been provided by the *Anchor Bible Dictionary*—though in a changed order. In this dictionary article, C. M. Tuckett provides a balanced and critical overview of the enormous literature that explores and defends the numerous Christian efforts to understand the Atonement—an overview that will provide a reliable framework for comparisons with the atonement explanations we have received from the Nephite prophets.[1]

The most personal of these explanations for the individual Christian is the teaching that sinners can be reconciled eternally to Christ and the Father through Christ's *atonement*. A second way of understanding the Atonement focuses on Christ's mission to bring light and knowledge to men in their ignorance, revealing himself and the Father to them, and teaching them how they can receive eternal life. Other more general theories of atonement have received greater attention in the interpretive literature. The teaching of early Christian leaders that the Atonement was the result of Christ's victory over Satan and the powers of evil was given new life and cut a very wide swath among twentieth-century interpreters. Because sacrificial language recurs in numerous references, equally prominent is the theory that the Atonement was a sacrifice of the sinless Son of God for the sins of the world. The fifth and possibly most prominent theory portrays the Atonement in terms of redemption understood as a ransom paid—or, more figuratively, of a rescue or deliverance from sin and the power of evil. There is scriptural language to support each of these interpretations, and most writers have tried to merge all of these together in theories dominated by one of these particular explanations. But over the last half century there has been a growing realization among Christian writers that all five explanations may have some basis in truth, even though they may not be reducible to one intellectually satisfying theory of atonement. The following discussion will emphasize the elements of these theories that have received the most reinforcement from Restoration scriptures and will identify corresponding teachings that are present in the Book of Mormon specifically.

1. Reconciliation

In Romans, Paul explains that reconciliation with God was made possible when "Christ died for us," that we may be "justified by his blood" and "saved from wrath through him." We are, in this way, "saved by his life." By his death, we "are reconciled to God," which atonement (reconciliation) enables us to "joy in God" (Romans 5:8–11). The family of Greek terms translated as *reconciliation* and *reconcile* (*katallassō*) indicates a complete or thorough change, reminding us of Christ's teaching to Nicodemus that a man must "be born again" before he can "see the kingdom of God" (John 3:3, 7). The letters of John extend the same theme by teaching that "everyone who believes that Jesus is the Christ is born of God," "overcomes the world," and does "not continue to sin." Even though "the whole world is under the control of the evil one," he "cannot harm him" (1 John 5:1, 4, 18–19; 3:9 NIV). Peter expands this teaching when he says the saints "have purified [their] souls in obeying the truth through the Spirit . . . : being born again . . . by the word of God" (1 Peter 1:22–23). Paul's focus on reconciliation continues in his second letter to the Corinthians as he describes "the ministry of reconciliation" given to the Christians by Christ and "the word of reconciliation" committed to them (2 Corinthians 5:18–20). He emphasizes the universality of the atonement of Christ to the Ephesians, explaining that unlike the law of Moses, the Atonement reconciles both Jews and Gentiles unto God, so that "both have access by one Spirit unto the Father" (Ephesians 2:15–18). By this act of reconciliation, God can bring former enemies into his fold.

The Nephite prophet Jacob ended his landmark sermon on the Atonement with a direct appeal to the language of reconciliation, calling upon his people to leave "the way of everlasting death" and to take up "the way of eternal life":

> Therefore cheer up your hearts and remember that ye are free to act for yourselves, to choose the way of everlasting death or *the way of eternal life*. Wherefore, my beloved brethren, *reconcile yourselves* to the will of God and not to the will of the devil and the flesh. And remember that after ye are *reconciled unto God* that it is only in and through the grace of God that ye are saved. Wherefore may God raise you from death by the power of the resurrection, and also from everlasting death by *the power of the atonement*, that ye may be received into the eternal kingdom of God, that ye may praise him through grace divine. (2 Nephi 10:23–25)[2]

In this passage, Jacob powerfully links the ancient doctrine of the two ways[3] to the doctrine of the Atonement that underlies "the way of eternal life." This understanding of the

Atonement is presented even more clearly in King Benjamin's explanation to the assembled Nephite people that "the law of Moses availeth nothing except it were through the atonement of [Christ's] blood" (Mosiah 3:15). Further, "the blood of Christ atoneth for their sins," and "there shall be no other name given nor no other way nor means whereby salvation can come unto the children of men" (Mosiah 3:16). As he further explains:

> The *natural man is an enemy to God* and has been from the fall of Adam and will be forever and ever but if he yieldeth to the enticings of the Holy Spirit and *putteth off the natural man and becometh a saint through the atonement* of Christ the Lord and becometh as a child, submissive, meek, humble, patient, full of love, willing to submit to all things which the Lord seeth fit to inflict upon him, even as a child doth submit to his father. (Mosiah 3:19)

Benjamin's people responded unanimously that they did believe his words "because of the Spirit of the Lord Omnipotent, which hath wrought *a mighty change* in us or in our hearts, that we have no more disposition to do evil but to do good continually" and expressed their desire "to enter into a covenant with our God to do his will and to be obedient to his commandments . . . all the remainder of our days" (Mosiah 5:2, 5). The king went on to explain that because of this covenant they had made, "ye shall be called the children of Christ, his sons and his daughters; for behold, this day he hath spiritually begotten you, for ye say that your hearts are changed through faith on his name; therefore ye are *born of him* and have become *his sons and his daughters*" (5:7). Benjamin credits this "mighty change" in the hearts of the people to a transformation worked by "the Spirit of the Lord" and to their willingness to make a covenant to take his name upon them and to obey him to the end of their lives. No longer enemies but "spiritually begotten" sons and daughters of Christ, his people are promised "everlasting salvation and eternal life" (5:15), conditional only upon their continued obedience to the Lord.

From this we learn that the "mighty change" described by Benjamin follows repentance that is grounded in a covenant of obedience, that it is a transformation effected by the Spirit, and that it is characterized as a new birth through which recipients become his sons and daughters. We further learn that it is a process made available to all men and women and that it is the only means by which sinners can be redeemed individually "from the gall of bitterness and bonds of iniquity" and, so reconciled, become heirs of the kingdom of God (Mosiah 27:26, 29). In a subsequent and more detailed recounting of this same experience, Alma said that the experience came after he repented and called upon Jesus Christ, who would "atone for the sins of the world," and that he had subsequently labored unceasingly to "bring souls unto repentance, . . . that they might also be born of God and be filled with the Holy Ghost" (Alma 36:17–18, 24). Alma made this personal experience the foundation of his signature sermon to the people of Zarahemla and tied it back to the experiences and teachings of his own father, Alma, and to Abinadi through whom Alma had been converted.

And now I ask of you: On what conditions are they saved? Yea, what grounds had they to hope for salvation? What is the cause of their being loosed from the bands of death, yea, and also the chains of hell? Behold, I can tell you: Did not my father Alma believe in the words which was delivered by the mouth of Abinadi? And was he not a holy prophet? Did he not speak the word of God and my father Alma believed them? And according to his faith there was *a mighty change* wrought in his heart. Behold, I say unto you that this is all true. And behold, he preached the word unto your fathers; and *a mighty change* was also wrought in their hearts, and they *humbled themselves* and *put their trust in the true and living God*. And behold, they were *faithful until the end*; therefore they were saved. And now behold, I ask of you, my brethren of the church: Have ye spiritually been born of God? Have ye received his image in your own countenances? Have ye experienced *this mighty change* in your hearts? Do ye *exercise faith in the redemption* of him who created you? Do you look forward with an eye of faith and view this mortal body raised in immortality and this corruption raised in incorruption, to stand before God to be judged according to the deeds which hath been done in the mortal body? (Alma 5:10–15)

These detailed accounts of the experience of the effects of the Atonement in the lives of repentant Nephites are consistent with the language of other prophets as reported throughout the Book of Mormon. The Atonement is consistently portrayed as the means by which this mighty change is made available to all who will repent—that they might be spiritually reborn and filled with joy in this life and prepared to be found worthy of eternal life when they meet the Lord at the Final Judgment.

2. Revelation

Although not widely recognized as a theory of atonement, there are significant interpretations of the New Testament that see Christ's accomplishments primarily focused on bringing mankind to a knowledge of God and of man's relationship to him. Jesus is repeatedly characterized by John as the bearer of light and knowledge, the one who reveals God's true nature and glory (John 1:14, 18). Through Jesus, light has come into the world, and by coming into that light, men can live by truth (John 3:16–21). Eternal life can be understood in terms of coming to know both Jesus and the Father, where *knowing* is understood in the more personal biblical sense of being acquainted with someone—and not in the abstract sense of theological definitions.

It is striking that the same Book of Mormon passages cited above for their explanations of the process by which repentant men and women can be reconciled to God through a spiritual rebirth include the assurance that knowledge of God is gained through that same process. For Alma, that divine knowing is so intimate that the spiritually reborn sons and daughters of God will have "received his image" in their countenances (Alma 5:14). Alma was given a vision of God in his heaven as part of the experience, but the personal experience in which he received the blessings of the Atonement gave him his understanding of the

Atonement. Because of the things which he had tasted and seen, he claimed to know of the Atonement and testified that "the knowledge which I have is of God" (Alma 36:26). In the same spirit, Benjamin foresaw a future day "when the knowledge of a Savior shall spread throughout every nation, kindred, tongue, and people," at which time "none shall be found blameless before God, . . . only through repentance and faith on the name of the Lord God Omnipotent" (Mosiah 3:20–21). Similarly, Benjamin's people rejoiced because their king "hath brought us to this great knowledge" and because they knew of the "surety and truth" of his words "because of the Spirit of the Lord Omnipotent, which hath wrought a mighty change in us" (5:4, 2).

The Nephite prophets oriented much of their teaching and prophesying to the Abrahamic covenant, and especially to the promise that through Abraham's seed all the nations of the earth would be blessed.[4] Setting out an explanation that would be repeated in many forms by his successors, Nephi taught his brothers that the knowledge of the gospel of their Redeemer would be the means by which the Lord would gather Abraham's seed in the last days and bring them back into his fold:

> And at that day shall the remnant of our seed *know* that they are of the house of Israel and that they are the covenant people of the Lord. And then shall they *know* and come to the *knowledge* of their forefathers and also to the *knowledge* of the gospel of their Redeemer, which was ministered unto their fathers by him. Wherefore they shall come to the *knowledge* of their Redeemer and the very points of his doctrine, that they may *know* how to come unto him and be saved. (1 Nephi 15:14)

It is even clearer in Book of Mormon teaching that the knowledge of the Redeemer and his gospel are essential in the actualization of the atonement of Jesus Christ in the lives of men and women on the earth.

3. Victory over Satan

A significant share of twentieth-century atonement studies emphasized the teachings of the early Christian fathers and scriptural passages that characterized mortal life in terms of a military struggle between the forces of good and evil.[5] Paul used this metaphor repeatedly and saw Christ's victory over Satan's armies in his death and resurrection, as illustrated in this key passage:

> And when you were dead in trespasses and the uncircumcision of your flesh, God made you alive together with him, when he forgave us all our trespasses, erasing the record that stood against us with its legal demands. He set this aside, nailing it to the cross. He disarmed the rulers and authorities and made a public example of them, *triumphing over them* in it. (Colossians 2:13–15 NRSV)

The author of Hebrews explicitly points to Christ's death as the key to that victory: "through death he might destroy the one who has the power of death, that is, the devil"

(Hebrews 2:14 NRSV). This corresponds closely to Jesus's saying that "now is the judgment of this world; now the ruler of this world will be driven out" (John 12:31 NRSV).

While this is not the most prominent Book of Mormon atonement theme, it is clearly stated by three Nephite prophets (Abinadi, Alma, and Mormon) and is often implicit in the teachings of others. From the time of Lehi, Nephites had understood the fallen and sinful state of mankind as the "captivity . . . of the devil" and had understood the plan of salvation as the means by which men could be liberated from that captivity (2 Nephi 2:27). In the words of Abinadi:

> He that persists in his own carnal nature and goes on in the ways of sin and rebellion against God, he remaineth in his fallen state, and the devil hath all power over him. Therefore he is as though there was no redemption made, being an enemy to God; and also is the devil an enemy to God. And now if Christ had not come into the world—speaking of things to come as though they had already come—there could have been no redemption. And if Christ had not risen from the dead or broken the bands of death—that the grave should have no *victory* and that death should have no sting—there could have been no resurrection. But there is a resurrection. Therefore the grave hath no *victory*, and the sting of death[6] is swallowed up in Christ. (Mosiah 16:5–8)

Centuries later, Mormon reiterates this teaching—echoing Abinadi's own words and phrases:

> Know ye that ye must come to the knowledge of your fathers and repent of all your sins and iniquities and believe in Jesus Christ, that he is the Son of God, . . . and by the power of the Father he hath risen again, whereby he hath gained the *victory over the grave*. And also in him is the sting of death swallowed up. And he bringeth to pass the resurrection of the dead, whereby man must be raised to stand before his judgment seat. And he hath brought to pass the redemption of the world. (Mormon 7:5–7)

Aaron may have been drawing on the same tradition when he taught the Lamanites that "the grave shall have no victory" inasmuch as "the sufferings and death of Christ atoneth for their sins" (Alma 22:14).

4. Sacrifice

Although the language of sacrifice permeates many of the New Testament passages and earliest Christian writings that relate to atonement, these do not present a unitary view of how Christ's sacrifice would accomplish an atonement. Paul's writings are the prime example. While he refers to the idea of sacrifice more than any other writer, he uses such a variety of different metaphors in the process that many scholars advise against looking for a unified theory in Paul's teachings on the Atonement. References to the "blood" of Christ are too easily linked to the idea of sacrifice as scholars now recognize that *blood* was another term for *death* and need have no direct connection to sacrifice per se, thus reducing the number of New Testament writings that should be read as references to sacrifice.

Another major problem with interpreting the references to Christ's sacrifice arises from the variety of understandings of sacrifice that Paul and his contemporaries inherited from their own Jewish traditions and from surrounding cultures. In Judaism and other ancient cultures, sacrifices were used in rituals establishing covenants between nations and between men and gods. Sacrifices could also be employed to express thanks to a deity for great blessings or as a means of commemorating great blessings of the past (i.e., Passover). Most attempts to understand the Atonement as a sacrifice invoke the Old Testament practice of sin offerings, but even this connection turns out to be problematic. Part of the problem is that Jewish scriptures and traditions include no rationale for sacrifice that would clarify what it means to say Christ sacrificed his life for the sins of others. Many ancient cultures understood sacrifices to be "propitiation," designed to allay the anger of an offended deity. While linking the Atonement to that tradition has been foundational for many Christians, it has seemed too problematic for others. What sense, they ask, could it make to see Jesus sacrificing himself to allay his own or the Father's anger for the sins of men?

A popular alternative has been to interpret the biblical terminology of sacrifice to mean that sacrifices can nullify or "expiate" past sins, implying that Jesus's life was sacrificed as a substitute for the lives of sinners. But this approach has its own problems. There appears to be no precedent in Jewish thought for the idea that one person's life might be sacrificed to expiate the sins of another. Some have pointed to the scapegoat tradition by which the sins of the people were ritually conferred on the head of one goat that would be then driven into the wilderness, while a second goat would actually be sacrificed. But the analogy breaks down when we note the obvious fact that the goat bearing sins as a substitute is not the one sacrificed. Still, the idea that Christ's sacrifice was expiation for sin seems to fit better with the scriptural language that consistently presents God as the actor and not the recipient of the sacrificial action.

The Epistle to the Hebrews presents the most developed and extensive explanation of Jesus as the sacrifice prefigured in the Jewish Day of Atonement. Here Jesus is portrayed as both the high priest and the sacrificial victim and the fulfillment of the prophetic dimension of the ancient ritual. But even here, our search for an explanation of Jesus's atonement for our sins comes up empty-handed, for the arguments of the author of Hebrews are actually focused on a different objective. His arguments are designed primarily to prove to his Jewish-Christian audience that the sacrifice of Jesus Christ brings the ancient tradition of sacrifices inaugurated through the law of Moses to a final conclusion (Hebrews 8:1–10:18). No more will God's people be expected to make sacrifices of animal lives. Rather, they should understand the sacrifice of Christ in covenantal terms because it provides the sacrificial launch of the new covenant as the law of Moses with its blood sacrifices is officially terminated. The author of Hebrews assumes, as do other writers, that the shedding of blood is required to expiate sins, but he does not explain sacrifice or substitution.

In his linguistic analysis of biblical sacrifice for the *Theological Dictionary of the New Testament*, Johannes Behm found the basis for the spiritualized concepts of sacrifice in the New Testament in the presuppositions of Old Testament writers.[7]

> The concept of sacrifice in the OT is rooted in the reality of the covenant order into which God's historical revelation has integrated the people of Israel. . . . In the sacrificial order of the old covenant God wills to have personal and active dealings with his people. Sacrifice, whether it be the gift of man to God, the expression of spiritual fellowship between God and man, or a means of atonement, is always orientated to the presence of God in grace and judgment.[8]

The prophets proclaimed against the materialistic sacrificial practices of their day because they betrayed the original purpose, which was to produce a "personal, spiritual encounter with the God of salvation."[9] As Paul and the author of Hebrews teach, the true meaning of sacrifice is displayed in the total self-giving of Christ that enables his people to give their own lives back to him. "To bring oneself, one's will, one's action, wholly to God, is the new meaning which the concept of sacrifice acquires" in the New Testament.[10]

The characterization of Christ's atonement as a sacrifice is introduced in the Book of Mormon first in the teachings of Lehi to his family:

> Wherefore redemption cometh in and through the Holy Messiah, for he is full of grace and truth. Behold, he offereth himself a sacrifice for sin, to answer the ends of the law unto all those which have a broken heart and a contrite spirit. And unto none else can the ends of the law be answered. (2 Nephi 2:6–7)

Amulek, who was taught by Alma, gives perhaps the clearest and most complete explanation:

> Behold, I say unto you that I do know that Christ shall come among the children of men to take upon him the transgressions of his people and that he shall atone for the sins of the world, for the Lord God hath spoken it. For it is expedient that an atonement should be made, for according to the great plans of the Eternal God there must be an atonement made or else all mankind must unavoidably perish. Yea, all are hardened; yea, all are fallen and are lost and must perish except it be through the atonement, which it is expedient should be made.
>
> For it is expedient that there should be *a great and last sacrifice*—yea, not a sacrifice of man, neither of beasts, neither of any manner of fowl—for it shall not be a human sacrifice, but it must be *an infinite and an eternal sacrifice*. . . .
>
> And then shall there be—or it is expedient there should be—a stop to the shedding of blood; then shall the law of Moses be fulfilled. Yea, it shall all be fulfilled, every jot and tittle, and none shall have passed away. And behold, this is the whole meaning of the law, every whit a pointing to that great and last sacrifice; and that great and last sacrifice will be the Son of God, yea, infinite and eternal. And thus he shall bring salva-

tion to all those who shall believe on his name, this being the intent of this last sacrifice, to bring about the bowels of mercy, which overpowereth justice and bringeth about means unto men that they may have faith unto repentance. (Alma 34:8–10, 13–15)

Like the author of Hebrews, both Lehi and Amulek see Christ's atonement as "a great and last sacrifice" that was sufficient to fulfill the demands of justice inherent in the law of Moses. Going further, the Nephite prophets saw the Atonement making possible the forgiveness of sins through the mercy of Christ's gospel, which required faith and repentance and not Mosaic sacrifices. Even when Jesus came to the Nephites after his resurrection, he did not refer to himself as the sacrifice, but instead instructed them that they were to replace the blood sacrifices they had been making under the law of Moses with sacrifices of their own broken hearts and contrite spirits:

And as many as have received me, to them have I given to become the sons of God. . . . For behold, by me redemption cometh, and in me is the law of Moses fulfilled. . . . And ye shall offer up unto me no more the shedding of blood. . . . And ye shall offer for a sacrifice unto me a broken heart and a contrite spirit. And whoso cometh unto me with a broken heart and a contrite spirit, him will I baptize with fire and with the Holy Ghost. (3 Nephi 9:17, 19–20)

The new gospel covenant instituted by Christ, through his atonement, would seem to focus on the same purpose as ancient sacrifice if we understand that being to recover an intimate relationship between God and his fallen children—bringing them back into his presence, or at least into a process that can lead to a full recovery of his presence.

5. Redemption

Less prominent in the New Testament than in either the Old Testament or the Book of Mormon is the notion that through his atonement Jesus redeemed all people from physical death and all those who would repent from their sins. One of the more common meanings for the New Testament language of redemption comes from the idea of ransoms paid to liberate enslaved peoples. This is reflected in English translations where Paul tells believers that they "were bought with a price" or where Mark tells us that Jesus's death was "a ransom for many" (1 Corinthians 6:20; 7:23; Mark 10:45 NRSV). While some interpreters believe strongly that Jesus's suffering and death are to be understood literally as a price paid to redeem us from hell, there are linguistic reasons to doubt this, and it has not been easy to identify to whom this price was paid. Characterizing it as a payment to God or to Satan leads to other difficult theological questions that have not been answered persuasively. Others have argued that a more reasonable interpretation of the New Testament language of redemption would focus on its more universal meanings of *rescue* or *liberation*, as exemplified historically in God's redemption of Israel from Egyptian slavery. This would seem to accord better with the larger range of statements in both the Old Testament and the Book of Mormon.[11]

The Hebrew Bible boasts as many as seventeen different terms that have been translated with some derivative of the English word *redeem*. While only a fraction of these have *ransom* or *redeem* as a principal meaning, almost all of them feature *deliver* or *save* as a principal meaning, including the name Joshua (*yeshuw'ah*), which was the name the angel prescribed to Joseph and Mary for their son Jesus: "She will bear a son, and you are to name him Jesus, for he will *save* his people from their sins" (Matthew 1:21 NRSV; compare Luke 1:31). Many of these terms can be used to mean *rescue* or *free/liberate*.

Scholars have recognized that one of the main Old Testament terms for *redeem* or *ransom* (*gā'al*) carries a special meaning in the familial contexts that pervade the Bible. As Laird Harris has explained:

> The primary meaning of this root is to *do the part of a kinsman* and thus to redeem his kin from difficulty or danger. It is used with its derivatives 118 times. One difference between this root and the very similar root *pādā* "redeem" is that there is usually an emphasis in *gā'al* on the redemption being the privilege or duty of a near relative.[12]

The classic example would be the story of Naomi, Ruth, and Boaz, who steps up as kinsman of Naomi's deceased husband to redeem the impoverished woman's property and to marry her widowed daughter-in-law and raise up children for her posterity. The term *gā'al* is used seven times in the negotiation between Naomi and Boaz as he accepts her request that he become the redeeming kinsman.

It may not be obvious to modern readers that ancient Israelites would also have seen themselves as God's kin and the Lord as their divine kinsman. Frank Moore Cross has forcefully reminded Bible readers that ancient Israel was a typical West Semitic tribal group with its social organization "grounded in kinship."[13] This kinship entailed a number of obligations, including protecting one's kinfolk, looking out for their welfare, and *playing the role of redeemer* to those in needy circumstances—"to love one's kinsman as himself, as his own soul."[14]

Like all such tribal societies, the Israelites saw their god Yahweh (Jehovah) as their divine kinsman, who fulfills the mutual obligations and receives the privileges of kinship. "He leads in battle, redeems from slavery, loves his family, shares the land of his heritage . . . , provides and protects. He blesses those who bless his kindred, curses those who curse his kindred. The family of the deity rallies to his call to holy war, 'the wars of Yahweh', keeps his cultus, obeys his patriarchal commands, maintains familial loyalty (*hesed*), loves him with all their soul, calls on his name."[15]

This kinship of Israelites with the Lord was further assured for all who would be part of Israel by the establishment of Yahweh's covenant with them. Nonkin were incorporated into Israel as kin through the covenants and rites of marriage and adoption. Periodic covenant renewal ceremonies refreshed this relationship to Yahweh for all the tribes and their members. In this way, all were reconfirmed as "the people of Yahweh."

The God of Israel adopts Israel as a "son" and is called "father," enters a marriage contract with Israel and is designated "husband," swears fealty oaths together with Israel, and enters into covenant, assuming the mutual obligations of kinship, taking vengeance on Israel's enemies, and going to war at the head of Israel's militia.

Marriage in ancient Israel may be described as entry into a mutual covenant of love, loyalty (*hesed*), and fidelity (*ĕmet*). In Ezekiel 16 Jerusalem is addressed as a beautiful woman of mixed ancestry. Yahweh came upon her and said, "I looked upon thee, and behold thy time was a time of love, and I spread my skirt over thee and covered thy nakedness, and I made oaths to thee and entered into a covenant with thee . . . and thou becamest mine."[16]

The strong sense of Yahweh as the divine kinsman helps us understand the redemption talk in these passages as Yahweh doing his duty as a kinsman—employing all his powers and resources to protect and bless—and to redeem his people. The iconic story of his redemption of Israel in Egypt is paired with his redemption of all peoples from the powers of Satan and from death.

Isaiah stands out in the Old Testament for the numerous references to the Lord as the Redeemer of Israel. He repeatedly quotes the Lord calling himself "the Redeemer of Israel," or otherwise refers to him in those terms. Every one of these twenty-three references uses *gāʾal*, the Hebrew term for a kinsman redeemer.[17] Psalms follows the same pattern. This emphasis on various forms of *redeem* in the atonement language of the Old Testament is magnified even more in the Book of Mormon, which features 118 instances, some of which occur in quotations of Isaiah. We have only the English translation of the Book of Mormon, and we can only speculate what the underlying language might have been. But all of these occurrences could fit comfortably with the implication of a kinsman redeemer and the associated phraseology of Isaiah that comes from his exclusive use of *gāʾal*. While, as is demonstrated above, the four other atonement concepts invoked in the New Testament also show up in some clear ways in the Book of Mormon, the language of redemption turns out to provide the most common atonement terminology. Of the thirty-one references to the plan of salvation, seventeen label it "the plan of redemption," and no other label occurs more than three times.

The Book of Mormon makes clear in two different ways that mankind's kinship relationship with the Lord is an essential dimension of his redeeming work and that we can understand that redemption as the Lord's performance of his duties and privileges as a kinsman redeemer. Much of this language in the Old Testament refers to the corporate redemption of Israel from time to time historically and, even more importantly, to the eventual gathering and redemption of all of Israel in the last days—as promised in numerous prophetic interpretations of the covenant of Abraham.[18] But, as the Nephite prophets explain from the beginning, God's promises to Abraham serve as instructive surrogates of the promises of salvation that he offers universally—to all men and women whether they be Israelites or Gentiles. And all face the same requirements for redemption—they must repent and covenant with the Lord to take his name upon them and to obey his commandments. As Nephi explained: "As many of the Gentiles as will repent are the covenant people of the Lord; and as many of the Jews as will not repent shall be cast off. For the Lord covenanteth with none save it be with them that repent and believe in his Son, which is the Holy One of Israel" (2 Nephi 30:2).

The second way the Lord emphasizes his kinship relationship with the redeemed arises from the covenant they make with him when they accept his gospel by repenting of their sins and being baptized as a witness of that covenant. Those who do so "with full purpose of heart" receive a remission of sins when the Father baptizes them with "fire and [with] the Holy Ghost," thereby redeeming them and making them his sons and daughters, as they are spiritually reborn (2 Nephi 31:13–14). In the words of Alma at the time he experienced this personally:

> I have repented of my sins and have been *redeemed* of the Lord. Behold, I am born of the Spirit. And the Lord said unto me: Marvel not that all mankind, yea, men and women—all nations, kindreds, tongues, and people—must be born again, yea, born of God, changed from their carnal and fallen state to a state of righteousness, being *redeemed* of God, becoming his sons and daughters. (Mosiah 27:24–25)

The Nephite Synthesis

Whereas scholars tend to emphasize the differences between the various accounts of the Atonement in the New Testament, the Book of Mormon endorses them all as integral aspects of "the great plan of redemption." Book of Mormon atonement explanations feature much of the same basic language seen in the New Testament. But rather than seeing these as competing explanations, the Nephite prophets seem to have understood each as one part of the larger story. This is most obvious in the lengthy atonement discourse of Jacob as preserved by Nephi in 2 Nephi 9–10, which may well have served as the model for all his successors.[19]

Jacob begins with the plan of salvation, or "the merciful plan of the great Creator." "For as death hath passed upon all men, . . . there must needs be a power of resurrection" (2 Nephi 9:6). Because of the Fall, "our flesh must waste away and die" (9:4), which makes the Resurrection necessary. But there was also a fundamental spiritual consequence, for "the fall came by reason of transgression"—which in turn cut men "off from the presence of the Lord" (9:6). Because physical death would be of "endless duration," Jacob saw that "an infinite atonement" would be required (9:7).[20] Without this "our spirits must become subject to that angel which fell from before the presence of the Eternal God and became the devil, to rise no more" (9:8).

Jacob here emphasizes the role of the devil, whose dominion over fallen men is undermined by the Resurrection:

> For behold, if the flesh should rise no more, our spirits must become subject to that angel which fell from before the presence of the Eternal God and became the devil, to rise no more. And our spirits must have become like unto him, and we become devils, angels to a devil—to be shut out from the presence of our God and to remain with the father of lies, in misery, like unto himself. (2 Nephi 9:8–9)

But because the Messiah will come to "redeem the children of men from the fall, . . . they have become free forever, . . . and they are free to choose liberty and eternal life through the great Mediator of all men, or to choose captivity and death according to the captivity and power of the devil" (2 Nephi 2:26–27).

Jacob characterizes this latter possibility as an "awful monster," which is "death and hell . . . [or] the death of the body and . . . the death of the spirit." But God has prepared "the way of deliverance," whereby "the bodies and the spirits of men will be restored one to the other" by "the power of the resurrection of the Holy One of Israel." This "power of the resurrection" causes that "hell must deliver up its captive spirits and the grave must deliver up its captive bodies." With "the spirit and the body . . . restored to itself again, . . . all men become incorruptible and immortal; and . . . they must appear before the judgment seat of the Holy One of Israel" to "be judged according to the holy judgment of God" (9:10–15).

Jacob's explication of the atonement of Jesus Christ draws heavily on the broader context of the plan of salvation as it was understood by the first generation of Nephite prophets. As an essential step in their progress toward eternal life in the presence of the Father, his spirit children were given physical bodies in a physical world. The Fall of Adam and Eve brought both physical and spiritual death into the world—deaths from which there was no escape. Their corrupted bodies would die and rot back into the dust, and they had no way to overcome the separation from the presence of the Father that resulted from the Fall. But God had foreseen all this, and his plan included a grand rescue or redemption by which those men and women who would choose to turn back from the way of the devil to follow the way of the Lord might be saved. The key was to overcome the finality of physical death. Jacob does not tell us how the sufferings and crucifixion of Jesus Christ could accomplish his resurrection. But when the Father raised him up from the grave, he instituted the general resurrection by which the spirits and bodies of all men and women would be reunited incorruptibly and would be brought before the judgment bar of Christ—at which time they would be rewarded according to the way they had chosen, according to their works.

Both the language and the logic of Jacob's explanations provide the model for all later Nephite prophets. Centuries later we find Abinadi adopting Jacob's distinctive phrasing in his own detailed teaching of the Atonement to the wicked priests of King Noah (Mosiah 15–16). Alma taught the words of Abinadi to his first converts "concerning the resurrection of the dead, and the redemption of the people which was to be brought to pass through the power and sufferings and death of Christ and his resurrection and ascension into heaven" (Mosiah 18:2). His son Alma continued with the same language, teaching the Nephites in Zarahemla of the great joy that comes "because of the resurrection of the dead, according to the will and power and deliverance of Jesus Christ from the bands of death" (Alma 4:14; compare 41:2). Later, his missionary companion Amulek presented one of the more complete discussions of the Atonement to the Zoramites, in which he also draws repeatedly on Jacob's formulations (Alma 34). And another four centuries later in his final comments, Mormon explains that "all men are redeemed, because the death of Christ bringeth to pass the resurrection, which bringeth to pass a redemption from an endless sleep, from which sleep all men shall be awoke by the power of God" (Mormon 9:13). So it is that the followers of Christ can "have hope through the atonement of Christ and the power of his resurrection, to be raised unto life eternal" (Moroni 7:41).

Just as the resurrection of Christ breaks the bands of death and raises all men to judgment before him, so has he given them a law or a commandment or "his words" by which they shall be judged (2 Nephi 9:17). Throughout the Book of Mormon, this law is referred to as "the way" or as the doctrine or the gospel of Jesus Christ. Just as "the plan of our God" describes all that the Father and the Son have done and will do to make eternal life possible for the children of men, the gospel spells out what men and women must do individually to receive this great blessing (9:13). As Jacob explains:

> He commandeth all men that they must repent and be baptized in his name, having perfect faith in the Holy One of Israel, or they cannot be saved in the kingdom of God. And if they will not repent and believe in his name and be baptized in his name and endure to the end, they must be damned, for the Lord God, the Holy One of Israel, hath spoken it. (2 Nephi 9:23–24)[21]

The recognition of Christ's sufferings as an essential dimension of his atonement is central to the teachings of all these Nephite prophets. Yet they offer a surprising variety of reasons why his suffering was necessary, reasons that can illuminate their understanding of the atonement itself. Jacob explains that he saw Christ's suffering and death leading to his resurrection and his role as judge of all men (2 Nephi 9:22). Benjamin thought Christ's suffering arose from "his anguish for the wickedness and abominations of his people" (Mosiah 3:7). Abinadi quoted Isaiah 53 to teach that Jesus bore our sorrows and was wounded and bruised for our iniquities. Abinadi saw God as the agent who used Christ's death and resurrection to gain the victory over death. He then gave the Son "power to make intercession for the children of men" because his experience would enable his "bowels of mercy" and fill him "with compassion toward the children of men." Abinadi explains that because Christ has broken the bands of death and taken men's transgressions upon himself, he can stand between them and justice, satisfying the demands of justice and redeeming his people (Mosiah 15:8–9). Alma later invoked this same phrasing and added the insight that by taking upon himself the infirmities of his people, Christ is "filled with mercy, according to the flesh, that he may know according to the flesh how to succor his people according to their infirmities" (Alma 7:12).

Conclusions

Like the New Testament writers, the Nephite prophets affirm repeatedly the facts of Christ's atonement and how through that atonement the Father and the Son have provided for the resurrection of all and the salvation and exaltation of all who will accept the invitation to repent and come unto Christ through obedience to his commandments—by enduring to the end. The Nephite sermons reference the power of the Father, the victory over death, the sufferings of Christ, and the notion of a divine kinsman redeeming his people from the captivity of the devil. Whereas these various features of the Atonement have been developed in Christian tradition as competing theories of atonement, the Nephite prophets understood them all as compatible pieces of one coherent explanation, which is fully elaborated by Jacob. Even so, many of the questions that can be asked about the inner workings of the Atonement remain unanswered. Nevertheless, as individuals who respond to the gospel invitation, we can each learn through our own experience that the Atonement described by those prophets does work with great power in our lives—refining our spirits and enabling us to bear the same testimony they have provided.

Noel B. Reynolds is a professor emeritus of political science at Brigham Young University.

Further Reading

Beilby, James, and Paul R. Eddy, eds. *The Nature of the Atonement: Four Views*. Downers Grove, IL: InterVarsity, 2006.

Finlan, Stephen. *Problems with Atonement: The Origins of and Controversy about the Atonement Doctrine*. Collegeville, MN: Liturgical Press, 2005.

Lane, Jennifer Clark. "The Lord Will Redeem His People: Adoptive Covenant and Redemption in the Old Testament and Book of Mormon," *Journal of Book of Mormon Studies* 2, no. 2 (1993): 39–62.

Spackman, T. Benjamin. "The Israelite Roots of Atonement Terminology." *BYU Studies Quarterly* 55, no. 1 (2016): 39–64.

Tuckett, C. M. "Atonement in the New Testament." In *Anchor Bible Dictionary*, edited by David Noel Freedman, 1:518–22. New York: Doubleday, 1992.

Notes

1. See C. M. Tuckett, "Atonement in the New Testament," *Anchor Bible Dictionary*, ed. David Noel Freedman (New York: Doubleday, 1992), 1:518–22.
2. Jacob returns to this theme twice after the passing of Lehi and Nephi. Compare Jacob 4:11 and 6:9. All quotations from the Book of Mormon are taken from the Yale critical text. See Royal Skousen, ed., *The Book of Mormon: The Earliest Text* (New Haven, CT: Yale University Press, 2009). Italics have been added to emphasize key terminology.
3. For a detailed treatment of the ancient doctrine of the two ways (the teaching contrasting the ways of God and Satan, life and death, light and darkness, etc.), see Noel B. Reynolds, "The Ancient Doctrine of the Two Ways and the Book of Mormon," *BYU Studies Quarterly* 56, no. 3 (2017): 49–78.
4. Noel B. Reynolds, "Understanding the Abrahamic Covenant through the Book of Mormon," *BYU Studies Quarterly* 57, no. 3 (2018): 39–79.
5. This approach was launched by the 1931 publication of Swedish theologian Gustaf Aulen's *Christus Victor: An Historical Study of the Three Main Types of the Idea of the Atonement*. The American edition was translated by A. G. Hebert and published by Macmillan.
6. Abinadi's phrase *sting of death* occurs in the same context as Paul's discussion of the Atonement does in 1 Corinthians 15:55 but has its own twist. Paul equates the sting with sin, which loses its painful effects

through Christ's victory over death. Abinadi specifies the endless "captivity of the devil" as the negative consequence of death that Christ's victory eliminates for the redeemed.

7. See Johannes Behm, "θυρεός," in *Theological Dictionary of the New Testament*, ed. Gerhard Kittel and Gerhard Friedrich, trans. Geoffrey W. Bromiley (Grand Rapids, MI: Zondervan, 2000), 3:180–90.

8. Behm, "θυρεός," 183.

9. Behm, "θυρεός," 183.

10. Behm, "θυρεός," 185–86.

11. See Jennifer Clark Lane, "The Lord Will Redeem His People: Adoptive Covenant and Redemption in the Old Testament and Book of Mormon," *Journal of Book of Mormon Studies* 2, no. 2 (1993), 39–62, for the earliest and most comprehensive application of this Old Testament concept of covenant and redemption in an interpretation of the teachings of the Book of Mormon prophets. While my analysis of atonement is largely independent of Lane's paper, I see the two as being in full agreement in their interpretations of the Book of Mormon.

12. See the full discussion in R. Laird Harris, Gleason L. Archer Jr., and Bruce K. Waltke, *Theological Wordbook of the Old Testament* (Grand Rapids, MI: Moody Press, 1980), 144–45.

13. See Frank Moore Cross, "Kinship and Covenant in Ancient Israel," first published as chapter 1 in his collected essays, *From Epic to Canon* (Baltimore, MD: Johns Hopkins University Press, 1998), 3–21, quotation on page 3. T. Benjamin Spackman has provided a helpful discussion of Cross's essay for Latter-day Saint readers in "The Israelite Roots of Atonement Terminology," *BYU Studies Quarterly* 55, no. 1 (2016): 39–64.

14. Cross, "Kinship and Covenant in Ancient Israel," 4.

15. Cross, "Kinship and Covenant in Ancient Israel," 7.

16. Cross, "Kinship and Covenant in Ancient Israel," 13, citing Ezekiel 16:8; compare Malachi 2:14 ("wife of my covenant").

17. See Isaiah 35:9; 41:14; 43:1, 14; 44:6, 22, 23, 24; 47:4; 48:17, 20; 49: 7, 26; 52:3, 9; 54:5, 8; 59:20; 60:16; 62:12; 63:4, 9, 16.

18. Noel B. Reynolds, "Understanding the Abrahamic Covenant through the Book of Mormon," *BYU Studies Quarterly* 57, no. 3 (2018): 39–74.

19. For the classic Latter-day Saint interpretation of the Atonement as taught in Jacob's sermon, see Robert L. Matthews, "The Atonement of Jesus Christ: 2 Nephi 9," in *The Book of Mormon: Second Nephi, The Doctrinal Structure*, ed. Monte S. Nyman and Charles D. Tate Jr. (Provo, UT: Religious Studies Center, Brigham Young University, 1989), 177–206.

20. Jacob's language reminds us that in the linguistic context of the Book of Mormon we should not be thinking of modern mathematical notions of infinity, but rather the earlier English usage that suggests enormous size or being limitless, or as Jacob says, "endless duration." It also applies without limits to all the peoples of the earth across all time.

21. For a brief discussion of the gospel of Jesus Christ and its relationship to the plan of salvation as these are taught in the Book of Mormon, see Noel B. Reynolds, "This Is the Way," *Religious Educator* 14, no. 3 (2013): 79–91; and Reynolds, "The Plan of Salvation in the Book of Mormon," *Religious Educator* (forthcoming).

21

The Crucifixion

Gaye Strathearn

A number of years ago some members of the Church heard that I was working on a paper about Christ's crucifixion.[1] They asked me why I was bothering with that topic: Why would I want to spend time studying the Crucifixion? Their questions highlighted for me how little we discuss the cross in classes, except perhaps to note that it took place. This modern situation is a long way from Brigham Young's direction to the missionaries that if they wanted to be successful on their missions they would need to have their minds "riveted—yes, I may say riveted—on the cross of Christ."[2] My response to my friends' questions was that although we may not often talk much about it, the cross was not just a historical event, it was a central part of Jesus's atoning sacrifice and is an important doctrine taught in our standard works. I have often thought about that exchange as I have continued to try to understand more fully the implications of the cross for my salvation.

In an effort to more fully understand and appreciate the importance of the cross and its doctrinal implications, I will discuss four aspects of crucifixion. First, I will discuss the literary and material culture evidence for crucifixion in the ancient world. In doing so we will be better placed to understand the descriptions on Jesus's crucifixion in the Gospel accounts. While many texts mention crucifixion, they generally do not provide detailed descriptions of it. Nevertheless, we will see that most of the elements mentioned in the Gospel accounts of Jesus's crucifixion are compatible with the nonbiblical texts and material culture. Second, I will discuss some of the medical research into the physical causes for Jesus's death on the cross. Given the variety of ways that crucifixions were performed in antiquity, the limited ancient sources, and the ethical limitations for modern research, it is difficult to do more than hypothesize the causes. Even so, important insight can be gleaned into the physical trauma. Third, I will discuss the doctrine of the cross as taught in both the New Testament and in our Restoration scripture. In doing so, we will see a consistent theme of the importance of the cross in the teachings of Christ's redemption of humanity. Finally, I will look at just one example of personal application of the doctrine of the cross. Throughout I will argue that the cross is anything but a marginal footnote—rather, it is an integral part of the Savior's atonement and is therefore something that deserves our attention and careful study.

Crucifixion in the Ancient World

The Gospel accounts of Jesus's crucifixion provide relatively few specific details. While there is some level of agreement among the accounts for certain aspects, there are also aspects unique to each Gospel. During his arraignment before Pilate, Jesus was scourged and mocked (Mark 15:15–17; Matthew 27:26–31; John 19:2; see also the Book of Mormon prophecies: 1 Nephi 19:9; 2 Nephi 6:9; Mosiah 3:9). According to John, Jesus then carried his cross to the place of execution (John 19:17), although the Synoptic Gospels record that Simon of Cyrene was conscripted to carry it (Mark 15:21; Matthew 27:32; Luke 23:26). The place of crucifixion was known as the Place of the Skull, variously identified by the Aramaic "Golgotha" (Mark 15:22; Matthew 27:33; John 19:17) or the Latin "Calvary" (Luke 23:33), which John places "nigh to the city" (19:20).

The Gospels are united in recording that Jesus was crucified along with two others (Mark 15:27; Matthew 27:38; Luke 23:33; John 19:18). None of the Gospel accounts of the Crucifixion make explicit mention of how he was attached to the cross, although in John 20:25 Thomas insists on seeing and touching "the print of the nails" in the hands of the resurrected Jesus.[3] All of the accounts, however, do note the derision of people who were watching the Crucifixion (Luke 23:35–37) or were passing by (Mark 15:29–32; Matthew 27:39–43).[4] They all record that Jesus was able to speak while he was on the cross (Mark 15:34, 37; Matthew 27:46, 50; Luke 23:43, 46; John 19:26–28, 30). Only John records that the Jews came to Pilate asking him to break the victims' legs so that their bodies would not remain on the cross during the Sabbath, although he notes that when the soldiers came to Jesus he was already dead, and that one of them pierced Jesus's side with a spear (John 19:31–34). All four Gospels record that Joseph of Arimathea asked Pilate for Jesus's body so that he could bury him (Mark 15:43–45; Matthew 27:57–59; Luke 23:50–53; John 19:38), but John alone identifies Nicodemus as the one who brought spices to prepare the body for burial (19:39–40). Only Matthew records that guards were posted at the tomb (27:62–66).

While scholars debate many of the specific details about Jesus's life and ministry, the historicity of his crucifixion is not in question. The writings of both Jewish and Roman historians, Josephus (AD 37–ca. 100) and Tacitus (ca. AD 56–120) confirm the Gospels' record that Jesus was crucified by Pilate.[5] As brief as the Gospels' details are, their combined accounts provide one of the most detailed accounts of any ancient crucifixion. Ancient sources frequently mention crucifixions taking place, but they rarely give extended details. Nevertheless, they can help readers of the New Testament better understand the nuances of Jesus's crucifixion.

Crucifixion has been defined as "execution by suspension," although generally it does not include "impalement or hanging."[6] The Persians seem to have invented the practice,[7] but many ancient groups, including the Romans and Jews, carried it out as a form of capital punishment.[8] Even though Christians generally have a set idea of what ancient crucifixion looked like, the term covered a wide range of practices. Seneca, a Roman philosopher (4 BC– AD 65), wrote, "Yonder I see crosses, not indeed a single kind, but differently contrived by different peoples."[9] Sometimes the suspension took place on a tree,[10] a pole,[11] or a variety of cross types, either the *crux commissa*, which is in the form of a "T" (e.g., the Puteoli and Paletine crucifixion graffiti),[12] or the *crux immissa*, also known as the "Latin cross," which has "the crossbar below the top of the stave but above the middle"[13]: † (the usual form used in Christian art). Usually victims were crucified while alive, but sometimes it was after they were dead.[14] Sometimes the victim was even crucified upside down.[15] We know that at least in some places the practice of crucifixion was closely regulated.[16]

In Roman times, this form of punishment was used for a variety of crimes, including arson, desertion, disobedience, piracy, theft, or murder.[17] But Josephus emphasizes that in Roman Judea the most frequent reason for crucifixion was political rebellion.[18] For example, in 4 BC the governor of Syria, Quintilius Varus, crucified two thousand Jews because they incited a rebellion after the death of Herod the Great.[19] On another occasion, he documents that Marcus Antonius Felix, the Roman procurator of Judea (AD 52–58), crucified a limitless number of brigands who had followed Eleazar in his rebellion against Rome.[20]

Although much of our artwork of Jesus's crucifixion portrays a fairly sanitized version of crucifixion, the cruelty of it was well known in the ancient world. Josephus describes it as a "most miserable death," a fact that is born out in the literature.[21] Seneca describes the suffering this way:

> Tell me, is Death so wretched as that? He asks for the climax of suffering; and what does he gain thereby? Merely the boon of a longer existence. But what sort of life is lingering death? Can anyone be found who would prefer wasting away in pain, dying limb by limb, or letting out his life drop by drop, rather than expiring once for all? Can any man be found willing to be fastened to the accursed tree, long sickly, already deformed, swelling with ugly tumours on chest and shoulders, and draw the breath of life amid long-drawn-out agony? I think he would have many excuses for dying even before mounting the cross![22]

We have a few accounts of individuals who survived the ordeal because they were taken down from the cross before death.[23] Its popularity as a form of capital punishment was fostered by the fact that the torture could be extended for long periods of time, it was humiliating, and its public nature served as a deterrent for others. One text attributed to a Roman rhetorician from Hispania named Quintilian (ca. 35–ca. 100 AD) says, "When we crucify criminals the most frequented roads are chosen, where the greatest number of people can look and be seized by fear."[24] This description corresponds with John's account that Jesus was crucified "nigh to the city" (19:20). The fact that there were passersby probably indicates that the site was close to a road of some kind.

Generally Roman citizens, especially the upper classes, were spared from enduring crucifixion. In fact, Cicero, an influential Roman orator and politician (106–43 BC), argues that not only should they not be subject to it but that it should be kept even from their "thought, eyes, and ears."[25] There were, however, some exceptions although they were strongly denounced by Cicero and the Roman historian Suetonius (ca. AD 69–after 122).[26] At the other end of the spectrum, however, slaves (both men and women), criminals, and foreigners were frequently put to death on a cross. It was so frequent that the phrase "*in (malam) crucem ire*," which can be translated literally as "go to an (evil) cross," became a slang expression for telling someone to "go to hell."[27] One gets a sense of the inevitability slaves must have felt about crucifixion from one's declaration in a play by the Roman playwrite Plautus (ca. 254–184 BC): "I know that the cross will be my tomb; there my ancestors have been laid to rest, my father, grandfather, great-grandfather, great-great-grandfather."[28]

By Roman times, some form of torture usually preceded crucifixion. These tortures most frequently included scourging,[29] but other techniques such as "fire and sword"[30] and "fire and hot metal plates"[31] are also noted in the descriptions.

John's account of Jesus carrying his own cross finds a parallel in the writings of a Greek biographer named Plutarch (AD 46–120). He records that "every criminal who goes to execution must carry his own cross on his back."[32] Scholars now believe that the term *cross* here is a reference to only part of the cross—the *patibulum*, or the horizontal part of the cross on which the victim's arms were extended. The vertical pole, in these cases, would have already been in place at the site of execution.[33] Other texts suggest that Plutarch may have overstated the fact when he said that everyone had to carry their cross. For example, the *lex Puteolana* ("laws of Puteoli"), which regulates how crucifixions were to be carried out, suggests that carrying the *patibulum* was optional—to be decided by the contractor in charge of the crucifixion: "*If* [the contractor] wants [the condemned slave] to bring the *patibulum* to the cross, the contractor will have to provide the wooden posts, chains, and cords for the floggers and floggers themselves" (ll. 8–9; emphasis added).[34] The floggers were used to goad the victim carrying the *patibulum* to continue moving to the place of execution. This was part of the torture and humiliation associated with crucifixion.

Once the victim arrived on-site, he or she was attached to the cross. In many of the literary accounts of crucifixion, the descriptions are often ambiguous about how this took place. Frequently they use language describing the victim as being "raised on a cross," being "lifted up" on a cross, or being "fixed" to the cross, but without giving specific details of how it took place. Some were clearly bound by ropes or, as the Pereire gem shows, with fetters.[35] In other cases, both nails and ropes were used.[36] But in some it is clear that they were attached with nails. Josephus describes two crucifixions where he specifically says that they were nailed to the cross. He records how Florus, the procurator of Judea from AD 64–66, crucified Romans

Pereire gem depiction of crucifixion.
© The British Museum.

Right anklebone with nail. *Jehoḥanan crucifixion.*
Courtesy of Kent P. Jackson.

of the equestrian order, who were Jews by birth: he "whipped, and nailed (Greek *proséloō*) [them] to the cross before his tribunal."[37] Likewise, in his description of Titus's siege of Jerusalem, he describes the soldiers capturing Jews who were trying to escape the siege: "So the soldiers out of the wrath and hatred they bore the Jews, nailed (Greek *proséloō*) those they caught. . . to the crosses."[38]

The only archaeological evidence we have for someone crucified in the first century is the remains of an individual named Jehoḥanan ben Ḥagqol, whose bones were found in an ossuary at Giv'at ha Mivtar in Jerusalem in 1968. We know that he was crucified because the nail was still in his right calcaneum (i.e., heel bone). When the nail was originally inserted, it must have hit a knot of wood because the tip of the nail is bent, and thus could not be removed. The position of the nail indicates that Jehoḥanan's feet were nailed on either side of the upright beam of the cross,[39] a position also indicated in the Puteoli crucifixion graffito of Alkimilla.[40] There was no evidence in the case of the Jehoḥanan remains that the bones of the arms or hands were nailed to the cross, so he may have been tied to the *patibulum*.[41] Therefore, Thomas's plea to "see in his hands the print of the nails, and put my finger into the print of the nails" of the resurrected Jesus (John 20:25) is consistent with what we know about crucifixion from the literary and material culture of the period.

Early Christian apologists Irenaeus and Tertullian both mention there was a seat (*sedile*) on the cross for Jesus's crucifixion, although that detail is not mentioned in the Gospel accounts.[42] Both the Puteoli and Palatine graffitos appear to include a *sedile* in their depictions of crosses.[43] These seats were not meant to relieve but to exacerbate the suffering of the victim.

In some cases, in an effort to heighten the shame of the punishment, the victim was crucified nude. The woman Alkimilla, for example, in the Puteoli crucifixion graffito is not clothed and Artemidorus Daldianus, a second-century-AD diviner from Ephesus, writes, "They are crucified naked (Greek *gymnoi*) and the crucified lose their flesh."[44] But the evidence is ambiguous because although the Greek word *gymnos* is generally translated as "naked," it can also be used to describe those who are "lightly clad, without an outer garment."[45] The Palatine graffito shows the victim wearing a short tunic. At least some early Christians believed that Jesus was crucified naked. In the second century AD, the bishop of Sardis named Melito (died ca. 180) lamented Jesus's crucifixion: "O frightful murder! O unheard of injustice! The Lord is disfigured

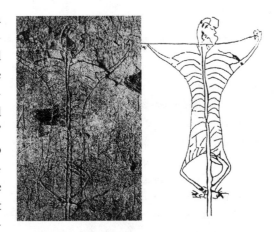

Puteoli graffito. *The Crucified Alkimilla.* Trajanic-Hadrianic era. Puteoli: Via Pergolesi 146, Taberna 5. West Wall. Drawing by Professor Antonio Lombatti. Courtesy of Antonio Lombatti.

and he is not deemed worthy of a cloak for his naked body, so that he might not be seen exposed. For this reason the stars turned and fled, and the day grew quite dark, in order to hide the naked person hanging on the tree, darkening not the body of the Lord, but the eyes of men."[46] Melito's lament is supported by the Pereire gem depicting Jesus naked on the cross. However, possibly in an attempt to preserve Jesus's modesty, the Acts of Pilate, a fourth-century text, states, "And Jesus went out from the praetorium, and the two malefactors with him. And when they came to the place, they stripped him and girded him with a linen cloth and put a crown of thorns on his head."[47]

Both Deuteronomy 21:22–23 and the Temple Scroll from the Dead Sea Scrolls (11Q19 LXIV 11–13) demand that those who "hang on a tree" should not be left there overnight. The body must be buried that day. Of course, this was not the normal practice with crucifixion. Its purpose was to extend the suffering for as long as possible. Once the victim had died, the bodies were usually left on the cross where their flesh was eaten by birds and wild animals[48] as a deterrent to all who saw them. Hence the slave's lament, mentioned above, that the cross would be his tomb, as it had been for his ancestors.[49]

All four Gospel accounts mention that Joseph of Arimathea came to Pilate and gained permission to take Jesus's body and bury it. By Roman times, this practice was permitted in some cases once death had been verified:

> The bodies of those who suffer capital punishment are not to be refused to their relatives; and the deified Augustus writes in the tenth book of his *de Vita Sua* that he also had observed this [custom]. Today, however, the bodies of those who are executed are not buried otherwise than if this had been sought and granted. But sometimes it is not

allowed, particularly [with the bodies] of those condemned for treason. . . . The bodies of executed persons are to be granted to any who seek them for burial.[50]

Philo, a Jewish philosopher living in Alexandria (20 BC–ca. AD 50), knew of men who had been crucified and were taken down from the cross and given to their families for burial prior to the emperor's birthday celebration.[51]

If, however, the person on the cross had not died before the end of the day, in order to comply with the mandate of Deuteronomy 21, other strategies were needed. John says that the soldier broke the legs of the other victims but did not need to do so to Jesus because he was already dead (19:31–33). That the Romans broke people's legs as a form of severe punishment is well attested,[52] but there is little evidence to suggest that it was associated with crucifixion—probably because crucifixion was not meant to be sped up.[53] There is, however, some support for John's description of the soldier piercing Jesus's side with a spear (19:34). Quintilian writes, "Crosses are cut down, the executioner does not prevent those who have been pierced from being buried."[54]

Many features included in the Gospels' accounts of Jesus's crucifixion are compatible with what we know about crucifixions from the literary and material culture of the ancient world. Although we may never know the full extent of Jesus's sufferings on the cross, these accounts more fully deepen our understanding of the sacrifice Jesus made for us. We will now turn our attention to trying to understand what it was about crucifixion that led to Jesus's death on the cross.

Cause of Death during Crucifixion

Modern researchers have tried to explain the physical causes for Christ's death on the cross. The process of discovery is made difficult by a number of factors: (1) crucifixion was performed in different ways, and these different methods may have influenced the pathophysiology leading to death; (2) we have only two types of sources from which to understand the effects of crucifixion: one archaeological discovery and literary texts, which provide only limited clues regarding the physiological effects of crucifixion; and (3) it is impossible to ethically re-create the process of crucifixion in order to study its physiological effects, although there are accounts of crucifixion from modern times.[55] One study attempted to humanely reconstruct crucifixion postures to study its effects on limited aspects of physiology, such as respiratory functioning, oxygen saturation, and blood pressure.[56] While this study resulted in serious questions about the role of asphyxiation as a cause of death, such attempts "cannot be considered directly comparable to crucifixion."[57]

Current thoughts suggest that a combination of medical factors, such as shock and trauma-induced coagulopathy, ultimately led to Christ's death on the cross. First, hypovolemic shock may have resulted from blood loss, dehydration, and tissue trauma. The scriptures record that during the physical and spiritual anguish that transpired in Gethsemane, Christ bled "at every pore" (Doctrine and Covenants 19:18; see also Luke 22:44) and that before his crucifixion he was subsequently beaten repeatedly and scourged. Profuse sweating and deprivation of fluids may also have contributed to his dehydration, as evidenced by the Savior crying out in thirst (John 19:28). Decreased blood perfusion to the bodily tissues may have resulted in a cascade of biochemical events further compromising organ functioning, including blood acidosis and a systemic inflammatory response. These changes associated with traumatic shock can lead to death within several hours. Trauma-induced coagulopathy, resulting in a blood-clotting deficit and bleeding diathesis, is an additional complication that could have further accelerated death.[58] Other medical hypotheses have included heart failure, syncope, asphyxia, arrhythmia plus asphyxia, and pulmonary embolism, any of which could have been present together, with none being the sole cause of death.[59]

With this overview of ancient crucifixion practices in relation to the Gospel accounts, and a brief summary of medical hypotheses about the possible causes of death with crucifixion, we are now in a place to understand the doctrinal aspects of crucifixion in our scriptural texts.

The Doctrine of the Cross

Jesus's teachings about the cross and discipleship

During his mortal ministry, Jesus frequently used the invitation to take up one's cross as a symbol for an invitation to discipleship (Matthew 10:38; 16:34; Mark 8:34; 10:21; Luke 9:23; 14:27). Just after Jesus had promised Peter that he would give to him the sealing keys, Jesus began to speak openly about his destiny to go to Jerusalem, where he would "suffer many things of the elders and chief priests and scribes, and be killed, and be raised again the third day" (Matthew 16:21; see also Mark 8:31; Luke 9:22). Peter immediately tried to assure his Master that this would not happen, to which Jesus responded by saying, "Get thee behind me, Satan: thou art an offence unto me: for thou savourest not the things that be of God, but those that be of men. Then said Jesus unto his disciples, If any man will come after me, let him deny himself, and take up his cross, and follow me" (Matthew 16:23–24). Luke, who uses a slightly different form of the verb (*arneomai*), adds, "Let him deny himself, and take up his cross *daily*, and follow me" (Luke 9:23; emphasis added). What does it mean to "take up our cross"?

In this context, it means that disciples must deny themselves. Both Matthew and Mark use the Greek word *aparneomai*, suggesting that discipleship entails the breaking of every link that ties people, even to themselves. It is about being able, like Jesus, to submit our will to the will of the Father (see Mosiah 15:7; Luke 22:42). Everyone who heard Jesus compare discipleship to the cross would have understood the impact of his teaching because of their familiarity with what crucifixion cost. His teachings were more than the abstract metaphor they are to modern readers because crucifixion was a very real part of their lives.

Becoming a disciple meant giving up everything—even our will—to follow Jesus. As Elder Neal A. Maxwell taught, our will is "really the only uniquely personal thing we have to place on God's altar."[60] Just as there was a cost for Jesus on Calvary, there is also a cost to be a disciple. In fact, in other settings, Jesus also taught, "And he that taketh *not* his cross, and followeth after me, *is not worthy of me*" (Matthew 10:38; emphasis added), and even more pointedly, "Whosoever doth not bear his cross, and come after me, *cannot* be my disciple" (Luke 14:27; emphasis added).

Such teachings must have become even more poignant to the earliest Christians as they watched their master arrested, scourged, humiliated, and crucified. How would they explain the paradox of their God being crucified? How would they transform "the offence [Greek *skandalon*] of the cross" (Galatians 5:11) into the doctrine of the cross that emphasized *the symbol of God's transformative power*? For this, in the New Testament, we are indebted to the teachings of Paul.

Paul's response to "the offence of the cross"

The accounts of Jesus's crucifixion in the four Gospels focus on the events of the trial and the subsequent crucifixion, with no attempt to discuss the significance of those events. In other words, the crucifixion accounts are generally more interested in the historical events than they are with the doctrinal implications. In Acts, the Crucifixion is at the heart of the teachings of Peter and John (2:23, 36; 4:10). Likewise, Paul reminds the Corinthians that he "determined not to know any thing among you, save Jesus Christ and him crucified" (1 Corinthians 2:2).

It is clear that the Christian message that Jesus, as Son of God, was crucified was troubling to both Jews and Gentiles. In his letter to the Galatians, Paul acknowledged that under the law of Moses, "cursed is every one that hangeth on a tree" (Galatians 3:13; see Deuteronomy 21:22–23).[61] We also know that some people mocked Christians for worshipping a God who was crucified. One example is the second-century Cynic philosopher Lucian, who once lived among Christians in the land of Israel. He later wrote a satire that mocked Christians who "have sinned by denying the Greek gods, and by worshipping that crucified sophist himself and living according to his laws." Further, Jesus was a man "whom they still worship—the man who was crucified in Palestine for introducing this new cult to the world."[62] In the literature we also see Christians and pagans in dialogue over the value of the Crucifixion. In the second century, Justin Martyr, a Christian apologist, acknowledged the charges: "It is for this that they charge us with madness, saying that we give the second place after the unchanging and ever-existing God and begetter of all things to a crucified man."[63] In the second or third century, Minucius Felix's *Octavius* tells of a pagan retort against Christians: "To say that a malefactor put to death for his crimes, and wood of the death-dealing cross, are objects of their veneration is to assign fitting altars to abandoned wretches and the kind of worship they deserve."[64] A graphic representation of the disdain that pagans had for the Christian worship of a crucified god is a graffito carved into plaster on a wall near the Palatine Hill in Rome that is probably dated from the second or third century.[65] It depicts a boy at the foot of a crucified man that has the head of a donkey. The crude inscription reads, "Alexamenos worships [his] God."[66]

It is probably this type of criticism of Christianity, what Paul calls "the offence of the cross," that he responds to as he emphasizes its importance. He acknowledges this type of taunt when he declares, "For the preaching of the cross is to them that perish foolishness; but unto us which are saved it is the power of God. . . . For the Jews require a sign, and the Greeks seek after wisdom: but we preach Christ crucified, unto the Jews a stumblingblock [Greek *skandalon*], and unto the Greeks foolishness" (1 Corinthians 1:18, 22–23).[67] In this passage, Paul reconfigures the traditional understanding of crucifixion from a symbol of shame into a symbol of the transformative *power of God*. He understands this power as the power to redeem the sinner and to transform him from the "old man" (Romans 6:6) into a new creature. President Joseph F. Smith describes this process as becoming "soldiers of the

Palatine graffito and drawing of the same. The inscription reads "Alexamenos worships [his] God."

Cross."[68] Thus Christ's crucifixion became the symbol of what must happen to all. Speaking of his own spiritual transformation, Paul taught the Galatians, "I am crucified with Christ: nevertheless I live; yet not I, but Christ liveth in me: and the life which I now live in the flesh I live by the faith of the Son of God, who loved me, and gave himself for me" (Galatians 2:20). He therefore glories in the cross: "But God forbid that I should glory, save in the cross of our Lord Jesus Christ, by whom the world is crucified unto me, and I unto the world" (6:14). Being crucified with Christ enables "that the body of sin might be destroyed, that henceforth we should not serve sin" (Romans 6:6). With that destruction of the body of sin through the cross, God is able to bring unity to the Church that is otherwise rife with enmity (Ephesians 2:16).

It is therefore not surprising that Paul weaves the cross throughout the fabric of his teaching. In 1 Corinthians he identifies two particular doctrines that are inseparably tied to the cross. In both cases he uses technical language for "the transmission of religious instruction": he *delivered* unto the saints what he had *received* of the Lord.[69] The first of the doctrines tied to the cross is that when the saints gather to partake of the Lord's Supper they are in effect "proclaiming [Greek *katangellō*] the Lord's death till he come" (1 Corinthians 11:26). In other words, individually and collectively they are standing as witnesses to proclaim their involvement in appropriating "the cross both for redemption and lifestyle as those who share Christ's death in order to share Christ's life."[70]

The second place where Paul weaves the cross into the doctrine that he received and delivered to the saints is with the Resurrection. "For I delivered unto you the most important things [Greek *en prōtois*] which I also received, how that Christ died for our sins according to the scriptures; and that he was buried, and that he rose again the third day according to the scriptures" (1 Corinthians 15:3–4). The most important things that Paul taught to the Corinthians were the Crucifixion and the Resurrection. Paul here chooses to use the Crucifixion as the symbol for Jesus's atoning sacrifice. For Paul and the early Christians, the cross was inseparably tied to the Resurrection (e.g., Romans 6:3–6; Galatians 2:20). Paul proclaims that he was willing to sacrifice everything that was once important to him "that I might know [Christ] and the power of the resurrection" and that to do this he would need to be "made conformable unto [Christ's] death [i.e., to be like Christ in his death; Greek *summorphizō*]" (Philippians 3:10). Without the events on the cross, there would have been no Resurrection, and without the Resurrection "then is our preaching vain, and your faith is also vain" (1 Corinthians 15:14). In other words, the Resurrection gave meaning to the cross, and the cross gave meaning to the Resurrection. They were two sides of the same coin. In the ancient Mediterranean, this combination of the cross and the Resurrection was something unique to Christianity: it transformed the fear and shame of crucifixion into a powerful doctrine and symbol of God's power to overcome the spiritual vicissitudes of life.

The doctrine of the cross in the Restoration

A *Newsweek* article once claimed that "Mormons do not . . . place much emphasis on Easter,"[71] meaning that we do not place much emphasis on celebrating Good Friday and the Crucifixion.[72] Our practice of emphasizing our distinctive teachings of Christ's suffering in Gethsemane seem to have begun when Elder Joseph Fielding Smith taught:

> It is impossible for us to comprehend the extent of his suffering when he carried the burden of the sins of the whole world, a punishment so severe that we are informed that blood came from the pores of his body, and this was before he was taken to the cross. The punishment of physical pain coming from the nails driven in his hands and feet, was not the greatest of his suffering, excruciating as that surely was. The greater suffering was the spiritual and mental anguish coming from the load of our transgressions which he carried.[73]

Later Elder Smith remarked, "It was in the Garden of Gethsemane that the blood oozed from the pores of his body. . . . That was not when he was on the cross; that was in the garden."[74] My point is *not* to devalue in any way the pivotal part that Gethsemane rightly plays in our theology. My intent is only to remind us that just as the early Christians understood the doctrine of the cross as being inseparably connected with the Resurrection, so our Restoration scripture teaches that it was also inseparably connected with Jesus's atoning and redeeming sacrifice.

Both the Book of Mormon and the Doctrine and Covenants repeatedly refer to Jesus's "sufferings and death" in association with their teachings on his atonement and redemption. In the Book of Mormon, this phrase is at the very heart of some important sermons. For example, when Alma the Younger was secretly preaching the words of Abinadi, he combined Jesus's sufferings, death, and resurrection in his discussion of the redemption of the people: "Yea, concerning that which was to come, and also concerning the resurrection of the dead, and the redemption of the people, which was to be brought to pass through the power, and *sufferings, and death of Christ*, and his resurrection and ascension into heaven" (Mosiah 18:2; emphasis added). The account of Aaron, the son of Mosiah, preaching to the Amalekites in the city of Jerusalem reads, "Now Aaron began to open the scriptures unto them concerning the coming of Christ, and also concerning the resurrection of the dead, and that there could be no redemption for mankind save it were through the death and sufferings of Christ, and the atonement of his blood" (Alma 21:9). Likewise, when he preached to King Lamoni's father, Aaron declared, "And since man had fallen he could not merit anything of himself; but the *sufferings and death of Christ* atone for their sins" (Alma 22:14; emphasis added). Finally, when Mormon wrote to his son Moroni, he implored that Christ's "sufferings and death . . . rest in your mind forever" (Moroni 9:25). In the Doctrine and Covenants, Jesus uses this phrase as he advocates with the Father on our behalf: "Father, behold the sufferings and death of him who did no sin, in whom thou wast well pleased; behold the blood of thy Son which was shed, the blood of him whom thou gavest that thyself might be glorified; wherefore Father, spare these my brethren that believe on my name, that they may come unto me and have everlasting life" (Doctrine and Covenants 45:4–5).

In addition to these passages that tightly connect Jesus's death with his sufferings, the Book of Mormon and Doctrine and Covenants on occasion use the cross as *the* symbol of Jesus's atonement. In Nephi's vision of the tree of life, he learns that the tree represents the love of God (1 Nephi 11:21–22). He then is shown some of the evidences of that love as he sees vignettes of Jesus's birth and mortal ministry. As part of that revelatory experience, Nephi "looked and beheld the Lamb of God, that he was taken by the people; yea, the Son of the everlasting God was judged of the world; and I saw and bear record. And I, Nephi saw that he was lifted upon the cross and slain *for the sins of the world*" (1 Nephi 11:32–33; emphasis added). The evidence of God's love for his children is that his Son was crucified for the sins of the world, a teaching remarkably similar to Jesus's teaching to Nicodemus: "And as Moses lifted up the serpent in the wilderness, even so must the Son of man be lifted up: that whosoever believeth in him should not perish, but have eternal life. For God so loved the world, that he gave his only begotten Son, that whosoever believeth in him should not perish, but have everlasting life. For God sent not his Son into the world to condemn the world; but that the world through him might be saved" (John 3:14–17). Thus, both the Bible and the Book of Mormon reinforce the central place of the cross as a symbol both of God's love and of Jesus's atoning sacrifice.

On day two of Jesus's visit to the Americas, he responded to a request from his disciples—"Tell us the name whereby we shall call this church" (3 Nephi 27:3)—by identifying two qualifications for the church: it must bear his name, and it must be "built upon [his] gospel" (27:5–10). Then he gave a definition of his gospel that included the following teaching about the cross: "And my Father sent me that I might be lifted up upon the cross; and after that I had been lifted up upon the cross, that I might draw all men unto me, that as I have been lifted up by men even so should men be lifted up by the Father, to stand before me, to be judged of their works, whether they be good or whether they be evil—and for this cause have I been lifted up; therefore, according to the power of the Father I will draw all men unto me, that they may be judged according to their works" (27:14–15).

What is important for our discussion is that when Jesus himself described his gospel and the Atonement, he described it in terms of the cross: "My Father sent me that I might be lifted up upon the cross" (27:14). Notice the purpose of his being lifted up on the cross: so that he could draw all men unto him to be judged.[75] The rest of his definition of the gospel then outlines what people must do to make sure that day of judgment is a day of rejoicing: repent, be baptized in his name, endure to the end, and be sanctified by the Holy Ghost, "that [they] may stand spotless before [him] at the last day" (27:20). Although in this passage being "lifted up" is associated with judgment, we have already noted that similar language in 1 Nephi 11 and John 3 use the phrase in association with God's love for his people. Being "lifted up" is also a frequent way to describe salvation (1 Nephi 16:2; Doctrine and Covenants 5:35; 9:14; 17:8).

The Doctrine and Covenants includes one of the most powerful scriptural passages about Jesus's atoning sacrifice in Gethsemane (19:16–19; see also Luke 22:44; Mosiah 3:7), but it also includes verses where redemption is specifically identified with the cross. In sections 53 and 54, Jesus declares to both Sidney Gilbert and Newel Knight that he "was crucified for the sins of the world" (53:2; 54:1), and the revelation to President Joseph F. Smith on the redemption of the dead teaches, "And so it was made known among the dead, both small and great, the unrighteous as well as the faithful, that redemption had been wrought through the sacrifice of the Son of God upon the cross" (138:35).

All these passages from our Restoration scripture support the biblical message of Paul that Jesus's crucifixion was an essential part of his atonement. The doctrine of the cross—that Jesus's death on Calvary was "for the sins of all men, who in Adam had fallen"[76]—has been taught by the Prophet Joseph Smith and our Restoration scripture.[77] The events on the cross are an essential part of our personal and collective redemption, and so Elder Jeffrey R. Holland has described Easter Friday as "atoning Friday with its cross."[78]

"The wounded Christ is the Captain of our souls"[79]

As important as this doctrinal understanding of the cross is, there is one more reason why understanding the cross more fully is important for modern Saints. When Jesus first came to the temple in Bountiful, the people were not initially sure who had appeared to them. Even though after the third time they finally understood the words of the Father, "Behold my Beloved Son, in whom I am well pleased, in whom I have glorified my name—hear ye him," when they saw Jesus descending out of heaven and standing in the midst of them, "they thought it was an angel that had appeared unto them" (3 Nephi 11:7–8). So Jesus declared to them:

> Behold, I am Jesus Christ, whom the prophets testified shall come into the world. And behold, I am the light and life of the world; and I have drunk out of that bitter cup which the Father hath given me, and have glorified the Father in taking upon me the sins of the world, in the which I have suffered the will of the Father in all things from the beginning. . . . Arise and come forth unto me, that ye may thrust your hands into my side, and also that ye may feel the prints of the nails in my hands and in my feet, that ye may know that I am the God of Israel, and the God of the whole earth, and have been slain for the sins of the world. (3 Nephi 11:10–11, 14)

Here stood the Son of God in a glorified, resurrected body; a body that was perfect in every way, except for the fact that, as prophesied by Zechariah (Zechariah 13:6), Jesus chose to retain the marks of his crucifixion. For the people of 3 Nephi, this retention was one of the tangible proofs that this being was not an angel but was in fact the Savior of the world. And after they each went forth one by one and "thrust their hands into his side, and did feel the prints of the nails in his hands and in his feet . . . they did cry out with one accord, saying, Hosanna! Blessed be the name of the Most High God! And they did fall down at the feet of Jesus, and did worship him" (3 Nephi 11:15–17). In this instance, the signs of the Crucifixion were a reason to rejoice!

Elder Holland suggests one reason why the marks of Jesus's crucifixion should also cause us to rejoice:

> When we stagger or stumble, [they are a reminder that] He is there to steady and strengthen us. In the end He is there to save us, and for all this He gave His life. However dim our days may seem, they have been a lot darker for the Savior of the world. As a reminder of those days, Jesus has chosen, even in a resurrected, otherwise perfect body, to retain for the benefit of His disciples the wounds in His hands and in His feet and in His side—signs, if you will, that painful things happen even to the pure and the perfect; signs, if you will, that pain in this world is *not* evidence that God doesn't love you; signs, if you will, that problems pass and happiness can be ours. . . . It is the wounded Christ who is the Captain of our souls, He who yet bears the scars of our forgiveness, the lesions of His love and humility, the torn flesh of obedience and sacrifice. These wounds are the principal way we are to recognize Him when He comes.[80]

Conclusion

Jesus's crucifixion on the cross is one of the central tenets of Christianity. Before the Battle of the Milvian Bridge (AD 312) when Constantine the Great saw the sign of the cross emblazoned in the sky with the Greek phrase "With this sign you shall conquer," he may have legitimized the cross as *the* symbol of Christianity, but he did not invent it. As we have noted, it was Jesus himself who linked the symbol of the cross with discipleship, and Paul is the first on record to transform the shame and humiliation of crucifixion into the symbol of God's transformative power. The cross was one element in the trilogy of that transformative power that takes place through Gethsemane, the cross, and the Resurrection. These elements do not stand alone but are interwoven with each other. Although Latter-day Saints may have for a time concentrated on Gethsemane and the Resurrection, such a focus does not do justice to our scriptural texts, which teach the importance of the cross in that trilogy, so much so that at times those scriptural texts even employ the cross as *the* symbol of the Atonement. As Paul taught the Romans, we are "reconciled to God by the death of his Son . . . , by whom we have now received the atonement" (Romans 5:10–11). Thus, there is much to be gained from a careful study of Jesus's crucifixion.

Gaye Strathearn is an associate professor in the Department of Ancient Scripture at Brigham Young University.

Further Reading

Bergeron, Joseph W. "The Crucifixion of Jesus: Review of Hypothesized Mechanisms of Death and Implications of Shock and Trauma-Induced Coagulopathy." *Journal of Forensic and Legal Medicine* 19 (2013): 113–16.

Chapman, David W. *Ancient Jewish and Christian Perceptions of Crucifixion.* Wissenschaftliche Untersuchungen zum Neuen Testament 244. Tübingen, Germany: Mohr Siebeck, 2008.

Cook, John Granger. *Crucifixion in the Mediterranean World.* 2nd ed. Wissenschaftliche Untersuchungen zum Neuen Testament 327. Tübingen, Germany: Mohr Siebeck, 2019.

Longenecker, Bruce W. *The Cross before Constantine: The Early Life of a Christian Symbol.* Minneapolis: Fortress, 2015.

Maslen, Matthew, and Piers D. Mitchel. "Medical Theories on the Cause of Death in Crucifixion." *Journal of the Royal Society of Medicine* 99 (2006): 185–88.

Millet, Robert L. *What Happened to the Cross? Distinctive LDS Teachings.* Salt Lake City: Deseret Book, 2007.

Notes

1. Gaye Strathearn, "Christ's Crucifixion: Reclamation of the Cross," *Religious Educator* 14, no. 1 (2013): 45–57, and reprinted with modifications in *With Healing in His Wings*, ed. Camille Fronk Olson and Thomas A. Wayment (Provo, UT: Religious Studies Center, Brigham Young University; Salt Lake City: Deseret Book, 2013), 55–79.

2. Brigham Young, *Journal of Discourses*, 26 vols. (London: Latter-day Saints' Book Depot, 1854–86), 12:33–34. See also Robert L. Millet, *What Happened to the Cross? Distinctive LDS Teachings* (Salt Lake City: Deseret Book, 2007), 113.

3. Two early Christian texts assume that Jesus was nailed to his cross. Ignatius, writes that he was "truly nailed (Greek *kathēlōmenon*) in the flesh for us under Pontius Pilate and Herod the tetrarch" (*To the Smyrnaeans* 1.2), and the Gospel of Peter says that after the Crucifixion, "the Jews drew the nails from the hands and feet of the Lord and laid him on the earth" (6.21).

4. However, Thomas's response to the apostles' report that they had seen the resurrected Jesus indicates that nails were used in his hands (John 20:25).

5. Josephus, *Jewish Antiquities* 18.63–64. For a discussion of the text-critical issues of this passage, see David W. Chapman, *Ancient Jewish and Christian Perceptions of Crucifixion*, Wissenschaftliche Untersuchungen zum Neuen Testament 2. Reihe 244 (Tübingen, Germany: Mohr Siebeck, 2008), 78–80; and Tacitus, *Annals* 15.44.

6. John Granger Cook, *Crucifixion in the Mediterranean World*, Wissenschaftliche Untersuchungen zum Neuen Testament 327 (Tübingen, Germany: Mohr Siebeck, 2014), 2.

7. J. Schneider, "σταυρός," in *Theological Dictionary of the New Testament*, ed. Gerhard Kittel and Gerhard Friedrich, trans. Geoffrey W. Bromiley, 10 vols. (Grand Rapids, MI: Eerdmans, 1971), 7:573.

8. Josephus records that on at least one occasion a Jew, Alexander Jannaeus, crucified eight hundred other Jews (*Jewish War* 1.96–98; *Antiquities* 13:379–380). It has been argued that the Nahum Pesher from the Dead Sea Scrolls makes reference to Alexander's crucifixions: "Its interpretation [of Nahum 2:13] concerns the Angry Lion [who filled his den with a mass of corpses, carrying out rev]enge against those looking for easy interpretations, who hanged living men [from the tree, committing an atrocity which had not been committed] in Israel since ancient times, for it is horrible for the one hanged alive from the tree" (4Q169 3–4 I 6–8). See Chapman, *Ancient Jewish and Christian Perceptions of Crucifixion*, 57–66.

9. Seneca, *Ad Marciam de consolatione* 20.3. Josephus also notes that crucifixions took place in different forms: "So the soldiers out of the wrath and hatred they bore the Jews, nailed those they caught, one after one way, and another after another, to the crosses, by way of jest; when their multitude was so great, that room was wanting for the crosses, and crosses wanting for the bodies" (*Jewish War* 5.451).

10. Deuteronomy 21:22; Galatians 3:13. For a discussion of Jewish interpretation of Deuteronomy 21:23 as attesting a form of crucifixion, see Chapman, *Ancient Jewish and Christian Perceptions of Crucifixion*, 117–47.

11. John Granger Cook shows an example on a flask made of African red slip ware depicting a criminal suspended on a stake and being attacked by wild beasts. In this case, the execution was a combination of crucifixion on a pole and being attacked by wild beasts. "Crucifixion as Spectacle in Roman Campania," *Novum Testamentum* 54 (2012): 77–80.

12. In a mock legal prosecution attributed to Lucian, the author argues that the cross (Greek *sTAUros*) receives its name from the Greek letter Tau: "Men weep and bewail their lot and curse Cadmus over and over for putting Tau into the alphabet, for they say that their tyrants, following his figure and imitating his build, have fashioned timbers in the same shape and crucify men upon them; and that it is from him that the sorry device gets its sorry name (*stauros, cross*). For all this do you not think that Tau deserves to die many times over? As for me, I hold that in all justice we can only punish Tau by making a T of him." *Consonants at Law: Sigma vs Tau, in the Court of the Seven Vowels* 12, English translation from A. M. Harmon in *The Works of Lucian*, 8 vols., Loeb Classical Library 14 (Harvard University Press, 1972), 1:408–9.

13. Bruce W. Longenecker, *The Cross Before Constantine: The Early Life of a Christian Symbol* (Minneapolis: Fortress, 2015), 12–13.

14. "They were accordingly scourged and subjected to torture of every description, before being killed, and then crucified" (Josephus, *Jewish War* 5.449).

15. "Some hang a man head downwards" (Seneca, *Ad Marciam de consolatione* 20.3); "some hang their victims with head toward the ground" (Josephus, *Jewish War* 5.451).

16. In 1956 a marble inscription (*lex Puteolana*) was found in a taberna (single room shop) close to the amphitheater of Puteoli, a municipality in Campania, Italy. It gives specific requirements for workers who were contracted to perform crucifixions: "Whoever will want to exact punishment on a male slave or female slave at private expense, as he [the owner] who wants the [punishment] to be inflicted, he [the contractor] exacts the punishment in this manner: if he wants [him] to bring the *patibulum* to the cross, the contractor will have to provide wooden posts, chains, and cords for the floggers and the floggers themselves. And anyone who will want to exact punishment will have to give four sesterces for each of the workers who bring the *patibulum* and for the floggers and also for the executioner. Whenever a magistrate exacts punishment at public expense, so shall he decree; and whenever it will have been ordered, the contractor must be ready to carry out the punishment, to set up stakes/crosses, and to provide for free (gratis) nails, pitch, wax, candles, and those things essential for such matters. Also if he will be commanded to drag [the cadaver] out with a hook, he must drag the cadaver itself out, the workers dressed in red, with a bell ringing, to a place where many cadavers will be" (lines 8–11). English translation from John Granger Cook, "Envisioning Crucifixion: Light from Several Inscriptions and the Palatine Graffito," *Novum Testamentum* 50, no. 3 (2008): 265–66.

17. See the list in the subject index under "crimes leading to crucifixion" in Cook, *Crucifixion in the Mediterranean World*, 518.

18. Cook, "Crucifixion and Burial," *New Testament* Studies 57 (2011): 197–98; and Chapman, *Ancient Jewish and Christian Perceptions of Crucifixion*, 78–86.

19. Josephus, *Antiquities* 17.295; *Jewish War* 2.75.

20. Josephus, *Jewish War* 2.253.

21. Josephus, *Jewish War* 7.203.

22. Seneca, *Epistles* 101.13–14, English translation by Richard M. Gummere in Loeb Classical Library 77 (Cambridge, MA: Harvard University Press, 1925), 3:164–65.

23. Herodotus records that one Sandoces was crucified by Darius because he was bribed to give an unjust judgment. When Darius found out that Sandoces had ably served the royal house, he changed his mind and ordered that Sandoces be taken down (7.194). Another example is Josephus's account of when he viewed a crucifixion and recognized three of the victims. He appealed to Titus to take them down. Although all three were cared for, he notes that "yet two of them died under the physician's hands, while the third recovered"

(*The Life of Flavius Josephus*, 420–421). In addition to these two examples, Ovid indicates that those who were being crucified still offered prayers in hope of surviving the ordeal (Ovid, *Letters from the Black Sea* 1.6.37–40). For a description, see Cook, *Crucifixion in the Mediterranean World*, 92–93.

24. Quintilian, *Declamations* 274.13, English translation in *Quintilian: The Lesser Declamations*, 2 vols., ed. and trans. D. R. Shackleton Bailey, Loeb Classical Library (Cambridge, MA: Harvard University Press, 2006), 1:259.

25. Cicero, *For Rabirius on a Charge of Treason* 5.16.

26. Cicero condemned Gaius Verres, the governor of Sicily, for not taking into account Publius Gavius's claims of citizenship when sentencing him to be crucified (*Against Verres* 2.5.157–62). For a discussion of Cicero's contempt for crucifying Roman citizens, see Cook, *Crucifixion in the Mediterranean World*, 62–74. Suetonius condemned Galba for crucifying a guardian who had poisoned his ward. This man also pleaded for a mitigating sentence because of his citizenship. Galba famously honored that citizenship by ordering the guardian's cross to be constructed higher than usual and painting it white (Suetonius, *Galba* 9). See also Josephus, *Jewish War* 2:308.

27. W. T. MacCary and M. M. Willcock, ed., *Plautus, Casina* (Cambridge: Cambridge University Press, 1976), 111. See also Cook, *Crucifixion in the Mediterranean World*, 52–53n9.

28. Plautus, *Miles Gloriosus* 372–73, trans. Wolfgang De Melo, Loeb Classical Library 163 (Cambridge, MA: Harvard University Press, 2011), 180–81.

29. Josephus, *Antiquities* 12.255–256; *Jewish War* 2.307; Dionysius of Halicarnasus, *Roman Antiquities* 5.51.3; 12.6.7; and Cicero, *Against Verres* 2.5.160–62.

30. Philo, *Flaccus* 10.84.

31. Cicero, *Against Verres* 2.5.163.

32. Plutarch, "On the Delays of Devine Vengeance," *Moralia* 7.554 A, B, trans. Philip H. De Lacy and Benedict Einarson, *Plutarch's Moralia*, 15 vols., Loeb Classical Library (Cambridge, MA: Harvard University Press, 1959), 7:215. See also the description in Chariton's romantic novel, *Chaereas and Callirhoe*, where Chaereas describes his ordeal of carrying a cross and being delivered to the executioner (4.3.5).

33. "Let him carry the gibbet [Latin *patibulum*] through the city and then let him be put on the cross" (Plautus, *The Charcoal Play*, 2).

34. Latin text with English translation in Cook, "Envisioning Crucifixion," 265–66 (see note 16 herein).

35. Xenophon of Ephesus says that using ropes was an Egyptian practice: "They raised the cross and bound him to it, tying his hands and feet tight with ropes." *The Story of Anithia and Habrocomes* 4.2.1, trans. Jeffrey Henderson, Loeb Classical Library 69 (Cambridge, MA: Harvard University Press, 2009), 311. The Acts of Andrew says that Andrew's feet and armpits were bound with ropes, without the use of any nails (148). The Pereire gem is, according to Roy D. Kotansky, "the earliest representation of the crucified Jesus, in any medium." "The Magic 'Crucifixion Gem' in the Britism Museum," *Greek, Roman, and Byzantine Studies* 57 (2017): 632. It shows the crucified Jesus being attached to the cross with fetters. This gem is difficult to date. Cook simply assigns it to a time "when the Romans were still practicing crucifixion" (*Crucifixion in the Mediterranean World*, 425). J. Spier and Felicity Harley, however, are more specific in their dating. They suggest that "the style of carving, material, and inscription are all typical of the large group of Greco-Roman magical amulets originating in Egypt and Syria during the second and third centuries." *Picturing the Bible: The Earliest Christian Art* (New Haven: Yale University Press, 2007), 228.

36. Pliny, *Natural History* 28.10.46.

37. Josephus, *Jewish War* 2.308.

38. Josephus, *Jewish War* 5.451. Philo uses the concept of nailing (Greek *prosēloō*) people to the cross as a metaphor in one of his philosophical discussions (*On Dreams That Are God Sent* 2.213).

39. Joseph Zias and Eliezer Sekeles, "The Crucified Man from Giv'at ha Mivtar: A Reappraisal," *Israel Exploration Journal* 35 (1985): 22–27.

40. The Puteoli crucifixion graffito is variously dated between the late first and mid-third century. Cook believes that it "is probably from the era of Trajan." Cook, *Crucifixion in the Mediterranean World*, 6.

41. Zias and Sekeles, "Crucified Man," 26–27.

42. Irenaeus writes, "The very form of the cross too has five extremities, two in length, two in breadth, and one in the middle, on which [last] the person rests who is fixed by the nails" (Irenaeus, *Against Heresies* 2.24.4). Likewise, Tertullian describes, "Every piece of timber which is fixed in the ground in an erect position is a part of a cross, and indeed the greater portion of its mass. But an entire cross is attributed to us, with its transverse beam, of course, and its projecting seat" (Tertullian, *Against the Nations* 1.12.3–4).

43. The Palatine graffito also has a board for the victim to stand on.

44. Artemidorus Daldianus, *Oneirokritika* 2.53. English translation from Cook, *Crucifixion in the Mediterranean World*, 192.

45. Walter Bauer, et al., *A Greek-English Lexicon of the New Testament and Other Early Christian Literature*, 3d ed., rev. and ed. Frederick W. Danker (Chicago and London: University of Chicago Press, 2000), s.v. γυμνος; and Cook, *Crucifixion in the Mediterranean World*, 192–93 and n. 149; and Raymond Brown, *The Death of the Messiah: From Gethsemane to the Grave. A Commentary on the Passion Narratives in the Four Gospels*, 2 vols., Anchor Bible Reference Library (New York: Doubleday, 1994), 2:952–53. My thanks to my colleague Nicholas J. Frederick for his help with this reference.

46. Melito of Sardis, *Peri Pascha* 97.

47. Acts of Pilate, 10:1. English translation in Whilhelm Schneemelcher, ed., *New Testament Apocrypha, Volume 1: Gospels and Related Writings,* rev. ed., trans. R. McL. Wilson (Louisville, KY: Westminster/John Knox, 1991), 512.

48. Suetonius, *The Life of Augustus* 13.1–2; Juvenal, *Satire* 14:77–78; and Acts of Andrew 148.

49. Plautus, *Miles Gloriosus* 372–73.

50. Corpus Iuris Civilis, *Pandectae* 48.24.1–3. English translation by Alan Watson in *The Digest of Justinian*, 4 vols. (Philadelphia: University of Pennsylvania Press, 2009), 4:377.

51. Philo, *Flaccus* 83. For a detailed discussion of the burial of crucified individuals, see Cook, "Crucifixion and Burial," 193–213.

52. For examples, see Suetonius, *The Life of Augustus* 67.2; Ammianus Marcellinus 14.9.8; and Polybius 1.80.13.

53. One late Christian text, the Acts of Andrew, does combine the ideas of breaking legs with crucifixion, although it is a negative example: the proconsul, Aegeates, sent Andrew "to be crucified, ordering his executioners to leave his sinews uncut [i.e., to leave his knees alone; *tas ankulas kataleiphthnai*], as he thought, that he might punish him more." English translation in Schneemelcher, *New Testament Apocrypha*, 2:147.

54. Pseudo Quintilian, *The Major Declamations* 6.9.

55. Cook, *Crucifixion in the Mediterranean World*, 430–35.

56. Frederick T. Zugibe, *The Crucifixion of Jesus: A Forensic Enquiry*, 2nd ed. (New York: M. Evans, 2005), 85–89, 107–22.

57. Joseph W. Bergeron, "The Crucifixion of Jesus: Review of Hypothesized Mechanisms of Death and Implications of Shock and Trauma-Induced Coagulopathy," *Journal of Forensic and Legal Medicine* 19 (2013): 114.

58. See the medical review by Bergeron, "Crucifixion of Jesus," 113–16.

59. Matthew Maslen and Piers D. Mitchell, "Medical Theories on the Cause of Death in Crucifixion," *Journal of the Royal Society of Medicine* 99 (2006): 185–88.

60. Neal A. Maxwell, "'Swallowed Up in the Will of the Father,'" *Ensign*, November 1995, 24.

61. In Jewish literature, crucifixion was seen as one type of Deuteronomy's "hanging on a tree." For a detailed discussion, see Chapman, *Ancient Jewish and Christian Perceptions of Crucifixion*, 117–77. Like Paul, a number of early Christian writers felt the need to reconcile Jesus's crucifixion with this passage in Deuteronomy (Justin Martyr, *Dialogue of Justin Martyr* 93–96; Irenaeus, *Against Heresies* 3.18; and Tertullian, *Against Marcion* 3.18; 5.3).

62. Lucian, *The Death of Peregrinus*, 13, 11, in *Lucian: Selected Dialogues*, trans. Desmond Costa (Oxford: Oxford University Press, 2005), 77.

63. Justin Martyr, *First Apology* 1.13.4. English translation in Cyril C. Richardson, ed., *Early Christian Fathers* (New York: Collier Books, Macmillan, 1970), 249.

64. Minucius Felix, *Octavius* 9.4. English translation by R. R. Glover and G. H. Rendall, Loeb Classical Library 250 (Cambridge MA: Harvard University Press, 1984), 337.

65. George M. A. Hanfmann, "The Crucified Donkey Man: Achaios and Jesus," in *Studies in Classical Art and Archaeology: A Tribute to Peter Heinrich von Blanckenhagen*, ed. Günter Kopcke and Mary B. Moore (Locust Valley, NY: J. J. Augustin, 1979), 205–7, pl. 55, 1.2; Peter Lampe, *From Paul to Valentinus: Christians at Rome in the First Two Centuries*, trans. Michael Steinhauser, ed. Marshall D. Johnson (Minneapolis: Fortress, 2003), 338; and G. H. R. Horsley, *New Documents Illustrating Early Christianity: A Review of the Greek Inscriptions and Papyri Published in 1979* (North Ryde, New South Wales: Ancient History Documentary Research Centre, Macquarie University, 1987), 137.

66. The charge that Christians worshipped a god with an ass's head is one that early Christian writers had to deal with. For example, see Tertullian, *To the Nations* 11, 14; and Minucius Felix, *Octavius* 9.3. Jews also had to deal with this type of charge. Josephus recounts that Apion claimed a man by the name of Zabidus entered their temple and "snatched up the golden head of the pack-ass." Josephus shows his disdain for the account by inserting the comment "as he facetiously calls it." Josephus, *Against Apion* 2.114, English translation by H. St. J. Thackeray, Loeb Classical Library 186 (Cambridge MA: Harvard University Press, 1926), 339.

67. For a detailed discussion of what Jews thought about crucifixion, see Chapman, *Ancient Jewish and Christian Perceptions of Crucifixion*, 211–62.

68. Joseph F. Smith, *Gospel Doctrine: Selections from the Sermons and Writings of Joseph F. Smith* (Salt Lake City: Deseret Book, 1986), 91.

69. Gordon D. Fee, in *The First Epistle to the Corinthians*, New International Commentary on the New Testament (Grand Rapids, MI: Eerdmans, 1987), 548. This is one of the few places where Paul seems to be quoting from the Jesus tradition. We do not know where or how he received this information.

70. Anthony C. Thiselton, in *The First Epistle to the Corinthians*, 887.

71. Kenneth L. Woodward, "What Mormons Believe," *Newsweek*, September 1, 1980, 70. It is a translation of the Greek word *pascha*, which is usually translated as *Passover*.

72. The word *Easter* is found only once in Acts 12:4 (KJV). It is a translation of the Greek word *pascha* or *Passover*, which is what many English translations prefer (NRSV, NIV, ESV).

73. Joseph Fielding Smith, *The Restoration of All Things* (Salt Lake City: Deseret Book, 1945), 199; see also Smith, *Seek Ye Earnestly* (Salt Lake City: Deseret Book, 1970), 119–21. I am grateful for the help of my colleague Robert L. Millet for bringing the quotations of the Restoration prophets to my attention.

74. Joseph Fielding Smith, *Doctrines of Salvation*, comp. Bruce R. McConkie (Salt Lake City: Bookcraft, 1954–56), 1:130. See also Bruce R. McConkie, *Doctrinal New Testament Commentary* (Salt Lake City: Bookcraft, 1979), 1:774–75.

75. Compare John 12:32–33, where Jesus says, "And I, if I be lifted up from the earth, will draw all men unto me. This he said, signifying what death he should die."

76. Joseph Smith—History, 1838–1856, volume C-1 [2 November 1838–31 July 1842], 1014, https://www.josephsmithpapers.org.

77. Many of the prophets have taught the importance of the cross. For example, see John Taylor, *The Gospel Kingdom: Selections from the Writings and Discourses of John Taylor* (Salt Lake City: Bookcraft, 1987), 114; Joseph F. Smith, *Gospel Doctrine*, 91; Heber J. Grant, Charles W. Penrose, and Anthony W. Ivins, in James R. Clark, *Messages of the First Presidency*, 6 vols. (Salt Lake City: Bookcraft, 1967), 5:208; Ezra Taft Benson, *Teachings of Ezra Taft Benson*, ed. Reed A. Benson (Salt Lake City: Bookcraft, 1988), 14; and Gordon B. Hinckley, Christmas devotional, December 8, 1996, as cited in *Church News*, December 14, 1996, 3–4.

78. Jeffery R. Holland, "None Were with Him," *Ensign*, May 2009, 88.

79. Jeffrey R. Holland, "Teaching, Preaching, Healing," *Ensign*, January 2003, 42.

80. Holland, "Teaching, Preaching, Healing," 42.

22

The Resurrection

Julie M. Smith

The New Testament is replete with material concerning the resurrection of Jesus Christ, from passing references to the grand event in the context of other concerns, to more developed discussions of its implications in the lives of the faithful, to accounts of appearances of the resurrected Jesus Christ. A closer look at material concerning the Resurrection in the New Testament shows that the authors agree on the reality and importance of the resurrection of Jesus Christ, but it also shows that they share the "good news" (i.e., gospel) of the Resurrection in distinct ways in order to emphasize various aspects of it.

The Resurrection in the New Testament Epistles

It is appropriate to begin this exploration with the Epistles since most of them were probably written before most of the Gospels. The Resurrection is mentioned with some frequency in the Epistles, and these references seem to fall into three categories.

First, some references are so brief as to seem to be made almost in passing, but they nonetheless make clear that belief in the resurrection of Jesus Christ is the core of the gospel message. For example, the closing lines of the Epistle to the Hebrews mention incidentally that God raised Jesus from the dead: "Now [may] the God of peace, that brought again from the dead our Lord Jesus, that great shepherd of the sheep, through the blood of the everlasting covenant, make you perfect in every good work to do his will" (Hebrews 13:20–21).[1] While these references do not shine much additional light on the nature or meaning of the

Resurrection, they do clearly show that the Resurrection was important to the writer and that its reality was accepted by the author (and presumably by the audience) without the need for extensive defense or explanation.

A second category of references uses the idea of the Resurrection as a reality that should shape the behavior of the writer and the audience but without engaging in the details of the history or doctrine of the Resurrection itself. For example, in 1 Corinthians 6:12–20 Paul tries to persuade his audience of the evils of sexual immorality. After anticipating and responding to justifications one might make in defense of licentiousness (6:12–14), Paul writes that "God hath both raised up the Lord, and will also raise up us by his own power" by way of introducing his own argument, which is that since "your bodies are the members of Christ," violations of the law of chastity would symbolically constitute involving the entire community in unrighteousness. Paul concludes that the fact of the Resurrection means that one should "glorify God in your body, and in your spirit, which are God's." In this instance Paul is not concerned with the history of the Resurrection nor with a deep doctrinal exploration of it, but rather with the simple fact of the resurrection of Jesus Christ as a prod to righteous behavior. Similarly, in 2 Corinthians 4:7–18 Paul describes the extensive challenges he faces and then explains he is able to persevere in faith because he knows that "he which raised up the Lord Jesus shall raise up us also by Jesus" (4:14). The reference to the Resurrection in this passage is a narrative turning point between Paul's complaint of his difficulties (4:7–12) and an explanation of his ability to avoid despair (4:15–18). Once again, Paul does not explore the details of history or doctrine but rather relies on belief in the Resurrection to influence behavior.[2] A similar instance occurs in Romans 10:9 when Paul writes, "If thou shalt . . . believe in thine heart that God hath raised him from the dead, thou shalt be saved," which, in its context, emphasizes that the root of belief in the gospel is belief in the resurrection of Jesus Christ.

The third and final category of resurrection references in the Epistles includes one longer passage, 1 Corinthians 15, that concerns the historical reality of the Resurrection and its theological implications. Paul begins by saying that he conveyed to the audience "first of all" (15:3) the message of Christ's death, burial, and resurrection. In this context "first of all" signals the importance (not necessarily the chronology) of this message and so constitutes Paul's belief in the prime relevance of the resurrection of Jesus Christ. In verse 4, when Paul mentions that Jesus "rose again," the Greek text uses a perfect tense verb, which is a verb tense that implies that this action is not simply an event in the past, but rather that it has an ongoing impact on the present. Additionally, Paul describes Jesus's return to life as "according to the scriptures," conveying his belief that the scriptures contain prophecies of Jesus's resurrection; here he may have specific passages in mind, or he may be alluding to a more universal sense in which the scriptures anticipate the Resurrection. Paul then describes resurrection appearances to Peter (KJV Cephas), the Twelve (this term would be understood as referring to the office, not the actual number, since the group would not have included Judas), five hundred people at once, James (the brother of Jesus), all of the apostles, and then to himself.

The reference to the fact that some of these witnesses were still living (15:6) constitutes a de facto invitation for Paul's audience to ask them about their witness of the resurrected Jesus. Scholars have long puzzled over why Paul's list of resurrection witnesses is not identical to those found in the Gospels, where Mary Magdalene alone (according to John 20:11) or with "the other Mary" (according to Matthew 28:1) or Cleopas and another disciple on the road to Emmaus (according to Luke 24:13) are the first to see the resurrected Jesus. One possibility for reconciling these texts is that Paul was simply unaware of these other resurrection appearances. A second possibility is that Paul (or his source of information) ignores the appearances to women since women's testimony was largely disregarded in the ancient world. Regardless of which explanation is better, the rhetorical effect of 1 Corinthians 15:1–11 is to emphasize the reality of the Resurrection and the role of eyewitnesses—points on which the other New Testament writers would wholeheartedly agree.

In 1 Corinthians 15:12–34, Paul shifts to address those in his audience who do not believe the dead can be resurrected. Here Paul does not equivocate but explains that if there is no resurrection, "then is our preaching vain, and your faith is also vain" and he would then be a "false witness." Ironically, the heretical beliefs of his audience provide Paul with a prime opportunity to emphasize the reality of the resurrection of the dead and, in particular, Jesus's resurrection. In 15:20 Paul considers Jesus's resurrection in the perspective of the grand sweep of history, from Adam (whose death is inverted in Christ's resurrection) to the end of time (when the last enemy, death, is subjugated). In these verses Paul once again makes clear the importance of the Resurrection, this time as the pivot point of history. Next comes the part of the passage most familiar to Latter-day Saint readers: the reference to baptism for the dead. In these verses (15:29–34) Paul returns to the earlier discussion of the reality of the Resurrection—contra those who argue against it—here pointing out that the practice of baptism for the dead (which they apparently do not object to) makes sense only if there is in fact a resurrection.

Verse 35 signals another shift, this time to details of the Resurrection based on the concerns of Paul's audience regarding resurrected bodies: "But some man will say, How are the dead raised up? and with what body do they come?" These questions probably reflect doubt that a physical resurrection can occur after a body has decomposed. Paul's answer begins with an analogy to a seed, implying that just as a seed is different from a plant, the resurrected body is different from a mortal body. Paul is perhaps relying on the "ancient idea that a seed put into the ground dies and is brought to life again miraculously as a plant"[3]; the fact that it is not biologically accurate to describe seeds as "dying" does not undermine Paul's analogy. The point is simply that the resurrected body is different from the mortal body, and thus the decay of the mortal body is not an obstacle to resurrection. As Paul explains in verse 53: "this corruptible [body] must put on incorruption, and this mortal [body] must put on immortality." In other words, the nature of resurrected bodies is sufficiently different from mortal bodies that the natural decay of the mortal body does not present an obstacle to resurrection. The passage concludes with Paul proclaiming that the Resurrection is a victory over death.

To summarize, the material concerning the Resurrection in the Epistles suggests that this event was key to the early Christians. They rarely felt the need (at least in the Epistles as we have them) to expound on the details of the Resurrection. The one exception to this is 1 Corinthians 15, where Paul addresses those who are concerned that the decay that accompanies death would make resurrection impossible. Paul assures his audience, through a variety of arguments, that the natural processes that follow death will not prevent resurrection.

The Resurrection in the Gospel of Mark

Close attention will be paid to the Gospel of Mark since it is the earliest canonical account of the life of Jesus Christ. Because Mark is, fundamentally, a *story*, teachings about the Resurrection often come through the narrative instead of through didactic statements. For example, Jesus's resurrection is foreshadowed in the story of the raising of Jairus's daughter (Mark 5:21–24, 35–43), with which it has obvious thematic similarities as well as some verbal similarities. These similarities emphasize the reality of the power to raise the dead as well as the stunned reaction of onlookers; they also prepare the audience to understand the reality of Jesus's resurrection at the end of the Gospel. Mark's audience would likely have approached the story of Jesus's death with the story of the raising of Jairus's daughter in mind and thus found hope even during the story's darkest moments. Likewise, Mark's story of the Transfiguration has many parallels with the Resurrection, most notably the glorified presence of Jesus. Because the text contains Jesus's admonition that the disciples are not to speak of the Transfiguration until after Jesus was raised from the dead (9:9), when the audience finally hears the story of the Transfiguration, they are implicitly learning that the Resurrection has in fact already happened—thus granting the disciples permission to speak of the Transfiguration. The presence of the story itself is thus a testimony of the reality of the Resurrection, and the content of the story, with its image of a glorified Jesus, is a hint at what that resurrection is like.

Another example of subtle teachings about the Resurrection embedded in the narrative of Mark occurs in 12:1–11, where Jesus shares a thinly veiled parable about wicked tenants: the death of the vineyard owner's son is vindicated (verses 10–11), anticipating Jesus's victory over death. Again, Mark's audience would have brought this hope of vindication with them to the story of Jesus's death and resurrection and thus been more likely to see the Resurrection as suggesting God's vindication of Jesus. There is one other brief reference to the coming resurrection in Mark: at the Last Supper, Jesus stated that after he is raised, he will go to Galilee (14:28). Most of the disciples did not understand the implications of Jesus's words, but Mark's audience learns that Jesus anticipated his death and resurrection. As was the case in the Epistles, these brief references do not develop the meaning or implications of the Resurrection but simply and powerfully attest to its reality.

Teachings about the Resurrection also come through several prophecies that Jesus made of his resurrection. The entire Gospel of Mark cleaves into three sections, and the structural backbone of the middle section (8:22–10:52) consists of three statements that Jesus makes of his death and resurrection; these occur in 8:31, 9:30–32, and 10:32–34. When Jesus states that he will rise "after three days (8:31)," the phrase implies "on the fourth day." Mark will later describe Jesus's rising as happening on the third day (16:1); the discrepancy may stem from the fact that in the Old Testament "three days" sometimes connotes an indeterminate but short amount of time, so it is possible that Jesus is speaking generally here and not specifically. There would then be some irony in the fact that Mark's audience was likely aware that Jesus's language was very close to being literally true with regard to how much time would elapse between his death and resurrection. It is also possible that his resurrection in fact occurred after three days when timed from his suffering and not from his death, as it is usually calculated. This approach may be of particular interest to Latter-day Saint readers, who emphasize Jesus's suffering in Gethsemane as much as—if not more so than—his suffering on the cross. In all three of these prophecies, Jesus mentions his rising from the dead but does so with incredible brevity, adding only the detail of the timing.

As with the Epistles, it appears that the fact of the Resurrection takes priority above commentary on its details or implications. Each prediction that Jesus made of his suffering, death, and resurrection is immediately followed by a mistaken claim made by the disciples (8:32–33; 9:33–34; 10:35–37) that, in turn, is immediately followed by Jesus's teachings about discipleship (8:34–9:1; 9:35–10:31; 10:38–45), and each of these discipleship teachings includes a paradoxical saying (8:35; 9:35; 10:43–44). This tight pattern suggests not only that these prophecies are important in their own right but also that they developed their meaning through this repetitive structure. Specifically, Jesus's teachings about his death and resurrection lead to misunderstandings by his followers that he then clarifies. The pattern of showing evidence of the disciples' misunderstanding immediately after each statement is extremely significant since it intertwines Jesus's mission with the theme of discipleship. In other words, understanding Jesus's identity is closely tied to behaving appropriately as disciples. The link between discipleship and prophecies also suggests that Jesus's suffering and death is the automatic outgrowth of living a certain way; thus discipleship and suffering are linked. These predictions, then, are not just about Jesus's identity but also about the identity of his disciples; the two are inseparably linked.

After each prophecy, Jesus addresses his disciples' misunderstanding; these teachings always contain a paradox, as in Mark 8:35, 9:35, and 10:43–44. Jesus makes clear in each case that the teaching applies to everyone, not just to the disciples who are present. The pattern implies that discipleship necessarily involves paradoxical elements. It is precisely these paradoxes that Jesus's disciples struggle to understand—they always favor one element of the paradox but cannot accept the other element.

While not concerned with Jesus's resurrection in particular but with the concept of resurrection in general, Jesus's conversation with the Sadducees in Mark 12:18–27 provides much insight into the topic of the Resurrection. In this encounter the Sadducees ask what will happen in the next life to a woman who had been married to seven men during her mortal life. Mark introduces the story by pointing out that the Sadducees "say there is no resurrection"; the inclusion of this detail indicates this is not a genuine question about marital status in the afterlife but rather an attempt to embarrass Jesus by pointing out the supposedly absurd consequences of a belief in the Resurrection.[4] What may strike Latter-day Saint readers as ironic about this incident is that the Sadducees seemingly assume that all marriages are eternal—Jesus does not. For our purposes, the key part of the passage occurs when Jesus tells the Sadducees they do not understand the scriptures or the power of God. At its most basic level, Jesus's statement means that resurrected life is different from earth life. Jesus states, "As touching the dead, that they rise: have ye not read in the book of Moses, how in the bush God spake unto him, saying, I am the God of Abraham, and the God of Isaac, and the God of Jacob? He is not the God of the dead, but the God of the living: ye therefore do greatly err" (12:26–27). Jesus's response indicates he was well aware that the Sadducees' question was not really about marriage but rather about resurrection.

Jesus then quotes from Exodus 3:6, where God is self-identifying to Moses to prepare him to return to the people: "Moreover [the Lord] said, I am the God of thy father, the God of Abraham, the God of Isaac, and the God of Jacob." If Abraham, Isaac, and Jacob had no longer existed at the time this was spoken, then it would have made no sense for God to mention their names. The fact that God does use them leads to the conclusion that Abraham, Isaac, and Jacob must have existed after death (as Jesus explains in the next verse) and thus implies there must be a resurrection. So the continued existence of the patriarchs after their deaths negates the Sadducees' belief that there was no resurrection. Simply put, Jesus is using God's reference to Abraham, Isaac, and Jacob after their deaths as evidence that those men continued to live on after their deaths. Jesus explains that, in a sense, there are no dead people: God can self-define in terms of Abraham, Isaac, and Jacob because they are still living. Significantly, Jesus's response to the Sadducees makes clear that this is not solely a dispute about one unusual (and perhaps hypothetical) case concerning a woman with seven husbands. To the extent that the Sadducees (or Mark's audience) understood that Jesus would die and be resurrected, it was important for Jesus to be able to defend the idea of resurrection; otherwise, his entire ministry would have been undermined. Thus what might initially seem like an implausible hypothetical situation was included in Mark's Gospel in order to provide Jesus with an opportunity to explain and defend the concept of resurrection in general and the possibility of his resurrection in particular.

The bulk of Mark's message about the Resurrection comes naturally in the narrative of Jesus's death and return to life. However, strong evidence suggests that the earliest versions of Mark's Gospel ended after 16:8, which means that there is no appearance of the resurrected Jesus in Mark's Gospel. This is not to imply that the resurrected Jesus did not appear to anyone but simply to suggest that that story did not appear in Mark's text. This may seem like the last story a writer would want to leave out of an account of Christ's life, but it is only by comparison with the other canonized Gospels that the lack of a resurrection appearance seems to be a problem: on its own Mark's Gospel has no inherent lack. Note that none of the canonized Gospels relate the actual Resurrection; they only tell of later appearances of the resurrected Jesus, and yet readers generally do not fault the Gospels for this lack.[5] Further, it is possible that members of Mark's audience would not have expected a resurrection appearance, but rather would have thought the empty-tomb scene adequately conveyed the reality of Jesus's resurrection, a rhetorical technique common in Hellenistic literature: "Indeed, it would have been the body's absence, not its presence, that would have signaled the provocative moment for the ancient reader."[6] And if Mark's aim was to motivate the audience to continue to tell the unfinished story of Jesus, then that goal was clearly accomplished since all of the endings later added—in Mark 16:9–20, in Matthew, and in Luke—witness to the success of Mark's strategy of spurring others to, in effect, continue the story themselves. Given that the entire point of the scene at the tomb is that death is not the end, it makes sense that the text does not show the end of Jesus's mission on earth.

But Mark does contain a powerful witness to the reality of the Resurrection even without an appearance of the resurrected Jesus Christ. The young man whom the women find in the tomb functions literarily as a symbol of the Resurrection before he even opens his mouth: Mark's audience would almost certainly have associated this young man at the tomb with the young man who fled arrest in Gethsemane (Mark 14:51–52) since the same Greek word (*neaniskos*) is used for them both (but used nowhere else in Mark) and in both cases their clothing is described. The young man in Gethsemane was dressed in a linen cloth (the same Greek word describes Jesus's burial shroud as "*the* linen cloth," not "*a* linen cloth") and ran away—sans clothing—when the authorities attempted to arrest him. He was initially described as following Jesus, with an unusual prefix on the verb for "following." The only other use of that combination is in Mark 5:37, where the idea of being a close disciple is mentioned, so the young man is presented as a close follower of Jesus—at least before he flees. That flight is a picture of shame: the cloth suggests he showed up with the intent of dying with Jesus but, under pressure, preferred the humiliation of running away naked rather than the pain of death. Jesus is crucified without clothing, just as the young man runs away without clothing, implying that Jesus is symbolically taking the young man's shame upon himself. When the young man reappears at the tomb, he is now wearing clothing associated with honor and glory—clothing described as being like Jesus's clothing at the Transfiguration (these are the only two instances in Mark where clothing is described as being white) and with the young man assuming a position of authority. In other words, he not only has been restored from shame but is now assuming an even more honorable position. In effect, Jesus has swapped roles with this young man and thus made the young man's restoration and glorification possible. In this symbolic presentation, the meaning of Jesus's resurrection is made clear through its effect on this young disciple.

The subtle but clear implication is that Jesus's death and resurrection has made this change possible for the young man. This picture of a young man restored from shame to glory is a key component of the meaning and impact of the Resurrection in Mark's Gospel. The two scenes with the young man show the effect of the Resurrection on the life of the disciple: Jesus's suffering, death, and resurrection make it possible for this young man to escape the shame of failed discipleship and to take on the role of authoritative messenger. He is, through the transformation that has happened to him, the primary resurrection witness in Mark's Gospel. Part of the puzzle of Mark's enigmatic ending is solved when the young man at the tomb is understood as a picture of the ideal disciple—failed, restored, glorified, and providing a template for the other disciples. In this light there is surely no lack—no sense of anything missing—from Mark's Gospel, because the power of the Resurrection is displayed even without an appearance of the resurrected Jesus Christ to any of the disciples.

When the young man in the tomb speaks, it is to announce the reality of the Resurrection and to commission the women to tell the other disciples. These women are given a special task as agents who extend Jesus's forgiveness and an invitation to follow him. Generally, women were not permitted to be witnesses under Jewish law, which means that in order for the disciples, Peter, and Mark's audience to accept the invitation to follow Jesus, they need to disregard the cultural norm of distrusting women's words. (In Luke's Gospel the scandal of women as early witnesses to the Resurrection is made very clear when Luke reports the men's reaction to the women's announcement: "their words seemed to them as idle tales, and they believed them not," Luke 24:11.) The final note of Mark's Gospel, in contrast, is that one cannot be a follower of Jesus—indeed, one will not be given the opportunity to follow Jesus—if one is not willing to listen to women and believe their words.

While some have discounted the reliability of the account of the Resurrection, it is important to realize that *if* the early church were to concoct or expand on an account of the Resurrection, the last thing it would have done would be to make women the sole witnesses to the reality of the Resurrection in light of the enormous cultural bias against the reliability of women's testimony. The fact that our earliest Gospel positions women as the only witnesses to the news of the Resurrection is, ironically, extremely strong evidence that the story happened as recounted in Mark.

In Mark's account Peter is mentioned separately from the disciples in the young man's charge ("tell his disciples and Peter," 16:7), perhaps suggesting he is distanced from the other disciples by his denial of Jesus. However, the implication of the young man's words is that Peter is invited to return to full fellowship by following Jesus to Galilee. Peter and the disciples who fled in fear are being given another chance to follow Jesus; it is evidence of mercy to specifically mention Peter and to make clear that the invitation applied to him as well, despite his earlier denial of Jesus. The promise of restoration to discipleship requires that the disciples act in faith by choosing to follow Jesus to Galilee. They are all expected to respond to the announcement of Jesus's resurrection. Interestingly, the Gospel ends with Mark's audience still in the tomb, left to contemplate, facing the reality that Jesus is no longer there. Those in Mark's audience are invited to seek their own resurrection appearance by choosing to follow Jesus. In a broader perspective, the Resurrection in Mark also functions as a token of vindication. Jesus was misunderstood, mocked, and disregarded at every point during his mortal life, and death by crucifixion was a supreme humiliation. Yet the Resurrection signals God's approval of Jesus's entire mission as set forth in Mark.

The picture of the Resurrection in Mark 16 is, in sum, character-driven, not focused on theological explication. In the young man, the audience sees the potential for the Resurrection to exchange shame for glory not just in Jesus but also in his followers; in the female witnesses, the audience sees the need to listen to women as authorized messengers; in the reference to Peter, the audience realizes that the resurrected Jesus is not going to turn his back even against one who turned against him.

The Resurrection in the Gospel of Matthew

Matthew follows Mark's outline rather closely (at least until after Mark 16:8, presumably because Mark ended at that point), so the material common to both Gospels will not be reiterated here. However, the differences contribute to a slightly different view of the Resurrection than that found in Mark's Gospel. For example, Matthew contains a scene absent in Mark that concerns the placing of guards at Jesus's tomb (Matthew 27:62–66); this scene would have further emphasized to Matthew's audience the reality of the Resurrection by allowing no opportunity for trickery on the part of Jesus's distraught disciples. Additionally, this story makes clear that Jesus's enemies understood and took seriously his prophecies that he would rise from the dead in a way that most of his disciples did not yet understand, which must have struck Matthew's audience as rather ironic. Further, the reference to the guards creates a five-part pattern in Matthew's text:[7]

1. Burial (27:57–61)
2. Placement of guards (27:62–66)
3. Women at the tomb (28:1–10)
4. Guards bribed (28:11–15)
5. Resurrection appearance (28:16–20)

This pattern echoes a similar five-part pattern in Matthew's account of Jesus's infancy (1:18–25; 2:1–12, 13–15, 16–18, 19–23), which also has positive material in the first, third, and fifth sections and negative stories in the second and fourth positions; it may also reflect the overarching structure of Matthew's Gospel, which presents five major discourses by Jesus (5–7; 10; 13; 18; 23–25)—each surrounded by narratives that enact the major themes of the discourse. These fivefold patterns may function to align Jesus with Moses (who was credited with writing the first five books of the Bible), but they also suggest that the material that is literally (and metaphorically) central to the resurrection story is not the appearance of the resurrected Jesus but rather the experience of the women at the tomb. Thus, there is more overlap with Mark's account—at least thematically—than one might initially suspect since both texts focus on the experience of the women at the tomb as central to the story of the Resurrection.

Matthew mentions an earthquake as the women approach the tomb (28:2); as a geophysical sign at the scene of Jesus's resurrection, this earthquake parallels the star that the magi followed (2:2). Together these signs signify the cosmological importance of Jesus's life and death. To Matthew, Jesus's resurrection is literally earthshaking. Matthew's scene at the tomb is similar to Mark's; the real difference comes in Matthew's inclusion of a scene depicting the resurrected Jesus appearing to the women (28:9–10) and then to the eleven disciples (28:16–20). The reference to the women holding Jesus's feet conveys both the physical reality of the Resurrection as well as their human affection for him. Perhaps most significant in the story of Jesus's appearance to the women is the note that they worshipped him; Matthew deftly conveys all that one would need to know about the status of the risen Jesus through the women's actions. As in Mark, the Resurrection vindicates Jesus's humiliating death.

Matthew also narrates the appearance of Jesus in Galilee, including the commission to preach the gospel to the world (Matthew 28:19–20). Jesus's words yield an interesting insight into the Resurrection via his statement "I am with you alway, even unto the end of the world." Here the words translated as "I am" are the same Greek words found in the Septuagint version (the ancient translation of the Bible into Greek) of Exodus 3:14, where God uses them in response to Moses's question about what God's name is: "Moses said unto God, Behold, when I come unto the children of Israel, and . . . they shall say to me, What is his name? what shall I say unto them? And God said unto Moses, I AM THAT I AM: and he said, Thus shalt thou say unto the children of Israel, I AM hath sent me unto you." It is significant that in this post-Resurrection appearance, Jesus is identifying himself with the God of the Old Testament. Yet the word order is skewed so that the text in Matthew reads literally "I with you am," emphasizing verbally the embeddedness of God with the people. Further, this passage forms a bookend with the material in the beginning of Matthew's Gospel where it was prophesied that Jesus's name would be "Emmanuel" (Matthew 1:23), which means "God with us." In sum, Matthew's scene emphasizes that the Resurrection makes it possible for Jesus to fulfill his mission as "God with us."

The Resurrection in the Gospel of Luke and in Acts

Luke's distinctive contribution to the story of the Resurrection is the narrative of the appearance of the risen Christ to two disciples on the road to Emmaus.[8] This is a very different resurrection appearance than those included in the other Gospels, primarily because the disciples do not recognize Jesus until he is no longer with them. One fascinating aspect of this narrative is how it interweaves into the appearance references to the Last Supper, the importance of scripture, the lack of understanding of the disciples, the provision of hospitality to a stranger, and the fulfillment of prophecy and thus recapitulates the important elements of Jesus's ministry in miniature and in the context of his resurrection. There is something provocative about the disciples' inability to recognize Jesus at first, and his self-revelation to them in the breaking of the bread is similarly intriguing, pointing to the importance of the sacrament of the Lord's Supper for its ability to "reveal" the Lord to his followers. The story conveys metaphorically that the risen Jesus Christ will be known to (all of) his followers through scripture, through hospitality, and through the reenactment of the Last Supper. The story of the appearance of the resurrected Lord to the disciples on the road to Emmaus thus becomes a template for how all future followers of Jesus will commune with him.

Luke's Gospel also contains an appearance of the resurrected Jesus Christ to another group of disciples (Luke 24:36–53). In some ways it is similar to Matthew's account, but Luke uniquely emphasizes several principles. First, the lack of understanding on the part of the disciples is emphasized (24:37). Additionally, the physical reality of the Resurrection is emphasized in Jesus's statement "Behold my hands and my feet, that it is I myself: handle me, and see; for a spirit hath not flesh and bones, as ye see me have" (24:39); Jesus also eats fish to confirm his corporality.[9] Luke's story also emphasizes the role of scripture (24:44–46) and the continued role of the temple (24:53) in ways unique to this account.

Historically, Luke has been regarded as having a particular concern for female followers of Jesus. But, interestingly, women are not central to Luke's material on the Resurrection: they may not be entirely absent (assuming that they are included in the group mentioned in Luke 24:33 and particularly if Cleopas's companion is female), but their role is not highlighted. And yet Luke has implicitly criticized those who would disregard the truthfulness of women's testimony (24:11). It is difficult to determine what to make of this de-emphasis on women's roles as resurrection witnesses in Luke's account.

The companion account to Luke's Gospel, the Acts of the Apostles, contains over a dozen references to the resurrection of Jesus Christ.[10] Most briefly emphasize the reality of the Resurrection and the frequency that the early Christians preached it without exploring details of its historical reality or theological implications. For example, in Peter's address on the day of Pentecost, he states that Jesus was raised up (Acts 2:24); the comment is brief and without historical or doctrinal elaboration, probably because the book of Acts positions itself as a historical record of the ministry of early church leaders, not as a detailed exploration of gospel doctrine. Nonetheless, the message is clear in Acts that the resurrection of Jesus Christ was absolutely central to early Christian belief and preaching. If there is one facet of the Resurrection that is emphasized in Acts, it is that Jesus was physically resurrected (see Acts 1:3; 2:31; 10:40–41); this meshes well with the material focusing on the physical reality of the Resurrection in Luke's Gospel discussed earlier in this chapter.

The Resurrection in the Gospel of John

One way in which John's account is different from the other Gospels is that Matthew, Mark, and Luke tend to emphasize that God raised Jesus from the dead (Mark 12:26; Luke 9:22), while John emphasizes that Jesus himself chose to lay down his life and take it up again (see John 10:17–18). Thus, Jesus's power is emphasized, and the Resurrection is positioned as something under his own control.

John presents miracles not as powerful acts (as the other Gospel writers do) but rather as signs, meaning there is a significant symbolic component to them. There are seven "signs" in John (note that John uses a different Greek term [*sēmeion*] than the other Gospel writers do to describe these miracles; John's usage emphasizes the symbolic connotations of the act while the other writers' term [*dunamis*] emphasizes the wondrous power of the act); the raising of Lazarus is the final sign. The sign inherent in the raising of Lazarus must surely include Jesus's power over life and death and is thus relevant to a discussion of the Resurrection. Interestingly, in John's text, Martha expresses solid faith in the Resurrection (John 11:24), but one that will occur "at the last day." Jesus responds that he is "the resurrection, and the life" and thus stresses the immediacy of the potential for resurrection owing to his unique nature. Martha has a faith in the Resurrection that is generic and future-oriented; Jesus instructs her that the Resurrection is, in some unexplained way, personally tied to him and thus specific and immediate. The statement "I am the resurrection" (11:25) is stunning on its face, and its position as Jesus's self-description in the middle of the seventh and climactic sign in John's Gospel catapults it to an even greater importance. Clearly, John wants to convey to the audience that the Resurrection is a key aspect of Jesus's mission and identity. Intriguingly, Jesus also weeps in this scene (11:35), creating a compelling portrait of Jesus as both extremely powerful and yet still responsive to human needs.

Earlier in the account of Lazarus's return to life, Jesus had stated that Lazarus's illness was not "unto death, but for the glory of God" (11:4). The audience has a moment of surprise—and perhaps worry—when Lazarus does in fact die; perhaps some wondered if Jesus were a false prophet. It is only the reality of Jesus's power over life and death that can solve this problem at the heart of the story, and thus the audience realizes that it is Jesus's power over death that shows "the glory of God."

But there is another layer to the story as well: it is in direct response to the raising of Lazarus that leads the authorities to plot Jesus's death (11:45–53). Thus, in terms of the narrative there is a very real sense in which Jesus trades his own life for Lazarus's life (especially since John notes that Jesus waited for two days before going to Lazarus, 11:6); now Jesus's comment about Lazarus's illness being for "the glory of God" has an even deeper resonance.

John's account of the Resurrection itself begins with Mary Magdalene at the entrance to Jesus's tomb. The picture of a woman weeping over an unexpected death is not new to John's audience: it would have recalled another Mary weeping at the death of Lazarus. The audience is thus primed to anticipate Jesus's resurrection. A great deal of the power of this account comes from one unusual detail: John 20:12 states that, as Mary looked into the tomb, she saw "two angels in white sitting, the one at the head, and the other at the feet, where the body of Jesus had lain." Jesus's body is, of course, gone. The angels are sitting (a present tense verb) in the place where the body had lain (imperfect verb). The image of angels at Jesus's head and feet is something of a fiction in the sense that his body is no longer there, but this image would have been a powerful one for John's audience—reminiscent of the ark of the covenant, which was covered in the golden mercy seat (Exodus 25:21) and had one angel on each end (25:19). The mercy seat was the place from which the Lord would meet the covenant people (25:21–22). When the tabernacle was built, the ark of the covenant was the only item in the holy of holies. Only the high priest, on one day each year, would enter that most sacred of spaces and pre-enact the atonement of Jesus Christ (Leviticus 16). The allusion to this event in John 20:12 is very striking: the very place where the Lord should appear is the place where his body is not. And yet the lack of a body *is* the message from the Lord—a message of the Resurrection.

As with the account of the disciples on the road to Emmaus, Mary does not initially recognize Jesus when he appears (John 20:14), but she later recognizes him in the moment when he speaks her name (20:16). John's audience would likely have interpreted this scene in light of Jesus's teaching that the sheep recognize the shepherd when he calls them by name (10:2–5, 14–16). The proximity of Jesus's comments regarding the sheep recognizing the shepherd to his statement that no one can take his life from him unless he chooses to sacrifice it (10:17–18) would have perhaps been recalled by John's audience and would have emphasized during this crucial scene of recognition that Jesus himself had chosen to be resurrected and thus controlled the process himself. The focal point of John's account is consequently on Jesus's power and authority.

John's account seems to diverge from Luke's account in one notable respect. In Luke's account Jesus, without preamble, invited the disciples to touch him (Luke 24:39), but in John's account, the invitation to Thomas to touch him suggests that it is a concession to Thomas's doubt and that it would have been preferable had it not been necessary: "blessed are they that have not seen, and yet have believed" (John 20:29). In terms of the literary presentation of the resurrection appearances, there is a significant difference in emphasis: Luke's account emphasizes the appropriateness of verifying the physical reality of the Resurrection while John's account suggests that the need to verify is a concession to lack of faith. Similarly, while Jesus eats fish in Luke's account, he does not do so in John's—even though Jesus is responsible for a miraculous catch of fish. The comparison of Luke's and John's accounts suggests the extent to which Luke wanted to emphasize the physical nature of the Resurrection, while John's concerns are elsewhere—primarily on Jesus's power and authority.

Conclusions

The various references to the resurrection of Jesus Christ in the New Testament make abundantly clear that it is one of the signal events taught by early church leaders. In some ways New Testament references to the Resurrection are more notable for what they do not contain than for what they do: there is precious little exploration of the details or implications of the Resurrection and far more concern with its factual, and often its physical, reality. The presence of eyewitnesses to the Resurrection is also a very important theme, and something that Peter specifically attests to in his preaching (Acts 5:32).

There are no canonized descriptions of the Resurrection itself; rather, the texts focus on the empty tomb and then on appearances of the resurrected Lord. The empty tomb scenes emphasize the physical reality of the Resurrection. The statement of the young man that "[Jesus] is risen" in Mark 16:6 conveys the simplicity and utter lack of adornment of the message. It is permitted to stand on its own; it is not elaborated, nor is it explained. Luke's Gospel, in particular, emphasizes the physical nature of Jesus's resurrection with Jesus's invitation to touch him and the inclusion of the detail that he ate fish. The stories of appearances by the resurrected Jesus provide an opportunity for him to give instruction to his disciples and for the disciples to become eyewitnesses to the reality of the Resurrection. Additionally, the appearance of the resurrected Jesus was an important counterpoint to the humiliating crucifixion, with the picture of Jesus's glory—not his suffering—becoming the last image of him in the minds of the Gospel audiences.

৯৯

Julie M. Smith is an independent scholar of the New Testament living near Austin, Texas.

Further Reading

J. Peter Hansen. "Paul the Apostle: Champion of the Doctrine of the Resurrection." *Go Ye into All the World: Messages of the New Testament Apostles*, edited by Reid L. Nielson and Fred E. Woods, 13–26. Salt Lake City: Deseret Book, 2002.

Eric D. Huntsman. *God So Loved the World: The Final Days of the Savior's Life*. Salt Lake City: Deseret Book, 2011.

Francis J. Moloney. *The Resurrection of the Messiah: A Narrative Commentary on the Resurrection Accounts in the Four Gospels*. New York: Paulist Press, 2013.

Notes

1. Other instances where the resurrection of Jesus Christ is mentioned tangentially include Romans 1:4; 4:24; 7:4; 8:11, 34; Ephesians 1:20; Galatians 1:1; 1 Thessalonians 1:10; Hebrews 6:2; 2 Timothy 2:8; and 1 Peter 1:3, 21.

2. Other instances where the Resurrection is mentioned in order to shape audience beliefs and behavior include Romans 6:1–14; 14:9; and 2 Corinthians 5:14.

3. Ben Witherington III, *Conflict and Community in Corinth: A Socio-Rhetorical Commentary on 1 and 2 Corinthians* (Grand Rapids, MI: Eerdmans, 1995), 307.

4. Interestingly, in the Old Testament the only generally accepted references to life after death are in Isaiah 26:19 and Daniel 2:2, although many other texts can be interpreted to refer to postmortal life.

5. Interestingly, the apocryphal Gospel of Peter does contain an account of the actual moment of resurrection; most scholars regard it as rather fanciful and unlikely to have a strong historical foundation.

6. Richard C. Miller, "Mark's Empty Tomb and Other Translation Fables in Classical Antiquity," *Journal of Biblical Literature* 129, no. 4 (2010): 767.

7. See Raymond Brown, "The Resurrection in Matthew (27:62–28:20)," *Worship* 64, no. 2 (March 1990): 159.

8. One disciple is identified as Cleopas (Luke 24:18); the other is not identified but could possibly be his wife (John 19:25).

9. Interestingly, there might be some difference between Luke's and Paul's perspectives on the resurrected body. Compare 1 Corinthians 15:50.

10. See Acts 1:3, 22; 2:30–31; 3:26; 4:2, 10, 33; 5:30–32; 10:40–41; 13:30, 37; 17:3, 18; 23:6; 25:19; 26:23.

Part 4

The Apostle Paul, General Epistles, and Revelation

23

The Life of the Apostle Paul
An Overview

Nicholas J. Frederick

"Few figures in Western history have been the subject of greater controversy than Saint Paul. Few have caused more dissension and hatred. None has suffered more misunderstanding at the hands of both friends and enemies. None has produced more animosity between Jews and Christians."[1]

These words, taken from a recent study of Paul by emeritus Princeton University professor John G. Gager, speak to the impact Paul has had in the roughly two thousand years since the emergence of the Christian faith. Paul continues to be the topic of much debate in the modern era, with books describing Paul as everything from the "real founder of Christianity"[2] to a "Jewish cultural critic."[3] While it may be close to impossible to retrieve the historical Paul from the pages of the New Testament, this chapter will attempt to construct a brief biographical overview of Paul and his life, synthesizing information from the book of Acts and from Paul's own letters while also remaining cognizant that there are several places where the New Testament sources are reticent or in disagreement.

The Early Life of Paul

The majority of Paul's life prior to his shift toward Christianity remains shrouded in mystery and must be reconstructed from the small glimpses given us through Paul's letters and Luke's history. One of the most important statements comes from Paul's letter to the Philippians, where he writes:

> Circumcised the eighth day, of the stock of Israel, of the tribe of Benjamin, an Hebrew of the Hebrews; as touching the law, a Pharisee; Concerning zeal, persecuting the church; touching the righteousness which is in the law, blameless. (Philippians 3:5–6)

While these may seem like small details, they are actually quite revealing. Paul's words suggest that religiously and ethnically he saw himself as a Jew. His descent through the tribe of Benjamin likely explains the origin of his actual name, Saul. While it is sometimes thought that *Saul* was Paul's name prior to becoming a Christian and that he took the name *Paul* after he became Christian, this is incorrect. *Saul* is a Hebrew name, and *Paul* a Roman name. The most notable member of the tribe of Benjamin was King Saul, the ruler who preceded David. While Saul is remembered somewhat negatively today, mainly owing to his improper offering of sacrifice and his acrimony toward David, he remained an important figure in Israelite history, and it is not surprising that Paul's Jewish parents would pass on that name to him. On the other hand, *Paul* means "short" or "small" in Latin and is a name likely connected with his family. Rather than being two names connected with two periods of his life, the names rather represent two cultural spheres. When Paul interacted with those of a Jewish background, he went by *Saul*; when his travels took him into gentile areas, he went by *Paul*.

Paul's statement that he was "circumcised the eighth day" tells us that his parents were observant Jews, a reflection that finds support in Acts 23, where Paul announces that "I am a Pharisee, the son of a Pharisee" (23:6). This suggests that Paul would have been raised in a devout Jewish home. Beginning at about age six, Paul would likely have begun studying the Law and the Prophets, probably committing several passages to memory. Quotations from the Hebrew Bible are strewn throughout Paul's letters, perhaps as a direct result of his early education. He probably used the Greek translation of the Hebrew Bible, the Septuagint, as his primary text, but his education likely included the study of Hebrew and Aramaic as well.[4]

This Jewish education would have come in addition to the regular education he would have received growing up in the Hellenistic atmosphere of the city of Tarsus, where Luke tells us Paul was born (Acts 21:39). Tarsus, located in the northeastern Mediterranean area of what is now south-central Turkey, was a prosperous city, full of both economic and intellectual opportunities for Jewish families seeking to establish themselves in the diaspora. Receiving an education in Tarsus would very likely have brought Paul into contact with not only the Greek alphabet and language but also the writings of those whose works were considered the pinnacle of Greek literary achievement, such as the epics of Homer and the tragedies of Sophocles and Euripides. This exposure to Greek literature may explain why Paul, when speaking at Athens on Mars' Hill, summons quotations from not one but two Greek poets, Epimenides and Aratus (see Acts 17:28).

In addition to his Jewish religious background and his Greek cultural background, Paul also appears to have been raised as a Roman citizen. While Paul himself never mentions his citizenship in his letters, Luke mentions it on multiple occasions (Acts 16:37–38; 22:25–28;

25:11). This citizenship was highly prized and would have entitled Paul to many important benefits, such as the three-part Roman name (*tria nomina*), exemption from ill-treatment at the hands of Jewish and Roman authorities, and the right to have a capital legal case brought before the Roman emperor himself. There were several ways one could obtain Roman citizenship. If one's father was a Roman citizen, then so were his children. One could be granted citizenship for military service or other favors to Rome. Likewise, one could also purchase it, although the price would be high and the practice prohibited (at least officially). Finally, slaves were given Roman citizenship at the time of their manumission from a Roman household. In Acts 22:28, Paul tells the Roman military tribune Claudius Lysias that he was born with his citizenship, meaning that his father would have been a Roman citizen as well. The two most likely scenarios are that either Paul's father (or perhaps grandfather) were manumitted slaves, or that someone in Paul's genealogical line had been granted citizenship based on service rendered to Rome. The origins of Paul's Roman citizenship may also help explain the roots of the name *Paulus*. If Paul's progenitors were manumitted slaves, they may have adopted the name of the person who granted them their freedom as a family name or nickname. Or perhaps, as others have suggested, *Paul* was selected simply because it was the closest sounding gentile name to *Saul*.[5]

At some point early in his education, Paul appears to have moved to Jerusalem. According to Acts, Paul was "yet brought up in this city at the feet of Gamaliel, and taught according to the perfect manner of the law of the fathers, and was zealous toward God, as ye all are this day" (Acts 22:3; compare 26:4). Depending on how the Greek participle *anatethrammenos* ("brought up") is understood, Paul could be seen as moving to Jerusalem with his family early in his life and thus receiving the majority of his education in Jerusalem, or he could be seen as receiving his primary education in Tarsus and then being sent to Jerusalem for more specialized education. Scholars remain divided as to when Paul made this move. Acts does contain the tantalizing detail that a nephew of Paul's, his "sister's son" (23:16), resided in Jerusalem during the time of his trial before the Sanhedrin, which may give weight to the idea that his family had moved to Jerusalem together. However, Acts also relays that Paul returned to Tarsus following his vision of the Savior, which could suggest existent family ties in Tarsus (9:30; 11:25). Perhaps the safest conclusion is that Paul "came to and settled in Jerusalem as a young adolescent and received his principal education there."[6] Keeping in mind the arbitrary nature of dating the events of Paul's life, especially the early events, this move likely occurred sometime between AD 15 and 25.

Acts further informs us that Paul received some of his education from Gamaliel (22:3). Gamaliel appears only once in the New Testament, as a leading Pharisee who offers a somewhat sympathetic take on the early Christian movement (Acts 5:34–40). Traditionally, there were two primary schools among the Pharisees, the school of Shammai and the school of Hillel. The school of Shammai tended to be a more conservative approach to the Judaism of the Pharisees, with Hillel being more liberal. Several of Jesus's teachings, such as his stance on divorce as recorded in Matthew 19:3, can be seen as negotiating these two positions. Gamaliel later became the leader of the school of Hillel (he may even have been Hillel's son or grandson) and is described by Luke as a *nomodidaskalos*, or "doctor of the Law" (Acts 5:34).[7] According to later Jewish tradition recorded in the Mishnah, "Since Rabban Gamaliel the elder died there has been no more reverence for the law; and purity and abstinence died out at the same time" (Soṭah 9:15). Gamaliel's emphasis on "reverence for the law" and "purity" may help us understand where Paul developed the zealousness for Judaism and its preservation that defines so much of his early career as a Christian antagonist.

There is also a fair amount of debate as to whether or not Paul was married. The only statement Paul himself ever makes regarding his marital situation comes in his discussion on marriage in 1 Corinthians 7. Paul writes, "I say therefore to the unmarried and widows, It is good for them if they abide even as I" (7:8). The implication is that Paul is currently not in a marital relationship. The question is whether he has always been single or whether he was once married but was single at the time he wrote 1 Corinthians. Several ancient Jewish sources indicate that it was unusual for men who were dedicated to study of the Torah to be unmarried, although there are exceptions.[8] One later piece of folklore claims that Paul was involved with the daughter of the high priest and that her rejection of Paul led to his animosity toward Judaism:

> Paul was a man of Tarsus and indeed a Greek, the son of a Greek mother and a Greek father. Having gone up to Jerusalem and having remained there a long time, he desired to marry a daughter of the (high?) priest and on that account submitted himself as a proselyte for circumcision. When nevertheless he did not obtain the girl, he became furious and began to write against circumcision, the Sabbath and the Law.[9]

This story contains a clear anti-Pauline bias, and it is unlikely to contain anything historical. However, in a provocative move, some of Paul's biographers have tentatively suggested that Paul was married but lost his wife and possibly children at some point before becoming a Christian;[10] it was this loss of family that angered Paul and sparked his persecution of Christianity. One scholar, Jerome Murphy-O'Connor, speculates:

> Jerusalem is sited in an earthquake zone, and it cannot have been immune to the domestic tragedies of fire and building collapse, which were so frequent at Rome. Had Paul's wife and children died in such an accident, or in a plague epidemic, one part of his theology would lead him logically to ascribe blame to God, but this was forbidden by another part of his religious perspective, which prescribed complete submission to God's will. If his pain and anger could not be directed against God, it had to find another target. An outlet for his pent-up desire for vengeance had to be rationalized.[11]

Paul's frustration at a perceived injustice in the loss of his family, combined with the importance placed on purity by Gamaliel and his school, may have kindled a fiery zeal within Paul that led him to pursue the path that first brought him directly into the pages of the New Testament, namely as an antagonist and persecutor of Christians. However, this scenario is entirely unsubstantiated and is pure speculation.

Paul the Persecutor (ca. AD 33)

Paul's role as persecutor of the nascent Christian movement is supported by both the accounts related in Acts and Paul's own epistles.[12] In the years following his vision of Jesus, Paul would write that "I persecuted the church of God" (1 Corinthians 15:9), "beyond measure I persecuted the church of God, and wasted it" (Galatians 1:13), and "concerning zeal, persecuting the church" (Philippians 3:6). It is difficult to know exactly what form these persecutory activities took and to what extent Paul went in punishing perceived violations. Paul is first introduced in Acts as being present and complicit in the execution of Stephen. While Paul was seemingly a minor character in the Stephen account, Luke's mention that the witnesses "laid down their clothes at a young man's feet, whose name was Saul" (Acts 7:58) suggests that Paul had already gained a stature or reputation as a punisher of Christians.[13] Following Stephen's stoning, Paul took the initiative and sought out permission from the high priest (Acts 9:2), or chief priests (Acts 26:12), to pursue, punish, and if necessary extradite Christians back to Jerusalem. One crucial point to understand here is that Paul appeared to have had no legal or judicial authority granted by Rome that would have allowed him to make arrests. Additionally, whatever legal or judicial authority the Jewish high priest and the Sanhedrin held probably did not extend outside Jerusalem. What Paul likely sought from the high priest and took to Damascus were letters condemning followers of Jesus and strongly recommending that any supporters be identified and strongly encouraged to deny any connections between Jesus and the Messiah. Paul relates in 2 Corinthians that "of the Jews five times received I forty stripes save one" (11:24), referring to judicial floggings in the synagogues (compare Deuteronomy 25:1–3). Paul and his supporters may have cowed synagogue leaders into inflicting a similar punishment if members of their synagogues chose not to retract their stance on Jesus's messianic role. To resist this punishment would have left the Christians open to the far more damaging punishment of excommunication from the synagogue. Paul may have even relied on the threat of a potential charge of blasphemy, which carried with it a punishment of death by stoning. How successful these threats were is unclear. While Paul may have been exaggerating when he wrote to the Galatians that he persecuted the Christians "beyond measure," it is difficult not to see his activities having real consequences. Arrests, beatings, violent assaults, home invasions—all are very real means through which Paul would have attempted to suppress the "heretical" Christians. In the words of one author, "Paul did real damage over a period of time impossible to estimate."[14]

Paul's Encounter with Jesus (ca. AD 34)

It was this charge to suppress Christianity that led Paul onto the road to Damascus. Separated from Jerusalem by about 135 miles, Damascus had a relatively large Jewish population and apparently had become a location for Christians to gather as well, as evidenced by Ananias's presence there. Paul set out with his letters and was apparently near the city when he encountered the resurrected Jesus. Luke records three versions of this visionary experience in Acts, and all three of them differ in certain respects (9:3–9; 22:6–14; 26:12–18). The two consistent elements throughout all three accounts are the bright light Paul saw and the loud voice he heard. While Paul does not explicitly say that he actually saw Jesus Christ in Acts, Paul's letters imply it.[15] The message relayed by Jesus was clear: the God that Paul had been following and the leader of those he had been persecuting were one and the same. Jesus's statement to Paul, "it is hard for thee to kick against the pricks" (Acts 26:14), is perhaps better rendered "It is hard to kick a cactus (especially when wearing open-toed sandals)."[16] The kingdom spoken of by Jesus was going to move forward, and for Paul to try to stop its growth would be as fruitless and senseless as trying to "kick a cactus."

It is common to speak of this visionary encounter as Paul's "conversion" to Christianity. However, it is unclear whether or not Paul would have seen himself being converted in the same sense in which we use the term today. He may have processed this experience as something closer to a commission or call. Before his vision, Paul was a zealous defender of the God of Israel and the covenant relationship that had been implemented between God and Israel (i.e., the law of Moses). Following his vision, Paul remained a zealous defender of the God of Israel and his covenant. What changed was his understanding of how Jesus fit into this schema. Paul essentially went from one form of Second Temple Judaism (Pharisaism) to another (Jesus-centered messianism). Jesus never tells Paul to get baptized or to join his church. He simply asks Paul why he has been persecuting him. However, it is notable that Paul is baptized shortly after regaining his sight (Acts 9:18).

Damascus, Arabia, and the "Missing Years" (ca. AD 34–47)

Being left blind as a result of his vision, Paul was led by his companions the rest of the way to Damascus, where he met Ananias, who subsequently healed Paul and may have performed his baptism (Acts 9:18). At this point, Paul's movements and whereabouts for the next decade of his life become very difficult to pin down with any kind of surety. Luke tells us that Paul was "certain days with the disciples which were at Damascus. And straightway he preached Christ in the synagogues" (9:19–20), suggesting that Paul remained in Damascus and preached. Luke also relays that Paul went straight from Damascus to Jerusalem, where he tried to join up with some of the other Christian disciples (9:26). However, Paul's own letters suggest a different series of events. In his letter to the Galatians, Paul writes that "I went into Arabia, and returned again unto Damascus. Then after three years I went up to Jerusalem to see Peter, and abode with him fifteen days" (Galatians 1:17–18). Luke's account of Paul's activities following his vision are clearly not all-inclusive, perhaps because Paul rarely spoke about them, or perhaps Paul's activities outside Jerusalem and its surrounding areas were not germane to Luke's focus on the Holy Land as the site of Christianity's founding and early growth.

Paul's reference to time spent in Arabia likely refers to the kingdom of the Nabateans, an area stretching from Damascus down into the Hijaz (modern Saudi Arabia). The king of the Nabateans at this time, Aretas IV (9 BC–AD 40; 2 Corinthians 11:32), was embroiled in a dispute with Herod Antipas, the tetrarch of Galilee, owing to the latter's divorcing of Aretas's daughter in order to marry Herodias.[17] Paul does not tell us why he first turned to Arabia.[18] Perhaps he needed time to think and consider what he had learned on the road to Damascus. Jesus's words were no doubt life changing for Paul and required a period of reorientation. Perhaps, like Moses and Jesus, he needed to pass through the wilderness, removed from his regular environment, to commune with God. Or perhaps he, demonstrating the zeal for truth that had defined his previous career as a persecutor, selected an area that had not been heavily proselytized by Christians and turned his efforts toward an area populated by non-Jews of Semitic origins. Whatever Paul's motivations for going to Arabia, he apparently did enough to rouse the ire of King Aretas IV. Paul writes in 2 Corinthians that "in Damascus the governor under Aretas the king kept the city of the Damascenes with a garrison, desirous to apprehend me: and through a window in a basket was I let down by the wall, and escaped his hands" (11:32–33). The implication is that Paul had done something to upset King Aretas (who was already frustrated with Jews because of the scandal of his daughter's divorce) and had then left Arabia and returned to Damascus. However, the governor of Damascus, likely acting under Aretas's orders, attempted to arrest Paul. Paul was then forced to flee Damascus in a humiliating fashion, by being lowered out of the city in a basket (Acts 9:25). It is only at this point that Paul returned to Jerusalem.

These small details preserved in Galatians and 2 Corinthians are significant for three specific reasons. First, they establish, for the first time, a historical date for an event in Paul's life. It is unlikely that Aretas would have been able to exercise influence over Damascus until near or after the death of the emperor Tiberius in AD 37 and the subsequent ascension of Gaius.[19] Taking into consideration the "three years" mentioned by Paul in Galatians, this would put Paul's experience on the road to Damascus around AD 34. While we have no direct information on when Paul was born, his vision of Jesus on the road to Damascus could have occurred when he was around thirty years old, putting his birth somewhere between AD 1 and 10.

The second and third reasons are what these experiences tell us about Paul's own self-perception and understanding of his mission and role within the nascent Christian movement, namely, that he considered his primary responsibility to proselytize to the Gentiles and that he would pursue this responsibility somewhat independent of the Jerusalem leadership. Paul mentions specifically that one of the things Jesus revealed to him was that "I might preach him among the heathen [*ethnos*]" (Galatians 1:16). He later remarks that a division of responsibilities between Jewish and gentile spheres was officially made between himself and Peter (Galatians 2:9). Paul's subsequent travels to cities such as Ephesus, Corinth, and Rome demonstrate that he took this responsibility seriously. Yet while Paul certainly viewed his missionary efforts as complementing what Peter and others were doing, he goes to great lengths to establish his own independence. He states that he preached for three years before he even met Peter, and emphasizes that his understanding of the gospel came straight from Jesus Christ, for after his vision "I conferred not with flesh and blood" (Galatians 1:16). Paul's sentiment is clear; he owes none of what he teaches to the influence of anyone other than Jesus.[20] Later on, in his letter to the church at Rome, Paul made a point to say that "so have I strived to preach the gospel, not where Christ was named, lest I should build upon another man's foundation" (Romans 15:20). Paul's normal method was to establish and build up churches in areas that had not already been evangelized by other Christians, and likewise he expected other Christians to not impose their ideas or directions upon his converts.[21]

This attitude, of course, raises a question about what exactly Paul means when he refers to himself as an apostle. While Latter-day Saints have a very definite idea of what it means to be an apostle, it is important to remember that the word literally means "one who is sent forth," and Paul's understanding of the title seems to come from that broad definition. Certainly Paul would include Peter and the eleven at Jerusalem as apostles, but he also includes himself, James (Acts 9:19), and those to whom the Lord appeared as well: "After that, he was seen of James; then of all the apostles" (1 Corinthians 15:7). In Romans, Paul also includes two otherwise unknown individuals, Junia and Andronicus, as being "among the apostles" (16:7). Paul's understanding of what qualified someone to be considered an apostle was whether or not he had personally encountered Jesus Christ: "Am I not an apostle? am I not free? have I not seen Jesus Christ our Lord? are not ye my work in the Lord?" (1 Corinthians 9:1; compare Acts 1:21–22). This does not mean that Paul could not have become part of the official quorum of the twelve apostles, only that his self-identification as an apostle should not be taken to mean that he was.[22] Additionally complicating the matter is the fact that apart from the selection of Matthias in Acts 1:21–26, the New Testament records no instances in which the body of the twelve apostles is reconstituted following the death of one of its members, making it difficult to draw firm parallels between this ancient organization and the modern quorum of today.

It is with this understanding of Paul that we should approach Paul's long-awaited return to Jerusalem following his escape from Damascus. Paul tells us that the purpose of this trip was to finally meet and become acquainted with Peter (Galatians 1:18). Acts adds the detail that Barnabas brought Paul to Peter and provided a recommendation of Paul's character and experiences since his vision. This introduction was likely necessitated because of Paul's prior reputation as a persecutor, which apparently had not dwindled in the three years he was away (Acts 9:26). Paul states that he spent fifteen days with Peter (Galatians 1:18). This time would not have been devoted to Paul's seeking a greater understanding of the gospel, as Paul appears to have felt like he understood all he needed to. Probably Paul approached Peter in order to get what he needed most, namely information from Peter on the life and ministry of the Savior from one who had witnessed it with his own eyes. During his time in Jerusalem, Paul also engaged in conversation and debate with some hellenized Jews, the result being that "they went about to slay him" (Acts 9:29). In a striking turn, Paul the persecutor had become Paul the persecuted. Clearly it was dangerous for Paul to remain in Jerusalem, so friends sent Paul to a place he likely hadn't seen in several years, his home of Tarsus (Acts 9:30). At this point the events of Paul's life become nearly impossible to trace. All Paul says is that "I came into the regions of Syria and Cilicia" (Galatians 1:21), and it is likely that some of the events Paul describes in 2 Corinthians 11:23–29 happened during this time in Tarsus.

This may also be the time during which Paul developed the craft and skill of a tentmaker or leatherworker, a trade that would be a great asset once he began his extensive missionary travels (Acts 18:3). What else Paul may have done during these missing years is impossible to know, and a lengthy period of time may have passed (ca. AD 37–46) before the details of Paul's life are picked up again.

Antioch (ca. AD 47)

Two significant events led to Paul's reemergence in the affairs of the Christian movement. First, Peter's groundbreaking vision recorded in Acts 10 gave divine sanction to the idea that circumcision was no longer a requirement for covenant membership. Prior to Acts 10, those who wished to become Christians essentially had to become Jews if they were not already, meaning that they had to agree to follow the law of Moses and be circumcised. After Peter's vision, however, this barrier to membership was removed, meaning that one could become a Christian without having to become a Jew first. It is hard to overstate just how controversial this decision was, and it is likely that the gradual realization of this new policy, especially after its affirmation in Acts 15, would have caused many to part ways with Christianity. Second, Stephen's harsh condemnation of the Jewish people in Acts 7 had earlier led to an increased persecution of the Christians (Acts 8:1; 11:19). Those fleeing persecution found a haven in the city of Antioch, the capital of the Roman province of Syria and at the time the third-largest city in the Roman Empire.[23] Antioch quickly became a center for Christian growth, particularly among the Gentiles, and it is here that Christians were first called "Christians" (Acts 11:26). Previously, those who adhered to the messianic movement surrounding Jesus had been called simply followers of "[the] way" (Acts 9:2), an enigmatic title that perhaps refers to the "way of Jesus" (John 14:6) or perhaps connotes the "other way" of being a Jew.

It was to Antioch that Barnabas, a Christian who hailed from Cyprus, traveled in about AD 47 at the behest of the Jerusalem leadership, likely to strengthen and support what was quickly becoming a significant group of followers. Perhaps realizing that the task at hand was more than one person could adequately handle, Barnabas took a detour to Tarsus with the express purpose of finding Paul. Together, they traveled to Antioch and spent "a whole year" teaching the new converts and likely evangelizing others (Acts 11:26). During Barnabas and Paul's tenure in Antioch, a prophet named Agabus arrived from Jerusalem and prophesied that a famine was imminent (see Acts 11:28). Recognizing the dangers that the lack of food presented and mindful of the Christians in Jerusalem, the disciples at Antioch gathered relief (likely financial) and sent it to Jerusalem with Barnabas and Paul, the second time Paul had been to Jerusalem since his vision. While in Jerusalem, Paul reports that he met privately with some of the church leaders, including Peter, James, and John, and that they extended to him and Barnabas "the right hand of fellowship" (Galatians 2:9). It was also at this meeting that it was formally decided that Paul and Barnabas would spearhead the mission to the Gentiles, while Peter would oversee the evangelizing of the Jews (2:9). Finally,

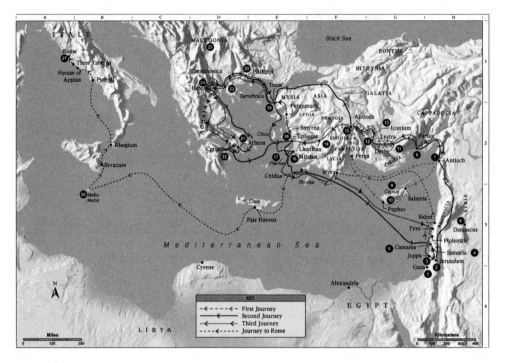

The Missionary Journeys of the Apostle Paul. © Intellectual Reserve, Inc.
Key: (1) Gaza (2) Jerusalem (3) Joppa (4) Samaria (5) Caesarea (6) Damascus (7) Antioch (in Syria)
(8) Tarsus (9) Cyprus (10) Paphos (11) Derbe (12) Lystra (13) Iconium (14) Laodicea and Colosse
(15) Antioch (in Pisidia) (16) Miletus (17) Patmos (18) Ephesus (19) Troas (20) Philippi (21) Athens
(22) Corinth (23) Thessalonica (24) Berea (25) Macedonia (26) Melita (27) Rome.

Peter reminded Paul and Barnabas to "remember the poor" (2:10), likely a reference to the famine and the relief Barnabas and Paul had brought from Antioch.[24]

Paul's First Mission (ca. AD 48–49)

Following their brief stay in Jerusalem, Barnabas and Paul returned to Antioch, taking with them a young man named John Mark, the nephew of Barnabas and future author of the Gospel of Mark (Acts 12:25). At some point after their return, the leaders of the church in Antioch, acting upon the inspiration of the Holy Ghost, selected Barnabas and Paul to begin moving the gospel out into the gentile world. They first traveled to the island of Cyprus, about sixty miles from Antioch, likely because Cyprus was Barnabas's home. After a short time spent preaching in Salamis, the missionaries arrived in Paphos, the imperial capital of Cyprus. Barnabas and Paul must have been making strides in their evangelizing efforts, because they were summoned to meet with Sergius Paulus, the Roman proconsul governing Cyprus. In the first of what would become several encounters between Paul's Christianity and the larger supernatural world, Paul was challenged by Sergius Paulus's deputy, a "sorcerer" and false prophet named Elymas (Acts 13:7–8). Elymas is described as a *magos*, a wise man or magician and may have filled the role of court astrologer. Elymas appears to have resented Sergius Paulus's interest in Barnabas and Paul and tried to turn him against the missionaries. But Paul, "filled with the Holy Ghost," blinded Elymas and denounced him as a "child of the devil" (13:9–11). The result of this encounter was that Sergius Paulus "believed, being astonished at the doctrine of the Lord" (13:12).

Following their time preaching in Cyprus, Barnabas and Paul decided to travel to the mainland of Asia Minor and continue their work. Traveling to Asia Minor may have been part of their plan all along, or perhaps their success with Sergius Paulus encouraged them to continue preaching. After landing in Perga, Barnabas and Paul headed for Pisidian Antioch, a city north of the Taurus Mountains. At this point, John Mark returned to Jerusalem, perhaps feeling that traveling through Asia Minor was more than he wanted to do (Acts 13:13). That Paul bore some resentment at John Mark's early departure becomes clear in events that follow the Council of Jerusalem the following year (15:37–40). In Pisidian Antioch, Barnabas and Paul entered a synagogue on the Sabbath and Paul proceeded to give a lengthy speech, his earliest recorded oration. Themes that become focal points in Paul's letters can be observed in this speech: God's role in directing history, the extension of the Abrahamic covenant to all believers, and the justification of the sinner that comes through faith in the Messiah's sacrifice. Not surprisingly, the Gentiles in Pisidian Antioch responded favorably to Paul's message, while the Jews raised up opposition to the missionaries by stirring up resentment among the city's elite, which forced the missionaries to leave the city.

The two missionaries headed next for Iconium, a prosperous city that lay about eighty miles from Pisidian Antioch. Again Barnabas and Paul preached in the synagogue, and this time they found success among both Jews and Gentiles. However, resistance was again stirred up against them, and again they were forced out of the city to avoid being stoned. From Iconium they travel to Lystra, about twenty-five miles to the south. In Lystra, Paul healed a man who had been a cripple since birth. This miracle did not escape the notice of the Lystrans, who concluded that Barnabas and Paul must be gods in disguise, specifically Zeus and Hermes.[25] The priest of Jupiter brought oxen and garlands to begin officiating in sacrifices to Barnabas and Paul, but they stopped him by speaking about the "living God" who created the "heaven, and earth, and the sea, and all things that are therein" (Acts 14:15). Unfortunately, this scene is quickly followed by the arrival of Jews from Pisidian Antioch and Iconium who had traveled a considerable distance (about one hundred miles in the case of those from Pisidian Antioch) simply to track down Barnabas and Paul. After convincing several of the Lystrans to join their efforts, the Jews stoned Paul and dragged him out of Lystra, where they dumped his body, presuming him to be dead. In a fascinating scene, the Lystrans who were sympathetic to Paul formed a circle around him, and Paul was healed to the point where he was able to stand up and even depart from Lystra the following day (see Acts 14:19–20). Following a brief trip to Derbe, Barnabas and Paul turned around and retraced their steps, visiting Lystra, Iconium, and Pisidian Antioch before finally sailing back home to Antioch, bringing their first mission to a close.

Paul's first mission included several key elements that would become part of the evangelizing process in Paul's subsequent missionary endeavors. First, Paul began his work in each city he visited by preaching in the local synagogues. He seemed to feel that even though his primary responsibility was to take the gospel to the Gentiles, he must first present it to the Jews (Acts 13:46–48). Second, Paul found success among the Gentiles but alienated the Jews, and the Jews remained Paul's frequent opponents throughout his ministry. As is typical, Paul obtained a sympathetic reaction from the Roman leaders he encountered. Generally when problems arose in the cities Paul visited, it was at Jewish instigation rather than from Roman interference. Third, Paul presented a message centered on God's role in initiating a new age through the death and resurrection of his Son. This age, Paul argued, is the time history hinges on, a turning point where the covenant is extended and the world prepares to enter into a new messianic period. Fourth, Paul's life as a missionary was not simply difficult; it was also dangerous. The stoning at Lystra is just one of several such threats Paul encountered over the next fifteen or so years until his eventual death in Rome.

Trouble in Antioch and the Council of Jerusalem (ca. AD 49)

Barnabas and Paul returned to Antioch only to find that trouble awaited them in the form of the "Judaizers," conservative Jewish-Christians who insisted that gentile converts to Christianity must be circumcised according to the law of Moses or "[they could not] be saved" (Acts 15:1). Peter's vision combined with Barnabas and Paul's evangelization efforts had clearly raised tensions in Jerusalem. Paul recorded an encounter in Galatians that may well have resulted from this tension or perhaps even exacerbated it.[26] Paul tells us that while he and Barnabas were in Antioch, it was customary to enjoy table fellowship with Gentiles. When Peter came to Antioch to visit, he also shared table fellowship with Gentiles. This all changed, however, when "certain [men] came from James" (Galatians 2:12). These men represented the conservative, orthodox faction of the Jerusalem church, and upon their arrival both Peter and surprisingly Barnabas separated themselves from the Gentiles, "fearing them which were of the circumcision" (2:12). The reactions of Peter and Barnabas are difficult to understand, especially after the events of Acts 10 and Acts 13–14. Perhaps they were concerned that table fellowship might be seen as scandalous to those in the Jerusalem church and make an already-tense situation worse. Or perhaps the concern was what those Jews outside the church would think if they heard that seemingly orthodox Jews like Peter and Barnabas were behaving in a contradictory manner, leading the Jews to begin persecuting converts and severely hampering evangelization. Paul, however, felt no such concerns: "But when I saw that they walked not uprightly according to the truth of the gospel, I said unto Peter before them all, If thou, being a Jew, livest after the manner of Gentiles, and not as do the Jews, why compellest thou the Gentiles to live as do the Jews?" (Galatians 2:14). For Paul, the issue of gentile circumcision had already been decided, and to suggest anything else, for whatever reason, was extremely problematic. Unfortunately, we don't have Peter's side of this debate, and Paul gave us no further information on how Peter and Barnabas took his public criticism.

It was perhaps this incident, or else others like it, that led to a gathering of important church leaders in Jerusalem around AD 49. The immediate issue was to finally resolve the vexing question of gentile circumcision, a matter that was causing "no small dissension and disputation" (Acts 15:2). Barnabas, Paul, and "certain other of them" traveled to Jerusalem from Antioch with Peter, James (the brother of Jesus), and "the apostles and elders" also in attendance (15:2). Peter spoke first, presenting a theological argument that the grace of the covenant that had been extended by God to the Jews for centuries had now been extended to the Gentiles. The Gentiles had received the Holy Spirit; they were also purified through faith. This was God's will, and the church would do well to embrace this shift in covenant understanding rather than resist it. Barnabas and Paul spoke next. Although Luke did not give a recounting of anything specific that they said, he did mention that they declared "what miracles and wonders God had wrought among the Gentiles" (15:12). Barnabas and Paul would have provided a valuable witness of the reality that God was now working among the Gentiles, a substantiation of Peter's theological position. Finally, James spoke and added an additional witness to Peter's words through the use of Amos 9:11–12. James argued that Amos's prophecy about the raising up of David's fallen tent had been fulfilled in the birth, death, and resurrection of Jesus Christ—he is David's heir, the Messiah. One of his primary reasons for coming when he did, James argued, was so that "the residue of men might seek after the Lord, and all the Gentiles" (Acts 15:17). James then delivered the final decision of the leadership: "Wherefore my sentence is, that we trouble not them, which from among the Gentiles are turned to God" (15:19).

Paul was no doubt thrilled at the decision reached at the Jerusalem conference.[27] The acceptance of Gentiles into the Christian church regardless of circumcision and other Jewish observances had been his position for some time. Armed with a letter from "the apostles and elders and brethren" that summarized the decision of the conference, Barnabas and Paul and a few associates traveled back to Antioch. After the letter had been read, the Christians "rejoiced for the consolation" (Acts 15:31). Likely encouraged by the results of both the conference and the reception in Antioch, Barnabas and Paul decided to undertake another mission to spread news of this milestone "in every city where we have preached the word of the Lord" (15:36). However, Barnabas wanted John Mark to accompany them. Paul, apparently still resentful after John Mark's departure during their first mission, "thought [it] not good to take him with them" (15:38). Sadly, the argument became heated enough that Barnabas and Paul split up, with Barnabas taking John Mark as a companion and Paul taking with him Silas, one of those who had accompanied Paul to Antioch to deliver the decision of the conference. Fortunately, Paul's letters hint at a future reconciliation with both Barnabas and John Mark (1 Corinthians 9:6; Colossians 4:10).

Accompanied by Silas, Paul first traveled "through Syria and Cilicia" (Acts 15:41) and later Derbe and Lystra, apparently revisiting the cities he and Barnabas had evangelized a few years earlier. There are likely two reasons why Paul decided to retrace his earlier steps rather than set out for new territory. First, Paul wanted to spread the news from town to town regarding the decision reached in the Jerusalem conference. It is quite likely that questions about circumcision and Jewish observance had arisen during his first mission, and now Paul had good news that brought his converts no small relief. Notably, it is during his time in Lystra that Paul met Timothy, a young man who would be invaluable to Paul's ministry in the coming years. Paul wanted Timothy to travel with him and Silas and even offered to circumcise Timothy. While this may seem strange based on the decision of the conference and Paul's own stance on circumcision, the decision was likely a practical one. As the uncircumcised son of a mixed marriage, Timothy would be regarded with suspicion by Jews and might then be a hindrance to further missionary efforts, especially since it was Paul's custom (at least according to Luke) to begin his evangelization in the synagogues upon reaching a new city. Paul's circumcision of Timothy should be seen as practical rather than theological.

A second reason why Paul may have chosen to retrace his earlier steps was the continued persistence of the Judaizers. As discussed earlier, "Judaizers" is the name given to the conservative faction of the Christian church, those who insisted on full conversion to Judaism for those wishing to worship as Christians. It was likely that this group (or one like them) was responsible for Peter's actions in Antioch, and it was likely the actions of this group that provided the impetus for the conference at Jerusalem. Acts 15:1 relates that "certain men which came down from Judea taught the brethren, and said, Except ye be circumcised after the manner of Moses, ye cannot be saved." It is quite possible that these "certain men" did not stop in Antioch but actually continued traveling to other places where the Christian message had been preached, including the congregations founded by Barnabas and Paul during their first mission. The Judaizers were apparently quite convincing because Paul soon received word that his converts had either been circumcised or at least were under the assumption that they needed to be. It is this situation that provides the occasion for Paul to write his epistle to the Galatians, a fiery invective against the Judaizers and all those who would listen to them. While the exact dating of this epistle remains the topic of much debate, the circumstances immediately preceding the Jerusalem conference seem to indicate that this is the most likely time period.[28] It is also possible that the Judaizers, finding themselves rebuffed in Jerusalem, began to more aggressively spread their message, which could also have taken them to Galatia. This would mean that Galatians was written shortly after the Jerusalem conference, perhaps while Paul and Barnabas were still in Antioch. Perhaps Paul's visit to his converts in Iconium and Lystra was to see how they had responded to his letter: Had they been convinced by his argument, or were the Judaizers still posing a threat? If either of these scenarios is correct, then Galatians would be Paul's earliest extant epistle, with a date of AD 49–50.

Paul's Second Mission (ca. AD 50–52)

After consolidating the concerns of the church in the cities of Galatia, Paul began what is generally referred to as his second mission. Whereas his first mission had been largely local and constrained to the cities in Galatia, this second mission took Paul through Asia Minor and into what we call Europe. Whether or not he initially planned to travel as far as he did is unknown, but two key spiritual experiences provided a sense of direction and scope for Paul as he ventured farther out into the gentile world. First, Luke tells us that Paul and Silas initially attempted to continue their travels north into Bithynia, but "the Spirit suffered them not" (Acts 16:7). Instead, Paul and Silas turned westward, toward Troas. Second, while in Troas, Paul experienced a dream or vision of a man in Macedonia who pled with Paul to "come over into Macedonia, and help us" (16:9). Paul immediately departed for Macedonia, convinced "that the Lord had called us for to preach the gospel unto them" (16:10). The inclusion of the first "we" passage in Acts 16:11 suggests that Luke joined Paul, Silas, and Timothy at this point.

From Troas, Paul and his party landed in Neapolis and traveled ten miles to Philippi, one of the most prosperous and important Roman colonies in Macedonia. In Philippi, Paul met and baptized Lydia and her household. Lydia's occupation as a "seller of purple" meant that she sold cloth or wool that had been dyed with rare and precious purple dye, which was difficult to obtain (purple dye was typically extracted from shellfish). This profession would have granted her a fair amount of financial success and prosperity, and thus it is no surprise that she offered herself as a hostess for Paul and his party. This success with Lydia was quickly tempered by an encounter between Paul and a young slave girl who served as a fortune-teller. Unlike Lydia, who appeared to be quite successful and financially independent, this girl was a slave who was completely dependent upon her masters. Even her body was not her own, as she was possessed to some degree by a spirit. However, the girl obviously recognized something special in Paul and his party and spent many days following them around and shouting, "These men are the servants of the most high God" (Acts 16:17). Paul, seemingly annoyed by this behavior, exorcised the spirit from the girl, freeing the girl but angering her masters, who were now faced with losing the financial benefits the girl had provided them.

What happened next is curious. The girl's masters complained to the Philippian authorities that Paul and Silas "do exceedingly trouble our city" (Acts 16:20). The response from the authorities was to take Paul and Silas, strip off their clothes, beat them with rods (a standard Roman punishment against those threating civil order), and finally cast them into prison. Additionally, their feet were held "fast in the stocks" (16:24), a measure that would greatly have increased their discomfort (compare 1 Thessalonians 2:2). Paul and Silas remained in prison throughout the night, patiently singing praises to God, until miraculously the doors of the prison opened up because of an earthquake. The reason this story is so curious is that Paul and Silas were both Roman citizens and therefore should have been exempt from this type of harsh punishment.[29] So why did Paul and Silas identify themselves as Roman citizens only *after* they had spent the night in prison? When the magistrates heard that Paul and Silas were citizens, they were justly fearful, for they could lose their positions as a result of this violation, and their attempt to quietly usher Paul and Silas out of Philippi is certainly understandable. Perhaps Paul felt that his suffering and persecution were part of the discipleship process—just as Jesus suffered, so should those who follow him suffer. Or perhaps Paul hoped that the magistrates would be more sympathetic toward his recent converts (now that he had an advantage over the magistrates), should any future trouble arise. Regardless, Paul and Silas departed from Philippi soon after. Paul's later letter to the Philippians indicates that this congregation was one he felt very close to, and it is clear he valued their friendship throughout his life.

From Philippi (where Paul apparently left Luke), Paul and his companions traveled west to Thessalonica, where again Paul ran afoul of the locals. As was his custom, Paul began by preaching in the synagogue of the Jews, where he preached three times. However, a group of Jews became annoyed at Paul's success, and in order to rid themselves of his presence they attempted to bring him to the city magistrates. Not finding Paul, they instead attacked a man named Jason, possibly because he was providing the house in which Paul was staying. Jason and his associates were forced to pay a bond or fine and were then released. Paul and his associates were quickly ushered out of the city and continued on their way toward Athens.

In Athens, the intellectual capital of the world, Paul continued his teaching and debates. Curious about what "new doctrine" (Acts 17:19) Paul was presenting, "certain philosophers" brought him before the court of the Areopagus, a venerable body located on the Hill of Ares, immediately southwest of the Acropolis. Here Paul was given the chance to explain Christian theology to an intellectual audience that included Stoics and Epicureans, an audience that would appreciate its novelty even if they rejected the message (17:18–32). Paul's subsequent speech is a masterstroke, one contrasting supposed Athenian piety with the truth about humanity, their origins, and their relationship to the true God. Without a knowledge and an understanding of God, Paul argued, even the intellectual elite, such as the Athenians, fall short. The Athenians, Paul argued, had created a God in their own image, rather than seeking to change themselves to match the image of God. While God may have acted with patience in the past, divine judgment is a reality for those who do not repent. However, when Paul brought up the topic of the Resurrection, his Greek audience lost interest and sent him on his way.

From Athens, Paul continued about forty miles west to Corinth, a port city that was the capital of the Roman province of Achaia. Unlike previous cities where he spent a short time and then moved on, Paul remained in Corinth for at least eighteen months and possibly even longer. While in Corinth, Paul continued his custom of preaching in the synagogue on the Sabbath and also plied his trade of working with leather. Paul lived for a time with two Jews who had come to Corinth from Rome, a husband and wife named Aquila and Priscilla, who practiced a similar trade (Acts 18:3). It is possible that Paul converted Aquila and Priscilla, although they may have been Christians before their expulsion from Rome because of the edict of the emperor Claudius.[30] It is likely during his time spent in Corinth that Paul wrote 1 and 2 Thessalonians, helping his Thessalonian congregation navigate through some difficult issues, such as persecution and the timing of Jesus's return. Paul apparently had a fair amount of success in Corinth, including the baptism of Crispus, the chief ruler of the synagogue, and his family. However, Paul once again incurred the resentment of the Jews living in Corinth, who brought Paul to Gallio, the proconsul of Achaia, on a trumped-up charge of being a lawbreaker.[31] Gallio saw through the charade and responded to the Jews that they should "look ye to it; for I will be no judge of such matters" (Acts 18:15). In a curious turn of events, Sosthenes, the leader of the synagogue, was taken and beaten in full view of Gallio, who "cared for none of those things" (18:17). Paul then left Corinth with Aquila and Priscilla, leaving Silas and Timothy behind to continue ministering to the Corinthians. After a brief stay in Ephesus, where Paul left Aquila and Priscilla, he returned to Jerusalem and then Antioch, concluding this second mission.

Paul's Third Mission (ca. AD 53–56)

Little time appears to have passed between Paul's return from his second mission and the beginning of his third mission (Acts 18:22–23). After his visit to Jerusalem, Paul again commenced his evangelization, similarly beginning in Antioch and moving to Galatia before finally arriving in Ephesus. Unlike Luke's account of Paul's second mission, which showed Paul traveling extensively throughout the Aegean, Paul's third mission was largely spent in Ephesus, a city Paul had briefly visited at the end of his second mission. In all, Paul spent approximately three years in Ephesus, by far his lengthiest stay in any one city during his missions (20:31). The abnormal period of time Paul spent in Ephesus could be attributed to the importance the city held in the ancient world. Ephesus was one of the largest cities in the Roman Empire, with a population approaching a quarter million. Nearly all communication throughout western Asia went through Ephesus, and Ephesus was also a commercial and cultural center. Of paramount importance was the worship of Diana, whose temple constructed outside the city walls was considered one of the seven wonders of the ancient world. If Paul was searching for a locale where he could spread his religious message far and wide, Ephesus provided the perfect environment.

Luke provides glimpses of what Paul did during those years in Ephesus. In addition to following his regular pattern of preaching in the Jewish synagogues, Paul also spent time in the "school of one Tyrannus," where presumably he gathered disciples and those interested in the Christian message and held various discussions (Acts 19:9). The result was that "all they which dwelt in Asia heard the word of the Lord Jesus, both Jews and Greeks" (19:10). Luke goes to great lengths to portray Paul's ministry as charismatic and inspired during this time. Handkerchiefs and aprons that touched Paul's body were used to heal various diseases and even to cast out devils. In a rather humorous aside, Luke tells of the seven sons of Sceva who also tried their hand at casting out devils but failed miserably when the evil spirit they were attempting to cast out "leaped on them, and overcame them, and prevailed against them, so that they fled out of that house naked and wounded" (19:16). This encounter resulted in many more embracing the message of Jesus Christ and bringing their magical texts together and burning them (19:19). Apparently, Paul became so successful at turning people away from their former religious beliefs that resentment began to build among those whose livelihood revolved around the selling of silver statues of Diana. These silversmiths rioted in protest and were subdued only when the Ephesian town clerk warned the rioters that their actions lacked legal foundation. While Luke portrays Paul's time in Ephesus as largely successful and without incident, it is possible that Paul was imprisoned for some time during his stay at Ephesus, as he mentions to the Corinthians that he "fought with beasts at Ephesus" (1 Corinthians 15:32).[32]

Perhaps concern for affairs in Corinth caused Paul to leave Ephesus. Paul had earlier sent Timothy and Erastus to Macedonia, and Timothy's return to Ephesus likely alerted Paul to the apostasy that had crept into the Corinthian branch. Paul had probably already written two letters to Corinth from Ephesus, one that did not survive (mentioned in 1 Corinthians 5:9–10) and one that did (1 Corinthians). However, Timothy's report made Paul realize that the situation required his actual presence. Luke reports that Paul traveled back to Greece, with stops in Troas and Macedonia. Once Paul arrived in Corinth, where he stayed for three months (Acts 20:3; likely the winter season), Paul realized just how far things had deteriorated. Mocked for his timid appearance and whiny voice, Paul left Corinth undermined and frustrated. He then likely wrote a letter he described as written "with many tears" (2 Corinthians 2:4), which is now lost. Paul sent this letter with Titus and likely continued traveling back through Macedonia and Troas; it was likely during that stay in Macedonia that Paul wrote part of 2 Corinthians (see 2:13). Fortunately, Titus appears to have been favorably received by the Corinthians, and he was even able to raise money for the collection while at Corinth (see 7:15). Happy to be reconciled, Paul wrote that he planned to visit Corinth a third time (12:14), although it is unknown whether or not he ever made a return visit to Corinth.

One of the reasons Paul may not have returned to Corinth was his eagerness to return to Jerusalem for Pentecost. Paul apparently avoided returning to Ephesus while traveling back from Greece because he worried that a stop in Ephesus would delay him from reaching Jerusalem in time. Pentecost may not have been Paul's only concern. He may have wanted to deliver the collection in conjunction with the festival, or he may have become excited about undertaking a possible voyage to Rome, a trip that had apparently been on his mind since his time in Ephesus (see Acts 19:21). It is likely that Paul began composing his epistle to the Romans during this time as a sort of introductory letter (see Romans 15:25–26) to what he appears to have fully expected to be part of a fourth mission. Paul did allow himself one brief stop at Miletus, a coastal town located about thirty miles from Ephesus. There, Paul gathered the elders of the church and delivered a warning that in the near future "grievous wolves enter in among you, not sparing the flock. Also of your own selves shall men arise, speaking perverse things, to draw away disciples after them" (Acts 20:29–30). Then, in Caesarea, despite a warning given him by the prophet Agabus that he would be bound and handed over to the Gentiles while in Jerusalem (21:11), Paul insisted on continuing his journey to Jerusalem.

Jerusalem and Imprisonment (ca. AD 57)

Paul arrived in a Jerusalem full of anxiety and unrest. Felix, the Roman procurator of Judea (ca. AD 52–60), was no friend of the Jews and had on several occasions shown little hesitation in killing those Jews who would not quietly submit to his rule.[33] Nationalistic attitudes ran high among the Jews, and Jewish resentment for Roman rule manifested itself in a general anti-Gentile sentiment. The celebration of Pentecost would have done nothing to diminish these views. About this time Luke records that accusations had been brought against Paul himself, namely that he was teaching Jews living in the diaspora to disregard the law of Moses and to refrain from circumcising their sons (Acts 21:20–21). When Paul met with James (the brother of Jesus), James asked Paul to prove his devotion to Judaism by accompanying a few Jews who were in the process of completing their Nazarite vows: according to the law, Paul would have needed to go through his own period of purification owing to his time spent in gentile territory (Numbers 19:11–13). James must have felt that this act would assuage any concerns about Paul's respect and devotion for Jewish law and tradition while away in the diaspora. To agree to such a proposal was not a guarantee of safety since Paul would have had to make his presence in the temple public and thus alert his enemies to his whereabouts. Paul nonetheless agreed, perhaps realizing that his reputation had put him in a precarious position or perhaps because he feared that the collection he and his colleagues had worked so hard to gather would be rejected if it came from someone who was viewed as anti-Jewish (Romans 15:30–31).

Unfortunately, James's plan did not work out. Luke relates that "the Jews which were of Asia" (Acts 21:27) stirred up the crowd by accusing Paul (falsely) of bringing Gentiles into the temple, a capital offense that would desecrate the temple. Paul was seized by an angry mob, dragged out of the temple, and nearly killed, an appropriate punishment (under the law) if Paul had in fact done what the mob accused him of. Fortunately, the Roman tribune Claudius Lysias, likely already on high alert because of the festival, intervened and rescued Paul with soldiers garrisoned in the nearby Antonia Fortress. Claudius Lysias was apparently under the impression that Paul was a revolutionary zealot, an Egyptian pseudo-Messiah who had led four thousand *sicarii* into the wilderness, and was thus surprised to learn not only that Paul could speak Greek but that he was also a citizen of Tarsus.[34] Paul requested to speak to the crowd and told them of his background, his vision, and his mission. Unsatisfied, the Jewish mob pushed for Paul's execution, and Claudius Lysias ordered Paul to be brutally scourged in order to extract more specific information about his identity and presence in Jerusalem. Recognizing that Roman law forbade the use of scourging, or *verberatio*, on a Roman citizen, Paul asked the centurion in charge of scourging him, "Is it lawful for you to scourge a man that is a Roman, and uncondemned?" (Acts 22:25). Alarmed at this revelation, Claudius Lysias ordered a cessation to Paul's punishment, although he continued to keep Paul in his custody.

Claudius Lysias thereupon ordered Paul to stand before the Sanhedrin. This move should not be understood as an attempt by Claudius Lysias to ignore his responsibilities and allow Jewish law to settle the dispute. Rather, it is more likely that Claudius Lysias needed further insight into why Paul and his Jewish opponents were engaged in such a heated religious dispute. Before the Sanhedrin, Paul maintained his innocence and successfully won over the Pharisees to his side by highlighting his pharisaic pedigree, although not before insulting Ananias, the high priest (Acts 23:1–9). Worried that the conflict between the Sadducees and the Pharisees over Paul's testimony might become violent, Claudius Lysias was forced once again to take Paul back into custody. Later that night the Lord appeared to Paul, comforting him: "Be of good cheer, Paul: for as thou hast testified of me in Jerusalem, so must thou bear witness also at Rome" (23:11). The following morning, likely frustrated at their inability to see Paul executed, a band of about forty Jews swore an oath that they would not eat or drink until they had killed Paul (Acts 12–13). They attempted to enlist the help of the chief priests and elders in contacting Claudius Lysias and asking him to return Paul for another hearing before the Sanhedrin, with the intent of killing Paul before he arrived. Alerted to this plot by a nephew of Paul's, Claudius Lysias realized that Paul would not be safe in Jerusalem and ordered him to be extradited to Caesarea Maritima to be interrogated by Antonius Felix, the Roman procurator (AD 52–60). The number of men sent to escort Paul, 470 (23:23), is extraordinary, but it may indicate the dedication Claudius Lysias had to ensure Paul's safe travel.

Before Felix and Festus (ca. AD 58–60)

Paul's trial before Felix took the form of a debate. Tertullus, a skilled prosecutor hired by the Jews, attempted to portray Paul as a seditious person intent on stirring up trouble for both the Jews and Rome. Paul responded by refuting Tertullus's accusations and reemphasizing his own beliefs in the God of Judaism and the law. When the debate was over, Felix declined to declare a verdict, instead stating that he would wait for Claudius Lysias to arrive. Paul was ordered to remain in custody but to have some liberties, such as the companionship of friends. However, Felix continued to delay his decision, ostensibly because he wanted to discuss Christianity and its beliefs with Paul, but Luke includes the more likely cause of the delay, namely that "he hoped also that money should have been given him of Paul" (Acts 24:26). Felix's holding out for a bribe is not surprising, given what is otherwise known about his character, although the act of taking bribes from prisoners was strictly prohibited according to the Roman *Lex Julia de pecuniis repetundis*. Rather than obtaining the quick release from prison he may have been expecting, Paul instead spent two years in captivity in Caesarea under the watch of Felix.

Likely owing to questionable administrative practices, Felix was removed from office in AD 60 and replaced by Porcius Festus (AD 60–62).[35] By all accounts a decent administrator, Festus initially acted impartially but likely underestimated the hatred Paul's Jewish opponents had for Paul. Festus rejected the Jewish appeal to transfer Paul to Jerusalem (where he would have been ambushed and killed along the way; see Acts 25:3) but invited Paul's opponents to travel to Caesarea and accuse Paul in person. However, once everyone gathered in Caesarea and both sides again pled their case, Festus sided with the Jews and asked Paul if he would be willing to travel to Jerusalem and be judged there. Festus likely had no knowledge of the Jewish plot to ambush Paul; rather, he was trying to please his constituency and thus was "willing to do the Jews a pleasure" (25:9). Well aware that certain death awaited him if he traveled to Jerusalem and sensing that Festus was more sympathetic to the Jews than to him, Paul again relied on his Roman citizenship. According to the Roman *Lex Julia de vi publica et privata*, a Roman citizen could at any time appeal (*provoco*) to the emperor to have his case heard, and that is what Paul did here: "I stand at Caesar's judgment seat, where I ought to be judged: to the Jews have I done no wrong, as thou very well knowest. For if I be an offender, or have committed any thing worthy of death, I refuse not to die: but if there be none of these things whereof these accuse me, no man may deliver me unto them. I appeal unto Caesar" (25:10–11).

Festus did not immediately send him to Rome. Rather, it was his responsibility to write up a report outlining the charges brought against Paul. Festus, being procurator only a short time, likely struggled with how to describe Paul's circumstances in a way that looked to be worth the emperor's time, rather than a silly cultural dispute that (at least in the emperor's eyes) any competent administrator should have been able to resolve. Thus, it is likely with a certain amount of relief that Festus welcomed Herod Agrippa II and his sister Bernice, who had arrived in Caesarea to welcome the new procurator. The last of the Hasmonean rulers over Judea, Herod Agrippa II would have been able to help Festus understand the complexities of Paul's circumstances. Paul again related his vision and offered a brief summary of his travels, including his capture in the temple. Festus was unimpressed with Paul's presentation and declared Paul to be mad. Herod Agrippa II was more sympathetic, and his famous response, "Almost thou persuadest me to be a Christian" (Acts 26:28), is ambiguous and could be read either respectfully or ironically. The important outcome of the encounter is that Herod Agrippa II declared that Paul "doeth nothing worthy of death or of bonds" and lamented that "this man might have been set at liberty, if he had not appealed unto Caesar" (26:31–32).

Paul's Imprisonment in Rome (ca. AD 60–62) and Execution (ca. AD 64)

Following his hearing with Herod Agrippa II, Festus agreed to send Paul to Rome to have his appeal heard. After a series of near-disastrous events that included a shipwreck and a viper's bite, Paul arrived in Rome. Luke records that he spent two years in Rome under some kind of confinement. Paul's case was likely not considered a serious offence by the Romans, and he was granted a lightened form of custody. Paul was allowed to dwell in a small, modest residence that he (or more likely his supporters) paid for (Acts 28:16), although he remained in the custody of a Roman soldier (28:16), perhaps even bound to the soldier by a chain (28:20). Unfortunately, Luke's account ends with Paul under arrest in Rome, leaving many questions unanswered. The likeliest scenario for what happened next is that Paul's case was dismissed, probably owing to the absence of his accusers. First Clement (5:5–7) mentions that Paul reached "the limits of the west," possibly suggesting that Paul achieved his goal of traveling to Spain (Romans 15:24, 28). However, on the way home from the west, Paul found himself once again in a difficult situation, one that he would not escape from. Eusebius wrote that after being released from his initial Roman imprisonment and undertaking an additional ministry, Paul came "a second time to the same city [and] suffered martyrdom under Nero."[36] Eusebius additionally relays the detail that Paul suffered death by beheading, the proper means of execution for a Roman citizen.[37] If this scenario is accurate, while Paul's death could have taken place as early as AD 62, it may have extended as late as AD 68 (the year of Nero's death).[38] Of course, it is also possible that Paul was executed during his first stay at Rome and Luke simply chose not to include that detail, which would likely place Paul's execution sometime between AD 62 and 64.

It is probable that 2 Timothy (if genuinely Pauline) preserves some of the last thoughts Paul ever recorded. In this revealing epistle, Paul laments that some of his colleagues, such as Demas, have left him, save Luke (4:10–11). His request that Timothy bring him the "cloak that I left at Troas with Carpus" (4:13) may reveal conditions indicative of a harsher imprisonment than his previous one (4:16). Yet Paul's ever-present optimism does not wane. Using a series of athletic metaphors, Paul confidently declares, "I have fought a good fight, I have finished my course, I have kept the faith" (4:7). In other words, Paul has wrestled a good match, he has run a good race, and he has maintained, through it all, his loyalty to and confidence in Jesus Christ.

With these words, Paul leaves his modern-day readers with a valuable archetype of discipleship. Over two (possibly three) decades of missionary work, Paul made no shortage of enemies, parted ways with friends and colleagues, wrote epistles fiery (Galatians) and contemplative (Philippians), and yet through it all he endured because of his faith. Paul's experiences tell us that the life of a disciple is not an easy one; it requires sacrifice and patience centered on the conviction that faith in Jesus Christ has not been misplaced or found wanting. As Paul (rather explicitly) writes to the Philippians, "I have suffered the loss of all things, and do count them but dung, that I may win Christ" (Philippians 3:8). Paul's legacy comes through to help his readers understand that life is hard and takes its toll, that true commitment can lead to a shortage of earthly satisfaction, and that obtaining a "crown of righteousness" (2 Timothy 4:8) is not about perfection, but about perseverance.

❧

Nicholas J. Frederick is an assistant professor in the Department of Ancient Scripture at Brigham Young University.

Further Reading

Latter-day Saint

Anderson, Richard Lloyd. *Understanding Paul.* Salt Lake City: Deseret Book, 1983. A work that was written more recently than Sidney Sperry's. It is more useful for engaging Paul's theology and the context of the epistles than as a study of Paul's life, but it is still a valuable resource for Latter-day Saints.

Hoskisson, Paul Y., ed. *The Apostle Paul, His Life and His Testimony: The 23rd Annual Sidney B. Sperry Symposium.* Salt Lake City: Deseret Book, 1994. A collection of essays, some scholarly, others devotional, devoted to the life of Paul and the issues that arise surrounding him in Acts and his letters.

Sperry, Sidney B. *Paul's Life and Letters.* Salt Lake City: Bookcraft, 1955. A classic Latter-day Saint treatment of Paul. It is heavily Protestant and somewhat outdated, but it is still useful, especially in its treatment of Paul's letters.

Wayment, Thomas A. *From Persecutor to Apostle: A Biography of Paul.* Salt Lake City: Deseret Book, 2006. A highly readable biography of Paul written by a Latter-day Saint and New Testament scholar. It is the best place to start for readers looking for a one-volume treatment of Paul's life.

Other

Dunn, James D. G. *Christianity in the Making, vol 2: Beginning from Jerusalem.* Grand Rapids, MI: Eerdmans, 2009. All three volumes in Dunn's Christianity in the Making series are must-reads, but this second volume masterfully navigates the primary and secondary literature on Paul to provide a cogent picture of Paul's role in the early Christian church.

Murphy-O'Connor, Jerome. *Paul: A Critical Life.* Oxford: Clarendon Press, 1996. An engaging and provocative biography of Paul by an outstanding New Testament scholar. Readers looking for an academic treatment of Paul's life from a non–Latter-day Saint perspective should begin here.

Schnelle, Udo. *Apostle Paul: His Life and Theology,* trans. M. Eugene Boring. Grand Rapids, MI: Baker Academic, 2003. A thorough treatment of Paul's life and thought for those who want something similar to Richard Lloyd Anderson's Understanding Paul but from a non–Latter-day Saint perspective.

Witherington III, Ben. *The Paul Quest: The Renewed Search for the Jew of Tarsus.* Downer's Grove, IL: InterVarsity, 1998. Witherington brings together all the arguments and issues involved in the search for the "historical Paul." A useful resource for those wanting to know more about what can and cannot be said about Paul himself.

Timeline for the Life of Paul

(Note: Because these dates are based on limited historical evidence and the text of the New Testament, this timeline should be seen as a *speculative* reconstruction of Paul's life.)

AD 1–10 (+/-5)	Paul's birth
30	Crucifixion of Jesus
31–33	Paul persecutes the Hellenists
34	Paul's "conversion"
34–37	Damascus and Arabia (the "missing years")
37	First visit to Jerusalem
37–46	Years spent in Syria and Cilicia
47	Paul and Barnabas preach in Antioch

48–49	Paul's first mission: Galatia
49	Council of Jerusalem (incident at Antioch either closely preceding or closely following the council)
50	Paul returns to Galatia (*Galatians*)
50–52	Paul's second mission: Corinth (*1* and *2 Thessalonians*)
53–56	Paul's third mission: Ephesus (*1* and *2 Corinthians, Romans*)
57	Return to Jerusalem and arrest
58–60	Imprisonment in Caesarea (*Philippians, Ephesians, Colossians*, and *Philemon*)
60–64	Imprisonment in Rome and execution (*Pastorals*)

Notes

1. John G. Gager, *Who Made Early Christianity? The Jewish Lives of the Apostle Paul* (New York: Princeton University Press, 2015), 17.

2. This has been the approach of some biographies of Paul aimed at popular audiences, such as A. N. Wilson, *Paul: The Mind of the Apostle* (New York: W. W. Norton, 1997); and Hyam Maccoby, *The Mythmaker: Paul and the Invention of Christianity* (New York: Harper and Row, 1986). However, the origin of the idea goes back to F. C. Baur, in particular *Paul: The Apostle of Jesus Christ: His Life and Works, His Epistles and Teachings* (London: Williams and Norgate, 1845).

3. Daniel Boyarin, *A Radical Jew: Paul and the Politics of Identity* (Berkeley: University of California Press, 1994).

4. For Paul's early education, see Jerome Murphy-O'Connor, *Paul: A Critical Life* (Oxford: Clarendon, 1996), 46–51.

5. For a discussion of the arguments for and against Paul being a Roman citizen, see Udo Schnelle, *Apostle Paul: His Life and Theology*, trans. M. Eugene Boring (Grand Rapids, MI: Baker Academic, 2003), 60–62. A classic study of Roman law and the New Testament is A. N. Sherwin-White, *Roman Society and Roman Law in the New Testament* (Oxford: Oxford University Press, 1963).

6. James D. G. Dunn, *Christianity in the Making, vol 2: Beginning from Jerusalem* (Grand Rapids, MI: Eerdmans, 2009), 335.

7. See Jacob Neusner, *The Rabbinic Tradition about the Pharisees before 70* (Leiden, Netherlands: Brill, 1971), 1:341–76.

8. From the Mishnah and Babylonian Talmud, see m. Yebamot 6:6; b. Yebamot 62b–63b; b. Qiddušin 29b; and b. Sanhedrin 36b. For a discussion of exceptions to this understanding, see John P. Meier, *A Marginal Jew: Rethinking the Historical Jesus*, vol. 1, *The Roots of the Problem and the Person*, The Anchor Bible Reference Library (New York: Doubleday, 1991), 336–41.

9. Epiphanius, *Refutation of All Heresies* 30.16.9.

10. "It is much more probable, however, that Paul cheerfully bowed to the expectation that young men should marry in their early twenties." Murphy-O'Connor, *Paul: A Critical Life*, 63.

11. Murphy-O'Connor, *Paul: A Critical Life*, 64–65.

12. Dating events in the life of Paul is a difficult task, and there are as many chronological timelines for the life of Paul as there are biographies. The dates presented here in this chapter represent my best estimation. For a discussion of the issues involved and other Pauline timelines, see Dunn, *Beginning from Jerusalem*, 497–512.

13. "The fact that the witnesses laid their clothes at Saul's feet suggests that he was already the acknowledged leader in the opposition to the early church." David G. Peterson, *The Acts of the Apostles* (Grand Rapids, MI: Eerdmans, 2009), 268. Compare Acts 4:35, 37; 5:2.

14. Murphy-O'Connor, *Paul: A Critical Life*, 67.

15. See Galatians 1:16; 1 Corinthians 9:1.

16. See Thomas A. Wayment, *From Persecutor to Apostle: A Biography of Paul* (Salt Lake City: Deseret Book, 2006), 41.

17. Josephus, *Antiquities* 18.109–115. It is the denouncement of this marriage by John the Baptist that provides the setting for his execution. Compare Matthew 14:3–12.

18. One possible link between Paul and Arabia is his comment in Galatians that Hagar represents "mount Sinai in Arabia" (Galatians 4:25). This opens up the intriguing possibility that Paul went to Arabia to visit Mount Sinai and find answers to his questions in a similar fashion as Moses did.

19. See Murphy-O'Connor, *Paul: A Critical Life*, 5–7.

20. "The only point Paul chose to make is that his time in Arabia further underlined his independence from the Jerusalem leadership; in Arabia there was no one whom he could have consulted." Dunn, *Beginning from Jerusalem*, 265.

21. Compare 1 Corinthians 3:10; 2 Corinthians 10:13–16.

22. For those who want to argue that Paul was a member of the quorum of the twelve apostles, the best textual evidence is Acts 14:4, 14 and Galatians 2:9.

23. Josephus, *Jewish War* 3.29.

24. It is important to note that at this juncture two possible sequences of events are introduced by Luke in Acts and Paul in Galatians. The first one, which I follow, is that the famine relief mentioned in Acts 11 is the same event discussed by Paul in Galatians 2:1–10. In support of this position is F. F. Bruce, who writes, "The view taken here is that it is to be identified with the visit of Acts 11:30, in the fourteenth year of Paul's conversion." F. F. Bruce, *The Epistle to the Galatians* (Grand Rapids, MI: Eerdmans, 1982), 108–9; see also Ben Witherington III, *The Acts of the Apostles* (Grand Rapids, MI: Eerdmans, 1998), 439–43. The other position is that Galatians 2:1–10 refers to the events mentioned in Acts 15. There are good arguments supporting both views. For an even-handed treatment of both positions, see Dunn, *Beginning from Jerusalem*, 446–70.

25. As recorded by Ovid in his charming collection of tales, *Metamorphoses*, Zeus and Hermes often would travel to earth in the guise of men as a test of hospitality. After several rejections, Zeus and Hermes found an acceptance in the house of the elderly couple Baucis and Philemon, who are rewarded for their hospitality by becoming priests in the temple of Zeus; see *Metamorphoses*, 8.611–724. This story apparently occurred nearby the city of Lystra, and it is likely that the inhabitants' reaction to Barnabas and Paul stems from their knowledge of this story.

26. Again, we experience questions in regard to the sequence of Paul's life as described in Galatians 2:11–14. Some scholars, such as F. F. Bruce, argue that the encounter between Peter and Paul in Antioch occurred between the first mission and the Council of Jerusalem, which issued the decree granting full membership to uncircumcised Gentiles. See Bruce, *Galatians*, 128–30; see also Ben Witheringon III, *Grace in Galatia* (Grand Rapids, MI: Eerdmans, 1998), 149–52. Others, such as Joseph A. Fitzmyer, argue that the encounter between Peter and Paul happened after the Council of Jerusalem (and presumably the decree); see Joseph A. Fitzmyer, *The Acts of the Apostles* (New Haven: Yale University Press, 1998), 541. Again, for a full discussion, see Dunn, *Beginning from Jerusalem*, 446–70. See also the work of David G. Peterson, who writes: "We cannot be certain when the next incident mentioned by Paul in Galatians 2:11–14 took place, though it is most likely to have been before the resolutions of the Jerusalem Council brought public agreement between Peter, James, Paul, and Barnabas on such matters" (Peterson, *Acts of the Apostles*, 420).

27. For more on the Jerusalem conference, including the events that led up to it and the outcomes that followed, see Robert J. Matthews, "The Jerusalem Conference," in *The Apostle Paul: His Life and Testimony*, ed. Paul Y. Hoskisson (Salt Lake City: Deseret Book, 1994), 96–109.

28. For a useful discussion of the issues surrounding the Epistle to the Galatians, including its dating, occasion, and audience, see Bruce, *Galatians*, 1–56. Bruce himself argues for an early date for Galatians, believing that a date sometime near the events of the Council of Jerusalem "would yield the most satisfactory correlation of the data of Galatians and Acts and the most satisfactory dating of Galatians" (55).

29. The *Lex Porcia de provocatione* specifically forbade the flogging of one who was a *civis romanus*, or a "Roman Citizen" (compare Livy, *Ab. Urb. Cond* 10.9.5). "In a Roman colony it appears that arrest, beating, and imprisonment were normal for aliens, but that it was potentially dangerous to give citizens the same treatment." Peter Garnsey, *Social Status and Legal Privilege in the Roman Empire* (Oxford: Oxford University Press, 1970), 268.

30. Suetonius records that Claudius expelled Jews from Rome because of uprisings resulting from "impulsore Chresto," which could mean that divisions over belief in Jesus Christ had led to these uprisings, or it could simply refer to someone named Chrestus who had no connection with Christianity (see Suetonius, *Divus Claudius* 25.4). Either way, Jews were likely banned from Rome somewhere around AD 49 and likely did not return until after the death of Claudius in AD 54.

31. Gallio's tenure as proconsul of Achaia can be firmly dated from spring AD 51 to spring AD 52. The majority of attempts at establishing a Pauline chronology use Gallio's proconsulship as a primary foundation.

32. For more on the argument for an Ephesian imprisonment, see Dunn, *Beginning from Jerusalem*, 777–80.

33. See Josephus, *Jewish War* 2.12.2; 2.13.4, 7. Compare Tacitus, *Historiae* 5.9; *Annales* 12.54.

34. See Josephus, *Jewish War* 2.13.5. Felix had been working on quelling the Egyptian's revolt and had largely been successful, although the Egyptian remained at large. Claudius Lysias appears to believe that the man he has apprehended, who had caused such a disturbance in the temple, was this Egyptian.

35. See Josephus, *Antiquities* 20.182.

36. Eusebius, *Ecclesiastical History* 2.22.2; compare 2 Timothy 4:16.

37. Eusebius, *Ecclesiastical History* 2.25.5; compare 1 Clement 5:7; Tertullian, *Prescription against Heretics* 36.

38. For a fuller discussion of these issues, see H. W. Tajra, *The Martyrdom of St. Paul: Historical and Judicial Context, Traditions, and Legends* (Tübingen, Germany: Mohr [Paul Siebeck], 1994).

24

The Epistles of the Apostle Paul
An Overview

Frank F. Judd Jr.

The book of Acts chronicles three separate missions of the apostle Paul: (1) he traveled through Cyprus and central Asia Minor (Acts 13:4–14; 28),[1] (2) he evangelized primarily in Greece (15:36–18:22), and (3) he revisited Greece and western Asia Minor (18:23–20:38). Since Paul felt a strong sense of stewardship over the church congregations that he established, he would periodically check up on them. For example, after evangelizing in central Asia Minor and traveling on to Derbe in eastern Asia Minor, Paul retraced his steps and returned to congregations he had previously established, "confirming the souls of the disciples and exhorting them to continue in the faith" (14:22). He also "ordained them elders in every church" and "commended them to the Lord" (14:23). As Paul commenced on his second mission, he returned to Derbe and Lystra (16:1–2) before traveling further to Greece and then Ephesus. On his third mission, Paul revisited areas he had evangelized during his second mission, in particular Ephesus (19:1–20) and locations throughout Greece (20:1–3).

When Paul was unable personally to revisit a particular group of saints, he sometimes sent others to inquire concerning their well-being. For instance, after he left Thessalonica and traveled to Athens, he sent Timothy back to instruct the saints and to give them comfort (1 Thessalonians 3:2). When Timothy returned, he thereupon reported to Paul concerning the "faith and charity" of the Thessalonian Christians and that they earnestly wanted to see Paul again (3:6). Similarly, when Paul was in Ephesus during his third mission, he sent Timothy and Erastus to visit the church congregations he had previously established in Greece, while "he himself stayed in Asia for a season" (Acts 19:22).

Sometimes, in lieu of personally returning or having one of his companions return to a congregation, Paul would simply send a letter.[2] After the composition was complete, Paul would then send the letter to its recipients. Since there was no real postal service for anyone but government officials in Paul's day, he would have the letter delivered by one or more of his trusted associates. When Paul wrote to the Colossians, for example, he informed them in the letter that he sent to them two of his faithful companions, Tychicus and Onesimus, in order to instruct them concerning what was happening with Paul as well as to gather information about their situation (Colossians 4:7–9). The implication is that Tychicus and Onesimus were the ones who actually delivered this letter to the Christians at Colossae, and following their visit they would return to Paul with the report. Since a large portion of the population of the Roman world was illiterate, including some members of his congregations, Paul instructed the Colossians to have this letter read out loud to the congregation: "And when this epistle is read among you, cause that it be read also in the church of the Laodiceans; and that ye likewise read the epistle from Laodicea" (4:16).[3]

Paul's letters preserved in the New Testament generally followed a customary outline.[4] They would typically begin with an introduction that identified the writer(s) and the addressee(s) and then expressed a greeting. For example, Paul's first letter to the Thessalonians begins, "Paul, and Silvanus, and Timotheus, unto the church of the Thessalonians . . ." and then declares, "Grace be unto you, and peace, from God our Father, and the Lord Jesus Christ" (1 Thessalonians 1:1). The body of the letter contained the main points of instruction the writer intended the recipients to understand. Letters would normally conclude with a farewell. Paul ended his first letter to the Thessalonians with one of his standard benedictions: "The grace of our Lord Jesus Christ be with you. Amen" (5:28).

There has been much discussion among scholars concerning the chronology of Paul's epistles. The New Testament contains Paul's letters in order according to size, beginning with the longest (Romans) and ending with the shortest (Philemon). This chapter, however, will present Paul's epistles in chronological order insofar as it is possible to determine: the earlier letters (Galatians, 1–2 Thessalonians, 1–2 Corinthians, and Romans), the later letters (Philippians, Ephesians, Colossians, and Philemon), and the last letters (1–2 Timothy and Titus). For each letter, this chapter will attempt to reconstruct the context in which the epistle was written and then outline some of the most important ideas contained within that particular epistle.

Galatians (ca. AD 49–50)

Rather than addressing a particular group of Christians in a particular city, Paul addressed this letter to "the churches of Galatia" (Galatians 1:2).[5] It is difficult to know precisely what groups of people Paul was referencing. The term *Galatia* could be used to describe the people who lived in the northern part of central Asia Minor, descendants of the Gauls who were under the rule of the last king of Galatia, Amynta, who died in 25 BC. But there is no record of Paul evangelizing this area. In fact, Acts 16:6 says that when Paul traveled through this area he was "forbidden of the Holy Ghost to preach the word." On the other hand, the term *Galatia* could refer to those who lived in the southern part of the Roman province of Galatia. This is the region that Paul and Barnabas visited on their first mission after sailing from Cyprus (Acts 13:14; 14:1, 6). But the term *Galatians* (Galatians 3:1), which Paul used to address his audience, would have been more appropriate for those in the north, who were ethnically Galatians, than for those in the south, who were living in the province of Galatia. Scholars are also divided concerning whether this epistle was written before the Jerusalem Council in Acts 15 (ca. AD 49) or afterward. Regardless, the Epistle to the Galatians is very likely one of Paul's earliest letters.

After a short greeting at the beginning of the Epistle to the Galatians, Paul dispensed with his typical well wishes and immediately declared, "I marvel that ye are so soon removed from him that called you into the grace of Christ unto another gospel" (1:6). Paul's concern was that the Christians in Galatia were listening to a group of people who came among them in order to "trouble" them and "pervert the gospel of Christ" (1:7). Paul was so upset that he called them "O foolish Galatians" (3:1). These individuals apparently tried to discredit Paul's authority as an apostle as well as his teachings that Gentiles did not need circumcision for salvation.[6]

Paul started his letter by defending his authority as an apostle of Jesus Christ. He declared that he was an apostle "not of men, neither by man, but by Jesus Christ" (1:1) and that immediately after his conversion he "conferred not with flesh and blood" (1:16). These statements do not deny his priesthood ordination through the proper priesthood channels (although we have no scriptural account of it), but rather they emphasize that Paul's authority came from God and he had the right as an apostle to receive revelation and teach doctrine: "The gospel which was preached of me is not after man. For I neither received it of man, neither was I taught it, but by the revelation of Jesus Christ" (1:11–12).

The issue in question concerned the requirements to become a true disciple of Jesus. While Paul was in Antioch, "false brethren" (Galatians 2:4)—called "Judaizers" by modern scholars—came among the gentile converts and taught the necessity of keeping the law of Moses for salvation. Naturally, Paul and Barnabas disagreed and traveled to Jerusalem to consult with Peter (2:1–2). Paul left the meeting with Peter feeling that they agreed on the issue, for, as Paul concluded, "Neither Titus, who was with me, being a Greek, was compelled to be circumcised" (2:3). Later, Peter visited Antioch and dined with Paul and his gentile converts, but when Judaizers from Jerusalem arrived, Peter removed himself "fearing them which were of the circumcision" (2:12).[7] Paul explained to the Galatians that Peter's example in this instance was hypocritical and sent the wrong message. From their meeting in Jerusalem, Peter understood that Jewish and uncircumcised gentile Christians were allowed to interact. But, as Paul explained, Peter's actions at dinner sent the message to gentile converts that they needed to become Jewish (i.e., circumcised) in order to be acceptable (2:14).

This is the introduction to Paul's famous discussion of salvation by faith apart from the requirements of the law of Moses.[8] Paul concluded: "A man is not justified by the works of the law, but by the faith of Jesus Christ" (Galatians 2:16); for if one could be saved by keeping the law of Moses, then the salvific work of Christ is meaningless: "Christ is dead in vain" (2:21). Salvation by means of the law of Moses required one to live it completely and perfectly, for as Moses himself taught: "Cursed is every one that continueth not in all things which are written in the book of the law" (3:10; compare Deuteronomy 27:26). But since nobody lived the law perfectly, as Paul concluded, "the just shall live by faith" (Galatians 3:11; compare Habakkuk 2:4).

If the law of Moses did not provide salvation, then why was it given in the first place? Paul explained: "it was added because of transgressions" (Galatians 3:19). A revelation through Joseph Smith clarifies that because of the rebellion of the Israelites, God "took Moses out of their midst, and the Holy Priesthood also; and the lesser priesthood continued" (Doctrine and Covenants 84:25–26). The ultimate purpose of the rituals of the law of Moses, according to Paul, was "to bring us unto Christ" (Galatians 3:24) as a schoolmaster. Similarly, the Nephites, explained Mormon, "did not suppose that salvation came by the law of Moses; but the law of Moses did serve to strengthen their faith in Christ" (Alma 25:16).

Paul encouraged the Galatians to "stand fast therefore in the liberty wherewith Christ hath made us free, and be not entangled again with the yoke of bondage" (Galatians 5:1). These gentile converts had been set free spiritually from the requirements of pagan religion (4:8–9). Since some of them were considering submitting to the law of Moses, Paul wondered why they "desire[d] again to be in bondage" (4:9), this time to the requirements of Jewish religion. Paul tried to impress upon the Galatians that Christ had come "to redeem them that were under the law" (4:5)—including both Jews with respect to the law of Moses and Gentiles with respect to their religious requirements.

What does God require from Christians if they are free from the demands of both Jewish and pagan religion? Paul concluded his letter with a heartfelt discussion of the importance of submitting to the Holy Spirit.[9] He counseled the Galatians: "Walk in the Spirit" (5:16), because "if ye be led of the Spirit, ye are not under the law" (5:18). And disciples who do so will be blessed with "the fruit of the Spirit," which is "love, joy, peace, longsuffering, gentleness, goodness, faith, meekness, [and] temperance" (5:22–23). For Christians, one of the primary purposes of following Christ through the Holy Spirit was to engender change in disciples in order to be like their Savior. Thus, as Paul closed his epistle to the Galatians, "in Christ Jesus neither circumcision availeth any thing, nor uncircumcision"; the goal was to become "a new creature" in Christ (6:15).

1–2 Thessalonians (ca. AD 50–52)

During his second mission, Paul left Philippi and traveled west along the Via Egnatia to Thessalonica, where he preached in the local synagogue and converted a number of people, including "devout Greeks" and "chief women" (Acts 17:1–4).[10] The descriptions "devout" and "God fearer," according to Joseph Fitzmyer, seem to be "quasi-technical phrases" that refer to Gentiles who were sympathetic toward Judaism, believed in one God, but did not submit to all the regulations of the law of Moses, such as circumcision for males.[11] A group of Jews, however, accosted a man named Jason for receiving Christians and accused them of doing things "contrary to the decrees of Caesar, saying that there is another king, one Jesus" (17:5–7). It became so dangerous for Paul that his converts sent him and Silas away to Berea and eventually, because these Thessalonian Jews continued to pursue them, to Athens (17:10–15).

Paul desired to return to Thessalonica and give assistance to his new converts but was unable to do so (1 Thessalonians 2:18). Because he was concerned about their welfare, Paul indicated that he sent Timothy back to Thessalonica in order "to establish [them], and to comfort [them] concerning [their] faith" (3:2). In the meantime, Paul left Athens and traveled west to Corinth (Acts 18:1). Timothy eventually returned and found Paul in Corinth, where, Paul reported, he "brought us good tidings of your faith and charity, and that ye have good remembrance of us always, desiring greatly to see us, as we also to see you" (1 Thessalonians 3:6). But there was apparently more to Timothy's report, for Paul decided to write a letter to the Christians at Thessalonica concerning questions they had and issues they were facing.[12] First Thessalonians is therefore, along with Galatians, probably one of Paul's earliest letters, possibly written from Athens during his second mission around AD 50. Second Thessalonians was probably composed not long after the first letter.[13]

Apparently, most of the converts in Thessalonica were Gentiles (Acts 17:4). Paul began his letter by mentioning that when he and his companions preached the gospel to them, they "turned to God from idols to serve the living and true God" (1 Thessalonians 1:9). This is the same message Paul and Barnabas preached during their first mission to the Gentiles in Lystra who attempted to offer sacrifice unto them after mistaking them for Greek gods. They declared: "Ye should turn from these vanities [i.e., idols] unto the living God" (Acts 14:15).

One of the issues that concerned Paul was the Thessalonian converts' attitudes toward self-reliance and temporal welfare. When Paul and his companions arrived in Thessalonica, they did not rely on the local congregation for temporal support, but they worked "night and day" because, as Paul concluded, "we would not be chargeable unto any of you" (1 Thessalonians 2:9). Not all the new converts, however, were following Paul's example of work, for Paul encouraged them "to do your own business, and to work with your own hands, as we commanded you" (4:11). It seems as though this issue persisted for some time after Paul wrote 1 Thessalonians, because in his second letter Paul reminded them once again that while in Thessalonica, the visiting disciples had worked to support themselves (2 Thessalonians 3:8) and taught them "if any would not work, neither should he eat" (3:10). The reason for this attitude among the members was probably not simply laziness. Rather, as we will see, it was possibly related to their expectation that Jesus would return soon, rendering, in their minds, regular daily work unnecessary.

During his original visit, Paul taught the Thessalonians to "serve the living and true God; and to wait for his Son from heaven, whom he raised from the dead, even Jesus, which delivered us from the wrath to come" (1 Thessalonians 1:9–10). It seems that church members in Thessalonica expected Jesus to return quite soon, for when some of their number died before that event took place, they were worried that those deceased members would miss out on important blessings. Paul attempted to calm their fears so that they would not be filled with sorrow "concerning them which are asleep" (i.e., dead) and not be like non-Christians who "have no hope" (4:13) in the Resurrection. Paul explained that those who "are alive and remain unto the coming of the Lord shall not prevent [i.e., have an advantage over] them which are asleep" (4:15) because when Christ returned, he would bring with him those righteous Christians who "sleep in Jesus" (4:14). Paul hoped that they would "comfort one another with these words" (4:18).

Paul's teachings did not completely resolve the issue, because in his second letter he warned the Thessalonians to not be troubled concerning the idea that "the day of Christ is at hand" (2 Thessalonians 2:2). It seems that the expectation of Christ's imminent return was fueled, at least in part, by letters that were forged in Paul's name: "letter[s] as from us" (2:2). Paul reassured them that there was going to be "a falling away" (2:3) before Christ returned. The King James translation "falling away" does not really give a good sense of the Greek word *apostasia* (English *apostasy*), which more accurately means "rebellion."[14] This rebellion, according to Paul, would consist of a "man of sin" who would sit "in the temple of God" and pretend to be God (2:3–4). Paul described this event in terms similar to the desecration of the Jewish temple in Jerusalem by the Seleucid king Antiochus IV around 168 BC. According to Paul, this apostasy was currently being held back from its full force, but it would eventually be destroyed when Christ returned (2:6–8).

1 Corinthians (ca. AD 52–56)

Paul visited Corinth during his second mission (Acts 18:1–18). Corinth was an important port city on the west side of the isthmus separating access to the Adriatic Sea to the west and the Aegean Sea to the east.[15] Here he met Aquila and Priscilla, who had come to Corinth from Rome and who were of the same profession (i.e., a "tentmaker" or, more generally, a leatherworker) as Paul (18:2–3). Paul preached in the local synagogue, and among his converts was "Crispus, the chief ruler of the synagogue" (18:8). Paul remained in Corinth for eighteen months (18:11). On one occasion a group of Jews brought him before the Roman governor Gallio, accusing Paul of persuading people "to worship God contrary to the law" (18:12–13). Gallio rebuked Paul's Jewish accusers, saying that if Paul had broken Roman law there would be consequences, but if it was a matter of Jewish law, "I will be no judge of such matters" (18:14–15).

Apparently, soon after leaving Corinth, Paul communicated with the converts in Corinth by means of a letter, for he stated in 1 Corinthians, "I wrote unto you in an epistle not to company with fornicators" (5:9). This letter either has not survived or, as some scholars have proposed, is partially preserved in 2 Corinthians 6:14–7:1, a section that interrupts the flow of the remainder of 2 Corinthians. Following the writing of this first letter, Paul learned that problems in Corinth were continuing. This information came to Paul by means of people who were "of the house of Chloe" (1 Corinthians 1:11) through a letter that members of the Corinthian congregation had written to him (7:1) and by three representatives (Stephanas,

Fortunatus, and Achaicus) who visited him from Corinth (16:17). In response, Paul wrote a second letter to them (preserved as our 1 Corinthians) in which he dealt with issues such as disunity and factions among them, immorality and their acceptance of such behavior, and lawsuits between the members (chapters 1–6) and then answered the questions that they asked him in their letter (chapters 7–16).[16]

Paul began the letter with his disapproval that many of them were separating into factions—various groups claiming to be followers of Paul, Apollos, Cephas, or Christ (1 Corinthians 1:12; compare 3:4).[17] He exhorted all of them to "be perfectly joined together in the same mind and in the same judgment" so there would "be no divisions among you" (1:10). Paul admitted that the core message of the gospel—"the preaching of the cross" (1:18), "Christ crucified" (1:23)—was a controversial one to others: "unto the Jews a stumbling-block, and unto the Greeks foolishness" (1:23).[18] The idea of a crucified messiah was offensive to Jews who expected someone powerful and triumphant, and it was silliness to Gentiles because that meant Christians worshipped a convicted criminal. But, Paul taught, "unto us which are saved it is the power of God" (1:18). This is because "the natural man receiveth not the things of the Spirit of God: for they are foolishness unto him: neither can he know them, because they are spiritually discerned" (2:14).

Another issue of concern to Paul was the proliferation of immoral behavior among the members; in particular, one member was apparently having sexual relations with his step-mother (1 Corinthians 5:1). If that were not bad enough, according to Paul, the attitude of the members toward this situation was indifferent: "And ye are puffed up, and have not rather mourned, that he that hath done this deed might be taken away from among you" (5:2). Paul instructed the church leaders to excommunicate the offending party (5:3, 5): "Purge out therefore the old leaven, that ye may be a new lump [of dough]" (5:7). In his first letter Paul had instructed them not to keep company with outsiders who participate in immoral behavior (5:9). Now, however, Paul intensified his prohibition to also include Christians who participate in this conduct: "any man that is called a brother" (5:11). This is because such association might have a lasting negative effect on disciples who were trying to shun this behavior, for "a little leaven leaveneth the whole lump" (5:6).

Paul concluded the beginning sections of his letter by warning the Corinthians against filing lawsuits against one another: "Now there is utterly a fault among you, because ye go to law one with another" (1 Corinthians 6:7). Paul was particularly concerned that they were employing non-Christians to judge matters between Christians (6:6). He would rather that the two parties either worked out the issue amicably between themselves or sought counsel from a fellow Christian because Old Testament scripture testified that believers will judge the world (6:1–5).

In chapter 7, Paul began to address questions from the letter they wrote to him: "Now concerning the things whereof ye wrote unto me" (1 Corinthians 7:1). The letter from the Corinthians had asserted: "It is good for a man not to touch a woman" (7:1), meaning that it advocated celibacy within marriage. Paul, on the other hand, instructed married couples to have normal marital relations ("due benevolence," 7:3).[19] In general, Paul's counsel was to follow his example and remain apart from a marriage relationship: "I say therefore to the unmarried and widows, It is good for them if they abide even as I" (7:8). Why would Paul encourage the Corinthians to avoid marriage? The Joseph Smith Translation clarifies this issue by specifying that Paul was referring to those who had been "called unto the ministry" (JST 1 Corinthians 7:29).[20] Paul reasoned that such individuals would thus be able to "attend upon the Lord without distraction" (1 Corinthians 7:35).

The next issue from the Corinthian letter to Paul concerned meat that had been "offered in sacrifice unto idols" (1 Corinthians 8:4; compare 8:1). The Corinthian Christians were primarily Gentiles (compare 12:2) and still had gentile friends and neighbors.[21] The heart of their concern was whether Christians were allowed to eat meat that had been offered to a pagan god. Paul's response covered two circumstances. First, if Christians were invited to a feast at a pagan temple, Paul concluded that it was permissible to attend and eat the meat because they "know that an idol is nothing in the world" (8:4) and that "meat commendeth us not to God: for neither, if we eat, are we the better; neither, if we eat not, are we the worse" (8:8; compare 10:27). The exception was if the Christian knew that someone would get the wrong impression and suppose that Christians advocated pagan sacrifice (8:7), thus becoming "a stumblingblock to them" (8:9; compare 10:28). In such a case Christians should refrain from eating, for as Paul declared, "If meat make my brother to offend, I will eat no flesh" (8:13; compare 10:31–32). Second, if the extra meat from the sacrifice subsequently was "sold in the shambles" (i.e., the market), Paul taught that Christians were allowed to purchase and eat it, but counseled them to not ask questions about the origin of the meat (10:25).

In the next chapter, Paul addressed the role of women.[22] It should be noted that the Greek words translated as "man" and as "woman" could also be translated as "husband" and as "wife," with the resulting understanding that what Paul said may apply better to roles within the family and not merely to issues of gender. Thus, Paul reasoned that just as the "head" (i.e., leader) of Jesus Christ is God the Father, so also "the head of every man [i.e., husband] is Christ; and the head of the woman [i.e., wife] is the man [i.e., her husband]" (1 Corinthians 11:3). If Paul were living today, he may have chosen his words more carefully to reflect Latter-day Saint emphasis on equality within marriage. Modern prophets and apostles have clarified the roles of husbands and wives: "Fathers and mothers are obligated to help one another as equal partners."[23] As Paul concluded: "Neither is the man without the woman, neither the woman without the man, in the Lord" (11:11).

Paul then returned to the questions the Corinthians posed in the letter "concerning spiritual gifts" (1 Corinthians 12:1).[24] According to Paul, just as the human body "hath many members" but "are one body" (12:12), so also "there are diversities of gifts," but they all come from "the same Spirit" (12:4). Paul pled with the Corinthians to seek after "the best gifts" (1 Corinthians 12:31) from the Spirit, who distributed them "to every man severally, as he [i.e., the Spirit] will" (12:11). For Paul, the greatest spiritual gift was charity (13:13), which the prophet Mormon defined as "the pure love of Christ" (Moroni 7:47), and exhorted people to "pray unto the Father with all the energy of heart, that ye may be filled with this love" (7:48).

One particular spiritual gift that the Corinthians were struggling with was speaking in tongues. Apparently, there were many in the congregation who were speaking in an unknown tongue, with the result that nobody could understand them. Paul preferred that people prophesy in a known tongue rather than speak in an unknown tongue, so that the congregation would receive knowledge and be edified (1 Corinthians 14:5–6; compare 14:19). Therefore, Paul required each person speaking in tongues to have an interpreter (14:27–28; compare 14:5, 13). He also instructed them to be in control because the spirit of prophecy is "subject to the prophets" (14:32)—or in other words, subject to those who are filled with the Spirit, and not the other way around—for, as Paul concluded, "God is not the author of confusion, but of peace" (14:33).

In 1 Corinthians, Paul included very important information about the mortal and post-mortal ministries of Christ. Since these epistles were likely written before the canonical Gospels were composed, Paul's letters probably contain the earliest references to these events.[25] First, Paul mentioned the Last Supper (11:23), in which Jesus taught that the elements of the bread and wine were symbolic of his death (11:26) and that disciples should reenact this ritual "in remembrance of me" (11:24–25).[26] In addition, Paul repeated one of the earliest formulaic or creedal statements of Christian belief: "Christ died for our sins according to the scriptures," and "he was buried" and "rose again the third day according to the scriptures" (15:3–4). Paul also referred to post-Resurrection appearances of the Savior not recorded elsewhere in the New Testament, including to a group of five hundred people and to the Lord's brother James (15:6–7).

These references led Paul into his discussion of topics of special interest to Latter-day Saints: baptism for the dead and resurrected bodies. Some members of the Corinthian congregation did not believe in the resurrection of the dead (1 Corinthians 15:12). In response, Paul referred to their practice of vicarious baptism: "Else what shall they do which are baptized for the dead, if the dead rise not at all? Why are they then baptized for the dead?" (15:29).[27] Paul then taught them about the difference between "terrestrial" (i.e., mortal or earthly) bodies and "celestial" (i.e., resurrected or heavenly) bodies (15:40)—the former full of corruption and the latter full of glory (15:42–44). For Latter-day Saints, the Joseph Smith Translation uses this discussion as a catalyst to teach about the different types of resurrected bodies: there are "also celestial bodies, and bodies terrestrial; but the glory of the celestial, one; and the terrestrial, another; and the telestial, another" (JST 15:40). In closing, Paul addressed their concern about "the collection for the saints" (16:1). He instructed them to gather together their weekly donations for the poor, which he would take with him to Jerusalem (16:2–3; compare Acts 11:29–30; Galatians 2:10).

2 Corinthians (ca. AD 53–56)

It is difficult to make complete sense of 2 Corinthians.[28] Within 2 Corinthians Paul digresses quite a bit, and his tone varies: chapter 7 is conciliatory, while chapters 10–13 are argumentative. Some scholars have proposed that 2 Corinthians is a compilation of a few different letters that were later combined into one. Even if 2 Corinthians is one unified letter, it is a very mixed letter. It takes some detective work to reconstruct the context that caused Paul to write this letter.[29] Paul originally visited Corinth during his second mission (Acts 18:1–17). Afterward, Paul wrote a letter counseling them to avoid fellowship with immoral people (mentioned in 1 Corinthians 5:9). Paul eventually wrote a second letter (1 Corinthians), in which he instructed the Corinthians to excommunicate an immoral member of their congregation (5:13). In that letter, Paul also told them he would soon visit them and deal with the problem if they refused to do so (4:18–21). This background helps one understand the context and purpose of 2 Corinthians.

Paul's original plan seems to have been to visit the Corinthians a second time, travel from Corinth to Macedonia (northern Greece), and then return through Corinth before heading to Jerusalem (2 Corinthians 1:15–16). But it appears that the second visit to Corinth did not go very well, and Paul changed his plans to return through Corinth (2:1, 5). Members of the Corinthian congregation were offended, but Paul defended his decision, saying that he refused to return in order "to spare you" (1:23; compare 13:2, 10). So instead, Paul wrote another letter to them in which he rebuked them and hurt the feelings of some in the congregation (7:8). The identity of this letter of rebuke is uncertain, but it may be 1 Corinthians or possibly 2 Corinthians chapters 10–13, which may have been later combined with other letters to make 2 Corinthians. Paul apologized for hurting their feelings (7:8; compare 2:4) but rejoiced that they "sorrowed to repentance" (7:9).

The Corinthians apparently followed Paul's counsel to excommunicate a wicked member of their congregation, but when writing 2 Corinthians, Paul determined that "sufficient to such a man is this punishment" (2:6) and now encouraged them "to forgive him, and comfort him" (2:7) and "confirm your love toward him" (2:8). Paul praised the Corinthians and compared them to an "epistle of Christ ministered by us, written not with ink, but with the Spirit of the living God" (3:3). He also acknowledged the challenges they all faced: "We are troubled on every side, yet not distressed; we are perplexed, but not in despair; persecuted, but not forsaken; cast down, but not destroyed" (4:8–9). He admitted that while in mortality disciples "groan" because they "earnestly" desire for the Resurrection and life with God (5:2–4). But God gave the gift of Jesus Christ to humanity in order to bring about "the ministry of reconciliation" (5:18). Through the vicarious atonement of his Son, humans may be "reconciled to God" (5:19–21).[30]

Paul reminded the Corinthians to avoid fellowship with anyone who may be involved in wickedness: "Be ye not unequally yoked together with unbelievers" (2 Corinthians 6:14; compare 1 Corinthians 5:9). And for those who may be involved with such individuals or behavior, Paul exhorted them using language from Isaiah 52:11: "Come out from among them, and be ye separate, saith the Lord, and touch not the unclean thing; and I will receive you" (2 Corinthians 6:17). A revelation to the early Latter-day Saints through the Prophet Joseph Smith repeated a similar Isaian plea (Doctrine and Covenants 133:5, 14). Paul's desire for these Christians was clear: "Let us cleanse ourselves from all filthiness of the flesh and spirit, perfecting holiness in the fear of God" (2 Corinthians 7:1).

The book of Acts records a prophecy of one Agabus concerning a famine "which came to pass in the days of Claudius Caesar" (Acts 11:28). It also states that disciples in the diaspora "determined to send relief unto the brethren which dwelt in Judea" (2 Corinthians 11:29), which was delivered thence "by the hands of Barnabas and Saul" (11:30). When Paul visited Jerusalem, Peter requested that he "remember the poor" (Galatians 2:10), which Paul indicated he was already eager to do. Collecting alms for the poor was a regular part of Paul's ministry. He reminded the Corinthians of the generosity of the saints in Macedonia (2 Corinthians 8:1–5), possibly a reference to the congregation in Philippi (Philippians 4:15–16). Accordingly, Paul taught the Corinthians to give generously, "not grudgingly, or of necessity: for God loveth a cheerful giver" (2 Corinthians 9:6–7; compare 1 Corinthians 16:2–3).

Earlier, Paul had told the members of the congregation, "I am the least of the apostles, that am not meet to be called an apostle, because I persecuted the church of God" (1 Corinthians 15:8–9). Paul wrote these words in humility, but some may have been using them to challenge Paul's authority and character (2 Corinthians 10:8–10). So in response, Paul felt compelled to "boast" (or assert) his authority, which was not outside his "measure" (or stewardship) as an apostle (10:13; compare Romans 11:13). In the King James Version, Paul referred to his critics as "the very chiefest apostles" (2 Corinthians 11:5; 12:11), a sarcastic reference to them as self-proclaimed "super-apostles" (NIV). He identified them as Jewish Christians: "Hebrews . . . Israelites . . . the seed of Abraham" (11:22) and exposed these pretenders as "false apostles, deceitful workers, transforming themselves into the apostles of Christ" (11:13).

It seems that these Judaizers were teaching that Paul was not a real apostle because he did not demonstrate all the "signs of an apostle" (2 Corinthians 12:12–13). Paul taught the Corinthians that he had an apostolic right to accept temporal assistance from members of the church, but he refused this assistance from the Corinthians (1 Corinthians 9:6, 12; compare 2 Thessalonians 3:8–9). Instead, he "robbed other churches" (2 Corinthians 11:8), meaning he accepted such assistance from them, specifically from the Christians in Macedonia (11:9). This perceived inconsistency apparently offended some of the Corinthians (11:7). Paul was earnestly trying to not burden the Corinthians with a demand for temporal support (11:8; 12:15–16). In what may be a sarcastic response, Paul apologized: "forgive me this wrong" (12:13). Paul closed the epistle by reminding the Corinthians that his written response to them was intended for their "edification" and not for their "destruction" (13:10).

Romans (ca. AD 53–56)

It is apparent that Paul wrote his epistle to the Romans before he ever visited Rome.[31] The book of Acts records that during his third mission, Paul traveled through Macedonia and Achaia (i.e., northern and central Greece) and was inspired to decide that after he returned to Jerusalem he should travel to Rome (Acts 19:21). In Acts, Paul also stated that his purpose in returning to Jerusalem was to "bring alms to my nation, and offerings" (24:17). In his epistle to the Romans, Paul indicated that he was currently bringing contributions from the Christians in Macedonia and Achaia "for the poor saints which are at Jerusalem" and that after he did so he would travel to Rome (Romans 15:25–28). The book of Acts also explains that as Paul traveled up the coast of Italy on his journey from Caesarea, "the brethren" (28:15) from Rome came to meet him. Thus, Paul was not Rome's first missionary, and Christianity was established there before he arrived. If Paul did not establish the church in Rome, why then did he write the Epistle to the Romans?

There are a number of reasons why Paul wrote this letter. Paul indicated that he wanted to share the gospel among those in Rome, so that he "might have some fruit among you also" (Romans 1:13). Typically, Paul desired to preach in locations where nobody else had preached before so that he would not "build upon another man's foundation" (15:20). Thus Paul's desire to preach among the Romans is noteworthy. In addition, Paul's declaration to the Romans that he was "not ashamed of the gospel of Christ" (1:16) is curious. It seems that Paul was responding to those in Rome who were critical of him, in particular concerning his missionary work among Gentiles, for he stated: "I have written the more boldly unto you . . . that the offering up of the Gentiles might be acceptable [to you]" (15:15–16). Why would Paul want the Romans to understand and accept him? One reason may be that he desired temporal assistance from them in order to get to Spain (15:24, 28). Christians in Rome would be less willing to help Paul if they did not accept his message, so Paul devoted a significant amount of space in this letter to explain his teachings about Gentiles and salvation.

Paul's audience in Rome consisted of both gentile and Jewish Christians. Although in later chapters Paul addressed ethnic Jews (Romans 4:1; 7:1), he began the letter by addressing Gentiles (1:5–6, 13).[32] To them Paul explained that ignorance of God's standards was not a valid excuse for bad behavior, for people were "without excuse" (1:20) because God had revealed basic truths to all humankind (1:18–20). In Book of Mormon terms, Paul was teaching something similar to what the prophet Mormon taught: "The Spirit of Christ is given to every man, that he may know good from evil; . . . wherefore ye may know with a perfect knowledge it is of God" (Moroni 7:16). Paul taught that God "will render to every man according to his deeds" (Romans 2:6). Jews who specifically had been taught the law of God through prophets and scriptures would be judged according to that standard (2:12), while Gentiles, who had received truths "by nature" and had "the law written in their hearts" or their "conscience" (2:14–15), would be judged according to that standard. And if Gentiles lived up to the standard taught by their conscience, they would be considered part of the covenant people (2:26).

Paul anticipated some questions from his audience. First, if both Jews and Gentiles could be saved, why did God have a covenant people? Paul's answer was that God had given Jews the responsibility of bringing forth the "oracles of God" (Romans 3:2), meaning the truths of God through revelation, prophets, or scripture. Second, if the Jews were chosen for such awesome responsibilities, did that mean they were better than other people? Paul responded with an emphatic no: "for all have sinned, and come short of the glory of God" (3:23; compare 3:9). Third, if all people were sinners, then how were they saved? Paul answered this question by teaching them about justification.[33] Justification means to be acquitted, or pronounced innocent with respect to the law. For Paul, there were two ways to be justified. The first might be termed justification by works: when one kept all the laws all the time. Concerning this Paul taught: "Moses describeth the righteousness which is of the law, That the man which doeth those things shall live by them" (10:5; compare Leviticus 18:5). In practical terms, however, this type of justification was impossible to achieve (3:20; compare Galatians 2:16; 2 Nephi 2:5). King Benjamin in the Book of Mormon similarly reasoned: "If ye should serve [God] with all your whole souls yet ye would be unprofitable servants. . . . Ye are still indebted unto him, and are, and will be, forever and ever" (Mosiah 2:20–24). If people cannot be justified by their own merits, how can they be justified? Paul summarized: "Therefore we conclude that a man is justified by faith without the deeds of the law" (Romans 3:28; compare Galatians 2:16). This is just as the Book of Mormon prophet Jacob taught: "Remember, after ye are reconciled unto God, that it is only in and through the grace of God that ye are saved" (2 Nephi 10:24; compare 25:23).

Paul used the example of Abraham to prove his point. If Abraham had been justified by works, Paul reasoned, he could boast in his own ability that he had earned salvation (Romans 4:2). But the story of Abraham in Genesis says that before Abraham performed the good work of circumcision, "he believed in the Lord; and [the Lord] counted it to him for righteousness [i.e., justification]" (Genesis 15:6). Thus, Paul pointed out that Abraham was justified while he was still uncircumcised, and that circumcision was a sign of the justification God had already bestowed upon Abraham because of his faith (Romans 4:10–11).

Another question Paul addressed concerned the role of good works in the process of justification. On the one hand, Paul taught the importance of doing good works: "For not the hearers of the law are just before God, but the doers of the law shall be justified" (Romans 2:13). On the other hand, however, Paul concluded that people are "justified by faith" (3:28). If a person was justified by faith, then why should he or she perform good works? Paul explained his answer by referring to the symbolism associated with baptism, which recalled the death of Jesus Christ, being symbolic of his burial and resurrection (6:3–5). But baptism was also reminiscent of the ending of a Christian's old life serving sin and the beginning of his or her new life as a disciple who does not serve sin (6:4–6). Thus, followers of Christ do good works not because they can earn salvation, but because they are new creatures in Christ who love and obey him, just as Jesus taught: "If ye love me, keep my commandments" (John 14:15; compare 2 Corinthians 5:17).[34]

Yet, as Paul admitted, there existed an internal struggle within every human heart: "For what I would, that I do not; but what I hate, that do I" (Romans 7:15), or in other words: "For I do not do what I want, but I do the very thing I hate" (7:15 NRSV). According to Paul, "I know that in me (that is, in my flesh,) dwelleth no good thing: for to will is present with me; but how to perform that which is good I find not. For the good that I would I do not; but the evil which I would not, that I do" (7:18–19). The Book of Mormon prophet Nephi lamented concerning this same struggle: "O wretched man that I am! Yea, my heart sorroweth because of my flesh; my soul grieveth because of mine iniquities . . . because of the temptations and the sins which do so easily beset me" (2 Nephi 4:17–18). How does one overcome this dilemma? Paul exclaimed as Nephi: "O wretched man that I am! who shall deliver me from the body of this death? I thank God [it is] through Jesus Christ our Lord" (Romans 7:24–25), through whom we become "more than conquerors" (8:37). "For," as Paul concluded, "the sufferings of this present time are not worthy to be compared with the glory which shall be revealed in us" (8:18).

Paul also perceived that his Roman audience did not fully understand what it meant to be a member of the covenant people, the house of Israel. Paul clarified his enigmatic statement "They are not all Israel, which are of Israel" (Romans 9:6) with the following explanation: "They which are the children of the flesh [or literal descendants of Abraham], these are not the children of God: but the children of the promise [or those who make and keep covenants] are counted for the seed" (9:8). This was likewise what Nephi taught: "As many of the Gentiles as will repent are the covenant people of the Lord; and as many of the Jews as will not repent shall be cast off; for the Lord covenanteth with none save it be with them that repent and believe in his Son" (2 Nephi 30:2; compare 3 Nephi 16:13).

Paul anticipated that some of the Roman Christians might conclude that the Lord loved the Gentiles but not his own people. Paul responded, "My heart's desire and prayer to God for Israel is, that they might be saved" (Romans 10:1). In order to achieve this, Paul said, he wanted to provoke his people to follow his example (11:13–14). But Paul said that they were "ignorant" of the way that God truly justified his people and were "going about to establish their own righteousness" (10:3). If, however, the law of Moses was not intended to provide a way for God's people to justify themselves by their own works, then what was the purpose of the law of Moses? Paul taught: "Christ is the end of the law for righteousness to every one that believeth" (10:4; compare Galatians 3:24). In other words, as Amulek taught in the Book of Mormon, "this is the whole meaning of the law, every whit pointing to that great and last sacrifice; and that great and last sacrifice will be the Son of God" (Alma 34:14). Thus the law of Moses did not provide salvation, but was given to teach about Christ, just as Abinadi taught: "It is a shadow of those things which are to come," but "redemption cometh through Christ the Lord" (Mosiah 16:14–15).

Paul warned the Gentiles among his audience, using imagery of grafting and the olive tree.[35] He stated that some of the natural branches of the tree of Israel had been "broken off" because of wickedness (Romans 11:17). This was similar to the imagery employed by the nonbiblical prophet Zenos, whose allegory has been preserved in the writings of the Book of Mormon prophet Jacob (Jacob 5:1–9). At the same time, however, Paul cautioned the gentile Christians: "For if God spared not the natural branches, take heed lest he also spare not thee" (Romans 11:21; compare 2 Nephi 30:2). And if the house of Israel did not continue in "unbelief," then "God is able to graft them [i.e., Israel] in again" (Romans 11:23). Paul informed his audience that Israel's "blindness" to the truth of the gospel would continue "until the fulness of the Gentiles be come in" (11:25). Modern revelation teaches that the house of Israel will remain in their state of unbelief "until the times of the Gentiles be fulfilled," when "a light shall break forth among" the house of Israel, which shall be "the fulness of [the] gospel" (Doctrine and Covenants 45:19, 25, 28). Nephi similarly clarified: "After the Gentiles had received the fulness of the Gospel, the natural branches of the olive tree, or the remnants of the house of Israel, should be grafted in, or come to the knowledge of the true Messiah, their Lord and their Redeemer" (1 Nephi 10:14). And thus Paul concluded that eventually "all Israel shall be saved" (Romans 11:26). Therefore, all disciples had a responsibility to "present [their] bodies a living sacrifice, holy, acceptable unto God" (12:1).

In the final chapters of Romans, Paul addressed some practical issues. First, he exhorted all Christians to "be subject unto the higher powers," for "the powers that be are ordained of God" (13:1). Paul was evidently referring to civic government, a concept he considered inspired of God and to which Christians ought to pay proper taxes (13:7). Using similar language, a modern revelation teaches: "Let no man break the laws of the land. . . . Wherefore, be subject to the powers that be, until he reigns whose right it is to reign, and subdues all enemies under his feet" (Doctrine and Covenants 58:21–22). The Joseph Smith Translation of Paul's exhortation, however, states that "there is no power *in the church* but of God" (JST Romans 13:1; emphasis added). Rather than always being considered a restoration of the original text, the Joseph Smith Translation sometimes functions as inspired application, alerting readers to additional insights not intended by the original writer.[36] Thus Paul counseled Christians to submit to secular government, and the Joseph Smith Translation adds the concept that Christians should submit to ecclesiastical government. Both lessons are true and relevant.

Second, Paul taught his audience about proper tolerance between the church members. Some issues within the church were open to personal choice. Some of the Roman Christians seem to have been vegetarians, possibly avoiding meat because they thought it might have been offered up as sacrifice to a pagan idol (compare Acts 15:20; 1 Corinthians 8:7). Paul's personal opinion was that this kind of prohibition was unnecessary (he referred to these Christians as "weak"), "for one believeth that he may eat all things: another, who is weak, eateth herbs [i.e., only vegetables]" (Romans 14:2). But Paul allowed all Christians personal choice in the matter and called for mutual tolerance: "Let not him that eateth [meat] despise him that eateth not; and let not him which eateth not [meat] judge him that eateth" (14:3). Paul also warned Christians who ate meat to not use their freedom to do so as an excuse to make others feel bad: "If thy [vegetarian] brother be grieved with thy meat [eating] . . . destroy not him with thy meat [eating]. . . . For the kingdom of God is not meat and drink; but righteousness, and peace, and joy in the Holy Ghost" (14:15, 17). Rather, they ought to be patient with those of a different opinion (15:1–2). Whether one ate meat or not, Paul declared, "we shall all stand before the judgment seat of Christ. . . . Let us not therefore judge one another any more" (14:10, 13).

Paul concluded his letter by recommending to the Christians in Rome a certain woman named Phebe, who was a "servant of the church which is at Cenchrea" (Romans 16:1).[37] Phebe seems to have held ecclesiastical authority as a "servant" (from the Greek word for "deaconess") in the church—possibly functioning similarly to a modern Relief Society general president. Paul encouraged the Roman Christians to "receive her in the Lord" and also to "assist her in whatsoever business she hath need of you" (16:2). It is interesting that at the end of Paul's many greetings, we find this interjection: "I Tertius, who wrote this epistle, salute you in the Lord" (16:22). This is evidence that Paul did not physically write all of his own letters, but rather that he used scribes, who wrote down Paul's instruction.[38] Tertius apparently also knew some of the Christians in Rome and sent his own personal greeting to them.

Philippians (ca. AD 58–62)

Paul visited Philippi on his second mission after "a man of Macedonia" appeared to him in a vision and pled for him to "come over into Macedonia, and help us" (Acts 16:9).[39] There he taught and baptized the first "European" converts: Lydia and her household (16:14–15). Paul and Silas were beaten and imprisoned for casting out an evil spirt from a girl who brought her masters financial gain (16:16–24). The next day, when the keeper of the prison said they were free to go, Paul reminded him that the magistrates had unjustly beaten and imprisoned Roman citizens (16:35–38). The magistrates were naturally very concerned about this and subsequently "came and besought them, and brought them out, and desired them to depart out of the city" (16:38–39).

Among those Paul addressed at Philippi were "the bishops and deacons" (Philippians 1:1). The modern organization of The Church of Jesus Christ of Latter-day Saints familiar to members is one bishop presiding over a single group, or ward, of members. But Paul's words reflect a very early ecclesiastical structure with a group of "bishops" (the Greek word for "overseers") and a group of "deacons" (the Greek word for "servants"). This later developed into the concept of a monepiscopacy, or one bishop per congregation (compare 1 Timothy 3:2; Titus 1:7).[40] Paul referred to his "bonds" (Philippians 1:7, 13) and was therefore in prison somewhere. Philippians is thus one of Paul's four so-called prison letters (including Ephesians, Colossians, and Philemon). Paul's experience in prison caused him to reflect on his innermost desires, whether he preferred to die and return to his heavenly home or to live and continue his missionary labors: "I am in a strait betwixt two, having a desire to depart, and to be with Christ; which is far better: Nevertheless to abide in the flesh is more needful for you" (1:23–24). Paul concluded, however, that he would "abide and continue with [them]" (1:25).

Paul employed an early Christian hymn to encourage the Philippians to follow the example of Jesus Christ.[41] According to Paul, Christ, who was originally "in the form of God" (Philippians 2:6), came to earth in "the form of a servant" (2:7). The emphasis of these phrases was on Christ's divine and mortal identities and natures rather than on merely his physical appearance. Christ "thought it not robbery to be equal with God" (2:6), meaning that he did not think that his premortal divine status was something he should selfishly hold on to. Rather, Christ came to earth and "made himself of no reputation" and "was made in the likeness of men" (2:7), or literally, "he emptied himself" of a certain measure of his premortal glory and "became mortal."[42] As a mortal man, Christ "humbled himself, and became obedient unto death, even the death of the cross" (2:8). These teachings on the incarnation were similar to what Nephi's angel referred to as "the condescension of God" (1 Nephi 11:26). Nephi saw in vision the birth of Christ into mortality (11:19–20) as well as his suffering and crucifixion (11:32–33). Modern revelation teaches that after Christ "descended below all things," he also "ascended up on high" (Doctrine and Covenants 88:6). Similarly, Paul taught that after Christ suffered death on the cross, "God also hath highly exalted him, and given him a name which is above every name" and that "every tongue should confess that Jesus Christ is Lord" (Philippians 2:9, 11).[43]

There seem to have been some among the Philippians who claimed authority because of their Jewish lineage and who desired others to submit to circumcision of the flesh (Philippians 3:3; compare Colossians 2:11). Paul countered this claim of Judaizers by emphasizing his own Jewish background: "Circumcised on the eighth day, of the stock of Israel, of the tribe of Benjamin, an Hebrew of the Hebrews; as touching the law, a Pharisee; concerning zeal, persecuting the church; touching the righteousness which is in the law, blameless" (Philippians 3:5–6). But Paul reminded them that a noteworthy Jewish heritage was not important in the eternal perspective: "What things were gain to me, those I counted loss for Christ" and "count them but dung, that I may win Christ" (3:7–8). Paul encouraged his audience to have the same perspective (3:15).

In conclusion, Paul exhorted the Philippians to focus on "whatsoever things are true, . . . honest, . . . just, . . . pure, . . . lovely, . . . [and] of good report" and having to do with "virtue . . . [and] praise" (Philippians 4:8). This is part of "the admonition of Paul" referred to in the thirteenth article of faith, which Latter-day Saints seek to emulate. Paul proudly acknowledged the generosity of the Philippians: "For even in Thessalonica ye sent once and again unto my necessity" (4:16). Paul had earlier informed the Corinthians about the generosity of "the churches of Macedonia" who, though they were in "deep poverty," freely gave in abundance (2 Corinthians 8:1–2). Paul was evidently referring to the Christians in Philippi. Paul ended his letter by sending greetings from "they that are of Caesar's household" (Philippians 4:22). Most scholars have understood this reference to mean that Paul was writing from prison in Rome, but it is at least possible that "Caesar's household" could also refer to the household of a local Roman governor elsewhere in the empire.[44]

Ephesians (ca. AD 58–62)

There are some difficult issues associated with this letter.[45] The book of Acts narrates how Paul called the elders of Ephesus to meet him in Miletus and then spoke to them of his three-year ministry among them and his great love and affection for them (20:17–20, 31). Yet, unlike his other letters, Paul did not send any personal greetings to specific individuals in this correspondence and hoped that the audience had heard of his service toward them (Ephesians 3:2). In addition, the phrase "at Ephesus" (1:1) is absent from some of the earliest manuscripts of this letter. These facts have caused some scholars to question the authenticity of this letter as well as its destination. But it is evident that Paul had great concern for the Christian communities to the east of Ephesus, such as Colossae and Laodicea, even though they had "not seen [his] face in the flesh" (Colossians 2:1). It is therefore reasonable to conclude that this letter was originally a circular letter Paul intended for the Christian congregations in and around Ephesus, similar to the nature of his letter to "the churches of Galatia" (Galatians 1:2). Paul's letter to the Ephesians was written while Paul was imprisoned (Ephesians 6:20), probably in Rome, but perhaps elsewhere.

Paul began this epistle by teaching his audience that they had been "sealed with that holy Spirit of promise" (Ephesians 1:13).[46] Modern revelation identifies the "Holy Spirit of promise" as the "Comforter," which the Lord promised his disciples "as is recorded in the testimony of John" (Doctrine and Covenants 88:3). In that Johannine account, Jesus clearly taught that the "Comforter" was "the Holy Ghost" (John 14:26). Paul identified this as "the earnest of our inheritance" (Ephesians 1:14; compare 2 Corinthians 1:22; 5:5). The earnest money was essentially a down payment, promising that the full amount would be paid at a future point. In antiquity, letters could be "sealed" with a wax or clay seal that was stamped with an insignia identifying the person who wrote the letter and indicating that the contents of the letter were approved by the writer. Paul explained that Christians were sealed by the Holy Ghost (Ephesians 1:13). Thus, if disciples were worthy to receive the Holy Ghost, it meant that they were approved of God, who gave them access to this precious down payment "until the redemption of the purchased possession" (1:14)—meaning until God paid in full and brought the righteous into his kingdom.[47]

There was evidently a conflict between some of the local Jewish and gentile Christians.[48] Paul reminded them that Jesus Christ "made both [Jews and Gentiles] one, and hath broken down the middle wall of partition between us" (Ephesians 2:14). He explained that this reconciliation was made possible through "the cross," or in other words, Christ and his atonement (2:16). The result was that Gentiles, some of whom may have previously felt as if they were outsiders, "are no more strangers and foreigners, but fellowcitizens with the saints, and of the household of God" (2:19). They became "fellowheirs" and "partakers of his promise in Christ by the gospel" (3:6). As Nephi testified, God "inviteth them all to come unto him and partake of his goodness; . . . and all are alike unto God, both Jew and Gentile" (2 Nephi 26:33). Paul testified of the unity of the church and its ordinances: "There is . . . one Lord, one faith, one baptism" (Ephesians 4:4–5) for both Jews and Gentiles. Ecclesiastical positions like apostles, prophets, and so forth were designed to help achieve this goal of unity—"for the perfecting of the saints" (4:11–12).[49]

This letter also contains counsel for its audience that is applicable in an everyday setting. Paul exhorted them to "have no fellowship with the unfruitful works of darkness, but rather reprove them" (Ephesians 5:11). He encouraged them to "be filled with the Spirit" (5:18). Paul then offered some practical advice. One way to shun the darkness and fill their lives with the Spirit, he stated, was by "speaking to yourselves in psalms and hymns and spiritual songs, singing and making melody in your heart to the Lord" (5:19; compare Colossians 3:16). Living one's life by following the inspiration received through the Holy Ghost was one way to "put on the whole armour of God, that [they] may be able to stand against the wiles of the devil" (Ephesians 6:11).

Colossians (ca. AD 58–62)

The ancient city of Colossae was located about 120 miles east of Ephesus. Paul and his companions spent considerable time evangelizing in and around Ephesus (Acts 19:10). Yet, it is apparent that Paul did not personally visit Colossae, for he included them in the category of those who "have not seen [his] face in the flesh" (Colossians 2:1). One of Paul's companions, Epaphras, was originally a member of the Colossian congregation (4:12). Epaphras informed Paul concerning the situation at Colossae, whereupon Paul wrote them a letter (1:7–8; compare 1:4). Paul wrote this letter while he was in prison somewhere (4:3), possibly in Rome. Colossae was devastated by an earthquake around the year AD 61. Since Paul made no mention of this disaster in the letter, he may have written this letter before that date.[50]

Paul warned the Colossians about those who were attempting to "beguile [them] with enticing words" (Colossians 2:4) and "spoil [them] through philosophy and vain deceit, after the tradition of men" (2:8). These false teachers seem to have been Judaizers who desired them to keep the regulations of the law of Moses, including circumcision and kosher food laws. Paul reminded the Colossians, "Ye are circumcised with the circumcision made without hands" (2:11), and warned them: "Let no man therefore judge you in meat, or in drink, or in respect of an holy day, or of the new moon, or of the sabbath days" (2:16). In addition, in Colossians 2:18 Paul alerted them concerning those who promised a reward for "voluntary humility" (i.e., living a celibate or ascetic lifestyle; compare 1 Corinthians 7:1) or "worshipping of angels" (i.e., venerating archangels; compare Jude 1:9).

Paul encouraged the Colossians to "let the word of Christ dwell in you richly in all wisdom; teaching and admonishing one another in psalms and hymns and spiritual songs, singing with grace in your hearts to the Lord" (Colossians 3:16). Thus, just as in his letter to the Philippians, Paul countered false notions by quoting an early Christian hymn.[51] This christological poem taught about the superiority of Jesus Christ, who was "the firstborn of every creature" (1:15), "the head of the body, the church," and "the firstborn from the dead; that in all things he might have the preeminence" (1:18).[52] Further, "by him were all things created" (1:15–16), and "he is before all things, and by him all things consist" (1:17), meaning that through Christ all life is sustained. This recalls the teachings of modern revelation that Christ is "in all and through all things. . . . This is the light of Christ . . . which is the same light that quickens your understandings; which light proceeds forth from the presence of God to fill the immensity of space—the light which is in all things, which gives life to all things" (Doctrine and Covenants 88:6–13). In sum, within Christ dwelt the "fulness" of divinity and power (Colossians 1:19; compare 2:9–10).

Paul taught the Christians in Colossae to "mortify therefore your members which are upon the earth" (Colossians 3:5). The King James Version phraseology can be confusing. Paul did not teach the Colossians to subject members of the church to humiliation, but rather to "put to death therefore what is earthly within you" (ESV)—such things as "anger, wrath, malice, blasphemy, [and] filthy communication out of your mouth" (3:8). Paul pled with them to "put off the old man with his deeds" (3:9) and to "put on the new man, which is renewed in knowledge after the image of [Christ] that created him" (3:10). This was as

King Benjamin taught the Nephites: "The natural man is an enemy to God . . . unless he yields to the enticings of the Holy Spirit, and putteth off the natural man and becometh a saint through the atonement of Christ the Lord, and becometh as a child, submissive, meek, humble, patient, full of love" (Mosiah 3:19).

Paul concluded his letter by instructing his audience that "when this epistle is read among you, cause that it be read also in the church of the Laodiceans; and that ye likewise read the epistle from Laodicea" (Colossians 4:16). This verse has important implications for understanding the earliest stages in the process of compiling the New Testament.[53] Eventually, congregations started to share letters. Some documents survived over time, such as the letter to the Colossians, while others did not, such as the letter to the Laodiceans. It is a safe assumption that they shared copies and kept the original letter for themselves. Over time, each community had its own collection of documents, which may have differed from another community's collection.

Philemon (ca. AD 58–62)

Paul's letter to Philemon is the shortest of the extant Pauline Letters.[54] Unlike the epistles directed to entire congregations discussed above, this letter was a personal correspondence with Philemon, a Christian slave owner, concerning Onesimus, his slave.[55] Since we know Onesimus was from Colossae (Colossians 4:9), it is likely that Philemon was as well. And since the church members met in his house (Philemon 1:2), it is possible Philemon was a leader of the Colossian congregation. Slavery was legal in the Roman Empire, but it was not based on race. People could become slaves if they were prisoners of war or as a punishment for crime. Further, individuals could sell themselves into slavery if they could not find a better occupation to support themselves. Some slaves and slave owners converted to Christianity. In his letters, Paul occasionally encouraged Christian "servants" (i.e., slaves) to obey their masters and Christian "masters" (i.e., slave owners) to be kind to their servants (compare Ephesians 6:5–9; Colossians 3:22; 4:1). A conflict between Philemon and Onesimus seems to have been the impetus for writing this letter.

It seems that Paul and Philemon knew each other before this incident (Philemon 1:19). Onesimus had run away from Philemon (1:15), possibly because he had stolen something (1:18). Eventually Onesimus met Paul in prison and was converted to Christianity (1:10). The name *Onesimus* meant "useful" or "profitable." Using a play on words, Paul mused to Philemon concerning Onesimus, "which in time past was to thee unprofitable, but now profitable to thee and to me" (1:11). As a runaway slave, Onesimus broke Roman law, which would have merited punishment, but Paul encouraged Philemon "to receive him [back] for ever" (1:15)—however, "not now as a servant, but above a servant, a brother beloved" (1:16). Possibly being concerned that Philemon might disregard his request, Paul reminded Philemon: "If thou count me therefore a partner, receive him as myself. If he hath wronged thee, or oweth thee ought, put that on mine account. . . . I will repay it: albeit I do not say to thee how thou owest unto me even thine own self besides" (1:17–19). It is evident that Paul expected to be released from prison sometime in the near future, for he instructed Philemon: "Prepare me also a lodging: for I trust that through your prayers I will be given unto you" (1:22).

1–2 Timothy and Titus (ca. AD 60–64)

Paul's letters to Timothy and Titus are almost certainly the last letters we have from the apostle. Timothy originally lived with his Jewish mother and Greek father in Lystra and was one of the early converts from Paul's first mission (Acts 16:1; compare 14:6–7). At the beginning of his second mission, Paul revisited the area, heard of Timothy's good reputation, and had him circumcised (16:2–3), presumably to avoid conflict when they entered synagogues. Thereafter, Timothy became one of Paul's important missionary companions, assisting Paul with the writing of many of his letters.[56] When Paul wrote his first letter to Timothy, we learn that Paul had left Timothy in charge of the church at Ephesus (1 Timothy 1:3).

Titus was also an early convert—a Gentile who apparently was in Antioch when Judaizers from Judea were preaching that gentile converts must be circumcised and keep the law of Moses (Acts 15:1; compare Galatians 2:1–3). Paul and Barnabas were so concerned about this that they took the uncircumcised Titus with them to Jerusalem as a kind of test case while they discussed the matter with church leaders, who agreed that gentile converts like Titus did not need circumcision (Galatians 2:1–3; compare Acts 15:2, 19). Titus, like Timothy, became an important missionary companion to Paul (2 Corinthians 8:23). In his letter to Titus, Paul indicated that he and Titus had been preaching together on the island of Crete and that he left Titus to continue the missionary work there (Titus 1:5).

Paul's letters to Timothy and Titus are often called the Pastoral Epistles.[57] This designation stems from the fact that these letters were from one "pastor" or shepherd (Paul) to another "pastor" or shepherd (Timothy and Titus) concerning "pastoring" or shepherding the church members over whom they had stewardship. Some scholars consider these letters pseudonymous—written by someone else in the name of Paul. Reasons for this conclusion include that these letters use vocabulary that is not found in Paul's earlier letters and that some of the issues addressed in these letters, such as warning against a form of Gnosticism (1 Timothy 6:20), reflect major issues of later second-century Christianity. While Latter-day Saints acknowledge these concerns, they can be resolved by recalling that Paul used scribes to compose his letters (compare Romans 16:22), which may account for differences in vocabulary, and that these letters were written toward the end of Paul's life, which could explain the references to issues that became more fully developed in later Christianity.[58]

Paul began his first letter to Timothy by cautioning him to not "give heed to fables and endless genealogies, which minister questions, rather than godly edifying" (1 Timothy 1:4; compare Titus 1:14; 3:9). When Latter-day Saints hear the word *genealogy*, they think of family history work, but this was not what Paul had in mind. Toward the end of this letter, Paul instructed Timothy to avoid "oppositions of science falsely so called" (1 Timothy 6:20). The word translated as "science" is the Greek word *gnosis*, which means "knowledge." Thus, Paul was concerned that some Christians were claiming and teaching special knowledge, which led to "oppositions," or in other words, disputations. The warning against myths and genealogies may be a reference to speculative stories and genealogies in Jewish apocryphal literature (Titus 1:14; 3:9). At least one issue that later Christian gnostics claimed special knowledge about was the origin of the universe and of divine beings. Paul's warning against "fables and endless genealogies" may also concern an early development of this line of gnostic speculation about the origins of divine beings.[59]

Paul counseled both Timothy and Titus concerning those who serve as bishops.[60] The word *bishop* comes from the Greek word *episkopos*, which means "overseer." Although one should not seek for position within the church, Paul praised those who desired sincerely to serve God and others within the church (1 Timothy 3:1). He taught Timothy and Titus that bishops should be examples of good personal behavior (3:2–3; Titus 1:7–9). According to Paul, a bishop should be "the husband of one wife" (1 Timothy 3:2; Titus 1:6). This was not a reference to polygamy. Rather, both the Savior as well as Paul cautioned against unnecessary divorce and remarriage for trivial reasons (compare Matthew 5:32; 19:9; 1 Corinthians 7:10). Thus, bishops should be a good example of fidelity within marriage, as well as of rearing faithful children (1 Timothy 3:4–5; Titus 1:6).

Paul explained that a bishop should not be a "novice" (1 Timothy 3:6), or new convert, which could cause him to be filled with pride or to become overwhelmed. And bishops should "have a good report of them which are without" (3:7), meaning those outside the church. In other words, bishops should maintain a good relationship with others in the community (3:2; Titus 1:8). Paul gave similar counsel to Timothy concerning deacons (a word meaning "servant"), who should be men of experience, rather than new converts, and examples of good personal behavior with respect to marriage and family (1 Timothy 3:8–12).[61]

Paul cautioned Timothy concerning things that would occur "in the latter times" (1 Timothy 4:1). While it is tempting to think that Paul was only describing events in our current day, one must remember that New Testament writers described their own days as "these last times" (1 Peter 1:20) and "these last days" (Hebrews 1:2). This is not to deny that there are applications of such teachings to our day. But one should understand that when Paul warned Timothy that "in the latter times some shall depart from the faith, . . . forbidding to marry, and commanding to abstain from meats" (1 Timothy 4:1, 3), he was referring to issues that were important to them in their own time and the near future. For example, we know that there were members of Paul's own congregations who encouraged others to live an ascetic lifestyle (Colossians 2:18) and who taught against marriage (JST 1 Corinthians 7:1) and against eating certain kinds of meat (1 Corinthians 8:7–9).

Paul also counseled Timothy concerning widows and church welfare. Paul authorized providing temporal support for widows who needed it so that the church members could "honour widows that are widows indeed" (1 Timothy 5:3)—meaning those widows who were examples of a worthy life (5:5, 10; compare Titus 2:3). But Paul also recommended the families of those widows to be the first ones to provide temporal welfare if they were in a position to do so, "for that is good and acceptable before God" (1 Timothy 5:4). This would allow the church to then step in and give temporal relief to those who do not have such support from their family (5:16).[62] Because the job market was not always favorable toward women in that day, Paul encouraged younger widows to seek to remarry so they could be part of a self-supporting family unit once again (5:11; compare Titus 2:4).

The general context and content of 2 Timothy are different from that of 1 Timothy and Titus. Paul informed Timothy that he was in prison in Rome (2 Timothy 1:16–17). The book of Acts narrates Paul's journey to Rome and concludes while Paul was still under house arrest awaiting trial (Acts 28:30–31). Before traveling to Rome, Paul informed the Roman saints of his desire to visit them and then to make his way to Spain (Romans 15:28). Although it is not recorded in the New Testament, early Christian tradition is that Paul was acquitted at his first trial, successfully traveled to Spain, and then was eventually imprisoned in Rome again and put on trial a second time.[63] The setting for 2 Timothy seems to be Paul's second imprisonment in Rome, awaiting trial. Thus, Paul's second letter to Timothy is probably the last letter we have from the apostle.

In this final correspondence, Paul lamented to Timothy: "At my first answer [i.e., trial] no man stood with me, but all men forsook me. . . . Notwithstanding the Lord stood with me, and strengthened me; . . . and I was delivered out of the mouth of the lion" (2 Timothy 4:16–17; compare 1 Corinthians 15:32).[64] It seems that Paul did not expect to be acquitted this time: "I am now ready to be offered, and the time of my departure is at hand" (2 Timothy 4:6). The great apostle Paul left Timothy with his final testimony: "I have fought a good fight, I have finished my course, I have kept the faith: henceforth there is laid up for me a crown of righteousness, which the Lord, the righteous judge, shall give me at that day" (4:7–8).

Conclusion

It is interesting to note that the book of Acts never mentions Paul writing letters. This seems strange to modern Christians because of how important we judge these texts to be: over half of the documents that make up the New Testament consist of Paul's letters. But when the narrative in the book of Acts ends, Paul is still alive and under house arrest in Rome (28:30–31). While Paul was alive, his letters were certainly important for the congregations to whom he addressed them, but they do not seem to have been viewed as critical for the church in general. If a Christian or a leader or a congregation wanted an answer to an important question, that person or an appointee could visit Paul and ask him directly. But when Paul and the other apostles began to die and disappear, there were no longer living and legitimate oracles to consult for revelation on difficult issues. Once this happened, all they had left were the letters that Paul and others had left behind. Latter-day Saints are thankful for the teachings and testimony left behind in the writings of the apostle Paul. It can be also be said, however, that Latter-day Saints are likewise thankful for the teachings and testimonies of modern living prophets and apostles today, who "are called even with that same calling with which he [Paul] was called" (Doctrine and Covenants 18:9) and who teach and counsel us today as Paul did nearly two millennia ago.

⟡

Frank F. Judd Jr. is an associate professor in the Department of Ancient Scripture at Brigham Young University.

Further Reading

Anderson, Richard Lloyd. *Understanding Paul*. Rev. ed. Salt Lake City: Deseret Book, 2007.

Blumell, Lincoln H. "Scribes and Ancient Letters: Implications for the Pauline Epistles." In *How the New Testament Came to Be*, edited by Kent P. Jackson and Frank F. Judd Jr., 208–26. Salt Lake City: Deseret Book, 2006.

Huntsman, Eric D. "The Occasional Nature, Composition, and Structure of Paul's Letters." In *How the New Testament Came to Be*, edited by Kent P. Jackson and Frank F. Judd Jr., 190–207. Salt Lake City: Deseret Book, 2006.

Millet, Robert L. "Walking in Newness of Life: Doctrinal Themes of the Apostle Paul." In *The Apostle Paul: His Life and His Testimony*, edited by Paul Y. Hoskisson, 132–50. Salt Lake City: Deseret Book, 1994.

Roetzel, Calvin J. *The Letters of Paul: Conversations in Context*. 6th ed. Louisville, KY: Westminster John Knox, 2015.

Sanders, E. P. *Paul: The Apostle's Life, Letters, and Thought*. Minneapolis: Fortress, 2015.

Wayment, Thomas A. *From Persecutor to Apostle: A Biography of Paul*. Salt Lake City: Deseret Book, 2006.

Notes

1. Helpful Latter-day Saint resources on Paul's life and letters include Richard Lloyd Anderson, *Understanding Paul*, rev. ed. (Salt Lake City: Deseret Book, 2007); and Thomas A. Wayment, *From Persecutor to Apostle: A Biography of Paul* (Salt Lake City: Deseret Book, 2006).

2. E. Randolph Richards, *Paul and First-Century Letter Writing: Secretaries, Composition, and Collection* (Downers Grove, IL: InterVarsity, 2004); and Lincoln H. Blumell, "Scribes and Ancient Letters: Implications for the Pauline Epistles," in *How the New Testament Came to Be*, ed. Kent P. Jackson and Frank F. Judd Jr. (Salt Lake City: Deseret Book, 2006), 208–26. Paul was educated (Acts 22:3) and therefore had the ability to write his own epistles (1 Corinthians 16:21). The evidence indicates, however, that the ever-busy Paul likely dictated his letters to scribes, probably for convenience. For instance, Paul's scribe for his epistle to the Romans sent personal greetings to the saints in Rome in the text of Paul's letter: "I Tertius, who wrote this epistle, salute you in the Lord" (Romans 16:22). After a scribe wrote out the body of the letter, Paul then ended his letters with a personal greeting written by himself: "The salutation of me Paul with mine own hand" (1 Corinthians 16:21). These handwritten testimonials contained expressions of Paul's affection for the recipients, but may also have functioned as a way to guard against forgery. Paul warned the Thessalonians to not be fooled "by letter as from us" (2 Thessalonians 2:2), meaning "letter as if it were written by us." Paul then emphatically wrote at the end of his letter: "The salutation of Paul with mine own hand, which is the token in every epistle: so I write" (2 Thessalonians 3:17).

3. This important verse also implies that by the time of this epistle, Christians were making multiple copies of Paul's letters and subsequently sharing them among the various congregations.

4. Eric D. Huntsman, "The Occasional Nature, Composition, and Structure of Paul's Letters," in Jackson and Judd, *How the New Testament Came to Be*, 190–207.

5. Helpful commentaries include Martinus C. de Boer, *Galatians: A Commentary* (Louisville, KY: Westminster John Knox, 2011); David A. deSilva, *The Letter to the Galatians* (Grand Rapids, MI: Eerdmans, 2018); and J. Louis Martyn, *Galatians* (New York: Doubleday, 1997).

6. Paul identifies himself as an apostle at the beginning of this letter (Galatians 1:1). The term *apostle* means "one who is sent forth" with authority to preach and minister. The issue of whether Paul was also a member

of the quorum of the twelve in addition to being an apostle is discussed in a different chapter of this volume. See also the discussion in David O. McKay, *Gospel Ideals: Selections and Discourses of David O. McKay* (Salt Lake City: Improvement Era, 1953), 250.

7. Gaye Strathearn, "Peter and Paul in Antioch," in *The Ministry of Peter, the Chief Apostle*, ed. Frank F. Judd Jr., Eric D. Huntsman, and Shon D. Hopkin (Salt Lake City: Deseret Book, 2014), 227–46.

8. Mark D. Ellison, "Paul and James on Faith and Works," *Religious Educator* 13, no. 3 (2012): 147–71; and Stephen E. Robinson, *Following Christ* (Salt Lake City: Deseret Book, 1995), 82–85.

9. Gaye Strathearn, "Law and Liberty in Galatians 5–6," in *Go Ye into All the World: Messages of the New Testament Apostles*, ed. Ray L. Huntington, Jerome M. Perkins, and Thomas A. Wayment (Salt Lake City: Deseret Book, 2002), 57–74.

10. For a discussion of the evidence in Acts, see Abraham J. Malherbe, *The Letters to the Thessalonians* (New York: Doubleday, 2000), 55–71.

11. Joseph A. Fitzmyer, *The Acts of the Apostles* (New York: Doubleday, 1998), 449–50.

12. Following the last verse of 1 Thessalonians in the King James Version is the following note: "The first epistle unto the Thessalonians was written from Athens." This conclusion is drawn from 1 Thessalonians 3:1–6 but does not take into account Acts 18:1–5, where it says that Paul traveled from Athens to Corinth before Timothy returned. These notes that follow Paul's letters in the King James Version are called "subscriptions" and were not part of the original letters. They were added by scribes many years later, and some of them are in error. On this, see Anderson, *Understanding Paul*, 71.

13. For recent commentaries, see M. Eugene Boring, *I & II Thessalonians: A Commentary* (Louisville, KY: Westminster John Knox, 2015); and Gordon D. Fee, *The First and Second Letters to the Thessalonians* (Grand Rapids, MI: Eerdmans, 2009).

14. Stephen E. Robinson, "Early Christianity and 1 Nephi 13–14," in *The Book of Mormon: First Nephi, The Doctrinal Foundation*, ed. Monte S. Nyman and Charles D. Tate Jr. (Provo, UT: Religious Studies Center, Brigham Young University, 1988), 178.

15. See Jerome Murphy-O'Connor, *St. Paul's Corinth: Texts and Archaeology* (Collegeville, MN: Liturgical Press, 1983).

16. For helpful commentaries, see Gordon D. Fee, *The First Epistle to the Corinthians*, rev. ed. (Grand Rapids, MI: Eerdmans, 2014); and Joseph A. Fitzmyer, *First Corinthians* (New York: Doubleday, 2008). For a recent Latter-day Saint commentary, see Richard D. Draper and Michael D. Rhodes, *Paul's First Epistle to the Corinthians* (Provo, UT: BYU Studies, 2015).

17. For historical background on many of the following issues, see Eric D. Huntsman, "'The Wisdom of Men': Greek Philosophy, Corinthian Behavior, and the Teachings of Paul," in *Shedding Light on the New Testament: Acts–Revelation*, ed. Ray L. Huntington, Frank F. Judd, Jr., and David M. Whitchurch (Provo, UT: Religious Studies Center, Brigham Young University, 2009), 67–97.

18. Jennifer Lane, "Jews and Greeks: The Broader Context for Writing the New Testament," in Jackson and Judd, *How the New Testament Came to Be*, 62–77.

19. Kent R. Brooks, "Paul's Inspired Teachings on Marriage," in Huntington, Perkins, and Wayment, *Go Ye into All the World*, 75–97.

20. See the discussions of this issue in Anderson, *Understanding Paul*, 102–4; Richard Neitzel Holzapfel and Thomas A. Wayment, *Making Sense of the New Testament: Timely Insights and Timeless Messages* (Salt Lake City: Deseret Book, 2010), 352–53; and David R. Seely, "'Is Christ Divided?' Unity of the Saints through Charity," in *Studies in Scripture, Vol. 6: Acts to Revelation* (Salt Lake City: Deseret Book, 1987), 66–67.

21. Eric D. Huntsman, "The Impact of Gentile Conversions in the Greco-Roman World," in *The Life and Teachings of the New Testament Apostles: From the Day of Pentecost through the Apocalypse*, ed. Richard Neitzel Holzapfel and Thomas A. Wayment (Salt Lake City: Deseret Book, 2010), 80–96.

22. Camille Fronk, "'Submit Yourselves . . . as unto the Lord,'" in Huntington, Perkins, and Wayment, *Go Ye into All the World*, 98–113; and Sherrie Mills Johnson, "Paul's Teachings in 1 Corinthians on Women," in Huntington, Judd, and Whitchurch, *Shedding Light on the New Testament*, 129–52.

23. "The Family: A Proclamation to the World," *Ensign*, November 1995, 129.

24. Robert C. Freeman, "Paul's Earnest Pursuit of Spiritual Gifts," in *The Apostle Paul: His Life and His Testimony*, ed. Paul Y. Hoskisson (Salt Lake City: Deseret Book, 1994), 34–46; and David M. Whitchurch, "The Unifying Power of Spiritual Gifts," in Huntington, Judd, and Whitchurch, *Shedding Light on the New Testament*, 98–127.

25. Richard Lloyd Anderson, "Paul's Witness to the Early History of Jesus' Ministry," in Hoskisson, *Apostle Paul*, 1–33.

26. Mark D. Ellison, "The Setting and Sacrament of the Christian Community," in Huntington, Perkins, and Wayment, *Go Ye into All the World*, 145–66.

27. Daniel B. Sharp, "Vicarious Baptism for the Dead: 1 Corinthians 15:29," *Studies in the Bible and Antiquity* 6 (2014): 36–66.

28. For helpful commentaries, see Frank J. Matera, *II Corinthians: A Commentary* (Louisville, KY: Westminster John Knox, 2003); and Margaret E. Thrall, *The Second Epistle to the Corinthians*, 2 vols. (Edinburgh, Scotland: T&T Clark, 1994–2000).

29. Seely, "Is Christ Divided?," 57–82.

30. Frank F. Judd Jr., "Jesus Christ: The Savior Who Knows," in *Celebrating Easter*, ed. Thomas A. Wayment and Keith J. Wilson (Provo, UT: Religious Studies Center, Brigham Young University, 2007), 113–36.

31. Helpful commentaries include Joseph A. Fitzmyer, *Romans* (New York: Doubleday, 1993); Robert Jewett, *Romans* (Minneapolis, MN: Fortress, 2007); and Douglas J. Moo, *The Letter to the Romans*, 2nd ed. (Grand Rapids, MI: Eerdmans, 2018).

32. James E. Faulconer, *Romans 1: Notes and Reflections* (Provo, UT: Foundation for Ancient Research and Mormon Studies, 1999).

33. Robert L. Millet, "Walking in Newness of Life: Doctrinal Themes of the Apostle Paul," in Hoskisson, *Apostle Paul*, 132–50.

34. Robinson, *Following Christ*, 65–90.

35. James E. Faulconer, "The Olive Tree and the Work of God: Jacob 5 and Romans 11," in *The Allegory of the Olive Tree*, ed. Stephen D. Ricks and John W. Welch (Provo, UT: Foundation for Ancient Research and Mormon Studies, 1994), 347–66.

36. On this, see Scott H. Faulring, Kent P. Jackson, and Robert J. Matthews, eds., *Joseph Smith's New Translation of the Bible: Original Manuscripts* (Provo, UT: Religious Studies Center, Brigham Young University, 2004), 8–11.

37. Camille Fronk Olson, *Women of the New Testament* (Salt Lake City: Deseret Book, 2014), 291–95.

38. See Blumell, "Scribes and Ancient Letters," 208–26.

39. For helpful commentaries, see Charles B. Cousar, *Philippians and Philemon* (Louisville, KY: Westminster John Knox, 2009); Paul A. Holloway, *Philippians* (Minneapolis, MN: Fortress, 2017); and John Reumann, *Philippians* (New York: Doubleday, 2008). See also Eduard Verhoef, *Philippi: How Christianity Began in Europe: The Epistle to the Philippians and the Excavations at Philippi* (New York: Bloomsbury, 2013).

40. Gaye Strathearn and Joshua M. Sears, "The Church of the First Century," in Holzapfel and Wayment, *Life and Teachings of the New Testament Apostles*, 35–62.

41. Thomas A. Wayment, "'Each Person Has a Hymn': The Creator-Savior Hymns," in *Thou Art the Christ, the Son of the Living God: The Person and Work of Jesus in the New Testament*, ed. Eric D. Huntsman, Lincoln H. Blumell, and Tyler J. Griffin (Salt Lake City: Deseret Book, 2018), 192–215.

42. On this interpretation, see Frank F. Judd Jr., "The Condescension of God According to Paul," in Huntington, Judd, and Whitchurch, *Shedding Light on the New Testament*, 181–83; and Nicholas J. Frederick and Frank F. Judd Jr., "The Revelation of Jesus Christ to Paul: Presenting a Deeper, Full Christology," in Huntsman,

Blumell, and Griffin, *Thou Art the Christ*, 224–25. There are various ways to express the nuances of verses 6–7. For other interpretations, see the discussion in Holloway, *Philippians*, 117–21.

43. See the discussion in Judd, "Condescension of God," 171–92.

44. On the different possibilities, see Holloway, *Philippians*, 19–24.

45. Helpful commentaries include Stephen E. Fowl, *Ephesians: A Commentary* (Louisville, KY: Westminster John Knox, 2012); and John Muddiman, *The Epistle to the Ephesians* (New York: Hendrickson, 2001).

46. Elder David A. Bednar, "Ye Must Be Born Again," *Ensign*, May 2007, 22; and Lawrence R. Flake, "Holy Spirit of Promise," in *Encyclopedia of Mormonism,* ed. Daniel H. Ludlow (New York: Macmillan, 1992), 2:651–52.

47. Stephen E. Robinson, *Believing Christ* (Salt Lake City: Deseret Book, 1992), 94–95.

48. Thomas A. Wayment, "Internal Divisions: Ephesians in Historical Context," in Huntington, Judd, and Whitchurch, *Shedding Light on the New Testament*, 153–70.

49. Grant Underwood, "The 'Same' Organization That Existed in the Primitive Church," in Huntington, Perkins, and Wayment, *Go Ye into All the World*, 167–86.

50. For recent commentaries, see Jerry L. Sumney, *Colossians: A Commentary* (Louisville, KY: Westminster John Knox, 2008); and R. McL. Wilson, *Colossians and Philemon* (London: T&T Clark, 2005).

51. Wayment, "'Each Person Has a Hymn,'" 192–94.

52. Clyde J. Williams, "The Preeminence of Christ," in *Studies in Scripture, Vol. 6: Acts to Revelation*, 136–45.

53. Richard D. Draper, "The Earliest 'New Testament,'" in Jackson and Judd, *How the New Testament Came to Be*, 260–91.

54. Helpful commentaries include Cousar, *Philippians and Philemon*; Joseph A. Fitzmyer, *The Letter to Philemon* (New York: Doubleday, 2000); Scot McKnight, *The Letter to Philemon* (Grand Rapids, MI: Eerdmans, 2017); and Wilson, *Colossians and Philemon*.

55. David R. Seely, "From Unprofitable Servant to Beloved Brother in Christ," in *Studies in Scripture, Vol. 6: Acts to Revelation*, 165–77.

56. See 1 Thessalonians 1:1; 2 Thessalonians 1:1; 2 Corinthians 1:1; Romans 16:21; Philippians 1:1; Colossians 1:1; and Philemon 1:1.

57. Helpful commentaries include Raymond F. Collins, *I & II Timothy and Titus* (Louisville, KY: Westminster John Knox, 2002); Luke Timothy Johnson, *The First and Second Letters to Timothy* (New York: Doubleday, 2001); and Philip H. Towner, *The Letters to Timothy and Titus* (Grand Rapids, MI: Eerdmans, 2006).

58. See the discussion in Blumell, "Scribes and Ancient Letters," 219–21.

59. See the discussion in Towner, *The Letters to Timothy and Titus*, 109–14. On the issue of protognostic speculation concerning the origin of divine beings, see Johnson, *First and Second Letters to Timothy*, 163.

60. Bruce A. Van Orden, "The Pastoral Epistles," in *Studies in Scripture, Vol. 6: Acts to Revelation*, 178–91.

61. In Paul's day, as well as in the early days of the Church in the latter days, deacons were adult men rather than boys around the age of twelve.

62. This is how the welfare program of The Church of Jesus Christ of Latter-day Saints works today: "We are carrying on a great welfare/humanitarian service. Our welfare program, as we know it today, was begun during the Great Depression, and puts tremendous emphasis on self-reliance. We try to teach our people to be self-reliant and, when they can't take care of their own needs, to enlist the help of their families. And when those needs cannot be met by the families, then the Church moves in to help them." Gordon B. Hinckley, *Teachings of Gordon B. Hinckley* (Salt Lake City: Deseret Book, 1997), 686.

63. Anderson, *Understanding Paul*, 355–57.

64. Paul was speaking figuratively here about being delivered from death at his first trial. As a Roman citizen, if Paul were convicted of a capital crime, he would have been beheaded rather than crucified or sent to wild beasts.

25

Hebrews and the General Epistles

Hebrews, James, 1–2 Peter, 1–3 John, and Jude

Lincoln H. Blumell, Frank F. Judd Jr., and George A. Pierce

Of the twenty-seven books that make up the New Testament, twenty-one are epistles. Additionally, letters can be found in Acts 15:23–29; 23:25–30 and Revelation 2–3 contains seven short letters addressed to churches in western Asia Minor. Thus, any reading of the New Testament necessarily involves a considerable engagement with letters. Beyond the thirteen letters attributed to Paul, which were either addressed to a specific branch of the church (1 and 2 Thessalonians, 1 and 2 Corinthians, Ephesians, Colossians, and Philippians), multiple church branches in the same geographic area (Galatians and Romans), or to an individual (1 and 2 Timothy, Titus, Philemon), there are eight additional letters in the New Testament. Seven of these eight letters are known by the designation "General Epistles." In this context "general" has to do with the fact that these letters are generally open or "universal" (Greek καθολικός, *katholikos*) and addressed to Christians at large rather than to a specific branch or individual.[1] While this designation is mostly accurate, there are of course exceptions within this rubric: both 2 and 3 John are addressed to a specific group or person; furthermore, while Hebrews, strictly speaking, is not counted as one of the General Epistles, it is "general" in the sense that it is addressed to Christians as a whole and not to a specific group. In this chapter these eight letters will be briefly surveyed in canonical order with various issues being specially addressed, such as their authorship and date, audience and genre, and content as well.

Hebrews

Authorship and date

The authorship of the Epistle to the Hebrews is a subject that has been in question since the second and third centuries AD. Readers of the KJV Bible will note that the title states, "The Epistle of Paul the Apostle to the Hebrews." Yet missing is the typical Pauline salutation, "Paul, an apostle of Jesus of Christ . . . ," that followed the standard epistolary formula of his time, which included name and position.[2] Various reasons for associating Hebrews with Paul have been offered, such as the closing benediction conferring grace to the audience, references to the author being in bonds (10:34; 13:3), the greeting of "they of Italy," and the mention of Timothy, Paul's mission companion. The subscription following the end of Hebrews in the KJV New Testament also states that the Epistle to the Hebrews was written "from Italy by Timothy," but one cannot necessarily assume that the Timothy in Hebrews is the same Timothy that accompanied Paul on his missionary journeys, since this statement is not corroborated in scripture and contradicts the author's report in 13:23—"Know ye that our brother Timothy is set at liberty; with whom, if he come shortly, I will see you."[3] Thus, it appears that Timothy was going to join the author and then visit the originally intended audience of Hebrews.

In addition to the absence of any self-identifying salutation at the beginning of the work, arguments against Pauline authorship include differences in a more expansive vocabulary, refined grammar, and employment of different rhetoric (using elements such as alliteration, catchwords, and repetitions) as compared to the Pauline corpus.[4] Absence of Pauline themes such as justification and sanctification, and the concentration on the high priesthood of Christ, which is missing from the Pauline Epistles, could also support a non-Pauline authorship. Other scholars have noted that the theme of the Resurrection is seemingly absent, and the understanding of faith differs from Paul's.[5] The most cited passage within Hebrews against Pauline authorship is: "How shall we escape, if we neglect so great salvation; which at the first began to be spoken by the Lord, and was confirmed unto us by them that heard him" (2:3), which scholars interpret as an indication that the author did not hear the gospel directly from Jesus but was a "second-generation" Christian, someone who had not had interaction with Christ but was taught by someone else.[6] These reasons do not provide insurmountable evidence against Pauline authorship of Hebrews, just as none of the evidence supporting such an authorship is overwhelming.

Since the third century AD, various church scholars and leaders have advanced diverse opinions about the author of Hebrews with alternative authors put forward such as Luke and Barnabas, or even Timothy, Priscilla and Aquilla, Clement of Rome, a disciple of Paul who transcribed his oral teachings, or some well-educated Hellenistic Jew who was learned in the Septuagint and converted to Christianity.[7] While not making a definitive statement about the Pauline authorship for the entire Epistle to the Hebrews, Joseph Smith did ascribe Hebrews 6:17 and 11:4 to Paul.[8] Subsequent Latter-day Saint General Authorities have employed the phrase "the writer of Hebrews" when citing the epistle.[9] For the Latter-day Saint, the value of the text is the doctrine contained therein, not necessarily the authorship—whether it be Paul, Luke, Barnabas, or someone else.

Issues surrounding authorship also complicate the dating of Hebrews. A general date range of AD 60–100 has been proposed to account for various points of argument about the date of composition. D. A. Carson and D. J. Moo note that although the phrase "confirmed unto us by them that heard him" has been used to argue for a "second generation" of Christians, this should be understood generationally and not chronologically.[10] The quotations of Hebrews in 1 Clement dated to ca. AD 96, based on a likely reference to persecutions under the Roman emperor Domitian, provide a date before which Hebrews could have been written. Further, if the Timothy mentioned in 13:23 is the companion of Paul in the New Testament, then the book would need to have been written in his lifetime, sometime during the second half of the first century AD. While some scholars have attempted to connect 12:4 ("Ye have not yet resisted unto blood") to the persecution of the church under the emperor Nero around AD 64, such specific details cannot be gleaned from the text, especially considering the various persecutions that the church endured from the Jews and the Romans from its founding. The strongest evidence for an early date (pre-AD 70) for Hebrews comes from its discussion of sacrifice and ritual of the high priest in present-tense verbs (see 10:1–2), and although that is associated with the tabernacle within the text, the descriptions of these elements would have had strong correlates with the Jerusalem temple, which operated until its destruction in AD 70. If the temple was already destroyed by the time that Hebrews was written, Carson and Moo posit that the author would have likely mentioned the temple's ruin and made different arguments about sacrifice in connection to Christ's work.[11] Finally, while some have associated the high Christology of Hebrews, discussed below, with later works like Luke–Acts or 1 Peter, commonly dated after AD 70, the Christology presented in Hebrews is similar to that of epistles considered to be pre-AD 70, such as 1 Corinthians, Philippians, or Colossians. Overall, while the evidence allows a general date of AD 60–100, it is likely that Hebrews was written before the destruction of the Jerusalem temple in AD 70.

Audience and genre

Throughout this chapter, Hebrews is categorized as an epistle. Although the expected epistolary formula of salutation and addressees typical of most other New Testament epistles is missing, Hebrews closes with a benediction, personal remarks, and a farewell typical of epistles in the Roman era. The designation of the work as an epistle has been nuanced by several observations and analyses of the missive's rhetorical structure. The rhetorical elements employed strongly suggest that the document is a sermon or group of sermons or teachings packaged as a letter to a particular, albeit unnamed, audience.[12] A number of locations have been suggested for the audience, including Jerusalem, Alexandria, Antioch, Bithynia and Pontus, Caesarea Maritima, Colossae, Corinth, Cyprus, Ephesus, Samaria, or Rome, with the last locale having the most scholarly support. The polished Greek of the epistle strongly suggests that the audience was composed of native Greek speakers rather than people having

Greek as a second language, and thus the audience could have been located anywhere within the Eastern Roman Empire. Like authorship, the destination of the Epistle to the Hebrews does not meaningfully contribute or detract from the theological message of the work.

Without a salutation, the audience of the Epistle to the Hebrews must remain somewhat unknown.[13] Despite this missing information, the original intended recipients were Christians who probably had some strong connections to Judaism either by being Jewish converts, having biological or cultural affinity, or being attracted to the ritual of the tabernacle as presented in the Septuagint. The author confronts the notion that these Christians would apostatize in the face of hardship. Regardless of their background, the author's purpose is to persuade the audience not to turn from Christianity toward Judaism or toward a more conservative Jewish Christianity but to endure hardship, recognize the superiority of Jesus Christ, rely on him as sacrifice and high priest, draw on the examples of faith found in the Old Testament, and avoid apostasy.

Content

The overarching message of Hebrews is the superiority of Jesus Christ above angelic messengers, human prophets, and the law of Moses with the attendant Levitical priesthood and sacrificial system. Christ's preeminence is repeatedly stressed throughout the document, warning its audience not to reject Christ in favor of other faith traditions.[14] The opening (1:1–4) of Hebrews evinces a high Christology and affirms his place as the ultimate divine revelation. This is followed by a discussion of the Son being superior to angels (1:5–14). The author of Hebrews argues that Christ's incarnation and sufferings afford him not only the right to receive glory and honor as the "captain," or originator and founder, of salvation but also the right to act as a high priest and provide reconciliation to God and succor for the believer in the midst of temptation (2:9–10, 16–18). The positions of Moses and Jesus are contrasted, also with the intention of illustrating Christ's supremacy, by noting that whereas Moses was a faithful servant in the household of God, Christ as the Son occupies a higher position (3:5–6). Even the "rest of the Lord" promised in the Old Testament is regarded as less than the rest that Christ promises, a rest that will parallel that of God's, which can be understood as the culminating act in the Creation (3:7–4:10; Genesis 2:2–3).[15]

The writer of Hebrews then reasons that Christ embodies a higher priesthood, provides a superior sacrifice, and initiates a better covenant with better promises. Continuing a theme briefly mentioned before the discussion of Moses, the author relates that Christ is a great high priest who can empathize with the human condition, enabling believers to "come boldly unto the throne of grace, . . . obtain mercy, and find grace to help in time of need" (4:14–16). Christ's status as a high priest is elevated above the Levitical priesthood by virtue of being a high priest "after the order of Melchisedec" (5:6, 10). After warning against spiritual immaturity and apostasy and encouraging his audience to persevere considering God's promised covenantal blessings, the author of Hebrews, quoting Psalm 110 and Genesis 14:18–20, draws on the character of Melchizedek as he appears in biblical literature to describe the nature of Christ's priesthood. In contrast to the historical figure of Melchizedek, who assuredly had an actual father and mother, likely had descendants, and had other relationships in his social context, Melchizedek as described in Genesis has no lineage: no father or mother is given for him there. After blessing Abraham and receiving Abraham's tithe in Genesis 14, nothing more about Melchizedek is related. Therefore, Melchizedek literarily had no beginning and had no end (compare JST Hebrews 7:3), a concept noted by the psalmist in Psalm 110, describing how David's Lord is to be "a priest for ever after the order of Melchizedek" (Psalm 110:4). Using this as a type, the author of Hebrews illustrates the eternal nature of Christ's priesthood. Since Christ was not from the tribe of Levi, he could not function as a high priest in a temporal sense within the tabernacle or temple. Yet in the spiritual sense, as the author of Hebrews shows, Christ's priesthood is eternal like that of Melchizedek's, and in this way he is superior to any of the earthly high priests that served in the tabernacle or temple.

This discussion of Melchizedek and the role of the high priest leads to a discussion of the permanency of Christ's sacrifice. In contrast to the sacrifices made under the Levitical system, his atoning sacrifice saves completely (Hebrews 7:25), and the sacrifices performed were a shadow of the new covenant and the new high priest (8:1–13). The superiority of Christ as both sacrifice and high priest is shown through the description of the Day of Atonement ritual in Hebrews 9. The author indicates that Christ's sacrifice of his own blood is borne by himself as the high priest into the heavenly tabernacle. Unlike an earthly high priest who would bring in the blood from sacrifices on the Day of Atonement, sprinkle the blood on the mercy seat on the ark of the covenant within the holy of holies, and then exit the most holy place, Jesus Christ entered the holy of holies in the heavenly tabernacle, presented his blood as a sacrifice at the mercy seat of God the Father, and then sat down enthroned at the right hand of the Father in heaven to serve as the believer's advocate. In this manner, Christ as sacrifice and high priest is continually present before the Father. The author then reinforces Christ's superiority in that the old sacrificial system foreshadowed Christ's ultimate sacrifice.

Following additional encouragement for the audience to continue in the Christian faith, the author of Hebrews then gives examples from scripture of people that maintain their faith in the face of adversity (11:1–40). The ultimate example of faith is Jesus Christ, who established the way to God by completing everything that was necessary for himself and believers to be able to return to the Father. The believer is further encouraged to consider trials a sign of discipline from a loving God. The writer of Hebrews then compares Zion to Sinai, encouraging his audience to continue steadfastly in the faith and serve God "acceptably with reverence and godly fear" (12:28).

The concluding chapter presents expectations for the readers of the document, including an injunction to follow the examples of those who brought them the gospel and other current leadership (13:1–8). Instead of the old sacrificial system, believers should now offer a sacrifice of praise and thanksgiving for what God has accomplished through Christ Jesus (see 13:9–16). The author closes with a request for prayer (13:18–19), a doxology (13:20–21), and some personal notes before giving a final benediction (13:22–25).

James

Authorship and date

The author of the Epistle of James identifies himself as "James, a servant of God and of the Lord Jesus Christ" (1:1). The author seems confident that readers will know who he is without further identification. The two most prominent people named James in the New Testament are the brother of John and the brother of Jesus. Although James the brother of John was an apostle, a member of Jesus's most trusted inner circle (Peter, James, and John), and the first martyr among the apostles (Acts 12:2, ca. AD 44), the author of this epistle is typically understood to be James the Lord's brother.[16] The brothers of Jesus were not disciples during their brother's mortal ministry (John 7:3–5). But the resurrected Jesus appeared to James (1 Corinthians 15:7), who eventually became a leader of the Jewish Christians in Jerusalem (Acts 15:13; 21:18; Galatians 1:18–19; 2:9).[17] It is possible that the Epistle of James was written during the mid to late 40s AD and was one of the earliest books of the New Testament to be written.

Audience and genre

The English name *James* translates the Greek name *Iakobos* (i.e. Jacob). James (or Jacob) addressed his epistle to "the twelve tribes which are scattered abroad" (1:1). This may have been intended to recall the patriarch Jacob (Israel) addressing his twelve sons before his death (Genesis 49:3–27) as well as the scattering of their descendants by the Assyrians and the Babylonians. In this light, James addressed those who were reconstituted Israel (diaspora Jews) or new Israel (Jewish converts).[18] As a leader of the Jewish Christians in Jerusalem, James would likely be viewed as having some authority over Jewish Christians in the diaspora. The Epistle of James is a sermon written in epistolary form. It begins like a typical letter, but it is addressed to a very general audience and contains none of the personal greetings we typically see in Paul's letters.

Content

The first chapter of James contains a number of exhortations. The most noteworthy of these for Latter-day Saints is the one that inspired the young Joseph Smith to seek divine guidance: "If any of you lack wisdom, let him ask of God, that giveth to all men liberally, and upbraideth not; and it shall be given him" (1:5).[19] Another of these sayings defined in a practical way what it means to worship God: "Pure religion and undefiled before God and the Father is this, To visit the fatherless and widows in their affliction, and to keep himself unspotted from the world" (1:27). The lack of reference to debates between gentile and Jewish Christians has persuaded some that this letter was written in the mid to late 40s AD, before church members began to deal with those issues.

The Epistle of James is probably most famous for its discussion of faith and works.[20] Some have viewed this discussion as a response to Paul's doctrine of salvation through faith and not by works (Ephesians 2:8–9). It would be more accurate, however, to understand this as a response to Christians who misinterpreted Paul's usage of the word *faith* to mean mere belief apart from obedience.[21] Paul himself responded to this kind of a misunderstanding: "Shall we continue in sin, that grace may abound? God forbid" (Romans 6:1–2). Paul understood, rather, that true faith in Christ was sincere belief in him coupled with sincere effort to keep his commandments (Romans 2:1–6). Addressing this misunderstanding of Paul's teachings, James reasoned: "Faith, if it hath not works, is dead, being alone. Yea, a man may say, Thou hast faith, and I have works: shew me thy faith without thy works, and I will shew thee my faith by my works" (2:17–18).

Another important issue addressed in the Epistle of James is self-control, directed in particular at those who "offend" others with their words (3:2).[22] James warned Christians: "The tongue is a fire, a world of iniquity. . . . It is an unruly evil, full of deadly poison" (3:6, 8). He taught that "the tongue is a little member" of the body that "boasteth great things" (3:5) and as a result "defileth the whole body" (3:6). James likened this tiny body part to horse bits that can "turn about their whole body" (3:3), ships that are "turned about with a very small helm" (3:4), and small sparks, for "how great a matter [i.e., a forest] a little fire kindleth" (3:5). He lamented that "out of the same mouth proceedeth blessing and cursing" and declared "these things ought not so to be" (3:10). Apparently there had been reports of "envying and strife" (3:16) among some groups of Christians. James encouraged these quarreling members to seek after "the wisdom that is from above" (3:17), which would fill them with "the fruit of righteousness" in order to "make peace" (3:18).

In addition, James discussed "wars and fightings among you" (meaning interpersonal rather than armed conflicts) that arose from "your lusts that war in your members" (4:1), meaning in the body. He had in mind those who broke the commandments that prohibited killing, coveting, and adultery (4:2–5) as well as those who "speaketh evil" against each other (4:11). In response, James exhorted those who participated in such conflicts to "submit yourselves therefore to God. Resist the devil, and he will flee from you" (4:7) and to "draw nigh to God, and he will draw nigh to you" (4:8).[23]

James seems to be aware of a version of the Sermon on the Mount that is similar to the one recorded in Matthew 5–7.[24] In his famous sermon, Jesus acknowledged the commandment in Leviticus 19:18 to "love thy neighbor" and taught people to also "love your enemies" (Matthew 5:43–44). James encouraged his audience to "do well" by keeping this "royal law" to love your neighbor as yourself (2:8). Later, he also warned anyone who "judgeth his brother" (4:11) and "judgeth another" (4:12), meaning his neighbor. An even more explicit connection between the Epistle of James and the Sermon on the Mount is found in James's counsel for Christians to "swear not, neither by heaven, neither by the earth, neither by any other oath; but let your yea be yea; and your nay, nay; lest ye fall into condemnation" (5:12). This recalled the teaching of Jesus from the Sermon on the Mount: "Swear not at all; neither by heaven; for it is God's throne: nor by the earth; for it is his footstool. . . . But let your communication be, Yea, yea; Nay, nay: for whatsoever is more than these cometh of evil" (Matthew 5:34–35, 37).

James concluded by encouraging his readers to follow the examples of Old Testament prophets. He reminded them that Job was "an example of suffering affliction, and of patience" (5:10). Specifically, James said that Christians should be patient, "for the coming of the Lord draweth nigh" (5:8). This explicit expectation of the imminent return of Christ, also seen in Paul's earliest epistles (compare 1 Thessalonians 1:10; 4:13–18), is another reason for an early dating of the Epistle of James. Finally, James closed his epistle by exhorting his audience to follow the example of Elijah, whose prayers initially caused the famine but then brought lifesaving rain for the Israelites (5:17–18). Similarly, Christians should pray in behalf of those who are sick, for "the effectual fervent prayer of a righteous man availeth much" (5:16).

1–2 Peter

Authorship and date

Both 1 and 2 Peter claim to be written by Peter, who was "an apostle of Jesus Christ" (1 Peter 1:1; 2 Peter 1:1).[25] Some scholars doubt that Peter, an Aramaic-speaking fisherman from Galilee, would have possessed the skills necessary to write such sophisticated letters in Greek and quote from the Septuagint.[26] But it is likely that Peter knew at least some Greek from interacting with Gentiles for his fishing business in Galilee as well as from his decades of preaching to non-Jews both at home (Acts 10:19–48) and, according to tradition, in Rome. It is also possible that Peter, like Paul, employed well-trained, Greek-speaking scribes who helped construct and edit these letters into their final, polished form.[27] According to early Christian tradition, Peter was executed in Rome during the reign of Nero sometime between AD 64 and 68.[28] Therefore, 1 and 2 Peter would have been composed before that time.

Audience and genre

First Peter is addressed to the "elect" (1:2) who are "strangers scattered throughout Pontus, Galatia, Cappadocia, Asia, and Bithynia" (1:1). There is no account of Peter visiting these locations in Asia Minor, but on the day of Pentecost he communicated with Jews "out of every nation under heaven" (Acts 2:5), including those whose homes were in "Cappadocia, in Pontus, and Asia" (2:9). On that day of miracles, three thousand were baptized (2:41). It is likely that some of them were from Asia Minor and subsequently took the gospel back home. This would help explain Peter's concern for those in this area.[29] Second Peter is addressed to faithful Christians: those who have received "precious faith with us through the righteousness of God and our Saviour Jesus Christ" (1:1). This epistle has much in common with an ancient farewell address, similar to the final words of Moses to the Israelites in Deuteronomy 31–33 or King Benjamin to the Nephites in Mosiah 2–5.[30] The two epistles begin like typical letters but are written to very general audiences and lack the personal greetings typical of Paul's epistles; they are therefore categorized as sermons in epistolary form.

Content

Peter began by reminding his audience that the resurrection of Jesus Christ should provide for Christians a "lively" (i.e., living or vibrant) hope in a future "inheritance incorruptible, and undefiled" that awaited them in heaven (1 Peter 1:3–4).[31] While on earth, however, Christians were to be "holy in all manner of conversation" (1:15), just as the ancient Israelites were commanded by the Lord, "Be ye holy; for I am holy" (1:16; compare Leviticus 11:44–45). This is made possible, explained Peter, through the Savior because of his atonement: "Ye were not redeemed with corruptible things, as silver and gold . . . but with the precious blood of Christ, as of a lamb without blemish and without spot" (1:18–19). Thus, Christians are "lively stones" and should become "a spiritual house" (i.e., a holy temple) with Jesus Christ as "the head of the corner" (i.e., the cornerstone, 2:5–7). And just as the Lord declared concerning his ancient covenant people, so he declared to his new covenant people their special status: "Ye are a chosen generation, a royal priesthood, an holy nation, a peculiar people" (2:9; compare Exodus 19:5–6).

Peter told his Christian audience that Gentiles "speak against you as evildoers" (1 Peter 2:12). Christians were sometimes accused of teaching and doing things that were against the laws or traditions of the empire (compare Acts 16:20–21). This may be why Peter then counseled his audience to "submit yourselves to every ordinance of man" (1 Peter 2:13). The phrase "ordinance of man" means a human institution, such as the government. This submission would also be to "the king" (i.e., the emperor) and to local "governors" (2:13–14).[32] By being good examples of proper behavior toward government, Peter declared, Christians could "put to silence the ignorance of foolish men" who thought they were disloyal (2:15). Proper behavior should also extend to relationships within one's own household, such as masters and servants (2:18), husbands and wives (3:1–7), elders and youth (5:5), and, in fact, everyone: "be ye all of one mind, having compassion one of another, love as brethren" (3:8).

Peter then employed references to the suffering of Christ as a point of entry into his teachings concerning the postmortal mission of Christ. Just as Christ suffered for the sins of those who are unjust, so he also "preached unto the spirits in prison; which sometime were disobedient" (1 Peter 3:19–20). During the time in the spirit world between Christ's crucifixion and resurrection, "the gospel was preached also to them that are dead, that they might be judged according to men in the flesh, but live according to God in the spirit" (4:6). Latter-day Saints are blessed with additional insights into these passages from a revelation in Doctrine and Covenants 138 given through President Joseph F. Smith in 1918.[33] According to this revelation, Christ did not personally preach to all the wicked spirits but appointed messengers from among the righteous spirits to spread the gospel message (Doctrine and Covenants 138:29–31).

By the time Peter wrote this epistle, Christians seem to have been suffering local persecution, for he reminded them not to consider it "strange concerning the fiery trial which is to try you, as though some strange thing happened unto you" (1 Peter 4:12).[34] Rather, persecuted disciples should "rejoice, inasmuch as ye are partakers of Christ's sufferings" (4:13). Followers of Christ should be "happy" because they bring glory to their Savior through their suffering (4:14). It is much better, explained Peter, that they remain true and "suffer as a Christian" rather than suffer as a result of sinful behavior (4:15–16). They should continue to do well as they "commit the keeping of their souls" to God (4:19).

First Peter concludes with Peter acknowledging that this epistle came to his readers "by Silvanus, a faithful brother unto you" (5:12). Silvanus was either the scribe whom Peter employed to write this epistle or possibly the emissary who delivered it. In addition, Peter sent greetings from "the church that is at Babylon" (5:13). Just as John in the book of Revelation, Peter seems to use the name *Babylon* as a code name for Rome (compare Revelation 16:19; 17:9). Finally, Peter sent greeting specifically from "Marcus my son" (1 Peter 5:13). This is very likely a reference to John Mark, whom Paul took as a companion on his first mission (Acts 12:25), and who, according to early Christian tradition, later became Peter's companion while in Rome.

Second Peter contains features that have caused scholars to identify it as an ancient farewell address.[35] Peter anticipated that his death would be soon: "shortly I must put off this my tabernacle" (1:14). He declared that while he was still "in this tabernacle" (1:13), he would "not be negligent" (1:12) to give counsel, which he intended his readers to remember following his "decrease" (1:15). He reminded Christians of the "exceeding great and precious promises" given to them whereby they "might be partakers of the divine nature" (1:4), taken by some scholars as support for the doctrine of theosis (or deification).[36] To receive such sacred blessings, he encouraged his audience to "add to your faith virtue; and to virtue knowledge; and to knowledge temperance; and to temperance patience; and to patience godliness; and to godliness brotherly kindness; and to brotherly kindness charity" (1:5–7). Latter-day Saints recognize similar language in a revelation given to Joseph Smith Sr. (Doctrine and Covenants 4:6).

Peter exhorted his readers to make their "calling and election sure; for if ye do these things, ye shall never fall" (2 Peter 1:10), and "an entrance shall be ministered unto you abundantly into the everlasting kingdom of our Lord and Saviour Jesus Christ" (1:11).[37] In connection with this, he recounted the eyewitness "of [Christ's] majesty" he received on the Mount of Transfiguration as a heavenly voice bore testimony of the Son of God (1:16–18; compare Matthew 17:1–5). Peter then reminded his audience that, if faithful, they could also receive a "more sure word of prophecy" that would be to them like "a light that shineth in a dark place" (2 Peter 1:19). The Prophet Joseph Smith taught that this more sure word included personal knowledge that one "is sealed up unto eternal life" (Doctrine and Covenants 131:5).

This is followed by repeated warnings against wickedness, with comparisons to various stories from the past, such as the hosts of heaven who were cast out in the premortal existence (2 Peter 2:4), those who lived at the time of Noah (2:5), the inhabitants of Sodom and Gomorrah (2:6), and the false prophet Balaam (2:15). Since the Epistle of Jude employs similar examples, they will be discussed below.

In the final chapter of 2 Peter, the apostle gave counsel concerning "scoffers" who will come forth "in the last days" (3:3). These individuals will make fun of Christians for their belief in the second coming of Jesus Christ. They will mock: "Where is the promise of his coming? for since the fathers fell asleep, all things continue as they were from the beginning of the creation" (3:4). While the words of Peter are certainly applicable to the modern day, they also were likely intended to instruct Christians of Peter's own day or the immediate future. Early Christians sometimes described their own time period as "the last days." For example, the writer of Hebrews taught his first-century audience: "God, who at sundry times and in divers manners spake in time past unto the fathers by the prophets, hath in *these last days* spoken unto us by his Son" (Hebrews 1:1–2; emphasis added). Likewise, Peter himself prefaced his first epistle by concluding that Jesus Christ "was foreordained before the foundation of the world, but was manifest in *these last times* for you" (1 Peter 1:20; emphasis added).

Whether for first-century saints or for Latter-day Saints, however, Peter's counsel is relevant. While he likely intended the numbers to be understood figuratively rather than literally, Peter reminded his readers that God's eternal timetable is different from the timetable of mortals: "be not ignorant of this one thing, that one day is with the Lord as a thousand years, and a thousand years as one day" (2 Peter 3:8). He reassured Christians who may have been concerned that Christ had not returned yet: "The Lord is not slack concerning his promise [to return]" (3:9), but the Second Coming will happen as unexpectedly "as a thief in the night" (3:10). In the meantime, Christians should continue waiting faithfully for, looking forward to, and preparing for that glorious day (3:12–14).

In conclusion, Peter mentioned the writings of "our beloved brother Paul" (3:15) and admitted that "all his epistles" contained "some things hard to be understood, which they that are unlearned and unstable wrest [i.e., distort], as they do also the other scriptures, unto their own destruction" (3:16).[38] Earlier, Peter had warned his readers that "no prophecy of the scripture is of any private interpretation" (1:20). It is significant to note from these references that by the time of the writing of 2 Peter, Paul's epistles had already begun to be collected together and were being referred to as scripture.

1–3 John

Authorship and date

None of the three Johannine letters contain the name *John* in the text, and 1 John is actually anonymous (like Hebrews) since the author never explicitly identifies himself. Nevertheless, it begins with the first person plural "we" (1:1), wherein the author proceeds to make the point that he (along with others) is a personal witness of the Lord, whom all of them have both seen and touched (1:1). Thus, from the beginning the author claims to be a special witness of the Lord Jesus (1:1–5). Additionally, 1 John contains a number of places that parallel what is found in the Gospel of John (1 John 1:1–4 parallel John 1:1–18; 1 John 3:11–17, 23; 4:7–21 parallel John 13:31–35), and overall the styles of 1 John and the Gospel of John are very similar. Finally, already by the second century, early Christians had taken the author to be the apostle John.[39] There are, therefore, good reasons to think that the apostle John was the source of this text.

In both 2 and 3 John the author identifies himself as the "elder" (*presbuteros*) in the first verse of each letter. The title could signify one of two possibilities: (1) the office of "elder" or "presbyter" within the early church or (2) a reference to his authoritative status and age. In 1 Peter 5:1, Peter also refers to himself as an "elder" and yet at the start of the same letter in 1 Peter 1:1 he refers to himself as an "apostle." Thus, the use of "elder" does not necessarily preclude the author of 2 and 3 John from being the apostle John, whom many early Christians supposed was the author.[40] Furthermore, in 2 John 1:4–6 there is a distinct parallel with John 13:34–35 (and 1 John 2:7–10), which could further reinforce the idea that John was the source of these two letters. On the other hand, modern scholarship has tended to distinguish the author of 2 and 3 John from the author of the Gospel of John.

As with most books in the New Testament, dating the Johannine Epistles is educated guesswork. There is nothing explicit within any of the letters that allows for a precise dating, and ascribing any date(s) always relies on a series of assumptions and constructs. One such construct is that the parallels between 1 John and the Gospel of John are taken as evidence that the former relies on the latter. Thus, it is commonly held that 1 John was written after the Gospel of John. In general, these letters have been dated to the last three decades of the first century (ca. AD 70–100), with the majority of scholarship opting for the last decade of the first century. By the first half of the second century, 1 John had already been cited by at least two different Christian authors and was thought by them to have been written while John was residing in Ephesus.[41]

Audience and genre

Though 1 John is designated among the New Testament epistles, in its literary form it lacks the trappings of a letter: the author never explicitly identifies himself at the beginning, which is typical in actual letters, and there is no address or greeting at the beginning and no valediction or conclusion at the end (compare 1 and 2 John). Overall, 1 John reads more like a homily or, perhaps, even an essay that was written to deal with a few different problems that had emerged in some early Christian congregations.[42] First John is addressed to those Christians who had stayed within the fold and who are called at various times "little children" (1 John 2:1, 12–13, 18, 28; 3:7, 18; 4:4; 5:21)—presumably people in fellowship with John and whom he regarded as his spiritual offspring.

Second John is addressed to the "elect lady and her children" (1:1). While this could be an actual woman and her children, the most common interpretation is that the "elect lady" refers to a local church and "her children" refers to its members. Thus, like certain of Paul's letters, 2 John appears to be directed to a specific branch of the church.

In 3 John the letter is addressed to a man named Gaius (1:1), who was a member of a local congregation. While the exact identification of Gaius is unknown, the author calls him "beloved" (1:1); includes him among his "children" (1:4), which is perhaps the author's designation of Christians who were in fellowship (compare 1 John 2:1); and reports that Gaius has walked "in truth" (1:4). Second and 3 John are the shortest two texts in the New Testament, and both read just like an actual letter with the constituent parts (2 John: verses 1–3 address and letter opening, verses 4–11 body of letter, verses 12–13 valediction and letter closing; 3 John: verses 1–4 address and letter opening, verses 5–12 body of letter, verses 13–15 valediction and letter closing).

Content

First John begins with the author's powerful witness of the Lord, specifically, that he has both "seen" and "handled" the Savior (1:1–3). This is immediately followed by an injunction that the true followers abide in "light" and have no part in "darkness" (1:5–7). Thus, the opening verses echo in various ways John 1:1–18, which discusses the incarnation by employing light and darkness imagery. First John continues with a discussion of sin and expiation, which comes through Jesus, whose "blood . . . cleanseth us from all sin" (1:7), who is an "advocate" (2:1; compare John 14:16), and who offered himself as a "propitiation for our sins" (2:2). Because of this, his followers can conquer and triumph over evil (2:12–17).

As 1 John proceeds, there is a preoccupation with certain people who "went out from us" (2:19). The context of this phrase suggests that these people had left both the fold of the faithful and had rejected the true faith in favor of adhering to different teachings regarding the person of Jesus. In this context these defectors are labeled "antichrists" on multiple occasions in 1 John (2:18, 22; 4:3), and once in 2 John 1:7, because they were denying (1) "that Jesus was the Christ" (2:22) and (2) that he had "come in the flesh" (4:2–3). Their denial that "he had come in the flesh" does not mean that they were contesting that Jesus ever actually existed, but rather that he actually had a corporeal body (i.e., flesh) during his ministry. Here it appears that this group was adhering to a form of what would later be called "docetism," from the Greek *dokeō* (δοκέω) meaning "to suppose, seem," and was alleging that Jesus only "seemed" or "appeared" to have flesh, while in reality he was just a spiritual being or phantasm during his lifetime.

What was at play in later conceptions of docetism was the belief that a divine being, such as Jesus, could not have had a corporeal body since this would necessarily imply that it would have been subject to pain, hunger, sickness, aging, and death. Thus, as Christianity spread in the second century, certain groups maintained that Jesus, a divine being, never had a physical body, only appeared as a phantasm, and never actually suffered and died. For these groups the central purpose of Jesus's mission had nothing to do with his salvific act of atonement, as he could not have actually suffered and died, and so they asserted that Jesus brought salvation in another way—mainly through the secret "knowledge" (Greek *gnōsis*) that he imparted. While it is not clear that those who "went out from us" in 1 John had completely adopted docetism (or were espousing "knowledge" as the way to salvation), their beliefs apparently had docetic elements. Thus, 1 John makes it clear from the very first that the author had actually "handled" (1:1) Jesus, which means that Jesus must have had a corporeal body and that those "antichrists" who had left the fellowship were in error. At the same time, the point is made in 1 John that it was the "blood of Jesus" that ultimately "cleanseth us from all sin" (1:7), highlighting the fact that Jesus both had a body (blood) and that his suffering and death enabled purification. A few verses later in 1 John 2:2 the point is made that Jesus offered himself as a "propitiation" for sin. The term translated "propitiation" is more clearly rendered "atoning sacrifice" and is from the Greek ἱλασμός (hilasmos), a term used in the Old Testament (LXX) in connection with the sacrifice on the Day of Atonement (Leviticus 25:9; Numbers 5:8). Thus, Jesus's salvific act was his atoning sacrifice that he could perform because he could suffer, bleed, and die, as he had a corporeal body.

First John continues with the theme of Jesus's corporal body in 1 John 5, but this has been obfuscated somewhat because of a well-known interpolation in the King James Bible. In 1 John 5:7–8 the KJV reads as follows: "For there are three that bear record in heaven, the Father, the Word, and the Holy Ghost: and these three are one. And there are three that bear witness in earth, the Spirit, and the water, and the blood: and these three agree in one." While these passages later evolved into a Trinitarian prooftext, with the erroneous insertion of "the Father, the Word, and the Holy Ghost: and these three are one" (see chapter 39 herein), the actual reading for these verses is "For there are three that bear record in heaven, the Spirit, and the water, and the blood: and these three agree in one." The reference here to spirit, water, and blood is tied to the testimony of Jesus and the fact that he had a body; both "water" and "blood" are explicitly mentioned together in John 19:34–35, when Jesus's dead body was on the cross and was pierced by the spear of the Roman soldier. Thus, a central theme of 1 John, in the face of those who had abandoned the faith and were denying the mortality and corporeality of Jesus, was that Jesus was mortal and had a corporal body, which enabled him to make an atoning sacrifice for sin.

Besides dealing with the recent apostasy, another overriding theme in 1 John is the subject of "love"—the Greek agapē (ἀγάπη). As in the farewell discourse of Jesus at the Last Supper and in the Intercessory Prayer in John 14–17, wherein "love" (agapē) becomes a hallmark of discipleship, so also in 1 John the attribute of love is the mark of a true disciple (2:10–11; 3:11, 14, 18, 23; 5:2). As 1 John concludes, there is an appeal to keep the true faith (5:1–13): Jesus is the Christ (5:1, 5); disciples must have love for each other and for God (5:2–3); and Jesus's death brought salvation (5:6–12). In the epilogue (5:14–21), followers are reminded once again about Christ's role in salvation; promised that if they pray, the Father will truly hear them; and told to keep themselves from idolatry.

Second John opens with "the elder" addressing "the elect lady and her children" (1:1) and expressing a hope that grace, mercy, and peace might abide in them from the Father and the Son (1:3). When the body of the letter opens in verse 4, the elder begins by commending the recipients since he has heard that they have continued to walk in truth (1:5–6) and that they have shown love to one another as they have been commanded (compare John 13:34–35). In verses 7–11, a warning is then given against deceivers, called antichrists, who were denying that Christ actually had a corporeal body while in mortality (see discussion above on 1 John), and an admonition is included that no one should associate with such people.

The letter concludes in verses 12–13, with the author expressing hope that he might soon be able to see the addressees personally, since he has much more to relate, and ends with a final salutation (compare 3 John 1:13–14).

Third John begins with "the elder" addressing an individual named Gaius, followed by a wish that Gaius might remain in health and prosperity (1:2). When the body of the letter commences in verse 3, the elder commends Gaius, just as he did the elect lady and her children (2 John 1:4), because he has heard that Gaius walks in the truth; the elder expresses joy on such account (3 John 1:4). In verses 5–8 Gaius is entreated to receive a group of traveling missionaries, with the author noting that Gaius's charitable reputation precedes him and showing how Gaius's charity would be helping with the work of evangelization. Proceeding to verses 9–11, the elder continues to encourage Gaius to show charity to the group of traveling missionaries by highlighting the negative example of a certain Diotrephes, who had not only refused the group but had also spoken malicious words against them and the elder. In verse 12 the elder commends a certain Demetrius, presumably the bearer of the letter, whom Gaius is to receive (compare Romans 16:1–2); and in verses 13–14 the elder concludes the letter by expressing hope that since he has much more to say, he plans to visit Gaius personally (compare 2 John 1:12–13). The letter ends with a salutation of peace (1:14).

Jude

Authorship and date

The author of the Epistle of Jude calls himself "the servant of Jesus Christ, and brother of James" (1:1). The Gospel of Mark records that Jesus had many brothers, two of whom were named James and Judah (Mark 6:3). Jude is traditionally identified as this Judah.[43] Later Christians remembered this brother of Jesus as Jude, rather than his Greek name Judas, possibly to avoid being associated with Judas Iscariot, who betrayed Jesus (Mark 3:19). As stated above, the brothers of Jesus were not disciples during their brother's mortal ministry (John 7:3–5). It is possible, however, that the resurrected Jesus appeared to his brother Jude, just as he had to James (1 Corinthians 15:7). Some have suggested that Jude was an apostle, but there is no solid foundation for such an identification.[44] Early Christian tradition holds that Jude was martyred ca. AD 65 in Beirut, within the Roman province of Syria. Whether or not this tradition is accurate, this epistle would have been written before Jude died.

Audience and genre

The Epistle of Jude was addressed to those who were "called" and "sanctified by God the Father, and preserved in Jesus Christ" (1:1). The identification of Judah the brother of Jesus as the author of this epistle suggests he became a figure of authority in the early church in the years following the death of Jesus Christ, just as did his brother James (Acts 15:13). This would help explain why Jude felt it was appropriate for him to write a letter of doctrine and counsel to a general audience of Christians. The Epistle of Jude is also a sermon written in epistolary form because in spite of its beginning like a typical letter, it is addressed to a very general audience and contains no personal greetings similar to those we find in Paul's letters.

Content

Jude pled with his Christian audience to "earnestly contend for the faith which was once delivered unto the saints" (1:3). The primary concern for Jude seems to be apostasy from within the church membership: "certain men crept in unawares" (1:4).[45] Specifically, he called these individuals "ungodly men" who were "turning the grace of our God into lasciviousness, and denying the only Lord God, and our Lord Jesus Christ" (1:4). In verse 8, Jude called them "filthy dreamers" (i.e., claiming false revelation) who "defile the flesh" (i.e., practice immorality). They also "despise dominion" (i.e., refuse to follow counsel from their leaders) and "speak evil of dignities" (i.e., rebel against church leaders).

Jude likened the circumstances of these apostates to various stories from the past. First, he reminded his audience of the fate of the first generation of Israelites who perished as a result of their rebellion in the wilderness (1:5; compare Numbers 14:35). Next, he recalled how a third of the hosts of heaven were cast out because they followed Satan (1:6; compare Revelation 12:9).[46] Third, he evoked the story of Sodom and Gomorrah, whose inhabitants were destroyed for their immorality (1:7; compare Genesis 19:24–25). Fourth, in verse 11 he stated that the apostates have "gone in the way of Cain," who killed his brother Abel (compare Genesis 4:8); run "greedily after the error of Balaam," who went with Balak in order to curse Israel for money (compare Numbers 22:6–22); and will perish just as "Core" (or Korah), who rebelled against the authority of Moses (compare Numbers 16:31–33).

Interestingly, Jude referred to two examples that are not contained in our current Bible nor in latter-day scripture, but rather in other ancient Jewish literature (i.e., The Assumption of Moses and the Book of Enoch).[47] First, he mentioned the story of "Michael the archangel," who disputed with the devil concerning "the body of Moses" and refused to accuse the devil but said, "The Lord rebuke thee" (1:9). This example reassured Jude's audience that even though apostates may seem to escape punishment for the time being, the Lord will eventually punish according to his own timetable those who rebelled against him. In a similar line of thought, Jude also quoted from a prophecy of Enoch concerning the Lord's coming "with ten thousand of his saints, to execute judgment upon all" (1:14–15). It is noteworthy that Jude referred to these stories as authoritative, though they are beyond what is contained in the traditional Jewish or Christian canon of scripture.

Lincoln H. Blumell is an associate professor in the Department of Ancient Scripture at Brigham Young University.

Frank F. Judd Jr. is an associate professor in the Department of Ancient Scripture at Brigham Young University.

George A. Pierce is an assistant professor in the Department of Ancient Scripture at Brigham Young University with a joint appointment to the BYU Jerusalem Center for Near Eastern Studies.

Further Reading

Epistle to the Hebrews

Bruce, F. F. *The Epistle to the Hebrews*. The New International Commentary on the New Testament. Grand Rapids, MI: Eerdmans, 1990.

Burge, Gary M., Lynn H. Cohick, and Gene L. Green. *The New Testament in Antiquity: A Survey of the New Testament within Its Cultural Contexts*. Grand Rapids, MI: Zondervan, 2009.

Carson, D. A., and Douglas J. Moo. *An Introduction to the New Testament*. Grand Rapids, MI: Zondervan, 2005.

Jobes, Karen H. Letters to the Church: A Survey of Hebrews and the General Epistles. Grand Rapids, MI: Zondervan, 2011.

Epistle of James

Ellison, Mark D. "Paul and James on Faith and Works." The Religious Educator 13, no. 3 (2012): 147–71.

Hauglid, Brian M. "'As the Body without the Spirit': James's Epistle on Faith and Works." In Go Ye into All the World: Messages of the New Testament Apostles, edited by Ray L. Huntington, Patty Smith, Thomas A. Wayment, and Jerome M. Perkins, 276–89. Salt Lake City: Deseret Book, 2002.

Jobes, Karen H. Letters to the Church: A Survey of Hebrews and the General Epistles. Grand Rapids, MI: Zondervan, 2011.

Epistles of Peter

Ball, Terry B. "Peter's Principles: An Approach to the First Epistle of Peter." In Go Ye into All the World: Messages of the New Testament Apostles, edited by Ray L. Huntington, Patty Smith, Thomas A. Wayment, and Jerome M. Perkins, 220–29. Salt Lake City: Deseret Book, 2002.

Jobes, Karen H. Letters to the Church: A Survey of Hebrews and the General Epistles. Grand Rapids, MI: Zondervan, 2011.

Judd, Frank F., Jr., Eric D. Huntsman, and Shon D. Hopkin, eds. The Ministry of Peter, the Chief Apostle. Salt Lake City: Deseret Book, 2014.

Skinner, Andrew C. "Peter—The Chief Apostle." In Go Ye into All the World: Messages of the New Testament Apostles, edited by Ray L. Huntington, Patty Smith, Thomas A. Wayment, and Jerome M. Perkins, 187–219. Salt Lake City: Deseret Book, 2002.

Epistles of John

Ellison, Mark D. "Preserving or Erasing Jesus's Humanity: Tensions in 1–2 John, Early Christian Writings, and Visual Art." In Thou Art the Christ, the Son of the Living God: The Person and Work of Jesus in the New Testament, edited by Eric D. Huntsman, Lincoln H. Blumell, and Tyler J. Griffin, 283–303. Provo, UT: Religious Studies Center, Brigham Young University; Salt Lake City: Deseret Book, 2018.

Kruse, Colin G. The Letters of John. Grand Rapids, MI: Eerdmans, 2000.

Lieu, Judith. The Second and Third Epistles of John. Edinburgh, Scotland: T&T Clark, 1986.

Ludlow, Victor L. "Light, Life, and Love in the Epistles of John." In The Testimony of John the Beloved, edited by Daniel K Judd, Craig J. Ostler, and Richard D. Draper, 113–24. Salt Lake City: Desert Book, 1998.

Epistle of Jude

Jobes, Karen H. Letters to the Church: A Survey of Hebrews and the General Epistles. Grand Rapids, MI: Zondervan, 2011.

Strathearn, Gaye. "The Overlooked Epistle of Jude." In Shedding Light on the New Testament: Acts—Revelation, edited by Ray L. Huntington, Frank F. Judd Jr., and David M. Whitchurch, 227–46 (Provo, UT: Religious Studies Center, Brigham Young University, 2009).

Notes

1. In certain quarters of Protestantism today, these epistles are sometimes called the "lesser epistles" since they are not regarded with as much theological esteem as the letters of Paul. This Protestant notion is largely the result of Martin Luther's low appraisal of certain of these letters.

2. For a full discussion of numerous positions for and against Pauline authorship of Hebrews, including Latter-day Saint General Authorities since Joseph Smith, see Terrence L. Szink, "Authorship of the Epistle to the Hebrews," in *How the New Testament Came to Be*, ed. Kent P. Jackson and Frank F. Judd Jr. (Provo, UT: Religious Studies Center, Brigham Young University; Salt Lake City: Deseret Book, 2006), 243–59.

3. Scholars consider this subscription and others associated with the New Testament epistles as part of an apparatus attributed to Euthalius, bishop of Sulca in Egypt, who added to these texts to further aid the reader. Although the inclusion of this material into various manuscript traditions varies, a general date range of AD fourth to seventh centuries is likely. In referring to the accuracy of Euthalius's work, Thomas Hartwell Horne noted that this man was "either grossly ignorant, or grossly inattentive." T. H. Horne, *An Introduction to the Critical Study and Knowledge of the Holy Scriptures* (London, England: T. Cadell, Strand, 1834), 2:76.

4. G. M. Burge, L. H. Cohick, and G. L. Green, *The New Testament in Antiquity: A Survey of the New Testament within Its Cultural Contexts* (Grand Rapids, MI: Zondervan, 2009), 390–95.

5. Bruce M. Metzger, *The New Testament: Its Background, Growth, and Content*, 3rd ed. (Nashville: Abingdon, 2003), 284.

6. D. A. Carson and D. J. Moo, *An Introduction to the New Testament* (Grand Rapids, MI: Zondervan, 2005), 604.

7. The earliest surviving manuscript of the Epistle to the Hebrews is dated to the third century AD and is placed among the Pauline Epistles after Romans. Eusebius preserved the statements of early church fathers such as Clement and Origen, who suggested that Paul is the author of the Epistle to the Hebrews but recognized the difficulties of that position. Clement proposed that owing to the similarities in Greek between Hebrews and Luke–Acts, Paul was the original author and the preserved Greek text is Luke's translation (see Eusebius, *Ecclesiastical History* 6.14.2). Origen suggested that one of Paul's disciples took notes on his sermons and teachings and compiled them together into the current form of Hebrews, but he refused to speculate on the actual author: "But who wrote the epistle in truth God knows" (Eusebius, *Ecclesiastical History* 6.25.14). Tertullian considered Hebrews to not be Pauline in origin but thought that Barnabas had written the epistle. Both Jerome and Augustine influenced the church into considering Hebrews to be authentically Pauline, although Augustine varied in his opinion throughout his life. Reformation leaders like Calvin and Luther also opposed the idea of Pauline authorship of Hebrews, rejecting the long-standing Catholic tradition. Carson and Moo, *Introduction to the New Testament*, 600–604.

8. In a letter to his uncle Silas Smith, Joseph discussed faith in the promises of God and drew on Hebrews 6:17–19, stating that "Paul said to his Hebrew brethren . . ." ("Letter to Silas Smith, 26 September 1833," p. 4, *The Joseph Smith Papers*, http://www.josephsmithpapers.org/paper-summary/letter-to-silas-smith-26-september-1833/3). Later, in teaching priesthood holders, Joseph Smith quoted Hebrews 11:4 and stated that Abel was sent from heaven to minister to Paul, indicating that Joseph attributed at least that portion of Hebrews to Paul (see "Instruction on Priesthood, 5 October 1840," pp. 4–5, *The Joseph Smith Papers*, http://www.josephsmithpapers.org/paper-summary/instruction-on-priesthood-4-october-1840/9). He had previously discussed Abel's plight as presented in Hebrews using the phrase "Paul in a letter to his Hebrew brethren" as part of a message to the Saints in Missouri published in *The Evening and the Morning Star* ("Letter to the Church, circa March 1834," p. 143, *The Joseph Smith Papers*, http://www.josephsmithpapers.org/paper-summary/letter-to-the-church-circa-march-1834/2).

9. See Szink, "Authorship of the Epistle to the Hebrews" for a detailed set of references to General Authority use of "writer of Hebrews."

10. Carson and Moo, *Introduction to the New Testament*, 605.

11. Carson and Moo, *Introduction to the New Testament*, 607; see also F. F. Bruce, *The Epistle to the Hebrews*, New International Commentary on the New Testament (Grand Rapids, MI: Eerdmans, 1990), 20–22; and G. W. Buchanan, *To the Hebrews*, Anchor Bible 36 (Garden City: Doubleday, 1972), 261.

12. Bruce, *Epistle to the Hebrews*, 389.

13. The title "To the Hebrews" is found on the earliest extant manuscript dated to the third century AD (Chester Beatty P[46]), and the second-century author Clement of Alexandria also referred to the work as "for Hebrews," suggesting that the early church used this title as a reference that likely reflected an earlier understanding of the composition of the original addressees.

14. Carson and Moo, *Introduction to the New Testament*, 597.

15. In its Genesis context, the "rest" that God enters on the seventh day of creation is not a period of inactivity; rather, "rest" for the deity as related to ancient Near Eastern thought, refers to the deity being enthroned in a temple after subduing chaos and establishing stability, peace, and order. J. H. Walton, *Ancient Near Eastern Thought and the Old Testament: Introducing the Conceptual World of the Hebrew Bible* (Grand Rapids, MI: Baker Academic, 2006), 196–99.

16. Dale Allison Jr., *James: A Critical and Exegetical Commentary* (New York: Bloomsbury T&T Clark, 2013), 3–31; and Luke Timothy Johnson, *The Letter of James* (New York: Doubleday, 1995), 92–110.

17. Gerald N. Lund, "I Have a Question," *Ensign*, September 1975, 36–37. See also Thomas A. Wayment, "The Continuing Influence of the Family of Jesus in Early Christianity," in *The Life and Teachings of the New Testament Apostles: From the Day of Pentecost Through the Apocalypse*, ed. Richard Neitzel Holzapfel and Thomas A. Wayment (Salt Lake City: Deseret Book, 2010), 134–56; and Richard Neitzel Holzapfel, "The Family of Jesus," in *The Life and Teachings of Jesus Christ: From the Transfiguration Through the Triumphal Entry*, ed. Richard Neitzel Holzapfel and Thomas A. Wayment (Salt Lake City: Deseret Book, 2006), 344–71.

18. Scot McKnight, *The Letter of James* (Grand Rapids, MI: Eerdmans, 2011), 59–68.

19. Steven C. Harper, *Joseph Smith's First Vision: A Guide to the Historical Sources* (Salt Lake City: Deseret Book, 2012), 26–27; and Craig K. Manscill, "'If Any of You Lack Wisdom': James's Imperative to Israel," in *Go Ye into All the World: Messages of the New Testament Apostles*, ed. Ray L. Huntington, Thomas A. Wayment, and Jerome M. Perkins (Salt Lake City: Deseret Book, 2002), 244–57.

20. Brian M. Hauglid, "'As the Body without the Spirit': James's Epistle on Faith and Works," in Huntington, Wayment, and Perkins, *Go Ye into All the World*, 276–89.

21. Mark D. Ellison, "Paul and James on Faith and Works," *Religious Educator* 13, no. 3 (2012): 147–71. See also Brian M. Hauglid, "The Epistle of James: Anti-Pauline Rhetoric or a New Emphasis?," in Holzapfel and Wayment, *Life and Teachings of the New Testament Apostles*, 157–70; and Stephen E. Robinson, *Following Christ* (Salt Lake City: Deseret Book, 1995), 82–85.

22. Charles Swift, "'The Tongue Is a Fire': The Symbolic Language of James 3," in *Shedding Light on the New Testament: Acts–Revelation*, ed. Ray L. Huntington, Frank F. Judd Jr., and David M. Whitchurch (Provo, UT: Religious Studies Center, Brigham Young University, 2009), 193–208.

23. David M. Whitchurch, "Discipleship and the Epistle of James," in Huntington, Wayment, and Perkins, *Go Ye into All the World*, 258–75.

24. John W. Welch, "Echoes from the Sermon on the Mount," in *The Sermon on the Mount in Latter-day Scripture*, ed. Gaye Strathearn, Thomas A. Wayment, and Daniel L. Belnap (Salt Lake City: Deseret Book, 2010), 333–35.

25. Andrew C. Skinner, "Peter—The Chief Apostle," in Huntington, Wayment, and Perkins, *Go Ye into All the World*, 187–219; and Brent L. Top, "Fallible but Faithful: How Simon the Fisherman Became Peter the Rock," in *The Ministry of Peter, the Chief Apostle*, ed. Frank F. Judd Jr., Eric D. Huntsman, and Shon D. Hopkin (Salt Lake City: Deseret Book, 2014), 1–12.

26. Lewis R. Donelson, *I & II Peter and Jude: A Commentary* (Louisville, KY: Westminster John Knox Press, 2010), 15–16; and John H. Elliott, *1 Peter* (New York: Doubleday, 2000), 118–30.

27. Frank F. Judd Jr., "The Case for Petrine Authorship of 1 Peter," in Judd, Hunstman, and Hopkin, *Ministry of Peter*, 247–65.

28. Larry R. Helyer, *The Life and Witness of Peter* (Downers Grove, IL: InterVarsity, 2012), 272–84; and Bart D. Ehrman, *Peter, Paul, & Mary Magdalene: The Followers of Jesus in History and Legend* (New York: Oxford University Press, 2006), 84–86.

29. Judd, "Petrine Authorship of 1 Peter," in Judd, Huntsman, and Hopkin, *The Ministry of Peter*, 248.

30. John W. Welch and Brent J. Schmidt, "Reading 2 Peter as a Farewell Text," in Judd, Huntsman, and Hopkin, *Ministry of Peter*, 317–35.

31. Terry B. Ball, "Peter's Principles: An Approach to the First Epistle of Peter," in Huntington, Wayment, and Perkins, *Go Ye into All the World*, 222–23.

32. Eric-Jon K. Marlowe, "'Honor the King': Submission to Civil Authority," in Judd, Huntsman, and Hopkin, *Ministry of Peter*, 283–96.

33. Scott C. Esplin, "Wondering at His Words: Peter's Influence on Knowledge of Salvation for the Dead," in Judd, Huntsman, and Hopkin, *Ministry of Peter*, 297–315; and M. Catherine Thomas, "Visions of Christ in the Spirit World and the Dead Redeemed," in *Sperry Symposium Classics: The New Testament*, ed. Frank F. Judd Jr. and Gaye Strathearn (Provo, UT: Religious Studies Center, Brigham Young University; Salt Lake City: Deseret Book, 2006), 354–72.

34. Sherrie Mills Johnson, "'Think It Not Strange Concerning the Fiery Trial,'" in Huntington, Wayment, and Perkins, *Go Ye into All the World*, 230–43.

35. Welch and Schmidt, "Reading 2 Peter as a Farewell Text," in Judd, Huntsman, and Hopkin, *Ministry of Peter*, 317–35.

36. James Starr, "Does 2 Peter 1:4 Speak of Deification?," in *Partakers of the Divine Nature: The History and Development of Deification in the Christian Traditions*, ed. Michael J. Christensen and Jeffrey A. Wittung (Grand Rapids, MI: Baker Academic, 2007), 81–94. See also Tad R. Callister, "Our Identity and Our Destiny," *Religious Educator* 14, no. 1 (2013): 1–17; Andrew C. Skinner, *To Become Like God: Witnesses of Our Divine Potential* (Salt Lake City: Deseret Book, 2016), 58–69; and Robert L. Millet, "God and Man," in *No Weapon Shall Prosper: New Light on Sensitive Issues*, ed. Robert L. Millet (Salt Lake City: Deseret Book, 2011), 345–78.

37. Robert L. Millet, "Make Your Calling and Election Sure," in Judd, Huntsman, and Hopkin, *Ministry of Peter*, 267–82; and Brian M. Hauglid, "Joseph Smith's Inspired Commentary on the Doctrine of Calling and Election," in Huntington, Judd, and Whitchurch, *Shedding Light on the New Testament*, 209–26.

38. Gaye Strathearn, "Peter and Paul in Antioch," in Judd, Huntsman, and Hopkin, *Ministry of Peter*, 227–46.

39. Irenaeus, *Against Heresies* 3.16.5.

40. Eusebius, *Ecclesiastical History* 2.23.25.

41. Papias in Eusebius, *Ecclesiastical History* 3.36.1–2; and Polycarp, *To the Philippians* 6.3; 7.1.

42. M. M. Culy, *I, II, III John: A Handbook on the Greek Text* (Waco, TX: Baylor University Press, 2004), xix–xx.

43. Peter H. Davids, *The Letters of 2 Peter and Jude* (Grand Rapids, MI: Eerdmans, 2006), 8–12; and Donelson, *I & II Peter and Jude: A Commentary*, 161–63.

44. Gaye Strathearn, "The Overlooked Epistle of Jude," in Huntington, Judd, and Whitchurch, *Shedding Light on the New Testament*, 228–31.

45. Alexander B. Morrison, *Turning Away from the Truth: A New Look at the Great Apostasy* (Salt Lake City: Deseret Book, 2005), 42–43; and Kent P. Jackson, "New Testament Prophecies of Apostasy," in Judd and Strathearn, *Sperry Symposium Classics: The New Testament*, 403–4.

46. Strathearn, "Overlooked Epistle of Jude," 237–40.

47. Strathearn, "Overlooked Epistle of Jude," 242–46.

26

The Book of Revelation
Following the Lamb

D. Jill Kirby

The Revelation (Apocalypse) of John is perhaps the least understood and most misunderstood part of the Bible. Violence, lurid imagery, and inscrutable descriptions of events seem to lie uneasily next to the Gospels and Epistles in the rest of the New Testament. Distracted readers may therefore miss the Apocalypse's profoundly prophetic message—God is redeeming his creation through Christ. Consistent with the witness of the rest of the New Testament, the central motif of salvific redemption is the slaughtered Lamb (Revelation 5:6, 9–10). However, it is the Lamb of 7:17 that speaks most strongly to disciples, for this Lamb is also going to "shepherd" (lead) his followers to the living water that gives eternal life. This paradoxical image, in which God's sheep are guided by a Shepherd-Lamb, is central to a coherent appreciation of John's message.[1] Despite all the bizarre interpretations offered for John's Apocalypse, his book is profoundly pastoral. It is about life and living as a disciple, projected against the backdrop of perhaps the greatest and grandest vision of the entire Bible.

However, to appreciate the "last things," readers must attend to first things. John's Revelation is not "a coded collection of secrets that will finally become intelligible at the end of time, for from the beginning it has been an open book designed to communicate with Christians on earth" (1:4; 22:10).[2] Nevertheless, Revelation was written almost two thousand years ago in a very different cultural setting, and some of its imagery is quite disturbing. Thus, we must attend to some significant literary features and the historical context before we move into its message.

Gender and Violence

Since many readers who might enjoy John's Revelation are understandably concerned about its violence, this will be the first topic. Readers may find these visions unsettling because of the raw carnage (e.g., 9:16–18; 19:17–18) or the targeting of women (2:20–23; 17:16), and other visions are alarming because God is not typically associated with calls for vengeance in the minds of most biblical readers (6:9–11), nor are the heavenly hosts often portrayed as celebrating the destruction of others (19:1–3).[3] There is no easy and complete response that settles these issues for all readers, and indeed, to engage the argument in any detail would consume this entire chapter. Four points will be made here, but interested readers should pursue this topic in the secondary literature.[4]

First, readers who question the propriety of imagery such as the martyrs' call for vengeance in 6:9–11 might hesitate to criticize unless they have experienced similarly crushing injustice. It is true that the visions of John's Revelation have been used to support ill-advised notions of "redemptive violence," but these arise from failure to appreciate that the Lamb conquered by his faithful witness, not through violence.[5] Similarly, the victims of oppression overcome through their own faithful witness, rather than adopting the violence of their oppressors.[6] Their desire for vengeance is addressed to God and left to his justice.

Second, the depictions of combat slaughter are as symbolic as much of the rest of John's imagery. For example, in 19:11–21 John narrates the premillennial destruction of evil. Initially, the heavens are opened to allow a rider on a white horse and his followers to descend. The rider is Christ, and he is said to be wearing a robe dipped in blood *before* the combat begins, suggesting that the blood is his own. He has many royal diadems, rather than a discrete number, as a challenge to the limited power of the dragon and the beast. Where one might expect to find a battle sword, he has a title, "KING OF KINGS, AND LORD OF LORDS" (19:16). This title expresses the superiority of his relationship with the rulers of the nations of the earth but is never part of his rapport with the saints. Although the rider has companions on white horses, their unspotted white clothing indicates that their battles have been fought and won—they have overcome and washed their robes in the blood of the Lamb. Only the rider will fight in this engagement; that is, "*he* doth judge and make war," then "*he* shall rule them with a rod of iron," and "*he* treadeth the wine press" (19:11, 15; emphasis added) of God's wrath. However, since his only weapon is a symbol, that is, a sword that comes from his mouth, the battle is one of words (19:15).[7] In effect, "the God who spoke the world into existence will, through the Word of God, speak evil into nonexistence."[8] The description of the carnage in 19:17–18, 21, then, symbolizes the completeness of the Lamb's victory, not how it is accomplished.[9] There are no real weapons, there is no real combat, and the saints never engage evil with violence.[10]

Third, God is very slow to execute justice on those who oppress the saints, but when he does so it has a poetic quality. The justice meted to the violent in Revelation is that they become victims of their own behaviors. For example, the whore is destroyed by the violence she used against others (17:16), teaching readers that "the city that thrives on the violence its rulers use against others will finally fall victim to these same destructive practices."[11] Yet, even this divine response to injustice is sometimes moderated. In the final plague septet, seven angels carrying vials containing the wrath of God leave heaven for the earth (15:5–8). One of the more horrific images follows from the mission of the third angel, whose vial turns potable water sources to blood (16:4–7). When his task is complete, he opines that God has given the wicked what they deserve: those who *killed* the saints have been *given blood to drink*. The souls of the martyrs, who asked for God's vengeance in 6:10, agree with the angel of the waters that this imbalance between crime and punishment is just and true (16:7). God's justice is more concerned with overcoming evil rather than destroying people. Even when Babylon finally falls, and with her all the cities of the nations, the suffering inhabitants still live, with time to repent (16:21).[12]

Finally, the most significant issue with the violence in John's Revelation is that it appears as if God and Christ have adopted the tactics of the beast rather than the qualities traditionally attributed to them. This concern is not addressed directly but is worked out in the narrative. The threatening scenes of the seals and the trumpets are interrupted to show the source and scale of divine mercy in the sealing of the 144,000, the redemption of multitudes seen before the throne of God and the Lamb, the safety of those who are inside the temple when John measures it, and the diminution of expected violence from the final earthquake (6:16–17; 7:1–17; 9:20–21; 10:1–11:12). Only when many have opted to worship God on the basis of the martyrdom and resurrection of the two witnesses does the seventh trumpet announce the end (11:13). Likewise, the tree of life over the river of life in the New Jerusalem is said to have leaves for the "healing of the nations" (22:2), which would not be needed if God had indeed executed justice as wholesale slaughter. Although God's warnings must be taken seriously, they should not be isolated from the ways in which their execution is delayed and moderated to facilitate needed lifestyle changes before the end comes.[13]

Genre

Revelation's genre is typically considered hybrid; that is, it has features of an epistle, a prophecy, and an apocalypse. The entire book, less the opening verses, is framed as a letter, to be carried by messengers from John to readers in the seven named churches (Ephesus, Smyrna, Pergamum, Thyatira, Sardis, Philadelphia, and Laodicea). John identifies his own work as a prophecy (1:3; 22:7, 10, 18–19), the only text to be explicitly identified with this genre in the Christian canon. He establishes continuity with Israel's prophets by repeatedly alluding to them without quoting any known version. However, he also creates his own prophetic vision by asserting that the promises made to ancient Israel will come to fruition through Christ's defeat of evil. John's auditors participate in this victory by doing as Jesus did, that is, bearing a faithful witness of God and Jesus in their own lives.[14]

Finally, John's narrative is an apocalypse. The classification of certain texts as apocalyptic literature was developed by Friedrich Lücke in his 1832 introduction to the Revelation of John. The texts he identified were Daniel, 4 Ezra, 1 Enoch, and the Sibylline Oracles, in addition to Revelation.[15] Although Revelation and 2 and 3 Baruch employ the term *apocalypse*, the generic description of an apocalypse is modern: "a genre of revelatory literature with a narrative framework, in which a revelation is mediated by an otherworldly being to a human recipient, disclosing a transcendent reality which is both temporal, insofar as it envisages eschatological salvation, and spatial insofar as it involves another, supernatural world."[16]

Texts regarded as apocalypses will have most, but not all, of the features described in the above definition. The key point is that an apocalypse reveals the *transcendent reality* of a future salvation or a supernatural world in some detail. By so doing, readers are alerted to the fact that there is more to life than the present, usually unpleasant circumstances, so to prosper they will need to adopt a longer, more complete perspective. The generic definition is often amended by the addition of a statement regarding the purpose of an apocalypse, typically to "interpret the present, earthly circumstances in light of the supernatural world and of the future, and *to influence both the understanding and behavior of the audience by means of divine authority*."[17] This modification is significant because it indicates that the insights of an apocalypse were written to be understood *and applied* by their audiences. Reading Revelation is not about decoding the future but about recoding oneself in the present to align more closely with God.

Symbolism

Symbolism is typical of apocalyptic literature, but John's symbolism is both pervasive and remarkable. The literary indications of a nonliteral interpretation include a linking of two totally different ideas, such as the identification of the Lamb as a shepherd (7:17), the use of words that formally indicate a nonliteral reading such as "mystery" (1:20) or "here is wisdom" (13:18), the impossibility of a literal interpretation such as "out of his mouth went a sharp, twoedged sword" (1:16), and most importantly the repeated use of the same expression in figurative contexts elsewhere in Revelation. In some cases, such as the identification of the Lamb (5:6) or the man-child who is caught up to heaven (12:5), symbols operate at the level of characterization, a point to which I will return in the following section. In others, such as the description of the New Jerusalem as a great, radiant cube coming down from heaven (21:10–16), what is created is a mental picture with dimensions that defy logical harmonization but are nonetheless meaningful.[18]

What is the purpose of this use of symbolic language? First, it was not meant to hide John's meaning from the Roman authorities, for John's readers would have easily connected a city personified as a woman resting on seven hills with Rome (17:9, 18).[19] Second, these symbols are evocative or tensive; that is, they can usually be identified with something in John's first-century world but that does not exhaust their meaning. Thus, the beast from the sea may be understood as the Roman cult of John's day that bent the indigenous religions of Asia Minor to its will, but its qualities are those of every oppressive organization throughout history.[20] In addition, this sort of language is particularly suited for describing ideas for which propositional language fails, such as the ultimate beginning or end of creation. Just as we can discern the *meaning* of our creation from Genesis without prejudice to the sciences or history, so too can John's nonpropositional communication convey the *meaning and goal* of existence without necessarily making any claim to scientific or historical verisimilitude. Just exactly *what* will happen remains to be seen, but the *why* and *how* are revealed and become the basis for concrete action in the present.[21]

One last important aspect of Revelation's symbolism is the use of numbers. Even casual readers are familiar with the way Revelation is structured by the number seven: there are seven letters, seven churches, seven seals, seven trumpets, and seven vials. However, many other instances of numerical symbolism are less obvious. Seven is associated with completeness, and there are seven beatitudes that together describe the proper response to John's narrative.[22] Since the world is envisioned with four corners, one way to indicate that Rome's mercantile interests exploited the entire world would be to name twenty-eight (4 x 7) items that are bought and sold (18:12–13). The title "Lord God Almighty" occurs seven times, as does "Christ," while "Lamb" appears twenty-eight times, but no such pattern exists for John's evil characters: the dragon, beast, and false prophet. Readers who wish to discover more of the intricacies of John's use of numerical symbolism have only to remember to count when they notice repetition.[23]

Narrative

Like the Gospels and Acts, John's Revelation is a narrative from 1:9–22:20, which means that readers must work with plot, setting, point of view, and so forth. However, for the present purpose, characterization and repetition are the most significant aspects of narrative. Like the apocalyptic chapters of Daniel, Revelation is written as a first-person narrative in which John is present in his own story as the narrator. Although John can see and hear beyond what is normal for a human, he is not omniscient and so receives instructions and explanations from characters such as the elders, a heavenly voice, or angels (5:4–5; 10:4; 17:7). John's duties as a narrator consist mostly of recording what he sees and hears regarding other characters and the events in which they are engaged.[24]

John uses repetition for characterization in a variety of ways, but three are significant for this chapter because we wish to see how John influences his readers to worship God and maintain their testimony of Jesus.[25] First, he uses repetition to emphasize some aspect of a character. For example, the whore is rarely mentioned without her wine, which reinforces distaste (16:19; 17:4; 18:6). Second, repetition creates webs of association in which characters are linked by their similarities.[26] For example, the two largest vertical webs are associated with the holiness of God and the deceptive nature of the dragon, both of whom sit at the pinnacle of their respective allegiances. God is characterized by repetition of *holy* in the *Trisagion*, sung by the four beasts: "Holy, holy, holy, Lord God Almighty / which was, and is, and is to come" (4:8). Although God's superior holiness is indicated by triple repetition, a feature of Semitic languages, Christ (3:7), the angels (14:10), the New Jerusalem (11:2; 21:2, 10), and the Saints ("holy ones") all share this same quality.[27] The dragon, on the other hand, is introduced as the deceiver of "the whole world" (12:9), and his comrades, the beast and the false prophet, as well as Babylon, are likewise deceptive (13:14; 19:20; 18:23). Naturally, the dragon's followers are those who are deceived (13:14; 20:8). John motivates lifestyle changes in his auditors because they are moved to question their own perceptions and alignments against the allegiances established by this repetition.

Finally, characters with contrasting allegiance are brought into conversation with each other through a combination of parallel and contrasting repetition. While the Lamb shares the power, authority, and throne of God (12:10), the beast shares that of the dragon (13:2). However, the Lamb's dignity and position are derived from God, the one "which was, and is, and is to come" (4:8), while the beast's situation will degenerate as the dragon's reach is curtailed by God (16:10). In this way John reveals the essential deception of the dragon's evil: he has nothing to offer that compares with God's gracious plans, he knows that his time is short, and yet he persists in deceiving humans (12:10–12). When Revelation's characters are "read" like this, rather than decrypted by asserting a singular association with persons or events in history, John's message becomes readily pertinent in multiple historical and cultural contexts.[28] The saints overcome the world when they are faithful witnesses of God's essential holiness, for which worship is rightfully due, while the dragon's fundamentally deceptive nature calls for rejection.

Historical Context

At the most basic level, knowing the historical context of an ancient narrative helps readers by suggesting the historical period and general cultural parameters that informed the author(s) and earliest audiences. This is essential to noticing, let alone interpreting, nearly every feature of ancient literature. The most significant elements of historical context are the author, the audience, and the date. Since John's Revelation does not appear to be pseudepigraphal or otherwise deliberately anachronized, we must closely attend to the internal evidence, that is, what the text itself says about these details. The audience is the seven churches identified in Revelation: Ephesus, Smyrna, Pergamum, Thyatira, Sardis, Philadelphia, and Laodicea (1:11), but John's use of the number seven may also be symbolic, indicating he had a wider audience in mind. In any case, most of the churches of Asia Minor at the end of the first century would have had some mix of Jewish and gentile Christians. The date at which the text reached its current form was probably late in the reign of Domitian (AD 81–96). The author identifies himself as John, locates himself within his audience as a "brother," affirms his testimony of Jesus and ascribes his present difficulties to it, and gives his location as the island of Patmos, off the coast of modern Turkey (1:9). Further details regarding his identity, if they were not already known, would have been provided to his audiences by the persons who carried his letter. He shows detailed awareness of the situation in the seven churches, suggesting that his choice of *brother* is accurate, at least as far as it goes. Although he never calls himself a prophet, he is commissioned at least twice to so serve (1:9–20; 10:1–11). Intriguingly, John refers to "prophets" several times as a group, alongside "saints" and "apostles" (16:6; 18:20). In addition, John is very familiar with the Hebrew Bible (Old Testament), and he rendered his revelation as an apocalypse in ways characteristic of Jewish apocalyptic, for which there are no known examples outside Palestine. He seems to know details of Jerusalem before AD 70 and writes as if Greek were his second language.[29]

Reading John's Revelation

With this background in mind, it is now appropriate to consider certain passages in some detail, as a pattern for reading the entire text. The initial vision of Christ in 1:9–20 and the letters to the seven churches (chapters 2–3) are foundational, so we will start with Christ among the churches. Then, since the saints must discern between true and false worship, it will help to look more closely at John's critique of Babylon. Third, we will ask what John thinks the saints must do to overcome and to enter the New Jerusalem, and finally we will look at the new creation and its glory in the New Jerusalem.

Christ among the churches

Although John has been introduced earlier, a second round of identification and association begins in 1:9. This time he emphasizes his status as a member of the churches to which he writes, thus creating an emotional bond between himself and those who will listen to his letter. The voice that commands John to write to the seven churches is that of Christ; the description that follows indicates Christ's relationship with the churches in the era between his resurrection and second coming.

The characterization of Christ in this vision reveals both his identity and role. His clothing discloses his status: a long robe and chest-high sash ("girt about the paps;" 1:13) indicate high social standing, as physical laborers wore short robes and a belt to bind up the robe.[30] Although John identifies the figure he sees as "one like unto the Son of man" (1:13), an allusion to Daniel 7:13, the white hair he describes is modeled after the image of God as the "Ancient of days" in Daniel 7:9. This distinctive conflation of the one like the Son of man and the Ancient of days from the same Danielic vision suggests that Christ is also to be thought of as divine.[31] Similarly, the depiction of his eyes as flames of fire and feet as polished metal reminds readers of the powerful figure in Daniel 10:5–6. The impression is strengthened by his speech, in which Christ claims for himself the divine description in Isaiah 44:6 that "I am the first, and I am the last" but distinguishes himself from God because he overcame death precisely by dying: "I am the first and the last: I am he that liveth, and was dead; and, behold, I am alive for evermore . . . and have the keys of hell and of death" (Revelation 1:17–18). The churches may likewise expect to transcend death, should their obligation as witnesses require it, because Christ has the keys of death and hell (1:18).[32]

Beyond his appearance, Christ is pictured as standing among the oil-burning lamps that represent the seven churches. This recalls the seven-branched lampstands standing before God in the Jerusalem temple and establishes a parallel.[33] The churches are now a worshipping community like that of ancient Israel: they worship Christ, and Christ is their protector and judge. He holds the angels that govern these churches in his right hand, which connotes control, favor, and security. Judgment is symbolized by the sword that comes from his mouth, and he speaks both praise and warning to the churches (Revelation 2–3). Thus, when the churches choose their relationship with Christ, they choose their future.[34]

The letters to the seven churches in chapters 2–3 have been sources of fruitful insight for almost two thousand years. Although on the surface they appear to be a distinctive section in John's Revelation, they are tightly bound to the larger narrative through repetition. Christ, the author of the letters, typically authenticates his judgment by identifying himself with one or more features of the initial vision of Christ among the seven lampstands (e.g., 1:13; 2:1). He likewise authenticates his promises of salvation by indicating that those who overcome will participate in the life of the New Jerusalem in one way or another (e.g., 2:7; 22:2). Between these two features, he delivers summary judgment. Three churches are both commended and warned: Ephesus, Pergamum, and Thyatira are all struggling with assimilation, albeit in different ways.[35] Two churches, Smyrna and Philadelphia, receive only praise, and it is these two churches that are experiencing persecution. Sardis and Laodicea, who are described as complacent, that is, without significant challenges, receive only condemnation. Although one can read each letter separately, they are also fruitfully read in the groups indicated, as we will now do.

The immediate problem in Ephesus, to whom the first letter was addressed, was discernment of false leaders and their similarly flawed teachings (2:2–3). The Ephesians seem to have been successful in rejecting false leaders, but in the process they have lost their "first love" (2:4). It is easy to understand how such discussions could degenerate into conflict, precisely because people cared deeply about the moral and theological implications of their choices.[36] Thyatira, likewise struggling with assimilation, presents the opposite picture (2:18–29). Its members are commended for their love but warned about their toleration of Jezebel, a woman who called herself a prophet (2:20). This is likewise easy to imagine, as people may be willing to do the right thing themselves but unwilling to engage in confrontation to motivate others (2:24–25).[37] Finally, the situation in Pergamum was somewhat different, for while Ephesus and Thyatira struggled with assimilation of unacceptable Christian practices, Pergamum was contending with assimilation to pagan behaviors (2:12–17). The pressure to participate in community social events that involved eating meat sacrificed to idols must have been immense for those seeking favorable business opportunities, marriages, and other civic contracts. Some resisted, thereby accepting the limitations, while others did not. [38] Read together, all three communities are fragmented by pressures to assimilate, although in different ways. The lesson is that disciples must maintain their loving relationships even while they learn the limits of their association with pagans and discriminate among Christian leaders.

The situation in the remaining four churches revolves around the presence or absence of a threat, and in each case the justice rendered is poetic. Smyrna and Philadelphia are both threatened, although not identically (2:10; 3:8–9). To the church in Smyrna, which faces death, Christ promises life (2:10), while to the church in Philadelphia, which faces loss of public esteem through slander, he grants his own love (3:9). On the other hand, Sardis and

Laodicea face no threat and seem to be thriving, but appearances are deceiving. Sardis shows a lively front but is, in fact, dead (3:1), while Laodicea claims to be rich and secure but is poor, blind, and naked (3:17). If Sardis does not wake up, she will find herself awakened by the unexpected return of Christ (3:3), while Laodicea must move away from tepid religion to buy what is needed from Christ (3:18). Christ's judgment, not that of society, is significant.[39]

Critique of Babylon

The quality that links Babylon to the other evil entities of Revelation is their deceptive intentions, so we begin with the truth: at the center of heaven is God's throne, and God is to be worshipped because of who he is (4:8) and what he has done as creator (4:11). In the midst of the throne, so likewise at the center of heaven, is the slain Lamb, and he is to be worshipped because he redeemed humanity (5:9–10). The dragon seems to have sought to frustrate God through destruction of the man-child (12:4), but his efforts were defeated by God. The dragon then attacked heaven itself, starting a war that will last until the Second Coming, but was foiled in his initial assault by an angelic army (12:7–8). The dragon was also expelled from heaven by means of the faithful witness of the saints: the dragon had been their accuser, but because the saints kept the testimony of Jesus, their robes were washed in the blood of the Lamb (22:14), leaving no need for an accuser in heaven (12:10–11).[40] Limited to the earth, the dragon's pursuit of the woman was similarly thwarted as the earth opened her mouth and swallowed the water he sent after the woman (12:15–16). Defeated three times, expelled from heaven, and stripped of his celestial army, the dragon stands angry and alone on the seashore (13:1). John's readers now know the truth: God and the Lamb are to be worshipped, and the dragon is not. Those who think that the dragon runs riotous because he is invincible will be tempted to give up, but those who realize that he has only limited power and time will resist.[41]

How does the dragon deceive? The dragon responds to his defeats by calling up two assistants, one from the sea, which John's audiences may have understood as Rome or the Roman cult, and one from the land, representing the local cults that supported Roman religiosity in their false worship (13:1, 11). John spends the whole of chapter 13 on the characterization of these two evil figures because by so doing he reveals the hidden nature of evil in all ages: it imitates God's goodness but ultimately points those who follow it toward death.[42] The most salient characteristics of the first beast is that, like Christ, it has suffered a mortal wound (13:3). However, Christ's death brought life, while the beast's life brings death (13:7–10). The second beast is said to have two horns like a lamb, but he is unlike the Lamb in that he turns those who listen to him away from God (13:13) and toward worship of the first beast in ways that permeate day-to-day existence (13:16–17). Although humans might find the beasts powerful and compelling, John's audiences know that the depredations of the two are limited (13:5). They must endure the persecution of the beasts, but their endurance will not be in vain if they remain faithful witnesses of the rightful worship of God and the Lamb (13:10).[43]

The last great evil figure in Revelation is both revealed and destroyed in chapter 17. One of the angels invites John to look more closely at a new female figure, identified by the angel as "the great whore" (17:1). John's earliest readers would have understood this character as a symbol for Rome (17:18), but her qualities are those of every oppressive power. From a distance, she looks like a fine lady, but her characterization includes elements of both the courtesan (fancy clothing and jewelry) and the tavern prostitute (multiple partners). Her corruption becomes even more clear when one approaches closely: she is drunk rather than sober, and her intoxicant is made of vile things.[44] Her description is antithetical to that of the cosmic woman (12:1) and the bride of the Lamb (21:9–11), for the whore's glory is a weak imitation of the woman clothed in the sun (12:1), and her association with the kings of the earth make her unfit for marriage (17:2). In addition, her position is unstable. She appears powerful, riding a beast with seven heads and ten horns, but this too is an illusion, and per- haps even satire, for the beast she rides is a grotesque parody of the horses of the imperial stable. This sort of imagery acts to convince John's audience that what appears glamorous and impressive is sordid and ridiculous.[45] After the arrogance of the ten kings leads to their defeat, they will react by destroying the whore (17:12–14, 16). Although she killed the saints and enslaved the whole earth, her victims do not rise and destroy her. Instead, her end comes through her closest associates because evil is its own worst enemy.[46]

While chapter 17 describes the whore and narrates her death, chapter 18 reveals the identity and nature of the evil that consorted with her by reporting on her funeral. Baby- lon's death is announced by a third mighty angel whose brightness highlights the twilight of Babylon (18:1). Since dirges were integral to funerals, a celestial voice reports three, sung by those who had once profited from Rome's exploitation.[47] The kings mourn Babylon, but they stand sufficiently far away to avoid giving aid or being unduly discomfited (18:9–10). The merchants mourn the loss of cargo, but one sees that their mercantile instincts are like those of the whore.[48] They have devalued human life by reducing it to merchandise that works the fields, fills the brothels, entertains in the arena, and maintains an illusion of a prosperous and virtuous community (18:12–13).[49] The last to speak are the sailors, and they are very candid in their self-interest (18:17–19). The final voice is again that of an angel, who makes three accusations: Babylon encouraged her merchants to exploit the earth for their own selfish purposes, she was deceptive in her engagements, and she *slaughtered* the prophets and saints. The condemnation of Babylon follows from her opposition to God and his ways.

Although John's earliest audiences would have heard a critique of Rome in these chap- ters, that identification does not exhaust this text for modern readers. The evil described here is typically labeled "empire" in honor of Rome's place in this narrative, but it neither began nor ended there. It is any nation, organization, or community that values wealth, ease, military power, cultural sophistication, and so forth over the Creator and his creation. Empire dominates, and it does so by enticing the elites with promises of more power. The common folk, even those who have been conquered, are likewise drawn to empire but by promises of physical and financial security (13:4; 16–17). Empire looks good from a dis- tance, which fuels its expansion (18:7–9). However, the reality is that empire is exploitative, for it *must* expand to feed the appetite of elites for wealth and novelty (18:11–14), and in the end it sets itself against God by destroying what he created (11:18).[50] The real outrage is its treatment of people, however, for it buys and sells humans as chattel and regards human life as a commercial commodity (18:13), while the Lamb redeemed humans, gave them dignity through a kingdom and priesthood, and set them on the path for a fullness of life in the New Jerusalem.[51] In short, empire is condemned for idolatry and injustice, the two sins most often charged to humanity in the Bible.[52] And since the saints are told to "come out" (18:4), readers are not free to assume that they do not share in the exploitative sins of empire.

Who is able to stand?

Given the critique of empire just offered, readers are justified in wondering who makes it to the New Jerusalem and how they do so. The short answer is that God has taken it upon himself to make it so; that is, salvation is an act of grace.[53] However, a longer response is worth considering, for the revelation of God's mercy and grace is largely carried in sections of the text that scholars call the "interludes" (embedded narratives) because they halt the forward progression of God's judgments. The most significant, in 7:1–17, indicates that God has offered a means of redemption for those who will seize it, and the rest of the interludes likewise depict divine grace still working within creation.[54]

The first interlude is part of the seal septet (6:1–8:4). One of the principal rhetorical functions of the first four seals and the first four trumpets is to shatter any illusions about being able to escape judgment.[55] The first four seals release war, violence, famine, pestilence, and death on humans (6:1–8). The first four trumpets strike the earth, its vegetation, the ocean, sources of fresh water, and the sky, darkening the sun, moon, and stars (8:7–12). In short, there is no place or nation to which one can flee for safety. The issue is put succinctly with the opening of the sixth seal (6:15–17): "And the kings of the earth, and the great men, and the rich men, and the chief captains, and the mighty men, and every bondman, and every free man, hid themselves in the dens and in the rocks of the mountains; and said to the mountains and rocks, Fall on us, and hide us from the face of him that sitteth on the throne, and from the wrath of the Lamb: for the great day of his wrath is come; and who shall be able to stand?"

Readers will notice that there are seven social classes listed, from kings to slaves, indicating that all of humanity poses this question. One response has already been given, for with the opening of the fifth seal the voices of the martyrs speak from under the altar in the heavenly temple, asking God for judgment. Nothing remains for them to do, and thus they are told simply to wait (6:9–11).[56] However, for those still on the earth, the question is so pertinent that the forward progress of John's vision is interrupted for an entire chapter (7:1–17).

As chapter 7 opens, four angels are prepared to release their destructive winds on the earth, the sea, and the trees. A fifth angel appears, carrying the seal of God, probably thought of as a signet ring, and warns the four angels to hold off until they have marked the servants of God on their foreheads with the seal (7:3). Those who can claim the dignity of this relationship with God will not face his displeasure. The text does not say what form the mark took, but it does indicate that those who serve God now belong to him, and they enjoy protection from the demonic armies of the trumpet cycle (9:4) but not from the depredations of the beast (13:7–10). John hears that 144,000 from the tribes of Israel have been so sealed (7:4), invoking the promises of Israel's prophets, but he sees an innumerable multitude from every nation, tribe, people, and language (7:9), indicating the universal fulfillment of these divine promises. According to an elder whose role is to explain the scene to John, the innumerable multitude who stand before the throne of God do so because they have "washed their robes, and made them white in the blood of the Lamb" (7:13–14), a repentance motif with implications for the title "servant of God." Finally, the interlude ends with a cascading chain of promises that likewise extend the assurances first made to Israel to the rest of humanity.[57]

The bride, the wife of the Lamb

The culmination of God's promises is presented by John in 21:1–22:5 as several significant eschatological passages from Israel's prophets are reprised, as are the promises to those who overcome in Revelation 2–3. This section is divided into three parts, each of which penetrates more deeply into the mystery of the final state of humans. The first part, 21:1–8, is focused on the broad details of the new creation. In 21:9–21, John accompanies an angel on a tour of the New Jerusalem, a symbolic city that represents both the redeemed and their society. Finally, John concludes with a description of the significant elements of the interior of the city and the final state of those humans who have overcome (22:1–5).[58] In all three sections, the emphasis has shifted from destruction to describing the profound renewal of the earth and those who inhabit it. This new earth, rather than traditional portrayals of heaven, becomes the final dwelling place of God, the Lamb, and humans.[59]

The description of the new heaven and earth in 21:1–8 echoes a similar declaration in Isaiah 65:17 and 66:22 and is announced in a chiasm centered on the New Jerusalem:

> *new* heaven and *new* earth (verse 1a)
>> the first heaven, earth and sea have *passed away* (verse 1b)
>>> the sea *exists no longer* (verse 1b)
>>>> the holy city descends (verse 2)
>>>> God dwells with humans (verses 3–4a)
>>> death *exists no longer* (verse 4b)
>> former things have *passed away* (verse 4b)
> God creates everything *new* (verse 5a)[60]

Two points are of immediate interest. First, the Greek word behind "new" is καινός, which has a sense of qualitative, rather than temporal, newness. This is a new reality accomplished by God's creative activity after the destruction of the old order.[61] Second, the obliteration of the sea follows from the roles of this body of water in the earlier chapters of John's vision. Foremost among them are the sea as the place from which the dragon summoned his evil helpers (13:1), the sea as the place of the dead (20:13), and the sea as the principal location of Babylon's evil mercantile activities (18:10–19). Thus, there will be no threat from Satan, no more death, and no further commercial exploitation.[62]

Verses 5–8 are often considered the theological climax of John's vision, as God speaks seven times from the throne, first to describe himself and his role, then to clarify the new situation in which humans find themselves. His announcement that he is making "*all things new*" (21:5; emphasis added) extends Isaiah's announcement that God was doing "*a new thing*" (Isaiah 43:19; emphasis added). The divine assurance that "it is done" (Revelation 21:6) indicates that God's plans end not with destruction but with creation, and God's self-identification as the "Alpha and the Omega, the beginning and the end" (21:6) means that the culmination of history is a person rather than an event. The remainder of this section describes the two eschatological alternatives for humans. They either enjoy a life in familial relationship with God and inherit his promises, an intimacy not offered before the new creation, or they inherit (have a share in) punishment (21:6–8). It is no accident that the vice list in 22:8 leads off with cowardice and faithlessness because those two traits would have led to compromise with evil. Beyond that, the abominable share the qualities of Babylon (17:4): murders take lives including those of the martyrs, whoremongers are unfaithful to their commitments, sorcerers reflect the activities of the beast (13:13–14), idolaters fail to worship correctly, and liars facilitate the deceptive behaviors of the dragon and his associates (12:9).[63] This depiction of the stark choice between life with God and the second death is another opportunity for John's listeners to examine their allegiance and behavior.

In the second section of John's description of the new creation, readers move in for a detailed view of the New Jerusalem. Just as John received an angelic invitation to see and understand the collapse of Babylon (17:1), so now he similarly views the descent from heaven of its antithesis, the New Jerusalem (21:9), once again indicating that readers are faced with a choice. And just as John measured the earthly temple in 11:1–2 with a reed, so now an angel measures the heavenly city with a golden reed (21:15) as John describes what he sees.[64] The initial and overwhelming impression is that the city reflects the beauty of God with its references to radiance and to gems, particularly jasper (4:3; 21:11, 18–19). The organization of the city alludes to, and extends, Ezekiel's description of the temple complex in Ezekiel 40–48. The twelve gates of the temple in Ezekiel 48:30–35 become the twelve gates of the New Jerusalem, although the focus in John's vision is on the ease of access to the city. The city is laid out "foursquare," just as was the temple in Ezekiel 42:15–20, although rather than a square, it is a cube and thus one degree of perfection greater than what was envisioned by Ezekiel, and its overall dimensions are significantly greater.[65] The conditions of life in the city are described by a series of alternating positive and negative statements. The city has no temple, no sun, no moon, no closed gates, and nothing defiled, abominable, or deceptive. From this, it follows that it has the presence and glory of God and the Lamb, no threats to peace or security, and citizens who are enrolled in the Lamb's book of life (Isaiah 60:3, 5, 11, 19). The implications of this for those so favored is elaborated upon in the final section.

John's last vision is narrowly focused on what appears to be the center section of the New Jerusalem (Revelation 22:1–5). No voices will speak because the richness of the imagery carries all that needs to be said. As has been the case throughout this section, John's vision redevelops images from the Old Testament. The river of life and the tree of life in the center of the tableau create the sense of a renewed Eden, although this time surrounded by a city in a joyful fusion of urban and rural imagery. The river, the first unpolluted stream in Revelation, flows from the throne of God and the Lamb, envisioned as a *bisellium* or dual throne, in an allusion to the water that flows from the temple in Ezekiel 47:1–12. The tree of life is probably growing over the top of the stream, in imitation of the sacred oasis in Greco-Roman literature. Its fecundity indicates that the citizens of the New Jerusalem will lack for nothing, and the notice that the leaves are for the healing of the nations stands in contrast to Babylon, which looted the nations for its own pleasure.[66]

Just as the physical description of the city centers on God and the Lamb, so too does the life of the humans who live there. All are marked as the servants of God by having his name on each of their foreheads, rather than just those males descended from Aaron. Although fully seeing God's face formerly brought death (Exodus 33:2), such intimacy is now simply part of life. Finally, the saints are said to "reign forever and ever," just as do God and the Lamb (Revelation 22:5; 11:15). No information is given regarding whom they rule over, but there is no question that the end of John's vision is not the end of all things, but rather a new beginning.[67]

Conclusion

John's Revelation is first and foremost a source of encouragement and insight. It is, to be sure, packaged in a combination of genres that are unfamiliar to many modern readers, expressed in symbolism that is best read with some background in first-century Christianity, and marked with violence that seems over-the-top to modern sensibilities. However, those who get past these surface features are confronted with the most profound prophetic call for authentic worship and pervasive reflection and repentance in the entire Bible as Babylon is thoroughly critiqued. John goes beyond the prophetic, however, to affirm that through the Lamb's selfless offering, God's creation will transcend death and hell, becoming a new creation in which evil is no longer present. To participate in this new creation, those who follow the Shepherd-Lamb can neither withdraw from this world, for they must be witnesses of the Lamb, nor assimilate to it, for they must come out (and stay out) of Babylon. Unfortunately, humans cannot extricate themselves from Babylon, which may be why the invitation to wash one's garments in the blood of the Lamb is among the last exhortations in the book (22:14). The sacrificial death of the Lamb, then, and the prophetic witness of those who follow him are the twin pillars of God's plan for the redemption of creation. In this sense, Revelation is indeed a blueprint of the future.

D. Jill Kirby is an assistant professor of religious studies at Edgewood College in Madison, Wisconsin.

Further Reading

Aune, David E. *Revelation 1–5*. Word Biblical Commentary 52A. Dallas: Word, 1997.

———. *Revelation 6–16*. Word Biblical Commentary 52B. Nashville: Nelson, 1998.

———. *Revelation 17–22*. Word Biblical Commentary 52C. Nashville: Nelson, 1998.

Bauckham, Richard. *The Theology of the Book of Revelation*. New York: Cambridge, 1993.

Carey, Greg. *Apocalyptic Literature in the New Testament*. Nashville: Abingdon, 2016.

Koester, Craig R. *Revelation: A New Translation with Introduction and Commentary*. Anchor Yale Bible Commentaries. New Haven: Yale, 2014.

Levine, Amy-Jill, ed., with Maria Mayo Robbins. *A Feminist Companion to the Apocalypse of John*. New York: T&T Clark, 2009.

Resseguie, James L. *The Revelation of John: A Narrative Commentary*. Grand Rapids, MI: Baker Academic, 2009.

Notes

1. The Greek phrase translated "lead them" in 7:17 is *poimanei autous*, literally "shepherd them." Notice of this paradoxical Shepherd-Lamb imagery is nearly ubiquitous in commentaries, and pasturing the divine flock is also predicated of God in Isaiah 49 and Psalm 23, but interested readers can begin with G. K. Beale, *The Book of Revelation* (Grand Rapids, MI: Eerdmans, 2013), 442.

2. Craig R. Koester, *Revelation and the End of All Things* (Grand Rapids, MI: Eerdmans, 2001), 40.

3. In fact, the phrase "how long" as a demand for vengeance is found at least fifty times in scripture, most often in the Psalms and in Jeremiah. See Wes Howard and Anthony Gwynther, *Unveiling Empire: Reading Revelation Then and Now* (Maryknoll, NY: Orbis, 1999), 142.

4. Some scholars have argued that the depiction of the violent end of the whore (17:16), as well as John's verbal assault on Jezebel (2:20–23), has hurt women. For an introduction to the argument, see Tina Pippin, "Eros and the End: Reading for Gender in the Apocalypse of John," *Semeia* 59 (1992): 193–210. See the larger commentary by Koester for more citations.

5. Michael J. Gorman, *Reading Revelation Responsibly: Uncivil Worship and Witness: Following the Lamb into the New Creation* (Eugene, OR: Cascade, 2011), 155–58.

6. Gorman, *Reading Revelation*, 150–51.

7. Koester, *End of All Things*, 175–79.

8. Gorman, *Reading Revelation*, 153.

9. Gorman, *Reading Revelation*, 152.

10. Gorman, *Reading Revelation*, 155. See also 1 Nephi 14, in which the saints are "armed with righteousness and with the power of God in great glory" rather than traditional weapons, while the nations of earth are beset with "wars and rumors of wars" (14:14–15).

11. Koester, *Revelation: A New Translation with Introduction and Commentary* (New Haven, CT: Yale University Press, 2014), 693–94.

12. Koester, *End of All Things*, 149–50.

13. Koester, *Revelation*, 307–8. More reflection on gendered and sexualized violence in Revelation may be found on pages 693–95.

14. Richard Bauckham, *The Theology of the Book of Revelation* (New York: Cambridge University Press, 2013), 144.

15. Frederick J. Murphy, *Apocalypticism in the Bible and Its World: A Comprehensive Introduction* (Grand Rapids, MI: Baker Academic, 2012), 5.

16. John J. Collins, *Apocalyptic Imagination: An Introduction to Jewish Apocalyptic Literature*, 2nd ed. (Grand Rapids, MI: Eerdmans, 2010), 5.

17. Adele Yarbro Collins, "Introduction: Early Christian Apocalypticism," *Semeia* 36 (1986): 7; emphasis added.

18. Beale, *Revelation*, 57.

19. Koester, *End of All Things*, 158, 159–60.

20. M. Eugene Boring, *Revelation* (Louisville, KY: Westminster John Knox, 2011), 55–56.

21. Boring, *Revelation*, 52. For example, in both Genesis and Revelation we learn our place in the rest of God's creation.

22. James L. Resseguie, *The Revelation of John: A Narrative Commentary* (Grand Rapids, MI: Baker Academic, 2009), 28–32. This source provides a relatively comprehensive introduction to numerical symbolism in Revelation. The significance of the seven beatitudes of Revelation is summarized in Gorman, *Reading Revelation*, 39.

23. Richard Bauckham, *The Climax of Prophecy: Studies on the Book of Revelation* (New York: T&T Clark, 1993), 29–37.

24. James L. Resseguie, *Narrative Criticism of the New Testament: An Introduction* (Grand Rapids, MI: Baker Academic, 2005), 121.

25. Janice Capel Anderson, *Matthew's Narrative Web: Over and Over and Over Again* (Sheffield, England: JSOT, 1994), 44.

26. James L. Resseguie, *Revelation Unsealed: A Narrative Critical Approach to John's Apocalypse*, vol. 32, *Biblical Interpretation Series*, ed. R. Alan Culpepper and Rolf Rendtorff (Boston: Brill, 1998), 124, 128, 142.

27. Leonard L. Thompson, *The Book of Revelation: Apocalypse and Empire* (New York: Oxford University, 1997), 78.

28. Resseguie, *Revelation Unsealed*, 103–4.

29. David E. Aune, *Revelation 1–5* (Grand Rapids, MI: Zondervan, 1997), xlix–l.

30. Koester, *Revelation*, 245.

31. Bruce M. Metzger, *Breaking the Code: Understanding the Book of Revelation* (Nashville, TN: Abingdon, 1993), 26–27.

32. Koester, *Revelation*, 254.

33. Koester, *Revelation*, 255.

34. Koester, *End of All Things*, 54.

35. Koester, *End of All Things*, 57, 63, 66.

36. Metzger, *Breaking the Code*, 32.

37. Koester, *End of All Things*, 60–61.

38. Koester, *End of All Things*, 57–62.

39. Koester, *End of All Things*, 56.

40. Koester, *End of All Things*, 122.

41. Koester, *End of All Things*, 123.

42. Gorman, *Reading Revelation*, 123–26.

43. Koester, *End of All Things*, 126–27.

44. Grant R. Osborne, *Revelation* (Grand Rapids, MI: Baker Academic, 2002), 611–12.

45. Koester, *End of All Things*, 156.

46. Koester, *End of All Things*, 161.

47. Osborne, *Revelation*, 644.

48. Koester, *End of All Things*, 165–66.

49. Metzger, *Breaking the Code*, 86.

50. Gorman, *Reading Revelation*, 145–47.

51. Koester, *End of All Things*, 79–80.

52. Gorman, *Reading Revelation*, 146.

53. Metzger, *Breaking the Code*, 96.

54. Koester, *Revelation*, 113.

55. Other readings are quite possible; see, for example, Doctrine and Covenants 77:7. My reading follows from interest in Revelation as a guide to living as a disciple in the present.

56. Koester, *End of All Things*, 87.

57. Koester, *End of All Things*, 90.

58. Resseguie, *Revelation*, 251.

59. Greg Carey, *Apocalyptic Literature in the New Testament* (Nashville: Abingdon, 2016), 130–31.

60. Aune, *Revelation*, 1114.

61. Osborne, *Revelation*, 729–30.

62. Beale, *Revelation*, 1041–42.

63. Koester, *Revelation*, 806–10.

64. This also echoes the measurements of the temple environs by a man who appeared "like bronze" in Ezekiel 40–41.

65. Osborne, *Revelation*, 747–55.

66. Koester, *Revelation*, 831–35.

67. Beale, *Revelation*, 1116.

Part 5

New Testament
Issues and Contexts

27

Understanding the Physical and Metaphysical Geography of the New Testament

George A. Pierce

The New Testament is replete with geographic place-names, terms, and imagery that provide details for the audiences of the various books. To help readers fully appreciate the efforts of the New Testament authors to include geographic details into their compositions, this chapter will discuss the importance of geography for scripture study, give an overview of the physical regions and sites of the New Testament with case studies that provide an awareness of the life setting of the text, and illustrate the metaphysical, or spiritual, geography of the New Testament. Those who study and teach the New Testament are encouraged to consider how geographic elements influence the interpretation and application of a story.

The question of the relevance of New Testament geographic details often arises for a modern reader given the separation of both time and distance from the original physical settings. In their assessment of the New Testament's historical geography, Anson Rainey and Steven Notley observe that "the narrative of the New Testament from its beginning to end assumes the reader is familiar with the physical setting that served as a stage for the unfolding drama."[1] While not intending to write works on geography or the natural world like Strabo (ca. 63 BC–AD 24) or Pliny the Elder (AD 23–79), the authors of the New Testament included geographic regional names, place-names, topographic indicators, and other elements to help situate their narratives of real people and real events within real locales for their audiences. The inclusion of such details by the New Testament authors presupposes that those places meant something to the original audience either within their sociopolitical context or as cognitive maps of past events associated with various places.

Given the importance of the regions and place-names associated with the Savior's ministry to the original audiences of the Gospels, an understanding of their geography aids in comprehending the events of the Savior's life and their significance. Thus, geography, history, and archaeology help establish and illuminate the context of the New Testament, and in turn, context may nuance the understanding and application of a text.[2]

Before we examine the physical geography of the New Testament, some aspects involving geographic statements within the text should be noted. First, the authors' own awareness of geographic reality (first- or secondhand) is apparent; that is, the authors connected events with places and included those places where necessary in their accounts. Throughout the New Testament, the intentional use of regional names or place-names is a purposeful element in the narrative, not merely filler material. Second, because the authors of the New Testament did not provide maps with their writings, movement had to be conveyed by description; the audiences were either familiar with the territories and places or relied on secondhand knowledge to fill in mental gaps. Certain textual components like those describing the maritime landscape such as the coastal zone (Mark 4:1; 5:21), bodies of water like the Mediterranean and the Sea of Galilee and their waves (Matthew 8:23–27; Mark 6:49; John 6:17–19; Acts 27), and ships (Matthew 8–9; 14:32–33; Mark 4:1, 36; John 21; James 3:4) would have been familiar even to those who did not live directly adjacent to the sea.

Third, for the ancient inhabitants of eastern Mediterranean lands, their orientation within the physical world was typically toward the east rather than the north, as privileged on modern maps. Directions within the New Testament are expressed as "up to Jerusalem" (found in the Gospels, Acts, and Galatians) or "down to Capernaum" (Luke 4:31) and refer to topographic situations and changes in elevation rather than any association with cardinal directions (e.g., up = northward and down = southward). Thus, at the end of Paul's second missionary journey, his travel from Ephesus to Jerusalem and Antioch as recorded in Acts 18:22 relates both of these directions: "And when he had landed at Caesarea, and gone up [in elevation to Jerusalem situated southeast of Caesarea], and saluted the church, he went down [in elevation] to Antioch [about 300 miles north of Jerusalem]." The references of "going up" to Jerusalem or descending from the holy city are more than directional or topographic because the concept of ascending was also ideological since one always "ascended" to the temple even from higher elevations. This concept is emphasized in Psalm 24:3–6 and the psalms of ascent (Psalms 120–34), which may be connected to pilgrims traveling to the Temple Mount or the Levitical priests ascending the fifteen steps between the Court of the Women and the Court of Israel at the temple.

Finally, the physical geography described serves to illustrate a theological geographic aspect to the text.[3] For example, Simon Peter's confession of Jesus as the Christ (Matthew 16:16) occurred at Caesarea Philippi, in the northernmost part of the Holy Land and near the upper limit of Israel's Old Testament border. Jesus then physically and theologically moved from the periphery of the Holy Land to the religious core of Judaism as he proceeded to Jerusalem to accomplish the Atonement.[4] Further, this theological geography includes place-names or references to Old Testament stories with place-names that illustrate why a place was holy. In this way the story of Jacob's dream in Genesis 28:10–22 explains the place-name *Bethel* as "the house of God," and Jesus makes an allusion to being the physical embodiment of this concept as he described "the angels of God ascending and descending upon the Son of man" (John 1:51). References to Old Testament places and events such as Sodom and Gomorrah (Matthew 11:23–24; Mark 6:11; Luke 10:12; Jude 1:7), the patriarchal narratives (Acts 7), or the Exodus and experience at Sinai (Hebrews 3:16; 11:27; Jude 1:5) in recorded speeches or within the written discourse acknowledged the church's heritage and tied the believers in Christ to the theology and salvation history of Israel. Likewise, the inclusion of tribal territories such as Zebulon and Naphtali and the subsequent quotation of Isaiah 9:1–2 in reference to the commencement of Jesus's ministry (Matthew 4:12–16) links the postexilic villages of Nazareth and Capernaum with Old Testament Israel through text and geography, deftly illustrating Jesus as the fulfillment of Isaiah's prophecy. Such elements of theological geography and references to Israel's past assume that the original audience had familiarity with the historical and prophetic material of the Hebrew Bible. These issues serve to inform the modern reader of the complex nature of geographic information gleaned from the New Testament.

Physical Geography

With their focus solely on the life, death, and resurrection of Jesus Christ, the Gospels are limited in their geographic scope to the area shaped by the kingdom of Herod the Great (ruled 39–4 BC).[5] As a vassal of Rome, Herod controlled territory bordered by the province of Syria to the north, the self-ruling cities of the Decapolis to the east, and the kingdom of the Nabateans to the south. Herod's reign extended over the regions with names familiar to the New Testament reader such as Galilee, Samaria, Perea (Transjordan; KJV "beyond the Jordan"), Judea, Idumea, and areas northeast of Galilee.[6] Herod's prolific construction projects included either renovations or new buildings at Samaria (called Sebaste in the Roman period), the creation of a port and Roman administrative center at Caesarea Maritima, fortresses and palaces at Masada and Herodium, and numerous other ventures at various sites. In Jerusalem, Herod oversaw the completion of fortifications, a palace, an aqueduct system, the expansion of the Temple Mount platform and colonnades, the construction of the Antonia Fortress adjacent to the Temple Mount enclosure, and renovations to the temple structure itself.

Geography serves as a structure for the sequence of Jesus's ministry as presented in the Synoptic Gospels. Jesus's birth in Bethlehem of Judea and childhood in Lower Galilean Nazareth are briefly mentioned in Matthew and Luke with Jesus's birth there fulfilling Micah's prophecy: "But thou, Beth-lehem Ephratah, though thou be little among the thousands of Judah, yet out of thee shall he come forth unto me that is to be ruler in Israel; whose goings forth have been from of old, from everlasting" (Micah 5:2). With minimal explanation, the allusion to Jesus's ancestor David by referring to Bethlehem, David's birthplace, as "the city of David" (Luke 2:4, 11) invites the audience to interpret the angelic proclamation that "the

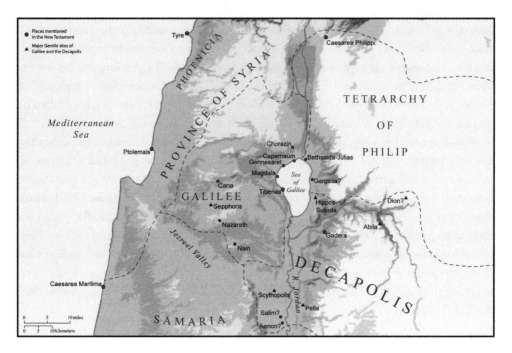

Regions and places in Galilee mentioned in the Gospels. Map by George A. Pierce.

Lord God shall give unto him [Mary's son] the throne of his father David: and he shall reign over the house of Jacob for ever; and of his kingdom there shall be no end" (1:32–33) in light of the promise made to David that "thine house and thy kingdom shall be established for ever before thee: thy throne shall be established for ever" (2 Samuel 7:16).[7] Little is said of Nazareth other than Matthew's association of the village with either the Hebrew *natzor* (one who is kept or protected, referring to the divine warnings and protection) or *nētzer* (branch) found in Isaiah 11:1, Jeremiah 23:5, and Zechariah 3:8.[8] Contempt for Nazareth's status as an obscure, unimportant locale, evinced by archaeology, is shown in Nathanael's statement "Can there any good thing come out of Nazareth?" (John 1:46) and the Pharisees' opinion "Search, and look: for out of Galilee ariseth no prophet" (John 7:52).[9] However, as George Adam Smith noted, the chief lesson of Nazareth lies in its position near major trade routes close to Sepphoris, a thriving gentile center, the temptations that the youth of Nazareth faced daily, the proximity of biblical events contrasted with the worldly power and consumption, and the possibility of emerging spotless in the face of such enticements.[10]

Apart from the birth and infancy narratives of Matthew and Luke, the Synoptic Gospels generally focus on Jesus's ministry in Galilee, a journey to northern cities such as Sidon and Caesarea Philippi, a later ministry in Judea and Perea, and a final period in Jerusalem before his death and resurrection.[11] In contrast, the Gospel of John, while including Galilean episodes, mainly concentrates on Jesus's ministry in Judea and Samaria.[12] While events at some inland villages such as Nazareth, Cana, and Nain are recounted,[13] all four Gospels associate the Savior's Galilean ministry with villages and towns surrounding the Sea of Galilee such

View of Caesarea Philippi. Courtesy of Lincoln H. Blumell.

as Capernaum (Matthew 4:13; 8:5; Mark 9:33; Luke 4:31), Chorazin (Matthew 11:21; Luke 10:13), Bethsaida (Matthew 11:21; Mark 6:45; 8:22; Luke 9:10; 10:13; John 1:44; 12:21), and "the country of the Gergesenes [Gadarenes/Gerasenes]" (Matthew 8:28–34; Mark 5:1–20; Luke 8:26–39), with Tiberias (John 6:1, 23) and Magdala (Matthew 15:39) employed as reference points and not places visited by the Savior.[14]

The northern sojourn in the Synoptic Gospels marks a turning point in Jesus's ministry from a concentration on preaching, teaching, and healing in the environs around the Sea of Galilee to his decision to go to Jerusalem to accomplish the Atonement. The highlight of the northern journey of Christ is clearly the confession of Peter at Caesarea Philippi. An understanding of the site and its monumental buildings adds a nuanced layer to the discussion between Jesus and his disciples and Peter's answer recorded in Matthew 16:13–19. The physical setting is given as "the coasts [i.e., region] of Caesarea Philippi," where Jesus asked the disciples about the prevailing public opinion of his identity with various responses given relating to Old Testament prophets such as Elijah, Jeremiah, or even John the Baptist. When the question was posed to the disciples, Peter responded, "Thou art the Christ, the Son of the living God" (Matthew 16:16), and Christ commended Peter for receiving revelation from God, then stated that his church would be built on the revelation that he is the Christ, promising keys of authority to Peter (Matthew 16:17–19). While the location may be quickly passed over in a reading of the text, the context of the discussion adds weight to the statements made. Caesarea Philippi was built by Herod Philip, the son of Herod the Great, in 2 BC at a sanctuary of the pagan deity Pan called Paneas (modern Banias), dated to the third century BC and situated near one of the headwaters of the Jordan River.[15] Herod the Great had built a temple to Caesar Augustus known as an *Augusteum* at the site. The worship of the emperor Augustus is closely tied to his autobiographical work, *Res Gestae Divi Augusti* ("The Deeds of the Divine Augustus"), a composition that documented the various acts and benefactions that Augustus performed in his lifetime, which would accord him the right of veneration and the status of a divine son of a divine father, Julius Caesar.[16] Thus, the difference between the Roman imperial cult, centered on Augustus and his deeds, and Jesus Christ and his gospel is clearly shown here at Caesarea Philippi. The disciples must make the choice as to which is more important: what their temporal context considers to be the works of a divine son or what spiritual revelation and the ministry of Christ have testified to them. The contrast between the world and Savior echoes into the modern era.

In addition to the confession of Jesus as the Christ in contrast to Augustus and his cult and the location being far removed from the core of Judaism, the location of Caesarea Philippi is also important since there Jesus announced his determination to go to Jerusalem "and suffer many things of the elders and chief priests and scribes, and be killed, and be raised again the third day" (Matthew 16:21). Because it was located near one of the headwaters of the Jordan River, military forces throughout time intent on invading the region, such as the Aramaeans, Assyrians, Babylonians, and others, would stop to replenish their water stores before campaigning southward through Galilee and into the Old Testament kingdoms of Israel and Judah. From Caesarea Philippi, Christ's prophecy of his passion and the events in the Synoptic Gospels intimate that Jesus would symbolically conquer the Holy Land as he moved south to Jerusalem. The Jerusalem known by Jesus would have been the epicenter of Jewish religious life with the central focus being the temple. With the conclusion in ca. AD 26 of renovations to the temple originally started by Herod the Great, the temple and its associated structures would have inspired the awe of visitors like the Galilean disciples recorded in Matthew 24:1. The sites associated with Christ's last days and the Atonement in and near Jerusalem such as the Upper Room, Gethsemane, Pilate's praetorium, Calvary, or the tomb may not have their exact locations identified and marked for modern visitors, and traditions associated with such sites require careful analysis.[17] Yet the significance of those events only adds to the centrality of Jerusalem within the biblical tradition as a place where Jehovah would set his name and establish a place to worship (Deuteronomy 12:11), where Jesus would suffer, die, and rise again (Matthew 16:21), and from which the apostolic church would grow and spread throughout the Roman Empire.

The expansion of the early church is predicted by the Savior in Acts 1:8: "Ye shall be witnesses unto me both in Jerusalem, and in all Judea, and in Samaria, and unto the uttermost part of the earth." Still steeped in Judaism, the church in Jerusalem had an affinity with the temple and found its converts in the Jews of the diaspora who returned to Jerusalem to celebrate the pilgrimage feasts such as Passover, the Feast of Weeks (Pentecost), or the Feast of Tabernacles and those from various parts of the Roman Empire who chose to stay in Jerusalem (Acts 2–7). Following the martyrdom of Stephen, the church spread from Jerusalem into parts of Judea and Samaria because of the missions of the apostles Peter and John and

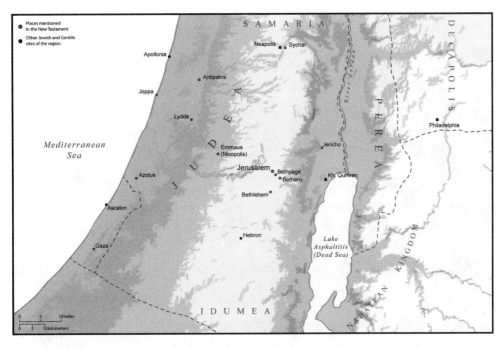

Regions and places surrounding Judea mentioned in the Gospels and Acts. Map by George A. Pierce.

others, including Philip, a deacon, who preached in Samaria and to the Ethiopian eunuch before ministering in coastal sites like Azotus (Old Testament Ashdod) and Caesarea Maritima (Acts 8). Coastal sites such as Jaffa and Caesarea also witnessed events connected to Peter and the spread of the gospel to the Gentiles (Acts 10). The rapid expansion of the church is documented within Acts as those who believe in Christ moved northward and westward because of persecution in Jerusalem and Judea. Congregations are noted in Damascus (Acts 9:2), Phoenicia (coastal Lebanon), Cyprus, and Syrian Antioch, where the followers of Jesus were first called Christians (Acts 11:19, 26).

The conversion of Saul, later known as the apostle Paul, marks the beginning of the next phase of church growth "unto the uttermost part of the earth." Following his conversion, baptism, a period of study in Arabia, and time in his hometown of Tarsus in Cilicia, Paul started to travel to preach the gospel in various regions of Cyprus, Asia Minor (modern Turkey), Macedonia, Greece, and eventually Italy. Paul's companions varied throughout the journeys (e.g., Barnabas, Mark, Timothy, Silas, and Luke), and the locales varied as well. He and his companion(s) visited towns, establishing congregations of believers, and revisited those flocks on subsequent journeys to give further instruction and encouragement. Further enlargement of the church is reflected in the addressees of other epistles such as "the twelve tribes scattered abroad" (James 1:1), "the strangers scattered throughout Pontus, Galatia, Cappadocia, Asia, and Bithynia" (1 Peter 1:1), and the seven churches in Asia Minor named in Revelation 1:11.

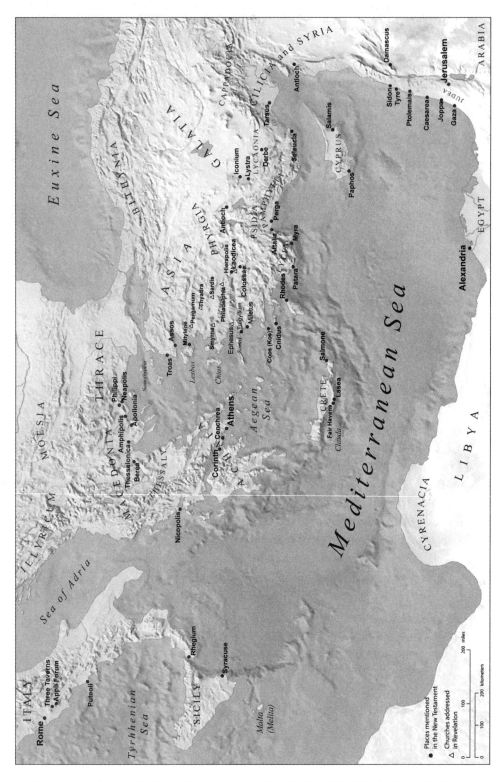

Regions and places in the Roman Empire mentioned in Acts–Revelation. Map by George A. Pierce.

Certain places that Paul visited are reflected in the titles of epistles found in the New Testament, such as Galatia, Colossae, Ephesus, Macedonian Philippi, Thessalonica, and Corinth. Here again, the history and culture of various places such as Thessalonica aids the modern reader in understanding the events that transpired at a certain site and how those events affected the missionary work of Paul and inspired epistles containing doctrinal teachings. In the Roman period, Thessalonica was considered the capital of Macedonia and a commercial hub along the *Via Egnatia*, an east–west route connecting Byzantium (later Constantinople, modern Istanbul) to Dyrrhachium on the Adriatic Sea (in modern Albania), the closest port to the Italian peninsula.[18] The city was founded in 315 BC and named after Alexander the Great's half sister. Thessalonica fell under Roman control in 168 BC, and the Romans dismantled the Macedonian aristocracy. Through deft political maneuvering, the city of Thessalonica found itself allied with victorious Roman powers in the turbulent years of the second and first centuries BC, siding with the Roman general Metellus against a local rebel named Andriscus, supporting Mark Antony and Octavian against Brutus and Cassius following Caesar's assassination, and backing Octavian in his civil war with Mark Antony. Thessalonica was awarded the status of being a "free city" without a Roman garrison and was able to govern itself according to its own laws and customs.[19] Inscriptions indicate the presence of Jews and Samaritans in Thessalonica and throughout Macedonia, a situation encountered by Paul on his second missionary journey (Acts 16:13; 17:1, 10).

According to his custom, Paul preached to the Jews in the synagogue at Thessalonica about Christ's sufferings and resurrection, and some Jews and Gentiles were converted to the gospel (Acts 17:1–4). The Jewish population that rejected Paul's message, aided by hired rabble, accused Paul and Silas, saying, "These that have turned the world upside down are come hither also; whom Jason hath received: and these all do contrary to the decrees of Caesar, saying that there is another king, one Jesus" (Acts 17:6–7), after which Paul and Silas were quickly sent to Berea. The accusations by the Jews reflect the culture of the city of Thessalonica in that the news of disturbances in places like Philippi had reached Thessalonica, and the city's status as a free city would be jeopardized if chaos ensued. The preaching of "another king, one Jesus" may have been interpreted as a prediction of the emperor's death, which was contrary to imperial decrees enacted by Augustus and Tiberius, and the beginning of a potential revolt against Rome aimed at restoring the Macedonian monarchy. These elements showcase the precarious nature of Paul's missionary efforts in navigating the history and culture of a place and the reaction of Jews unpersuaded by Paul's preaching, and how the gospel spread despite opposition and the necessity to move hastily to other towns. Because of his brief time with the Thessalonians, the epistles that he wrote, considered to be some of the earliest written portions of the New Testament, contain foundational teachings for the early Christians about the Second Coming.

Metaphysical Geography

The Bible begins and ends with cosmic geography, namely Eden and the New Jerusalem, and the New Testament contains numerous references to metaphysical geography, considered as real as physical locations within the text.[20] While the scope of this chapter precludes a lengthy discussion, the concepts of darkness and light, heaven and hell as literal places, and the reality of the kingdom of heaven or kingdom of God on earth are evident throughout the New Testament. The central message of Jesus Christ in the Gospels, echoed by the authors of the Epistles, is the establishment of the kingdom of heaven, sometimes referred to as the kingdom of God (Matthew 4:17, 23).[21] This kingdom is depicted as a metaphysical reality "promised to them that love him" (James 2:5) and a fulfillment of prophecies concerning the gathering of Israel (Isaiah 52:7–12) and the establishment of an everlasting kingdom (Zechariah 14:9–17). The author of Hebrews described it as "a kingdom which cannot be moved" (Hebrews 12:28), and Peter stated that it would be an "everlasting kingdom of our Lord and Saviour Jesus Christ" (2 Peter 1:11). While the expectation of the Jewish populace during Jesus's ministry equated the appearance of the Messiah with the establishment of a physical kingdom of God, the reality presented by Christ was a kingdom that would need incubation and growth and be fully realized at his Second Coming. The coming of the kingdom is a process and not an event.

Salvation is pictured as moving from darkness into light (1 Peter 2:9; 1 John 2:8–11), and perseverance can be seen in the encouragement to dwell in the light (1 Timothy 6:16). The place of rest or reward designated as heaven, found throughout the New Testament, is augmented by titles such as "heavenly places" (Ephesians 1:3, 20; 2:6), "paradise" (Luke 23:43), or features like "mansions" (John 14:2). These environs are contrasted with places of imprisonment, punishment, or judgment such as "perdition" (1 Timothy 6:9), "hell" (Matthew 16:18; 23:33; Luke 10:15), "the deep" (Romans 10:7), "mist of darkness" (2 Peter 2:17), "everlasting chains under darkness" (Jude 1:6), "outer darkness" (Matthew 8:12), and "prison" (1 Peter 3:19). While most mentions of hell as a place of punishment use the Greek words *gehenna* (originally Aramaic) or *hades*, 2 Peter 2:4 describes the work of Christ in the spirit world and states that Christ visited Tartarus, the Greek name given to the abyss of torment and suffering for the wicked in the underworld, and this is the only place in the New Testament where this specific location in the netherworld is used. The specificity of this statement in 2 Peter augments the description of the gospel being preached "to them that are dead" in 1 Peter 4:6. The use of the place-name *Tartarus* implies the extent to which the gospel was preached—not merely in the spirit world, the abode of the dead or the grave, but also in the lowest parts of the underworld to spirits being punished or imprisoned in "chains of darkness."[22]

Conclusion

Geography in the New Testament is more than extraneous detail given by the authors to entertain the audience. Each place-name, physical or metaphysical, was purposefully included to evoke a cultural memory, inform about the sociopolitical or economic condition at the time of the event, or inspire action to achieve or continue in the faith. The Gospels reveal the ministry and atoning sacrifice of Jesus Christ within the regions of Judea, Samaria, and Galilee while also establishing the reality of the theological kingdom of heaven and the expectations of its citizenry. Starting from a kernel in Jerusalem, geographic notations within Acts and the Epistles show the rapid growth of the church through the mid-first century AD as the message of the gospel was accepted by Jews and Gentiles across the Eastern Roman Empire. These elements should not be ignored by the modern reader but should serve as an impetus to understand the context of the narrative, which in turn affects the interpretation and application of the narrative. By connecting to the geography of the New Testament, the modern reader should gain further admiration and appreciation for the events and people that have most affected the history of the world and an increased devotion to the Savior and his gospel.

⤳

George A. Pierce is an assistant professor in the Department of Ancient Scripture at Brigham Young University with a joint appointment to the BYU Jerusalem Center for Near Eastern Studies.

Further Reading

Aharoni, Yohanan. *The Land of the Bible*, trans. A. Rainey. Philadelphia, PA: Westminster, 1976.

Avi-Yonah, Michael. *The Holy Land: A Historical Geography from the Persian to the Arab Conquests 536 B.C. to A.D. 640*, trans. A. Rainey. Jerusalem: Carta, 1972.

Notley, R. Steven. *In the Master's Steps: The Gospels in the Land*. Jerusalem: Carta, 2015.

Rainey, Anson F., and R. Steven Notley. *The Sacred Bridge: Carta's Atlas of the Biblical World*. Jerusalem: Carta, 2006.

Notes

1. Anson F. Rainey and R. Steven Notley, *The Sacred Bridge: Carta's Atlas of the Biblical World* (Jerusalem: Carta, 2006), 349.
2. Adrian Curtis, *Oxford Bible Atlas*, 4th ed. (Oxford: Oxford University Press, 2007), 4.
3. Curtis, *Oxford Bible Atlas*, 7.
4. Gary M. Burge, Lynn H. Cohick, and Gene L. Green, *New Testament in Antiquity: A Survey of the New Testament within Its Cultural Contexts* (Grand Rapids, MI: Zondervan, 2009), 189.
5. Several names are typically used to describe the entire region, such as *Israel, Palestine, Syria-Palestine*, or others. Names such as *Israel* or *Palestine* are misleading and historically inaccurate. The Galilee was neither part of the Roman province of Syria nor the province of Judea until the former kingdom of Herod was incorporated into a newly created province of Syria-Palestine by the emperor Hadrian in AD 135 following the Bar Kokhba revolt. Hadrian chose the name *Palestine* on the basis of the association with the Philistines who were forcibly exiled from the territory in the sixth century BC.

6. The extents of this area are nearly those of the kingdom of Israel during the reigns of David and Solomon as described in the Old Testament. The Hasmonean dynasty gradually incorporated these areas into their Jewish kingdom following the successful revolt against the Seleucids in 164 BC.

7. Luke's reference to Bethlehem as the "city of David," while connecting Jesus to David via Bethlehem, stands in contrast to the Old Testament usage of the phrase translated as "city of David." That particular epithet refers specifically to the Jebusite stronghold called the "fortress of Zion" conquered by David and made into a royal residence until Solomon built a separate palace (see 2 Samuel 5:7, 9; 1 Kings 3:1).

8. Rainey and Notley, *Sacred Bridge*, 349–50.

9. For the paucity of first century AD remains at Nazareth, see Vassilios Tzaferis and Bellarmino Bagatti, "Nazareth," in *The New Encyclopedia of Archaeological Excavations in the Holy Land*, vol. 3, ed. E. Stern (New York: Simon and Schuster, 1993), 1103–6.

10. George Adam Smith, *The Historical Geography of the Holy Land*, 4th ed. (New York: George H. Doran, 1896), 432–35.

11. D. A. Carson and Douglas J. Moo, *An Introduction to the New Testament*, 2nd ed. (Grand Rapids, MI: Zondervan, 2005), 77, 134, 169–72, and 198.

12. Carson and Moo, *Introduction to the New Testament*, 257.

13. For recent work identifying Cana of Galilee as modern Khirbet Qana, see C. Thomas McCullough, "Searching for Cana: Where Jesus Turned Water into Wine," *Biblical Archaeology Review* 41, no. 6 (November/December 2015): 31–39.

14. The site of the miracle of the swine, in which Jesus cast out unclean spirits from one or two persons into a herd of pigs, is located at Gergesa in Matthew 8, Gerasa in Mark 5, and Gadera in Luke 8. The location of Gergesa (modern Kursi) has been more accepted than Gadera or Gerasa based on the topography and proximity to the Sea of Galilee, a position that has been maintained since the third century AD. See "Origen's Commentary on the Gospel of John," in *The Anti-Nicene Fathers: The Writings of the Fathers Down to AD 325*, vol. 9, ed. A. Menzies (New York: Charles Scribner's Sons, 1906), 371.

15. Zvi Ma'oz, "Banias," in *The New Encyclopedia of Archaeological Excavations in the Holy Land*, vol. 1, ed. E. Stern (New York: Simon and Schuster, 1993), 136–43, and Vassilios Tzaferis, "Banias," in *The New Encyclopedia of Archaeological Excavations in the Holy Land*, vol. 5, ed. E. Stern (Jerusalem: Carta, 2008), 1587–92.

16. Alison E. Cooley, ed., *Res Gestae Divi Augusti* (Cambridge: Cambridge University Press, 2009).

17. For differing viewpoints on the location of the Crucifixion and the tomb of Jesus, see Gabriel Barkay, "The Garden Tomb—Was Jesus Buried Here?," *Biblical Archaeology Review* 12, no. 2 (March/April 1986): 40–53, 56–57; and Jeffrey R. Chadwick, "Revisiting Golgotha and the Garden Tomb," *Religious Educator* 4, no. 1 (2003): 13–48.

18. H. L. Hendrix, "Thessalonica," in *Anchor Bible Dictionary*, vol. 6, ed. D. N. Freedman (New York: Doubleday, 1992), 523–27.

19. Burge, Cohick, and Green, *New Testament in Antiquity*, 280–81.

20. Curtis, *Oxford Bible Atlas*, 3–4.

21. The kingdom of heaven is mentioned fifty-five times in Matthew, twenty times in Mark, forty-six times in Luke, and five times in John; Burge, Cohick, and Green, *New Testament in Antiquity*, 155.

22. It should be noted that according to Joseph F. Smith, Christ did not personally visit the "wicked and disobedient who had rejected the truth" but organized messengers from among the righteous dead to share the gospel with those in darkness (Doctrine and Covenants 138:29–30).

28

The Use of the Old Testament in the New Testament

Daniel O. McClellan

If *remember* is the most important word in the scriptures, then one of the most important functions of scripture is to serve as a repository for "social memory," or the shared understanding a group has of its collective past and its identity.[1] This conceptualization of scripture certainly aligns well with many of the rhetorical goals expressed by the authors and editors of the Book of Mormon, as well as with their own application of scripture. Indeed, Nephi's statement that he "did liken all scriptures unto us, that it might be for our profit and learning" (1 Nephi 19:23) reflects a deeper insight into the function of scripture than Latter-day Saints might generally be aware.[2] Social memory is relevant to a community only to the degree that it informs and gives meaning to their experiences and their identity, so for scripture to remain relevant, a group must constantly renegotiate between its sacred past and the circumstances, needs, and contexts of its present. Likening the scriptures is not a single event but an ongoing process of making meaning.

The texts of the New Testament function not only to narrate the life and teachings of Jesus Christ and his earliest followers but also to renegotiate the relationship of those followers to their own ideological and scriptural heritage within the Jewish faith. They assert a shared history and ideology and a place in the macronarrative of God's dealings with humanity. This was accomplished through the rereading of Jewish scripture through the interpretive lenses of Christ's life, death, and resurrection, as well as the formation of his church. The more Jewish scripture could be integrated into the telling of those events, the stronger the link to that sacred past and the stronger the claim for viewing Christianity as the fulfilment of all that which Judaism looked forward to and all it waited upon.[3] Sometimes this integration was explicit, and the authors preceded quotations with introductory formulae such as "as it is written . . ." (1 Corinthians 2:9) or "it is written in the prophets . . ." (John 6:45), while more frequently paraphrase or allusion was employed to give rich scriptural flavor and add semantic layers for those who had eyes to see and ears to hear.

As a result of this framing of the life and teachings of Christ and his church, as well as the need to anchor the Christian gospel to the bedrock of early Judaism, the latter's sacred texts—including, but not limited to, those that would become our Old Testament—exercised a profound influence on the shape and message of the New Testament. While this may seem a rather basic observation, its application to a close study of the New Testament raises a number of important questions and reveals many complexities with which Latter-day Saints do not often engage. For example, there are quite significant differences between some of the New Testament's quotations of the Old Testament and the sources of those quotations within the version of the Old Testament to which we today assign authority. Additionally, the New Testament sometimes quotes texts and traditions that do not appear to come from the Old Testament at all. In other places, different authors interpret the same Old Testament text in very different ways.

The goal of this chapter is to consider some of the dynamics associated with the New Testament's engagement with the Old Testament (hereafter OT) and discuss how those dynamics might influence our approaches to reading the New Testament (hereafter NT) and applying its messages. The chapter will begin with an introduction to the nature and function of scripture in the first century AD, while the bulk of the chapter will briefly examine the ways that the books of Matthew, John, Acts, Hebrews, and Revelation quote, dialogue with, or otherwise engage early Jewish scripture.[4] Each author approaches Jewish scripture in their own unique manner, using the texts in a variety of ways to frame their presentation of the gospel for their particular audiences and rhetorical goals. A better understanding of these dynamics will enhance the readers' abilities not only to engage in more meaningful study of the NT text but also to more fully liken the scriptures unto themselves.

Scripture in First-Century Judaism

The concept of scripture was quite a bit more broad and vague in the first century than it is now. No concept of canon at all related to our own modern one existed at the time the NT was being composed, and while there was within the NT a rough grouping of sacred texts into the Law and the Prophets (and sometimes the Psalms),[5] the boundaries of those categories do not appear to have been clearly delineated.[6] There was quite a bit more textual fluidity at that time as well. Many biblical books circulated in slightly different versions, while some more foundational texts like Genesis were expounded upon, paraphrased, and rewritten in an effort to increase their relevance and value to then-contemporary communities.[7]

In addition, many other texts written during the previous two centuries—a period of considerable literary production within Judaism—were considered historical and authoritative.[8]

Alongside texts we now identify as biblical, a number of apocryphal and pseudepigraphical texts have been found among the Dead Sea Scrolls, with no indication they were considered any less genuine or inspired.[9] There were around two dozen different manuscripts of the pseudepigraphical 1 Enoch discovered among the Dead Sea Scrolls, making it the third most represented text at Qumran, outnumbered only by the Psalms and Deuteronomy. There is evidence that the authors of the NT had a similar approach to these texts. As just one example, the author of Jude directly quotes from the book of 1 Enoch (1 Enoch 1:9) in Jude 1:14, attributing the quote to the prophet Enoch.[10] As a result of these circumstances in first-century Judaism, the NT authors had a far wider range of texts, versions, and traditions influencing their perspectives and from which they could quote or draw inspiration.[11]

The methods of engagement with scripture were also quite distinct in the first century. Early Jewish scriptures were not grouped together into delineated collections and bound into books, but kept on individual scrolls, with smaller and related books sometimes consolidated on a single scroll. This meant there was no standardized order of books, and some authors might have access to only a select few books. While scribes and Jewish leaders could access and read these scrolls, only around 10 percent of the population is estimated to have been literate.[12] Encountering the scriptures was not commonly a private and silent matter but a public and auditory one. Most people only heard scripture as it was read out loud, usually from an Aramaic or Greek translation. The story in Luke 4:16–20 of Jesus's synagogue reading may have been representative of the exposure Jewish people of the day would have had to the scriptures. This story reveals another fascinating aspect of scripture: if we compare Luke 4:18–19 to Isaiah 61:1–2, we note some differences in what the texts say. Most critically, the reference to the recovery of sight to the blind is completely absent in the OT passage.

That reference is found, however, in a Greek translation of Isaiah, and this leads us to another factor contributing to early Christian perspectives on the OT: the NT authors—who were writing in Greek—relied overwhelmingly on Greek translations of the Jewish scriptures.[13] As a result of many factors, including textual variation and translation technique, these translations often reflected readings that differed from the Hebrew manuscripts upon which most modern translations of the Bible are based. By the first century AD, these Hebrew manuscripts show signs of being harmonized with each other and with the textual tradition that would become known as the Masoretic Text (hereafter MT).[14] While fragments of Greek manuscripts of OT books have been discovered among the Dead Sea Scrolls and in other places, the earliest extant collections of Greek translations of the entire OT are Christian collections dating to the fourth and fifth centuries AD, and they include apocryphal and other books, and order the texts in different ways. In this chapter I will use the designation "Septuagint" (abbreviated "LXX") to refer generally to Greek translations of the OT and other Jewish scripture, but the term was originally used to refer specifically to the Greek translation of the Pentateuch, or the first five books of Moses. I will occasionally refer to the "Old Greek" (or "OG") as well as to later revisions of the Septuagint.[15]

As a result of the NT authors' reliance on the LXX, it was widely considered by early Christians to be more accurate than the Hebrew. In fact, some even accused Jewish scribes of altering the Hebrew text in an effort to obscure the Christian ideologies that they found in so many places in the Greek.[16] It was not until after Jerome's translation of the OT into Latin in the early fifth century AD that that preference shifted toward the Hebrew text.[17] Our modern preference for the Hebrew version is a product of that shift and is a departure from the preferences of the authors of the NT. Neither should be given unilateral priority, however. In some places the LXX preserves older and more reliable readings than are found in the MT, while in others it preserves demonstrably later and secondary readings. In still other places, a firm conclusion eludes scholars.[18]

As this brief review has hopefully made clear, scripture in the first century AD was a fluid and dynamic category that differed greatly from the concept as we understand it today. There is still much conceptual and text-critical work left for scholars to do, but in the meantime, it enriches our study of the scriptures to be aware of these dynamics and their influence on the authors of the NT. This will hopefully equip the reader to approach the NT with constructive and informed questions in mind about the authors' assumptions about the scriptures, their rhetorical goals, and their methods for achieving them. I now turn to the examination of individual books of the NT and their engagement with Jewish scripture.

Matthew

The Gospel attributed to Matthew by the second century AD is canonically first but chronologically second (Mark was most likely written first). The Gospel of Matthew is among the most thoroughly and intentionally embedded in the Jewish scriptural tradition. One of the primary rhetorical priorities of the author of Matthew was to assert the centrality of Jewish tradition to the gospel preached by Christ and to embed Christ's mission in that tradition. By the time of the composition of Matthew in the late first century AD, missionary work had extended well beyond Judea and the composition of the church was becoming increasingly gentile. Matthew's Gospel reasserts the Jewish embeddedness of Christ by presenting Jesus through the lenses of the OT, framing him as a new Moses who came not to destroy the law, but to fulfill it (Matthew 5:17–18; compare Luke 16:16–17). Despite the concern for the Jewishness of Jesus, the author also highlights the tension between Christ's fulfilment of the law and the existing Jewish hierarchy and its traditions; the scribes, Pharisees, and chief priests are the primary antagonists in Matthew, while non-Israelite supplicants are held up as exemplifying faith over and against the unbelief of Israel (Matthew 8:10; 15:24–28).

One of the ways the Gospel of Matthew links Jesus to Jewish tradition is with OT imagery and titles, most notably "Christ," the Greek translation of the Hebrew משיח (māšîaḥ, "anointed"; compare Daniel 9:25). One of the more curious Matthean titles in reference to Jesus is "Son of man" (Matthew 24:30; compare Mark 14:21; Luke 9:22; John 6:27), which occurs exclusively in the OT in reference to humans (most commonly the prophet Ezekiel; see 2:1; 6:2; 8:5; 11:2). In Hebrew, "son of" can be used to refer to a member of a group or class, so "son of man" simply means "human."[19] In the NT, however, it functions as a title for the

Messiah (Matthew 24:27; Mark 2:10; Luke 9:22; John 6:27).[20] There is no clear explanation for the difference between the OT and the NT usage of this title.

A close look at Matthew's OT sources helps clarify the picture considerably. In referencing the Son of man, Matthew 24:30 quotes from Daniel: "And then shall appear the sign of the Son of man in heaven: and then shall all the tribes of the earth mourn, and they shall see the Son of man coming in the clouds of heaven with power and great glory." Daniel 7:13 reads, "I saw in the night visions, and, behold, one like the Son of man came with the clouds of heaven, and came to the Ancient of days, and they brought him near before him." The English translations do not make the quotation clear, but the Greek phrase ἐπὶ τῶν νεφελῶν τοῦ οὐρανοῦ (*epi tōn nefelōn tou ouranou*, "upon the clouds of heaven") is identical in Matthew and the Old Greek translation of Daniel, suggesting Matthew is drawing from the OG of Daniel 7. The "one like the Son of man" in Daniel would be better translated "one like a son of man" (Aramaic: כבר אנש, *kəbar ĕnāš*), or in other words, someone who looked like a human. The second half of Daniel 7:13 says (in Aramaic) that this human-looking figure "came to the Ancient of days" (ועד-עתיק יומיא מטה), but the Greek translation to which the author of Matthew had access does not have the expected preposition ἕως (*heōs*, "to," or "until"), it has ὡς (*hōs*, "as"), reading ὡς παλαιὸς ἡμερῶν παρῆν (*hōs palaios ēmerōn parēn*), "*as* the Ancient of days he came." This suggests the identification of the Son of man with the Ancient of Days.[21]

That passage of Daniel is not quoted in Matthew, but the context certainly would have been influential in the borrowing of the rest of verse 13. Whatever the reason for the peculiar rendering of the Aramaic preposition "to" in Greek, the translation seems to have resulted in the conflation of an originally unidentified human-looking figure with the Ancient of Days, which contributed to the association of the title "Son of man" with the divine Ancient of Days. The messianic use of this title would have been in circulation primarily among Greek speakers who did not have access to the Hebrew or to those who preferred the messianic implications of the Greek tradition.[22]

One of the centerpieces of the rhetorical campaign of the Gospel of Matthew is Jesus's fulfillment of OT prophecy. The first assertion of this fulfillment occurs where the author evokes Isaiah 7:14 in Matthew 1:22–23: "Now all this was done, that it might be fulfilled which was spoken of the Lord by the prophet, saying, Behold, a virgin shall be with child, and shall bring forth a son, and they shall call his name Emmanuel, which being interpreted is, God with us." The Hebrew word translated "virgin" in the King James Version of Isaiah 7:14 is עלמה (*'almah*), which means "young woman" and does not necessarily have any semantic association with virginity. The author of Matthew is quoting from the Greek translation of Isaiah, however, which renders עלמה with the Greek παρθένος, a term more clearly (although not exclusively) associated with virginity.[23] While the original Hebrew in no way precludes reading the text as a reference to virgin birth, the LXX rendering makes that interpretation much easier and incentivizes the author of Matthew to give preference to that text.

In some places, the author's reliance on the LXX guided them into rather unusual rhetorical territory. Matthew 21, which narrates Jesus's final entry into Jerusalem before his death, provides an interesting example of this. When Jesus and his disciples reached the Mount of

Olives, he instructed them to go find an ass and a colt to bring to him. The author explains that this was done in order to fulfill the words of the prophet Zechariah, and then quotes the following (Matthew 21:5): "Tell ye the daughter of Sion, Behold, thy King cometh unto thee, meek, and sitting upon an ass, and a colt the foal of an ass."[24] Matthew 21:6–7 then describe Christ's fulfillment of the prophecy: "And the disciples went, and did as Jesus commanded them, and brought the ass, and the colt, and put on them their clothes, and they set *him* thereon."

What is peculiar about this passage is that it describes Jesus being placed upon two animals at the same time. It is not quite as explicit in English, but the Greek phrase translated "thereon" in the King James Version (KJV) is ἐπάνω αὐτῶν (*epanō autōn*), which means "upon *them*." This peculiar story results from the author's reliance on the Greek translation of Zechariah. In the Hebrew of Zechariah 9:9, the final clause is an appositional phrase: ורכב על־חמור ועל־עיר בן־אתנות (*vərōkēb ʿal-ḥămôr vəʾal-ʿayir ben-ʾătōnôt*), which might be more helpfully translated ". . . and riding upon a donkey, *that is* a colt, the offspring of a jenny."[25] The Greek translation used a simple conjunction that easily obscured the apposition and led to the misunderstanding that two animals are in view. The author of Matthew was so concerned with presenting Jesus as exactly fulfilling OT prophecy that he closely followed the literal Greek translation and described Jesus entering Jerusalem simultaneously astride two animals. The other Gospels narrate this scene with a single colt (Mark 11:7; Luke 19:35; John 12:14–15). Note also that a footnote in the Latter-day Saint editions of the Bible quotes a Joseph Smith Translation revision that reads, ". . . and brought the *colt*, and put on *it* their clothes; *and Jesus took the colt and sat* thereon; *and they followed him*." Joseph Smith recognized the problem but, without knowing the underlying reason, resolved it by simply revising the text of Matthew.

John

John is unique among the Gospels, both in its narrative and its ideology. It is the only Gospel that discusses Christ's premortal identity and oneness with God, but it also has only a fraction of the OT quotations found in the other Gospels.[26] Rather than quote from the OT directly, the author(s) of John prefer to weave allusions to the imagery and symbols of the OT into their presentation of Christ's life, mission, and identity.[27] Among the more significant allusions to the OT in John are the seven "I am" statements the authors use to frame Jesus's self-identity and tie his mission to God's own agency and authority (John 6:35; 8:12; 10:7, 11; 11:25; 14:6; 15:1), as well as other uses of the Greek ἐγώ εἰμι (*egō eimi*), "I am." These statements appeal to an important means of divine self-identification used in the OT. When Moses asked God in Exodus 3 what name he should give to the Israelites when they ask who sent him, the response is "I AM THAT I AM: and he said, Thus shalt thou say unto the children of Israel, I AM hath sent me unto you" (3:14). The Hebrew rendered "I am that I am" reads אהיה אשר אהיה (*ʾehyeh ʾăšer ʾehyeh*), or "I will be what I will be," which is a folk etymology that ties the divine name YHWH to the verbal root "to be" (היה, HYH).

The Greek translation of this passage turns the folk etymology into a complete sentence by rendering ἐγώ εἰμι ὁ ὤν (*egō eimi ho ōn*), or "I am the one who is." Elsewhere in the LXX, the Greek phrase ἐγώ εἰμι is also used to translate the Hebrew אני הוא (*ănî hû'*, "I am he"), which is another method of self-identification used by the Lord.[28] For instance, in Deuteronomy 32:39, the Lord states, "See now that I, *even* I, *am* he (אני הוא), and *there is* no god with me" (compare Isaiah 41:4; 43:10; 44:6). In light of this, Jesus's use of the Greek ἐγώ εἰμι can be understood to function as an assertion of a special relationship with the God of the OT, YHWH (or Jehovah).[29] This is particularly emphatic in John 8:58, in which Jesus asserts, "Before Abraham was, I am." In order for the rhetorical force of this rather ungrammatical statement to land, we must read "I am" not as a predication of existence but as one of God's titles. Jesus is saying that the great "I Am" existed before Abraham, at the same time asserting some kind of identification with him.

While this rhetorical identification has long facilitated the identification of Christ with God within mainstream Christian communities, the sense is more likely an assertion of access to divine agency. The divine name YHWH was considered a vehicle for divine agency within early Judaism, and so to possess it was to possess the authority to exercise God's power. The clearest example of this is found in Exodus 23:20–21, in which God deputizes his angel to exercise divine prerogatives:[30] "Behold, I send an Angel before thee, to keep thee in the way, and to bring thee into the place which I have prepared. Beware of him and obey his voice, provoke him not; for he will not pardon your transgressions: for my name is in him."[31] By appealing to this tradition, the authors of John are closely linking Christ with the God of Israel and with other significant divine figures of the OT.

Jesus's quotation of Psalm 82 in John 10 is well-known among Latter-day Saints but primarily as a prooftext for humanity's divine heritage.[32] The rest of the psalm, which narrates the judgment and condemnation of the unjust gods, rather complicates the rhetorical value of the Latter-day Saint reading, but that does not appear to be how the psalm or its quotation in John were intended to be understood anyway. Jesus's use of the psalm is clearly meant to undercut the condemnation of his claim to unity with God, but its precise rhetorical function is unclear. Jesus states in John 10:30, "I and my Father are one," which enrages some gathered Jewish people who immediately undertake to stone him. When asked why, they respond that even though Jesus is a human, he makes himself out to be a god.[33] At this point, Jesus quotes the psalm: "Is it not written in your law, I said, Ye are gods? If he called them gods, unto whom the word of God came, and the scripture cannot be broken; say ye of him, whom the Father hath sanctified, and sent into the world, Thou blasphemest; because I said, I am the Son of God?" (John 10:34–36).

On the surface, the quotation appears to defend Christ's divinity on the grounds that at least some humans were explicitly called "gods" in the scriptures.[34] This seems a rather weak defense, but a closer look at how the psalm was read during this period reveals quite a bit more nuance and significance, particularly for Latter-day Saints. The key is to understand who, precisely, was thought to have been called "gods." The passage refers obliquely to "them," which suggests there was a common interpretation of the psalm in circulation at the time the text was written that did not require elaboration—the hearers would have understood who they were. Originally, the psalm referred to the gods of the nations who were neglecting their duty to administer justice within their assigned stewardships on behalf of the poor and the needy.[35] We find several rabbinic texts from shortly after the time of Christ, however, interpreting Psalm 82 as a reference to the Israelites at Sinai.[36] According to this reading, when the Israelites received the law of Moses (compare "unto whom the word of God came"), they were freed from the power of the angel of death and effectively rendered immortal (compare "ye are gods"). Upon their sinning with the golden calf, however, they were condemned to mortality (compare Psalm 82:7: "But ye shall die like men, and fall like one of the princes"). This reading recontextualized the psalm in a way that was relevant to the self-identity of the community at the time—it "likened" the scriptures unto them.

Christ's appeal to the psalm employed that likening to highlight his identity as the very "Word of God." If the Israelites were made divine by the reception of that word, how much more divine is that very Word himself, sanctified by the Father and sent into the world? If anyone has a legitimate claim to divinity, it is the Word of God. This reading of John 10:34–36 fits comfortably within the authors' emphasis on Christ's identity as God's Word (compare John 1:1–14) but also with their insistence that those who believe on the Son will be given power to become the "sons of God" (compare John 1:12). Those authors did not read Psalm 82 the way today's Latter-day Saints read it, nor did they read it the way it was likely originally intended to be understood, but they did employ a popular contemporary reading to assert Christ's divinity as well as the divine potential of all humanity.

Acts

The author of Luke–Acts shows close familiarity with the vocabulary and phraseology of the OT, and particularly the LXX, quoting most heavily from Greek translations of the Psalms, the minor prophets, Isaiah, and the Pentateuch. This section will discuss two examples of this engagement, specifically Stephen's summary of Jewish history in Acts 7 and James's quotation of Amos 9 in Acts 15.

Stephen's speech before the Sanhedrin in Acts 7:2–53 is the longest speech in the book of Acts, and it draws repeatedly from the unique terminology of the LXX.[37] In the speech, Stephen responds to accusations of blasphemy against the law and the temple by selectively recounting the history of Judaism's dealings with God independent from the law and the temple, from Abraham down to the construction of the first temple. In his recounting, Stephen highlights the many different ways the will of God was made known to the patriarchs apart from the law, as well as the disobedience of the Israelites in general to that will, particularly as mediated by Moses, the giver of the law. Stephen relativizes the temple as well, insisting "the most High dwelleth not in temples made with hands" (Acts 7:48). He concludes by turning the accusations around and indicting the members of the Sanhedrin themselves: "Which of the prophets have not your fathers persecuted? and they have slain them which shewed before of the coming of the Just One; of whom ye have been now the betrayers and murderers: who have received the law by the disposition of angels, and have not kept it" (Acts 7:52–53).

In recounting the history in this way, Stephen uses Israelite history as a framework for interpreting the early church's relationship to God and to Judaism. This gives meaning to Christianity's confrontation with Jewish leadership and also inserts Christians into the biblical narrative, insisting they are actors in the same drama. Christ fills the role of the prophets, mediating God's will to his people. Stephen and the other Christians are those who followed God's will as mediated through his prophets, while the members of the Sanhedrin play the role of the wicked Israelites who disobeyed and persecuted the prophets in direct contradiction to the will of God. It is not Stephen who stands in opposition to God, but the Jewish leaders who blithely prioritize the law and the temple over God's own will.

Acts 15 contains a fascinating quotation from the LXX.[38] In this chapter, Paul and Barnabas have come to Jerusalem to investigate a disagreement regarding whether or not gentile converts to Christianity must keep the law of Moses by being circumcised. During the debate, Peter reminds the audience of his revelation regarding taking the gospel to the Gentiles (Acts 10:9–16) and Paul and Barnabas then share their experiences preaching to the Gentiles. At this point, James gives his testimony, declaring that Peter's experience agrees with "the words of the prophets" (Acts 15:15). In verses 16–17 he quotes from what appears to be the book of Amos: "After this I will return, and will build again the tabernacle of David, which is fallen down; and I will build again the ruins thereof, and I will set it up: that the residue of men might seek after the Lord, and all the Gentiles, upon whom my name is called, saith the Lord, who doeth all these things." In verses 19–20 James concludes, "Wherefore my sentence is, that we trouble not them, which from among the Gentiles are turned to God: but that we write unto them, that they abstain from pollutions of idols, and from fornication, and from things strangled, and from blood." This satisfied the gathered apostles and elders, who sent letters to the scattered congregations announcing the consensus.

A look at the version of Amos 9:11–12 from the Hebrew manuscripts reveals some important differences from the version quoted by James, though. Here is the text from the KJV: "In that day will I raise up the tabernacle of David that is fallen, and close up the breaches thereof; and I will raise up his ruins, and I will build it as in the days of old: that they may possess the remnant of Edom, and of all the heathen, which are called by my name, saith the Lord that doeth this."

Our main concern is the way Amos 9:12 is represented in Acts 15:17. Instead of referring to the "remnant of Edom," the version in Acts refers to the "residue of men," which reflects a reading of the Hebrew אדום (ʾedôm, "Edom") as אדם (ʾadam, "humanity"). Additionally, the verb has changed from "possess" to "seek after," which suggests a reading of the Hebrew יירשׁ (yîršû, "they will possess") as ידרשׁ (yīdrəšû, "they will seek after"). These are the readings found in the Septuagint translation, but in addition to deviating from the Hebrew text, the LXX also introduces a grammatical problem. In the Hebrew, "the remnant of Edom" is the direct object of the verb "possess." With the Septuagint reading, however, the "residue of men" becomes the subject of the transitive verb "seek after," leaving that verb without a direct object. What will the "residue of men" seek after? In the Septuagint, the clause is simply left incomplete, but in Acts 15:17, an object is provided: "the Lord."

These two different readings produce vastly different messages. The Hebrew version of Amos 9:11–12 refers to the military conquest of Edom and other lands around Israel, which would not have served the rhetorical goals of the author of Acts. The Greek translation quoted in Acts 15 fits comfortably with the rhetorical purposes for which it was cited, namely to suggest the prophetic foretelling of the extension of the gospel beyond the house of Israel to the Gentiles. Either James was familiar with and chose to quote from the Greek translation, or the author of Acts put those words in his mouth. Either way, the Septuagint was a better ideological fit for the missionary interests of the developing Christian church.

Hebrews

Regarding the book of Hebrews, biblical scholar George Guthrie has asserted that it "packs more of the Old Testament into its complex discourse than any other New Testament writing."[39] Indeed, the text quotes the OT seven times in the first chapter alone (and each time from the LXX), and some of these quotations differ significantly from their Hebrew sources.[40] In some cases in Hebrews, these differences clarify confusing passages from our OT. For instance, in Hosea 14:2, Israel is exhorted to turn to the Lord and to "say unto him, Take away all iniquity, and receive us graciously: so will we render the calves of our lips." The phrase "calves of our lips" seems to have something to do with some manner of offering or sacrifice of prayer or praise, but it is quite unusual, even for the OT. The Hebrew word rendered "calves" here is פרים (*pārîm*), which means "bulls," but without the final consonant, the word פרי (*pərî*) means "fruit." This reading makes more sense and is the one found in the LXX. Hebrews 13:15 appears to quote the LXX: "By him therefore let us offer the sacrifice of praise to God continually, that is, the fruit of our lips giving thanks to his name."

Chapter 11 of Hebrews is a famous explanation of and exhortation to faith that appeals to a number of narratives and traditions about the heroes of Jewish history. The author mentions Noah, Abraham, Isaac, Jacob, Joseph, Moses, and many others.[41] In Hebrews 11:35–37, the author states, "Women received their dead raised to life again: and others were tortured, not accepting deliverance; that they might obtain a better resurrection: and others had trial of cruel mockings and scourgings, yea, moreover of bonds and imprisonment: they were stoned, they were sawn asunder, were tempted, were slain with the sword: they wandered about in sheepskins and goatskins; being destitute, afflicted, tormented."

Two references are of interest for us. First, verse 35b refers to those who did not accept deliverance from torture in the interest of obtaining a "better resurrection." Second, verse 37 refers to someone being "sawn asunder." Neither of these two references fit with the stories from our OT, which raises the question of the traditions to which the author is referring.

Fortunately, this mystery is not terribly difficult to solve. The first reference is to the book 2 Maccabees, which is found in the Apocrypha (or what Catholics often call the deutero-canonical books) and was included in the early uncial manuscripts like Sinaiticus (fourth century) and Alexandrinus (fifth century).[42] Second Maccabees recounts historical events related to the Jewish revolt against Antiochus IV Epiphanes during the 160s BC. It expands on the narrative from the first seven chapters of the book of 1 Maccabees, filling in some additional detail, including a well-known narrative about the martyrdom of a mother and her seven sons, which is likely the source of the reference in Hebrews 11:35. According to that narrative, Antiochus arrested the mother and her seven sons and threatened to torture them if they do not eat pork. One by one, they refused and were tortured to death. Several of the sons declared that while Antiochus will have nothing but divine punishment to look forward to, they look forward to a glorious resurrection as a result of dying for the law:[43]

2 Maccabees 7:9	2 Maccabees 7:14
And when he was at his last breath, he said, "You accursed wretch, you dismiss us from this present life, but the King of the universe will raise us up to an everlasting renewal of life, because we have died for his laws."	When he was near death, he said, "One cannot but choose to die at the hands of mortals and to cherish the hope God gives of being raised again by him. But for you there will be no resurrection to life!"

The reference in Hebrews 11 to one "sawn asunder" comes from an early Jewish composition known as the *Martyrdom of Isaiah*, incorporated into a Christian text known as the *Martyrdom and Ascension of Isaiah*. In the first chapter of this work, the prophet Isaiah prophesies of his death (*Martyrdom and Ascension of Isaiah* 1:9):[44] "He will cause many in Jerusalem and Judah to desert the true faith, and Beliar will dwell in Manasseh, and by his hands I will be sawed in half."

The martyrdom itself is narrated in the fifth chapter (*Martyrdom and Ascension of Isaiah* 5:1, 14): "Because of these visions, therefore, Beliar was angry with Isaiah, and he dwelt in the heart of Manasseh, and he sawed Isaiah in half with a wood saw. . . . And while Isaiah was being sawed in half, he did not cry out, or weep, but his mouth spoke with the Holy Spirit until he was sawed in two."

These narratives were written during the persecutions of Antiochus IV Epiphanes and were intended to exhort Jewish people to remain faithful in the face of those persecutions. Prior to these stories, champions of faith like Daniel and his companions were miraculously saved by the intercession of God, but these martyrdoms marked a new motif in which the faithful were not saved but looked forward to recompense on the other side of the veil. Isaiah asserts to Hezekiah that he will receive "the inheritance of the Beloved" (*Martyrdom and Ascension of Isaiah* 1:13), while the mother and her seven sons look forward to resurrection to a glorious life. While neither text would ultimately be included in the canon that would develop centuries later, they were considered authoritative and historically accurate among some early Christians, and they provided powerful examples of faith to which the author of Hebrews could appeal in his exhortation of Christians to endure persecution.

Revelation

The book of Revelation narrates John's vision of the eschaton, or end times, given by Jesus while John was exiled on the island of Patmos. As is conventional with the genre of apocalypse,[45] the book of Revelation is oriented toward the future, but the imagery and the themes of the book are drawn directly from the OT and Judaism's sacred past, even while it avoids directly quoting from scripture. The clearest allusions to the OT are to the books of Isaiah, Ezekiel, Daniel, and the Psalms, but imagery and paraphrases are also drawn from the minor prophets and from the historical books of Samuel and Kings. In places, the author is clearly drawing from a Greek translation. For instance, the author paraphrases Psalm 2:9 in Revelation 2:27, 12:5, and 19:15, but instead of stating God will "break them with a rod of iron," the text reflects the Greek rendering, "rule them with a rod of iron." Elsewhere, the references fall closer to the Hebrew versions than to any known Greek versions. The author clearly seeks to reflect a Hebrew background in some places (e.g., Revelation 16:16), but because the paraphrases may indicate quotation from memory, and because we know other Greek translations to which we do not have access were in circulation, it is difficult to reach a conclusion.

The biblical imagery in Revelation is employed in an effort not only to more firmly tie Christianity's future to its Jewish past, but also to reframe the understanding of both in light of Christ's mission and what Christians were experiencing contemporaneously. One of the central concerns of the book of Revelation is to overturn the Christian expectation of political autonomy. For instance, the author draws from the OT imagery of power and rule in stating that John *heard* an elder state that the "Lion of the tribe of Judah" (see Genesis 49:9–10) and the "Root of David" (see Isaiah 11:1) has conquered ("prevailed" in the KJV), but when John looks for himself, what he sees is a slain lamb. The elders literally change their tune: "And they sung a new song, saying, Thou art worthy to take the book, and to open the seals thereof: for thou wast slain, and hast redeemed us to God by thy blood" (Revelation 5:9). This unexpected fulfillment replaces the symbol of David and a mighty lion with a slaughtered lamb, rhetorically asserting that victory for God and his people is achieved through sacrifice, not through military or political power.

Toward the end of Revelation, the author appropriates and rearranges the final chapters of Ezekiel to again renegotiate the significance of OT prophecy in light of Christ's victory over sin and death. In Ezekiel 37, the prophet sees a vision of a valley of dry bones and prophesies of resurrection, the gathering of Israel, the reestablishment of Davidic kingship, and the foundation of God's temple in the midst of his people for all time. Chapters 38–39 narrate the battle of Gog, with birds feasting on the dead, and 40–48 describe the temple and its ordinances and surroundings. The author of Revelation rearranges things slightly, beginning with the birds feasting on the dead in Revelation 19, followed by the resurrection of the dead in chapter 20, and then the battle of Gog and Magog. After God's victory, the New Jerusalem is described in terms related to Ezekiel's, although the city is a thousand times larger and there is no temple; rather than be confined to a physical structure, the presence of God and the Lamb will pervade the whole city.

Conclusion

As this brief discussion has hopefully demonstrated, the OT and the social memory it facilitated were critical to the success of the rhetorical goals of the authors of the NT and foundational in early Christianity's development of its identity. Each author had their own goals and concerns, but some general observations can be made. Writing in Greek, NT authors had easier access to Greek translations of the Jewish scriptures, which had been translated within the previous two centuries and were much more closely aligned with the ideological lenses through which they were interpreting the OT themselves. There was also a much broader corpus from which they could draw. Much of the influential literature of Greco-Roman period Judaism was composed originally in Greek. This produced a natural bias toward the Greek translations (but the importance of the Hebrew heritage of Judaism was certainly not lost on them). The "Son of man" traditions from Daniel and Enoch had increased messianic expectations in the century or so preceding the birth of Christ, particularly in their Greek translations, so those texts became increasingly significant in understanding Christ's mission and in renegotiating Christianity's relationship to its Jewish past. The foundational narratives of creation, Sinai, and exile remained influential frameworks, however, and the promise of restoration took on new significance for a group that had come to understand the kingdom of God not to constitute a literal political entity, but a community of believers worshipping the God of heaven. Related prophecies were reinterpreted accordingly.

Latter-day Saints read the NT for a variety of reasons, but certainly understanding our sacred past and our relationship to it is high on the list. Being aware of the dynamics associated with the NT authors' own negotiations with their own sacred past significantly complicates our reading, but the challenge is certainly worth the effort. A better understanding of the rhetorical goals and methods of the authors of the NT helps us get closer to their messages and also helps us to better understand the processes involved in likening the scriptures to ourselves, which should improve our engagement with scripture across all the methods we may employ and help us to better understand the mission of the Savior and apply his teachings.

Daniel O. McClellan is a scripture translation supervisor for The Church of Jesus Christ of Latter-day Saints and a PhD student in theology and religion at the University of Exeter.

Further Reading

Jobes, Karen H., and Moisés Silva. *Invitation to the Septuagint*. 2nd ed. Grand Rapids, MI: Baker Academic, 2015.

Kaiser, Walter C., Jr., Darrell L. Bock, and Peter Enns. *Three Views on the New Testament Use of the Old Testament*. Grand Rapids, MI: Zondervan, 2008.

Law, Timothy Michael. *When God Spoke Greek: The Septuagint and the Making of the Christian Bible*. Oxford: Oxford University Press, 2013.

Ludlow, Jared W. "Paul's Use of Old Testament Scripture." In *How the New Testament Came to Be*, edited by Kent B. Jackson and Frank F. Judd Jr., 227–42. Provo, UT: Religious Studies Center, Brigham Young University; Salt Lake City: Deseret Book, 2006.

Moyise, Steve. *The Old Testament in the New: An Introduction*. 2nd ed. London: Bloomsbury, 2015.

Notes

1. This oft-repeated sentiment is an extrapolation from President Spencer W. Kimball's famous statement that the most important word in the dictionary may well be "remember": "When you look in the dictionary for the most important word, do you know what it is? It could be 'remember.' Because all of (us) have made covenants . . . our greatest need is to remember. That is why everyone goes to sacrament meeting every Sabbath day—to take the sacrament and listen to the priests pray that (we) 'may always remember him and keep his commandments which he has given (us).' . . . 'Remember' is the word." Spencer W. Kimball, "Circles of Exaltation," address to religious educators, Brigham Young University, June 28, 1968, 8.

2. For an excellent discussion of some of the ways this "likening" takes place in the Book of Mormon's use of Isaiah, see Joseph M. Spencer, "Isaiah 52 in the Book of Mormon: Notes on Isaiah's Reception History," *Relegere* 6, no. 2 (2016): 189–217.

3. See Luke 24:44: "All things must be fulfilled, which were written in the law of Moses, and in the prophets, and in the psalms, concerning me."

4. I have of necessity been selective regarding what texts to evaluate. Unless otherwise noted, all Bible passages will be quoted from the 2013 Latter-day Saint edition of the KJV.

5. Matthew 5:17; 7:12; Luke 16:16. Luke 24:44 refers to that which was "written in the law of Moses, and in the prophets, and in the psalms."

6. Josephus asserts a tripartite division of authoritative texts that total twenty-two books, which does not quite match the number of books in the traditional canon. Different attempts have been made to fit the modern canon into this number, but such approaches beg the question. For a helpful discussion, see Steve Mason, "Josephus and His Twenty-Two Book Canon," in *The Canon Debate*, ed. Lee Martin MacDonald and James A. Sanders (Peabody, MA: Hendrickson, 2002), 110–27.

7. See Hanne von Weissenberg, Juha Pakkala, and Marko Marttila, eds., *Changes in Scriptures: Rewriting and Interpreting Authoritative Traditions in the Second Temple Period* (Berlin: de Gruyter, 2011). As a single example, the targumim were Aramaic translations of biblical texts from the turn of the era that frequently altered and added to the biblical narratives. Joseph Smith's revision of the Bible closely aligns with the practice of targumic expansion and exposition. Unfortunately, the implications of this observation have yet to be fully teased out by Latter-day Saint scholars.

8. For excellent discussions of the concepts of "scripture" and "canon" and their development in early Christianity, see Bruce M. Metzger, *The Canon of the New Testament: Its Origin, Development, and Significance* (Oxford: Clarendon Press, 1987); MacDonald and Sanders, eds., *The Canon Debate*; Lee Martin MacDonald, *The Biblical Canon: Its Origin, Transmission, and Authority* (Peabody, MA: Hendrickson, 2007); Michael J. Kruger, *The Question of Canon: Challenging the Status Quo in the New Testament Debate* (Downers Grove, IL: InterVarsity Press, 2013). On the Septuagint as canon, see Simon Crisp, "The Septuagint as Canon," *Bible Translator* 67, no. 2 (2016): 137–50. See also Timothy Michael Law, *When God Spoke Greek: The Septuagint and the Making of the Christian Bible* (Oxford: Oxford University Press, 2013).

9. "Pseudepigrapha" means "false writings" and is used in biblical studies to refer to texts spuriously attributed to well-known figures from Jewish and Christian history.

10. See Edward Mazich, "'The Lord Will Come with His Holy Myriads': An Investigation of the Linguistic Source of the Citation of 1 Enoch 1,9 in Jude 14b–15," *Zeitschrift für die neutestamentliche Wissenschaft* 94, no. 3–4 (2003): 276–81; Nicholas J. Moore, "Is Enoch Also among the Prophets? The Impact of Jude's Citation of 1 Enoch on the Reception of Both Texts in the Early Church," *Journal of Theological Studies* 64,

no. 2 (2013): 498–515. For a translation of the book of Enoch, see George W. E. Nickelsburg and James C. VanderKam, *1 Enoch: A New Translation* (Minneapolis, MN: Augsburg, 2004).

11. On the influence of the Greek translation of the Hebrew Bible on the formation of the Christian scriptures, see Law, *When God Spoke Greek*.

12. For a fascinating discussion of literacy during Jesus's life, see Craig A. Evans, *Jesus and His World: The Archaeological Evidence* (Louisville, KY: Westminster John Knox, 2012), 63–88. For earlier periods, see Shira Faigenbaym-Golovin et al., "Algorithmic Handwriting Analysis of Judah's Military Correspondence Sheds Light on Composition of Biblical Texts," *Proceedings of the National Academy of Sciences of the United States of America* 113, no. 17 (2016): 4,664–69.

13. These Greek translations began to appear in the late third or early second century BC as new generations of Jewish practitioners in Egypt and elsewhere could not adequately comprehend the scriptures in Hebrew. The traditional story from the pseudepigraphical *Letter of Aristeas* of seventy-two elders from the twelve tribes of Israel translating the Torah at the request of Ptolemy II Philadelphus is not historical. For recent analyses of the *Letter of Aristeas*, see Sylvie Honigman, *The Septuagint and Homeric Scholarship in Alexandria: A Study in the Narrative of the* Letter of Aristeas (London: Routledge, 2003); Erich S. Gruen, "The *Letter of Aristeas* and the Cultural Context of the Septuagint," in *Die Septuaginta – Texte, Kontexte, Lebenswelten*, ed. Martin Karrer and Wolfgang Kraus, WUNT 219 (Tübingen: Mohr Siebeck, 2008), 134–56; Benjamin G. Wright III, *The Letter of Aristeas: 'Aristeas to Philocrates' or 'On the Translation of the Law of the Jews'* (CEJL; Berlin: de Gruyter, 2015). On the Septuagint in the New Testament, see Mogens Müller, "The Septuagint as the Bible of the New Testament Church," *Scandinavian Journal of the Old Testament* 7, no. 2 (1993): 194–207; R. Timothy McLay, *The Use of the Septuagint in New Testament Research* (Grand Rapids, MI: Eerdmans, 2003).

14. For good overviews of the state of the Old Testament in the early centuries AD and the development of the Masoretic Text, see Emanuel Tov, *Textual Criticism of the Hebrew Bible*, 3rd ed. (Minneapolis, MN: Fortress, 2012); Ernst Würthwein and Alexander Achilles Fischer, *The Text of the Old Testament: An Introduction to the Bibla Hebraica*, 3rd ed., trans. Erroll F. Rhodes (Grand Rapids, MI: Eerdmans, 2014).

15. For a helpful discussion of the history of the term "Septuagint," see Jennifer M. Dines, *The Septuagint* (London: T&T Clark, 2004), 1–9. For introductions to the Septuagint, see Natalio Fernández Marcos, *The Septuagint in Context: Introduction to the Greek Version of the Bible*, trans. Wilfred G. E. Watson (Leiden: Brill, 2000); Dines, *The Septuagint*; Karen H. Jobes and Moisés Silva, *Invitation to the Septuagint*, 2nd ed. (Grand Rapids, MI: Baker Academic, 2015).

16. Most famously, Origen (an Alexandrian Christian theologian who died around AD 253/4) referred to the Septuagint as "our scriptures," and the Hebrew version as "the Jewish scriptures." Origen, *Epistula ad Africanum* 5. He also produced a six-column text known as the *Hexapla* that put side-by-side the Hebrew text, a Greek transliteration of that Hebrew text, and four versions of the Septuagint. It had annotations in the text to identify places where Origen believed the text to have been altered either by omission or addition.

17. See Dennis Brown, "Jerome and the Vulgate," in *A History of Biblical Interpretation. Volume 1: The Ancient Period*, ed. Alan J. Hauser and Duane F. Watson (Grand Rapids, MI: Eerdmans, 2003), 355–79; Paul B. Decock, "Jerome's Turn to the Hebraica Veritas and His Rejection of the Traditional View of the Septuagint," *Neotestamentica* 42, no. 2 (2008): 25–22.

18. These dynamics are complex and are scattered around the scholarship, but for the best discussions, see Anneli Aejmelaeus, *On the Trail of the Septuagint Translators. Collected Essays Revised and Expanded Edition* (Leuven: Peeters, 2007); Emanuel Tov, *Textual Criticism of the Hebrew Bible*, 3rd ed., rev. (Minneapolis: Fortress, 2011), 127–41; Emanuel Tov, *Textual Criticism of the Hebrew Bible, Qumran, Septuagint: Collected Essays*, vol. 3 (Leiden: Brill, 2015).

19. On this usage, see Paul Joüon and Takamitsu Muraoka, *A Grammar of Biblical Hebrew* (Rome: Editrice Pontificio Istituto Biblico, 2006), §129*j*.

20. On the history of this usage, see Delbert Burkett, *The Son of Man Debate: A History and Evaluation* (Cambridge: Cambridge University Press, 2000); Benjamin E. Reynolds, "The 'One Like a Son of Man' according

to the Old Greek of Daniel 7,13–14," *Biblica* 89, no. 1 (2008): 70–80; Mogens Müller, *The Expression 'Son of Man' and the Development of Christology* (London: Equinox, 2008); Leslie W. Walck, *The Son of Man in the Parables of Enoch and in Matthew* (London: T&T Clark, 2011).

21. See McLay, *Use of the Septuagint in New Testament Research*, 156–58.

22. One can see this conflation of the Son of man and the Ancient of Days in the combination of their imagery in the description of Christ from Revelation 1:7, 13–14.

23. See Rodrigo de Sousa, "Is the Choice of ΠΑΡΘΕΝΟΣ in LXX Isa. 7:14 Theologically Motivated?," *Journal of Semitic Studies* 53, no. 2 (2008): 211–32.

24. This differs slightly from the prophecy preserved in the KJV's version of Zechariah 9:9: "Rejoice greatly, O daughter of Zion; shout, O daughter of Jerusalem: behold, thy King cometh unto thee: he *is* just, and having salvation; lowly, and riding upon an ass, and upon a colt the foal of an ass."

25. In an appositional phrase, a noun is usually followed by another noun or adjective that restates, describes, specifies, or provides more information about the first—for instance, "I'm a better golfer than my brother, Dave." In that sentence, "Dave" is in apposition to the phrase "my brother" and serves to provide more information about that phrase.

26. The Westcott-Hort list of OT references lists 124 for Matthew, 70 for Mark, 109 for Luke, and only 27 for John.

27. I refer to plural authors of John in light of John 21:24, which reads in the KJV, "This is the disciple which testifieth of these things, and wrote these things: and we know that his testimony is true." A Johannine community is clearly responsible for the final form of the text. Rather than attempt to decouple the disciple's own testimony from the editorial or authorial work of that community, I simply assume multiple authors. For a recent discussion of authorship, see Craig R. Koester, *Revelation: A New Translation with Introduction and Commentary*, AYB 38a (New Haven, CT: Yale University Press, 2014), 65–71.

28. For a helpful examination of this Hebrew phrase in Jewish and Christian literature, see Catrin H. Williams, *I am He: The Interpretation of 'Anî Hû' in Jewish and Early Christian Literature* (Tübingen: Mohr Siebeck, 2000).

29. "Jehovah" represents the combination of the vowels from the Hebrew word for "lord" (אדני, *'ădonāy*; used as a substitute for pronouncing the divine name) and the consonants from the divine name, יהוה, by a thirteenth-century-AD Spanish monk named Raymundo Martini. While scholars today transliterate the divine name YHWH, when this combination became popular and was regularly printed, the *yod* was transliterated as /j/ when appearing as a consonant, and the *waw* was transliterated as /v/. (Martini originally wrote the name "Yohoua.")

30. This passage is likely an attempt to make sense of many earlier biblical passages where the identity of God and his angel appear confused or conflated (e.g., Genesis 16:7–13; 21:17–19; 22:11–18; 31:11–13; Exodus 3:2–6; Numbers 22:22–35; Judges 6:11–23; 13:3–23). For more on the possession of the divine name and the angel of the Lord, see Jarl E. Fossum, *The Name of God and the Angel of the Lord* (Tübingen; Mohr Siebeck, 1985).

31. The fact that this passage appears to give the angel the authority to forgive or not forgive sins is not insignificant. Another tacit assertion of Jesus's possession of the divine name, and therefore divine power, is found in Mark 2:5–12, in which Christ asserts the divine prerogative to forgive sins, which the scribes scoff is something God alone can do. Exodus 23:21 is likely lurking in the background of this story. See Daniel Johansson, "'Who Can Forgive Sins but God Alone?' Human and Angelic Agents, and Divine Forgiveness in Early Judaism," *Journal for the Study of the New Testament* 33, no. 4 (2011): 351–74.

32. See, for instance, Boyd K. Packer, "The Pattern of Our Parentage," in Conference Report, October 1984, 68; Tad R. Callister, "Our Identity and Our Destiny," *Brigham Young University 2012-2013 Speeches* (Provo, UT: Brigham Young University, 2013), 3–4.

33. The KJV renders "thou, being a man, makes thyself God," which suggests Jesus is claiming to be God the Father himself. The Greek does not have the definite article, however, and "divine," or "a god" is a more likely interpretation of the Jewish accusation.

34. For the many different approaches to this passage, see James A. Emerton, "The Interpretation of Ps lxxxii in John x," *Journal of Theological Studies* 11 (1960): 329–32; James S. Ackerman, "The Rabbinic Interpretation

of Psalm 82 and the Gospel of John," *Harvard Theological Review* 59, no. 2 (1966): 186–91; Anthony Hanson, "John's Citation of Psalm LXXXII Reconsidered," *New Testament Studies* 13 (1966): 363–67; Jerome H. Neyrey, "'I Said: You Are Gods': Psalm 82:6 and John 10," *Journal of Biblical Literature* 108, no. 4 (1989): 647–63; Mark D. Nispel, "Christian Deification and the Early Testimonia," *Vigiliae Christianae* 53 (1999): 289–304; Carl Mosser, "The Earliest Patristic Interpretations of Psalm 82, Jewish Antecedents, and the Origin of Christian Deification," *Journal of Theological Studies* 56 (2005): 30–74; Michael Heiser, "Jesus's Quotation of Psalm 82:6 in John 10:34: A Different View of John's Theological Strategy" (paper presented at the Pacific Northwest Regional Meeting of the Society of Biblical Literature, May 13, 2011, Spokane, WA). See also Daniel O. McClellan, "Psalm 82 in Contemporary Latter-day Saint Tradition," *Interpreter* 15 (2015): 79–96.

35. On this reading, see Simon B. Parker, "The Beginning of the Reign of God: Psalm 82 as Myth and Liturgy," *Revue Biblique* 10, no. 4 (1995): 532–59; Robert P. Gordon, "The Gods Must Die: A Theme in Isaiah and Beyond," in M. N. van der Meer et al., eds., *Isaiah in Context: Studies in Honour of Arie van der Kooij on the Occasion of His Sixty-Fifth Birthday* (Leiden: Brill, 2010), 53–55; David Frankel, "El as the Speaking Voice in Psalm 82:6–8," *Journal of Hellenic Studies* 10 (2010), jhsonline.org/Articles/article_144.pdf; Peter Machinist, "How Gods Die, Biblically and Otherwise: A Problem of Cosmic Restructuring," in *Reconsidering the Concept of Revolutionary Monotheism*, ed. B. Pongratz-Leisten (Winona Lake, IN: Eisenbrauns, 2011), 189–240; James M. Trotter, "Death of the אלהים in Psalm 82," *Journal of Biblical Literature* 131, no. 2 (2012): 221–39; Brent A. Strawn, "The Poetics of Psalm 82: Three Critical Notes along with a Plea for the Poetic," *Revue Biblique* 121, no. 1 (2014): 21–46; Ellen White, *Yahweh's Council: Its Structure and Membership* (Tübingen: Mohr Siebeck, 2014), 24–33; Daniel McClellan, "The Gods-Complaint: Psalm 82 as a Psalm of Complaint," *Journal of Biblical Literature* 137, no. 4 (2018): 833–51.

36. Tanḥuma B. 9; ʿAbodah Zarah 5a; Midrash Rabbah Exodus 32:7.

37. For more on the textual and linguistic background of this passage, see Richard I. Pervo, *Acts: A Commentary* (Hermeneia; Minneapolis: Fortress, 2009), 171–93.

38. For discussions of this passage, see McLay, *Use of the Septuagint in New Testament Research*, 17–30; Wolfgang Kraus, "The Role of the Septuagint in the New Testament: Amos 9:11–12 as a Test Case," in *"Translation If Required": The Septuagint in Retrospect and Prospect*, ed. Robert J. V. Hiebert (SCS 10; Atlanta, GA: Society of Biblical Literature, 2010), 171–90; W. Edward Glenny, "The Septuagint and Apostolic Hermeneutics: Amos 9 in Acts 15," *Bulletin for Biblical Research* 22, no. 1 (2012): 1–26.

39. George H. Guthrie, "Hebrews' Use of the Old Testament: Recent Trends in Research," *Currents in Biblical Research* 1, no. 2 (2003): 271.

40. Hebrews 1:5a (Psalm 2:7); Hebrews 1:5b (2 Samuel 7:14//1 Chronicles 17:13); Hebrews 1:6 (Deuteronomy 32:43); Hebrews 1:7 (Psalm 103:4); Hebrews 1:8–9 (Psalm 44:7–8); Hebrews 1:10–12 (Psalm 101:26–29); and Hebrews 1:13 (Psalm 109:1). See Susan Docherty, "The Text Form of the OT Citations in Hebrews Chapter 1 and the Implications for the Study of the Septuagint," *New Testament Studies* 55, no. 3 (2009): 355–65.

41. There is no reliable evidence for Pauline authorship of Hebrews. For a thorough review of the scholarship on authorship, see Clare K. Rothschild, *Hebrews as Pseudepigraphon: The History and Significance of the Pauline Attribution of Hebrews*, WUNT 235 (Tübingen: Mohr Siebeck, 2009).

42. For a recent and very helpful commentary on 2 Maccabees, see Daniel R. Schwartz, *2 Maccabees*, CEJL (Berlin: de Gruyter, 2008).

43. The following quotations are taken from the NRSV.

44. The translation is from M. A. Knibb, "Martyrdom and Ascension of Isaiah," in *The Old Testament Pseudepigrapha*, ed. James H. Charlesworth, 2 vols. (New Haven, CT: Yale University Press, 1983), 2:157, 163–64.

45. For an insightful recent discussion of this genre, see John J. Collins, "The Genre Apocalypse Reconsidered," *Zeitschrift für Antikes Christentum* 20, no. 1 (2016): 21–40.

29

Women and the World of the New Testament

Catherine Gines Taylor

The New Testament is a rich resource for learning about the women who walked beside Jesus during his ministry, who served as patrons and key actors within the early church, and who spread the good news of salvation after Christ's death and resurrection. Thinking critically about women's roles in the Roman world of the New Testament is a task taken up by multiple academic disciplines and within the complexities of Christianity.[1] Thoughtful, faithful, analytical readers look to female exemplars in scripture and material culture to help both women *and* men utilize the narratives of women in their own devotional practices. New Testament women are presented in distinct scriptural accounts that underscore profoundly symbolic and archetypal meanings. Our understanding of these meanings is enhanced through the practice of careful reading, scriptural exegesis, and hermeneutics. These rigorous practices expand the way we see and understand women in ever-growing and capacious ways.

Women in scripture are presented to us by their writers through a variety of lenses. We read their stories and narratives and often wish that our limited view of them was more informed or that we could see further than the distance offered by the text. Paying attention to the language and imagery of archetypes is important in studying scripture precisely because they speak directly to our understanding in both individual and communal ways.[2] This chapter focuses on a few specific archetypes of New Testament women that signify their position and power, while also considering the *realia* of lived religious experience for women. It is also important to examine the models for women who were not in traditional positions of power or who were marginalized. This kind of close reading and thinking requires a courageous and self-critical willingness to revisit the texts that we know so well. We must imagine, consider, and investigate these narratives so that they may open our hearts and minds.

While much has been written about the many women, both named and unnamed, who appear in pages of the New Testament, this study will uniquely contribute by underscoring their roles, their voices, and their archetypal examples. From patronizing familial networks to the propertied women of Paul's letters, women played pivotal roles in scripture and the successes of earliest Christianity. One of the best ways to understand the scriptural context of New Testament women is through the material culture that belongs to the age. This chapter will combine text and, at times, images from the earliest Christian sources.

This chapter is divided into three sections. The first section presents two case studies in which the narratives of two women in the New Testament, Mary (the mother of Jesus) and Tabitha, are presented within the context of early Christian art. The purpose of this section is to demonstrate how well-known and lesser-known scriptural stories were received by early Christians in ways that may surprise our modern reading of those same stories. The second section gives an illustrative sampling of named but lesser-known women in the New Testament whose stories present compelling questions and spark interest in further investigation. Finally, the third section focuses on unnamed women in the New Testament whose archetypal symbolism helps the reader understand them in sophisticated ways beyond their narratives. While this chapter can in no way provide a comprehensive look at all New Testament women, it will explore some ways in which gender is ordered, represented, and patterned within the scriptural and historical narrative.

Contextual Case Studies

As a primary case study, we should begin by illuminating the account of Mary as she is introduced to us in the moment of Annunciation.[3] Canonical sources for the Annunciation are found in Luke and Matthew. The account in Luke details the angel Gabriel's assignment by God to appear to Mary in the city of Nazareth in Galilee to proclaim her as favored and blessed and to deliver a message. After his initial salutation, Gabriel presents a succinct and powerful message: "Behold, thou shalt conceive in thy womb, and bring forth a son, and shalt call his name Jesus. He shall be great, and shall be called the Son of the Highest; and the Lord God shall give unto him the throne of his father David; and he shall reign over the house of Jacob for ever; and of his kingdom there shall be no end" (Luke 1:31–33). Gabriel answers Mary's concerns and generally describes the holy event that will occur. He gives her a witness sign in the pregnancy of her cousin Elizabeth, who was called barren. Mary's incredulity and fears are allayed in the infinite possibilities of God, and she submits to the will of the Lord. This glorious dialogue is secondary to the nucleus of the message: Christ is the Son of God, who will be born in the flesh to his mother, Mary, through the royal bloodlines of Judah, and who is the King of kings, reigning over the household of celestial and terrestrial inheritance forever and without end. The message of Gabriel has been celebrated and

analyzed over centuries; however, the iconography of the Annunciation has not been
considered in association with the reception
of the most important part of the announcement, that the household of kings, royal and
divine, would receive its heir apparent on
earth through Mary's flesh and would be favored within the household construct of the
materfamilias ("mother of the family").

As early as the second century, there was
both curiosity and confusion regarding the
role of Mary. We have good reason to suspect that the apocryphal texts that detail the
extracanonical details of Mary's life were for-
mulated as popular tales in the early church
and became well enough known to be written
down by the second century (see chapter 19
herein).[4] The degree to which the stories and
tales that became Christian apocrypha are
evidence of the earliest Marian cult cannot
be overemphasized. The iconography of the
Virgin Annunciate engaged in the domestic
task of spinning naturally developed out of
ancient iconographies that already celebrated
motherhood and the pious Matron.

Figure 1. Annunciation, Pignatta Sarcophagus,
Ravenna, Italy, 5th century AD.
Author's photograph.

Apocryphal writings on the Annunciation "display great literary and theological imagination, . . . and, of course, it was these stories that not only reproduced the folk traditions about
Mary and developing Mariology, but in themselves also fueled that theology."[5] The infancy
narrative found in the Protevangelium of James, originally composed in the second century, is
the only known surviving textual source available to readers of the fifth century that incorporates spinning as a dominant symbol in the Annunciation story. A fifth-century sarcophagus
named for the Pignatta family, today in Ravenna, Italy, features the Virgin Mary in the guise
of the spinning Roman matron. She is seated on a low stool, drawing woolen roves vertically
to her distaff from a large woven basket (fig. 1).[6] Her pose is characteristically classical as she
sits in profile facing the angel Gabriel.[7] The Virgin wears a simple stola with her palla wrapped
around her shoulders and draped over her head, demonstrating her traditional piety and modesty. Mary's gaze is directed simultaneously toward her handiwork and Gabriel.[8]

The Protevangelium of James provides the noncanonical sequence of events that sur-
rounds the birth of Mary to Joachim and Anna as well as the early life of the Virgin. In these
earliest Annunciation motifs, text and image intersect in both formal and intimate ways,
informing and legitimizing each other. These narratives become typical examples of divine

intervention, but amid the seemingly impossible miracles that surround the Virgin as she is prepared for her role, it is also possible to find suggestions of the common and ordinary. For example, it is Mary's lot to spin the purple and the scarlet for the temple veil, combining the mundane act of spinning with sacred material. Mary's task does not fall to her by accident. She is the sole legal heir to her father's inheritance, he being a rich man and a direct descendant of the royal line of David. She is specifically taken before the chief priests at her birth and receives "a supreme blessing which cannot be superseded,"[9] the undefiled daughters of the Hebrews serve her, and her parents take her at the age of three to the temple for the priest to bless her, saying, "The Lord has magnified your name among all generations."[10] Her genealogy was known, and the whole house of Israel revered her; she was to the second-century Christians of the Roman world *the* archetypal *materfamilias*, the mother as a rightful sovereign and legally powerful figure within the household.

Mary as the spinning Annunciate was the Christian archetype of exemplary womanhood, marriageability, motherhood, and fertility well before she was given the exclusive title *Theotokos*, or "God-bearer," by the church in AD 431 at Ephesus and later described as "Mother of God" (*mētēr theou*) in ecclesiastical texts.[11] Averil Cameron has pointed out that Christology was the center point around which the figure of Mary developed and attracted interest, popular devotion, and early images.[12] Though references to Mary in Gospel accounts were limited to events like the Annunciation, Visitation, Nativity, Adoration of the Magi, and the Flight into Egypt, other ideas about Mary and her role grew out of nonexplicit and apocryphal traditions, many of which were developing before the fifth century.[13]

As a second case study in scriptural reception, we can also look to the less familiar account of Tabitha from Acts 9, who was raised from the dead by Peter in similitude of Christ's raising the daughter of Jairus.[14] The story of Peter in Tabitha's house has traditionally been used to highlight the widow's experience in the early church or to illustrate charitable love within early Christian communities. Tabitha gives us insight into the archetypal complexity of the philanthropic rescuer in her own community and the capacity of widows who also acted as mothers and providers to those in need. Again, little attention has been given to the reception of early Christian images that address the iconography of Peter and the household of Tabitha. Peter's interaction with Tabitha is found at an interdisciplinary crossroads, where Acts 9 meets the earliest visual representations of Peter in Tabitha's house.

Luke introduces us to the woman called Tabitha, whose Aramaic name, translated into Greek, is "Dorcas," with both names meaning "gazelle." Tabitha's character has been associated with the gazelle as a symbol of a nurturer or life giver. It is easy to see how Peter's attentions to Tabitha accentuated her acts as symbols of love, compassion, service, and graciousness, and as a type of proselyte for the new community of Christians. This narrative was useful in expanding Christianity's borders beyond Jewish believers to gentile converts. It is important for us to examine how the image of Peter raising Tabitha was depicted in the earliest years of the church and its specific historicity for the fourth century.

A fourth-century Roman style sarcophagus gives us an excellent example today at the Church of Ste. Madeleine in Saint Maximin, France (fig. 2). On the left end, we find the scene with Peter raising Tabitha in a well-appointed room complete with draperies, a luxurious bed, an architectural column, and a pipe organ. Figures of the poor are diminutively small and kneel or sit near the side of the bed. Two women, widows, are standing behind Tabitha with their gaze and gestures directed toward her. Tabitha is proportionately large and fills the picture plane. Her dress is a simple stola and her head remains uncovered, though her hair is neatly coiffed and prepared for burial. Tabitha is depicted here as a type of crossroads figure as demonstrated in the varied figures she is shown helping. Besides the two widows standing behind Tabitha's bed, we find three smaller figures representing the poor

Figure 2. Raising of Tabitha, Sarcophagus, Church of Ste. Madeleine, Saint Maximin, France, 4th century AD. Giuseppe Wilpert. Rome: Pontificio Istituto di Archeologia Cristiana, 1929. Plate CXLV, no.7.

in the foreground next to Tabitha's bed. Indeed, they are small, according to the standards of hierarchy of scale, precisely because they are poor and are of a distinctively different social class in comparison to Tabitha and the stately, matronly widows. Tabitha's left hand rests on the head of the small female figure at her left who supports a seated, naked figure with her hands and right knee. The third kneeling figure is set apart from these and reaches out to touch the hem of Peter's garment, an act in similitude of the woman with an issue of blood touching Christ's garment. This third figure wears a peculiar head covering, akin to the Phrygian cap of foreign magi, often shown wearing similar hats in artistic representations of the Adoration of the Magi. The widows and the woman with the naked boy are easy to situate into the Levitical laws regarding the care of the widows and the fatherless. However, the inclusion of the Phrygian-capped figure indicates that Tabitha's generosity was considered, within the fourth century, to include the foreign poor as well, a notion that coincides with the nature of diverse port cities like Joppa and the conversion of Gentiles.

While we typically focus on Peter's raising Tabitha from the dead as a miracle with the convenient effect of conversion, we have long hesitated in defining the role Tabitha occupied in performing acts of charity, specifically by bestowing goods and clothing on the widows and less fortunate of Joppa. There is some discussion that Tabitha was likely a widow herself, but one who had means to maintain her household and expand her philanthropic reach to her community. That Peter goes to Tabitha's house to raise her is not just to demonstrate her ability as a non-Jewish proselyte to expand the cause of Christianity but also to normalize a new type of patron within the early church, that of the *Matrona*.

Choosing Christ Jesus: Named Women in the New Testament

When we talk about women in scripture, we often think first of named women who offer significant examples or embodiments of traits and characteristics, some of which resonate with us. In many ways, women in scripture provide personified archetypes or depictions of our own reality that, in addition to what we learn by historical and theological analysis, can be read as valuable and insightful to our own practice and devotion. We rarely talk about what it means to view women in the New Testament through the lens of archetypal models or how that perspective might shape our own practical and devotional lives. As Latter-day Saints, it is imperative that we increase our grasp of iconographic types for women in scripture so that we can recognize the competence and influence of women within the full scope of their power, holiness, and humanity. Particularly for Latter-day Saint women, how we understand scriptural accounts involving women helps shape the way we reflect the text into our own personal narrative. If we are serious in our consideration of these women, if they matter to us, we must do the work it takes to know them.

Named women within the New Testament embody multifaceted roles including that of matron, businesswoman, head of household, wise woman, prophetess, and philanthropist. These positions are often ignored in favor of the traditional roles of virginal maid, wife, and mother. If we confine ourselves to archetypes that embrace only the roles or symbolism that we find comfortable, or that have been promoted as culturally normative, we will find ourselves not only limited but also incomplete.

There are a number of named women in the New Testament who are not well known, or who fall too easily into the shadow of more illustrious actors. However, there is a synergistic familiarity that comes with careful attention to women like Anna, Joanna, Lydia, Phoebe, Prisca, and Rhoda alongside women who are more often discussed, like the Marys, Martha, and Elizabeth. Even someone as well known as Mary, the mother of Jesus, may find herself featured in significant accounts like the wedding at Cana that are often unremembered in favor of her role in the Nativity. Without attempting to provide an encyclopedic accounting, commentary, and biography for all of the named women in the New Testament, I will consider only an illustrative sample of women who are not often highlighted or studied with much care.

Anna

Many of us can clearly imagine the prophetess Anna as a matronly, exemplary, wise woman abiding in God's temple. The Gospel of Luke pays careful attention to widows and women generally, perhaps revealing his benevolent concern for the poor and oppressed.[15] As a widow, Anna may have been part of an order of consecrated elderly women who enjoyed social respectability within the Jewish world,[16] even if they were also very poor and reliant on the welfare of those who made offerings in the temple or gave alms. As a prophetess, she reflects the "tradition of Miriam, Deborah, and Huldah, and she foreshadows the honorable Christian calling held by, among others, the daughters of Philip (Acts 21:9)."[17] Anna's experience in Luke 2:36–38 closely parallels that of Simeon's from Luke 2:25–35. Simeon recognizes Jesus as the Christ and praises God. Simeon's words are included in the story, but even though Anna is recognized as a prophetess, devoted to temple worship and prayer, her voice is only mentioned; her words are absent. Luke pairs Anna with Simeon in a way typical to his practice of using both male and female characters, like Zechariah and Elizabeth, in his narrative.[18] Simeon speaks words of praise and consolation to Mary and Joseph, but Anna's audience is different; her audience is *all* who seek the Savior. She, like Elizabeth, initiates a new messianic pronouncement as she "began to praise God and to speak about the child to all who were looking for the redemption of Jerusalem" (Luke 2:38 NRSV).

Joanna

As an attestation for active, female disciples of Jesus, Luke 8:3 is remarkable. The verse names three women who, by presumably independent will and means, joined Jesus and presumably used their resources to provide for the community of believers. We are introduced to Joanna by reference to her husband, Chuza, whose title *epitropos* may indicate that he managed property for Herod.[19] Joanna's husband is mentioned without indicating if he is a believer, thereby giving us pause to consider that perhaps Chuza is very lenient about his wife's movements and beliefs, or like other "rebel" women from the noncanonical Acts of Apostles, Joanna has taken her dowry or her independent means and left her home to follow Jesus.[20] Joanna takes on the archetype of a rather unorthodox truth seeker. Her consecrated piety, which perhaps lay outside traditional social structures, demonstrated Joanna's humility and her utter devotion to act in favor of spiritual discipleship.

Joanna is also second in the list of women in Luke 24:10 who witness the empty tomb. Whereas Mark 16:1–8 indicates an angelic commission for the women witnesses to tell the apostles, Luke 24 adds subtlety to the story by placing the initiative with the women themselves to go and tell.[21] Matthew 28:9 nuances the account even further when Jesus suddenly meets the women on their way. The women take hold of Jesus's feet and worship him before also receiving the commission to go and tell. In all cases, Joanna, Mary Magdalene, Mary the mother of James, Salome, and "other women" are given the role of first messengers, envoys, even *apostoloi* or apostles,[22] commissioned to tell the good news.

Lydia

Lydia is a woman living in Philippi, a Roman province in Macedonia, whom Paul meets and baptizes near the beginning of his ministry, along with her entire *oikos*, during his first journey. The late antique Roman household, the Latin *domus* or the Greek *oikos*, extended beyond the nuclear family and often included "several generations, a large number of slaves, other dependents and even unrelated clients."[23] The household was the essential locus for the spread of early Christianity, and the first churches were associated with the organized house church and the assembly of the Christian community. One of the most powerful examples of this phenomenon in the apostolic period is found within the household of Lydia, mentioned in Acts 16. Lydia is first encountered among other women who gathered at "a place of prayer" (16:13–15 NRSV), a location in which it was proper and appropriate for women to hear Paul preach.

Lydia's name has caused some scholars to question her historicity. The region of Lydia in Asia Minor was where the city called Thyatira, Lydia's hometown, was located. This connection caused some to think that she was a fictitious figure with her name adopted by Luke as a personification of this place.[24] However, it is at Philippi where Paul and Lydia meet. Philippi is home to the Dionysian cult and polytheistic goddess worship. Many women gather there for worship purposes. Placing Lydia and her conversion at Philippi makes a theological statement,[25] especially when that statement is directed toward converting women who are possibly participating in these mystery cults. Shelly Matthews has further studied the historicity of women like Lydia—identifying real women and finding them in scripture between the lines of narrative. Rather than conceding that Lydia's narrative is fictional, she points to Paul's letters that reveal women as primary hosts for house churches.[26] Matthews finds the pattern of fiscally independent women who support Paul to be an attestation of Lydia's reality. Furthermore, what she finds most suspect in the narrative is that such a woman as Lydia is presented only as a "convert accommodating Paul and his mission, and not as a missionary/leader in her own right."[27] Archetypally, Lydia demonstrates how religious piety *and* independent work were not mutually exclusive.

Phoebe

At the end of Paul's epistle to the Romans (16:1–2), we are introduced to a woman called Phoebe. She is commended by Paul, as a *diakonos*, or deacon, from a regional church at Cenchreae, to the hospitality of the saints in Rome.[28] Phoebe's title, *deacon*, is sometimes translated as "servant" (KJV, NIV), but Paul clearly uses the term in Greek, without gendered distinctions, to also refer to his own ministry of preaching and teaching within the church.[29] Paul asks that the Roman believers welcome and aid Phoebe in part because he is under obligation to her as his patron or benefactor. Phoebe was probably the person who carried the letter, which would arguably become one of the most important books in the New Testament.[30] As a patron, Phoebe provides funds for the church and may also publicly represent believers within the church. Significantly, Phoebe is also described as *prostatis*, the feminine form of a noun that means "one who stands before" and can be interpreted as leader, or in this context is likely emphasizing her role as patron.[31] Both designations are evidenced in association with women during late antiquity. For example, a stele from Jerusalem with an epigraph dating to the second half of the fourth century reads, "Sophia, a deacon, a second Phoebe."[32]

Paul clearly identifies women like Phoebe as part of his circle of coworkers. She has work to do in Rome and is independent enough to accomplish it of her own accord. Some scholars have suggested that she may have been traveling "to or through Rome as a missionary or Church worker."[33] Paul acknowledges Phoebe's role as a patron and as a teacher, but he also describes her as an archetypal networker, someone who enhances the unity of the church by sharing information. She is a mentor and advocate with Paul and carries words and wisdom to the nascent church.

Prisca

Among Paul's coworkers in Christ Jesus, Priscilla is mentioned six times in the New Testament as *Prisca*, the diminutive name form of *Priscilla* (Acts 18:2–3, 18–19, 24–26; Romans 16:3–5; 1 Corinthians 16:19; 2 Timothy 4:19). Acts contextualizes the circumstances of Paul's meeting with Prisca and her husband Aquila by establishing that they, and other Jews, have left Rome under the orders of Claudius.[34] Paul finds both work and hospitality in the household of Prisca and Aquila in part because they too dealt in the textile trade. After a considerable time, Paul, Prisca, and Aquila travel to Ephesus, where they part ways but are not forgotten by Paul. He further addresses their efforts and the church that met in their house. We come to know Prisca as she traveled with her husband, spreading the gospel to Rome, Ephesus, and Corinth. One encounter that demonstrates Prisca's perceptive and authoritative wisdom is found in connection with the preaching of another believer, Apollos the Alexandrian.[35] After moving on from their ministry in Corinth, Prisca and Aquila seem to be functioning like Barnabas, Timothy, Silas, and other Pauline missionaries.[36] Their teaching roles naturally take them to the synagogue at Ephesus, where they cross paths with Apollos, a well-educated and effective orator. He had "been instructed in the way of the Lord and spoke as one stirred up by the Spirit" (Acts 18:25 CEB). Prisca and Aquila hear him and bring him into their circle of friends, and Prisca takes the authoritative initiative to instruct him privately and "more accurately" in God's way (Acts 18:26 NRSV).

Questions had arisen in Ephesus and Corinth among believers concerning baptism, ways of staying in the path, and gifts of the Spirit (see Acts 19:1–10 NRSV). Prisca, as an educated businesswoman, uses her benevolent influence, wisdom, and authority to protect and teach others. She is loyal in her relationships and faithful in her pioneering enterprises that sustain the spread of the good news to many people. Although the account of Prisca and Aquila in Acts has been approached with some caution because some scholars believe it may include highly idealized narratives,[37] further attestations in Romans, 1 Corinthians, and 2 Timothy underscore the fact that Prisca's name and her work were known and respected, even highly esteemed, by communities of Christian believers. For Prisca and Aquila to be able to perform as itinerant preachers and welcome congregants into their house church may speak to the success of their business enterprises as well as to their capacity to sustain a prominent and well-funded missionary effort.

Prisca is a missionary, but she is also a wife. Naming Prisca first in the pair is significant and may point to her status as a propertied *materfamilias* and to the status of her family according to Roman social constructs.[38] The vision of household dynamics glimpsed in these few verses reflects a sense that, at least in some early Christian communities, egalitarian attitudes toward women existed within marriage.[39] These structures also held up under the scrutiny of Roman law, whereby women of property or family were designated as the *materfamilias* and head of household.[40] Prisca's devotion and dedication to her vocational work are matched by external supports in many facets of her life. Her husband partners with her in devotion, she enjoys the friendship and contemplative notice of the apostle Paul, and she finds herself as an organizational and economic life force in relationship with her community.

Without diminishing their contribution as a secondary force, we must also acknowledge the wave of named women who were also known as "workers in Christ Jesus." Prisca and Aquila join a number of named New Testament women who are faithful evangelists, workers in the Lord, and devotees: the many Marys—not including Mary the mother of Jesus and Mary Magdalene ([Mary 1] John 11:1–33; 12:1–8; [Mary 2] John 19:25; 20:1–18; [Mary 3] Matthew 27:56; [Mary 4] John 19:25; [Mary 5] Acts 12:12; [Mary 6] Romans 16:6)—Tryphaena and Tryphosa (Romans 16:12), Lois (2 Timothy 1:5), Eunice (2 Timothy 1:15), Persis (Romans 16:12), and Junia (Romans 16:7). Paul also admonishes two other women called Euodia and Syntyche in Philippians 4:2–3 to be of "the same mind in the Lord" because they have also "struggled beside me in the work of the gospel." This critical mass of named women takes up a significant role in the building up of the church. They are visionary seekers, they challenge social systems in favor of spiritual communion, they are empathetic with their fellow believers, and they displayed an uncanny openness to the powerful life force of the Spirit. Examining the textual and historical context for these women helps us to reconstruct the stories of those who have been consistently overlooked in our study of the Bible and the earliest Christian church.

Sustained in Christ Jesus: Unnamed Women of the New Testament

Unnamed women in the New Testament are easily recognizable within archetypal constructs, partly because they are explicitly known according to their symbolic modalities. Unnamed women fall into patterned categories that describe their familial relationships, their social position, their sexual status, their bodily state of being, and their actions or behaviors. Nearly all unnamed women are categorized according to their physicality, their essential bodies, and the external manifestations of their internal selves. Rarely are we privy to their thoughts or words. Unnamed men in the New Testament may also fall into these same categories, but they often have the capacity to act with social independence. For example, the rich man from Mark 10:25, the good Samaritan from Luke 10:36, and even the crippled beggar at the temple gate in Acts 3:1–10 act or speak in ways independent of customary gendered restrictions. Unnamed men also speak for themselves or others when they interact with Jesus, like the centurion and his servant from Matthew 8:5, 9 or the father of the boy with a spirit from Mark 9:14–29. As unnamed women speak less often than men, it is imperative that we examine and enumerate the ways that they are archetypally present in the New Testament and then consider the ways their stories illuminate and complicate the way we understand them. We must never lose sight of the fact that their narratives were connected to communities and that the way we read them can reflect our own receptive biases.

Unnamed women and familial relationships

Unnamed women are often described in relation to men as mother, daughter, wife, widows, mother-in-law, daughter-in-law, and so forth. Although many women are only noted by their familial affiliations, they still exerted influence without words. One example that leads us to consider these connections is the mother-in-law of Simon Peter, whom Jesus heals from a fever in Mark 1:30. She, as proof of her cure, immediately begins serving the men gathered in the tradition of hospitality. We must also acknowledge the woman absent from the narrative, Peter's wife, who is caring for her mother within her marital household, most likely because she is widowed.[41] Widows, virgins, and celibates are often noted for their extraordinary circumstances within the early church. Widows, wise women, and virgins are sometimes archetypally associated with visionaries and prophetesses, like Philip's four daughters, who in Acts 21:9 reflect the prophecy in Joel 3. Even in their silence, Philip's daughters are still noted for their devotional relationship to the believers.[42] Unfortunately, these women and other women in Acts, even those with considerable familial affiliations, for the most part, do not speak.[43] Even if his exclusion is not deliberate, Luke has left us without a record of their prophetic words. We must concede that, without language, women may lack public credibility. Even in the case of the household slave, Rhoda, who speaks the truth and brings news of Peter's liberation from prison, she is not believed (see Acts 12:12–15 NRSV). Beverly Roberts Gaventa has underscored the fact that mothers, daughters, wives, and widows in the Acts of the Apostles may not have words or may be absent altogether, but some do, especially in the case of virgins and widows, manage to act independently and in alignment with God's relentless fulfillment of his promises.[44]

Marital status and familial relationships define women in the ancient Greco-Roman world. The lived constructs of marriage in the first-century Mediterranean world are surprisingly diverse because they depend on the social and religious laws and customs held by many different groups of people. Marriage under Augustan Roman law reforms applies to Roman citizens.[45] These laws formalize the rights of women, based on their fertility, to maintain their own property independent of their husbands, allowing women under certain circumstances to divorce.[46] Gender parity is an issue that Paul addresses, particularly for unmarried women in 1 Corinthians 7:32–33, who are anxiously concerned with the Lord's work in contrast to married women who necessarily have other kinds of material responsibilities.[47]

Unnamed women defined by their sexual status

Some unnamed women are defined by their sexual status in the New Testament. They include the woman who is looked at lustfully (Matthew 5:28), the adulterous woman (John 8:3–11), divorced women (Matthew 5:31–32; 19:3–9; Mark 10:2–12; Luke 16:18), prostitutes (Matthew 21:31–32; Luke 15:30; 1 Corinthians 6:15–16), those who had been married multiple times (Matthew 22:23–30; Mark 12:18–25; Luke 20:27–36), bridesmaids (Matthew 25:1–13), unmarried women (1 Corinthians 7), those who take part in unnatural intercourse (Romans 1:26), and virgins (Luke 1–2; 1 Corinthians 7). Sexualized language, image, and metaphor are used largely and almost exclusively in connection with women, their bodies, and their behaviors. For example, adulteresses, as discussed in John 8:3–11 and generally in James 4:1–13, are read as actors who operate within the larger christological condemnation of disloyal, unchaste behavior.[48] Social constructs surrounding female sexuality had very real-life effects when it came to marriage expectations, pregnancy, sexual behaviors, coercion, and even rape. We would do well to read these sexual archetypal descriptions with some compassion, some mercy, and the clear realization that the male partner is often absent from the narrative. Often, women privileged their material, spiritual, social, and physical security over their own power, will, and ability to act and were prone to both the social stigma and physical consequences of the behavior of themselves and others.

Whereas issues of purity laws are the focus of sexual behaviors, especially as we take our cue from unnamed women, we must recognize and deliberately consider the way we read narratives that harm or exclude women for merely being female. The anonymity of unnamed women, in its most frustrating guise, perpetuates the objectification of women designated by their sexual actions by proclaiming a judgment akin to damnation. Even if the sinning female from these narratives is forgiven, the hermeneutics of imagination may perpetuate her as an exile within the biblical context and, perhaps, beyond.

We must further complicate our thinking toward unnamed women in the New Testament who are reduced to their sexual identity. It is to our advantage to ask questions like the following: How does women's sexuality determine control over their bodies by others or demonstrate control over their own bodies and possessions? What burdens and advantages does reality place upon the lives of married, single, divorced, and ascetic women? What issues arise around health and cleanliness laws specific to women? Does pointing out special cases of healing for women unduly highlight their vulnerable positioning for shame? These questions can be particularly helpful because they help us recognize the complex nature of these women who are otherwise relatively passive in the restorative accounts of their bodies.

On the other hand, desexualizing women can be detrimental. By denying their specifically female sexual power in creation, we find that women are transmuted into anonymity or rhetorically into the male domain where all of mankind become men and sons. The devaluation of marriage, motherhood, and other creative capacities for sexually engaged women within the familial dynamic can also remove women's power from the long-held mother archetype of the *creatrix*.

Unnamed women and social relationships

Unnamed women are also categorized in the New Testament as social outsiders and insiders. Outsiders like the Canaanite woman (Matthew 15:21–28) and the Samaritan woman at the well (John 4:1–42) were faced with initial social resistance in their narratives but were also instrumental in drawing former outsiders into the larger covenant community.[49] The responsibility to hold faith in divine promise is also relevant for unnamed Greek women, "outsiders" who were also believers, as well as the unnamed "insider" companions to male disciples and apostles. Unnamed women were often described according to their social status. At one end of the spectrum were women of elect status, leading women, and at the other end, slaves. Unnamed women within the community of believers also acted in roles concerning civic action and well-being. For example, the woman, a widow, who in Luke 18:20 pleads or acts as an advocate for herself against an unjust judge is recognized for her strength and persistence as she is successful in her case. Others within the community tended to the physical needs of others, especially the most vulnerable, generally in the role of a nurse (Matthew 24:19; Mark 13:17; Luke 21:23; 1 Thessalonians 2:7).

To find women participating in socially and theologically instructive ways, it is sometimes useful to incorporate imaginative and inquisitive ways of reading the scriptural narrative. For example, Elaine Wainwright asks important questions regarding Jesus's interaction with the Syro-Phoenician woman. She demands of us as readers to consider the anonymity of her possessed daughter, whose ailment is at the center of the narrative.[50] The interpersonal conversation takes place in the border region between Israel and Tyre/Sidon, a place of marginalization.[51] Jesus initially ignores the woman's plea to heal her daughter, citing her ethnic designation as a Canaanite in order to argue that "it is not fair to take the children's food and throw it to the dogs" (Matthew 15:26 NRSV). From her position of vulnerability, she still bravely replies as an advocate for her ill, foreign daughter, "Yes, Lord, yet even the dogs eat the crumbs that fall from their masters' table" (Matthew 15:27 NRSV), and is ultimately blessed with a healing miracle.

The sociality of unnamed women was also intricately connected to their bodily state of being. For example, the woman who hemorrhages, the bent woman, and various iterations of pregnant, laboring, and nursing women provide very clear images of women whose social narrative is specifically bound to their bodies. Many of these accounts are acutely essentialist, meaning that the narrative is wholly dependent on their female bodies. Their physical circumstances are framed in ways connected with shame, issues of gendered cleanliness, and the commodification of their sexuality. These women have endured over time, not because they merely tolerated their circumstances or survived them but because they were extraordinary actors who, in spite of their bodies, autonomously reached beyond their physical circumstances. Their stories are not necessarily different from many other women around them who could have also been exemplars, but they are prioritized into the New Testament text in ways that call our attention to their bodies in specific ways, often as a contrast point for Christ's healing touch.

Women's social actions were also connected bodily to gendered expectations regarding hospitality, work, patronage, and household chores. New Testament women were socially connected to acts of hospitality. They were the actors who fed others, washed others, prepared meals, and leavened the bread of life and their communities. Parables often feature domestic tasks accomplished by women who sweep, provide sustenance, even offer coins. Women's affiliation with hospitality is deeply connected to their role as patrons to the disciples. Without question, women were at hand within the household, acting as and staying with the disciples of Jesus in shared fellowship.

Unnamed women and holy or devotional acts

The largest group of unnamed women are those identified by their actions. Holy and devotional acts are underscored in the New Testament by the accounts of women who anoint, praise, teach, lament, pray, and prophesy. Women take action as true believers; they are baptized, persecuted, and devoted (at places of prayer). They are witnesses to Jesus's resurrection and are called deacons, profess reverence, and are moved on by the Holy Spirit.

We sometimes understand women's devotional practices in the early church through the reaction of men toward them rather than from an explicit record of the acts themselves. For example, in 1 Corinthians 11:5 it is clear from Paul's letter that women in the Corinthian church prayed and prophesied publicly, a tradition that "may perhaps go back to the example of Prisca"[52] as a founding missionary in Corinth. Paul argues in behalf of these women and stresses that a woman should have *exousia*, or authority, over her own head and "appeals to the new church order marked by mutual interdependence of men and women."[53] In the same chapter (11:14–16 NRSV), Paul also adds ambiguity to his former statements by expressing the persistence of nature and custom in the acceptable quality of women's devotions, the subordination of which is traditionally emphasized over other interpretations.[54] This has led many scholars to argue for one of these two perspectives, rather than seeing the productive tension inherent in Paul's own arguments.[55]

Apart from arguing for the official capacities of women in devotional settings, there are also customary circumstances in which women were primary actors. Women who anoint, female messengers, and women who participate in rites of death and burial come immediately into view as we examine the events surrounding Christ's passion, crucifixion, death, burial, and resurrection. Women in the New Testament perform holy acts that indicate a high level of perception, foreknowledge, or intuitive understanding of coming events.

The realms of hospitality and death are simultaneously the domains of women. The act of the anointing woman, recorded anonymously in the Synoptic Gospels and named as Mary the sister of Martha and Lazarus in the Gospel of John, is not outside her office, even if its enactment is somewhat unconventional. Dennis McDonald prioritizes female participation and its significance by underscoring the anointing act as one that moves beyond hospitality into the realm of prophetic seership.[56] The woman acts from recognition of Jesus's forthcoming passion, and she does so without the need of an exterior revelatory sign. MacDonald compares the varied story of the woman anointing Jesus with ointments, oils, and tears to the account of the nurse Eurycleia, who recognizes Odysseus's feet as she washes them on his return to Ithaca.[57] This trope of recognition is presented as a specifically female act of wisdom and is enacted in moments of birth, death, and rebirth—all realms where women stand at the gates, attend, participate, and witness.

Unnamed women are dominantly present at the cross as well as in the burial and resurrection accounts. Their presence was credible to the audience of the New Testament, which illuminates the acceptability of women within rituals and practices of mourning, watching, waiting, and lamenting the dead. Carolyn Osiek has highlighted the incongruities of the New Testament world, where apotheosis accounts and messianic rhetoric were crucial to the communal memory of first-century believers, and yet when that message was first delivered by women, they were not believed.[58]

Unnamed women and unholy or profane actions

In addition to unnamed women being associated with holy acts, there are also those who are anonymously associated with tale-tellers, silly women, and even the false female prophetess Jezebel, who is typified and vilified in Revelation 2:20. The term *Jezebel* is, of course, associated with the Israelite queen from 1 Kings 16 who encourages her husband, King Ahab, to abandon the worship of Jehovah in favor of the deities Baal and Asherah. Women who speak falsely are first presented in the example of Sapphira, the first female speaker in Acts, whose words are lies and who is struck dead (Acts 5:1–11). Women as tale-tellers are a problem because their words are viewed as being in conflict with the true faith. The Pastoral Epistles of 1 and 2 Timothy and Titus include warnings relevant to the last days. Part of their rhetoric warns against "false teachings," adhering to extreme behaviors like asceticism or celibacy, and believing legends or old wives' tales rather than gospel teachings.[59] The practice of describing women as tellers of tales was dually problematic for the early church, which collectively set its hope in the living God. First, by associating these practices specifically with women, the writer(s) immediately connects women with irrational and emotional superstitions in opposition to men's spiritual or rational mind. Secondly, the common refrain from 1 Timothy 5:13, describing women as "gossips and busybodies," aligns women's idle nonsense against sayings that are "sure and worthy of full acceptance" within the gospel framework from 1 Timothy 4:9. By associating women with the foolish woman as an archetype, we can naturally focus on her naïveté, but we would be wise to also consider that those who ultimately find a path of mature thinking, even the path of Woman Wisdom, begin with questioning, simple discourse, and new experience.

By gendering authoritative voices, there is a clear bias against women's "silly" narratives. Even though there were legitimate concerns over correct teachings perpetuated amongst the faithful, this diminutive name-calling is rhetorically dismissive. As mentioned in 2 Timothy 3:6 within the context of the apocalyptic discussion of the last days, silly women are those who are most vulnerable to false teachers. They are swayed by their desires and never arrive "at a knowledge of the truth" (3:6).[60] The struggle for authentic instruction, especially within the nascent church at Ephesus, indicates both the growing nature of the congregation and the fact that the church was conceptually faced with the prospect of apocalyptic finality. Time is perceived as essentially short, and women who professed proper and correct reverence for God are put in high contrast with women, personified or real, who are traditionally denigrated for their silly ways.

Conclusions

In thinking through the experiences of New Testament women, we should focus attention on the fact that they were holy, nurturing, humble, and submissive as well as decisive, revelatory, intuitive, resilient, powerful, and fallible human beings. It is not the intention of this study to use gender as a tool of categorization, especially if it limits and marginalizes women as other or differentiates or separates them from the powerful discourses within scripture. Each of the women discussed here contributes to a larger, more holistic way of comprehending women in the world of the New Testament.

Suggesting specific archetypal meanings for New Testament women is not meant to be the definitive or final word on the matter. This kind of examination attempts instead to be helpful in highlighting patterns and characteristics in the text. The entirety of each scriptural account and all iterations of commentary for each woman would be impossible to convey here. However, when we encounter their pericopes, it is useful to consider these New Testament women, if not from all perspectives, at least from broader vantage points. What we are offered, as faithful and conscientious readers, is an intimately deep, and often surprising, engagement with the expansive lives of women whose devotion, in many ways, reflects that of modern women.

❧

Catherine Gines Taylor is the Hugh W. Nibley Fellow at the Neal A. Maxwell Institute for Religious Scholarship at Brigham Young University.

Further Reading

Bauckham, Richard. *Gospel Women: Studies of the Named Women in the Gospels.* Grand Rapids, MI: Eerdmans, 2002.

Joynes, Christine E., and Christopher C. Rowland, eds. *From the Margins 2: Women of the New Testament and Their Afterlives.* Sheffield, England: Sheffield Phoenix, 2009.

McCabe, Elizabeth A., ed. *Women in the Biblical World.* Lanham, MD: University Press of America, 2009.

Meyers, Carol, Toni Craven, and Ross S. Kraemer, eds. *Women in Scripture: A Dictionary of Named and Unnamed Women in the Hebrew Bible, the Apocryphal/Deuterocanonical Books, and the New Testament.* Grand Rapids, MI: Eerdmans, 2000.

Olson, Camille Fronk. *Women of the New Testament.* Salt Lake City: Deseret Book, 2014.

Spencer, F. Scott. *Salty Wives, Spirited Mothers, and Savvy Widows: Capable Women of Purpose and Persistence in Luke's Gospel.* Grand Rapids, MI: Eerdmans, 2012.

Notes

1. Volumes of commentaries, dictionaries, and academic studies are available. See, for example, Richard Bauckham, *Gospel Women: Studies of the Named Women in the Gospels* (Grand Rapids, MI: Eerdmans, 2002); Christine E. Joynes and Christopher C. Rowland, eds., *From the Margins 2: Women of the New Testament and Their Afterlives* (Sheffield, England: Sheffield Phoenix, 2009); Elizabeth A. McCabe, ed., *Women in the Biblical World* (Lanham, MD: University Press of America, 2009); Carol Meyers, Toni Craven, and Ross S. Kraemer, eds., *Women in Scripture: A Dictionary of Named and Unnamed Women in the Hebrew Bible, the Apocryphal/Deuterocanonical Books, and the New Testament* (Grand Rapids, MI: Eerdmans, 2000); and Camille Fronk Olson, *Women of the New Testament* (Salt Lake City: Deseret Book, 2014).

2. Archetypes are patterns or models from which copies, examples, or imitations can be derived. The origin of archetypes is ancient and dates back to the forms within Platonic thought. Archetypal criticism is used

in the assessment of literature and art and is expansive and useful when considering symbolic language in scripture. See, for example, Carl Jung, *Man and His Symbols* (Garden City, NY: Doubleday, 1964).

3. Compare Catherine C. Taylor, "The *Pignatta Sarcophagus*: Late Antique Iconography and the Memorial Culture of Salvation," *Biblical Reception* 3 (2014): 30–56.

4. David R. Cartlidge and J. Keith Elliott, *Art and the Christian Apocrypha* (London: Routledge, 2001), 1–20.

5. J. K. Elliott, *A Synopsis of the Apocryphal Nativity and Infancy Narratives* (Leiden, Netherlands: Brill, 2006), ix.

6. The combination of images on this sarcophagus, including the Annunciation scene, may indicate that this imagery was specifically chosen by or for a particular client rather than being part of the typical decorative repertoire readily available in the workshop.

7. This pose is commonly seen in numismatic evidence as female members of the imperial household take on this seated profile or three-quarter pose demonstrating *pudicitia*, or modest virtue.

8. All facial features have been weathered or worn away, yet her face remains in profile without indication of any sideward or forward glance.

9. Protevangelium of James 6.2, in J. K. Elliott, *The Apocryphal New Testament* (Oxford: Oxford University, 2005), 59.

10. Protevangelium of James 7.2 in Elliott, *Apocryphal New Testament*, 60.

11. Ioli Kalavrezou, "Images of the Mother: When the Virgin Mary Became *Meter Theou*," *Dumbarton Oaks Papers* 44 (1990): 165–72.

12. Averil Cameron, "The Early Cult of the Virgin," in *Mother of God: Representations of the Virgin in Byzantine Art*, ed. Maria Vasilake (Milan, NY: Skira, 2000), 3.

13. Elliott, *Apocryphal New Testament*, 48–51.

14. Compare Catherine C. Taylor, "Peter in the House of Tabitha: Late Antique Sarcophagi and Christian Philanthropy," in *The Ministry of Peter, the Chief Apostle*, ed. Frank F. Judd Jr., Eric D. Huntsman, and Shon D. Hopkin (Provo, UT: Religious Studies Center, Brigham Young University; Salt Lake City: Deseret Book, 2014), 191–210.

15. Bonnie Bowman Thurston, *The Widows: A Women's Ministry in the Early Church* (Minneapolis: Fortress, 1989), 23.

16. Thurston, *Widows*, 24.

17. Thurston, *Widows*, 25.

18. Thurston, *Widows*, 23.

19. Richard I. Pervo, "Joanna," in Meyers, Craven, and Kraemer, *Women in Scripture*, 102–3.

20. Pervo, "Joanna," 103.

21. Pervo, "Joanna," 103.

22. Bauckham, *Gospel Women*, 109–202.

23. Eric D. Huntsman, *Jesus Christ and the World of the New Testament* (Salt Lake City: Deseret Book, 2006), 161.

24. Valerie Abrahamsen, "Lydia," in Meyers, Craven, and Kraemer, *Women in Scripture*, 111.

25. Abrahamsen, "Lydia," 111.

26. Shelly Matthews, "Elite Women, Public Religion, and Christian Propaganda," in *A Feminist Companion to the Acts of the Apostles*, ed. Amy-Jill Levine (London: T&T Clark, 2004), 130–33.

27. Matthews, "Elite Women," 132.

28. Elizabeth McCabe, "A Reevaluation of Phoebe in Romans 16:1–2 as a *Diakonos* and *Prostatis*: Exposing the Inaccuracies of English Translations," in McCabe, *Women in the Biblical World*, 99.

29. McCabe, "Reevaluation of Phoebe," 99–101.

30. Brian Dodd, *Problem with Paul* (Downer's Grove, IL: InterVarsity, 1996), 23.

31. Richard B. Hays, "Paul on the Relation between Men and Women," in *A Feminist Companion to Paul*, ed. Amy-Jill Levine (London: T&T Clark, 2004), 144.

32. McCabe, "Reevaluation of Phoebe," 100.

33. Jouette M. Bassler, "Phoebe," in Meyers, Craven, and Kraemer, *Women in Scripture*, 135.

34. Jouette M. Bassler, "Prisca," in Meyers, Craven, and Kraemer, *Women in Scripture*, 136.

35. Ross Shepard Kraemer, *Her Share of the Blessings* (Oxford: Oxford University Press, 1992), 144.

36. F. Scott Spencer, "Women 'of the Cloth' in Acts: Sewing the Word," in Levine, *Feminist Companion to the Acts of the Apostles*, 152.

37. Dennis MacDonald, "Lydia and Her Sisters as Lukan Fictions," in Levine, *Feminist Companion to the Acts of the Apostles*, 105–10.

38. Bassler, "Prisca," 137.

39. T. J. Wray, *Good Girls, Bad Girls of the New Testament: Their Enduring Lessons* (Lanham, MD: Rowman & Littlefield, 2016), 193.

40. Kate Cooper, "Household and Empire: The Materfamilias as *Miles Christi* in the Anonymous *Handbook for Gregoria*," in *Household, Women, and Christianities, in Late Antiquity and the Middle Ages*, ed. Anneke B. Mulder-Bakker and Jocelyn Wogan-Browne (Turnhout, Belgium: Brepols, 2006), 91–108.

41. Ross Kraemer, "Mother-in-Law of Simon (Peter)," in Meyers, Craven, and Kraemer, *Women in Scripture*, 422.

42. Beverly Roberts Gaventa, "What Ever Happened to Those Prophesying Daughters?," in Levine, *Feminist Companion to the Acts of the Apostles*, 60.

43. Gaventa, "What Ever Happened," 58–60.

44. Gaventa, "What Ever Happened," 60.

45. Susan Treggiari, *Roman Marriage: Iusti Coniuges from the Time of Cicero to the Time of Ulpian* (Oxford: Clarendon Press, 2002), 3–37.

46. Treggiari, *Roman Marriage*, 435–83.

47. Sheila Briggs, "Married Women (and Men), Unmarried Women (and Men), and Women (and Men) Married to Unbelievers," in Meyers, Craven, and Kraemer, *Women in Scripture*, 471–74.

48. Adele Reinhartz, "Adulterous Woman," in Meyers, Craven, and Kraemer, *Women in Scripture*, 454–55.

49. See, for example, Gale R. O'Day, "Surprised by Faith: Jesus and the Canaanite Woman," in *Feminist Companion to Matthew*, ed. Amy-Jill Levine (Sheffield, England: Sheffield Academic, 2001), 114–25; and Elaine Wainwright, "Not without My Daughter: Gender and Demon Possession in Matthew 15:21–28," in Levine, *Feminist Companion to Matthew*, 126–37.

50. Wainwright, "Not without My Daughter," 132–34.

51. Wainwright, "Not without My Daughter," 132.

52. Margaret M. Mitchell, "Women Praying and Prophesying," in Meyers, Craven, and Kraemer, *Women in Scripture*, 476.

53. Mitchell, "Women Praying and Prophesying," 476.

54. Mitchell, "Women Praying and Prophesying," 477.

55. Mitchell, "Women Praying and Prophesying," 477.

56. Dennis MacDonald, "Renowned Far and Wide," in *A Feminist Companion to Mark*, ed. Amy-Jill Levine (Sheffield, England: Sheffield Phoenix, 2001), 135.

57. MacDonald, "Renowned Far and Wide," 128–31.

58. Carolyn Osiek, "The Women at the Tomb: What Are They Doing There?," in Levine, *Feminist Companion to Matthew*, 214–20.

59. Lucinda A. Brown, "Women Tale Tellers," in Meyers, Craven, and Kraemer, *Women in Scripture*, 491.

60. Lucinda A. Brown, "'Silly' or Little Women," in Meyers, Craven, and Kraemer, *Women in Scripture*, 494.

30

Family, Marriage, and Celibacy in the New Testament

Mark D. Ellison

The institution of the family forms an important, complex backdrop to the New Testament and Christian origins. The family (Greek *oikos/oikia*, "house" or household) is both the context for many activities of the early church and the subject of diverse New Testament teachings.[1] After the Resurrection, followers of Jesus met to worship in homes in gatherings called "house churches" that would have included a host family joined by other individuals and families. Christian worship developed within this household setting, and members of the faith community used familial imagery and terminology to describe themselves—believers were "brothers" and "sisters," and the church, long before it constructed buildings, was the household of God (*oikos theou*), God's family (1 Timothy 3:15; 5:1–2). The gospel of Christ spread through networks of houses, kinship relations, and other social connections, and sometimes entire households converted together (Acts 16:15, 34). Among Jesus's teachings and stories that early Christians remembered, retold, and recorded were many that related to the household setting, family relationships, marriage, and wedding feasts. The apostles and others who authored New Testament books wrote counsel applying the gospel to life in the home.

As Latter-day Saint readers encounter these teachings, they may sometimes meet challenges. For one, they may be surprised by the diverse perspectives the New Testament presents on the subjects of family and marriage. Some precepts will be familiar, such as the commandment to honor one's father and mother, warnings against sexual sin and immorality, or teachings that marriage is ideally permanent, part of the divine plan from the beginning, a symbol of the relationship of Christ and the church, and a requirement for bishops. Others may seem puzzling when compared to current Latter-day Saint teachings and practices. For example, in contrast to the esteem and importance given to family, marriage, and childbearing among Latter-day Saints, some New Testament passages approach these subjects with ambivalence. Some passages subvert familial roles and loyalties, and some even praise the unmarried state for the opportunity it gave for undivided dedication to God. The presence of such differences should perhaps not be too surprising, given the different culture and circumstances of the first century. It can be easy, however, to overlook or forget how foreign the biblical world was, in certain respects, in comparison to our own. The task of reading ancient scripture requires efforts to step into the ancient world and understand teachings on their own terms, in their own cultural context.[2]

An important consideration for Latter-day Saint readers to bear in mind is that, according to the Doctrine and Covenants, some of our distinctive doctrines and practices have their origins in modern revelations that were not known in any previous age (see Doctrine and Covenants 121:26–27; 124:41; 128:18).[3] While we tend to think of the Restoration as "bringing back that which was lost," some revelations concern "things which never have been revealed from the foundation of the world," reserved for "this, the dispensation of the fulness of times" (Doctrine and Covenants 128:18).[4] Therefore, we should not expect to find them in the New Testament, whose authors addressed needs of an earlier age, within the religious and cultural framework of that age.

It is also important to recognize that New Testament teachings on family and marriage come to us in somewhat fragmentary form. None of the books of the New Testament was meant to serve as a treatise on the subject of family, marriage, or celibacy; rather, teachings on these subjects appear incidentally as authors address larger concerns, writing at various times, in diverse locales, facing different situations.

Family and marriage as conceived in the ancient Mediterranean world of the New Testament reflected the circumstances, traditions, and attitudes of that time and place, some of which would be quite uncomfortable or even morally offensive to modern readers. Lack of privacy, physical violence, slavery, male authoritarianism, and misogyny were cultural realities.[5] Against this backdrop, New Testament authors did share a conviction that the gospel of Jesus Christ should have a transforming, refining, ennobling effect on the private lives and personal relationships of all believers. Even so, the very real problems in their cultural environment call for caution and discernment in understanding New Testament teachings and evaluating their application in our own age. For example, readers may detect tension between current Latter-day Saint teachings and ancient attitudes on gender. The Church of Jesus Christ of Latter-day Saints currently emphasizes that marriage is "a partnership of equals, with neither person exercising dominion over the other,"[6] yet two New Testament passages state "the husband is the head of the wife" (Ephesians 5:23; see 1 Corinthians 11:3), and another describes the wife as "the weaker vessel" (1 Peter 3:7). The voices of women are to be valued and sought in the modern Church,[7] but two New Testament passages instruct women to remain silent at church (1 Corinthians 14:34–35; 1 Timothy 2:11–12).[8]

Past Latter-day Saint authorities have attempted to soften such passages by qualifying them somewhat,[9] but more recently Church leaders have opted not to quote them but rather to cite passages that emphasize equality and partnership over male domination in the home.[10] Some New Testament statements about family and marriage may simply reflect ancient attitudes and do not necessarily represent teachings essential to the gospel. We can be charitable readers and, as we are invited to do with the Book of Mormon, recognize that in the New Testament "if there are faults they are the mistakes of men," and choose to "condemn not the things of God," but "give thanks unto God that he hath made manifest unto you our imperfections, that ye may learn to be more wise than we have been" (title page of the Book of Mormon; Mormon 9:31).

Another factor that helps to explain the complexity of New Testament teachings on family, marriage, and celibacy is that they appear in writings of the formative period of the early church. Christ had come, ministered, died, and risen; all the books of the New Testament represent efforts to understand these transformative events and their implications in the lives of Jesus's followers. They and their world were forever changed—but what did that mean in practice? When it came to being "in the world but not of the world," some New Testament texts emphasized being "not of the world" and challenged social norms associated with family and marriage, while others (written at other times in different circumstances) emphasized being "in the world" and took more traditional stances toward family and marriage.

This chapter proceeds with the belief that if the multifaceted New Testament teachings on family, marriage, and celibacy are appreciated in their historical context and evaluated in light of the totality of the gospel, they can be of enduring value in our day and may be a resource for strengthening individuals, couples, and families and fostering inclusiveness among all the diverse members of the latter-day "household of God." Our "household" includes married couples who are trying to build a harmonious home life, and parents—some married, some single—who are working to raise believing children in frequently adverse conditions. What could the Saints of former days teach us about how the gospel of Christ affected their approach to family life in their own, often challenging circumstances? Our "household" also includes single members of whom Church teaching requires chastity, who may feel a deep need for scriptural role models and resources that speak to their life situation. Further, our church family includes childless adults who, with their unmarried brothers and sisters, at times feel grieved or marginalized in a church culture that gives superlative emphasis to childrearing, family, and marriage. What could the richness of New Testament teachings do for these members, and for the whole "body of Christ" (1 Corinthians 12:12–31)? This chapter does not take up these questions directly but poses them for the reader to contemplate. In what follows, this chapter touches occasionally on Latter-day Saint perspectives while it aims primarily to describe how family, marriage, and celibacy were understood in the New Testament world and how New Testament authors taught about these subjects. It does so, mindful that engagement with the past better equips us in the present (see Doctrine and Covenants 88:78–80; 93:53).

Customs and Cultural Background

Ancient Mediterranean households typically consisted of not only parents and children but also extended family such as cousins, elderly relatives, or the parents' adult siblings and their spouses.[11] In Galilean villages the picture of family is of this group of relatives who live and work together: a house and fields shared by brothers, sisters, mother, father, and children (Mark 10:29). Wealthy households throughout the Roman world included other dependents such as employees, slaves, freed slaves, and clients who sought the patronage of the head of the household. Individual households belonged to larger families of kinship connections. Family members generally valued group identity over individual identity and worked to advance their collective honor and well-being.

Marble funerary relief with portrait of a family group, 2nd–3rd century AD. The Metropolitan Museum of Art, metmuseum.org, Fletcher Fund, 1949.

In Roman society, the household's oldest living male was the *pater familias*, the head of the household and its estate, who wielded considerable authority (*patria potestas*, the father's power over his descendants and dependents). Roman law gave fathers "the power of life and death"—in theory the authority to imprison, enslave, beat, or even kill a descendant, but in practice a mostly symbolic principle that generally upheld the father's position yet was curbed by various social and legal restraints.[12] Nevertheless, defying a father's will was a serious matter. In such an authoritarian society, it could be difficult for individuals who heard the gospel message to choose to become a follower of Jesus; early Christian literature contains plentiful references to the potential discord caused when families included both believers and unbelievers.[13] This condition seems anticipated in Jesus's statement "I came not to send peace, but a sword. For I am come to set a man at variance against his father, and the daughter against her mother, and the daughter in law against her mother in law. And a man's foes shall be they of his own household" (Matthew 10:34–36).[14] Such circumstances may partially explain why Jesus, Paul, and other early Christians subordinated familial loyalties to the higher duty disciples owed to God and the faith community. Followers of Jesus frequently had to choose between the two.

Marriages typically were arranged between fathers of the bride and groom. Jews often married within kin groups.[15] People usually married not because they were in love (a modern motive), but because their fathers regarded the match as advantageous to the families and the couple.[16] This did not preclude a husband and wife from developing a genuinely loving, caring relationship; marital affection and harmony were widely valued ideals. The authority of fathers was tempered by their knowledge that the marriage's success depended largely on the willingness of both bride and groom and by consent requirements in Roman law.

A first stage in the formation of marriage was the betrothal, which often included negotiation of a dowry (a contribution of money or property from the bride's family to the new household). The betrothal period (which could vary in length) concluded with a formalization of marriage celebrated by wedding ceremonies and festivities. These were private affairs in the sense that they were not conducted under governmental authority (nor church authority, for centuries) but were celebrated by families in their homes and communities, with friends and relatives. Under Roman law, marriages could be formed without a ceremony, but celebrations and some rites were typical, foremost being the *deductio*—the leading of the betrothed woman from her father's house into the house of her husband. A description of this part of a wedding celebration appears in the apocryphal book of 1 Maccabees, written in the late second or early first century BC. In "celebrating a great wedding," members of two well-to-do families conducted the bride from her home "with a large escort" in "a tumultuous procession with a great amount of baggage; and the bridegroom came out with his friends and his brothers to meet them with tambourines and musicians" (1 Maccabees 9:37–39 NRSV; compare the parable of the ten virgins, Matthew 25:1–13). The wedding feast would typically take place at the groom's house; the celebrations might include songs, music, love poems, and dancing (Matthew 22:1–14; Luke 14:15–24; John 2:1–11).

Jewish weddings appear to have included prayers or blessings pronounced upon the bride and groom (compare Genesis 24:60).[17] In the apocryphal book Tobit (written in the late third to early second century BC), part of a nuptial prayer refers to Adam and Eve as the archetypal married couple and role models for the newlyweds Tobias and Sarah (Tobit 8:4–8). Jesus also referred to the first parents when teaching about marriage (Matthew 19:3–6; Mark 10:2–9). When Christians in fourth-century Rome developed a practice of having a priest or bishop pronounce a blessing upon a marrying couple (an early stage in the development of Christian marriage rites), the blessing used the words spoken to Adam and Eve, "Be fruitful, and multiply" (Genesis 1:28), a practice that early Christians inherited from Jewish custom.[18] The concept of marriage as a covenant is attested in postexilic Judaism: "The Lord was a witness between you and the wife of your youth; . . . she is your companion and your wife by covenant" (Malachi 2:14 NRSV).[19]

For first marriages, Roman women tended to wed after age fifteen, while men usually married after twenty-five; in the eastern Mediterranean both bride and groom were usually in their teens.[20] The age disparity in Roman marriage meant that from the outset of marriage, men might be financially established and their authority emphasized. Yet it also meant that husbands often predeceased their wives, leaving many widows. A widow's circumstances and ability to subsist could be precarious (Deuteronomy 27:19; Ruth 1; Mark 12:41–44) but need not be; some widows in the Greco-Roman world were quite wealthy and exercised considerable influence as heads of households. In the New Testament, women like Lydia (Acts 16:14–15), Phoebe (Romans 16:1–2), and Chloe (1 Corinthians 1:11) seem to have been heads of households who used their resources to host Christian congregations and serve important roles in the church.

A life expectancy of less than twenty-five years exerted an inexorable pressure for marriage and reproduction, which took a toll on women—it was not uncommon for women to die when giving birth in their late teens or early twenties.[21] Child mortality was high—"by the time a child reached the age of ten, half of his or her birth cohort were dead"—but if a child survived its first few years, life expectancy might rise to about forty years.[22] Only wealthy families could afford tutors or schoolmasters for their children; literacy hovered around 10–15 percent (but may have been a little higher in Jewish communities).[23] Thus, most people who became familiar with books of the Bible would have done so by hearing them read aloud in community worship, in the synagogue, or in house churches.

In Roman society unwanted infants were sometimes exposed (abandoned outdoors), and either died or were taken in by adults, often as slaves. By contrast, Jesus's sayings about children (e.g., Matthew 18:3–6; 19:14) "suggested that children were spiritually valuable persons who could even be exemplary."[24] Influenced by these teachings, early Christians strongly opposed infanticide, abortion, and exposure of infants and encouraged the adopting of abandoned children.[25]

Adoption of adults was also a practice in Roman society, particularly among imperial elites who sought to secure heirs and advance their dynasties; Julius Caesar famously adopted Octavian, who, as Augustus, adopted Tiberius. First-century Christians would have been aware that adopted sons, especially among nobility, were far from second-class members of a family but were full and honored heirs. Paul drew on the imagery of adoption as he wrote to the saints in Rome about the meaning of being a "child of God": "All who are led by the Spirit of God are children of God. For you did not receive a spirit of slavery to fall back into fear, but you have received a spirit of adoption. When we cry, 'Abba! Father!' it is that very Spirit bearing witness with our spirit that we are children of God, and if children, then heirs, heirs of God and joint heirs with Christ" (Romans 8:14–17 NRSV). For Paul and many scriptural authors, a "child of God" was what a person *became* by entering the gospel covenant and living "in Christ" (compare John 1:12; Mosiah 5:7), not what a person *is* as a preexistent spirit; the premortal existence of humanity is a doctrine articulated most clearly in latter-day scripture (see Doctrine and Covenants 93:23; Abraham 3:22–23) but not unambiguously taught in the Bible. "In the Roman worldview, sonship did not primarily point *backward* to begetting, but *forward* to inheritance, often through the medium of adoption";[26] for this reason, Paul found the imagery of adoption an apt way of illustrating the idea of *becoming* a "child of God" in Christ.

Many households included slaves. Slaves constituted an estimated 10 percent of the 50–60 million people in the empire, and perhaps 17 percent of the population closer to Rome.[27] The Greek word for "slave," *doulos*, appears over one hundred times in the New Testament, but it is translated "servant" in the King James Version, obscuring the reality of slavery as an institution in the New Testament world.[28] Slavery in the Roman Empire was not based on race or nationality; one became a slave as a prisoner of war, as a kidnapping victim, as punishment for a crime, by being abandoned or sold by one's parents, being born to slave parents, or selling oneself to escape debt or poverty. Slavery was not always lifelong; a slave's freedom could be purchased for a ransom price (compare Mark 10:45), and masters might free their slaves. Slaves were vulnerable to physical and sexual abuse, and some served in brutally harsh settings. Others, however, worked in professions, were educated, and filled positions of trust for their masters, exercising authority and enjoying relatively comfortable circumstances. Many freed slaves (*liberti*) became quite wealthy and influential members of society (Acts 6:9).

New Testament writings attest the presence of slaves and masters among the members of the church. Slavery was so enmeshed in ancient society that New Testament authors took it for granted rather than questioning or criticizing it as an institution. However, Paul stands out remarkably in encouraging a unity among the saints that would transcend social divisions: "There is no longer Jew or Greek, there is no longer slave or free, there is no longer male and female; for all of you are one in Christ Jesus" (Galatians 3:28 NRSV; compare Colossians 3:11). In one case Paul encouraged a Christian householder to receive back his escaped slave "no longer as a slave but more than a slave, a beloved brother" (Philemon 1:16 NRSV).[29] The metaphor of slavery figures in many New Testament sayings (e.g., John 8:34; Galatians 4:22–5:1). In his mortal ministry, Christ emptied himself of his divine status and took the form of a slave (Philippians 2:7). Both Jesus and Paul referred to discipleship as being the Lord's "servant" or "slave" (e.g., Matthew 10:24; 24:45–51; Luke 17:7–10; Romans 1:1), but both also taught that the relationship with God is better understood as that of a child to a father rather than that of a slave to a master (Matthew 6:9; John 20:17; Galatians 4:6–7).

Under Roman law, fully legal marriage was available only to free persons who were citizens or belonged to another legally recognized category.[30] From a legal standpoint, all other marriages between noncitizens or between slaves would have been regarded as a form of concubinage. However, as historian Carolyn Osiek points out, "the unfavorable connotations attached to terms like 'concubinage' today did not apply. Concubinage was simply a marital union not fully recognized under the restrictive marriage legislation of Rome." Some early Christians may have been citizens (such as Paul, Acts 22:25–29), but many would not have been, and their marriages "were recognized by local law and by community custom."[31]

Celibacy—abstinence from marriage and sexual relations—was practiced by various groups throughout the broader Mediterranean and Near East. Though family, marriage, and childbearing were honored in Jewish tradition, Judaism in the first century also included a few groups of people who practiced sexual renunciation, for life or for limited periods, in pursuit of a holy way of life. These included the Qumran community, some Essenes (probably the same group) described by Pliny the Elder and Josephus, and the celibate male and female Therapeutae mentioned by Philo.[32] The Old Testament nowhere commands a practice of lifelong celibacy but does mention temporary abstinence for the ritual purity needed to participate in acts of worship (e.g., Exodus 19:10–15; Leviticus 15:18–23). By the first century, this connection between sexual abstinence and religious activity had developed into an opinion among some that a prophetic vocation required lifelong continence.[33]

Roman culture also had its own ambiguities regarding family and marriage. On one hand, Roman law and philosophy promoted marriage and family as crucial to the sustaining of society: Augustan legislation penalized adultery and bachelorhood and promoted legitimate childbearing; the first-century-AD Stoic Musonius Rufus taught the necessity of sound households, stating, "Whoever destroys human marriage destroys the home, the city, and the whole human race."[34] Yet divorce was easy to obtain, and marriage bonds among Romans remained weak.[35] Roman society also had its own ascetic expressions: sexual renunciation was seen as key to forming religious specialists (such as the Vestal Virgins, priestesses in the Roman state religion), and sexual restraint was regarded as an essential element in the philosophical way of life (some philosophers denied themselves marriage and reproduction, while others taught that sexual intercourse in marriage was proper only for the procreation of children).

Anxieties about the body, ritual purity, and sexuality and the exploration of alternatives to traditional ways of life were to a degree characteristic of late ancient society. In this milieu, the writings of the New Testament are generally typical of the age in preserving both teachings that affirm marital and familial relationships, and others that challenge them in certain ways.

Family, Marriage, and Celibacy in the Gospels

Some passages in the Gospels firmly uphold the institution of the family with its attendant loyalties. In his conversation with the rich young man, Jesus listed "Honor thy father and mother" among the commandments to keep in order to inherit eternal life (Matthew 19:16–22; Mark 10:17–22; Luke 18:18–23). While on the cross, Jesus placed his mother in the care of his disciple John (John 19:25–27), showing concern for her well-being even in his extremity and exemplifying the duty to care for a widowed mother (evidently Joseph had died by this point).[36] Curiously, however, Jesus did not commit his mother to the care of his surviving brothers, but to his disciple, leaving the reader to wonder whether this might have been due to the disbelief of Jesus's brothers (John 7:5) or to the idea that his followers composed a new kind of family.

The majority of Jesus's sayings on the subject of family tend to subordinate traditional familial roles and loyalties to the role disciples hold in the kingdom, with its priorities. When Jesus's mother and brothers arrived at Capernaum where he was teaching, he used the opportunity to ask the crowd, "Who are my mother and my brothers?" Identifying his listeners as his family, he told them, "Whoever does the will of God is my brother and sister and mother" (Mark 3:31–35 NRSV; see Matthew 12:46–50; Luke 8:19–21).[37] On occasions Jesus bluntly told individuals that following him had to take priority over such duties as burying a deceased parent or bidding family members farewell (Luke 9:59–62; Matthew 8:21–22). Whoever left houses, brothers or sisters, father or mother, children, or fields for Christ's sake would receive a hundredfold reward and inherit eternal life (Matthew 19:29; Mark 10:29–30; Luke 18:29–30).[38] An arresting statement in Luke, "Whoever comes to me and does not hate father and mother, wife and children, brothers and sisters, yes, and even life itself, cannot be my disciple" (Luke 14:26 NRSV), is expressed more softly yet perhaps closer to the intended meaning in Matthew: "Whoever loves father or mother more than me is not worthy of me; and whoever loves son or daughter more than me is not worthy of me" (Matthew 10:37 NRSV).[39]

On the subject of marriage, once again the reader encounters teachings that uphold the institution and others that challenge people's thinking in certain ways. Jesus's approval of marriage is clear in his attendance at the Cana wedding feast (John 2:1–12) and particularly in his response to a question about divorce. As related in Matthew, some Pharisees approached Jesus with the question, "Is it lawful for a man to divorce his wife for any cause?" (Matthew 19:3 NRSV). The phrasing reflects debate between two schools of thought among first-century Pharisees; followers of the Jewish sage Shammai forbade divorce except for adultery, while followers of the sage Hillel permitted divorce for a wide variety of reasons (including if a woman burnt her husband's dinner!).[40] In response, Jesus redirected focus from permissible reasons for divorce to the original aim of marriage, referring to the creation story in Genesis as a basis for teaching that since husband and wife are "what God has joined together," marriage ought to be permanent:

> He answered, "Have you not read that the one who made them at the beginning 'made them male and female' [Genesis 1:27], and said, 'For this reason a man shall leave his father and mother and be joined to his wife, and the two shall become one flesh' [Genesis 2:24]? So they are no longer two, but one flesh. Therefore what God has joined together, let no one separate."[41] (Matthew 19:4–6 NRSV; compare Mark 10:6–9)

In later centuries, this saying, with its affirmation of the original place of marriage and sexuality in God's creation, proved valuable for Christians seeking to defend the goodness of marriage against extreme ascetics whose teachings demeaned marriage and childbearing.[42] It also figured in the development of a doctrine of marital indissolubility (permanence)—a teaching that "helped to define Christian identity in a world where marital stability was not always cherished."[43]

Mark records that Jesus went on to teach: "Whoever divorces his wife and marries another commits adultery against her; and if she divorces her husband and marries another, she commits adultery" (Mark 10:11 NRSV). Other New Testament passages indicate that the early church recognized legitimate reasons for divorce and did not view every case of remarriage as adultery (Matthew 5:32; 19:9; 1 Corinthians 7:15),[44] but what may have struck Mark's earliest readers as most surprising was Jesus's statement that the man who divorces his wife commits adultery *against her*. In the ancient world, adultery was viewed as an offense *against a man*—a crime against either the husband of a married woman or against the father of an unmarried woman who "belonged" to her father until she married and thereafter "belonged" to her husband. By teaching that a man's adultery was an offense *against his wife*, Jesus placed the husband under "the same moral obligation as the wife" and "raised the dignity and status of women."[45] A wife did not simply "belong" to her husband like a possession, but each belonged to the other and had mutual claim on the other's fidelity (1 Corinthians 7:3–4).

In Matthew these teachings on marriage and divorce are immediately followed by an exchange that affirms a single life as a worthy spiritual vocation for some individuals. When the disciples remark that if divorce is so serious, "it is better not to marry," Jesus states: "Not everyone can accept this teaching, but only those to whom it is given. For there are eunuchs who have been so from birth, and there are eunuchs who have been made eunuchs by others, and there are eunuchs who have made themselves eunuchs for the sake of the kingdom of heaven. Let anyone accept this who can" (Matthew 19:10–12 NRSV).[46] The reference to those "who have made themselves eunuchs for the sake of the kingdom of heaven" is best understood not as a literal reference to emasculation, but as a figurative reference to voluntary celibacy that uses the same kind of hyperbole Jesus employed in such sayings as "If your right eye causes you to sin, tear it out" and "If your right hand causes you to sin, cut it off" (Matthew 5:29–30 NRSV).[47] Since the saying is followed by references to Peter and the other disciples having left everything (including family, if only temporarily) in order to follow Jesus, it may figuratively describe the disciples during the time they traveled with Jesus.[48]

The New Testament gives no indication that Jesus himself was married.[49] Because marriage was so common at the time, it is possible that Jesus was married and that the Gospel writers simply never mentioned it. The marital status of the apostles is not mentioned in the Gospels except in the case of Peter, whose mother-in-law was healed by Jesus (Mark 1:29–31 and parallels; compare 1 Corinthians 9:5). On the other hand, the idea that Jesus might have had a wife, as it has surfaced in popular culture in recent years, is based on texts that are of dubious historical value or are outright fictions.[50] At times some Latter-day Saints have assumed that Jesus must have been married, but the reasons typically given are quite debatable, and Church spokespersons have stated that it is *not* a Church doctrine that Jesus was married.[51] During his ministry Jesus had no home of his own (Matthew 8:20; Luke 9:58), and it is not unreasonable to guess that his sacrifice of home and property extended also to marriage so that he might give single-minded devotion to his atoning mission (see Luke 12:50). Certainly in the period following the New Testament, early Christians remembered Jesus as celibate.[52] Ultimately, Latter-day Saints need not be unsettled to learn either that Jesus was not, or was, married; as some Latter-day Saint scholars have observed, the Gospel authors focused on Christ's redemptive mission, not his marital status.[53]

Another challenging passage occurs when a group of Sadducees poses a question to Jesus regarding a woman who had had seven husbands, asking whose wife she would be in the Resurrection (Matthew 22:23–32; Mark 12:18–27; Luke 20:27–38). Jesus answers, "When they shall rise from the dead, they neither marry, nor are given in marriage; but are as the angels which are in heaven" (Mark 12:25; compare Matthew 22:30; Luke 20:34–36). Some Christian writers from the second century forward took this to mean that the next life would be a nonconjugal state in which marriage would no longer exist—a view that has prevailed in traditional Christianity to the present day.[54] However, both Latter-day Saint and non–Latter-day Saint commentators have drawn attention to the ambiguity in Jesus's response, with its reference to there being no *creation* of marriages, rather than no *existence* of marriage, in the age to come. For example, non–Latter-day Saint New Testament scholar Ben Witherington observed that Jesus's statement that "no new marriages will be initiated in the eschatological state" is "surely not the same as claiming that all existing marriages will disappear in the eschatological state."[55] Since the Sadducees did not believe in resurrection (Matthew 22:23), their question was not a serious inquiry, but was meant to ridicule and was unlikely to have elicited much detail from Jesus about conditions in the Resurrection (Matthew 7:6). The people Jesus referred to when he said "*they* neither marry nor are given in marriage" appear to be Sadducees ("there were *with us* seven brethren"; Matthew 22:25; emphasis added), perhaps limiting the scope of Jesus's response, which might be paraphrased (as Gaye Strathearn has proposed): "If, as you believe, there is no resurrection, then obviously the wife will not belong to any of the brothers because *you don't even believe that there will be a resurrection.*"[56] The Sadducees' question also presupposed a practice of levirate marriage (in which a widow without offspring might marry her late husband's brother, Deuteronomy 25:5–6)—a practice that created a temporal marriage to address needs raised by death but was unneeded in the next world in which death would no longer exist.[57] Both the practice of levirate marriage and the Sadducees' disbelief in resurrection seem to correspond to the teaching in Doctrine and Covenants 132:15–16 that when a man marries a woman merely for "so long as he is in the world and she with him," it is "not of force when they are dead." But if first-century hearers understood Jesus's saying in this sense, that nuance was lost on later Christian writers.

Intriguingly, literary and archaeological evidence show that early Christians anticipated that spouses would reunite after death. Tertullian (third century AD) wrote that believing spouses would continue to be "bound" to each other in the Resurrection.[58] An inscription on the tomb of a twenty-two-year-old woman named Bassa (fourth century AD) speaks comfort to her bereaved husband Gaudentius with assurance of their affectionate reunion in heaven: "Sweet husband, most closely bound to me forever, drive off your tears, the noble court of heaven is pleasant. . . . You will be saved, I confess, and will come to the kisses of Bassa."[59] The sarcophagus of a couple named Catervius and Severina (fourth century AD) portrays the pair receiving a crown of glory from the hand of God (1 Peter 5:4; 2 Timothy 4:8) directly beneath an inscription blessing them to "rise together among the blessed with the help of Christ."[60] John Chrysostom

Sarcophagus relief with portrait of Flavius Julius Catervius and Septimia Severina, late 4th century, Cathedral of San Catervo, Tolentino. © Mark D. Ellison.

(fourth century AD) assured a young widow whose husband had died after just five years of marriage, "You shall depart one day to join the same company with him, not to dwell with him for five years as you did here, nor for 20, or 100, nor for a thousand or twice that number but for infinite and endless ages."[61] Early Christians do not seem to have understood these reunions as "eternal marriage" or "eternal family" in the same sense that modern Latter-day Saints do (in the Roman world, the concepts of "marriage" and "family" were tied to many concerns of this world such as the production of legitimate heirs who would inherit possessions). However, the hopes early Christians expressed for heavenly reunions and living together eternally show that they did not believe Jesus's answer to the Sadducees implied a dissolution of loving marital and familial bonds after death.

Family, Marriage, and Celibacy in the Undisputed Letters of Paul

Paul's writings also display a complex attitude toward family and marriage.[62] In some passages Paul sought to reinforce the stability of marriage among church members. First Thessalonians—likely the earliest-written book of the New Testament—includes Paul's instruction to know how "to control your own body (KJV "possess his vessel") in holiness and honor," which might alternatively be understood as to take unto himself a wife in holiness and honor. In this context Paul teaches against fornication (Greek *porneia*, sexual sin) and uncontrolled passion (1 Thessalonians 4:3–5 NRSV; compare 1 Corinthians 6:15–20; 9:25). Yet Paul's teaching of self-control was balanced by a resistance of ascetic extremism. Responding to church members at Corinth who thought it was "well for a man not to touch a woman," Paul discouraged sexual abstinence within marriage except perhaps for temporary, mutually agreed-on periods of prayer; otherwise, husband and wife were to show each other consideration and deference in matters of sexual intimacy (1 Corinthians 7:1–5).[63] Paul also reiterated Jesus's teaching against divorce and encouraged believers not to divorce an unbelieving spouse so long as each consented to remain married, promising that believers would have a sanctifying, saving influence on their unbelieving spouse and children (7:10–16). Nevertheless, when people had a choice to marry, Paul's counsel was to marry "in the Lord"—to wed a fellow Christian (7:39).

On the other hand, Paul expressed the wish that the Corinthians would be as he was, unmarried and sexually continent (1 Corinthians 7:8–9).[64] Clarifying that he was giving his personal opinion, Paul taught that it would be preferable for the unwed not to marry (unless their passions were strong) and pointed to the free, unencumbered devotion to God possible in the unmarried state (7:6–40). Paul stated that his reason for this counsel was because "the appointed time has grown short" and "the present form of this world is passing away" (7:29, 31 NRSV). The plain sense of his rationale, as written, is that he was anticipating an imminent return of Christ and the apocalyptic end of the current age of the world, with all its attendant tribulations. Given this "impending crisis," he wanted the saints at Corinth "to be free from anxieties," able to give undivided attention to "the affairs of the Lord" and pleasing the Lord rather than being anxious about pleasing a spouse (1 Corinthians 7:26, 32–35 NRSV). Underlying Paul's thought may have been Jesus's teachings about the tribulations to come and how those days would be particularly difficult for any who were with child or caring for an infant (Matthew 24:19).

Historian David G. Hunter comments: "It is fair to say that in 1 Corinthians 7 Paul failed to provide a truly positive rationale for Christian marriage. Ultimately he presented marriage as merely a defense against illicit desire. 'By this essentially negative, even alarmist strategy,' Peter Brown has observed, 'Paul left a fatal legacy to future ages.'"[65] Part of that legacy was the development of a tradition that virginity was of greater religious merit and would earn a greater eternal reward than a life that included marriage and childbearing (compare 1 Corinthians 7:38).

One means by which Latter-day Saints have avoided this legacy is the Joseph Smith Translation of 1 Corinthians 7:29, which alters the meaning of the passage by narrowing its audience, "*But I speak unto you who are called unto the ministry,*" and redefining the shortness of time as that remaining until those addressed "*shall be sent forth unto the ministry.*" Thus, the unwed state was preferable for those embarking on full-time missionary journeys but not necessarily for everyone. It is not clear from the JST whether this represents a restoration of original intent (if not original text) or an inspired, prophetic reframing of the ancient text that harmonizes it with Restoration scripture and makes it applicable to the latter-day Church.[66] In any case, there is no insurmountable theological problem with the plain reading of the received text of 1 Corinthians 7, including Paul's expectation of an imminent return of Christ. Latter-day Saints believe that apostles may hold personal opinions and that "not every statement made by a Church leader, past or present, necessarily constitutes doctrine."[67]

Often quoted in Latter-day Saint discussions of marriage, 1 Corinthians 11:11 does not deal primarily with marriage in its original context within the epistle. Rather, the statement "neither is the man without the woman, neither the woman without the man, in the Lord" occurs in the course of a larger passage (1 Corinthians 11:2–16), notoriously difficult and much debated, regarding women in worship settings. Paul affirms that women pray and prophesy in Christian worship (1 Corinthians 11:5) yet is concerned that they wear proper hair coverings. The discussion is marked by tension between hierarchical and egalitarian views of gender. On one hand, the sequence of creation in Genesis (Genesis 2:7, 21–22) leads Paul to say, "The husband is the head of his wife" (1 Corinthians 11:3 NRSV). On the other hand, Paul turns around and challenges this notion as he states that man also comes through woman (is born of woman) and neither is without the other in the Lord (1 Corinthians 11:11–12).[68] Though Paul's overriding intention appears to have been to encourage unity in the church (1 Corinthians 11:18), his statement about the mutual interdependence and reciprocity of woman and man "in the Lord" certainly has application in marriage. Both in marriage and in the Church family, men and women are "intended to learn from, strengthen, bless, and complete each other."[69]

Family, Marriage, and Celibacy in Later Epistles

Embedded in a number of New Testament books are texts listing instructions to various members of early Christian households—wives and husbands, children and parents, slaves and masters. Called "household codes" by scholars, these texts bear similarity to passages in Greek and Hellenistic Jewish literature promoting social stability by extolling ordered, well-managed homes in which family members fill their roles in proper relationship to each other.

The earliest of the New Testament household codes appear in Colossians 3:18–4:1, 1 Peter 2:13–3:12, and Ephesians 5:21–6:9 (which derives from the code in Colossians). The codes in the Pastoral Epistles (1 Timothy 2:8–15; 5:1–22; 6:1–10; Titus 2:1–10) are of a later date, and since they add other members of the congregation such as widows, elders, bishops, and deacons, they might be called "congregational codes" written for the house church setting.[70] All but the code in 1 Peter are attributed to Paul, but on the basis of key differences between these texts and the undisputed epistles of Paul, most New Testament scholars believe they were written by followers of Paul in his name, potentially after his lifetime.[71] In any case, these codes represent a more traditionalist strand of teaching that upholds existing social structures and hierarchies in the ancient household. They seem to reflect a setting in which expectations of an imminent Second Coming had begun to fade, and the charged apocalypticism underlying the Synoptic Gospels and Pauline Epistles was moderating. Christian communities across the Mediterranean world were coming to terms with the long-term project of building up the church and establishing themselves within society. This required defending against charges of being countercultural or seditious; one can see an anxious desire for peaceful social integration in the counsel to honor the emperor, pray for kings and other authority figures, be subject to rulers, live a quiet, peaceful life, avoid disputes, and be courteous to everyone (1 Peter 2:17; 1 Timothy 2:1–2; Titus 3:1–2). This assimilating expression of New Testament–era Christianity included affirming the norms of traditional households. However, the New Testament household codes made some important modifications to existing norms.

For example, the codes redescribed familial relationships by emphasizing mutual deference to counterparts and reorienting individuals to each other in view of each person's relationship to Deity: wives were to be subject to their husbands *as unto the Lord* (Ephesians 5:22–24, 33; Colossians 3:18; 1 Peter 3:1, 5–6); children were to obey their parents *in the Lord* (Ephesians 6:1–3; Colossians 3:20); slaves were to be subject to their masters *as unto Christ* (Ephesians 6:5–8; Colossians 3:22–25; 1 Peter 2:18–25); husbands were not to treat a wife harshly but to be considerate of her, honor her, and love her *as Christ loved the church* and gave himself for it (Ephesians 5:25–33; Colossians 3:19; 1 Peter 3:7); fathers were not to provoke their children to anger, but bring them up in the discipline and instruction *of the Lord* (Ephesians 6:4; Colossians 3:21); masters were to treat slaves justly and fairly knowing that both they and their slaves had the same *Master in heaven* (Ephesians 6:9; Colossians 4:1). Thus, while the household codes reinforced the order and patriarchal authority valued in the broader society, they also urged their readers to rethink their household roles in light of the gospel of Christ. The traditionally subordinate members of each pair—wives, children, and slaves—are addressed first, "as persons in their own right endowed with dignity," showing that they "also have a significant role to play."[72] The counsel to wives in 1 Peter 3:1–6 runs counter to the ancient custom that a wife should fear her husband and adopt the worship of his gods; rather, the believing woman's faith might win over her unbelieving husband. The instruction in Ephesians 5:22 for wives to be subject to their husbands appears only after the preliminary statement in Ephesians 5:21 that *all* household members—husbands and wives alike—should "be subject to one another out of reverence for Christ" (Ephesians 5:21 NRSV). In fact, the verb *hypotassō*, "to submit, to subject," does not appear at all in verse 22 but is "borrowed" from verse 21; the sense of the two verses is "Submit yourselves to each other, wives to your husbands . . . ," and so on through the household, with instructions specifying ways for each member to manifest that mutual submission.[73] Though Christian households continued to be quite patriarchal and hierarchical, these modifications urged them toward greater equality and respect for each individual.[74]

The material on marriage in Ephesians 5:22–33 is of special significance; here marriage serves as analogy for the relationship between Christ and the church, and the reverse is also true—Christ and the church serve as a model for the loving relationship that ought to exist between husband and wife.[75] This is described as "a great mystery" (Greek *mysterion*, Latin *sacramentum*, Ephesians 5:32)—language that influenced the gradual development of marriage as a sacrament in Christian tradition.[76]

In the Pastoral Epistles, one encounters a different set of concerns centered on false teachings and dissidents (1 Timothy 1:3, 19; 4:1, 7; 6:3–5; 2 Timothy 4:3–4).[77] Certain rebellious teachers were contradicting sound doctrine and upsetting entire households or house churches (Titus 1:9–11). A particular characteristic of some of the false teachings was their asceticism—forbidding to marry, fasting and abstaining from certain foods, and promoting rigorous bodily discipline (1 Timothy 4:3, 8). In response, the Pastorals emphasized the goodness of God's creation (1 Timothy 4:4–5); required that bishops, deacons, and elders be married, though only once (1 Timothy 3:2, 12; Titus 1:5–6); and urged church leaders to teach sound doctrine (1 Timothy 4:6; Titus 2:1).

Some scholars hold that the Pastorals were written to counter folktales, teachings, and practices of the kind that eventually were recorded in the apocryphal Acts of Paul and Thecla.[78] This second-century text relates the tale of a young woman named Thecla who, upon hearing the ascetic teaching of Paul, becomes fiercely loyal to the apostle and determines to live her life as a virgin, greatly upsetting her mother, not to mention her fiancé. Tumult ensues, and the tales of Thecla's deeds and travels portray her as defiant of male Roman authorities yet repeatedly delivered from death by miraculous means. She baptizes herself and ultimately becomes a healer and a revered holy woman. In contrast, the Pastoral Epistles oppose the renunciation of marriage (1 Timothy 4:3–5), express concern about "profane myths and old wives' tales" (1 Timothy 4:7 NRSV), sound an alarm about women led astray by teachers of falsehoods who infiltrate Christian households (2 Timothy 3:6–8), counsel women to be silent and submit to male authority (1 Timothy 2:11–15),[79] and urge loyalty to family (1 Timothy 5:8). Together, the Pastoral Epistles and the Acts of Paul and Thecla provide a glimpse at a period of controversy over how church members were to be different from the world, how the gospel was to affect private life, what roles men and women were to play in the church, and how the legacy of Paul was to be remembered. The Pastorals also give evidence of attempts to prevent interpreting earlier teachings about the value of celibacy for *some* people, in *some* circumstances, as the superior or preferred way of life for *all* people.[80]

Family, Marriage, and Celibacy in Christian and Latter-day Saint Tradition

New Testament scholar Luke Timothy Johnson observed that over the centuries, Christian traditions have responded in different ways to what he calls "the complex witness of the New Testament concerning marriage, family, and sexuality." Some radical ascetic sects renounced marriage; Roman Catholicism upheld both celibacy and marriage as honorable vocations but regarded virginity as the holier path; Protestantism viewed marriage and family more positively, "in a more direct continuity with the Old Testament and the order of the first creation," but lost connection with aspects of New Testament teaching.[81]

Where do Latter-day Saints stand regarding these New Testament teachings? Certainly Restoration scripture and teachings of Latter-day Saint prophets have dramatically influenced our outlook. We have come to understand marriage and family as divinely ordained, central to the developmental purposes of mortal life, and potentially eternal (Doctrine and Covenants 49:16–17; 131:1–4; 132:19). In these respects, Latter-day Saint theology surpasses what can be found in the New Testament, and for many these teachings and practices are among the most cherished aspects of Latter-day Saint identity and purpose. Yet the question remains what value we might still gain from the complex, perhaps wonderfully nuanced record of our New Testament forebears. If we are to turn our hearts to our fathers and mothers, including our spiritual ancestors of the early church, what might we learn from them? If we without them cannot be complete (see Doctrine and Covenants 128:15), in what ways might the multifaceted witness of the New Testament make us more complete?

Perhaps in the New Testament we hear the testimony of different voices, much as we do in modern Latter-day Saint testimony meetings, each with its own truth to tell. Some voices seem to tell us of a time when family structures were so rigid that they needed to be challenged. Some voices tell us of the ways Christ transformed and elevated their understanding of all their family relationships. Some invite us to expand our concept of family. And some testimonies remind us that even apart from family relationships, the individual follower of Christ holds a role of dignity and honor as God's child and an heir in the eternal household of God.

⚬

Mark D. Ellison is an associate professor in the Department of Ancient Scripture at Brigham Young University.

Further Reading

Campbell, Ken M., ed. *Marriage and Family in the Biblical World*. Downers Grove, IL: InterVarsity, 2003. Essays on marriage and family in the ancient Near East, ancient Israel, the Greco-Roman world, Second Temple Judaism, and the New Testament. The collection is of uneven quality—the chapter on the Roman world distills excellent historical scholarship, while the chapter on New Testament views has some valuable material but is less historical and descriptive than confessional and prescriptive as it defends a conservative evangelical position.

Holzapfel, Richard N., Eric D. Huntsman, and Thomas A. Wayment. *Jesus Christ and the World of the New Testament*. Salt Lake City: Deseret Book, 2006. A plentifully illustrated guide to cultural, historical, and textual insights on the New Testament by three Latter-day Saint scholars. Households and marriage are discussed on pages 161, 205, 210–211, 243, 248, 307.

Hunter, David G. *Marriage and Sexuality in Early Christianity*. Minneapolis: Fortress, 2018. This is an updated version of *Marriage in the Early Church* (1992), containing selected early Christian texts on the subject of marriage, from the New Testament to the eighth century, translated into English, with introductory essays.

Johnson, Luke Timothy. "The Complex Witness of the New Testament Concerning Marriage, Family, and Sexuality." In *Contested Issues in Christian Origins and the New Testament: Collected Essays*, 659–78. Leiden, Netherlands: Brill, 2013. A concise but substantive scholarly survey of the complexity of New Testament teachings on marriage, family, and sexuality.

Maier, Harry O. "The Household and its Members." In *New Testament Christianity in the Roman World*, by Harry O. Maier, 134–73. Oxford: Oxford University Press, 2018. A discussion of the characteristics of households and household members in the Greco-Roman world that are "foreign" to us, and how understanding these differences illuminates key New Testament texts. Skillfully draws insights from archaeology and ancient literary sources.

Moxnes, Halvor, ed. *Constructing Early Christian Families: Family as Social Reality and Metaphor*. London: Routledge, 1997. A multiauthored volume examining the social institution of the family in the New Testament world and the ways familial metaphors expressed the early church's self-understanding.

Osiek, Carolyn, and David L. Balch. *Families in the New Testament World: Households and House Churches*. Louisville, KY: Westminster John Knox, 1997. A landmark study that examines households, marriage, celibacy, gender roles, and family life in the New Testament with insights from the fields of archaeology, cultural anthropology, and social history.

Notes

1. In the Greek of the New Testament, several terms denote various aspects of "family." The term *patria* refers to lineage (Luke 2:4; Acts 3:25; Ephesians 3:15), as can *genos* (Acts 4:6), which also refers more broadly to nationality or race (Mark 7:26; Acts 4:36; 7:13, 19; 13:26; 17:28–29; Philemon 3:5; 1 Peter 2:9). The most frequently used term is *oikos* or *oikia*, "house," meaning not just the physical structure of a dwelling place but also its inhabitants—the household or (extended) family. The Latin terms *domus* and *familia* correspond roughly to the Greek *oikos* and *oikia*, denoting "household," its members, and its property; for a discussion, see Harry O. Maier, *New Testament Christianity in the Roman World* (Oxford: Oxford University Press, 2018), 146–48.

2. Biblical scholar Susan Calef observes that throughout the history of reading and interpreting the Bible, there has been a tendency for interpreters to project "their own understanding of family onto New Testament teachings about the subject": Susan A. Calef, review of Halvor Moxnes, ed., "Constructing Early Christian Families: Family as Social Reality and Metaphor," *Journal of Religion* 80, no. 1 (2000): 122.

3. Craig L. Blomberg and Stephen E. Robinson, *How Wide the Divide? A Mormon and an Evangelical in Conversation* (Downers Grove, IL: InterVarsity, 1997), 94. Latter-day Saint scholar Stephen Robinson observes,

"The LDS need to do a better job of identifying correctly which of their beliefs originate in the Bible and which originate from modern revelation."

4. For further discussion of a broader view of "Restoration," see Philip L. Barlow, "To Mend a Fractured Reality: Joseph Smith's Project," *Journal of Mormon History* 38, no. 3 (2012): 28–50.

5. For a discussion of this topic, see Carolyn Osiek, "Family Matters," in *Christian Origins: A People's History of Christianity*, vol. 1, ed. Richard A. Horsley (Minneapolis: Fortress, 2005), 201–20.

6. lds.org/topics/marriage.

7. M. Russell Ballard, "Strength in Counsel," *Ensign*, November 1993; and Russell M. Nelson, "A Plea to My Sisters," *Ensign*, November 2015.

8. Instead of "it is not permitted unto them [women] to speak," JST 1 Corinthians 14:34 changes the wording to "it is not permitted unto them to *rule*." No such JST change is made to 1 Timothy 2:11–12.

9. For example, Spencer W. Kimball, "Home: The Place to Save Society," *Ensign*, January 1975, 2–10.

10. Compare the lack of references to the above passages in recent general conference talks to the many recent references to 1 Corinthians 11:11; see scriptures.byu.edu.

11. Greek and Latin had no term for "family" as commonly understood today—i.e., the coresident, nuclear family of husband, wife, and children; see Halvor Moxnes, "What Is Family? Problems in Constructing Early Christian Families," in *Constructing Early Christian Families: Family as Social Reality and Metaphor*, ed. Halvor Moxnes (London: Routledge, 1997), 20–21.

12. See Bruce W. Frier and Thomas A. J. McGinn, *A Casebook on Roman Family Law* (Oxford: Oxford University Press, 2004), 191–92.

13. For example, Matthew 10:34–37; 1 Corinthians 7:12–17; Justin Martyr, *Second Apology* 1–2; Acts of Paul and Thecla 8–16; The Martyrdom of Perpetua and Felicity 1.1–2; 2.1–2.

14. As Bruce W. Young observes, it is doubtful that Jesus rejoiced in the conflicts he knew would come; see his "Following Christ in Times of War: Latter-day Saints as Peacemakers," in *Common Ground, Different Opinions: Latter-day Saints and Contemporary Issues*, ed. Justin F. White and James E. Faulconer (Salt Lake City: Greg Kofford Books, 2013), 201.

15. See Tobit 4:12–13.

16. For a study of the transition from ancient models of marriage to marriage based primarily on "love," see Stephanie Coontz, *Marriage, a History: From Obedience to Intimacy, or How Love Conquered Marriage* (New York: Viking, 2005).

17. Kenneth Stevenson, *Nuptial Blessing: A Study of Christian Marriage Rites* (New York: Oxford University Press, 1983), 13.

18. See Ambrosiaster, *Quaestiones veteris et novi testamenti* 127.2–3, CSEL 50, 399–400; *Comm. in 1 Cor 7:40*, CSEL 81/2, 90; *Comm. in 1 Tim 3:12*, CSEL 81/3, 268; Innocent I, *Epistula* 4.6.9; David G. Hunter, "'On the Sin of Adam and Eve': A Little-Known Defense of Marriage and Childbearing by Ambrosiaster," *Harvard Theological Review* 82, no. 3 (1989): 287–88; and David G. Hunter, "Sexuality, Marriage, and the Family," in *The Cambridge History of Christianity*, vol. 2, *Constantine to c. 600*, ed. Augustine Casiday and Frederick W. Norris (Cambridge: Cambridge University Press, 2008), 591–92. It is not known whether Jewish marriage customs described in the Talmud represent first-century practices; see Mark Searle and Kenneth W. Stevenson, *Documents of the Marriage Liturgy* (Collegeville, MN: Liturgical Press, 1992), 3.

19. Jewish tradition held "the view of marriage as a covenant between husband and wife which is entered into and lived out within the larger covenantal relationship of God and Israel. The couple in some sense embody that larger relationship." Searle and Stevenson, *Documents of the Marriage Liturgy*, 25.

20. Susan Treggiari, *Roman Marriage: Iusti Coniuges from the Time of Cicero to the Time of Ulpian* (New York: Oxford University Press, 1991), 400.

21. Peter Brown, *The Body and Society: Men, Women, and Sexual Renunciation in Early Christianity*, 20th anniversary ed. (New York: Columbia University Press, 2008), 6, 24–25; compare Leonard V. Rutgers, "Cata-

combs and Health in Christian Rome," in *Children and Family in Late Antiquity: Life, Death, and Interaction*, ed. Christian Laes, Katariina Mustakallio, and Ville Vuolanto (Leuven, Belgium: Peeters, 2015), 35–52.

22. Osiek, "Family Matters," 205; of course, some individuals lived much longer than the average life expectancy; Polycarp, bishop of Smyrna, was eighty-six when he was martyred in the mid-second century: *The Martyrdom of Polycarp* 9.3. Compare Maier, *New Testament Christianity*, 156: "Half of all children died before the age of two [and] parents needed to conceive five to seven children to assure surviving heirs and material support in their old age. However, in poor families, three children at most could be supported."

23. William Harris, *Ancient Literacy* (Cambridge: Harvard University Press, 1989). Jewish communities in the first century AD may have had higher than average literacy rates, at least in the ability to read (if not write); see Harry Y. Gamble, *Books and Readers in the Early Church: A History of Early Christian Texts* (New Haven, CT: Yale University Press, 1995), 7; Maier, *New Testament Christianity*, 160–61; and Josephus, *Against Apion* 2.204.

24. David G. Hunter, "Children," in *Encyclopedia of Early Christianity*, 2nd ed., ed. Everett Ferguson (New York: Garland, 1998), 236.

25. Didache 2.2; Justin Martyr, *First Apology* 29; *Letter to Diognetus* 5.6; Athenagoras, *A Plea for the Christians* 35.6; Apostolic Constitutions 4.1.1–2.

26. Michael Peppard, *The Son of God in the Roman World: Divine Sonship in Its Social and Political Context* (New York: Oxford University Press, 2011), 4. Peppard discusses adoption in the Roman world and adoption imagery in the New Testament.

27. Frier and McGinn, *Roman Family Law*, 14; and Maier, *New Testament Christianity*, 161.

28. The KJV also uses the word *servant* to translate the Greek word *diákonos*, which connotes one who serves food, waits upon, attends to, or ministers to another, and is the source of the word *deacon*. The one time the English word *slave* appears in the KJV (Revelation 18:13), it translates the Greek *sōma*, literally "body," reflecting how a slave was a commodity—a body to be owned, worked, and exploited.

29. See 1 Corinthians 7:21–24; Galatians 3:28; Philemon; Ephesians 6:5–9; Colossians 3:22–4:1; 1 Timothy 6:1–2; 1 Peter 2:18–25; see the discussion in Maier, *New Testament Christianity*, 161–68.

30. Such as Junian Latins or peregrines (foreigners who were permanent residents); see Frier and McGinn, *Roman Family Law*, 31–33. In AD 212 Emperor Caracalla granted Roman citizenship to practically all free persons.

31. Osiek, "Family Matters," 211; compare Maier, *New Testament Christianity*, 146. Epitaphs commemorate the length of *contubernium* marriages to the day, implying that such relationships were at least sometimes formed on a specific date and probably with some form of ceremony; see Karen K. Hersch, *The Roman Wedding: Ritual and Meaning in Antiquity* (New York: Cambridge University Press, 2010), 33n70, citing K. R. Bradley, *Slaves and Masters in the Roman Empire: A Study in Social Control* (New York: Oxford University Press, 1987), 49n12.

32. Pliny, *Natural History* 5.17.73; Josephus, *Antiquities* 18.1.1, 6; *Jewish War* 2.8.2; Philo, *De vita contemplativa* 3.33; 8.68.

33. John the Baptist, for example, seems to have been unmarried. For a discussion of this subject and its relevance to Christianity, see Geza Vermes, *Jesus the Jew: A Historian's Reading of the Gospels* (Philadelphia: Fortress, 1973), 99–102.

34. Musonius Rufus, frag. 14, trans. Cora E. Lutz, "Musonius Rufus: The Roman Socrates," *Yale Classical Studies* 10 (1947): 93.

35. See Kate Cooper, *The Fall of the Roman Household* (Cambridge: Cambridge University Press, 2007). Cooper notes that the transformation of marriage among Christians eventually resulted in an "increased hold of the marriage bond," xi.

36. See Tobit 4:3. Jesus showed similar compassion in restoring to life the only son of a widow at Nain (Luke 7:11–17).

37. The use of familial terminology to refer to the relationships between nonrelated members of a group is called "fictive kinship" in the field of anthropology; early Christians are a classic example of fictive kinship. For a discussion, see Maier, *New Testament Christianity*, 171–73.

38. The King James Version adds "or wife" after "father or mother" in Matthew 19:29 and Mark 10:29. Some early manuscripts don't have "or wife" in Matthew 19:29, though some do, including Codex Sinaiticus; no early manuscripts have "or wife" in Mark 10:29.

39. Luke 11:27–28, too, may be read as a prioritization of discipleship over familial roles. See Warren Carter and Amy-Jill Levine, *The New Testament: Methods and Meanings* (Nashville: Abingdon, 2013), 69; and Julie M. Smith, *Search, Ponder, and Pray: A Guide to the Gospels* (Salt Lake City: Kofford Books, 2014), 88–89.

40. *Talmud Bavli* (Babylonian Talmud) Gittin 90a.

41. The earliest versions of Jesus's teaching on divorce appear to prohibit it unconditionally (Mark 10:11–12; 1 Corinthians 7:10–11; compare Luke 16:18); later versions in Matthew give an exception for sexual immorality (*porneia*; Matthew 5:31–32; 19:9). This exception may have been assumed by Jesus and his first hearers and added later for clarification; see Bruce J. Malina and Richard L. Rohrbaugh, *Social-Science Commentary on the Gospel of John* (Minneapolis: Fortress, 1998), 16–18. For current Latter-day Saint application of this teaching, see Dallin H. Oaks, "Divorce," *Ensign*, May 2007, 71.

42. For example, Irenaeus, *Against Heresies* 1.28.1; and Methodius, *Symposion e peri hagneias* 2.1; Clement of Alexandria, *Paedagogus* 2.10.

43. David G. Hunter, *Marriage in the Early Church* (Minneapolis: Fortress, 1992), 3.

44. Compare Dallin H. Oaks, "Divorce," *Ensign*, May 2007, 70-73.

45. Walter W. Wessel, "Mark," in *The Expositor's Bible Commentary* (Grand Rapids, MI: Regency, 1984), 8:712; see also Julie M. Smith, *The Gospel according to Mark: A New Rendition*, BYU New Testament Commentary series (Provo, UT: BYU Studies, 2019).

46. Though most New Testament scholars understand "this teaching" (Matthew 19:11) to refer to celibacy (i.e., not marrying, as stated in Matthew 19:10), some argue that it may refer to remaining unmarried after divorce (implied in Matthew 19:9); see Quentin Quesnell, "Made Themselves Eunuchs for the Kingdom of Heaven (Mt 19, 12)" *Catholic Biblical Quarterly* 30, no. 3 (1968): 335–58.

47. Bruce R. McConkie proposed that the eunuchs Jesus mentioned were apparently "men who in false pagan worship had deliberately mutilated themselves in the apostate notion that such would further their salvation." *Doctrinal New Testament Commentary* (1965–73), 1:549. Jesus, however, referred not to pagan practices but to those whose celibacy was "for the kingdom of heaven's sake"; he never used the phrase "the kingdom of heaven" with reference to pagan notions of afterlife. Regarding Jesus's use of figurative language, the Gospels take a dim view of Jesus's hearers who understand his words too literally and fail to grasp their higher, symbolic import (see, e.g., Mark 8:14–21; John 3:1–12; 4:5–14; 6:22–66).

48. See Matthew 19:27–30; Mark 10:28–30. The disciples apparently had not abandoned their families permanently but were away from them as they traveled with Jesus; according to 1 Corinthians 9:5, in later years some disciples traveled with their spouses. It is also possible that Jesus meant the statement as a self-reference—that, for the special purposes of his mission, he himself had forgone marriage and was living a celibate life "for the sake of the kingdom of heaven"; see Josef Blinzler, "Eisin eunouchoi," *Zeitschrift für die Neutestamentliche Wissenschaft und die Kunde der Älteren Kirche* 48 (1957): 254–70.

49. New Testament texts mention Jesus's mother, father, brothers, and sisters, but the only "wife" or "bride" of Christ is metaphorical—the church (Ephesians 5:31–32; 2 Corinthians 11:2–4; Revelation 21:2, 9–10; 22:17).

50. Recent popular speculation that Jesus was married has been fueled by Dan Brown's novel *The Da Vinci Code* and by the papyrus fragment called "The Gospel of Jesus's Wife," which has been shown to be a modern forgery. See Karen L. King, "Jesus said to them, 'My wife . . . ': A New Coptic Papyrus Fragment," *Harvard Theological Review* 107, no. 2 (2014): 131–59; Ariel Sabar, "The Unbelievable Tale of Jesus's Wife," *Atlantic*, July–August 2016; and Ariel Sabar, "Karen King Responds to 'The Unbelievable Tale of Jesus's Wife'"

Atlantic, June 16, 2016, https://www.theatlantic.com/politics/archive/2016/06/karen-king-responds-to-the
-unbelievable-tale-of-jesus-wife/487484/. For a discussion of this subject by three Latter-day Saint scholars,
see Richard Neitzel Holzapfel, Andrew C. Skinner, and Thomas A. Wayment, *What Da Vinci Didn't Know:
An LDS Perspective* (Salt Lake City: Deseret Book, 2006), especially 37–50.

51. Examples of Latter-day Saint arguments that Jesus was married include the following: (a) Orson Hyde, who
speculated that Jesus was married on the evidence of the wedding of Cana (John 2:1–11) and the reference
in Isaiah 53:10 to the Servant's "seed" (in *Journal of Discourses*, 2:82). However, Jesus attended the wedding
as a guest, not a groom (John 2:2), and the Book of Mormon interprets Christ's "seed" as prophets who
have taught of Christ and those who have believed them (Mosiah 15:11–15). See fairmormon.org/answers
/Jesus_Christ/Was_Jesus_married. (b) The claim that since Judaism held marriage and childbearing in high
regard and rabbis were usually married, it would have been scandalous for Jesus not to have been married.
For an example of this argument, see D. Kelly Ogden and Andrew C. Skinner, *Verse by Verse: The Four Gospels* (Salt Lake City: Deseret Book, 2006), 108–9. This argument, however, oversimplifies the Judaism of the
first century, which included groups of people who practiced sexual renunciation in pursuit of a holy way
of life (as discussed above). John the Baptist may have been unmarried. (c) The claim that since Doctrine
and Covenants 131:1–4 teaches that marriage is required for the highest degree of heavenly reward, Christ
must have been married; see a variation of this in Ogden and Skinner, *Verse by Verse*, 108–9. Though theoretically possible, this reasoning fails to consider the utterly unique character of Christ's mortal mission and
the possibility that it might have required a single-minded devotion including a celibate life (see Matthew
19:12; Luke 12:50). Examples of Church spokespersons who have clarified that it is *not* a Church doctrine
that Jesus was married include Charles W. Penrose, "Peculiar Questions Briefly Answered," *Improvement
Era*, September 1912, 1042, "We do not know anything about Jesus Christ being married. The Church has
no authoritative declaration on the subject"; Dale Bills, quoted in "LDS do not endorse claims in 'Da Vinci,'"
Deseret News, May 17, 2006, "The belief that Christ was married has never been official church doctrine. It
is neither sanctioned nor taught by the church. While it is true that a few church leaders in the mid-1800s
expressed their opinions on the matter, it was not then, and is not now, church doctrine."

52. For example, Clement of Alexandria (ca. AD 160–215), who wrote quite positively about marriage and
family life, mentions ascetic sects who justified their renunciation of marriage on the grounds that they
were "imitating the Lord who neither married nor had any possession in this world," an argument that
would have gained no traction without widespread memory that Jesus had been single; *Stromata* 3.6.49, *The
Library of Christian Classics*, vol. 2, *Alexandrian Christianity*, trans. and ed. Henry Chadwick (Philadelphia:
Westminster Press, 1954), 62–63; Tertullian, *Monogamy* 5 (written c. AD 217), stated that Christ "was entirely unwedded"; trans. S. Thelwall, *Ante-Nicene Fathers*, vol. 4, ed. Alexander Roberts and James Donaldson (Buffalo, NY: Christian Literature Publishing Co., 1885), 62; Methodius (d. about AD 311), *Symposion e
peri hagneias* 1.4–5, referred to Christ as "first and chief of virgins" who "preserved the flesh which He had
taken upon Him incorrupt in virginity"; *Ante-Nicene Fathers*, vol. 6, trans. William R. Clark, ed. Alexander
Roberts and James Donaldson (Buffalo, NY: Christian Literature, 1886), 312–13.

53. Holzapfel, Skinner, and Wayment, *What Da Vinci Didn't Know*, 37–50.

54. See, for example, Clement of Alexandria, *Christ the Educator* 1.4.3; Tertullian, *To His Wife* 1.1.4; Jerome,
Epistulae 75.2; M. Colleen McDannell and Bernhard Lang, *Heaven: A History* (New Haven, CT: Yale Univer-
sity Press, 1988), 24–32; Dyan Elliott, *Spiritual Marriage: Sexual Abstinence in Medieval Wedlock* (Princeton,
NJ: Princeton University Press, 1993), 39; and Nicola Denzey, *The Bone Gatherers: The Lost Worlds of Early
Christian Women* (Boston: Beacon, 2007), 58–59.

55. Ben Witherington, *The Gospel of Mark: A Socio-Rhetorical Commentary* (Grand Rapids, MI: Eerdmans,
2001), 328; with thanks to Gaye Strathearn, "Teaching the Four Gospels: Five Considerations," *Religious
Educator* 13, no. 2 (2012): 106n51. Compare James E. Talmage, *Jesus the Christ*, 548: "In the resurrection
there will be no marrying nor giving in marriage; for all questions of marital status must be settled before
that time."

56. Strathearn, "Teaching the Four Gospels," 97, emphasis in the original.

57. Witherington, *Gospel of Mark*, 328; by the first century, levirate marriage does not seem to have been practiced any longer.

58. Tertullian, *Monogamy* 10.

59. ICUR 5.14076: "Dul[c]is in aeternum mihimet iun[tissi]me coniux, / Ex[c]ute iam lacrimas, placuit bona [r]egia caeli ... Sospes eris fateor v[. . . . . o]scula Bassae"; final line as reconstructed by Antonio Ferrua: "Sospes eris fateor u[enies et ad o]scula Bassae"; trans. Dennis Trout, "Borrowed Verse and Broken Narrative: Agency, Identity, and the (Bethesda) Sarcophagus of Bassa," in *Life, Death, and Representation: Some New Work on Roman Sarcophagi*, ed. Jaś Elsner and Janet Huskinson (Berlin: DeGruyter, 2010), 341–43; and Friedrich Wilhelm Deichmann, Giuseppe Bovini, and Hugo Brandenburg, *Repertorium der christlich-antiken Sarkophage, Bd 1 Rom und Ostia* (Wiesbaden, Germany: Franz Steiner, 1967), 229–30, Taf. 85, no. 556.

60. CIL IX 5566 = ILS 1289 = CLE 1560a = ILCV 98b = ICI X 22b, "surgatis pariter cristo praestante beati"; Jutta Dresken-Weiland, *Repertorium der christlich-antiken Sarkophage, zweiter Band: Italien mit einem Nachtrag Rom und Ostia, Dalmatien, Museen der Welt* (Mainz am Rhein, Germany: Verlag Philipp von Zabern, 1998), 52–53, no. 148; and Aldo Nestori, *Il Mausoleo e il Sarcofago di Flavivs Ivlivs Catervivs a Tolentino* (Citta del Vaticano: Pontificio Instituto di Archeoogia Cristiana, 1996).

61. John Chrysostom, *To a Young Widow* 3.188–201; *Nicene and Post-Nicene Fathers*, Series I (Grand Rapids: Eerdmans, 1983), trans. W. R. W. Stephens, 9:123. Additional examples in early Christian literature and archaeology discussed in Mark D. Ellison, "Visualizing Christian Marriage in the Roman World" (PhD diss., Vanderbilt University, 2017), 193–224.

62. The undisputed letters of Paul are Romans, 1–2 Corinthians, Galatians, Philippians, 1 Thessalonians, and Philemon; for a discussion of authorship of the epistles traditionally attributed to Paul, see a modern commentary or study bible, such as the book introductions to each epistle in *The New Oxford Annotated Bible, College Edition*, 4th ed. (New York: Oxford University Press, 2010).

63. JST 1 Corinthians 7:1–2 clarifies the implicit question and answer in these verses: "Now concerning the things whereof ye wrote unto me, *saying*: It is good for a man not to touch a woman. Nevertheless, *I say*. . . ." JST 1 Corinthians 7:5 changes the KJV "Defraud ye not one the other" to "*Depart* ye not one *from* the other. . . ."

64. In 1 Corinthians 9:5–12, Paul states that he and his missionary companions "have the right to be accompanied by a believing wife," as other apostles, but that they "have not made use of this right." The possibility that he was married but simply not traveling with his wife on his missionary journeys is unlikely given how Paul presents himself as a role model for continent, unmarried believers in 1 Corinthians 7. The implication is that Paul was not married at the time he wrote the epistle. If he had been married previously, he was apparently either widowed or divorced at the time he wrote 1 Corinthians.

65. David G. Hunter, *Marriage, Celibacy, and Heresy in Ancient Christianity: The Jovinianist Controversy* (New York: Oxford University Press, 2007), 89; citing Peter Brown, *The Body and Society: Men, Women, and Sexual Renunciation in Early Christianity* (New York: Columbia University Press, 1988), 55.

66. See Scott H. Faulring, Kent P. Jackson, and Robert J. Matthews, eds., *Joseph Smith's New Translation of the Bible: Original Manuscripts* (Provo, UT: Religious Studies Center, Brigham Young University, 2004), 8–11, which explains that the JST is not necessarily the restoration of original text, but may represent the restoration of original ideas, clarifications for modern readers, efforts to harmonize text with other scriptural passages or revelations, or inspired teachings that were not written at all by ancient authors.

67. D. Todd Christofferson, "The Doctrine of Christ," *Ensign*, May 2012, 88; and "Approaching Mormon Doctrine," http://www.mormonnewsroom.org/article/approaching-mormon-doctrine.

68. This paragraph draws in part from Mark D. Ellison, "Adam in the New Testament," bibleodyssey.org/people /related-articles/adam-in-the-new-testament.aspx.

69. David A. Bednar, "We Believe in Being Chaste," *Ensign*, May 2013, 41–42.

70. David L. Balch, "Household Codes," in David N. Freedman, ed., *Anchor Bible Dictionary* (New York: Doubleday, 1992), 3.318.

71. But see Lincoln H. Blumell, "Scribes and Ancient Letters: Implications for the Pauline Epistles," in *How the New Testament Came to Be* (Salt Lake City: Deseret Book, 2006), 208–26.

72. Osiek, "Family Matters," 216.

73. The New Living Translation gives this sense by rendering the two verses: ". . . submit to one another out of reverence for Christ. For wives, this means submit to your husbands as to the Lord."

74. For example, 1 Peter 3:7 illustrates both vestiges of patriarchy and aspects of egalitarianism: the wife is "the weaker vessel," but husband and wife together are "joint-heirs of the grace of life."

75. Hunter, *Marriage in the Early Church*, 5; this nuptial metaphor is an extension of that found in many Old Testament passages that describe the Lord's relationship with Israel in terms of marriage, as a covenant; for example, Ezekiel 16:8.

76. See Philip L. Reynolds, *How Marriage Became One of the Sacraments: The Sacramental Theology of Marriage from Its Medieval Origins to the Council of Trent* (Cambridge: Cambridge University Press, 2016).

77. Some of the teachings of concern, in addition to those discussed, involved early forms of Gnosticism (1 Timothy 6:20, the falsely called knowledge [*gnōsis*]) and Judaism/Judaizing (Titus 1:10, 14).

78. For example, Dennis MacDonald, *The Legend and the Apostle: The Battle for Paul in Story and Canon* (Philadelphia: Westminster, 1983); and Stephen J. Davis, *The Cult of Saint Thecla: A Tradition of Women's Piety in Late Antiquity* (Oxford: Clarendon, 2001), 8–18.

79. The teaching in 1 Timothy 2:14 that it was Eve, not Adam, who was deceived, stands in contrast to Paul's teaching in Romans 5:12–21 that places blame on Adam for the Fall. Many scholars regard the similar teaching in 1 Corinthians 14:33b–36 as a later interpolation since it interrupts the flow of the text, appears elsewhere in some manuscripts, contradicts Paul's approval of women participating in worship in 1 Corinthians 11:5, and seems to be an attempt to insert later views into this earlier letter.

80. For a discussion of how the canonization of the Pastoral Epistles promoted an interpretation of Paul that rejected compulsory celibacy and favored marriage, see Hunter, *Marriage, Celibacy, and Heresy*, 92–96. The tensions between marriage and celibacy are seen elsewhere in the New Testament too: marriage is honorable in Hebrews (Hebrews 13:4), while a redeemed multitude in John's Apocalypse are virgins (see Revelation 14:1–4, though this may be symbolic).

81. Luke Timothy Johnson, "The Complex Witness of the New Testament Concerning Marriage, Family, and Sexuality," in *Contested Issues in Christian Origins and the New Testament: Collected Essays* (Leiden, Netherlands: Brill, 2013), 659–78.

31

Nonverbal Communication in the New Testament

David M. Calabro

Nonverbal communication includes all aspects of the communication process other than words. In normal face-to-face communication, nonverbal communication plays a vital role in interpretation; a simple request, for instance, is vastly different if it is said with clenched fists or while gently holding the addressee's hand. Scripture reports only a small fraction of the nonverbal communication that would have taken place in the actual events, leaving a great deal to the reader's imagination; even so, a close reading of scripture reveals a considerable repertoire of nonverbal signs that add meaning to the text. An example of such a sign is Jesus's gesture when he raises the daughter of Jairus: "He took the little girl by the hand and said to her, *Talitha, koum!* meaning, 'Little girl, arise!'" (Mark 5:41).[1]

Categories of nonverbal communication include kinesics (the use of hand gestures, body postures, facial expression, and gaze), haptics (the use of touch), vocalics or paralanguage (the use of nonspeech sounds and voice inflection), proxemics (the communicative use of physical closeness and distance), chronemics (the communicative use of timing), physical appearance, objectics (the use of "artifacts" or physical objects to communicate), and olfactics (communication through scent). However, opinions vary on the relationship between these categories and on what should and should not be included in nonverbal communication.[2] For the present purposes, it is useful to adopt Fernando Poyatos's division of communication into three components: language, kinesics, and vocalics.[3] In particular, the focus here will be on hand gestures, gazes, postures, and vocalics—those elements of nonverbal communication that are explicitly described in the New Testament text.

Older studies, particularly entries on gestures in Bible dictionaries before the 1990s, tend to associate biblical nonverbal communication with the uncontrolled emotion of "Oriental" peoples. This is evident, for example, in the following statement made in 1909 by W. Ewing:

> The Oriental is a natural expert in appropriate and expressive gesture. To his impulsive and emotional temperament, attitude and action form a more apt vehicle for thought and feeling than even speech. . . . Conversation is accompanied by a sort of running commentary of gestures. Easterns conduct argument and altercation at the pitch of their voices: emphasis is supplied almost wholly by gestures. These are often so violent that an unskilled witness might naturally expect to see bloodshed follow.[4]

Statements such as this are of questionable value. Not only are they based on impressions of modern rather than ancient Near Eastern cultures, but the impressions themselves are superficial, lacking long-term insider knowledge of the cultures. The statements certainly are not based on the New Testament text, which reports only a modest quantity of gestures. It is true that many people in the Near East and in Mediterranean countries communicate with a wider range of movement than is typical for middle-class northern European culture, and this may have been true also in the days of Jesus and the apostles. Some gestures reported in the New Testament, such as prostration (see chapter 32 herein) and the lifting of the hands in prayer, involve a high degree of movement and tend to confirm this assumption. However, this was not necessarily true for all parts of society and for all social situations. The surprise for modern Western readers is that the appropriate gestures for a given situation are different from our own culture. For instance, it is in the most sacred situations of worship, situations that we might associate with tranquil passivity, that the gestures with the highest degree of movement occur. The same observation holds for the volume and tempo of speech—people in New Testament times were not necessarily always conducting "argument and altercation at the pitch of their voices," but the situations in which loud voices were appropriate, such as prayer, may appear unusual to modern readers.

Another issue that underlies many studies of nonverbal communication in the New Testament is that of identifying the most relevant context for Jesus's and the apostles' gestures. Surveys of gestures in Bible dictionaries tend to assume a continuity between Old and New Testament body language.[5] Some other studies, however, dwell exclusively on comparisons with Greco-Roman nonverbal communication.[6] This issue is related to the historicity of the Gospels and Acts. If the actions of Jesus and the apostles spring primarily from the imagination of the writers, then there is a possibility that the most relevant context is that of an early Christian culture that was hellenized and largely gentile. But if the accounts report the gestures of Jesus and the apostles with a reasonable degree of historical accuracy, then one should look to a Semitic background. The abundant evidence of Aramaic and Hebrew linguistic influence in the Gospels lends support to the second possibility.[7] The problem of Jesus's gestures is similar to that of reconstructing Jesus's *ipsissima verba*, or the precise words that he spoke. Ultimately, both of these things—Jesus's actions as well as his words—

are impossible to reconstruct in complete detail on the basis of sources at hand; they must instead be reconstructed in broad strokes with the help of comparative research.

The present article assumes (1) that the Gospel accounts and Acts present an essentially realistic description of Jesus's and the apostles' gestures, and (2) that the primary background of these gestures is that of the Semitic culture of the working class in Roman Palestine during the early first century AD. This view finds support in the continuity of gestures described in ancient Near Eastern sources, the Hebrew Bible, the Dead Sea Scrolls, and the New Testament. To be sure, Hellenistic culture also exerted a strong influence on the society in which Jesus lived, and this probably included the emulation of Greek gestures and manners of speaking among the elite elements of society. The members of the Herodian ruling family, some religious leaders such as the Sadducees, publicans such as the apostle Matthew, and Roman citizens such as Paul certainly fell into this category. But for the working-class families of Jesus and most of the apostles, as well as the majority of those among whom Jesus ministered, the body language most often employed would be the same that had been passed down from ancient generations of Semitic ancestors.

After the New Testament itself, the most important primary sources for the study of nonverbal communication in the New Testament are the Old Testament, the Apocrypha, the pseudepigrapha, the Dead Sea Scrolls, rabbinic literature (including the Mishnah, the later but more extensive Palestinian Talmud, and the Aramaic translations of the scriptures known as the Targums), and early Christian writings. Jewish and early Christian iconography helps to shed light on some gestures. Our necessary reliance on these ancient sources means that we are limited to certain kinds of body language that were thought to be important enough to record in writing or to memorialize in art, such as gestures used in performing miracles and in ritual. This, of course, represents only a small fraction of the nonverbal signs that Jesus and those around him must have used when they communicated. Nevertheless, the gestures that are mentioned in the New Testament record are an important witness to the faith of early believers, who sought not only to hear the words of Jesus and his apostles but also to know and emulate their actions.

The discussion that follows progresses from gestures employing individual body parts to postures of the whole body and finally to vocalics. The gestures are organized according to the body part that performs the gesture: first the hands, including the extending of one hand, the extending of two hands, and gestures involving physical contact with another person; then other parts of the body, including the eyes and the lips.

Raising the Right Hand in Oath

In Revelation 10:5–6, John sees an angel who with one foot on the earth and the other on the sea, raises his right hand and swears that certain signs are about to be fulfilled. The Greek expression used here is *airō tēn cheira tēn dexian eis ton ouranon*, "lift up the right hand toward heaven." The raising of the right hand in oath is frequently attested in the Hebrew Bible (Genesis 14:22–23; Exodus 6:8; Numbers 14:30; Deuteronomy 32:40–41; Ezra 10:18–19;

Nehemiah 9:15; Job 31:21–22; Psalm 106:26–27; Ezekiel 20:5–6, 15, 23, 28, 42; 36:7; 44:12; 47:14). David Seely provides a thorough discussion of this gesture in his article "The Raised Hand of God as an Oath Gesture."[8]

Many have noted the similarity between Revelation 10:5–6 and Daniel 12:7, in which an angel lifts both hands toward heaven and swears that certain signs will be accomplished at a specified time. This suggests that the imagery of the passage in John's revelation is influenced by the Daniel passage.[9] However, the angel lifts only one hand here, while in Daniel 12:7 it is explicit that both the right and the left hands are used. So even if the imagery is influenced by the Daniel passage, the gesture itself bears independent witness to a one-handed oath gesture.

Other sources indicate that raising the hand in oath was also a common practice in the Holy Land around the time of the New Testament. In a scroll of Genesis and Exodus from the Dead Sea Scrolls (4QGen-Exod[a]), the phrase *nś 'ty 't ydy* "I lifted up my hand" in Exodus 6:8 is replaced by the word *nšb 't[y]* "I swore." In Targum Neofiti (an Aramaic translation of the Hebrew Bible, dating to sometime in the first four centuries AD), the translation adds the word *bšbw 'h* "in oath" to phrases describing the lifting of the hand in Genesis 14:22 and Deuteronomy 32:40. These expansions are likely intended to prevent confusion with other hand-lifting gestures that have other meanings. Thus, even though it is a heavenly being that performs the gesture in Revelation 10:5–6, the gesture would have been easily recognizable to John the Revelator.

The raising of the hand in oath remains a common practice in the Near East today.[10] The current form of the gesture, with the hand raised approximately to the square, the palm facing forward, is found in iconography from the time of the Old Testament and likely represents the New Testament–period form of the gesture as well.[11]

Extending the Hand to Speak

Five passages in the book of Acts describe a gesture using one hand in the context of addressing a group of people. Three different Greek idioms are used, the first two of which use the same verb: *kataseiō tē cheiri* "motion with the hand," *kataseiō tēn cheira* "wave the hand," and *ekteinō tēn cheira* "extend the hand." The instances are as follows:

Reference	Greek idiom	Complete phrase	Larger context
Acts 12:17	*kataseiō tē cheiri*	"he motioned to them with his hand to be silent"	Peter speaking to a small group of saints gathered at a woman's house in Jerusalem, he having just appeared after his deliverance from prison.
Acts 13:16	*kataseiō tē cheiri*	"he motioned with his hand"	Paul at a synagogue, addressing the congregation after the rulers of the synagogue have invited men of the congregation to speak.

Reference	Greek idiom	Complete phrase	Larger context
Acts 19:33	*kataseiō tēn cheira*	"he waved his hand"	Alexander (a Jew) attempting to address a rioting crowd in a theater in Ephesus; his speech is cut off by the people's shouting.
Acts 21:40	*kataseiō tē cheiri*	"he motioned with his hand to the people"	Paul addressing an angry crowd on the stairs between the temple and the Roman fortress in Jerusalem; the gesture is followed immediately by the people becoming silent, after which Paul speaks to them in Hebrew/Aramaic.
Acts 26:1	*ekteinō tēn cheira*	"he extended his hand"	Paul addressing King Agrippa after the king has given him permission to speak.

In each case, the phrase mentioning the gesture is immediately followed by a phrase describing speech (or, in the case of Acts 19:33, an attempt to speak).

Some interpreters consider the gesture in all of the passages above to be the same. According to Burke, the phrases with *kataseiō* all describe "the gesture a public speaker uses either to gain the crowd's attention or quiet it down before beginning his speech," and the instance with *ekteinō* in Acts 26:1 refers to "the same motion."[12] The New International Version (NIV) echoes this interpretation by rendering all three phrases consistently as "he motioned (with his hand)." However, some other translations, including the New Revised Standard Version (NRSV) and the New Jerusalem Bible (NJB), distinguish between the two verbs that are used, rendering only the instances with *kataseiō* as the motion for silence.[13]

On a basic level, the gesture descriptions and the contexts in which they occur point to a single gesture. All the passages describe a person lifting one hand toward a group of people immediately before delivering a speech. However, as Ray Birdwhistell has shown in studies of modern gesture, it is possible for a single gesture to have multiple forms or modulations. For example, one can modify a military salute by exaggerating it, performing it in a casual way, performing it stiffly, or holding it longer or shorter.[14] This seems to be the case with the speech gesture. One can discern two forms corresponding to the verbs *kataseiō* "motion, wave" and *ekteinō* "extend," the one denoting movement and the other a static pose. The different verbs also correspond to a crucial difference in context. Where *kataseiō* is used, the speaker does not already have the attention of the audience, and the text sometimes mentions the quieting down of the audience as a purpose or a result of the gesture. In the one case where *ekteinō* is used, the speaker (Paul) already has his audience's attention and has just been given permission to speak. The two idioms in Acts 19:33 and 26:1, one with *kataseiō* and the other with *ekteinō*, are so similar otherwise that one suspects the difference of verb to be significant, especially since we are dealing with a single composition. Thus, it seems that the speech gesture, although basically one gesture, has one form involving rapid movement to gain the attention of the audience and a more static form for addressing an audience that is already listening.

The literature on this speech gesture generally places it in a Greco-Roman context.[15] In favor of this view is the fact that Jesus is never described as performing this gesture (the idiom *ekteinō tēn cheira* describes a gesture Jesus performs before speaking in Matthew 12:49, but the context indicates that this is more of a pointing gesture than a rhetorical accompaniment to speech), and those who perform it are mostly hellenized Jews (Peter in Acts 12:17 is an exception to this). However, it is also possible to put the gesture in a Semitic context. In Proverbs 1:24, the personified Lady Wisdom says, "I called, but you refused; I extended my hand, but none heeded." The Hebrew gesture idiom, *nāṭâ yād*, is a precise equivalent to the Greek *ekteinō tēn cheira*. The expected outcome of the gesture, "giving heed," corresponds to the results following the use of the gesture in such passages as Acts 21:40 (in particular, the refusal to give heed recalls Acts 19:33). The Greek translation of Proverbs 1:24 in the Septuagint renders the gesture idiom as *exeteinon logous* "I spoke at length" (literally "I extended words"), showing that this Israelite gesture was understood as one of rhetorical speech. Returning to the examples of the gesture in Acts, the ones who perform it are consistently Jews, and Paul does it while speaking Aramaic. Peter does it when addressing Jewish Christians in Jerusalem. In Acts 19:33–34, the crowd recognizes that Alexander is a Jew before he starts speaking, which casts doubt on the idea that his gesture is Greek; in fact, it may be Alexander's gesture that gives away his Jewish identity.

Lifting the Hands in Prayer

In 1 Timothy 2:8, the author expresses to Timothy his wish "that the men in every place should pray lifting up pure hands, free of anger or disputation." The gesture idiom here is *epairō cheiras* "lift up the hands." Although the date of 1 Timothy is disputed (proposals range from ca. AD 65 to ca. AD 100), the earliest date is near the end of Paul's ministry, so those who are to lift their hands in prayer would be mostly gentile converts—particularly at Ephesus, where Timothy was the bishop. Nevertheless, as a sanctioned ritual action, this gesture may be rooted in earlier Jewish Christian practice.

Lifting both hands in prayer is perhaps the best-attested ritual gesture of antiquity. The gesture is found both in iconography and in texts from the Holy Land, starting in the Middle Bronze Age (ca. 2000–1500 BC) and continuing throughout late antiquity. The Hebrew Bible contains twenty-two occurrences of the gesture, denoted by six different Hebrew idioms, the most common of which are *pāraś kappayim* "spread the hands" and *nāśā' yādayim* "lift up the hands." Discussion of the biblical examples and of the parallels in inscriptions and iconography from the biblical world appears in works by Mayer Gruber, Othmar Keel, and David Calabro.[16]

The gesture of lifting both hands in prayer is also found in the Apocrypha (2 Maccabees 3:20; 14:34; 15:12, 21; 3 Maccabees 2:1; 5:25; Tobit 3:11; Sirach 48:20), as well as in many ancient pseudepigraphic texts. One instance found in 1 Enoch 84:1 is particularly comparable to the one in 1 Timothy: "Then I lifted up my hands in righteousness and blessed the Holy and Great One." There are references to this gesture in 1 Clement 2:3; 29:1, attesting to the practice of prayer with uplifted hands in the early Christian church. John Tvedtnes has assembled further sources on this gesture, although even this represents only a fraction of the textual and iconographic sources bearing witness to this gesture.[17]

In this gesture, the hands were raised in front of the shoulders, or sometimes high above the head, the palms facing forward. This is identical to the gesture, known from ancient Near Eastern iconography, of a supplicant approaching a king; it is likely that the use of this gesture in prayer comes from a notion that prayer is similar to approaching a king with a petition (see Luke 18:1–8).[18] The gesture was also understood symbolically as an exposure of the hands and heart to divine examination (see Isaiah 1:15; Psalm 24:3–4).[19] Ralph F. Wilson contrasts the expression of "openness, invitation, surrender" inherent in the lifting of hands with "childhood instruction to fold little hands in prayer, . . . to keep them out of mischief"—a gesture that, from the ancient Israelite standpoint, would have opposite connotations.[20]

In Judaism, the lifting of hands in prayer was gradually replaced during the first two centuries AD by a posture of standing with the hands clasped in front, which was understood symbolically as the attitude of a servant before a master.[21] In western Christianity, the lifting of hands continued until about the thirteenth century AD, when it yielded to the gesture of joining the hands in front of the torso, a gesture similar to that of a vassal taking vows before a suzerain.[22]

Lifting the Hands to Bless

According to Luke 24:50, Jesus, addressing his disciples immediately before his ascension into heaven, "lifted up his hands and blessed them." The Greek idiom here, *epairō tas cheiras*, is practically identical to that in 1 Timothy 2:8; but the context indicates a different gesture, one associated with the blessing of a congregation instead of prayer by a congregation.

A two-handed blessing gesture like the one in Luke 24:50 is mentioned in Leviticus 9:22, in which Aaron lifts up both hands to bestow a blessing on the Israelites. Another instance is found in Sirach 50:20, in which the high priest Simon blesses the congregation at the temple with uplifted hands. The Mishnah and Talmud contain information on the circumstances in which the priest would or would not perform the priestly blessing, and on the ways in which this ritual action differed when performed at the temple in Jerusalem and when performed in other places (Mishnah Berakhot 5:4; Taʿanit 4:1; Megillah 4:3–7; Tamid 7:2; Talmud Bavli Taʿanit 26b).

From the descriptions in the rabbinic sources, it seems that the priestly blessing gesture around the time of Jesus was performed with the palms facing forward, both hands being raised to the height of the shoulders (except when a priest other than the high priest would perform the gesture at the temple, in which case the priest would raise his hands above his head). The gesture is still performed by Kohanim (descendants of Aaron) in Jewish synagogues; it is not known when the distinctive finger articulation of the modern gesture, with the thumbs touching and the fingers of each hand forming a V shape, came into practice.

Laying On of Hands for Healing and Blessing

Many passages in the Synoptic Gospels (Matthew, Mark, and Luke) describe Jesus healing people by the laying on of hands or by other forms of touch:

Instance	Matthew	Mark	Luke
healing people and casting out devils	—	—	4:40 "he laid his hands on each of them"
healing a leper	8:3 "he extended his hand and touched him"	1:41 "he extended his hand and touched him"	5:13 "he extended his hand and touched him"
Jairus asking Jesus to heal his daughter	9:18 "lay your hand upon her"	5:23 "lay your hands on her"	—
healing two blind men (first instance)	9:29 "he touched their eyes"	—	—
healing sick people in Nazareth	—	6:5 "he laid his hands on them"	—
healing a deaf man	—	7:32–33 "that he might lay his hand on him, . . . he put his fingers into his ears, and he spat and touched his tongue"	—
healing a blind man	—	8:22–23, 25 "that he might touch him, . . . he spit on his eyes and laid his hands on him. . . . He laid his hands on his eyes again"	—
healing a crippled woman	—	—	13:13 "he laid his hands on her"
blessing little children	19:13, 15 "that he might lay his hands on them and pray, . . . he laid his hands on them"	10:13, 16 "that he might touch them, . . . he laid his hands on them and blessed them"	Luke 18:15 "that he might touch them"
healing two blind men (second instance)	20:34 "he touched their eyes"	—	—

The most frequent phrase in this context is "lay hands on" (in Greek, *epitithēmi tas cheiras*). The part of the body on which the hands are laid is not usually specified; although we may tend to think of laying hands on the head of the person being blessed, the account of the healing of the blind man in Mark 8:22–23, 25 indicates that the idiom could describe contact with the afflicted part of the body. People asking Jesus to heal in Matthew 9:18 and Mark 7:32 refer to only one hand, but whenever Jesus actually performs the gesture, the phrase includes both hands (also note that the parallel to Matthew 9:18 in Mark 5:23 refers to both hands). In some instances, the text uses the more ambiguous word *touch* (Greek *haptō*).

In Mark 16:18, as part of Jesus's commission to his disciples after his resurrection (a portion not found in the earliest manuscripts of Mark), he explains that those who are baptized "shall lay hands on the sick, and they shall recover." This is fulfilled in Acts 9:12, 17, in which Ananias lays hands on Paul to restore Paul's sight (note that the KJV has the singular *hand* in verse 12, but the Greek here has the plural, with no significant textual variation). Paul also uses the laying on of hands to heal a man of fever and dysentery on the island of Malta (Acts 28:8). Although the laying on of hands was carried out by mortal men, the early saints believed that there was also an action on the part of God, "extending the hand to heal" (see Acts 4:30).

Some studies have pointed out parallels with Greek sources in which gods and human wonder-workers heal others through touch.[23] However, these similarities do not preclude a Hebrew background for healing and blessing by the laying on of hands in the New Testament. The Old Testament accounts of the miracles of Elijah and Elisha include examples of reviving the dead through touch, although the form of touch in these instances is dissimilar to the New Testament examples (1 Kings 17:21; 2 Kings 4:34–35). More similar from the standpoint of gesture form is the practice of laying hands on another's head to bestow a blessing. We find this gesture in the story of Jacob blessing his grandsons Ephraim and Manasseh, in which Jacob lays one hand on each child's head (Genesis 48:14, 17–18). In the book of Jubilees, Rebekah lays both her hands on Jacob's head to give him a matriarchal blessing (Jubilees 25:11–15). This gesture of laying hands on another's head has a healing function in an Aramaic text from the Dead Sea Scrolls known as the Genesis Apocryphon, which tells of Abraham praying for the afflicted pharaoh and laying hands on his head, after which the pharaoh recovers from his affliction (1QapGen ar 20.21–22, 28–29).

Laying On of Hands for Confirmation and Ordination

Several passages in Acts and in the New Testament epistles also refer to the laying on of hands (using the same Greek idiom, *epitithēmi tas cheiras*) in the context of bestowing the Holy Ghost, ordaining to an office, or setting apart for a mission:

> Acts 6:6: Apostles "appointing" (Greek *kathistēmi*, Acts 6:3) seven men to administer to the temporal needs of the church

> Acts 8:17–19: Peter and John bestowing the Holy Ghost on Samaritan believers

> Acts 13:3: Saul and Barnabas being "set apart" (Greek *aphorizo*, Acts 13:2) for a mission

> Acts 19:6: Paul bestowing the Holy Ghost on baptized believers in Ephesus

> 1 Timothy 4:14; 2 Timothy 1:6: Paul and a group of Ephesian elders bestowing "a gift (of God)" on Timothy, possibly a reference to Timothy's setting apart as bishop of Ephesus

In addition, in Hebrews 6:2, we find mention of "the doctrine of laying on of hands," indicating that this was not just a customary practice but an established part of church teachings.

The laying on of hands in the Old Testament also occurs in the context of ordination or setting apart. It is this gesture by which the Israelites set apart the Levites for their service (Numbers 8:10), and by which Moses appointed Joshua as his successor (Numbers 27:18; Deuteronomy 34:9). The gesture was also performed on sacrificial animals (Exodus 29:10, 15, 19, and fourteen other verses in Leviticus, Numbers, and 2 Chronicles), on the scapegoat on the Day of Atonement (Leviticus 16:21), and on a person accused of blasphemy (Leviticus 24:14). Some previous studies have argued that there were two different gestures, namely a one-handed gesture used on the sacrificial animal and a two-handed gesture used in other contexts; more recent research, however, indicates that the gesture in all these cases employed both hands.[24] This same gesture of the laying on of hands was also used in early Judaism to ordain a rabbi, as described in rabbinic sources.[25]

Scholarly discussions of the laying on of hands as it appears in the Old and New Testaments most frequently describe it as a gesture of transfer: the hands are understood as a medium by which power, spiritual gifts, and authority are channeled from the one performing the gesture to the one receiving it. For instance, Luke Timothy Johnson, discussing Paul's reference to the laying of hands on Timothy (1 Timothy 4:14; 2 Timothy 1:6), states that it is a "ritual gesture for the transmission of power and the bestowal of authority."[26] This understanding is in harmony with Old Testament passages such as Leviticus 16:21 and Numbers 27:16–20. The latter passage also supports an interpretation of the gesture as one of appointing the recipient to a particular status or role, which agrees with Acts 6:3, 6; 13:2–3. Further, the connection with the laying on of hands in the Old Testament means that the rites of confirmation, ordaining, and setting apart in the early church would recall the Jewish rite of sacrifice, which early Christians understood as a type of Christ's sacrifice for sin (Hebrews 10:1–13).[27]

The Healing Handclasp

In addition to healing by the laying on of hands, Jesus often raised others from death or sickness with a handclasp. The Greek idiom is *krateō tēs cheiros* "grasp by the hand," denoting a firm, sustained handclasp (without any other connotation of movement, unlike the various forms of the modern Western "handshake"). In Mark 1:31, Jesus heals Peter's mother-in-law of fever by taking her by the hand and lifting her up (the parallel passage in Matthew 8:15 mentions only touching her hand, while the other parallel in Luke 4:39 does not mention a gesture at all but merely the rebuking of the fever). When Jesus visits the dead daughter of Jairus, he takes the girl by the hand and says to her in Aramaic, *Talitha, koum!* "Little girl, arise!" (Matthew 9:25; Mark 5:41; Luke 8:54). Also relevant, perhaps, is an instance in which Jesus casts an evil spirit out of a boy, and while the boy is then lying down as if dead, Jesus takes him by the hand and lifts him up (Mark 9:27). One can suppose that the boy had gone unconscious and Jesus brought him out of this state with the handclasp as a separate act of healing. Finally, in Acts 3:7, Peter emulates the Master in healing a crippled beggar, taking him by the right hand and lifting him up.

Self-Lowering Gestures

The gestures of grasping another's feet and washing another's feet may be grouped together because they both involve a very low posture relative to the other person, being therefore similar to prostration (see below). These two gestures were generally performed by women toward men in ancient Israelite society. The first, grasping another's feet, occurs in Matthew 28:9, in which Mary Magdalene and Mary the mother of James, having met Jesus, "came and took hold of his feet, and they prostrated themselves before him." This is comparable to the gesture of the Shunammite woman whose son died, who then beseeched Elisha by grasping his feet (2 Kings 4:27).

In ancient Israel, the washing of the feet of guests was a hospitality rite generally delegated to female servants. If the household had no female servant, water would be provided for the guest to wash his or her own feet (see Genesis 18:4; 19:2; 24:32; 43:24; Judges 19:21; 1 Samuel 25:41; 2 Samuel 11:8; Song of Solomon 5:3). This custom seems to have continued into New Testament times. Thus, Jesus pointed out to his host, "You gave me no water for my feet, but she has washed my feet with her tears and wiped them with her hair" (Luke 7:44). Paul mentions washing the saints' feet (in other words, giving hospitality to members of the church) as one of the characteristics of a righteous widow (1 Timothy 5:10). It may be that Peter's initial objection to Jesus's washing of his feet (John 13:5–9) was a reaction not just to Jesus's humility but to the fact that he was acting in what was traditionally a woman's role.

Rending the Garments

In Matthew 26:65 and the parallel passage in Mark 14:63–64, after Jesus testifies to the Sanhedrin that they will see him sitting on the right hand of God, the high priest tears his own clothes, saying, "He has blasphemed!" Similarly, in Acts 14:14, Paul and Barnabas, after having performed a healing miracle in Lystra, realize that the people believe them to be gods and are about to sacrifice to them; the two missionaries then rend their garments and cry out to the people to desist.

Rending the garments is a well-known sign of grief in the Old Testament. A dramatic example is found in 2 Samuel 13:31, which describes King David tearing his clothes on hearing that his son Absalom has slain all his other sons. The tearing of the clothes at the hearing of blasphemy is a related custom, expressing intense shock like that of hearing for the first time about the death of a loved one. We see this in Numbers 14:6, in which Joshua and Caleb tear their clothes when they hear the people murmur against Moses.

Another illustration of this custom comes from the Palestinian Talmud:

Rabbi Simeon ben Laqish was riding in the street. There met him a Samaritan who went along blaspheming, and each time Rabbi Simeon would rend his garment. This happened again and again, until finally Rabbi Simeon got down from his donkey, struck the Samaritan on the chest, and said to him: "Wicked one! Does your mother have clothing sufficient for me?" Thus it was customary to tear one's clothes against blasphemy; this custom still survives.[28]

Lifting the Eyes to Heaven

In addition to lifting the hands, prayer often involved lifting the eyes toward heaven. The Gospels describe Jesus looking up to heaven when blessing the loaves and fishes that miraculously multiply (Matthew 14:19; Mark 6:41; Luke 9:16). He also lifts his eyes toward heaven as he heals a deaf man (Mark 7:34) and as he begins his intercessory prayer (John 17:1). This contrasts with the penitent publican who, considering himself unworthy, will not lift his eyes to heaven as he prays (Luke 18:13).

The lifting of the eyes in prayer is attested in the Old Testament—for example, in Psalm 123:1: "To you I lift up my eyes, O you who sit enthroned in heaven." It is also found in the Apocrypha (2 Maccabees 15:34; 4 Maccabees 6:26; Tobit 3:12).

This gesture obviously differs from the modern custom of praying with the eyes closed. As the contrast between Jesus's prayer and that of the publican shows, the lifting of the eyes expresses confidence in God's favor toward the person doing the gesture. The choice to lift or to lower the eyes thus presupposes an evaluation of one's current status before God.

Kissing

Kissing in first-century Roman Palestine was a common practice in situations of greeting and leave-taking; the kiss could be exchanged between members of the same gender and did not carry the romantic implications that it does in some cultures today. However, it did carry implications of friendliness and fellowship. In the parable of the prodigal son, the father runs to his returning son and kisses him, a purely nonverbal exchange that leaves no doubt of the father's readiness to welcome his son (Luke 15:20). The kiss by which Judas betrays Jesus is accompanied by the words "Greetings, Master!" (Matthew 26:49; compare Mark 14:45; Luke 22:47). In Acts 20:37, the Ephesian elders kiss Paul as he takes leave of them, weeping as they do so. Paul exhorts various congregations in his epistles to "greet one another with a holy kiss" (Romans 16:16; 1 Corinthians 16:20; 2 Corinthians 13:12; 1 Thessalonians 5:26), and Peter also exhorts people similarly (1 Peter 5:14).

Kissing as a gesture of greeting or leave-taking is also frequently attested in the Old Testament and the Apocrypha (Genesis 29:11, 13; 31:28; 32:1; 33:4; 45:15; 48:10; 50:1; Exodus 4:27; Ruth 1:9, 14; Tobit 5:17; 7:6; 10:12). Gruber points out, however, that the examples in the Old Testament are generally between close relatives.[29] For instance, three of the instances of kissing in greeting are between brothers (Genesis 33:4; 45:15; Exodus 4:27). This could provide a key to understanding the "holy kiss" exchanged between Christians: after being brought into the church as children of God, Christians greet one another as siblings.

Although specific evidence of the form of the kiss used in greeting and leave-taking is lacking, it may have been similar to the light kiss on the cheeks used in similar contexts in southern Europe and in Latin America today. It would thus differ from the romantic kiss on the lips (Song of Solomon 1:2; 7:9).

Standing to Pray

Postures of prayer in the New Testament include standing, kneeling, and prostration. The standing posture is attested in Matthew 6:5; Mark 11:25; and Luke 18:11, 13. It is also found in the Old Testament (Psalm 106:30; Jeremiah 18:20; Nehemiah 9:2). In later Judaism, this becomes the posture of the Jewish *'Amidah* ("standing") prayer. The symbolism of this posture, as explained in rabbinic literature, points to the posture of a servant before his master, ready to serve.[30]

Standing to Read or Exhort

In modern Western culture, standing is the usual posture for any situation of public speaking. This posture was used for some of the same situations in the Jewish culture of Roman Palestine, but not for all such situations. In particular, one would stand to read from a text or to deliver a testimony, defense, or exhortation. Thus, Jesus stands to read from the book of Isaiah at a synagogue in Nazareth (Luke 4:16) and to deliver the Sermon in the Plain, a sermon in Luke similar to the Sermon on the Mount in Matthew (Luke 6:17). Paul also stands to deliver his witness of the doctrine of Christ (Acts 13:16; 21:40). This is comparable to the Old Testament, in which, for example, Jeremiah stands at the city gate to exhort people (Jeremiah 7:2; 17:19), and Ezra stands to read from the Torah before the congregation (Nehemiah 8:4).

Sitting to Teach or Expound

While standing was used for some kinds of public address, sitting was the expected posture for the teaching or expounding of doctrine. Thus, after standing to read from Isaiah at the synagogue in Nazareth, Jesus sits down to expound on what he has read (Luke 4:20). It is also in a sitting posture that Jesus delivers the Sermon on the Mount (Matthew 5:1). The difference between the sitting posture of the Sermon on the Mount and the standing posture of the Sermon in the Plain corresponds to a difference in the overall tone of the two discourses. The Sermon on the Mount contains numerous quotations of legal sayings from scripture, which Jesus then comments on, all of which reinforces the impression that this is an expounding of doctrine. By contrast, the Sermon in the Plain lacks these references to scripture and is easily interpreted as more of a hortatory sermon. In Matthew 13:1–2, Jesus delivers a series of parables, sitting first on the shore and then, when the multitude becomes too great, on a boat a short distance from the shore. According to Matthew 26:55, Jesus sat daily to teach in the temple.

Kneeling and Prostration

The typical postures of supplication were kneeling (*gonupeteō, tithēmi ta gonata*) and prostration (*proskuneō, piptō epi prosōpon, piptō pros/para tous podas, prospiptō*). There is no discernible difference in function between the two postures, although it would be logical to assume that prostration, with the face all the way to the ground, was a more intense form of self-lowering than mere kneeling. Both postures are attested for those who approached Jesus to beseech him:

Petitioner	Matthew	Mark	Luke
leper	8:2 *proskuneō*	1:40 *gonupeteō*	5:12 *piptō epi prosōpon*
man possessed by demons	—	5:6 *proskuneō*	8:28 *prospiptō*
Jairus	9:18 *proskuneō*	5:22 *piptō pros tous podas*	8:41 *piptō para tous podas*
Canaanite woman	15:25 *proskuneō*	7:25 *prospiptō pros tous podas*	—
father of epileptic boy	17:14 *gonupeteō*	—	—
wife of Zebedee	20:20 *proskuneō*	—	—

The verb *proskuneō* is usually rendered as "worship" in the KJV, and some other translations (NIV, NRSV) render the word as "kneel." Both of these translations lead to misunderstanding of the text, as the correct meaning of the verb, when used in reference to a physical posture, is "prostrate oneself before."[31] Gruber posits that Matthew consistently mentions kneeling in this context, and that Luke consistently mentions falling on the face, while Mark mentions both postures; however, this is based on the understanding of *proskuneō* as "kneel."[32] With the correct understanding of the verb, only the story of the leper shows a difference in posture in the parallel accounts: Mark 1:40 has *gonupeteō* "kneel," while the parallels in Matthew 8:2 and Luke 5:12 mention prostration.

As attitudes of supplication, kneeling and prostration were also appropriate for prayer. As with the lifting of the hands, the use of these postures in prayer indicates a notion that prayer is like bringing a petition before a king. Both Matthew 26:39 and Mark 14:35 mention Jesus prostrating himself with his face to the ground as he prayed in Gethsemane, "My Father, if it is possible, let this cup pass from me; nevertheless not as I will, but as you will." The parallel in Luke 22:41 mentions Jesus kneeling and does not mention prostration. This is not necessarily a conflict in the sources, as Jesus could obviously have done both—indeed, prostration typically includes kneeling.

The New Testament records several examples in which a person, having witnessed a miracle, comes to Jesus with prostration. In these cases, the function of the posture seems to be that of worship (which is the meaning of the verb *proskuneō* when used in an abstract sense); it expresses the recognition of Jesus's divinity. In Matthew 14:33, some of Jesus's disciples prostrate themselves to him after seeing him walk on the water. Peter, James, and John prostrate themselves to Jesus after seeing his glory and hearing the voice of the Father bear witness of the Son (Matthew 17:6). A leper whom Jesus has cleansed "falls upon his face" at the feet of Jesus and thanks him (Luke 17:16). The blind man who has been healed prostrates himself to Jesus after Jesus testifies of his divine sonship (John 9:38). Kneeling may have the same function in Romans 14:11 and Philippians 2:10, where Paul states that "every knee shall bow, and every tongue confess" when we appear before Christ to be judged.

The Old Testament contains many examples of kneeling (1 Kings 8:54; Daniel 6:10; Psalm 95:6) and especially of prostration (Genesis 18:2; Exodus 34:8; Nehemiah 8:6; Ezekiel 44:4) in contexts that are closely analogous to those in the New Testament, including supplication, prayer, and worship.[33] Kneeling and prostration are also found in the context of prayer in 2 Maccabees 3:20–21 and 3 Maccabees 2:1.

The most obvious formal feature of kneeling and prostration is the lowering of the body. This communicates the basic idea of declaring one's own status to be low relative to another person, which is appropriate for beseeching as well as for worship.

Groaning and Weeping

The Gospels record Jesus sighing (Mark 7:34; 8:12), groaning (John 11:33, 38), and weeping (Luke 19:41; John 11:35), all expressions of sorrow or pity. There is no record in the Gospels of Jesus laughing, although he does speak of his own joy in John 15:11. Others "laughed him to scorn" (Matthew 9:24; Mark 5:40; Luke 8:53).

In several passages, Jesus speaks of "weeping and gnashing of teeth" in the context of the punishment of the wicked (Matthew 8:12; 13:42, 50; 22:13; 24:51; 25:30; Luke 13:28). The gnashing of teeth (Greek *brugmos tōn odontōn*) in these passages is a sign of intense physical or emotional pain. Elsewhere it is an expression of rage, as when the members of the Sanhedrin gnash their teeth at Stephen after hearing his testimony (Acts 7:54).

Loud Voices

In several instances while making a speech, Jesus is said to "cry" or "call out" the words he is speaking. One passage in Luke uses the Greek word *phōneō* in this context, while the few instances in John use the verb *krazō*; both verbs have to do with calling out in a loud voice. The things Jesus says immediately after his voice raises include the following:

Luke 8:8: "he who has ears to hear, let him hear" (expounding a parable)

John 7:28: "you know me, and you know where I am from" (teaching in the temple)

John 7:37: "if any man thirst, let him come to me, and drink"

John 12:44: "he that believes in me believes not in me but in him who sent me"

Whitney Shiner points out the contrast between some modern portrayals of a soft-spoken Jesus and the volume that would be necessary to preach in an ancient environment:

> Even when the scene specifies a large crowd, we often think of Jesus speaking as if he were in a rather intimate setting. Movie portrayals of Jesus also perpetuate this image, since even the most lavish spectacle movies do not hire and costume ten thousand extras for crowd scenes and the close-ups of Jesus speaking bring him closer to the viewer. No movie Jesus could ever be heard in the crowds the Gospels report.[34]

But we should be careful not to overgeneralize this statement. While Jesus must have used a loud voice while speaking in public (and the same would be true for Peter, Paul, and other apostles and missionaries), this does not necessarily apply to other situations. In private situations reported in the Gospels, it is those who are beseeching Jesus who cry out, and his response seems to be softer in contrast (Mark 10:47–52 is representative).

Conclusion

This brief survey shows that gestures and other nonverbal signs have a story to tell. They carry information about the culture of the speaker as well as reflecting the speaker's communicative intentions, even if we who read the text centuries later may not grasp the full import in the same way that a member of the ancient society would. Paying attention to nonverbal signs is one way in which modern readers can glimpse the multiple layers of meaning of the scriptural text.

⌖

David M. Calabro is curator of Eastern Christian and Islamic manuscripts at the Hill Museum and Manuscript Library at St. John's University.

Further Reading

Burgoon, Judee K., David B. Buller, and W. Gill Woodall. *Nonverbal Communication: The Unspoken Dialogue.* New York: McGraw-Hill, 1996.

Calabro, David M. "Gestures of Praise: Lifting and Spreading the Hands in Biblical Prayer." In *Ascending the Mountain of the Lord: Temple, Praise, and Worship in the Old Testament*, edited by David R. Seely, Jeffrey R. Chadwick, and Matthew J. Grey, 105–21. Provo, UT: Religious Studies Center, Brigham Young University; Salt Lake City: Deseret Book, 2013.

———. "A Reexamination of the Ancient Israelite Gesture of Hand Placement." In *Sacrifice, Cult, and Atonement in Early Judaism and Christianity: Constituents and Critique*, edited by Henrietta L. Wiley and Christian A. Eberhart, 99–124. Atlanta: SBL, 2017.

Ehrlich, Uri. *The Nonverbal Language of Prayer: A New Approach to Jewish Liturgy*. Tübingen, Germany: Mohr Siebeck, 2004.

Shiner, Whitney. *Proclaiming the Gospel: First-Century Performance of Mark*. Harrisburg, PA: Trinity, 2003.

Notes

1. To accurately reflect the Greek gestural idioms, which are often rendered inconsistently in modern translations, I use my own translations of the Greek except where otherwise noted. Likewise, the translations from Aramaic and Hebrew are my own.
2. See Judee K. Burgoon, David B. Buller, and W. Gill Woodall, *Nonverbal Communication: The Unspoken Dialogue* (New York: McGraw-Hill, 1996), 18–19.
3. Fernando Poyatos, *New Perspectives in Nonverbal Communication: Studies in Cultural Antrhopology, Social Psychology, Linguistics, Literature and Semiotics* (New York: Pergamon, 1983), 175–214.
4. W. Ewing, "Gestures," in *Dictionary of the Bible*, ed. James Hastings (Edinburgh, Scotland: T&T Clark), 201.
5. David G. Burke, "Gesture," in *The International Standard Bible Encyclopedia*, ed. Geoffrey W. Bromiley (Grand Rapids, MI: Eerdmans, 1982), 2:449–57; and Mayer I. Gruber, "Gestures," in *The Harper Collins Bible Dictionary*, ed. Paul J. Achtemeier (San Francisco: Harper Collins, 1996), 372–73.
6. Whitney Shiner, *Proclaiming the Gospel: First-Century Performance of Mark* (Harrisburg, PA: Trinity Press International, 2003), 127–42.
7. The literature on this topic is extensive; as a starting place, see Matthew Black, *An Aramaic Approach to the Gospels and Acts* (Oxford: Clarendon, 1967).
8. David Seely, "The Raised Hand of God as an Oath Gesture," in *Fortunate the Eyes That See: Essays in Honor of David Noel Freedman in Celebration of His Seventieth Birthday*, ed. Astrid B. Beck et al. (Grand Rapids, MI: Eerdmans, 1995), 411–21.
9. Eugene P. McGarry, "The Ambidextrous Angel: Inner-Biblical Exegesis and Textual Criticism in Counterpoint," *Journal of Biblical Literature* 124, no. 2 (2005): 212–14.
10. Robert A. Barakat, "Arabic Gestures," *Journal of Popular Culture* 6 (1973): 772.
11. See David M. Calabro, "Ritual Gestures of Lifting, Extending, and Clasping the Hand(s) in Northwest Semitic Literature and Iconography" (PhD diss., University of Chicago, 2014), 393–493.
12. Burke, "Gesture," 453.
13. The NIV, NRSV, and the NJB often clarify the interpretation of the passages with *kataseiō*, adding the phrase "for silence" even when it is not present in the Greek.
14. See Ray L. Birdwhistell, *Kinesics and Context* (Philadelphia: University of Pennsylvania Press, 1970), 79–80.
15. See, for example, Ernst Fuchs, "*Ekteinō*," in *Theological Dictionary of the New Testament* (Grand Rapids, MI: Eerdmans, 1964), 2:460, 463; many sources cite Quintilian's Latin treatise on oratorial technique, *Institutio oratoria*, 11:3:84ff.
16. Mayer I. Gruber, *Aspects of Nonverbal Communication in the Ancient Near East* (Rome: Biblical Institute, 1980), 1:22–50; Othmar Keel, *The Symbolism of the Biblical World: Ancient Near Eastern Iconography and the Book of Psalms* (New York: Crossroad, 1985), 307–23; David M. Calabro, "Gestures of Praise: Lifting and Spreading the Hands in Biblical Prayer," in *Ascending the Mountain of the Lord: Temple, Praise, and Worship in the Old Testament*, ed. David R. Seely, Jeffrey R. Chadwick, and Matthew J. Grey (Provo, UT: Religious Studes Center, Brigham Young University; Salt Lake City: Deseret Book, 2013), 105–21.
17. See John Tvedtnes, "Temple Prayer in Ancient Times," in *The Temple in Time and Eternity*, ed. Donald W. Parry and Stephen D. Ricks (Provo, UT: Foundation for Ancient Research and Mormon Studies, 1999), 81–84.
18. See David M. Calabro, "Prayer, Jewish," in *The Encyclopedia of Ancient History*, ed. Roger S. Bagnall et al. (London: Wiley-Blackwell, 2012), 10:5505–7.
19. Tvedtnes, "Temple Prayer," 84; and Calabro, "Gestures of Praise," 117.

20. Ralph F. Wilson, "Lifting Hands in Worship," *Paraclete* (1986): 6–7.

21. Uri Ehrlich, *The Nonverbal Language of Prayer: A New Approach to Jewish Liturgy* (Tübingen, Germany: Mohr Siebeck, 2004), 110–19.

22. See Gerhart B. Ladner, "The Gestures of Prayer in Papal Iconography of the Thirteenth and Early Fourteenth Centuries," in *Didascaliae: Studies in Honor of Anselm M. Albareda*, ed. Sesto Prete (New York: B. M. Rosenthal, 1961), 245–75; and Jean-Claude Schmitt, *La raison des gestes dans l'occident médiéval* (Paris: Gallimard, 1990), 295–97.

23. Eduard Lohse, "*Kheir*," in *Theological Dictionary of the New Testament* (Grand Rapids, MI: Eerdmans, 1974), 9:425.

24. See David M. Calabro, "A Reexamination of the Ancient Israelite Gesture of Hand Placement," in *Sacrifice, Cult, and Atonement in Early Judaism and Christianity: Constituents and Critique*, ed. Henrietta L. Wiley and Christian A. Eberhart (Atlanta: SBL, 2017), 99–124. As explained in that article, some biblical passages (such as Leviticus 1:4) seem to mention only one hand, but this is due to an error in the vowel markings that were added to the Hebrew text around AD 700.

25. Lohse, "*Kheir*," 429.

26. Luke Timothy Johnson, *The First and Second Letters to Timothy: A New Translation with Introduction and Commentary* (New York: Doubleday, 2001), 345.

27. See Calabro, "Reexamination."

28. J. T. Marshall, *Manual of the Aramaic Language of the Palestinian Talmud: Grammar, Vocalized Text, Translation and Vocabulary* (Eugene, OR: Wipf and Stock, 2009), no. 114.

29. Gruber, "Gestures," 373.

30. Ehrlich, *Nonverbal Language of Prayer*, 113.

31. Danker, *Greek-English Lexicon*, 882–83.

32. Gruber, "Gestures," 373.

33. See further Gruber, *Aspects of Nonverbal Communication*, 90–143.

34. Shiner, *Proclaiming the Gospel*, 129.

32

Ritualized Prostration in the New Testament

Andrew C. Smith

One of the prominent and recurring actions within sections of the New Testament is the "falling at the feet," the "falling on the ground," or the "worship" before someone, in most cases either God or Jesus.[1] Generally identified as a form of prostration, most of the cases of this action are signified by the usage of the Greek word *proskuneō*, though other words are also used to describe the same type of action. This action, while culturally, socially, and politically significant in the ancient world and in many cultures in the modern world, strikes Western (particularly American) audiences as odd, strange, or foreign. This strangeness is largely a function of the fact that Western cultures have developed, adopted, and accepted differing norms for the expression of social and religious messages and values. This chapter will elucidate the usage of the action of ritual prostration within the New Testament world by, first, establishing certain methods for the understanding of rituals and ritualized action and, second, comparing and contextualizing the connection and dependence of prostration in the New Testament with its precedents in the Old Testament. This chapter will then move beyond these to analyze the usage of the words of prostration in order to appreciate the ways prostration was utilized in New Testament times and by the authors of the New Testament in their respective works.

Understanding Rituals and Ritualized Action in Scriptural Texts

To understand what ritualized prostration may have meant and why it appears so prevalently in both the Old and New Testaments, it is necessary to think more broadly about ritual actions within human societies. Every culture and religious system has its set of ritual actions—whether called "ordinances," "sacraments," or something else—that fill an important role. Beyond distinctly religious ritual actions, every community is likewise undergirded by a variety of more common ritual actions that assist in communication between individuals within that community and with individuals of other communities. Such ritual actions can change over time, their importance within society ebbing and flowing or being replaced outright by other (similar or completely different) rituals. Such rituals can also be used in many different ways depending on the message that participants wish to send. Consider, for instance, the handshake. While being a basic ritual of greeting and extending polite overtures of friendliness, it can also send a variety of different social messages if done in a different way: it can be simply formulaic or without feeling, it can be warm and inviting, or it can be cold and vapid. It can be embellished and expanded with the addition of other ritualized actions (embraces, back-patting, shoulder-gripping, elaborate series of hand slaps and motions, and so forth). Its deliberate omission sends messages of offense, while overdoing it (e.g., squeezing too hard with the hand) can act as a passive-aggressive means of asserting superiority. Or it may not be the norm at all, with other ritual actions—for instance, bowing of the head in many contemporary Eastern cultures—filling the same social need (though obviously also differing in import and message). In any case, such a simple physical gesture can be seen as an intensely complex interaction, with the potential for a vast amount of social and symbolic messaging and signification encoded in a simple physical gesture. Yet, despite its complexity, most messages are readily apparent to all of us. They go without being said. We can automatically understand their importance and interpret them largely correctly. Beyond that, we unconsciously assume that others are able to read such messages clearly as well. However, such an assumption is not always warranted, as someone from one culture may not automatically understand the nuances of messages sent by specific actions related to handshakes in another culture.

Such is the case for prostration in the ancient world. Mostly foreign to modern Western audiences, prostration (or the variety of physical postures that could fit under such an umbrella term), as an intentionally ritualized action, sent specific messages about the social interaction taking place. However, without proper contextualization and understanding of its place within the society of the New Testament and its authors, modern audiences might struggle to appreciate or fully understand the social interactions taking place. In the last few decades, ritual studies as a scholarly and academic field has arisen as a way of studying and presenting methods for the analysis of these complex interactions.[2]

The ritual action of prostration in the biblical world can most effectively be classified as a ritual of exchange or communion, meaning a ritual action in which an individual either presents a request or simply seeks to engage with or demonstrate dependency with the object of the prostration (most often God, but also other humans).[3] While in some cases prostration is being used in other ways, the majority of the cases in both the Old and New Testaments are used in this way.[4] While we can assume this represents how prostration appeared in the culture and context of ancient Israel, we must also remember that our analysis of the rituals can be complicated by the standard issues of dealing with ancient texts.[5] We must also recognize that in many cases biblical authors presume that their original audience automatically understood what they were presented: the significance went without being said. With this last thought in mind, we recognize that prostration in the New Testament and its world is dependent on and derived from the ways it was used in the Old Testament and its world.

Contextualizing Prostration in the Old and New Testaments

Prostration in the Old Testament is largely represented by the word *yištaḥăweh/hištaḥăwah*, which appears 170 times in the Hebrew text.[6] This word is regularly understood to mean "to bow down"; however, its morphological stem form is rather irregular within Biblical Hebrew, potentially affecting notions of what the term originally meant and how it was understood.[7] Whatever the case may be regarding its etymological development, what is clear about the term is that "the unusual shape of the word hints at its extraordinary cultural significance."[8] This word is also translated as "worship" in many, but not all, cases in the King James Version.[9] However, a focus on the "inward attitude" or "worship" aspects of prostration does not fully represent the range of situations and purposes of *hištaḥăwah* in the biblical text, something also noted in the usage of *proskuneō* in the New Testament.[10] While the majority of usages of *hištaḥăwah* (68 percent) are directed toward Deity or other numinous personages, a significant minority of its usages (32 percent) are directed at other mortals.[11] The distinction between mortal or numinous objects forms the major characteristic that interpreters and translators use to distinguish between prostration as worship or veneration and prostration as social or hierarchical homage or honoring. However, the same word is used in both cases, and it should not be assumed that the earliest authors and audiences necessarily always made a distinction between the two uses. Indeed, there are a couple of instances in which the division between mortal and numinous recipients is deliberately obscured, with prostration done simultaneously to the king and to God (1 Chronicles 29:20 and Psalm 45:11).

No single characteristic or element dominates the literary presentation of prostration in the Old Testament. Rather, the usage of this term, befitting the large-scale diachronic development of the Old Testament (i.e., the fact that the contents of the Bible were written across hundreds of years, in many different locations, by different authors, in different contexts, for different purposes), can only be seen as quite variegated, representing a multivalent perspective on its meaning and purpose, as it appears in many different contexts.[12] As such, there are many different ways one can analyze prostration and its uses.[13] Herein, we will focus only on its ritual character, its directionality, and certain literary aspects connected to those characteristics.

As noted, the major category of ritual into which most of the examples of prostration in the Old Testament (84 percent) fall is that of rites of exchange or communion.[14] However, to truly represent how prostration was viewed, it is necessary to further subdivide this category, on the basis of the division presented above with prostration used with both numinous beings and other mortals as the object. In this case, 70 percent of the uses of prostration as a ritual of exchange or communion are directed toward numinous beings, while 30 percent are directed to other mortals. The conception of prostration throughout the composition of the Old Testament held fairly steady with the point that, as a ritual, prostration could be used as both a ritual of request or exchange with a mortal (mainly the king, but also others of high social standing) and a ritual of exchange and communion with God.[15]

Analysis of Prostration in the New Testament

Relying on this basis for the use of prostration culturally and religiously in the Old Testament, the New Testament authors also prominently place prostration as a meaningful action relaying specific sociocultural and religiopolitical messages to their original audiences. As mentioned, these messages are largely presented via the term *proskuneō* ("to worship, pay homage, show reverence; to prostrate"). However, there are also a number of other terms that present the same type of action. These words, not appearing anywhere as often as *proskuneō*, include *piptō* ("to fall, collapse; to bow down; to die"), *katapiptō* ("to fall down"), and *gonupeteō* ("to fall upon one's knees, to kneel before").[16] In the case of the Gospels, it appears in some instances the author's word choice was deliberate to change materials from previously written Gospels to better present specific literary aims, themes, and messages.[17] Likewise, in some cases, it has been surmised that (more than likely) the authors deliberately presented a form of prostration without using any of these words.[18]

While scattered throughout the New Testament, references to prostration are largely localized in two main sections of writing: the Gospels and Revelation. Prostration is found to a lesser degree elsewhere in the New Testament. It appears in Acts ten times (as both *proskuneō* and *piptō*) in the context of Stephen's self-defense, Paul's conversion,[19] the worship of the Ethiopian eunuch, and the conversion of Cornelius.[20] But it only appears twice (once as *piptō* and once as *proskuneō*) in the writings of Paul (both in the same verse, 1 Corinthians 14:25) and once in the Epistle to the Hebrews (Hebrews 11:21).[21]

However, within the Gospels, prostration appears most frequently, deliberately, and meaningfully in Matthew and John. While appearing in Mark and Luke, it does so less frequently and almost incidentally when compared to the thematic and deliberate manner with which it is used in Matthew.[22] Matthew, on the other hand, uses prostration frequently and obviously enough that it can be considered a deliberate theme (or subtheme) within his Gospel, particularly as connected to his themes of Jesus as the anointed Davidic King of Israel and as Immanuel ("God with us").[23] This is very different from the way that *proskuneō* appears and is used in the Gospel of John. In John, rather than being spread throughout the text, mention of prostration is concentrated and focused mainly within one pericope, the discussion between Jesus and the Samaritan woman (in John 4).[24]

In the book of Revelation, prostration occurs largely in two contexts, determined mostly by the object of the action. Prostration is mostly directed toward either the Lord or the beast.[25] For instance, "the four and twenty elders fall down before him that sat on the throne, and worship [*proskunēsousin*] him that liveth for ever and ever, and cast their crowns before the throne" (Revelation 4:10). On the other hand, "they worshipped [*prosekunēsan*] the dragon which gave power unto the beast; and they worshipped [*prosekunēsan*] the beast, saying, Who is like unto the beast? who is able to make war with him?" (Revelation 13:4). In line with this, considered literarily, Revelation's usage of prostration is most closely reflective of the ways that prostration is seen in the Old Testament.[26]

The occurrences of prostration in the Gospels, whether repeated or unique, are much more prominent. Prostration occurs prominently in the narratives of some of the most important events in Jesus's life (particularly in Matthew): in the wise men and Herod pericope (Matthew 2), in the temptation narrative (Matthew 4; Luke 4), after walking on water (Matthew 14:13), the Mount of Transfiguration (Matthew 17:6),[27] and with requests for healing or other boons from various individuals throughout the Gospels.[28] Prostration also occupies a prominent place in the narratives of Jesus's passion, his suffering, death, and resurrection. It occurs in an ironic form with the mockery of the Roman soldiers who dress Jesus up in royal colors and crown of thorns and bow before him (Mark 15:19; Matthew 27:29).[29] Then Jesus is also presented as prostrating as "he went a little further and fell on his face, and prayed" (Matthew 26:39; compare Mark 14:35). In both the cases presenting Jesus as falling prostrate in Gethsemane, the word of prostration is *piptō*.[30] Prostration is also thematically correlated and connected to the Resurrection, particularly the actions of those witness to it (see Matthew 28:9, 17; Luke 24:52–53).

Prostration appears only in a couple of places in the parables and direct teachings of Jesus. The discussion between Jesus and the Samaritan woman in John 4 is of distinct interest since it presents an instance of prostration as more devoted (or being more prescriptively defined in Jesus's prophecy of a coming time) to an internal motivation, unencumbered by physical location or (perhaps) by physical posture (John 4:23–24). Prostration appears in only one of the parables of Jesus, that of the unmerciful servant (Matthew 18:23–35).

Given the aggregate occurrences of prostration in the New Testament in light of the ritual studies methods above, it is clear that, as in the Old Testament, the majority (99 percent) of prostrations occur as rites of exchange or communion, meaning a ritual action in which an individual either presents a request or simply seeks to engage with or demonstrate dependency on the object of prostration (most often God, but also other humans).[31] These numbers accord very well with the overall numbers and presentation of prostration from the Old Testament. In terms of literary analysis, the basic presentation of prostration in the New Testament fits roughly with that of the Old Testament, again indicating the genealogical connection between the cultures and peoples of the New and Old Testaments.

However, considering the difference between numinous and mortal objects of prostration, the New Testament occurances of prostration revolve around an aspect not found in the Old Testament: the incarnation of the Lord Jesus Christ. In the Old Testament, the ratio is about 2 to 1, with 68 percent of the instances of prostration directed at a numinous being (mostly God), while 32 percent are directed at other mortals. The New Testament, however, adds a different wrinkle: the consideration of whether or not Jesus is mortal or numinous, or both.[32] Thirty percent of the prostrations in the New Testament are directed at the mortal Jesus.[33] Otherwise, 63 percent of the prostrations are directed at numinous beings, and only 5 percent are directed at specifically mortal recipients.[34] Thus, depending on the theological line one were to take, if Jesus was considered only a mortal, New Testament prostration vis-à-vis its object would look very similar to that of the Old Testament (roughly 63 percent numinous, 35 percent mortal). However, if one accepts Jesus as numinous, then the ratios skew very differently (93 percent numinous and 5 percent mortal).

The ambiguity of Jesus's status combined with the presentation and issues related to prostration in the Old Testament suggests that the Gospel of Matthew is using prostration deliberately for a literary purpose, namely as a vehicle of dramatic irony to heighten the dramatic tension in its presentation of Jesus as both King and Holy One of Israel. We have already seen how prevalent and deliberately placed prostration is in the Gospel of Matthew. With the thirteen occurrences of *proskuneō*,[35] five uses of *piptō*,[36] and additional two instances of *gonupeteō*,[37] the Gospel of Matthew is surpassed in sheer volume of usage only by the book of Revelation. The emphasis on prostration in the Gospel of Matthew can also be seen in the way that the author introduces changes to the materials taken from the Gospel of Mark in its literary composition.[38] Three changes are specifically apparent. The first is that Matthew inserts into the story of Jesus walking on water an instance of prostration not found in Mark. At the point in the narrative when Jesus gets into the boat, Matthew inserts, "They that were in the ship came and worshipped [*prosekunēsan*] him, saying, Of a truth thou art the Son of God" (Matthew 14:33).[39] The second and third changes involve a shift in which word is used for prostration. As has been noted, after Jesus's scourging, the Roman soldiers mock him by prostrating before him. However, there is a significant difference here in the fact that while Mark uses *proskuneō* to describe their action (Mark 15:19), Matthew changes this word to *gonupeteō* (Matthew 27:29). It seems that Matthew was loath to use such a positive and theologically significant word (that he was using thematically) to describe the humiliation and mockery of the Roman soldiers. The last change involves a shift in the other direction. In Mark 5:22, Jairus prostrates to Jesus to ask for help healing his daughter; the word used is *piptō*. In Matthew's telling of the story, the word is changed to *proskuneō* (in Matthew 9:18). These changes and the number of times prostration is highlighted throughout the Gospel of Matthew make it clear that the author wanted these actions noted by the audience and was specific and deliberate in his placement of them.

Considering all the instances of prostration in Matthew specifically, it becomes clear that Matthew is deliberately playing on the social and religious uses of prostration as exhibited and established in the Old Testament. In the Old Testament, prostration was considered a normative action in showing respect to, honoring, and entreating the king or someone else of specifically high social standing. However, it was much more commonly utilized as a ritual of exchange or communion with Deity. From this perspective, the usage of prostration throughout the Gospel of Matthew is used as a deliberate example of situational or dramatic irony.[40] Dramatic irony, understood as illuminating "the duality of the difference between what appears to be happening and what is actually happening"[41] and specifically involving the "privileged status of the reader in knowing more than the characters"[42] in the story, has been noted as used frequently in ancient texts to characterize the relationship between the human and the divine.[43] Simply put, Matthew's presentation of prostration generally sets the characters as prostrating to Jesus while thinking of him as either a man of high power or (at the most) as the true king of Israel, while the reading audience knows more than they do—that he is the Holy One of Israel. In this case, Matthew's ironic presentation of prostration is firmly situated in the ambiguous and dichotomous uses of prostration as directed at either mortals or numinous beings in the Old Testament. However, without recognizing that aspect of its use, the irony of prostration in Matthew is not as recognizable.

In a more literary turn, it is also clear that Matthew distinctly utilizes the three stages of dramatic irony: installation, exploitation, and resolution. First, in the installation phase, Matthew informs his audience of something that the other characters will not or do not know about or recognize. In this case, it is clear from the very beginning that Jesus is both the prophesied King of Israel and "Emmanuel" ("God with us"), established as such by Matthew's prophecy-fulfillment formulas and Annunciation narrative (Matthew 1:18–25) and the narrative of the arrival of the wise men and their subsequent prostration before the infant (Matthew 2:1–12).[44] In this manner it is communicated clearly to the reading audience that Jesus is more than simply a man but literally "God with us." This knowledge, however, is used to increase the tension experienced by the audience (the exploitation stage) throughout the rest of the Gospel as others come and ironically prostrate before Jesus without knowing that while they may consciously be doing so to the King (or at least someone who has high social status or must be entreated to use his power), they are also doing so before God. The audience is left to wonder how and when the truth will become known. This is further intensified by the general situational irony present in all of the Gospels as "salvation is accomplished through the apparent defeat of the Messiah."[45] Finally, in the resolution stage, Matthew's Gospel ends with specifically nonironic prostrations, as the women (Matthew 28:9) and the disciples (Matthew 28:17) all prostrate before the risen Lord, who authoritatively declares himself as fully divine: "All power is given unto me in heaven and in earth" (Matthew 28:18).

Conclusion

Prostration as a ritualized action held an important place socially, politically, and religiously to various peoples throughout the ancient world. As such, it formed an important element of the religious lives of the authors and original audiences of the Old and New Testaments.

To understand the importance and use in the latter, it is vital to have an understanding of its use in the former. Approaching prostration within these scriptural texts from the perspective of ritual studies can help illuminate how and why prostration was used historically and literarily. Doing so carefully can help us understand these specific actions whose meaning and intent were so deeply ingrained in the culture of these people that it went without being said or the authors didn't feel the need to spell it out. For Latter-day Saints, understanding and seeing the different cultural ways of expressing humility, honor, respect, and communion with God in scripture can have important ramifications. It is, of course, important for understanding the scriptures. But it is also important as the Church continues to rise out of obscurity and become a truly global religion. We can see, appreciate, and understand the differences of expression that all of God's children exhibit in their relationships with him.

❧

Andrew C. Smith was an instructor of Religious Education at Brigham Young University when this chapter was written.

Further Reading

On ritual

Bell, Catherine. *Ritual: Perspectives and Dimensions.* New York: Oxford University Press, 2009. The most accessible and in-depth introduction to ritual studies, covering major theories and theorists, as well as methods of analysis of rituals.

Belnap, Daniel L., ed. *By Our Rites of Worship: Latter-day Saint Views on Ritual in Scriptures, History, and Practice.* Provo, UT: Religious Studies Center, Brigham Young University; Salt Lake City: Deseret Book, 2013. The only substantial volume on ritual within a Latter-day Saint context; important reading for all Latter-day Saints interested in the rituals and ordinances they perform.

Klingbeil, Gerald A. *Bridging the Gap: Ritual and Ritual Texts in the Bible.* Winona Lake, IN: Eisenbrauns, 2007. An introduction to the study of ritual as applied broadly to the Bible, illuminating various rituals and ritualized actions, with a bibliography of other resources for further study.

On prostration specifically

Bowen, Matthew L. "'They Came and Held Him by the Feet and Worshipped Him': Proskynesis before Jesus in Its Biblical and Ancient Near Eastern Context." *Studies in the Bible and Antiquity* 5 (December 2013): 63–89. Another look at prostration as seen in the Bible and ancient Near East, with a different methodological approach.

Fretheim, Terrence. "חוה." In *New International Dictionary of Old Testament Theology and Exegesis*, 2:42–44. Grand Rapids, MI: Zondervan, 1997. An overview of the usage and importance of the major word for prostration (*yištaḥăweh/hištaḥăwah*) as used in the Old Testament.

Greeven, H. "προσκυνέω." In *Theological Dictionary of the New Testament* 6:758–66. Grand Rapids, MI: Eerdmans, 1999. An overview of the usage and importance of the major word for prostration (*proskuneō*) in the Greek world and the New Testament.

Notes

1. The notion of "worship" and what that term means is vague and difficult to pin down; it actually may have distinctly Protestant Christian discursive overtones related to discomfort with ritual (particularly Catholic

ritual) in general and a firmly embedded body-spirit dualism that may not apply or obtain for certain ancient peoples. Thus, its usage as translation for any of the words of prostration discussed may obscure rather
than enlighten what the original authors intended.

2. While many approaches, methods, and perspectives have been developed, one of the most versatile and
   powerful for helping in understanding the socioreligious rituals within scripture (only part of which will
   be used herein) is the approach found in Catherine Bell, *Ritual: Perspectives and Dimensions*, rev. ed. (New
   York: Oxford University Press, 2009). Bell also contributed to and helped develop the field of ritual studies
   with a more theoretical volume focused on how to understand ritual anthropologically, sociologically, and
   from a history of religions perspective. See Catherine Bell, *Ritual Theory, Ritual Practice* (New York: Oxford
   University Press, 1992). For an example of ritual analysis directly applicable to Latter-day Saint religious
   ritual, see Daniel Belnap, ed., *By Our Rites of Worship: Latter-day Saint Views on Ritual in Scripture, History,
   and Practice* (Provo, UT: Religious Studies Center, Brigham Young University; Salt Lake City: Deseret Book,
   2013).

3. As Bell states, these are rituals in which "people make offerings to a god or gods with the practical and
   straightforward expectation of receiving something in return. . . . Direct offerings may be given to praise,
   please, and placate divine power, or they may involve an explicit exchange by which human beings provide
   sustenance to divine powers in return for divine contributions to human well-being." Bell, *Ritual*, 108. However, she also notes that this exchange can be conceived of as either concrete (expecting, for instance, a good
   harvest) or rather abstract (with notions of grace or redemption). As she notes, "In ritual, it is probably safe
   to say that no act is purely manipulative or disinterested. Ritual acts of offering, exchange, and communion
   appear to invoke very complex relations of mutual interdependence between the human and the divine."
   Bell, *Ritual*, 109. Bell's usage of *divine* is broader than we might colloquially use, including categories of
   beings we might not include, such as demons.

4. Bell's typology for rituals involves six categories (which are not considered mutually exclusive—i.e., a given
   ritual may fit into more than one category at one and the same time). As she states, "In most societies, rituals
   are multiple and redundant. They do not have just one message or purpose. They have many and frequently
   some of these messages and purposes can modify or even contradict each other." Bell, *Ritual*, 136. Her
   six categories are rituals of exchange/communion, rites of passage/transition, calendrical/commemorative
   rites, rites of fasting/feasting/festival, rites of affliction, and political rites. Prostration in the New Testament
   never appears as a rite of passage/transition (rites that accompany important life events, e.g., birth or transition to adulthood, and so forth; for more, see Bell, *Ritual*, 94–102) nor as a calendrical or commemorative
   rite (rites commemorating special historical or mythological events; for more, see Bell, *Ritual*, 102–8). Likewise, only one instance of prostration can possibly be seen as a rite of affliction (rituals meant to rectify or fix
   a disrupted relationship, etc.; for more on these, see Bell, *Ritual*, 115–20); this occurs in 1 Corinthians 14:25.

5. For instance, issues of provenance, preservation, incomplete information, textual development across time,
   and the potential for rituals to be used as literary objects by the authors of the text.

6. Similar to the case in the New Testament, there are other words utilized that also present the same or similar
   actions. These include words related to the Hebrew roots *qdd, npl, kr ʾ*. While such words are important for
   the consideration of the presentation of prostration as a whole, they appear much less frequently. As such,
   here we will consider the usage of *hištaḥăwah* as representative.

7. In short, the discovery of the Ugaritic verb *ḥwy* caused an etymological reevaluation to consider *hištaḥăwah*
   as being derived from the root *ḥwy* in Hebrew (with the root meaning of "to live"), rather than from the root
   šḥh (meaning "to bow down"). In either case, however, the term still has the same denotation or meaning in
   its usage. For more on the detailed analysis of these debates and their ramifications, see H. D. Preuss, "חוה
   Ḥwh; הִשְׁתַּחֲוָה Hishtachavāh," in *Theological Dictionary of the Old Testament*, ed. G. Johannes Botterweck and
   Helmer Ringren, trans. John T. Willis (Grand Rapids, MI: Eerdmans, 1980); and Terence E. Fretheim, "חוה,"
   in *New International Dictionary of Old Testament Theology and Exegesis* (Grand Rapids, MI: Zondervan,
   1997).

8. Bruce K. Waltke and Michael Patrick O'Connor, *An Introduction to Biblical Hebrew Syntax* (Winona Lake, IN: Eisenbrauns, 1990), 361.

9. This translation is largely upheld because "strictly speaking . . . the verb merely designates a gesture as part of a more inclusive action; but it comes to refer also to the inward attitude thus expressed." Preuss, "Hishtachavāh," 249.

10. See H. Greeven, "Προσκυνέω," in *Theological Dictionary of the New Testament*, ed. Gerhard Kittel and Gerhard Friedrich, trans. Geoffrey W. Bromiley (Grand Rapids, MI: Eerdmans, 1999), 6:758.

11. "Numinous personages" is here intended to be broadly defined as immortal beings to whom are attributed supernatural powers (or powers beyond that of normal, mortal humans). It should be recognized that in the ancient world there was much more flexibility in defining who and what fell into such a category.

12. Illustrating the variety of its usages are the following: prostration is what Abraham tells his servants he and his son Isaac will do on the mountaintop (Genesis 22:5), while also being what Abraham does to interact with the Hittites while buying the cave for Sarah's burial (Genesis 23:7, 12). The Israelites and their leaders prostrate in response to Moses's message and signs of deliverance (Exodus 4:31) as well as after the Passover instructions are given (Exodus 12:27), and the command is given a number of times that the Israelites are not to bow to other gods (Exodus 20:5; 23:24; 34:14; Leviticus 26:1) but are to prostrate to Jehovah (Exodus 24:1; 33:10). However, Moses also declares that the magicians of Pharaoh will bow to him (Exodus 11:8), and he himself prostrates before his father-in-law (Exodus 18:7). In the Psalms, *hištaḥăwah* is used repeatedly to illustrate interaction with deity (e.g., Psalms 5:7; 22:27, 29; 29:2 passim) but is used in many other books as the appropriate and expected means of interacting with kings and other honored mortals (e.g., to David in 1 Samuel 25:23, to Solomon in 1 Kings 1:53, and to Haman in Ruth 3:2, 5).

13. For instance, a nondenotative literary analysis can focus on a number of factors surrounding the usage of *hištaḥăwah*: connotative attribution (or the feeling with which it is used), the grammatical person (who is doing the prostration—an individual, or undertaken communally), and the direction or object of the prostration (to whom or to what is it done).

14. This is, by far, the largest category of those from Bell's typology. Prostration is not utilized at all in the Old Testament in a manner that could be categorized as a rite of passage/life cycle. There is only one instance (0.5 percent of the total instances) that can be labeled as a commemorative or calendrical rite (Deuteronomy 26:10), only four (2 percent) instances that fall within the category of rites of feasting, fasting, and festivals (Nehemiah 9:3; 2 Chronicles 29:28, 29, and 30), and twelve (7 percent) that can be considered rites of affliction (Genesis 33:3, 6, 7, 10; Exodus 11:8; 34:8; Numbers 22:31; Job 1:20; Nehemiah 9:3; 2 Chronicles 29:28–30). After rites of exchange and communion, prostration as used as a political rite is the next largest category, with thirty-four instances (20 percent).

15. In the ancient world (as in the modern world), the line between rituals of communion and exchange can be fuzzy or ill-defined. Communion is understood as making contact or connection, while exchange involves giving something in exchange for something else. For example, offering sacrifice or one's loyalty to God to ensure a specific blessing (e.g., a bountiful harvest or protection from enemies). These are not, however, the only ways that prostration as a ritualized action appears. Viewing its usage holistically in the Old Testament, a number of categorizations or classifications outside those presented by Bell suggest themselves. These include seeing its usage as being a rite of respect or honoring (31 percent of its instances), rite of thanksgiving or gratitude (20 percent), a rite of praise (11 percent), a rite of salutation (5 percent), a rite of hospitality (1 percent), or even as a rite of mourning (0.5 percent).

16. For each of these, see their respective entries in William D. Mounce, *The Analytical Lexicon to the Greek New Testament* (Grand Rapids, MI: Zondervan, 1993). Or consult James Strong, John R. Kohlenberger, and James A. Swanson, *The Strongest Strong's: Exhaustive Concordance of the Bible* (Grand Rapids, MI: Zondervan, 2004). Likewise, there are plenty of online resources or Bible study programs that are useful in this regard. It should be noted that the denotative and idiomatic meaning of *piptō* is much broader than that of the other words, as it can mean "to fall" (i.e., to happen or occur as well as to drop or collapse) as well as

"to die." Thus, not all of its uses represent a specific act of prostration, and even some of those that arguably do represent a type or form of prostration may deliberately use *piptō* for its idiomatic connotations of death mixed with a potential symbolic prostration meaning—for example, the experience of Ananias and Sapphira in Acts 5 (who literally die but are symbolically presented as prostrating while so doing) or the experience of Jesus in Gethsemane in Mark 14:35 and Matthew 26:39 (who literally is prostrating but is presented symbolically as dying). The use of *katapiptō* is similar in its broader meaning. However, because of its infrequency, it is not as influential or is potentially meant deliberately. The word appears only three times in the New Testament, only one of which (Acts 26:14) resonates with prostration.

17. On the individual nature and voices of the four Gospels, see Gaye Strathearn and Frank F. Judd Jr., "The Distinctive Testimonies of the Four Gospels," *Religious Educator* 8, no. 2 (2007): 59–85.

18. For instance, the anointing and kissing of the feet of Jesus by the sinful woman in Luke 7. For an analysis of this experience as a type of prostration, see Matthew L. Bowen, "'They Came and Held Him by the Feet and Worshipped Him': Proskynesis before Jesus in Its Biblical and Ancient Near Eastern Context," *Studies in the Bible and Antiquities* 5 (December 2013): 80–82. While it is clear that there are symbolic resonances in this case, arguments can be made against such (or at the least that the author did not want the connection to be made overtly) because of the lack of any prostration word as well as the fact that she is described explicitly as standing (Luke 7:37–38).

19. While Paul is willing to describe some of his actions with *proskuneō* (see Acts 24:11), in the three accounts of his conversion story *piptō* and *katapiptō* are used (Acts 9:4; 10:25; 26:14). This may be because, literarily, the narrator of the first account and Paul (while personally telling the other two) desired to have more idiomatic implications of death present in the usage of *piptō* while retaining the image of prostration as the proper reaction to contact with divinity.

20. Cornelius's prostration is the outlier in this category, as it is the only prostration to a human in the non-Gospels and non-Revelation materials. In general, prostration to other humans is done relatively infrequently in the New Testament, occurring only three times (Matthew 18:26; Acts 10:25; Revelation 3:9), excluding those prostrations directed toward the mortal Jesus, given the theological point of view of the Gospel writers that Jesus was divine. This point, of course, could be debated in the Gospel of Mark, given its relatively low Christology, but prostration does not play as large a point in Mark's Gospel as it does in the Gospels of Matthew and John, who present a much higher Christology. Even then, in Matthew 18:26, the prostration presented is ambiguous in this regard because it occurs in a parable directed to a human king who is likened to the ruler of the kingdom of heaven and who has been traditionally identified with Jesus.

21. The instances of prostration occurring in 1 Corinthians 10:25 and Hebrews 11:21 seem to be mainly incidental references to the action, without major literary importance within those specifics texts.

22. Prostration appears in Mark twice as *proskuneō* (5:6; 15:19), twice as *piptō* (5:22; 14:35), and twice as *gonupeteō* (1:40; 10:17). Luke uses *proskuneō* three times (4:7; 4:8; 24:52) and *piptō* three times (5:12; 8:41; 17:16).

23. While these themes and concepts appear in the other Gospels, arguably Matthew uses them in a much more overt and central manner. On this, see Mark L. Strauss, *Four Portraits, One Jesus: A Survey of Jesus and the Gospels* (Grand Rapids, MI: Zondervan, 2007), 239–42. For other background, see Richard Neitzel Holzapfel, Eric D. Huntsman, and Thomas A. Wayment, *Jesus Christ and the World of the New Testament* (Salt Lake City: Deseret Book, 2006), 62–77.

24. *Proskuneō* appears twelve times in John, with ten occurrences in John 4:20–24. The other two occurrences are in John 9:38 (describing a blind man who was healed) and 12:20 (describing the Greeks in Jerusalem for the Passover). *Piptō* appears only twice in John 11:32 (Mary falling at Jesus's feet) and 18:36 (with the guard accompanying Judas falling to the ground when Jesus announced who he was via invocation of the divine name in the garden).

25. There are important exceptions to this, including one instance of prostration to humans (the church at Philadelphia; Revelation 3:9) and a number directed toward an angel (Revelation 19:10; 22:8). It should be

noted that in both of the cases with the angel, the one prostrating (John) is rebuked for doing so and told to prostrate before God instead.

26. On the question of numinous beings, this delineation follows the typology established in the ancient world wherein beings not explicitly understood as mortal would be understood as numinous or "divine," be they angels, demons, or God.

27. Prostration is not recounted in the versions of the event in Mark 9:2–10 and Luke 9:28–36.

28. The mother of the sons of Zebedee approaches and prostrates before Jesus on behalf of her sons (Matthew 20:20); the Gadarene demoniac prostrates before Jesus before asking him not to torment him and to allow him to enter into the swine (Mark 5:6). This is a common occurrence with others requesting healing—for example, Jairus prostrates to ask for healing for his daughter (Matthew 9:18; compare Mark 5:22, Luke 8:41), the woman of Canaan prostrates to ask for the same for her daughter (Matthew 15:25), the man with the possessed son also prostrates to beseech Jesus for help (Matthew 17:14), and a leper beseeches Jesus for healing while prostrating (Luke 5:12). Once prostration even occurs as a gesture of gratitude or thanksgiving *after* a healing (Luke 17:15–16).

29. The Matthew reference is, significantly, not *proskuneō* but *gonupeteō*. Mark uses *proskuneō* in his account.

30. Prostration in this case seems to be presented as a ritual of exchange ("O my Father, if it be possible, let this cup pass from me: nevertheless not as I will, but as thou wilt"; Matthew 26:39), but by using *piptō* rather than *proskuneō*, the authors distance themselves from the full theological and literary import of such a word while also retaining the imagery and symbolism of prostration combined with *piptō*'s connotations of death.

31. The one exception is found in John 18:36. Interestingly, however, given the very public display being shown as well as the intense sociopolitical context of the New Testament's composition, it is easy to see a vast majority of the instances (87 percent) also being read as entailing an "emphasis on the public display of religio-cultural sentiments. . . . [with individuals] express[ing] publicly—to themselves, each other, and sometimes outsiders—their commitment and adherence to basic religious values," and thus falling into the category of rites of feasting, fasting, and festivals. Bell, *Ritual: Perspectives and Dimensions*, 120. Admittedly, this is a debatable understanding based on the interpretation and viewpoint of the reader. It could easily be understandable for a reader to take a narrower view of what constitutes the feasting, fasting, and festival category and concluding that none of these are such. The major sticking point is the general performative nature of these rituals: they are almost all done in public, within the gaze of others—did the actors intend them to be a publicly overexpression of their devotion, belief, or faith in Jesus to fulfill requests or do something else? It seems in most cases that most readers would answer yes to such questions. Likewise, 44 percent of the occurrences can also potentially be seen as overt political statements or political rites. These specific instances are labeled "political" insofar as each of them has distinct messages of either rejection of secular authority or recognition of Jesus as having numinous religious or theological political authority.

32. It is, of course, recognized that this distinction and debate about it have been important theologically since the earliest days of the Christian era. The viewpoint for this chapter is that Jesus was both mortal and numinous during his mortal ministry.

33. This, of course, excludes those directed at him after his resurrection, when it is clear that he is (1) not mortal anymore and (2) is fully divine or numinous.

34. In the New Testament, the category of numinous beings includes not only God but also the eleven instances directed to the beast and/or the dragon in the book of Revelation, as well as those instances with Satan as the object in the temptation narratives. The other few instances remaining are not fully specified or even implied by context and thus are left out.

35. These are found in Matthew 2:2, 8, 11; 4:9, 10; 8:2; 9:18; 14:33; 15:25; 18:26; 20:20; 28:9, 17.

36. Two of these are found in tandem (describing the same subject and action) with instances of *proskuneō*, in Matthew 2:11 and 4:9. The other three stand on their own and are found in 17:6, 18:29, and 26:39.

37. These two instances are in Matthew 17:14 and 27:29.

38. On the reliance of Matthew on Mark, for a general introduction see Holzapfel, Huntsman, and Wayment, *Jesus Christ and the World of the New Testament*, 50–51. It should be noted that other scholars see the opposite relationship, that is, Markan reliance on Matthew. For more in-depth introduction to the debates and hypotheses related to the "Synoptic problem," see Strauss, *Four Portraits, One Jesus*, 44–55.

39. This story also appears in John 6:15–21 but is not told in Luke. In John there is no mention of prostration either.

40. Irony, in all of its forms (dramatic, verbal, character, and so forth), is a concept of distinct importance in all of the Gospels to one extent or another and has been examined in many different ways. The Gospels of Mark and John have been shown to use irony in a variety of ways. Likewise, the Gospel of Matthew has been examined for irony in various ways. However, I am not aware of anyone discussing the usage of prostration as ironic. For an introduction to irony as presented in the Gospels, see Strauss, *Four Portraits, One Jesus*, 77–78, 177, 304–5. For more in-depth discussions of irony, both more broadly in the Greek and in the ancient world as well as more specifically in the Gospel of Matthew, see Karl McDaniel, *Experiencing Irony in the First Gospel: Suspense, Surprise and Curiosity* (London: Bloomsbury, 2013); and InHee C. Berg, *Irony in the Matthean Passion Narrative* (Minneapolis: Fortress, 2014).

41. Berg, *Irony in the Matthean Passion Narrative*, 88.

42. Berg, *Irony in the Matthean Passion Narrative*, 93.

43. See Berg, *Irony in the Matthean Passion Narrative*, 4–5.

44. Likewise, the contrast with Herod, who also declares intent to prostrate before the new king (Matthew 2:8) but obviously doesn't really intend to, sets up two groupings for categorizing those who do prostrate, a categorization known by the audience but that the characters themselves do not recognize.

45. Strauss, *Four Portraits, One Jesus*, 77.

33

Worship and Ritual Practices in the New Testament

Erik Odin Yingling

The period from the first century AD to the middle of the second century AD has occasionally been called the dark period of Christian worship practices.[1] Details of Christian liturgy in this period, unlike later centuries, are not described in any systematic fashion. In fact, during the apostolic era the document that most closely resembles a "Church Handbook of Instructions"—a rulebook called the Teaching of the (Twelve) Apostles or simply the Didache (the "Teaching")—did not make it into the books of the New Testament.[2] The alleged darkness of the historical sources from this period, however, should not prevent us from gleaning insights from the texts of the New Testament and other early Christian writings, even as these insights remain open to revision. While the New Testament authors and their respective communities did not always agree on the details of Christian worship, their texts do describe a diversity of practices that we can explore. This chapter surveys some of these rituals and worship practices, namely prayer, hymn singing, sacramental meals, the ritual kiss, discernment practices, baptism, footwashing, and foot dusting.

Prayer Practices

In the New Testament, daily prayer in Jerusalem occurred at regular intervals associated with both home and temple. In the book of Acts we read that prayer happened at the third, sixth, and ninth hours (Acts 2:15; 3:1; 10:9, 30–31). This corresponded to the temple sacrifices in the morning (about 9:00 a.m.), main meal of the day (about noon), and evening sacrifice (about 3:00 p.m.).[3] Worshippers would stand outside the sanctuary praying as the priest offered incense upon the altar (compare Luke 1:10).

The repetitive hourly aspects of prayer may have been an opportunity as well as a challenge. Jesus warned against vain or empty repetitions but encouraged his followers to persist in prayer until their request was granted (Matthew 6:7). He refers, for instance, to an unjust judge who eventually favored a relentless widow (Luke 18:1–5). On another occasion, Jesus told a parable of a (seemingly annoyed) neighbor who finally answered his acquaintance's request. This was due to the petitioner's "importunity" or shameless persistence (Luke 11:8).[4] We can see this persistence exemplified in the verses that immediately follow this parable: "So I say to you: Keep asking, and it will be given you. Keep searching, and you will find. Keep knocking, and the door will be opened for you, because everyone who keeps asking will receive, and the person who keeps searching will find, and the person who keeps knocking will have the door opened" (Luke 11:9–10 ISV).[5] In other words Jesus taught the disciples that they should not give up if their prayers were not answered initially but that they should continue to exercise their faith. In the parable the neighbor's petitions were effective because they were relentless and urgent. This emphasis on persistent prayer fits within the Jerusalem culture of habitual prayers repeated three times a day.

In addition to the metaphorical direction of the petitioner's prayer, ancient prayer practices were often directed toward a physical location or object. In Greek the very linguistic root of prayer refers to praying "toward" something.[6] It was common, for instance, for Jews to pray toward Jerusalem or its temple (1 Kings 8:38). In other instances, a worshipper would direct eyes and voice upward toward heaven (Mark 6:41; John 11:41; 17:11). The body could also be situated so as to "elevate" its posture, as the petitioner would stand up and uplift the hands in prayer (1 Timothy 2:8; Luke 24:50).

As an expression of humility, prayer could also be directed away from the sky and toward the earth. Biblical accounts mention worshippers who kneel and others who even fall to the ground in prayer (Mark 14:35; Luke 22:41; 1 Kings 8:54; Acts 20:36). Such actions are in harmony with the word translated as "worship" in the New Testament, since the verb προσκυνέω (*proskuneō*) often referred to prostrating oneself before the feet of a ruler or the image of a god.[7] Although Jesus often prayed looking up to heaven, he also praised the idea of praying while looking down at the ground (Mark 6:41; John 11:41; 17:1). In one parable Jesus praised a man who "would not lift up so much as his eyes unto heaven." Instead of lifting his hands up in prayer, the man struck his chest with his hands (Luke 18:13). The gesture of praying with uplifted hands, or the *orans* posture, was a common posture for prayer among Jews, Christians, and pagans of the ancient world (fig. 1).

Throughout history, the *orans* posture has been interpreted in many different ways. Like other sacred rituals, it has been given various meanings as well as functions. In other words, people have inquired what this ritual might teach, or what changes this ritual might effect in the spiritual or physical world. In the Psalms we learn that raising hands in prayer mirrored the smoke of temple incense that ascended as a petition to God (Psalm 141:2). In the New Testament, praying with uplifted hands, moreover, signified that one prayed without

Figure 1. A woman praying in the *orans* posture. Catacomb of Callixtus, Rome, early 4th century. Wikimedia Commons.

doubt or anger (1 Timothy 2:8). Put differently, the *orans* posture was a sign that one had forgiven others and had faith that God would answer the petition. In other scriptural passages the *orans* performs various functions. In some instances, sacred buildings or people were blessed or consecrated with uplifted hands. Thus, Solomon dedicates the temple while praying in the *orans* posture, and Jesus "blesses" or "consecrates" his disciples before his ascension with the same gesture (1 Kings 8:22–38; Luke 24:50–51).[8] During the ascension we might also wonder if Luke intends to associate the spreading of hands with the parting of the heavenly veil. As Jesus extends his crucified hands, the heavenly veil begins to part and Jesus ascends to heaven (Luke 24:50–51). It is also worth noting that in the following centuries some early Christians soon began to associate the *orans* posture with Jesus's outstretched arms on the cross. One such reference comes from the second-century Odes of Solomon: "I expanded my hands: and I sanctified [them] to my Lord: For the expansion of my hands is his sign. And my expansion is the upright wood."[9]

Hymn Singing

During the New Testament era, a strict categorical boundary between hymns, prayers, and scripture readings did not exist. Praising God could refer to prayer as well as to song (Acts 16:25; Hebrews 13:15). Teaching could take the form of songs, and reading psalms could be called singing "hymns and spiritual songs" (Colossians 3:16; Ephesians 5:19). Spiritual songs also might have been impromptu performances inspired by the Spirit. Alternatively, since silent reading was much less common in the ancient world, "reading" could transform into a vocal or even musical activity.[10]

For some time, scholars have argued that there are hymns embedded within the text of the New Testament. Given overlap between scripture reading and hymn singing, this is a much-debated and entangled question. A number of possibilities have been put forward thus far (e.g., Philippians 2:5–11; Colossians 1:15–20; 1 Peter 3:18–22; 1 Timothy 3:16).[11] Such hymns express ideas such as Christ's incarnation, crucifixion, ministry to spirits in prison, and exaltation in heaven. Of these proposed hymns, the one that commands perhaps the most attention is found in Philippians 2:5–11:

> Let this mind be in you, which was also in Christ Jesus: who, being in the form of God, thought it not robbery to be equal with God: but made himself of no reputation, and took upon him the form of a servant, and was made in the likeness of men: and being found in fashion as a man, he humbled himself, and became obedient unto death, even the death of the cross. Wherefore God also hath highly exalted him, and given him a name which is above every name: that at the name of Jesus every knee should bow, of things in heaven, and things in earth, and things under the earth; and that every tongue should confess that Jesus Christ is Lord, to the glory of God the Father.

The above hymn presents the congregation with a broad picture of Christ's role in the plan of salvation and human potential. Jesus sets the example by descending below all things, ultimately to rise above all things and become like his Father. Through Christ's abasement, he is exalted and every knee bows and every tongue confesses his name.

In addition to the hymn in Philippians, there may be no better place to consult than the choral hymns found in the book of Revelation, or "Apocalypse." Among others, scholar Leonard Thompson has argued that the heavenly liturgy in John's visions is a reflection of "the actual practice of the primitive church."[12] Lucetta Mowry is even bolder, concluding that "we may have [in the Apocalypse] the earliest known form of a Christian service of worship, possibly the Eucharist."[13] Even critics of this viewpoint acknowledge Revelation's unique place as one of the most liturgical books in the New Testament.[14] In spite of the numerous debates that will continue over this text, there seems to be a critical consensus forming over the past half century as to its liturgical character. Alan Cabaniss summarizes this view: "It is coming to be generally recognized that the author of the Apocalypse presents his visions, at least in part, against the background or within the framework of the church liturgy of the latter years of the first century."[15]

Such declarations are supported by a number of factors. While Mowry is correct in pointing out that the hymns in Revelation can mirror early Jewish and Christian liturgies, the most compelling evidence is found within the text itself.[16] For instance, John's visions occur during the Sunday worship services, or the "Lord's day" (Revelation 1:10).[17] Though John is in exile and thus cannot be present with his congregations, his letter was likely intended to inform their own worship services. Moreover, in early Christian worship services, one of the likely duties of the prophet was to present an "apocalypse," or a "revelation," to the congregation (1 Corinthians 14:26).[18] John's "apocalypse" similarly was probably read in church. The text begins by invoking the congregation's leader "that readeth" as well as the worshippers "that hear the words" of the revelation (Revelation 1:3). John's visions, moreover, present us with a picture of worship that is not confined to heaven alone. Heaven and earth coalesce while earthly figures, both living and dead, join the angelic rites.[19] The worship service includes the seer himself, angels, angels who were once prophets, elders, living creatures, martyrs, and the 144,000.[20] Finally, it seems fitting to ask, If John were concerned only with worship in heaven, why would he be so intent on criticizing certain worship practices on earth that he believed to be in error? (Revelation 2:14, 20; 9:20; 13:4, 8, 15; 16:2). It seems more likely that John's criticisms, and his vision of the heavenly liturgy, were meant to provide ideals for actual worship practices in the early church.

Such practices are alluded to in a number of places in the book of Revelation. Scholars have recognized the presence of eight hymns within the text (4:8, 11; 5:9–14; 7:9–12; 11:15–18; 12:10–12; 15:3–4; 16:5–7; 19:1–8).[21] In essence the songs take the form of short praises offered to the "Lord God" or "the Lamb." They praise the holiness of God as Creator and the Lamb as Redeemer and offer thanks for being made kings and priests unto God. Such hymns often occur in the context of the heavenly temple and occur around God's throne and the nearby altar.

In the ancient world, choruses were often highly ritualized just as they appear to be in the book of Revelation. As in some Jewish choruses, the worshippers in John's vision join together in a circle or series of circles. In the first century, worshippers in certain Jewish worship services formed choral circles and moved about "wheeling and counterwheeling." They sang antiphonally (i.e., with the call and response or repeating the words of the leader of the circle) and moved their hands and feet.[22] In some Jewish sources, the angelic choir forms a circle around the heavenly throne, and Enoch takes the role of the celestial choirmaster.[23] In John's vision the choruses likewise form "in a circle around the throne"[24] and its altar. These rings unite the angels, the living, and the dead in communion with God (Revelation 4:6; 5:11; 7:11). Their duty is to give glory to God, and as such they become, as it were, embodied extensions of the glorious halo of colored light that also encircles the throne.[25] The sound of the chorus becomes a type of aural glory that parallels the visual halo of colored light that glorifies God on his throne.

In the setting of a house church, these circles might have formed around a choirmaster, who would sing "in the middle of the assembly" (Hebrews 2:12, my translation).[26] Scholars also have noticed the antiphonal character of the hymns in John's Revelation.[27] Almost like a musical dialogue, one group within the chorus sings forth certain lines of praise, and in response another group breaks forth in singing or chanting the "amen" in affirmation (Revelation 5:9–14; 7:11–12; compare 1 Corinthians 14:15–16). At other times one part of the chorus praises God (or the Lamb) and another responds in turn with ritual actions such as prostrations (Revelation 4:8–11; 7:9–11). Prostrating, sitting, and standing are all part of the repertoire of actions performed in the circle (4:4; 11:6).

Such ritual actions were also augmented by a pageantry of sacred objects, scents, and dress. Those in the circle don white clothing, wear wreaths, and often hold objects in their hands such as palm branches or incense bowls. Sometimes the chorus takes an intermission so that prayer and incense can be offered at the altar. In one such instance, an angelic priest walks into the center of the silent circle and approaches the altar, cupping a golden censer in his hand. He then offers the prayers of the saints as "the smoke of the incense, which came with the prayers of the saints, ascended up before God out of the angel's hand" (Revelation 8:4). At other times incense is offered during the hymn. In the circle, for instance, those who sing the "new song" about becoming "kings and priests" cup in their hands incense bowls, "which are the prayers of the saints" (5:9–10). Taken together, what we see within the circle of the chorus is a very close relationship between praise, prayers, song, and the smell of incense. All these factors come together to glorify God's name.

Within the heavenly chorus, the name of God is particularly important in the worship services. The attitude one adopts toward divine names is linked to the power of prophecy and distinguishes between the righteous and unrighteous. In the vision, the antagonists are said to blaspheme God's name; meanwhile, the faithful sing praises to his name (Revelation 13:6; 16:9, 11, 21). There are also references to the names of Christ and the saved being so sacred that no one can know their names except themselves (2:17; 19:12). As the chorus encircles the altar, it often praises God, whose name transcends past, present, and future time (4:8; 11:17). As such, God is able to reveal the prophetic truths of the vision to John and all those who sing in the heavenly chorus. Those in the circle praise the Lamb and thus have "testimony of Jesus," which is "the spirit of prophecy" (19:10).

It should also be mentioned that such hymns might have been situated in the context of the sacramental meal.[28] Those who sing in the chorus are those who have passed beyond the "door" into the throne room (Revelation 4:1, 8–11). Such individuals who "open the door" are said to "sup with [the Lamb]" (3:20). In another instance John records that those who worship God are invited to the "marriage supper of the Lamb" (19:9).

Sacramental Meals

Sacramental meal practices were at the core of early Christian worship and were intended to keep alive the memory of Jesus and his teachings. From the earliest point in the Last Supper tradition, the emblems of bread and wine were associated with Jesus's words "this do in remembrance of me" (1 Corinthians 11:24; Luke 22:19). For those whose memory of Jesus had faded, it could be reawakened "in breaking of bread" (Luke 24:35). At first the early Christians sought to keep this memory alive by breaking bread "daily" and offering prayer (Acts 2:42, 46). However, daily gatherings seem to have been an ideal that was not easily maintained, for later in the same book we find Christians breaking bread "the first day of the week" (i.e., Sunday; Acts 20:11).

Regardless of when the disciples gathered, scholars generally believe that this meal was both an ordinance and a real meal.[29] Just like Passover was both an ordinance and an actual supper, so too was Christian communion. Meal practices seem to have continued during

Jesus's resurrection ministry. As Jesus explained his doctrine further, his invitation was to "come and dine" (John 21:12). While we cannot know all the details of these early meal practices, New Testament accounts mention sacred meals that included items such as bread, wine, fish, honeycomb, and the like (Luke 24:39–43; John 21:12–13). It is also clear that early Christian meals were sacred rites, since they required personal introspection and worthiness and had symbolic significance (1 Corinthians 11:24–30). They also included activities such as preaching and praying as the members ate "their meat with gladness and singleness of heart" (Acts 2:46).

However, these ideals of unity or "singleness of heart" were not always realized. Paul laments that the "Lord's Supper" was profaned through divisions and contentions in the Corinthian church. Some members left the meals hungry (probably the poor), while others ate and drank in excess to the point of intoxication (1 Corinthians 11:20–21).[30] For Paul the function of the sacrament was not only to memorialize the death of Jesus, but it also had other, expanded meanings. It was supposed to symbolize the idea that the members of the church had become the "members" of Christ's body since they had ingested emblems of his body and blood (12:12). Each member of the body of Christ should thus act in harmony with one another. Whether the members were Jews, Gentiles, slaves, or freeborn, all drank from the same cup and thus were "made to drink into one Spirit" (12:13). Paul taught that although they each had different spiritual gifts, the most important gift members should bring to the meeting was that of charity and love (12:12–31; 13:1–8). One of the ways this principle of love was enacted in worship services was through the exchange of a ritual kiss.

The Ritual Kiss

Although it may seem peculiar to many modern minds, the ritual kiss was one of the central practices of early Christian worship. One expert in this area, Michael Penn, has remarked, "Along with rites such as baptism and a common meal, kissing is part of the earliest strata of Christian practice."[31] Others scholars have lamented that despite the critical role kissing played in the worship services, "modern historians of the early Christian gathering mostly ignore it."[32]

Indeed, the kiss is actually found at the linguistic heart of the action of worship. At the very root of the Greek verb for worship προσκυνέω (*proskuneō*) is the action of the kiss (κυνέω/*kuneō*).[33] In the New Testament, individuals "worship" Christ by offering gifts, falling down at his feet, holding them, and even kissing them (Matthew 2:2, 8–11; 18:26; 28:9; Luke 7:38).

In Paul's letters there is a concern to keep worship and the ritual kiss pure or "holy" (Romans 6:16; 1 Corinthians 16:20; 2 Corinthians 13:12; 1 Thessalonians 5:26). This emphasis on holiness and propriety was likely critical. For a variety of reasons, even some rather conservative scholars[34] think that the New Testament ritual kiss was given and received on the mouth (try holding a grudge in that position!). It should be remembered, however, that no New Testament texts describe the details of this practice, so we cannot be totally certain of this assessment. What we do know is that later anti-Christian critics accused the worship services of eliciting immorality and that later Christian leaders soon began to lay out very strict rules for kissing during worship.[35]

Even during the New Testament period, there is evidence that church leaders were trying to protect worship services from such corruption. For his part, Paul was concerned that a number of breaches in chastity had occurred in the context of worship. In veiled symbolism, Paul hints that such improprieties began by allowing fornicators to participate in the "Passover" practices of Christians (1 Corinthians 5:1, 9–13). Peter also hints at certain "blemishes," who had "eyes full of adultery" during the worship feasts (2 Peter 2:13–14). Jude calls such people "spots" who "crept in unawares" into the "feast of charity" and turned the "grace of our God into lasciviousness" (Jude 1:12, 4). Now, the question arises, If the ritual kiss presented so many problems, why was it practiced in the first place?

As is evidenced in other New Testament passages, the ritual kiss was ideally supposed to quell contention and bring about unity and forgiveness among the congregation (as were other rites). It should be remembered that Christians considered themselves spiritual family members and that it was common for family members in Greco-Roman society to exchange such kisses (Romans 16:13–16; Ephesians 3:15).[36] It was through the ordinances of the gospel, and the power of the Spirit, that Christians believed they had been united as one family in Christ as the seed of Abraham (Galatians 3:27–29). In a culture in which greetings could reinforce harsh social hierarchies—such as groveling and kissing the feet, hands, or knees—the Christian kiss of love was intended to transcend these divisions and establish a family of equals. As expressed by one scholar: "This practice expressed the mutual closeness of people who came from different social classes and was intended to transcend gender, religious, national, and ethnic divisions among people who believed that they were one in Christ."[37] According to this logic, slaves, masters, Jews, Gentiles, males, and females saluted one another on equal terms through the rites of the gospel. For Paul, such a cultural and spiritual revolution seems to have been worth the risk, even as he emphasized that the kiss should be kept "holy" (1 Corinthians 12:13; Colossians 3:11).

In the Synoptic Gospels, we also learn that the kiss might have played an important role in the close circle of disciples that followed Jesus. Perhaps this provided the precedent for the later liturgical use of the kiss among early Christians. In the Gospel narratives, the kiss of Judas follows the account of Jesus's sacrament meal with his disciples. The kiss may possibly have been a sign of fellowship among the group, for Jesus hails Judas as "friend" in response to the kiss (Matthew 26:50). On the other hand, it should also be mentioned that the term *friend* could also invoke a moment of social tension (22:12). In the nighttime shadows of the Garden of Gethsemane, it also seems that it was not easy to differentiate between the appearance of Jesus and his disciples. Thus, Matthew and Mark record that Judas needed a "sign" (*semeion*) or "token" (*sussēmon*) to reveal Christ to the mob (26:48; Mark 14:44). The gesture revealed the identity of each person. Jesus was identified as "master" and Judas as "friend" and betrayer (Matthew 26:48–50; Luke 22:47–48; Mark 14:44–45). The kiss, then, became an important means of discernment.

Discernment and Worship

Discernment played an important role in the worship life of the early Christian church. It was critical to figure out which spiritual influences and doctrine belonged and which did not belong in the worship services. The New Testament era was a contentious time in which various teachers, apostles, and prophets competed for the hearts of the followers of Jesus. In the New Testament, we read of false teachers, false brethren, false Christs, false apostles, false prophets, and even one false prophetess (Mark 13:22; 2 Corinthians 11:13; Galatians 2:4; 2 Peter 2:1; 1 John 4:1; Revelation 2:20). Because prophecy was a common gift exercised during worship services, it is not surprising that the warning against false prophets is particularly common.

So how were early Christians taught to discern between true and false leaders? In an interesting turn from conventional thinking about prophecy, Jesus taught that true prophets were revealed more through their actions than by their prophetic words (Matthew 7:15–24). Although words were important, emphasis was placed on proper action. Likewise, Paul defended his right to be an apostle because he had seen Christ (1 Corinthians 9:1; 11:1) and imitated his example by showing forth "signs and wonders and mighty deeds" (2 Corinthians 12:12). An analysis of deeds was critical in the process of discernment. Paul warned against wolflike church leaders who would abandon their function as lay ministers and gobble up the goods of their flocks (Acts 20:28–34). While the early church received various donations, lay ministers acted as a safeguard against corruption.

Some of the most detailed information about discernment during the apostolic era comes from the "handbook" called the Didache. These keys for discernment come in the form of practical guidelines and policies relevant for this era and culture. In particular, the text demonstrates a concern for prophets, who apparently had abused the generosity of the community in the past. Such prophets would prophesy "Give me money!" or demand that a meal be prepared for them (Didache 11.9, 12). True prophets, on the other hand, would labor to support their own needs and did not act as merchants "trading on Christ" (12.5). True teachers ought to teach the Christian gathering to love one another, to love God, to fast, to pray, to baptize, to partake of the sacrament, and to keep the other commandments of God (1–10). Such genuine apostles and prophets should "be welcomed as if [they] were the Lord" and be given the best hospitality the community could offer (11.4; 13.1–7). Though the general rule was simple—"If any prophet teaches the truth, yet does not practice what he teaches, he is a false prophet"—it was actually much more complex and nuanced (11.10). Once a prophet was tested and found to be a true prophet, his behavior need not be perfect, and could even seem to be quite rough: "But any prophet proven to be genuine who does something with a view to portraying in a worldly manner the symbolic meaning of the church (provided he does not teach you to do all that he himself does) is not to be judged by you, for his judgment is with God. Besides the ancient prophets also acted in a similar manner" (11.11).

Thus, the Didache urges the members of the church not to be overly judgmental of true prophets, who are allowed to have human frailties and who sometimes even break cultural codes of holiness. If the prophet was otherwise proven to be true, then the members should leave the judgment of the prophet up to God, knowing that God had occasionally asked biblical prophets to transgress certain norms in order to achieve a greater good (e.g., Hosea 1:2).[38]

The early church was also given keys to discern true messengers from heaven. When Jesus first appeared after his resurrection, we read that "[the eleven disciples] worshipped him: but some doubted" (Matthew 28:17). The passage seems to indicate that it is possible to worship God while still questioning, seeking, and even doubting. Moreover, it implies that Thomas was not the only one who initially had questions. Luke states that the disciples "were terrified and affrighted, and supposed they had seen a spirit" and began to have questioning thoughts in their hearts (Luke 24:37–38). To help the disciples discern the truth, Jesus invited them to put their fingers in his wounded hands and feet. Most famously, Jesus invited Thomas to "reach hither thy finger" and feel the nail prints in his hands and the wound in his side. Matthew calls such actions a gesture of "worship" (Matthew 28:9). In another New Testament passage these keys for discernment have been translated as "proofs," "tokens," "evidences" or "sure signs" of the resurrected Jesus (Acts 1:3).[39] John stated that there were "many other signs" that the resurrected Christ demonstrated, but these were not all written in his book (John 20:30).

Elsewhere in the New Testament, however, we can read about other keys of discernment. In some New Testament accounts, heavenly beings disguise themselves before mortals. Such passages hint at a connection between hospitality, worship, and discernment. The Epistle to the Hebrews mentions the importance of entertaining strangers for "thereby some have entertained angels unawares" (13:2; compare Genesis 18:1–8). Or in a slightly different fashion, the hospitality of Cleopas revealed a certain "stranger" to be the risen Christ through the breaking of bread (Luke 24:13–32).

Today such ideas are expressed during worship services, as congregations sing the popular hymn "A Poor Wayfaring Man of Grief." In the hymn, the singer meets an unknown wandering stranger and serves him through various acts of hospitality and service. Such service eventually leads to the moment of revelation:

> Then in a moment to my view
> The stranger started from disguise.
> The tokens in his hands I knew;
> The Savior stood before mine eyes.[40]

This hymn thus brings together the keys for discernment mentioned in the New Testament accounts of disguised heavenly messengers, including service, hospitality, and the revelation of Jesus's hands. The hymn is particularly influenced by Jesus's parable of the sheep and the goats and implies that those who have devoted their lives "to the least" will ultimately comprehend the tokens in Jesus's hands and see past Christ's "disguise" (Matthew 25:31–46).

Baptism

The Greek verb βαπτίζω (*baptizō*) means to "dip" or "plunge" someone into water.[41] In the New Testament the practice of baptism by immersion seems to be implied, because Jesus came "out of the water" after the rite was performed (Mark 1:10; compare Romans 6:3–6). The Synoptic Gospels agree that the purpose of John's baptism was to bring about repentance and the remission of sins (Mark 1:4; Matthew 3:11; Luke 3:3), even as the Gospel of John focuses its attention on "the Lamb of God, which taketh away the sin of the world" (John 1:29). The Gospel of John also likens baptism to being born again. This second birth has a dual meaning in the Greek text, since the word ἄνωθεν (*anōthen*) can mean "again" or "above."[42] In the text Nicodemus is confused because he thinks he must literally be "born again" but doesn't understand that he must actually be spiritually reborn, or born from above (John 3:3–7). It should be noticed that elsewhere in the Gospel of John, the word ἄνωθεν (*anōthen*) means "above" (3:31; 19:11, 23).

In other New Testament writings baptism takes on yet other meanings. For Paul, baptism was participation in the body of Christ. Most famously, Paul compared baptism to the crucifixion, death, and resurrection of Christ (Romans 6:3–6). Such symbolism works best when the initiate is baptized by immersion and thus can stand in the water, receive a water burial, and then rise again. Paul also taught that those who were "baptized into Christ have put on Christ" (Galatians 3:27). Christ was thought of, then, as the new clothing or tunic that the initiate would "put on" after getting soaked in the water. Is it possible that Paul's crucifixion symbolism may be hiding in the metaphor of clothing? We might wonder if Paul, who himself had worked with fabrics, had recognized that the tunic was roughly a cross-shaped item that one could "put on" (Acts 18:3). The tunic not only took the shape of a cross when it was belted about the body (as an ancient T-shirt), but also when it was not worn, unbelted, and laid flat upon the ground (figs. 2–3).[43]

Perhaps Paul endowed the tunic with new christological meanings and associated it with the new clothing the initiate put on after being immersed in baptism. For Paul, baptism was a ritual act in which the initiate performed the role of Christ in salvation history.

Those who were baptized and received the Spirit became "body parts" or "members" of Christ's own body (1 Corinthians 12:12–27; Romans 12:4–6). Thus, the body parts should not envy nor contend with one another since they were all necessary. If one body part began to suffer, this would be felt throughout the whole body (12:25–26). Through ordinances the members were also united with the Spirit. Although the gift of the Spirit bestowed a diversity of gifts among the members of Christ, the members were all joined to "the same Spirit" (12:4). After baptism, the members likely would drink from a single sacramental cup and thus "drink into one Spirit" (12:13).[44] We can see that baptism, reception of the Spirit, and drinking from a common cup were meant to unite the members into the body of Christ: "There is one body, and one Spirit, . . . one Lord, one faith, one baptism" (Ephesians 4:4–5). In baptism all became "Christ," so there "is neither Jew nor Greek, there is neither bond nor free, there is neither male nor female: for ye are all one in Christ Jesus" (Galatians 3:27–28).

Figure 2. Tunic framed as if worn, 4th–7th century AD, Kharga Oasis, Byzantine Egypt. Courtesy of Metropolitan Museum of Art of New York, 33.10.48.

Figure 3. Tunic spread out on a flat surface, likely from the 5th century AD, said to be from Akhmim, Egypt. Courtesy of Metropolitan Museum of Art of New York 26.9.8.

The Washing and Dusting of the Feet

One of these rites is the washing of the feet. After Jesus had eaten the Passover supper with his disciples, the Gospel of John recounts that Jesus washed the feet of his disciples (13:2). In contemporary scholarship, footwashing has been called "the sacrament that almost made it."[45] In comparison with the popularity of the ordinance of communion in the Christian world at large, footwashing has historically been neglected in the Christian tradition (though there are a number of exceptions to this rule).[46] Nonetheless, the textual evidence seems to support the notion that this was more than just an example of humility on Jesus's part. Jesus told Peter, "If I wash thee not, thou hast no part with me" (13:8). In this passage the Greek word μέρος (*meros*) refers to words such as *place, portion, lot*, or *destiny* and frequently invokes the fate of the saved or the damned (Matthew 24:51; Luke 12:46; 15:12; Revelation 21:8; 22:19).[47] The idea that only the feet needed to be washed for a person to be "clean every whit" suggests that the cleansing was believed to be physical as well as spiritual in nature (John 13:10).

While it is true that footwashing was a common gesture of hospitality in the home, it was also performed in the house of God. Originally Moses was commanded to take off his shoes before approaching God on the holy mount, for he stood on holy ground (Exodus 3:5). Afterward, when the tabernacle was constructed, the priests were commanded to wash their hands and feet before approaching the altar (Exodus 30:18–21; 40:30–31). A number of first-century sources indicate that footwashing was required for priests before serving at the temple altar. For the Alexandrian Jew Philo, "men are sanctified when washed with water," and "one should not enter with unwashed feet on the pavement of the temple of God."[48] Furthermore, Philo believed that walking on the temple pavement was "highly symbolic":

> By the washing of the feet is meant that his steps should no longer be on earth but tread the upper air. For the soul of the lover of God does in truth leap from earth to heaven and wing its way on high, eager to take its place in the ranks and share the ordered march of sun and moon and the all-holy, all-harmonious host of other stars, marshalled and led by the God Whose Kingship none can dispute or usurp, the kingship by which everything is justly governed.[49]

In short, the washing of the feet allegorized, for Philo, the salvific ascension of the soul through the heavens to join God amid the cosmos. While we cannot be certain that early Christians viewed Jesus's footwashing through this cosmological lens, the text of the Gospel of John supports the general idea that Jesus's footwashing was a sacred ordinance related to salvation. After Jesus had washed the disciples' feet, he then commanded them to "wash one another's feet" (13:14). This last command might indicate that there were certain early Christian communities that believed it was important to continue the practice of the washing of the feet (compare Luke 7:38, 44, 47–48; 1 Timothy 5:9–10).[50]

In a somewhat related manner, the New Testament also mentions the dusting of feet. If members of a household refused to receive the missionaries into their home, then as a consequence they also declined to perform common hospitality rituals such as footwashing

(Acts 13:51). In such settings, the disciples were forced to dust off their own feet, which had become dirty from their many travels on dusty roads. There was also a symbolic dimension to foot dusting. Inasmuch as footwashing could convey principles such as hospitality, forgiveness, and even salvation in God's kingdom, foot dusting signified the opposite. The feet were dusted as a testimony against such households in the Day of Judgment (Luke 9:5; Mark 6:11; Matthew 10:14–15). In this context, the feet of God's servants became, as it were, vicarious feet for God, whose feet were a symbol of his judgment (1 Corinthians 15:25; Ephesians 1:22; Romans 16:20). As odd as it may seem to modern people—whose feet live in comparative luxury—the mere foot could invoke some of the weightiest spiritual issues of the New Testament era.

Conclusions

Throughout this chapter, we have glimpsed a few aspects of Christian worship practices and rituals during the New Testament era. We have seen a variety of rituals both similar to and different from those practiced in our own day. My hope is that contemporary readers will be positively motivated by these examples. Although we have seen a diversity of rites and worship practices, their common aim seems to have been to point people toward principles such as faith, dedication, unity, and love for God and others. History, then, can be an aid for those who seek such ideals. However, what history can give us in the present era is only part of its value.

What a history of such rituals takes from us may also be of equal benefit. It takes a gesture of empathy to place ourselves in the position of people whose ways and culture may seem removed from our own. The long-dead people of the past take real patience and toil to learn their stories. With our head stuffed in old books, we often find ourselves taking that dusty extra mile with individuals who can no longer give anything physical in return (Matthew 5:41–42). For those readers who enjoyed walking a first mile of early Christian liturgy, I invite you to continue to explore new pathways by consulting the sources in the notes.

⁓

Erik Odin Yingling is a PhD student at Stanford University in art history, holding degrees from Yale and BYU, where he studied Christian liturgy and the ancient Near East.

Further Reading

Alikin, Valerij A. *The Earliest History of the Christian Gathering: Origin, Development and Content of the Christian Gathering in the First to Third Centuries*. Leiden, Netherlands: Brill, 2011.

Bradshaw, Paul F., and Maxwell E. Johnson. *The Eucharistic Liturgies: Their Evolution and Interpretation*. London: SPCK, 2012.

Brown, Matthew B. *The Gate of Heaven: Insights on the Doctrines and Symbols of the Temple*. American Fork, UT: Covenant Communication, 1999.

Hurtado, Larry W. *At the Origins of Christian Worship: The Context and Character of Earliest Christian Devotion*. Grand Rapids, MI: Eerdmans, 2000.

O'Loughlin, Thomas. *The Didache: A Window on the Earliest Christians.* New York: Perseus, 2011.

Taylor, Nicholas. "Baptism for the Dead (1 Cor. 15:29)?" *Neotestamentica* 36 (2002): 111–20.

Trumbower, Jeffrey A. *Rescue for the Dead: The Posthumous Salvation of Non-Christians in Early Christianity.* New York: Oxford University Press, 2001.

Wainwright, Geoffrey, and Karen B. Westerfield Tucker. *The Oxford History of Christian Worship.* Oxford: Oxford University Press, 2006.

Notes

1. Lucetta Mowry, "Revelation 4–5 and Early Christian Liturgical Usage," *Journal of Biblical Literature* 71, no. 2 (1952): 84.

2. Text and commentary found in Michael W. Holmes, Joseph Barber Lightfoot, and John Reginald Harmer, *The Apostolic Fathers: Greek Texts and English Translations* (Grand Rapids, MI: Baker Academic, 2007), 334–44; and Frank Hawkins, "The Didache," in *The Study of the Liturgy*, ed. Cheslyn Jones, Geoffrey Wainwright, and Edward Yarnold (London: SPCK, 1978), 55–56.

3. Maxwell E. Johnson, "The Apostolic Tradition," in *The Oxford History of Christian Worship*, ed. Geoffrey Wainwright and Karen B. Westerfield Tucker (New York: Oxford University Press, 2006), 60.

4. The King James Version translates ἀναίδεια (*anaideia*) as "importunity," but it can also be translated with words such as *shamelessness* or *impertinence*. See the relevant entry in Frederick W. Danker and Walter Bauer, *A Greek-English Lexicon of the New Testament and Other Early Christian Literature* (Chicago: University of Chicago Press, 2014).

5. International Standard Version. The Greek continuous or progressive aspect of the present tense allows for the translation "keep on asking" and so forth. Moreover, the neighbor's persistence suggests that this progressive aspect is most appropriate.

6. The verb προσεύχομαι (*proseuchomai*) is divided into two parts. The prefix *pros* means "toward," and *euchomai* means to "pray" or "wish."

7. See entry for προσκυνέω in Henry George Liddell et al., *A Greek-English Lexicon* (Oxford: Clarendon, 1996); commentary found in Thomas Allen Seel, *A Theology of Music for Worship Derived from the Book of Revelation* (Metuchen, NJ: Scarecrow, 1995), 34–37.

8. Note that the same verb εὐλογέω (*eulogeo*) is also in the Passover rite. Jesus "blesses" or "consecrates" the bread and wine. See entry for εὐλογέω in Joseph Henry Thayer, trans. *A Greek-English Lexicon of the New Testament Being Grimm's Wilke's Clavis Novi Testamenti* (Grand Rapids: Baker Book House, 1977).

9. See Lawrence J. Johnson, *Worship in the Early Church: An Anthology of Sources* (Collegeville, MN: Liturgical Press, 2009), 1:62.

10. Jesper Svenpro, "Archaic and Classical Greece: The Invention of Silent Reading," in *A History of Reading in the West*, ed. Guglielmo Cavallo and Roger Chartier (Amherst: University of Massachusetts Press, 2003), 50–52.

11. Others include 1 Peter 1:18–22; 2:21–25 and Romans 1:3–4. Robert J. Karris, *A Symphony of New Testament Hymns: Commentary on Philippians 2:5–11, Colossians 1:15–20, Ephesians 2:14–16, 1 Timothy 3:16, Titus 3:4–7, 1 Peter 3:18–22, and 2 Timothy 2:11–13* (Collegeville, MN: Liturgical Press, 1996), 5; and Jack T. Sanders, *The New Testament Christological Hymns: Their Historical Religious Background* (Cambridge: Cambridge University Press, 2004), vii–viii.

12. Leonard Thompson, "Cult and Eschatology in the Apocalypse of John," *Journal of Religion* 49, no. 4 (1969): 347, 343.

13. Mowry, "Revelation 4–5," 84.

14. Josephine Massynbaerd Ford, "The Christological Function of the Hymns in the Apocalypse of John," *Andrews University Seminary Studies* 36, no. 2 (1998): 207.

15. Allen Cabaniss, "A Note on the Liturgy of the Apocalypse," *Interpreter's Forum* 7, no. 1 (1953): 79; see also Andrea Spatafora, "Heavenly Liturgy and Temple in the Apocalypse," *Theoforum* 46 (2015): 186.

16. Mowry, "Revelation 4–5," 78–79.

17. Otto A. Piper, "The Apocalypse of John and the Liturgy of the Ancient Church," *American Society of Church History* 20, no. 1 (1951): 19.

18. Thompson, "Cult and Eschatology," 344.

19. Mowry, "Revelation 4–5," 10–11.

20. See Revelation 4:10–11; 5:11–14; 6:9–10; 22:8–9; and Mowry, "Revelation 4–5," 10–11.

21. Spatafora, "Heavenly Liturgy," 186.

22. Note the connection made between Passover and such dances in Jean Daniélou, *Philo of Alexandria* (Cambridge: James Clarke, 2014), 8.

23. Andrei A. Orlov, "Celestial Choirmaster: The Liturgical Role of Enoch-Metatron in 2 Enoch and the Merkabah Tradition," *Journal for the Study of the Pseudepigrapha* 14, no. 1 (2004): 3–29, esp. 19–20.

24. Translation is mine. The phrase κύκλῳ τοῦ θρόνου (*kuklō tou thronou*) is used in Revelation 4:6; 5:11; 7:11. Throughout the chapter passages that are quoted in Greek are taken from Eberhard Nestle et al., *Novum Testamentum Graece* (Stuttgart: Deutsche Bibelgesellschaft, 2015). See entry for κύκλῳ in Liddell, *A Greek-English Lexicon*.

25. The same language is used for the circle of elders as for the "circle" of prismatic light that forms a halo around the divine throne. In both cases the phrase κυκλόθεν τοῦ θρόνου (*kuklothen tou thronou*) is used (Revelation 4:3–4). That these are circles can be seen from the discussion above and the linguistic similarities discussed in the previous footnote.

26. "I will sing in the middle of the assembly": ἐν μέσῳ ἐκκλησίας ὑμνήσω (*en meso ekklesias humneso*).

27. Mowry, "Revelation 4–5," 77–78; and Ford, "Christological Function of the Hymns," 208, 213, 215, 217, 220.

28. Cheslyn Jones and Geoffrey Wainwright, *The Study of Liturgy* (London: SPCK, 2008), 168.

29. Valerij A. Alikin, *The Earliest History of the Christian Gathering: Origin, Development and Content of the Christian Gathering in the First to Third Centuries* (Leiden, Netherlands: Brill, 2011), 108.

30. Alikin, *Earliest History of the Christian Gathering*, 104.

31. Michael Philip Penn, *Kissing Christians Ritual and Community in the Late Ancient Church* (Philadelphia: University of Pennsylvania Press, 2013), 19.

32. Alikin, *Earliest History of the Christian Gathering*, 256.

33. See relevant entries for προσκυνέω and κυνέω in Liddell, *Greek-English Lexicon*.

34. Larry W. Hurtado, *At the Origins of Christian Worship: The Context and Character of Earliest Christian Devotion* (Grand Rapids, MI: Eerdmans, 2000), 43.

35. Hurtado, *At the Origins of Christian Worship*, 43.

36. Hurtado, *At the Origins of Christian Worship*, 43–44.

37. Alikin, *Earliest History of the Christian Gathering*, 256.

38. See discussion in Holmes, *Apostolic Fathers*, 363n11.1.

39. See entry for τεκμήριον in Liddell, *Greek-English Lexicon*.

40. James Montgomery, "A Poor Wayfaring Man of Grief," in *Hymns* (Salt Lake City: The Church of Jesus Christ of Latter-day Saints, 1985), no. 29.

41. See entry for βαπτίζω in Bauer, *Greek-English Lexicon*.

42. See ἄνωθεν in Liddell, *Greek-English Lexicon*.

43. Bissera Pentcheva, "Cross, Tunic, Body: Theology through the Phenomenology of Light," in *La stauroteca di Bessarione. Atti delle giornate internazionali di studio La stauroteca di Bessarione*, ed. Peter Schreiner Valeria Poletto (Venice: Istituto veneto di scienze, lettere e arti; Gallerie dell'Accademia; Istituto ellenico; Centro tedesco di studi veneziani, 2018), 257–79.

44. Sacramental references usually mention one singular cup: 1 Corinthians 10:16; Matthew 26:27; Mark 14:23; Luke 22:17.

45. Robert M. Herbold, "Footwashing and Last Things," *Christian Century* 9 (1983): 205; and John Christopher Thomas, *Footwashing in John 13 and the Johannine Community* (Sheffield, England: JSOT, 1991), 180ff.

46. It is practiced among Catholics and the Orthodox (Eastern and Oriental) on the Thursday of Holy Week, but the rite is not usually practiced amongst Protestants. Exceptions to this include Seventh-day Adventists, Anabaptists, the Church of God (Anderson, Indiana), and some Baptist denominations.

47. See entry for μέρος in Liddell, *Greek-English Lexicon*.

48. See discussion and primary source citations in Alan R. Kerr, *The Temple of Jesus' Body: The Temple Theme in the Gospel of John* (London: Sheffield Academic, 2002), 290.

49. Kerr, *Temple of Jesus' Body*, 291.

50. Carol A. Newsom, Sharon H. Ringe, and Jacqueline E. Lapsley, *Women's Bible Commentary* (London: SPCK, 2014), 600. Sacramental references usually mention one singular cup (1 Corinthians 10:16; Matthew 26:27; Mark 14:23; Luke 22:17).

34

Baptism in the New Testament

Seth S. Larsen

Most Christians today view baptism as an essential part of their faith tradition and the initial step toward following Jesus Christ and receiving a remission of their sins. Furthermore, they often view baptism as a sacred act, a sacrament, a rite, or an ordinance that is necessary to obtain salvation. For Latter-day Saints, baptism plays a critical role in initiating the process of justification and sanctification, "elements of a single divine process that qualifies us to live in the presence of God the Father and Jesus Christ."[1] While many suppose that baptism had its origins in the baptism performed by John the Baptist, Latter-day Saints believe that baptism "was not a new rite introduced by John the Baptist and adopted by Christ and his followers."[2] Rather, we hold the unique perspective that baptism has been a vital part of God's salvific plan for his children from the very beginning.

Through modern revelation, Latter-day Saints understand that the ordinance of baptism was introduced first to Adam sometime after the Fall. After being expelled from the Garden of Eden and God's presence, Adam heard the voice of the Lord instructing and commanding him, saying: "If thou wilt turn unto me, and hearken unto my voice, and believe, and repent of all thy transgressions, and be baptized, even in water, in the name of mine Only Begotten Son, who is full of grace and truth, which is Jesus Christ, the only name which shall be given under heaven, whereby salvation shall come unto the children of men, ye shall receive the gift of the Holy Ghost, asking all things in his name, and whatsoever ye shall ask, it shall be given you" (Moses 6:52). With this initial commandment and instruction to Adam, the Lord explained the rich, profound, and beautiful symbolism connected to this redeeming rite:

That by reason of transgression cometh the fall, which fall bringeth death, and inasmuch as ye were born into the world by water, and blood, and the spirit, which I have made, and so became of dust a living soul, even so ye must be born again into the kingdom of heaven, of water, and of the Spirit, and be cleansed by blood, even the blood of mine Only Begotten; that ye might be sanctified from all sin, and enjoy the words of eternal life in this world, and eternal life in the world to come, even immortal glory; for by the water ye keep the commandment; by the Spirit ye are justified, and by the blood ye are sanctified. . . .

And now, behold, I say unto you: This is the plan of salvation unto all men, through the blood of mine Only Begotten, who shall come in the meridian of time. . . .

And it came to pass, when the Lord had spoken with Adam, our father, that Adam cried unto the Lord, and he was caught away by the Spirit of the Lord, and was carried down into the water, and was laid under the water, and was brought forth out of the water. And thus he was baptized, and the Spirit of God descended upon him, and thus he was born of the Spirit, and became quickened in the inner man. And he heard a voice out of heaven, saying: Thou art baptized with fire, and with the Holy Ghost. This is the record of the Father, and the Son, from henceforth and forever; and thou art after the order of him who was without beginning of days or end of years, from all eternity to all eternity. Behold, thou art one in me, a son of God; and thus may all become my sons. Amen. (Moses 6:59–60, 62, 64–68)

The Lord also made it clear that as long as children were born into a fallen and sinful world their parents were commanded to "teach these things freely" unto their children (Moses 6:58).

Although there are no direct references in the Old Testament indicating that the posterity of Adam kept this commandment, Joseph Smith and the scriptures of the Restoration make it clear that the ordinance of baptism was performed throughout antiquity. Joseph Smith taught:

[T]he ancients who were actually the fathers of the church in the different ages, when the church flourished on the earth, . . . were initiated into the kingdom by baptism, for it is self evident in the scripture—God changes not. . . . [T]herefore, as Noah was a *preacher* of righteousness he must have been *baptised*. . . . In the former ages of the world, before the Saviour came in the flesh, "the saints" were baptised in the name of Jesus Christ to come . . . that they might be buried in baptism like him, and be raised in glory like him, that as there was but *one* Lord, *one* faith, *one* baptism, and *one* God and father of us all, even so there was but *one* door to the mansions of bliss.[3]

The pre-Christian-era portion of the Book of Mormon—more than three-quarters of the book—contains many references to baptism and, according to Elder Bruce R. McConkie, "some of the best information we have relative to this eternal law."[4] The Book of

Mormon makes it clear that the people were both living the fullness of the law of Moses and performing baptism by immersion.

If one steps away from the lens of the Restoration and looks strictly at the religious cultures surrounding the emergence of Christianity, it is easy to see that the use of water played an important role in the purification and initiation rites of those religious cultures. In fact, such rites and even immersion were common practices in the religious culture of the Greeks and Romans, especially among the various mystery religions.[5] Often these washings were a preliminary preparation for initiation into the mystery religions, but occasionally ideas of rebirth or forgiveness were associated with these washings.[6]

It is also well known that the Jews performed a variety of purification and initiation rites associated with water and immersion. These Jewish washings, especially Jewish proselyte baptisms, have been considered by many as the antecedents to the mode of John's baptism, and all of them—Greco-Roman, Jewish, and John's immersion rites—have been considered by one scholar or another to be the antecedents for Christian baptism.[7] As mentioned above, Latter-day Saints understand and believe the origin of Christian baptism stems from Adam; however, similarities one may find in other immersion rites become superficial when the basic but significant differences between those rites and that of Christian baptism are recognized. For the purposes of this chapter, we will explore baptism as it is found in the New Testament only.

John the Baptist

In the New Testament, the first baptismal experience one will come across is that of John, who was given the appropriate title "'Baptist' (*Baptistēs*) or 'the Baptizer' (*o Baptizōn*, 'the one immersing')."[8] John was the son of Zacharias and Elizabeth, who were both of the priestly lineage of Aaron and through whom John inherited the right to officiate in the Aaronic priesthood.[9] According to Doctrine and Covenants 84:28, John was ordained to this priesthood by an angel when he was only eight days old. His mission was foretold by Isaiah, Lehi, Malachi, and Gabriel.[10] John (the Baptist) seems to have been aware of these prophecies and sought security, confidence, and strength in them (John 1:23). Jesus—who was himself the ultimate beneficiary of John's prophetic work—had high compliments for his older cousin. He told a multitude of Jews that John was "a burning and a shining light" (5:35), and at another time Jesus said, "Verily I say unto you, Among them that are born of women there hath not risen a greater than John the Baptist" (Matthew 11:11).

According to the Prophet Joseph Smith, John the Baptist was not great on account of the miracles he performed, because he performed no miracles. Rather, John the Baptist was the greatest born among women for three reasons: first, he was trusted with the divine mission of preparing the way before the face of the Lord; second, he was trusted and required to baptize Christ and to be a witness of the Holy Ghost descending upon him; and third, "John at that time was the only legal administrator holding the keys of power. . . . The keys, the kingdom, the power, the glory had departed from the Jews; and John, the son of Zachariah, by the holy anointing and decree of heaven, held the keys of power at the time."[11] With these great responsibilities, John the Baptist stood in a very peculiar position at a very unique time. He was the "last legal administrator of the old dispensation, the first of the new; he was the last of the old prophets, the first of the new," Elder McConkie wrote. "With him ended the old law, and with him began the new era of promise. He is the one man who stood, literally, at the crossroads of history; with him the past died and the future was born."[12]

The Lord tells us that John was to *overthrow the kingdom of the Jews, and to make straight the way of the Lord before the face of his people, to prepare them for the coming of the Lord, in whose hand is given all power*" (Doctrine and Covenants 84:28; emphasis added). For years the wicked, corrupt, and greedy leadership of the Jews had focused more on growing their wealth—especially through corrupting the temple economy—and expanding their power than they had on leading Israel in truth and righteousness according to God's law. Thus, in this state of apostasy, the Jews had become a kingdom unto themselves. To overthrow the kingdom of the Jews and reestablish the kingdom of God, a major spiritual revolution would need to happen.[13] John the Baptist understood the role he was to play, and he performed it to perfection. Naturally, such a prophetic mission would create unwanted disruption, especially among the established ruling class of the Jews. But John did not back down, hesitate, or share his message quietly. He went about as foretold by the prophet Isaiah and confirmed by all the Gospels, "crying" in the wilderness (Isaiah 40:3; compare Matthew 3:3; Mark 1:3; Luke 3:4; John 1:23).

John's command to repent and prepare for the coming Messiah, and his demand that Israel produce evidence to show their sincerity, generated no small stir. As Matthew records, "then went out to him Jerusalem, and all Judea, and all the region round about Jordan, and were baptized of him in Jordan, confessing their sins" (Matthew 3:5–6). John's cry of repentance did not just reach the downtrodden masses of Judea, it had also reached the powerful and wealthy Jewish leadership, and apparently it raised questions within their circles as to whether or not he was the Messiah. The Gospel of John records that while John was baptizing in Bethabara beyond the Jordan, the Pharisees "sent priests and Levites from Jerusalem to ask him, "Who art thou?"—and after discovering that he was not the Messiah, they asked him, "Why baptizest thou then?" (John 1:19, 25). John answered this question using Isaiah's prophecy, saying that he was "making straight the way of the Lord" (1:23).

The fact that John was not in Jerusalem or inviting the people to the temple may shed some light on the religious state that Israel and its leaders were in. Israel had looked beyond the symbolism the law of Moses was intended to create. According to John, many in Jewish leadership were abusive and corrupt: a "generation of vipers" who were going to be "hewn down" (Matthew 3:7, 10). John's baptism was to make crooked Israel straight again and to prepare them to receive their God.

First, John's baptism offered the Israelites an opportunity to truly repent and receive forgiveness of their sins. John's baptism "was doubtless preceded by an exhortation by John, and the people were baptized 'confessing their sins'" (Mark 1:5; Matthew 3:6).[14] Israel as a people had broken God's law and had gone astray; thus, because of their disobedience, they were under the condemnation of law. However, through John's baptism Israel could become justified, or in other words pardoned from the punishment of the broken law. Accepting John's baptism meant Israel could stand blameless or without sin so that when the Lord came with his baptism of fire they could be sanctified, or in other words made holy and clean as he is holy and clean.[15] Everett Ferguson, an authority on baptism in the early church, states that the baptism of John "was a conversion baptism but not a variation of proselyte baptism; its premise was repentance, and its purpose was the forgiveness of sins; it was not the basis of a new Israel or to join a new community (the goal was a renewal of Israel)."[16]

Second, it is possible that John may have been trying to restore the law of Moses in its purity and entirety by reintroducing the baptismal ordinance, which had been lost over time through various stages of apostasy. It is clear from Jesus's interaction with Nicodemus, who was a ruler among the Jews, that the Jewish people and their leadership no longer knew about or understood baptism. The idea of baptism as a rebirth was perplexing to Nicodemus. The Book of Mormon makes it clear that baptism fits perfectly within the framework of the law of Moses; the ordinance of baptism—much like animal sacrifice within the law of Moses—acted as a symbolic reference to Christ's atonement. Just as Christ died, was buried in the tomb, and resurrected the third day, the proselyte symbolically dies in Christ, giving up the old life of sin, and is buried with Christ in the water; and as Christ came forth from the tomb, so the proselyte comes forth out of the water a new creature in Christ (Romans 6:1–6). The prophetic authors of the Book of Mormon mention forty-three times that they lived the law of Moses, and they mention baptism ninety times. A restoration of the full law of Moses would therefore prepare Israel for the Lord's coming among them and for the reception of the fullness of his gospel.

Many scholars have sought to link John's baptism to earlier and contemporary Jewish purification and cleansing washings, proselyte baptism, and the baths of the Essenes and others.[17] The similarities have led some scholars to view such washings as antecedents of John's baptism. Both Jewish washings and John's baptism contain a theme of purification or cleansing. Many Jewish washings—like John's—were performed by immersion. Jewish proselyte baptism was an initiation rite for Gentiles who were converting to Judaism, and John's baptism was also a conversion or reconversion for Israel's people.

However, there are distinct differences that disconnect John's baptism from these Jewish washings as possible antecedents. John's baptism was a onetime event. Most of the Jewish washings were a ceremonial purification rite that would be performed when needed throughout one's lifetime. John's baptism was focused on repentance and the forgiveness of sins to prepare Israel for the coming of their Lord. Thus, John's baptism was an eschatological purification rite rather than a ceremonial one.[18] Jewish proselyte baptism was an initiation rite for Gentiles seeking to join the Israelite community.[19] John held priesthood keys and personally administered his baptism, whereas Jewish proselyte baptism and other purification baths or washings were a self-immersion (often with two or three witnesses).[20] As Ferguson notes, "This practice provides the most plausible explanation for the description of John as 'the Baptist': He was doing something different, or else the designation would not have distinguished him."[21]

The Baptism of Jesus Christ

Immediately after introducing John and his baptism, the New Testament Gospels record unique but similar accounts of Christianity's most important baptism—the baptism of Jesus Christ. This important event marks a major transition between the baptism and ministry of John and the baptism and ministry of Jesus Christ—a transition that John was cognizant would happen if he fulfilled his role as the forerunner of Christ. When John's disgruntled disciples reported the increase of Jesus's popularity and followers, John taught them, "He that hath the bride is the bridegroom: but the friend of the bridegroom, which standeth and heareth him, rejoiceth greatly because of the bridegroom's voice: this my joy therefore is fulfilled. *He must increase, but I must decrease*" (John 3:29–30; emphasis added).

Matthew's account of Jesus's baptism is the longest of all four Gospel accounts, comprising all of five verses. It emphasizes John's humble hesitancy to fulfill his sacred mission of baptizing the Son of God: "I have need to be baptized of thee," Matthew records John as saying, "and comest thou to me?" (Matthew 3:14).[22] Jesus responds, "Suffer it to be so now: for thus it becometh us to fulfil all righteousness" (3:15), and this might be meant to answer more than just John's anxieties. Perhaps Matthew, with his clear understanding of the necessity of baptism, included this interchange between the Baptist and the Christ to answer the questions that some would have concerning a sinless Messiah receiving "the baptism of repentance for the remission of sins" (Mark 1:4). It appears the Book of Mormon prophet Nephi felt the need to address the same issue in his record and did so in detail:

> And now, I would ask of you, my beloved brethren, wherein the Lamb of God did fulfil all righteousness in being baptized by water? Know ye not that he was holy? But notwithstanding he being holy, he showeth unto the children of men that, according to the flesh he humbleth himself before the Father, and witnesseth unto the Father that he would be obedient unto him in keeping his commandments. Wherefore, after he was baptized with water the Holy Ghost descended upon him in the form of a dove. And again, it showeth unto the children of men the straitness of the path, and the narrowness of the gate, by which they should enter, he having set the example before them. And he said unto the children of men: Follow thou me. (2 Nephi 31:6–10)

Nephi's expounding of the phrase "fulfill all righteousness"—and one could argue Matthew used the phrase in the same manner—explains that Jesus was not receiving John's baptism for a remission of sins, for he was sinless. Rather, Jesus was baptized to (1) show mankind that although he was the all-powerful Jehovah in the flesh, he was humble before his Father; (2) witness to or covenant with his Father that he would be obedient; (3) show mankind the strictness, exactness, and discipline required to enter the kingdom of God; and (4) show, as Christ himself taught, that baptism is necessary for salvation (John 3:5).

"To fulfill all righteousness," writes Elder McConkie, "is to perform every ordinance, keep every commandment, and do every act necessary to the attainment of eternal life."[23] If Jesus's commanding invitation was to follow him, we should know what he did and how he did it.

Luke's account of Jesus's baptism is the shortest among the Synoptic Gospels, only two verses in all. This is a little surprising following Luke's attention to detail leading up to this important event. Although it is short, Luke does preserve important details not found in the other Gospels. For instance, only Luke mentions that the heavens being opened and the Spirit descending were a result of Jesus praying (3:21). Luke's description of the Holy Ghost's appearance at Jesus's baptism is also unique. Matthew, Mark, and John each mention the Spirit descending upon Jesus "like a dove" (Matthew 3:16; Mark 1:10; John 1:32), but Luke records that "the Holy Ghost descended in a *bodily shape* like a dove" (3:22; emphasis added) and retains the eternal truth concerning the Godhead as found in Doctrine and Covenants 130:22. Speaking of the Spirit's descent at Christ's baptism, Joseph Smith taught:

> The sign of the dove was instituted before the creation of the world, a witness for the Holy Ghost, and the devil cannot come in the sign of a dove. The Holy Ghost is a personage, and is in the form of a personage. It does not confine itself to the *form* of the dove, but in *sign* of the dove. The Holy Ghost cannot be transformed into a dove; but the sign of a dove was given to John to signify the truth of the deed, as the dove is an emblem or token of truth and innocence.[24]

The Gospel of John suggests the same idea for the role the Holy Ghost played at the baptism of Jesus. John (the Beloved) records the Baptist as saying: "He that sent me to baptize with water, the same said unto me, Upon whom thou shalt see the Spirit descending, and remaining on him, the same is he which baptizeth with the Holy Ghost" (John 1:33).

Baptism in the Gospels

On the subject of baptism, the Synoptic Gospels are generally quite sparse, with just a few subtle references. Perhaps the most significant comes at the end of the Gospel of Matthew. After the Resurrection and forty-day ministry, and just before his ascension into heaven, the Lord gave his apostles a charge: "Go ye therefore, and teach all nations, baptizing them in the name of the Father, and of the Son, and of the Holy Ghost" (Matthew 28:19). This commission was taken seriously by the apostles, and accounts of their many baptisms can be read in the Acts of the Apostles and in the epistles of Paul. However, those accounts were not the first experience Jesus's disciples had with baptism.

In the Fourth Gospel, John records a fascinating insight concerning Jesus, his disciples, and baptism. In John 3 we see that the ministries of the Baptist and Jesus overlap. Jesus, along with his disciples, went into the land of Judea for precisely the same reason John the Baptist was there, namely to baptize, "because there was much water there" (3:23). It is clear that John was fulfilling his prophetic mission to prepare the way before the Lord; as one of the Baptist's disciples reported, "Rabbi, he that was with thee beyond Jordan, to whom thou barest witness, behold, the same baptizeth, and all men come to him" (3:26). John 4:1 mentions that news had made it to the Pharisees that Jesus had "made and baptized more disciples than John," and apparently this made them uneasy. As the Joseph Smith Translation for verses 2–4 clarifies: "They sought more diligently some means that they might put him to death; for many received John as a prophet, but they believed not on Jesus. Now the Lord knew this, though he himself baptized not so many as his disciples; for he suffered them for an example, preferring one another" (JST John 4:2–4). These verses make it clear that Jesus was indeed performing the ordinance of baptism himself but primarily gave that responsibility to his disciples so they could be an example.[25]

Although Jesus, his disciples, and early Christian leaders also baptized in water unto repentance, the baptism they were performing had minor but significant differences in comparison to the baptism of John. For one, those who received Christian baptism would have taken upon themselves Christ's name. In addition to this a promise was added "that in due course [Christ's] converts would be baptized by the Spirit."[26] It is most likely that because of these small but vital differences, Jesus and his disciples were not only baptizing new followers but rebaptizing John's disciples that were listening to and obeying the Baptist's message and invitation to follow the Lamb of God, including Andrew and John (John 3:36–37). John the Baptist himself taught his disciples that "I indeed have baptized you with water; but he shall not only baptize you *with water*, but with fire, and the Holy Ghost" (JST Mark 1:8; emphasis added). Acts 19:1–7 provides an example of a group of John the Baptist's disciples receiving Christian baptism some two decades after the Resurrection:

> And it came to pass, that, while Apollos was at Corinth, Paul having passed through the upper coasts came to Ephesus: and finding certain disciples, he said unto them, Have ye received the Holy Ghost since ye believed? And they said unto him, We have not so much as heard whether there be any Holy Ghost. And he said unto them, Unto what then were ye baptized? And they said, Unto John's baptism. Then said Paul, John verily baptized with the baptism of repentance, saying unto the people, that they should believe on him which should come after him, that is, on Christ Jesus. When they heard this, they were baptized in the name of the Lord Jesus. And when Paul had laid his hands upon them, the Holy Ghost came on them; and they spake with tongues, and prophesied. And all the men were about twelve.

It seems evident from these verses that those who had been baptized and were disciples of John were rebaptized in the name of Christ.

The Gospel of John contains another important story dealing with baptism: John 3:3–5. These verses are the foundational authority for Christian baptism for one main reason—they record the Lord himself teaching about the purpose and necessity of baptism. In these verses, the Lord teaches that through baptism one is born anew, reborn from above or spiritually reborn, through the dual cleansing and sanctifying powers of baptism in the water and from the Spirit (John 3:3, 5).[27] Thus, Jesus brings together the two elements of baptism that were separate in John's baptism.[28] Jesus boldly emphasized to the Pharisaic teacher and ruler Nicodemus that baptism is prerequisite to seeing and gaining entrance into the kingdom of God. The teachings of Christianity's central figure in these verses make it essential for those who claim to be Christ-centered in their faith, and for all who are seeking after him, to be born anew through the waters of baptism and the reception of the Holy Ghost.

Baptism in the Acts of the Apostles

Acts preserves much regarding the role baptism played in the early church and what Christian baptism—baptism of water and the Spirit—looked like in the earliest days of the primitive church. In this section we will look at two insightful pericopes dealing with baptism: the day of Pentecost and Philip's ministry in Samaria.

The day of Pentecost

Fifty days after Passover was the Jewish celebration of Pentecost, also known as "the feast of harvest" (Exodus 23:16), "the feast of weeks" (Exodus 34:22; Deuteronomy 16:10), or "the day of the firstfruits" (Numbers 28:26). The day of Pentecost marks the day in which the Lord's promised endowment of the Holy Ghost was fulfilled. Elder Bruce R. McConkie wrote: "During his mortal ministry our Lord gave his disciples the gift of the Holy Ghost, which is the right to the constant companionship of that member of the Godhead based on faithfulness (John 20:22). But as long as Jesus was with them, the actual enjoyment of the gift was withheld (John 7:39; 14:26; 15:26–27; 16:7–15; Acts 1:8). Fulfilment of the promise came on the day of Pentecost."[29]

It is important to understand that there were different groups of people interacting in various ways with the spiritual outpouring on that day. Gathered together were the disciples of the Lord experiencing the gifts of the Spirit (Acts 2:4). Then there were those witnessing this miraculous event who felt the influence of the Spirit and stood in amazement as they heard God's word in their own language (2:7–8). There were also those who mocked (2:13). It was to these last two groups that Peter bore a powerful witness of Christ, causing those gathered to be "pricked in their heart" and to ask what they needed to do (2:37). Peter's response to their question provides insight into the process of conversion in the early church and gives us some understanding as to what baptism looked like in first-century Christianity: "Then Peter said unto them, Repent, and be baptized every one of you in the name of Jesus Christ for the remission of sins, and ye shall receive the gift of the Holy Ghost. . . . Then they that gladly received his word were baptized: and the same day there were added unto them about three thousand souls" (2:38, 41). From these verses, it appears that baptism was a necessary part of following Jesus Christ in the post-Resurrection church. According to Peter's invitation, it appears that a proselyte must show or manifest faith in Jesus Christ and his teachings and repentance in order to be baptized and gain entrance into Christ's church. Like the baptism of John, first-century baptism brought a remission of sins but was performed in the name of Christ and was followed by the proselyte receiving the gift of the Holy Ghost by the laying on of hands (8:17).

Philip's ministry in Samaria

Acts 8:5–19 contains the account of Philip—one of the "seven men of honest report, full of the Holy Ghost and wisdom" (6:3)—ministering in Samaria and provides additional insight into first-century baptism. The account states that Philip "preached Christ unto them. And the people with one accord gave heed unto those things which Philip spake, hearing and see- ing the miracles which he did" (8:5–6). Their belief increased to the point that "they believed Philip preaching the things concerning the kingdom of God, and the name of Jesus Christ, they were baptized, both men and women" (8:12). The main insight from this story is gained from the following verses:

> Now when the apostles which were at Jerusalem heard that Samaria had received the word of God, they sent unto them Peter and John: who, when they were come down, prayed for them, that they might receive the Holy Ghost: (for as yet he was fallen upon none of them: only they were baptized in the name of the Lord Jesus.) Then laid they their hands on them, and they received the Holy Ghost. (8:14–17)

There are many things we can learn from this account. First, there were some in the first century who, like Philip, held the priesthood authority to baptize with water and had pow- erful faith to work many miracles but did not have the power or authority to confer the gift of the Holy Ghost. This power seems to have rested with the apostles during at least part of the first century. Second, the gift of the Holy Ghost was bestowed by the laying on of hands, something Latter-day Saints would find familiar to their baptismal experience. Third, this account emphasizes the important two-part nature of baptism that Christ taught to Nico- demus. The Samaritan Saints believed and were baptized with water, but their baptism was complete only when Peter and John came and bestowed the gift of the Holy Ghost.

Baptism in the Pauline Epistles

The letters of the apostle Paul, although they are very time- and context-specific, are im- portant early Christian texts because they provide a window through which we can observe the earliest forms of Christianity after the resurrection of Jesus Christ. "The apostle Paul is a central figure for the study of Christian baptism," writes Ferguson. "His own experience and the evidence of his letters show baptism to have been practiced from the earliest days of the church."[30]

Galatians 3:26–27

In his letter to the Galatians, Paul expounded on the purposes for the law of Moses and the role it played in pointing Israel to Christ. Paul refuted the claims made by the Judaizers—

Christians who believed and taught that in order to become Abraham's seed and gain salvation, one needed to conform to the law of Moses by explaining that Abraham's seed were individuals of faith.[31] It was faith in Christ that connected one to the promises of Abraham, not the law. God's law acts as a guide or schoolmaster to help us learn of Christ and become more like him. However, because of our inability to keep the law perfectly, it is the law that condemns us. The law itself has no power to save; Christ alone saves. Christ, through his atonement, allows us to be justified by obedience to the law. We are sanctified and saved through faith in Christ. Faith in Christ is expressed through the act of baptism. As Paul stated, "Ye are all the children of God by faith in Christ Jesus. For as many of you as have been baptized into Christ have put on Christ" (Galatians 3:26–27).

The phrase "baptized into Christ" more accurately means baptized in the name of Christ. Beasley-Murray explains: "The *Eis Xriston* ('into Christ') is to be understood as an abbreviation of the common *Eis to onoma tou Xristou* ('in the name of Christ') and therefore has the meaning of baptism with reference to Christ, for dedication to and appropriation by Christ."[32] Thus, through baptism one receives or takes upon himself or herself a new name and becomes part of a new family—the family of Christ. King Benjamin taught: "I would that ye should take upon you the name of Christ, all you that have entered into the covenant with God that ye should be obedient unto the end of your lives. And it shall come to pass that whosoever doeth this shall be found at the right hand of God, for he shall know the name by which he is called; for he shall be called by the name of Christ" (Mosiah 5:8–9). Elder McConkie explained this process in this manner:

> Those accountable mortals who then believe and obey the gospel are born again; they are born of the Spirit; they become alive to the things of righteousness or of the Spirit. They become members of another family, have new brothers and sisters, and a new Father. They are the sons and daughters of Jesus Christ. They take upon them his name in the waters of baptism and certify anew each time they partake of the sacrament that they have so done; or, more accurately, in the waters of baptism power is given them to become the sons of Christ, which eventuates when they are in fact born of the Spirit and become new creatures of the Holy Ghost.[33]

The second half of Paul's statement is striking, powerful, and beautiful, but it naturally produces feelings of humility and inadequacy when one begins to understand its implications in daily life. "For as many of you as have been baptized into Christ have *put on Christ*" (Galatians 3:27; emphasis added). In other words, by taking upon oneself Christ's name through baptism, one has chosen to take upon himself or herself the appearance of Christ that comes through the endowment of the Spirit. For Latter-day Saints, this comes through living a Christlike life. As the Book of Mormon prophet Alma stated while questioning the people of the church in Zarahemla: "And now behold, I ask of you, my brethren of the church, have ye spiritually been born of God? Have ye *received his image in your countenances*?" (Alma 5:14; emphasis added). Ferguson writes, "Baptism places one into Christ, so that one is now clothed with Christ, having put him on as one puts on clothing. This has the effect of bringing to one the benefits that are Christ's, making one what Christ is—true descendant of Abraham, heir of the promises, son God, recipient of the Spirit."[34]

1 Corinthians 15:29

According to 1 Corinthians 15, there were some among the saints in Corinth that were either doubting, or even possibly teaching against, the reality of the Resurrection (both Christ's and the coming one of all humanity). To combat such views, in 1 Corinthians 15 Paul made a progressive, rational argument for the reality of Christ's, and thus all mankind's, bodily resurrection:

> But if there be no resurrection of the dead, then is Christ not risen: and if Christ be not risen, then is our preaching vain, and your faith is also vain. Yea, and we are found false witnesses of God; because we have testified of God that he raised up Christ: whom he raised not up, if so be that the dead rise not. For if the dead rise not, then is not Christ raised: and if Christ be not raised, your faith is vain; ye are yet in your sins. Then they also which are fallen asleep in Christ are perished. If in this life only we have hope in Christ, we are of all men most miserable. (15:13–19)

It is in this context—Paul's argument for the reality of the Resurrection—that he says, "Else what shall they do which are baptized for the dead, if the dead rise not at all? why are they then baptized for the dead?" (15:29). In other words, Paul is arguing, "There is no point for saints to perform baptisms for those who have died if those who have died won't live again; and if the dead won't live again, then Christianity is a lie." Paul's purpose was not to teach about baptism, or even baptism for the dead, or to support the doctrines of the latter-day church (though he is citing vicarious baptism); rather, Paul was defending the reality and validity of bodily resurrection.[35] Why perform vicarious baptisms, as the Corinthians were doing, if there will be no resurrection of the dead?

Romans 6:1–11

One of Paul's most well-known explanations of baptism is in his epistle to the Romans. Paul powerfully and beautifully connects the purpose that baptism serves in the conversion process and its relationship to Christ and his atonement. After explaining justification through the grace of Christ, Paul asks a question that transitions the topic to baptism: "Shall we continue in sin, that grace may abound? God forbid. How shall we, that are dead to sin, live any longer therein?" (6:1–2). Then he explains, "Know ye not, that so many of us as were baptized into Jesus Christ were baptized into his death? Therefore we are buried with him by baptism into death: that like as Christ was raised up from the dead by the glory of the Father, even so we also should walk in newness of life" (6:3–4). Paul's use of the phrase "know ye not" indicates that this portion of his message was—or should be—known among the early Christians, namely that those baptized in the name of Christ were baptized into his death.[36]

It is also interesting to note that Paul once again uses the same recognized abbreviated phrase "baptized into Jesus Christ" in this passage as he used in his epistle to the Galatians.

For Paul, baptism is more than just a necessary rite to follow Christ; rather, through baptism one participates with Christ in his atonement. Through baptism, one is buried with Christ into death. "Knowing this," Paul writes, "that our old man is crucified with him, that the body of sin might be destroyed, that henceforth we should not serve sin" (6:6). Paul also taught that baptism was in "the likeness of [Christ's] resurrection" (6:5); one is raised up from the watery grave to "walk in newness of life" (6:4). Baptism, for Paul, was not simply an entrance rite into the kingdom of God but an entrance into a new life in Christ. "Therefore," Paul wrote to the Corinthian saints, "if any man be in Christ, he is a *new creature*: old things are passed away; behold, all things are become new" (2 Corinthians 5:17; emphasis added). This is also supported in his previous teachings on baptism found in Galatians.

There are other references to baptism in the epistles of Paul. In his letter to the Colossians, Paul makes a comparison between the law of circumcision and baptism and the role they both play in putting off the natural man and becoming a new being and forsaking sin (2:11–13). In his letter to Titus, Paul teaches that Christ through his mercy saves us "by the washing of regeneration, and renewing of the Holy Ghost" (3:5), which again presents baptism as a rite that restores one to purity and establishes or releases the divinity planted within each of us. These references reveal that, for Paul, baptism was vital to one's progression of faith and relationship to Christ and ultimately to one's eternal potential. Also, the many symbolic connections found within the Christian baptismal rite had very real applications to life and eternity and very real blessings to be received by the recipient.

Conclusion

After the Pauline Epistles, there are only a few scattered references to baptism in the remaining New Testament books.[37] From this cursory study, a few things seem clear: (1) baptism, as taught by Christ and later his disciples, was necessary for salvation; (2) Christian baptism must include two parts in order to be complete: the baptism of water and the baptism of the Spirit; (3) Christians manifested their faith in Jesus Christ by being baptized; (4) through baptism, one received a remission of sins; (5) through baptism, one took the name of Christ as well as the responsibility to be a new person, a Christlike person; (6) baptism was necessary to gain entrance into the church of Christ and be numbered among the disciples; and (7) baptism in the first century was more than just an entrance rite; in fact, it was deeply symbolic and connected the participant to Christ and the blessings associated with him—namely, becoming the seed of Abraham and inheriting the blessings and covenant promises of Abraham.

Seth S. Larsen is an instructor in the Seminaries and Institutes program of The Church of Jesus Christ of Latter-day Saints.

Further Reading

Beasley-Murray, G. R. *Baptism in the New Testament*, 11–31. New York: St. Martin's, 1963.

Christofferson, D. Todd. "Justification and Sanctification." *Ensign*, June 2001.

Ferguson, Everett. *Baptism in the Early Church: History, Theology, and Liturgy in the First Five Centuries*. Grand Rapids, MI: Eerdmans, 2009.

Gavin, F. *The Jewish Antecedents of the Christian Sacraments*, 26–58. New York: KTAV, 1969.

McConkie, Bruce R. *Doctrinal New Testament Commentary*. 3 vols. Salt Lake City: Bookcraft, 1965–73.

Notes

1. D. Todd Christofferson, "Justification and Sanctification," *Ensign*, June 2001, 18.
2. Bruce R. McConkie, *Mormon Doctrine*, 2nd ed. (Salt Lake City: Bookcraft, 1966), 52, s.v. "Baptism."
3. *Times and Seasons*, September 1, 1842, 903–5, *The Joseph Smith Papers*, http://www.josephsmithpapers .org/paper-summary/times-and-seasons-1-september-1842/9. See also Doctrine and Covenants 20:23–28, which affirms that the righteous posterity of Adam did, in fact, keep this commandment.
4. McConkie, *Mormon Doctrine*, 72.
5. Everett Ferguson, *Baptism in the Early Church: History, Theology, and Liturgy in the First Five Centuries* (Grand Rapids, MI: Eerdmans, 2009), 25–37.
6. Ferguson, *Baptism in the Early Church*, 29.
7. G. R. Beasley-Murray, *Baptism in the New Testament* (New York: St. Martin's Press, 1963), 11–31; Arthur Darby Nock, "Early Gentile Christianity and Its Hellenistic Background," in *Essays on the Trinity and the Incarnation*, ed. A. E. J. Rawlinson (London: Longmans, Green & Co., 1928), 51–156; reprinted in Zeph Stewart, ed., *Arthur Darby Nock: Essays on Religion and the Ancient World* (Oxford: Oxford University Press, 1986), 49–133; and F. Gavin, *The Jewish Antecedents of the Christian Sacraments* (repr., New York: KTAV, 1969), 26–58. Gavin makes strong claims that Christianity is a morphed form of Judaism, especially Christian baptism. He argues that it is the same as Jewish proselyte baptism.
8. Ferguson, *Baptism in the Early Church*, 83.
9. Discourse, 22 January 1843, as reported by Wilford Woodruff, p. [6], *The Joseph Smith Papers*, http://www .josephsmithpapers.org/paper-summary/discourse-22-january-1843-as-reported-by-wilford-woodruff/3.
10. Isaiah 40:3; 1 Nephi 10:7–10; Malachi 3:1 (according to the Lord, in Matthew 11:10, John the Baptist fulfilled Malachi's prophecy); and Luke 1:13–22.
11. Joseph Smith, Discourse, 29 January 1843, as reported by Willard Richards–B, p. [2], *The Joseph Smith Papers*, http://www.josephsmithpapers.org/paper-summary/discourse-29-january-1843-as-reported-by-willard -richards-b/1.
12. Bruce R. McConkie, *Doctrinal New Testament Commentary* (Salt Lake City: Bookcraft, 1965–73), 1:113.
13. Steven C. Harper, *Making Sense of the Doctrine and Covenants: A Guided Tour through Modern Revelations* (Salt Lake City: Deseret Book, 2008), 296.
14. C. H. H. Scobie, *John the Baptist* (Philadelphia: Fortress, 1964), 90–91.
15. For a detailed explanation of justification and sanctification and their relationship to one another, see Christofferson, "Justification and Sanctification."
16. Ferguson, *Baptism in the Early Church*, 89.
17. Gavin, *Jewish Antecedents of the Christian Sacraments*; Scobie, *John the Baptist*, 93–102; and Joan E. Taylor, *The Immerser: John the Baptist within Second Temple Judaism* (Grand Rapids, MI: Eerdmans, 1997), 15–48. Taylor makes a strong argument that John and his baptism should not be linked to the Essenes.

18. Ferguson, *Baptism in the Early Church*, 88.
19. Some have pointed out that the report in Luke 3:14 that soldiers had responded to John's message might indicate that John baptized Gentiles, but Jewish soldiers who enforced the work of the tax collectors cannot be ruled out.
20. Ferguson, *Baptism in the Early Church*, 81.
21. Ferguson, *Baptism in the Early Church*, 88.
22. This emphasis found in the Gospel accounts of John's declaration that the one coming after him was greater than he and provided a superior baptism may be countering the possible embarrassment felt by later Christians in that Jesus, superior to John, was baptized by the lesser Jewish prophet. The fact that each Gospel author includes this event despite the possible embarrassment strongly supports the historicity of Jesus's baptism. Ferguson, *Baptism in the Early Church*, 100.
23. McConkie, *Doctrinal New Testament Commentary*, 1:123. Ferguson writes: "Righteousness was an important concept for Matthew. It often refers to God's saving activity, but here it likely means to obey God's plan. In receiving baptism Jesus identified with the people of Israel to whom John addressed his message and started on a path that led to the cross. He also set an example of obedience for others." Ferguson, *Baptism in the Early Church*, 102.
24. Joseph Fielding Smith, *Teachings of the Prophet Joseph Smith* (Salt Lake City: Deseret News, 1938), 276. Compare to Joseph Smith, Discourse, 29 January 1843, as reported by Franklin D. Richards, p. [13], *The Joseph Smith Papers*, http://www.josephsmithpapers.org/paper-summary/discourse-29-january-1843-as-reported-by-franklin-d-richards/3.
25. Concerning these very verses, Elder McConkie wrote, "Contrary to the false teachings and traditions of sectarianism Jesus personally performed water baptisms so that in all things he might be the great Exemplar. Without question he also performed all other ordinances essential to salvation and exaltation." McConkie, *Doctrinal New Testament Commentary*, 1:148.
26. McConkie, *Doctrinal New Testament Commentary*, 1:146.
27. The Lord taught Alma the Younger this same thing as well: "Marvel not that all mankind, yea, men and women, all nations, kindreds, tongues and people, must be born again; yea, born of God, changed from their carnal and fallen state, to a state of righteousness, being redeemed of God, becoming his sons and daughters; and thus they become new creatures; and unless they do this, they can in nowise inherit the kingdom of God" (Mosiah 27:25–29).
28. Beasley-Murray, *Baptism in the New Testament*, 230–31.
29. McConkie, *Mormon Doctrine*, 818, s.v. "Day of Pentecost."
30. Ferguson, *Baptism in the Early Church*, 146.
31. Beasley-Murray, *Baptism in the New Testament*, 146–47.
32. Beasley-Murray, *Baptism in the New Testament*, 147.
33. McConkie, *Doctrinal New Testament Commentary*, 2:471–72.
34. Ferguson, *Baptism in the Early Church*, 148.
35. It might be helpful for Latter-day Saints to understand that Joseph Smith and the early Saints of the Restoration would not have read or understood 1 Corinthians 15:29 as anything other than Paul arguing for the reality of the Resurrection until Joseph received his January 1836 revelation. It was through this revelation that Joseph first learned that his brother Alvin, and all who have died without the gospel who would have received it in mortality had they been given the chance, would not be denied the rewards of the gospel in the life to come. The reception of this revelation led to much discussion, pondering, and additional revelation surrounding the performance of proxy ordinances, the earliest being baptism for the dead. Most likely, the Prophet and Saints would not have recognized or made a connection with this verse until sometime during or after the restoration of the doctrine of vicarious ordinances. See also Matthew McBride, "Letters on Baptism for the Dead," in *Revelations in Context: The Stories behind the Sections of the Doctrine and Covenants*, https://history.lds.org/article/doctrine-and-covenants-baptisms-for-the-dead?lang=eng.

36. Ferguson, *Baptism in the Early Church*, 156.

37. One is in 1 Peter 3:20, a verse that produces a fascinating perspective of the events surrounding Noah, his family, the Flood, and the ark. Often, it is the ark of Noah that is viewed as the object providing salvation to Noah and his family, but verse 20 states that they were "saved by water." For Noah and his family, the danger was not the Flood. Of course, God needed to preserve them from the Flood to fulfill his covenants and eternal purposes, but for the righteous death is sweet, and Noah as well as his family would eventually die. The real danger was spiritual death; it was the wicked and worldly influences that surrounded them. With this perspective in mind, it was the water of baptism that saved them from the real danger of spiritual death.

35

Plants in the New Testament

Terry B. Ball

The New Testament is rich in botany and agriculture. Nearly a hundred verses of the New Testament speak of plants or use agricultural terms. More than twenty different plant taxa are mentioned by name, and the text abounds with references to plant parts and products such as seeds, branches, flowers, and oil. The Savior and New Testament writers regularly used botanical and agricultural imagery to illustrate and teach their messages. This study will therefore discuss plants and botanical terms mentioned in the New Testament in an effort to help modern readers better understand life during New Testament times and the teachings of the text.

Biblical botany has generated a considerable corpus of research and much debate in academia over the years. Michael Zohary, the renowned botanist of the Near East, summarized the challenges faced by the discipline when he observed that "owing to inadequate knowledge of the native plants and the tendency, in dubious cases, to assign to the plants of the Bible names familiar to the translators, inaccuracies and confusion abound in the translations."[1] Accordingly, in this study of New Testament plants and botanical terms, I will not attempt to give a thorough review of the debates over the identity and proper translation of each plant species or terms discussed. Doing so would require a volume of considerable length. Rather, in dictionary format,[2] I will list and discuss each plant, plant part, or product found in the King James Version of the New Testament, focusing only on the current, most accepted opinions about identification and translation and the botany associated with each. I will then review the context in which each term is used and share insights on how the botany associated with the suggested identification or translation of the term can inform one's understanding of the text in which it is used.[3] Any exegesis that accompanies each entry will largely derive from my own understanding.

KJV Botanical Term

Aloes (*aloē*, ἀλόη, 1x): A plant or plant product that was mixed with myrrh and used for preparing bodies for burial in Jesus's time. Nicodemus brought "about an hundred pound weight" (ca. 75 US pounds) of the mixture to help Joseph of Arimathea prepare the crucified Christ for burial by wrapping the body in linen layered with the "spices" (John 19:38–40). The exact species from which "aloes" were derived has been a matter of debate. Aloe is also mentioned in the Old Testament, typically in the context of being mixed with myrrh to make a desirable fragrance (Song of Solomon 4:14; Proverbs 7:17; Psalm 45:8; compare Numbers 24:6). Most agree the Old Testament aloe is derived from some species of *Aquillaria*, most likely *Aquillaria agallocha*, which is native to East Africa and northern India and commonly known as eaglewood, or perhaps *Santalum album* (sandalwood), which is likewise native to India. Wood and extracts from both species were highly prized for making fragrances. Some feel that because both the Old Testament and New Testament aloes were used in combination with myrrh, they are likely the same species, but most conclude that the New Testament aloe used to prepare the body of Christ was more likely derived from *Aloe succortrina*, a true aloe that is native to the island of Socotra (Arabian Sea), because the oil extracted from the fleshy, succulent leaves of the plant has a long history of use for embalming in ancient Egypt and elsewhere. Being both rare and imported, any of these possible species for the source of the aloes used to prepare Christ's body for interment would have been very costly. The large amount of the precious commodity donated by Nicodemus indicates the respect he must have held for Jesus. Thus, worshipful men offered precious plant products both to welcome Christ into the world and to bid him farewell (Matthew 2:11; John 19:39).

Anise (*anēthon*, ἄνηθον, 1x): A plant tithed in New Testament times. The Greek term translated as "anise" in the KJV likely does not refer to the common anise, *Pimpinella anisum*. Though it is a valuable plant cultivated in temperate climates to be used as a condiment and spice, it does not appear to have been planted in Bible lands during New Testament times. Rather, the Greek *anēthon* more likely refers to the common dill, *Anethum graveolens*. This versatile member of the carrot family has been cultivated in the Levant from Neolithic times and grows wild there as well. Leaves of the plants were, as today, a popular pickling agent, and the aromatic seeds and seed oil were used as a flavoring and medicinally as a carminative. The Talmud requires tithes to be paid on the greens, stems, and pods of dill.[4] Christ endorsed the payment of tithes in "anise" but condemned those who did so as a show of piety while omitting the "weightier matters of the law" such as "judgment [justice], mercy, and faith" (Matthew 23:23).

Barley (*krithē*, κριθή, 3x): A cereal crop domesticated and cultivated since Neolithic times throughout much of the ancient Near East. Barley continues to be an important cereal crop throughout much of the world today. The most common species of cultivated barley, *Hordeum vulgare*, includes both two-rowed and six-rowed varieties, differentiated by the number of fertile or grain-producing flowers found on the seed spike. Anciently, barley, along with wheat, constituted the primary cereal staples from Egypt through the Levant to Mesopotamia and Asia Minor. Though barley makes inferior flour and bread compared to wheat, being lower in gluten protein, it was still widely grown because it tolerates a much wider range of climates and soil types and ripens much earlier than wheat.

In New Testament times, barley loaves were the common or poor man's fare. Thus, it is not surprising that the peasant "lad," whose donation fed the five thousand, had but five barley loaves of bread (John 6:9, 13), nor that three measures of barely could be purchased for the price of one measure of wheat (Revelation 6:6).

Bramble (*batos*, βάτος, 1x); bush (*batos*, βάτος, 4x): A thorny bush, most likely *Rubus sanguineus* or *Rubus ulmifolius*, both native to the Holy Land and commonly called "holy bramble" or "wild blackberries." These *Rubus* species are evergreens with long, typically intertwining branches armed with sharp, hooked prickles and often growing in dense thickets. They produce a small, edible, black-colored berry.

Christ illustrated the truth that one can discern a person's nature by what that person produces when he explained that one does not gather grapes from a bramble bush (Luke 6:44). New Testament writers used this same Greek word for bramble to refer to the burning bush out of which God spoke to Moses (Mark 12:26; Luke 20:37; Acts 7:30, 35).

Briers: *See* Thistle.

Cinnamon (*kinamōmon*, κινάμωμον, 1x): A spice and perfume made from the inner bark or extracted oil of the Ceylon cinnamon tree, *Cinnamomum zeylanicum*, native to Ceylon and India. The inner bark is stripped from the younger shoots of mature trees and rolled and dried into cylinders, or "quills," for trade. The dried quills can be ground into spice. Cinnamon oil can be extracted from both the bark and the mature fruit of the tree.

In biblical times, cinnamon was a costly and prized import. It was a principal component of the "holy anointing oil" Moses was commanded to make for anointing the tabernacle, its furnishings, and those who ministered therein (Exodus 30:22–33) and was used by the temptress to perfume her bed (Proverbs 7:17; compare Song of Solomon 4:14). John the Revelator foresaw that the merchants of the earth would mourn the fall of worldly Babylon, for it was an important market for their cinnamon (Revelation 18:10–15).

Corn (*sitos*, σῖτος, 1x; *kokkos*, κόκκος, 1x); corn fields (*sporimos*, σπόριμος, 3x); ears of corn (*stachus*, στάχυς, 4x); treading out corn (*aloaō*, ἀλοάω, 2x); grain (*kokkos*, κόκκος, 1x): *Corn* is a generic term used in the KJV for cereal grains such as wheat and barley. Corn in the KJV Bible should not to be confused with New World corn or maize (*Zea mays*).

The Pharisees accused Christ's disciples of breaking the law when on a Sabbath day while passing through fields of "corn" (grain), they plucked "ears of corn" to eat (Matthew 12:1; Mark 2:23; Luke 6:1; compare Mark 4:28). In speaking of his impending death, Christ explained to his disciples that unless a "corn," or kernel of wheat, is placed in the ground and dies, it cannot bring forth fruit (John 12:24). In reviewing the history of Israel's rejection of God and his covenants, Stephen recounted how Jacob sent their forefathers to Egypt during a famine because he had heard there was "corn" (grain), there (Acts 7:12). As he justified the necessity of receiving material support for their ministry from the people of the church, Paul reminded them that just as the law of Moses prohibited the muzzling of the oxen that "treadeth out the corn," or threshed the grain, so too those in the service of God should not be denied sustenance from those among whom they labored (1 Corinthians 9:9; compare 1 Timothy 5:18).

Cummin (*kuminon*, κύμινον, 1x): *Cuminum cyminium*, a member of the carrot family. Cummin has a long history of cultivation and use in the Near East. Ground seeds from the plant are used as a flavoring for breads, soups, and other dishes, and oil extracted from the seeds can be used in perfumes. It was used medicinally as an antispasmodic and was thought to be good for the eyes.

Cummin was one of the plants tithed under Mosaic law. Christ accused certain scribes and Pharisees of punctiliously paying "tithe of . . . cummin" while neglecting the more important virtues such as justice, mercy, and faith (Matthew 23:23).

Figs (*sukon*, σῦκον, 3x); **fig tree** (*sukē*, συκῆ, 16x); **unripe figs** (*olunthos*, ὄλυνθος, 1x): The common fig, *Ficus carica*. Figs have long grown both wild and cultivated in orchards and private residences throughout Bible lands, and they have been an important staple in the Levant from as early as Neolithic times, throughout the biblical era, and into modern times. Fig plants vary in shape from shrubs to trees, depending on growing conditions and varieties. In nature they rely on a symbiotic relationship with a species of wasp for pollination, though varieties exist that require no fertilization to produce fruit. In the Mediterranean climate, figs can yield two crops of fruit each year: winter figs that are ripe by June and summer figs that ripen in August or September. Ripe winter figs may persist on a tree even when summer figs are just beginning to form. Because of their high sugar content, fig fruits can be dried and stored for long periods of time. Anciently, dried fig cakes were regularly prepared to be used between fruitless seasons.

Figs are the first plant mentioned by name in the Bible (Genesis 3:7) and find frequent reference thereafter. They are listed as one of the seven species that characterized the land of Israel (Deuteronomy 8:8). Abigail sent two hundred fig cakes to appease David for her husband's ill-advised arrogance (1 Samuel 25:3–18), and Isaiah prescribed "a lump of figs" to treat King Hezekiah's near-fatal boil (2 Kings 20:7).

Christ used figs to teach his disciples. To illustrate that false prophets cannot bring forth good works, he rhetorically asked if men gather figs (*sukon*) of thistles (Matthew 7:15–20; compare James 3:12). In the Olivet Discourse, he used a parable of a fig tree (*sukē*) to invite his disciples to be observant of the signs of his millennial return, explaining that just as they know summer is imminent when they see a fig tree put forth new branches and leaves, so too they can know his return is at hand when they see the prophecies he had just shared with them fulfilled (Matthew 24:32–33). On one of his final journeys from Bethany to Jerusalem, Christ cursed a barren fig tree, which subsequently withered and died, to provide a manifestation not only of his power but also the power that his disciples could exercise through faith and prayer (Matthew 20:19–22; Mark 11:12–14, 20–24). John used the imagery of unripe figs (*olunthos*) falling from a tree in a strong wind to illustrate how the stars would fall from heaven as part of the natural catastrophes that would accompany the opening of the sixth seal (Revelation 6:13).

Flax (*linon*, λίνον, 1x); linen (*linon*, λίνον, 1x); linen cloth (*sindón*, σινδών, 5x); fine linen (*bussos*, βύσσος, 5x); linen clothes (*othonion*, ὀθόνιον, 5x): The common flax, *Linum usitatissimum*. Flax is perhaps the oldest source of plant textile fibers. Cloth made from flax is best known as linen, a term derived from the Greek *linon*. It is an annual herb that grows up to three feet tall and has long narrow leaves and showy blue flowers. Cultivation of flax for textiles likely originated in the Near East and is thought to have begun as early as the late Neolithic period.

Linen is mentioned throughout the Bible, first appearing as the fine fabric in which Pharaoh dressed Joseph as he appointed him second in command over Egypt (Genesis 41:37–42). Fine linen could be regarded as a sign of wealth and materialism (e.g., Luke 16:19; Revelation 18:12, 16), while pure and white linen clothed angels and saints (e.g., Revelation 15:6; 19:8, 14). In the KJV the Greek *linon* is translated as "flax" only once, when Matthew explains how, when Jesus charged those whom he had healed to not speak of the miracle, he was fulfilling a prophecy of Isaiah, wherein the prophet foretold that the mortal Messiah's passing would be so quiet, gentle, and unnoticed that it would not even "quench" a "smoking flax" (Matthew 12:14–20). In this context the "smoking flax" should be understood as a smoldering linen wick—one that even the smallest stir of wind could extinguish. Linen is likely the fabric that constituted the "swaddling clothes" that warmed and bound up the newborn Christ (Luke 2:7, 12) and certainly the fabric in which he was buried (Matthew 27:59; Mark 15:46; Luke 23:53; 24:12; John 19:40; 20:5–7).

Frankincense (*libanos*, λίβανος, 2x): The aromatic oleo-gum resins extracted from the resin ducts found in the bark of several species of trees in the genus *Boswellia*, including *B. sacra* (found in Arabia and Somalia), *B. papyrifera* (found in Northeast Africa), *B. frereana* (found in Somalia), and *B. serrata* (found in India). Anciently, the precious gum resin produced by these trees was used in a myriad of ways. For example, it was burnt alone or mixed with other materials to make incense for votive and ceremonial purposes; burnt as a fumigant to cleanse and reduce odors; powdered to make fragrant talc and cosmetics; and burnt, chewed, eaten, or powdered to treat a wide variety of maladies such as infertility, bags under the eyes, hemorrhoids, broken bones, and gout. Owing to the remote and very restricted habitat in which the trees grow, the tightly controlled and costly import of the gum resin, and the demand for the product, frankincense was typically a rare and expensive commodity. It often commanded fabulous prices in the markets of the Roman Empire, at times equated with that of gold, and was considered a gift worthy of emperors and kings.

The wise men from the East brought frankincense as a gift for the infant Jesus (Matthew 2:11), not only reflecting the stature and reverence they felt the child deserved, but also significantly enriching the humble peasant family. John the Revelator describes the weeping and wailing that will arise from merchants that deal with costly commodities such as frank-incense when they realize that the sudden fall of worldly and extravagant Babylon deprives them of a market lustful for their precious wares (Revelation 18:10–15).

Gall (*cholé*, χολή, 2x): Likely bitter herbs or some other bitter substance. True gall is ac-tually the bile produced in the bile ducts of animals and is very bitter. Hence, *gall* has become associated with bitterness (e.g., Acts 8:23). Matthew records that Christ was offered "vinegar to drink mingled with gall" (Matthew 27:34), while Mark's parallel account reports he was offered "wine mingled with myrrh" (Mark 15:23), suggesting that the gall Matthew spoke of was actually a bitter herb such as myrrh.

Grain: *See* Corn.

Grapes (*staphulē*, σταφυλή, 3x); **vine** (*ampelos*, ἄμπελος, 9x); **vinegar** (*oinos*, οἶνος, 1x; *oxos*, ὄξος, 5x); **vineyard** (*ampelón*, ἀμπελών, 20x); **vineyard, dresser of** (*ampelourgos*, ἀμπελουργός, 1x); **wine** (*oinos*, οἶνος, 30x); **wine, given to** (*paroinos*, πάροινος, 2x); **wine, excess of** (*oinophlugia*, οἰνοφλυγία, 1x); **wine, new** (*gleukos*, γλεῦκος, 1x): The common grape, *Vitis vinefera*. The grape is a shrubby deciduous vine that sends forth from its base many long, sprawling, and climbing branches that can, under ideal circumstances, reach up to thirty feet in length and grow up to twelve feet in a year. The leaves are typically fist-sized and shaped with three to five large, toothed lobes, but size and shape can vary consider-ably. The bee-pollinated flowers mature into delicious berries that grow in clusters and can vary widely in size, color, texture, and flavor depending on variety and edaphic conditions. Grapes grow marvelously in Bible lands, with reports of plum-sized grapes growing in clus-ters that average ten to twelve pounds not uncommon. Fresh grapes, raisins, and wine have been primary components of both the sustenance and economy of the people in the Levant since the dawn of history.

Planting a vineyard was one of Noah's earliest acts after leaving the ark (Genesis 9:20), and grapes are listed among the seven species that characterize the bounties of the promised land (Deuteronomy 8:7–8). The annual grape harvest during biblical times was a season of great rejoicing as the fruit was gathered and then eaten fresh, dried into raisins, or, most commonly, processed into wine by treading out the fruit's sweet juice in the winepress or vat. Vocabulary associated with grapes and viticulture abounds in the Bible, such as *vines*, *vineyards*, *wine*, *vinegar*, *winevat*, *winefat*, *winepress*, *vinedressers*, *winebibbers*, and *being drunken with wine*. Flourishing vines were a type for divine favor (e.g., Amos 9:13), and dif-ficulties in viticulture a sign of divine displeasure and punishment (e.g., Isaiah 5:1–6; 16:10).

In the New Testament, John indicates that Christ began the miracles of his ministry with the transforming of water into wine at the wedding in Cana (John 2:1–11). Christ mentioned vines and wine regularly in his teachings. He identified himself as the "true vine" and his disciples as "the branches" that would be pruned (purged) to bring forth more fruit or taken away if unproductive. He promised that those branches that would "abide" in him would be empowered and made fruitful, but they would be cast off and burned if they did not (John 15:1–8). Vineyards provided the setting for several of Christ's parables, including the parable of the laborers hired throughout the day (Matthew 20:1–16), the parable of the two sons (Matthew 21:28–32), the parable of the wicked husbandmen (Matthew 21:33–41; Mark 12:1–9; Luke 20:9–16), and the parable of the barren fig tree (Luke 6:1–10), in which figs and grapes were cultivated together, a common practice even today. In the parable of the good Samaritan, the rescuer poured a mixture of wine and oil into the victim's wounds to treat them (Luke 10:30–34). In the Sermon on the Mount, Jesus taught that one could identify false prophets by their actions and teachings, or "fruits," explaining that one does not gather "grapes of thorns" (Matthew 7:16; compare Luke 6:44; James 3:12).

In explaining to John the Baptist's disciples why his followers did not observe the fasting practices of the Pharisees, Christ reminded the questioners that one does not put "new wine" into "old bottles" lest the bottles break and the wine be lost (Matthew 9:14–17; Mark 2:18–22; Luke 5:33–39). The wine bottles in this metaphor were made of partially tanned animal skins that, when new, are pliable and elastic but become dry and brittle with age. If one were to put new wine into old bottles, the gas given off as the wine fermented would burst the brittle containers. Accordingly, new wine is stored only in new, supple bottles that can expand as the liquor ferments. The metaphor illustrates that just as the rigid teachings of the Pharisees could not accommodate Christ's gospel, Christ's disciples need not conform to Pharisaical practices.

As Jesus instituted the sacrament at the Last Supper, he used wine ("fruit of the vine") to represent his "blood of the new testament" shed "for the remission of sins" (Matthew 26:27–29; compare Mark 14:23–25; Luke 22:17–18). On the cross, Jesus was offered vinegar after earlier refusing vinegar mixed with gall according to Matthew (Matthew 27:34, 48) and wine mixed with myrrh according to Mark (Mark 15:23, 36; compare Luke 23:36; John 19:29–30). *Vinegar* in these passages refers to sour or acidic wine that was a common drink among the Roman soldiers. Gall is an excretion of the liver and myrrh a bitter-tasting oleo-gum-resin produced by *Commiphora* sp. (see "Myrrh" herein). Some speculate that the "gall" or "myrrh" in these accounts may actually refer to wormwood (see "Wormwood" herein) or some other bitter substance, but whatever constituted the concoction, its purpose seems to have been to dull the senses of the one being crucified, perhaps suggesting why the atoning Christ refused to drink the mixture but partook of the unmixed "vinegar" (actually sour wine).

Those following Nazarite vows, such as John the Baptist, were prohibited from partaking of any product of the vine (Luke 1:15; compare Luke 7:33; Numbers 6:1–3). On the day of Pentecost some thought those speaking in different languages were drunk, being "full of new wine" rather than the gift of tongues (Acts 2:13). Paul counseled the faithful Romans to not drink wine if it would cause others to stumble or be offended (Romans 14:21) and the Ephesians to "be not drunk with wine" (Ephesians 5:18; compare 1 Peter 4:3). He admonished that bishops and deacons should not be given to wine, but that a little wine could be helpful for the stomach and certain infirmities (1 Timothy 3:3, 8; 5:23; Titus 1:7).

In Revelation, an angel warned John that those who "worship the beast" would drink the "wine of the wrath of God," and a subsequent angel likened the wicked to ripened clusters of grapes that would be gathered and trodden in the winepress of the wrath of God when the "Son of man" appeared (Revelation 14:10–20). Ultimately, Babylon would receive the "wine of the fierceness of [God's] wrath" for imbibing in the wine of her fornication (Revelation 16:19; 17:2; compare Revelation 18:3, 13).

Grass (*chortos*, χόρτος, 10x); hay (*chortos*, χόρτος, 1x): *Grass* is a general term for species of Poaceae, a large and nearly worldwide family of monocot plants. The Greek *chortos* can also refer to hay or herbage in general. With its wide variety of climates and ecosystems, the Holy Land today supports over four hundred species of grass, though some are recent imports to the region. While luxuriant meadows and pastures of grass are rare and typically must be maintained through human cultivation or grow near water sources, hardy wild grasses can be found throughout the land, from the dry deserts of the Negev, through the rolling hills of the Shephelah, in the rugged mountains of the Judean wilderness, among the forests of Bashan, and, most abundantly, in the more fertile and wet northern environs. In the harsher and drier climates, many grass species go through their entire life cycle in a very short period of time, sprouting as precipitation permits, maturing, dropping their seeds, and then disappearing from the landscape in a matter of weeks.

Jesus used the imagery of such transient grass—"which to day is, and to morrow is cast in the oven" but which, like "the lilies of the field," is beautifully clothed by God—to encourage his followers to trust that God will likewise clothe them (Matthew 6:28–31; compare Luke 12:27–28). James similarly likened the fleeting nature of wealth to grass that withers in the sun (James 1:10–11), and so Peter also, quoting imagery from Isaiah, assured that, like grass, the "glory of man" will fade and wither, "but the word of the Lord endureth forever" (1 Peter 1:24–25; compare Isaiah 40:6–8). The five thousand miraculously fed with five loaves and two fishes sat on grass as they received their portion from the disciples (Matthew 14:19–20; John 6:9–12). John the Revelator saw "all green grass" burnt up at the sounding of an angel's trumpet, while the devouring locusts unleashed by another angel's trumpet were commanded to not hurt "the grass of the earth" as they attacked those that did not have "the seal of God in their foreheads" (Revelation 8:1–7; 9:1–4). Paul listed *hay*, perhaps referring to dried grass used to fill chinks in walls, as one of the possible building materials that individuals might use to build upon the foundation of Jesus Christ, warning that whatever they built upon that foundation would eventually be tested by fire to their great loss or reward (1 Corinthians 3:10–15).

Hay: *See* Grass.

Herbs (*lachanon*, λάχανον, 4x; *botané*, βοτάνη, 1x): A general term for herbs, garden plants, or vegetables. Jesus likened the future of the kingdom of heaven to a mustard plant that, though it grows from the "least" or smallest "of all seeds," eventually matures into the "greatest among herbs" (Matthew 13:31–32; compare Mark 4:31–32). Christ chastised the Pharisees for piously paying tithes in herbs while ignoring important virtues such as justice and love (Luke 11:42). Paul admonished the Romans not to dispute with nor despise one who "eateth herbs" (meaning vegetarians), thinking such a diet is required by the law (Romans 14:1–3). To the Hebrews, Paul explained that those who fall away are like poor soil that does not benefit from the rains of heaven and bears only "thorns and briars" that will be burned, while those who stay true to the faith are like good earth that "drinketh in the rain" and brings forth "herbs" for those who tend it, thus obtaining the blessing of God (Hebrews 6:4–9).

Hyssop (*hussópos*, ὕσσωπος, 2x): Likely *Origanum syriacum*, the Syrian hyssop or marjoram, but the identification is not certain. In some biblical contexts, *hyssop* may refer to other taxon or be a generic term for a group of plants. The Syrian hyssop grows among shrubs, typically in stony ground. Shrubby at the base and more herbaceous at the top, the plant can grow up to three feet tall and has hairy branches and thick, oblong to elliptical, hairy leaves. It is known as *za'atar* among the Arabs and is used in teas and as a spice.

In the Old Testament, hyssop is used in purification rites as a brush for sprinkling water and sacrificial blood (e.g., Exodus 12:22; Leviticus 14:4, 6, 52) and as a purifying agent (e.g., Psalm 51:7; Leviticus 14:52). Paul reminded the Hebrews that the blood Moses sprinkled, using hyssop, over the people, the tabernacle, and the book of the law was a type for the redeeming blood shed by Christ (Hebrews 9:11–20). John records that at one point during the Crucifixion, Christ was offered a vinegar-sopped sponge "upon hyssop" (John 19:29). Matthew and Mark have the sponge being placed on a "reed" (Matthew 27:48; Mark 15:36), which leads some to conclude that the hyssop in John's context may refer to the long stem of a reed grass (see "Reed" herein), such as Sorghum (*Sorghum bicolor*) or Giant Reed (*Arundo donax*).

Lilies (*krinon*, κρίνον, 2x): Likely a general term referring to several species of wildflowers, especially the crown anemone (*Anemone coronaria*). There are two true lilies reported to grow in Bible lands, the Madonna, or white lily (*Lilium candidum*), and the Chalcedonian, or red martagon lily (*Lilium chalcedonicum*). Both, however, are relatively rare and restricted to mountainous regions and thus not likely candidates for the "lilies of the field" that Jesus used to illustrate the effortless beauty of God's creation and the care he gives it (Matthew 6:28–30; see Luke 12:27–28). In contrast, the crown anemone is a common and beautiful wildflower that produces brilliant scarlet flowers that, along with other showy native flowers, fill the fields of the Holy Land with an explosion of color in early spring and then fade as summer heat desiccates the land. Jesus encouraged his disciples to trust in God's care by reasoning with them that if God would clothe the transitory grass and lilies of the field in such splendor, "how much more will he clothe you . . . ?" (Luke 12:27–28; see Matthew 6:28–30).

Linen: *See* Flax.

Mint (*héduosmon*, ἡδύοσμον, 2x): Likely horse mint (*Mentha longifolia*). Several mint species are native to Bible lands, with horse mint being the most common. It is a large species of mint that can grow up to three feet tall; produces relatively small, toothed, lanceolate to oblong leaves on stems covered with tiny hairs; and has small lilac-colored flowers clustered in terminal spikes. Mints are typically found growing along watercourses, swamps, and ditches. The delightful aroma and flavor of mints that derive from their essential oils have made them a popular condiment and flavoring for meats, soups, salads, and teas. Horse mint was also prized for its medicinal properties used in infusions as a carminative, stimulant, and mild analgesic. Along with anise and cummin, mint was one of the plants tithed under Mosaic law. Christ chastised certain scribes and Pharisees for dutifully paying tithes on these commodities but ignoring the more important virtues of justice, mercy, and faith (Matthew 23:23; compare Luke 11:42).

Mustard (*sinapi*, σίναπι, 5x): Likely black mustard (*Brassica nigra*). Historically, the taxonomic identity of the New Testament "mustard" has been an issue of considerable debate. The white mustard (*Sinapis alba*), the charlock mustard (*Sinapis arvensis*), and even non-mustards such as the toothbrush tree (*Salvadora persica*) and the pokeberry (*Phytolacca decandra*) have all been proposed as possible identities for the plant. Today, however, most conclude that black mustard is the likely taxon of Jesus's mustard parables, for it is a common and conspicuous herb that grows abundantly in the wild and was cultivated in the Galilee during New Testament times. Black mustard has been reported to grow up to ten feet and typically reaches three to six feet in height. It produces large leaves, mostly at the base, and, at the ends of its many branches, a plethora of small, brilliant yellow flowers that mature into many-seeded elongated siliques. The tiny seeds are ground to produce the mustard powder and oil used since biblical times as a flavoring, condiment, and medicament.

Jesus likened the future growth of "the kingdom of Heaven" to a mustard grain or seed that, though small at first, even "the least of all seeds," matures to be "the greatest among herbs," even becoming a "tree" in which birds can "lodge" (Matthew 13:31–32; compare Mark 4:31–32; Luke 13:19). Hyperbole is perhaps involved in this parable, for though the seeds are small, they are not the smallest or "least" among seeds. Moreover, being an annual herb, black mustard is not a true tree. Still, the mature plants can be large and sturdy enough to support the small birds that forage on the seeds. Using a mustard seed as a proverbial type for the incredibly small, Jesus promised his disciples that even if they could have only as much "faith as a grain of mustard," they would still have the power to "remove" a "mountain," a proverbial type for the incredibly large (Matthew 17:20; compare Luke 17:6).

Myrrh (*smurna*, σμύρνα, 2x); myrrh, mingled with (*smurnizó*, σμυρνίζω, 1x): The aromatic oil/gum resin extracted from various species of *Commiphora* such as the African myrrh (*C. myrrha*), the Abyssinian myrrh (*C. abyssinica*), or the Indian myrrh (*C. kataf*). *Commiphora* are native to Arabia, Somalia, and Ethiopia. They are typically thick-branched shrubs or small trees that thrive in rocky and relatively arid soil. Along their robust branches, small leaves, divided into three tiny egg-shaped leaflets, nestle among stout thorns. Like other members of the Burseraceae family, such as frankincense, *Commiphora* species produce an oily gum resin that, though bitter to the taste, is highly priced for its aromatic, cosmetic, and medicinal properties. Ancient Egyptians burned myrrh resin in their temples, used it to make perfumes, and embalmed their dead with it.

In biblical times, myrrh was a precious trade commodity (e.g., Genesis 37:25; 43:11), a component of the "holy anointing oil" (Exodus 30:23–25), and an enticing perfume (e.g., Proverbs 7:17; Psalm 45:8; Song of Solomon 1:13). Myrrh appears at both the birth and death of Jesus. It was among the costly gifts brought by the wise men to honor and enrich the Christ child and his family (Matthew 2:11). Three decades later, while suffering upon the cross, Christ refused to drink the analgesic "wine mingled with myrrh" offered by his tormentors (Mark 15:23). The grieving Joseph and Nicodemus layered costly myrrh and aloes within the linen wrappings used to bind the Savior's body for the tomb (John 19:39).

Oil: *See* Olive tree(s).

Ointment: *See* Olive tree(s).

Olive tree(s) (*elaia*, ἐλαία, 3x); **olive berries** (*elaia*, ἐλαία, 1x); **olives, Mount of** (*oros tōn Elaiōn*, ὄρος τῶν Ἐλαιῶν, 7x; *orous tōn Elaiōn*, Ὄρους τῶν Ἐλαιῶν, 2x); **Olivet** (*Elaiōn*, Ἐλαιῶν, 1x); **oil** (*elaion*, ἔλαιον, 11x); **ointment** (*muron*, μύρον, 13x): The common olive, *Olea europea*. The olive is a magnificent tree that thrives even in the rocky and poorer soils of the Bible lands. It typically grows fifteen to twenty-five feet high, and the gnarled trunks of the oldest trees can exceed three feet in diameter. Gray to blue-green, oblong to elliptical leaves cover its many branches, and its small white flowers mature into one-seeded drupes, typically about one inch in length. The slow-growing trees can live for centuries, producing fruit even when the trunks are hollow and the larger branches ancient. The tenacious and tortured appearance of the oldest olive trees seems to characterize the Holy Land's people, culture, history, geography, and ecology.

Cultivated olives, those producing the best fruit, are propagated by grafting and from biblical times until today are found throughout the country in large commercial olive-yards, small village orchards, and private home gardens. The earliest archaeological evidence of olive use currently dates to the fourth millennium BC. Anciently the olive harvest was an important family and community activity. Ripe fruit was gathered in the autumn by beating on the limbs of the trees with sticks and placing the fallen fruit into baskets. Then various kinds of heavy, cleverly engineered stone and wooden implements were used to crush the drupes and press and separate the precious oil from the mash.

Arguably, no other plant has played a greater role in the sustenance, economy, and daily life of biblical people. Its fruit was eaten from ripe and cured to green and pickled. Its wood was prized by craftsmen for its hardness, beauty, and polished luster. Most importantly, its versatile oil permeated the daily life of every individual. It was used to make holy ointments to anoint kings and priests; burned in lamps to provide light for households, businesses, and the temple; poured on the sick for anointing; used as a base and solvent for perfumes, spices, cosmetics, medicines, incenses, and aromatics; applied as a dressing for skin and hair; and copiously consumed when used in food preparation, flavoring, and cooking.

Thus, as one might expect, olives and olive products are mentioned throughout the Bible. For example, in the Old Testament a dove brought an olive leaf to Noah to inform him that the waters of the deluge had abated (Genesis 8:11), and the olive was one of the seven species that characterized the promised land (Deuteronomy 8:8). Most, if not all, biblical references to oil, ointment, or anointing indicate the use of olive oil. Thus, Jacob poured olive oil over the memorial pillar he constructed at Bethel (Genesis 28:18). Likewise, the tabernacle and later the temple were continuously illuminated by the burning of pure olive oil (Exodus 27:20), and olive oil even constituted an essential part of many kinds of offerings (e.g., Leviticus 2:1–7, 15; 6:21).

Similarly, in the New Testament olives and olive products are regularly mentioned. For example, oil was used to anoint the sick (Mark 6:13; James 5:14), and Paul taught that God anointed the Son "with the oil of gladness" (Hebrews 1:8–9). It likely was an olive oil–based ointment that at least one or perhaps two devout women used to anoint Jesus as they reverenced and worshipped him in preparation for his "burial" (Matthew 26:6–13; Mark 14:3–9; Luke 7:36–50; John 12:1–9),[5] and the good Samaritan used oil medicinally as he poured it into the wounds of the newfound neighbor he rescued on the road to Jericho (Luke 10:29–37). Oil is also mentioned as a trade good in parables and visions (e.g., Luke 16:6; Revelation 6:6; 18:13) and was the critical commodity in Christ's parable of the ten virgins who were awaiting the arrival of the tarrying bridegroom. The five foolish virgins who failed to bring extra olive oil appear to represent those of the faithful who wish to rejoice with the Messiah when he returns but fail to be adequately vigilant and prepared for his delayed coming. The olive oil itself perhaps symbolizes the obedience, service, study, and devotion requisite to knowing and being known by the Lord. Such oil cannot be borrowed from another or acquired at a moment's notice, but rather must be obtained before his coming through individual effort (Matthew 25:1–13).

Olive trees are also used metaphorically in the New Testament. Paul likened Israel to an olive tree and the gentile converts to wild branches grafted into its roots (Romans 11:17–24). Similarly, the two prophets who minister shortly before the appearance of the Messiah are identified as the "two olive trees" of Zechariah's vision (Revelation 11:3–4; compare Zechariah 4:11–14). Interestingly, James uses the absurdity of expecting a fig tree to produce olives to the foolishness of the faithful not controlling their tongues (James 3:2–18).

Considering the import of olives and olive products in the lives of biblical peoples, it seems appropriate that the Mount of Olives, so named for the olive orchards on its slopes, was the location for the beginning of Christ's triumphal entry (Matthew 21:1–16; Mark 11:1–14; Luke 19:29–40), the site where he taught his disciples of the future trials and triumphs of his kingdom (Matthew 24:3–51; Mark 13:3–37; compare Luke 21:37), the background for his atoning suffering, and the location of his ascension (Matthew 26:30–46; Mark 14:26–42; Luke 22:39–46; Acts 1:9–12).

Olivet: *See* Olive tree(s).

Palm (*phoinix*, φοῖνιξ, 2x): The date palm, *Phoenix dactylifera.* The date palm is one of the most ancient and characteristic of all fruit trees in the Holy Land. Typically growing thirty to sixty feet tall, its unbranched trunk terminates in an explosion of fibrous pinnate fronds six to nine feet long. Female trees produce huge clusters, often weighing thirty to fifty pounds, of single-seeded fruits that are prized for their sweet, fleshy pulp. The archaeological evidence for date cultivation dates back to about 4000 BC in the Levant. Historically, every part of the date tree was used. Date fronds were used for thatching and fence building. The fibrous leaves were formed into household utensils, and also used for weaving mats and baskets. The massive trunks provided timber for fences and rafters. Rope was made from date tree fibers. Most importantly, the fruit and honey derived from it were important parts of the biblical diet.

Moses identified dates, referring to their "honey," as one of the seven species that were indicative of the bounty of the promised land (Deuteronomy 8:8). Carvings of date leaves and trunks were used as architectural embellishment on Solomon's temple (1 Kings 6:29, 32; compare Ezekiel 40:31). Jericho is called the "city of palm trees" (Deuteronomy 34:3), and the Hebrew word for dates, *Tamar,* was a common name for biblical places and persons (e.g., Genesis 14:7; 38:6; 2 Samuel 13:1; 2 Chronicles 8:4). "Bethany," the home of Martha, Mary, and Lazarus and site of some of the Savior's most moving experiences (e.g., John 11–12), means "the house of dates." During the Feast of Tabernacles, the covenant people were instructed to take "boughs of goodly trees," including "branches of palm trees, . . . [and] rejoice before the Lord your God seven days" (Leviticus 23:40). Thus, the waving of palm fronds became a practice of rejoicing and praise. Today Christians celebrate "Palm Sunday," commemorating Christ's triumphal entry into Jerusalem, wherein those praising him "took branches of palm trees, and went forth to him" crying "Hosanna: Blessed is the King of Israel" (John 12:13). John saw in vision great multitudes from every nation, kindred, people, and tongue likewise holding "palms in their hands" as they worshipped God and the "Lamb" (Revelation 7:9).

Reed (*kalamos,* κάλαμος, 11x): A generic term for exceptionally tall, slender grass species that generally grow in water or marshy ground. They typically have robust stems that are often hollow or segmented. Depending on context, the Greek root *kalamos,* translated as "reed" in the KJV, can refer to an actual reed plant, a reed pen, a reed staff, or a reed measuring rod. Several species of grasses native to Bible lands fit the description of reeds. Four species of the common reed, *Phragmites* sp., grow in the Levant, with *Phragmites australis* being the most abundant. They are common in swamps and marshy areas where they range from three to fifteen feet in height. The hollow and jointed canes produced by these reeds were used for mats, pens, walking sticks, hedges, and even home construction. The giant reed grass, *Arundo donax,* is an especially large reed that can grow up to twenty feet tall and has stems as thick as three inches in diameter. Along the Jordan River and some coastal regions of the Dead Sea, it can grow in nearly impenetrable thickets. Its canes have historically been used for such items as measuring rods, walking sticks, fishing rods, and musical pipes. Durrah or Indian millet, *Sorghum bicolor,* is another reedlike grass that typically grows up to six feet tall in the Holy Land. The stems have a thick pith, like sugarcane, but it is not sweet. It is cultivated both in the lowlands and mountains as a summer crop that does not need irrigation. Its globular seeds, also known as Jerusalem corn, have historically been used for animal feed and to make a coarse bread and meal. Cattails (*Typha* sp.), though not grasses, are another genus of reedlike plants native to the Holy Land. These aquatic or semiaquatic species can grow nine to twelve feet tall and have long sticklike fruiting stems. Their leaves are used in basketwork and mat making.

Jesus implied that John the Baptist was not a "reed shaken with the wind," perhaps indicating that he was not one moved to-and-fro by every gust of adversity or popular culture—he was not a waverer (Matthew 11:7; Luke 7:24). Matthew saw in Jesus's charge to those he healed to "not make him known" a fulfillment of Isaiah's messianic servant prophecy wherein the prophet described the ministry of the servant as being so nurturing, compassionate, and quiet in passing that it would not break a "bruised" or fragile reed (Matthew 12:15–20; compare Isaiah 42:1–3). When the thin siliceous walls of reeds are bruised, even the smallest gust of wind can topple them over. In mocking the kingship of Jesus, the Roman soldiers, in Matthew's record, put "a reed in his right hand" to imitate a king's scepter (Matthew 27:29–30), while Mark indicates they smote him upon the head with it (Mark 15:19). Later, a reed was used to hoist a sponge soaked in vinegar (sour wine) to the lips of the suffering Savior on the cross (Matthew 27:48; Mark 15:36). In his apocalyptic vision, John was given a reed measuring rod to measure the temple and its altar and worshippers, with the measuring seeming to be an assurance of protection in the face of impending danger (Revelation 11:1). Later in the revelation, he talked with an angel holding a golden reed, which the angel used to measure the city, gates, and walls of the New Jerusalem (21:15–16). In this case, the measuring appears to illustrate the beauty and proportions of the glorious city.

Spices (*aroma*, ἄρωμα, 4x; *amomon*, ἄμωμον, 1x): A generic term for aromatic or sweet herbs. Nicodemus and Joseph of Arimathea layered spices, including aloes and myrrh, in the linen wrapped around the body of Christ to prepare him for burial (John 19:38–40). After the Sabbath, Mary Magdalene, Salome, and Mary the mother of James brought more spices intending to further "anoint him" (Mark 16:1; compare Luke 23:56; 24:1). Considering that Nicodemus and Joseph of Arimathea had already prepared Jesus's body with "an hundred pound weight," approximately 75 US pounds, of spices, the mourning women seemed to want to add their spices, not out of necessity but rather out of love and adoration. The use of such extravagant amounts of spices in royal burials is attested by Josephus (*Antiquities* 17.199; compare 2 Chronicles 16:14) and perhaps indicates that the faithful individuals preparing Jesus for burial recognized his royal station.

Spikenard (*nardos*, νάρδος, 2x): Likely the nard plant *Nardostachys jatamansi* and the oil derived from it. A native of Nepal and other parts of the Himalayas, spikenard is a short, hairy, perennial herb that produces small clusters of white to pink blossoms. An aromatic oil is produced throughout the plant and is especially abundant and fragrant in its roots. The oil was used anciently in perfumery and incense making, though modern tastes typically find its aroma unappealing. Mixed with other oils, a spikenard ointment was used to treat nervous disorders. Because of its distant origin, it was a costly commodity in the New Testament lands, typically imported in sealed alabaster containers that were broken open only for special occasions. Mary's anointing of Jesus's feet with the precious ointment, followed by the wiping of them with her hair, is one of the most intimate and tender expressions of love and devotion in all scripture (John 12:1–6; compare Mark 14:3–7; Matthew 26:6–13).

Sycamine (*sukaminos*, συκάμινος, 1x): Though its name is similar in sound in both Greek and English renditions, the biblical "sycamine" or mulberry tree (*Morus* sp.) should not be confused with the "sycomore" or sycamore fig tree (*Ficus sycomorus*) discussed below. While many species of mulberry exist throughout the world, historically two have been cultivated in Mediterranean countries: the white mulberry (*Morus alba*), originating in China and grown for its leaves that feed silkworms, and the black mulberry (*Morus nigra*), originating in Persia and cultivated for its berrylike fruit that has a sweet and sour flavor. Whereas the white mulberry is a more recent introduction into Bible lands, it is thought that the "sycamine" that Christ taught could be "plucked up" and "planted in the sea" if one had sufficient faith (Luke 17:6) was the black mulberry. Because it grows upward of thirty feet tall, with a thick crown and rigid branches, the moving of a black mulberry tree by any means would be a formidable task.

Sycomore (*sukomōrea*, συκομωραία, 1x); The sycamore fig, *Ficus sycomorus*, not to be confused with the common sycamore (*Platanus occidentalis*), the English sycamore (*Acer pseudoplatanus*), or the biblical sycamine (*Morus nigra*). In the same genus as the common fig, this robust evergreen tree produces copious quantities of figs in clusters along all of its parts, including both old and new branches and even on its trunk. Though the fruit is inferior in quality and flavor to the common fig, it is still sweet and so prodigiously produced that it was widely consumed anciently, especially among the poor. In order for the tree to produce ripe, edible figs, each wasp-fertilized fruit must be individually pierced or incised by hand at just the right stage of development, a task accomplished by sycamore tenders such as the prophet Amos (Amos 7:14). The trees can be massive, upward of forty feet tall, with trunk circumference reaching twenty feet and crowning canopies 120 feet in diameter, thus providing a perfect perch from which short spectators such as Zacchaeus could rise above the crowds to observe the passing of Jesus (Luke 19:1–6).

Tares (*zizanion*, ζιζάνιον, 8x): The bearded darnel, *Lolium temulentum*. This noxious weed grass grows exclusively in grainfields and is propagated annually by being harvested with the grain and resown with the next planting of the contaminated seed. A poisonous fungus can infect the seeds of darnel, rendering flour made from darnel-contaminated grain toxic. Consuming the contaminated flour reportedly can cause a state of drunkenness, blindness, or even death. Once mature plants produce seed heads, darnel and wheat can be easily distinguished from each other, but before going to seed, they are very similar in appearance. Moreover, the actual grains produced in the seed heads of wheat and darnel are very similar and difficult to separate after threshing. Thus, in the parable of the wheat and the tares (see Matthew 13:24–30), the fact that an enemy had sown tares in the field was not recognized until the blades had "brought forth fruit" (Matthew 13:26). While the unripe tares could have been uprooted immediately upon discovery, the wise householder feared doing so would uproot the unripe wheat as well. To avoid damaging the wheat, he instructed his servants to wait until the time of the harvest, when both the tares and wheat would be fully ripe, and only then to gather out and burn the tares first before bringing the wheat to the barn. This was certainly a labor-intensive strategy, but the only safe means whereby the wheat could be protected and cleansed of the contaminants. The parable warns that the "kingdom of heaven," which in this context appears to refer to the church, may include "tares" who are emissaries of the adversary placed to masquerade as devout members but who in truth harm the whole. The parable assures that the adversary's efforts to pollute the kingdom will come to naught when they are exposed by their ripened "fruits" and gathered for destruction while the good grain is gathered for preservation.

Thistle (*tribolos*, τρίβολος, 1x); briers (*tribolos*, τρίβολος, 1x): Thistle is a generic term for herbaceous plants from the Composite family that are armed with sharp prickles and spines. Many species of thistle grow in Bible lands, including globe thistle (*Echinops viscocus*), golden thistle (*Scolymus maculatus* and *Scolymus hispanicus*), holy thistle (*Silybum marianum*), Spanish thistle (*Centaurea iberica*), and Syrian thistle (*Notobasis syriaca*). Thistles are typically considered noxious weeds and a manifestation of the curse that came upon the ground because of the fall from Eden (Genesis 3:17–18). Christ taught that one can identify false prophets by their "fruits," meaning the results of what they say and do, illustrating the point with the observation that one does not gather figs from thistles (Matthew 7:16; compare Luke 6:44). The Epistle to the Hebrews warns that if those "once enlightened" with the "heavenly gift" fall away, it is "impossible" to "renew them again" through repentance, for in their apostasy they "crucify to themselves the Son of God afresh, and put him to open shame," just as earth or soil that has been blessed with the gift of rain from heaven but still brings forth "briers" rather than good herbs is cursed and will ultimately be burned (Hebrews 6:4–8).

Thorn(s) (*akantha*, ἄκανθα, 14x; *skolops*, σκόλοψ, 1x); thorns, of (*akanthinos*, ἀκάνθινος, 2x): A generic term for a stiff, sharp-pointed straight or curved process projecting from the stems, branches, or other parts of a plant. Zohary notes that more than seventy species of plants that produce thorns or spines grow in Bible lands and that the combined twenty Old and New Testament terms for thorns, thistles, nettles, briers, brambles, burrs, cockles, and so forth are often misidentified or arbitrarily translated in the Bible. To avoid incorrect identification, he recommends translating all such terms simply as "thorns" or "thistles" collectively.[6] Thorn-bearing species in the Levant include the evergreen Christ thorn tree (*Ziziphus spina-christi*). It can grow up to thirty feet tall and produces two short but sharp thorns, one straight the other curved, at the base of each leaf. The Christ thorn is so named for its popularity as the source for the "crown of thorns" placed by the soldiers on the Savior's head as they mocked his kingship (Matthew 27:27–31; Mark 15:17; John 19:2–3, 5), but the thorns produced by both it and its close relative, the shrubby lotus thorn (*Ziziphus lotus*), are hardly formidable. Likewise, the thorns produced by another shrubby plant that is also commonly called Christ thorn, *Paliurus spina-christi*, though sharp, are comparatively short and less than impressive. Moreover, though the flexible vines of the shrub can be readily woven into a wreath, the plant is not common around Jerusalem. A more likely candidate from which the crown of thorns would have been made is the heavily armed shrub thorny burnet (*Sacropoterium spinosum*), which is common around Jerusalem and has long been used as a protective hedge in the region. The thorns on thorny burnet are robust, long, and dense, formed as branchlets that dry and harden after flowering. Other common thorn-bearing species include herbs and shrubs such as bramble (*Rubus sanguineus*), gray nightshade (*Solanum incanum*), spiny zilla (*Zilla spinosa*), gundelia (*Gundelia tournefortii*), Syrian acanthus (*Acanthus syriacus*), buckthorn (*Rhamnus palaestina*), and boxthorn (*Lycium europaeum*), as well as trees such as pomegranate (*Punica granatum*) and acaia species (*Acacia nilotica, A. seyal, A. tortilis*).

Generally, in the New Testament thorns are used to illustrate the negative. In teaching that men should be judged by their fruits, meaning their words and works, Christ rhetorically asked, "Do men gather grapes of thorns . . . ?" (Matthew 7:16; see Luke 6:44). In the parable of the sower and the soils, he likened thorns to the "care of this world" and the "deceitfulness of riches" that can "choke" the faith and productivity out of those who "heareth the word" (Matthew 13:3–9, 18–23; see Mark 4:3–20; Luke 8:5–15). Paul lamented, but came to appreciate, what he learned from an unidentified "infirmity" that he called a "thorn in the flesh, the messenger of Satan" that buffeted and humbled him (2 Corinthians 12:7–9). To the Hebrews, he explained that heavenly watered soil that yet produces thorns is to be rejected, cursed, and burned just as are those who apostatize after having tasted the "heavenly gift" (Hebrews 6:4–8).

Vine: *See* Grapes.

Vinegar: *See* Grapes.

Vineyard: *See* Grapes.

Wheat (*sitos*, σῖτος, 12x): Wheat (*Triticum* sp.) was and is today the most important cereal crop cultivated in Bible lands. It truly is the staff of life in the Levant and the first of the seven species Moses listed to illustrate the bounties of the promised land (Deuteronomy 8:8). Wheat was first domesticated in the ancient Near East during Neolithic times and has been cultivated ever since. Though wheat taxonomy and history are topics of considerable debate and confusion among scholars, it appears that the winter wheats durum (*Triticum durum*) and emmer (*Triticum dicoccum*) were the most important species utilized during New Testament times. Both were dry farmed (grown without irrigation); sown at the beginning of the winter rains in September and October; and harvested, threshed, and winnowed during early summer, typically in late June or July. Other wheats that are or have been cultivated in the region include einkorn (*Triticum monococcum*) and bread wheat (*Triticum aestivum*). The native wild emmer (*Triticum dicoccoides*) may have also been utilized during early biblical times, though its easily shattered and hulled seeds would have been difficult to process. The Greek term *sitos* is a generic term for any kind of cereal grain but typically is understood to refer to wheat. In the KJV it is translated as "wheat" in every instance (e.g., Acts 27:38; Revelation 6:6; 18:13) except once where it is rendered "corn" (Acts 7:12).

In New Testament times, harvesting wheat required several labor-intensive processes. First the dry, ripe wheat stalks were cut close to the ground and tied into sheaves. The sheaves were then laid flat on a threshing floor, an area of hard-beaten and compacted earth or bare rock, and then ground and pulverized, typically by pulling a threshing sledge or driving a heavy cart over them (see Isaiah 28:26–28). The threshing would knock the seeds from the seed heads and grind all the rest of the plant material into chaff. Then on a windy day the mixture of chaff and grain would be thrown into the air using a winnowing fork, causing the lighter chaff to blow away and the clean, heavier seeds to fall back to the floor. An alternative to waiting for a windy day for winnowing was to aggressively wave a winnowing fan over the mixture of threshed seeds and chaff on the threshing floor. The wind created by the fan would blow away the lighter chaff, leaving the heavier purged or clean seeds in place to be gathered and stored for use. After winnowing, the useless but highly combustible chaff was disposed of in fires that were extraordinarily intense and sometimes explosive. John the Baptist used winnowing imagery as he described the Messiah as one "mightier" than he, "whose fan is in his hand, and he will thoroughly purge his floor, and gather his wheat" while the chaff would be burned with unquenchable fire (Matthew 3:11–12; Luke 3:17). Christ likewise referred to the rigors of harvesting, threshing, and winnowing wheat to warn Peter of Satan's desire to "sift" him as wheat (Luke 22:31). He also used wheat imagery in some parables. In the parable of the wheat and the tares, the householder's enemy sowed tares in the wheat field in an effort to pollute and spoil the crop, just as the adversary places or entices some members of the Church to do it harm (see Matthew 13:24–30; see also "Tares" herein). In the parable of the unjust steward, the deceitful man attempted to endear himself to one of his master's debtors by fraudulently allowing the debtor to write off 80 percent of his debt of wheat, apparently hoping the debtor would return the favor in some way when the steward's master fired him for his wasteful practices (Luke 16:1–12). Christ attempted to help Philip and Andrew understand the blessings that would result from his impending death, as well as the necessity of it, by explaining, "Except a corn of wheat fall into the ground and die, it abideth alone: but if it die, it bringeth forth much fruit" (John 12:24). The imagery likely made sense to the two disciples when they came to understand that Christ's death and resurrection brought forth the resurrection of all humankind (1 Corinthians 15:20–23, 35–38).

Wine: *See* Grapes.

Wormwood (*apsinthos,* ἄψινθος, 1x): A generic name for a group of aromatic, often woody species of *Artemisia* closely related to sagebrush. White wormwood (*Artemisia herba-alba*) is the common wormwood of the Holy Land. It is a dwarf, heavily branched shrub that has small, hairy, dissected leaves in the rainy season and scale-like leaves in the summer. The plant has a bitter taste and has been used medicinally as an antiseptic and antispasmodic. A bitter tea made from wormwood was used to treat intestinal worms, hence its common name. At the sounding of the third angel's trumpet during the seventh seal, John the Revelator saw a star "called Wormwood" that fell upon the waters of the earth, causing a third part of them to become "wormwood" and "bitter" (Revelation 8:11; compare Jeremiah 23:15; Amos 5:7), apparently representing the bitter troubles, calamites, and disasters that will unfold in that apocalyptic era.

⁓

Terry B. Ball is a professor in the Department of Ancient Scripture at Brigham Young University.

Further Reading

Miller, Anthony G., and Miranda Morris. *Plants of Dhofar, the Southern Region of Oman: Traditional, Economic and Medicinal Uses.* Diwan of the Royal Court, Sultanate of Oman: The Office of the Adviser for Conservation of the Environment, 1988.

Moldenke, Harold N., and Alma L. Moldenke. *Plants of the Bible*. Waltham, MA: Chronica Botanica, 1952.

Nicholson, Paul T., and Ian Shaw. *Ancient Egyptian Materials and Technology*. Cambridge: Cambridge University Press, 2000.

Swenson, Allan A. *Plants of the Bible and How to Grow Them*. New York: Carol, 1994.

Walker, Winifred. *All the Plants of the Bible*. New York: Harper and Brothers, 1957.

Zohary, Michael, and Naomi Feinbrun-Dothan. *Flora Palestina*. Parts 1–4. 2nd ed. Jerusalem: Israel Academy of Sciences and Humanities, 2015.

Zohary, Michael. *Plants of the Bible*. Cambridge: Cambridge University Press, 1982.

Notes

1. Michael Zohary, *Plants of the Bible* (Cambridge: Cambridge University Press, 1982), 13–14.
2. The terms or names for each entry below are listed in alphabetical order and are drawn solely from the King James Version of the Bible. The parenthetical information following each entry term presents first a transliteration of the Greek root from which the term was translated, followed by the root as it is written in Greek, and then a count of how many times the root is translated with the entry term in the KJV. For example, under the first entry, "Aloes," the parenthetical information "*aloe*, ἀλόη, 1x" indicates that "aloes" in the KJV is translated from a form of the Greek root *aloe*, written ἀλόη in Greek, and translated one time as "aloes" in the KJV.
3. Botanical information found under each entry was gathered from the following volumes: Anthony G. Miller and Miranda Morris, *Plants of Dhofar, The Southern Region of Oman: Traditional, Economic and Medicinal Uses* (Diwan of the Royal Court, Sultanate of Oman: The Office of the Adviser for Conservation of the Environment, 1988); Harold N. Moldenke and Alma L. Moldenke, *Plants of the Bible* (Waltham, MA: Chronica Botanica, 1952); Paul T. Nicholson and Ian Shaw, *Ancient Egyptian Materials and Technology* (Cambridge: Cambridge University Press, 2000); Allan A. Swenson, *Plants of the Bible and How to Grow Them* (New York: Carol, 1994); Winifred Walker, *All the Plants of the Bible* (New York: Harper and Brothers, 1957); Michael Zohary and Naomi Feinbrun-Dothan, *Flora Palestina*, parts 1–4, 2nd ed. rev. (Jerusalem: Israel Academy of Sciences and Humanities, 2015); and Michael Zohary, *Plants of the Bible* (Cambridge: Cambridge University Press, 1982), 13–14.
4. Jacob Neusner, ed., *The Talmud of the Land of Israel*, vol. 7: *Maaserot*, trans. Martin S. Jaffee (Chicago: The University of Chicago Press, 1987), 190–91.
5. All of the Gospels record the anointing of Jesus with costly ointment by a woman while he was at a house. The details among the accounts vary concerning who anointed him, what part of his body was anointed, when he was anointed, and what was said at the time, which has led some to conclude that Jesus was anointed on two different occasions, once by a woman known to be a sinner and later by Mary the sister of Lazarus and Martha. Others hold that the anointing was a single event that the Gospel authors simply recall differently.
6. Zohary, *Plants of the Bible*, 153.

36

Clothing and Textiles in the New Testament

Kristin H. South and Anita Cramer Wells

"For I was an hungred, and ye gave me meat: I was thirsty, and ye gave me drink: I was a stranger, and ye took me in: naked, and ye clothed me" (Matthew 25:35–36). With these words, Jesus reminded his disciples of the importance of kindness to others while also listing the basic necessities of life—food, water, shelter, and clothing. These elements are so fundamental to daily functioning that it is all too easy to assume they have always been the same as they are today, an oversight that limits fuller understanding of scriptural teachings and events. Such is the case with ancient clothing culture, the subject of this chapter. Fortunately, textual and archaeological discoveries allow us to better visualize and appreciate the surprisingly rich sartorial context of the New Testament. This chapter will outline what is known from the biblical era about clothing and show how this knowledge can inform our study of the New Testament.

Clothing, including nontextile items such as jewelry, footwear, and even armor, receives numerous mentions in the New Testament, indicating its importance as a marker of status, both worldly and spiritual. When Jesus counseled his disciples to regard the body as more than its raiment (Matthew 6:25), he was acknowledging the common human tendency to judge others—and ourselves—on the basis of the clothing we wear. Modern social science has shown that clothing is, in fact, one of the most direct and accurate markers of social standing (4 Nephi 24–25) and that we notice it immediately when meeting someone new.

The role of clothing as a way of displaying social status is ubiquitous in New Testament usage: when reading that John the Baptist wore clothing made of coarse camel hair with a leather belt (Mark 1:6), we can surmise quickly that not only his clothing but also his prophetic vision, his blunt honesty, and his role in society would be opposite that of those "clothed in soft raiments" who were "gorgeously apparelled" (Luke 7:25). Likewise, when the father wished to welcome his wayward son home, he clothed him in the best robe available, along with a ring and a pair of shoes (15:22). The striking change in the appearance of this desperate young man would have clearly shown to all who saw him that he had returned to his status as a son of the household instead of being the servant among pigs that his riotous living had reduced him to.

Because clothing serves such an important function in marking our place in society, we can often forget that its visual cues provide symbolic understanding: there is nothing inherent in the placement of precious stones and metal on one's head that creates a king, but the crown is a universal symbol of royalty nonetheless. When a mocking crowd adorned Christ in a costly dyed robe, along with a crown of thorns and a reed for a scepter (Matthew 27:29; John 19:2, 5), their intention to subvert and twist the symbolism of royalty was immediately apparent.

This chapter begins with a summary of what is known of actual clothing from New Testament times, then discusses what was distinctive about the clothing of the Jews from whom the earliest Christians were drawn. It then surveys how clothing references give added meaning to New Testament teachings and events, including the crucifixion, burial, and resurrection of Christ.

Ancient Evidence

Despite the many references to textiles in scripture, actual evidence of ancient clothing culture can be difficult to locate. This is due in part to the antiquity of the time, two millennia ago, but also to the fragile nature of clothing. With regular use, cloth breaks down and is eventually discarded or reused in other forms, such as cleaning cloths, pillows, rugs, or filling materials (hence Isaiah's prophecy that the earth would "wax old like a garment," Isaiah 51:6). The life cycle of clothing is acknowledged in a parable in Matthew 9:16 (compare Mark 2:21) when Jesus asked rhetorically if a person would attempt to mend an old piece of cloth by patching it with a new piece. The obvious answer is predicated on the realization that the organic materials constituting cloth soften and lose their strength over time and that such an attempt to combine the strong new cloth with a weakened older one would lead to an even larger hole. In a more general sense, Jesus was referencing the mundane and familiar in order to point out the futility of attempting to categorize him and his movement in old ways. He was the new cloth or the new wine (Matthew 9:17; Mark 2:22) whose ministry and mission required new understanding.

The first line of inquiry into ancient clothing culture, then, must come from the biblical sources themselves and from other associated writings that describe and define ancient wardrobe options. In addition, while archaeological remains are scanty, they do exist and have played an extremely important role in opening up the study of ancient clothing. Artistic representations from the time can also shed light on ancient customs, as can modern parallels if used cautiously.

Ancient Textile Terminologies

Because the New Testament has come down to us in Greek, a look at the original Greek terms translated as "cloak," "robe," and so on can also be useful. Many of these terms have now been matched to actual archaeological finds, so we have direct knowledge of the type of clothing Jesus meant when he urged his followers to give to a litigious neighbor his cloak [*himation*] as well as his already-taken coat [*chiton*] (Matthew 5:40).

The *himation* (spelled *cloke* in the King James translation) was a billowing outer garment worn by both men and women. For men, it was usually draped over the left shoulder and under the right arm in order to keep that arm more easily accessible, while women wore it fastened at the shoulder with a brooch. The classical *himation* of Greco-Roman use was a large rectangular piece of cloth worn wrapped around the body, but a local fashion (illustrated in the burial statues of Palmyra, in Syria, and in the Fayum portraits in Egypt) was a more tightly fitted *himation*, often with woven-in patterns such as a large H along one end or the shape of the Greek letter *gamma* (Γ) in each of the four corners. The Roman *pallium* for men or *palla* for women was an adaptation of the *himation*, a colorful mantle that could have several colors in striped or checked patterns. Women might wear it as the *himation* or bring it across the back of the head to cover their hair as well. With this context, Jesus's admonition to give away one's cloak betrays an astonishing generosity: a *himation* was laboriously handwoven, and its size and corresponding amount of thread made it an expensive item.

The most common element of daily clothing was the *chiton*. Originally a Semitic term (*k-t-n*, Hebrew *kuttoneth*), the English term *cotton* is ultimately derived from this word. In antiquity, however, a *chiton* was a sleeveless tunic of linen or wool, woven in one or two pieces, with narrow colored stripes (*clavi*) down either side from the shoulder to the bottom end of the garment. A *chiton* could be of any color, and examples from eastern Mediterranean lands include red, purple, blue, green, yellow, pink, peach, and orange.

Starting in the third century AD, a new fashion emerged, and people took to wearing tunics with long, wide sleeves (*dalmatica*) or with long, tight sleeves (*sticharion*). Both types were usually woven in separate sections with the sleeves sewn onto the tunic.

Women were expected to cover their hair in public (1 Corinthians 11:5–6). The Hebrew *ma'aforet* is the same as Latin *ma-*

This bronze miniature from the 1st to 2nd century shows a Roman woman covered in a *himation*, including part of it draped over her head. Its generous size allows it to envelop her and conceal her inner layers of clothing.

This image of nailless sandals, from 4th-century Egypt, shows the multiple layers of leather that were used to make sandals in Judea as well.

fortium (Greek *mafortus*) and seems to reference a piece of cloth meant to be worn as a veil or headdress both for women and for priests. They could be dyed as well and were usually mentioned in wedding dowries as part of an ensemble that also included a *dalmatic*. So commonly were the two items mentioned together that they came to be known by a compound word: *dalmaticomafortus*. This combination was most commonly known in the eastern Mediterranean world and hence is a strong candidate for the most usual wardrobe of New Testament women. Arab women at this time were often veiled across the face, while Greek and Hebrew women covered only their hair. Egyptian Christian women of the following centuries were often buried with their hair plaited and covered in netlike sprang headgear made of green, yellow, and red wool, which they would have worn in life too.

According to both written tradition and archaeology, Jewish footwear consisted of multiple layers of leather pressed and stitched together with leather thongs to form a nailless sandal. This was in distinction from the sandals worn by members of the Roman military, whose metal hobnails made a loud clatter as one approached and also left a distinctive footprint in the dust. The prohibition on wearing sandals with nails thus protected the population in times of danger by letting them know when a soldier was approaching. When John the Baptist declared himself unworthy to loosen or bear the shoes of his cousin Jesus (e.g., Mark 1:7; Acts 13:25), he was probably speaking of these nailless sandals.

Archaeological Textile Finds

This extreme fragility of cloth and its tendency to deteriorate over time makes it difficult to state with certainty what New Testament–era clothing would have looked like. The problem is true of organic materials in general: in many parts of the world, only stone monuments and pottery fragments remain to attest to the lifestyles of ancient peoples. Luckily, however, the dry, arid climate of ancient Judea has allowed some textiles to be preserved, most notably in areas beyond the rush of regular human interference. Important instances of such preservation have been discovered at infrequently used caves (Qumran, the Cave of Letters), a desert cemetery on the banks of the Dead Sea (Khirbet Qazone), and the famous hill fortress of Masada.

The Bar Kokhba revolt of AD 132–35 set Jewish revolutionaries against the ruling Roman authorities. Barred from entry into Jerusalem, many Jews fled to live and hide in high, barren caves near the Dead Sea. Christianized Jews, too, although not participating fully in the revolt—how could they view Bar Kokhba as the Messiah when they already believed in Christ?—were punished by Roman authorities and denied entrance to Jerusalem, but the documents in the caves indicate it was the participants in the revolution and their family members who hid in the caves. Thus, we are examining the wardrobes of Mosaic law-observant Jews when we look at the clothing from the Cave of Letters and Murabba'at. The burial site of Khirbet Qazone, very nearby on the other side of the Dead Sea, contains a population buried in very similar items of clothing. Dated to the first to third centuries AD, the site appears to have served predominantly Nabatean but also Jewish populations.

What we find at each of these sites is clothing of a high quality, consistent in type across religious and national divides. At Khirbet Qazone, the major types of clothing included tunics, mantles, and scarves or veils for women, plus some possible loincloths. Nearly all were made of wool. The veils were made in bright colors—yellow, pink, scarlet—and two of the tunics were apricot colored, showing that women's clothing went far beyond the undyed hues of browns and beige. At the Cave of Letters, another burial site, an entire cache of items that constituted a woman's personal belongings was found, including a mirror, cosmetics, weaving items, and articles that an astute scholar has recognized as a brassiere (*strophion*) and ragged cloths for use during menstruation.

Textiles at Murabba'at employed twill techniques and crepe, colored with apricot, yellow, green, blue, brown, and red dyes. The finds also included a rug fragment of a type described by Athenaeus, a Greek-speaking Egyptian of the third century AD, as the height of luxury: purple, with loops of wool on both sides.[1] Regardless of original quality, the finds in this most desperate of habitable places had been patched and reused. Some linen was torn to strips, which in some cases appeared to have blood on them.

"Desperate" also describes the famous last stand of rebels at the hilltop fortress Masada in AD 73. Excavations there in the 1960s revealed numerous textiles. These pieces include fragments of a variety of objects of daily wear: socks, hairnets, tunics, mantles, and cloaks, but the conquering Romans seem to have made off with everything of real value.

Textile finds from more distant surrounding areas, such as the deserts of Jordan and Syria and the wealthy and well-preserved neighboring region of Egypt, provide additional clues to the cloth options of the day. The spice route that brought myrrh and frankincense up from the south of the Arabian Peninsula included several fortified way stations at which excavators have discovered fabric remains that shed light on the textile culture of the wealthy Nabatean traders who frequented the route. At 'En Rahel, a Negev way station in use from the mid-second century BC to the first century AD, textile fragments of goat hair, wool, and camel hair were all found. A ring-shaped cushion found at 'En Rahel would have been placed on the head to facilitate the carrying of jars and other burdens. Sha'ar Ramon and Mo'a, two other points in the Negev along the Incense Route in use from the first to the third centuries AD, also included a large majority of wool textiles, with additional pieces of goat hair and camel hair. Linen, the most common textile fabric in neighboring Egypt, is represented in very few pieces at these sites but does exist. Additional finds of textile-making implements—thread, fleece, and spindle whorls—show that weaving and spinning were performed on-site.

In sum, the literary and archaeological evidence indicates that clothing options in ancient eastern Mediterranean lands during New Testament times were fairly limited and mirrored those of other ethnicities and nationalities throughout the Greco-Roman sphere of influence. Both men and women wore shapeless but colorful rectangular tunics, often with two narrow stripes of color as the only decoration. The tunics were complemented with outer cloaks or mantles and, in the case of women, veils or headscarves. Intimate underlayers of linen could include loincloths and brassieres plus more closely fitted tunics. Religious differences in clothing among the Jewish population, called for in the Mosaic law, are discussed below. Christians, however, dressed very much like their neighbors.[2]

Artistic Representation

In addition to literary and direct archaeological evidence, scholars look to ancient art to see how people represented themselves. However, because of Jewish religious restrictions on creating potentially idolatrous artwork, there is a dearth of direct biblical information. Yet wall paintings in the synagogue and house church at Dura-Europos in Syria, statuary throughout the ancient world, and mosaics at Ravenna, Italy, provide useful and interesting information about ancient fashion and society, often clarifying textual references and showing how textiles were meant to be worn.

Dura-Europos, on the eastern edge of modern-day Syria, was excavated in the 1930s and yielded evidence for the earliest-known Christian house church, from the mid-third century. It contained multiple frescoes on Christian themes, such as Jesus healing a paralytic, the Good Shepherd, and the three Marys visiting Christ's tomb. Although fashion is not the intentional topic of the frescoes, they reveal what Christians in the third century wore, or what they considered appropriate for people in Christ's time to have worn. The clothing of the women always goes to their feet, while the men are usually dressed in typical Greco-Roman fashions—shorter tunics with cloaks. Frescoes in the nearby synagogue show people in current fashions but also portray men in Persian-style fitted tunics over trousers, perhaps archaizing the stories from the past that were depicted on the walls.

Ravenna became the capital of the western Roman Empire in AD 402, after the emperors had declared Christianity the official religion of the empire. Art-filled buildings appropriate to a capital and to a center of Christian worship were built in the following two centuries and have been preserved, creating a legacy of historic importance. The clothing depicted on the walls at Ravenna is rich in color and design, as might be expected of the rulers of a vast and still-powerful empire. Christian figures are depicted in lush, well-preserved detail. The mosaics at Ravenna reveal an upper-class strata of society who wore richly decorated, colorful, and flowing pieces of clothing, along with jewelry and decorative hair ornaments. As such, they serve better to demonstrate a hierarchical ideal than to detail everyday wear.

Modern Parallels

Another potentially interesting source of information about ancient clothing is the parallels we can draw from the modern lifestyles of those in the region who continue to live according to traditional—often nomadic—patterns of life. Such parallels, however, must be drawn with great caution. Just because a way of life appears old or unusual to our eyes is no promise of its antiquity. Nevertheless, it does appear to be true that some aspects of life in the region have not changed significantly since ancient times. One example

Image of Haman leading Mordecai before the thrones of Ahasuerus and Esther. From the synagogue at Dura-Europos. Note the varieties of clothing shown, including short tunics or *chitons*, long outer *himations*, and Ahasuerus dressed in the Persian style, with long trousers beneath his tunic.

is the nomadic lifestyle of those who herd sheep and goats throughout the area. Because of the frequent scriptural allusions to Christ as the Good Shepherd and Christian followers as his flock, some biblical scholars have made much of the parallels between modern shepherding practices and what they may illuminate about ancient times.

One such report, of note for textile studies, comes from a nineteenth-century British vicar who observed Palestinian shepherds wearing a flowing tunic-style robe that they could secure at the waist with the addition of a belt, creating a pocket in which to carry a baby lamb

Mosaic at Ravenna.

against their own bodies. This image of a loving shepherd, cuddling a lamb close to his heart, carries obvious resonance with the Good Shepherd as described in Isaiah 40:11: "He shall gather the lambs with his arm, and carry them in his bosom."

In addition, literary, archaeological, artistic, and ethnographic evidences can provide a surprising amount of factual detail about ancient clothing practices despite the fragility of textile remains.

"Strength and Honor": Women's Work with Fibers and Dyes

Around the world throughout history, the making and shaping of textiles has been the work of women. This was true in ancient Israel as well. Among the idealized traits of a faithful Israelite wife were her abilities to work the raw materials of fibers into completed, dyed cloth available for household use or sale: "She seeketh wool, and flax, and worketh willingly with her hands. . . . She layeth her hands to the spindle, and her hands hold the distaff. . . . She is not afraid of the snow for her household: for all her household are clothed with scarlet. She maketh herself coverings of tapestry; her clothing is silk and purple. . . . She maketh fine linen, and selleth it; and delivereth girdles unto the merchant." As a result of all of this industry and wisdom, "strength and honour are her clothing" (Proverbs 31:13, 19, 21–25).

Because wool takes dye very readily and linen does not, brightly colored ancient clothing was most often made of wool. (Silk, which also dyes easily and can accept bright and brilliant hues, was far more expensive and difficult to obtain.) According to some ancient sources and modern archaeological finds, weavers of Judea became well known for their work in wool, developing a distinctive method of dyeing and weaving their wool to create shaded bands of color that started out lightly dyed at the edges and gradually moved to intensely colored in the centers of the bands.

Linen was the everyday fiber of the ancient Mediterranean world. The Mishnah, a collection of oral rabbinic tradition from the third century AD, describes the preparation of flax and the weaving and use of linen, making a local origin for most everyday linen likely. It also specifies that people might expect to obtain their wool from Judea and their linen from Galilee while noting that fine Egyptian or Indian linen was required as part of the uniform of the high priest. Of the two, the more expensive was Egyptian linen.

Fine Egyptian linen, also known as "byssos" or "king's linen," was produced, at least during pharaonic times, in Egyptian temples and reserved for priests, kings, and statues of the gods. Made from the finest underripe green flax, this is surely the linen that was used in the ancient Israelite temples as well. Marking great wealth and status, it was distinguished from everyday clothing by the degree of its refinement. Ancient cloth from Egypt, now in museums around the world, demonstrates why this might have been so: Egyptian linen could be woven to an extremely fine standard, with high thread counts and individual strands so thin that the gauzy cloth was insubstantial enough to see through. Latin sources referred to such linen as *linea nebula* ("misty linen") or *ventus textilis* ("woven wind" or "woven air").

Such cloth would have been confined to the upper strata of society because of the expense of making it and its impractical nature. The wearing or use of such fine linen, like costly purple garments, would have been a very visible social marker, much coveted among the status seekers of antiquity. Church father Tertullian, in the early third century AD, instructed women to shun the costly garments popular in his time and instead to clothe themselves in "the silk of uprightness, the fine linen of holiness, [and] the purple of modesty."[3]

Everyday linen, however, was a more substantial cloth that grew softer and more absorbent with every washing. In the world of the Bible, as in European societies for centuries following, linen was the fiber of choice for soft, odor- and stain-repellent undergarments, and today the word *linens* refers to bedding, regardless of the fiber of their make. Linen is made from the soft, flexible inner fibers of the flax plant (*Linum usitatissimum*). These fibers are made available through the retting process (*ret* is related to the word *rot*) by which the plant is soaked in water long enough for the tough outer fibers to be softened and loosened, after which they are stripped to obtain the flexible inner fibers. When Rahab of Jericho hid the Israelite spies on her roof in Joshua 2:6, she was able to do so because her roof contained multiple bundles of flax soaking in the sun. We thus learn that Rahab was involved in that most ancient of female professions, the preparation of flax fiber for weaving linen.

Although available for import from India and experimentally grown as early as 700 BC by Sennacherib in Nineveh, cotton never became a regular aspect of biblical clothing culture. Literary evidence for its use in Palestine, at Jericho, has been dated only to AD 575, but several archaeological findspots next to the Dead Sea demonstrate its existence there in small quantities in the Roman era. Similar in feel and use to linen, cotton eventually became the most common fiber for daily use in modern times, but in biblical and classical antiquity, linen and wool were far and away the most common sartorial staples.

According to Proverbs 31:22, an honorable Israelite wife could also have worked in purple. In reality, purple was a very costly and rare dye, the use of which was limited to elites. When Jesus wanted to stereotype a wealthy man in his parable of Luke 16:19, he declared that a "certain rich man" habitually dressed in "purple and fine linen." The purple mentioned here is the expensive and scarce royal purple, obtained by combining the glands of thousands of *murex* snails to harvest the pigment-rich bromine they secrete. It is of note that Lydia, an early convert at Philippi, was a seller of such purple dye, or of cloth that had been treated with it (Acts 16:14). As such, she would have been accustomed to dealing with a wealthy clientele and was probably quite prosperous herself.

Royal purple, also called true purple, Tyrian purple, Phoenician purple, or imperial dye, was one of very few dyes known to antiquity that would keep its color over multiple washings and exposure to sunlight. This colorfastness, combined with the brilliance of the color itself, made it extremely valuable, while the difficulty of obtaining it raised its expense and desirability to the point that Roman rulers firmly proscribed its use, allowing only those of very high social standing to wear no more than narrow bands of purple in carefully defined areas. Archaeological finds in Egypt have shown, however, that even low-ranking officers, some soldiers, and possibly their civilian companions did make use of it as a display of affluence and influence.

If sumptuary laws could be proclaimed, however, they could also be circumvented. False purple was very popular among those who could not afford true purple, or whose social circumstances did not allow their use of it. This imitation dye, created by the combination of a red (usually madder) and a blue (plant-derived indigo) resembled true purple. In one cemetery in Egypt, filled with Christians from the third to sixth centuries, for instance, false purple *clavi* (vertical stripes) are the most common color in use apart from undyed wool and linen.

Facility with textiles continued to be a mark of a woman's good character into New Testament times. The disciple Tabitha was praised for all "the coats and garments" (Acts 9:39) she had made in her lifetime for the widows, evidence of the good works that provoked a miraculous resuscitation from the dead by Peter.

Laying the Warp: Old Testament Continuities

Because the Jewish people of the New Testament era attempted to live the Mosaic law, any view of clothing in the time of Jesus must be filtered through the lens of their religious past. Throughout the Old Testament, clothing performed important symbolic and social functions that the people of the New Testament understood and referenced.

The Bible starts with a creation account that depicts Deity covering the bare planet earth with water and land, plants and animals. The sky is accessorized with heavenly bodies and glowing lights. God clothed his creation from the beginning; light and water both are seen as garments for the earth in the imagery of Psalm 104. In reference to this event, the Lord even asks Job, "Where wast thou when I . . . made the cloud a garment thereof, and thick darkness a swaddlingband for it?" (Job 38:4, 9). Humankind was the next adornment to come, and Job described that creation in wardrobe terms: "Thou hast clothed me with skin and flesh" (10:11). Yet that naked state of innocence in the garden eventually gave way to millennia of fashion choices. From Adam and Eve's attempt to make leaf aprons that the Lord replaced with garments (of skin, symbolizing the sacrifice of the Lamb, but the Hebrew word for "skin" (*'or*) is also a homophone with the Hebrew word for "light") to the specifications for priestly clothing in the Israelite temple thousands of years later, how humans covered their mortal body mattered in the Bible and to God.

The law of Moses specified some clothing guidelines that were important in both the Old and New Testaments: tassels must be present on coat corners for men, clothing should not be woven of mixed fabrics (*sha'atnez*), and cross-dressing was forbidden. Numbers 15:38 and Deuteronomy 22:12 specifically required Jewish men to wear tassels on the corners of their garments with an interwoven blue thread. During New Testament times, this injunction was fulfilled by the addition of tassels (*tzitzit*) to the four corners of the *himation*, or outer mantle. The prayer shawl (*tallit*) developed in postbiblical times as a way of continuing to keep this commandment even after men stopped wearing four-cornered clothing layers.

Such archaeological details are difficult to trace in the ancient world, but at Masada a small fragment of cloth with the special woven-in blue (*tekhelet*) of these shawls has been found, and a bundle apparently meant to be used as tassels came from the Cave of Letters.

Another evidence of people keeping to the Mosaic law comes from the excavations at Masada: in every instance, clothing fragments were made of a single type of thread: either linen or wool, but never a mix (*sha ʿatnez*) of the two. Combinations of linen and wool were common in the ancient world (and the homespun "linsey-woolsey" of recent centuries continued this tradition) but were forbidden in Mosaic law: Leviticus 19:19 and Deuteronomy 22:11 both prohibit the mixing of wool and linen. The clothing at Masada seems to have avoided such mixing, despite being of high quality and including items imported from regions beyond Judea. At the Cave of Letters, textiles were found in which the weaver's mark, a small design sewn with woolen thread onto linen cloth, had been picked out, in order to preserve the single-type purity of the cloth. Both of these finds demonstrate that Jews of the period of the New Testament observed the rule of avoiding the mixture of diverse types of threads. Christians, however, especially once Christianity had moved beyond its Judaic origins by accepting non-Jewish converts, had no such Mosaic scruples: many early Christian burials in Egypt contain cloth of mixed wool and linen, most often using linen as the warp and colored wool as the weft threads.

The archaeological jackpot at Qumran, site of the find of the Dead Sea Scrolls, less famously included linen wrappings for the sacred books. The majority of each wrapping was undyed, but the portions with blue dye may have had a protective or symbolic meaning. The prohibition on mixed threads was applied here as well, with the result that the color was a less intense hue owing to the resistance of linen to dyestuffs. Once these purpose-woven cloths had been used to protect sacred books, they could no longer simply be discarded, so they were placed in the caves with the scriptures and subsequently preserved in the undisturbed dry heat.

Apparently, gendered clothing distinctions mattered enough in the law that cross-dressing was prohibited (Deuteronomy 22:5). Such a prohibition makes it clear that according to the law, a person's gender could be—and should be—distinguished by his or her clothing. By New Testament times, men's and women's clothing differed not in type (a tunic for either was constructed in the same way) but in color and length. Women wore more brightly colored garments, while men were expected to dress in more muted tones. Women's hair should always be covered, while men's did not have to be. A woman's tunic extended to her feet, while a working man's tunic was only knee-length. When men wore longer tunics, it signaled higher status, beyond the roles of daily work. Thus, Jesus criticized the scribes "which love to go in long clothing" (Mark 12:38) as part of their assumption of social superiority, while the "long white garment" (16:5) of the angel waiting in Christ's tomb and Christ's postmortal description as one "clothed with a garment down to the foot" (Revelation 1:13) indicated a supernatural being whose situation was beyond mortal cares. In comparison, when the prophet Elijah ran before King Ahab, he first "girded up his loins" (1 Kings 18:46), whereby he tucked the tail of his tunic inside his belt to be able to move easily without his clothing getting in the way. The concept of having loins girded, thus ready for movement and labor, contrasts with the long robes of the rulers and would-be rulers whose wealth and status and clothing choices were meant for leisure.

Jesus and his followers knew the Old Testament well, and aspects of clothing culture run through all of those stories. From the little coat that Hannah sewed and delivered annually to her prophet son Samuel at the temple (1 Samuel 2:19) to Tamar's symbolic act of tearing her royal "garment of divers[e] colours" once she had been raped (2 Samuel 13:18–19), and from King David's change of clothes signifying the end of mourning his baby's death (12:20) to his high-flying linen ephod that distressed his wife Michal (6:14), biblical clothing communicated messages beyond function for warmth and protection. Clothing was used to delineate status, as disguise to hide status or alter relationships, as part of a legal setting, and to show emotions and interactions with the divine.

As in most societies, the cost, quality, and style of clothing indicated rank in the biblical world. When Haman was asked to imagine the highest honor possible for King Ahasuerus to bestow, his first suggestion was that "the royal apparel be brought which the king useth to wear" (Esther 6:8), which was then ironically put on his nemesis, Mordecai. Clothing Daniel "with scarlet" (Daniel 5:29) and a gold necklace announced his role as third ruler in Belshazzar's kingdom. In Tamar's situation referenced above, a virgin in the king's court was allowed to wear a special garment that showed her marital eligibility, and tearing and removing that was a reflection of Tamar's physical attack and changed situation. For teenage Joseph, his prime position as firstborn son of Jacob's favorite wife, Rachel, was clearly demonstrated by Jacob's homemade gift of "a coat of many colours" (Genesis 37:3; the Hebrew word indicates a decorated, possibly long-sleeved robe). This coat, later to be mutilated by the brothers as part of their deceit, led to Joseph's kidnapping and eventual future in Egypt. When David cut off a corner of King Saul's robe rather than assassinate him (1 Samuel 24:4–11), he sent a message about his respect for authority but also about Saul's vulnerability and David's mercy. War failure was even vividly shown by wardrobe decisions: once when the Israelites lost a battle, the victors shamed the soldiers by shaving half their beards and sending them home with their clothes half cut off (2 Samuel 10:4).

Since clothing was such a societal marker, its misuse was frequent in scripture as an act of deception. In the early patriarch stories of Genesis, this comes up generation after generation: Jacob used his brother Esau's clothes to confuse his aging and blind father, Isaac, into giving him the birthright blessing (Genesis 27:27). Then Jacob himself was hoodwinked at his wedding when "in the morning, behold, it was Leah" instead of Rachel (29:25). Joseph's brothers put goat's blood on his coat to make Jacob think his son was dead (37:31–32). Tamar conceived twins by her father-in-law Judah, Joseph's brother, when she posed as a harlot by removing her widow's garments and covering herself with a veil (38:14). Royalty occasionally preferred not to be known as such: King Josiah disguised himself as a common soldier to participate in battle, which led to his untimely death (2 Chronicles 35:22); King Saul "disguised himself, and put on other raiment" to consult a witch (1 Samuel 28:8); and King Jeroboam's wife was sent to the prophet Ahijah in a futile disguise (1 Kings 14:2). The

Israelite settlers were deceived into a problematic treaty by an entire group's clothing when the neighboring Gibeonites pretended to have journeyed from a distant land wearing old shoes and old garments (Joshua 9:4–6). The Book of Mormon account also begins with a story rooted in Jerusalem and this pattern of biblical clothing disguise when Nephi "took the garments of Laban and put them upon [his] own body" (1 Nephi 4:19), which, on that dark evening, fooled not only Laban's servant Zoram but also Nephi's own brothers.

Functioning as part of communal customs, clothing was a component of ancient legal transactions and covenantal relationships. Jonathan gave David his robe, garments, and weapons (1 Samuel 18:3–4) to cement their covenant of friendship. Boaz covered Ruth with his skirt and gave up his shoe in both a personal promise and a legal testimony that demonstrated his intention to marry her (Ruth 3:9; 4:7). After Joseph lost his coat and family, his story continued in Egypt, where another chapter of his story pivoted on the evidence of a lost garment that Potiphar's wife held up as proof that he had attempted to seduce her (Genesis 39:12). Clothing is also detailed in the Old Testament as part of war plunder, obligatory donations, and prison uniforms (Jeremiah 52:33).

Beyond earthly social mores and authority, clothing played a part in interactions with the divine. Moses removed his shoes to show reverence (Exodus 3:5), and temple clothing was a vital part of worship and holiness. Passover celebrations were to be eaten while dressed for departure (12:11), which makes the angel's instructions to Peter in Acts 12:8 to dress hastily on that Passover occasion even more relevant. The Lord showed his power through clothing: making wardrobes last miraculously through the forty years of wilderness wandering (Deuteronomy 8:4) and preserving lives and clothing to emerge unscathed from Nebuchadnezzar's fiery furnace (Daniel 3:21, 27). Prophets used clothing items to symbolize the fate of nations: Jeremiah followed the Lord's instructions to wear an unwashed linen belt and then hide it (Jeremiah 13:1–11), and Isaiah spent three years dressed like a slave at the Lord's command (Isaiah 20:2–3).

Clothing could also be used as a vehicle to express strong internal emotions. When the prophet Elijah's mantle descended on Elisha at his departure, it was an indication of the transfer of prophetic authority (2 Kings 2:12–14), and Elisha tore his own clothes in mourning and to symbolize that his former position was no more. With this powerful way to show grief, at least ten Old Testament characters tore their clothes, both men and women, from Reuben to King David to Mordecai to Athaliah. In the New Testament this occurs as well, when Paul and Barnabas, both raised as Jews, rend their clothes to protest false worship in Lystra (Acts 14:14). Joel 2:13 prefigured Christ's message of internal change rather than mere external compliance, urging the people to "rend your heart, and not your garments, and turn unto the Lord your God."

Priestly Robes

Not only was clothing part of interactions with the divine, it had elements spelled out by God particularly for those interactions. Priests were substitutes for Deity in the temples, so their appearance was intended to be otherworldly, and every object in the temple, including clothing, was set apart and sanctified only for temple usage. Guidance for the priestly wardrobe is extensive in the law of Moses. While little is written about the clothing required for later priests in Herod's temple, they would have followed the ancient prescriptions as closely as possible. Thus the following guidelines, written centuries earlier, would have applied to Caiphas, Annas, and Zacharias as they carried out their various temple duties.

Exodus 28 proclaims that the clothes of the priests were to be for glory and beauty, and details how the ordinary priest was to wear a hat, belt, pants, and tunic, with the high priest adding the breastplate, ephod, robe, and golden headband to the outfit. The pants and tunic were made of white linen, the hat was a fabric strip wound around the head, and the belt was woven with four threads: fine white linen, blue, purple, and scarlet. The sleeveless robe was woven of blue threads with a hem of decorative pomegranates and golden bells. The expensive golden breastplate would have served to mark out the priest wearing it as a singularly important servant of God. He symbolically carried the twelve tribes of Israel before the Lord by means of the named jewels adorning it. The headband was fastened in place by blue thread and read "holiness to the Lord," dedicating the priest and the people to God.

Rules dictated how the priestly clothing was to be treated, laundered (imagine how the required animal sacrifices would have soiled the white robes), and recycled, with elaborate symbolism and tradition growing up around each element of that process. The priests' clothing was first worn after a ritual anointing and blessing (Exodus 40:13). The high priest was forbidden from going about with a bare head or from tearing his clothes (Leviticus 21:10); it is thus intriguing that Matthew records that during Jesus's trial the high priest broke that law and "rent his clothes" as he charged Christ with blasphemy (Matthew 26:65). Ezekiel foresaw a future heavenly temple where the priests were clothed only in linen, with no wool allowed (Ezekiel 44:17). Of course, Jesus as the great High Priest was prefigured by these images and ideas.

The priestly religious regalia symbolized righteousness, majesty, and divine power, as a number of scriptures indicate: "Let thy priests be clothed with righteousness" (Psalm 132:9); "Thou [Lord] art clothed with honour and majesty" (Psalm 104:1); "[God] hath clothed me with the garments of salvation, he hath covered me with the robe of righteousness" (Isaiah 61:10). Ezekiel used clothing as a metaphor for God's magnificent bounty and care as the Lord symbolically dressed and provided for his adulterous bride Jerusalem: "I clothed thee also with broidered work, and shod thee with badgers' skin, and I girded thee about with fine linen, and I covered thee with silk" (Ezekiel

While the Bible does not specify every aspect of the high priest's wardrobe, this recent replication follows as many details as are given in the Old Testament descriptions.

16:10). And Isaiah reassured the mourners in Zion that restoration would bring "the garment of praise for the spirit of heaviness" (Isaiah 61:3), allowing a wardrobe shift to indicate the promised joy. This idea is carried forward into the New Testament, as everyone who overcomes the world would be "clothed in white raiment" (Revelation 3:5), making one and all heavenly priests.

Apart from the temple priests, other groups of highly religious Jews who wanted to distinguish themselves from one another did so in part through their apparel. Essenes dressed in simple white linen clothing, perhaps likening themselves to a community of temple priests. The aristocratic Sadducees, purportedly descendants of the priestly Zadokites, would have donned ritual robes if serving in temple duties. Pharisees, the fraternity to which Paul belonged and whose descendants became the Jews of rabbinic times, wore clothing that was distinctive and recognizable, and even criticized by Jesus: "They make large their phylacteries [*tefillin*], and enlarge the borders of their garments" (Matthew 23:5). Tefillin, leather straps connecting miniature boxes of scripture to be worn on the body, were created as the literal way to honor Deuteronomy 6:4–9 and keep the law before one's eyes and next to one's heart continually.

Temple Veil

When the ancient temple was built, Exodus 26 specified its various curtains of fine-twined linen, goat's hair, embroidered hangings, and especially a blue, purple, and scarlet veil made of "fine-twined linen of cunning work" (26:31) that would delineate and protect the holy of holies as sacred space. It was embroidered with cherubim, angelic figures. The temple veil was about sixty feet high and thirty feet wide. This is the veil that was torn in half from top to bottom at Jesus's crucifixion (Matthew 27:51), symbolizing that through Christ's death, the presence of God was now accessible to all (Hebrews 6:19–20). Doctrine and Covenants 101:23 suggests that the Lord himself is still veiled, or covered, until the Second Coming, at which time he will be revealed in all his power and majesty.

New Testament Threads from Christ's Life

From the babe in swaddling bands to his burial in linen clothes in the garden tomb, Jesus was clothed in a physical body that wore particular fabrics. Clothing is an element of his sermons, his parables, his miracles, his transfiguration, his crucifixion and resurrection, and his glorified return in "dyed garments" (Doctrine and Covenants 133:46).

Mary "wrapped him in swaddling clothes" (Luke 2:7), which were not the rags of Nativity art but rather narrow bands common to all well-cared-for infants, made for that purpose and perhaps even embroidered with lineage identifications.[4] Such swaddling bands foreshadowed his eventual ministry of binding up the broken and also his burial, when his body was wrapped in linen and laid in a tomb.

A powerful healing miracle recorded by three Gospel writers (Matthew 9:20–22; Mark 5:27–30; Luke 8:43–46) pertained to Jesus's clothes. The woman with an issue of blood had faith that "if I may touch but his clothes, I shall be whole" (Mark 5:28). Luke adds the detail that she "came behind him, and touched the border of his garment" (Luke 8:44). This border was likely the wool tassel fringe (*tzitzit*) required by Numbers 15:38 to remind Jews of the law. Such an identification allows for the beautiful fulfillment of the prophecy in Malachi 4:2 that the Lord will bring "healing in his wings" (*wings* is from the Hebrew word *kanaph*, which also means "border of a garment"). This woman may have been remembering the miraculous power found in Elijah's mantle (2 Kings 2:8), later echoed in Paul's healing miracles of Acts 19:12, where "handkerchiefs or aprons" were brought from his body to the sick (and repeated by Joseph Smith with his red silk handkerchief in Nauvoo).

For the peasant fishermen who accompanied Jesus to the Mount of Transfiguration, the change in his raiment there was unforgettably otherworldly. Matthew described it as "white as the light" (17:2), Luke records that it was "white and glistering (Greek *exastrapto*: "to flash out like lightning, be radiant," 9:29), and Mark says that "his raiment became shining, exceeding white as snow" (9:3). Of his modern encounters with heavenly beings, Joseph Smith recorded that their "brightness and glory defy all description" (Joseph Smith—History 1:17).

Burial Garments

Textiles play multiple roles in the central event of the New Testament, the crucifixion and resurrection of Christ. From dressing Christ as a king, ironically proclaiming his true status through their mockery (John 19:2–5), to soldiers gambling over who would be allowed to keep his clothing (Luke 23:34; John 19:23–24), to the angelic heralds in "shining garments" (Luke 24:4) announcing Christ's resurrection, the everyday reality of the importance of clothing was never forgotten, even in this most mournful—and joyful—of moments.

Christ's triumphal entry into Jerusalem on Palm Sunday, at the start of his momentous holy week, had important textile details: he sat upon a young donkey covered with two of his disciples' garments as a saddle (Luke 19:35) and was welcomed by multitudes who lay down palm branches and "spread their garments in the way" (Matthew 21:8). Later, he performed a tender symbolic service to his apostles when he "laid aside his garments; and took a towel, and girded himself" (John 13:4) to prepare to wash their feet. This towel (Greek *lention*) was a linen cloth of a type worn by servants but also used to cover nakedness during crucifixion, thus prefiguring his upcoming death.

As part of his trial and its related torment, Jesus's clothes were again removed. His scourged, bloody body was dressed in royal mockery, with a purple or scarlet robe described by Luke as "gorgeous" (23:11) and a braided crown of thorns (Matthew 27:28–29; Mark 15:17; John 19:2–3). Mark reports that after the mockery, "they took off the purple from him, and put his own clothes on him" (15:20) en route to the crucifixion. However, these were again removed at the cross and the soldiers cast lots to divide his clothing. Jesus had an unusual coat (*chiton*), described by John as "without seam, woven from the top throughout" (19:23). A Judean tunic was usually woven of two pieces held together at the shoulders, but this kind Jesus wore was more common in Egypt and required the use of a wider loom. The prophecy in Psalm 22:18 was thus fulfilled: "They part my garments among them, and cast lots upon my vesture."

In the first century AD, the final burial could take place right after death ("primary" burial) or be delayed until only the bones remained ("secondary" burial). Primary burial was an especially costly business, requiring not only a full sepulchre for the body, rather than a smaller ossuary for the bones alone, but also the expense of linen in which to wrap the person being buried. Burials described in the New Testament are primary, with an accompanying need for linen to wrap and complete the burial.

After his death, Jesus was buried in a borrowed tomb. On this point, all four Gospels agree. Details of the wrapping of the body, however, differ. In preparation for burial, Joseph of Arimathea wrapped Jesus's body in a "clean linen cloth" according to Matthew 27:59. This description is notable for what it does not say: the tomb itself is described, in the following phrase, as "new," but the linen is merely clean. Mark, however, states that Joseph of Arimathea went out "and he bought fine linen . . . and wrapped him in the linen" (15:46). Bought for the occasion by a man of wealth, this linen would most likely have been new. Luke cannot settle the question: he does not state anything more definite than that linen was used for the wrapping (23:53). John, however, gives a new set of details: whether new or used, the linen was accompanied by a significant quantity of unguents and spices. Jesus's close followers then "wound [his body] in linen clothes with the spices" (19:39–40). John ends this recital of facts with this tantalizing but incomplete editorial: all of this was done "as the manner of the Jews is to bury."

The burial of Lazarus gives us a little more information: according to John 11:44, Lazarus (and presumably all people buried after "the manner of the Jews") had his hands and feet "bound . . . with graveclothes" and his face covered with a "napkin." The "napkin" that covered the face was a simple towel. The Greek *soudarion* refers to the equivalent of a modern handkerchief: a cloth used for wiping away sweat and blowing the nose. The graveclothes (*keiria*) mentioned here could have been purpose-woven for use in burial—the term implies narrow linen bands used to bind up a corpse after it has been wrapped in shrouds—or torn strips of linen taken from existing cloth. Parallels of both kinds have been found in great quantities in Egyptian burials.[5]

When Lazarus miraculously returned to life, he was still bound hand and foot with his burial wrappings, and presumably came stumbling and blind from the tomb. Jesus, on the other hand, had a thorough transformation. Thus, clothing culture enriches the symbolism that brackets the birth and death of Christ: he was wrapped in linen both in birth and in death, and his resurrection included a complete change of his earthly body into something transcendent, accompanied by a total change of garb. His burial clothes remained in the tomb, neatly folded and left behind (John 20:6–7; Luke 24:12). The angelic visitors who guarded the tomb and informed its visitors of Christ's whereabouts were notably arrayed in shining white garments. Could such brilliant white garb (Matthew 28:3) be an extension and symbolic transformation of the undyed linen of burial clothing?

Conclusions

Clothing is personal yet social. It both reflects and creates our social identity. Wardrobe variations, from top to bottom, from inner to outer layers, from season to season and year to year, are layered and multifaceted, but we, as humans bound by social traditions, know how to understand the many unspoken messages sent by each variation. These highly visible signals allow us to classify people by age, gender, status, career, wealth, and historical era.

Clothing is superficial yet universal. James recognized the ungodly but common tendency to use those very social signifiers listed above as indications of a person's complete worth. He warned his church assembly not to afford more "respect of persons" to those wearing "goodly apparel" than those in "vile raiment" (2:1–4). Isaiah likewise warned against extravagant artifice in women's adornment (3:16–24), and similar apostolic concern is found in 1 Timothy 2:9. Galatians 3:27 pleads with the newly converted to avoid all divisions and distinctions, but rather to "put on Christ."

Clothing is essential yet fleeting. Job wryly noted, "Naked came I out of my mother's womb, and naked shall I return thither" (1:21), but for each step in between, the proper clothing for every occasion is socially assigned. This short survey has shown that in New Testament times, despite a more limited wardrobe vocabulary than is available in modern times, people were able to discern sharp social divides based on sartorial distinctions. Jesus, in his teachings, parables, and symbolic actions, made frequent and effective use of these common threads.

Clothing is eternal yet ever changing. Throughout history, images of scriptural people have been clothed in the wardrobe ideas of the time that the art was made. This human tendency attests to the changeable nature of fashion but also to our impulse to "liken all scriptures unto us" (1 Nephi 19:23). When we can see scripture characters dressed like us, we can use their clothing to symbolically ascribe to them attributes that dress naturally conveys: modesty and moderation, affluence and arrogance, poverty and humility, and occupation, marital, or spiritual status. Adorned in clothing like us, they are more readily understood in our time and in our terms. Perhaps, in this way, we naturally follow Christ's admonition to clothe the stranger: by placing historical, scriptural strangers in a familiar setting, we come to understand and love them as our neighbors. The ultimate promise of eternal life and of the New Testament is that God will clothe us, if we seek first his kingdom and righteousness, more gloriously than Edenic garments of skin and more beautifully than the lilies of the field (Matthew 6:28–34).

‒‒‒‒

Kristin H. South is an archaeologist specializing in ancient textiles and is a member of the History Department at The Waterford School in Sandy, Utah.

Anita Cramer Wells is an early-morning seminary teacher and volunteer editor at Book of Mormon Central.

Further Reading

Barag, Dan, et al. *Masada*. Israel Exploration Society, 1994. The official report for the excavations at Masada, including an extensive and authoritative section on the textiles.

Gaspa, Salvatore et al. *Textile Terminologies from the Orient to the Mediterranean and Europe, 1000 BC to 1000 AD*. Zea E-Books, 2017. Excellent articles explaining the connection between ancient terms and the clothing they referenced.

Geikie, Cunningham. *The Holy Land and the Bible: A Book of Scripture Illustrations Gathered in Palestine*. Vol. 1. J. B. Alden, 1888. "Modern" nineteenth-century observations of daily life in the Holy Land.

Markoe, Glenn, ed. *Petra Rediscovered: The Lost City of the Nabataeans*. Harry N. Abrams in association with the Cincinnati Art Museum, 2003. Excavations at Khirbet Qazone and the textile finds there.

Nielsen, Donna B. *The Holy Child Jesus: Notes on the Nativity*. CD-ROM. Discussion of swaddling bands.

Schrenk, Sabine, ed. *Textiles in Situ: Their Find Spots in Egypt and Neighbouring Countries in the First Millennium CE*. Abegg-Stiftung, 2006. Articles on excavated textiles from the Cave of Letters, the Negev, and southern Jordan.

Sebesta, Judith L., and Larissa Bonfante, eds. *The World of Roman Costume*. University of Wisconsin Press, 2001. Josephus, Talmud, and Midrash references.

South, Kristin H., and Kerry Muhlestein. "Regarding Ribbons: The Spread and Use of Narrow Purpose-Woven Bands in Late-Roman Egyptian Burials." In *Drawing the Threads Together: Textiles and Footwear of the First Millennium AD from Egypt*. Tielt, Belgium: Lannoo, 2013. Discussion of archaeological finds from early Christian burials in Egypt.

Notes

1. Athenaeus, *Deipnosophistae* 5.26.
2. *Letter to Diognetus* 6.4.
3. Tertullian, *On the Apparel of Women* 2.13.
4. The NRSV renders Luke 2:7 as "band of cloth."
5. Purpose-woven burial tapes in Egypt were sometimes made of a mixture of undyed and red-stained linen. Such red and undyed burial tapes came to be directly associated with Christian burials in Nubia by the sixth century AD and may have symbolically referenced blood or had a connection with the "scarlet thread" that saved Rahab and her family (Joshua 2:18). In the modern Christian (Coptic) church in Egypt, a red ribbon plays an important symbolic role in baptisms and marriages.

Part 6
The Text of the New Testament

37

Textual Criticism and the New Testament

Thomas A. Wayment

Simply stated, New Testament textual criticism is the practice of attempting to recover the earliest attainable text and is sometimes associated with the idea of recovering the "original" text of the New Testament. This effort is necessary given the fact that the surviving ancient copies of the Greek New Testament contain numerous differences called textual variants.[1] What is intended by the term *original* is a matter of dispute, and for the sake of this discussion, it will refer to the most original version of the Greek text of the New Testament that is recoverable by modern methods of study. That is not the same as recovering the original text exactly as it was written by Matthew, Mark, or Luke, for example. The modern reader who is not deeply interested in such detailed academic matters will be confronted with a sense of unease that such discussions are at times arcane and seemingly irrelevant. But the larger questions such as *Is the New Testament accurately translated?* or *How does such an effort alter faith in any significant way?* are simply too complex to answer thoroughly in a single study. Answers to such questions, however, can be based on the study of textual criticism, and the simple answers are that the KJV Bible now in common use has errors and textual limitations, while the answer to the second question is that textual criticism has the potential to raise questions about biblical accuracy that can affect faith.

In brief terms, textual criticism is the study of the existing manuscripts of the Bible, for which there are nearly six thousand New Testament manuscripts in Greek. Those manuscripts, which are handwritten copies dating from the second century to the Middle Ages, contain thousands of differences in wording, spelling, and the actual text they contain. Thus, it falls to the text critic to sift through the differences, determine which changes are errors, spurious additions, and unintentional mistakes, and then offer an informed opinion regarding what is the earliest recoverable text of the New Testament.[2] Over the course of the last several centuries, scholars have developed a set of tools to aid them in sifting through the variants in these texts. One particularly important way that scholars assess these differences is through a genealogical approach that assigns the various manuscripts each to a family of texts, and then subsequent decisions are made on the basis of whether a particular family of manuscripts is judged to be more reliable than another family of texts.

In 2006 Carl Griffin and Frank Judd Jr. surveyed the principles and practices of New Testament textual criticism for a Latter-day Saint audience, offering the suggestion that Latter-day Saint scholars could productively approach the topic of study through the principles of "reasoned eclecticism" (defined below).[3] That essay was published in tandem with a study that described the variety and difficulties associated with the nearly six thousand New Testament manuscripts, the four major textual families, and the hundreds of thousands of textual variants, thus giving Latter-day Saint audiences access to quality descriptions of the problems and challenges facing translators, New Testament scholars, and those working on textual issues.[4] Both of these studies are descriptive in their approach and offer general surveys of the importance of these issues for Latter-day Saints. Those studies, when combined with the wealth of high-quality general studies on the topic, provide an opportunity to move the conversation forward in at least one important way, by discussing the implications of the practice for Latter-day Saint sacred scripture. Therefore, this study will first briefly describe the relevant issues that shape the conversation and then offer a focused discussion regarding why New Testament textual criticism should be an essential consideration for Latter-day Saints.

Textual Criticism, Text Families, Unique Readings

The assumption that a translation of the New Testament exists as an authoritative and accurate rendering of what Jesus and his disciples taught and did is problematic largely because our knowledge of that time period is characterized by gaps in the historical record. It is well known that the books of the New Testament were not written while Jesus was alive and that some of them were written decades after his death.[5] To further complicate matters, copies of copies of those writings exist in fragmentary form beginning first in the mid to late second century, and then in complete form for most books only in the fourth century. That is not to say that an accurate text of the New Testament is hopelessly lost, or even that the text is so questionable as to be unreliable, but rather that there are significant gaps in our knowledge of how the text was copied and transmitted.

The text of the New Testament is witnessed by approximately 135 papyrus fragments of mostly individual New Testament books ranging in size from a small postage stamp–sized fragment to larger fragments that span over seventy-five pages.[6] These copies are described by their writing material, papyrus, and they are generally the earliest copies that survive. Beginning in the late fourth and early fifth century, a number of complete or nearly complete manuscripts, known today as codices, survived that contain the New Testament. The most important are Codices Sinaiticus (fourth century), Alexandrinus (fifth century), Vaticanus (fourth century), and Ephraemi Rescriptus (fourth century). These texts—the papyri and the four great codices—form the basis of nearly all text-critical discussions. When these manuscripts align in the way they preserve the text, it is exceptionally difficult to argue that they do not contain the most reliable text of the New Testament that can be recovered through modern tools of study.

A major challenge in the process of determining the most accurate version of the text is the realization that even within this framework of reliable manuscripts, there is evidence that each individual case has to be weighed on its own merits. A simple example illustrates this issue. In Matthew 27, Pilate presented two men to the crowd with the intent that the crowd could choose to release one prisoner and at the same time condemn the other. The name of the second individual is Jesus Barabbas according to some manuscripts, whereas others report his name simply as Barabbas. The textual critic must weigh the quality of the different manuscripts, assess whether one version is perhaps more original, and then offer a suggestion as to which version of the name should be included in translations. In other words, a modern translation of the Bible cannot simply translate Codex Sinaiticus, for example, as though it preserved the most original text of the New Testament. The reason for this is that even Codex Sinaiticus has its limitations and textual ambiguities, and it also contains a number of books that never made it into the official canon of the Church. The weighing of differences in the sources introduces the opportunity for human judgment and reasoning to make the final determination. Most scholars today advocate for this type of approach, and it is what Griffin and Judd argued for in promoting "reasoned eclecticism," the term used by scholars to designate the method of determining the most reliable text that relies on each individual situation to consider the quality of the texts that preserve it, the history of the passage, and other historical factors.

In a general sense, this is a reasonable way forward for arriving at a point where the reader can be relatively confident that the most reliable text has been recovered to the extent possible. There will always be limitations in this methodology, but often they do not radically change the way the message of the New Testament authors is understood in the cases where ambiguity remains. For example, in Matthew 8:28 it will probably always remain unclear whether Jesus went to the Gadarenes or the Gergesenes because there are so many different spellings of the village and so much confusion in the Greek manuscripts regarding the village in question, but apart from historical and archaeological interest, the difference has almost no significance for the meaning of this passage.[7] However, as will be discussed later, the pursuit of the most reliable text of the New Testament presents the Latter-day Saint reader with unique challenges and hurdles.

Some of the Most Significant Textual Problems

Perhaps the most important examples of textual dispute in the New Testament, where the text is in serious question because the Greek manuscripts preserve differences of wording between them and the interpretation is markedly affected, are worthy of brief consideration. Several of these passages are either removed from the text entirely in modern translations, like the New International Version (NIV) or New Revised Standard Version (NRSV), or are placed in double brackets "[[…]]" to indicate that they are included in the translation only with hesitation. On the basis of the surviving textual tradition, some of these are no longer considered serious points of debate because the tools of textual criticism can offer compelling solutions. Others remain more difficult to decide because the manuscript evidence is more ambiguous.

In no particular order, the following are some of the most significant textual variation units or passages. At the end of Matthew 27:49, a number of early and important manuscripts add the sentence "And another [soldier] took a spear and pierced him in the side, and water and blood flowed out." Typically, a textual critic would look at the various manuscripts that contain this extra passage, consider their dates, determine if the reading is also present in the papyri, and then offer a judgment concerning its authenticity. But considering only the quality of the manuscripts that preserve this reading—several of the most reliable manuscripts preserve it (Sinaiticus, Vaticanus, and others)—would warrant its inclusion into the text, and the manuscripts that omit it are certainly inferior (Alexandrinus, Bezae, Freer, and others). This example demonstrates how the quality of texts alone cannot be the sole consideration in some situations. In this example, the fact that the additional verse is nearly a verbatim quotation from John 19:34 likely indicates that scribes attempted to harmonize Matthew's account to John's, and therefore the additional verse is considered secondary.

John 5:3–4 contains what is almost certainly a scribal addition to the story of the man who was healed at the pool of Bethesda. According to the King James translation, the familiar text reads, "In these lay a great multitude of impotent folk, of blind, halt, withered, waiting for the moving of the water. For an angel went down at a certain season into the pool, and troubled the water: whosoever then first after the troubling of the water stepped in was made whole of whatsoever disease he had." There is almost no doubt today that the words included in parentheses are spurious, and they are preserved only in very late and less reliable Greek manuscripts. Their weak textual support is a strong indicator that they are not original to John 5.[8] This is particularly obvious when the better manuscripts that omit this passage are compared to the weaker ones that include it. The addition to the text was probably introduced by a well-meaning scribe who wanted to supply a reason why the sick and ill would lie around the pool of Bethesda waiting to be healed.

One of the more complicated instances of textual variation is the story of the woman taken in adultery, or the *Pericope adulterae*. In its current form and position, the story is preserved in the majority of modern translations in John 7:53–8:11, but it is either placed in brackets or in notes. This text is familiar to Latter-day Saint readers because it is preserved in the King James translation. Most Greek manuscripts of the New Testament do not preserve this passage, and the quality of manuscripts that do not contain it is almost overwhelming. The passage has only moderately good textual support in a single manuscript of the Western tradition in Codex Bezae. All other important witnesses omit the story entirely or place the passage in another position such as after Luke 21:38, before John 7:37, or after John 21:25.[9] With this story, however, a number of scholars have argued that it may potentially preserve an account from the life of Jesus, although not recorded originally in John 7:53.[10] In this example, the textual evidence is insufficient to make a decision based solely on texts, primarily because some early Christian authors appear to have known a version of this story that may have been slightly different from the one recorded in John. Thus, the suggestion is that while it was not recorded in the Gospels, other Christians knew it was a story that could be traced back to the life of Jesus.

According to a significant number of manuscripts, the Gospel of Mark ended without reporting the different visits to the tomb or the appearance of the resurrected Lord, thus ending in what appears to be mid-story. The ending of Mark may be one of the most difficult textual problems because so much is at stake with the ending. Specifically, Mark may have ended his account without telling any of the resurrection experiences told in the other Gospels. At least two potentially original endings have emerged, known simply as the shorter and longer endings of Mark. To confuse matters, the shorter ending is often included with the longer ending.[11] The shorter ending states tersely, "They reported to those around Peter what they had been commanded to report. After these things, Jesus himself sent from the east to the west through them the holy and imperishable preaching of eternal salvation. Amen."[12] Although the two most respected manuscripts end following Mark 16:8 (Codices Sinaiticus and Vaticanus), the longer ending—the version translated in the King James Version—has moderately good support. The arguments for and against the longer or shorter endings can become quite technical, and the modern arguments seem to have evolved along the lines of whether a book could end mid-sentence or whether the story of Jesus's resurrection was first reported with such an abbreviated ending.[13] Ultimately, the solution will not be reached without further evidence, but the text-critical discussion shows a willingness to be flexible when the manuscript evidence indicates one solution and scholars have pushed back against it with the hope of recovering the validity of the longer ending of Mark.[14]

A rather simple text-critical question arises with the potential forgery of a verse that was inserted into the text of the New Testament with a specific interest in promoting a distinct doctrinal position. In 1 John 5:7–8, only a few extremely late Greek manuscripts contain the words, "[7] in heaven, the Father, the Word, and the Holy Ghost: and these three are one. [8] And there are three that bear witness in earth." The textual evidence against these words is almost overwhelming, with only a late fourteenth-century Greek manuscript as the primary piece of evidence to support it.[15] Interestingly, these forged words found their way into the King James translation and have thereby become well known despite the fact that they were clearly forged.

One text-critical issue that has developed into a rather heated discussion at times is the story of Gethsemane as told in Luke 22:43–44. According to the King James translation, the verses in question report, "[43] And there appeared an angel unto him from heaven, strengthening him. [44] And being in an agony he prayed more earnestly: and his sweat was as it were great drops of blood falling down to the ground." Many scholars have seen these two verses as questionable, both because there is good manuscript evidence against them and because they appear to have a clear doctrinal interest, and therefore they may have been added to the New Testament by someone who wished to shape the meaning of the story.[16] The major manuscript evidence in support of these verses is generally later, although the verses are contained in one early uncial manuscript (0171), and most notably they were included in Codex Sinaiticus and then removed by a later scribe.[17] From a text-critical standpoint, this would amount to only marginally good textual support.

There are literally hundreds of text-critical issues in the New Testament, and this brief discussion of them has admittedly been subjective. Some less noteworthy examples are the question of whether Jesus was moved with compassion or anger in Mark 1:41. The manuscript evidence supports the idea that he felt compassion, but scholars have questioned whether believers would have been embarrassed by the possibility that Jesus felt anger. Luke 23:34 reports the saying "Father, forgive them, for they know not what they do," a reading that has some questionable support, and in fact the texts that omit these words are typically much more reliable than the ones that preserve it. Finally, John 1:18 refers to Jesus as the "only begotten Son" or, according to other manuscripts, the "only begotten God" or "the only begotten. God." The textual traditions for the two readings are nearly equal in reliability, and therefore it is difficult to resolve.[18] Many more examples could be cited and discussed, but the purpose of this discussion has been to demonstrate that the tools of textual criticism can in certain instances make a reasonable argument for the most reliable text of the New Testament while at other times, they can only arrive at general propositions for the restoration or recovery of the original text.

The Lord's Prayer—A Test Case

For Latter-day Saints, a second and third form of the New Testament text exist in some instances—the Book of Mormon and the Joseph Smith Translation of the Bible.[19] Although these sources are limited in what they quote from the New Testament, the quotations that are contained in them nevertheless present some challenges for the Latter-day Saint textual critic.[20] Looking at any point of intersection between these texts raises important questions about the ways that Latter-day Saints view the reliability of the New Testament text and the authenticity of the Book of Mormon text. This vantage point in turn raises important questions about the Joseph Smith Translation and how it is used in interpreting the Bible and recovering the most original text of the New Testament.

Perhaps the most difficult text-critical challenge with respect to these three texts is found in the Lord's Prayer as recorded in Matthew 6:9–13, 3 Nephi 12:9–13, and the Joseph Smith Translation of Matthew 6:9–13. In particular, there is a significant textual variant in Matthew 6:13 that is easily resolved on text-critical grounds alone, but not as easily when Restoration scriptural texts are considered. The passage in question, using the language of the King James translation, reads, "For thine is the kingdom, and the power, and the glory, for ever. Amen" (Matthew 6:13). For the text critic working independently of the Book of Mormon, the texts that omit this portion of Matthew 6:13 are impressive both in their reliability and range, and apart from the Greek manuscripts, the phrase is also omitted in Latin manuscripts and some of the Coptic versions.[21] This evidence would be considered overwhelming by most text critics of the New Testament. The phrase is included in a number of later manuscripts that are typically viewed as less reliable because of their later dating.[22] Most modern translations do not print the phrase in the text because the issue seems easily resolved, and scholars typically assume that the phrase was added to the Lord's Prayer when the passage began to be read in worship services.[23] It was added as a formal ending to the prayer where the Lord is praised emphatically, and the congregants and cantor could share in praising God.

The Book of Mormon, however, preserves the phrase exactly as it is used in the King James translation. The phrase is altered slightly in the Joseph Smith Translation, where the Prophet added an additional "and ever" to the end: "For thine is the kingdom, and the power, and the glory, forever and ever. Amen." In light of these findings, the question then becomes whether the Book of Mormon should be used to establish the original text of the New Testament, or whether it should be viewed as secondary or independent to the New Testament. In another way of looking at the question, the issue is whether the Joseph Smith Translation and the Book of Mormon should be used in a New Testament text-critical discussion at all. One of the challenges in connecting these discussions is that the authenticity of the Book of Mormon text and the Joseph Smith Translation becomes connected to the transmission of the Greek New Testament. In the example under consideration, the passage from Matthew 6:13 is not defensible on historical grounds as belonging to the most original text of the New Testament, and Latter-day Saint textual critics would then be forced to argue for an indefensible position in order to preserve the concept of the authenticity of the Book of Mormon passage.

Initially, it may seem simple enough to propose that the Book of Mormon preserves a second historical event where the prayer was repeated in a new setting with different wording and potentially new meaning. That would be possible, theoretically, although such a solution would create difficulties in explaining how a late Byzantine (fourth to fifteenth centuries AD) passage from a Greek text made its way into the Book of Mormon historical setting. Strangely, in this situation the Book of Mormon would be the first text to record the reading, and then one would have to suppose that Byzantine copyists came up with the exact same reading several hundred years later. Looking closer at the issue, the Book of Mormon also offers several other variations from the King James Version, with the omission of "Thy kingdom come" in Matthew 6:10 and "Give us this day our daily bread" in 6:11. The Joseph Smith Translation further complicates the matter by introducing nineteen changes to the King James translation.

A couple of important features emerge from the comparison, ones that can perhaps guide the Latter-day Saint conversation on the matter. First, when compared side by side, the Joseph Smith Translation, in this example, appears to be a commentary rather than a textual revision.

Matthew 6 (KJV)	Matthew 6 (JST)
9 Our Father which art in heaven, Hallowed be thy name. 10 Thy kingdom come. Thy will be done in earth, as it is in heaven. 11 Give us this day our daily bread. 12 And forgive us our debts, as we forgive our debtors. 13 And lead us not into temptation, but deliver us from evil: For thine is the kingdom, and the power, and the glory, for ever. Amen.	9 Our Father **who** art in heaven, Hallowed be thy name. 10 Thy kingdom come. Thy will be done **on** earth, as it is **done** in heaven. 11 Give us this day our daily bread. 12 And forgive us our **trespasses**, as we forgive **them who trespass against us**. 13 And **suffer** us not **to be led** into temptation, but deliver us from evil: For thine is the kingdom, and the power, and the glory, forever **and ever**. Amen.

In the above example, the bolded text isolates the meaningful differences between the two texts. The most substantial changes are the shift from "debts" to "trespasses" and the change in verb form from "lead us not into temptation" to "suffer us not to be led into temptation." Matthew's wording regarding "debts" is universally agreed upon by all Greek manuscripts, and seems to convey the idea that believers should acknowledge their indebtedness to others and through that recognition forgive others with the hope that they too will be forgiven. The Joseph Smith Translation text is closer to the wording of Luke 11:2, which speaks of sin instead of debts, but the shift from debts to trespasses in Matthew is an obvious interpretation of the meaning based on a text-critical approach to the passage. The other major difference centers on the issue of whether God would lead a person into temptation, which the Joseph Smith Translation changes so that God holds the power to permit a person to be led into temptation by someone else, but God is not directly responsible for leading a person into temptation.[24] Such a change again appears to represent an interpretive interest.

A different picture emerges when the same comparison is made between the Book of Mormon and the King James text.

3 Nephi 13	Matthew 6 (KJV)
9 Our Father who art in heaven, hallowed be thy name. 10 Thy will be done on earth as it is in heaven. 11 And forgive us our debts, as we forgive our debtors. 12 And lead us not into temptation, but deliver us from evil. 13 For thine is the kingdom, and the power, and the glory, forever. Amen.	9 Our Father which art in heaven, Hallowed be thy name. 10 **Thy kingdom come.** Thy will be done in earth, as it is in heaven. 11 **Give us this day our daily bread.** 12 And forgive us our debts, as we forgive our debtors. 13 And lead us not into temptation, but deliver us from evil: For thine is the kingdom, and the power, and the glory, for ever. Amen.

A different set of questions arises from this comparison, particularly the issue of why the Book of Mormon text omits "Give us this day our daily bread" and the invocation "thy kingdom come." Given the differences between the two texts, one would have to imagine a historical setting where the Book of Mormon audience would not need to pray for daily food and also would not be encouraged to pray for the coming of the kingdom of God. Such a pursuit could imagine two distinctly different settings and historical situations, but the overarching question of recovering the most reliable text of the Greek New Testament, the question that this study has engaged, would still remain unanswered.

Moving Forward

As has hopefully been demonstrated, Latter-day Saints face unique challenges when confronting text-critical problems when Restoration scripture also provides a comparative passage of scripture. Joseph Smith and subsequent leaders have not provided guidance on this issue that would clarify how such questions are to be answered, and yet those very questions have become the focus of critics of the Book of Mormon.[25] Also, it has hopefully been demonstrated that the tools of textual criticism are often sufficient to handle the challenge of dealing with the recovery of the most reliable text of the Greek New Testament. But those same tools are not sufficient to handle the question of when there are Greek manuscripts and modern scriptural texts that exist only in translation. In other words, text-critical tools were not designed to handle questions about similarities between the Greek New Testament, the Book of Mormon, and the Joseph Smith Translation. If textual criticism is the only tool that can be brought to this discussion, then the Book of Mormon text will continually appear anachronistic as a historical document because its original text cannot be compared against the Greek New Testament productively. One simple reason for this is that the original text of the Book of Mormon could potentially be translated in dramatically different ways using modern scholarly tools and approaches. Additionally, prophetic inspiration exists between the original Book of Mormon text and its English translation, and the fact will always remain that the language of inspiration had significant overlaps with the language of the King James translation because that was the religious language of the Prophet Joseph Smith.

Instead of looking at these questions text critically, it will be helpful for Latter-day Saint scholars to maintain a continued interest in the issue of the recovery of the most reliable text of the New Testament using the traditional tools of text criticism, while also developing a nuanced approach to the way the Book of Mormon engages ancient texts, both the Old and New Testament. There is little doubt that the Book of Mormon frequently draws on the language of the New Testament, sometimes quoting its language verbatim (compare Mosiah 16:10 to 1 Corinthians 15:53), but to see this as an issue that raises questions either about the authenticity of the Book of Mormon or about the most reliable text of the Greek New Testament is to overlook what it means to translate a text through inspiration. Without sidetracking this discussion into the question of whether the Book of Mormon translation was done word for word or whether concepts and phrases were given to Joseph Smith, who then rendered them using his own language, this study will engage the question of how Book of Mormon quotations of the New Testament should not force Latter-day Saint scholars to argue for a revision of biblical texts when the Book of Mormon contains alternative readings.[26]

In his dissertation, Latter-day Saint scholar Nicholas Frederick tackled this question, arguing that Joseph Smith cited the opening verses of the Gospel of John throughout the translation of the Book of Mormon in new and creative ways.[27] Joseph's engagement with the Bible was both interpretive and thoughtful, suggesting that the Book of Mormon, in part, expresses the intellectual collision of biblical texts that already existed in Joseph Smith's mind through his cultural upbringing, and that those texts were revised through a process that can be described as inspiration. Joseph saw new ideas emerging from old texts, and it seems he did not limit his interests to texts that had been written by the time Lehi and his family departed to the New World. Instead, scripture was part of Joseph Smith's vocabulary, and it became part of the Nephite vocabulary through his translation of their ancient texts.

Although the suggestion that Joseph Smith creatively adapted texts may cause some consternation among Latter-day Saint exegetes, the reality of the matter is that without advocating for the creative and inspirational use of biblical texts, the Book of Mormon will appear anachronistic in several instances. One could also argue that the language of the King James translation is the language that God revealed to Joseph. The solution to that problem is beyond recovery because the original text of the Book of Mormon is not present for examination. Two important solutions arise from the approach advocated in this study. First, Latter-day Saint scholars are free to engage questions of the most reliable text of the Bible, and to suggest that the most reliable text of the Bible may depart from what is quoted in the Book of Mormon. This is the situation that exists with the Lord's Prayer. The most original form of the prayer in Matthew is easily recoverable on the basis of text-critical considerations, and the Book of Mormon is different from that text. Second, the Book of Mormon can be interpreted to be in conversation with the Bible, where the language of a modern translation conveys the extent of that conversation.

Returning to the Lord's Prayer in the Book of Mormon and the Joseph Smith Translation, the Book of Mormon version lacks the request for the coming of the kingdom of God. It also lacks the request for daily bread. Unlike the New Testament version of the prayer, the Book of Mormon experience follows a period of extreme wickedness (see 3 Nephi 8–9), so much so that many people were destroyed before the visit of Jesus Christ. In direct contrast to the setting in Matthew, where disciples had shown interest in Jesus and his teachings, the Book of Mormon setting is one of rebuke, followed by the preservation of a righteous remnant. In that light, the reading of the Lord's Prayer may indicate that the Book of Mormon people were either too wicked to ask for such things, and instead their most important request was for forgiveness, or that the kingdom had already come to them, in which case they no longer needed to ask for it. Perhaps in anticipation of feeding the Nephites until they were full (3 Nephi 18:4), Jesus did not teach them to pray for food, since he would later that day visually demonstrate a miraculous feeding.

Conclusion

It is hoped that this study has demonstrated two important ideas regarding the text of the New Testament. First, the most recoverable text of the Greek New Testament is an attainable goal, one that can be used productively in many instances to produce a sound and reliable text that can inform modern translations of the Bible. A corollary of this discussion is that the translation of the New Testament as presented in the King James Bible is not without its limitations. This study presented some of the most challenging instances of textual variation, but there are hundreds of additional examples. That is not to say that the King James Version is too flawed to convey the word of God, only that in certain cases where there are known text-critical issues it should be used with caution. Second, this study has attempted to engage the thorny question of how Latter-day Saint scholars of the Bible can engage the challenge of recovering the most reliable text of the New Testament when the Book of Mormon or other Restoration scripture also quotes those same biblical passages.

The use of the Bible in the Book of Mormon is a topic that has only recently been engaged openly, and this study has suggested that the Book of Mormon uses the Bible creatively and through inspiration. Those approaches do not provide sufficient grounds for Latter-day Saint exegetes to revise their quest to establish the most reliable text of the New Testament. Instead, recovering the most reliable text of the New Testament can in turn help determine the source texts that were used in the creation of Book of Mormon narratives, and subsequently help identify places where inspiration shaped and expanded passages adopted from the Bible.

⌖

Thomas A. Wayment is a professor of classical studies at Brigham Young University.

Further Reading

Frederick, Nick. "What Has Moroni to Do with John?" *Religious Educator* 14, no. 3 (2013): 93–109.

Griffin, Carl W., and Frank F. Judd Jr. "Principles of New Testament Textual Criticism." In *How the New Testament Came to Be*, edited by Kent P. Jackson and Frank F. Judd Jr., 78–92. Provo, UT: Religious Studies Center, Brigham Young University; Salt Lake City: Deseret Book, 2006.

Holmes, Michael W. "Reasoned Eclecticism in New Testament Textual Criticism." In *The Text of the New Testament in Contemporary Research*, edited by Bart D. Ehrman and Michael W. Holmes, 336–60. Grand Rapids, MI: Eerdmans, 1995.

Metzger, Bruce, and Bart Ehrman. *The Text of the New Testament: Its Transmission, Corruption, and Restoration*. 4th ed. New York: Oxford University Press, 2005.

Vaganay, Léon, and Christian-Bernard Amphoux. *An Introduction to New Testament Textual Criticism*. Translated by Jenny Heimerdinger. 2nd ed. London: Cambridge University Press, 1991.

Notes

1. Compare Eldon J. Epp, "It's All about the Variants: A Variant-Conscious Approach to New Testament Textual Criticism," *Harvard Theological Review* 100 (2007): 275–308.

2. The process for the Old Testament is inherently different and will not be discussed in this study.

3. Carl W. Griffin and Frank F. Judd Jr., "Principles of New Testament Textual Criticism" in *How the New Testament Came to Be*, ed. Kent P. Jackson and Frank F. Judd Jr. (Provo, UT: Religious Studies Center, Brigham Young University; Salt Lake City: Deseret Book, 2006), 78–92.

4. Carol F. Ellertson, "New Testament Manuscripts, Textual Families, and Variants" in Jackson and Judd, *How the New Testament Came to Be*, 93–108.

5. President Hinckley noted the same phenomenon in general conference. See Gordon B. Hinckley, "The Great Things Which God Has Revealed," *Ensign*, April 2005, 82.

6. The longest New Testament papyrus is the Bodmer papyrus (P[46]), and it contains portions of Romans, 1–2 Corinthians, Galatians, Philippians, Ephesians, Colossians, 1 Thessalonians, and Hebrews. It dates to the beginning of the second century AD.

7. Mark 5:1 calls them Gerasenes, although some texts for Mark call them Gadarenes (Alexandrinus), Gergystenes (Freer), and Gergesenes (Sinaiticus); Luke 8:26 calls them Gerasenes, although other texts of Luke call them Gergsenes (Sinaiticus) and Gadarenes (Alexandrinus and Freer).

8. Blumell carefully describes how such spurious verses came to be included in the King James translation. See Lincoln H. Blumell, "The Text of the New Testament," in *The King James Bible and the Restoration*, ed. Kent P. Jackson (Provo, UT: Religious Studies Center, Brigham Young University; Salt Lake City: Deseret Book, 2011), 61–74.

9. Two papyri, 66 and 75, plus Sinaiticus and Vaticanus.

10. See Daniel B. Wallace, "Reconsidering 'The Story of the Woman Taken in Adultery Reconsidered,'" *New Testament Studies* 39 (1993): 290–96; Bart D. Ehrman, "Jesus and the Adulteress," *New Testament Studies* 34 (1988): 24–44; and Thomas A. Wayment, "The Woman Taken in Adultery and the History of the New Testament Canon," in *The Life and Teachings of Jesus Christ: From the Transfiguration through the Triumphal Entry* (Salt Lake City: Deseret Book, 2006), 372–97.

11. Although both endings are included in some manuscripts, the ones that do so are very late and are considered to be too late to potentially convey the most original recoverable text.

12. Translation from the New English Translation.

13. Thomas A. Wayment, "The Endings of Mark and Revelation," in Jackson, *The King James Bible and the Restoration*, 75–94. M. Clayton Croy, *The Mutilation of Mark's Gospel* (Nashville: Abingdon, 2003), 137–63, contends that the abbreviation of the Gospel of Mark may have occurred because the last page of the codex containing it was lost. See P. W. van der Horst, "Can a Book End with a Gar? A Note on Mark XVI:8," *Journal of Theological Studies* 23 (1972): 121–24; and K. R. Iverson, "A Further Word on Final Gar (Mark 16:8)," *Catholic Biblical Quarterly* 68 (2005): 79–94.

14. Some scholars have connected the discussion of the endings of the Gospel of Mark with the authenticity of the Book of Mormon. Connecting the two discussions is problematic for many reasons, first because the issue of the ending cannot be solved convincingly for a broad audience, and second because the authenticity of the Book of Mormon exists independently of the Greek text. Parallels in language between the two more than likely represent the Prophet's religious vocabulary that came through in the translation process.

15. Bruce M. Metzger, *A Textual Commentary on the Greek New Testament*, 2nd ed. (New York: United Bible Societies, 2000), 647–49.

16. The classic study on this passage is in B. D. Ehrman and M. A. Plunkett, "The Angel and the Agony: The Textual Problem of Luke 22:43–44," *Catholic Biblical Quarterly* 45 (1983): 401–16.

17. Interestingly, Lincoln H. Blumell has argued that believing Christians removed the verses out of embarrassment for what the verses said about Jesus's humanity; see "Luke 22:43–44: An Anti-Docetic Interpolation or an Apologetic Omission?," *TC: A Journal of Biblical Textual Criticism* 19 (2014): 1–35. See also Thomas A. Wayment, "A New Transcription of POxy 2383 (P69)," *Novum Testamentum* 50 (2008): 351–57. See also Pasquale Orsini and Willy Clarysse, "Early New Testament Manuscripts and Their Dates: A Critique of Theological Palaeography," *Ephemerides Theolgoicae Lovanianses* 88 (2012): 466.

18. Paul R. McReynolds, "John 1:18 in Textual Variation and Translation," in *New Testament Textual Criticism: Its Significance for Exegesis: Essays in Honor of Bruce M. Metzger*, ed. Eldon Epp and Gordon Fee (Oxford: Clarendon, 1981), 105–7.

19. The Doctrine and Covenants should not be overlooked as a source for quotation of the New Testament and what that might mean for the recovery of the original text of the New Testament.

20. The question of whether the Book of Mormon quotes from the New Testament can be a challenging issue for the historicity of the Book of Mormon. However, the Book of Mormon clearly uses a form of the Sermon on the Mount (see Matthew 5–7 and 3 Nephi 12–14) that is almost identical to the King James translation of those chapters in Matthew.

21. The most important manuscripts to support this reading are Codex Sinaiticus and Codex Vaticanus.

22. The most impressive of the manuscripts to include the passage is Codex Washingtonianus (fifth century AD).

23. Metzger, *Textual Commentary on the Greek New Testament*, 13–14.

24. Greek scribes were not bothered by the insinuation of God leading a person into temptation, because the Greek word used here means both *temptation* and *trial*. Thus, for the Greek reader, God was leading a person into trial and not temptation by the devil.

25. For example, see Wesley P. Walters, *The Use of the Old Testament in the Book of Mormon* (Salt Lake City: Utah Lighthouse Ministry, 1990).

26. For a discussion of the various translation methods used by Joseph Smith, see Richard S. Van Wagoner and Steven C. Walker, "Joseph Smith: The Gift of Seeing," *Dialogue: A Journal of Mormon Thought* 15 (1982): 46–68; and more recently Gerrit J. Dirkmaat and Michael Hubbard MacKay, *From Darkness unto Light: Joseph Smith's Translation and Publication of the Book of Mormon* (Provo, UT: Religious Studies Center, Brigham Young University, 2015). Brant Gardner offers a historical overview of the question of literal and equivalent translation practice in Brant A. Gardner, *The Gift and Power: Translating the Book of Mormon* (Salt Lake City: Greg Kofford Books, 2011).

27. Nicholas Frederick, *The Bible, Mormon Scripture, and the Rhetoric of Allusivity* (New Jersey: Farleigh Dickenson University Press, 2016).

38

The King James Translation of the New Testament

Lincoln H. Blumell and Jan J. Martin

The King James Version of the Bible (hereafter KJV) is arguably the most celebrated book in the English-speaking world. It has had an enormous impact on the English language and has done more to fix particular expressions in the minds of English speakers than any other book.[1] Though it was first published over four hundred years ago (1611), the KJV is still in print today and in spite of its archaic language and text-critical shortcomings remains the Bible that more Americans choose to read than any other English translation.[2] The perpetual attraction of the KJV appears to be its language, which is at once ordinary and elevated, allowing it to ring in the ears and linger in the mind of its readers.

For English-speaking members of The Church of Jesus Christ of Latter-day Saints, the KJV is a familiar friend. The Church has used the KJV since the days of Joseph Smith. However, it was not until the 1970s that a practical need for a Latter-day Saint edition of the KJV became apparent, and it was not until 1979 that a Latter-day Saint edition of the KJV was published.[3] Surprisingly, even with the availability and use of the Latter-day Saint edition, it was only as recently as May 1992 that the Church officially declared the KJV to be *the* Bible for English speakers.[4] The Church's current handbook for leaders (2010) declares, "English-speaking members should use the Latter-day Saint edition of the King James Version of the Bible. . . . Although other versions of the Bible may be easier to read, in doctrinal matters, latter-day revelation supports the King James Version in preference to other English translations."[5] This statement clearly explains the reason the Church continues to use the KJV when many other Christian churches have abandoned it for modern translations. It also frankly acknowledges that the King James Bible's sixteenth-century language may present difficulties for the modern reader.

There are essentially two fundamental challenges with the English of the KJV: accessibility and accuracy. An accessible text uses language that its readers easily understand. Unfortunately, the sixteenth-century English of the KJV can make comprehension difficult in places. An accurate translation of a text uses a second language to carefully represent the original language as closely as possible. Since the publication of the KJV in 1611, there have been important advances in understanding Biblical Hebrew and Greek and numerous discoveries of additional biblical manuscripts that have provided important textual variations and clarifications (see chapter 37 herein). Unfortunately, the KJV text does not reflect these advances and in places is simply an inaccurate translation.

This chapter, therefore, will address the accessibility and accuracy of the King James English in the Latter-day Saint edition of the Bible, particularly in the New Testament. First, it will begin with a brief history of the translation of the KJV, illustrating the book's textual ancestry. Second, it will demonstrate the composite nature of the KJV text by tracing the origins of each part of one New Testament passage. Third, it will illustrate why the KJV translators chose a heightened form of English by comparing a passage from the KJV New Testament with the same one taken from three other modern translations. Fourth, it will demonstrate challenges with accessibility using two examples of archaic words that are present in both the Old and New Testaments. Finally, the last part of this chapter will include a section, in tabular form, of fifty passages in the KJV New Testament that are translated incorrectly and will provide a more accurate rendering of these passages so that readers of the KJV will be better able to navigate their way through its New Testament translation.

Translating the King James Bible

In January 1604, King James VI and I, king of Scotland, England, and Ireland, gathered religious leaders to Hampton Court in an attempt to establish religious uniformity throughout his kingdoms.[6] In the midst of the debates, James unexpectedly ordered the making of a new translation of the Bible. At the time of the conference, England was in the uncomfortable position of using two different Bibles: the Bishops' Bible (1568) and the Geneva Bible (1560). The Bishops' Bible, published by a group of English bishops under the patronage of Queen Elizabeth I, was at the time the only one authorized for use in the church. Unfortunately, the bishops who produced the Bishops' Bible were somewhat deficient in Hebrew and Greek scholarship and wrote in awkward, Latinate English. Consequently, the Bishops' Bible never became popular, and lay people did not use it for study at home. The Geneva Bible, on the other hand, was published by a group of Protestant scholars living in exile during the reign of Mary I (1553–58). This translation had considerably more scholarly merit, and it also contained tables, marginalia, concordances, and a plethora of study aids for the benefit of the lay readership. It was an extremely successful English Bible and became the most popular version for private use, but King James refused to accept it as the Bible for the Church of

England because he particularly disliked the antimonarchist sentiments in the book's annotations.

King James's solution to the religious divisions among his subjects was to make a uniform translation of the English Bible. Following the meeting at Hampton Court, where the king announced his intentions, efforts immediately turned to gathering a body of scholars who could provide the translation. By June 30, 1604, forty-seven of an intended fifty-four translators were appointed and were drawn from the ranks of England's foremost scholars. They were divided into six committees called "companies": two from Cambridge, two from Oxford, and two from Westminster, with each company assigned to translate a different section of the Bible. Under the direction of King James, fourteen rules were put in place to guide the companies as they carried out their translations; a fifteenth rule was added later. Because these guidelines were so central to the translation, they are listed here in their entirety:[7]

1. The ordinary Bible read in the Church, commonly called the Bishops' Bible, to be followed, and as little altered as the truth of the original will permit.

2. The names of the prophets, and the holy writers, with the other names in the text, to be retained, as near as may be, accordingly as they are vulgarly used.

3. The old ecclesiastical words to be kept, viz.: as the word "Church" not to be translated "Congregation" etc.

4. When a word hath diverse significations, that to be kept which hath been most commonly used by the most of the Ancient Fathers, being agreeable to the propriety of the place, and the Analogy of Faith.

5. The division of the chapters to be altered either not at all, or as little as may be, if necessity so require.

6. No marginal notes at all to be affixed, but only for the explanation of the Hebrew or Greek words, which cannot without some circumlocution so briefly and fitly be expressed in the text.

7. Such quotations of places to be marginally set down as shall serve for fit reference of one Scripture to another.

8. Every particular man of each company to take the same chapter or chapters, and having translated or amended them severally by himself where he think good, all to meet together, confer what they have done, and agree for their parts what shall stand.

9. As one company hath dispatched any one book in this manner, they shall send it to the rest to be considered of seriously and judiciously, for His Majesty is very careful for this point.

10. If any company, upon the review of the book so sent, shall doubt or differ upon any place, to send them word thereof, note the place and withal send their reasons, to which if they consent not, the difference to be compounded at the general meeting, which is to be of the chief persons of each company, at the end of the work.

11. When any place of especial obscurity is doubted of, letters to be directed by authority to send to any learned man in the land for his judgement of such a place.

12. Letters to be sent from every Bishop to the rest of his clergy, admonishing them of this translation in hand, and to move and charge as many as being skilful in the tongues have taken pains in that kind, to send his particular observations to the company, either at Westminster, Cambridge or Oxford.
13. The directors in each company to be the Deans of Westminster and Chester for that place, and the King's Professors in the Hebrew and Greek in each University.
14. These translations to be used where they agree better with the text than the Bishops' Bible, viz.: Tyndale's, Matthew's, Coverdale's, Whitchurch's [Great Bible], Geneva.
15. Besides the said directors before mentioned, three or four of the most ancient and grave divines, in either of the universities not employed in the translating, to be assigned by the Vice-Chancellors, upon conference with the rest of the heads, to be overseers of the translations as well Hebrew as Greek, for the better observation of the 4th rule above specified.[8]

To facilitate the translation process, and in accordance with instruction number 1, forty folio-sized unbound 1602 Bishops' Bibles were distributed to the translators to work from. By design, the new Bible was a revision of previous Bibles rather than a new translation. The Bishops' Bible was the core text. Working from it, the translators examined the other Bibles, particularly the Hebrew and Greek originals for the Old and New Testament respectively, and selected what they felt were the right words for every verse. Even though only a few of the translators' papers have survived, they still provide invaluable insights into the process of translation.[9]

Today, this kind of approach to Bible translation is typical, but in the early 1600s, this scheme was incredibly innovative. Because the KJV is effectively a revision of the Bishops' Bible, which is itself a revision of earlier English Bibles, the KJV is not the fixed and stable work of one collection of translators. Thus, its reputation as the hallmark of all English Bibles is misleading. As the KJV translators themselves explained, "wee never thought from the beginning, that we should neede to make a new Translation, nor yet to make of a bad one a good one . . .

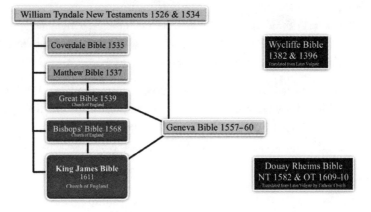

Table 1. King James Bible predecessors.

but to make a good one better, or out of many good ones, one principall good one."[10] The "good one" that they were going to improve was the Bishops' Bible of 1568. The "many good ones" were the Bibles made by a handful of predecessors. Thus, the KJV has a textual ancestry.

Even though the followers of the Oxford theologian John Wycliffe (1320–84) translated the Latin Vulgate Bible into an excessively literal Middle English in the late fourteenth century, William Tyndale (1494–1536) is the true father of the English Bible. Tyndale, an exiled, reform-minded English priest with an extraordinary gift for languages, was the first person to translate the New Testament into English from Greek source texts (1526). Likewise, he was also the first person to translate portions of the Old Testament into English from the Hebrew source text. He completed the Pentateuch in 1530 and Jonah in 1533. Joshua–2 Chronicles was published posthumously in 1537.[11] Because of his arrest in Antwerp on charges of heresy (May 1535) and his subsequent martyrdom (October 1536), Tyndale was unable to translate the complete Old Testament. Nevertheless, as the diagram shows, all English translations of the Bible produced between 1535 and 1611, including those authorized by the English Church (Great Bible, Bishops' Bible, King James Bible), were substantially based on Tyndale's work. Even the Catholic translators of the Douay–Rheims Bible (1582) referred to Tyndale, though their base text was the Latin Vulgate Bible rather than Greek source text. Because Tyndale was a deeply thoughtful translator who sought to bring his work as close to the literal meaning of the Greek as he could, his translations top the list of the prescribed additional resources that the KJV translators were supposed to use.[12] Nevertheless, the KJV translators owe an immense debt to all of their English predecessors because they contributed heavily to the development of an English way of expressing biblical material.

One illustration, taken from Matthew 1:18–20, is sufficient to demonstrate the way the KJV translators combined portions of earlier English Bible translations to form the King James text.

> *Now* the birth of Jesus Christ was on this wise: When *as* his mother Mary was **espoused** to Joseph, before they came together, she was found with child *of* the Holy Ghost.
>
> Then Joseph her husband, being a *just* man, and *not willing* to make *her a publick* example, was minded to put her away **privily**.
>
> But while he **thought on** *these things*, behold, the angel of the Lord appeared unto him in a dream, saying, Joseph, <u>thou</u> son of David, fear not to take unto thee Mary thy wife: for that which is conceived in her is of the Holy Ghost.

The large majority of this passage was taken directly from Tyndale's 1534 New Testament. However, portions of it were borrowed from other translations. The two <u>underlined</u> words were copied from Myles Coverdale's 1535 Bible. The *italicized* words were taken from the Geneva Bible. The bold words are all that remain of the base text, the Bishops' Bible. The only word that may be original to the KJV translators is espoused.[13] This sample shows that Tyndale provided the basis of the King James text. However, it also demonstrates the amount of revision the KJV translators did and how carefully they selected from the other versions of the Bible that were available to them. This passage also indicates how much of the Bishops' Bible had to be changed.

The translators began the actual work on the project sometime in the fall of 1604. They took three years to complete the preliminary phases of revision/translation before circulating their work for review by other companies. It would take approximately two more years (1608–9) before the general committee would be selected, made up of one representative from each of the six companies. This committee met at Stationers' Hall in London for nine months in 1610 to carefully review the whole translation and discuss unresolved disputes between variant translations. John Bois, who participated in this final review and kept meticulous notes of part of the proceedings, indicated just how impassioned some of the discussions became. Ward Allen summarizes:

> Bois notes discussions at 453 places in the Epistles. If his notes are complete, the general meeting deliberated each day over some thirty-two readings. We know from Bois that the members of the meeting engaged in arguments, which were sometimes violent, consulted dictionaries, pored over and discussed current and antique theologians, traced textual variations, studied classical authors to settle questions of diction, thought about style, composed in places original readings. We know from the tenth rule that the meeting deliberated over questions which were so difficult that the translators themselves had reached a deadlock over correct answers.[14]

The final outcome resulted in the KJV text familiar to us today. For example, the marginal annotations for Luke 1:57 demonstrate the stages of the translation process. The Bishops' Bible reads, "Elizabeths time came that she should bee delivered, and she brought forth a sonne." The first revision made the following change: "Now Elizabeths time was fulfilled that she should bee delivered, and she brought forth a sonne." One last change made by the Stationers' Hall group brings the text into the form familiar to King James Version readers: "Now Elizabeths full time came, that she should bee delivered, and shee brought forth a sonne."[15] Hundreds, if not thousands, of similar such changes produce a text that echoes familiarity to many Bible readers of today.

The first edition of the KJV came quietly and without fanfare from the press of Robert Barker, the king's printer, in 1611.[16] The large, heavy volume, measuring approximately eleven by sixteen inches, was designed to sit impressively on a church lectern where it could be read aloud to the congregation. The text was printed in two columns per page, with cross-references in the interior and exterior margins and brief chapter summaries placed before the first verse of each chapter. In addition to the actual biblical text, a decorative title page was affixed that contained the following inscription: "THE HOLY BIBLE, Conteyning the Old Testament, and the New. Newly translated out of the originall tongues: & with the former Translations diligently compared and revised, by his Maiesties speciall Comandement. Appointed to be read in Churches. Imprinted at London by Robert Barker, Printer to the Kings most Excellent Maiestie. Anno Dom. 1611." Following the title page, there was a three-page dedication of the work to King James, "the Most High and Mightie Prince," followed by the translators' preface, calendars of church festivals, prayers and lessons with

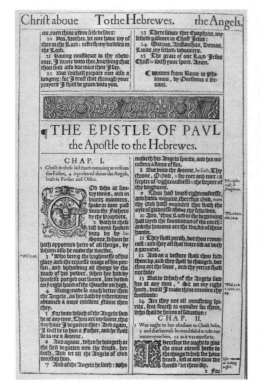

1611 King James Bible, opening of the Epistle to the Hebrews. Public domain.

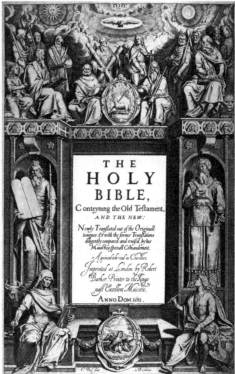

Title page, 1611 King James Bible. Public domain.

readings for various church services, a map of the Holy Land, a table of contents listing the books of the Bible and the number of chapters, and thirty-four pages of biblical genealogies.

The Language of the King James Bible

While no record exists of King James's opinion of the KJV, Hugh Broughton, a Puritan Hebrew scholar who had been excluded from the companies of translators, did not approve. He boldly and passionately declared that the translation "bred in me a sadness that will grieve me while I breath. It is so ill done. Tell his Maiest[y] that I had rather be rent in pieces with wild horses, then any such translation by my consent should be urged upon poor Churches. . . . The new edition crosseth me. I require it to be burnt."[17] One reason that Broughton was so dramatically opposed to the translation was because he felt that the English was out of date.[18] He was right. The English of the 1611 KJV was derived, at least in part, from English that was common sixty or seventy years earlier. However, the translators had a good reason for using a style of English that was not contemporary.

In the preliminaries to the 1611 KJV, Miles Smith, a member of the final revision committee, explained that a good translation opened "the window, to let in the light" and put "aside the curtain, that we may look into the most Holy place."[19] In other words, the language of the Bible needed to be plain, dignified, and understandable to lay people. However, it should also be rich, resonant and appropriate for a holy place. The language needed to reach up to the sublimity of God while also reaching down to the vulgarity of man.[20] One modern author stated it this way: "Not everyone prefers a God who talks like a pal or a guidance counselor. Even some of us who are nonbelievers want a God who speaketh like—well, God."[21]

One comparative illustration will demonstrate the difference in the KJV's heightened language. James 1:5 is well known to Latter-day Saints and much beloved because of its connection to the Prophet Joseph Smith and the First Vision. The chart below compares the KJV translation with three modern translations.

King James Bible (KJB)	New Revised Standard Version (NRSV)	New International Version (NIV)	Common English Version (CEB)
If any of you lack wisdom, let him ask of God, that giveth to all men liberally, and upbraideth not; and it shall be given him.	If any of you is lacking in wisdom, ask God, who gives to all generously and ungrudgingly, and it will be given you.	If any of you lacks wisdom, you should ask God, who gives generously to all without finding fault, and it will be given you.	But anyone who needs wisdom should ask God, whose very nature is to give to everyone without a second thought, without keeping score. Wisdom will certainly be givent to those who ask.

New Revised Standard Version—Published in 1989 by the National Council of Churches
New International Version—Published in 1978 by the Committee on Bible Translation
Common English Version—Published in 2011 by the Common English Bible Committee

Table 2. Translation comparison of James 1:5.

It is easy to see from this comparison what the KJV translators so thoroughly understood. The seventeenth-century phraseology feels richer and more capable of carrying complex and multiple meanings than most twentieth- and twenty-first-century translations do. Flattened language, language that is submissive to its audience, loses some, if not all, of its ability to move, challenge, chastise, and inspire.[22] It is true that the language of the KJV can be strange and difficult in places, but strange does not mean incomprehensible and difficult does not always mean detrimental.

The most noticeable and substantial archaic aspects of the King James language are the verb forms (*hath, doeth, shalt, begat*, etc.) and the pronouns (*thee, thy, thou, thine*, etc.). Fortunately, these are very manageable with careful attention and a little practice. However, two other types of words can significantly obscure the meaning of the text for a modern reader: (1) English words that are no longer in use today and (2) English words that have changed in meaning over time. The second type occurs much more often in the KJV than the first, but it is worth providing examples of both.

Obsolete English Words and English Words with Altered Meanings

Of the roughly twelve thousand different words that make up the KJV text fewer than 1 percent are archaic, and even fewer than 1 percent are obsolete. Thus, the large majority of the language in the KJV is accessible to the modern English speaker. However, the obsolete and archaic words should not be ignored, which is why the Latter-day Saint edition of the KJV sometimes provides clarifying footnotes. One example of an obsolete word is the word *assay*, which means "to try to do, attempt, or venture."[23] It appears six times in the KJV, three times in the Old Testament, and three times in the New Testament, but because *assay* is not currently in use in everyday speech, its meaning may be obscure to most modern readers. A student of the New Testament will encounter *assay* for the first time in Acts 9:26, when Saul comes to Jerusalem after his conversion to Christ: "And when Saul was come to Jerusalem, he assayed to join himself to the disciples: but they were all afraid of him, and believed not that he was a disciple." Unfortunately, there is no explanatory footnote next to *assay* to aid the reader in understanding its meaning. The same is also true for the two other passages where it appears in the New Testament: Acts 16:7 and Hebrews 11:29. The only place in the Latter-day Saint edition of the KJV where it does have an explanatory footnote is in the Old Testament. In Deuteronomy 4:34, Moses exhorts the children of Israel to keep the commandments. He asks, "Or hath God assayed to go and take him a nation from the midst of another nation, by temptations, by signs, and by wonders, and by war, and by a mighty hand, and by a stretched out arm, and by great terrors, according to all that the Lord your God did for you in Egypt before your eyes?" A superscript *a* next to *assayed* correctly states in the footnote that the word means "attempted." With this explanation, an inaccessible term suddenly becomes accessible. However, this is true only for those who study the Deuteronomy verse. Unfortunately for readers, no cross-references connect this helpful footnote to any of the later passages where *assay* appears in the Old or New Testaments.

A similar problem occurs with words whose meanings have changed over time. For example, the word *reins* appears fifteen times in the KJV, fourteen in the Old Testament, and once in the New Testament. When first encountering this word, a modern reader will likely assume that *reins* is the plural of *rein*, which means "a long narrow strap attached to the bridle or bit of a horse or other animal."[24] However, applying the "long narrow strap" definition to any verse where *reins* appears results in a completely different meaning from what was intended. *Reins* is actually an archaic word that refers to "the region of the kidneys" and represents the "seat of the feelings or affections."[25] This use of *reins* is no longer part of everyday speech. This time, the only helpful footnote for *reins* is in the New Testament. Thus, readers who encounter *reins* for the first time in the Old Testament will struggle to make sense of it because there are no cross-references linking the Old Testament passages to the explanatory footnote in the New Testament. *Reins* appears in Revelation 2:23 during a recitation of what will happen to a seductress named Jezebel. The verse states, "And I will kill her children with death; and all the churches shall know that I am he which searcheth the reins and hearts: and I will give unto every one of you according to your works." A superscript *b* next to *reins* explains that it represents a Greek word meaning "desires and thoughts." Though it is certainly helpful to know what the underlying Greek meaning is, the footnote does relatively little to assist the reader in understanding the English meaning of *reins*. The footnote also fails to explain why this form of *reins* is an appropriate English equivalent for the Greek word. Thus, even with the helpful insight about the Greek term, *reins* could remain an unfamiliar and difficult English word for many readers. It is evident from these two examples that some words in the KJV are inaccessible to a modern reader unless explanatory help is given. Though the Latter-day Saint edition of the KJV does supply needed assistance, improvements could be made to the frequency of clarification and to the type of clarification provided.

KJV Translation and the New Testament

When the KJV was first printed in 1611, it contained a translators' preface near the beginning that was written by Miles Smith, a member of the final revision committee. In that eleven-page introduction, "The Translators to the Reader," he stated, "So hard a thing it is to please all, even when we please God best, and do seek to approve ourselves to every one's conscience."[26] The preface set forth the reasoning behind the making of the new translation: the translators believed that the Bible was God's word and that it should be available in the language of the people. Even in translation, Smith wrote, the words of scripture are of great worth: "If we be ignorant, they will instruct us; if out of the way, they will bring us home; if out of order, they will reform us; if in heaviness, comfort us; if dull, quicken us; if cold, inflame us. . . . Love the Scriptures, and wisdom will love thee." To help allay concerns about the accuracy and value of the translation, Smith added the following:

> We affirm and avow, that the very meanest [most humble] translation of the Bible in English, set forth by men of our profession . . . containeth the word of God, nay, is the word of God. As the King's speech which he uttered in Parliament, being translated into *French, Dutch, Italian*, and *Latin*, is still the King's speech, though it be not interpreted by every translator with the like grace. . . . No cause therefore why the word translated should be denied to be the word, or forbidden to be current, notwithstanding that some imperfections and blemishes may be noted in the setting forth of it.[27]

As evinced by "The Translators to the Reader," the KJV translators were aware that there were "some imperfections and blemishes" in their new Bible. Even though many of them were excellent scholars in their own right and relied on some of the best scholarly tools available in their day, the translation sometimes falls short of accurately conveying the sense of the underlying Greek, as it is easy to miss every idiom, subtlety, and nuance.[28] This is especially the case with the Greek text of the New Testament. By the time of the KJV translation, the Greek language in the New Testament source texts had not been spoken for over a millennium. While the translation appearing in the New Testament of the KJV is mostly accurate, perhaps at times even exemplary, there are nonetheless places where the translation misses the original meaning of the text or where the rendering is almost unintelligible—at least by twenty-first-century standards. Therefore, to help the reader of the KJV New

Testament better understand the actual text and what the first-century authors were trying to convey, we have provided below a list of fifty instances, presented in canonical order, where the translation needs to be either corrected or revised. We have by no means offered an exhaustive list of New Testament corrections, nor have we treated any passages where text-critical factors are at play but have focused only on the actual translation of the underlying Greek text. Our only purpose here is to help the reader better understand the original meaning of the text in places where the KJV has translation problems or errors.

	Passage	KJV Translation	Explanation and Better Translation
1.	Matthew 5:15; Mark 4:21; Luke 8:16; 11:33, 36; Revelation 18:23; 22:5	**"candle"**	In these passages the Greek word is λύχνος (*luchnos*), which has the literal meaning "lamp." Here Jesus is not talking about candles, which would be anachronistic, but about oil lamps.
2.	Matthew 6:25, 31, 34	**"take no thought"**	The Greek verb used here is μεριμνάω (*merimnaō*), which means "be anxious, or unduly concerned." Thus, the counsel given by Jesus in this section of the Sermon on the Mount is to "not be anxious" or "unduly concerned" about worldly things when the apostles were on the Lord's errands.
3.	Matthew 10:4	"Simon the **Ca-naanite**, and Judas Iscariot, who also betrayed him."	The Greek term for the KJV *Canannite* is κανανίτης (*kananitēs*, or more probably κανανάιος), and it is simply a Greek rendering of the Hebrew קנאה (*qn'h*), which has the meaning "zeal." Thus, it should read "Simon the Zealot" (see Luke 6:15 and Acts 1:3).
4.	Matthew 13:21; compare Mark 6:25; Luke 17:7; 21:9	"Yet hath he not root in himself, but dureth for a while: for when tribulation or persecution ariseth because of the word, **by and by** he is offended."	The phrase "by and by" is a translation of the Greek adverb εὐθέως (*eutheōs*), which means "immediately" or "at once." Thus, "immediately he is offended." Compare Mark 4:17.
5.	Matthew 17:24	"And when they were come to Capernaum, they that received tribute *money* came to Peter, and said, Doth not your master pay **tribute**?"	The Greek word used here is δίδραχμον (*didraxmon*) and literally means "double drachma." In the Greek rendering of the Old Testament (LXX), this term is used in Exodus 30:11–16 to signify the "half shekel" temple tax that was to be paid annually by all males twenty years and older. In this verse the same meaning applies: "Does your master pay the temple tax?" The KJV rendering "tribute" misses the point.
6.	Matthew 22:17 (compare Matthew 22:19; Mark 12:14; Luke 20:22)	"Tell us therefore, What thinkest thou? Is it lawful to give **tribute** unto Caesar, or not?"	In these verses the Greek word is κῆνσος (*kēnsos*), from which our English word *census* is derived. The meaning is not "tribute" but rather a certain kind of "tax," namely the "poll tax" or "capitation tax" that all non-Roman citizens were obliged to pay. Thus, the question being asked Jesus was whether it was lawful to pay "taxes." This was a loaded question because openly declaring that Roman taxes should not be paid was a punishable offense under Roman law.

7.	Matthew 23:24	"*Ye* blind guides, which **strain** at a gnat, and swallow a camel."	The Greek verb is διϋλίζω (*diulizō*) and means "filter out" or "strain out." Thus, a better rendering is "strain **out** a gnat."
8.	Matthew 27:34 (compare Matthew 27:48; Mark 15:36; Luke 23:36; John 19:29–30)	"They gave him **vinegar** to drink mingled with gall: and when he had tasted *thereof*, he would not drink."	The Greek word is ὄξος (*oxos*) and instead of *vinegar*, which is a lexical possibility, the best rendering is "sour wine" or "ordinary wine." Thus, "They gave him sour wine to drink." This type of wine was considered of a lower quality than ordinary "wine" (οἶνος; *oinos*) because it had moved along in the fermentation process and was considerably more bitter; nevertheless, it had not yet fermented to the extent that it had become "vinegar"—from an alcohol to an acetic acid. Anciently, people did not drink vinegar because it was not palatable. This kind of "sour wine" was known to have been commonly imbibed by Roman soldiers.
9.	Mark 5:30 (compare Luke 6:19; 8:46)	"And Jesus, immediately knowing in himself that **virtue** had gone out of him, turned him about in the press, and said, Who touched my clothes?"	The Greek word is *power* (δύναμις; *dunamis*). The present usage of *virture* may have come from Latin influence of *virtus* that has the meaning of "power."
10.	Mark 6:20	"For Herod feared John, knowing that he was a just man and an holy, and **observed** him; and when he heard him, he did many things, and heard him gladly."	The Greek verb is συντηρέω (*suntēreō*) and properly means "preserve together" or "keep safe from damage or loss." In this verse the point is being made that Herod Antipas initially "protected" John or "kept him safe" from the threats of Herodias, who desired to have John killed (compare Mark 6:17–19).
11.	Luke 2:1	"And it came to pass in those days, that there went out a decree from Caesar Augustus, that all the world **should be taxed**."	The Greek verb used here is ἀπογράφω (*apographō*) and has the principal meaning of "to register" or "to enroll." Thus, the "decree" of Augustus was "that all the world should be registered." Here it is referring to a census registration that would serve as the basis for later taxation.
12.	Luke 4:13	"And when the devil had ended all the temptation, he departed from him **for a season**."	The Greek phrase is ἄχρι καιροῦ (*arxi kairou*) and has the more accurate meaning of "until an opportune time." The Greek καιρός has the meaning of "right time" or "right moment." Thus, Luke is stating that after the devil withdrew from Jesus during the temptations, he would return at an opportune time—when the devil thought Jesus might be vulnerable to temptation.
13.	Luke 22:32	"But I have prayed for thee, that thy faith fail not: and **when thou art converted**, strengthen thy brethren."	The Greek verb is ἐπιστρέφω (*epistrephō*), and though it can have the meaning of "conversion," it literally means "to be turned" or "returned." Thus, Peter is to strengthen the brethren after he has "returned."

14.	John 5:39	"**Search** the scriptures; for in them ye think ye have eternal life: and they are they which testify of me."	The Greek verb is ἐραυνάω (*eraunaō*), and though it does mean "search" or "examine," as implied in the KJV translation, it is to be taken in another mood. Whereas the KJV translators took it in the imperative mood, the Greek mood is the indicative, which is not a command but a statement of fact: "You are searching the scriptures." Thus, the meaning of the verse is not that Jesus is commanding his Jewish interlocutors to "search the scriptures" but rather, "You are searching the scriptures because you think that in them you have eternal life; and it is they that are testifying of me."
15.	John 14:18	"I will not leave you **comfortless**: I will come to you."	The Greek word is ὀρφανός (*orphanos*), literally "orphan." Therefore, "I will not leave you as orphans."
16.	John 20:17	"Jesus saith unto her, **Touch me not**; for I am not yet ascended to my Father: but go to my brethren, and say unto them, I ascend unto my Father, and your Father; and *to* my God, and your God."	The Greek verb is ἅπτω (*haptō*) and means "to touch" or "to hold." Here it appears in the imperative mood with the middle voice, meaning that the action is already occurring. Thus, instead of "Touch me not," a better rendering would be "Stop holding on to me." This is actually a very tender moment in John where upon recognizing the risen Christ Mary takes hold of him (compare Matthew 28:7).
17.	Acts 1:20	"For it is written in the book of Psalms, Let his habitation be desolate, and let no man dwell therein: and his **bishoprick** let another take."	This verse quotes from Psalm 69:25 (LXX 68:26) and 109:8 (LXX 108:8). The term *bishoprick* (from LXX Ps 108:8) comes from the Greek ἐπισκοπή (*episkopē*) that just means "office" or "leadership." Thus, "and his office let another take." When this psalm is translated in the KJV, it is rendered as follows: "Let his days be few; *and* let another take his office."
18.	Acts 1:22	"Beginning from the baptism of John, unto that same day that he was taken up from us, must one be **ordained** to be a witness with us of his resurrection."	This word does not appear in the Greek; the KJV supplies the word *ordained* from the Tyndale translation, but the Greek only says that it was necessary for one of these "to become a witness of his resurrection with us." The focus here was on providing scriptural authority for taking Judas's office away as well as installing his replacement, who was already known to the Lord.
19.	Acts 5:30	"The God of our fathers raised up Jesus, **whom ye slew and hanged on a tree**."	This phrase does not have the conjunction *and* in Greek; the verb for "hanged" is κρεμάννυμι (*kremannumi*) and is a participle with the interpretive force being "whom you slew by hanging him on a tree."
20.	Acts 7:45	"Which also our fathers that came after brought in with **Jesus** into the possession of the Gentiles, whom God drave out before the face of our fathers, unto the days of David."	While the Greek proper name is Ἰησοῦς (*iēsous*), or Jesus, the actual person being meant here is Joshua—the successor of Moses. As Jesus and Joshua share the same name, although it is rendered differently in English, Joshua is meant here (compare Hebrews 4:8).

21.	Acts 12:4	"And when he had apprehended him, he put *him* in prison, and delivered *him* to four quaternions of soldiers to keep him; intending after **Easter** to bring him forth to the people."	The Greek word here is πάσχα (*pascha*), which means "Passover." This is an anachronism in the KJV translation in which "Easter" is rendered instead of "Passover."
22.	Acts 14:12	"And they called Barnabas, **Jupiter**; and Paul, **Mercurius**, because he was the chief speaker."	Here the Greek actually reads "Zeus" (Ζεύς; *zeus*) and "Hermes" (Ἑρμῆς; *hermēs*) respectively. *Jupiter* and *Mercury* are the Roman equivalents of *Zeus* and *Hermes*. It is unclear what motivated the translators to render them in the way they did.
23.	Acts 17:22	"Then Paul stood in the midst of Mars' hill, and said, *Ye men of Athens, I perceive that in all things ye are* **too superstitious.**"	The Greek adjective is δεισιδαίμων (*deisidaimōn*) and in a pejorative sense means "superstitious." In this instance, Paul is not trying to criticize the Athenians but rather commend them for their religiosity so as to present his message. Thus, a better rendering of the term here is "very devout" or perhaps "very religious," used in a complimentary way.
24.	Acts 19:24, 27–28, 34–35	"**Diana**"	Here the Greek reads "Artemis" (Ἄρτεμις; *artemis*). *Diana* is the Roman equivalent; see Acts 14:12 above.
25.	Acts 19:37	"For ye have brought hither these men, which are neither **robbers of churches**, nor yet blasphemers of your goddess."	The Greek word is ἱερόσυλος (*hierosulos*) and literally means "a temple robber."
26.	Acts 20:28	"Take heed therefore unto yourselves, and to all the flock, over the which the Holy Ghost hath made you **overseers**, to feed the church of God, which he hath purchased with his own blood."	The Greek term here is ἐπίσκοπος (*episkopos*), which can have as one of its principal meanings "overseer," but also means "bishop." Every other time the term is found in the New Testament the KJV renders it "bishop": Philippians 1:1; 1 Timothy 3:2; Titus 1:7; 1 Peter 2:25. Thus, a more consistent translation here would be "bishops."
27.	Acts 27:17	"Which when they had taken up, they used helps, undergirding the ship; and, fearing lest they should fall into the **quicksands**, strake sail, and so were driven."	The Greek word translated as "quicksands" is Σύρτις (*surtis*) and is actually the name of two shallow gulfs in the Mediterranean Sea. According to the Greek geographer Strabo (2.5.20), there was the "Greater Syrtis," the modern Gulf of Sirte off the coast of Libya, and the "Lessor Syrtis," the modern Gulf of Gabes off the coast of Tunisia. Here the "Greater Syrtis" is being referenced. Thus, a more accurate translation would be: "fearing they would run aground on the sand-bars of Syrtis."
28.	Acts 28:11	"And after three months we departed in a ship of Alexandria, which had wintered in the isle, whose sign was **Castor** and **Pollux**."	The Greek word is διόσκουροι (*dioskouri*) and literally means "sons of Zeus." These were the twin brothers Castor and Pollux. A rendering closer to the Greek would be something like "with the Twin Brothers as its figurehead."

29.	Acts 28:13	"And from thence **we fetched a compass**, and came to Rhegium: and after one day the south wind blew, and we came the next day to Puteoli."	The Greek verb is περιέρχομαι (*perierxomai*) and means "to go around or about." In a nautical context, it means "to sail around or about"; thus, "From there we sailed about and came to Rhegium."
30.	Romans 11:32	"For God **hath concluded** them all in unbelief, that he might have mercy upon all."	The Greek verb rendered "concluded" is συγκλείω (*sygkleiō*), which has the principal meaning of "shutting in," "to confine," or "to imprison." Thus, God "confined" all in disobedience.
31.	1 Corinthians 1:18	"For the preaching of the cross is to **them that perish** foolishness; but unto us **which are saved** it is the power of God."	In Greek these are participial phrases, so a better rendering is "For the preaching of the cross is to them **who are perishing** foolishness; but to us **who are being saved** it is the power of God."
32.	1 Corinthians 4:4	"For **I know nothing by myself**; yet am I not hereby justified: but he that judgeth me is the Lord."	The entire sense of this phrase is distorted in the KJV translation. The verb σύνοιδα (*sunoida*) can mean "to know," but a more precise meaning is "to be conscious of." The reflexive "by myself" is better rendered "against myself." Thus, "For I am conscious of nothing against myself."
33.	1 Corinthians 13:12	"For now we see through a **glass**, darkly; but then face to face: now I know in part; but then shall I know even as also I am known."	The Greek word is ἔσοπτρον (*esoptron*), and the principal meaning is "mirror": "For now we see in a mirror dimly." Ancient mirrors were made from flat pieces of metal that were polished and capable of a dim reflection.
34.	1 Corinthians 15:19	"If in this life only we have hope in Christ, we are of all men most miserable."	The rendering of this passage is somewhat confusing in the KJV. In this part of 1 Corinthians 15, Paul is making the point that the Corinthians' "faith" is not in vain regarding the Resurrection and here seems to be subordinating mere "hope" in Christ to genuine "faith" in Christ. Thus, "If in this this life we have only hoped in Christ, we are more miserable than all other people."
35.	1 Corinthians 16:22	"If any man love not the Lord Jesus Christ, let him be **Anathema Maranatha**."	The phrase "Anathema Maranatha" (ἀνάθεμα μαράνα θά; *anathema marana tha*) is a Greek phonetic rendering of an Aramaic phrase, like the ones that sometimes appear in the Gospels: Matthew 27:46; Mark 5:41; 7:34. But in this case no translation is given. The approximate meaning of the phrase "Anathema Maranatha" is "accursed, our Lord, come!" With the addition of the third person Greek imperative command "let him be" (ἤτω; *ētō*), the meaing of this Greek/Aramaic phrase is "Let him be accursed! Our Lord, come!"

36.	Galatians 5:12	"I would they were even **cut off** which trouble you."	The Greek verb is ἀποκόπτω (*apokoptō*) and has the meaning of "cutting or hewing off." Whenever this verb is used elsewhere in the New Testament it always refers to a literal "cutting off" (Mark 9:43, 45; John 18:10, 26; Acts 27:32). In this verse it appears in the middle voice, which has a reflexive sense, so that it means "to cut oneself off." Used is this way it often means "to castrate oneself" or "make oneself a eunuch." Thus, in this verse Paul is chiding his opponents who are clamoring for circumcision and hyperbolically asserts that they should carry this to its logical conclusion: "I would that those who are troubling you would even emasculate/castrate themselves!"
37.	Galatians 6:11	"Ye see how large a **letter** I have written unto you with mine own hand."	The Greek word here is γράμμα (*gramma*), which has the principal meaning "writing" or an "alphabet letter." In this verse Paul is not trying to point out how large a letter he has written in terms of length (compare Romans, 1 Corinthians, and 2 Corinthians), but rather the size or font in which individual letters have been written. Thus, the verse should be rendered: "You see how large letters I am writing to you with my own hand." As this comes near the very end of the letter, Paul is simply pointing out that he is now personally writing the letter (subscribing) and explaining the sudden change in font size. The implication is that Galatians 1:1–6:10 was written by a scribe or amanuensis and that Paul is now adding a personal touch by writing himself (compare Romans 16:22).
38.	Philippians 2:7	"But made himself of **no reputation**, and took upon him the form of a servant, and was made in the likeness of men."	The Greek verb is κενόω (*kenoō*) and principally means "to empty" or "to pour out." Thus, the reading should be "But [Jesus] emptied himself, and took upon him the form of a servant." Here Paul is discussing the condescension of Christ and asserting that as part of this process he "emptied himself" of his premortal glory and became mortal.
39.	Philippians 3:20	"For our **conversation** is in heaven; from whence also we look for the Saviour, the Lord Jesus Christ."	The Greek word is πολίτευμα (*politeuma*) and means "citizenship"; thus, "For our citizenship is in heaven."
40.	Philippians 3:21	"Who shall change our **vile** body, that it may be fashioned like unto his glorious body, according to the working whereby he is able even to subdue all things unto himself."	The Greek word is ταπείνωσις (*tapeinōsis*) and means "humble" or "low estate." Thus, a better translation would be something like "Who shall change our humble body, that it may be fashioned like his glorious body." The point being made is that our present mortal bodies are much lower than Christ's resurrected body.
41.	1 Thessalonians 5:3	"For when they shall say, Peace and safety; then sudden destruction cometh upon them, as **travail** upon a woman with child; and they shall not escape."	The Greek word rendered "travail" is ὠδίν (*ōdin*), and though it has the general meaning of "anguish" or "pain," it is specifically used in the context of "birth pangs" or "labor pains" when a woman is about to give birth. The imagery being invoked here is that the "sudden/unexpected destruction" will come just as "labor pains of a pregnant woman" suddenly appear.

42.	Hebrews 4:8	"For if **Jesus** had given them rest, then would he not afterward have spoken of another day."	This should read "Joshua" and not "Jesus." See note to Acts 7:45 above.
43.	Hebrews 9:7	"But into the second *went* the high priest alone once every year, not without blood, which he offered for himself, and *for* the **errors** of the people."	The Greek term is ἀγνόημα (*agnoēma*) or "a sin of ignorance"; thus, "which he offered for himself and for the sins of the people committed in ignorance."
44.	Hebrews 10:23	"Let us hold fast the profession of *our* **faith** without wavering; (for he *is* faithful that promised;)"	The Greek word here is ἐλπίς (*elpis*) and means "hope"; thus, "Let us hold fast to the profession of our hope without wavering."
45.	1 Timothy 5:8	"But if any provide not for his own, and specially for those of his own house, he hath denied the faith, and is worse than **an infidel**."	Rather simply "an unbeliever" (ἄπιστος; *apistos*).
46.	1 Timothy 6:20	"O Timothy, keep that which is committed to thy trust, avoiding profane *and* vain babblings, and oppositions of **science** falsely so called."	The Greek word is γνῶσις (*gnōsis*) and means "knowledge." Thus, "and oppositions of what is falsely called 'knowledge.'" Here the passages is seemingly referring to the teaching of Gnosticism.
47.	James 3:2	"For in many things **we offend** all. If any man offend not in word, the same *is* a perfect man, *and* able also to bridle the whole body."	The Greek verb is πταίω (*ptaiō*) and means "to stumble" or "to fail." Thus, it should read "For in many things we completely stumble."
48.	1 Peter 2:9	"But ye *are* a chosen generation, a royal priesthood, an holy nation, **a peculiar people**; that ye should shew forth the praises of him who hath called you out of darkness into his marvellous light."	The phrase "a peculiar people" is based on the Greek phrase λαὸς εἰς περιποίησιν (*laos eis peripoiēsin*), which literally means "a people for [God's] possession." It does not mean that God's people are weird or strange but that they are God's very own people or possession. The English word *peculiar* is derived from the Latin *peculiaris* that means "of one's own property" or "private property." First Peter 2:9 is quoting Exodus 19:5.

49.	Revelation 17:6	"And I saw the woman drunken with the blood of the saints, and with the blood of the martyrs of Jesus: and when I saw her, I wondered with great **admiration**."	The Greek word is θαῦμα (*thauma*) and means "wonder or amazement." John was not in "admiration" of the "great whore" (Revelation 17:1) but rather in "wonder" or "amazement" when he saw this vision of her; thus, "I wondered with great amazement."
50.	Revelation 19:17	"And I saw an angel standing in the sun; and he cried with a loud voice, saying to all the fowls that fly in the midst of heaven, Come and gather yourselves together unto the **supper of the great God**."	In this phrase the adjective *great* (μέγα; *mega*) does not modify *God* but rather *supper*, so it should instead read "the great supper of God."

Lincoln H. Blumell is an associate professor in the Department of Ancient Scripture at Brigham Young University.

Jan J. Martin is an assistant professor in the Department of Ancient Scripture at Brigham Young University.

Further Reading

Blumell, Lincoln H. "A Text-Critical Comparison of the King James New Testament with Certain Modern Translations." *Studies in the Bible and Antiquity* 3 (2011): 67–127.

Bray, Gerald. *Translating the Bible: From William Tyndale to King James.* Oxford: Latimer Trust, 2010.

Burke, David G., John F. Kutsko, and Philip H. Towner, eds. *The King James Version at 400. Assessing Its Genius as Bible Translation and Its Literary Influence.* Atlanta, SBL, 2013.

Campbell, Gordon. *Bible: The Story of the King James Version, 1611–2011.* Oxford: Oxford University Press, 2010.

Jackson, Kent P., ed. *The King James Bible and the Restoration.* Provo, UT: Religious Studies Center, Brigham Young University, 2011.

Norton, David. *The King James Bible: A Short History from Tyndale to Today.* Cambridge: Cambridge University Press, 2011.

Notes

1. Gordon Campbell, *Bible: The Story of the King James Version, 1611–2011* (Oxford: Oxford University Press, 2010), 1; and David Crystal, *The King James Bible and the English Language* (Oxford: Oxford University Press, 2010), 7.
2. Philip Goff, Arthur E. Farnsley II, and Peter J. Thuesen, "The Bible in American Life" (New York: Oxford University Press, 2017), 10.

3. Fred E. Woods, "The Latter-day Saint Edition of the King James Bible," in *The King James Bible and the Restoration*, ed. Kent P. Jackson (Provo, UT: Religious Studies Center, Brigham Young University; Salt Lake City: Deseret Book, 2011), 260–76.

4. "First Presidency Statement on the King James Version of the Bible," *Ensign*, August 1992, 80.

5. The Church of Jesus Christ of Latter-day Saints, *Handbook 2: Administering the Church* (Salt Lake City: The Church of Jesus Christ of Latter-day Saints, 2010), 180.

6. James ruled in Scotland as James VI from July 24, 1567, and then in England and Ireland as James I from 24 March 1603 until his death.

7. This list is taken from Norton, *King James Bible*, 86–89; see also Alfred W. Pollard, ed., *Records of the English Bible: The Documents Relating to the Translation and Publication of the Bible in English, 1525–1611* (New York: Oxford University Press, 1911), 53–55.

8. It appears that guideline 15 was added at a later time.

9. See Ward Allen, ed., *Translating the New Testament Epistles, 1604–1611: A Manuscript from King James's Westminster Company* (Ann Arbor, MI: University Microfilms International for Vanderbilt University Press, 1977), xxviii; see also Norton, *King James Bible*, 94–106.

10. King James Version original preface (1611), www.kjvbibles.com/kjprevace.htm.

11. Norton, *King James Bible*, 7.

12. In the prologue to his 1525 New Testament translation, Tyndale asked others who were learned in languages to send him suggestions if they "perceive in eny places that I have not attained the very sence of the tonge or meanynge of the scripture or have not geven the right englysshe worde." In William Tyndale, *The New Testament* (Cologne: Peter Quentell, 1525), sig. Aii^r.

13. Norton, *King James Bible*, 36, 40; Norton notes that *espoused* is also used in Richard Taverner's Bible (1539), and this may have been where the KJV translators got it from, though it is also possible that the KJV translators thought of it themselves.

14. Allen, *Translating the New Testament Epistles*, xxiv.

15. Quoted in Allen, *Translating the New Testament Epistles*, xxix.

16. Campbell, *Bible: The Story of the King James Version*, 86, 108.

17. Hugh Broughton, *A censure of the late translation for our churches sent unto a right worshipfull knight, attendant upon the king* (Middleburg: R. Schilders, 1611), STC (2nd ed.) / 3847, Early English Books Online, https:/eebo.chadwyck.com.

18. Broughton, *A censure*, sig. aiv^v.

19. King James Version original preface.

20. Adam Nicholson, *God's Secretaries: The Making of the King James Bible* (New York: HarperCollins, 2003), 227–33.

21. Charles McGrath, "Why the King James Bible Endures," *New York Times*, April 23, 2011, www.nytimes.com/2011/04/24/weekinreview/24mcrath.html.

22. Nicholson, *God's Secretaries*, 153, 236.

23. Oxford English Dictionary Online, www.oed.com, s.v. "assay."

24. Oxford English Dictionary Online, s.v. "rein."

25. Oxford English Dictionary Online, s.v. "reins."

26. "The Translators to the Reader," vii. Spelling and capitalization are modernized in this quotation and in those that follow. A good reproduction is found in Erroll F. Rhodes and Liana Lupas, eds., *The Translators to the Reader: The Original Preface of the King James Version of 1611 Revisited* (New York: American Bible Society, 1997), 27.

27. "The Translators to the Reader," xii.

28. To put it another way, reading the Greek New Testament in translation is like watching a movie in black and white, whereas reading it in the original is like watching the same movie in high definition.

39

The Greek New Testament Text of the King James Version

Lincoln H. Blumell

According to the explicit instructions of King James that the translation of the Bible he patronized be based on manuscripts written in the original languages of the Bible (see chapter 38 herein)—Hebrew for the Old Testament and Greek for the New Testament—the two committees assigned the task of providing a translation for the New Testament employed the Greek texts of the day.[1] The Greek text that was ultimately used as the basis for the KJV New Testament was one produced by the French Calvinist Theodore de Beza (1519–1605).

From Beza Back to Erasmus

Beza came from a prominent Catholic family at Vézelay in Burgundy and had studied law at Orleans before settling in Paris, where he began a career as a lawyer in 1539. Though he would earn a reputation as a capable litigator, his real passion was for classical literature, and he would eventually earn some notoriety for publishing a collection of Latin poetry in 1548. Shortly after the publication of this work, he fell seriously ill. When he recovered, he took it as a sign of divine providence and abandoned his legal career in favor of ecclesiastical pursuits. Later that same year, he went to Geneva and joined the Calvinist movement and formally renounced the Catholic faith. In 1549 he became a professor of Greek at the academy in Lausanne, and in 1558 Calvin invited him to return to Geneva so he could hold a professorship at the newly founded academy.

During Beza's time as a professor of Greek at Lausanne, he became interested in the New Testament—so interested, in fact, that he determined to publish his very own edition. First, in 1556 he published an annotated Latin edition of the New Testament, and then in 1565 he added a Greek text. Over the course of the next forty years, Beza would go on to publish nine different editions of the Greek New Testament.[2]

The translators of the King James Bible made extensive use of Beza's 1588–89 and 1598 editions.[3] In these editions, Beza provided the text of the New Testament in three columns: in the left the Greek, in the middle a Latin translation of the Greek, and in the right the Latin Vulgate. For his Greek text, Beza was principally indebted to an earlier Greek text produced by Stephanus, who was in turn dependent on Erasmus; consequently, Beza's text was virtually the same as these earlier editions. However, it should be noted that Beza did attempt with his editions to find older Greek manuscripts upon which to base his Greek text. At times Beza did consult the Peshitta, a Syriac translation of the Bible,[4] for various readings, and he also would consult what has since come to be known as the Codex Bezae.[5] This ancient codex, which came into Beza's possession sometime after 1562, dated to the fifth or sixth century and contained on the left-hand page the Greek text in a single column and on the right-hand page the Latin text in a single column.[6] Additionally, it also appears that Beza consulted a second ancient manuscript, Codex Claromontanus, which he had found in Clermont, France. This codex, like Codex Bezae, dated to the fifth or sixth century and contained the Pauline Epistles written in parallel columns of Greek and Latin.[7] Unfortunately, however, because these two manuscripts differed in many respects from the generally received Greek text of the time, Beza tended not to include the variant Greek readings in his actual text but merely mentioned the variants in his annotations.[8] Consequently, some of these variants, which clearly had an ancient pedigree, never made their way into the KJV translation since they were not in Beza's Greek text but were confined to the notes. Therefore, even though Beza would consult the Syriac Peshitta, Codex Bezae, and Codex Claromontanus, his editions of the Greek New Testament were virtually identical to an earlier Greek New Testament published by Stephanus that was based on much later manuscript evidence (i.e., the Greek New Testament text of Erasmus, discussed below).

Robert Estienne (1503–59), more commonly known by the Latin form of his name, Stephanus, was a famous Parisian printer and publisher who had a penchant for printing classical and ecclesiastical literature. Besides producing his famous *Thesaurus Linguae Latinae* in 1532, which was used for many subsequent centuries, he also published a number of Bibles.[9] He published three editions of the Latin Vulgate (1528, 1532, and 1540) and two editions of the Hebrew text of the Old Testament (1539 and 1544–46). After 1544 he turned his attention primarily to publishing Greek texts and during his lifetime published four different editions of the Greek New Testament (1546, 1549, 1550, and 1551). In his first two editions, he relied principally on the earlier Greek New Testament text published by Erasmus but also, to a lesser extent, on the text published under the direction of Francisco Ximenes de Cisneros, which is known as the Complutensian Polyglot. His third edition (1550) was noteworthy because it was the first Greek edition of the New Testament to include a critical apparatus noting textual variants and alternative readings for select passages.[10] His fourth and final version (1551), the one that Beza principally relied on for his editions of the Greek New Testament, was also very noteworthy because, for the first time, Stephanus introduced versification into the New Testament. His versification was subsequently followed and applied in the KJV New Testament, and it is used in virtually all Bibles today.[11]

As Stephanus's New Testament editions relied heavily on the Greek New Testament produced by Erasmus and, to a lesser extent, on an edition produced under Francisco Ximenes de Cisneros, it is worthwhile to discuss these two editions. However, of these two earlier editions, Erasmus's is by far the most important, at least for the purposes of the present study. It essentially formed the basis of almost all subsequent Greek New Testaments published in the sixteenth century because it was the first widely used Greek New Testament text to appear after the invention of the printing press.[12] Consequently, the

Title page, 4th edition of New Testament (1551). Robert Estienne. Public domain.

Greek text underlying the King James Bible is essentially the text produced by Erasmus, even though it came to the KJV translators via Stephanus and Beza.

Desiderius Erasmus (1466–1536), the famous Dutch humanist from Rotterdam, was ordained a Catholic priest in 1492. Shortly thereafter, he decided to pursue a doctorate in theology and in 1495 went to the University of Paris. During the course of his studies in Paris, he determined to seriously take up the study of ancient Greek since the majority of early Christian literature was written in Greek. As he became more immersed in the study of ancient Greek, he felt he could best pursue his interests elsewhere. So he left Paris in 1499 without finishing his doctorate and eventually enrolled at Cambridge. After only one year, he left, again without obtaining his doctorate, and moved to Italy to pursue his study of ancient Greek. At the time, Italy was the real center of Greek learning because a number of scholars had left Constantinople and relocated to Italy when Constantinople fell into Muslim hands in 1453. Erasmus would receive his doctorate at the University of Turin in 1506.

In 1511 Erasmus returned to Cambridge, where he would hold a professorship in Greek. This lasted only about three years, however, because the promised financial support for this position never fully materialized. In the summer of 1514, Erasmus left for Basel, Switzerland, where he was approached by a well-known printer named Johannes Froben about the possibility of producing a Greek New Testament.[13] Erasmus did not immediately agree to the project and returned to Cambridge in the spring of 1515. However, when a mutual friend, Beatus Rhenanus, approached Erasmus on behalf of Froben with a promise that if he should produce a text Froben would pay him handsomely, Erasmus readily agreed.[14] By the summer, Erasmus was back in Basel, and work was promptly undertaken on the project.

Erasmus hoped there might be some readily available manuscripts of the Greek New Testament in Basel that he could use. However, the only manuscripts he could find required some degree of correcting, and there was no one manuscript that contained the entire New Testament. In total, Erasmus used seven different manuscripts to create his edition of the New Testament, and all but one of them were owned by the Dominican Library in Basel.[15] The manuscripts were all minuscules, meaning that they were written in the cursive, lower-case Greek script common in medieval manuscripts.

The manuscripts relied on by Erasmus may be outlined as follows:[16]

1. Codex 1^{eap}, a minuscule containing the entire New Testament except for Revelation, dated to about the twelfth century.
2. Codex 1^{r}, a minuscule containing the book of Revelation except for the last six verses (Revelation 22:16–21), dated to the twelfth century.
3. Codex 2^{e}, a minuscule containing the Gospels, dated to the twelfth century.
4. Codex 2^{ap}, a minuscule containing Acts and the Epistles, dated to the twelfth century or later.
5. Codex 4^{ap}, a minuscule containing Acts and the Epistles, dated to the fifteenth century.
6. Codex 7^{p}, a minuscule containing the Pauline Epistles, dated to the eleventh century.
7. Codex 817^{e}, a minuscule containing the Gospels, dated to the fifteenth century.

^{e} = Gospels (Evangelists), ^{a} = Acts, ^{p} = Pauline Epistles, ^{r} = Revelation

In total, then, Erasmus had three manuscripts of the Gospels and Acts, four manuscripts of the Pauline Epistles, and one manuscript of Revelation. Since Erasmus was in such a hurry, he simply submitted Codex 2^{e} and 2^{ap} to the printer, compared these two manuscripts with the others, and wrote in any corrections or emendations for the printer in the margins or between the lines of the two manuscripts.

Remarkably, it took Erasmus only a couple of months to finish his edition, and by October 1515 the manuscript was headed to the press. Part of the reason for the extreme haste with which the project was undertaken was that the printer, Johannes Froben, was aware that another version of the Greek New Testament, the Complutensian Polyglot, was also going to be published, and he wanted to ensure that his version came out first. The production of the Complutensian Polyglot was overseen by cardinal primate of Spain Francisco Ximenes de Cisneros (1436–1517).[17] It was printed in 1514, but it was not sanctioned by the pope until 1520 and consequently was not published and widely circulated until 1522. Since Erasmus's copy was the first printed Greek New Testament on the market, it became the standard text.

By March 1516 the first edition of Erasmus's Greek New Testament was printed; it was entitled *Novum Instrumentum Omne*.[18] The book was a Greek-Latin diglot printed with two columns per page: the Greek text always in the left-hand column and the Latin text always in the right-hand column. The annotations were printed following the text.[19] Owing to the extreme haste with which the first edition of Erasmus's Greek New Testament was produced and printed, it was loaded with various typographical errors, literally numbering in the hundreds. Besides the typographical errors, however, there were other serious problems with the first edition. These errors arose directly from Erasmus's haste and use of inferior (late) biblical manuscripts. For example, the manuscript that he relied on for the book of Revelation lacked the final page on which was written the last six verses (Revelation 22:16–21). To remedy this problem, Erasmus simply used the Latin Vulgate and translated these verses back into Greek. However, the translation supplied by Erasmus was different in many respects from earlier Greek texts and subsequently had the effect of altering and changing certain Greek readings. Elsewhere, when Erasmus ran into difficulties with these Greek manuscripts, he simply provided his own Greek translation based on the Latin text and subsequently introduced a number of Greek variants into the New Testament that were previously unattested in the Greek.[20]

In 1519 a second edition was produced[21] in which a number of typographical emendations were made, and again in 1522 a third edition was published in which a few substantive changes were made. Perhaps the most significant change between the second and third editions was the insertion of what

Title page, 1516 edition of Erasmus's *Novum Instrumentum omne*. Public domain.

The last page of Erasmus's Greek New Testament (Revelation 22:8–21). Public domain.

has come to be known as the "Johannine Comma," comprising 1 John 5:7b–8a: "[7a]For there are three that bear record [b]*in heaven, the Father, the Word, and the Holy Ghost: and these three are one.* [8a]*And there are three that bear witness in earth,* [b]the Spirit, and the water, and the blood: and these three agree in one" (KJV, emphasis added). In the first and second editions of Erasmus's Greek New Testament, he did not include either verse 7b or 8a because they were not found in any Greek manuscript of the New Testament he had consulted. Thus, 1 John 5:7–8 read: "[7]For there are three that bear record: [8]the Spirit, and the water, and the blood: and these three agree in one." However, he came under increasing fire from a number of ecclesiastical quarters because these verses were long thought to be important Trinitarian prooftexts. Erasmus therefore remarked that if he could find them in a single Greek manuscript, he would include them in a subsequent edition. A Greek manuscript suddenly appeared with these verses, so he included them in his third edition. Scholars have long recognized that this particular manuscript, which dates to the sixteenth century, was produced for the very purpose of including these verses![22] It is evident that verses 7b and 8a were not original but were later added to 1 John to promote Trinitarian theology.[23]

By the time of Erasmus's fourth edition in 1527, which proved to be the definitive edition (although a fifth and final edition came out in 1535), some of the more serious text-critical problems with his manuscript were finally addressed. By this time the Complutensian Polyglot was available, so Erasmus judiciously made use of it and corrected certain readings that he had either created via his Latin-to-Greek translations or were the result of the generally inferior nature of the manuscripts he had consulted in Basel to create his Greek text. Notwithstanding the many improvements that were made in the fourth edition, a number of problems still persisted, but because Erasmus's Greek New Testament was the first widely accessible copy of the New Testament, it gained natural popularity that gave it a status of prominence. In fact, the Greek text of Erasmus would eventually become the standard Greek text of the New Testament for the next two hundred years because it was largely transmitted by Stephanus and Beza. In a 1633 edition of the Greek New Testament produced by two Dutch printers, Bonaventure and Abraham Elzevir, which was basically a reprint of Beza's 1565 edition, they made the following remark in the preface: *Textum ergo habes, nunc ab omnibus receptum, in quo nihil immutatum aut corruptum damus* ("Therefore you have [dear reader] the text, now received by all, in which we give nothing changed or corrupted").[24] From this remark, the Greek text produced by Bonaventure and Elzevir, which came via Erasmus to Stephanus and then to Beza, came to be regarded for many centuries as the *Textus Receptus*, the received or standard text of the New Testament.

Conclusion

While the King James Bible effectively set the standard for all subsequent English translations of the Bible and its New Testament translation was regarded with special reverence for many years, it has come under increasing criticism in the past century. The central criticism leveled at the King James New Testament has not so much to do with the actual English translation, though it is not without some problems, but rather with the textual basis of the Greek subtext. The textual basis for the King James New Testament is essentially a handful of late Greek manuscripts that range in date from the twelfth to the fifteenth century and that were known to Erasmus during the time he put together his Greek New Testament. Over the course of the last four hundred years, a number of Greek manuscripts, as well as fragments of other manuscripts, have been discovered that predate by over one thousand years the "Erasmian" text used by the translators of the King James New Testament. In fact, complete copies of the Greek New Testament have been discovered that date to the fourth century (i.e., Codex Vaticanus and Codex Sinaiticus).[25] One of the most significant contributions of these "newly" discovered texts is that they sometimes contain readings for various verses that differ markedly from those found in the King James Version. These textual variants, as they are called, are significant because in many cases it is near certain they more accurately represent the original text of the New Testament.

Consequently, the King James New Testament, which was produced long before many of these manuscripts came to light, contains some readings that are clearly secondary interpolations not attested in the oldest and most reliable New Testament manuscripts. While this is clearly a shortcoming of the King James New Testament, these textual discrepancies do not substantially affect more than twenty to thirty verses in the entire New Testament, and in only about five or six of them do these variants significantly alter the meaning of a verse or passage. Therefore, the shortcomings of the King James New Testament should not be exaggerated; all the same, neither should they be disregarded and ignored.

In the table that follows, I provide twelve passages that serve to highlight some of the most significant textual variants that either affect the KJV text of the New Testament or have generated scholarly discussion regarding New Testament variants.

Passage	KJV Translation	Text-Critical Issue
1. Matthew 24:36	"But of that day and hour knoweth no *man*, no, **not the angels of heaven, but my Father only**."	On the basis of ancient manuscript evidence, it strongly appears that a phrase was later dropped out of this verse so that the second half should read: ". . . not the angels of heaven, **nor the Son**, but only the Father." Thus, originally, it was more emphatic that in mortality Jesus did not yet know the exact timing of the Second Coming. As the verse presently reads in the KJV, this is already evident from a close reading.
2. Matthew 26:28	"For this is my blood of the **new** testament, which is shed for many for the remission of sins."	There is relatively strong support from ancient witnesses that the adjective *new* (καινή, *kainē*) was added to Matthew 26:28. While Luke 22:20 does employ the adjective (thus "new testament," better rendered "new covenant"), as does 1 Corinthians 11:25 (compare Jeremiah 31:31–34), it was not what Matthew wrote. However, in light of the references in Luke and Paul, it is certainly not wrong to call it a "new covenant."
3. Mark 9:29; compare Matthew 17:21	"And he said unto them, This kind can come forth by nothing, but by prayer **and fasting**."	On the basis of ancient textual witnesses, it seems quite likely that the phrase "and fasting" (Greek καὶ νηστείᾳ, *kai nēsteia*) was later added to the verse. Thus, it is probably best to omit this phrase. Compare Mark 9:29 NRSV: "He said to them, 'This kind can come out only through prayer.'"
4. Mark 16:9–20	"**⁹ Now when *Jesus* was risen early the first *day* of the week, he appeared first to Mary Magdalene, out of whom he had cast seven devils. ¹⁰ *And* she went and told them that had been with him, as they mourned and wept. ¹¹ And they, when they had heard that he was alive, and had been seen of her, believed not. ¹² After that he appeared in another form unto two of them, as they walked, and went into the country. ¹³ And they went and told *it* unto the residue: neither believed they them. ¹⁴ Afterward he appeared unto the eleven as they sat at meat, and upbraided them with their unbelief and hardness of heart, because they believed not them which had seen him after he was risen. ¹⁵ And he said unto them, Go ye into all the world, and preach the gospel to every creature.**	Mark 16:9–20, known as the longer ending, is absent from a number of early and important ancient manuscripts. Thus, it is commonly thought that Mark ended at 16:8. However, the longer ending is nonetheless attested in some important ancient witnesses. Additionally, there are two other endings of Mark, little known outside of scholarship, that are also attested. The shorter or intermediate ending adds material equivalent to about 1–2 verses after 16:8 and is attested in a few eighth-century manuscripts: "But they reported briefly to Peter and those with him all that they had been told. And after this Jesus himself sent out by means of them, from east to west, the sacred and imperishable proclamation of eternal salvation." There is likewise another longer ending attested in a fifth-century manuscript: "And they excused themselves, saying, 'This age of lawlessness and unbelief is under Satan, who does not allow the truth and power of God to prevail over the unclean things of the spirits. Therefore reveal your righteousness now'—thus they spoke to Christ. And Christ replied to them, 'The term of years of Satan's power has been fulfilled, but other terrible things draw near. And for those who have sinned I was

		16 He that believeth and is baptized shall be saved; but he that believeth and is baptized shall be saved; but he that believeth not shall be damned. **17** And these signs shall follow them that believe; In my name shall they cast out devils; they shall speak with new tongues; **18** They shall take up serpents; and if they drink any deadly thing, it shall not hurt them; they shall lay hands on the sick, and they shall recover. **19** So then after the Lord had spoken unto them, he was received up into heaven, and sat on the right hand of God. **20** And they went forth, and preached every where, the Lord working with them, and confirming the word with signs following. Amen.	delivered over to death, that they may return to the truth and sin no more, that they may inherit the spiritual and imperishable glory of righteousness that is in heaven.'" While there are four different endings of Mark attested, the two best-attested endings are those ending at Mark 16:8 or 16:20 (the one presently in the KJV).[26]
5.	Luke 22:43–44	"**43** And there appeared an angel unto him from heaven, strengthening him. **44** And being in an agony he prayed more earnestly: and his sweat was as it were great drops of blood falling down to the ground."	These verses are absent in some important ancient manuscripts while they are present in others. Thus, some modern Bibles either omit these verses altogether or place them in brackets to highlight their questionable character. However, the ancient manuscript evidence is such that the verses are attested in the earliest manuscripts before they are then omitted by later manuscripts. Likewise, we know from ancient Christian writings that in the middle of the fourth century AD, in the wake of the Council of Nicaea, some Christians adhering to the Nicene Creed began to purposely omit these verses from their copies of the scriptures (see Epiphanius, *Ancoratus* 31.3–5). Thus, these verses should be regarded as authentic but suppressed and deleted by some later Christians.[27]
6.	John 5:3–5	"**3** In these lay a great multitude of impotent folk, of blind, halt, withered, **waiting for the moving of the water. 4 For an angel went down at a certain season into the pool, and troubled the water: whosoever then first after the troubling of the water stepped in was made whole of whatsoever disease he had.** **5** And a certain man was there, which had an infirmity thirty and eight years."	John 5:3b–4 is missing from most modern translations because there is almost no textual support from any ancient manuscripts. At some point verses 3b–4 were added to explain why the water was "troubled" (or "stirred up") in verse 7. Since the pool of Bethesda was a mineral spring, the stirring of the water was caused by air being released up through the water. It is clear therefore that someone added the story about the angel long after the Gospel of John was written, and it is best to read the story without this angelic explanation.

| 7. | John 7:53–8:11 | "⁵³ **And every man went unto his own house. ¹ Jesus went unto the mount of Olives. ² And early in the morning he came again into the temple, and all the people came unto him; and he sat down, and taught them. ³ And the scribes and Pharisees brought unto him a woman taken in adultery; and when they had set her in the midst, ⁴ They say unto him, Master, this woman was taken in adultery, in the very act. ⁵ Now Moses in the law commanded us, that such should be stoned: but what sayest thou? ⁶ This they said, tempting him, that they might have to accuse him. But Jesus stooped down, and with** *his* **finger wrote on the ground,** *as though he heard them not.* **⁷ So when they continued asking him, he lifted up himself, and said unto them, He that is without sin among you, let him first cast a stone at her. ⁸ And again he stooped down, and wrote on the ground. ⁹ And they which heard** *it,* **being convicted by** *their own* **conscience, went out one by one, beginning at the eldest,** *even* **unto the last: and Jesus was left alone, and the woman standing in the midst. ¹⁰ When Jesus had lifted up himself, and saw none but the woman, he said unto her, Woman, where are those thine accusers? hath no man condemned thee? ¹¹ She said, No man, Lord. And Jesus said unto her, Neither do I condemn thee: go, and sin no more.**" | The entire story of the woman taken in adultery in John 7:53–8:11 is almost certainly an interpolation since it appears in only one known manuscript before the eighth century: Codex Bezae of the fifth or sixth century. Likewise, in later manuscripts it is sometimes placed after John 7:36 or 7:44, at the end of the Gospel (i.e., after John 21:25), or after Luke 21:38, which suggests it was not original to this section of John. Because a story about Jesus forgiving a woman of sins was known by Christians already in the second century (Papias in Eusebius, *Ecclesiastical History* 3.39.17), and this is the only time in the Gospels such a story is told, there is perhaps some ancient basis for it. Nevertheless, its placement here in John is clearly an interpolation, and it is likely that there are elements of the story that are clearly secondary.²⁸ |
| 8. | 1 John 5: 7–8 | "⁷ For there are three that bear record **in heaven, the Father, the Word, and the Holy Ghost: and these three are one. ⁸ And there are three that bear witness in earth,** the Spirit, and the water, and the blood: and these three agree in one." | The entire bolded section comprising 1 John 5:7b–8a is an interpolation and not part of the original text. This famous interpolation, often referred to as the "Johannine Comma," was added to Greek manuscripts in the sixteenth century and first appears in a Latin manuscript in the eighth century. Someone inserted the phrase to serve as a Trinitarian prooftext. In this section of 1 John, the point is being made that Jesus had a corporeal body, and it has nothing to do with the Godhead (Father, Word, and Holy Ghost). Modern Bibles have universally omitted this passage so that it reads: "⁷ There are three that testify: ⁸ the Spirit and the water and the blood, and these three agree" (1 John 5:7–8 NRSV). |

9.	Acts 23:9	"And there arose a great cry: and the scribes *that were* of the Pharisees' part arose, and strove, saying, We find no evil in this man: **but** if a spirit or an angel hath spoken to him, **let us not fight against God**."	The last phrase of this verse appears to have been added on the basis of the ancient manuscript evidence. Thus, the second half of this verse is better rendered as follows: "We find no evil in this man: what if a spirit or an angel spoke to him?"
10.	1 Peter 2:2	"As newborn babes, desire the sincere milk of the word, **that ye may grow thereby:**"	Early manuscripts widely preserve the following reading: "that you may grow thereby **unto salvation**." It therefore appears that the phrase "unto salvation" (εἰς σωτηρίαν, *eis sōtērian*) was lost at some point.
11.	Revelation 22:14	"Blessed *are* **they that do his commandments**, that they may have right to the tree of life, and may enter in through the gates into the city."	The reading "they that do his commandments" is attested only in very late manuscripts, whereas the earliest widely attested reading is "Blessed are **those who wash their robes**." Because the Greek phrase "that do his commandments" (οἱ ποιοῦντες τὰς ἐντολὰς) could look like the phrase "who wash their robes" (οἱ πλύνοντες τὰς στολὰς), perhaps the rendering represents a simple misreading that was perpetuated in later manuscripts. For "robes washed," see also Revelation 7:14.
12.	Revelation 22:19	"And if any man shall take away from the words of the book of this prophecy, God shall take away his part out of the **book of life**, and out of the holy city, and *from* the things which are written in this book."	The phrase "book of life" is an error that appears in the KJV because Erasmus made an error in his Greek version of the New Testament. The reading here should instead be "tree of life." When Erasmus provided the last six verses of Revelation, he relied on a copy of the Latin Vulgate in which a scribe had mistakenly miscopied the correct word *ligno* ("tree") as *libro* ("book").

Appendix: Ancient Texts of the New Testament

In what follows, I provide a brief overview of the principal ancient manuscripts that preserve the Greek text of the New Testament. These texts form the basis on which scholars today attempt to determine and reconstruct the earliest readings of the New Testament.

Codex Alexandrinus

A fifth-century-AD codex that contains every book in the New Testament except portions of Matthew (chapters 1–24), John (chapters 6–8), and 2 Corinthians (chapters 4–12). This codex also includes 1 and 2 Clement as well as the majority of the Septuagint (LXX).[29] It is called Codex Alexandrinus because its earliest known location was the city of Alexandria in Egypt. It is written with capital Greek letters (uncial script) and is laid out with two columns per page. Cyril Lucar, Patriarch of Alexandria during the early part of the seventeenth century, sent this Bible as a gift to King James I of England. James died (in March 1625) before it arrived, and so it was instead presented to his successor, Charles I, in 1627. Today it is housed in the British Library.

Codex Bezae

A fifth- or sixth-century codex that contains many of the books in the New Testament with the exception of Matthew 1, 6–9, and 27; Mark 16; John 1–3; Acts 8–10 and 22–28; Romans 1; James; 1 and 2 Peter; 1, 2, and 3 John; Jude; and Revelation. In various places, this Bible contains a number of unique readings that are not attested elsewhere, though many of these readings probably represent later interpolations to the various New Testament books. This ancient Bible is a Greek and Latin diglot, meaning that it contains on the left-hand page the Greek text in a single column and on the right-hand page the Latin text in a single column. It is called the Codex Bezae because it once belonged to Theodore Beza, a sixteenth-century French reformer, who donated it to Cambridge University in 1581. This Bible is still in the possession of Cambridge University.

Codex Sinaiticus

A fourth-century codex that contains complete copies of every book in the New Testament. It also contained the Epistle of Barnabas and *The Shepherd of Hermas* along with the Septuagint. It could even potentially be one of the fifty Bibles commissioned by Constantine in the year AD 331 and produced under the direction of Eusebius of Caesarea. This Bible is written with four Greek columns per page. It was discovered by Constantin Tischendorf in the 1850s at St. Catherine's Monastery in the Sinai (hence the name Codex Sinaiticus), and he subsequently took it back to St. Petersburg. In 1933 this codex was purchased by the British government for £100,000.00. This codex is presently housed in the British Library.

Codex Vaticanus

A fourth-century codex that contains complete copies of all the books in the New Testament with the exception of part of the Epistle to the Hebrews (chapters 9–13), all the Pastorals (Titus and 1 and 2 Timothy), and Revelation. Like Codex Sinaiticus, it may have even been one of the fifty Bibles commissioned by Constantine and produced under the direction of Eusebius of Caesarea. It is written with capital Greek letters (uncial script) and is laid out with three columns of text per page. It is called the Codex Vaticanus because it is in the possession of the Vatican Library.

Codex Vaticanus, page with ending of Luke and beginning of John. Public domain.

Papyri

Various papyri discovered in Egypt that date between the second and sixth centuries AD help supplement our knowledge of the text of the New Testament, as such fragments preserve the earliest attestations of select New Testament passages. To date, there are about 138 known New Testament papyrus fragments (numbered $\mathfrak{P}^1$, $\mathfrak{P}^2$, $\mathfrak{P}^3$, and so forth) that range in length from fragments containing a verse or two to entire codices containing a certain book of the New Testament. These fragments are very useful for the textual history of the New Testament since they are the earliest evidence we have and can predate the oldest ancient Bibles (mentioned above) by as many as 200–250 years. Notable fragments include $\mathfrak{P}^{52}$, a small fragment that contains John 18:31–33 on one side and 18:37–38 on the other and dates to the first half of the second century AD (earliest known piece of the New Testament); and $\mathfrak{P}^{46}$,

Page from $\mathfrak{P}^{46}$, end of Romans and start of Hebrews (ca. AD 200). Courtesy University of Michigan.

the oldest substantial New Testament manuscript that dates to ca. AD 200 and contains many of Paul's letters; and $\mathfrak{P}^{66}$, a virtually complete codex of John's Gospel that dates to ca. AD 200.[30]

Lincoln H. Blumell is an associate professor in the Department of Ancient Scripture at Brigham Young University.

Further Reading

Blumell, Lincoln H. "A Text-Critical Comparison of the King James New Testament with Certain Modern Translations." *Studies in the Bible and Antiquity* 3 (2011): 67–127.

Brandt, Pierre-Yves. "Manuscrits grecs utilisés par Erasme pour son édition de Novum Instrumentum de 1516." *Theologische Zeitschrift* 54 (1998): 120–24.

Burke, David G., John F. Kutsko, and Philip H. Towner, eds. *The King James Version at 400. Assessing Its Genius as Bible Translation and Its Literary Influence*. Atlanta: SBL, 2013.

De Jonge, Henk Jan. "*Novum Testamentum a nobis versum*: The Essence of Erasmus' Edition of the New Testament." *Journal of Theological Studies* 35 (1984): 394–413.

Elklertson, Carol F. "New Testament Manuscripts, Textual Families, and Variants." In *How the New Testament Came to Be*, edited by Kent P. Jackson and Frank F. Judd Jr., 93–108. Provo, UT: Religious Studies Center, Brigham Young University; Salt Lake City: Deseret Book, 2006.

Metzger, Bruce, and Bart Ehrman. *The Text of the New Testament: Its Transmission, Corruption, and Restoration*. 4th ed. New York: Oxford University Press, 2005.

Notes

1. A very similar version of this chapter was first published by the author in "The Text of the New Testament," in *The King James Bible and the Restoration*, ed. Kent P. Jackson (Provo, UT: Religious Studies Center, Brigham Young University, 2011), 61–74. I thank the Religious Studies Center for permission to use this piece as the basis for the present chapter.

2. A tenth and final edition of Beza's Greek New Testament was published posthumously in 1611. Only four of the editions published by Beza (1565, 1582, 1588–89, and 1598) were independent editions, as the others were simply smaller reprints. See Bruce Metzger and Bart Ehrman, *The Text of the New Testament: Its Transmission, Corruption, and Restoration*, 4th ed. (New York: Oxford University Press, 2005), 151–52.

3. See F. H. A. Scrivner, ed., *The New Testament in Greek: According to the Text Followed in the Authorised Version Together with the Variations Adopted in the Revised Version* (Cambridge: Cambridge University Press, 1908), vii.

4. In 1569 a Syriac translation of the New Testament was first published by Immanuel Tremellius. In Beza's subsequent editions (post-1569), he consulted the Syriac. On Tremellius's Syriac New Testament, see Kenneth Austin, *From Judaism to Calvinism: The Life and Writings of Immanuel Tremellius* (Aldershot, England: Ashgate, 2007), 125–44.

5. This codex was subsequently named after Beza. The reason for the different spelling, Bezae instead of Beza, is that it reflects the Latin genitive case, which typically expresses possession. *Codex Bezae* literally means "Codex of Beza." In 1581 Beza donated this Bible to Cambridge University, where it remains to this day.

6. This codex contains most of the books in the New Testament, with the exception of Matthew 1, 6–9, and 27; Mark 16; John 1–3; Acts 8–10 and 22–28; Romans 1; James; 1 and 2 Peter; 1, 2, and 3 John; Jude; and Revelation. It is believed that before coming into Beza's hands, this codex had come from Lyon, France. On the history of Codex Bezae, see David C. Parker, *Codex Bezae: An Early Christian Manuscript and Its Text* (Cambridge: Cambridge University Press, 1992), 46–48.

7. This codex contains the Pauline Epistles. The first seven verses of Romans (in Greek) are missing because of a lacuna. Additionally, Romans 1:27–30 and 1 Corinthians 14:13–22 are the additions of later hands. The ordering of the Pauline Epistles is standard, and Hebrews is placed after Philemon. On this codex, see Kurt Aland and Barbara Aland, *The Text of the New Testament: An Introduction to the Critical Editions and to*

the *Theory and Practice of Modern Textual Criticism*, trans. Erroll F. Rhodes (Grand Rapids, MI: Eerdmans, 1995), 110.

8. Metzger and Ehrman, *Text of the New Testament*, 151.

9. For an in-depth biographical sketch of Stephanus, see Elizabeth Armstrong, *Robert Estienne, Royal Printer: An Historical Study of the Elder Stephanus* (Cambridge: Cambridge University Press, 1954).

10. Since his critical apparatus contained a number of textual variants, it created a stir in Paris and provoked a series of severe attacks from the Sorbonne. To escape the hostilities the following year (1551), he moved to Geneva, where he would later become a Calvinist.

11. The chapter divisions as we know them today were first introduced in the thirteenth century by Stephen Langton.

12. There are a couple of reasons why it took over half a century after the invention of the printing press in the middle of the fifteenth century for a printed edition of the Greek New Testament to appear. First, since Latin was the official ecclesiastical language of the church and Jerome's Vulgate was regarded as *the* biblical text, Greek was initially seen as secondary in importance. Second, Greek fonts were more difficult to manufacture than Latin fonts, especially since Greek required a number of diacritical marks. See Metzger and Ehrman, *Text of the New Testament*, 137–38.

13. There may have been earlier negotiations between Froben and Erasmus about producing a Greek edition of the New Testament, but this is not certain. See Metzger and Ehrman, *Text of the New Testament*, 142.

14. Metzger and Ehrman, *Text of the New Testament*, 142.

15. One manuscript that contained Acts and the Pauline Letters (Codex 2[ap]) was obtained from the family of Johann Amerbach of Basel. See William W. Combs, "Erasmus and the Textus Receptus," *Detroit Baptist Seminary Journal* 1 (Spring 1996): 45.

16. On these manuscripts, see Metzger and Ehrman, *Text of the New Testament*, 142–44; Pierre-Yves Brandt, "Manuscrits grecs utilisés par Erasme pour son édition de Novum Instrumentum de 1516," *Theologische Zeitschrift* 54 (1998): 120–24; Aland and Aland, *Text of the New Testament*, 4–6; and C. C. Tarelli, "Erasmus's Manuscripts of the Gospels," *Journal of Theological Studies* 44 (1943): 155–62. Codex 1[eap] simply means that this codex contained [e] (Gospels [= evangelists]), [a] (Acts), and [p] (Pauline Letters).

17. Though Francisco Ximes de Cisneros originally conceived of the project and played a critical role in its publication, there were numerous other scholars who helped out. When the project was completed, it occupied six volumes. The first four volumes covered the Old Testament, the fifth volume covered the New Testament, and the sixth and final volume contained various Hebrew, Aramaic, and Greek dictionaries and study aids. While the fifth volume was completed and printed in 1514, its publication and dissemination had to wait until 1517, when the four volumes of the Old Testament were completed. As a set, its publication was further delayed until Pope Leo X sanctioned it in 1520. Thus, it did not begin to be distributed widely before 1522. The name of this Bible is derived from the Latin name of the town Alcalá (Latin *Complutum*), where it was printed. The word *polyglot* is of Greek origin and simply refers to any book that contains a side-by-side version of different languages of the same text. For the Old Testament, the pages contained the Hebrew text, Jerome's Latin Vulgate, and the Greek Septuagint in three parallel columns. For the New Testament, there were simply the Greek and Latin texts in parallel columns. For a more detailed treatment of this Bible, see Julián Martín Abad, "The Printing Press at Alcalá de Henares, The Complutensian Polyglot Bible," in *The Bible as Book: The First Printed Editions*, ed. Kimberly Van Kampen and Paul Saenger (New Castle, DE: Oak Knoll, 1999), 101–18; and Metzger and Ehrman, *Text of the New Testament*, 138–42.

18. Erasmus chose the phrase *Novum Instrumentum* instead of *Novum Testamentum* because he believed that the word *Instrumentum* better conveyed the idea of a decision put down in writing than did the word *Testamentum*, which "could also mean an agreement without a written record." Henk Jan de Jonge, "*Novum Testamentum a nobis versum*: The essence of Erasmus' Edition of the New Testament," *Journal of Theological Studies* 35 (1984): 396n5. In the second edition of Erasmus's Greek New Testament, he would change the title to *Novum Testamentum*.

19. De Jonge, "*Novum Testamentum a nobis versum*," 395, describes the first edition as follows: "The Latin and Greek texts of the Gospels and Acts fill pages 1–322, the texts of the Epistles and Revelation pages 323–4 and a second series of pages numbered from 1 to 224. Immediately after this, the *Annotationes* fill pages 225–675." It was designed more as a new Latin translation than a Greek one, where the Greek came to be used to support his various Latin readings.

20. Metzger and Ehrman, *Text of the New Testament*, 145. In 1518 the Venetian printer Aldus Manutius issued a Greek New Testament that was essentially a copy of Erasmus's first edition. In fact, it so closely copied Erasmus's text that many of the typographical errors were simply reprinted. Somewhat ironically, in later years Erasmus would not infrequently defend certain of his readings by reference to the Aldine version without realizing that this version was simply a copy of his own text.

21. All told, between the first and second editions about 3,300 copies were produced. See Metzger and Ehrman, *Text of the New Testament*, 145. When Luther issued his German translation of the New Testament in 1522, he relied principally on Erasmus's 1519 edition.

22. This manuscript, known today as Codex Montfortianus or as Codex Britannicus by Erasmus, dates to the early sixteenth century. It contains the entire Greek New Testament written in minuscule script with one column per page. It has long been recognized that this manuscript was basically produced to induce Erasmus to include the Johannine Comma, since he had said he would do so if he found a Greek manuscript containing those verses. It is currently housed at Trinity College in Dublin. See Aland and Aland, *Text of the New Testament*, 129.

23. On the dubious nature of the Johannine Comma, see Bruce Metzger, *A Textual Commentary on the Greek New Testament*, 2nd ed. (New York: United Bible Societies, 1994), 647–49; and Michael Welte, "Earliest Printed Editions of the Greek New Testament," in Van Kampen and Saenger, *Bible as Book*, 120–21.

24. Quoted in Metzger and Ehrman, *Text of the New Testament*, 152.

25. Codex Vaticanus is a fourth-century codex that contains complete copies of all the books in the New Testament (see appendix). It may be noted, however, that Erasmus might have known about Codex Vaticanus even though he did not use it in any substantial way in the making of his Greek New Testament. In his *Annotationes in Novum Testamentum*, when defending his omission of the Johannine Comma (1 John 5:7b–8a) in the first two editions of his Greek New Testament, Erasmus reports that he had the librarian of the Vatican consult a very ancient copy of the Greek New Testament and that it did not contain these verses: "To this Paolo Bombasio, a learned and blameless man, at my enquiry described this passage [1 John 5:7–8] to me word for word from a very old codex from the Vatican library, in which it does not have the testimony 'of the father, word, and spirit.' If anyone is impressed by age, the book was very ancient; if by the authority of the Pope, this testimony was sought from his library." Translation of the Latin text is my own. Latin text taken from Anne Reeve and M. A. Screech, eds., *Erasmus' Annotations on the New Testament: Galatians to the Apocalypse* (Leiden, Netherlands: Brill, 1993), 770.

26. For a more in-depth discussion of the endings of Mark, see Lincoln H. Blumell, "A Text-Critical Comparison of the King James New Testament with Certain Modern Translations," *Studies in the Bible and Antiquity* 3 (2011): 89–95. This article can be accessed online at http://www.lincolnhblumell.com/wp-content/uploads /2012/02/2011-Studies-in-the-Bible-and-Antiquity-20113.pdf.

27. For an in-depth discussion of these verses, see Lincoln H. Blumell, "Luke 22:43–44: An Anti-Docetic Interpolation or an Apologetic Omission?," *TC: A Journal of Biblical Textual Criticism* 19 (2014): 1–35. This article can be accessed online at http://www.lincolnhblumell.com/wp-content/uploads/2012/02/2014-TC-Journal -of-Biblical-Textual-Criticism-Luke-22.pdf.

28. For a more in-depth discussion of this passage, see Blumell, "A Text-Critical Comparison," 107–13.

29. The Septuagint, or LXX as it is commonly known, is simply the Greek translation of the Hebrew Bible.

30. For a useful introduction to the various New Testament papyri, see Philip W. Comfort and David Barret, eds., *The Text of the Earliest New Testament Greek Manuscripts: New and Complete Transcriptions with Photographs* (Wheaton, IL: Tyndale House, 2001).

40

Joseph Smith's Translation of the New Testament

Kent P. Jackson

Few non–Latter-day Saints are aware that Joseph Smith created a revision of the Bible.[1] Based on the King James translation, which was the common English Bible of his time, Joseph Smith's revision was the result of a significant undertaking of time and effort to provide a better translation for the members of the Church. A revelation of December 1830 states in God's words that through the Prophet's work with the Bible, "the scriptures shall be given, even as they are in mine own bosom, to the salvation of mine own elect" (Doctrine and Covenants 35:20). Passages like that enabled him and his contemporaries in the Church to understand that the Bible revision was an important part of his calling. They called it the "New Translation," but most Latter-day Saints today know it as the "Joseph Smith Translation" (JST).[2]

The New Translation plays a significant role in Latter-day Saint beliefs. In this chapter I will summarize some of the major features of the New Testament portion in an effort to help us better understand the nature of the textual changes the Prophet made and how those changes enhance our reading of the New Testament.

The Translation

Joseph Smith taught that we believe in the Bible "as far as it is translated correctly" (Articles of Faith 1:8). In his day, among the meanings of the word *translate* were "carry or remove from one place to another" and "transfer; to convey from one to another." Thus, the word *translation* fits well with Joseph Smith's work on the Bible, which was not a rendering from other languages but a reformulation and transformation from one state to another.[3] For us as Latter-day Saints, it is one of the important evidences to the divine mission of the Lord's prophet.

Joseph Smith began his revision of the Bible in the summer of 1830, starting at its first chapter. At Genesis 24:41 the following spring, he temporarily put the Old Testament aside and began to revise the New Testament. He worked on the New Testament until late July 1832, when he finished the book of Revelation. The Prophet rarely wrote the translation himself but dictated the text to his scribes. They recorded his New Testament revision on 217 pages of folded paper, approximately 8 × 13 inches in dimension. In addition, he made further changes in later passes through the dictated material. Working as Joseph Smith's scribes were four of his closest associates: Sidney Rigdon, John Whitmer, Jesse Gause, and Frederick G. Williams. All four men held important positions in the Church. John Whitmer had served as scribe and copyist since the fall of 1830 and was one of the Church's earliest leaders. Rigdon, Gause, and Williams were counselors in the First Presidency. When Gause left the Church, Williams replaced him as counselor and simultaneously as scribe for the Bible revision.

Two significantly different scribal procedures were used in the New Testament revision. For Matthew 1 through John 5, Joseph Smith dictated the text in full. For the rest of the New Testament, he dictated chapter and verse numbers and then only the changed words, simultaneously marking in his printed Bible the insertion points for those words. This method anticipated that in the typesetting process, the marked printed Bible would serve as a guide for the location of the revised wordings.

The two methods produced different results. Per verse of scripture, many more changes are found in the sections in which the Prophet dictated the text in full. Thus, for example, Matthew, Mark, and Luke each have many more changes than John.[4] The nature of the changes is different as well, with the Synoptic Gospels having many more small, clarifying, textual changes than are found elsewhere in the New Testament.

Testimonies

Joseph Smith named the Gospels of Matthew and John *testimonies*, but not the Gospels of Mark and Luke.[5] We do not know why. Perhaps he viewed the two apostolic records as having special witnessing power because they were the recollections of members of the ancient twelve. Yet all four of the Gospels in the New Translation contain an enhanced testimony of Jesus compared to their corresponding passages in the Bible. In the New Translation, Jesus is more divine, his words are more clear, and the testimonies of the writers are more direct than in the Bible. This prompted early researcher Robert J. Matthews to see in the New Translation what he called "a greater portrayal of the Master," and indeed it is.[6]

Providing Clarity and Understanding

We have no way of knowing exactly what Joseph Smith had in mind with any particular revision he made in his Bible translation, so we must discuss potential reasons with caution. Because the Book of Mormon teaches that after the writing of the New Testament "many plain and precious things" would be "taken away" from the Bible (1 Nephi 13:28), it seems likely that a prophetic correction of the Bible would include material that had become lost. Also, because Joseph Smith stated that "much instruction has been given to man since the beginning which we [now] have not,"[7] it is not too much to assume that a prophetic Bible translation would add such material to the restored text.

Some parts of the Prophet's Bible revision are new revealed texts with unique content. Moses 1 and the Enoch material in Moses 6–7 are the prime examples. Most of the JST, however, consists of changes made to existing words in the King James translation, usually on the level of a verse (revising a word or two) or on the level of a short collection of verses (revising an ongoing thought in a discourse or narrative).

By sheer numbers, the majority of changes do not add new content but revise existing content to make the Bible more understandable for modern readers. Smaller changes that make it more understandable include replacing personal pronouns with names or nouns, replacing archaic vocabulary and grammar with more contemporary forms, changing the wording to add clarity, and removing italics. The example that follows illustrates the kinds of small changes the Prophet made in abundance. In this transcription, the replacement words appear in bold type, and the deleted words from the King James translation follow, inside brackets. The spelling is standardized to current usage.

Mark 9:19–21 (JST Mark 9:5)[8]

> **Jesus** [KJV, *He*] **spoke unto** [KJV, *answereth*] him and **said** [KJV, *saith*], O faithless generation, how long shall I be with you? **How** [KJV, *how*] long shall I suffer you? **Bring** [KJV, *bring*] him unto me. And they brought him unto **Jesus.** [KJV, *him:*] **And** [KJV, *and*] when **the man** [KJV, *he*] saw him, **immediately** [KJV, *straightway*] **he was torn by the spirit** [KJV, *the spirit tare him*]; and he fell on the ground, and wallowed foaming. And **Jesus** [KJV, *he*] asked his father, How long **a time is it** [KJV, *is it ago*] since this came unto him? And **his father** [KJV, *he*] said, **When** [KJV, *Of*] a child.

Easily noticed in this passage are the instances in which pronouns (*he* and *him*) are replaced with names. In addition, sometimes a pronoun is replaced with an identifying noun, as in *the man* replacing *he*, and *his father* replacing *he*. There are many pronoun replacements like these in Joseph Smith's revision of the New Testament. In most cases, they respond to the tendency of the Gospel writers to use phrases like "And he said unto him." Although the Prophet never explained the revisions he made, we can observe that these pronoun replacements make the text more precise and understandable. Wordings of this variety are hardly unique, and modern translators often make similar decisions in translation. The highly respected New Revised Standard Version, for example, employs this technique to remove ambiguities and make the text read better, just as Joseph Smith did.[9]

The text above shows examples of old or obsolete vocabulary being replaced with more modern words. The Prophet replaced the word *straightway* with the more contemporary *immediately*. Throughout the New Testament, he replaced many archaic grammatical forms as well, such as *said* in place of *saith*. That common change in the New Translation is more than simply modernizing the grammar, as it changes a present-tense verb to past tense, which makes the narrative flow more smoothly. A similar change was made in the same clause, with the present-tense *answereth* being replaced by a verb in the past tense. The Prophet's rejection of *answereth* also reflects the discomfort that other Bible readers have had with the verb *answer* being used (instead of something like *respond*) when no question was asked. He replaced *answereth* or *answered* in other places in the New Testament as well. The archaic past tense *tare* was replaced by a passive verb form. Other changed archaisms in the New Testament, though not in the example above, include changing *that* and *which* to *who* when referring to humans and changing *ye* to *you*. Near the end of the passage, the Prophet provided replacements for the two awkward phrases "How long is it ago since" and "Of a child."

Although the manuscripts of Joseph Smith's New Testament revision show much effort to modernize, it must be emphasized that this process was not done universally or consistently. There are places where archaisms were not noted and revised. In some parts of the translation, editorial changes like these are more common than in other parts, suggesting that the Prophet had modernization of the text on his mind some days more than others.

In our example above from Mark 9, another subtle change is also visible. As the Prophet dictated the text, his scribes included very little capitalization and punctuation, simply recording his words as he uttered them. Sometime later, he and his clerks went through the text and added these features to prepare the manuscript for publication. The text above shows some differences from the King James Version that modernize the punctuation. It has a sentence-ending period where the King James has a colon, and it capitalizes two words following question marks to create new sentences. These changes make the text look more contemporary and more natural than the corresponding text in the King James translation. But it should be pointed out that the punctuation and capitalization inserted on the manuscripts are very inconsistent.

Another structural difference is not visible in the above example but is clear on the manuscript pages. Everything in the text belongs to a single verse. In fact, what we have today in Mark 9:16–27 was all one verse in Joseph Smith's translation—Mark 9:5. When the Prophet and his scribes created the verse breaks for the JST, they rejected the short verses of the King James Bible and created long verses based on the content. This is one of many evidences for his preference for scriptures to have paragraph-length verses, rather than the intrusive verse breaks found in the traditional Bible.[10]

Italics in the Bible were a printing fashion from the sixteenth century. They were used primarily to identify words not in the original languages but necessary for the English translation.[11] Linguists and translators today recognize that including the words themselves was almost always justified, but italicizing them was unnecessary, confusing, and often inaccurate. It is clear that Joseph Smith and his contemporaries viewed the KJV's italics with suspicion.[12] Lending evidence for this view is the fact that a disproportionate number of revisions on the JST manuscripts are found in locations where the King James translators italicized words. Although the Prophet deleted or revised many of the italicized words, in other cases he kept the words themselves by simply reading them to his scribes, intending them to be printed without italicization. No italics were to be used in Joseph Smith's Bible translation.

It is instructive to note that our example above has more than a dozen word changes and yet none are noted in the footnotes or appendix of the Latter-day Saint editions of the Bible. The reason is that the JST revisions that were chosen for such inclusion were those that were of doctrinal or historical importance,[13] whereas the changes in our selection are restricted to adding clarity to the text. Yet because the Prophet made so many changes of this sort, it is clear that he considered the modernizing and clarifying of the text to be important, even though it was not done consistently. All of these changes—including doing away with the italics, creating larger paragraphs, modernizing words and grammar, and rewording passages to make them more understandable—lead me to conclude that although Joseph Smith loved the Bible, he did not have the kind of affection for the King James translation itself that others in the Church have had since his time.

Matthew 24

Joseph Smith's translation of Matthew 24 provides clarity and understanding on a much larger scale. It is the only part of the New Testament translation that has been included in the Latter-day Saint canon, and it is known today as Joseph Smith—Matthew in the Pearl of Great Price.[14] Sometime between mid-April and mid-June 1831, the Prophet and his scribe Sidney Rigdon revised the chapter, which contains Jesus's great prophecy of future events. The prophecy is often called the "Olivet Discourse," named after the Mount of Olives, where Jesus delivered the sermon to his apostles.[15] There are versions of it in Matthew 24, Mark 13, and Luke 21. Because Joseph Smith—Matthew has a unique history textually, and because of its standing in the Latter-day Saint scriptures, it deserves special attention here.

The Olivet Discourse is distinctive in many ways and presents interpretive challenges to readers. At the beginning of the account, Jesus's disciples ask him two questions. The first, "When shall these things be?" (Matthew 24:3), has to do with his prediction regarding the temple—"There shall not be left here one stone upon another, that shall not be thrown down" (Matthew 24:2). The second question was "What shall be the sign of thy coming, and of the end of the world?" (Matthew 24:3).

In each of the Synoptic Gospels, the account of what follows seems to view the two questions as one, with Jesus answering them simultaneously. Hence the primary interpretive challenge is this: Did Jesus (or the early Christians who preserved and arranged the accounts) believe that the destruction of the temple and Jesus's second coming would take place at the same time? Or would these two events be separated by many years? Some commentators have chosen the first option, while conservative Christians, with the benefit of two thousand years of hindsight, see the events as separate. Joseph Smith's translation does as well.

On March 7, 1831, during the time when the Prophet was still translating Genesis, he received a revelation that is an alternative narration of the Olivet Discourse. The revelation, now section 45 of the Doctrine and Covenants, has much language in it that reflects the content of Matthew 24. Near the end of it, God tells Joseph Smith to set aside the Old Testament translation and work on the New Testament instead: "It shall not be given unto you to know any further concerning this chapter [Matthew 24], until the New Testament be translated, and in it all these things shall be made known; wherefore I give unto you that ye may now translate it, that ye may be prepared for the things to come" (Doctrine and Covenants 45:60–61). The next day, he began his revision of the New Testament, and about two or three months later, he arrived at Matthew 24.

Joseph Smith's text of Matthew 24 is a remarkable chapter-length revision that dramatically reinvents the entire chapter and does so without adding much new material. In my opinion, it is the masterpiece of revised existing text in the New Translation. In his revision of this chapter, the Prophet changed it in such a way that the two questions the disciples asked are answered in separate sections of the discourse. The questions themselves are recast so there is no ambiguity about their meaning: "Tell us when shall these things be which thou has said concerning the destruction of the temple, and the Jews" and "What is the sign of thy coming, and of the end of the world, or the destruction of the wicked, which is the end of the world?" (Joseph Smith—Matthew 1:4). Jesus answers the two questions consecutively. The first, dealing primarily with circumstances in the first century AD, is answered in verses 5–21a. The second, dealing with the end times, is answered in verses 21b–55. The tools for bringing this about are (a) relocation, with some passages moved to new places, and (b) repetition, with some passages appearing in both sections. Thus "wars and rumors of wars," kingdoms fighting against kingdoms, famines, pestilences, and earthquakes are moved later in the chapter in a last-days setting. Verses about abounding iniquity are repeated, showing it to be a characteristic of both time periods. The outcome is a near seamless narrative of Jesus's words, with a text that comes alive in ways that would have been impossible without the inspired prophetic hand of Joseph Smith.

The only evidence we possess for how Joseph Smith—Matthew was prepared is what is preserved on the original manuscripts. The earliest text is on a document labeled "New Testament Manuscript 1" (NT1), which Joseph Smith dictated in its entirety to Sidney Rigdon. In general, few editorial changes were written on that manuscript after the original dictation. Yet there were several refinements made on the pages that contain Matthew 24. This suggests to me that Joseph Smith felt that this chapter was of particular importance.

John Whitmer, in his assignment to assist Joseph Smith by "transcribing"—that is, by making copies of the translations and revelations (Doctrine and Covenants 47:1)—made a duplicate of NT1, which archivists have labeled "New Testament Manuscript 2" (NT2). That document became the final New Testament manuscript that would be continued through the book of Revelation and prepared for publication. The Prophet and his scribe made an additional pass through Matthew 24 on that manuscript, refining it even further.

The two rounds of refinements made to the text of Matthew 24 after its original dictation are important, but the basic text was put in place with the original dictation, including the relocation and duplication of passages. The later edits, however, brought additional clarity to help the text better communicate its intended message. Latter-day Saints can view all these efforts—from the original dictation through the final refining process—as parts of the Lord's intended work.

The resulting text is one of the gems of the Restoration. Doctrine and Covenants 45:61 tells the Church that this chapter's revised translation would be given to help Latter-day Saints prepare "for the things to come." It is not the only revelation in the Latter-day Saint canon about end-time events, but no other exceeds it in its clarity. It is our most systematic and understandable prophecy of the last days. Early Church members knew of its importance, as is shown in the fact that as early as 1835 it was published separately as a broadside—a one-sheet document for posting and distribution. Included in it was the entirety of Matthew 24 from the New Translation, along with the final verse of chapter 23, which helps introduce it.[16]

While serving as president of the British Mission in 1851, Elder Franklin D. Richards apparently had a copy of the Matthew 24 broadside in his possession, or a copy of a copy. When he compiled his mission booklet that year, *The Pearl of Great Price*, he included the Matthew 24 translation among the other selections. In 1880, when a newly revised edition was canonized, Joseph Smith's translation of Matthew 24 was accepted with the rest of the book as scripture, and it continues as scripture in the Pearl of Great Price today.

Mark 13

Mark 13 is Mark's version of the Olivet Discourse, considered by most scholars to have been the original from which Matthew prepared his own rendition. The two are quite similar, and Matthew's is characteristically longer. Joseph Smith's translation of Mark's version illustrates a different means of providing a revised text—namely, copying it from an already-existing source. The evidence shows that when he and Sidney Rigdon arrived at Mark 13, they simply copied the revised text of Matthew 24 into the place of Mark 13 rather than creating a new translation of the Mark account. This again suggests that they understood the Matthew revision to be of special importance, and the Prophet likely believed that because he already had an inspired translation of the Olivet Discourse, he did not need to retranslate the Mark account. After some introductory sentences unique to Mark, they copied all but the first and last passages of the Matthew account from NT2 into the place of Mark 13. Because this transcription was made before later revisions were added both in Matthew and in Mark, the texts are not quite identical now.

The Mark 13 text was created probably near December 1831. It would not be the last time Joseph Smith would create a New Translation text by copying from a translation he had already done. When he arrived at Isaiah 29 a year or so later, he did not provide a new rendering of it but copied 2 Nephi 27—Nephi's revelation and commentary on Isaiah 29—from the 1830 Book of Mormon onto the New Translation manuscript.[17]

New Text

Although most of Joseph Smith's Bible translation consists of the revision of existing words from the King James Version, as in the examples above, in some places the Prophet created what I would call "new text"—text that does not have a counterpart in our current Bible. The New Testament translation has some important examples. I will present two here that I consider to be especially notable because they illustrate some of the ways Joseph Smith's translation interacts with the existing text and the existing biblical message.

Matthew 2:[24] (JST Matthew 3:9)[18]

Using the chapter designations of traditional Bibles, this text appears at the end of Matthew 2, which has twenty-three verses. But the entire passage is Matthew 3:9 in the Joseph Smith Translation.[19] In the text below, I have modernized the spelling and punctuation.

> And it came to pass that Jesus grew up with his brethren and waxed strong and waited upon the Lord for the time of his ministry to come. And he served under his father, and he spake not as other men, neither could he be taught, for he needed not that any man should teach him. And after many years, the hour of his ministry drew nigh.

This lovely little passage discreetly and cautiously fills in thirty years of Jesus's life. It is notable for its brevity, yet it shows that even before Jesus's ministry began, he was unlike any other human. It is a complementary narrative to the account in Luke of twelve-year-old Jesus in the temple in Jerusalem, where the Prophet revised the text to read that the learned doctors there "were hearing him and asking him questions," rather than the other way around as preserved in the Bible.[20]

Luke 3:2–6 (JST Luke 3:2–4)[21]

In this passage, John the Baptist begins his work as forerunner by bearing testimony of Jesus and his mission. The King James text is in the left column and Joseph Smith's translation in the right. For the New Translation, I have standardized the spelling, provided modern punctuation, and retained the Prophet's original paragraph-size verses.[22]

King James Translation

Annas and Caiaphas being the high priests, the word of God came unto John the son of Zacharias in the wilderness.

And he came into all the country about Jordan, preaching the baptism of repentance for the remission of sins;

As it is written in the book of the words of Esaias the prophet, saying, The voice of one crying in the wilderness, Prepare ye the way of the Lord, make his paths straight.

Every valley shall be filled, and every mountain and hill shall be brought low; and the crooked shall be made straight, and the rough ways shall be made smooth;

And all flesh shall see the salvation of God.

Joseph Smith's Translation

Now in this same year, the word of God came unto John the son of Zacharias in the wilderness. And he came into all the country about Jordan, preaching the baptism of repentance for the remission of sins, as it is written in the book of the prophet Esaias. And these are the words, saying, The voice of one crying in the wilderness, Prepare ye the way of the Lord, and make his paths straight.

For behold and lo, he shall come, as it is written in the book of the prophets, to take away the sins of the world and to bring salvation unto the heathen nations, to gather together those who are lost which are of the sheepfold of Israel, yea, even her dispersed and afflicted, and also to prepare the way and make possible the preaching of the gospel unto the Gentiles.

And to be a light unto all who sit in darkness unto the uttermost parts of the earth, to bring to pass the resurrection from the dead and to ascend up on high, to dwell on the right hand of the Father until the fullness of time and the law and the testimony shall be sealed and the keys of the kingdom shall be delivered up again unto the Father, to administer justice unto all, to come down in judgment upon all, and to convince all the ungodly of their ungodly deeds which they have committed; and all this in the day that he shall come, for it is a day of power, yea, every valley shall be filled, and every mountain and hill shall be brought low, the crooked shall be made straight, and the rough ways made smooth, and all flesh shall see the salvation of God.

This noteworthy passage inserts a messianic prophecy from John the Baptist into the middle of a prophecy from Isaiah. Much like Nephi's commentary and revelation on Isaiah 29 in 2 Nephi 27, this text weaves themes and vocabulary familiar from Isaiah into John's own revelation of Jesus and his ministry—framed at the beginning and the end with the text of Isaiah 40:3–5. John prophesies that Jesus would take away the sins of the world, bring salvation to Israel and the Gentiles, be a light to the world, bring about the Resurrection, ascend to the Father until the fulness of time, come again, and administer justice and judgment. The setting in the New Testament is most significant: after the birth and childhood

716   Kent P. Jackson

narratives, Joseph Smith's revision of the Gospel of Luke begins with a remarkable proclamation of Jesus's mission that summarizes his divine work of salvation.

Pure Intelligence and Prophetic Agency

Some unique characteristics of Joseph Smith's revised New Testament text can be seen in Matthew 26, which he translated twice.[23] He translated it in June 1831 with Sidney Rigdon assisting as scribe and again about three months later with John Whitmer as scribe. The translations were written on different manuscripts, and Whitmer was apparently unaware of the earlier translation. The best evidence is that Joseph Smith, owing to the passage of time and other concerns during the intervening summer, simply forgot that he had translated the chapter already.

These translations are important because they provide us with the means to evaluate how Joseph Smith's translation process worked, at least in this particular case. When my coauthor Peter Jasinski and I examined closely the two translations, we observed that in most cases where significant content was added to the text, it was added in both translations. But what we found remarkable was that even though the same new thoughts were added to both translations, those thoughts were usually not expressed in the same words, and they were often inserted in different locations in the text, sometimes a few lines apart.[24] From that evidence, we concluded the following:

> Joseph Smith taught that the Holy Ghost gives us "pure intelligence," which serves in "expanding the mind [and] enlightening the understanding."[25] Under "the Spirit of Revelation," "you feel pure Intelligence flowing unto you" that can "give you sudden strokes of ideas."[26] Perhaps it would be reasonable to propose that as Joseph Smith worked his way through Matthew 26, dictating the text to his scribe Sidney Rigdon in spring 1831 and again to his scribe John Whitmer the next fall, impressions came to his mind in the form of pure intelligence, enlightened understanding, and sudden strokes of ideas—but not necessarily in exact words. Responding to those impressions, the Prophet himself supplied the words that corrected the problem or emphasized the point or otherwise caused the verse to express the ideas that the Lord wanted it to communicate. This suggestion may explain why the duplicate translations are verbally different.[27]

Modern readers of Joseph Smith's revised New Testament text do not know how all its revisions were brought about. But to me, the conclusions we reached by examining the duplicate translations may be among the most important clues to the nature of the New Translation in general—revelation of pure intelligence coupled with prophetic agency in the selection of English words. This may not be the model everywhere in the New Translation, because elsewhere in it I see what I consider to be evidence of explicit verbal inspiration. Nor is it, in my view, the model for the English translation of the Book of Mormon, which was a preexisting text revealed visibly to Joseph Smith in English words. But the two translations of Matthew 26 suggest that in some matters relative to the New Translation, the Prophet was inspired with ideas, but it was his responsibility to provide words to express those ideas.

‒‒‒

Kent P. Jackson is a professor emeritus in the Department of Ancient Scripture at Brigham Young University.

Further Reading

Faulring, Scott H., Kent P. Jackson, and Robert J. Matthews, eds. *Joseph Smith's New Translation of the Bible: Original Manuscripts*. Provo, UT: Religious Studies Center, Brigham Young University, 2004.

————, eds. "New Testament Revision 1." The Joseph Smith Papers, http://www.josephsmithpapers.org/paper -summary/new-testament-revision-1/1.

————, eds. "New Testament Revision 2." The Joseph Smith Papers, http://www.josephsmithpapers.org/paper -summary/new-testament-revision-2/1.

Matthews, Robert J. "A Greater Portrayal of the Master." *Ensign*, March 1983, 6–13.

Notes

1. For the Bible translation in general, see Kent P. Jackson, "How We Got the Book of Moses," rev. version, in *By Study and by Faith: Selections from the* Religious Educator, ed. Richard Neitzel Holzapfel and Kent P. Jackson (Provo, UT: Religious Studies Center, Brigham Young University, 2009), 136–47; and Kent P. Jackson, "New Discoveries in the Joseph Smith Translation of the Bible," rev. version., in Holzapfel and Jackson, *By Study and by Faith*, 169–81. The original documents are published in Scott H. Faulring, Kent P. Jackson, and Robert J. Matthews, eds., *Joseph Smith's New Translation of the Bible: Original Manuscripts* (Provo, UT: Religious Studies Center, Brigham Young University, 2004); and Scott H. Faulring and Kent P. Jackson, eds., *Joseph Smith's Translation of the Bible: Electronic Library* (Provo, UT: Brigham Young University Press, 2011).

2. The title "Joseph Smith Translation" was adopted in preparation for the English Latter-day Saint edition of the Bible in 1979. The title *Inspired Version* is best applied only to the printed edition published by the Community of Christ (formerly the Reorganized Church of Jesus Christ of Latter Day Saints) beginning in 1867.

3. Noah Webster, *An American Dictionary of the English Language* (New York: Converse, 1828), s.v. "translate" and "translation." The idea of changing words from one language to another is also listed among the definitions.

4. Robert J. Matthews, *"A Plainer Translation": Joseph Smith's Translation of the Bible—A History and Commentary* (Provo, UT: Brigham Young University Press, 1975), 425.

5. New Testament Manuscript 2, folio 1 (NT2.1), page 1; NT2.2, pages 8, 45; and NT2.4, page 105. See Faulring, Jackson, and Matthews, *Joseph Smith's New Translation of the Bible*, 235, 314, 359, and 442.

6. Robert J. Matthews, "A Greater Portrayal of the Master," *Ensign*, March 1983, 6–13.

7. "The Elders of the Church in Kirtland, to Their Brethren Abroad," *The Evening and the Morning Star* 2, March 1834, 143.

8. This passage comes from NT2.2, pages 25–26. See Faulring, Jackson, and Matthews, *Joseph Smith's New Translation of the Bible*, 335–36. In that publication, I identified the second word in the quote as *spake*, but I am uncertain now if it is *spake* or *spoke*. For the differences in the verse numbers, see the discussion below.

9. Every one of the following examples from the New Revised Standard Version was also revised similarly by Joseph Smith. "**Jesus** [Greek, *He*] asked the father" (Mark 9:21); "Then **Joseph** [Greek, *he*] bought a linen

cloth" (Mark 15:46); "Then all the people of the surrounding country of the Gerasenes asked **Jesus** [Greek, *him*] to leave them" (Luke 8:37); and "**Jesus** [Greek, *He*] said" (Luke 22:34).

10. Other evidence for this preference includes the long paragraphs in the editions of the Book of Mormon published in Joseph Smith's lifetime, the lengthy paragraphs in the revelations when they were first published in the Doctrine and Covenants, the long paragraphs in the Matthew 24 broadside (see below), and the long verses in the first publication of the Book of Abraham. The biblical verse numbers were invented by a French printer in the sixteenth century. The practice of turning each verse into a separate paragraph has long since been abandoned in modern translations, in which content-based paragraphs are used with the verse numbers inserted as superscripts within the paragraphs. See Kent P. Jackson, Frank F. Judd Jr., and David Rolph Seely, "Chapters, Verses, Punctuation, Spelling, and Italics," in *The King James Bible and the Restoration*, ed. Kent P. Jackson (Provo, UT: Religious Studies Center, Brigham Young University; Salt Lake City: Deseret Book, 2011), 101–3.

11. For discussion of the use of italics in the scriptures in general, see Jackson, Judd, and Seely, "Chapters, Verses, Punctuation, Spelling, and Italics," 108–12.

12. See the discussion and the sources cited in Kent P. Jackson, "The King James Bible and the Joseph Smith Translation," in Jackson, *King James Bible and the Restoration*, 202–3.

13. Personal communication from Robert J. Matthews to the author.

14. It includes Matthew 24 and the last verse of chapter 23. From the Old Testament translation, the Pearl of Great Price includes Genesis 1:1–6:13 as the Book of Moses.

15. Matthew 25 is the continuation of the Olivet Discourse with parables about being prepared for Jesus's coming.

16. See Peter Crawley, *A Descriptive Bibliography of the Mormon Church, Volume One, 1830–1847* (Provo, UT: Religious Studies Center, Brigham Young University, 1997), 60–61.

17. See Royal Skousen, "Textual Variants in the Isaiah Quotations in the Book of Mormon," in *Isaiah in the Book of Mormon*, ed. Donald W. Parry and John W. Welch (Provo, UT: FARMS, 1998), 387–88.

18. NT2.1, pages 3–4. See Faulring, Jackson, and Matthews, *Joseph Smith's New Translation of the Bible*, 239.

19. In the appendixes of the Latter-day Saint editions of the Bible, this passage is identified as "JST Matthew 3:24–26." This is not the JST reference, however, but the reference from the 1944 edition of the *Inspired Version*, published by the Reorganized Church of Jesus Christ of Latter Day Saints. The verse divisions and punctuation in the Latter-day Saint footnotes and appendix are not from the JST manuscripts but from that RLDS printing. When preparing the *Inspired Version*'s first edition in 1867, the RLDS publications committee ignored Joseph Smith's verse divisions and created their own.

20. NT2.3, page 51. See Faulring, Jackson, and Matthews, *Joseph Smith's New Translation of the Bible*, 371–72.

21. NT2.3, pages 51–52. See Faulring, Jackson, and Matthews, *Joseph Smith's New Translation of the Bible*, 372–73.

22. Labeled "JST, Luke 3:4–11" in the appendixes of the Latter-day Saint editions of the Bible. See note 19. The text in the English Bible appendix contains a minor difference in the second paragraph (*who are of the sheepfold* instead of *which are of the sheepfold*) and an error a few words later (*the dispersed* instead of *her dispersed*). The first was an editing decision made in the preparation of the 1867 RLDS *Inspired Version*, and the second appears to be a typographical error made in that edition.

23. He also translated 2 Peter 3:4–6 twice, but our discussion here will focus on the Matthew chapter. For a detailed discussion, see Kent P. Jackson and Peter M. Jasinski, "The Process of Inspired Translation: Two Passages Translated Twice in the Joseph Smith Translation of the Bible," *BYU Studies* 42, no. 2 (2003): 35–64.

24. Jackson and Jasinski, "Two Passages Translated Twice," 59.

25. Andrew F. Ehat and Lyndon W. Cook, eds., *The Words of Joseph Smith: The Contemporary Accounts of the Nauvoo Discourses of the Prophet Joseph* (Provo, UT: Religious Studies Center, Brigham Young University, 1980), 4.

26. Ehat and Cook, *Words of Joseph Smith*, 5.

27. Jackson and Jasinski, "Two Passages Translated Twice," 61–62.

41

The New Testament in the Doctrine and Covenants

Nicholas J. Frederick

The Doctrine and Covenants and the King James Bible share an undeniable relationship. Canonized in 1835, the Doctrine and Covenants consists chiefly of a written record of Joseph Smith's revelations, most of which were received and recorded between 1828 and 1838. Like the Book of Mormon, the revelations and other texts canonized in the Doctrine and Covenants do not simply mimic King James language, adopting a familiar idiom to express innovative ideas. Rather, the revelations frequently quote from or allude to specific passages from the King James Bible, carefully integrating the words of Old and New Testament prophets into the revealed words of a modern one. As one scholar has observed, Joseph Smith's revelations "are full of biblical phrases and images, and they echo KJV idiom. The biblicism is sometimes deliberate, with direct allusions to biblical prophecy or concepts, and sometimes (apparently) unconscious—biblical words woven into the fabric of a new narrative having its own coherence."[1] The purpose of this chapter is to examine how the Doctrine and Covenants has adopted the language of the New Testament and adapted it into a nineteenth-century religious, specifically Latter-day Saint, context.[2] I will begin by examining the three New Testament texts that make the largest contribution to the text of the Doctrine and Covenants, namely the Gospel of Matthew, the Gospel of John, and the book of Revelation. I will then offer a short, heavily descriptive discussion of how the remaining New Testament texts are used in the Doctrine and Covenants.[3] Following this examination, I will offer some concluding observations on the place of the New Testament as a whole in the Doctrine and Covenants.

The Gospel of Matthew

Along with the Gospel of John and the book of Revelation, the Gospel of Matthew is one of the most frequently alluded to texts in the Doctrine and Covenants,[4] with the total number of allusions surpassing well over one hundred. Perhaps not surprisingly, the majority of these allusions come from Matthew's five prominent sermons. Matthew's Gospel is conveniently constructed around five lengthy discourses (the Sermon on the Mount in Matthew 5–7, the charge to the apostles in Matthew 10, the discourse on the kingdom in Matthew 13, the discourse on the church in Matthew 18, and the Olivet Discourse in Matthew 24–25), likely intended to link the Gospel with Moses and his five books.[5] The Matthean sermon that gets the most attention is the Olivet Discourse in Matthew 24–25. Not only is it alluded to about forty times throughout the Doctrine and Covenants, it plays a prominent role in the construction of at least two key eschatological revelations, Doctrine and Covenants 29 and 45. The Olivet Discourse is Matthew's rendition of Jesus's teachings to the Twelve Apostles on the Mount of Olives shortly before his crucifixion (compare Mark 13; Luke 21:5–37). In Matthew 24 Jesus lays out the signs preceding the destruction of Jerusalem and his eventual return. Matthew 25 contains parables of judgment, including the familiar stories of the ten virgins, the parable of the talents, and the parable of the sheep and the goats. It is fitting, then, that in two revelations (29 and 45) heavily concerned with future events such as the gathering of Israel, the Second Coming, the Millennium, and the Resurrection and Judgment, the language of Matthew 24–25 would play a significant role.

The allusion to Matthew 24:6 in Doctrine and Covenants 45:35 provides a useful example of how the Doctrine and Covenants utilizes the language of the New Testament.

> And I said unto them: *Be not troubled, for, when all these things shall come to pass*, ye may know that the promises which have been made unto you shall be fulfilled. (Doctrine and Covenants 45:35)

> And ye shall hear of wars and rumours of wars: see that *ye be not troubled: for all these things must come to pass*, but the end is not yet. (Matthew 24:6)

There are two important observations to be made here. First, the insertion of the phrase "And I said unto them" links this revelation, given in 1831, with Jesus's Olivet Discourse, given about eighteen hundred years earlier. These two discourses are being explicitly coupled together. Second, very rarely does the Doctrine and Covenants simply insert allusions to the New Testament in a word-for-word manner. The revelations maintain a careful balance between maintaining enough of the New Testament's language to preserve the phrasal link with it, while at the same time changing enough of the language so that the allusion works within its new context almost seamlessly. Doctrine and Covenants 45:35 moves the "ye" farther into the phrase while changing "must come" to "shall come." Additionally, the entire last phrase of Doctrine and Covenants 45:35, "ye may know that the promises which have been made unto you shall be fulfilled," is completely changed from Matthew's version.

An additional layer of complexity is revealed two verses later, in Doctrine and Covenants 45:37–38. At first glance, these two verses appear to continue the Matthean appropriation observed in Doctrine and Covenants 45:35:

> Ye look and behold the fig trees, and ye see them with your eyes, and ye say when they begin to shoot forth, and their *leaves* are yet *tender, that summer is* now *nigh* at hand. Even so it shall be in that day when they shall see all these things, then shall they know that the hour is nigh. (Doctrine and Covenants 45:37–38)

> Now learn a parable of the fig tree: When his branch is yet *tender*, and putteth forth *leaves*, ye know *that summer is nigh*. (Matthew 24:32)

The sharing of language such as "tender," "leaves," and "that summer is nigh," in addition to the explicit allusions to Matthew 24 in Doctrine and Covenants 45:35, initially indicates that this is another example of the Doctrine and Covenants's allusion to Matthew 24. But consider these verses from Luke's Gospel:

> And he spake to them a parable; *Behold the fig tree*, and all the trees; *when they now shoot forth*, ye see and know of your own selves *that summer is now nigh at hand*. So likewise ye, *when ye see these things* come to pass, *know* ye *that the* kingdom of God is nigh at hand. (Luke 21:29–31)

It is clear from a comparison with Doctrine and Covenants 45:37–38 that Luke's Gospel is evoked even more than Matthew's:

> Ye look and *behold the fig trees*, and ye see them with your eyes, and ye say *when they begin to shoot forth*, and their leaves are yet tender, *that summer is now nigh at hand.* Even so it shall be in that day *when they shall see all these things*, then shall they *know that the* hour *is nigh.* (Doctrine and Covenants 45:37–38)

This allusion to Luke 21 in the text of Doctrine and Covenants 45 is a striking one. The revelation explicitly alludes to Jesus's speaking on the Mount of Olives and then appropriates Matthew's language from that sermon. But where Doctrine and Covenants 45 could simply maintain Matthew's language from Matthew 24:32 in Doctrine and Covenants 45:37–38, instead the revelation alludes to *Luke's* Gospel, drawing both Gospels and their language into the context of Doctrine and Covenants 45. This high level of adoption and adaptation from multiple sources in a single *pericope* is not unique to Doctrine and Covenants 45. This type of allusivity is present throughout the Doctrine and Covenants.

Two other Matthean stories that play an important role in the Doctrine and Covenants are John the Baptist's words in Matthew 3 and Jesus's discussion with Peter in Matthew 16. Matthew 3 narrates John the Baptist's fiery denunciation of the arrogance of the Jews and their presumption of salvation simply because of their lineage. John warns that a change is coming, that God's judgment is imminent: "And now also the axe is laid unto the root of the trees: therefore every tree which bringeth not forth good fruit is hewn down, and cast into the fire" (Matthew 3:10). John's opening declaration of "Repent ye: for the kingdom of heaven is at hand. . . . Prepare ye the way of the Lord, make his paths straight" (Matthew 3:2–3) is alluded to several times in the Doctrine and Covenants (33:10; 39:19; 42:7; 65:1; 133:17). The phrases "in whom thou wast well pleased" (45:4) and "in/with whom I am well pleased" (50:37; 51:3; 61:35) could be allusions to God's declaration at Jesus's baptism (Matthew 3:17). John's prediction that the chaff will be burned with "unquenchable fire" (Matthew 3:12) is possibly alluded to in Doctrine and Covenants 43:33; 63:34, 54; and 101:66.[6] Finally, the most explicit allusion to Matthew 3 comes in Doctrine and Covenants 97:7, where Matthew 3:10 is repeated nearly word for word: "The ax is laid at the root of the trees; and every tree that bringeth not forth good fruit shall be hewn down and cast into the fire."[7] Notable here is the inclusion of the phrase "I, the Lord, have spoken it" following the allusion to Matthew. John the Baptist's words in Matthew 3:10 have now become Jesus's words in Doctrine and Covenants 97:7.

The significance of Matthew 16 is that it represents the only chapter in the Gospels that explicitly mentions a church and thus becomes a useful text to draw on when discussing the restored church. Matthew 16 finds Jesus questioning the Twelve Apostles as to his identity, a question that is answered through Peter's declaration of Jesus as "the Son of the living God" (Matthew 16:16). Jesus subsequently bestows the "keys of the kingdom" (16:19) on Peter, accompanied by the promises that "upon this rock I will build my church" (16:18) and "whatsoever thou shalt bind on earth shall be bound in heaven" (16:19). All these phrases are alluded to in the Doctrine and Covenants. In Doctrine and Covenants 1, the Lord states that "power is given" to his servant in order to "seal both on earth and in heaven" (1:8). In two early revelations, the Lord promises that "if ye are built upon my rock, they [earth and hell] cannot prevail" (6:34) and "whosoever is of my church, and endureth of my church to the end, him will I establish upon my rock, and the gates of hell shall not prevail against them" (10:69). Perhaps most significantly, when the Lord formally introduces himself in Doctrine and Covenants 42:1, he does so using the same title Peter uses for Jesus in Matthew 16:16: "Hearken, O ye elders of my church, who have assembled yourselves together in my name, even Jesus Christ the Son of the living God, the Savior of the world; inasmuch as ye believe on my name and keep my commandments."

The Gospel of John

The second of the three most prominent New Testament texts in the Doctrine and Covenants is the Gospel of John. Although there are not necessarily as many allusions to John's Gospel as there are to Matthew's, the Doctrine and Covenants appropriates John's Gospel in a complex and fascinating way. Two revelations in particular, Doctrine and Covenants 7 and 93, focus specifically on the *text* of the Gospel of John itself. Doctrine and Covenants 7, received in April 1829, claims to be part of a record written by John himself and serves to clarify one of the more enigmatic elements of John 21, namely the fate of the "beloved disciple." In John's Gospel, Peter asks Jesus what will happen to the "beloved disciple," a title that is generally, although not universally, seen as referring to John.[8] Jesus responds, "If I will that he tarry till I come, what is that to thee? follow thou me" (John 21:22). This saying is the biblical source for the tradition that John is still on the earth. While translating the Book of Mormon, Oliver Cowdery and Joseph Smith debated the meaning of Jesus's words to Peter, and "they mutually agreed to settle it by the Urim and Thummim."[9] Accordingly, Joseph received Doctrine and Covenants 7, a first-person text that was "translated from parchment, written and hid up by himself," referring to John.[10] Doctrine and Covenants 7, then, is positioned as a record that predates the Gospel of John and contains a lengthier version of Jesus's discussion with Peter and John than that preserved in the biblical Gospel of John.

While Doctrine and Covenants 7 offers an expanded treatment of the ending of John's Gospel, Doctrine and Covenants 93, a revelation received in May 1833, deals with the beginning of John's Gospel. Doctrine and Covenants 93 begins by evoking Johannine language such as "I am in the Father, and the Father in me, and the Father and I are one" and "I was in the world and made flesh my tablernacle, and dwelt among the sons of men" (93:3–4). After this brief explication on the divinity of Jesus Christ, John and his record are explicitly mentioned: "And John saw and bore record of the fulness of my glory, and the fulness of John's record is hereafter to be revealed" (93:6). Notably, much of the Johannine language in Doctrine and Covenants 93:7–17 parallels specific language from the prologue of John's own Gospel (John 1:1–18). Phrases such as "in the beginning the Word was," "the world was made by him," "in him was the life of men and the light of men," and "full of grace and truth" are quite familiar to readers of John's Gospel. As with Doctrine and Covenants 7, Doctrine and Covenants 93 presents a portion of John's Gospel that seems to predate the current "Gospel of John."

However, Doctrine and Covenants 93 goes one step further and, instead of using the earlier text of John to answer a question, uses the earlier text of John to present new theological insights into the nature of Jesus Christ himself. In the Gospel of John, Jesus was seen as God (1:1–5), as Jehovah come down from heaven (John 8:58), a pillar of fire that "dwelt" or "tented" in a fleshy form among humanity. The Trinitarian Christianity of Joseph Smith's time that saw no significant distinction between the Father and Son was based on certain passages in John. Doctrine and Covenants 93, however, uses language from John's Gospel to teach just the opposite idea. According to Doctrine and Covenants 93, Jesus was not always God, because he "received not of the fulness at first," but in fact progressed "grace to grace" until he "received a fulness" (93:12–13). Using this innovative Christology constructed from the language of John's Gospel, the remainder of Doctrine and Covenants 93 tackles topics such as the premortal life, the essence of spirits, and the eternal nature of elements. One of the main points of Doctrine and Covenants 93 is that humans, who had a beginning similar to Jesus, can progress as he did, grace to grace, until they themselves may "receive of the fulness."

In addition to its focus on the text of John's Gospel, the Doctrine and Covenants also utilizes that Gospel in another unique manner, namely as a voice for Jesus. In several of the revelations, when Jesus speaks, he speaks using the language and verbiage of John's Gospel. For example:

> Behold, I am Jesus Christ, the Son of God. I am the same that came unto mine own, and mine own received me not. I am the light which shineth in darkness, and the darkness comprehendeth it not. (Doctrine and Covenants 6:21; compare John 1:5, 11)

> Behold, I am Jesus Christ, the Son of God. I came unto mine own, and mine own received me not. I am the light which shineth in darkness, and the darkness comprehendeth it not. I am he who said—Other sheep have I which are not of this fold—unto my disciples, and many there were that understood me not. (Doctrine and Covenants 10:57–59; compare John 1:5, 11; 10:16)

> My son Orson, hearken and hear and behold what I, the Lord God, shall say unto you, even Jesus Christ your Redeemer; the light and the life of the world, a light which shineth in darkness and the darkness comprehendeth it not; who so loved the world that he gave his own life, that as many as would believe might become the sons of God. Wherefore you are my son. (Doctrine and Covenants 34:1–3; compare John 1:4–5, 12; 3:16)

John's unique language and nuanced portrayal of Jesus provided an ideal voice for Jesus Christ, a voice that illustrated the depth of Jesus's mission and the breadth of his realm.

The Book of Revelation

While the language and imagery of the book of Revelation is prominent throughout the Doctrine and Covenants, there are four sections in particular—Doctrine and Covenants 29, 76, 77, and 88—in which Revelation plays a more significant role. The first of these, Doctrine and Covenants 29, carefully explores the reality and purpose of individual agency. Received in September 1830, this section is a particularly stunning eschatological text, carefully exploring the reality and purpose of agency and how the exercising of that agency affects the fate of humanity at the Resurrection and the Judgment. A large part of the revelation is devoted to the second coming of Jesus Christ and includes, in intense and breathtaking language, the events and signs preceding his arrival. The signs of Jesus's coming include the sun being "darkened," the moon turning to "blood," and stars falling from the heaven (Doctrine and Covenants 29:14; compare Revelation 6:12–13).[11] A "great hailstorm" will destroy the "crops of the earth" (29:16; compare Revelation 8:7; 11:19), and the wicked will receive their just punishment, for "the cup of mine indignation is full" (29:17; compare Revelation 14:10). Doctrine and Covenants 29 describes, in gruesome detail, how flies and maggots will feast on the flesh of the wicked, until "their flesh shall fall from off their bones, and their eyes from their sockets" (29:19). Afterward, the "fowls of the air shall devour them up" (29:20; compare Revelation 19:21). The source of this wickedness on the earth, Doctrine and Covenants 29 reveals, is the "great and abominable church, which is the whore of all the earth" (29:21;

compare Revelation 17:1; 19:2).[12] This section then describes the eventual fate of the earth, including the Millennium (29:22; compare Revelation 20:3, 7) and the creation of a "new heaven and a new earth" (29:23; compare Revelation 21:1). Finally, Doctrine and Covenants 29 turns to the role played by agency in the premortal life and in the Garden of Eden. The revelation describes how Satan managed to sway "a third part of the hosts of heaven" (29:36; compare Revelation 12:4) and then "was thrust down, and thus came the devil and his angels" (29:37; compare Revelation 12:9). Naturally, the language of an apocalyptic text such as the book of Revelation would provide valuable imagery and language for Joseph Smith's own eschatological revelations.

Unique among all of Joseph Smith's canonized revelations, Doctrine and Covenants 77 serves as a question and answer session between Joseph Smith and the Lord. The setting for the reception of Doctrine and Covenants 77 is Joseph's continuing work on the translation of the Bible. Joseph Smith's history states that "about the first of March, in connection with the translation of the scriptures, I received the following explanation of the Revelations of Saint John."[13] Perhaps Joseph read through Revelation and gathered together a series of questions, or perhaps Doctrine and Covenants 77 represents a collation of questions and answers Joseph received as he was translating. Among other things, Joseph is instructed about the possible meanings of the "sea of glass" (77:1; compare Revelation 4:6), the book "sealed with seven seals" (77:6–7; compare Revelation 5:1), the sealing of the 144,000 (77:11; compare Revelation 7:4), and the identity of the two witnesses who lie dead in the streets of Jerusalem for three and a half days (77:15, compare Revelation 11:8). The information Joseph receives reveals a very pragmatic approach to the book of Revelation, one that demystifies one of the Bible's most mystical texts. Rather than being a text full of abstruse imagery, ambiguous events, and language that seems to hazily recede the harder it is studied, Doctrine and Covenants 77 suggests a text that has distinct answers to its questions and a clear reality behind its symbols. The twenty-four elders who surround God's throne are simply Christian missionaries who lived during the first century AD and then dwelt in paradise. The events described in Revelation are literal, played out during one of the thousand-year periods of time symbolized by the seven "seals." From this perspective, it is not surprising that Joseph would later claim that "Revelation is one of the plainest books God ever caused to be written," while at the same time expressing frustration that the book of Revelation was "a constant source of speculation amongst the elders, causing a division of sentiment and opinion in relation to it."[14]

Doctrine and Covenants 76 and 88 are, in the words of historian Richard L. Bushman, two of the "revelations of exaltation." Doctrine and Covenants 76 records the account of a vision shared by Joseph Smith and Sidney Rigdon in 1832 in which they beheld different kingdoms of glory and received additional insights on the fates of both the righteous and the wicked. Doctrine and Covenants 88 is primarily a revelation aimed at establishing a setting for educating and instructing missionaries. Yet the revelation goes far beyond these practicalities, yielding "a cohesive compound of cosmology and eschatology united by the attempt to link the quotidian world of the now to the world beyond."[15] The language and imagery present in the book of Revelation was utilized in both Doctrine and Covenants 76 and 88 in order to describe revelations. In Doctrine and Covenants 76, the language of the book of Revelation was used largely to discuss Satan and the fate of those who follow him:[16]

> And while we were yet in the Spirit, the Lord commanded us that we should write the vision; for we beheld *Satan, that old serpent, even the devil*, who rebelled against God, and sought to take the kingdom of our God and his Christ. (76:28)

> And he laid hold on the dragon, *that old serpent*, which is *the Devil*, and *Satan*, and bound him a thousand years. (Revelation 20:2; compare 12:9)

> Wherefore, he *maketh war with the saints* of God, and encompasseth them round about. (76:29)

> And it was given unto him to *make war with the saints*, and to overcome them: and power was given him over all kindreds, and tongues, and nations. (Revelation 13:7)

> These are they who shall go away *into the lake of fire and brimstone*, with *the devil* and his angels. (76:36)

> And *the devil* that deceived them was cast *into the lake of fire and brimstone*, where the beast and the false prophet are. (Revelation 20:10; compare 19:20)

> These are they who are liars, and *sorcerers*, and adulterers, and *whoremongers, and whosoever loves and makes a lie*. (76:103)

> For without are dogs, and *sorcerers*, and *whoremongers*, and murderers, and idolaters, *and whosoever loveth and maketh a lie*. (Revelation 22:15)

Part of Doctrine and Covenants 88 is a description of events that will precede the Second Coming. Again, the book of Revelation provides much of this language.

> And *angels shall fly through the midst of heaven, crying with a loud voice*, sounding the trump of God, saying: Prepare ye, prepare ye, O inhabitants of the earth; for the judgment of our God is come. Behold, and lo, the Bridegroom cometh; go ye out to meet him. (88:92)

> And I beheld, and heard an *angel flying through the midst of heaven, saying with a loud voice*, Woe, woe, woe, to the inhabiters of the earth by reason of the other voices of the trumpet of the three angels, which are yet to sound! (Revelation 8:13).

And another angel shall sound his trump, saying: That great church, the mother of abominations, that *made all nations drink of the wine of the wrath of her fornication*, that persecuteth the saints of God, that shed their blood. (88:94)

And there followed another angel, saying, Babylon is fallen, is fallen, that great city, because she *made all nations drink of the wine of the wrath of her fornication*. (Revelation 14:8)

And there shall be *silence in heaven for the space of half an hour*; and immediately after shall the curtain of heaven be unfolded, as a scroll is unfolded after it is rolled up, and the face of the Lord shall be unveiled. (88:95)

And when he had opened the seventh seal, there was *silence in heaven about the space of half an hour*. (Revelation 8:1)

The book of Revelation provided a valuable vocabulary for Joseph Smith to draw on as he composed his revelations—several of them outline a detailed eschatological vision shared by John's apocalypse. The importance of the book of Revelation is further suggested by Doctrine and Covenants 77, the only biblical book to receive its own question-and-answer revelation.

Having considered these texts, I will, in the remainder of this chapter, provide shorter glimpses of the New Testament documents that are not integrated into the Doctrine and Covenants as thoroughly as Matthew, John, and Revelation.

The Gospel of Mark

Perhaps the clearest use of the Gospel of Mark in the Doctrine and Covenants comes in the form of several passages taken from Mark 16:

And he said unto them, *Go ye into all the world, and preach the gospel to every creature*. (Mark 16:15)

And if they desire to take upon them my name with full purpose of heart, they are called to *go into all the world to preach my gospel unto every creature*. (Doctrine and Covenants 18:28)

For, verily, the sound must go forth from this place into all the world, and unto the uttermost parts of the earth—*the gospel must be preached unto every creature*, with signs following them that believe. (Doctrine and Covenants 58:64)

Go ye into all the world, preach the gospel to every creature, acting in the authority which I have given you, baptizing in the name of the Father, and of the Son, and of the Holy Ghost. (Doctrine and Covenants 68:8)

> *He that believeth and is baptized shall be saved; but he that believeth not shall be damned.* (Mark 16:16)

> *And he that believeth and is baptized shall be saved, and he that believeth not shall be damned.* And he that believeth shall be blest with signs following, even as it is written. (Doctrine and Covenants 68:9–10)

> *And these signs shall follow them that believe*; In my name shall they *cast out devils*; they shall speak with new tongues; they shall take up *serpents*; and if they drink any *deadly thing*, it shall not hurt them; they shall lay hands on *the sick*, and they shall recover. (Mark 16:17–18)

> Require not miracles, except I shall command you, except *casting out devils, healing the sick*, and against poisonous serpents, and against *deadly poisons*. (Doctrine and Covenants 24:13)

> For, verily, the sound must go forth from this place into all the world, and unto the uttermost parts of the earth—the gospel must be preached unto every creature, *with signs following them that believe.* (Doctrine and Covenants 58:64)

> But, behold, faith cometh not by signs, *but signs follow those that believe.* (Doctrine and Covenants 63:9)

> *And these signs shall follow them that believe.* (Doctrine and Covenants 84:65)

> *And these signs shall follow him*—he shall *heal the sick*, he shall *cast out devils*, and shall be delivered from those who would administer unto him *deadly poison.* (Doctrine and Covenants 124:98)

This usage of Mark 16:15–18 is noteworthy because these verses make up part of what is commonly referred to as the "long ending" of Mark. Some scholars believe that Mark's Gospel ended at 16:8: "And they went out quickly, and fled from the sepulchre; for they trembled and were amazed: neither said they any thing to any man; for they were afraid." This ending may have been viewed as too ambiguous, so another ending was added by later copyists using an assortment of phrases from Matthew, Luke, and John. This ending is the current Mark 16:9–20 in the King James Bible.[17] There are at least two possible ways to view the inclusion of this ending of Mark's Gospel in Joseph Smith's revelations: Mark 16:9–20 is, contrary to scholarly arguments, actually part of Mark's Gospel and not a later addition, or more likely, the presence of parts of the long ending of Mark in Joseph Smith's revelations is due to adopting the language of the King James Bible, of which Mark 16:9–20 is a part.[18]

Luke–Acts

There are fewer specific chapters or themes from Luke's writings that are repeatedly incorporated into the revelations than there are from Matthew, John, and Revelation. One possible exception to this is Luke 16, the parable of the unjust steward. Allusions to Luke 16 appear in revelations associated with stewardship and the law of consecration:

> And he called him, and said unto him, How is it that I hear this of thee? *give an account of thy stewardship*; for thou mayest be no longer steward. (Luke 16:2)

> And also, my servants who are abroad in the earth should send forth *the accounts of their stewardships* to the land of Zion. (Doctrine and Covenants 69:5; compare 70:4; 72:3)

> And I say unto you, *Make to yourselves friends of the mammon of unrighteousness*; that, when ye fail, they may receive you into everlasting habitations. (Luke 16:9)

> And now, verily I say unto you, and this is wisdom, *make unto yourselves friends with the mammon of unrighteousness*, and they will not destroy you. (Doctrine and Covenants 82:22)

There are also a couple of significant allusions to Luke 21, Luke's version of Matthew's Olivet Discourse:

> And then shall they see the Son of man *coming in a cloud with power and great glory*. (Luke 21:27)

> For behold, verily, verily I say unto you, the time is soon at hand, that I shall *come in a cloud with power and great glory*. (Doctrine and Covenants 34:7)

> And when these things begin to come to pass, then look up, and *lift up your* heads; for *your redemption draweth nigh*. (Luke 21:28)

> *Lift up your* hearts and be glad, *your redemption draweth nigh*. (Doctrine and Covenants 35:26)

The promise that the Saints will be endowed "with power from on high" in Doctrine and Covenants 38 adopts the same language the resurrected Jesus used when making the same promise to his apostles:

> And, behold, I send the promise of my Father upon you: but tarry ye in the city of Jerusalem, until *ye be endued with power from on high*. (Luke 24:49)

> Wherefore, for this cause I gave unto you the commandment that ye should go to the Ohio; and there I will give you my law; and there *you shall be endowed with power from on high*; . . . see that all things are preserved; and when men *are endowed with power from on high* and sent forth, all these things shall be gathered unto the bosom of the church. (Doctrine and Covenants 38:32, 38)

Significantly, Jesus follows up this promise that his apostles will be "endued with power from on high" with the instruction "that they should not depart from Jerusalem, but wait for the promise of the Father, which, saith he, ye have heard of me" (Acts 1:4). Although Luke says nothing further about what the "promise of the Father" might be, Doctrine and Covenants 95 provides some clarification, one that links it with temple ritual:

> Yea, verily I say unto you, I gave unto you a commandment that you should build a house, in the which house I design to endow those whom I have chosen with power from on high; for *this is the promise of the Father* unto you; therefore I command you to tarry, even as mine apostles at Jerusalem. (Doctrine and Covenants 95:8–9)

In both Doctrine and Covenants 6 and 35 the Lord poignantly addresses his followers as his "little flock," a phrase appearing in Luke 12:

> *Fear not, little flock*; for it is your Father's good pleasure to give you the kingdom. (Luke 12:32)

> Therefore, *fear not, little flock*; do good; let earth and hell combine against you, for if ye are built upon my rock, they cannot prevail. (Doctrine and Covenants 6:34)

> *Fear not, little flock*; the kingdom is yours until I come. Behold I come quickly; even so. Amen. (Doctrine and Covenants 35:27)

The warning that "unto whom much is given much is required" in Doctrine and Covenants 82 is an allusion to Luke 12:

> But he that knew not, and did commit things worthy of stripes, shall be beaten with few stripes. *For unto whomsoever much is given, of him shall be much required*: and to whom men have committed much, of him they will ask the more. (Luke 12:48)

> *For of him unto whom much is given much is required*; and he who sins against the greater light shall receive the greater condemnation. (Doctrine and Covenants 82:3)

Finally, the description of John the Baptist given in Doctrine and Covenants 84 alludes to the words Gabriel uses when he addresses Zacharias about John's birth:

> For he shall be great in the sight of the Lord, and shall drink neither wine nor strong drink; and he shall *be filled with the Holy Ghost, even from his mother's womb*. (Luke 1:15)

> Which gospel is the gospel of repentance and of baptism, and the remission of sins, and the law of carnal commandments, which the Lord in his wrath caused to continue with the house of Aaron among the children of Israel until John, whom God raised up, *being filled with the Holy Ghost from his mother's womb*. (Doctrine and Covenants 84:27)

The language of the book of Acts is used in a similar fashion. Doctrine and Covenants 38 serves as God's introduction to the Saints in Fayette and includes the instruction that they be gathered to Ohio in order that the Abrahamic covenant could begin to be fulfilled. Woven into this revelation is a phrase from Peter's address to Cornelius:

> Then Peter opened his mouth, and said, Of a truth I perceive that God is *no respecter of persons.* (Acts 10:34)

> And for your salvation I give unto you a commandment, for I have heard your prayers, and the poor have complained before me, and the rich have I made, and all flesh is mine, and I am *no respecter of persons.* (Doctrine and Covenants 38:16)

Doctrine and Covenants 45, the Lord's latter-day restatement of the Olivet Discourse, contains a phrase from Paul's sermon on Mars' Hill:

> For in him we *live, and move, and have our being*; as certain also of your own poets have said, For we are also his offspring. (Acts 17:28)

> Hearken, O ye people of my church, to whom the kingdom has been given: hearken ye and give ear to him who laid the foundation of the earth, who made the heavens and all the hosts thereof, and by whom all things were made which *live, and move, and have a being.* (Doctrine and Covenants 45:1)

Doctrine and Covenants 45:41 is noteworthy, as it is indicative of Restoration scripture's tendency to quote a New Testament (or perhaps Book of Mormon) quotation of an Old Testament passage (Acts 2:19), rather than the Old Testament passage itself (Joel 2:30):[19]

> And I will shew wonders in heaven above, and signs in the earth beneath; *blood, and fire, and vapour of smoke.* (Acts 2:19)

> And they shall behold *blood, and fire, and vapors of smoke.* (Doctrine and Covenants 45:41)

> And I will shew wonders in the heavens and in the earth, *blood, and fire, and pillars of smoke.* (Joel 2:30)

Finally, one of the longer allusions to the book of Acts comes in Doctrine and Covenants 86, a revelation in which the Lord explains the parable of the wheat and the tares. The language of 86:10 clearly draws on Peter's sermon before the Sanhedrin in Acts 3:

> Whom the heaven must receive *until the times of restitution of all things, which God hath spoken by the mouth of all his holy prophets since the world began.* (Acts 3:21)

> Therefore your life and the priesthood have remained, and must needs remain through you and your lineage *until the restoration of all things spoken by the mouths of all the holy prophets since the world began.* (Doctrine and Covenants 86:10)

Romans

Paul's epistle to the Roman church may be his longest and most theologically complex epistle, but its language is given very little attention in the Doctrine and Covenants, with only a few allusions strewn through the revelations. Doctrine and Covenants 24 contains the injunction to "magnify thine office," a short allusion that could come from Romans 11.[20]

> For I speak to you Gentiles, inasmuch as I am the apostle of the Gentiles, I *magnify mine office*. (Romans 11:13)

> *Magnify thine office*; and after thou hast sowed thy fields and secured them, go speedily unto the church which is in Colesville, Fayette, and Manchester, and they shall support thee; and I will bless them both spiritually and temporally. (Doctrine and Covenants 24:3; compare 24:9; 66:11)

One of the more significant New Testament allusions appears in Doctrine and Covenants 54, a revelation addressing Leman Copley's violation of his covenant in refusing to yield his land to the Saints. Part of the revelation contains an allusion to Romans 4, Paul's explanation of why covenant promises cannot be gained through adherence to Jewish lineage alone, removed from faith. That both passages discuss the implications of covenant adherence suggests that the use of a New Testament passage can be determined by similar contexts as much as by the appropriate language:

> For if they which are of the law be heirs, *faith is made void, the promise made of none effect*. (Romans 4:14)

> And as the covenant which they made unto me has been broken, even so *it has become void and of none effect*. (Doctrine and Covenants 54:4)

A similar awareness of context is present in Doctrine and Covenants 52, a revelation concerning twenty-four elders who are called as missionaries, with each pair instructed to go their own separate way:

> Yea, verily I say, let all these take their journey unto one place, in their several courses, and one man *shall not build upon another's foundation*, neither journey in another's track. (Doctrine and Covenants 52:33)

The language is similar to that of Paul in Romans 15, who stated that he made an effort not to establish churches or baptize converts where another missionary had already begun to work:

> Yea, so have I strived to preach the gospel, not where Christ was named, lest I *should build upon another man's foundation*. (Romans 15:20)

Again, this passage demonstrates a contextual awareness that goes beyond simply adopting language.

1 and 2 Corinthians

At least three sections of the Doctrine and Covenants, sections 46, 74, and 76, rely heavily on the language of 1 Corinthians. Doctrine and Covenants 46, a revelation concerning the proper conduct of church meetings, includes the lengthiest description of spiritual gifts found in the Doctrine and Covenants:

> And again, to some it is given by the Holy Ghost to know the *differences of administration*, as it will be pleasing unto *the same Lord*. . . . And again, it is given by the Holy Ghost to some to know the *diversities of operations*, whether they be of God, that *the manifestations of the Spirit may be given to every man to profit withal*. And again, verily I say unto you, *to some is given, by the Spirit of God, the word of wisdom. To another is given the word of knowledge*, that all may be taught to be wise and to have knowledge. And again, to some it is given to have *faith* to be healed. And to others it is given to have faith *to heal*. And again, to some is given *the working of miracles*; And to others it is given to *prophesy*; and to others *the discerning of spirits*; and again, it is given to some to speak with *tongues*; and *to another* is given *the interpretation of tongues*. And all these gifts come from God, for the benefit of the children of God. (Doctrine and Covenants 46:15–26)

This lengthy description is modeled after Paul's description of spiritual gifts in 1 Corinthians:

> And there are *differences of administrations*, but *the same Lord*. And there are *diversities of operations*, but it is the same God which worketh all in all. But *the manifestation of the Spirit is given to every man to profit withal*. For *to one is given by the Spirit the word of wisdom; to another the word of knowledge* by the same Spirit; to another *faith* by the same Spirit; to another the gifts of *healing* by the same Spirit; to another *the working of miracles*; to another *prophecy*; to another *discerning of spirits*; to another divers kinds of *tongues; to another the interpretation of tongues*; but all these worketh that one and the selfsame Spirit, dividing to every man severally as he will. (1 Corinthians 12:5–11)

Like Doctrine and Covenants 77, section 74 is constructed around a question regarding a New Testament text, in this case 1 Corinthians 7:14, and the question of the spiritual status of children. After quoting 1 Corinthians 7:14, the Lord reveals to Joseph that when Paul wrote that "the unbelieving husband is sanctified by the wife, and the unbelieving wife is sanctified by the husband; else were your children unclean, but now are they holy," what he meant was that "a believer should not be united to an unbeliever; except the law of Moses should be done away among them" (Doctrine and Covenants 74:1, 5). In other words, children who have not reached the age of accountability have need neither of circumcision (Paul's world) nor infant baptism (Joseph Smith's world).

Finally, Doctrine and Covenants 76 contains Joseph Smith's and Sidney Rigdon's majestic vision of the heavens. Doctrine and Covenants 76 terms the three kingdoms of glory "celestial," "terrestrial," and "telestial," comparing them to the glory of the "sun," "moon," and "stars":

> These are they whose *bodies* are *celestial*, whose *glory* is that of the *sun*, even the *glory* of God, the highest of all, whose *glory* the *sun* of the firmament is written of as being typical. (Doctrine and Covenants 76:70)

> Wherefore, they are *bodies terrestrial*, and not *bodies celestial*, and differ in *glory* as the *moon* differs from the *sun*. (Doctrine and Covenants 76:78)

> And the *glory* of the *telestial* is one, even as the *glory* of the *stars* is one; for as one *star* differs from another *star* in *glory*, even so differs one from another in *glory* in the *telestial* world. (Doctrine and Covenants 76:98)

Doctrine and Covenants 76 adopts the language and imagery of Paul's discussion of resurrected bodies in 1 Corinthians 15:

> There are also *celestial bodies*, and *bodies terrestrial*: but the glory of the celestial is one, and the glory of the terrestrial is another. There is one *glory* of the *sun*, and another *glory* of the *moon*, and another *glory* of the *stars*: for one star differeth from another star in glory. (1 Corinthians 15:40–41)

This similarity in language and imagery tends to affect how Latter-day Saints read 1 Corinthians today, viewing Paul as also speaking about three kingdoms of glory rather than about two different types of bodies (incorruptible bodies in heaven and corruptible bodies on the earth).

The language of 2 Corinthians does not appear as frequently in the text of the Doctrine and Covenants as does 1 Corinthians, but there are a couple of notable allusions, particularly to 2 Corinthians 11–12. In these two chapters Paul defends his apostolic calling against a group of challengers he refers to as the "very chiefest apostles" (2 Corinthians 11:5). Nowhere else in his epistles is Paul as emotionally exposed as he is in these two chapters, opening up about everything from his struggles as a missionary to his personal encounter with Jesus. At least three allusions from this part of 2 Corinthians appear in the Doctrine and Covenants. The first comes from part of Joseph Smith's poignant letter penned while in Liberty Jail.[21]

> In journeyings often, in perils of waters, *in perils of robbers*, in perils by mine own countrymen, in perils by the heathen, in perils in the city, in perils in the wilderness, *in perils* in the *sea*, *in perils among false brethren*. (2 Corinthians 11:26)

> If thou art called to pass through tribulation; if thou art *in perils among false brethren*; if thou art *in perils among robbers*; if thou art *in perils* by land or by *sea*. (Doctrine and Covenants 122:5)

The second allusion comes from Joseph's vision of the afterlife that he received in January 1836, now canonized as Doctrine and Covenants 137:

> I knew a man in Christ above fourteen years ago, (*whether in the body, I cannot tell; or whether out of the body, I cannot tell*: God knoweth;) such an one caught up to the third heaven. (2 Corinthians 12:2)

> The heavens were opened upon us, and I beheld the celestial kingdom of God, and the glory thereof, *whether in the body or out I cannot tell.* (Doctrine and Covenants 137:1)

The third allusion comes much earlier in two revelations from 1829, Doctrine and Covenants 17 and 18:[22]

> And he [Jesus] said unto me, *My grace is sufficient for thee*: for my strength is made perfect in weakness. (2 Corinthians 12:9)

> And if you do these last commandments of mine, which I have given you, the gates of hell shall not prevail against you; for *my grace is sufficient for you*, and you shall be lifted up at the last day. (Doctrine and Covenants 17:8)

> And now I speak unto you, the Twelve—Behold, *my grace is sufficient for you.* (Doctrine and Covenants 18:31)

Here the Lord repeats the words he spoke to Paul almost two thousand years earlier to the Three Witnesses (Doctrine and Covenants 17) and to the future Twelve Apostles (Doctrine and Covenants 18). The language of 1 and 2 Corinthians contributes language to some key doctrinal elements while also providing Joseph with a text he can draw on to make sense of his own personal struggles.

Galatians, Ephesians, Philippians, Colossians

The language of the Doctrine and Covenants hardly draws on Paul's letter to the Galatians, with the exception of Galatians 6, which appears three times:[23]

> Brethren, if a man *be overtaken in a fault*, ye which are spiritual, restore such an one in the spirit of meekness; considering thyself, lest thou also be tempted. (Galatians 6:1)

> Any member of the church of Christ transgressing or *being over taken in a fault*, shall be dealt with according as the scriptures directs. (Doctrine and Covenants 20:80)

> Be not deceived; God is not mocked: *for whatsoever* a man *soweth, that shall* he *also reap*. (Galatians 6:7)

> Fear not to do good, my sons, *for whatsoever* ye *sow, that shall* ye *also reap*. (Doctrine and Covenants 6:33)

> And let us *not be weary in well doing*: for in due season we shall reap, if we faint not. (Galatians 6:9)

> Wherefore, *be not weary in well-doing*, for ye are laying the foundation of a great work. And out of small things proceedeth that which is great. (Doctrine and Covenants 64:33)

The same is true for Philippians and Colossians, which both appear only sparingly:

> Who shall change our vile body, that it may be fashioned like unto his glorious body, according to the working whereby he is able even to *subdue all things unto himself.* (Philippians 3:21)

> I, having accomplished and finished the will of him whose I am, even the Father, concerning me—having done this that I might *subdue all things unto myself.* (Doctrine and Covenants 19:2)

> For by him were all things created, that are in heaven, and that are in earth, visible and invisible, whether they be *thrones, or dominions, or principalities, or powers:* all things were created by him, and for him. (Colossians 1:16)

> All *thrones and dominions, principalities and powers,* shall be revealed and set forth upon all who have endured valiantly for the gospel of Jesus Christ. (Doctrine and Covenants 121:29)

> And everything that is in the world, whether it be ordained of men, by *thrones, or principalities, or powers,* or things of name, whatsoever they may be, that are not by me or by my word, saith the Lord, shall be thrown down, and shall not remain after men are dead, neither in nor after the resurrection, saith the Lord your God. (Doctrine and Covenants 132:13)

Of these four epistles, Ephesians receives the most representation in the Doctrine and Covenants. A few short quotations come from Ephesians 1 and 4:

> Having predestinated us unto the adoption of children by Jesus Christ to himself, according to *the good pleasure of his will.* (Ephesians 1:5)

> And to them will I reveal all mysteries, yea, all the hidden mysteries of my kingdom from days of old, and for ages to come, will I make known unto them *the good pleasure of my will* concerning all things pertaining to my kingdom. (Doctrine and Covenants 76:7)

> That in the *dispensation* of *the fulness of times* he might *gather together in one all things* in Christ, *both which are in heaven, and which are on earth*; even in him. (Ephesians 1:10)

> Unto whom I have committed the keys of my kingdom, and a *dispensation* of the gospel for the last times; and for *the fulness of times*, in the which I will *gather together in one all things, both which are in heaven, and which are on earth.* (Doctrine and Covenants 27:13)

> For *the perfecting of the saints, for the work of the ministry*, for the edifying of the body of Christ. (Ephesians 4:12)

> The above offices I have given unto you, and the keys thereof, for helps and for governments, for *the work of the ministry* and *the perfecting of my saints.* (Doctrine and Covenants 124:143)

Doctrine and Covenants 27:15–18 contains one of the lengthiest and clearest adoptions of a New Testament passage, in this case Paul's discussion of the armor of God from Ephesians 6:13–17:

> Wherefore take unto you the whole armour of God, *that ye may be able to withstand* in the evil day, and having done all, to stand. Stand therefore, having your loins girt about with truth, and having on the breastplate of righteousness; and your feet shod with the preparation of the gospel of peace; above all, *taking the shield of faith, wherewith ye shall be able to quench all the fiery darts of the wicked. And take the helmet of salvation, and the sword of the Spirit*, which is the *word* of God. (Ephesians 6:13–17)

> Wherefore, lift up your hearts and rejoice, and gird up your loins, and *take upon you my whole armor, that ye may be able to withstand the evil day, having done all*, that ye may be able *to stand. Stand, therefore, having your loins girt about with truth, having on the breastplate of righteousness, and your feet shod with the preparation of the gospel of peace*, which I have sent mine angels to commit unto you; *taking the shield of faith wherewith ye shall be able to quench all the fiery darts of the wicked; and take the helmet of salvation, and the sword of my Spirit*, which I will pour out upon you, and my *word* which I reveal unto you, and be agreed as touching all things whatsoever ye ask of me, and be faithful until I come, and ye shall be caught up, that where I am ye shall be also. Amen. (Doctrine and Covenants 27:15–18)

1 Thessalonians

As with Galatians, Philippians, and Colossians, Paul's two epistles to the Thessalonian church receive little attention in the Doctrine and Covenants, with only a few allusions to 1 Thessalonians and none (at least that I could find) to 2 Thessalonians:

> Then *we* which are alive and remain *shall be caught up* together with them *in the clouds, to meet* the Lord in the air: and so shall *we ever be with the Lord.* (1 Thessalonians 4:17)

> That when the trump shall sound for the dead, *we shall be caught up in the cloud to meet* thee, that *we* may *ever be with the Lord.* (Doctrine and Covenants 109:75)

1 Timothy, 2 Timothy, and Titus

First Timothy, 2 Timothy, and Titus, often known collectively as the "Pastoral Epistles" owing to the emphasis on ecclesiology, appear sparingly throughout the Doctrine and Covenants, with only a few clear allusions to 1 and 2 Timothy and perhaps one to Titus:

> I will therefore that men pray every where, *lifting up holy hands, without wrath and doubting.* (1 Timothy 2:8)

> And in this place let them lift up their voice and declare my word with loud voices, *without wrath or doubting, lifting up holy hands* upon them. For I am able to make you holy, and your sins are forgiven you. (Doctrine and Covenants 60:7)

> Now the Spirit speaketh expressly, that in the latter times some shall depart from the faith, giving heed to *seducing spirits, and doctrines of devils.* (1 Timothy 4:1)

> But ye are commanded in all things to ask of God, who giveth liberally; and that which the Spirit testifies unto you even so I would that ye should do in all holiness of heart, walking uprightly before me, considering the end of your salvation, doing all things with prayer and thanksgiving, that ye may not be *seduced by* evil *spirits, or doctrines of devils,* or the commandments of men; for some are of men, and others of devils. (Doctrine and Covenants 46:7)

> *Forbidding to marry,* and commanding *to abstain from meats,* which God hath created to be received with thanksgiving of them which believe and know the truth. (1 Timothy 4:3)

> And again, verily I say unto you, that whoso *forbiddeth to marry* is not ordained of God, for marriage is ordained of God unto man . . . and whoso forbiddeth *to abstain from meats,* that man should not eat the same, is not ordained of God. (Doctrine and Covenants 49:15, 18)

> But they shall proceed no further: for their *folly shall be manifest* unto all men, as theirs also was. (2 Timothy 3:9)

> Let such beware and repent speedily, lest judgment shall come upon them as a snare, and their *folly shall be* made *manifest,* and their works shall follow them in the eyes of the people. (Doctrine and Covenants 63:15; compare 35:7; 136:19)

Henceforth there is laid up for me *a crown of righteousness*, which the Lord, the righteous judge, shall give me at that day: and not to me only, but unto all them also that love his appearing. (2 Timothy 4:8)

For a trump shall sound both long and loud, even as upon Mount Sinai, and all the earth shall quake, and they shall come forth—yea, even the dead which died in me, to receive *a crown of righteousness*, and to be clothed upon, even as I am, to be with me, that we may be one. (Doctrine and Covenants 29:13; compare 25:15)

That the aged men be *sober*, grave, *temperate*, sound in *faith*, in *charity*, in *patience*. (Titus 2:2)

Admonish him in his faults, and also receive admonition of him. Be patient; be *sober*; be *temperate*; have *patience, faith*, hope and *charity*. (Doctrine and Covenants 6:19)

The Epistle to the Hebrews

The Epistle to the Hebrews plays a much larger role in the Doctrine and Covenants than most of the New Testament epistles, in terms of both how often Hebrews is alluded to as well as how clear the allusions are:

Are they not all *ministering* spirits, sent forth to *minister for them who shall be heirs of salvation*? (Hebrews 1:14)

Therefore I will make him as flaming fire and a *ministering* angel; he shall *minister for those who shall be heirs of salvation*. (Doctrine and Covenants 7:6)

For the *word* of God *is quick, and powerful, and sharper than any twoedged sword*, piercing even *to the dividing asunder* of soul and spirit, and of the *joints and the marrow*. (Hebrews 4:12)

Behold, I am God; give heed unto my *word*, which *is quick and powerful, sharper than a two-edged sword, to the dividing asunder of* both *joints and marrow*. (Doctrine and Covenants 6:2; compare 11:2; 12:2; 14:2; 33:1)

These all died in faith, not having received the promises, but having seen them afar off, and were persuaded of them, and embraced them, *and confessed* that *they were strangers and pilgrims on the earth*. (Hebrews 11:13)

And confessed they were strangers and pilgrims on the earth. (Doctrine and Covenants 45:13)

Doctrine and Covenants 76 in particular draws extensively on the language of Hebrews, suggesting that Joseph Smith found in Hebrews a vocabulary he could use to describe what he viewed in his vision of the afterlife and the three degrees of glory:

> If they shall fall away, to renew them again unto repentance; seeing they *crucify to themselves* the Son of God afresh, *and put him to an open shame.* (Hebrews 6:6)

> Having denied the Holy Spirit after having received it, and having denied the Only Begotten Son of the Father, having *crucified* him *unto themselves and put him to an open shame.* (Doctrine and Covenants 76:35)

> Whither the forerunner is for us entered, even Jesus, made an high *priest* for ever *after the order of Melchisedec.* (Hebrews 6:20)

> And are *priests* of the Most High, *after the order of Melchizedek,* which was after the order of Enoch, which was after the order of the Only Begotten Son. (Doctrine and Covenants 76:57)

> But ye *are come unto mount Sion, and unto the city of the living God, the heavenly* Jerusalem, and to an innumerable company of angels. (Hebrews 12:22)

> These are they who *are come unto Mount Zion, and unto the city of the living God, the heavenly* place, the holiest of all. (Doctrine and Covenants 76:66)

> To the general assembly and church of the firstborn, which are written in heaven, and to God the Judge of all, and to the spirits of *just men made perfect,* and to *Jesus the mediator of the new covenant,* and to the blood of sprinkling, that speaketh better things than that of Abel. (Hebrews 12:23–24)

> These are they who are *just men made perfect* through *Jesus the mediator of the new covenant,* who wrought out this perfect atonement through the shedding of his own blood. (Doctrine and Covenants 76:69)

> Are they not all *ministering spirits,* sent forth to minister *for them* who *shall be heirs of salvation?* (Hebrews 1:14)

> And also the telestial receive it of the administering of angels who are appointed to minister for them, or who are appointed to be *ministering spirits for them;* for they *shall be heirs of salvation.* (Doctrine and Covenants 76:88)

The Epistle of James

Unlike some of the other shorter letters, the Epistle of James does have a fair amount of representation in the Doctrine and Covenants:

> If any of you *lack wisdom, let him ask of* God, that *giveth* to all men *liberally, and upbraideth not*; and it shall be given *him.* (James 1:5)

> Therefore, he *that lacketh wisdom, let him ask of* me, and I will *give* him *liberally and upbraid him not.* (Doctrine and Covenants 42:68; compare 46:7)

Every good gift and every perfect gift is *from above*, and cometh down *from the Father of lights*, with whom is no variableness, neither shadow of turning. (James 1:17)

For ye know that there is no unrighteousness in them, and that which is righteous cometh down *from above, from the Father of lights*. (Doctrine and Covenants 67:9)

Pure religion and undefiled before God and the Father is this, to visit the fatherless and widows in their affliction, and to *keep himself unspotted from the world*. (James 1:27)

And that thou mayest more fully *keep thyself unspotted from the world*, thou shalt go to the house of prayer and offer up thy sacraments upon my holy day. (Doctrine and Covenants 59:9)

Ye ask, and receive not, because ye *ask* amiss, *that ye may consume it upon your lusts*. (James 4:3)

For verily I say unto you, they are given for the benefit of those who love me and keep all my commandments, and him that seeketh so to do; that all may be benefited that seek or that ask of me, that *ask* and not for a sign *that they may consume it upon their lusts*. (Doctrine and Covenants 46:9)

Behold, the hire of the labourers who have reaped down your fields, which is of you kept back by fraud, crieth: and the cries of them which have reaped are entered *into the ears of the Lord of sabaoth*. (James 5:4)

That the cry of the saints, and of the blood of the saints, shall cease to come up *into the ears of the Lord of Sabaoth*, from the earth, to be avenged of their enemies. (Doctrine and Covenants 87:7)

1 and 2 Peter

The clearest example of text from the two epistles of Peter comes from two allusions made to 2 Peter 1:5–7, Peter's discussion of how to make one's calling and election sure.[24]

And beside this, giving all *diligence*, add to your *faith* virtue; and to *virtue* knowledge; and to *knowledge* temperance; and to *temperance* patience; and to *patience* godliness; and to *godliness* brotherly kindness; and to *brotherly kindness charity*. (2 Peter 1:5–7)

And faith, hope, charity and love, with an eye single to the glory of God, qualify him for the work. Remember *faith, virtue, knowledge, temperance, patience, brotherly kindness, godliness, charity*, humility, *diligence*. (Doctrine and Covenants 4:5–6)

The decisions of these quorums, or either of them, are to be made in all righteousness, in holiness, and lowliness of heart, meekness and long-suffering, and in *faith*, and *virtue*, and *knowledge, temperance, patience, godliness, brotherly kindness* and *charity*. (Doctrine and Covenants 107:30)

There are a few more subtle allusions to 1 and 2 Peter as well:

> Wherefore *gird up* the *loins* of your mind, *be sober*, and hope to the end for the grace that is to be brought unto you at the revelation of Jesus Christ. (1 Peter 1:13)

> Now I give no more unto you at this time. *Gird up* your *loins* and *be sober*. Even so. Amen. (Doctrine and Covenants 73:6)

> The elders which are among you I exhort, who am also an elder, and a witness of the sufferings of Christ, and also a *partaker of the glory* that shall *be revealed*. (1 Peter 5:1)

> Verily I say unto you, blessed are you for receiving mine everlasting covenant, even the fulness of my gospel, sent forth unto the children of men, that they might have life and be made *partakers of the glories* which are to *be revealed* in the last days, as it was written by the prophets and apostles in days of old. (Doctrine and Covenants 66:2)

> But the day of the Lord will come as a thief in the night; in the which the heavens shall pass away with a great noise, and the *elements shall melt with fervent heat*, the earth also and the works that are therein shall be burned up. (2 Peter 3:10)

> And also that of *element shall melt with fervent heat*; and all things shall become new, that my knowledge and glory may dwell upon all the earth. (Doctrine and Covenants 101:25)

> Wherefore, beloved, seeing that ye look for such things, be diligent that ye may be found of him in peace, *without spot, and blameless*. (2 Peter 3:14)

> And that ye might escape the power of the enemy, and be gathered unto me a righteous people; *without spot and blameless*. (Doctrine and Covenants 38:31)

> But *grow in grace, and in the knowledge of* our Lord and Savior Jesus Christ. To him be glory both now and for ever. Amen. (2 Peter 3:18).

> Behold, ye are little children and ye cannot bear all things now; ye must *grow in grace and in the knowledge of* the truth. (Doctrine and Covenants 50:40)

1, 2, and 3 John

The language of the Johannine epistles appears briefly in the Doctrine and Covenants, with a couple of allusions to 1 John, one possible allusion to 2 John, and no allusions to 3 John:

> If we confess our sins, he is faithful and just to forgive us our sins, *and to cleanse* us *from all unrighteousness*. (1 John 1:9)

> That he came into the world, even Jesus, to be crucified for the world, and to bear the sins of the world, and to sanctify the world, *and to cleanse* it *from all unrighteousness*. (Doctrine and Covenants 76:41)

My little children, these things write I unto you, that ye sin not. And if any man sin, we have an *advocate with the Father*, Jesus Christ the righteous. (1 John 2:1)

Lift up your hearts and be glad, for I am in your midst, and am your *advocate with the Father*; and it is his good will to give you the kingdom. (Doctrine and Covenants 29:5; compare 45:3; 62:1)

The elder unto the *elect lady* and her children, whom I love in the truth; and not I only, but also all they that have known the truth. (2 John 1:1)

Behold, thy sins are forgiven thee, and thou art an *elect lady*, whom I have called. (Doctrine and Covenants 25:3).

The Epistle of Jude

Jude, itself a very short letter, appears only a couple of times in the Doctrine and Covenants:

Yet Michael the archangel, when contending with the devil he disputed about the body of Moses, durst not bring against him a *railing accusation*, but said, The Lord rebuke thee. (Jude 1:9)[25]

Not with *railing accusation*, that ye be not overcome, neither with boasting nor rejoicing, lest you be seized therewith. (Doctrine and Covenants 50:33)

And others save with fear, pulling them *out of the fire, hating even the garment spotted by the flesh*. (Jude 1:23)

Crying repentance, saying: Save yourselves from this untoward generation, and come forth *out of the fire, hating even the garments spotted with the flesh*. (Doctrine and Covenants 36:6)

Final Observations

In his study of the book of Revelation, David A. deSilva noted how carefully John adopted Old Testament language and imagery throughout the book of Revelation:

By recontextualizing the content of authoritative prophecy, John subtly invites these Scriptures to lend their authority to his own visions. If the words of the prophets and psalms were inspired in their original contexts, they remain recognizable as inspired material in the new context. . . . John gives the texts new shape, referents, and direction, but the older texts lend their power to that new shape. His frequent weaving in of small phrases and descriptions known from Daniel or other prophetic or apocalyptic literature . . . enhances the hearers' impression that they are hearing another authoritative vision, another species of the same genre, as it were.[26]

This description could just as easily apply to Joseph Smith's use of the New Testament within the revelations canonized as the Doctrine and Covenants. By adopting the language of a familiar scriptural text, Joseph invites the New Testament texts to "lend their authority" to his nineteenth-century scripture. Additionally, Joseph, like John, does not merely copy the New Testament into his revelations. He also gives the New Testament "new shape, referents, and direction" in fascinating ways that open up entirely new methods of interpretation. Rather than being surprised or even turned off by how much of the New Testament appears in the Doctrine and Covenants, Latter-day Saints should actively seek out and study these types of biblical interactions, recognizing that this type of biblical deconstruction and reconstruction is exactly what inspired prophets tend to do. Nephi's statement that the Lord speaks "the same words unto one nation like unto another" (2 Nephi 29:8) suggests that similarity in language between scriptural texts may be ultimately attributable to the same God using the same language to instruct different people in different times.

On a more technical level, while much more could be done regarding how the language of the New Testament influenced the verbiage of the Doctrine and Covenants, this brief examination does allow us to draw some preliminary observations: (1) Of the twenty-seven New Testament texts, twenty-four are clearly and identifiably present in the Doctrine and Covenants—only 2 Thessalonians, 3 John, and Philemon are absent. (2) It is clear that the New Testament plays a significant role in the language of the Doctrine and Covenants, as there are hundreds of clear, indisputable allusions to the New Testament strewn throughout. (3) Some New Testament texts are used more than others, with some barely appearing at all. While length could be one factor, it is not the only factor (see Acts or Romans) since the familiarity of certain New Testament texts or passages to a nineteenth-century audience must also be considered. (4) In some cases, the purpose of the integration of New Testament texts is to provide a familiar language or idiom to the revelations, with the original context of the New Testament passage being of little importance. (5) However, some New Testament texts, such as Matthew, Revelation, and John, provide more than just a familiar idiom—they also play a role in how key doctrinal ideas are described, even providing a voice for Jesus Christ. In the case of these three texts (and likely Hebrews as well, because of its prominent role in Doctrine and Covenants 76), the language and context of the New Testament should be part of any exegetical study of the Doctrine and Covenants.

Appendix: Allusions to the New Testament within the Doctrine and Covenants

This list is not meant to be all-inclusive of every single allusion to the New Testament in the Doctrine and Covenants. Rather, it is intended to give readers a more specific sense of how interconnected these two texts are and provide substantial textual references for those desiring further study. While this list is primarily the result of my own research and study of the Doctrine and Covenants, I also relied on the work of Ellis T. Rasmussen, "Textual Parallels to the Doctrine and Covenants and Book of Commandments as Found in the Bible" (master's thesis, Brigham Young University, 1951), and Lois Jean Smutz, "Textual Parallels to the Doctrine and Covenants (Sections 65–133) as Found in the Bible" (master's thesis, Brigham Young University, 1971), as well as the recent publication by Thomas A. Wayment, *The New Testament: A New Translation for Latter-day Saints* (Provo, UT: Religious Studies Center, Brigham Young University; Salt Lake City: Deseret Book, 2018).

Matthew
Matt 3:2/D&C 39:19; 42:7
Matt 3:2–3/D&C 33:10
Matt 3:3/D&C 65:1
Matt 3:10/D&C 52:18; 97:7
Matt 3:12/D&C 101:65–66
Matt 3:17/D&C 45:4; 50:37; 51:3
Matt 4:16/D&C 57:10
Matt 4:17/D&C 39:19; 42:7
Matt 5:5/D&C 56:20; 59:2; 88:17
Matt 5:7/D&C 54:6
Matt 5:8/D&C 56:18; 97:16
Matt 5:13/D&C 101:40; 103:10
Matt 5:28/D&C 42:23; 63:16
Matt 5:32/D&C 42:74
Matt 6:14/D&C 82:1
Matt 6:20/D&C 6:27
Matt 6:25/D&C 84:81
Matt 6:28/D&C 84:82
Matt 6:29/D&C 84:82
Matt 6:33/D&C 11:23; 106:3
Matt 6:34/D&C 84:84
Matt 7:2/D&C 1:10
Matt 7:6/D&C 41:6
Matt 7:7/D&C 4:7; 6:5; 11:5; 12:5;
    14:5; 49:26; 66:9; 75:27; 88:63
Matt 7:13/D&C 132:25
Matt 7:14/D&C 132:22
Matt 7:24/D&C 11:24
Matt 7:25/D&C 90:5
Matt 7:27/D&C 90:5
Matt 8:12/D&C 19:5; 101:91;
    133:73
Matt 10:7/D&C 39:19
Matt 10:9-10/D&C 24:18
Matt 10:11/D&C 24:15
Matt 10:14/D&C 24:15; 60:15;
    75:20
Matt 10:15/D&C 75:21–22
Matt 10:19/D&C 24:6; 84:85
Matt 10:22/D&C 53:7

Matt 10:38/D&C 56:2
Matt 10:39/D&C 98:13; 103:27
Matt 10:40/D&C 39:5, 22; 112:20
Matt 10:42/D&C 58:28; 84:90
Matt 11:14/D&C 77:9
Matt 11:24/D&C 75:21–22
Matt 11:29/D&C 32:1; 54:10
Matt 12:20/D&C 52:11
Matt 12:31/D&C 132:27
Matt 12:32/D&C 132:27
Matt 13:11/D&C 6:7; 42:65; 63:23;
    64:5; 107:19
Matt 13:30/D&C 86:7
Matt 13:38/D&C 86:2
Matt 13:39/D&C 86:3
Matt 13:40/D&C 86:7
Matt 15:26/D&C 41:6
Matt 16:18/ D&C 6:34; 10:69; 17:8;
    18:5; 21:6; 33:13; 98:22; 128:10
Matt 16:19/D&C 1:8; 7:7; 90:2;
    124:93; 127:7; 128:8, 10; 132:46
Matt 16:24/D&C 23:6
Matt 16:27/D&C 1:10; 65:5; 76:111;
    101:65.
Matt 17:12/D&C 49:6
Matt 18:6/D&C 54:5; 121:22
Matt 18:16/D&C 6:28
Matt 18:18/D&C 1:8; 124:93; 127:7;
    128:8, 10; 132:46
Matt 18:19–20/D&C 6:32
Matt 18:20/D&C 32:3; 61:36; 75:11
Matt 19:30/D&C 29:30
Matt 20:1/D&C 88:70, 74
Matt 20:6–9/D&C 33:3
Matt 20:16/D&C 29:30; 95:5;
    121:34
Matt 22:13/D&C 19:5; 101:91;
    133:73
Matt 22:14/D&C 95:5
Matt 22:21/D&C 63:26
Matt 23:12/D&C 112:3

Matt 23:33/D&C 121:23
Matt 23:34/D&C 63:31
Matt 23:37/D&C 10:65; 29:2; 43:24
Matt 24:2/D&C 45:20
Matt 24:6/D&C 45:26, 35
Matt 24:7/D&C 45:33
Matt 24:12/D&C 45:27
Matt 24:27/D&C 43:22
Matt 24:29/D&C 29:14
Matt 24:30/D&C 45:16, 44
Matt 24:32/D&C 35:16; 45:37
Matt 24:33/D&C 45:63; 110:16
Matt 24:34/D&C 45:21;
Matt 24:36/D&C 39:21; 49:7
Matt 24:42/D&C 133:11
Matt 24:43/D&C 104:86
Matt 24:44/D&C 51:20
Matt 24:45/D&C 51:19; 72:4
Matt 24:48/D&C 45:26
Matt 25:1/D&C 133:10
Matt 25:1–13/D&C 33:17
Matt 25:6/D&C 88:92; 133:10
Matt 25:21/D&C 51:19; 117:10
Matt 25:23/D&C 52:13
Matt 25:25/D&C 60:2, 13
Matt 25:40/D&C 42:38
Matt 25:41/D&C 29:28; 76:44
Matt 25:46/D&C 76:44
Matt 26:29/D&C 27:5
Matt 27:52/D&C 88:97
Matt 28:3/D&C 20:6
Matt 28:18/D&C 93:17
Matt 28:19/D&C 68:8
Matt 28:20/D&C 24:8, 10; 62:9;
    132:49

Mark
Mark 1:4/D&C 107:20
Mark 4:25/D&C 60:3
Mark 6:11/D&C 75:20–22
Mark 9:42/D&C 121:22

Mark 9:44/D&C 76:44

Mark 9:46/D&C 76:44

Mark 9:48/D&C 76:44

Mark 13:11/D&C 84:85

Mark 13:24/D&C 34:9

Mark 13:37/D&C 82:5

Mark 14:38/D&C 31:12

Mark 14:62/D&C 49:6

Mark 16:15/D&C 18:28; 68:8

Mark 16:15–17/D&C 58:64

Mark 16:16–17/D&C 68:9–10

Mark 16:17–18/D&C 24:13; 35:9; 124:98

Mark 16:17/D&C 24:13; 63:9; 84:65, 67; 124:98

Mark 16:18/D&C 84:71–72

Luke

Luke 1:6/D&C 136:4

Luke 1:13/D&C 27:7

Luke 1:15/D&C 84:27

Luke 1:17/D&C 27:7

Luke 2:9/D&C 76:19

Luke 2:10/D&C 31:3

Luke 3:3/D&C 107:20

Luke 3:9/D&C 97:7

Luke 9:5/D&C 75:20

Luke 10:7/D&C 84:79; 106:3

Luke 10:12/D&C 75:21-22

Luke 10:20/D&C 50:30

Luke 11:9/D&C 66:9; 75:27; 88:63

Luke 11:10/D&C 75:27

Luke 11:34/D&C 88:67

Luke 11:50/D&C 29:46; 35:18; 128:18

Luke 12:30/D&C 84:83

Luke 12:32/D&C 6:34; 29:5; 35:27

Luke 12:42/D&C 72:17; 78:22; 101:61; 104:75; 136:27

Luke 12:48/D&C 82:3

Luke 14:11/D&C 101:42; 112:3

Luke 16:2/D&C 69:5; 70:4; 72:3

Luke 16:9/D&C 82:22

Luke 17:2/D&C 121:22

Luke 17:4/D&C 98:40

Luke 18:1–5/D&C 101:81–84

Luke 21:19/D&C 101:38

Luke 21:24/D&C 45:25, 30

Luke 21:26/D&C 45:26

Luke 21:27/D&C 34:7

Luke 21:28/D&C 35:26

Luke 21:29–31/D&C 45:37–38

Luke 21:30/D&C 45:37

Luke 21:31/D&C 45:38

Luke 22:31/D&C 52:12

Luke 24:39/D&C 129:2

Luke 24:49/D&C 38:32, 38; 95:8–9; 105:33

John

John 1:1/D&C 93:7, 8

John 1:2/D&C 93:21

John 1:3/D&C 93:10

John 1:4/D&C 93:9

John 1:5/D&C 6:21; 10:58; 11:11; 34:2; 39:2; 45:7, 29; 88:49

John 1:9/D&C 84:46; 93:2

John 1:11/D&C 6:21; 10:57; 11:29; 39:3; 45:8

John 1:12/D&C 11:30; 34:3; 39:4; 42:52; 66:1

John 1:13/D&C 63:10

John 1:14/D&C 66:12; 76:23; 93:11

John 1:16/D&C 93:12, 20

John 1:18/D&C 67:11; 76:13

John 1:32/D&C 93:15

John 1:34/D&C 93:6

John 1:47/D&C 41:11

John 3:5/D&C 5:16

John 3:16/D&C 34:3; 49:5

John 3:19/D&C 10:21; 29:45

John 4:14/D&C 63:23

John 4:34/D&C 60:16

John 4:42/D&C 42:1

John 7:34/D&C 29:29

John 8:11/D&C 6:35; 24:2

John 8:12/D&C 10:70; 11:28; 12:9; 39:2; 45:7

John 8:23/D&C 63:59

John 10:16/D&C 10:59

John 10:27/D&C 38:22

John 12:36/D&C 106:5

John 13:10/D&C 38:10

John 13:20/D&C 39:5; 84:36–37

John 14:2/D&C 98:18

John 14:3/D&C 98:18

John 14:10/D&C 93:3, 20

John 14:11/D&C 93:3, 20

John 14:15/D&C 42:29; 46:9; 124:87

John 14:16/D&C 88:3

John 14:30/D&C 127:11

John 15:16/D&C 14:8; 88:64; 101:27

John 16:12/D&C 50:40

John 16:16/D&C 84:119

John 16:21/D&C 136:35

John 16:23/D&C 14:8; 101:27

John 16:33/D&C 50:41; 61:36

John 17:3/D&C 132:24

John 17:11/D&C 29:13; 50:41

John 17:12/D&C 50:42

John 17:21/D&C 35:2

John 20:23/D&C 132:46

John 21:22/D&C 7:4

John 21:23/D&C 7:4

Acts

Acts 1:3/D&C 97:14

Acts 1:4/D&C 95:9

Acts 2:4/D&C 14:8

Acts 2:5/D&C 64:42

Acts 2:19/D&C 45:41

Acts 2:38/D&C 49:13, 14; 137:6

Acts 2:40/D&C 36:6

Acts 3:21/D&C 27:6; 86:10

Acts 4:12/D&C 18:23

Acts 7:55/D&C 107:56

Acts 8:21/D&C 49:2

Acts 9:5/D&C 121:38

Acts 10:4/D&C 112:1

Acts 10:34/D&C 38:16

Acts 13:32/D&C 19:29; 62:5; 96:7

Acts 17:28/D&C 45:1

Acts 18:24/D&C 100:11

Acts 22:16/D&C 39:10

Acts 24:16/D&C 135:4

Acts 26:13/D&C 110:3

Acts 26:14/D&C 121:38

Acts 26:16/D&C 14:8

Romans

Romans 1:16/D&C 68:4

Romans 4:14/D&C 54:4

Romans 6:4/D&C 76:51

Romans 8:28/D&C 90:24; 98:3;
    100:15; 105:40

Romans 9:22/D&C 76:33

Romans 9:28/D&C 52:11

Romans 11:13/D&C 24:3, 9; 66:11

Romans 11:36/D&C 93:10

Romans 15:20/D&C 52:33

1 Corinthians

1 Cor 1:12/D&C 76:99

1 Cor 1:27/D&C 1:19; 35:13

1 Cor 3:2/D&C 19:22

1 Cor 3:17/D&C 93:35

1 Cor 3:21/D&C 76:59

1 Cor 3:22/D&C 76:59, 99

1 Cor 4:5/D&C 123:13

1 Cor 6:19/D&C 18:32

1 Cor 7:14/D&C 74:1

1 Cor 9:17/D&C 27:13; 110:12, 16

1 Cor 10:13/D&C 64:20

1 Cor 12:5–11/D&C 46:15–26

1 Cor 12:7–8/D&C 46:12

1 Cor 12:21/D&C 84:109

1 Cor 12:31/D&C 46:8

1 Cor 13:13/D&C 4:5; 12:8; 18:19

1 Cor 15:25/D&C 49:6; 58:22;
    76:106

1 Cor 15:29/D&C 127:6; 128:16

1 Cor 15:40–41/D&C 76:70–71,
    96–98

1 Cor 15:40/D&C 76:78

1 Cor 15:44/D&C 29:43; 88:27–28

1 Cor 15:46–48/D&C 128:14

1 Cor 15:51–52/D&C 43:32; 63:51;
    101:31

1 Cor 16:7/D&C 137:7

1 Cor 16:9/D&C 112:19

2 Corinthians

2 Cor 4:17/D&C 63:66

2 Cor 5:17/D&C 29:24; 63:49

2 Cor 6:6/D&C 121:41

2 Cor 11:14/D&C 128:20; 129:8

2 Cor 11:26/D&C 122:5

2 Cor 12:2–3/D&C 137:1

2 Cor 12:9/D&C 17:8; 18:31

2 Cor 13:1/D&C 6:28; 128:3

Galatians

Gal 5:1/D&C 88:86

Gal 6:1/D&C 20:80

Gal 6:7/D&C 6:33

Gal 6:9/D&C 64:33

Ephesians

Eph 1:4/D&C 124:33, 41; 127:2;
    128:5, 8; 132:5, 63

Eph 1:5/D&C 76:7

Eph 1:10/D&C 27:13; 138:48

Eph 1:13/D&C 76:53; 88:3;
    124:124; 132:7, 18–19

Eph 3:21/D&C 76:112

Eph 4:2/D&C 118:3

Eph 4:12/D&C 124:143

Eph 4:30/D&C 124:124

Eph 6:13/D&C 27:15

Eph 6:14/D&C 27:16; 38:9

Eph 6:14–17/D&C 27:16–18

Eph 6:16/D&C 3:8; 27:17

Philippians

Phil 2:10/D&C 88:79

Phil 2:10–11/D&C 88:104

Phil 3:21/D&C 19:2

Colossians

Col 3:14/D&C 88:125

1 Thessalonians

1 Thess 1:9/D&C 20:19

1 Thess 4:16–17/D&C 45:45

1 Thess 4:17/D&C 27:18; 109:75

1 Thess 5:2/D&C 45:19; 106:4

1 Thess 5:4/D&C 106:5

1 Timothy

1 Tim 2:8/D&C 60:7

1 Tim 3:16/D&C 19:10

1 Tim 4:1/D&C 46:7

1 Tim 4:3/D&C 49:15, 18

1 Tim 6:10/D&C 1:3

2 Timothy

2 Tim 3:9/D&C 35:7; 63:15; 136:19

2 Tim 4:8/D&C 25:15; 29:13

Titus

Titus 2:2/D&C 6:19

Hebrews

Heb 1:3/D&C 138:40

Heb 1:14/D&C 7:6; 76:88; 138:59

Heb 2:18/D&C 62:1

Heb 3:13/D&C 45:6

Heb 4:12/D&C 6:2; 11:2; 12:2; 14:2;
    33:1

Heb 5:6 (see also 6:20; 7:11, 17,
    21)/D&C 76:57; 107: 9, 29, 71,
    73, 76; 124:123

Heb 6:6/D&C 76:35

Heb 7:3/D&C 78:16; 84:17

Heb 7:16/D&C 84:27

Heb 8:12/D&C 38:14; 58:42

Heb 10:7/D&C 99:5

Heb 11:6/D&C 63:11

Heb 11:13/D&C 45:13

Heb 12:22/D&C 76:66–67

Heb 12:22-23/D&C 138:12

Heb 12:23/D&C 76:54, 71, 94,
    102; 77:11; 78:21; 88:5; 93:22;
    107:19; 129:3

Heb 12:24/D&C 76:69; 107:19

Heb 12:26/D&C 84:118

James

James 1:5/D&C 42:68; 46:7

James 1:17/D&C 67:9

James 1:27/D&C 59:9

James 3:1/D&C 82:3

James 4:3/D&C 46:9

James 5:4/D&C 87:7; 95:7; 98:2

James 5:8/D&C 106:4

James 5:14/D&C 42:44

1 Peter

1 Peter 1:13/D&C 73:6

1 Peter 1:19/D&C 131:5

1 Peter 1:22/D&C 88:123

1 Peter 3:18/D&C 67:11

1 Peter 3:18–20/D&C 138:7–9

1 Peter 3:19/D&C 76:73

1 Peter 3:19-20/D&C 138:28

1 Peter 4:6/D&C 88:99; 138:10,
    30, 34

1 Peter 4:13/D&C 66:2

1 Peter 5:1/D&C 66:2

2 Peter

2 Peter 1:5–7/D&C 4:5–6; 107:30–31

2 Peter 1:8/D&C 107:31

2 Peter 2:4/D&C 38:5

2 Peter 3:12/D&C 101:25

2 Peter 3:14/D&C 38:31

2 Peter 3:16/D&C 10:63

2 Peter 3:18/D&C 50:40

1 John

1 John 1:9/D&C 76:41

1 John 2:1/D&C 29:5; 32:3; 45:3;
   62:1; 110:4

1 John 3:2/D&C 130:1

2 John

2 John 1:1/D&C 25:3

Jude

Jude 1:7/D&C 76:105

Jude 1:9/D&C 50:33

Jude 1:15/D&C 99:5

Jude 1:23/D&C 36:6

Jude 1:25/D&C 20:4

Revelation

Rev 1:1/D&C 88:79

Rev 1:6/D&C 76:56

Rev 1:8/D&C 19:1; 35:1; 38:1; 45:7;
   54:1; 61:1; 63:60; 68:35; 75:1;
   84:20

Rev 1:14–16: D&C 110:3

Rev 1:18/D&C 110:4

Rev 2:17/D&C 130:11

Rev 3:10/D&C 124:124

Rev 4:4/D&C 77:5

Rev 4:6/D&C 77:1–3

Rev 4:8/D&C 77:4

Rev 4:10/D&C 77:5

Rev 5:1/D&C 77:6–7

Rev 5:3/D&C 88: 79, 104

Rev 5:13/D&C 76:119; 88: 79, 104;
   124:101

Rev 6:1/D&C 77:7

Rev 6:9/D&C 135:7

Rev 6:12/D&C 29:14; 45:42; 77:10

Rev 6:14/D&C 88:95

Rev 7:1/D&C 77:8

Rev 7:2/D&C 77:9

Rev 7:4/D&C 77:11

Rev 7:9/D&C 7:3; 10:51; 11:21;
   42:58; 77:8, 11; 88:103; 98:33,
   34; 133:37

Rev 8:1/D&C 77:12; 88:95

Rev 8:2/D&C 77:12

Rev 8:5/D&C 88:90

Rev 8:13/D&C 88:92; 133:36

Rev 10:5/D&C 88:110

Rev 10:8/D&C 77:14; 88:110

Rev 11:3/D&C 77:15

Rev 12:4/D&C 29:36

Rev 12:6/D&C 33:5; 86:3

Rev 12:9/D&C 29:37

Rev 12:9/D&C 76:28; 88:110

Rev 13:7/D&C 76:29

Rev 14:1/D&C 133:18

Rev 14:2/D&C 133:22

Rev 14:6/D&C 7:3; 10:51; 11:21;
   36:5; 42:58; 77:8, 11; 88:103;
   98:33, 34; 133:36, 37

Rev 14:7/D&C 88:104; 133:38

Rev 14:8/D&C 35:11; 88:94, 105

Rev 14:10/D&C 29:17; 43:26; 115:6

Rev 14:13/D&C 59:2; 63:48–49;
   124:86

Rev 15:2/D&C 130:7

Rev 15:3/D&C 76:114

Rev 16:6/D&C 88:94

Rev 18:3/D&C 35:11

Rev 19:2/D&C 29:21

Rev 19:9/D&C 58:11

Rev 19:12/D&C 110:3

Rev 19:15/D&C 76:107; 88:106

Rev 19:20/D&C 76:36

Rev 20:2/D&C 45:55; 76:28;
   88:110

Rev 20:2–3/D&C 43:31

Rev 20:3/D&C 29:22; 88:111

Rev 20:6/D&C 63:18; 76:64

Rev 20:7/D&C 29:22

Rev 20:10/D&C 76:36

Rev 20:12/D&C 128:6–7; 137:9

Rev 20:14/D&C 63:17

Rev 21:1/D&C 29:23

Rev 21:4/D&C 88:116; 101:29

Rev 21:5/D&C 1:37

Rev 21:6/D&C 19:1; 35:1; 38:1;
   45:7; 54:1; 61:1; 63:60; 68:35;
   75:1; 84:20

Rev 21:8/D&C 63:17

Rev 21:27/D&C 132:19

Rev 22:13/D&C 19:1; 35:1; 38:1;
   45:7; 54:1; 61:1; 63:60; 68:35;
   75:1; 84:20

Rev 22:15/D&C 76:103

Rev 22:17/D&C 10:66

Rev 22:18–19/D&C 20:35

Rev 22:20/D&C 33:18

Nicholas J. Frederick is an assistant professor in the Department of Ancient Scripture at Brigham Young University.

Further Reading

Barlow, Philip. *Mormons and the Bible: The Place of the Latter-day Saints in American Religion.* 2nd ed. Oxford: Oxford University Press, 2013. Successfully situates the composition of Mormon scripture within a nineteenth-century context, with a specific section (pages 21–26) dealing with the Bible in the Doctrine and Covenants.

Huntsman, Eric D. "The King James Bible and the Doctrine and Covenants." In *The King James Bible and the Restoration*, edited by Kent P. Jackson, 182–96. Provo, UT: Religious Studies Center, Brigham Young University, 2007. A good resource for exploring the nineteenth-century context of the language of the King James Bible and how it is used in the Doctrine and Covenants.

Frederick, Nicholas J. "Using the Gospel of John to Understand the Text of the Revelations." In *You Shall Have My Word: Exploring the Text of the Doctrine and Covenants*, edited by Scott C. Esplin, Richard O. Cowan, and Rachel Cope, 205–19. Provo, UT: Religious Studies Center, Brigham Young University; Salt Lake City: Deseret Book, 2012. This paper studies quotations and allusions from the Gospel of John in the Doctrine and Covenants, specifically looking at how knowledge of the context of John's Gospel can add to an understanding of Latter-day Saint scripture.

Notes

1. Philip Barlow, *Mormons and the Bible: The Place of the Latter-day Saints in American Religion*, 2nd ed. (Oxford: Oxford University Press, 2013), 25.

2. The technical name for the study of how two or more texts interact is "intertextuality." It has become common in biblical studies to use intertextuality in studying the impact of the Old Testament on the New Testament. Important to this type of intertextual study are the works of Richard B. Hays, *Echoes of Scripture in the Letters of Paul* (New Haven, CT: Yale University Press, 1989), and *The Conversion of the Imagination: Paul as Interpreter of Israel's Scripture* (Grand Rapids, MI: Eerdmans, 2005), as well as the recent publication of G. K. Beale and D. A. Carson's massive work, *Commentary on the New Testament Use of the Old Testament* (Grand Rapids, MI: Baker Academic, 2007). While the majority of intertextual studies that address Latter-day Saint scripture center on the Book of Mormon and its relationship to the Bible, some intertextual work has been done involving the Bible and the Doctrine and Covenants. Two important master's theses exploring the textual connections are Ellis T. Rasmussen, "Textual Parallels to the Doctrine and Covenants and Book of Commandments as Found in the Bible" (master's thesis, Brigham Young University, 1951), and Lois Jean Smutz, "Textual Parallels to the Doctrine and Covenants (Sections 65–133) as Found in the Bible" (master's thesis, Brigham Young University, 1971). Other works include Eric D. Huntsman, "The King James Bible and the Doctrine and Covenants," in *The King James Bible and the Restoration*, ed. Kent P. Jackson (Provo, UT: Religious Studies Center, Brigham Young University, 2007), 182–96; Terry B. Ball and Spencer S. Snyder, "Isaiah in the Doctrine and Covenants," in *You Shall Have My Word: Exploring the Text of the Doctrine and Covenants*, ed. Scott C. Esplin, Richard O. Cowan, and Rachel Cope (Provo, UT: Religious Studies Center, Brigham Young University; Salt Lake City: Deseret Book, 2012), 108–33; Nicholas J. Frederick, "Using the Gospel of John to Understand the Text of the Revelations," in Esplin, Cowan, and Cope, *You Shall Have My Word*, 205–19; and Lisa Olsen Tait, "Gathering the Lord's Words into One: Biblical Intertextuality in the Doctrine and Covenants," in Esplin, Cowan, and Cope, *You Shall Have My Word*, 92–107.

3. It is not my intent to pinpoint and analyze every single location in the Doctrine and Covenants where there might be an intertextual connection with the New Testament. Rather, I will focus on the places in the Doctrine and Covenants where there is a *clear* and *established* quotation or allusion to the New Testament. In other words, this chapter does not focus on themes or words but on connections on the phrasal level. In order to determine which possible passages fit these requirements, I employed a series of criteria similar to the ones I outlined in my article "Evaluating the Interaction between the New Testament and the Book of Mormon: A Proposed Methodology," *Journal of Book of Mormon Studies* 24 (2015): 1–30.

4. For convenience's sake, this chapter will use "allusion" or "alluded to" to refer to intertextual connections between the Doctrine and Covenants and the New Testament.

5. In Matthew's Gospel, Jesus is the "new Moses," and much of Matthew's Gospel is constructed around parallels between the two figures. See Dale C. Allison Jr., *The New Moses: A Matthean Typology* (Eugene, OR: Wipf and Stock, 2013).

6. The same phrase appears three times in the Book of Mormon (Mosiah 2:38; Alma 5:52; and Mormon 9:5), suggesting another possible source for the phrase in the Doctrine and Covenants, although it could be argued that the source for all three Book of Mormon passages is Matthew 3:12 anyway.

7. It is also possible that the source for this passage is Luke 3:9.

8. This uncertainty stems from the fact that the Gospel of John never reveals the identity of the "beloved disciple." Notably, Doctrine and Covenants 7 solves this mystery as well, as John is identified as "my beloved" in verse 1.

9. Michael Hubbard MacKay et al., eds., *Documents, Volume 1: July 1828–June 1831*, vol. 1 of the Documents series of *The Joseph Smith Papers*, ed. Dean C. Jessee, Ronald K. Esplin, Richard Lyman Bushman, and Matthew J. Grow (Salt Lake City: Church Historian's Press, 2013), 48.

10. See Book of Commandments 6. While the entirety of Doctrine and Covenants 7 is generally understood as having come from the parchment of John, the phrase "and for this cause the Lord said unto Peter" seems out of place in John's narrative. I would suggest that this phrase could be read as a parenthetical insertion made by the translator of the parchment or by Joseph Smith himself as a means of indicating that the remainder of Doctrine and Covenants 7:4 is the answer to the question posed by Smith and Cowdery.

11. This description is likely also informed by Joel 2:31 and Matthew 24:29.

12. The direct source for Doctrine and Covenants 29:21 is likely 1 Nephi 22:13 / 2 Nephi 28:18, but the Book of Mormon's description is likely itself an allusion to Revelation 17:1 and 19:2.

13. Joseph Smith History, 1838–1856, vol. A–1, 192; accessible at josephsmithpapers.org.

14. See discourse delivered on April 8, 1843, recorded in *The Words of Joseph Smith*, ed. Lyndon W. Cook and Andrew F. Ehat (Orem, UT: Grandin Book, 1991), 183–88.

15. Richard L. Bushman, *Joseph Smith: Rough Stone Rolling* (New York: Alfred A. Knopf, 2005), 206.

16. One exception to this is Doctrine and Covenants 76:119, which appropriates language from Revelation 5:13 to describe a benediction to God.

17. "Thus, on the basis of good external evidence and strong internal considerations it appears that the earliest ascertainable form of the Gospel of Mark ended with 16:8." Bruce M. Metzger, *A Textual Commentary on the Greek New Testament*, 2nd ed. (Stuttgart: Deutsche Bibelgesellschaft, 2002), 105. For a fuller discussion of the issues involved with Mark's ending, see Robert H. Stein, *Mark* (Grand Rapids, MI: Baker Academic, 2008), 733–37; and R. T. France, *The Gospel of Mark* (Grand Rapids, MI: Eerdmans, 2002), 685–88.

18. Moreover, the long ending of Mark appears on at least two occasions in the Book of Mormon: Mormon 9:22–24 and Ether 4:18. The former, Mormon 9:22–24, is an exact quotation of Mark 16:15–18. It is possible that the Doctrine and Covenants is drawing on the language of the Book of Mormon, but the Book of Mormon is clearly drawing on Mark 16.

19. The direct source of this allusion could be 1 Nephi 22:18: "Behold, my brethren, I say unto you, that these things must shortly come; yea, even *blood, and fire, and vapor of smoke* must come; and it must needs be upon the face of this earth; and it cometh unto men according to the flesh if it so be that they will harden their hearts against the Holy One of Israel." However, 1 Nephi appears to be drawing on Acts 2:19 for its language, so the ultimate source of the language in Doctrine and Covenants 45:41 would indirectly be Acts 2:19 anyway.

20. The only other places where *magnify* and *office* appear together are Jacob 1:19 and 2:2.

21. Coincidentally or not, another allusion to 2 Corinthians appears prominently in Doctrine and Covenants 121:41 (compare 2 Corinthians 6:6), the first part of Joseph's Liberty Jail correspondence.

22. This allusion could also be to Ether 12:26–27 and Moroni 10:32, but, again, those three would be alluding to 2 Corinthians 12:9.

23. Galatians 5:1 does appear in Doctrine and Covenants 88:86.

24. This statement does not take into account Doctrine and Covenants 138, which explicitly quotes 1 Peter 3:18–20 and 4:6 in 138:7–10. It was a reading of these verses from 1 Peter that led to Joseph F. Smith's vision of the spirit world on October 3, 1918.

25. This could also be from 2 Peter 2:11. There is significant overlap between Jude and portions of 2 Peter.

26. David A. deSilva, *Seeing Things John's Way: The Rhetoric of the Book of Revelation* (Louisville: Westminster John Knox, 2009), 148–49.

Part 7
After the New Testament

42

Christianity in the Second Century

Luke Drake

Imagine that two thousand years from now a group of historians want to understand Latter-day Saint history and culture from 1918 to 2018. Suppose, however, that the only resources these historians have available to them are a copy of the April general conference report from 1975; several posts from a variety of blogs and from Facebook (with comments); a few dozen copies of sacrament meeting talks from Church members in Bolivia, Ghana, Indonesia, and Argentina; an excerpt from a sermon given by Chieko Okazaki; a handful of articles from the *Salt Lake Tribune*; a letter from the First Presidency discussing safety in Church activities; an op-ed on California's Proposition 8 from the *New York Times*; a collection of talks given by President Boyd K. Packer; and a Sunday School manual in Spanish that was published in 1940. If these were the only resources that these future people had at their disposal, what sort of portrait could and would they draw of The Church of Jesus Christ of Latter-day Saints in the twentieth and twenty-first centuries? In what ways would their understandings of Latter-day Saint religion and culture be incomplete? What questions would be ultimately unanswerable?

In some ways, scholars of second-century Christianity (AD 100–200) face a similar predicament. What we can say about Christianity in this period is the product of a relatively sparse amount of surviving historical evidence. For example, other than several dozen ancient writings, no Christian archaeological evidences survive from the first or second century—no buildings, no paintings, no sculptures, no pottery, nothing.[1] Our only surviving evidences of Christian groups in this period are literary in nature: some letters, some fictional texts, some Christian regulatory handbooks, some sermons that would have been delivered in a worship setting, some Christian critiques of Jews and pagans, and so on.[2] What this means for us is that in order to tell the story of second-century Christianity, we must take an extremely close and critical look at the surviving literature of the period and then do our best to extrapolate cautiously from that literature in order to find answers to our questions. In fact, we may even have to acknowledge that some questions cannot be readily answered based on the extant evidence.

Therefore, while the questions that this chapter will address are seemingly simple, answering them is at times complicated and challenging. What would life have been like for a Christian in the second century? What did second-century Christians believe about God and Jesus and humankind's relationship to the divine? How did these early Christians practice their Christianity? What were their churches and church services like? Were they persecuted? If not, why do we hear so much about early Christian persecutions? If so, how did they respond to these persecutions? What was the role of women in Christian communities? What was the status of scripture? For the past couple of centuries, brilliant scholars (largely from, but not limited to, Europe and the United States) have devoted themselves to answering these questions by means of the handful of literary evidences that survive from this time. In this chapter I will briefly discuss several questions in turn, addressing only the broadest strokes of scholarship.

What Did Second-Century Christians Believe?

One of the characteristics of second-century Christianity is the remarkable degree of diversity that we find on any number of theological issues.[3] Questions regarding the nature of God and of Jesus, the contours of scripture, religious practice, church authority structures, the role of women, and so forth were variously answered and contested by Christian groups throughout the empire. In other words, when considering the question What did second-century Christians believe? we must likewise ask, Which Christians? When? Where?

To give a sense of the significance and complexity of the diverse beliefs and practices in this period, let's examine just a few theological questions that were under dispute (these questions would reverberate for centuries) and examine only a few of the ways they were addressed within just one city, Rome. The questions to be considered are: What was the nature of Jesus Christ? More specifically, to what degree was he human? To what degree was he divine? What sort of body did he have, and what were the implications of Christ's body for his followers (and their respective bodies)?

While Christians were very much in the minority when compared to their non-Christian and Jewish counterparts in the middle of the second century AD,[4] they appear to have achieved a solid foothold in the empire's capital, Rome.[5] Among the Christians who lived in Rome at this time were three important intellectual figures—Marcion, Valentinus, and Justin Martyr—each of whom disagreed strongly with one another on the question of Christ's nature and whose theological views very likely represented a significant number of

Christians in Rome at that time. To demonstrate the variety of ways in which second-century Christians understood their theology, we shall briefly examine the belief systems of each of these three figures.

Marcion (active ca. AD 140–150)

Marcion was a wealthy Christian shipowner from Asia Minor who moved to Rome and immediately became an influential part of the Christian cause, in part through a generous donation of money that he made to the Roman church.[6] By AD 144, however, he appears to have been expelled from his congregation, and his financial offerings were allegedly returned to him. Marcion's expulsion, it seems, was connected to his position on a number of theological issues. In a book that he entitled *Antitheses,* Marcion made the case that the God of the Jewish scriptures, the creator of this material realm, was *not* the same God as the God of Jesus. For whereas the God of the Jewish scriptures was wrathful, the God of Jesus was merciful and forgiving; whereas the God of Jewish scripture ordered the destruction of entire populations of people, the God of Jesus instructed his disciples to love one's enemies. Marcion, in effect, was proposing the existence of not one God, but *two*: a lower God, as depicted in the Old Testament and that was worshipped by the Jews, and a higher God, as revealed by the teachings of Jesus, to whom true Christians devoted themselves.

Marcion's differentiation, then, between the true God of Jesus and the wrathful God of Jewish scripture affected how he perceived the nature of Jesus and his role in human salvation. Jesus, according to Marcion, had *not* come to the world on behalf of the God of the Jewish scriptures but rather to redeem humanity *from* the God of the Jewish scriptures. Furthermore, because the God of the Jewish scriptures had created the material realm, and because Jesus had nothing to do with that God, Jesus, then, had nothing to do with the material realm. As such, for Marcion, Jesus was a fully divine being, sent from the true God, who only *appeared* to have a material body. Jesus only *appeared* to eat, drink, and suffer in the flesh. As a fully divine being, he did not actually participate in these material activities. Christianity then, for Marcion, entailed abandoning the lesser deity of Judaism (including renouncing the Old Testament)[7] and worshipping the true God that had sent Jesus to this material realm. Marcion's message and evangelizing activities were profoundly influential, attracting large numbers of adherents throughout the empire, especially in Asia Minor (modern-day Turkey).

Valentinus (ca. AD 100–ca. 175)

Valentinus was a creative Christian teacher, philosopher, and writer, probably trained in Alexandria, Egypt, and active in Rome in the middle of the second century.[8] In Rome he founded his own school of Christian thought, which would go on to produce a large number of Christian philosophical figures in later decades. Valentinus's theological system (often described as "gnostic") is far too complicated to discuss here—indeed, there are relatively few scholars who are capable of treating Valentinus's material with the sort of philosophical rigor that it demands—but we can, at the very least, make mention of a few of his views on the nature of Jesus.[9]

Valentinus taught that salvation was attained by knowledge of, or acquaintance with, the Father, God. The messenger that brought this saving knowledge, or *gnosis*, to humanity was the Word, or the Son, Christ, who took on a body in the form of Jesus of Nazareth. In other words, Valentinus argued that Christ was entirely divine and that he incorporated a body, albeit one of a superior nature to those of everyday men and women. Most famously, perhaps, Valentinus is said to have opined on Jesus's divine essence in this way: "He was continent, enduring all things. Jesus digested divinity: he ate and drank in a special way. . . . He had such a great capacity for continence that the nourishment in him was not corrupted; for he did not experience corruption."[10] While discussions of Jesus's digestive processes may seem strange or even inappropriate to readers today, it reflects a deep concern held by many ancient people regarding the nature of God, the body, material existence, and so forth. It appears that, for Valentinus, Jesus was endowed with a special sort of body—one made up of fiery materials that were capable of destroying whatever food the body took in.[11]

Justin Martyr (ca. AD 100–165)

Justin Martyr[12] was born to Greek parents in Samaria and also had the very rare opportunity to be educated in the Greek philosophical tradition. At some point in the early second century, he converted to Christianity and eventually arrived in Rome, where he (like Valentinus) started his own Christian philosophical school. Justin wrote several works after becoming a Christian, a handful of which survive today.

Justin also made his own particular case for the nature of Christ—a case that will sound much more familiar to contemporary Christian readers since it resembles some of what was codified in later Christian centuries. Like Marcion and Valentinus, he proclaimed that Jesus was a divine being. Unlike his two contemporaries, however, Justin also advocated for Jesus's full humanity: he was born into flesh and blood, he developed from infancy into manhood, he ate real food, he suffered, and he eventually experienced death. Jesus was *both* human and divine.[13] Justin's view, to some degree, would eventually become the dominant view held by most Christians in later centuries.

My purpose in offering this comparative overview of a few theological positions of these three ancient Christian is to make the very simple point that the belief systems of second-century Christians cannot be reduced to one set of beliefs. In fact, these three viewpoints represent only a fraction of the positions held by Christians in the second century on a single set of theological questions regarding the nature of Christ. We have evidences of competing positions held by other Christians at the same time in different locations: some Christians, for instance, believed that Jesus was born as a mortal but later *became* God's Son at the time of his baptism on account of his extraordinary degree of righteousness. Still others believed that "Jesus" and "the Christ" were entirely separate entities: Jesus was a mortal man who became inhabited by "the Christ," a divine entity that lived within the mortal tabernacle of Jesus for the duration of its divine ministry. Shortly before the Crucifixion, the immortal Christ departed from the mortal Jesus, leaving him to die on the cross. The list goes on.

Scholars have written countless books attempting to lay out the manifold religious views and practices of second-century Christians: everything from early Christian views on the divine realm, salvation, church organization, ritual practice, sexual ethics, the role of women, and so forth.[14] The point in all of this, then, is that the category of "Christian" in the second century is a capacious one, comprising a variety of beliefs and practices depending, in part, on where one lived and on the traditions and sensibilities of one's particular Christian community.

An Aside on Early Christian Diversity

As an aside, it may be tempting for Latter-day Saints to presume that the diversity of thought and practice that we see in second-century Christianity was simply the product of a kind of general apostasy, understood as the consequence of people sinfully turning away from the original teachings of the apostles. This is a view maintained by many contemporary Christians, that is, that the Christian movement in the apostolic age—as reflected in the New Testament—was unified in its theology and practice and that second-century Christianity represents the proliferation of aberrant and schismatic beliefs.[15] In other words, many Christians today suppose that in the era of the New Testament, the early disciples of Jesus had all the answers on what a Christian should do and believe and that this early system was altered by the introduction of false ideas in later centuries.

In order to gain a more sophisticated picture of the historical situation, contemporary readers should remember a few things. First, the answers to many of the theological questions faced by second-century Christians were not at all obvious, in part because many of them were never addressed in the early years of the "Jesus movement." Paul, for instance, wrote several letters that were viewed by many second-century Christians as authoritative; none of these letters, however, offer an extended treatise on the nature of Jesus.

Second, contemporary Christians should likewise remember that at this time there was no universally fixed canon of scripture and that different Christians in different places had access to a different set of authoritative texts and oral traditions to inform their faith and practice. For instance, suppose you were a second-century convert living in North Africa who had access to only the Gospel of Mark, a Gospel that says nothing about a virgin birth and provides no description of any kind of Jesus's resurrected body. What would you deduce about the nature of Jesus? It seems reasonable that you might interpret Jesus's baptismal scene as the moment in which Jesus was called to be the Son of God. Imagine, then, another Christian living in Rome. Suppose this Christian has access to the letters of Paul, in which Paul states that Jesus was born "in the likeness of sinful flesh" (Romans 8:3) and that the resurrected body is a "spiritual body" (1 Corinthians 15:44). One can imagine how this Christian might be more likely to embrace a notion of Jesus that is phantasmal, in which Jesus only *appeared* to take on flesh. Finally, suppose a third Christian living in Ephesus ascribes particular value to the Gospel of John, in which the Word is said to have become flesh (John 1:14) and in which Thomas seems to verify the fleshly nature of Jesus's resurrected body (20:26–28). One can see how this Christian might have deduced that Jesus was a being that took on flesh and that his resurrection was a bodily resurrection (though how he or she might have understood "bodily" would have been contingent on a host of other variables).

To be clear, I am not saying that Valentinus, Marcion, and Justin had access only to biblical materials that supported their theological positions. Rather, I am suggesting that often these second-century Christians were faced with questions that had either not been asked or had not been universally resolved by the followers of Jesus in the decades following the apostolic era and that their efforts to answer them in ways that stayed faithful to their religious traditions yielded a variety of conclusions.[16] In this way, second-century Christians were not so different from the early apostles: it is clear from the New Testament writings that Paul had disagreements with his authoritative contemporaries (e.g., James, Peter) on matters regarding salvation and the Mosaic law; it only follows that he and other Christians of his era disagreed on other theological matters as well.

Finally, contemporary readers would do well to remember the near impossibility of Christian unity in light of the tremendous challenge to intercongregational communication posed by vast geographic distances. It should therefore not be surprising to find that an ancient assembly in Carthage (North Africa) harbored beliefs about God, scripture, and revelation that were at variance with the beliefs of their contemporaries in distant Syria. We must remember that today we have the great advantage of Church communication that happens almost instantaneously and that there is a worldwide effort at Church headquarters to produce, distribute, and translate correlated manuals and materials to ensure that the same things are being taught in all congregations around the globe. These sorts of communicative and administrative mechanisms were not in place in the second century AD.[17]

What Did Christian Worship in the Second Century Look Like?

Because there was no mechanism by which early Christians could be completely correlated or unified on all aspects of their religious beliefs, there was no singular, universal model for Christian worship at this time: an assembly of Christians in Rome would have expressed their devotion in ways that were both similar to and different from neighboring assemblies *in the same city*, let alone an assembly in faraway Cyprus. With this in mind, we can begin to flesh out what the scant amount of surviving literature from this period tells us about second-century Christian worship.

House churches

To begin, it is important to remember that, as noted above, we have no surviving archaeological evidence of second-century Christian religious practice: so far as we know, there were no buildings in the second century that were *exclusively* dedicated to Christian worship. Where, then, did early Christians engage in their religious practice? It appears that they met in what scholars have come to call "house churches"—the homes of wealthy members of the local congregation that could accommodate more than a handful of people. Early Christians likely met in the homes of their more affluent neighbors in order to celebrate their religion and venerate their God together (much like members of the Church did at the start of this dispensation and continue to do so in certain places around the world where the Church is relatively new). In other words, in a given city, it is likely that a variety of house churches would hold worship meetings independently from one another. The size of the assembly would have been constrained by the size of the home they met in, and in the earlier stages of Christian history it is likely that the leader of the meetings was the owner of the home.[18]

Baptism

For most Christians, water baptism was a necessary ritual act by which one entered into the Christian community.[19] The way in which baptism was carried out likely depended, in part, on the time and place in which it was performed. One surviving literary reference entitled the Didache (or "Teachings") lays out a particular perspective for how baptism should be performed:

> [After you have reviewed a set of prescribed ethical positions with the potential convert,] baptize in the name of the Father and of the Son and of the Holy Spirit in running water. But if you have no running water, then baptize in some other water; and if you are not able to baptize in cold water, then do so in warm. But if you have neither, then pour water on the head three times in the name of Father and Son and Holy Spirit. And before the baptism let the one baptizing and the one who is to be baptized fast, as well as any others who are able. Also, you must instruct the one who is to be baptized to fast for one or two days beforehand. (Didache 7.1–4)[20]

Again, there is no reason to believe that this set of instructions would have been followed in all areas of the ancient world. It simply shows that at least some second-century Christians were interested in codifying what they viewed as the correct, authorized mode of baptism.

Many of our sources indicate that there was a preparatory period prior to baptism in which one renounced sin and received doctrinal instruction. Some ancient texts indicate that the prospective Christian was to be baptized in the nude.[21] He or she would then emerge from the water and be given a white robe. Some communities even fed the newly baptized person milk and honey.[22] Others concluded the baptismal ritual with prayers and a kiss (Justin Martyr, *First Apology* 65.1–2).[23] Among some second-century Christians, it became customary to anoint the baptized person with oil;[24] for others this was done before baptism.[25] Tertullian, a powerful Christian authority in North Africa, attests that hands were laid on the newly baptized Christian as a way of "invoking and inviting the Holy Spirit."[26] In many ancient Christian texts, baptism is called a "seal," invoking the image of a wax seal that was used to secure the contents of a document. We should note that Christian baptism was not a practice invented by early Christians but rather had its origins in Jewish religious practice—Christians took over and elaborated the practice from Jewish tradition and instilled in it new theological meaning.[27]

Sunday gatherings: Reading, sermons, prayers, Eucharist[28]

Most Christians gathered together on Sundays to engage in weekly worship, although we have evidence of some Christians who continued to worship on Saturdays (i.e., Sabbath), in accordance with the commands in the Old Testament. While the particularities of these gatherings would have varied according to time and place, an ancient anecdote will suffice to paint a broad picture. Justin Martyr, in *First Apology* 67, records that Christians gathered on Sunday, the day on which Jesus Christ had risen from the dead. A reader within the community read from the "memoirs of the apostles" or "the writings of the prophets" for as long as time permitted.[29] The group then listened to a sermon given by the presiding authority, in which they were often exhorted and instructed on how to live.[30] The congregation then rose and prayed together, after which "bread and a cup of water and [a cup] of wine mixed with water"[31] were administered to the group, over which the presiding authority prayed once more. Deacons carried a portion of the eucharistic meal to those who were unable to attend. Resources were also collected by the presiding authority from those who could afford to donate in order to take care of orphans, widows, refugees, the sick, the poor, the imprisoned, or any other Christian in need.

The role of women

Based on what we have seen thus far, it should come as no surprise that the role of women within the early Christian assembly was a contested one. We should note that, by and large, ancient ideologies of gender in the Roman world were unfavorable to women, depicting them, more or less, as underdeveloped men. Many Christian congregations imbibed this worldview wholesale, imagining women as mentally and morally weak, as relatively incapable of public leadership, and as a continual source of sexual danger to those around them.[32]

That said, among other Christian communities of the second century it is abundantly clear that women played prominent roles in the spiritual formation and growth of the group: they served in leadership roles, received revelation, prophesied, enjoyed spiritual gifts, and were viewed as powerful, charismatic leaders and teachers.[33] As we see in nearly all ideological disputes between Christian groups, each side made vigorous appeals to scripture in order to defend their respective theological positions.

To What Degree Were Christians Persecuted? How Did Christians Respond to Persecution?

A popular misconception today is the idea that all early Christians lived in perpetual fear and hiding under the impending threat of persecution and execution at the hands of Roman officials. The nature of the Christian situation, however, appears to have been less extreme, although certainly marked by the suffering and death of some at various times and places. The Roman Empire was generally tolerant of the religious activities of those who lived within it so long as these activities were not deemed seditious. Furthermore, the empire possessed a sophisticated legal system, and early Christians would have largely enjoyed the same rights and privileges as their pagan and Jewish contemporaries. They would have had equal access to many of the commercial, political, and social opportunities that their neighbors did and would have participated according to their own interests and capabilities.

This is not to say, however, that Christian beliefs and practices were viewed favorably by many of their non-Christian and Jewish contemporaries—quite the contrary, as we shall see below. Nor is it the case that many early Christians did not experience serious episodes of persecution, beginning even in the New Testament era (see 1 Peter 4:12). Some Christians were tortured and others were violently killed on account of their religious convictions. Such persecutions, it appears, were local and occasional in nature, not universal and systematic (at least until the third and fourth centuries). In other words, it was possible for a group of Christians in Gaul (modern-day France) to suffer death by torture at the same time that a group of Christians in Rome enjoyed the eucharistic meal. In fact, the first instance of official, empire-wide persecution did not occur until the year AD 250 under the emperor Decius.[34] All known prior episodes of persecution were local or regional and were the product of *ad hoc* concerns.

An example of local persecution: Nero

One of the earliest and most famous instances of local persecution occurred under the rule of the Roman emperor Nero. In the year AD 64, a fire broke out in the city of Rome. Many contemporary Romans believed that the emperor Nero had purposefully caused the fire to facilitate one of his building projects. In order to draw unwanted attention away from himself, Nero accused and subsequently tortured Christians of the city, publicly blaming them for the act of destruction.

This episode is instructive for a few reasons. First, we should note the *local* nature of the persecution: Nero persecuted Christians in Rome and in Rome alone. Second, we should note the *logic* of the persecution: Nero persecuted the Christians of the city in order to deflect the blame for the act of arson from himself. In other words, in this episode Christians were not persecuted for their religious beliefs per se. Rather, they were persecuted because of imperial corruption—Nero needed someone to blame, and early Christians fit the bill. Fifty years later, the Roman historian Tacitus claimed that Nero specifically targeted the

Christians because they were generally hated by the people of Rome (for more on this, see "Charges against Early Christians," below).[35]

It is not uncommon for some contemporary commentators to describe this event as the first evidence of imperial persecution. Such a statement, however, can be misleading; for while it is true that an emperor was behind the decree, it tends to imply that the persecution was universal, which it was not. Nero's persecution against the Christians was a local event, stimulated by local concerns.[36] That said, it is likely that Nero's actions set a precedent for local and regional administrators who, over the course of the next two centuries, sporadically engaged in violent activity against their Christian contemporaries for a variety of cited reasons.

Charges against early Christians

Early Christian and non-Christian literature of the period records several charges that were brought against Christians in these local and regional disputes. Christians were accused, for instance, of adhering stubbornly to foolish doctrines (resurrection, incarnation) and for venerating a crucified criminal. They were accused of disrupting the family, such as when a new convert renounced her biological family in the name of her faith. Some early critics, seizing on the Christian ritual practices of the Eucharist and the holy kiss among members of the congregation, charged Christians with practicing cannibalism (devouring the flesh and blood of Christ) and incest (mingling sexually with those they called "brother" and "sister").[37] Because some Christian groups congregated at night, they were occasionally accused of plotting revolutionary political activities. Christians were likewise criticized by some of their Jewish contemporaries regarding a range of mostly theological issues: Christians were condemned, for instance, for abandoning the law of God as outlined in scripture (circumcision, Sabbath observance, and so forth) and for following a false Messiah and a magician.[38]

Interestingly, Christians were even accused of *atheism*, which, in an ancient context, did not imply that Christians didn't believe in God but rather that they failed to show proper piety to *all* the gods, including the cult of the emperor. In the ancient world, one maintained a proper relationship with the gods by offering sacrifices and libations (wine offerings) to them in their temples. The gods were pleased by the sacrifices of the local populace and generously provided things like good crops, moderate weather, and protection against barbarian enemies (*pax deorum*, or "the peace of the gods"). The emperor himself was considered by many to be a god, and sacrifices were likewise offered to him and other imperial figures in many parts of the empire to ensure continued peace in the land. Those early Christians who had converted to the Christian movement now found themselves in a precarious social situation: by refusing to offer sacrifices to the gods and emperors at feasts and in local temples, they risked being seen as disrespectful to both local cults as well as to the Roman state. To refuse to offer sacrifices could be interpreted not only as an affront to powerful deities—hence threatening divine displeasure—but also as a political statement against the empire.

Because of this, Christians were viewed by some as antisocial, treasonous, and blasphemous, and their religious practices were seen as the source of local calamities.[39]

This sense of suspicion toward this upstart religious movement at times materialized into episodes of mob violence. In more severe cases, regional administrators would get involved, especially when they had reason to believe that Christians were guilty of crimes that were contrary to Roman law and culture (treason, cannibalism, and so forth). In rare cases, emperors became involved in regional disputes regarding Christians. Such a case occurred in ca. AD 112, when the emperor Trajan approved the execution of Christians in Asia Minor who refused to offer sacrifices to his cult image and to deny their Christianity.[40] Similarly, at the end of the second century, Marcus Aurelius approved the regional persecution of Christians in Lyons and Vienne.[41] Christian responses to the critiques and violence leveled against them were, obviously, diverse and in accordance to personal propensities. For the sake of simplicity, we'll consider two broad Christian responses to pagan opposition: martyrdom and apologetics.

Martyrdom

In approximately AD 110, a Christian bishop of Antioch named Ignatius was arrested and transported to the capital of Rome in order to face trial and execution for a crime that is unknown to us today. In one of his most powerful (and, for some, unsettling) remarks to the Christians that he would leave behind, he said, "I am willingly dying for God, unless you hinder me. I urge you, do not become an untimely kindness to me. Allow me to be bread for the wild beasts; through them I am able to attain to God" (Ignatius, *Romans* 4.1).[42] While certainly not representative of all Christians of his day, Ignatius represents an illustrative example of one response to persecution that flourished in the second and third centuries AD: that of the Christian martyr who willingly and eagerly looked forward to dying on behalf of the Christian cause. Notice that Ignatius does not simply accept the prospect of a painful death—he demands it: "May I have the full pleasure of the wild beasts prepared for me; I pray they will be found ready for me. Indeed, I will coax them to devour me quickly—not as happens with some, whom they are afraid to touch. And even if they do not wish to do so willingly, I will force them to do it" (Ignatius, *Romans* 5.2).

In the second and third centuries and in tandem with the local and regional persecutions of the period, we see the emergence of literature that celebrates the activity of Christian martyrs.[43] In these literary works, male and female Christian martyrs are depicted as the paragons of Greek masculinity: resolved in their convictions, unflinching in the face of excruciating pain, anxious to meet a noble death, all on account of their devotion to Christ and their Christian identities.[44]

Within some Christian communities, martyrs come to be seen as religious figures with particularly potent spiritual capacities: martyrs were said to possess the ability to see visions, to perform miracles, and to atone for sins. In one text written at the turn of the third century, a bishop and a presbyter are seen to be pleading at the feet of a female martyr, indicating perhaps that for some Christians, the martyr was at the pinnacle of church hierarchy.[45] Christian theology regarding both the martyr's relationship to the living as well as the martyr's larger role within the divine plan would develop in subsequent centuries, particularly after the Christianization of the Roman Empire.

Martyr narratives, both oral and written, no doubt served an important function for early Christians in the face of real or perceived persecution. For those Christians who faced physical torment from local antagonists, martyr narratives provided models for righteous suffering and gave assurances of eternal rewards in spite of earthly agonies and humiliations. For those Christians who faced the perceived threat of persecution, such stories would have served as sources of inspiration and solidarity within their small, second-century house churches. The deaths of certain key figures, especially when displayed in a heavenly light, no doubt fueled the imagination and strengthened the bonds between the members of Christian communities.[46]

Apologetics

Opposition to Christian communities did not always take the form of physical violence. Many learned, non-Christian elites viewed Christians and their cult in the same way that they perceived other religious groups that they deemed as foreign:[47] at best, as the product of silly superstitions or, at worst, a cancer that threatened the religious, economic, and political fabric that differentiated Rome from barbarian nations. These literary attacks on Christians and Christianity often took the form of brief asides (e.g., the Roman historian Tacitus's reference to Christianity as "a most mischievous superstition," *Annals* 15) as well as full treatises (e.g., the pagan philosopher Celsus's scathing anti-Christian volume, *True Doctrine*), in which Christians were systematically mocked or charged with a litany of allegations.

By the middle of the second century a literary class of Christians emerged, armed with the rhetorical and philosophical training necessary to combat the intellectual attacks made against the fledgling Christian movement: these figures are known today as early Christian *apologists*. The term *apologist* derives from the Greek word *apologia*, which means "defense" or "a speech in defense of" something. Hence, when one speaks of an early Christian apologist, or of early Christian apologetics, or of an early Christian apology, one is not referring to Christians who were apologizing for their religion (in the sense of saying, "I'm sorry for being a Christian"); rather, these were Christians who were actively defending their religion, often employing scathing attacks of their own against the philosophical and theological positions of their pagan and Jewish opponents.

We have apologetic literature that survives from the second century onward, designed to meet the attacks made by the cultured critics of earliest Christianity, as well as to make reasoned cases for the superiority of the Christian religion to its pagan and Jewish counterparts.[48] The ways in which Christian apologists defended their religion varied according to their circumstances and rhetorical skill. Some sought to leverage pagan and Jewish history, philosophy, and culture on behalf of their reasoned defense of Christianity and, by so doing, to demonstrate that Christian beliefs and practices were in harmony with, and even the paragon of, the more virtuous aspects of pagan or Jewish tradition. Justin Martyr, for instance, argued in his defense against pagan critics that Christians' belief in Christ (the Word, Greek *logos*) was, in fact, the zenith of an ancient tradition practiced by the Greek philosopher Socrates.[49] Others sought to defend Christianity by claiming absolute Christian exclusivity: Christian doctrine and practice, they argued, had nothing to do with the systems of this world. Such a position allowed them to condemn every aspect of the pagan and Jewish cultural systems that surrounded them.[50] The apologetic tradition continued until Christianity had become the dominant religious force in the ancient Mediterranean.[51]

What Contributions Did (and Can) Second-Century Christianity Make to the Restored Gospel?

This question has many answers—far too many for this short chapter. For our purposes, I will mention only two, along with an accompanying observation. First, contemporary Latter-day Saints—like all Christians—owe the survival of their religious textual heritage (e.g., the New Testament) to the largely uncelebrated efforts of second-century Christians who protected and preserved the literature of the first century. Early members of the "Jesus movement" wrote the foundational literature of Christianity, including some of its finest gems: Luke's parable of the prodigal son (Luke 10), Matthew's discussion of sheep and goats (Matthew 25), Paul's discourse on charity (1 Corinthians 13), and James's invitation to seek wisdom from God (James 1:5–6), among others. It was second-century Christians, however, who preserved the literature for later generations, both by making these texts a central component of their religious practice, as well as by painstakingly reproducing new manuscripts to carry the tradition. Consider the logistics: in order for a Christian community to have a copy of the Gospel of John, someone in the congregation had to obtain an older manuscript and reproduce it, word for word, by hand. The second-century Christians who did this were not professional scribes: they were average people who dedicated long hours to the preservation of what they saw as sacred. Whatever inspiration contemporary Latter-day Saints derive from ancient scripture is owed, in part, to the unsung efforts of nameless second-century Christians who ensured that their tradition was not lost (the same can be said of the often unrecognized labor of the Christian copyists who followed them).

Second, several doctrinal innovations or clarifications emerged in the second century that have informed or align with Latter-day Saint thought and practice today. These doctrines are often attributed to the earliest disciples of Jesus (i.e., to writers of the New Testament, or to Jesus himself), though our first clear evidences of them tend to emerge in the second century. The nature of Jesus as a being who is both human and divine, as discussed above, can be seen as one of these doctrines. Latter-day Saint understandings of Jesus align with a theological position that has its roots in second-century reflections on Jesus.[52] Additionally, since the inception of The Church of Jesus Christ of Latter-day Saints, prophets have urged Church members to "seek for truth wherever [one] might find it."[53] By this view, the restoration of gospel fullness would include the quest for new and refined truths scattered throughout the writings of these Christian ancestors; in addition to sifting through their writings to find examples of shared beliefs and practices, there is great value (perhaps, sometimes, more value) in reading early Christian literature with the trust that it contains religious truth that we have not yet fathomed or appreciated—like forgotten treasures hidden in a field (see Matthew 13:44; Gospel of Thomas 109).

Finally, one should remember that, while we have already noted that Christians were not universally persecuted by imperial edict in the second century, it was nonetheless no easy task to be a Christian at that time. The Christians who preserved scripture, who received revelation about the nature of God and his gospel, and who laid the foundation for later Christian generations did so amid remarkable social risk and uncertainty. They were in the vast minority, subject to periodic regional persecutions, and considered by their non-Christian counterparts to be a foreign and laughable cult. Some were tortured and others killed on account of their faith. Latter-day Saints of the twenty-first century should feel a similar sort of appreciation for these ancient pioneers as they rightfully do for their nineteenth-century counterparts: both groups laid the foundations for the spiritual communion that Latter-day Saints enjoy today.

Conclusion

Although generally overshadowed in popular discussions of early Christian history by the towering influence of the New Testament and later fourth-century councils and creeds, second-century Christianity produced some of the most influential figures, innovations, and literature of Christian tradition. Within these decades we find many of the seeds that blossomed into Christian orthodoxy in subsequent centuries, shaping the West and the world as we know it. Historically, Latter-day Saints have felt little need to devote attention to this period of time—or worse, have even relegated the activities of second-century Christians entirely to the category of "apostate."[54] Casting light on the virtuous efforts and accomplishments of these early figures not only demonstrates the debt owed by contemporary Christians (including Latter-day Saints) to these spiritual pioneers, but also serves as a reproof for our uncritical judgment of the past. The darkness that we ascribe to these early years of Christian history may, at times, reflect our failure to perceive the radiant, faithful contributions of the saintly men and women who preceded us.

⟲

Luke Drake is a doctoral student of ancient Mediterranean religions in the Department of Religious Studies at the University of North Carolina at Chapel Hill.

Further Reading

Chadwick, Henry. *The Early Church*. Harmondsworth, England: Penguin, 1968.

Ehrman, Bart D. *After the New Testament, 100–300 C.E.: A Reader in Early Christianity.* 2nd ed. Oxford: Oxford University Press, 2015.

Grant, Robert M. *Greek Apologists of the Second Century.* Philadelphia: Westminster, 1988.

Kraemer, Ross. *Her Share of the Blessings: Women's Religions among Pagans, Jews, and Christians in the Greco-Roman World.* New York: Oxford University Press, 1992.

Lewis, Nicola Denzey. *Introduction to Gnosticism: Ancient Voices, Christian Worlds.* New York: Oxford University Press, 2013.

Lampe, Peter. *From Paul to Valentinus: Christians at Rome in the First Two Centuries.* Minneapolis: Fortress, 2003.

MacMullen, Ramsay. *Christianizing the Roman Empire.* New Haven, CT: Yale University Press, 1984.

McGowan, Andrew B. *Ancient Christian Worship: Early Church Practices in Social, Historical, and Theological Perspective.* Grand Rapids, MI: Baker Academic, 2014.

Notes

1. The earliest surviving building that was exclusively used for Christian worship dates to the middle of the third century and is located in Syria (Dura-Europos). See Susan B. Matheson, *Dura-Europos: The Ancient City and the Yale Collection* (New Haven, CT: Yale University Art Gallery, 1982), 28–31. For a brief discussion of other early Christian archaeological remains, see Frank Trombley, "Overview: The Geographical Spread of Christianity," in *The Cambridge History of Christianity: Origins to Constantine* (Cambridge: Cambridge University Press, 2006), 304.

2. Though we have in our possession several dozen "texts" from the second century, we should be clear that in most cases these texts are preserved in manuscripts that, in fact, date to periods much later than the second century. In other words, while certain surviving literary evidences date to the second century (these are mostly scraps of old papyrus), most of these texts are preserved in documents that are later copies of earlier second-century originals. For instance, the *Letter to Diognetus* is an important text written in the second century that gives us insight into how some second-century Christians defended themselves against their intellectual opponents (see discussion on apologetics below). The earliest surviving copy of this text, however, is a handwritten manuscript that was made in the thirteenth century—over one thousand years after the original was written!

3. As we see represented in the first-century witnesses of the New Testament, though perhaps to a lesser degree.

4. Several erudite scholars have attempted to tackle this question over the last several decades. Rodney Stark, *The Rise of Christianity: How the Obscure, Marginal Jesus Movement Became the Dominant Religious Force in the Western World in a Few Centuries* (Francisco, CA: HarperSanFrancisco, 1997), offers an effective overview of the question and addresses the work and assumptions of previous scholars. Stark's work has not been without its critics. See, for instance, a few sample critiques and Stark's response to these in the *Journal of Early Christian Studies* 6, no. 2 (Summer 1998): 161–267.

5. The history of Christianity in Rome can be dated to the middle of the first century, as evidenced in both the New Testament (Romans 16) and Roman history (e.g., Emperor Nero's persecution of Roman Christians in AD 64 as recorded in the works of the Roman historians Tacitus, *Annals* 15.44, and Suetonius, *Nero* 61.1–2). Later evidences indicate that Christians continued to thrive in the city, as seen in early Christian texts such as *1 Clement,* the Shepherd of Hermas, and Ignatius's *Letter to the Romans.*

6. The classic work on Marcion's biography and theology was written in German by Adolf von Harnack in 1924. It has been translated into English on multiple occasions, such as in *Marcion: The Gospel of the Alien God* (Eugene, OR: Wipf and Stock, 2007). For a subtle and recent treatment of Marcion, see Judith Lieu, *Marcion and the Making of a Heretic: God and Scripture in the Second Century* (New York: Cambridge University Press, 2015).

7. In addition to repudiating Jewish scripture, Marcion seems to have advocated a Christian canon that exclusively comprised edited versions of the Gospel of Luke and ten of the letters of Paul. Marcion's editions of

these texts apparently omitted positive references to Jewish scripture and to the Jewish God—literary details that Marcion attributed to the errors of later copyists. Furthermore, Marcion seems to have removed the first two chapters of the Gospel of Luke (Jesus's birth narrative) on account, perhaps, of his belief that Jesus only *appeared* to have a physical body.

8. Later Christians who were vehemently opposed to Valentinus's thought nonetheless conceded that he was a "brilliant mind" (Jerome, *On Hosea* 2.10) (Tertullian, *Against the Valentinians* 4).

9. For introductory material on Valentinus and translated works, see Bentley Layton, *The Gnostic Scriptures: A New Translation with Annotations and Introductions* (New York: Doubleday, 1995), 267–80; Ismo Dunderberg, "The School of Valentinus," in *A Companion to Second-Century Christian "Heretics,"* ed. Antti Marjanen (Leiden, Netherlands: Brill, 2008), 64–100; Peter Lampe, *From Paul to Valentinus: Christians at Rome in the First Two Centuries* (Minneapolis: Fortress, 2003), 292–318. See also the excellent interview with Einar Thomassen in Miguel Conner, *Voices of Gnosticism: Interviews with Elaine Pagels, Marvin Meyer, Bart Ehrman, Bruce Chilton and Other Leading Scholars* (Dublin: Bardic, 2011), 103–17.

10. Layton, *Gnostic Scriptures*, fragment 3, 239.

11. However, for an alternative interpretation of this fragment's meaning from one of the premiere scholars on the subject, see Einar Thomassen, *The Spiritual Seed: The Church of the 'Valentinians'* (Leiden, Netherlands: Brill, 2006), 457–60.

12. In the Christian tradition, and in academic works, Justin is frequently referred to as "Justin Martyr," not because "Martyr" is a surname but because it indicates that he died as a martyr, around AD 165.

13. See Justin Martyr, *Dialogue with Trypho* 48, trans. Thomas B. Falls (Washington, DC: Catholic University Press, 2003), 73: "Christ existed as God before all ages, and then he consented to be born and become man."

14. Again, it is important to remember that relatively little ancient material actually survives from this period. In other words, the diversity that we see is the product of a highly fragmentary historical record. Imagine all that has been lost!

15. Even some Christians in the second century maintained this view in light of the diversity of Christian belief and practice. See, for instance, Hegesippus (ca. AD 110–80): "Until then the church remained a pure and uncorrupted virgin, for those who attempted to corrupt the healthful rule of the Savior's preaching, if they existed all, lurked in obscure darkness. But when the sacred band of the Apostles and the generation of those to whom it had been vouchsafed to hear with their own ears the divine wisdom had reached the several ends of their lives, then the federation of godless error took its beginning through the deceit of false teachers," as cited in Eusebius, *Ecclesiastical History* 3.32.7–8, trans. Kirsopp Lake (Cambridge, MA: Harvard University Press, 1926).

16. Many introductory textbooks on early Christian history employ a set of terms to distinguish these "varieties" of early Christianity: those who subscribed to the belief system espoused by Marcion are referred to as "Marcionites," those who subscribed to the belief system of Valentinus are referred to as "Valentinians," those who subscribed to the belief system espoused by Justin Martyr are referred to as "proto-orthodox," and so forth. I have chosen not to use these terms for a handful of reasons, one of which is that they are not ancient and would have been foreign to the Christians that they describe: no ancient "Marcionite" would have thought of herself as a "Marcionite," but rather as a Christian.

17. The letters of Paul represent an early attempt to unify the thoughts and practices of faraway Christian assemblies. Similar letters and texts were written in the second century with the same purpose in mind. Nothing, however, was done on the same scale anciently as contemporary Latter-day Saint correlation efforts.

18. Romans 16 is evidence of this phenomenon in the first century. At the end of this letter, Paul sends his greetings to several individuals who appear to represent multiple house churches in Rome.

19. For discussions on early Christian views on baptism, see Andrew B. McGowan, *Ancient Christian Worship: Early Church Practices in Social, Historical, and Theological Perspective* (Grand Rapids, MI: Baker Academic, 2014), 135–82; and David Brakke, *The Gnostics: Myth, Ritual, and Diversity in Early Christianity* (Cambridge, MA: Harvard University Press, 2010), 74–82.

20. Bart D. Ehrman, trans., *The Apostolic Fathers* (Cambridge, MA: Harvard University Press, 2003).

21. *Apostolic Tradition* 21.3. For third- and fourth-century witnesses, see *Acts of Xanthippe and Polyxena* 21 and Cyril of Jerusalem, *Mystagogical Catecheses* 2.2. For a fuller discussion that addresses both early Christian literature and artwork, see Robin M. Jensen, *Baptismal Imagery in Early Christianity: Ritual, Visual, and Theological Dimensions* (Grand Rapids, MI: Baker Academic, 2012), 167–69. Conversely, Laurie Guy has argued that Christian "nakedness" in these texts probably refers to wearing undergarments that afforded modesty but that were otherwise inappropriate for normal public interactions. See Guy, "'Naked' Baptism in the Early Church: The Rhetoric and the Reality," *Journal of Religious History* 27, no. 2 (2003): 133–42.

22. Tertullian, *On the Soldier's Crown* 3.3; *Against Marcion* 1.14.3.

23. The Christian tradition of giving one another a holy kiss can be traced back to the letters of Paul (Romans 16:16; 1 Corinthians 16:20; 2 Corinthians 13:12; 1 Thessalonians 5:26; see also 1 Peter 5:14). Interestingly, Paul and the author of 1 Peter see no need to justify or explain this ancient activity, and so we can assume that it was a relatively common practice by the middle of the first century within the communities to whom these letters were sent. By the second century, we see this practice continued in the writings of a few prominent Christian authors. For more on this, see Michael Philip Penn, *Kissing Christians: Ritual and Community in the Late Ancient Church* (Philadelphia: University of Pennsylvania Press, 2013).

24. See Tertullian, *On Baptism* 6–8.

25. See Acts of Thomas 26–27, 49, 120–21.

26. Tertullian, *On Baptism* 8.

27. See Adela Y. Collins, "The Origins of Christian Baptism," in *Living Water, Sealing Spirit*, ed. Maxwell E. Johnson (Collegeville, MN: Liturgical Press, 1995), 35–57.

28. The term *Eucharist* comes from the Greek word for "thanksgiving" (*eucharistia*). Originally this term probably referred to the prayer of thanksgiving that one offered before a meal. As Christianity spread, it came to signify the Christian ritual practice of eating and drinking together in memory and celebration of Jesus (what Latter-day Saints refer to as "the sacrament").

29. It is tempting to suppose that "memoirs of the apostles" is a reference to the Gospels of Matthew, Mark, Luke, and John. Ultimately we cannot be certain of the texts to which Justin is referring, since in the second century there was no fixed Christian canon. Were these memoirs the canonical Gospels as we know them today? Were they ancient variations of these texts? Something else altogether? The "writings of the prophets," on the other hand, is taken to be a clear reference to texts from the Old Testament.

30. A few of these early sermons survive to this day. For a sense of what a second-century sermon might have sounded like, see *2 Clement* and Melito of Sardis's "On the Passover."

31. An early manuscript of Justin's *Apology* omits the phrase "and [a cup] of wine mixed with water" in the description of the eucharistic meal. This has led some scholars to believe that the original reading was simply "bread and water." Several ancient texts likewise mention eucharistic meals consisting of bread and water, including Acts of Paul 25–27 (with vegetables), the Vercelli Acts of Peter 2, and the Acts of Thomas 121, 152. For further discussion and more examples (Eucharists of milk, cheese, and fish), see Andrew McGowan, *Ascetic Eucharists: Food and Drink in Early Christian Ritual Meals* (Oxford: Clarendon, 1999), 89–250.

32. See Elizabeth A. Clark, "Devil's Gateway and Bride of Christ: Women in the Early Christian World," in *Ascetic Piety and Women's Faith: Essays on Late Ancient Antiquity* (Lewiston: Edwin Mellen, 1986), 23–60.

33. See, for instance, the multiple roles that women play within Christian communities in the Acts of Paul and Thecla. For a compelling account of female martyrs from AD 202, see The Martyrdom of Perpetua and Felicity. For a discussion of an early Christian group in which women participated in public prophecy and church office, see Christine Trevett, *Montanism: Gender, Authority, and the New Prophecy* (Cambridge: Cambridge University Press, 1996).

34. There were three empire-wide edicts of Christian persecution issued by three Roman emperors—Decius (AD 249–50), Valerian (AD 257–60), and Diocletian (AD 303–13)—though each of these differed in their methods and aims. Decius, for instance, simply required that all citizens of the empire demonstrate that

---

they had offered sacrifices to the gods before authorized officials. Diocletian, on the other hand, appears to have believed that Christians were inhibiting communication between the empire and the gods and ordered that Christian books and churches be destroyed, that Christian meetings be banned, and that all citizens be required to offer sacrifice under penalty of death. Much has been written about these persecutions. A pithy overview of the persecutions in the context of early Christian history can be found in Henry Chadwick, *The Early Church* (Harmondsworth: Penguin, 1968).

35. According to Tacitus, "Therefore, to scotch the rumour, Nero substituted as culprits, and punished with the utmost refinements of cruelty, a class of men, loathed for their vices, whom the crowd styled Christians. . . . Vast numbers were convicted, not so much on the count of arson as for hatred of the human race. And derision accompanied their end: they were covered with wild beasts' skins and torn to death by dogs; or they were fastened on crosses, and, when daylight failed were burned to serve as lamps by night." *Annals* 15.44, trans. John Jackson (Cambridge, MA: Harvard University Press, 1937).

36. The same might be said of the persecutions of Christians in Asia Minor under the reign of the Roman emperor Domitian (AD 90s), as well as later regional persecutions, which we will discuss below.

37. See Athenagoras, *Plea Regarding the Christians*.

38. See Justin Martyr, *Dialogue with Trypho*.

39. Tertullian, a brilliant and pugnacious Christian from North Africa, wrote the following, most likely at the very end of the second century: "As a justification of their hatred, . . . they [pagans] consider that the Christians are the cause of every public calamity and every misfortune of the people. If the Tiber rises as high as the city walls, if the Nile does not rise to the fields, if the weather will not change, if there is an earthquake, a famine, a plague—straightway the cry is heard: 'Toss the Christian to the lion!'" *Apology* 40.1–2, trans. Rudolph Arbesmann (Washington, DC: Catholic University Press, 1977).

40. See Pliny's letter to Trajan, and Trajan's response, in Bart D. Ehrman, *After the New Testament 100–300 CE: A Reader in Early Christianity*, 2nd ed. (Oxford: Oxford University Press, 2015), 29.

41. All of that being said, it should be remembered that for as many who had problems with Christians and their beliefs in the second century, there were just as many (and probably many more) in the empire who had either never heard of the burgeoning Christian cult, or that knew too little to have an opinion about them.

42. Bart D. Ehrman, trans., *The Apostolic Fathers* (Cambridge, MA: Harvard University Press, 2003).

43. The term *martyr* comes from the Greek word *martus*, which anciently meant "witness," such as in a legal sense or with respect to anyone who can testify of something. For Christians in the second century, *martus* came to mean one who dies for the faith. This use of the term is remarkable, since it seems to gesture both toward the spectacle of execution (wild beasts, gladiators, executioners, etc.), as well as to the testimony being offered by the one being willingly executed.

44. The classic compendium of early and later Greek and Latin accounts of Christian martyrs is Herbert Musurillo, *The Acts of the Christian Martyrs* (Oxford: Clarendon, 2000). This type of literature was not exclusive to Christians. See, for instance, 4 Maccabees, a Jewish text with similar themes and concerns.

45. The passage in question can be found in The Martyrdom of Perpetua and Felicitas 13. This remains one of the most interesting martyr narratives to survive from antiquity.

46. Unsurprisingly, it is likewise clear in our early literature that not all Christians chose the path of martyrdom when faced with violent persecution. Those who denied the faith in the face of suffering were referred to by some early Christians as the "lapsed." The question of the status of a Christian who compromised his or her religious values in order to avoid being slaughtered became one of great importance, particularly in the third century AD.

47. Other foreign cults, which were often vilified by Greek and Latin elites, included the mystery cults of Isis (Egyptian mother goddess), Mithras (Persian God of Light), and Cybele (mother goddess of Anatolia, i.e., in modern-day Turkey). It is important to note, however, that while these cults were often disparaged by elite figures, they likewise enjoyed great popularity in certain elite and non-elite pagan circles.

48. Christians did not invent this mode of argumentation. Before the emergence of Christianity, we have examples of apologetic literature written by Jews in defense of Judaism, and pagans in defense of their philosophical traditions.

49. Hence, when Justin defends Christians against the charge of atheism, he notes that five hundred years earlier the Greeks had charged Socrates with the same crime before his execution. Justin argues, in essence, that Socrates was a sort of proto-Christian because he lived according to the "word/reason" (*logos*), and the word (*logos*) is Christ. Justin Martyr, *First Apology* 46.

50. See, for instance, the *Letter to Diognetus* 5: "Christians are right to keep their distance from the thoughtlessness and deception common to both groups, and from the fussiness and pride of the Jews. But as for the mystery of the Christians' own religion, don't expect to be able to learn this from a human. . . . [Christians] live in their own countries, but only as aliens; they participate in everything as citizens, and endure everything as foreigners. Every foreign country is their fatherland, and every fatherland is foreign. . . . They live on earth, but their citizenship is in heaven."

51. For a more detailed introduction to the Greek apologetic tradition, see Robert M. Grant, *Greek Apologists of the Second Century* (Philadelphia: Westminster, 1988). For the Latin West, see Nicholas L. Thomas, *Defending Christ: The Latin Apologists before Augustine* (Turnhout, Belgium: Brepols, 2011).

52. See Justin Martyr, *Dialogue with Trypho* 48; and Tertullian, *On the Flesh of Christ* 5.

53. Dieter F. Uchtdorf, "What Is Truth?," Church Educational System devotional, January 2013. Consider also the remarks of John Taylor: "We are open to truth of every kind, no matter whence it comes, where it originates, or who believes in it." *The Gospel Kingdom: Selections from the Writings and Discourses of John Taylor*, ed. G. Homer Durham (Salt Lake City: Improvement Era, 1941), 93, as cited in *Teachings of Presidents of the Church: John Taylor* (Salt Lake City: The Church of Jesus Christ of Latter-day Saints, 2001), 213.

54. Recent efforts by some Latter-day Saint authors have begun to demonstrate shared traditions and the collective debt that Latter-day Saints owe to some of these ancient figures. See Fiona and Terryl Givens, *The Christ Who Heals: How God Restored the Truth That Saves Us* (Salt Lake City: Deseret Book, 2017). See also the recent efforts to reexamine Latter-day Saint notions of apostasy in Miranda Wilcox and John D. Young, *Standing Apart: Mormon Historical Consciousness and the Concept of Apostasy* (New York: Oxford University Press, 2014).

43

The Canonization of the New Testament

Daniel Becerra

By the end of the first century AD, all of the twenty-seven documents that now constitute the New Testament were written and had begun to circulate among early Christians. However, it was not until centuries later that these texts were collectively named as part of the authoritative body of Christian scripture. The process by which this occurred is called "canonization." The term *canon* comes from the Greek word *kanōn*, meaning "measuring rod" or "measuring stick," and was frequently applied in the ancient church to the collection of texts that informed the beliefs and practices of the Christians who read them.[1] While the terms *scripture* and *canon* are often used interchangeably, there is a subtle yet important distinction between the two: *scripture*, as the term is commonly used by scholars, denotes the inspired and authoritative status of a written document, whereas *canon* typically refers to a defined list of such documents.[2] This distinction is significant because Christians did not begin to create, much less agree upon, such lists until long after the death of Jesus Christ (ca. AD 30). Thus, for several centuries, the earliest Christians considered many texts to be scriptural but had no commonly accepted canon.

To reconstruct the process by which twenty-seven early Christian documents became the official scripture of the church, modern scholars rely on different sources of evidence.[3] These include first of all the actual use of these writings by early Christian authors. By noting the frequency and manner of their citations by ecclesiastical leaders, for example, scholars infer the value that the earliest Christians attached to them. Second, scholars also rely on explicit statements and decisions made by both individual Christian authors and ecclesiastical councils relating to the authority of various writings. And finally, the contents and arrangements of ancient manuscript collections also tend to reflect which texts were most important to early Christians.[4]

Broadly speaking, the process of canonization occurred in three overlapping stages:

1. In the first and second centuries, there was no formally closed group of authoritative Christian literature. The four Gospels, several Pauline letters, 1 Peter, and 1 John were widely used and highly regarded by many early Christians. On the other hand, Hebrews, 2 Peter, 2–3 John, James, Jude, and Revelation held less prominence and authority in Christian communities throughout the Roman Empire.

2. In the second through early fourth centuries, additional Christian writings were composed and read alongside the aforementioned documents. Debates regarding the authoritative status of newly composed texts, such as the Shepherd of Hermas, as well as the literature that would eventually constitute the New Testament, continued well into the fourth century. While there still did not exist any formally closed canon during this period, the scope of the church's authoritative writings was beginning to solidify as individual texts began to be consciously grouped into collections. One reason for this growing canon-consciousness was encounters with teachings and texts deemed heretical by early church leaders.

3. In the fourth and fifth centuries, early Christians struggled earnestly to define and distinguish between authoritative and nonauthoritative texts. During this period many lists of canonical books were drafted by church leaders. The first such list to advocate the exclusive use of the twenty-seven books that now compose the New Testament was written in the year AD 367. This list was later ratified by several church councils in subsequent years, effectively closing the New Testament canon for many Christians.

The purpose of this chapter is to trace the contours of this centuries-long canonization process in more detail by discussing four related topics: (1) the authoritative texts and teachings of the earliest Christians; (2) factors leading to the selection and closure of the canon; (3) the criteria by which canonicity was determined; and (4) important canon lists.

The Authoritative Texts and Teachings of the Earliest Christians

The scriptures of Israel and teachings of Jesus

At its inception, Christianity was a largely Jewish movement, meaning that Jesus and the majority of his earliest followers were Jews. The New Testament records that Jesus and the apostles quoted extensively from Old Testament[5] books like Deuteronomy, the Psalms, Isaiah, and others, thus demonstrating that the early church considered the scriptures of Israel—albeit in their Greek translation—to be one authoritative source for moral instruction as well as determining matters of doctrine and practice.[6] In contrast to their Jewish neighbors, however, the followers of Jesus understood the Jewish scriptures to be fulfilled primarily in the life and mission of Jesus of Nazareth. Although no known Christian writings were produced until the decades following Jesus's death, the earliest Christians preserved the teachings and acts of Jesus in memory and passed them on orally.[7] These teachings were understood to have the highest authority in Christian communities and constituted the basis for Christian discipleship.

Beginning in the middle of the first century, about twenty years after Jesus's death, Christians began to produce their own writings, which gradually increased in variety and number to include Gospels, letters, narratives of apostolic "acts," and other genres of literature. Throughout the second and third centuries, Christians across the Roman Empire treasured such texts—not all of which would be included in the New Testament—even though no church council had formally legitimized or mandated their exclusive use. These documents informed the worship, preaching, and teaching of many Christian communities.

The canonization of the New Testament texts may be profitably understood not so much as a process of collecting these documents individually, but as assembling smaller collections of texts. The four major components of the New Testament include three such "minicollections": a collection of letters attributed to Paul, a collection of four Gospels, and a collection of what are commonly referred to as "universal" (or "catholic") epistles, so named on account of their general rather than specific intended audience. Only the books of Acts and Revelation stand apart from these three collections. It will be helpful at this point to provide a brief overview of when these four different components of the New Testament began to take shape.[8]

The letters of Paul

Paul's letters are almost certainly the earliest surviving Christian documents—although not all were written at the same time—and were tailored to the particular circumstances of the persons and communities to whom they were individually addressed.[9] Paul, therefore, did not likely anticipate that his letter to the Thessalonians, for example, would be read by those in Corinth, or his letter to Philemon read by Timothy and Titus.[10] Furthermore, the thirteen letters traditionally attributed to Paul and currently in the New Testament were certainly not the only ones he wrote to Christian communities. In 1 Corinthians 5:9, for example, Paul mentions a letter he had sent previously to the saints at Corinth. Ephesians 3:3 alludes to an earlier, but lost, letter to the Ephesians. Elsewhere Paul similarly mentions a letter he sent to saints at Laodicea (Colossians 4:12). None of these documents, however, survive today.

The earliest evidence that Paul's letters were being compiled and read together as a single collection comes from the beginning of the second century, making Paul's writings not only the first to be composed but the first to be gathered into a collection.[11] While the earliest such collection included only ten of Paul's letters (excluding 1 and 2 Timothy and Titus), by the end of the second century, collections containing all thirteen letters of Paul were common in Christian communities.[12] The book of Hebrews, however, was viewed with suspicion even into later centuries on the grounds that many Christians doubted that Paul wrote it, not least because the letter itself does not claim to have been written by the apostle.[13]

The four Gospels

The four Gospels were likely written in the second half of the first century to (1) preserve and testify of the teachings and acts of Jesus, which up to this point were primarily, if not exclusively, transmitted through word of mouth; and (2) adapt and apply these traditions to the particular circumstances in which Christian communities found themselves (hence the distinctive character of each Gospel).[14] Two of the Gospels are attributed to apostles of Jesus (Matthew and John), while the other two (Mark and Luke) are attributed to men who were followers of Jesus and companions of apostles, but not apostles themselves (see Acts 12:25; 2 Timothy 4:11).[15]

The current scholarly consensus is that the Gospel of Mark was written first, being composed in the midsixties to early seventies AD, some three to four decades after the death of Jesus, and fifteen to twenty years after the earliest surviving letter of Paul was written. The Gospels of Matthew and Luke followed shortly after, being written in the seventies and eighties respectively, and reflect significant reliance on Mark's Gospel as a source. The Gospel of John was likely composed sometime between AD 80 and 100.

As with the letters of Paul, the four Gospels were originally addressed to individual Christian communities and thus were not at first read as a collection. It is not until the end of the second century that evidence emerges of Christians reading them together and arguing for their exclusive use. The earliest such evidence is a statement from a bishop and theologian named Irenaeus (ca. AD 180), who argues that the Gospels can be neither "more or less in number" than four.[16] Before the second century, the Gospel of John seems to have been the least widely used in some regions, perhaps, as some scholars have argued, because of its differences in substance, style, and outline from other, more popular Gospels.[17]

The collection of four Gospels gained wide acceptance by the mid-third century, although the order in which the books were placed differed in some regions. Christian communities in the Western Roman Empire, for example, preferred the order Matthew, John, Luke, Mark, apparently privileging those Gospels written by apostles. Because of the vast distances that separated Christian inhabitants of the Roman Empire, as well as their general cultural diversity, it was not uncommon for Christian communities in different geographic regions—some of which might be thousands of miles apart—to favor some texts above others, or even to highly value texts rejected in, or unknown to, other congregations.[18]

The Universal Epistles

The third minicollection included in the New Testament comprises the letters 1 and 2 Peter, 1–3 John, James, and Jude. Because these letters are not addressed to particular communities or individuals, they are commonly referred to by scholars as the "Universal" or "Catholic" Epistles. The term *catholic* derives from the Greek word *katholikos*, which means "universal," referring to the general rather than specific intended audience of these epistles. All seven letters were likely written in the latter half of the first century. Early on, however, only 1 John and 1 Peter were widely read by Christians; the other five letters were still used but only regionally. One of the reasons for this was that some early Christians questioned the apostolic authorship of these letters. The Universal Epistles were not likely being read together as a collection until the third century.[19]

Acts of the Apostles and Revelation

The Acts of the Apostles and the book of Revelation are the only two documents to stand outside the three minicollections that compose the New Testament and have their own history of acceptance. The book of Acts and the Gospel of Luke are two volumes of the same work and were both written by Luke in the late first century. Whereas the Gospel records the ministry of Jesus, Acts records the first missionary efforts of Jesus's apostles. In contrast to Luke's Gospel, however, the book of Acts did not gain wide popularity until the end of the second century.

The book of Revelation is what is known as an "apocalypse," from the Greek word *apocalypsis*, meaning "uncovering," and is a genre of literature that claims to disclose something hidden, often being revealed by heavenly beings in symbolic language and frequently pertaining to the end of the world (see chapter 26 herein). By the end of the first century, Revelation was widely read, although more so in Christian communities in the Western Roman Empire than in the East. Reasons for its slower acceptance as scripture in the East, which didn't occur until the late fourth century, include disputes over the apostolic origins of the book and disagreements regarding whether the events described therein should be understood literally or symbolically.[20]

Other authoritative texts

While all of the above-mentioned texts would eventually become part of the New Testament canon, they were not the only writings valued by Christians in the early centuries of the church. Numerous other letters, gospels, acts, and apocalypses were read and considered authoritative in Christian communities across the Roman Empire. Many letters, for example, were sent from early church leaders to diverse Christian individuals and communities. These were intended to provide their addressees with instruction regarding Christian living and, like Paul's letters, were tailored to the individual circumstances of those to whom they were written. Some of these documents, however, were also disseminated widely and read beyond their original intended audience. First Clement and the Epistle of Barnabas are two examples of letters that were considered broadly authoritative but that ultimately were not included in the New Testament. First Clement was written in the late first century and is attributed to Clement, the third bishop of Rome. Addressed to the saints in Corinth, the letter attempts to resolve disputes among the clergy and congregation in that community.[21] The Epistle of Barnabas was likely written sometime between AD 70 and 135 and is attributed to

Paul's missionary companion, Barnabas. It addresses Christianity's relationship with Judaism and argues that Christians are the true inheritors of God's covenant with Israel.[22]

In addition to letters, there were numerous gospels composed. Gospels attributed to Peter, Thomas, Judas, Mary, and Philip, for example, were circulated and read in some, although not all, Christian communities (see chapter 19 herein). While these gospels purport to have been written by followers of Jesus, modern scholars and many early Christians generally agree that such was not the case. It was not uncommon in the ancient world for such "pseudonymous" (i.e., falsely named) texts to be written by one person and attributed to another on the grounds that the author understood his work to be inspired by, in honor of, or true to the mind and teachings of the person for whom he named it.[23] Whether and to what degree such authors were trying to intentionally deceive their readers is a matter of debate.[24] Additionally, another text popular in the Eastern Roman Empire until the fourth century was the Diatessaron, which harmonized the four Gospels into a single coherent narrative. The Diatessaron was written sometime in the second century and attributed to an author and theologian named Tatian.

Numerous accounts of the missionary endeavors, or "acts," of the apostles were also written in the second century, including the Acts of John, Acts of Peter, Acts of Andrew, Acts of Paul, and Acts of Thomas. These works were composed anonymously, circulated independently of one another, and claim to record the deeds of Jesus's apostles as they spread his message throughout the known world. Many of the stories contain accounts of miracles such as healings, exorcisms, and raising the dead. While these stories were certainly popular in some Christian communities, many ancient Christians also viewed them with suspicion, not least on account of some of their "unorthodox"[25] theological content, which is one of the primary reasons they were never included in the canon. Modern scholars generally do not view these texts as historically reliable accounts of what Jesus's apostles actually did.

Texts of the same genre as the book of Revelation were also widely read by Christians in the second century. The Apocalypse of Peter, for example, purports to have been written by the apostle Peter—a claim ultimately rejected by both many ancient Christians and modern scholars—and records a conversation between the resurrected Christ and Peter in which Jesus describes the destruction of the world, final judgment, and destinies of the righteous and wicked. The Shepherd of Hermas, another apocalyptic text, was written in the early second century by a man named Hermas and contains a series of visions and parables delivered by an angel. These texts teach principles relating to ethical life and the Final Judgment. Although viewed as scripture by many early Christians, the Shepherd of Hermas was ultimately excluded from the canon because its author was not an apostle.

Factors Leading to the Selection and Closure of the Canon

As a large number of Christian texts were being composed in the first and second centuries, Christians became increasingly aware of the need to delimit the number and scope of their authoritative literature. This was a complex process that not only spanned centuries but varied in pace among the different regions of the Roman Empire. Scholars have argued that a number of social, technological, and theological factors contributed to the selection and closure of New Testament canon.[26] The most prominent of these include the following.

Creation of the codex

Before the end of the first century, Christians likely copied their sacred texts on scrolls made of papyrus (2 John 12; compare 2 Timothy 4:13), a paperlike material made from the papyrus plant, which was indigenous to Egypt. The maximum length of a single scroll was about thirty feet, which was roughly enough space to fit the Gospel of Luke and the book of Acts.[27] Parchment, a writing material made from animal skin (typically sheep, goats, and calves), was also sometimes used by Christians, although less frequently given that it was more expensive to produce.[28] One technological development that facilitated the eventual gathering of authoritative books together in a single volume was the invention of the codex, or leaf-book, which closely resembles a modern book. When Christians adopted the codex form of book for their scriptural writings, this allowed them to gather many more documents into a single volume. This format would also eventually help standardize the order of the New Testament books.

Marcion

Another likely influence on the formation of the canon was a man named Marcion (see chapter 19 herein). Marcion was a wealthy Christian shipowner living in Rome in the mid-second century. He believed that the God of the Old Testament could not possibly be the same loving and merciful God described by the Gospels. Consequently, he sought to establish a collection of authoritative writings that removed any mention of what he understood to be a cruel and vengeful deity. His efforts led to what some scholars have called the first verifiable—although eventually rejected—canon of the New Testament. Marcion's canon included only the Gospel of Luke and ten letters of Paul, which were all edited to exclude any mention of the Jewish scriptures and the God described therein. Marcion gained a substantial following in the second and third centuries, but he was ultimately excommunicated for his views. In responding to the teachings of Marcion, early church leaders were impelled to become more reflective about the scope of the church's scriptures and the degree to which they might be subject to alteration.

Gnosticism

Gnosticism, derived from the Greek word *gnosis* and meaning "knowledge," is a broad term used by scholars to designate groups of Christians who claimed to possess special knowledge that would enable them to gain a higher degree of salvation than anyone else.[29] While gnostic Christians valued most of the same literature as other Christians, they also produced their own texts that they claimed contained secret teachings of Jesus and the apostles. Some of these include the Gospel of Philip, Gospel of Mary, and Gospel of Thomas, the last of which claims to record secret sayings delivered by Jesus to the apostle Thomas. Many early Christian authorities criticized gnostic Christians not only for their use of these books but for the way they interpreted more widely accepted writings like the Gospel of John. One bishop's response to such interpretative practices was to establish what he referred to as a "rule of faith," which was founded on the teachings of the more traditional texts, like the four Gospels and writings of Paul, and intended to be a standard by which proper Christian teaching could be determined. Numerous other early authorities would follow suit, condemning the esoteric writings of the gnostics as heretical; in the process they advocated for the exclusive use of many of the texts that would eventually compose the New Testament.

Montanism

Another second-century influence on the closure of the canon was a movement led by a man named Montanus (ca. AD 170). This movement emerged in Asia Minor and spread throughout the Roman Empire. Montanus and his associates, two women named Prisca and Maximilla, believed themselves to be inspired instruments of the Holy Spirit and adhered to what they understood to be the true form of Christianity. They taught that other Christians lacked spiritual gifts and that the Heavenly Jerusalem would soon descend and be located in the small town of Pepuza, the same place where the three resided, spoke in tongues, and uttered prophecies that were recorded for their followers. The larger church strongly opposed the prophetic messages of the Montanists and was faced with the question of how new revelations should be treated in light of existing information revealed in scriptural texts. As a step toward the adoption of a more fixed canon, many Christian authorities at this time emphasized the absolute authority of apostolic writings for determining matters of faith and adjudicating the continuing activity of the Holy Spirit in the church.

Persecution

The persecution of Christians by the Roman government was another factor that likely contributed to the finalization of the canon. Christians in the Roman Empire experienced sporadic persecution from the mid-first century to early fourth century. In AD 303, during what is commonly known as "the Great Persecution," the emperor Diocletian (AD 284–305) issued an order that all Christian scriptures were to be confiscated and burned. Accordingly, when imperial authorities demanded the surrender of these documents, Christian believers (primarily the clergy) were forced to decide which books to hand over and which to try to save. Many faithful individuals hid copies of those most valued texts and handed over writings considered less authoritative in order to placate the Romans and avoid punishment. Persecution, therefore, offered early Christians another occasion to make deliberate judgments regarding which texts they held in highest regard.

Emperor Constantine

Finally, several decades following the Great Persecution, when Christians were free to worship relatively unmolested in the Roman Empire, the emperor Constantine (AD 306–337) ordered fifty deluxe copies of the scriptures to be made in an effort to organize and promote Christian worship in his new capital, Constantinople. These copies were intended to furnish Christian churches in the region and encourage uniformity in belief and practice. The production of these codices suggests that the matter of which books were most valued was close to settled by the fourth century. Although it is a minority opinion, some scholars argue that at least two surviving New Testament manuscripts—Codex Vaticanus and Codex Sinaiticus—may have been among Constantine's original fifty copies, or were perhaps influenced by them.[30] The survival of Constantine's codices notwithstanding, scholars posit that if these deluxe copies included the current twenty-seven books of the New Testament, then this likely would have had a profound impact on the eventual finalization and acceptance of the canon as it exists today.[31]

Criteria for Canonicity

During the second through the fourth centuries, as early Christians sought to define and distinguish between authoritative and nonauthoritative texts, there were primarily three criteria by which canonicity was determined: apostolicity, orthodoxy, and widespread use.

Apostolicity

Arguably the most important criterion for church leaders was a text's apostolicity, meaning its authorship by or close connection with an apostle. The Shepherd of Hermas, for example, was a popular book but was ultimately denied entry to the canon in part because it was not written by an apostle. The Gospels of Mark and Luke, on the other hand, while not written by apostles, were nevertheless validated because of the authors' close associations with Peter and Paul.[32] In accordance with this criterion, texts accepted into the canon were typically composed at an earlier date than those that were excluded, reflecting a preference for books written by eyewitnesses to Jesus Christ's ministry. The books of Hebrews, Revelation, 2–3 John, James, and Jude were slow to be formally accepted on a large scale owing to some doubts regarding their apostolic origins.

Orthodoxy

Another criterion was a text's conformity with a tradition of fundamental Christian beliefs. This tradition of orthodoxy, although it developed over time, was understood to have been received from the apostles and passed down from generation to generation. It was also sometimes referred to by early Christian authors as the "rule of faith," "canon of truth," and "ecclesiastical canon."[33] These phrases encompassed widely-held beliefs relating to things like the nature of the Godhead, the reality of the incarnation, suffering, and resurrection of

Jesus, the creation and redemption of humankind, proper scriptural interpretation, and the rituals of the church. The texts known as the Gospel of Peter and Gospel of Thomas, to name two examples, were rejected on the grounds that their portrayal of Christ was incongruent with this inveterate tradition of orthodoxy.

Widespread use

Another criterion for canonicity was a text's widespread and continuous usage, especially by respected Christian authorities and in the large metropolitan centers of the Roman Empire, such as Rome, Ephesus, Antioch, Alexandria, and Constantinople. The broad use of a text implied its value for determining matters of faith and practice on a large scale and thus its relevance to the church beyond specific regional locales. For example, the Eastern Church's high valuation of the book of Hebrews influenced the West to adopt it, while the Western Church's usage of Revelation led to its acceptance in the East. Because the popularity and liturgical use of a book frequently led to its formal acceptance, canonization should be understood not only as a process by which authority is conferred but as a means of recognizing already-authoritative literary works.

Canon Lists

It wasn't until the fourth and fifth centuries that the majority of lists of authoritative books were drafted. During this time, early Christian leaders arguably did not impose anything new on the church, but rather formally ratified what was already widely accepted. Three of the most important lists that attest to the establishment of the New Testament canon as it exists today are the Muratorian Canon, the canon of Eusebius, and Athanasius's thirty-ninth *Festal Letter*.[34]

Muratorian Canon

The Muratorian Canon is a fragmentary document named after Ludovico Muratori, the man who discovered it in the eighteenth century. Scholars disagree on when it was written, estimating its date of composition to be sometime between the second and fourth centuries. The document contains a list of twenty-four books accepted for reading in the church. These include the four Gospels, Acts, thirteen letters of Paul, Jude, and 1–2 John. It likewise includes two books that would never become canonical (Wisdom of Solomon and Apocalypse of Peter) and excludes five that would (Hebrews, 1 and 2 Peter, James, and 3 John). Finally, the document also explicitly rejects several other books: Shepherd of Hermas, two letters falsely attributed to Paul (one to the Laodiceans and another to the Alexandrians), and other unnamed writings of heterodox groups.

Canon of Eusebius

Another canon list comes from an ancient church historian named Eusebius (ca. AD 260–339) and was written in the early fourth century. Eusebius divides his list of books into four categories. The first category enumerates twenty-one books accepted without qualification in the church: the four Gospels, Acts, fourteen letters of Paul, 1 John, and 1 Peter. He adds, however, that the book of Revelation may also be used if desired. The second category lists books that were commonly used but whose authority was still under dispute at the time: James, Jude, 2 Peter, and 2–3 John. Eusebius notes that some Christians would place the books of Revelation and Hebrews in this category as well. The third category contains books Eusebius considers illegitimate: Acts of Paul, the Shepherd of Hermas, the Apocalypse of Peter, the Epistle of Barnabas, and the Didache (also known as "Teaching of the Twelve Apostles"). The final category lists those books deemed heretical and thus to be completely rejected. These include gospels attributed to Peter, Thomas, and Matthias, to name a few, as well as books claiming to record the acts of Andrew, John, and other apostles.

Athanasius's thirty-ninth Festal Letter

The first canon list to name all twenty-seven books of the New Testament as exclusively authoritative was written by Athanasius, who was the bishop of Alexandria, Egypt, and a prominent theologian. His thirty-ninth *Festal Letter* was sent out on Easter of the year AD 367 and recommended a list of canonical books to church members in North Africa. This list was later ratified by the Council of Carthage in AD 397 and subsequent councils as well.[35] Athanasius concludes his letter with a statement regarding the value of these books for Christians: "These [books] are fountains of salvation, so that they who thirst may be satisfied with the living words they contain. In these alone is proclaimed the doctrine of godliness."[36]

New Testament canons today

The acceptance of Athanasius's *Festal Letter* by most Christians should not overshadow the fact that there still does not exist a single universally agreed-upon New Testament canon. In fact, given the diversity of Christianity in both ancient and modern times, no canon list ever produced has been binding on all those who claim to be Christian. The modern Syrian Orthodox and Chaldean Syrian churches for example, reject 2 Peter, 2–3 John, Jude, and Revelation. The Greek Orthodox Church likewise rejects the book of Revelation. On the other hand, the Ethiopian Church, in addition to the commonly accepted twenty-seven books of the New Testament, also includes the Shepherd of Hermas, two letters of Clement, and a collection of church law called the *Apostolic Constitutions* in its canon.[37]

Conclusion

The canonization of the New Testament was a long and complicated process, and numerous factors led to the formation of what is now arguably the most beloved volume of Christian scripture. By understanding the history of the canon, Latter-day Saints should not only gain a greater appreciation for this remarkable book of scripture but find themselves deeply indebted to those ancient Christians who faithfully recorded, preserved, defended, and transmitted the teachings of Jesus and his earliest followers.

☙

Daniel Becerra is a PhD candidate in Duke University's graduate program in religion (early Christianity).

Further Reading

Gamble, Harry. "Canon, New Testament." In *Anchor Bible Dictionary*, edited by David Noel Freedman, 1:852–61. New York: Doubleday, 1992.

Jackson, Kent P., and Frank F. Judd Jr., eds. *How the New Testament Came to Be*. Provo, UT: Religious Studies Center, Brigham Young University; Salt Lake City: Deseret Book, 2006.

McDonald, Lee M. *The Formation of the Christian Biblical Canon*. Peabody, MA: Hendrickson, 1995.

McDonald, Lee M., and James A. Sanders, eds. *The Canon Debate*. Peabody, MA: Hendrickson, 2002.

Metzger, Bruce M. *The Canon of the New Testament: Its Origin, Development, and Significance*. New York: Oxford University Press, 1997.

Notes

1. The word wasn't applied to Christian writings in the sense of an authoritative collection of texts until the fourth century. Before that point, it referred more to a set of governing Christian beliefs, something akin to the Articles of Faith in the modern Church of Jesus Christ of Latter-day Saints.

2. Some scholars, however, understand the word *canon* in a much more capacious sense, as referring to normative texts, beliefs, and traditions, even before such things become formally ratified through conscious deliberation and ecclesiastical mandates.

3. For a brief introduction to prominent issues relating to the formation of the biblical canon more broadly, see Lee Martin McDonald and James A. Sanders, "Introduction," in *The Canon Debate*, ed. Lee McDonald and James Sanders (Peabody, MA: Hendrickson, 2002), 3–17. For issues relating specifically to the New Testament, see Harry Gamble, "The New Testament Canon: Recent Research and the Status Quaestionis," in McDonald and Sanders, *Canon Debate*, 267–94.

4. Those manuscripts and collections that survive to the present tend to be those whose contents were circulated most widely. The earliest of such collections date to about the fourth century. See Harry Gamble, "Canon, New Testament," in *The Anchor Bible Dictionary*, ed. David Noel Freedman (New York: Doubleday, 1992), 1:853.

5. Some scholars believe, however, that Christianity did not inherit a fixed canon from Judaism, for Judaism had not yet fully set limits on its scripture in the first century. See Gamble, "Canon," 853.

6. See, for example, Jared Ludlow, "Paul's Use of Old Testament Scripture," in *How the New Testament Came to Be*, ed. Kent P. Jackson and Frank F. Judd Jr. (Provo, UT: Religious Studies Center, Brigham Young University; Salt Lake City: Deseret Book, 2006), 227–42.

7. One early Christian author named Papias (ca. AD 60–130) alludes to this process of oral transmission, saying, "But if anyone ever came who had been a follower of the elders, I inquired into the words of the elders— what Andrew, Peter, Philip, Thomas, James, Matthew, or any other of the Lord's disciples had said, and what

Ariston and the elder John, the Lord's disciples, said. For I did not think that information from books would profit me as much as the word of a living and surviving voice." See Eusebius, *Ecclesiastical History* 3.39.4. It is also possible that a collection of Jesus's sayings and other teachings was composed and circulated at a very early date. Scholars refer to this hypothetical written source for some of the Gospels as "Q," a shorthand for the German word *Quelle*, meaning "source."

8. For the format and content of following summary, I am indebted to Gamble's helpful article in the *Anchor Bible Dictionary*: "Canon," 852–61.

9. For a brief introduction to Paul's letters and the reasons they were written, see Eric Huntsman, "The Occasional Nature, Composition, and Structure of Paul's Letters," in Jackson and Judd, *How the New Testament Came to Be*, 190–207.

10. One exception to this is the letter to the Colossians, in which the author explicitly states that it should be read by the saints in Laodicea (Colossians 4:16).

11. Second Peter, which may have been written toward the end of the first century, refers to a collection of Pauline Letters; see 2 Peter 3:15–16.

12. Gamble, "Canon," 853–54.

13. For a brief introduction to issues relating to authorship of Hebrews, see Terrence Szink, "Authorship of the Epistle to the Hebrews," in Jackson and Judd, *How the New Testament Came to Be*, 243–59.

14. Gamble, "Canon," 854; Thomas A. Wayment, "First-Century Sources on the Life of Jesus," in *How the New Testament Came to Be*, 109–22.

15. Authorship is a complex phenomenon and involves not only the telling a story but conscious choices regarding what to include in one's account as well as how to present that information to the reader. Accordingly, some scholars have highlighted the role of the Gospel authors as editors. For one example, see Gaye Strathearn, "Matthew as an Editor of the Life and Teachings of Jesus," in Jackson and Judd, *How the New Testament Came to Be*, 141–56.

16. Irenaeus, *Against Heresies* 3.11.8.

17. Gamble, "Canon," 855.

18. Unlike today, in which the ease of travel and communication across large distances, as well as a centralized ecclesiastical authority, promote uniformity in worship, doctrine, and practice, in the ancient church there existed more regional variety with respect to such things.

19. Evidence for this comes from a fourth-century Christian author and historian, Eusebius, who says that these seven letters were being read publicly in many churches. See Eusebius, *Ecclesiastical History* 2.23.25.

20. Gamble, "Canon," 855.

21. Michael Holmes, ed., *The Apostolic Fathers: Greek Texts and English Translations*, 3rd ed. (Grand Rapids, MI: Baker Academic, 2007), 33–43.

22. Holmes, *Apostolic Fathers*, 370–75.

23. K. Aland, "The Problem of Anonymity and Pseudonymity in Christian Literature of the First Two Centuries," *Journal of Theological Studies* 12 (1961): 39–49. For the implications of pseudonymity for understanding the formation of the New Testament, see Kent D. Clarke, "The Problem of Pseudonymity in Biblical Literature and Its Implications for Canon Formation," in McDonald and Sanders, *Canon Debate*, 440–68. For one Latter-day Saint perspective on this issue, see also Stephen E. Robinson, "Lying for God: The Uses of the Apocrypha," in *Apocryphal Writings and the Latter-day Saints*, ed. C. Wilfred Griggs (Provo, UT: Religious Studies Center, Brigham Young University, 1986), 133–54.

24. Thomas A. Wayment, "False Gospels: An Approach to Studying the New Testament Apocrypha," in Jackson and Judd, *How the New Testament Came to Be*, 292–303.

25. At this point the boundaries of orthodoxy were still being established and were thus somewhat more fluid than in later centuries.

26. For a more detailed discussion of these factors, see Everett Ferguson, "Factors Leading to the Selection and Closure of the New Testament Canon: A Survey of Some Recent Studies," in McDonald and Sanders, *Canon Debate*, 295–320.

27. Bruce Metzger, *The Canon of the New Testament: Its Origin, Development, and Significance* (New York: Oxford University Press, 1997), 108–9. However, this is a debated point. David Brack argues, "Considering the size of Luke and Acts, it would be too unwieldy to glue both papyri into one papyrus roll, and Luke's preface makes clear that there were two rolls. See *Luke's* Legato *Historiography: Remembering the Continuity of Salvation through Rhetorical Transitions* (Eugene, OR: Pickwick, 2017), 26.

28. For more on the early Christian production of texts, see Lincoln H. Blumell, "Scripture as Artifact," in *The Oxford Handbook of the Early Christian Interpretation of Scripture* (forthcoming).

29. For a more detailed treatment of the relationship of Gnosticism and the canon, see Pheme Perkins, "Gnosticism and the Christian Bible," in McDonald and Sanders, *Canon Debate*, 355–71.

30. Kirsopp Lake, "The Sinaitic and Vatican Manuscripts and the Copies sent by Eusebius to Constantinople," *Harvard Theological Review* 11 (1918): 32–35; and T. C. Skeat, "The Use of Dictation in Ancient Book-Production," *Proceedings of the British Academy* 42 (1956): 195–97.

31. Lee McDonald, *The Formation of the Christian Biblical Canon* (Peabody, MA: Hendrickson, 1995), 188; and Metzger, *Canon of the New Testament*, 205.

32. According to Eusebius, Papias identifies Mark as Peter's interpreter. See Eusebius, *Ecclesiastical History* 3.39.15–16. See also Acts 12:25 and 2 Timothy 4:11.

33. Metzger, *Canon of the New Testament*, 252.

34. For additional lists see "Appendix D: Lists and Catalogues of New Testament Collections," in McDonald and Sanders, *Canon Debate*, 591–97.

35. Though there had been general agreement for centuries, the Roman Catholic Church did not formally establish its canon of scripture until the sixteenth century at the Council of Trent.

36. Athanasius, *Festal Letter* 39.6.

37. Alexander B. Morrison, "Plain and Precious Things: The Writing of the New Testament," in Jackson and Judd, *How the New Testament Came to Be*, 25.

Contributors

Grant Adamson is a lecturer in the Department of Religious Studies and Classics at the University of Arizona. He did his graduate work at Rice University (MA, PhD) and Brigham Young University (MA). He specializes in early Christianity and the ancient Mediterranean, having published with Acumen/Routledge, Brill, the *Bulletin of the American Society of Papyrologists*, Macmillan, and Oxford.

Terry B. Ball is a professor of ancient scripture at Brigham Young University. He is a former dean of Religious Education and chair of the Department of Ancient Scripture at BYU. Before joining the faculty at BYU, he spent ten years as a seminary and institute teacher in the Church Educational System. He received his BS from BYU in botany and education. His MA is from BYU in ancient Near Eastern studies, and his PhD from BYU in archaeobotany with an emphasis in the ancient Near East. He has taught and traveled extensively in the Holy Land, including teaching at the BYU Jerusalem Center for Near Eastern Studies. In addition to teaching and researching in ancient scripture, he is an active researcher in the field of archaeobotany.

Daniel Becerra is a PhD candidate in Duke University's graduate program in religion (early Christianity). He holds a master of theological studies from Harvard Divinity School. His primary research interests concern moral formation in late antiquity (ca. second–seventh centuries CE), particularly within Christian ascetic contexts. His most recent published works can be found in the journals *Studia Patristica*, *Studies in the Bible and Antiquity*, and *The Bulletin of the American Society of Papyrologists*.

Daniel L. Belnap is an associate professor in the Department of Ancient Scripture at Brigham Young University. He received graduate degrees in Northwest Semitics from the University of Chicago. He specializes in Hebrew Bible and ancient Near East religion, with interest in ritual studies. He has published one book, *Fillets of Fatling and Goblets of God: The Use of Meal Events in the Ritual Imagery in the Ugaritic Mythological and Epic Texts* (Gorgias

Press, 2008), as well as numerous articles. He also edited *By Our Rites of Worship: Latter-day Saint Views of Ritual in Scripture, History, and Practice* (RSC/Deseret Book, 2013).

Lincoln H. Blumell is an associate professor in the Department of Ancient Scripture at Brigham Young University. He holds graduate degrees from the University of Calgary, University of Oxford, and University of Toronto. He specializes in early Christianity and Greek and Coptic papyrology and epigraphy. He has published two books, *Lettered Christians: Christians, Letters, and Late Antique Oxyrhynchus* (Brill, 2012), *Christian Oxyrhynchus: Texts, Documents, and Sources* (Baylor University Press, 2015), with Thomas A. Wayment, and has a third book in press, *Didymus the Blind's Commentary on the Psalms 26:10–29:2 and 36:1–3* (Brepols, *Corpus Christianorum Series Graeca*). He is also the author of numerous articles.

Matthew L. Bowen is an assistant professor of religious education at Brigham Young University–Hawaii. He holds a PhD from the Catholic University of America in Washington, DC, in biblical studies. He specializes in scriptural narratology, poetics, and onomastics. He is the author of numerous articles and the recent book *Name as Key-Word: Collected Essays on Onomastic Wordplay and the Temple in Mormon Scripture* (Interpreter/Eborn Books, 2018). Another volume, *Deuter-Onomastics: Names as Polemical Themes in the Deuteronomistic History*, will be forthcoming from Gorgias Press.

David M. Calabro is curator of Eastern Christian and Islamic Manuscripts at the Hill Museum and Manuscript Library at St. John's University. He received a PhD in Near Eastern languages and civilizations from the University of Chicago. His research focuses on nonverbal communication, ritual, and religious narrative in the Near East. His book *Hands Lifted to Heaven: Ritual Gestures in Northwest Semitic Literature and Art* is forthcoming from Penn State University Press/Eisenbrauns.

Jason R. Combs is an assistant professor in the Department of Ancient Scripture at Brigham Young University. He holds graduate degrees from Yale Divinity School, Columbia University, and the University of North Carolina at Chapel Hill. He specializes in the cultural history of early Christianity with particular emphasis on religious experience. He has published articles in academic journals including the *Journal of Biblical Literature*, *Early Christianity*, and *The Bulletin of the American Society of Papyrologists*.

Luke Drake is a doctoral student of ancient Mediterranean religions in the Department of Religious Studies at the University of North Carolina at Chapel Hill. He has a master of theological studies from Harvard Divinity School in New Testament and early Christianity and a BA in English from Brigham Young University.

Mark D. Ellison, associate professor in the BYU Department of Ancient Scripture, earned a PhD in early Christianity and early Christian art from Vanderbilt University and an MA in religious studies (archaeology and the Bible) from the University of South Florida. He researches intersections of early Christian literature, art, and practices, with special attention to early Christian families, worship, and the lived experience of ordinary people in late antiquity. With Professor Robin M. Jensen (University of Notre Dame), he is the coeditor of *The Routledge Handbook of Early Christian Art*. His dissertation, "*Visualizing Christian Marriage in the Roman World*," examines the self-representation of married Christians in late Roman visual art and inscriptions. Before joining the BYU faculty, he worked for Seminaries and Institutes of Religion as a teacher, coordinator, and instructional designer.

Alan Taylor Farnes is an independent scholar of New Testament manuscripts whose research primarily focuses on how scribes copied the New Testament text. He was recently awarded a PhD from the University of Birmingham in the UK, specializing in New Testament textual criticism. He holds a graduate degree from Duke University and earned his undergraduate degree from Brigham Young University. His dissertation studied the scribal habits of New Testament scribes, focusing specifically on New Testament manuscripts that are known copies of other known New Testament manuscripts. Alan has presented at international conferences on textual criticism, papyrology, and the Synoptic problem.

Nicholas J. Frederick is an assistant professor in the Department of Ancient Scripture at Brigham Young University. He received his PhD in the history of Christianity from Claremont Graduate University. He is the author of two books, *The Bible, Mormon Scripture, and the Rhetoric of Allusivity* (Fairleigh Dickinson University Press, 2016) and *Joseph Smith's Seer Stones* (Religious Studies Center, 2016). His primary area of study is exploring the intertextual relationship between the Bible and Restoration scripture. He is in the preliminary phrases of writing a third book exploring more broadly the relationship between the New Testament and the Book of Mormon.

John Gee is the William (Bill) Gay Research Professor and senior research fellow at the Neal A. Maxwell Institute for Religious Scholarship at Brigham Young University. He is a generalist with a specialty in Greco-Roman Egypt and the author of two books and over a hundred articles covering a wide variety of religious, historical, and scriptural topics, including New Testament manuscript history, ancient marriage contracts and document sealing practices, and the New Testament's use of the Roman legal system. He has served as the editor of a multilingual, peer-reviewed international professional journal and as section chair for the Society of Biblical Literature.

Bryce Gessell is a PhD student in the history and philosophy of science at Duke University. His research is on the mind-body problem, and how discoveries in brain anatomy and physiology influence theories in psychology, both historically and in modern science. His work has appeared in venues like *Biology and Philosophy*, *Philosophy of Science*, *British Journal for the History of Philosophy*, and *Teorema*. He has an MA degree from Tufts University and a BA degree from Brigham Young University, both in philosophy.

Tyler J. Griffin is an associate teaching professor of ancient scripture at Brigham Young University. He holds degrees in electrical engineering and instructional technology from Utah State University. Prior to coming to BYU, he taught institute for seven years and seminary for eight years before that. Much of his research time is devoted to developing interactive digital learning apps for the New Testament and the Book of Mormon. He has worked with the Church's Motion Picture Studios to develop a 3D interactive mockup of Jerusalem in the first century. He is also active in researching effective pedagogical techniques and teacher development.

Trevan G. Hatch is the ancient scripture, religious studies, and philosophy specialist in the Harold B. Lee Library at Brigham Young University, and he is also an adjunct instructor in the Department of Ancient Scripture. Trevan earned a BA in history at Brigham Young University, an MA in Jewish studies with an emphasis in rabbinic literature at Baltimore Hebrew University/Towson University, and a PhD in sociology of religion at Louisiana State University. He is finishing a second doctoral degree in Jewish studies with an emphasis in Bible and early Judaism at the Spertus Institute of Jewish Studies in Chicago. He also studied at two universities in Israel: Hebrew University of Jerusalem and the University of the Holy Land. Hatch is the author of *Stranger in Jerusalem: Seeing Jesus as a Jew* (Wipf & Stock, 2019) and is coediting *Divine Jealousy: What Latter-day Saints Can Learn from Jews* (Greg Kofford Books, with Jewish scholar Dr. Leonard Greenspoon at Creighton University).

Eric D. Huntsman is a professor of ancient scripture at Brigham Young University, where he also directs the Ancient Near Eastern Studies program in the Kennedy Center for International Studies. After majoring in classical Greek and Latin at BYU, he received his MA and PhD in ancient history from the University of Pennsylvania. He taught classics at BYU from 1994 to 2003, where his work focused on women in imperial Rome. Since transferring to the Department of Ancient Scripture, he has published a number of articles and chapters on the New Testament and especially Johannine literature. In addition to his more academic work, he has published widely for a broader Latter-day Saint audience, his most recent book being *Becoming the Beloved Disciple: Coming unto Christ through the Gospel of John* (Cedar Fort, 2018).

Kent P. Jackson is a professor emeritus of ancient scripture at Brigham Young University. He has a BA in ancient studies from BYU and an MA and PhD in ancient Near Eastern studies from the University of Michigan. He joined the faculty of Brigham Young University in 1980. His research interests include Latter-day Saint scripture, doctrine, and history, with emphasis on the intersection of the restored Church of Jesus Christ and the Bible. He has authored or edited *Joseph Smith's Commentary on the Bible*; *Joseph Smith's New Translation of the Bible: Original Manuscripts*; *The Book of Moses and the Joseph Smith Translation Manuscripts*; and *The King James Bible and the Restoration*. Dr. Jackson is a former associate dean of religion and former associate director of the Brigham Young University Jerusalem Center for Near Eastern Studies.

Frank F. Judd Jr. is an associate professor of ancient scripture at Brigham Young University. He received a PhD in New Testament from the University of North Carolina at Chapel Hill. His scholarly interests include the New Testament, archaeology and historical geography of the Bible, and Latter-day Saint interpretation of scripture. He has authored or edited *How the New Testament Came to Be*, *The Essential New Testament Companion*, and *The Ministry of Peter, the Chief Apostle*. Dr. Judd has served at the BYU Jerusalem Center for Near Eastern Studies multiple times, both as a teacher and most recently as associate director.

D. Jill Kirby is an assistant professor of religious studies at Edgewood College in Madison, Wisconsin. She holds a PhD from the Catholic University of America. Her current research interests include early Christian apocalyptic literature, especially the book of Revelation, and reception history of apocalyptic literature in the English/Scottish Reformation.

Seth S. Larsen is an instructor in the Seminaries and Institutes program of The Church of Jesus Christ of Latter-day Saints. He holds a BA from BYU in Ancient Near Eastern Studies with an emphasis in the Greek New Testament. During this time, he learned Greek and studied the Gospels of Matthew, Mark, and John, as well as many gnostic and early Christian texts in the Greek language. He is currently writing a master's thesis for a graduate degree in Religious Education. During his graduate studies he has written on baptism in the first two centuries.

Jared W. Ludlow is a professor in the Department of Ancient Scripture at Brigham Young University. Before 2006, he spent six years teaching religion and history at BYU–Hawaii. He received his bachelor's degree from BYU in Near Eastern studies, his master's degree from UC–Berkeley in biblical Hebrew, and his PhD in Near Eastern religions from UC–Berkeley and the Graduate Theological Union. His primary research interests are in ancient Judaism and early Christianity.

Jan J. Martin is an assistant professor in the Department of Ancient Scripture at Brigham Young University. She holds a graduate degree from BYU and two additional graduate degrees from the University of York, UK. She specializes in sixteenth-century English Bible translation and has a particular interest in the development of the language of English theology. She has published several articles on William Tyndale and his influence on the developing text of the English Bible.

Joshua M. Matson is a PhD candidate in religions of western antiquity at Florida State University, a teacher at the Tallahassee Institute of Religion, and a research associate with the *Scripta Qumranica Electronica* project. He holds an MA in biblical studies from Trinity Western University and a BA in ancient Near Eastern studies from Brigham Young University. His research focuses on the Dead Sea Scrolls; he specializes in materially and textually reconstructing fragmentary manuscripts. His most recent publications include "The Fourth Gospel and Expectations of the Jewish Messiah," in *Thou Art the Christ, the Son of the Living God: The Person and Work of Jesus in the New Testament*, and "Where the World, Babel, and Zion Meet: Redefining the Mormon People at the 1964–65 Mormon Pavilion," in the *Journal of Mormon History* (2018).

Daniel O. McClellan is a scripture translation supervisor for The Church of Jesus Christ of Latter-day Saints and a PhD student in theology and religion at the University of Exeter. He has graduate degrees from the University of Oxford and from Trinity Western University. His research focuses on cognitive linguistics, the cognitive science of religion, and the conceptualization of deity in the Bible. His most recent publications can be found in the *Journal of Biblical Literature, Biblical Interpretation*, and *Method Today: Redescribing Approaches to the Study of Religion* (Equinox, 2018).

Robert L. Millet is a professor emeritus of ancient scripture, Brigham Young University. During his three decades of teaching at BYU, Dr. Millet served as chair of the Department of Ancient Scripture, dean of Religious Education, and Richard L. Evans Professor of Religious Understanding. He is the author or editor of more than seventy books and 190 articles, book chapters, and reviews. Dr. Millet has codirected the Latter-day Saint–evangelical theological dialogue since 2000 and has been engaged in similar dialogues with the Church of the Nazarene and Community of Christ. He and his wife, Shauna, have six children and twelve grandchildren and reside in Orem, Utah.

George A. Pierce is an assistant professor in the Department of Ancient Scripture at Brigham Young University with a joint appointment to the BYU Jerusalem Center for Near Eastern Studies. He holds graduate degrees from Wheaton College, the University of York (UK), and the University of California, Los Angeles. He specializes in the archaeology of the southern Levant, historical geography of the Holy Land, and computer applications in archaeology. He has published on historical geography and regional settlement patterns of the Dothan Valley, biblical Negev, western Galilee, southern Philistia, and the central coastal plain of Israel.

Dana M. Pike is a professor of ancient scripture and ancient Near Eastern studies at Brigham Young University. He earned a BS degree in archaeology from BYU and a PhD in Hebrew Bible and ancient Near Eastern studies from the University of Pennsylvania. Since coming to BYU over two decades ago, Pike has taught two years at the BYU Jerusalem Center, has worked as one of the international editors of the Dead Sea Scrolls (coeditor of *DJD XXXIII*), and has researched and published on the Bible, the scrolls, and the Book of Mormon. He teaches courses on the Old Testament, the New Testament, and the history and culture of ancient Israel. He is currently serving as department chair of ancient scripture. He is a coauthor of *Jehovah and the World of the Old Testament* (Deseret Book, 2009).

Noel B. Reynolds, a professor emeritus of political science at Brigham Young University, received both graduate degrees from Harvard University. While his academic research, publication, and teaching has mainly focused on topics in legal philosophy, he has also taught and published extensively on religious topics. He served as an editor for Macmillan's *Encyclopedia of Mormonism* and has published multiple edited volumes and has written numerous articles on the Book of Mormon and other topics of interest to Latter-day Saints, including most recently "The Gospel according to Mormon," in the *Scottish Journal of Theology*. He was also the producer of *The Dead Sea Scrolls Electronic Edition*, published in 2005 by Brill. He served many years as president or director of FARMS both before and after it became a research institute of BYU.

David Rolph Seely is a professor of ancient scripture at Brigham Young University. He earned his undergraduate degree in Greek and an MA in classics from BYU and a PhD from the University of Michigan in ancient and biblical studies. He is a member of the international team of scholars that translated and published the Dead Sea Scrolls and published, together with Professor Moshe Weinfeld, the *Barkhi Nafshi* hymns from Qumran. He has coauthored *Jehovah and the World of the Old Testament* with Richard Neitzel Holzapfel and Dana M. Pike and *Solomon's Temple in Myth and History* with William J. Hamblin.

Avram R. Shannon is an assistant professor of ancient scripture at Brigham Young University. He earned a MSt in Jewish studies from the University of Oxford and a PhD in Near Eastern languages and cultures from Ohio State University. He specializes in early rabbinic literature and ancient Mediterranean religions. He has published articles on the definition of ritual in ancient Judaism and on the comparison of Jewish Midrash with the Joseph Smith Translation.

Andrew C. Skinner is a professor of ancient scripture and ancient Near Eastern studies at Brigham Young University. A former dean of Religious Education (2000–2006) and founding executive director of the Neal A. Maxwell Institute for Religious Scholarship at BYU (2006–8), he served as chair of the Department of Ancient Scripture and as Richard L. Evans Professor of Religious Understanding (2010–13). In addition, he has taught several times at BYU's Jerusalem Center for Near Eastern Studies and served as its academic director. He is a member of the Dead Sea Scroll Foundation advisory board and of the international group reediting and retranslating the scrolls. He is the author or coauthor of twenty-one books, including *The Savior's Final Week* and *To Become Like God*, as well as over two hundred articles on religious and historical topics in journals, encyclopedias, and edited volumes. He is also the editor or coeditor of seven volumes. Dr. Skinner holds academic degrees from the University of Colorado, Iliff School of Theology, Harvard University, and the University of Denver and pursued graduate studies at Hebrew University in Jerusalem.

Andrew C. Smith earned his PhD from Claremont Graduate University, specializing in Qur'anic studies and comparative scriptural studies. He is particularly interested in the study of ritual within scripture. His doctoral dissertation dealt with prostration in the Hebrew Bible/Old Testament and the Qur'an. His article "Furthering Prostration in the Hebrew Bible: A Non-Denotative Analysis of Hištaḥăwah" was published in the *Journal for the Study of the Old Testament*. He has also written and published articles related to the Book of Mormon and Latter-day Saint scripture.

Julie M. Smith graduated from the University of Texas at Austin with a BA in English and from the Graduate Theological Union in Berkeley, CA, with an MA in biblical studies. She is on the executive board of the Mormon Theology Seminar and on the steering committee for the BYU New Testament Commentary, for which she is writing an article on the Gospel of Mark. She is the author of *Search, Ponder, and Pray: A Guide to the Gospels* and the editor of and contributor to *As Iron Sharpens Iron: Listening to the Various Voices of Scripture* and *Apocalypse: Reading Revelation 21–22*. She also blogs for *Times & Seasons*, where she is the book review editor.

Kristin H. South is a member of the History Department at The Waterford School in Sandy, Utah. She has earned graduate degrees from Yale University in Near Eastern Languages and Civilizations and in archaeology from Brigham Young University. Since 1998, she has participated in excavations at Fag el Gamus, an early Christian site in Egypt, with the BYU Egypt Excavation Project and she regularly publishes finds of archaeological textiles from that site. She has also excavated at other Roman and Byzantine sites in Jordan and Syria, and has completed conservation and analysis of museum collections of archaeological textiles.

Gaye Strathearn is an associate professor in the Department of Ancient Scripture at Brigham Young University. She earned a BA in physical therapy from the University of Queensland, a BA and MA in Near Eastern studies from BYU, and a PhD in religion with an emphasis on the New Testament from Claremont Graduate University. She has published *He Will Give You Rest: Christ's Invitation and Promise* with Richard Neitzel Holzapfel (Deseret Book, 2010), edited six volumes, and written more than thirty articles or book chapters for Latter-day Saint audiences on a variety of New Testament topics.

Catherine Gines Taylor is the Hugh W. Nibley Fellow at the Neal A. Maxwell Institute for Religious Scholarship at Brigham Young University. Dr. Taylor specializes in late antique Christian art history and iconography. She holds graduate degrees from BYU and the University of Manchester. Her research interests focus on the interdisciplinary study of art, scripture, lay piety, patronage, and patristic texts. More specifically, her research centers on images of women in early Christian contexts. Her monograph, *Late Antique Images of the Virgin Annunciate Spinning*, was published by Brill in 2018. Other publications include "The Pignatta Sarcophagus: late antique iconography and the memorial culture of salvation" (Sheffield Phoenix Press, 2015); "Burial Threads: A Late Antique Textile and the Iconography of the Virgin Annunciate Spinning" (Oxbow, 2015). Dr. Taylor's current research investigates the typologies of Susanna and Wisdom on sarcophagi and other funerary monuments.

Michael R. Trotter is a doctoral student of Christianity in antiquity at the Department of Theological Studies at Saint Louis University. He holds undergraduate and graduate degrees from Brigham Young University in ancient Near Eastern studies and classics with an emphasis in early Christianity. He specializes in early Christian understandings of the devil, New Testament textual criticism, and Greek papyrology. His coauthored publications include "P.Oxy. LXIV 4405: An Early Witness to a System of Textual Division at Oxyrhynchus" (*Journal of Juristic Papyrology*, 2016) and "Three New Fragments from the J. Rendel Harris Collection (Birmingham)" (*Analecta Papyrologica*, 2016). He was also a key contributor to *Didymus the Blind's Commentary on Psalms 26:10–29:2 and 36:1–3* (Brepols, 2019).

Thomas A. Wayment is a professor of classical studies at Brigham Young University. He earned a PhD in New Testament Studies from the Claremont Graduate School. Since that time he has been employed at Brigham Young University, where previously served as a professor of ancient scripture and publications director of the Religious Studies Center. He has published widely on New Testament topics, and his current research focuses on the textual foundations of Christianity.

John W. Welch is the Robert K. Thomas Professor of Law in the J. Reuben Clark Law School at Brigham Young University, where he teaches legal courses on biblical law, Greek and Roman law, and law in the New Testament and Book of Mormon. He holds graduate degrees from BYU and Duke. He served as editor-in-chief of *BYU Studies* from 1991 to 2018 and has authored or edited several books, including *Chiasmus in Antiquity* (Gerstenberg, 1981), *Masada and the World of the New Testament* (BYU Studies, 1997), *Charting the New Testament* (FARMS, 2002), and *The Sermon on the Mount in the Light of the Temple* (Ashgate, 2009). His wide-ranging publications include works on the early Christian interpretations of the parable of the good Samaritan, fear and magic in the trial of Jesus, and textual relations between the Sermon on the Mount and the Didache. He is an author and editor in the BYU New Testament Commentary.

Anita Cramer Wells received her bachelor's degree in Near Eastern Studies from BYU, where she studied biblical Hebrew and worked as a researcher for FARMS. She received a master's degree in library and information science from Drexel University, teaches early-morning seminary, and volunteers as an editor for Book of Mormon Central. Her published works on scripture include "Bare Record: The Nephite Archivist, The Record of Records, and the Book of Mormon Provenance" (*Interpreter*, 2017) and the children's book *Nephi, Nephi, The Scriptures Are True!* (Deseret Book, 2004).

Erik O. Yingling researches Christian ritual, art, and phenomenology. He is a PhD student at Stanford University in art history, holding degrees from Yale and BYU, where he studied Christian liturgy and the ancient Near East. Some of his publications include "The Ghost in the Glass: Reflecting on Reflections and the Death Mask of Leland Stanford Jr.," in *Faults and Traces: Some Stanford Ghost Stories* (Cantor Center for the Visual Arts, 2016); "A New Coptic Epitaph from the Petrie Museum of Egyptian Archaeology" (*Bulletin of the American Society of Papyrologists*, 2016, with Lincoln H. Blumell); and "Singing with the Savior: Reconstructing the Ritual Ring-dance in the Gospel of the Savior" (*Apocrypha*, 2013).

Index

false gods versus one true,
197–201
holiness of, in Revelation, 470
in Judaism versus Greco-Roman religion, 197–201
love of, 89–90, 257
Marcion on, 755, 778
and mediation through prayer,
284–85
name of, in choral hymn of
Revelation, 591
Paul's teachings on, 408
reconciliation with, 279–80,
343–45, 431
revealed to people on earth,
282–83, 345–46
throne of, 474
worshipping, 451, 474
gods
Greco-Roman, 198, 200–201,
417n25, 426, 685, 762
human beings as, 89, 503–4
one true God versus false,
197–201
Gog, 508
gold coins, 214
Golden Rule, 92
gold rings, 220
Gospel of Truth, discovery of,
327
Gospels. *See* Infancy Gospel of
Thomas; John, Gospel of; Luke,
Gospel of; Mark, Gospel of;
Mary, Gospel of; Matthew, Gospel of; noncanonical Gospels;
Peter, Gospel of; Philip, Gospel
of; Synoptic Gospels; Thomas,
Gospel of
grace, 90, 93, 169–70,
273–74n16, 279, 284–85, 343,
405, 431, 449, 476
grain, 23, 211–12, 214, 219–20,
621–22, 635–36
grapes, 624–26
grass, 626
great whore, in Revelation, 475,
689
Grébant, M., 327
Greco-Roman religion, 194,
206–7
gentiles and gentile missions,
194–96
New Testament references to,
197–206
purification and initiation
rites, 605

sacrifices to idols, 198, 426,
762
story of Zeus and Hermes,
200–201, 417n25, 685
**Greek New Testament, 691–703,
705n12**
Greek philosophy, 178, 190–91
ancient, 179–81
encountered by Paul, 181–82
Epicureans / Epicureanism,
184–86
Hellenistic, 181–87
Roman philosophy and, 188
Stoics / Stoicism, 184,
186–87
groaning, 569

H

Hadrian, 495n5
halakhic texts, 125–26
Haman, 649
hand(s)
extending, to speak, 558–60
healing handclasp, 564–65
laying on of, 562–64, 612,
759
lifting, in prayer, 560–61,
587–88
lifting, to bless, 561
raising right, 557–58
Hasmonean, origin of name,
18n6
Hasmonean dynasty, 12–17,
55, 74
head tax (poll tax), 146, 211,
682
healing(s)
of blind man, 308
of centurion's servant, 256
laying on of hands for,
562–63
of man at pool of Bethesda,
662
of man blind from birth, 308
through handclasp, 564–65
of woman with issue of blood,
652–53
heart, change of, 344
heathen, 207n4
heavenly messengers. *See* angels
Hebrews, Epistle to, 446
allusions to, in Doctrine and
Covenants, 739–40
Atonement in, 348

audience and genre of,
448–49, 464n13
content of, 449–50
dating and authorship of,
447–48, 463n7
midrash and understanding,
132–35
rabbinic literature and,
128–29
use of Old Testament in,
506–7
hedonism, 185
Hegesippus, 768n15
hell, 494
Hellenism, 9–10, 138n50
hematidrosis, 268
heqeš, 94, 100
herbs, 626–27
ḥerem, 34n34
Hermas, 777, 780
hermeneutics. *See* Jewish
hermeneutics
Hermes, 200–201, 417n25,
685
Herod, 15–16, 46–47, 74
Herod Agrippa I, 16, 151–52,
158–59n56, 200
Herod Agrippa II, 16–17, 152,
154, 159n70, 413
Herod Antipas, 16, 48, 79, 144,
151, 164, 173, 254, 269
Herodian dynasty, 15–17
Herod of Chalcis, 159n70
Herod Philip, 144–45, 164,
489–90
Herod's Palace, 46–47, 52n15,
233
Herod's temple, 55–56
cleansing of, 82, 254, 314
clothing of high priest at, 62
construction of, 143
destruction of, 67–68,
235–38, 294
festivals at, 61–62, 64
in first-century Judaism and
Christianity, 65–67
in narratives of Jesus's life
and ministry, 63–65
role in early church, 274n27
symbolism in, 63, 64
Temple Mount, 56–58
temple worship at, 58–61
Herod the Great, 142–45, 164,
231, 274n25, 487
Hexapla, 511n16
Hezekiah, 44

Citation Index